MANAGERIAL ECONOMICS

EIGHTH EDITION

Christopher R. Thomas

University of South Florida

S. Charles Maurice

Texas A&M University
Late Professor Emeritus

McGraw-Hill
Irwin

Boston   Burr Ridge, IL   Dubuque, IA   Madison, WI   New York   San Francisco   St. Louis
Bangkok   Bogotá   Caracas   Kuala Lumpur   Lisbon   London   Madrid   Mexico City
Milan   Montreal   New Delhi   Santiago   Seoul   Singapore   Sydney   Taipei   Toronto

 **McGraw-Hill Irwin**

MANAGERIAL ECONOMICS
Published by McGraw-Hill/Irwin, a business unit of The McGraw-Hill Companies, Inc., 1221 Avenue of the Americas, New York, NY, 10020. Copyright © 2005, 2002, 1999, 1995, 1992, 1988, 1985, 1981 by The McGraw-Hill Companies, Inc. All rights reserved. No part of this publication may be reproduced or distributed in any form or by any means, or stored in a database or retrieval system, without the prior written consent of The McGraw-Hill Companies, Inc., including, but not limited to, in any network or other electronic storage or transmission, or broadcast for distance learning.

Some ancillaries, including electronic and print components, may not be available to customers outside the United States.

This book is printed on acid-free paper.

2 3 4 5 6 7 8 9 0 DOC/DOC 0 9 8 7 6 5 4

ISBN 0-07-287174-1

Vice president and editor-in-chief: *Robin J. Zwettler*
Publisher: *Gary Burke*
Executive sponsoring editor: *Lucille Sutton*
Developmental editor: *Katie Crouch*
Editorial assistant: *Rebecca Hicks*
Marketing manager: *Martin D. Quinn*
Senior media producer: *Anthony Sherman*
Project manager: *Laura Griffin*
Senior production supervisor: *Rose Hepburn*
Designer: *Adam Rooke*
Supplement producer: *Matthew Perry*
Senior digital content specialist: *Brian Nacik*
Cover image: *© 2003 Imagebank*
Typeface: *10/12 Palatino*
Compositor: *GAC Indianapolis*
Printer: *R. R. Donnelley*

Library of Congress Cataloging-in-Publication Data

Thomas, R. Christopher.
 Managerial economics / Christopher R. Thomas, S. Charles Maurice. — 8th ed.
  p. cm.
 Rev. ed. of: Maurice, S. Charles. Managerial economics. 7th ed.
 Various multi-media instructional aids are available to supplement the text.
 Includes index.
 ISBN 0-07-287174-1 (alk. paper)
 1. Managerial economics. I. Maurice, S. Charles. Managerial economics. II. Title
HD30.22.M39 2005
338.5′024′658—dc22

                                                                    2003067269

www.mhhe.com

To Don and Sherry

ABOUT THE AUTHORS

Christopher R. Thomas

Christopher R. Thomas is currently associate professor of economics at University of South Florida. He worked for two years as an energy economist at Oak Ridge National Laboratory before joining the faculty at USF in 1982. He now teaches managerial economics at the undergraduate level and in two executive training programs, a traditional executive M.B.A. program and an executive M.B.A. program for physicians that draws doctors nationwide. Professor Thomas has published numerous articles on government regulation of industry and antitrust issues in *Quarterly Journal of Economics, Journal of Law and Economics, Southern Economic Journal, Journal of Economics and Business, Quarterly Review of Economics and Business,* and *Journal of Economic Education.* He serves as a policy associate at the Center for Economic Policy Analysis at University of South Florida. Professor Thomas lives with his wife and daughter in Tampa, Florida, where he enjoys playing tennis.

S. Charles Maurice

Chuck Maurice was professor emeritus of economics at Texas A&M University. He spent 30 years in the Department of Economics at Texas A&M, where he served as department head from 1977 through 1981 and held the Rex B. Grey University Professorship of Free Enterprise from 1981 through 1985. Professor Maurice published numerous articles on microeconomic theory in the top economic journals. He co-wrote two scholarly books on natural resource depletion: *The Doomsday Myth* and *The Economics of Mineral Extraction.* He also wrote with Charles Ferguson, and later, Owen Phillips, the widely used intermediate-level microeconomics textbook *Economic Analysis,* which was published from 1971 to 1996. Professor Maurice retired to Gainesville, Florida, where he lived until his death in the spring of 1999.

PREFACE

WHY MANAGERIAL ECONOMICS?

Over the past dozen or so years, business school curriculum committees have taken steps to strengthen the analytical and critical thinking skills of business students. While the trend toward stronger academic training in business schools stems from a number of factors, one of the most compelling reasons for doing so is, quite simply, that employers of business school graduates are demanding better thinkers. Many of us who teach economics to business students believe that training in economics not only helps business students better understand and predict the economic forces shaping real-world business decisions but also serves to develop and strengthen overall analytical skills of students of all majors.

Most business schools require students to take several courses in economics. Managerial economics, which is often one of these courses, brings together topics in microeconomics that can be applied to business decision making to create a valuable way of thinking about markets and business decisions. The objective of *Managerial Economics* is to help business students become architects of business strategy rather than simply middle managers plodding along the beaten path of others.

PEDAGOGICAL HIGHLIGHTS

The Eighth Edition of *Managerial Economics* maintains all of the pedagogical features that have made previous editions successful. These features follow.

Emphasis on the Economic Way of Thinking

The primary goal of this book has always been, and continues to be, to teach students the economic way of thinking about business decisions. *Managerial Economics* develops critical thinking skills and provides students with a logical way of analyzing business decisions.

Easy to Learn and Teach From

Managerial Economics has always been a self-contained book that requires no previous training in microeconomics. While maintaining a rigorous style, this book is designed to be one of the easiest books in managerial economics from which to teach *and* learn. Rather than parading students quickly through every interesting or new topic in microeconomics and industrial organization, *Managerial Economics* instead carefully develops and applies the most *useful* concepts for business decision making.

Dual Sets of End-of-Chapter Questions

To promote the development of analytical and critical thinking skills, which most students probably do not know how to accomplish on their own, two different kinds of problem sets are provided for each chapter. Much like the pedagogy in mathematics textbooks, which employ both "exercises" and "word problems," *Managerial Economics* provides both Technical Problems and Applied Problems.

- **Technical Problems**—Each section of a chapter is linked (by an icon in the margin) to one or more Technical Problems specifically designed to build and reinforce a particular skill. The Technical Problems provide a step-by-step guide for students to follow in developing the analytical skills set forth in each chapter. The answers to all of the Technical Problems are provided at the end of the text, so the Technical Problems

v

serve as an integrated workbook within the text. The narrow focus of each Technical Problem accomplishes two things: (1) It encourages students to master concepts by taking small "bites" instead of trying to "gulp" the whole chapter at once, and (2) it allows students to pinpoint any areas of confusion so that interaction with the instructor—in the classroom or in the office—will be more productive. When students finish working the Technical Problems, they will have practiced all of the technical skills required to tackle the Applied Problems.

- **Applied Problems**—Following the Technical Problems, each chapter has a set of Applied Problems that serve to build critical thinking skills as well as business-decision-making skills. These problems, which are much like the "word problems" in a math textbook, are a mix of stylized business situations and real-world problems taken from *Business Week,* the *Economist, The Wall Street Journal,* and other business news publications. Business students frequently find classroom discussion of the Applied Problems to be among the most valuable lessons of their entire business training. Answers to Applied Problems are only available in the *Instructor's Resource Manual.*

The clarity of exposition, coupled with the integrated, step-by-step process of the Technical Problems, allows students to learn most of the technical skills before coming to class. To the extent that technical skills are indeed mastered before class, instructors can spend more time in class showing students how to *apply* the economic way of thinking to business decision making.

Flexible Mathematical Rigor

Starting with only basic algebra and graph-reading skills, all other analytical tools employed in the book are developed within the text itself. The *Student Workbook* contains an 18-page tutorial review of the basic algebra and graphing skills needed to work the problems in the text. This tutorial, entitled

"Review of Fundamental Mathematics," contains numerous mathematical exercises with answers.

While calculus is not a part of any chapter, instructors wishing to teach a calculus-based course can do so by using the Mathematical Appendixes at the end of most chapters. The Mathematical Appendixes employ calculus to analyze some of the key topics covered in the chapter. Most appendixes have a set of Mathematical Exercises that requires calculus to solve, and the answers to the Mathematical Exercises are available in the *Instructor's Resource Manual.* A "Brief Review of Derivatives and Optimization" is also provided in the *Instructor's Resource Manual* and in the student area of the website for this book (www.mhhe.com/economics/thomas8). This six-page tutorial covers the concept of a derivative, the rules for taking derivatives, unconstrained optimization, and constrained optimization.

Self-Contained Empirical Analysis

The Eighth Edition continues to offer a self-contained treatment of statistical estimation of demand, production, and cost functions. While this text avoids advanced topics in econometrics and strives to teach students only the fundamental statistical concepts needed to estimate demand, production, and cost, the explanations of statistical procedures nonetheless maintain the rigor found in the rest of the book. For those instructors who do not wish to include empirical analysis in their courses, the empirical content can be skipped with no loss of continuity.

Wide Audience

Managerial Economics is appropriate for undergraduate courses in managerial economics (or courses in applied microeconomics) and for M.B.A. and executive M.B.A. level courses. The self-contained nature of the book can be especially valuable in night classes or executive M.B.A. courses where students may have limited opportunity to meet with an instructor for help outside class.

SUPPLEMENTS

The following supplemental materials are available for the Eighth Edition.

Student Workbook

The *Student Workbook* provides students with chapter reviews and many extra problems with answers. Each chapter of the *Student Workbook* has five sections: Essential Concepts, Study Problems, Matching Definitions, Multiple-Choice/True-False, and Homework Exercises. As previously mentioned, the *Student Workbook* also provides a tutorial on business mathematics, which includes numerous exercises with answers.

Instructor's Resource Manual

The *Instructor's Resource Manual* contains answers to the Applied Problems, answers to the problems in the Mathematical Appendixes, and answers to the Homework Exercises in the *Student Workbook*.

Test Bank (Softcover and CD)

The *Test Bank* offers multiple-choice and fill-in-the-blank questions that closely match the Technical Problems in each chapter. The *Test Bank* is available both in softcover and on CD (Microsoft Word 2002) for easy compilation of exams.

Student Statistix 8 CD

As in the previous edition, *Managerial Economics* can be packaged with a CD that contains the Student Edition of *Statistix 8,* a popular Windows-based statistical software package. This software provides students with many easy-to-use statistical procedures including two-stage least-squares. The CD also contains all of the data sets used in this book—there are 12 of these. I have written and class-tested a tutorial, which is available on the website of the text, showing students how to use this software to work the problems in *Managerial Economics.*

PowerPoint Slides

All of the graphs contained in this edition of *Managerial Economics* are also available a *PowerPoint* slides on CD, as well as on the book website.

www.mhhe.com/economics/thomas8

The McGraw-Hill website for *Managerial Economics* supplies support material and information for both instructors and students. The website contains the following instructional materials: (1) chapter summaries and key terms, (2) 20 multiple-choice questions for each chapter with instant grading, (3) Special Topic Modules (STMs) covering linear programming in production analysis and investment or capital budgeting decisions, (4) Illustrations "retired" from previous editions, (5) Consulting Projects for take-home exercises requiring statistical analysis to make business decisions, (6) a brief tutorial on using *Statistix 8* to work problems in *Managerial Economics,* and (7) a six-page calculus review called "Brief Review of Derivatives and Optimization." The password-protected Instructor's site includes the *Instructor's Resource Manual* and downloadable PowerPoint slides.

NEW FEATURES IN THE EIGHTH EDITION

This edition of *Managerial Economics* represents a rather significant reorganization. And, as with all revisions, I have updated and revised material throughout the book to make improvements in clarity and content.

Previous users will notice several organizational changes. For one thing, I have moved several chapters to new locations. Optimization theory is now covered in Chapter 3, while the chapter on demand elasticity has been moved to Part II, Demand Analysis. I have also combined several chapters: Demand estimation and forecasting are now covered in a single chapter and strategic decision making now takes one chapter instead of two. Also, the chapter on multiple plants, markets, and products has been reorganized and renamed. Chapter 14, "Advanced Techniques for Profit Maximization," now covers two additional topics that have been moved from earlier parts of the book: cost-plus pricing and strategic entry deterrence.

Perhaps a more important organizational change involves my decision to move some topics from the textbook to the dedicated McGraw-Hill website for the book. I have moved the chapter on investment decisions (capital budgeting) to the website, creating Special Topic Module 2. Many users observed that business students are required to take courses in finance that cover investment and capital budgeting analysis. So, beginning with this edition, this topic joins linear programming as a stand-alone Special Topic Module on the McGraw-Hill website. Hopefully, moving these topics to the website will pass the market test, which will make room in future editions for coverage of some new topics. As always, any advice or comments from adopters are valued and encouraged.

In addition to the changes in organization, the following revisions have been undertaken to improve clarity and coverage in the Eighth Edition:

- As previously discussed, strategic decision making in oligopoly markets is now covered in a single chapter, instead of two chapters as in the last edition. In the process of combining the two chapters, numerous improvements have been made: The process of identifying dominant, dominated, and Nash equilibrium cells in payoff tables has been simplified and unified; the discussion of trigger strategies has been shortened and simplified; the discussion of cartels now emphasizes the incentive to cheat on price-fixing arrangements (rather than how cartels make pricing and output decisions); and a new subsection on facilitating practices has been added.

- Eleven Illustrations from the last edition (all of which can still be found on the website at "Illustrations from Previous Editions") have been retired, and 25 percent of the Illustrations in this edition are either new or revised.

- The chapter on optimization theory has been substantially revised to emphasize the main idea of the chapter: using marginal analysis to make optimal decisions. The graphical analysis has been improved, and average cost has been added to the discussion of costs that are irrelevant in decision making (joining sunk and fixed costs).

- In the chapter on demand elasticities, the "Calculating Price Elasticity of Demand" section has been substantially revised to simplify, as much as possible, the methodology for computing point and interval elasticities. Computation of price, income, and cross-price elasticities in the case of linear demand functions is now fully developed in this chapter.

- Short-run and long-run costs are now related utilizing a short-run expansion path, which clarifies why output adjustments are more costly to accomplish in the short run than in the long run.

- Discussion of cost-plus pricing has been substantially improved and moved to the newly organized Chapter 14. My executive M.B.A. students continue to show great interest in this pricing technique. In this edition, the problems with cost-plus pricing, both theoretical and practical, are given greater attention. I have added some applied analysis with an example to show why, in the special case of constant costs, cost-plus pricing is no better and no easier than using the $MR = MC$ rule to find the profit-maximizing price. And, of course, in all other cases, cost-plus pricing fails to give the optimal price.

- As in all revisions, I have added a number of new Technical and Applied Problems throughout the book.

A WORD TO STUDENTS

One of the primary objectives in writing this book is to provide you, the student, with a book that enhances your learning experience in managerial economics. However, the degree of success you achieve in your managerial economics course will depend, in large measure, on the effectiveness of your study. I would like to offer you this one tip on studying: Emphasize *active* study rather than *passive* study. Passive study activities are those that do not require you to think for yourself. Reading the text, reviewing class notes, and listening to lectures are "passive" in nature because the authors of your textbook or your instructor are providing the analytical guidance for you. You are simply following someone else's analytical thought process, working only hard enough to agree with the authors or instructor.

In contrast, "active" study techniques require you to think and reason for yourself. For example, when you close your book and put aside your lecture notes and try to explain a concept to yourself—perhaps sketching on a pad the graph or mathematical demonstration of a result—only then are you creating the path of logical analysis for yourself. The better you can explain the "how" and "why" of key concepts, the more thorough will be your understanding. Of course, some passive study is necessary to become familiar with the material, but genuine understanding and ability to use the decision-making skills of managerial economics require emphasis on active, rather than passive, study techniques.

ACKNOWLEDGMENTS

Many of the best ideas for improving a textbook come from colleagues, adopters, reviewers, and students. This revision was no exception. I would particularly like to thank my colleagues Celina Jozsi, Carole Green, Barbara Caldwell, Jim Lasseter, Victoria Perk, Betilde Rincon, and Mark Wilson at University of South Florida and Glen Archibald at University of Mississippi for their comments and valuable advice. In addition, Michael Welker at Franciscan University provided valuable assistance in developing self-test questions for the textbook website. I also benefited tremendously from ideas provided by the following reviewers:

Krishna Rao Akkina, Kansas State University

E. Woodrow Eckhard, University of Colorado–Denver

Bob Harmel, Midwestern State University

Carl A. Kogut, University of Louisiana–Monroe

Jacob Kurien, Rockhurst University

A. Seddick Meziani, Montclair State University

Edward Millner, Virginia Commonwealth University

John Ruggiero, University of Dayton

Farhad Saboori, Albirght College

Lawrence Southwick Jr., State University of New York at Buffalo

Neil Younkin, St. Xavier University

I am especially lucky to have had the opportunity to work again with Lucille Sutton and Katie Crouch, my editorial team at McGraw-Hill/Irwin. They offered their considerable experience and knowledge, making it a pleasure, once again, to revise this textbook. I also benefited greatly from the assistance provided by Laura Griffin, who ably served as project manager on this edition.

As always, I encourage faculty and students to communicate any comments or suggestions to my editors at McGraw-Hill or to me directly at cthomas@coba.usf.edu. Your feedback is much appreciated.

Christopher R. Thomas
Tampa, Florida
September 15, 2003

BRIEF CONTENTS

CONTENTS

- ## PART II DEMAND ANALYSIS 163

CHAPTER 5 Theory of Consumer Behavior 164

CHAPTER 6 Elasticity and Demand 208

CHAPTER 7 Demand Estimation and Forecasting 248

■ PART III   PRODUCTION AND COST ANALYSIS   309

CHAPTER 8   Production and Cost in the Short Run   310

CHAPTER 9   Production and Cost in the Long Run   343

CHAPTER 10   Production and Cost Estimation   393

- ## PART V ADVANCED MANAGERIAL DECISION MAKING 573

CHAPTER 14 Advanced Techniques for Profit Maximization 574

CHAPTER 15 Decisions under Risk and Uncertainty 629

ON THE WEBSITE Special Topic Module 2: Investment Decisions

ILLUSTRATIONS IN THE EIGHTH EDITION

PART 1

Some Preliminaries

CHAPTER

1

Managers, Profits, and Markets

Student of managerial economics: Will I ever use this?
Professor: Only if your career is successful.

Succeeding in the world of business, no matter how you slice it, means winning in the marketplace. From CEOs of large corporations to managers of small, privately held companies—and even nonprofit institutions such as hospitals and universities—managers cannot expect to succeed in business without a clear understanding of how market forces create both opportunities and constraints for business enterprises. Economic forces in the marketplace determine the demand for products, the prices of resources and costs of production, the number of rival firms, the nature of pricing strategies, and ultimately the profitability of business investments.

Publishers roll out dozens of new books each year touting the latest strategy *du jour* from one of the year's most "insightful" business gurus. The never-ending parade of new business "paradigms" and buzzwords might lead you to believe that successful managers must constantly replace outdated analytical methods with the latest fad in business decision making. While it is certainly true that managers must constantly be aware of new developments in the marketplace, the economic way of thinking about business decision making is timeless. Managerial economics provides a systematic, logical way of analyzing business decisions—both today's decisions and tomorrow's.

Instead of presenting a detailed list of rules for specific decision-making problems, such as how to design a successful automobile advertising campaign or how to obtain venture capital, managerial economics addresses the larger economic forces that shape both day-to-day operations and long-run planning decisions. Managerial economics focuses on the application of *microeconomic* theory to business problems. Microeconomics is the study and analysis of the behavior of individual segments of the economy: individual consumers, workers and owners of resources, individual firms, industries, and markets for goods and services. Microeconomics is concerned with topics such as how consumers choose the goods and services they purchase and how firms make hiring, pricing, production, advertising, research and development, and investment decisions.

Business publications such as *The Wall Street Journal, Business Week, The Economist, Forbes,* and *Fortune* regularly cover the many stories of brilliant and disastrous decisions made by executive managers. Although luck often plays a role in the outcome of some of these stories, in many of them, the manager's understanding—or lack of understanding—of fundamental economic relations accounts for the difference between success and failure in business decision making. Although economic theory is not the only tool used by successful managers, it is a powerful and essential tool. The objective of this text is to show you how managers can use economic analysis in making decisions that will achieve the firm's goals—usually the maximization of profit.

While this text focuses on making profitable business decisions, the principles and techniques set forth also offer valuable advice for managers of nonprofit organizations such as foundations, universities, hospitals, and government agencies. The manager of a hospital's indigent-care facility, for example, may wish to know how to minimize the cost of treating a community's indigent patients while maintaining a satisfactory level of care. A university president, facing a strict budget set by the state board of regents, may want to enroll and teach as many students as possible subject to meeting the budget constraint. Although profit maximization is the primary objective addressed in this text, the economic way of thinking about business decision making provides all managers with a powerful set of tools and insights for furthering the goals of their firms or organizations.

1.1 MANAGERIAL ECONOMICS AND ECONOMIC THEORY

A large part of this text is devoted to the use of economic theory in addressing business-decision-making problems. We want to explain briefly how and why economic theory is used to analyze business problems. No doubt you have heard statements such as "That's OK in theory, but what about the real world?" or "I don't want ivory-tower theorizing; I want a practical solution." Practical solutions to challenging real-world problems are seldom found in cookbook formulas, superficial rules of thumb, or simple guidelines. Profitable solutions generally require that people understand how the real world functions, which is often far too complex to comprehend without making the simplifying assumptions used in theories. Theory allows people to gain insights into complicated problems by using

ILLUSTRATION 1.1

Managerial Economics
The Right ℞ for Doctors

A number of universities offer M.B.A. programs designed specifically for medical doctors. The majority of the doctors enrolled in these specialized programs are seeking to develop the business-decision-making skills they need to manage private and public medical clinics and hospitals.

As a group, doctors in these M.B.A. programs tend to be intelligent high-achievers who are in a hurry to learn something useful. They recognize their high opportunity costs of attending class rather than attending to patients, and they are understandably most interested in courses that will quickly teach them practical business skills. In managerial economics, they have found many valuable tools for business decision making and have been quick to apply the principles and tools of managerial economics to a variety of business problems in medicine. Some of the more interesting of these applications, all of which are topics you will learn about in this text, are discussed here:

• *Irrelevance of fixed costs in decision making:* Nearly all the physicians admitted to making some decisions based on fixed costs. A director of a radiation oncology department complained that many of her hospital's administrative costs are included as part of the incremental costs of treating additional patients. While the hospital prided itself in moving toward a marginal cost pricing structure for services, the accounting department's calculation of marginal cost was inflated by fixed administrative costs.

• *Price discrimination:* A doctor specializing in vasectomies wanted to increase revenue by engaging in price discrimination. After a lengthy discussion about the legality of charging different prices for medical services, he decided to promote his vasectomy clinic by placing a $40-off coupon in the local newspaper's TV guide. He believes that only lower-income patients will clip the coupon and pay the lower price.

• *Advertising dilemma:* After a class discussion on the advertising dilemma in oligopoly markets, a doctor who specializes in LASIK eye surgery expressed her relief that none of the other three LASIK surgeons in her small town had shown any interest in advertising their services. She decided it would not be wise for her to begin running radio ads.

• *Linear trend forecasting:* Several physicians used linear trend analysis to forecast patient load. An administrator of a hospital's emergency room services found that using "day-of-week" dummy variables, he could offer hospital administrators statistical evidence—instead of his casual observation—that certain days of the week tend to be (statistically) significantly busier than others.

simplifying assumptions to make sense out of confusion, to turn complexity into relative simplicity. By abstracting away from the irrelevant, managers can use the economic way of thinking about business problems to make predictions and explanations that are valid in the real world, even though the theory may ignore many of the actual characteristics of the real world.

Using economic theory is in many ways analogous to using a road map. A road map abstracts away from nonessential characteristics and concentrates on what is relevant for the task at hand. Suppose you want to drive from Tampa to Atlanta. If you have never made that trip before, you would probably want a map. Suppose you could have either an ordinary road map or a NASA satellite photograph of the region between Tampa and Atlanta. The satellite photograph is an exact representation of the real world; it shows every road, tree, building, cow, and river between

- *Strategic entry deterrence:* A doctor in New Orleans decided to open new clinics in Baton Rouge and Morgan City. No other clinics like his are currently operating in these two cities. In order to discourage other doctors from opening similar clinics, he plans to price his services just slightly above average total cost but significantly below the price that would maximize profit under monopoly.

- *Profit maximization vs. revenue maximization:* A doctor with a 25 percent ownership interest in a pharmaceutical supply firm realized during class that his sales manager is probably selling too many units, since the manager's compensation is based substantially on commissions. The doctor plans to recommend raising drug prices to sell fewer units and to begin paying the sales manager a percentage of profit.

- *Economies of scale and scope:* Hospital managers perceive the current trend toward "managed care" to be forcing hospitals to reduce costs without reducing quality. Economies of scale and scope, to the extent that such economies exist, offer an attractive solution to the need for cost reduction. Hospital administrators in the class were especially interested in empirical methods of measuring economies of scale in order to plan for future expansion or contraction.

- *Cost-minimizing input combination:* One doctor who owns and manages a chain of walk-in clinics decided to reduce the employment of M.D.s and increase the employment of R.N.s on the basis of classroom discussion of cost minimization. Apparently, for many of the procedures performed at the clinic, experienced nurses can perform the medical tasks approximately as well as the physicians, as long as the nurses are supervised by M.D.s. The doctor-manager reasoned that even though M.D.s have higher marginal products than R.N.s, the marginal product per dollar spent on R.N.s exceeded the marginal product per dollar spent on M.D.s.

Business publications report that doctors with M.B.A. degrees are becoming increasingly powerful in the medical profession as hospitals, health maintenance organizations, and other types of health care clinics hire them to manage the business aspect of health care. Some doctors, as well as the American Medical Association, are opposed to blending business and medical values. Given the nature of the applications of managerial economics cited here, it appears that a course in managerial economics offers doctors insights into the business of medicine that they would not usually get in medical school. Many doctors think this knowledge is good medicine.

Tampa and Atlanta. While the NASA photo would be amusing to look at, its inclusion of everything makes it inferior to a traditional road map in its ability to guide you to Atlanta. The road map abstracts from reality by eliminating nonessential information and showing only the important roads between Tampa and Atlanta. The simpler map gives a much clearer picture of how to get to Atlanta than the NASA photograph.

Likewise, the economic approach to understanding business decision making reduces business problems to their most essential components. Understanding the fundamentals of business decision making provides a way of thinking and analyzing problems that can be applied in a wide range of situations. The tools of analysis that you will learn in managerial economics will apply to today's decisions as well as to decisions you will face in the future.

1.2 MEASURING AND MAXIMIZING ECONOMIC PROFIT

As mentioned earlier, the primary purpose of this text is to show managers how to make decisions that will generate the most profit for their businesses. Profit serves as the score in the "game" of business. It's the amount by which revenues exceed costs. And when costs exceed revenues, the resulting negative profits, or losses, signal owners in no uncertain terms that they are reducing their wealth by owning and running unprofitable businesses. The success of managers' decisions is judged according to a single overriding concern: Are managers' decisions creating higher or lower profits? Managers who can make the largest possible profits not only enrich the owners of firms—and managers are often part or full owners of firms they manage—but they also create for themselves a reputation for profitable decision making that can be worth millions of dollars in executive compensation. Thus it is crucial for managers to understand how the "score" is calculated and how to achieve the highest possible score without getting sidetracked by issues that don't affect the score. It is essential that managers never forget that the goal of the firm is to maximize economic profits. Nothing else matters in the world of business as much as profit does because the value of a business and the wealth of its owners are determined solely by the amount of profits the firm can earn.

After hearing so much news lately about scandals over financial reporting errors, as well as several spectacular cases of management and accounting fraud—think Enron and WorldCom—you probably won't be surprised when we explain it this section why "profits" reported in corporate financial statements generally overstate the profitability of firms. The tendency for overstating profits examined in this section, however, has nothing to do with accounting mistakes or fraud. Indeed, the reason accounting reports of profit (which accountants may call net income, net earnings, or net profit, depending on the circumstances) poorly reflect the actual profitability of firms can be explained by examining the generally accepted accounting practices set forth by professional accounting associations subject to approval from government agencies. Before we can explain why financial accounting procedures overstate business profitability, we must first show you how to measure the economic costs businesses incur when using resources to produce goods or services.

Economic Cost of Using Resources

opportunity cost
What a firm's owners give up to use resources to produce goods or services.

market-supplied resources
Resources owned by others and hired, rented, or leased in resource markets.

As you know, businesses produce the goods or services they sell using a variety of resources or productive inputs. Many kinds of labor services and capital equipment inputs may be employed along with land, buildings, raw materials, energy, financial resources, and managerial talent. The economic cost of using resources to produce a good or service is the *opportunity cost* to the owners of the firm using those resources. The **opportunity cost** of using any kind of resource is what the owners of a business must give up to use the resource.

The method of measuring opportunity costs differs for various kinds of inputs used by businesses. Businesses utilize two kinds of inputs or resources. One of these categories is **market-supplied resources,** which are resources owned by others and hired, rented, or leased by the firm. Examples of resources purchased from others include labor services of skilled and unskilled workers, raw materials purchased in resource markets from commercial suppliers, and capital equipment rented or leased from equipment suppliers. The other category of resources is **owner-supplied resources.** The three most important types of owner-supplied resources are money provided to the business by its owners, time and labor services provided by the firm's owners, and any land, buildings, or capital equipment owned and used by the firm.

owner-supplied resources
Resources owned and used by a firm.

Businesses incur opportunity costs for *both* categories of resources used. Thus, the **total economic cost** of resources used in production is the sum of the opportunity costs of market-supplied resources and the opportunity costs of owner-supplied resources. Total economic cost, then, represents the opportunity cost of all resources used by a firm to produce goods or services.

total economic cost
Sum of opportunity costs of market-supplied resources plus opportunity costs of owner-supplied resources.

The opportunity costs of using *market-supplied* resources are the out-of-pocket monetary payments made to the owners of resources. The monetary payments made for market-supplied inputs are also known as **explicit costs.** For example, one of the resources Dell Computer Co. needs to manufacture its Dimension 8300 model personal computer is an Intel Pentium 4 microprocessor chip. This chip is manufactured by Intel Corp., and Dell can purchase one for $300. Thus Dell's opportunity cost to obtain the computer chip is $300, the monetary payment to the owner of the input. We want to emphasize here that explicit costs are indeed opportunity costs; specifically, it's the amount of money sacrificed by firm owners to get market-supplied resources.

explicit costs
Monetary opportunity costs of using market-supplied resources.

In contrast to explicit costs of using market-supplied resources, there are no out-of-pocket monetary or cash payments made for using owner-supplied resources. The opportunity cost of using an *owner-supplied* resource is the best return the owners of the firm could have received had they taken their own resource to market instead of using it themselves. These nonmonetary opportunity costs of using a firm's own resources are called **implicit costs** because the firm makes no monetary payment to use its own resources. Even though firms do not make explicit monetary payments for using owner-supplied inputs, the opportunity costs of using such inputs are not zero. The opportunity cost is only equal to zero if the market value of the resource is zero, that is, if no other firm would be willing to pay anything for the use of the resource.

implicit costs
Nonmonetary opportunity costs of using owner-supplied resources.

Even though businesses incur numerous kinds of implicit costs, we will focus our attention here on the three most important types of implicit costs mentioned earlier: (1) the opportunity cost of cash provided to a firm by its owners, which accountants refer to as **equity capital;** (2) the opportunity cost of using land or capital owned by the firm; and (3) the opportunity cost of the owner's time spent managing the firm or working for the firm in some other capacity. For more than 70 years, these implicit costs have been the center of controversy over how accountants should measure the costs of using owner-supplied resources. We will have more to say about this issue in our later discussion of measuring business profit, as well as in Illustration 1.2. Let's first look at examples of each of these implicit costs.

equity capital
Money provided to businesses by the owners.

ILLUSTRATION 1.2

The Sarbanes-Oxley Act
Will It Close the GAAP between Economic and
Accounting Profit?

The spectacular crash of Enron in the fall of 2001 was
the largest scandal in a recent series of corporate scandals that included such large firms as WorldCom,
Sunbeam, Waste Management, Xerox, and Global
Crossing, all of which involved executive malfeasance
and manipulation of financial statements. Congress re-
acted during the summer of 2002 by passing the Sarbanes-Oxley Act, which gave the federal government
substantial new authority to regulate the auditing of
corporate financial statements with the aim of reducing fraudulent reports of accounting profits. While Sarbanes-Oxley primarily focuses on detecting and
preventing fraud via improved auditing, the act has
also rekindled interest in a long-standing conceptual
disagreement between economists and accountants
concerning how to properly measure profits. As we
have emphasized in this chapter, accountants follow
reporting rules known as generally accepted accounting principles, or GAAP, which do not allow most
kinds of implicit costs of owner-supplied resources to
be deducted from revenues. Failure to deduct these
implicit costs causes accounting measures of profit—

variously called net earnings, earnings after tax, net income, operating profit, and net profit on financial
statements—to overstate economic profit, which subtracts all costs of resources used by businesses.

A number of authorities in the fields of finance and
accounting believe Sarbanes-Oxley focuses too much
attention and regulatory effort on reducing fraud. They
believe the real problem stems from accounting rules
that poorly measure the profitability of businesses.
Robert Bartley, one of several experts who have recently contributed their opinions on the subject, offers
the following observation:

> For while there has been some cheating and corner-
> cutting, the real problem with corporate reporting is con-
> ceptual. EPS, the familiar earnings per share [accounting
> profit divided by the number of outstanding shares of
> common stock], is supposed to measure corporate profit,
> as determined by GAAP, or generally accepted account-
> ing principles. But economists have long recognized that
> profit is . . . by no means the same thing as accounting
> profit.[1]

This same concern is amplified by G. Bennett Stewart
in his commentary on the Sarbanes-Oxley Act:

> The real problem [causing the recent accounting scan-
> dals] is that earnings and earnings per share (EPS), as

Initially, and then later as firms grow and mature, owners of businesses—single
proprietorships, partnerships, and corporations alike—usually provide some
amount of money or cash to get their businesses going and to keep them running.
This equity capital is an owner-supplied resource and entails an opportunity cost
equal to the best return this money could earn for its owner in some other investment of comparable risk. Suppose, for example, investors use $20 million of their
own money to start a firm of their own. Further suppose this group could take the
$20 million to the venture capital market and earn a return of 12 percent annually
at approximately the same level of risk incurred by using the money in its own
business. Thus the owners sacrifice $2.4 million (= 0.12 × $20 million) annually by
providing equity capital to the firm they own. If you don't think this is a real cost,
then be sure to read Illustration 1.2.

Now let's illustrate the implicit cost of using land or capital owned by the firm.
Consider Alpha Corporation and Beta Corporation, two manufacturing firms that
produce a particular good. They are in every way identical, with one exception:
The owner of Alpha Corp. rents the building in which the good is produced; the

measured according to GAAP, are unreliable measures of corporate performance and stock-market value. Accountants simply are not counting what counts or measuring what matters.[2]

We have discussed in this chapter how to measure the implicit costs of several kinds of owner-supplied resources not presently treated as costs under GAAP: owners' financial capital (i.e., equity capital), physical capital, land, and time spent managing their firms. While all of these types of implicit costs must be treated as costs to bring accounting earnings in line with economic profits, it is the opportunity cost of equity capital, according to Stewart, that generates the greatest single distortion in computing accounting profit:

> The most noteworthy flaw in GAAP is that no charge is deducted from [revenues] for the cost of providing . . . shareholders with a . . . return on their investment . . . The most significant proposed adjustment of GAAP is to deduct the cost of equity capital from net income [i.e., accounting profit]. Failure to deduct it is a stupendous earnings distortion.[3]

He goes on to explain that in 2002 the 500 firms that comprise the Standard and Poor's (S&P) stock index employed about $3 trillion of equity capital, which, at a 10 percent annual opportunity cost of equity capital, represents a resource cost to businesses of $300 billion ($0.10 \times 3 trillion). To put this cost, which GAAP completely ignores, into perspective, Stewart notes that the sum total of all accounting profit for the S&P 500 firms in 2002 was just $118 billion. After subtracting this opportunity cost of equity capital from aggregate accounting profit, the resulting measure of economic profit reveals that these 500 businesses experienced a loss of $182 billion in 2002. As you can now more fully appreciate, the GAAP between economic and accounting profit creates a sizable distortion that, if corrected, can turn a seemingly profitable business, along with its CEO, into a big loser!

[1]Robert L. Bartley, "Thinking Things Over: Economic vs. Accounting Profit," *The Wall Street Journal,* June 2, 2003, p. A23.

[2]G. Bennett Stewart III, "Commentary: Why Smart Managers Do Dumb Things," *The Wall Street Journal,* June 2, 2003, p. A18.

[3]Ibid.

owner of Beta Corp. inherited the building the firm uses and therefore pays no rent. Which firm has the higher costs of production? The costs are the same, even though Beta makes no explicit payment for rent. The reason the costs are the same is that using the building to produce goods costs the owner of Beta the amount of income that could have been earned had the building been leased at the prevailing rent. Since these two buildings are the same, presumably the market rentals would be the same. In other words, Alpha incurred an explicit cost for the use of its building, whereas Beta incurred an implicit cost for the use of its building.[1] Regardless of whether the payment is explicit or implicit, the opportunity cost of using the building resource is the same for both firms.

-----

[1]Alternatively, Beta's sacrificed return can be measured as the amount the owner could earn if the resource (the building) were sold and the payment invested at the market rate of interest. The sacrificed interest is the implicit cost when a resource is sold and the proceeds invested. This measure of implicit cost is frequently the same as the foregone rental or lease income, but if they are not equal, the true opportunity cost is the *best* alternative return.

We should note that the opportunity cost of using owner-supplied inputs may not bear any relation to the amount the firm paid to acquire the input. The opportunity cost reflects the current market value of the resource. If the firm paid $1 million for a plot of land two years ago but the market value of the land has since fallen to $500,000, the implicit cost now is the best return that could be earned if the land is sold for $500,000, not $1 million (which would be impossible under the circumstances), and the proceeds are invested. If the $500,000 could be invested at 6 percent annually, the implicit cost is $30,000 (= 0.06 × $500,000) per year. You should be careful to note that the implicit cost is *not* what the resource could be sold for ($500,000) but rather it is the best return sacrificed each year ($30,000).

Finally, consider the value of firm owners' time spent managing their own businesses. Presumably, if firm owners aren't managing their businesses or working for their firms in other capacities, they could obtain jobs with some other firms, possibly as managers. The salary that could be earned in an alternative occupation is an implicit cost that should be considered as part of the total cost of production because it is an opportunity cost to these owners. The implicit cost of an owner's time spent managing a firm or working for the firm in some other capacity is frequently, though not always, the same as the payment that would be necessary to hire an equivalent manager or worker if the owner does not work for the firm.

We wish to stress again that, even though no explicit monetary payment is made for the use of owner-supplied resources, $1 worth of implicit costs is no less (and no more) of an opportunity cost of using resources than $1 worth of explicit costs. Consequently, both kinds of opportunity costs, explicit and implicit opportunity costs, are added together to get the total economic cost of resource use. We now summarize this important discussion on measuring the economic costs of using resources in a principle:

▣ **Principle** The opportunity cost of using resources is the amount the firm gives up by using these resources. Opportunity costs can be either explicit costs or implicit costs. Explicit costs are the costs of using market-supplied resources, which are the monetary payments to hire, rent, or lease resources owned by others. Implicit costs are the costs of using owner-supplied resources, which are the greatest earnings forgone from using resources owned by the firm in the firm's own production process. Total economic cost is the sum of explicit and implicit costs.

Figure 1.1 illustrates the relations set forth in this principle. Now that we have shown you how to measure the cost of using resources, we can explain the difference between economic profit and accounting profit.

Economic Profit versus Accounting Profit

economic profit
The difference between total revenue and total economic cost.

Economic profit is the difference between total revenue and total economic cost. Recall from our previous discussion that total economic cost measures the opportunity costs of *all* the resources used by the business, both market-supplied and owner-supplied resources, and thus:

$$\text{Economic profit} = \text{Total revenue} - \text{Total economic cost}$$
$$= \text{Total revenue} - \text{Explicit costs} - \text{Implicit costs}$$

FIGURE 1.1
Economic Cost of Using
Resources

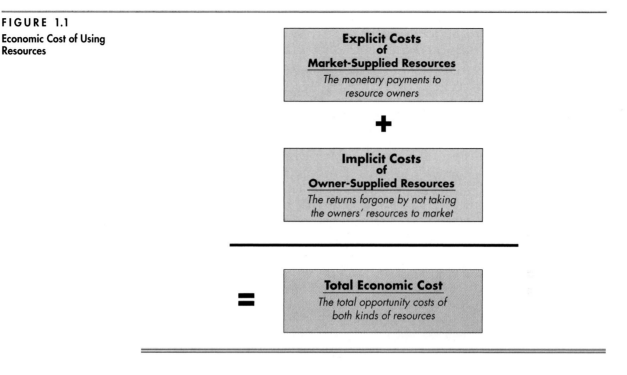

Economic profit, when it arises, belongs to the owners of the firm and will increase the wealth of the owners. When revenues fail to cover total economic cost, economic profit is negative, and the loss must be paid for out of the wealth of the owners.[2]

When accountants calculate business profitability for financial reports, they follow a set of rules known as "generally accepted accounting principles" or GAAP. If you have taken courses in accounting, you know that GAAP provides accountants with detailed measurement rules for developing accounting information presented in financial statements, such as balance sheets, cash flow statements, and income statements. The Securities and Exchange Commission (SEC) along with the Financial Accounting Standards Board (FASB), a professional accounting organization, work together to construct the detailed rules of GAAP. To understand the importance of GAAP for our present discussion, you only need to know that GAAP rules do not allow accountants to deduct most types of implicit costs for the purposes of calculating taxable accounting profit.

----

[2]In Part IV of this text, we will continue our examination of economic profit. There we discuss how economic profit serves as an inducement for new firms to enter markets when profits are positive and for existing firms to exit markets when profits are negative. And, in Chapter 11, we will explain why firms earning zero economic profit are said to be earning just a "normal" profit.

accounting profit
The difference between total revenue and explicit costs.

Accounting profit, then, differs from economic profit because accounting profit does not subtract from total revenue the implicit costs of using resources. **Accounting profit** is the difference between total revenue and explicit costs:

Accounting profit = Total revenue − Explicit costs

Depending on the type of financial statement and where it appears in a statement, accounting profit goes by a variety of names such as income, net income, operating income, net profit, earnings, or net earnings.

As you can see, when firms employ owner-supplied resources, the resulting implicit costs are not subtracted from total revenue and the accounting profits reported in financial statements overstate business profitability. All three types of implicit costs discussed earlier are ignored by accountants.[3] We want to stress, however, that when financial accountants omit these implicit costs from financial reports, they are following generally accepted rules set forth by the FASB and SEC. The practice of omitting most kinds of implicit costs, which can be quite large for many firms, is widely recognized by managers, shareholders, government officials, and financial analysts, who make lucrative careers converting the information in financial accounting statements into measures more closely resembling economic profit (see Illustration 1.2).

Business owners, of course, must bear all costs of using resources, both explicit and implicit, regardless of which costs may be deducted for accounting purposes. Since all costs matter to owners of a firm, you should now clearly understand why maximizing economic profit, rather than accounting profit, is the objective of the firm's owners. And, as we explain in the following section, the value of a firm is determined by the amount of economic profit, rather than accounting profit the firm is expected to earn in the current period and all future periods. As you now see, it is economic profit that matters in business decision making, so in the rest of this chapter and in later chapters whenever we refer to "profit," we will mean *economic* profit. We will now summarize the relation between economic and accounting profits in a principle:

Principle Economic profit is the difference between total revenue and total economic cost:

Economic profit = Total revenue − Total economic cost

= Total revenue − Explicit costs − Implicit costs

Accounting profit differs from economic profit because accounting profit does not subtract from total revenue the implicit costs of using resources:

Accounting profit = Total revenue − Explicit costs

 Since the owners of firms must cover the costs of all resources used by the firm, maximizing economic profit, rather than accounting profit, is the objective of the firm's owners.

---

[3]One of the implicit costs that accountants do deduct when computing accounting profit is the cost of depreciation of capital assets, which is the reduction in the value of capital equipment from the ordinary wear and tear of usage. As you may know from taking accounting courses, businesses have several methods to choose from when computing depreciation costs, and some of these methods tend to overstate the actual value of depreciation in the early years of equipment ownership.

Notice to students: The arrows in the left margin throughout this text are directing you to work the enumerated Technical Problems at the end of the chapter. Be sure to check the answers provided for you at the end of the book *before* proceeding to the next section of a chapter. We have carefully designed the Technical Problems to guide your learning in a step-by-step process.

Maximizing the Value of the Firm

As we stressed in the preceding discussion and principle, owners of a firm, whether the shareholders of a corporation or the owner of a single proprietorship, are best served by management decisions that seek to maximize the profit of the firm. In general, when managers maximize economic profit, they are also maximizing the value of the firm, which is the price someone will pay for the firm. How much will someone pay for a firm? Suppose you are going to buy a business on January 1 and sell it on December 31. If the firm is going to make an economic profit of $50,000 during the year, you are willing to pay no more than $50,000 (in monthly payments matching the flow of profit) to own the firm for that year. Since other potential buyers are *also* willing to pay up to $50,000, the firm likely sells for very nearly or exactly the amount of the economic profit earned in a year.

When a firm earns a stream of economic profit for a number of years in the future, the **value of a firm**—the price for which it can be sold—is the present value of the future economic profits expected to be generated by the firm:

value of a firm
The price for which the firm can be sold, which equals the present value of future profits.

$$\text{Value of a firm} = \frac{\pi_1}{(1 + r)} + \frac{\pi_2}{(1 + r)^2} + \cdots + \frac{\pi_T}{(1 + r)^T} = \sum_{t=1}^{T} \frac{\pi_t}{(1 + r)^t}$$

where π_t is the economic profit expected in period t, r is the risk-adjusted discount rate, and T is the number of years in the life of a firm.[4] Since future profit is not known with certainty, the value of a firm is calculated using the profit *expected* to be earned in future periods. The greater the variation in possible future profits, the less a buyer is willing to pay for those risky future profits. The risk associated with not knowing future profits of a firm is accounted for by adding a **risk premium** to the (riskless) discount rate. A risk premium increases the discount rate, thereby decreasing the present value of profit received in the future, in order to compensate investors for the risk of not knowing with certainty the future value of profits. The more uncertain the future profits, the higher the risk-adjusted discount rate used by investors in valuing a firm, and the more heavily future profits will be discounted.

risk premium
An increase in the discount rate to compensate investors for uncertainty about future profits.

---

[4]Since a dollar of profit received in the future is worth less than a dollar received now, multi-period decision making employs the concept of present value. Present value is the value at the present time of a payment or stream of payments to be received (or paid) some time in the future. The appendix at the end of this chapter reviews the mathematics of present value computations, a topic usually covered in an introductory course in finance or accounting.

ILLUSTRATION 1.3

Is Baseball Going Broke?
Accounting Profits vs. Market Values

During the summer of 2000, a "Blue Ribbon Panel" commissioned by Major League Baseball issued its final report on the financial health of the league's 30 baseball teams. The panel reached the bleak conclusion that Major League Baseball is going broke because teams located in large, profitable geographic markets attract and keep top players while teams located in small, unprofitable markets cannot attract and keep the best players. According to the panel, the resulting lopsided distribution of talented players makes baseball games less competitive and less exciting for baseball fans. The panel concluded that only a significant increase in revenue sharing—baseball's arrangement requiring rich, successful teams to give some of their revenue to financially troubled, losing teams—will prevent fans from losing interest in the sport.

Two statistics editors at *Forbes* magazine, Michael Ozanian and Kurt Badenhausen, criticized the Blue Ribbon Panel's conclusion that baseball is going broke.

In a commentary in *The Wall Street Journal*, they argued that the panel's concern about the future profitability of baseball teams is misleading for two reasons. First, the panel based their analysis on accounting profits of the major league teams. Ozanian and Badenhausen worried that accounting profit can be manipulated too easily. They quoted baseball's current president Paul Beeston, who said, "Under generally accepted accounting principles, I can turn a $4 million profit into a $2 million loss and I can get every national accounting firm to agree with me." Second, the baseball panel should have examined the trend in the *market values* of Major League Baseball teams rather than *past* accounting profits in order to get an accurate picture of the financial *prospects* for major league team owners.

Ozanian and Badenhausen noted that team values increased from an average value of $115 million per team in 1995 to $233 million per team in 2000. According to their calculations, not a single team decreased in market value. They attributed rising team values to new stadiums and escalating fees for television broadcast privileges. As an example of this trend, they noted

◻ **Principle** The value of a firm is the price for which it can be sold, and that price is equal to the present value of the expected future profits of the firm. The larger (smaller) the risk associated with future profits, the higher (lower) the risk-adjusted discount rate used to compute the value of the firm, and the lower (higher) will be the value of the firm.

The Equivalence of Value Maximization and Profit Maximization

Owners of a firm want the managers to make business decisions that will maximize the value of the firm, which, as we discussed in the previous subsection, is the sum of the discounted expected profits in current and future periods. As a general rule, then, a manager maximizes the value of the firm by making decisions that maximize expected profit in each period. That is, single-period profit maximization and maximizing the value of the firm are usually equivalent means to the same end: Maximizing profit in each period will result in the maximum value of the firm, and maximizing the value of the firm requires maximizing profit in each period.

◻ **Principle** If cost and revenue conditions in any period are independent of decisions made in other time periods, a manager will maximize the value of a firm (the present value of the firm) by making decisions that maximize profit in every single time period.

that the owners of the San Francisco Giants, who suffered $94 million in negative accounting profits over the 1995–2000 period, saw the team's value increase by 12 percent going into the 2000 season—the season in which the team began playing in its new Pacific Bell Park. "Based on asset appreciations, the national pastime resembles a growth industry, not one in dire straits," asserted Ozanian and Badenhausen.

As we explain in this chapter, the market value of a firm—the price for which it can be sold—is the present value of the *future* economic profits buyers expect the firm to generate. You can be sure that buyers of baseball teams pay careful attention to all factors that might affect future economic profits of baseball teams. If the prices of teams are rising (falling), then buyers' expectations about future economic profits in baseball are also rising (falling).[a] Thus the current market value of a baseball team is unrelated to the team's accounting (or economic) profit in past years.

Baseball is no different from any other industry. The prospect of declining economic profits in the future will cause market values of firms to decrease (for a given risk-adjusted discount rate). If reports that team values increased during the five-year period 1995–2000 are correct, it would be difficult to believe Major League Baseball is going broke. In short, one should be suspicious of gloomy forecasts for an industry if many of the firms in the industry are experiencing rising market values. Baseball's Blue Ribbon Panel seems to have struck out swinging at an accounting profit curve ball.

[a]The market value of a baseball team can also change if buyers change the discount rate they use to compute the present value of future profits. In the present situation, the sources of higher profits—new stadiums and rising television broadcast fees—might also reduce the risk associated with future profits, so that buyers would likely use a *lower* risk-adjusted discount rate to compute the value of baseball teams. Lower risk-adjusted discount rates would then further increase team values.

Source: Michael K. Ozanian and Kurt Badenhausen, "Commentary: Baseball Going Broke? Don't Believe It," *The Wall Street Journal*, July 27, 2000, p. A24.

The equivalence of single-period profit maximization and maximizing the value of the firm holds only when the revenue and cost conditions in one time period are independent of revenue and costs in future time periods. When today's decisions affect profits in future time periods, price or output decisions that maximize profit in each (single) time period will not maximize the value of the firm. Two examples of these kinds of situations occur when (1) a firm's employees become more productive in future periods by producing more output in earlier periods—a case of learning by doing—and (2) current production has the effect of increasing cost in the future—as in extractive industries such as mining and oil production. Thus, if increasing current output has a positive effect on future revenue and profit, a value-maximizing manager selects an output level that is *greater* than the level that maximizes profit in a single time period. Alternatively, if current production has the effect of increasing cost in the future, maximizing the value of the firm requires a *lower* current output than maximizing single-period profit.

Despite these examples of inconsistencies between the two types of maximization, it is generally the case that there is little difference between the conclusions of single-period profit maximization (the topic of most of this text) and present value maximization. Thus single-period profit maximization is generally the rule for managers to follow when trying to maximize the value of a firm.

1.3 SEPARATION OF OWNERSHIP AND CONTROL

When the manager of a firm is also the owner of a business, what is good for the owner is, of course, good for the manager. But most large business organizations are run by professional management teams that possess little or no equity ownership in the business. When the owners and managers are not the same people, conflicts can arise between the firm's owners and its managers.

These conflicts arise because of differences between the objectives of the owners and the managers. As already explained, owners want managers to maximize the value of the firm, which is usually accomplished by maximizing profit. Managers, when they have little or no ownership in a business, may pursue objectives that are not compatible with earning the maximum possible amount of profit for the owners. One profit-reducing objective managers are thought to pursue is the consumption of excessive or lavish perquisites. It is an unusual manager indeed who would not like to have the company pay for a lavish office, memberships in the most exclusive country clubs, extraordinary levels of life and health insurance, a limousine and chauffeur, and, if possible, a Challenger corporate jet. Another profit-reducing objective of managers is the pursuit of market share. Some managers are driven to have the firm be the largest, rather than the most profitable, firm in its industry. While maximizing the growth rate of a firm might be consistent with maximizing profit in some situations, as a general rule, pricing and output decisions that create the biggest, fastest-growing companies do not also maximize the value of the firm. In many industries, the most profitable firms are not the largest or fastest-growing ones, as Illustration 1.4 shows.

The Principal–Agent Problem

principal–agent problem
The conflict that arises when the goals of management (the agent) do not match the goals of the owner (the principal).

A principal in an agreement contracts with an agent to perform tasks designed to further the principal's objectives. A **principal–agent problem** arises when the agent has objectives different from those of the principal, and the principal either has difficulty enforcing the contract with the agent or finds it too difficult and costly to monitor the agent to verify that he or she is furthering the principal's objectives. Although there are a multitude of examples of the principal–agent problem in society, we are concerned here with the owner–manager problem, particularly as it applies to the corporate form of business organization. In corporations, shareholders are obviously the principals, and the managers are the agents.

moral hazard
Exists when either party to an agreement has an incentive not to abide by all provisions of the agreement and one party cannot cost effectively monitor the agreement.

The agency problem occurs because of moral hazard. **Moral hazard** exists when either party to an agreement has an incentive not to abide by all the provisions of the agreement *and* one party cannot cost effectively find out if the other party is abiding by the agreement or cannot enforce the agreement even when that information is available. Although moral hazard arises in a large number of principal–agent agreements in business, we are concerned here only with moral hazard in the case of the firm's management working for shareholders.

You may be wondering why the shareholders don't simply tell the managers to maximize the value of the firm and, if they don't comply, replace them with new managers. This process is a lot more complex and difficult than it appears at first glance. A large, modern corporation is an extremely complicated institution. The upper management of such a firm is much more familiar with the functioning of the corporation than most or even all of the stockholders. Stockholders would not even know, in many cases, whether management is or is not attempting to maximize the value of the firm or its profits, especially when business is good and the price of the stock is rising. Stockholders get most of their information about the performance of the firm from the managers themselves.

In the case of large corporations, any given shareholder typically holds a relatively small proportion of the total outstanding stock. Stockholders are generally broadly diversified and would have difficulty organizing into a group that could actually affect the firm's policies. Furthermore, an individual stockholder would probably not have the incentive to find the necessary information about the firm and then attempt to monitor management. The cost of obtaining and processing the required information would be huge, while the benefits to an individual shareholder would be small, even if the monitoring were successful. Shareholders usually have diversified portfolios in which no individual stock looms particularly large, relative to their total holdings. They frequently don't have much of an interest in one particular stock. Therefore, the owners of large corporations have a difficult time policing the managers.

Corporate Control Mechanisms

The discussion of agency problems is not meant to imply that shareholders are completely helpless in the face of managers who aren't doing what the shareholders expect them to do. Rules of corporate governance give shareholders rights that allow them to control managers directly through control measures and indirectly through the board of directors, whose responsibility it is to monitor management. Shareholders themselves, and in partnership with the board of directors, may choose from a variety of mechanisms for controlling agency problems. In addition to the governance methods available to shareholders, several forces outside the firm can also force managers to pursue maximization of the firm's value. We will review only briefly a few of the most important types of mechanisms that can intensify a manager's desire to maximize profit.

Stockholders often try to solve the agency problem by tying managers' compensation to fulfilling the goals of the shareholders. Managers have a greater incentive to make decisions that further the goals of shareholders when managers themselves are shareholders. Equity ownership is considered one of the most effective mechanisms for corporate control, so much so that some professional money managers and large institutional investors refuse to invest in firms whose managers hold little or no equity stake in the firms they manage.

ILLUSTRATION 1.4

Managerial Strategy
Maximize Profit or Maximize Market Share?

Although sports and war metaphors are common in business conversation and management seminars, managers may be reducing the value of their firms by placing too much emphasis on beating their competitors out of market share rather than focusing on making the most profit for their shareholders. In a recent study of managerial strategy, Professors J. Scott Armstrong at the University of Pennsylvania's Wharton School and Fred Collopy at Case Western Reserve University advise CEOs to "keep their eyes on profits, not market share." Armstrong and Collopy discovered that, instead of maximizing profit, many managers make decisions with an eye toward performing well relative to their competitors—a decision-making point of view they refer to as "competitor-oriented."

In their nine-year study of more than 1,000 experienced managers, Armstrong and Collopy found that managers are more likely to abandon the goal of profit maximization when they have greater amounts of information about the performance of their rivals. In the study, managers were asked to choose between two pricing plans for a new product—a low-price and a high-price strategy—and were told the five-year present value of expected profits associated with each strategy. The table in the next column presents two of the "treatments" that were administered to different groups of subjects.

The "base" treatment gives the manager no information about how a rival firm will fare under the two plans, while the "beat" treatment allows the manager to know how a decision will affect a rival. In the base treatment, almost all managers, as expected, chose the most profitable strategy (high price). When given

Net Present Value of Expected Profit over Five Years

	Low-price strategy	High-price strategy
Base treatment:		
Your firm	$40 million	$ 80 million
Beat treatment:		
Your firm	40 million	80 million
Rival firm	20 million	160 million

information about the rival firm's profit, subjects could see the impact of their decision on their rival, and many managers abandoned profit maximization. In the beat treatment, 60 percent chose not to maximize profit (low price). To address the possibility that the subjects were considering longer-term profits, Armstrong and Collopy changed the payoffs to *20-year* present values. The results were the same.

Armstrong and Collopy believe the abandonment of profit as the firm's objective is a consequence of managers having information about a competitor's performance. They discovered that exposing managers to techniques that focus on gaining market share increased the proportion of subjects who abandoned profit maximization. They also found that "executives who had taken strategic-management courses were more likely to make decisions that harmed profitability." These results are impressive because they have been repeated in more than 40 experiments with more than 1,000 subjects.

To see if firms that seek to maximize market share (competitor-oriented firms) tend to be less profitable *over the long run* than firms that pursue profit without concern for market share, Armstrong and Collopy

The members of the board of directors are agents of the shareholders charged with monitoring the decisions of executive managers. But just as managers are agents for owners, so too are directors, and agency problems can arise between directors and shareholders. Many observers believe that the value of the board's monitoring services is enhanced by appointing outsiders—directors not serving on the firm's management team—and by linking directors' compensation to the value

tracked the performance of two groups of firms over a 54-year period. The group of firms that made pricing decisions based on competitor-oriented goals, such as increasing market share, were consistently less profitable over the 54-year period than the group that made pricing decisions to increase profit without regard to market share. Furthermore, companies pursuing market share were found to be less likely to survive: "Four of the six companies that focused strictly on market share (Gulf, American Can, Swift, and National Steel) did not survive. All four profit-oriented companies (DuPont, General Electric, Union Carbide, and Alcoa) did."

Armstrong and Collopy conclude that the use of competitor-oriented objectives is detrimental to profitability: "We believe that microeconomic theory, with its emphasis on profit maximization, is the most sensible course of action for firms; that is, managers should focus directly on profits." To encourage managers to keep their focus on profit and *not* on market share, they offer the following specific advice:

- Do not use market share as an objective.
- Avoid using sports and military analogies because they foster a competitor orientation.
- Do not use management science techniques that are oriented to maximizing market share, such as portfolio planning matrices and experience curve analysis.
- Design information systems to focus attention on the firm's performance, as measured by profits.
- Beware that improvements in the ability to measure market share—specifically through scanner data collected at checkouts—may lead to a stronger focus on market share and less focus on profitability.

In a recent book examining the business strategies of Southwest Airlines, the authors of the book focus on the decisions made by the airline's CEO, Herb Kelleher. In a section titled "Say Nuts to Market Share," Kelleher explains the role that market share plays at Southwest Airlines. Kelleher says

> Market share has nothing to do with profitability . . . Market share says we just want to be big; we don't care if we make money doing it . . . That is really incongruous if profitability is your purpose.

The book goes on to say that Kelleher believes "confusing the two concepts (increasing profit and increasing market share) has derailed many firms that were otherwise on track in fulfilling their fundamental purpose (maximizing profit and firm value)." Perhaps it was only a coincidence, but we should mention that the value of Southwest Airlines tripled during the early to mid-1990s.

As we emphasize in this chapter, shareholders wish to see the value of the firm maximized. A manager bent on being the biggest airline or biggest auto rental agency may fail to be the most profitable airline or auto rental agency. Between advances in shareholders' willingness and ability to fire CEOs and the active market for corporate control (mergers, acquisitions, and takeovers), a manager who fails to pursue primarily the maximization of profit may have a short career.

Sources: J. Scott Armstrong and Fred Collopy, "Competitor Orientation: Effects of Objectives and Information on Managerial Decisions and Profitability," *Journal of Marketing Research*, May 1996, pp. 188–99; "The Profitability of Winning," *Chief Executive*, June 1, 1994, p. 60; Kevin Freiberg and Jackie Freiberg, *Nuts!: Southwest Airlines' Crazy Recipe for Business and Personal Success* (New York: Broadway Books, 1995), p. 49.

of the firm. The effectiveness of a board of directors is undermined when business decisions are so complex that the board cannot reliably judge whether a decision furthers shareholder interests and when the CEO plays a strong role in selection of the board members.

Another method of creating incentives for managers to make value-maximizing decisions involves corporate policy on debt financing. A policy that emphasizes

ILLUSTRATION 1.5

Do Profits Matter in the Information Age?

In 1999 many economists and most financial analysts were confounded by skyrocketing values of firms in the high-technology sector of the U.S. economy. The year-long run-up in market valuations of Internet companies, the so-called dot-coms, as well as some new software firms resulted in a stock market "bubble" in which many of these high-technology firms traded at values far exceeding the present values of their expected future profits. Amazingly, some of these highly valued dot-coms had never earned any revenues at all. The "bubble" seemed to undermine fundamental economic principles governing the market values of firms. Practically every day in the news, a financial guru offered another explanation for the "new economics" of the Information Age.

During this dot-com frenzy on Wall Street, investment bankers and venture capitalists frequently clamored, "Profits don't matter anymore." Pursuit of market share was hailed as the replacement for old-fashioned, outdated pursuit of profit. Greg Bohlen of investment house J. C. Bradford & Co. summed up the "new thinking" about surviving on the Web in a *Wall Street Journal* article: "When you're in a fast-paced world (and) the barriers to entry are very low, profits don't matter—it becomes market share." For some analysts, the idea that profits matter to owners of firms seemed destined to become one more case of road kill on the Information Superhighway.

For nearly a year, instructors of economics and finance faced inquisitive students who asked, "Why don't profits matter anymore?" Students were told that Internet firms and other high-tech firms were no different from other firms: Either economic profit would become a more certain part of these firms' futures or their market valuations would fall. If the dot-coms continued making losses without any realistic prospects for future profits, investors would eventually revise downward their expectations about future economic profits, and the firms' values would fall.

By the end of 1999, prospects for economic profits failed to materialize for many, if not most, of the Internet firms that experienced huge increases in their market values. In mid-April 2000 the "bubble" finally burst. *The Wall Street Journal* described the jolting experience of Red Hat Software, Inc., a distributor of Linux operating-system software: "Like many high-flying tech (firms), Red Hat has been crushed . . . Its Friday 4 P.M. price of $25.0625 was 84 percent off its high. Among the reasons cited by Wall Street analysts: Losses widened to $19.2 million . . . "

Rather than view the sharp declines in firms' values as a natural adjustment process for correcting situations in which the present value of expected future profits does not justify current market valuations, many financial analysts instead interpreted the collapse in high-technology stock prices as something new and seemingly different. William Glynn, director of Southeast Interactive Technology Funds, said in *The Wall Street Journal:* "The world has changed. Your concept company? Forget it. Your company with no revenue that had a valuation of $30 million? Today it's worth half that." The author of *The Wall Street Journal* article also seemed to view the April crash as a fundamental change in the economic order of markets: "Remember that world (in which profits don't matter)? It has vanished now. Profits suddenly matter a lot, especially to the dot-coms and software companies whose shares were crushed in the great April sell-off. Sadly, many of the companies . . . are still profitless . . . "

We want to emphasize that the decisive April 2000 sell-off of technology firms was not a change in the way the world works. It was no surprise that sharp stock price declines punished firms that remained profitless or that earned less profit than expected. The only surprise was the rather long period of time that investors tolerated economic losses before they adjusted downward their expectations of future profits. As we told you at the beginning of this chapter, economic principles and analytical methods do not quickly become outdated. Expected future profits continue to matter, even in this Information Age.

Source: Bernard Wysocki Jr., "The Outlook," *The Wall Street Journal,* May 1, 2000, p. 1.

financing corporate investments with debt rather than equity—selling shares of common stock to raise financial capital—can further the interests of shareholders in several ways. First, debt financing makes bankruptcy possible, since firms cannot go bankrupt if they have no debt. Thus managers who value their employment have an additional incentive to increase profitability in order to lower the probability of bankruptcy. Second, managers face less pressure to generate revenues to cover the cost of investments if the payments are dividends to shareholders, which they can choose to defer or neglect altogether, rather than if the payments are installments on a loan. Finally, lenders have an incentive to monitor managers of firms that borrow money from them. Thus banks and other lenders may make it difficult for managers to consume excessive perks or make unprofitable investments.

Corporate takeovers are also an important possible solution to the conflict between shareholders and managers who do not maximize the value of the firm. If the value of the firm is less with the present set of managers than it would be with another, there is a profit incentive for others to acquire the firm and replace the management team with a new set of managers. For example, if the firm has a poorly designed compensation scheme that fails to motivate managers to maximize profits, another company, or group of corporate raiders, believing its management could do a better job, might take over the firm by purchasing enough shares to take control. Even though most of the media, many politicians, and certainly the managers of the takeover targets dislike takeovers, frequently called "hostile," takeovers act as a check on the power of incompetent managers to create inefficiency and also on the power of managers who are less interested in maximizing profits, since they are not major owners, than they are in expanding their corporate domain. Thus takeovers can sometimes resolve to some extent the conflict between managers and shareholders.

1.4 MARKET STRUCTURE AND MANAGERIAL DECISION MAKING

As we mentioned earlier, managers cannot expect to succeed without understanding how market forces shape the firm's ability to earn profit. A particularly important aspect of managerial decision making is the pricing decision. The structure of the market in which the firm operates can limit the ability of a manager to raise the price of the firm's product without losing a substantial amount, possibly even all, of its sales.

Not all managers have the power to set the price of the firm's product. In some industries, each firm in the industry makes up a relatively small portion of total sales and produces a product that is identical to the output produced by all the rest of the firms in the industry. The price of the good in such a situation is not determined by any one firm or manager but, rather, by the impersonal forces of the marketplace—the intersection of market demand and supply, as you will see in the next chapter. If a manager attempts to raise the price above the market-determined

price-taker
A firm that cannot set the price of the product it sells, since price is determined strictly by the market forces of demand and supply.

price-setting firm
A firm that can raise its price without losing all of its sales.

market power
A firm's ability to raise price without losing all sales.

price, the firm loses all its sales to the other firms in the industry. After all, buyers do not care from whom they buy this identical product, and they would be unwilling to pay more than the going market price for the product. In such a situation, the firm is a **price-taker** and cannot set the price of the product it sells. We will discuss price-taking firms in detail in Chapter 11, and you will see that the demand curve facing a price-taking firm is horizontal at the price determined by market forces.

In contrast to managers of price-taking firms, the manager of a **price-setting firm** does set the price of the product. A price-setting firm has the ability to raise its price without losing all sales because the product is somehow differentiated from rivals' products or perhaps because the geographic market area in which the product is sold has only one, or just a few, sellers of the product. At higher prices the firm sells less of its product, and at lower prices the firm sells more of its product. The ability to raise price without losing all sales is called **market power,** a subject we will examine more thoroughly in Chapters 13 and 14. Before we discuss some of the differing market structures to be analyzed in later chapters of this text, we first want you to consider the fundamental nature and purpose of a market.

What Is a Market?

market
Any arrangement through which buyers and sellers exchange anything of value.

A **market** is any arrangement through which buyers and sellers exchange final goods or services, resources used for production, or, in general, anything of value. The arrangement may be a location and time, such as a commercial bank from 9 A.M. until 6 P.M. on weekdays only, an agricultural produce market every first Tuesday of the month, a trading "pit" at a commodity exchange during trading hours, or even the parking lot of a stadium an hour before game time when ticket scalpers sometimes show up to sell tickets to sporting events. An arrangement may also be something other than a physical location and time, such as a classified ad in a newspaper or a website on the Internet. You should view the concept of a market quite broadly, particularly since advances in technology create new ways of bringing buyers and sellers together.

Markets are arrangements that reduce the cost of making transactions. Buyers wishing to purchase something must spend valuable time and other resources finding sellers, gathering information about prices and qualities, and ultimately making the purchase itself. Sellers wishing to sell something must spend valuable resources locating buyers (or pay a fee to sales agents to do so), gathering information about potential buyers (e.g., verifying creditworthiness or legal entitlement to buy), and finally closing the deal. These costs of making a transaction happen, which are additional costs of doing business over and above the price paid, are known as **transaction costs.** Buyers and sellers use markets to facilitate exchange because markets lower the transaction costs for both parties. To understand the meaning of this seemingly abstract point, consider two alternative ways of selling a used car that you own. One way to find a buyer for your car is to canvass your neighborhood, knocking on doors until you find a person willing to pay a price

transaction costs
Costs of making a transaction happen, other than the price of the good or service itself.

you are willing to accept. This will likely require a lot of your time and perhaps even involve buying a new pair of shoes. Alternatively, you could run an advertisement in the local newspaper describing your car and stating the price you are willing to accept for it. This method of selling the car involves a market—the newspaper ad. Even though you must pay a fee to run the ad, you choose to use this market because the transaction costs will be lower by advertising in the newspaper than by searching door to door.

Different Market Structures

market structure
Market characteristics that determine the economic environment in which a firm operates.

Market structure is a set of market characteristics that determines the economic environment in which a firm operates. As we now explain, the structure of a market governs the degree of pricing power possessed by a manager, both in the short run and in the long run. The list of economic characteristics needed to describe a market is actually rather short:

- *The number and size of the firms operating in the market:* A manager's ability to raise the price of the firm's product without losing most, if not all, of its buyers depends in part on the number and size of sellers in a market. If there are a large number of sellers with each producing just a small fraction of the total sales in a market, no single firm can influence market price by changing its production level. Alternatively, when the total output of a market is produced by one or a few firms with relatively large market shares, a single firm can cause the price to rise by restricting its output and to fall by increasing its output, as long as no other firm in the market decides to prevent the price from changing by suitably adjusting its own output level.

- *The degree of product differentiation among competing producers:* If sellers all produce products that consumers perceive to be identical, then buyers will never need to pay even a penny more for a particular firm's product than the price charged by the rest of the firms. By differentiating a product either through real differences in product design or through advertised image, a firm may be able to raise its price above its rivals' prices if consumers find the product differences sufficiently desirable to pay the higher price.

- *The likelihood of new firms entering a market when incumbent firms are earning economic profits:* When firms in a market earn economic profits, other firms will learn of this return in excess of opportunity costs and will try to enter the market. Once enough firms enter a market, price will be bid down sufficiently to eliminate any economic profit. Even firms with some degree of market power cannot keep prices higher than opportunity costs for long periods when entry is relatively easy.

Microeconomists have analyzed firms operating in a number of different market structures. Not surprisingly, economists have names for these market structures: perfect competition, monopoly, monopolistic competition, and oligopoly.

Although each of these market structures is examined in detail later in this text, we briefly discuss each one now to show you how market structure shapes a manager's pricing decisions.

In *perfect competition,* a large number of relatively small firms sell an undifferentiated product in a market with no barriers to the entry of new firms. Managers of firms operating in perfectly competitive markets are price-takers with no market power. At the price determined entirely by the market forces of demand and supply, they decide how much to produce in order to maximize profit. In the absence of entry barriers, any economic profit earned at the market-determined price will vanish as new firms enter and drive the price down to the average cost of production. Many of the markets for agricultural goods and other commodities traded on national and international exchanges closely match the characteristics of perfect competition.

In a *monopoly* market, a single firm, protected by some kind of barrier to entry, produces a product for which no close substitutes are available. A monopoly is a price-setting firm. The degree of market power enjoyed by the monopoly is determined by the ability of consumers to find imperfect substitutes for the monopolist's product. The higher the price charged by the monopolist, the more willing are consumers to buy other products. The existence of a barrier to entry allows a monopolist to raise its price without concern that economic profit will attract new firms. As you will see in Chapter 12, examples of true monopolies are rare.

In markets characterized by *monopolistic competition,* a large number of firms that are small relative to the total size of the market produce differentiated products without the protection of barriers to entry. The only difference between perfect competition and monopolistic competition is the product differentiation that gives monopolistic competitors some degree of market power; they are price-setters rather than price-takers. As in perfectly competitive markets, the absence of entry barriers ensures that any economic profit will eventually be bid away by new entrants. The toothpaste market provides one example of monopolistic competition. The many brands and kinds of toothpaste are close, but not perfect, substitutes. Toothpaste manufacturers differentiate their toothpastes by using different flavorings, abrasives, whiteners, fluoride levels, and other ingredients, along with a substantial amount of advertising designed to create brand loyalty.

In each of the three market structures discussed here, managers do not need to consider the reaction of rival firms to a price change. A monopolist has no rivals; a monopolistic competitor is small enough relative to the total market that its price changes will not usually cause rival firms to retaliate with price changes of their own; and, of course, a perfectly competitive firm is a price-taker and would not change its price from the market-determined price. In contrast, in the case of an *oligopoly* market, just a few firms produce most or all of the market output, so any one firm's pricing policy will have a significant effect on the sales of other firms in the market. This interdependence of oligopoly firms means that actions by any one firm in the market will have an effect on the sales and profits of the other firms. As you will see in Chapter 13, the strategic decision making in oligopoly markets is the most complex of all decision-making situations.

Globalization of Markets

globalization of markets
Economic integration of markets located in nations around the world.

During the 1990s, businesses in many nations experienced a surge in the **globalization of markets,** a phrase that generally refers to increasing economic integration of markets located in nations around the world. Market integration takes place when goods, services, and resources (particularly people and money) flow freely across national borders. Despite the current excitement in the business press over the present wave of globalization, the process of integrating markets is not unique to the 1990s, but rather it is an ongoing process that may advance for some period of time and then suffer setbacks. The last significant wave of globalization lasted from the late 1800s to the start of World War I. During that period, expansion of railroads and the emergence of steamships enabled both a great migration of labor resources from Europe to the United States as well as a surge in flow of goods between regional and international markets. Even though some governments and some citizens oppose international economic integration, as evidenced by a number of antiglobalization protests, most economists believe the freer flow of resources and products can raise standards of living in rich and poor nations alike.

The movement toward global markets in the last decade can be traced to several developments. During this period North American, European, and Latin American nations successfully negotiated numerous bilateral and multilateral trade agreements, eliminating many restrictions to trade flows among those nations. And, during the late 1990s, 11 European nations agreed to adopt a single currency—the euro—to stimulate trade on the continent by eliminating the use of assorted currencies that tends to impede cross-border flows of resources, goods, and services. Adding to the momentum for globalization, the Information Age rapidly revolutionized electronic communication, making it possible to buy and sell goods and services over a worldwide Internet. As noted in Illustration 1.6, *Microsoft Office* software has become something of an international language for businesses, as companies around the world communicate using *Excel* spreadsheets and documents created in *Word* and *PowerPoint*. All of these developments contributed to reducing the transaction costs of bringing buyers and sellers in different nations together for the purpose of doing business.

As you can see from this discussion, globalization of markets provides managers with both an opportunity to sell more goods and services to foreign buyers as well as a threat from increased competition by foreign producers. This trend toward economic integration of markets changes the way managers must view the structure of the markets in which they sell their products or services, as well as the ways they choose to organize production. Throughout the text, we will point out some of the opportunities and challenges of globalization of markets.

ILLUSTRATION 1.6

Internet Spurs Globalization of Services

Since 1999 antiglobalization protestors in Seattle, Washington, D.C., Quebec, and Genoa have directed criticism at multinational corporations—as well as their governments, the World Trade Organization, the International Monetary Fund, and World Bank—for moving manufacturing operations to countries with low wages. While the protestors express deep concern that workers in poorer countries will be "exploited" by multinational corporations and be forced to work in sweatshops for "unfair" wages, the more basic fear among protestors seems to be an understandable concern that they will lose their jobs as manufacturing moves to other countries. In the next chapter, Illustration 2.3 takes a closer look at how globalization has affected manufacturing industries in the United States.

In a recent article in *The Wall Street Journal*, Douglas Lavin explains that antiglobalization protestors have overlooked a more significant shift in services: "Thanks largely to the fact that a decent education, *Microsoft Office*, and the Internet are all as useful in Manila as in Minneapolis, the service sector has gone (global)."[a] The worldwide Internet now makes possible for services what railroads and steamships made possible for manufactured goods: Services can be produced anywhere in the world and "delivered" digitally via terrestrial, broadband, fiber-optic cables, or high-capacity satellites in geosynchronous orbits to end-users most anywhere in the world. Every imaginable kind of service is now experiencing globalization: from accounting services, claims processing, credit evaluation, and answering customer service questions on 1-800 telephone numbers to data entry, software coding, and even gambling. Businesses in the United States, Britain, Spain, Hong Kong, and France currently lead the way in outsourcing services to workers in other countries, such as India, the Philippines, Jamaica, Ghana, Hungary, and the Czech Republic.

As Lavin emphasizes in his article, the Internet "explosion" coupled with vast improvements in telecommunications technology enabled the service sector to join the process of globalization. Because many Third World nations can afford the infrastructure investments required to access the Internet—even when better roads and bridges may be too costly—Lavin predicts globalization of the service sector could create a significant improvement in living standards in poorer nations. Furthermore, by providing multinational corporations with the ability to buy inexpensive services, globalization tends to increase productivity, which tends to push wages up in the home countries of these corporations. We think Lavin's message for the antiglobalization protestors is worth repeating:

> Protestors argue that globalization exploits the poorest of the poor. Tell that to the thousands of well-paid accountants working for Arthur Andersen in the Philippines or engineers working for Cisco in India . . . Tell that to people in Manila or New Delhi who for the first time, independent of their choice of residence, can trade internationally what's long been untradeable: education, skill and dedication.

Economists have long recognized that when two parties voluntarily engage in trade, both parties gain. Globalization of services made possible by the Internet provides an opportunity for such trades: Businesses can reduce their costs, and hundreds of thousands of workers in low-income nations can earn higher wages.

[a]This Illustration draws heavily from the article by Douglas Lavin, "Globalization Goes Upscale," in *The Wall Street Journal*, Feb. 1, 2002, p. A 21.

1.5 SUMMARY

Managerial economics provides a systematic, logical way of analyzing business decisions that focuses on the economic forces that shape both day-to-day decisions and long-run planning decisions. Managerial economics applies microeconomic theory—the study of the behavior of individual economic agents—to business problems in order to teach business decision makers how to use economic analysis to make decisions that will achieve the firm's goal: the maximization of profit.

Economic theory helps managers understand real-world business problems by using simplifying assumptions to abstract away from irrelevant ideas and information and turn complexity into relative simplicity. Like a road map, economic theory ignores everything irrelevant to the problem and reduces business problems to their most essential components.

The opportunity cost of using resources to produce goods and services is the amount the firm's owner gives up by using these resources. Opportunity costs are either explicit opportunity costs or implicit opportunity costs. Explicit costs are the costs of using market-supplied resources, which equal the monetary payments to hire, rent, or lease resources owned by others. Implicit costs are the costs of using owner-supplied resources, which are the best earnings forgone from using resources owned by the firm in the firm's own production process. Total economic cost is the sum of explicit and implicit costs. Economic profit is the difference between total revenue and total economic cost:

Economic profit = Total revenue − Total economic cost

= Total revenue − Explicit costs − Implicit costs

Accounting profit differs from economic profit because accounting profit does not subtract from total revenue the implicit costs of using resources:

Accounting profit = Total revenue − Explicit costs

Thus accounting profit will be larger than economic profit for firms using owner-supplied resources. Since all costs matter to owners of a firm, maximizing economic profit is the objective of the firm's owners.

The value of a firm is the price for which it can be sold, and that price is equal to the present value of the expected future profits of the firm. The risk associated with not knowing future profits of a firm is accounted for by using a higher risk-adjusted discount rate to calculate the present value of the firm's future profits. The larger (smaller) the risk associated with future profits, the higher (lower) the risk-adjusted discount rate used to compute the value of the firm, and the lower (higher) will be the value of the firm. In the absence of any agency problems, the objective of a manager is to maximize the value of the firm. A manager will maximize the value of a firm by making decisions that maximize profit in every single time period, unless cost and/or revenue conditions in any period depend upon decisions made in other time periods.

In firms where the managers are not also the owners, the managers are agents of the owners, or principals. A principal–agent problem exists when the agent has objectives different from those of the principal, and the principal either has difficulty enforcing agreements with the agent or finds it too difficult and costly to monitor the agent to verify that he or she is furthering the principal's objectives. Agency problems arise because of moral hazard. Moral hazard exists when either party to an agreement has an incentive not to abide by all the provisions of the agreement *and* one party cannot cost effectively find out if the other party is abiding by the agreement or cannot enforce the agreement even when the information is available.

In order to address agency problems, shareholders can employ a variety of corporate control mechanisms. Shareholders can reduce or eliminate agency problems by (1) requiring that managers hold a stipulated amount of the firm's equity, (2) increasing the percentage of outsiders serving on the company's board of directors, and (3) financing corporate investments with debt instead of equity. Corporate takeovers also create an incentive for managers to make decisions that maximize the value of a firm.

The structure of the market in which a firm operates can limit the ability of managers to increase the price of the firm's products. In some markets, firms are price-takers. In these markets prices are determined not by managers but by market forces that cannot be controlled. In other markets, managers of price-setting firms possess some degree of market power and can raise price without losing all their sales.

A market is any arrangement that enables buyers and sellers to exchange goods and services, usually for money payments. A market may be a location at a certain time, a newspaper advertisement, a website on the Internet, or any other arrangement that works to bring buyers and sellers together. Markets exist to reduce transaction costs, the costs of making a transaction.

A market structure is a set of market characteristics that determines the economic environment in which a firm operates: (1) the number and size of the firms operating in the market, (2) the degree of product differentiation, and (3) the likelihood of new firms entering. A perfectly competitive market has a large number of relatively small firms selling an undifferentiated product with no barriers to entry. A monopoly market is one in which a single firm, protected by barriers to entry, produces a product that has no close substitutes. In a monopolistically competitive market, a large number of relatively small firms produce differentiated products without any barriers to entry. Finally, in an oligopoly market, there are only a few firms experiencing interdependence—each firm's pricing decision affects all other firms' profits—with varying degrees of product differentiation and barriers to entry.

TECHNICAL PROBLEMS

1. For each one of the costs below, explain whether the resource cost is explicit or implicit, and give the annual opportunity cost for each one. Assume the owner of the business can invest money and earn 10 percent annually.

    a. A computer server to run the firm's network is leased for $6,000 per year.

    b. The owner starts the business using $50,000 of cash from a personal savings account.

    c. A building for the business was purchased for $18 million three years ago but is now worth $30 million.

    d. Computer programmers cost $30 per hour. The firm will hire 200,000 hours of programmer services this year.

    e. The firm owns a 1955 model Clarke-Owens garbage incinerator, which it uses to dispose of paper and cardboard waste. Even though this type of incinerator is now illegal to use for environmental reasons, the firm can continue to use it because it's exempt under a "grandfather" clause in the law. However, the exemption only applies to the current owner for use until it wears out or is replaced. (*Note:* The owner offered to give the incinerator to the Smithsonian Institute as a charitable gift, but managers at the Smithsonian turned it down.)

2. During a year of operation, a firm collects $175,000 in revenue and spends $80,000 on raw materials, labor expense, utilities, and rent. The owners of the firm have provided $500,000 of their own money to the firm instead of investing the money and earning a 14 percent annual rate of return.

    a. The explicit costs of the firm are $_____. The implicit costs are $_____. Total economic cost is $_____.

    b. The firm earns economic profit of $_____.

    c. The firm's accounting profit is $_____.

    d. If the owners could earn 20 percent annually on the money they have invested in the firm, the economic profit of the firm would be _____ (when revenue is $175,000).

3. Over the next three years, a firm is expected to earn economic profits of $120,000 in the first year, $140,000 in the second year, and $100,000 in the third year. After the end of the third year, the firm will go out of business.

    a. If the risk-adjusted discount rate is 10 percent for each of the next three years, the value of the firm is $_____. The firm can be sold today for a price of $_____.

b. If the risk-adjusted discount rate is 8 percent for each of the next three years, the value of the firm is $_____. The firm can be sold today for a price of $_____.

4. Fill in the blanks:

a. Managers will maximize the values of firms by making decisions that maximize _____ in every single time period, so long as cost and revenue conditions in each period are _____.

b. When current output has the effect of increasing future costs, the level of output that maximizes the value of the firm will be _____ (smaller, larger) than the level of output that maximizes profit in a single period.

c. When current output has a positive effect on future profit, the level of output that maximizes the value of the firm will be _____ (smaller, larger) than the level of output that maximizes profit in the current period.

APPLIED PROBLEMS

1. At the beginning of the year, an audio engineer quit his job and gave up a salary of $175,000 per year in order to start his own business, Sound Devices, Inc. The new company builds, installs, and maintains custom audio equipment for businesses that require high-quality audio systems. A partial income statement for Sound Devices, Inc., is shown below:

	2004
Revenues	
Revenue from sales of product and services	$970,000
Operating costs and expenses	
Cost of products and services sold	355,000
Selling expenses	155,000
Administrative expenses	45,000
Total operating costs and expenses	$555,000
Income from operations	$415,000
Interest expense (bank loan)	45,000
Legal expenses to start business	28,000
Income taxes	165,000
Net income	$177,000

To get started, the owner of Sound Devices spent $100,000 of his personal savings to pay for some of the capital equipment used in the business. In 2004, the owner of Sound Devices could have earned a 15 percent return by investing in stocks of other new businesses with risk levels similar to the risk level at Sound Devices.

a. What are the total explicit, total implicit, and total economic costs in 2004?

b. What is accounting profit in 2004?

c. What is economic profit in 2004?

d. Given your answer in part c, evaluate the owner's decision to leave his job to start Sound Devices.

2. A doctor spent two weeks doing charity medical work in Mexico. In calculating her taxable income for the year, her accountant deducted as business expenses her round-trip airline ticket, meals, and a hotel bill for the two-week stay. She was surprised to learn that the accountant, following IRS rules, could not deduct as a cost of the trip the $8,000 of income she lost by being absent from her medical practice for two weeks. She asked the accountant, "Since lost income is not deductible as an expense, should I ignore it when I make my decision next year to go to Mexico for charity work?" Can you give the doctor some advice on decision making?

3. When Burton Cummings graduated with honors from the Canadian Trucking Academy, his father gave him a $350,000 tractor-trailer rig. Recently, Burton was boasting to some fellow truckers that his revenues were typically $25,000 per month, while his operating costs (fuel, maintenance, and depreciation) amounted to only $18,000 per month. Tractor-trailer rigs identical to Burton's rig rent for $15,000 per month. If Burton was driving trucks for one of the competing trucking firms, he would earn $5,000 per month.

   a. How much are Burton Cummings's explicit costs per month? How much are his implicit costs per month?

   b. What is the dollar amount of the opportunity cost of the resources used by Burton Cummings each month?

   c. Burton is proud of the fact that he is generating a net cash flow of $7,000 (= $25,000 − $18,000) per month, since he would be earning only $5,000 per month if he were working for a trucking firm. What advice would you give Burton Cummings?

4. Explain why it would cost Andre Agassi or Venus Williams more to leave the professional tennis tour and open a tennis shop than it would for the coach of a university tennis team to do so.

5. An article in *The Wall Street Journal* discusses a trend among some large U.S. corporations to base the compensation of outside members of their boards of directors partly on the performance of the corporation. "This growing practice more closely aligns the director to the company. [Some] companies link certain stock or stock-option grants for directors to improved financial performance, using a measure such as annual return on equity."

   How would such a linkage tend to reduce the agency problem between managers and shareholders as a whole? Why could directors be more efficient than shareholders at improving managerial performance and changing their incentives?

6. An article in *The Wall Street Journal* reported that large hotel chains, such as Marriott, are tending to reduce the number of hotels that they franchise to outside owners and increase the number the chain owns and manages itself. Some chains are requiring private owners or franchisees to make upgrades in their hotels, but they are having a difficult time enforcing the policy. Marriott says this upgrading is important because "we've built our name on quality."

   a. What type of agency problem is involved here?

   b. Why would Marriott worry about the quality of the hotels it doesn't own but franchises?

   c. Why would a chain such as Marriott tend to own its hotels in resort areas, such as national parks, where there is little repeat business, and franchise hotels in downtown areas, where there is a lot of repeat business? Think of the reputation effect and the incentive of franchises to maintain quality.

7. *Fortune* magazine reported that SkyWest, an independent regional airline, negotiated a financial arrangement with Delta and United to provide regional jet service for the two

major airlines. For its part of the deal, SkyWest agreed to paint its jets the colors of Delta Connection and United Express and to fly routes specified by the two airlines. In return, Delta and United agreed to pay SkyWest a predetermined profit margin and to cover most of the regional airline's costs. *Fortune* explained that while the deal limited the amount of profit SkyWest could earn, it also insulated the smaller airline from volatility in earnings since Delta and United covered SkyWest's fuel costs, increased its load factor (the percentage of seats occupied), and managed its ticket prices.

Fortune suggested that Wall Street liked the deal because SkyWest's market valuation increased from $143 million to $1.1 billion after it began its service with the two major airlines. Explain carefully how this arrangement with Delta and United could have caused the value of SkyWest to increase dramatically even though it limited the amount of profit SkyWest could earn.

8. Diplomatic tensions over the war with Iraq and patriotic fervor led the state legislature in South Carolina to initiate a resolution boycotting French products. But before the resolution could become law, South Carolina lawmakers abruptly changed their minds and never followed up on the measure. Can you explain this unexpected change of heart by legislators?

▣   MATHEMATICAL APPENDIX   Review of Present Value Calculations

The concept of present value is a tool used to determine the value of a firm, which is the present value of expected future profits to be earned. In Chapters 1 and 13 of this text, you will find it useful to be able to calculate present values. Even if you have not already studied present value analysis in your finance or accounting classes, this short presentation will provide you with the basic computational skills needed to calculate the present value of a stream of expected profit to be received in future periods.

Present Value of a Single Payment in the Future

The payment you would accept today rather than wait for a payment (or stream of payments) to be received in the future is called the *present value* (*PV*) of that future payment (or stream of payments). Suppose, for example, that a trustworthy person promises to pay you $100 a year from now. Even though you are sure you will get the $100 in a year, a dollar now is worth more than a dollar a year from now. How much money would you accept now rather than wait one year for a guaranteed payment of $100? Because of the time value of money, you will be willing to accept less than $100; that is, the present value of a $100 payment one year from now is *less* than $100. The process of calculating present value is sometimes referred to as *discounting* since the present value of a payment is less than the dollar amount of the future payment.

To properly discount the $100 future payment, you must first determine the opportunity cost of waiting for your money. Suppose that, at no risk, you could earn a return of 6 percent by investing the money over a one-year period. This 6 percent return is called the *risk-free discount rate* since it determines the rate at which you will discount future dollars to determine their present value, assuming you bear no risk of receiving less than the promised amount. In Chapter 18, we will show you how to determine the appropriate risk premium to add to the risk-free discount rate when the future payment involves a degree of risk. For now, you need not be concerned about adjusting for risk.

Given that you can earn 6 percent (with no risk) on your money, how much money do you need now—let's denote this amount as $X—in order to have exactly $100 a year from now? Since $X(1.06) is the value of $X in one year, set this future value equal to $100:

$$\$X(1.06) = \$100$$

It follows that the amount you must invest today ($X) is $94.34 (= $100/1.06) in order to have $100 in a year. Thus the present value of $100 to be received in one year is $94.34 now. In other words, you would accept $94.34 now, which will grow to $100 in one year (at a 6 percent annual discount rate).

Now suppose that the $100 payment comes not in one year but after two years. Investing $X at 6 percent would yield $X(1.06) at the end of year 1 and [$X(1.06)] (1.06) = $X(1.06)^2$ at the end of year 2. For an investment to be worth $100 in two years,

$$\$X(1.06)^2 = \$100$$

The amount you must invest today in order to have $100 at the end of two years is $89 [= $100/(1.06)^2]. Thus the present value of $100 in two years with a discount rate of 6 percent is $89.

Clearly a pattern is emerging: The present value of $100 in one year at 6 percent is

$$PV = \frac{\$100}{(1.06)} = \$94.34$$

The present value of $100 in two years at 6 percent is

$$PV = \frac{\$100}{(1.06)^2} = \$89$$

Therefore, the present value of $100 to be received in t years (t being any number of years) with a discount rate of 6 percent is

$$PV = \frac{\$100}{(1.06)^t}$$

This relation can be made even more general to determine the present value of some net cash flow (NCF) to be received in t years at a discount rate of r. Net cash flow is the cash received in time period t, net of any costs or expenses that must be paid out of the cash inflow. Also note that if the discount rate is 6 percent, for example, r is expressed as 0.06, the decimal equivalent of 6 percent.

Relation The present value (PV) of $NCF to be received in t years at a discount rate of r is

$$PV = \frac{\$NCF}{(1 + r)^t}$$

As illustrated above, the present value of a cash flow declines the further in the future it is to be received—for example, the present value of $100 at 6 percent was $94.34 in one year and only $89 in two years. As should be evident from the more general statement of present value, the present value of a cash flow is inversely related to the discount rate—for example, the present value of $100 to be received in two years is $89 with a discount rate of 6

percent but only $85.73 [= $100/(1.08)^2] with a discount rate of 8 percent.

Relation There is an inverse relation between the present value of a cash flow and the time to maturity: The present value of a cash flow to be received in t years is greater than that for the same cash flow to be received in $t + i$ years. There is an inverse relation between the present value of a cash flow and the discount rate.

Present Value of a Stream of Payments

So far we have considered the present value of a single payment. We now extend present value analysis to consider the value of a stream of payments in the future. Suppose your trustworthy friend promises to pay you $100 in one year and $100 in two years. Using 6 percent as the risk-free discount rate for the first year, the present value of the first payment would be

$$PV = \frac{\$100}{(1.06)} = \$94.34$$

At the 6 percent discount rate, the present value of the second payment would be

$$PV = \frac{\$100}{(1.06)^2} = \$89$$

Thus the present value of the two-period stream of cash flows is

$$PV = \frac{\$100}{(1.06)} + \frac{\$100}{(1.06)^2} = \$94.34 + \$89 = \$183.34$$

From the preceding, you should be able to see that the present value of a stream of net cash flows is equal to the sum of the present values of the net cash flows. We can state this more precisely in the following:

Relation The present value of a stream of cash flows, where NCF_t is the cash flow received or paid in period t, is given by

$$PV = \frac{\$NCF_1}{(1 + r)} + \frac{\$NCF_2}{(1 + r)^2} + \frac{\$NCF_3}{(1 + r)^3} + \cdots + \frac{\$NCF_T}{(1 + r)^T}$$

$$= \sum_{t=1}^{T} \frac{\$NCF_t}{(1 + r)^t}$$

where r is the discount rate, and T is the life span of the stream of cash flows.

MATHEMATICAL EXERCISES

1. Using a discount rate of 6.5 percent, calculate the present value of a $1,000 payment to be received at the end of

   a. One year

   b. Two years

   c. Three years

2. What is the present value of a firm with a five-year life span that earns the following stream of expected profit? (Treat all profits as being received at year-end.) Use a risk-adjusted discount rate of 12 percent.

Year	Expected profit
1	$10,000
2	20,000
3	50,000
4	75,000
5	50,000

3. The *National Enquirer* reported that, in their divorce settlement, Burt Reynolds offered Loni Anderson $10 million spread evenly over 10 years but she instead demanded $5 million now. If the appropriate discount rate is 8 percent, which alternative is better for Burt and which for Loni? What if the discount rate is 20 percent?

CHAPTER 2

Demand, Supply, and Market Equilibrium

A s we emphasized in Chapter 1, successful managers understand how market forces create both opportunities and constraints for profitable decision making. Such managers understand the way markets work, and they are able to predict the prices and production levels of the goods, resources, and services that are relevant to their businesses. The production manager of a soft-drink bottler could use new information about sugar production, such as government approval of a potent new fertilizer for growing sugar cane, to predict the future price of sugar and then make changes in syrup inventories. The owner–manager of a home-appliance manufacturing firm would want to use information about new home construction to make future production plans. This chapter presents one of the most powerful tools of economics for analyzing the way market forces determine prices and production in competitive markets—supply and demand analysis.

Even though supply and demand analysis is deceptively simple to learn and apply, it is widely used by highly experienced—and well-paid—market analysts and forecasters. You will see that such analysis provides a useful framework for processing market and other economic information to make decisions that affect the profitability of the business. And you will come across the concepts set forth in this chapter again and again throughout the rest of the text.

This chapter focuses primarily on the way markets for consumer goods and services function, although the basic concepts apply also to markets for resources, such as labor, land, raw materials, and capital equipment. Supply and demand analysis applies principally to markets characterized by many buyers and sellers and markets in which a homogeneous or relatively nondifferentiated good or service is sold. As we stated in the previous chapter, such markets are called competitive markets. In competitive markets, individual firms are price-takers because prices are determined by the impersonal forces of the marketplace—demand and supply. As you will see in this chapter, each firm in a competitive market is so small relative to the total market demand that it can sell all the output it wishes to sell at the going market-determined price. Thus competitive firms have no reason to actively try to win customers away from any other firm. For this reason, perfectly competitive markets promote the least amount of interfirm rivalry of any market structure. As you will see later in the text, managers of firms in monopolistically competitive markets and oligopoly markets can increase their firms' profits by beating some of their rivals out of sales.

We begin the analysis of competitive markets by describing the buyer side of the market—called the *demand side* of the market. Next we describe the seller side—called the *supply side*. We then combine the demand side with the supply side to show how prices and quantities sold are determined in a market. Finally, we show how forces on the demand side or the supply side of the market can change and thereby affect the price and quantity sold in a market.

2.1 DEMAND

quantity demanded
The amount of a good or service consumers are willing and able to purchase during a given period of time (week, month, etc.).

The amount of a good or service that consumers in a market are willing and able to purchase during a given period of time (e.g., a week, a month) is called **quantity demanded.** Although economists emphasize the importance of price in purchasing decisions, as we will do, they also recognize that a multitude of factors other than price affect the amount of a good or service people will purchase. However, in order to simplify market analysis and make it manageable, economists ignore the many factors that have an insignificant effect on purchases and concentrate only on the most important factors. Indeed, only six factors are considered sufficiently important to be included in most studies of market demand.

This section develops two types of demand relations: (1) *generalized demand functions*, which show how quantity demanded is related to product price and five other factors that affect demand, and (2) *ordinary demand functions*, which show the relation between quantity demanded and the price of the product when all other variables affecting demand are held constant at specific values. As you will see in this chapter, ordinary demand functions are derived from generalized demand functions. Traditionally, economists have referred to ordinary demand functions simply as *demand functions* or *demand*. We shall follow this tradition.

The Generalized Demand Function

The six principal variables that influence the quantity demanded of a good or service are (1) the price of the good or service, (2) the incomes of consumers, (3) the prices of related goods and services, (4) the tastes or preference patterns of consumers, (5) the expected price of the product in future periods, and (6) the number of consumers in the market. The relation between quantity demanded and these

generalized demand function
The relation between quantity demanded and the six factors that affect quantity demanded: $Q_d = f(P, M, P_R, \mathcal{T}, P_e, N)$.

six factors is referred to as the **generalized demand function** and is expressed as follows:

$$Q_d = f(P, M, P_R, \mathcal{T}, P_e, N)$$

where f means "is a function of" or "depends on," and

Q_d = quantity demanded of the good or service
P = price of the good or service
M = consumers' income (generally per capita)
P_R = price of related goods or services
$\mathcal{T}$ = taste patterns of consumers
P_e = expected price of the good in some future period
N = number of consumers in the market

The generalized demand function shows how all six variables *jointly* determine the quantity demanded. In order to discuss the *individual* effect that any one of these six variables has on Q_d, we must explain how changing just that one variable *by itself* influences Q_d. Isolating the individual effect of a single variable requires that all other variables that affect Q_d be held constant. Thus whenever we speak of the effect that a particular variable has on quantity demanded, we mean the individual effect *holding all other variables constant.*

We now discuss each of the six variables to show how they are related to the amount of a good or service consumers buy. We begin by discussing the effect of changing the *price* of a good while holding the other five variables constant. As you would expect, consumers are willing and able to buy more of a good the lower the price of the good and will buy less of a good the higher the price of the good. Price and quantity demanded are negatively (inversely) related because when the price of a good rises, consumers tend to shift from that good to other goods that are now relatively cheaper. Conversely, when the price of a good falls, consumers tend to purchase more of that good and less of other goods that are now relatively more expensive. Price and quantity demanded are inversely related when all other factors are held constant. This relation between price and quantity demanded is so important that we discuss it in more detail later in this chapter and again in Chapter 5.

Next, we consider changes in *income*, again holding constant the rest of the variables that influence consumers. An increase in income can cause the amount of a commodity consumers purchase either to increase or to decrease. If an increase in income causes consumers to demand more of a good, when all other variables in the generalized demand function are held constant, we refer to such a commodity as a **normal good.** A good is also a normal good if a decrease in income causes consumers to demand less of the good, all other things held constant. There are some goods and services for which an increase in income would reduce consumer demand, other variables held constant. This type of commodity is referred to as an **inferior good.** In the case of inferior goods, rising income causes consumers to demand *less* of the good, and falling income causes consumers to demand *more* of the good. Some examples of goods and services that might be inferior include mobile homes, shoe repair services, generic food products, and used cars.

normal good
A good or service for which an increase (decrease) in income causes consumers to demand more (less) of the good, holding all other variables in the generalized demand function constant.

inferior good
A good or service for which an increase (decrease) in income causes consumers to demand less (more) of the good, all other factors held constant.

Commodities may be *related in consumption* in either of two ways: as substitutes or as complements. In general, goods are *substitutes* if one good can be used in the place of the other; an example might be Toyotas and Chryslers. If two goods are substitutes, an increase in the price of one good will increase the demand for the other good. If the price of Toyotas rises while the price of Chryslers remains constant, we would expect consumers to purchase more Chryslers—holding all other factors constant. If an increase in the price of a related good causes consumers to demand more of a good, then the two goods are **substitutes.** Similarly, two goods are substitutes if a decrease in the price of one of the goods causes consumers to demand less of the other good, all other things constant.

Goods are said to be *complements* if they are used in conjunction with each other. Examples might be cameras and film, lettuce and salad dressing, or baseball games and hot dogs. A decrease in the price of tickets to the baseball game will increase demand for hot dogs at the game, all else constant. If the demand for one good decreases when the price of a related good increases, the two goods are **complements.** Similarly, two goods are complements if a decrease in the price of one of the goods causes consumers to demand more of the other good, all other things constant.[1]

Expectations of consumers also influence consumers' decisions to purchase goods and services. More specifically, consumers' expectations about the future price of a commodity can change their current purchasing decisions. If consumers expect the price to be higher in a future period, demand will probably rise in the current period. On the other hand, expectations of a price decline in the future will cause some purchases to be postponed—thus demand in the current period will fall. An example of this can be seen in the automobile industry. Automakers often announce price increases for the next year's models several months before the cars are available in showrooms in order to stimulate demand for the current year's cars.

A change in consumer tastes can change demand for a good or service. Obviously, taste changes could either increase or decrease consumer demand. While consumer tastes are not directly measurable (as are the other variables in the generalized demand function), you may wish to view the variable $\mathcal{T}$ as an index of consumer tastes; $\mathcal{T}$ takes on larger values as consumers perceive a good becoming higher in quality, more fashionable, more healthful, or more desirable in any way. A decrease in $\mathcal{T}$ corresponds to a change in consumer tastes away from a good or service as consumers perceive falling quality, or displeasing appearance, or diminished healthfulness. Consequently, when all other variables in the generalized demand function are held constant, a movement in consumer tastes toward a good or service will increase demand and a movement in consumer tastes away from a good will decrease demand for the good. A change in consumer tastes or preferences occurs

substitutes
Two goods are substitutes if an increase (decrease) in the price of one of the goods causes consumers to demand more (less) of the other good, holding all other factors constant.

complements
Two goods are complements if an increase (decrease) in the price of one of the goods causes consumers to demand less (more) of the other good, all other things held constant.

---

[1]Not all commodities are either substitutes or complements in consumption. Many commodities are essentially independent. For example, we would not expect the price of lettuce to significantly influence the demand for automobiles. Thus we can treat these commodities as independent and ignore the price of lettuce when evaluating the demand for automobiles.

when, for example, the *New England Journal of Medicine* publishes research findings that show a higher incidence of cancer among people who regularly eat bacon. This causes the demand for bacon to decrease (the taste index $\mathcal{T}$ declines), all other factors remaining constant.

Finally, an increase in the number of consumers in the market will increase the demand for a good, and a decrease in the number of consumers will decrease the demand for a good, all other factors held constant. In markets that experience a growth in the number of buyers—such as the health care industry as the population matures or Florida during the tourist season—we would expect demand to increase.

The generalized demand function just set forth is expressed in the most general mathematical form. Economists and market researchers often express the generalized demand function in a more specific mathematical form in order to show more precisely the relation between quantity demanded and some of the more important variables that affect demand. They frequently express the generalized demand function in a linear functional form. The following equation is an example of a linear form of the generalized demand function:

$$Q_d = a + bP + cM + dP_R + e\mathcal{T} + fP_e + gN$$

where Q_d, P, M, P_R, $\mathcal{T}$, P_e, and N are as defined above, and a, b, c, d, e, f, and g are parameters.

The intercept parameter a shows the value of Q_d when the variables P, M, P_R, $\mathcal{T}$, P_e, and N are all simultaneously equal to zero. The other parameters, b, c, d, e, f, and g, are called **slope parameters:** They measure the effect on quantity demanded of changing one of the variables P, M, P_R, $\mathcal{T}$, P_e, or N while holding the rest of these variables constant. The slope parameter b, for example, measures the change in quantity demanded per unit change in price; that is, $b = \Delta Q_d / \Delta P$.[2] As stressed earlier, Q_d and P are inversely related, and b is negative because ΔQ_d and ΔP have opposite algebraic signs.

The slope parameter c measures the effect on the amount purchased of a one-unit change in income ($c = \Delta Q_d / \Delta M$). For normal goods, sales increase when income rises, so c is positive. If the good is inferior, sales decrease when income rises, so c is negative. The parameter d measures the change in the amount consumers want to buy per unit change in P_R ($d = \Delta Q_d / \Delta P_R$). If an increase in P_R causes sales to rise, the goods are substitutes and d is positive. If an increase in P_R causes sales to fall, the two goods are complements and d is negative. Since $\mathcal{T}$, P_e, and N are each directly related to the amount purchased, the parameters e, f, and g are all positive.[3]

slope parameters
Parameters in a linear function that measure the effect on the dependent variable (Q_d) of changing one of the independent variables (P, M, P_R, $\mathcal{T}$, P_e, and N) while holding the rest of these variables constant.

---

[2]The symbol "Δ" means "change in." Thus if quantity demanded rises (falls), then ΔQ_d is positive (negative). Similarly, if price rises (falls), ΔP is positive (negative). In general, the ratio of the change in Y divided by the change in X ($\Delta Y / \Delta X$) measures the change in Y per unit change in X.

[3]Since consumer tastes are not directly measurable as are the other variables, you may wish to view $\mathcal{T}$ as an index of consumer tastes that ranges in value from 0, if consumers think a product is worthless, to 10 if they think the product is extremely desirable. In this case, the parameter e shows the effect on quantity of a one-unit change in the taste index ($\mathcal{T}$), and e is positive.

▣ **Relation** When the generalized demand function is expressed in linear form:

$$Q_d = a + bP + cM + dP_R + eT + fP_e + gN$$

the slope parameters (b, c, d, e, f, and g) measure the effect on the amount of the good purchased of changing one of the variables (P, M, P_R, T, P_e, and N) while holding the rest of the variables constant. For example, b ($= \Delta Q_d/\Delta P$) measures the change in quantity demanded per unit change in price holding M, P_R, T, P_e, and N constant. When the slope parameter of a specific variable is positive (negative) in sign, quantity demanded is directly (inversely) related to that variable.

Table 2.1 summarizes this discussion of the generalized demand function. Each of the six factors that affect quantity demanded is listed, and the table shows whether the quantity demanded varies directly or inversely with each variable and gives the sign of the slope parameters. Again let us stress that these relations are in the context of all other things being equal. An increase in the price of the commodity will lead to a decrease in quantity demanded as long as the other variables—income, the price of related commodities, consumer tastes, price expectations, and the number of customers—remain constant.

A generalized demand function always includes price as a variable but may not always include every one of the other five variables shown in Table 2.1. Market analysts sometimes omit consumer tastes and price expectations, since these variables may not be important in every situation. The number of customers may also be disregarded in formulating a generalized demand equation when the number of consumers in a particular market does not change. For example, the demand for local telephone service is not likely to be sensitive to the expected price of telephone service. Households will not choose to disconnect their telephones this month on the basis of a belief that local telephone rates are going to fall next month. Consumer tastes may also have little impact on demand for local telephone service, since fashion generally plays little or no role in determining telephone demand. In a small town that experiences only an inconsequential change in the number of telephone customers, N does not play an important role in determining the variation in Q_d and need not be included in the generalized demand

---

TABLE 2.1

Summary of the Generalized (Linear) Demand Function
$Q_d = a + bP + cM + dP_R + eT + fP_e + gN$

Variable	Relation to quantity demanded	Sign of slope parameter
P	Inverse	$b = \Delta Q_d/\Delta P$ is negative
M	Direct for normal goods	$c = \Delta Q_d/\Delta M$ is positive
	Inverse for inferior goods	$c = \Delta Q_d/\Delta M$ is negative
P_R	Direct for substitute goods	$d = \Delta Q_d/\Delta P_R$ is positive
	Inverse for complement goods	$d = \Delta Q_d/\Delta P_R$ is negative
T	Direct	$e = \Delta Q_d/\Delta T$ is positive
P_e	Direct	$f = \Delta Q_d/\Delta P_e$ is positive
N	Direct	$g = \Delta Q_d/\Delta N$ is positive

function. For these reasons, the generalized linear demand function can sometimes be simplified to include just three variables from Table 2.1:

$$Q_d = a + bP + cM + dP_R$$

Although it is not always appropriate to use this simplified version of the generalized demand function, the three-variable demand function does provide a reasonable model of consumer demand in many applications.

Demand Functions

demand function (demand)
A table, a graph, or an equation that shows how quantity demanded is related to product price, holding constant the five other variables that influence demand.

The relation between price and quantity demanded per period of time, when all other factors that affect consumer demand are held constant, is called a **demand function** or simply **demand.** Demand gives, for various prices of a good, the corresponding quantities that consumers are willing and able to purchase at each of those prices, all other things held constant. The "other things" that are held constant for a specific demand function are the five variables other than price that can affect demand. A demand function can be expressed as an equation, a schedule or table, or a graph. We begin with a demand equation.

A demand function can be expressed in the most general form as the equation

$$Q_d = f(P)$$

which means that the quantity demanded is a function of (depends on) the price of the good, holding all other variables constant. A demand function is obtained by holding all the variables in the generalized demand function constant except price. For example, using a three-variable demand function,

$$Q_d = f(P, M', P'_R) = f(P)$$

where the prime on the variables M and P_R means that those variables are held constant at some specified amount no matter what value the product price takes.

☐ **Relation** A demand function expresses quantity demanded as a function of product price only: $Q_d = f(P)$. Demand functions—whether expressed as equations, tables, or graphs—give the quantity demanded at various prices, holding constant the effects of income, price of related goods, consumer tastes, expected price, and the number of consumers. Demand functions are derived from generalized demand functions by holding all the variables in the generalized demand function constant except price.

To illustrate the derivation of a demand function from the generalized demand function, suppose the generalized demand function is

$$Q_d = 1,800 - 20P + 0.6M - 50P_R$$

To derive a demand function, $Q_d = f(P)$, the variables M and P_R must be assigned fixed values. Suppose consumer income is $20,000 and the price of a related good is $250. To find the demand function, the fixed values of M and P_R are substituted into the generalized demand function:

$$Q_d = 1,800 - 20P + 0.6(20,000) - 50(250)$$
$$= 1,800 - 20P + 12,000 - 12,500$$
$$= 1,300 - 20P$$

Thus the demand function is expressed in the form of a linear demand equation, $Q_d = 1,300 - 20P$. The intercept parameter, 1,300, is the amount of the good consumers would demand if price is zero. The slope of this demand function $(= \Delta Q_d/\Delta P)$ is -20 and indicates that a \$1 increase in price causes quantity demanded to decrease by 20 units. Although not all demand functions are linear, you will see later in the text that the linear form is a frequently used specification for estimating and forecasting demand functions.

This linear demand equation satisfies all the conditions set forth in the definition of demand. All variables other than product price are held constant—income at \$20,000 and the price of a related good at \$250. At each price, the equation gives the amount that consumers would purchase at that price. For example, if price is \$50,

$$Q_d = 1,300 - (20 \times 50) = 300$$

or if price is \$40,

$$Q_d = 1,300 - (20 \times 40) = 500$$

demand schedule
A table showing a list of possible product prices and the corresponding quantities demanded.

A **demand schedule** (or table) shows a list of several prices and the quantity demanded per period of time at each of the prices, again holding all variables other than price constant. Seven prices and their corresponding quantities demanded are shown in Table 2.2. Each of the seven combinations of price and quantity demanded is derived from the demand function exactly as shown above. (You may check this for yourself.)

demand curve
A graph showing the relation between quantity demanded and price when all other variables influencing quantity demanded are held constant.

As noted, the final method of showing a demand function is a graph. A graphical demand function is called a **demand curve.** The seven price–quantity-demanded combinations in Table 2.2 are plotted in Figure 2.1, and these points are connected with the straight line D_0, which is the demand curve associated with the demand equation $Q_d = 1,300 - 20P$. This demand curve meets the specifications of the definition of demand. All variables other than price are held constant. The demand

TABLE 2.2
The Demand Schedule for the Demand Function
$D_0: Q_d = 1,300 - 20P$

Price	Quantity demanded
\$65	0
60	100
50	300
40	500
30	700
20	900
10	1,100

FIGURE 2.1

A Demand Curve:
$Q_d = 1{,}300 - 20P$

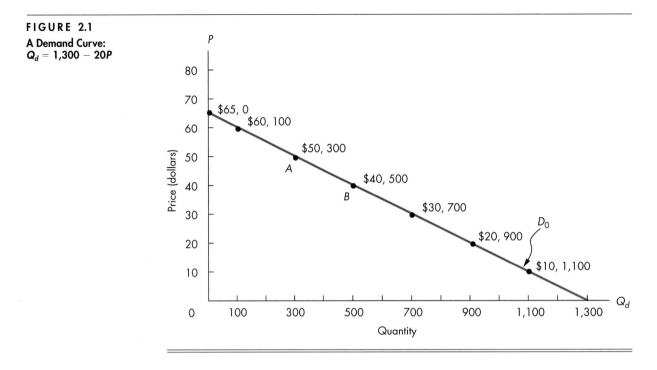

inverse demand
function
The demand function when
price is expressed as a
function of quantity
demanded: $P = f(Q_d)$.

curve D_0 gives the value of quantity demanded (on the horizontal axis) for every value of price (on the vertical axis).

Note that in the graph of the demand equation, $Q_d = 1{,}300 - 20P$, the independent variable P is plotted along the vertical axis and the dependent variable Q_d is plotted along the horizontal axis. This switch is traditional among economists. Thus the equation plotted in the figure is the inverse of the demand equation and is called the **inverse demand function** since price is expressed as a function of quantity demanded: $P = 65 - 1/20Q_d$.[4] The vertical intercept is 65, indicating that at a price of $65, consumers will demand zero units of the good. The horizontal intercept is 1,300, which is the maximum amount of the good buyers will take when the good is given away ($P = 0$). The slope of the graphed inverse demand is $-1/20$, indicating that if quantity demanded rises by one unit, price must fall 1/20 of a dollar (or 5 cents). This inverse, as you can see, yields price–quantity combinations identical to those given by the above demand equation.

---

[4]Recall from high school algebra that the "inverse" of a function $Y = f(X)$ is the function $X = g(Y)$, which gives X as a function of Y, and the same pairs of Y and X values that satisfy $Y = f(X)$ also satisfy the inverse function $X = g(Y)$. In other words, both equations express the same relation between Y and X. For example, for the equation $Y = 10 + 2X$, the inverse function, $X = 1/2Y - 5$, is found by solving algebraically for X in terms of Y.

Although demand is generally interpreted as indicating the amount that consumers will buy at each price, sometimes managers and market researchers wish to know the highest price that can be charged for any given amount of the product. As it turns out, a point on a demand curve can be interpreted in either of two ways: (1) the maximum amount of a good that will be purchased if a given price is charged or (2) the maximum price that consumers will pay for a specific amount of a good. Consider, for example, point *A* ($50, 300) on the demand curve in Figure 2.1. If the price of the good is $50, the maximum amount consumers will purchase is 300 units. Equivalently, $50 is the highest price that consumers can be charged in order to sell 300 units. Sometimes $50 is called the demand price for 300 units, and each price on demand can be called the **demand price** for the corresponding quantity on the horizontal axis.

demand price
The maximum price consumers will pay for a specific amount of a good.

The Law of Demand

Before moving on to an analysis of changes in the variables that are held constant when deriving a demand function, we want to reemphasize the relation between price and quantity demanded, which was discussed earlier in this chapter. In the demand equation, the parameter on price is negative; in the demand schedule, price and quantity demanded are inversely related; and in the graph, the demand curve is negatively sloped. This inverse relation between price and quantity demanded is not simply a characteristic of the specific demand function discussed here. This inverse relation is so pervasive that economists refer to it as the **law of demand.** The law of demand states that quantity demanded increases when price falls and quantity demanded decreases when price rises, other things held constant.

law of demand
Quantity demanded increases when price falls, and quantity demanded decreases when price rises, other things held constant.

Economists refer to the inverse relation between price and quantity demanded as a law, not because this relation has been proved mathematically but because examples to the contrary have never been observed. If you have doubts about the validity of the law of demand, try to think of any goods or services that you would buy more of if the price were higher, other things being equal. Or can you imagine someone going to the grocery store expecting to buy one six-pack of Pepsi for $2.50, then noticing that the price is $5, and deciding to buy two or three six-packs? You don't see stores advertising higher prices when they want to increase sales or get rid of unwanted inventory.

The principal reason for the inverse relation between price and quantity demanded is that all goods have substitutes. When the price of one good rises, consumers can shift some of their purchases to other goods that serve a similar function. The only electric company in a city faces competition from the gas company in many uses. Even when AT&T was the only long-distance telephone company, people could substitute mail for telephone calls, and now AT&T faces intense competition from other long-distance phone companies. We believe it will be difficult for you to think of a product that you are now consuming for which there is absolutely no available substitute.

change in quantity demanded
A movement along a given demand curve that occurs when the price of the good changes, all else constant.

Once a demand function, $Q_d = f(P)$, is derived from a generalized demand function, a **change in quantity demanded** can be caused only by a change in price. The other five variables that influence demand in the generalized demand function (M, P_R, $\mathcal{T}$, P_e, and N) are fixed in value for any particular demand equation. A change in price is represented on a graph by a movement along a fixed demand curve. In Figure 2.1, if price falls from $50 to $40 (and the other variables remain constant), a change in quantity demanded from 300 to 500 units occurs and is illustrated by a movement along D_0 from point A to point B.

▣ **Relation** For a demand function $Q_d = f(P)$, a change in price causes a change in quantity demanded. The other five variables that influence demand in the generalized demand function (M, P_R, $\mathcal{T}$, P_e, and N) are fixed in value for any particular demand equation. On a graph, a change in price causes a movement along a demand curve from one price to another price.

Shifts in Demand

When any one of the five variables held constant when deriving a demand function from the generalized demand relation changes value, a new demand function results, causing the entire demand curve to *shift* to a new location. To illustrate this extremely important concept, we will show how a change in one of these five variables, such as income, affects a demand schedule.

increase in demand
A change in the demand function that causes an increase in quantity demanded at every price and is reflected by a rightward shift in the demand curve.

We begin with the demand schedule from Table 2.2, which is reproduced in columns 1 and 2 of Table 2.3. Recall that the quantities demanded for various product prices were obtained by holding all variables except price constant in the generalized demand function. If income increases from $20,000 to $20,500, quantity demanded increases *at each and every price,* as shown in column 3. When the price is $30, for example, consumers will buy 700 units if their income is $20,000 but will buy 1,000 units if their income is $20,500. In Figure 2.2, D_0 is the demand curve associated with an income level of $20,000, and D_1 is the demand curve after income rises to $20,500. Since the increase in income caused quantity demanded to increase *at every price,* the demand curve shifts to the right from D_0 to D_1 in Figure 2.2. Everywhere along D_1 quantity demanded is greater than along D_0 for equal prices. This change in the demand function is called an **increase in demand.**

decrease in demand
A change in the demand function that causes a decrease in quantity demanded at every price and is reflected by a leftward shift in the demand curve.

A **decrease in demand** occurs when a change in one or more of the variables M, P_R, $\mathcal{T}$, P_e, or N causes the quantity demanded to decrease at every price and the

TABLE 2.3 **Three Demand Schedules**	(1) Price	(2) D_0: $Q_d = 1,300 - 20P$ Quantity demanded ($M = \$20,000$)	(3) D_1: $Q_d = 1,600 - 20P$ Quantity demanded ($M = \$20,500$)	(4) D_2: $Q_d = 1,000 - 20P$ Quantity demanded ($M = \$19,500$)
	$65	0	300	0
	60	100	400	0
	50	300	600	0
	40	500	800	200
	30	700	1,000	400
	20	900	1,200	600
	10	1,100	1,400	800

determinants of demand
Variables that change the quantity demanded at each price and that determine where the demand curve is located: M, P_R, $\mathcal{T}$, P_e, and N.

change in demand
A shift in demand, either leftward or rightward, that occurs only when one of the five determinants of demand changes.

demand curve shifts to the left. Column 4 in Table 2.3 illustrates a decrease in demand caused by income falling to $19,500. At every price, quantity demanded in column 4 is less than quantity demanded when income is either $20,000 or $20,500 (columns 2 and 3, respectively, in Table 2.3). The demand curve in Figure 2.2 when income is $19,500 is D_2, which lies to the left of D_0 and D_1.

While we have illustrated shifts in demand caused by changes in income, a change in any one of the five variables that are held constant when deriving a demand function will cause a shift in demand. These five variables—M, P_R, $\mathcal{T}$, P_e, and N—are called the **determinants of demand** because they determine where the demand curve is located. A **change in demand** occurs when one or more of the determinants of demand change. Think of M, P_R, $\mathcal{T}$, P_e, and N as the five "demand-shifting" variables. The demand curve shifts to a new location only when one or more of these demand-shifting variables changes.

☐ **Relation**   An increase in demand means that, at each price, more is demanded; a decrease in demand means that, at each price, less is demanded. Demand changes, or shifts, when one of the determinants of demand changes. These determinants of demand are income, prices of related goods, consumer tastes, expected future price, and the number of consumers.

The shifts in demand illustrated in Figure 2.2 were derived mathematically from the generalized demand function. Recall that the demand function D_0 ($Q_d = 1,300 - 20P$) was derived from the generalized demand function

$$Q_d = 1,800 - 20P + 0.6M - 50P_R$$

where income and the price of a related good were held constant at values of $M = $20,000$ and $P_R = 250. When income increases from $20,000 to $20,500, the new

FIGURE 2.2
Shifts in Demand

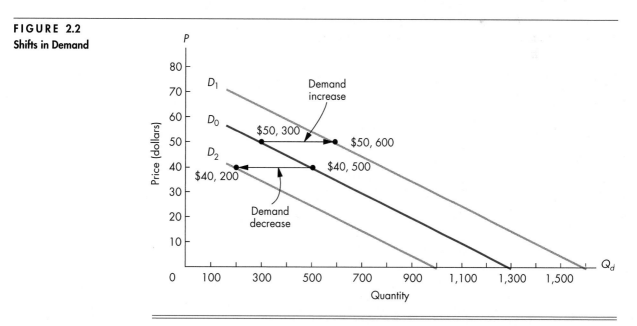

demand equation at this higher income is found by substituting $M = \$20,500$ into the generalized demand function and solving for the new demand function:

$$D_1: Q_d = 1,800 - 20P + (0.60 \times 20,500) - 12,500$$
$$= 1,600 - 20P$$

In Figure 2.2, this demand function is shown by the demand curve D_1. At every price, quantity demanded increases by 300 units ($1,600 = 1,300 + 300$). Each of the quantities in column 3 of Table 2.2 was calculated from the new demand equation $Q_d = 1,600 - 20P$. As you can see, every quantity in column 3 is 300 units larger than the corresponding quantity in column 2. Thus the increase in income has caused an increase in demand.

When income falls from $\$20,000$ to $\$19,500$, demand shifts from D_0 to D_2. We leave the derivation of the demand function for D_2 as an exercise. The procedure, however, is identical to the process set forth above.

From the preceding discussion, you may have noticed that the direction in which demand shifts when one of the five demand determinants changes depends on the sign of the slope parameter on that variable in the generalized demand function. The increase in income caused quantity demanded to rise for all prices because $\Delta Q_d / \Delta M (= +0.6)$ is positive, which indicates that a $1 increase in income causes a 0.6-unit increase in quantity demanded at every price level. Since income increased by $500 in this example, quantity demanded increases by 300 units ($= 500 \times 0.6$). Thus when the slope parameter on M is positive in the generalized demand function, an increase in income causes an increase in demand. As explained earlier, when income and quantity demanded are positively related *in the generalized demand function*, the good is a normal good. If the parameter on M is negative, an increase in income causes a decrease in demand, and the good is an inferior good.[5]

Consider now the slope parameter on the price of a related good. Returning once more to the previous numerical example, recall that the slope parameter for P_R in the generalized demand function is equal to -50, which means that a $1 increase in the price of the related good causes quantity demanded to decrease by 50 units at every product price. In other words, an increase in the price of the related good causes the demand curve to shift to the left. As explained earlier, when P_R and Q_d are inversely related in the generalized demand function, the two goods are complements. Had the parameter for P_R been positive, the price of the related good and quantity demanded would be directly related, an increase in the price of the related good would shift demand to the right, and the two goods would be substitutes.

---

[5]It is only correct to speak of a change in income affecting *quantity demanded* when referring to the generalized demand function. Once income has been held constant to derive a demand function, a change in income causes a change in demand (a shift in the demand curve), not a change in quantity demanded. The same distinction holds for the other determinants of demand P_R, $\mathcal{T}$, P_e, and N.

TABLE 2.4
Summary of Demand Shifts

Determinants of demand	Demand increases[a]	Demand decreases[b]	Sign of slope parameter[c]
1. Income (M)			
Normal good	M rises	M falls	$c > 0$
Inferior good	M falls	M rises	$c < 0$
2. Price of related good (P_R)			
Substitute good	P_R rises	P_R falls	$d > 0$
Complement good	P_R falls	P_R rises	$d < 0$
3. Consumer tastes ($\mathcal{T}$)	$\mathcal{T}$ rises	$\mathcal{T}$ falls	$e > 0$
4. Expected price (P_e)	P_e rises	P_e falls	$f > 0$
5. Number of consumers (N)	N rises	N falls	$g > 0$

[a]Demand increases when the demand curve shifts rightward.
[b]Demand decreases when the demand curve shifts leftward.
[c]This column gives the sign of the corresponding slope parameter in the generalized demand function.

For $\mathcal{T}$, P_e, and N, the slope parameters are all positive in the generalized demand function, and an increase in any one of these variables causes demand to increase. A decrease in either $\mathcal{T}$, P_e, or N causes a decrease in demand. Table 2.4 summarizes this discussion for all five of the determinants of demand.

2.2 SUPPLY

quantity supplied
The amount of a good or service offered for sale during a given period of time (week, month, etc.).

The amount of a good or service offered for sale in a market during a given period of time (e.g., a week, a month) is called **quantity supplied,** which we will denote as Q_s. The amount of a good or service offered for sale depends on an extremely large number of variables. As in the case of demand, economists ignore all the relatively unimportant variables in order to concentrate on those variables that have the greatest effect on quantity supplied. In general, economists assume that the quantity of a good offered for sale depends on six major variables:

1. The price of the good itself.
2. The price of the inputs used to produce the good.
3. The prices of goods related in production.
4. The level of available technology.
5. The expectations of the producers concerning the future price of the good.
6. The number of firms or the amount of productive capacity in the industry.

generalized supply function
The relation between quantity supplied and the six factors that jointly affect quantity supplied: $Q_s = g(P, P_I, P_r, T, P_e, F)$.

The Generalized Supply Function

The **generalized supply function** shows how all six of these variables *jointly* determine the quantity supplied. The generalized supply function is expressed mathematically as

$$Q_s = g(P, P_I, P_r, T, P_e, F)$$

The quantity of a good or service offered for sale (Q_s) is determined not only by the price of the good or service (P) but also by the prices of the inputs used in production (P_I), the prices of goods that are related in production (P_r), the level of available technology (T), the expectations of producers concerning the future price of the good (P_e), and the number of firms or amount of productive capacity in the industry (F). The symbol g is used as "a function of" to distinguish the supply relation from the generalized demand function.

Now we consider how each of the six variables is related to the quantity of a good or service firms produce. We begin by discussing the effect of a change in the price of a good while holding the other five variables constant. Typically, the higher the price of the product, the greater the quantity firms wish to produce and sell, all other things being equal. Conversely, the lower the price, the smaller the quantity firms will wish to produce and sell. Producers are induced by higher prices to produce and sell more, while lower prices tend to discourage production. Thus price and quantity supplied are, in general, directly related.

An increase in the price of one or more of the inputs used to produce the product will obviously increase the cost of production. If the cost rises, the good becomes less profitable and producers will want to supply a smaller quantity at each price. Conversely, a decrease in the price of one or more of the inputs used to produce the product will decrease the cost of production. When cost falls, the good becomes more profitable and producers will want to supply a larger amount at each price. Therefore, an increase in the price of an input causes a decrease in production, while a decrease in the price of an input causes an increase in production.

substitutes in production
Goods for which an increase in the price of one good relative to the price of another good causes producers to increase production of the now higher-priced good and decrease production of the other good.

Changes in the prices of goods that are related in production may affect producers in either one of two ways, depending on whether the goods are substitutes or complements in production. Two goods, X and Y, are **substitutes in production** if an increase in the price of good X relative to good Y causes producers to increase production of good X and decrease production of good Y. For example, if the price of corn increases while the price of wheat remains the same, some farmers may change from growing wheat to growing corn, and less wheat will be supplied. In the case of manufactured goods, firms can switch resources from the production of one good to the production of a substitute (in production) commodity when the price of the substitute rises. Alternatively, two goods, X and Y, are **complements in production** if an increase in the price of good X causes producers to supply more of good Y. For example, crude oil and natural gas often occur in the same oil field, making natural gas a by-product of producing crude oil, or vice versa. If the price of crude oil rises, petroleum firms produce more oil, so the output of natural gas also increases. Other examples of complements in production include nickel and copper (which occur in the same deposit), beef and leather hides, and bacon and pork chops.

complements in production
Goods for which an increase in the price of one good, relative to the price of another good, causes producers to increase production of both goods.

technology
The state of knowledge concerning the combination of resources to produce goods and services.

Next, we consider changes in the level of available technology. **Technology** is that state of knowledge concerning how to combine resources to produce goods and services. An improvement in the state of technology generally results in one or more of the inputs used in making the good to be more productive. As we will show you in Chapters 8 and 9, increased productivity allows firms to make more of a good or service with the same amount of inputs or the same output with fewer inputs. In either case, the cost of producing a given level of output falls when firms use better technology, which would lower the costs of production and increase the supply of the good to the market, all other things remaining the same. Even though measuring technology is rather complicated, you can view advances in technology as leading to lower costs and greater supply of the good.

A firm's decision about its level of production depends not only on the current price of the good but also upon the firm's *expectation* about the future price of the good. If firms expect the price of a good they produce to rise in the future, they may withhold some of the good, thereby reducing supply of the good in the current period.

Finally, if the number of firms in the industry increases or if the *productive capacity* of existing firms increases, more of the good or service will be supplied at each price. For example, the supply of air travel between New York and Hong Kong increases when either more airlines begin servicing this route or when the firms currently servicing the route increase their capacities to fly passengers by adding more jets to service their New York–Hong Kong route. Conversely, a decrease in the number of firms in the industry or a decrease in the productive capacity of existing firms decreases the supply of the good, all other things remaining constant. As another example, suppose a freeze in Florida decreases the number of firms by destroying entirely some citrus growers. Alternatively, it might leave the number of growers unchanged but decrease productive capacity by killing a portion of each grower's trees. In either situation, the supply of fruit decreases. Thus changes in the number of firms in the industry or changes in the amount of productive capacity in the industry are represented in the supply function by changes in F.

As in the case of demand, economists often find it useful to express the generalized supply function in linear functional form:

$$Q_s = h + kP + lP_I + mP_r + nT + rP_e + sF$$

where Q_s, P, P_I, P_r, T, P_e, and F are as defined earlier, h is an intercept parameter, and k, l, m, n, r, and s are slope parameters. Table 2.5 summarizes this discussion of the generalized supply function. Each of the six factors that affect production is listed along with the relation to quantity supplied (direct or inverse). Let us again stress that, just as in the case of demand, these relations are in the context of all other things being equal.

supply function
A table, a graph, or an equation that shows how quantity supplied is related to product price, holding constant the five other variables that influence supply.

determinants of supply
Variables that cause a change in supply (i.e., a shift in the supply curve).

Supply Functions

Just as demand functions are derived from the generalized demand function, supply functions are derived from the generalized supply function. A **supply function** shows the relation between Q_s and P holding the **determinants of supply** (P_I, P_r, T, P_e, and F) constant:

$$Q_s = g(P, P_I', P_r', T', P_e', F') = g(P)$$

TABLE 2.5
Summary of the Generalized (Linear) Supply Function
$Q_s = h + kP + lP_I + mP_r + nT + rP_e + sF$

Variable	Relation to quantity supplied	Sign of slope parameter
P	Direct	$k = \Delta Q_s/\Delta P$ is positive
P_I	Inverse	$l = Q_s/\Delta P_I$ is negative
P_r	Inverse for substitutes in production (wheat and corn)	$m = \Delta Q_s/\Delta P_r$ is negative
	Direct for complements in production (oil and gas)	$m = \Delta Q_s/\Delta P_r$ is positive
T	Direct	$n = \Delta Q_s/\Delta T$ is positive
P_e	Inverse	$r = \Delta Q_s/\Delta P_e$ is negative
F	Direct	$s = \Delta Q_s/\Delta F$ is positive

change in quantity supplied
A movement along a given supply curve that occurs when the price of a good changes.

where the prime means the determinants of supply are held constant at some specified value. Once a supply function $Q_s = g(P)$ is derived from a generalized supply function, a **change in quantity supplied** can be caused only by a change in price.

Relation   A supply function expresses quantity supplied as a function of product price only: $Q_s = g(P)$. Supply functions give the quantity supplied for various prices, holding constant the effects of input prices, prices of goods related in production, the state of technology, expected price, and the number of firms in the industry. Supply functions are derived from generalized supply functions by holding all the variables in the generalized supply function constant except price.

To illustrate the derivation of a supply function from the generalized supply function, suppose the generalized supply function is

$$Q_s = 50 + 10P - 8P_I + 5F$$

Technology, the prices of goods related in production, and the expected price of the product in the future have been omitted to simplify this illustration. Suppose the price of an important input is $50, and there are currently 90 firms in the industry producing the product. To find the supply function, the fixed values of P_I and F are substituted into the generalized supply function:

$$Q_s = 50 + 10P - 8(50) + 5(90)$$
$$= 100 + 10P$$

The linear supply function gives the quantity supplied for various product prices, holding constant the other variables that affect supply. For example, if the price of the product is $20,

$$Q_s = 100 + 10(20) = 300$$

or if the price is $50,

$$Q_s = 100 + 10(50) = 600$$

supply schedule
A table showing a list of possible product prices and the corresponding quantities supplied.

A **supply schedule** (or table) shows a list of several prices and the quantity supplied at each of the prices, again holding all variables other than price constant.

TABLE 2.6

The Supply Schedule for the Supply Function S_0:
$Q_s = 100 + 10P$

Price	Quantity supplied
$65	750
60	700
50	600
40	500
30	400
20	300
10	200

FIGURE 2.3

A Supply Curve:
$Q_s = 100 + 10P$

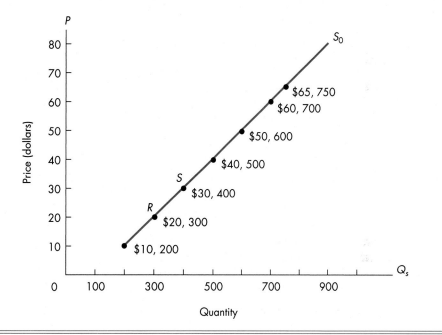

supply curve
A graph showing the relation between quantity supplied and price, when all other variables influencing quantity supplied are held constant.

inverse supply function
The supply function when price is expressed as a function of quantity supplied: $P = f(Q_s)$.

Table 2.6 shows seven prices and their corresponding quantities supplied. Each of the seven price–quantity-supplied combinations is derived, as shown earlier, from the supply equation $Q_s = 100 + 10P$, which was derived from the generalized supply function by setting $P_I = \$50$ and $F = 90$. Figure 2.3 graphs the **supply curve** associated with this supply equation and supply schedule. As with demand curves, price is shown on the vertical axis and quantity on the horizontal axis. Thus the equation plotted in the figure is the inverse of the supply equation and is called the **inverse supply function:** $P = -10 + 1/10Q$. The slope of this inverse supply equation graphed in Figure 2.3 is $\Delta P/\Delta Q_s$, which equals $1/10$ and is the reciprocal of the slope parameter $k (= \Delta Q_s/\Delta P = 10)$.

In the supply equation $Q_s = 100 + 10P$, the intercept parameter is a positive number, which would seem to indicate that producers are willing to offer 100 units to consumers when the price is zero. As we will show in a later chapter, and as your intuition tells you now, producers usually quit producing if price falls below some minimum level. You can think of $10 in Figure 2.3 as the lowest price for which production will occur. Mathematically speaking, we might say the supply equation describes supply only over the range of prices $10 or greater ($P \geq \$10$). We will show in later chapters how to find the price level below which production ceases.[6]

supply price
The minimum price necessary to induce producers voluntarily to offer a given quantity for sale.

Any particular combination of price and quantity supplied on a supply curve can be interpreted in either of two equivalent ways. A point on the supply schedule indicates either (1) the maximum amount of a good or service that will be offered for sale at a specific price or (2) the minimum price necessary to induce producers voluntarily to offer a given quantity for sale. This minimum price is sometimes referred to as the **supply price** for that level of output.

change in quantity supplied
A movement along a given supply curve that occurs when the price of the good changes, all else constant.

As in the case of a demand function, once a supply equation, $Q_s = g(P)$, is derived from a generalized supply function, a **change in quantity supplied** can be caused only by a change in price. A change in quantity supplied represents a movement along a given supply curve. Consider the supply curve S_0 in Figure 2.3. If product price rises from $20 to $30, the quantity supplied increases from 300 to 400 units, a movement from point R to point S along the supply curve S_0.

▣   **Relation**   For a supply function $Q_s = g(P)$, a change in price causes a change in quantity supplied. The other five variables that affect supply in the generalized supply function (P_I, P_r, T, P_e, F) are fixed in value for any particular supply function. On a graph, a change in price causes a movement along a supply curve from one price to another price.

Shifts in Supply

As we differentiate between a change in quantity demanded because of a change in price and a shift in demand because of a change in one of the determinants of demand, we must make the same distinction with supply. A shift in supply occurs only when one of the five determinants of supply (P_I, P_r, T, P_e, F) changes value. An increase in the number of firms in the industry, for example, causes the quantity supplied to increase at every price so that the supply curve shifts to the right, and this circumstance is called an **increase in supply.** A decrease in the number of firms in the industry causes a **decrease in supply,** and the supply curve shifts to the left. We can illustrate shifts in supply by examining the effect on the supply function of changes in the values of the determinants of supply.

increase in supply
A change in the supply function that causes an increase in quantity supplied at every price, and is reflected by a rightward shift in the supply curve.

decrease in supply
A change in the supply function that causes a decrease in quantity supplied at every price, and is reflected by a leftward shift in the supply curve.

_____

[6]When the intercept parameter is negative in a supply function, the supply curve intersects the price axis at a price greater than zero. (You will verify this in Technical Problem 7.) In such cases, the price at which the supply curve intersects the price axis represents the minimum price below which production ceases.

TABLE 2.7
Three Supply Schedules

(1) Price	(2) S_0 Quantity supplied $Q_s = 100 + 10P$ ($P_I = \$50, F = 90$)	(3) S_1 Quantity supplied $Q_s = 250 + 10P$ ($P_I = \$31.25, F = 90$)	(4) S_2 Quantity supplied $Q_s = -200 + 10P$ ($P_I = \$50, F = 30$)
$65	750	900	450
60	700	850	400
50	600	750	300
40	500	650	200
30	400	550	100
20	300	450	0
10	200	350	0

FIGURE 2.4
Shifts in Supply

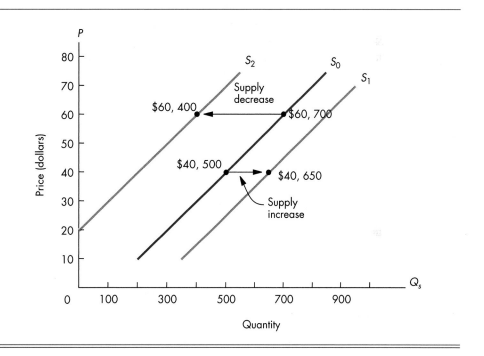

Table 2.6 is reproduced in columns 1 and 2 of Table 2.7. If the price of the input falls to $31.25, the new supply function is $Q_s = 250 + 10P$, and the quantity supplied increases *at each and every price* as shown in column 3. This new supply curve when the price of the input falls to $31.25 is shown as S_1 in Figure 2.4 and lies to the right of S_0 at every price. Thus the decrease in P_I causes the supply curve to shift rightward, illustrating an increase in supply. To illustrate a decrease in supply, suppose the price of the input remains at $50 but the number of firms in the industry decreases to 30 firms. The supply function is now $Q_s = -200 + 10P$, and

TABLE 2.8
Summary of Supply Shifts

Determinants of supply	Supply increases[a]	Supply decreases[b]	Sign of slope parameter[c]
1. Price of inputs (P_I)	P_I falls	P_I rises	$l < 0$
2. Price of goods related in production (P_r)			
Substitute good	P_r falls	P_r rises	$m < 0$
Complement good	P_r rises	P_r falls	$m > 0$
3. State of technology (T)	T rises	T falls	$n > 0$
4. Expected price (P_e)	P_e falls	P_e rises	$r < 0$
5. Number of firms or productive capacity in industry (F)	F rises	F falls	$s > 0$

[a]Supply increases when the supply curve shifts rightward.
[b]Supply decreases when the supply curve shifts leftward.
[c]This column gives the sign of the corresponding slope parameter in the generalized supply function.

quantity supplied decreases *at every price* as shown in column 4. The new supply curve in Figure 2.4, S_2, lies to the left of S_0 at every price. Thus the decrease in the number of firms causes a decrease in supply, which is represented by a leftward shift in the supply curve. You can think of P_I, P_r, T, P_e, and F as the five "supply-shifting" variables.

□   **Relation** An increase in supply means that, at each price, more of the good is supplied; a decrease in supply means that, at each price, less is supplied. Supply changes (or shifts) when one of the determinants of supply changes. These determinants of supply are the price of inputs, the price of goods related in production, the state of technology, the expected price in the future, and the number of firms or the amount of productive capacity in the industry.

As in the case of demand, the direction in which a supply curve shifts when one of the determinants of supply changes value depends on the sign of the slope parameter in the generalized supply function. In the above example, when the input price falls to \$31.25, quantity supplied increases for every price because the slope parameter for P_I is negative ($l = -8$). Thus a fall in the price of the input causes an increase in supply. Table 2.8 summarizes this discussion of shifts in supply.

2.3 MARKET EQUILIBRIUM

market equilibrium
A situation in which, at the prevailing price, consumers can buy all of a good they wish and producers can sell all of the good they wish. The price at which $Q_d = Q_s$.

Demand and supply provide an analytical framework for the analysis of the behavior of buyers and sellers in markets. Demand shows how buyers respond to changes in price and other variables that determine quantities buyers are willing and able to purchase. Supply shows how sellers respond to changes in price and other variables that determine quantities offered for sale. The interaction of buyers and sellers in the marketplace leads to **market equilibrium.** Market equilibrium is a situation in which, *at the prevailing price,* consumers can buy all of a good they wish and producers can sell all of the good they wish. In other words, equilibrium occurs when price is at a level for which quantity demanded equals quantity

TABLE 2.9
Market Equilibrium

Price	S_0 Quantity supplied $(Q_s = 100 + 10P)$	D_0 Quantity demanded $(Q_d = 1{,}300 - 20P)$	Excess supply (+) or excess demand (−) $(Q_s - Q_d)$
	(1)	(2)	(3)	(4)
$65	750	0	+750
60	700	100	+600
50	600	300	+300
40	500	500	0
30	400	700	−300
20	300	900	−600
10	200	1,100	−900

equilibrium price
The price at which $Q_d = Q_s$.

equilibrium quantity
The amount of a good bought and sold in market equilibrium.

excess supply (surplus)
Exists when quantity supplied exceeds quantity demanded.

excess demand (shortage)
Exists when quantity demanded exceeds quantity supplied.

market clearing price
The price of a good at which buyers can purchase all they want and sellers can sell all they want at that price. This is another name for the equilibrium price.

supplied. In equilibrium, the price is called **equilibrium price** and the quantity sold is called **equilibrium quantity.**

To illustrate how market equilibrium is achieved, we can use the demand and supply schedules set forth in the preceding sections. Table 2.9 shows both the demand schedule for D_0 (given in Table 2.2) and the supply schedule for S_0 (given in Table 2.6). As the table shows, equilibrium in the market occurs when price is $40 and both quantity demanded and quantity supplied are equal to 500 units. At every price above $40, quantity supplied is greater than quantity demanded. **Excess supply** or a **surplus** exists when the quantity supplied exceeds the quantity demanded. The first three entries in column 4 of Table 2.9 show the excess supply or surplus at each price above $40. At every price below $40, quantity supplied is less than quantity demanded. A situation in which quantity demanded exceeds quantity supplied is called **excess demand** or a **shortage.** The last three entries in column 4 of the table show the excess demand or shortage at each price below the $40 equilibrium price. Excess demand and excess supply equal zero only in equilibrium. In equilibrium the market "clears" in the sense that buyers can purchase all they want and sellers can sell all they want at the equilibrium price. Because of this clearing of the market, equilibrium price is sometimes called the **market clearing price.**

Before moving on to a graphical analysis of equilibrium, we want to reinforce the concepts illustrated in Table 2.9 by using the demand and supply functions from which the table was derived. To this end, recall that the demand equation is $Q_d = 1{,}300 - 20P$ and the supply equation is $Q_s = 100 + 10P$. Since equilibrium requires that $Q_d = Q_s$, in equilibrium,

$$1{,}300 - 20P = 100 + 10P$$

Solving this equation for equilibrium price,

$$1{,}200 = 30P$$

$$P = \$40$$

FIGURE 2.5

Market Equilibrium

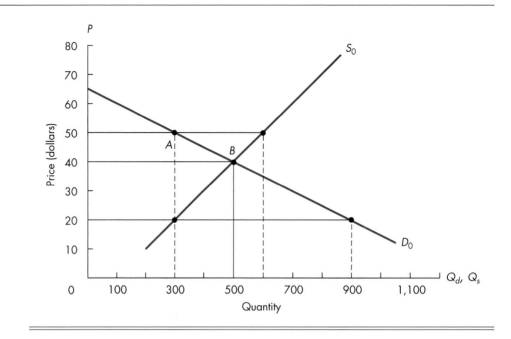

At the market clearing price of $40,

$$Q_d = 1{,}300 - (20 \times 40) = 500$$
$$Q_s = 100 + (10 \times 40) = 500$$

As expected, these mathematically derived results are identical to those presented in Table 2.9.

According to Table 2.9, when price is $50, there is a surplus of 300 units. Using the demand and supply equations, when $P = 50$,

$$Q_d = 1{,}300 - (20 + 50) = 300$$
$$Q_s = 100 + (10 \times 50) = 600$$

Therefore, when price is $50,

$$Q_s - Q_d = 600 - 300 = 300$$

which is the result shown in column 4.

To express the equilibrium solution graphically, Figure 2.5 shows the demand curve D_0 and the supply curve S_0 associated with the schedules in Table 2.9. These are also the demand and supply curves previously shown in Figures 2.1 and 2.3. Clearly, $40 and 500 units are the equilibrium price and quantity. Only at a price of $40 does quantity demanded equal quantity supplied.

Market forces will drive price toward $40. If price is $50, producers want to supply 600 units while consumers only demand 300 units. An excess supply of 300 units develops. Producers must lower price in order to keep from accumulating unwanted inventories. At any price above $40, excess supply results, and producers will lower price.

If price is $20, consumers are willing and able to purchase 900 units, while producers offer only 300 units for sale. An excess demand of 600 units results. Since their demands are not satisfied, consumers bid the price up. Any price below $40 leads to an excess demand, and the shortage induces consumers to bid up the price.

Given no outside influences that prevent price from being bid up or down, an equilibrium price and quantity are attained. This equilibrium price is the price that clears the market; both excess demand and excess supply are zero in equilibrium. Equilibrium is attained in the market because of the following:

□ **Principle** The equilibrium price is that price at which quantity demanded is equal to quantity supplied. When the current price is above the equilibrium price, quantity supplied exceeds quantity demanded. The resulting excess supply induces sellers to reduce price in order to sell the surplus. If the current price is below equilibrium, quantity demanded exceeds quantity supplied. The resulting excess demand causes the unsatisfied consumers to bid up price. Since prices below equilibrium are bid up by consumers and prices above equilibrium are lowered by producers, the market will converge to the equilibrium price–quantity combination.

A final point about market equilibrium should be made before moving on to changes in equilibrium in the next section. It is crucial for you to understand that in the analysis of demand and supply there will never be either a permanent shortage or a permanent surplus as long as price is allowed to adjust freely to the equilibrium level. In other words, assuming that market price adjusts *quickly* to the equilibrium level, surpluses or shortages do not occur in free markets. In the absence of impediments to the adjustment of prices (such as government-imposed price ceilings or floors), the market is always assumed to clear. This assumption greatly simplifies demand and supply analysis. Indeed, how many instances of surpluses or shortages have you seen in markets where prices can adjust freely? The duration of any surplus or shortage is generally short enough that we can reasonably ignore the adjustment period for purposes of demand and supply analysis.

2.4 CHANGES IN MARKET EQUILIBRIUM

qualitative forecast
A forecast that predicts only the direction in which an economic variable will move.

quantitative forecast
A forecast that predicts both the direction and the magnitude of the change in an economic variable.

If demand and supply never changed, equilibrium price and quantity would remain the same forever, or at least for a very long time, and market analysis would be extremely uninteresting and totally useless for managers. In reality, the variables held constant when deriving demand and supply curves do change. Consequently, demand and supply curves shift, and equilibrium price and quantity change. Using demand and supply, managers may make either qualitative forecasts or quantitative forecasts. A **qualitative forecast** predicts only the *direction* in which an economic variable, such as price or quantity, will move. A **quantitative forecast** predicts both the *direction* and the *magnitude* of the change in an economic variable.

ILLUSTRATION 2.1

Do Buyers Really Bid Up Prices?

We have emphasized that when a surplus exists, unwanted inventories accumulate and sellers lower prices. And when there is a shortage, consumers, unable to buy all they want at the going price, bid up the price. It's easy to see that a surplus would induce sellers to lower the price. But do consumers actually bid up the price during a shortage?

Over the past two decades, housing markets in the United States have experienced two periods of rapidly increasing demand that created temporary shortages accompanied by episodes of consumers' bidding up the prices of homes. The predictable nature of consumer bidding wars is illustrated by two newspaper reports.

In spring 1986, an article in *The Wall Street Journal* described how the bidding process actually took place first in housing markets in Boston and upstate New York, then appeared later in most of the Northeast, suburbs of Chicago, Detroit, Minneapolis, parts of Ohio, and major California cities. Lured by lower mortgage interest rates, a huge influx of home buyers began offering sellers $100 to $45,000 extra for scarce houses in desirable suburbs or prestigious urban neighborhoods. While overbidding wasn't the norm, it occurred in 25 percent of home sales in some booming areas. As the *WSJ* noted, "Its pervasiveness is helping to drive house prices sky high," and "there is too much overbidding to hold down prices."

The article reported several specific examples. A New York couple offered $2,000 above the $181,000 asking price for a New Jersey home that needed a new furnace, a new paint job in the garage, and extensive bathroom repairs. They made the offer to win a bidding war with two other buyers. And they said they were happy because they knew people who had paid as much as $10,000 above the asking price. An Alexandria, Virginia, lawyer, after she was outbid for another home, paid $170,000 for a $167,000 house that needed $25,000 in repairs. A real estate agent in Albany, New York, said that one-fourth of the homes in the area priced between $65,000 and $170,000 sold for more than the asking price.

More recently, in August 1997, an article in *The New York Times* reported that relatively low mortgage interest rates and growing stock portfolios were combining to promote the return of bidding wars in affluent areas of northern New Jersey, Los Angeles, the San Francisco Bay area, and Boston: "Competing buyers [are] push[ing] selling prices well beyond the asking price." One 30-something couple chose to pay $17,600 more than the asking price for a Bergen County, New Jersey, home rather than let another couple get the home for just $10,000 over the asking price.

Translated into demand and supply, when interest rates fell and stock market portfolios swelled in value, the demand for homes in many areas of the United States increased substantially. Quantity demanded exceeded quantity supplied at the old equilibrium price. Consumers, not able to get all the houses they wanted at that price bid the price up. Not until the new price reaches the new higher equilibrium will overbidding cease.

Sources: Charles Bagli, "Home Buyers Find the Bidding Wars Are Back," *The New York Times*, Aug. 13, 1997; Joann S. Lublin, "Eager Home Buyers Bid Up Prices in Rising Numbers of Hot Markets," *The Wall Street Journal*, Mar. 7, 1986.

For instance, if you read in *The Wall Street Journal* that Congress is considering a tax cut, demand and supply analysis enables you to forecast whether the price and sales of a particular product will increase or decrease. If you forecast that price will rise and sales will fall, you have made a qualitative forecast about price and quantity. Alternatively, you may have sufficient data on the exact nature of demand and supply to be able to predict that price will rise by $1.10 and sales will fall by 7,000 units. This is a quantitative forecast. Obviously, a manager would get more information from a quantitative forecast than from a qualitative forecast. But managers may not always have sufficient data to make quantitative forecasts. In many

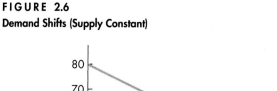

FIGURE 2.6
Demand Shifts (Supply Constant)

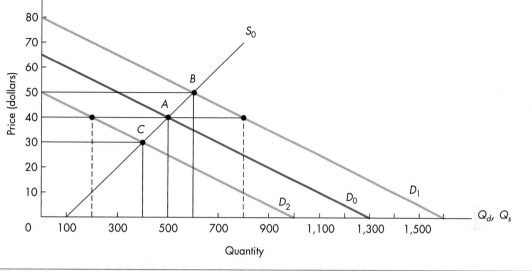

instances, just being able to predict correctly whether price will rise or fall can be extremely valuable to a manager.

Thus an important function and challenging task for managers is predicting the effect, especially the effect on market price, of specific changes in the variables that determine the position of demand and supply curves. We will first discuss the process of adjustment when something causes demand to change while supply remains constant, then the process when supply changes while demand remains constant.

Changes in Demand (Supply Constant)

To illustrate the effects of changes in demand when supply remains constant, we have reproduced D_0 and S_0 in Figure 2.6. Equilibrium occurs at $40 and 500 units, shown as point A in the figure. The demand curve D_1, showing an increase in demand, and the demand curve D_2, showing a decrease in demand, are reproduced from Figure 2.2. Recall that the shift from D_0 to D_1 was caused by an increase in income from $20,000 to $20,500. The shift from D_0 to D_2 resulted from the decrease in income from $20,000 to $19,500.

Begin in equilibrium at point A. Now let demand increase to D_1 as shown. At the original $40 price, consumers now demand 800 units with the new demand. Since firms are still willing to supply only 500 units at $40, a shortage of 300 units results. As described in the previous section, the shortage causes the price to rise to a new equilibrium, where quantity demanded equals quantity supplied. This new equilibrium, where D_1 crosses S_0, occurs when the price is $50 and the quantity sold is 600 units (point B). Therefore the increase in demand increases both equilibrium price and quantity.

To illustrate the effect of a decrease in demand, supply held constant, we return to the original equilibrium at point A in the figure. Now we decrease the demand to D_2. At the original equilibrium price of $40, firms still want to supply 500 units, but now consumers want to purchase only 200 units. Thus there is a surplus of 300 units at $40. As already explained, a surplus causes price to fall. In this example, the market returns to equilibrium only when the price decreases to $30 and the quantity sold is 400 (point C). Therefore the decrease in demand decreases both equilibrium price and quantity. We have now established the following principle:

□ **Principle** When demand increases and supply is constant, equilibrium price and quantity both rise. When demand decreases and supply is constant, equilibrium price and quantity both fall.

Changes in Supply (Demand Constant)

To illustrate the effects of changes in supply when demand remains constant, we reproduce D_0 and S_0 in Figure 2.7. The supply curve S_1, showing an increase in supply, and the supply curve S_2, showing a decrease in supply, are reproduced from Figure 2.4. Recall that the shift from S_0 to S_1 was caused by a decrease in the price of an input from $50 to $31.25. The shift from S_0 to S_2 resulted from a decrease in the number of firms in the industry from 90 to 30.

FIGURE 2.7
Supply Shifts (Demand Constant)

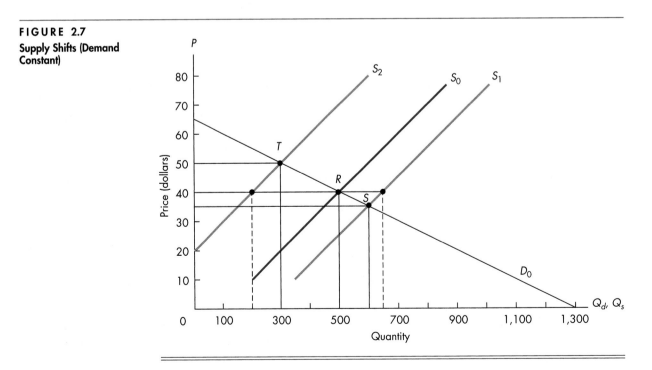

Begin in equilibrium at point R. Let supply first increase to S_1 as shown. At the original \$40 price consumers still want to purchase 500 units, but sellers now wish to sell 650 units, causing a surplus or excess supply of 150 units. The surplus causes price to fall, which induces sellers to supply less and buyers to demand more. Price continues to fall until the new equilibrium is attained at a price of \$35 and a quantity sold of 600 units (point S). At this new equilibrium, quantity demanded equals quantity supplied. Thus when supply increases and demand remains constant, equilibrium price will fall and equilibrium quantity will increase.

To demonstrate the effect of a supply decrease, we return to the original input price, \$50, to obtain the original supply curve S_0 and the original equilibrium at $P = \$40$ and $Q = 500$ units (point R). Let the number of firms in the industry decrease from 90 to 30, causing supply to shift from S_0 to S_2 in Figure 2.7. At the original \$40 price, consumers still want to buy 500 units, but now sellers wish to sell only 200 units, as shown in the figure. This leads to a shortage or excess demand of 300 units. Shortages cause price to rise. The increase in price induces sellers to supply more and buyers to demand less, thereby reducing the shortage. Price will continue to increase until it attains the new equilibrium at a price of \$50 and 300 units of output being sold (point T). At the new equilibrium, S_2 intersects D_0 and quantity supplied equals quantity demanded. Therefore, when supply decreases while demand remains constant, price will rise and quantity sold will decrease. We have now established the following principle:

Principle   When supply increases and demand is constant, equilibrium price falls and equilibrium quantity rises. When supply decreases and demand is constant, equilibrium price rises and equilibrium quantity falls.

Simultaneous Shifts in Both Demand and Supply

To this point, we have examined changes in demand or supply holding the other curve constant. In both cases, the effect on equilibrium price and quantity can be predicted. In situations involving both a shift in demand and a shift in supply, it is possible to predict either the direction in which price changes or the direction in which quantity changes, *but not both*. When it is not possible to predict the direction of change in a variable, the change in that variable is said to be **indeterminate.** The change in either equilibrium price or quantity will be indeterminate when the direction of change depends upon the relative magnitudes of the shifts in the demand and supply curves.

indeterminate
Term referring to the unpredictable change in either equilibrium price or quantity when the direction of change depends upon the relative magnitudes of the shifts in the demand and supply curves.

In Figure 2.8, D and S are, respectively, demand and supply, and equilibrium price and quantity are P and Q (point A). Suppose demand increases to D' and supply increases to S'. Equilibrium quantity increases to Q', and equilibrium price rises from P to P' (point B). Suppose, however, that supply had increased even more to the dashed supply S'' so that the new equilibrium occurs at point C instead of at point B. Comparing point A to point C, equilibrium quantity still increases (Q to Q''), but now equilibrium price *decreases* from P to P''. In the case where both demand and supply increase, a *small* increase in supply relative to demand causes price to rise, while a *large* increase in supply relative to demand causes price to fall.

FIGURE 2.8

Simultaneous Shifts: Demand and Supply Both Increase

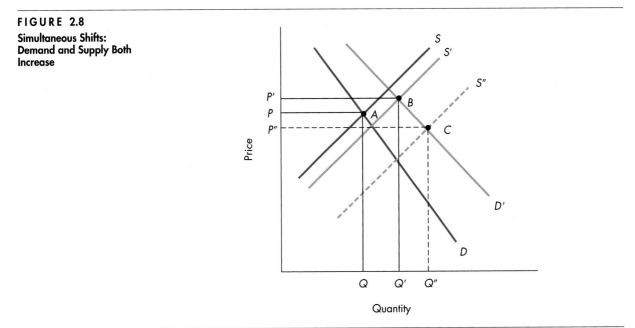

In the case of a simultaneous increase in both demand and supply, equilibrium output always increases, but the change in equilibrium price is indeterminate.

When both demand and supply shift together, either (1) the change in quantity can be predicted and the change in price is indeterminate or (2) the change in quantity is indeterminate and the change in price can be predicted. Figure 2.9 (page 63) summarizes the four possible outcomes when demand and supply both shift. In each of the four panels in Figure 2.9, point *C* shows an alternative point of equilibrium that reverses the direction of change in one of the variables, price or quantity. You should use the reasoning process set forth above to verify the conclusions presented for each of the four cases. We have established the following principle:

▣ **Principle** When demand and supply both shift simultaneously, if the change in quantity (price) can be predicted, the change in price (quantity) is indeterminate. The change in equilibrium quantity or price is indeterminate when the variable can either rise or fall depending upon the relative magnitudes by which demand and supply shift.

Predicting the Direction of Change in Airfares: A Qualitative Analysis

Suppose you manage the travel department for a large U.S. corporation and your sales force makes heavy use of air travel to call on customers. The president of the corporation wants you to reduce travel expenditures for 2004. The extent to which you will need to curb air travel in 2004 will depend on what happens to the price of air travel. If airfares fall in 2004, you can satisfy the wants of both the president,

FIGURE 2.9
Summary of Simultaneous Shifts in Demand and Supply: The Four Possible Cases

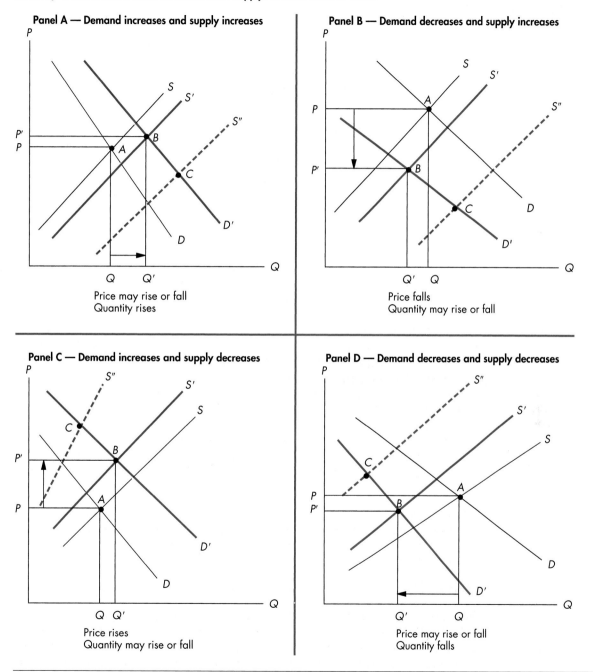

Panel A — Demand increases and supply increases

Price may rise or fall
Quantity rises

Panel B — Demand decreases and supply increases

Price falls
Quantity may rise or fall

Panel C — Demand increases and supply decreases

Price rises
Quantity may rise or fall

Panel D — Demand decreases and supply decreases

Price may rise or fall
Quantity falls

ILLUSTRATION 2.2

For Sale by Owner: One Kidney, Like-New Condition . . .

An acute shortage of human organs for transplantation has recently focused international attention on what appears to be an urgent need to increase charitable organ donations worldwide. The root of the current crisis can be traced, at least in part, to the development in 1986 of cyclosporine, a drug designed to inhibit organ and tissue rejection. Combined with increasing sophistication in tissue matching and advances in surgical techniques, the introduction of cyclosporine dramatically increased the success rates for many kinds of organ transplants. As survival rates increased and prices for transplants began to fall, demand for donated organs increased to levels that greatly exceeded the number of organs supplied through voluntary organ donations.

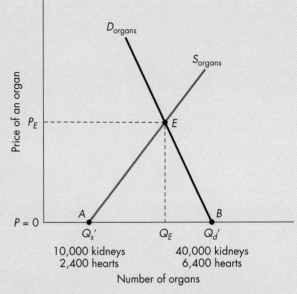

In 1995, U.S. doctors performed 2,400 heart transplant operations while 4,000 patients waited for hearts to be donated, 731 of whom died waiting. The situation was worse for kidneys: 10,000 kidney transplants were performed, 30,000 patients waited, and 1,375 died waiting for a kidney donation. For lung and liver transplants, 290 and 674 patients, respectively, died waiting for organs. In the United States and in most western European nations, the shortage of organs has placed the tremendous ethical burden of deciding who most deserves transplants squarely on the shoulders of the medical profession. The futile liver transplant for baseball legend Mickey Mantle highlighted the ethical dilemma in the United States.

Until recently, most medical professionals believed the best solution to the worsening shortage of organs was to encourage governments to promote vigorously an increase in the supply of organ donations. Educating citizens about the need to carry donor cards, strengthening laws to enforce the donation wishes of the deceased (families frequently overrule a deceased family member's organ donation decision), legalizing elective ventilation to increase organ-harvest rates (keeping brain-dead people alive with respirator machines), and even using animal organs are some of the options doctors hope will increase the supply of organs for transplantation. Unfortunately, the supply of organs appears stuck at inadequate levels while demand for organs continues to rise rapidly, and the shortage worsens each year.

As we explained in this chapter, shortages of any good arise when the price of the good is not allowed to rise to the market clearing level. Try not to squirm as we treat human organs as economic goods no different from wheat. This Illustration shows how the laws of demand and supply can explain why there is a shortage of human organs and how to eliminate the shortage. Gary Becker, the 1992 Nobel laureate in economics, proposed in a recent *Business Week* column, "There aren't enough livers, hearts, and kidneys to go around, so why not increase the [quantity] suppl[ied] by offering money to donors?" In the United States, the Transplant Act of 1984 makes it a felony to buy or sell organs. America's medical policy makers are now ready to consider relaxing the law to allow some form of financial incentives for organ donation. Despite this new willingness to try financial incentives, doctors remain fearful that cash payments for organs could backfire and decrease the quantity of organs supplied. *The Wall Street Journal* reports that physicians who in the past refused to consider financial reimbursement are now having second thoughts. One doctor is quoted: "Frankly, I'm against financial incentives. But I'm for saving lives, and therefore I'm for whatever it takes to save lives."

The accompanying figure shows an upward-sloping supply of donated organs, reflecting the observation that as the financial incentives for organ donation rise, so too does the number of organs donated. At a price of zero, the quantity of organs donated is Q_s' (point A) and the quantity demanded is Q_d' (point B). The shortage of human organs is measured by the distance between points A and B in the figure. In 1995, as noted above, "conscientious" citizens donated 10,000 kidneys as 30,000 patients waited for organs, and a shortage of 20,000 kidneys resulted. For heart transplants, a shortage of 1,600 hearts existed in 1995. As organ demand continues to shift rightward and organ supply remains stagnant, the shortage of organs (as measured by the distance between A and B) will only get much larger.

If millions of people die each year, why isn't point A located to the *right* of point B instead of to the *left* of it? In every country where citizens have been polled, surveys find an overwhelming willingness to donate organs. But as Kurtz and Saks report in their 1996 study, "The public has yet to put its 'organs' where its mouth is." Efforts to encourage organ donation as the "right thing to do" have so far caused only minimal rightward shifts in the organ supply curve. People's reluctance to designate themselves legally as organ donors can be attributed partly to procrastination and partly to anxiety harbored by some potential donors that, in the event of an accident, emergency room medical treatment might be less aggressive for accident victims whose driver's licenses are stamped "organ donor." In matters of one's own life, most people tend to be quite reluctant to take risks for free. As we show in a later chapter, people who have an aversion to risk require compensation in order to accept voluntarily a risky proposition. The higher the price offered for donated organs, the greater the number of people willing to stamp "organ donor" on their drivers' licenses.

At a price of P_E in the figure, the market for organs clears. Anyone willing and able to pay the market clearing price P_E will get an organ without a lengthy wait. When the price of donated organs rises to P_E, doctors and health care administrators no longer must make the dreadful decision of which patients get organs and which patients remain on the waiting list. The impersonal forces of the market allocate the scarce organs to the recipients most willing and able to pay for a donated organ. In the figure, those patients with demand prices—the maximum price a consumer would be willing and able to pay for a donated organ—at or above P_E choose to buy an organ at the market-determined price. Those patients between Q_E and point B with demand prices below P_E will not choose to buy an organ.

Many doctors, and indeed all compassionate citizens, are concerned that relying on market prices to allocate scarce organs leaves some patients without organs. Some patients choose not to pay for a new organ because even with a new organ, they judge their posttransplant life expectancy to be too short and tenuous to justify the price and discomfort of the transplant operation. Some patients between Q_E and B would have higher demand prices, and thus purchase an organ, if only their incomes were higher. Not all these people are poverty cases; some are simply people unwilling to strap their families with large medical bills. For potential recipients who truly represent poverty cases, compassionate donors could be allowed to designate that their organs go to the pool of indigent patients, where organs are allocated by a lottery system.

As long as the number of desired organs exceeds the number of donated organs—the quantity demanded exceeds the quantity supplied at a price of zero—the shortage of organs can be eliminated by letting the price of donated organs rise to the market clearing price. While not everyone who wants an organ for nothing will get one, at the market clearing price, more people get organs than would be the case if no financial incentives were offered (Q_E is greater than Q_s').

Sources: Gary Becker, "How Uncle Sam Could Ease the Organ Shortage," *BusinessWeek*, Jan. 20, 1997, p. 18; "Buddy Can You Spare a Lung?" *The Economist*, Jan. 25, 1997, p. 19; Prerna Mona Khanna, "Scarcity of Organs for Transplant Sparks a Move to Legalize Financial Incentives," *The Wall Street Journal*, Sept. 8, 1992, p. B1; Sheldon F. Kurtz and Michael J. Saks, "The Transplant Paradox: Overwhelming Public Support for Organ Donation v. Under-Supply of Organs," *The Journal of Corporation Law*, Summer 1996, pp. 768–803.

FIGURE 2.10
Demand and Supply for Air Travel

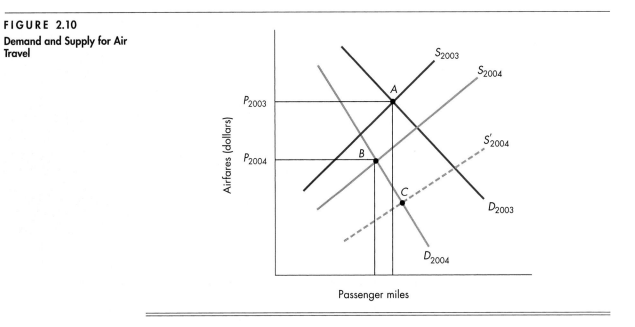

who wants expenditures cut, and the sales personnel, who would be hurt by travel restrictions. Clearly, you need to predict what will happen to airfares in 2004. You have recently read in *The Wall Street Journal* about the following two events that you expect will affect the airline industry in 2004:

1. A number of new, small airlines have recently entered the industry and others are expected to enter in 2004.
2. Videoconferencing is becoming a popular, cost-effective alternative to business travel for many U.S. corporations. The trend is expected to accelerate in 2004 as telecommunications firms begin cutting prices on teleconferencing rates.

We can use Figure 2.10 to analyze how these events would affect the price of air travel in 2004. The current demand and supply curves in the domestic market are D_{2003} and S_{2003}. Equilibrium airfare in 2003 is denoted P_{2003} at point A in Figure 2.10.

An increase in the number of airlines causes supply to increase. The increase in supply is shown in Figure 2.10 by the shift in supply to S_{2004}. Since videoconferencing and air travel are substitutes, a reduction in the price of videoconferencing causes a decrease in demand. The decrease in demand is shown in Figure 2.10 by the shift in demand to D_{2004}. Thus you must analyze a situation in which demand and supply shift simultaneously. The decrease in demand combined with the increase in supply leads you to predict a fall in airfares in 2004 to P_{2004} (point B in Figure 2.10). While you can predict that airfares will definitely fall when demand decreases and supply increases, you cannot predict whether equilibrium quantity will rise or fall in this situation (supply could instead shift to S'_{2004} in Figure 2.10). The change in quantity is indeterminate. The predicted fall in airfares is good news for you but bad news for the financially troubled airline industry.

This analysis of the air travel market is an example of qualitative analysis. You predicted only the *direction* of the price change, not the magnitude of the change. Managers are certainly interested in whether price will increase or decrease. They are also interested in *how much* price will increase or decrease. Determining how much price will rise involves quantitative analysis. To carry out quantitative analysis, either you must be given the exact specification of the market demand and supply equations or you must estimate them from market data. In later chapters we will show you how to estimate demand and supply from market data. We will look now at an example of quantitative analysis where the demand and supply equations have already been estimated for you.

Advertising and the Price of Potatoes: A Quantitative Analysis

The Potato Growers Association of America estimates that next year the demand and supply functions facing U.S. potato growers will be

$$Q_d = 28 - 0.04P$$
$$Q_s = -2 + 0.16P$$

where quantity demanded and quantity supplied are measured in trillions of hundredweight (a measure equal to 100 pounds) per year, and price is measured in cents per hundredweight. First, we predict the price of potatoes next year and how many potatoes will be sold. The market clearing price is easily determined by setting quantity demanded equal to quantity supplied and solving algebraically for equilibrium price:

$$Q_d = Q_s$$
$$28 - 0.04P = -2 + 0.16P$$
$$30 = 0.20P$$
$$150 = P_E$$

Thus the equilibrium price of potatoes next year will be 150 cents ($1.50) per hundredweight. The equilibrium level of potato production is determined by substituting the market price of 150 cents into either the demand or the supply function to get Q_E:

$$Q_d = Q_s = Q_E$$
$$28 - (0.04 \times 150) = -2 + (0.16 \times 150) = 22$$

Thus the equilibrium output of potatoes will be 22 trillion hundredweight per year.

Even though that's a lot of potatoes, the Potato Growers Association plans to begin a nationwide advertising campaign to promote potatoes by informing consumers of the nutritional benefits of potatoes. The association estimates that the

ILLUSTRATION 2.3

Did Globalization Kill U.S. Manufacturing?

As we discussed in Chapter 1, globalization of markets brings together buyers and sellers in various countries by weakening, or eliminating entirely, import quotas, tariffs, and other kinds of government restrictions on trade between nations. An article in *Business Week* commented on the recent emergence of global markets: "International trade has mushroomed, becoming a daily part of life for all the world's consumers and workers. Beyond a doubt, there is a consensus among the vast majority of economists, policymakers, and executives that open markets are a boon for growth, and that no country can thrive in the long run unless it is a full part of the global economy." In spite of the largely positive appraisal of globalization by those in government, academics, and business, some Americans believe instead that manufacturing firms in the United States have been harmed by global competition.

Doomsayers began predicting the demise of U.S. manufacturing even before official enactment in 1994 of the North American Free Trade Agreement (NAFTA), the multilateral agreement by the United States, Canada, and Mexico that significantly reduced trade barriers between the three nations. Ross Perot, a candidate in the 1992 presidential election, and labor union officials predicted that passage of NAFTA would cause a substantial relocation of U.S. manufacturing activity to Mexico. "When you've got a seven-to-one wage differential between the United States and Mexico, you will hear the giant sucking sound," Perot said in 1993 in reference to his vision of manufacturing plants being sucked out of the United States into countries with lower labor costs. It seemed "obvious" that low wages in Mexico, China, and India would throw millions of factory workers in America out of work as manufacturers shed productive capacity by shutting down plants and downsizing remaining production facilities.

To see how the doomsayers' outlook on globalization leads them to predict a decline in output for U.S. manufacturers, we can apply the tools of demand and supply developed in this chapter. In the figure, Panel A shows the effect of declining productive capacity on equilibrium output for a manufactured good. The decline in productive capacity predicted by Ross Perot and some labor unions causes the supply-shifting variable F (the number of firms or the amount of productive capacity) to decrease and the supply curve for the

manufactured good shifts leftward from S_0 to S_1 in Panel A. The decrease in supply causes equilibrium output of the good manufactured in the United States to decrease from Q_0 to Q_1. The doomsayers predicted that the reduced output of manufactured goods in the United States would force the displaced factory workers into jobs paying lower wages. In their view, the United States would become a nation of service-oriented hamburger flippers unable to produce manufactured goods for itself. As it turns out, the predicted demise of U.S. manufacturing industries did not happen.

A recent article in *Fortune* magazine presented statistical evidence debunking the "big myth about U.S. manufacturing" that global competition caused a contraction of output in U.S. manufacturing industries. The following statistics presented in the article show the sustained importance of manufacturing in the U.S. economy:

- Manufacturing output in the United States has never been higher.
- Manufacturing accounts for about 17 percent of U.S. gross domestic product (GDP), the same percentage as in 1977.
- In 1998 U.S. manufacturing output was worth $1.43 trillion, 42 percent higher than in 1992.
- U.S. manufacturers produce 50 percent more output than Japan, and 33 percent more than the United Kingdom, France, and Germany combined.

Why, then, did manufacturing expand rather dramatically in the United States even though labor costs are much lower in many foreign countries? How can we explain the absence of the "giant sucking sound" that so worried the doomsayers?

We can identify several events that caused supply and demand for goods manufactured in the United States to increase as illustrated in Panel B of the figure. On the supply side of the market for manufactured goods, U.S. manufacturing has benefited from a sharp and steady increase in productivity for the past 20 years. Over this period, falling interest rates and lower levels of inflation coupled with tax incentives for investment in new plant and equipment—including substantial investments in computers and information management technologies—combined to improve the state of technology in U.S. manufacturing. The

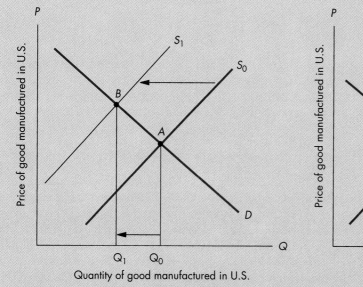

Panel a

Panel b

improvement in technology causes the supply-shifting variable T to increase and the supply of manufactured goods then shifts from S_0 to S_1 in Panel B as both capital and labor in manufacturing become more productive. While manufacturing now employs a declining fraction of the U.S. workforce, the *Fortune* article notes that this is not a problem since "a country's manufacturing prowess isn't measured by the number of people working in factories. If it were, China and India would be the world's leaders." Indeed, increased output from a smaller number of workers indicates strong gains in the productivity of inputs.

On the demand side of the market for goods manufactured in the United States, two factors contributed to the increase in demand. First, when foreign governments lifted trade restrictions, the demand-shifting variable N increased, as more foreign buyers were then able to buy goods made in the United States. Also, during periods of rising income levels around the world (demand-shifting variable M increased), demand for U.S. manufactured goods increased because nearly all goods exported from the United States are normal goods to customers in other countries. The increases in N and M combined to increase demand for goods manufactured in the United States. Panel B shows the combined effects as a rightward shift in demand from D_0 to D_1. The simultaneous increases in both demand and supply for the manufactured good cause the equilibrium output to increase. The effect of globalization on

the equilibrium price of the manufactured good is indeterminate because the price of the manufactured good can rise, fall, or stay the same when both demand and supply increase.

Globalization of world markets for manufactured goods has certainly not "killed" manufacturing industries in the United States. While doomsayers are probably correct that some manufactured goods can be produced at lower cost in foreign countries where unskilled labor is much cheaper, advances in U.S. productivity coupled with increased demand for goods made in the United States—particularly high-end manufactured goods that require highly skilled labor—have led to a boom rather than a bust in U.S. manufacturing. We should emphasize, however, that the impact of globalization on U.S. manufacturing might have looked more like the doomsayers' prediction in Panel A had U.S. manufacturing industries not invested heavily to improve the state of technology in manufacturing. We discuss the relation between productivity of inputs and costs of production in much more detail in later chapters.

Sources: Michael J. Mandel and Paul Magnusson, "Global Growing Pains," *BusinessWeek*, Dec. 13, 1999; Philip Siekman, "The Big Myth about U.S. Manufacturing," *Fortune*, Oct. 2, 2000, p. 244 [C, D, E]; for Ross Perot quote, see Charles Zewe, "Three Years Later, NAFTA's Effects Still Debated," CNN Interactive (CNN.com), posted June 30, 1997.

advertising campaign, which will make consumers want to eat more potatoes, will increase demand to

$$Q_d = 40 - 0.05P$$

Assuming that supply is unaffected by the advertising, you would obviously predict that the market price of potatoes will rise as a result of the advertising and the resulting increase in demand. However, to determine the actual market clearing price, you must equate the new quantity demanded with the quantity supplied:

$$40 - 0.05P = -2 + 0.16P$$

$$P_E = 200$$

The price of potatoes will increase to 200 cents ($2.00) with the advertising campaign. Consequently, the prediction is that the national advertising campaign will increase the market price of potatoes by 50 cents per hundredweight. This is an example of a quantitative forecast since the forecast involves both the magnitude and the direction of change in price. To make a quantitative forecast about the impact of the ads on the level of potato sales, you simply substitute the new market price of 200 cents into either the demand or the supply function to obtain the new Q_E:

$$Q_d = Q_s = Q_E$$
$$40 - (0.05 \times 200) = -2 + (0.16 \times 200) = 30$$

2.5 CEILING AND FLOOR PRICES

Shortages and surpluses *can* occur after a shift in demand or supply, but as we have stressed, these shortages and surpluses are sufficiently short in duration that they can reasonably be ignored in demand and supply analysis. In other words, markets are assumed to adjust fairly rapidly, and we concern ourselves only with the comparison of equilibriums before and after a shift in supply or demand. There are, however, some types of shortages and surpluses that market forces do not eliminate. These are more permanent in nature and result from government interferences with the market mechanism, which prevent prices from freely moving up or down to clear the market.

Typically these more permanent shortages and surpluses are caused by government imposing legal restrictions on the movement of prices. Shortages and surpluses can be created simply by legislating a price below or above equilibrium. Governments have decided in the past, and will surely decide in the future, that the price of a particular commodity is "too high" or "too low" and will proceed to set a "fair price." Without evaluating the desirability of such interference, we can use demand and supply curves to analyze the economic effects of these two types of interference: the setting of minimum and maximum prices.

ceiling price
The maximum price the government permits sellers to charge for a good. When this price is below equilibrium, a shortage occurs.

If the government imposes a maximum price, or **ceiling price,** on a good, the effect is a shortage of that good. In Panel A of Figure 2.11, a ceiling price of $1 is set on some good X. No one can legally sell X for more than $1, and $1 is less than the equilibrium (market clearing) price of $2. At the ceiling price of $1, the maximum

FIGURE 2.11
Ceiling and Floor Prices

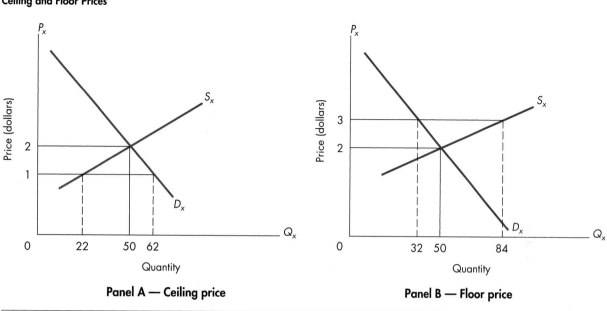

Panel A — Ceiling price

Panel B — Floor price

amount that producers are willing to supply is 22 units. At $1, consumers wish to purchase 62 units. A shortage of 40 units results from the imposition of the $1 price ceiling. Market forces will not be permitted to bid up the price to eliminate the shortage because producers cannot sell the good for more than $1. This type of shortage will continue until government eliminates the price ceiling or until shifts in either supply or demand cause the equilibrium price to fall to $1 or lower. It is worth noting that "black" (illegal) markets usually arise in such cases. Some consumers are willing to pay more than $1 for good X rather than do without it, and some producers are willing to sell good X for more than $1 rather than forgo the extra sales. In most cases the law is not a sufficient deterrent to the illegal trade of a good at prices above the ceiling.

Alternatively, the government may believe that the suppliers of the good are not earning as much income as they deserve and, therefore, sets a minimum price or **floor price.** You can see the results of such actions in Panel B of Figure 2.11. Dissatisfied with the equilibrium price of $2 and equilibrium quantity of 50, the government sets a minimum price of $3. Since the government cannot repeal the law of demand, consumers reduce the amount they purchase to 32 units. Producers, of course, are going to increase their production of X to 84 units in response to the $3 price. Now a surplus of 52 units exists. Because the government is not allowing the price of X to fall, this surplus is going to continue until it is either eliminated by the government or demand or supply shifts cause market price to rise to $3 or higher. In order for the government to ensure that producers do not illegally sell their

floor price
The minimum price the government permits sellers to charge for a good. When this price is above equilibrium, a surplus occurs.

surpluses for less than $3, the government must either restrict the production of X to 32 units or be willing to buy (and store or destroy) the 52 surplus units.

This section can be summarized by the following principle:

▢ **Principle**   When the government sets a ceiling price below the equilibrium price, a shortage or excess demand results because consumers wish to buy more units of the good than producers are willing to sell at the ceiling price. If the government sets a floor price above the equilibrium price, a surplus or excess supply results because producers offer for sale more units of the good than buyers wish to consume at the floor price.

For managers to make successful decisions by watching for changes in economic conditions, they must be able to predict how these changes will affect the market. As we hope you have seen, this is precisely what economic analysis is designed to do. This ability to use economics to make predictions is one of the topics we will emphasize throughout the text.

2.6 SUMMARY

In this chapter we presented the basic framework of demand and supply analysis. The market was divided into two different groups of participants: consumers and producers. Demand analysis focuses on the behavior of consumers, while supply analysis examines the behavior of producers. The demand and supply curves together determine the price and output that occur in a market. The impact of changing market circumstances on equilibrium price and output is determined by making the appropriate shifts in either demand or supply and comparing equilibriums before and after the change.

The generalized demand function specifies how the quantity demanded of a good is related to six variables that jointly determine the amount of a good or service consumers are willing and able to buy. By holding constant the five determinants of demand—income, the price of related goods, consumer tastes, expected price, and the number of consumers—and letting only the price of the good vary, a demand function is derived. The law of demand states that quantity demanded and price are inversely related, all other variables influencing demand held constant. Whenever the price of a good changes, a "change in quantity demanded" occurs, which is represented by a movement along a fixed demand curve. A point on the demand curve shows either the maximum amount of a good that will be purchased if a given price is charged or the maximum price consumers will pay for a specific amount of the good.

The five determinants of demand (M, P_R, $\mathcal{T}$, P_e, and N) are also called the demand-shifting variables because their values determine the location of the demand curve. If any of these five variables changes, the demand curve shifts either leftward (demand decreases) or rightward (demand increases), and a change in demand is said to have occurred. Table 2.4 summarizes how demand curves shift when each of the determinants of demand changes value.

For producers, the generalized supply function shows how six variables—the price of the product, the price of inputs, the prices of goods related in production, the state of technology, the expected price of the good, and the number of firms or amount of productive capacity—jointly determine the amount of a good or service producers are willing to supply. Quantity supplied and price are directly related, all other variables influencing supply held constant. When the price of a good changes, a change in quantity supplied occurs, which is represented by a movement along a fixed supply curve. A point on the supply curve shows either the maximum amount of a good that will be offered for sale at a given price or the minimum price (the supply price) necessary to induce producers voluntarily to offer a particular quantity for sale.

The five determinants of supply (P_I, P_r, T, P_e, and F) are also called the supply-shifting variables because their values determine the location of the supply curve. If any one of these five variables changes, the supply curve shifts either leftward (supply decreases) or rightward (supply increases), and a change in supply is said to have occurred. Table 2.8 summarizes how supply curves shift when each of the determinants of supply changes value.

The equilibrium price and quantity in a market are determined by the intersection of demand and supply curves. At the point of intersection, quantity demanded equals quantity supplied, and the market clears. Since the location of the demand and supply curves is determined by the five determinants of demand and the five determinants of supply, a change in any one of these 10 variables will result in a new equilibrium point. When demand increases and supply remains constant, price and quantity sold both rise, as shown by the movement from point A to B in Figure 2.6. A decrease in demand, supply constant, causes both price and quantity sold to fall, as shown by the movement from point A to C. When supply increases and demand remains constant, price falls and quantity sold rises, as shown by the movement from point R to S in Figure 2.7. A decrease in supply, demand constant, causes price to rise and quantity sold to fall, as shown by the movement from point R to T.

When both supply and demand shift simultaneously, it is possible to predict either the direction in which price changes or the direction in which quantity changes, but not both. The change in equilibrium quantity or price is said to be indeterminate when the direction of change depends upon the relative magnitudes by which demand and supply shift. The four possible cases for simultaneous shifts in demand and supply are summarized in Figure 2.9.

Demand and supply analysis allows managers to make either qualitative or quantitative forecasts. A forecast is qualitative in nature when only the direction of change in market equilibrium is predicted. If enough quantitative information is available, managers can make quantitative forecasts to predict both the direction and magnitude of changes in equilibrium values of price and quantity. Never underestimate the value of qualitative forecasts. Correctly predicting the direction of change in price or sales can be an extremely valuable skill for any manager.

Sometimes the government imposes either a ceiling price or a floor price, which interferes with the market mechanism and prevents price from freely moving up or down to clear the market. When government sets a ceiling price below the equilibrium price, a shortage results because consumers wish to buy more of the good than producers are willing to sell at the ceiling price. If government sets a floor price above the equilibrium price, a surplus results because producers offer for sale more of the good than buyers wish to purchase at the higher floor price.

In this chapter we had two purposes. The first was to show you how managers can use economic theory to make predictions about the effect of exogenous events upon prices. We attempted to show what to expect about price and quantity in specific markets when certain variables change or are expected to change. As we will show in later chapters, the ability to make correct forecasts under difficult conditions separates good (successful) managers from those who are not so good (unsuccessful).

The second purpose was to prepare you for the material we will present in the following chapters. These chapters will show how demand and supply functions are derived from the behavior of consumers and firms and how these functions can be estimated. A thorough understanding of the material set forth in this chapter is essential to developing the ability to use and interpret demand and supply estimations and make accurate forecasts about the future.

TECHNICAL PROBLEMS

1. The generalized demand function for good A is

$$Q_d = 600 - 4P_A - 0.03M - 12P_B + 15\mathcal{T} + 6P_e + 1.5N$$

where Q_d = quantity demanded of good A each month, P_A = price of good A, M = average household income, P_B = price of related good B, $\mathcal{T}$ = a consumer taste index ranging in value from 0 to 10 (the highest rating), P_e = price consumers expect to pay next month for good A, and N = number of buyers in the market for good A.

   a. Interpret the intercept parameter in the generalized demand function.

   b. What is the value of the slope parameter for the price of good A? Does it have the correct algebraic sign? Why?

    c. Interpret the slope parameter for income. Is good *A* normal or inferior? Explain.

    d. Are goods *A* and *B* substitutes or complements? Explain. Interpret the slope parameter for the price of good *B*.

    e. Are the algebraic signs on the slope parameters for $\mathcal{T}$, P_e, and *N* correct? Explain.

    f. Calculate the quantity demanded of good *A* when $P_A = \$5$, $M = \$25,000$, $P_B = \$40$, $\mathcal{T} = 6.5$, $P_e = \$5.25$, and $N = 2,000$.

2. Consider the generalized demand function:

$$Q_d = 8,000 - 16P + 0.75M + 30P_R$$

    a. Derive the equation for the demand function when $M = \$30,000$ and $P_R = \$50$.

    b. Interpret the intercept and slope parameters of the demand function derived in part *a.*

    c. Sketch a graph of the demand function in part *a.* Where does the demand function intersect the quantity-demanded axis? Where does it intersect the price axis?

    d. Using the demand function from part *a,* calculate the quantity demanded when the price of the good is $1,000 and when the price is $1,500.

    e. Derive the inverse of the demand function in part *a.* Using the inverse demand function, calculate the demand price for 24,000 units of the good. Give an interpretation of this demand price.

3. The demand curve for good *X* passes through the point $P = \$2$ and $Q_d = 35$. Give two interpretations of this point on the demand curve.

4. Recall that the generalized demand function for the demand curves in Figure 2.2 is

$$Q_d = 1,800 - 20P + 0.6M - 50P_R$$

    a. Derive the demand function for D_2 in Figure 2.2. Recall that for D_2 income is $19,500 and the price of the related good is $250.

    b. Beginning with the demand curve D_2, suppose a decrease in income causes consumers to be willing and able to purchase 300 fewer units at each price. Sketch this new demand curve and label it D_3. What is the equation for D_3? By how much must income fall to cause the shift from D_2 to D_3?

5. Using a graph, explain carefully the difference between a movement along a demand curve and a shift in the demand curve.

6. What happens to *demand* when the following changes occur?

    a. The price of the commodity falls.

    b. Income increases and the commodity is normal.

    c. Income increases and the commodity is inferior.

    d. The price of a substitute good increases.

    e. The price of a substitute good decreases.

    f. The price of a complement good increases.

    g. The price of a complement good decreases.

7. Consider the generalized supply function:

$$Q_s = 60 + 5P - 12P_I + 10F$$

where Q_s = quantity supplied, P = price of the commodity, P_I = price of a key input in the production process, and F = number of firms producing the commodity.

    a. Interpret the slope parameters on P, P_I, and F.

    b. Derive the equation for the supply function when $P_I = \$90$ and $F = 20$.

    c. Sketch a graph of the supply function in part *b.* At what price does the supply curve intersect the price axis? Give an interpretation of the price intercept of this supply curve.

    d. Using the supply function from part *b,* calculate the quantity supplied when the price of the commodity is $300 and $500.

    e. Derive the inverse of the supply function in part *b.* Using the inverse supply function, calculate the supply price for 680 units of the commodity. Give an interpretation of this supply price.

8. Suppose the supply curve for good X passes through the point $P = \$25$, $Q_s = 500$. Give two interpretations of this point on the supply curve.

9. The following generalized supply function shows the quantity of good X that producers offer for sale (Q_s):

$$Q_s = 19 + 20P_x - 10P_I + 6T - 32P_r - 20P_e + 5F$$

where P_x is the price of X, P_I is the price of labor, T is an index measuring the level of technology, P_r is the price of a good R that is related in production, P_e is the expected future price of good X, and F is the number of firms in the industry.

    a. Determine the equation of the supply curve for X when $P_I = 8$, $T = 4$, $P_r = 4$, $P_e = 5$, and $F = 47$. Plot this supply curve on a graph.

    b. Suppose the price of labor increases from 8 to 9. Find the equation of the new supply curve. Plot the new supply curve on a graph.

    c. Is the good related in production a complement or a substitute in production? Explain.

    d. What is the correct way to interpret each of the coefficients in the generalized supply function given above?

10. Using a graph, explain carefully the difference between a movement along a supply curve and a shift in the supply curve.

11. Other things remaining the same, what would happen to the *supply* of a particular commodity if the following changes occur?

    a. The price of the commodity decreases.

    b. A technological breakthrough enables the good to be produced at a significantly lower cost.

    c. The prices of inputs used to produce the commodity increase.

    d. The price of a commodity that is a substitute in production decreases.

    e. The managers of firms that produce the good expect the price of the good to rise in the near future.

    f. Firms in the industry purchase more plant and equipment, increasing the productive capacity in the industry.

12. The following table presents the demand and supply schedules for apartments in a small U.S. city:

Monthly rental rate (dollars per month)	Quantity demanded (number of units per month)	Quantity supplied (number of units per month)
$300	130,000	35,000
350	115,000	37,000
400	100,000	41,000
450	80,000	45,000
500	72,000	52,000
550	60,000	60,000
600	55,000	70,000
650	48,000	75,000

a. If the monthly rental rate is $600, excess _____ of _____ apartments per month will occur and rental rates can be expected to _____.

b. If the monthly rental rate is $350, excess _____ of _____ apartments per month will occur and rental rates can be expected to _____.

c. The equilibrium or market clearing rental rate is $_____ per month.

d. The equilibrium number of apartments rented is _____ per month.

13. Suppose that the demand and supply functions for good X are

$$Q_d = 50 - 8P$$

$$Q_s = -17.5 + 10P$$

a. What are the equilibrium price and quantity?

b. What is the market outcome if price is $2.75? What do you expect to happen? Why?

c. What is the market outcome if price is $4.25? What do you expect to happen? Why?

d. What happens to equilibrium price and quantity if the demand function becomes $Q_d = 59 - 8P$?

e. What happens to equilibrium price and quantity if the supply function becomes $Q_s = -40 + 10P$ (demand is $Q_d = 50 - 8P$)?

14. Determine the effect upon equilibrium price and quantity sold if the following changes occur in a particular market:

a. Consumers' income increases and the good is normal.

b. The price of a substitute good (in consumption) increases.

c. The price of a substitute good (in production) increases.

d. The price of a complement good (in consumption) increases.

e. The price of inputs used to produce the good increases.

f. Consumers expect that the price of the good will increase in the near future.

g. It is widely publicized that consumption of the good is hazardous to health.

h. Cost-reducing technological change takes place in the industry.

15. Suppose that a pair of events from problem 14 occur simultaneously. For each of the pairs of events indicated below, perform a qualitative analysis to predict the direction of change in either the equilibrium price or the equilibrium quantity. Explain why the change in one of these two variables is indeterminate.

a. Both *a* and *h* in problem 14 occur simultaneously.

b. Both *d* and *e* in problem 14 occur simultaneously.

    c. Both *d* and *h* in problem 14 occur simultaneously.

    d. Both *f* and *c* in problem 14 occur simultaneously.

16. Suppose that the generalized demand function for good *X* is

$$Q_d = 60 - 2P_x + 0.01M + 7P_R$$

where

    Q_d = quantity of *X* demanded
    P_x = price of *X*
    M = (average) consumer income
    P_R = price of a related good *R*

    a. Is good *X* normal or inferior? Explain.

    b. Are goods *X* and *R* substitutes or complements? Explain.

    Suppose that M = \$40,000 and P_R = \$20.

    c. What is the demand function for good *X*?

    Suppose the supply function is

$$Q_s = -600 + 10P_x$$

    d. What are the equilibrium price and quantity?

    e. What happens to equilibrium price and quantity if other things remain the same as in part *d* but income increases to \$52,000?

    f. What happens to equilibrium price and quantity if other things remain the same as in part *d* but the price of good *R* decreases to \$14?

    g. What happens to equilibrium price and quantity if other things remain the same, income and the price of the related goods are at their original levels, and supply shifts to $Q_s = -360 + 10P_x$?

17. In problem 12, suppose the city council decides rents are too high and imposes a rent ceiling of \$400.

    a. The ceiling on rent causes a _____ of _____ apartments per month.

    b. How many *more* renters would have found an apartment in this city if the ceiling had not been imposed?

    Suppose that instead of imposing a ceiling price, the city council places a floor price of \$600 on rental rates.

    c. The floor price on rent causes a _____ of _____ apartments per month.

18. Use the following graph to answer these questions.

    a. What are the equilibrium price and quantity?

    b. What is the effect of a ceiling price of \$40?

    c. What is the effect of a floor price of \$50? A floor price of \$70?

    d. Suppose income increases and consumers are willing and able to buy 100 more units at each price. Construct the new demand curve and label it D_1. What are the new equilibrium price and quantity?

    e. Suppose input prices fall and suppliers are willing to offer for sale 200 more units at each price. Construct the new supply curve, and label it S_1. Suppose instead that when input prices fall, supply price falls by \$20 for each level of output. Verify that the new supply curve is exactly the same in either case. What are the new equilibrium price and output when the supply and demand curves are D_1 and S_1?

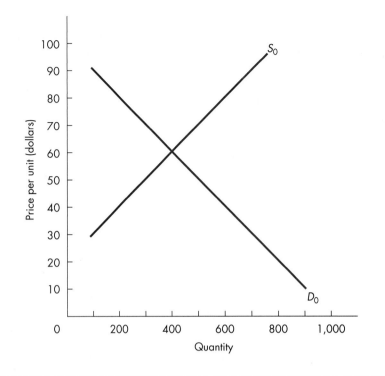

APPLIED PROBLEMS

1. Suppose you are the manager of a California winery. How would you expect the following events to affect the price you receive for a bottle of wine?
   a. The price of comparable French wines decreases.
   b. One hundred new wineries open in California.
   c. The unemployment rate in the United States decreases.
   d. The price of cheese increases.
   e. The price of a glass bottle increases significantly due to new government antishatter regulations.
   f. Researchers discover a new wine-making technology that reduces production costs.
   g. The price of wine vinegar, which is made from the leftover grape mash, increases.
   h. The average age of consumers increases, and older people drink less wine.

2 Citrus Speculation and Forecasting, Inc., has been hired by a private consortium of orange growers to predict what will happen to the price and output of oranges under the conditions below. What are your predictions? For each part, sketch a graph showing the appropriate demand and supply analysis.
   a. A major freeze destroys a large number of the orange trees in Florida.
   b. The scientists in the agricultural extension service of the University of Florida discover a way to double the number of oranges produced by each orange tree.
   c. The American Medical Association announces that drinking orange juice can reduce the risk of heart attack.

    d. The price of grapefruit falls.

3. Evaluate the following statements using graphical analysis. Provide a brief narrative explanation of your graph to support your evaluation. Make sure the axes and curves in your graphs are properly labeled.

    a. "When demand for home heating oil increases, a shortage of heating oil will occur."

    b. "A decrease in the supply of random access memory (RAM) chips for personal computers causes a shortage of RAM chips."

4. Several economics faculty members were standing in line in the student union cafeteria for lunch. One was heard to say, "I sure wish the union would raise their food prices." The others agreed. What in the world would motivate such a wish?

5. Rising jet fuel prices recently led most major U.S. airlines to raise fares by approximately 15 percent. Explain how this substantial increase in airfares would affect the following:

    a. The demand for air travel.

    b. The demand for hotels.

    c. The demand for rental cars.

    d. The supply of overnight mail.

6. The famous Swedish economist Assar Lindbeck remarked in his book on rent controls, "Rent control appears to be the most efficient technique presently known to destroy a city—except for bombing." Rent controls place price ceilings on rents at levels below equilibrium rental rates for the stated purpose of making housing more affordable for low-income families. Using demand and supply analysis, answer the following questions:

    a. How does imposing rent controls affect the number of housing units available to low-income families?

    b. Under rent controls, can all low-income families get rent-controlled housing?

    c. Who gains from rent controls? Who loses?

    d. Why would Professor Lindbeck think rent controls are destructive?

    e. Can you think of an alternative policy to make plenty of housing available to low-income families that would not be subject to the problems of rent controls?

7. Suppose you are a stock market analyst specializing in the stocks of theme parks, and you are examining Disneyland's stock. *The Wall Street Journal* reports that tourism has slowed down in the United States. At Six Flags Magic Mountain in Valencia, California, a new Viper roller coaster is now operating and another new ride, Psyclone, will be opening this year. Using demand and supply analysis, predict the impact of these events on ticket prices and attendance at Disneyland. As reported in *The Wall Street Journal*, Disneyland slashed ticket prices and admitted that attendance was somewhat lower. Is this consistent with your prediction using demand and supply analysis? In light of the fact that both price and output were falling at Disneyland, is the law of demand being violated in the world of fantasy?

8. The Council on Economic Priorities recently published "Shopping for a Better World," a guide that rates 168 companies on their social performance. The aim of the council is to "make progressive policies profitable" by informing consumers about such questions as which pasta producer also makes cigarettes, which companies have women in executive management positions, which companies give to charity, and so on. Using demand and supply analysis, explain how disseminating this type of information can translate into higher profits for "socially responsible" firms.

9. California voters, in an attempt to halt the rapid increase in the state's automobile insurance rates, approved Proposition 103. The measure proposes to roll back auto insurance rates by 20 percent and freeze them for at least a year. Using a graph, show the impact of Proposition 103 on the market for automobile insurance in California. As the costs of providing insurance continue to rise, what do you predict will happen over time in the California market for auto insurance? How would your prediction change if Proposition 103 is defeated?

10. *The Wall Street Journal* reported that recent law school graduates were having a very difficult time obtaining jobs in the legal profession. Many law schools said that 10 to 20 percent of their graduates still had not found jobs. The historical average had been 6 to 8 percent. Many recent graduates were taking jobs outside law at much lower wages than were typically paid to beginning lawyers. Based on this information, what would be your prediction about lawyers' salaries for the future? The next year? The next six years?

11. Construct a graph showing equilibrium in the market for movie tickets. Label both axes and denote the initial equilibrium price and quantity as P_0 and Q_0. For each of the following events, draw an appropriate new supply or demand curve for movies, and predict the impact of the event on the market price of a movie ticket and the number of tickets sold in the new equilibrium situation:

    a. Movie theaters double the price of soft drinks and popcorn.

    b. A national video rental chain cuts its rental rate by 25 percent.

    c. Cable television begins offering pay-per-view movies.

    d. The screenwriters' guild ends a 10-month strike.

    e. Kodak reduces the price it charges Hollywood producers for motion picture film.

12. An article in *Business Week* reported the discovery of a new processing technology that makes it economically feasible to turn natural gas into a liquid petroleum that yields superclean gasoline, diesel fuel, or any other product derived from crude oil. This discovery represents 770 billion barrels of oil equivalent, "enough to slake the world's thirst for oil for 29 years."

    a. Using demand and supply analysis, explain why this new process will *not* cause a surplus of crude oil. If no surplus is created, then what will be the impact of this process on the market for crude oil?

    b. Had this process *not* been discovered, explain why we still would have had "enough" crude oil to meet the growing worldwide demand for crude oil.

13. Many cities have experienced a substantial decrease in the amount of garbage being collected after they changed from levying a tax on each household to pay for the pickup to charging a fee for each bag or can picked up. Would this have been the result of a change in demand? If so why, or if not, why not? If not, what was the probable reason?

14. Firewood prices in places from northern California to Boston and suburban New Jersey have remained steady even though the supply of firewood has been diminished by environmental restrictions on cutting. *The Wall Street Journal* reports that sales of gas fireplaces are outpacing sales of wood-burning hearths and that "people are burning less and less wood." Use supply and demand analysis to show why firewood prices are not rising while the quantity of firewood burned is declining. (*Hint:* Allow for simultaneous shifts in the demand and supply of firewood.)

15. *Business Week* recently declared, "We have entered the Age of the Internet," and observed that when markets for goods or services gain access to the Internet, more consumers and more businesses participate in the market. Use supply and demand analysis to predict the effect of e-commerce on equilibrium output and equilibrium price of products gaining a presence on the Internet.

☐   **MATHEMATICAL APPENDIX**   **Demand and Supply—The Linear Case**

This appendix presents a mathematical analysis of demand and supply when both demand and supply are linear functions. The analytic tools required in this appendix, as well as in the mathematical appendixes in later chapters, are basic high school algebra and some fundamental concepts from calculus. The student workbook that accompanies this textbook provides a brief review of the mathematical tools employed in the mathematical appendixes in this book.

The Generalized Linear Demand Function

The linear form of the generalized demand function can be expressed as

$$(1) \qquad Q_d = a + bP + cM + dP_R$$

where Q_d is the quantity demanded per unit of time, P is the price per unit of the good or service, M is a measure of consumer income, and P_R is the price of the good or service related in consumption. To keep mathematical notation and expressions as simple as possible, only two of the five demand-shifting variables discussed in Chapter 2 are included in equation (1). The parameters a, b, c, and d have the following algebraic signs:

  a: The intercept parameter gives the value of Q_d if P, M, and P_R are all equal to zero simultaneously. Since quantity demanded must be a nonnegative value, a is restricted to being greater than or equal to zero ($a \geq 0$).

  b: The slope parameter for the price of the good, b, measures the rate of change in Q_d as price changes, holding the other variables that affect Q_d constant. Consequently, b can be interpreted as the partial derivative $\partial Q_d / \partial P$. The law of demand stipulates that Q_d and P are inversely related, thus b must be negative ($b < 0$).

  c: The slope parameter for consumer income, c, measures the rate of change in Q_d as income changes, holding all other variables constant. If the good or service is normal (inferior), then $\partial Q_d / \partial M$ will be positive (negative).

  d: The slope parameter for the price of a related good or service, d, measures the rate of change in Q_d as P_R changes, all else constant. If the related good or service is a substitute (complement), then $\partial Q_d / \partial P_R$ will be positive (negative).

Each of the partial derivatives (b, c, and d) is constant because the demand function is linear in functional form.

The Generalized Linear Supply Function

The linear form of the generalized supply function can be expressed as

$$(2) \qquad Q_s = h + kP + lP_I + sF$$

where Q_s is the quantity supplied per unit of time, P is the price per unit of the good, P_I is the price of an input used in producing the good, and F is the number of firms in the industry. Again to keep mathematical expressions simple, we include only two of the five supply-shifting variables discussed in Chapter 2. The parameters h, k, l, and s have the following signs:

  h: The intercept parameter gives the value of Q_s if P, P_I, and F are all equal to zero simultaneously. The intercept parameter for the generalized supply curve (h) does not have any particular economic interpretation and can be positive, negative, or zero.

  k: The slope parameter for the price of the good, k, measures the rate of change in Q_s as price changes, holding the other variables that affect Q_s constant. Consequently, k can be interpreted as the partial derivative $\partial Q_s / \partial P$, and k cannot be negative ($k \geq 0$).

  l: The slope parameter for the price of an input, l, measures the rate of change in Q_s as the price of the input changes, holding all other variables constant. All other things equal, an increase (decrease) in input prices causes producers to decrease (increase) the amount of the good offered for sale, and thus $\partial Q_s / \partial P_I$ is negative.*

  s: The slope parameter for the number of firms, s, measures the rate of change in Q_s as the number of firms changes, holding all other variables constant. All other things equal, an increase in the number of firms causes the amount of the good offered for sale to increase, and thus $\partial Q_s / \partial F$ is positive.

————

  *In most cases, more than one input price influences quantity supplied. For example, if three inputs are used in production, the generalized linear supply function can be expressed as $Q_s = h + kP + l_1 P_{I1} + l_2 P_{I2} + l_3 P_{I3} + sF$. The slope parameters l_1, l_2, and l_3 are all negative.

As for the linear demand function, each of the partial derivatives (k, l, and s) is constant because the supply function is linear in form.

Derivation of Demand and Supply Functions

When all variables other than P are held constant in the generalized demand and supply functions, the ordinary demand and supply functions can be expressed as a function of price only:

$$(3) \qquad Q_d = f(P)$$
$$(4) \qquad Q_s = g(P)$$

To obtain demand and supply equations (3) and (4), respectively, all the variables other than P—often referred to as "shift variables"—are set equal to constant values (M', P'_R, P'_I, and F') in the generalized demand and supply functions:

$$Q_d = a + bP + cM' + dP'_R$$
$$Q_s = h + kP + lP'_I + sF'$$

The constant terms in each function may be grouped together as

$$(5),\,(6) \quad A = a + cM' + dP'_R \quad \text{and} \quad H = h + lP'_I + sF'$$

which form the intercept parameters of the ordinary demand and supply functions:

$$(3') \qquad Q_d = f(P) = A + bP$$
$$(4') \qquad Q_s = g(P) = H + kP$$

When a change in M or P_R causes the value of A to change, a new demand equation results, and the graph of the demand equation—called the demand curve—shifts parallel to the original demand curve. (Why is the shift parallel?) For supply, a change in P_I or F causes H to change, and the supply curve shifts parallel to the original supply curve. It should be clear from inspecting equations (5) and (6) that shifts in demand or supply curves happen when changes in the values of one (or more) of the shift variables occur.

Inverse Demand and Supply Functions

The inverse of a function $y = f(x)$ can be expressed as $x = f^{-1}(y)$. Using this notation, the inverse demand and supply functions can be expressed as

$$(7) \qquad P = f^{-1}(Q_d) = -\frac{A}{b} + \frac{1}{b}Q_d$$

$$(8) \qquad P = g^{-1}(Q_s) = -\frac{H}{k} + \frac{1}{k}Q_s$$

When following the convention in economics of plotting P on the vertical axis and Q_d and Q_s on the horizontal axis, the demand and supply curves represent the *inverse* demand and supply equations. When price is graphed on the vertical axis and quantity on the horizontal axis, $-A/b$ and $-H/k$ are the price (vertical) intercepts for the demand and supply curves, respectively. The slopes of the demand and supply curves, when P is on the vertical axis and Q_d and Q_s are on the horizontal axis, are $1/b$ and $1/k$, respectively.

Market Equilibrium

The price at which the market reaches equilibrium or "clears" is the price for which $Q_d = Q_s$. To find the equilibrium price, set $Q_d = Q_s$ and solve for P_E:

$$(9) \qquad A + bP_E = H + kP_E$$

$$P_E = \frac{A - H}{k - b} = P_E(b, k, A, H)$$

To solve for equilibrium output, Q_E, substitute P_E into either $Q_d = f(P)$ or $Q_s = g(P)$. Substituting equation (9) into (3') yields the solution for Q_E:

$$(10) \qquad Q_E = A + bP_E = A + b\left(\frac{A - H}{k - b}\right)$$

$$= \frac{Ak - bH}{k - b} = Q_E(b, k, A, H)$$

The equilibrium values of both price and quantity are determined by the slopes of both demand and supply as well as the values of *all* the shift parameters in demand *and* supply.

Calculating the Change in P_E and Q_E

In this section, changes in equilibrium price and quantity are examined using the total differentials of P_E and Q_E. Three situations are examined: (1) demand shifts while supply remains unchanged, (2) supply shifts while demand remains unchanged, and (3) both demand and supply shift simultaneously. All three situations can be analyzed using the following total differentials of equations (9) and (10):

$$(11) \quad dP_E = \frac{\partial P_E}{\partial A} \frac{\partial A}{\partial M'} dM' + \frac{\partial P_E}{\partial A} \frac{\partial A}{\partial P'_R} dP'_R$$

$$+ \frac{\partial P_E}{\partial H} \frac{\partial H}{\partial P'_I} dP'_I + \frac{\partial P_E}{\partial H} \frac{\partial H}{\partial F'} dF$$

$$(12) \quad dQ_E = \frac{\partial Q_E}{\partial A} \frac{\partial A}{\partial M'} dM' + \frac{\partial Q_E}{\partial A} \frac{\partial A}{\partial P'_R} dP'_R$$

$$+ \frac{\partial Q_E}{\partial H} \frac{\partial H}{\partial P'_I} dP'_I + \frac{\partial Q_E}{\partial H} \frac{\partial H}{\partial F'} dF$$

A shift in demand (supply constant)

When one of the two demand-shifting variables in equation (3) changes value, demand shifts and new equilibrium values for price and quantity result. Suppose a change in income causes demand to shift while supply remains constant. This situation can be imposed on the differentials of P_E and Q_E by noting that $dP'_R = dP'_I = dF' = 0$, and thus for the linear demand and supply equations

$$(13) \quad dP_E = \frac{\partial P_E}{\partial A} \frac{\partial A}{\partial M'} dM' = \frac{1}{k - b} c\, dM'$$

$$(14) \quad dQ_E = \frac{\partial Q_E}{\partial A} \frac{\partial A}{\partial M'} dM' = \frac{k}{k - b} c\, dM'$$

Since $k - b$ is positive, dP_E and dM' have the same sign when the good is normal ($c > 0$). If the good is inferior, ($c < 0$), dP_E and dM' have opposite signs. Similarly for dQ_E, $k/(k - b)$ is positive, and thus Q_E and M' move in the same (opposite) direction when the good is normal (inferior).

Recall that the shift in demand from D_0 to D_1 in Figure 2.6 is caused by an increase in income from $20,000 to $20,500. Thus $dM' = 500$. Substituting the values of the slope parameters for price from the demand and supply equations ($b = -20$ and $k = 10$) and the slope parameter for income ($c = 0.6$) into the differentials (13) and (14) yields

$$dP_E = \frac{1}{10 - (-20)} \times 0.6 \times 500 = +10$$

$$dQ_E = \frac{10}{10 - (-20)} \times 0.6 \times 500 = +100$$

Moving from point A to B in Figure 2.6 requires an increase in equilibrium price of $10 and an increase in equilibrium quantity of 100 units.

A shift in supply (demand constant)

When one of the two supply-shifting variables in equation (4) changes value, supply shifts and new equilibrium values for price and quantity result. Suppose a change in the price of an input causes supply to shift while demand remains constant. This situation can be imposed on the differentials of P_E and Q_E by setting $dP'_R = dM' = dF' = 0$, and thus for the linear demand and supply equations

$$(15) \quad dP_E = \frac{\partial P_E}{\partial H} \frac{\partial H}{\partial P'_I} dP'_I = -\frac{1}{k - b} l\, dP'_I$$

$$(16) \quad dQ_E = \frac{\partial Q_E}{\partial H} \frac{\partial H}{\partial P'_I} dP'_I = -\frac{b}{k - b} l\, dP'_I$$

Since $-[1/(k - b)]$ is negative and l is negative, dP_E and dP'_I always have the same sign. When demand is constant, an increase (decrease) in the price of an input price always increases (decreases) the equilibrium price of the good or service. The opposite result holds for the change in Q_E. Since $-[b/(k - b)]$ is positive and l is negative, Q_E and P'_I move in opposite directions.

Simultaneous changes in both demand and supply

In this section one demand-shifting variable and one supply-shifting variable both change values simultaneously. Examination of the appropriate total differentials reveals that the direction of change in one of the equilibrium variables P_E or Q_E can be determined (with information about whether a good is normal or inferior or a substitute or complement good), but the direction of change in the other equilibrium variable cannot be determined—its change is indeterminate.

Turning first to a general analysis, suppose income increases while the price of a key ingredient falls, and all other things remain constant. The appropriate total differentials are found by setting $dP'_R = dF' = 0$ in equations (11) and (12):

$$(17) \quad dP_E = \frac{\partial P_E}{\partial A} \frac{\partial A}{\partial M'} dM' + \frac{\partial P_E}{\partial H} \frac{\partial H}{\partial P'_I} dP'_I$$

$$= \frac{1}{k - b} \times c \times dM' + -\frac{1}{k - b} \times l \times dP'_I$$

$$(18) \quad dQ_E = \frac{\partial Q_E}{\partial A} \frac{\partial A}{\partial M'} dM' + \frac{\partial A}{\partial H'} \frac{\partial H}{\partial P'_I} dP'_I$$

$$= \frac{k}{k - b} \times c \times dM' + -\frac{b}{k - b} \times l \times dP'_I$$

FIGURE 2A.1

Simultaneous Shifts in Demand and Supply: $dM' = 500$ and $dP'_I = -18.75$

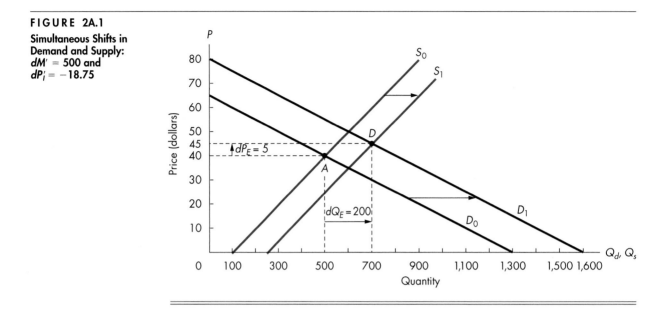

To illustrate the application of these two differentials, consider the generalized demand and supply functions presented in Chapter 2 and graphed in Figures 2.4 and 2.6. Let income increase from $20,000 to $20,500 ($dM' = 500$). Also let the price of the input decrease from $50 to $31.25 ($dP'_I = -18.75$). You know from reading Chapter 2 that when both demand and supply increase (as they do here), the change in equilibrium price will be indeterminate and the change in equilibrium quantity will be positive.

To verify that the change in P_E depends on the magnitude of the changes in M' and P'_I, first find the signs of the coefficients for dM' and dP'_I. Since the good is normal in this example, c is positive, $c/(k - b)$ is positive, and the expression $c/(k - b)\, dM'$ is positive. Since l is negative, $-l/(k - b)$ is positive, and the expression $-l/(k - b)\, dP'_I$ is negative. The two terms in the differential have opposite signs, and the differential dP_E cannot be signed. It follows that the change in P_E is indeterminate and depends upon the relative magnitudes of dM' and dP'_I.

It is easy to verify that the change in Q_E is definitely positive. Since c is positive, $ck/(k - b)$ is positive, and the expression $ck/(k - b)\, dM'$ is positive. Since l is negative,

$-lb/(k - b)$ is negative, and the expression $-lb/(k - b)$ dP'_I is positive. Both terms in dQ_E are positive, so dQ_E is definitely positive regardless of the magnitudes of the changes in M' and P'_I.

Using the parameter values from D_0 and S_0, the changes in P_E and Q_E can be calculated as

$$dP_E = \frac{0.6}{10 - (-20)}(500) + -\left(\frac{-8}{10 - (-20)}\right)(-18.75)$$
$$= 10 + -5 = 5$$

$$dQ_E = \frac{0.6 \times 10}{10 - (-20)}(500) + -\left(\frac{-8 \times 20}{10 - (-20)}\right)(-18.75)$$
$$= 100 + 100 = 200$$

Figure 2A.1 shows the initial equilibrium point A and the simultaneous shifts in demand and supply that result in new equilibrium point D. As the figure shows, the simultaneous shifts from D_0 to D_1 and from S_0 to S_1 result in a $5 increase in equilibrium price and a 200-unit increase in equilibrium quantity.

MATHEMATICAL EXERCISES

1. For linear demand and supply functions, changes in the values of any of the determinants of demand (M, P_R, $\mathcal{T}$, P_e, N) or determinants of supply (P_I, P_r, T, P_e, F) cause *parallel* shifts in demand or supply, respectively. Explain why these shifts are always parallel for linear demand and supply functions.

2. The generalized demand and supply functions for a good are determined to be

$$Q_d = 400 - 25P + 0.4M + 24P_R$$
$$Q_s = 48 + 12P - 20P_I + 20F$$

   a. Initially $M = \$61{,}140$ and $P_R = \$6$. Find the equation for the demand function, D_0.
   b. Find the inverse demand function.
   c. Initially $P_I = \$25$ and $F = 22$. Find the equation for the supply function, S_0.
   d. Find the inverse supply function.
   e. If a price ceiling of $600 is imposed, does a shortage or surplus result? How much?
   f. Solve for P_E and Q_E.
   Now let the number of firms increase to 133.
   g. Find the new supply function. What is the new equilibrium?
   h. Calculate the change in P_E and Q_E using differentials. Comparing parts f and g, do the values of dP_E and dQ_E match the change in equilibrium values of price and output?

3. Consider the generalized demand and supply functions for good X:

$$Q_d = 800 - 2P - 0.01M + 16P_y$$
$$Q_s = 50 + 4P - 40P_I + 51F$$

   a. Good X is a(n) _____ good. Goods X and Y are _____.
   Suppose income is initially $20,000, the price of good Y is $10, the price of the input is $25, and the number of firms producing good X is 20.
   b. Write the equations for demand and supply. What are price and quantity in initial equilibrium?
   Now let the price of the related good Y increase to $50 and the price of the input increase to $36. Assume these two events occur simultaneously.
   c. Find algebraic expressions for dP_E and dQ_E. Determine the algebraic signs of dP_E and dQ_E. Which panel in Figure 2.9 represents this situation?
   d. Calculate numerical values for the change in P_E and Q_E using the differentials from part c. Now find the new equilibrium price and quantity. Do the computed values of dP_E and dQ_E match the change in price and quantity between parts b and c?

CHAPTER

3

Marginal Analysis for Optimal Decisions

Making optimal decisions about the levels of various business activities is an essential skill for all managers, one that requires managers to analyze benefits and costs to make the best possible decision under a given set of circumstances. In December 2000, as Ford Motor Company began producing its redesigned and reengineered 2002 Explorer, Ford's new CEO Jacques Nasser decided that the first 5,000 units rolling off assembly lines would not be delivered immediately to Ford dealer showrooms, even as potential buyers waited anxiously to get the new model. Instead, all of the new vehicles were parked in lots outside factories while quality control engineers examined 100 of them for defects in assembly and workmanship. The intense, 24-hour-a-day inspection process continued for three months, delaying the launch of the highly profitable new Explorer until April 2001. While no one could blame Ford's executives for wanting to minimize costly product recalls—Ford was still recovering from a massive $3 billion recall of its original Explorer that had a tendency to roll over—many auto industry analysts, car buyers, and owners of Ford dealerships nonetheless thought Ford was undertaking too much quality control. Nasser assured his critics that choosing to add three months of quality control measures was optimal, or best, under the circumstances. Apparently, he believed the benefit of engaging in three months of quality control effort (the savings attributable to preventing vehicle recalls) outweighed the cost of the additional quality control measures (the loss and delay of profit as 5,000 new Explorers spent three months in factory parking lots).

As you can see, Ford's CEO, weighing costs and benefits, made a critical decision that three months, rather than two months or four months, and a sample of 100 vehicles, rather than 50 vehicles or 300 vehicles, were the optimal or best levels of these two quality control decisions for launching the redesigned Explorer. We don't have enough information about Ford's costs and benefits of quality control to tell you whether Nasser succeeded in making the optimal decision for Ford. We can, however, tell you that in April 2003, *Consumer Reports* ranked the overall reliability of Ford automobiles dead last—and Ford Motor Company had a new CEO.[1]

As mentioned above, a manager's decision is optimal if it leads to the best outcome under a given set of circumstances. We will show you in this chapter that finding the best solution involves applying the fundamental principles of optimization theory. These principles of optimal decision making turn out to be nothing more than a formal presentation of commonsense ideas that you already apply, probably without knowing it, in your own everyday decisions. Managerial decisions entail choosing levels of various business activities—for example, the number of workers to hire, the amount of output to produce, the amount to spend on advertising, and so on—with the goal of maximizing or minimizing some business measure, such as revenues, costs, profits, or the value of the firm. Making these kinds of optimizing decisions is what managerial economics is all about.

In this chapter you will learn how to use a rather simple, yet powerful, method for finding the optimal level of business activities, or any kind of activity for that matter. This analytical technique, which economists refer to as "marginal analysis," forms the foundation of the theories of profit maximization, production, input choice, and even consumer behavior. The idea behind using marginal analysis in business decisions is this: When a manager contemplates whether a particular business activity needs adjusting, either up or down, to reach the best value, the manager needs to estimate how changing the business activity will affect both the benefits the firm receives from the activity and the costs the firm incurs from engaging in the activity. If changing the level of business activity causes benefits to rise by more than costs rise, or, alternatively, costs to fall by more than benefits fall, then the net benefit the firm receives from the activity will rise. Under these circumstances, managers will continue adjusting the activity level until no further net gains are possible, which means the activity has reached its optimal value or level.

This reasoning forms the fundamental logic for making optimal decisions. Managers benefit from understanding this logic because it enables them to make better decisions while avoiding some rather common types of business decision errors. We begin the analysis of optimal decision making by explaining some terminology that you will encounter in this chapter and throughout a large part of the text. We then derive two rules for making optimal decisions. If you thoroughly understand both rules, you should have little difficulty with the theories that are developed later in the text.

---

[1]See Joann Muller, "Putting the Explorer under the Microscope," *BusinessWeek*, Feb. 12, 2001, and Kathleen Kerwin, "Can Ford Pull Out of Its Skid?" *BusinessWeek*, Mar. 31, 2003.

3.1 CONCEPTS AND TERMINOLOGY

objective function
The function the decision maker seeks to maximize or minimize.

Before we begin to develop the theory of optimizing behavior, we must present some concepts and terminology with which you should be familiar in order to understand the development and application of the principles of optimization. In addition to their use in this chapter, these concepts are used throughout the text when setting forth theoretical concepts.

Optimizing behavior on the part of a decision maker involves trying to maximize or minimize an *objective function*. For a manager of a firm, the **objective function** is usually profit, which is to be maximized. For a consumer, the objective function is the satisfaction derived from consumption of goods, which is to be maximized. For a city manager seeking to provide adequate law enforcement services, the objective function might be cost, which is to be minimized. For the manager of the marketing division of a large corporation, the objective function is usually sales, which are to be maximized. In other words, the objective function measures whatever it is that the particular decision maker wishes to either maximize or minimize.

maximization problem
An optimization problem that involves maximizing the objective function.

minimization problem
An optimization problem that involves minimizing the objective function.

If the decision maker seeks to maximize an objective function, the optimization problem is called a **maximization problem**. Alternatively, if the objective function is to be minimized, the optimization problem is called a **minimization problem**. As a general rule, when the objective function measures a benefit, the decision maker seeks to maximize this benefit and is solving a maximization problem. When the objective function measures a cost, the decision maker seeks to minimize this cost and is solving a minimization problem.

activities or choice variables
Variables that determine the value of the objective function.

The value of the objective function is determined by the level of one or more **activities** or **choice variables**. For example, the value of profit depends on the number of units of output produced and sold. The production of units of the good is the activity that determines the value of the objective function, which in this case is profit. The decision maker controls the value of the objective function by choosing the levels of the activities or choice variables.

discrete choice variables
A choice variable that can take only specific integer values.

continuous choice variables
A choice variable that can take any value between two end points.

The choice variables in the optimization problems discussed in this text will at times vary *discretely* and at other times vary *continuously*. A **discrete choice variable** can take on only specified integer values, such as 1, 2, 3, . . . , or 10, 20, 30, . . . Examples of discrete choice variables arise when benefit and cost data are presented in a table, where each row represents one value of the choice variable. In this text, all examples of discrete choice variables will be presented in tables. A **continuous choice variable** can take on any value between two end points. For example, a continuous variable that can vary between 0 and 10 can take on the value 2, 2.345, 7.9, 8.999, or any one of the infinite number of values between the two limits. Examples of continuous choice variables are usually presented graphically but are sometimes shown by equations. As it turns out, the optimization rules differ only slightly in the discrete and continuous cases.

In addition to being categorized as either maximization or minimization problems, optimization problems are also categorized according to whether the decision maker can choose the values of the choice variables in the objective function

unconstrained optimization

An optimization problem in which the decision maker can choose the level of activity from an unrestricted set of values.

constrained optimization

An optimization problem in which the decision maker chooses values for the choice variables from a restricted set of values.

marginal analysis

Analytical technique for solving optimization problems that involves changing values of choice variables by small amounts to see if the objective function can be further improved.

from an unconstrained or constrained set of values. **Unconstrained optimization** problems occur when a decision maker can choose *any* level of activity he or she wishes in order to maximize the objective function. In this chapter, we show how to solve only unconstrained *maximization* problems since all the *unconstrained* decision problems we address in this text are maximization problems.[2] **Constrained optimization** problems involve choosing the levels of two or more activities that maximize or minimize the objective function subject to an additional requirement or constraint that restricts the values of *A* and *B* that can be chosen. An example of such a constraint arises when the total cost of the chosen activity levels must equal a specified constraint on cost. In this text, we examine both constrained maximization and constrained minimization problems.

As we show later in this chapter, the constrained maximization and the constrained minimization problems have one simple rule for the solution. Therefore, you will only have one rule to learn for all constrained optimization problems.

Even though there are a huge number of possible maximizing or minimizing decisions, you will see that all optimization problems can be solved using a single analytical technique, called *marginal analysis*. **Marginal analysis** involves changing the value(s) of the choice variable(s) by a small amount to see if the objective function can be further increased (in the case of maximization problems) or further decreased (in the case of minimization problems). If so, the manager continues to make incremental adjustments in the choice variables until no further improvements are possible. Marginal analysis leads to two simple rules for solving optimization problems, one for unconstrained decisions and one for constrained decisions. We turn first to the unconstrained decision.

3.2 UNCONSTRAINED MAXIMIZATION

net benefit

The objective function to be maximized: $NB = TB - TC$.

Any activity that decision makers might wish to undertake will generate both benefits and costs. Consequently, decision makers will want to choose the level of activity to obtain the maximum possible *net benefit* from the activity, where the **net benefit** (*NB*) associated with a specific amount of activity (*A*) is the difference between total benefit (*TB*) and total cost (*TC*) for the activity:

$$NB = TB - TC$$

Net benefit, then, serves as the objective function to be maximized, and the amount of activity, *A*, represents the choice variable. Furthermore, decision makers can choose *any* level of activity they wish, from zero to infinity, in either discrete or continuous units. Thus we are studying *unconstrained* maximization in this section.

---

[2]As it turns out, an unconstrained *minimization* problem can be transformed into an unconstrained *maximization* problem just by multiplying the objective function by −1. The value of the choice variable that minimizes the objective function is exactly equal to the value of the choice variable that maximizes the objective function (after it has been multiplied by −1).

ILLUSTRATION 3.1

Is Cost–Benefit Analysis Really Useful?

We have extolled the usefulness of marginal analysis in optimal decision making—often referred to as *cost–benefit analysis*—in business decision making as well as decision making in everyday life. This process involves weighing the marginal benefits and marginal costs of an activity while ignoring all previously incurred or sunk costs. The principal rule is to increase the level of an activity if marginal benefits exceed marginal costs and decrease the level if marginal costs exceed marginal benefits. This simple rule, however, flies in the face of many honored traditional principles such as "Never give up" or "Anything worth doing is worth doing well" or "Waste not, want not." So you might wonder if cost–benefit analysis is as useful as we have said it is.

It is, at least according to an article in *The Wall Street Journal* entitled "Economic Perspective Produces Steady Yields." In this article, a University of Michigan research team concludes, "Cost–benefit analysis pays off in everyday living." This team quizzed some of the university's seniors and faculty members on such questions as how often they walk out on a bad movie, refuse to finish a bad novel, start over on a weak term paper, or abandon a research project that no longer looks promising. They believe that people who cut their losses this way are following sound economic rules: calculating the net benefits of alternative courses of action, writing off past costs that can't be recovered, and weighing the opportunity to use future time and effort more profitably elsewhere.[a]

The findings: Among faculty members, those who use cost–benefit reasoning in this fashion had higher salaries relative to their age and departments. Economists were more likely to apply the approach than professors of humanities or biology. Among students, those who have learned to use cost–benefit analysis frequently are apt to have far better grades than their SAT scores would have predicted. The more economics courses the students had taken, the more likely they were to apply cost–benefit analysis outside the classroom. The director of the University of Michigan study did concede that for many Americans cost-benefit rules often appear to conflict with traditional principles such as those we previously mentioned. Notwithstanding these probable conflicts, the study provides evidence that decision makers can indeed prosper by following the logic of marginal analysis and cost–benefit analysis.

[a]"Economic Perspective Produces Steady Yield," *The Wall Street Journal*, Mar. 31, 1992.

The Optimal Level of Activity (A*)

We begin the analysis of unconstrained maximization with a rather typical set of total benefit and total cost curves for some activity, *A*, as shown in Panel A of Figure 3.1. Total benefit increases with higher levels of activity up to 1,000 units of activity (point *G*); then total benefit falls beyond this point. Total cost begins at a value of zero and rises continuously as activity increases. These "typical" curves allow us to derive general rules for finding the best solution to all such unconstrained problems, even though specific problems encountered in later chapters sometimes involve benefit and cost curves with shapes that differ somewhat from those shown in Panel A. For example, total benefit curves can be linear. Total cost curves can be linear or even *S*-shaped. And, as you will see in later chapters, total cost curves can include fixed costs when they take positive values at zero units of activity. In all of these variations, however, the rules for making the best decisions do not change. By learning how to solve the optimization problem as set forth in Figure 3.1, you will be prepared to solve all variations of these problems that come later in the text.

FIGURE 3.1
The Optimal Level of Activity

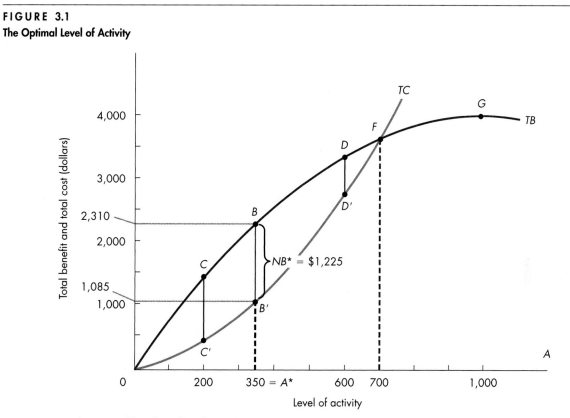

Panel A — Total benefit and total cost curves

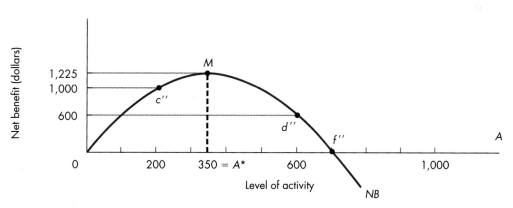

Panel B — Net benefit curve

optimal level of activity
The level of activity that maximizes net benefit (A*).

The level of activity that maximizes net benefit is called the **optimal level of activity**, which we distinguish from other levels of activity with an asterisk: A^*. In Panel A of Figure 3.1, net benefit at any particular level of activity is measured by the vertical distance between the total benefit and total cost curves. At 200 units of activity, for example, net benefit equals the length of line segment CC', which happens to be $1,000 as shown in Panel B at point c''. Panel B of Figure 3.1 shows the net benefit curve associated with the TB and TC curves in Panel A. As you can see from examining the net benefit curve in Panel B, the optimal level of activity, A^*, is 350 units, where NB reaches its maximum value. At 350 units in Panel A, the vertical distance between TB and TC is maximized, and this maximum distance is $1,225 (= NB^*).[3]

Two important observations can now be made about A^* in unconstrained maximization problems. First, the optimal level of activity does not generally result in maximization of *total* benefits. In Panel A of Figure 3.1, you can see that total benefit is still rising at the optimal point B. As we will demonstrate later in this book, for one of the most important applications of this technique, profit maximization, the optimal level of production occurs at a point where revenues are not maximized. This outcome can confuse managers, especially ones who believe any decision that increases revenue should be undertaken. We will have much more to say about this later in the text. Second, the optimal level of activity in an unconstrained maximization problem does not result in minimization of total cost. In Panel A, you can easily verify that total cost isn't minimized at A^* but rather at zero units of activity.

Finding A^* in Figure 3.1 seems easy enough. A decision maker starts with the total benefit and total cost curves in Panel A and subtracts the total cost curve from the total benefit curve to construct the net benefit curve in Panel B. Then, the decision maker chooses the value of A corresponding to the peak of the net benefit curve. You might reasonably wonder why we are going to develop an alternative method, marginal analysis, for making optimal decisions. Perhaps the most important reason for learning how to use marginal analysis to make decisions is that economists regard marginal analysis as "the central organizing principle of economic theory."[4] The graphical derivation of net benefit shown in Figure 3.1 serves only to *define* and *describe* the optimal level of activity; it does not explain *why* net benefit rises, falls, or reaches its peak. Marginal analysis, by focusing only on the changes in total benefits and total costs, provides a simple and complete explanation of the underlying forces causing net benefit to change. Understanding precisely what causes net benefit to improve makes it possible to set forth simple rules for deciding when an activity needs to be increased, decreased, or left at its current level.

---

[3]You might, at first, have thought the optimal activity level was 700 units since two curves in Panel A of Figure 3.1 intersect at point F, and this situation frequently identifies "correct" answers in economics. But, as you can see in Panel B, choosing 700 units of activity creates no more net benefit than choosing to do nothing at all (i.e., choosing $A = 0$) because total benefit equals total cost at both zero and 700 units of activity.

[4]See Robert B. Ekelund, Jr., and Robert F. Hébert, *A History of Economic Theory and Method*, 4th ed. (New York: McGraw-Hill, 1997), p. 264.

We are also going to show that using marginal analysis to make optimal decisions ensures that you will not consider irrelevant information about such things as fixed costs, sunk costs, or average costs in the decision-making process. As you will see shortly, decision makers using marginal analysis can reach the optimal activity level using only information about the benefits and costs *at the margin*. For this reason, marginal analysis requires less information than would be needed to construct *TB*, *TC*, and *NB* curves for all possible activity levels, as in Figure 3.1. There is no need to gather and process information for levels of activity that will never be chosen on the way to reaching *A**. As we explain later, if the decision maker is currently at 199 units of activity, information about benefits and costs is only needed for activity levels from 200 to 351 units. The optimal level of activity can be found without any information about benefits or costs below 200 units or above 351 units. We are now ready to develop the logic of marginal analysis for unconstrained maximization problems.

Marginal Benefit and Marginal Cost

marginal benefit (MB)
The change in total benefit caused by an incremental change in the level of an activity.

marginal cost (MC)
The change in total cost caused by an incremental change in the level of an activity.

In order to understand and use marginal analysis, you must understand the two key components of this methodology: marginal benefit and marginal cost. **Marginal benefit** is the change in total benefit caused by an incremental change in the level of an activity. Similarly, **marginal cost** is the change in total cost caused by an incremental change in activity. Dictionaries typically define "incremental" to mean "a small positive or negative change in a variable." You can think of "small" or "incremental" changes in activity to be any change that is small *relative* to the total level of activity. In most applications it is convenient to interpret an incremental change as a one-unit change. In some decisions, however, it may be impractical or even impossible to make changes as small as one-unit. This causes no problem for applying marginal analysis as long as the activity can be adjusted in relatively small increments. We should also mention that "small" refers only to the change in *activity level*; "small" doesn't apply to the resulting changes in total benefit or total cost, which can be any size.

Marginal benefit and marginal cost can be expressed mathematically as

$$MB = \frac{\text{Change in total benefit}}{\text{Change in activity}} = \frac{\Delta TB}{\Delta A}$$

and

$$MC = \frac{\text{Change in total cost}}{\text{Change in activity}} = \frac{\Delta TC}{\Delta A}$$

where the symbol "Δ" means "the change in" and A denotes the level of an activity. Since "marginal" variables measure rates of change in corresponding "total" variables, marginal benefit and marginal cost are also slopes of total benefit and total cost curves, respectively.

The two panels in Figure 3.2 show how the total curves in Figure 3.1 are related to their respective marginal curves. Panel A in Figure 3.2 illustrates the procedure for measuring slopes of total curves at various points or levels of activity. Recall from your high school math classes or a pre-calculus course in college that the

FIGURE 3.2
Relating Marginals to Totals

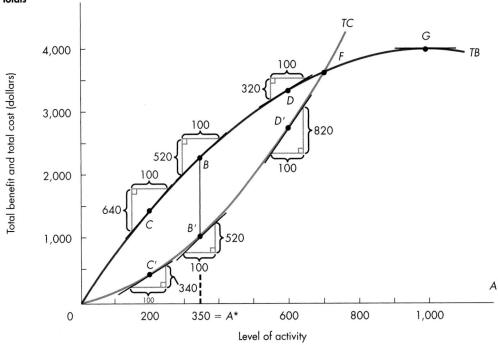

Panel A — Measuring slopes along TB and TC

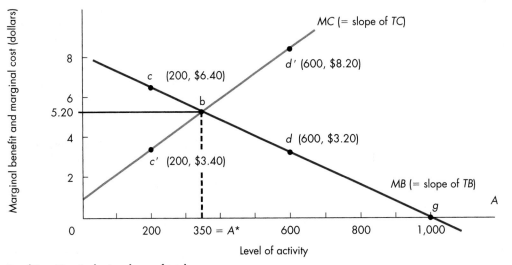

Panel B — Marginals give slopes of totals

slope of a curve at any particular point can be measured by first constructing a line tangent to the curve at the point of measure and then computing the slope of this tangent line by dividing the "rise" by the "run" of the tangent line.[5] Consider, for example, the slope of *TB* at point *C* in Panel A. The tangent line at point *C* rises by 640 units (dollars) over a 100-unit run, and total benefit's slope at point *C* is $6.40 (= $640/100). Thus the marginal benefit of the 200th unit of activity is $6.40, which means adding the 200th unit of activity (going from 199 to 200 units) causes total benefit to rise by $6.40.[6]

You should understand that the value of marginal benefit also tells you that subtracting the 200th unit (going from 200 to 199 units) causes total benefit to *fall* by $6.40. Since the slope of *TB* at point *C* is $6.40 per unit change in activity, marginal benefit at point *c* in Panel B is $6.40. You can verify that the same relation holds for the rest of the points shown on total benefit (*B*, *D*, and *G*), as well as for the points shown on total cost (*C′*, *B′*, and *D′*). We summarize this important discussion in a principle:

□ **Principle** Marginal benefit (marginal cost) is the change in total benefit (total cost) per unit change in the level of activity. The marginal benefit (marginal cost) of a particular unit of activity can be measured by the slope of the line tangent to the total benefit (total cost) curve at that point of activity.

At this point, you might be concerned that constructing tangent lines and measuring slopes of the tangent lines presents a tedious and imprecise method of finding marginal benefit and marginal cost curves. As you will see, the marginal benefit and marginal cost curves used in later chapters are obtained without drawing tangent lines. It is quite useful, nonetheless, for you to be able to visualize a series of tangent lines along total benefit and total cost curves in order to see why marginal benefit and marginal cost curves, respectively, are rising, falling, or even flat. Even if you don't know the *numerical* values of the slopes at points *C*, *B*, *D*, and *F* in Figure 3.2, you can still determine that marginal benefit in Panel B must slope downward because, as you can tell by looking, the tangent lines along *TB* get flatter (slopes get smaller) as the activity increases. Marginal cost, on the other hand, must be increasing in Panel B because, as you can tell by looking, its tangent lines get steeper (slope is getting larger) as the activity increases.

---

[5]When a line is tangent to a curve, it touches the curve at only one point. For smooth, continuous curves, only one line can be drawn tangent to the curve at a single point. Consequently, the slope of a curve at a point is unique and equal to the slope of the tangent line at that point. The algebraic sign of the slope indicates whether the variables on the vertical and horizontal axes are directly related (a positive algebraic slope) or inversely related (a negative algebraic slope). For a concise review of measuring and interpreting slopes of curves, see "Review of Fundamental Mathematics" in the *Student Workbook* that accompanies this text.

[6]When interpreting numerical values for marginal benefit and marginal cost, remember that the values refer to a particular unit of activity. In this example, marginal benefit equals $6.40 for the 200th unit. Strictly speaking, it is incorrect, and sometimes confusing, to say "marginal cost is $6.40 for 200 units." At 200 units of activity, the marginal benefit is $6.40 *for the last unit of activity undertaken* (i.e., the 200th unit).

FIGURE 3.3

Using Marginal Analysis to Find A*

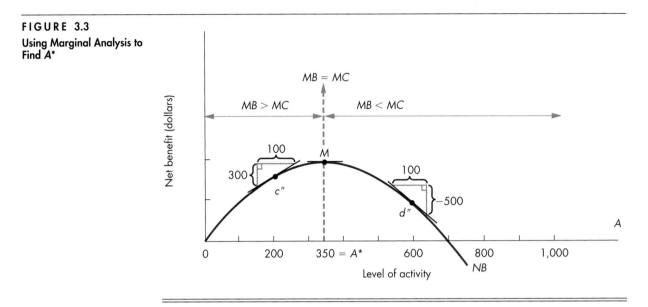

Finding Optimal Activity Levels with Marginal Analysis

As we stated earlier, the method of marginal analysis involves comparing marginal benefit and marginal cost to see if net benefit can be increased by making an incremental change in activity level. We can now demonstrate exactly how this works using the marginal benefit and marginal cost curves in Panel B of Figure 3.2. Let's suppose the decision maker is currently undertaking 199 units of activity in Panel B and wants to decide whether an incremental change in activity can cause net benefit to rise. Adding the 200th unit of activity will cause both total benefit and total cost to rise. As you can tell from points c and c' in Panel B, TB increases by more than TC increases ($6.40 is a larger increase than $3.40). Consequently, increasing activity from 199 to 200 units will cause net benefit to rise by $3 (= $6.40 − $3.40). Notice in Figure 3.3 that, at 200 units of activity (point c''), net benefit is rising at a rate of $3 (= $300/100) per unit increase in activity, as it must since MB equals $6.40 and MC equals $3.40.

After increasing the activity to 200 units, the decision maker then reevaluates benefits and costs at the margin to see whether another incremental increase in activity is warranted. In this situation, for the 201st unit of activity, the decision maker once again discovers that MB is greater than MC, which indicates the activity should be further increased. This incremental adjustment process continues until marginal benefit and marginal cost are exactly equal at point M ($A^* = 350$). As a practical matter, the decision maker can make a single adjustment to reach equilibrium, jumping from 199 units to 350 units in one adjustment of A, or make a series of smaller adjustments until MB equal MC at 350 units of activity. In any

ILLUSTRATION 3.2

Are Hybrid Gasoline-Electric Cars Optimal?
Analysis at the Margin

Heightened concern about U.S. dependence on imported petroleum, particularly Middle Eastern oil, has fueled the interest of both policymakers and consumers in new, fuel-saving technologies for automobiles. While Bush Administration officials and environmentalists wrangle over which new automotive technology is best for America in the long run, auto buyers can now make the switch from gasoline cars to so-called hybrid cars that get their power from a combination of electric batteries coupled with a relatively small gasoline-powered engine.

Honda Motor Co. offers two models of such gas-electric cars—the Insight and the hybrid version of its Civic—and Toyota Motor Corp. covers the hybrid niche of the auto market with its Prius. The initial sales of hybrid autos proved disappointing for both automakers. Then the run-up in gasoline prices surrounding the war in Iraq stimulated interest and sales in the U.S. auto market. Toyota's sales of its Prius increased 29 percent in 2002, and Honda saw sales of its

hybrid Civic jump 32 percent in February 2002. In spite of this recent interest, hybrids account for only a bite-sized piece of the U.S. car market.

Beginning in 1993, the Clinton-Gore Administration initiated a $1.5 billion government research program called "Partnership for a New Generation of Vehicles" with the primary objective of developing a gas-electric car that could achieve 80 miles per gallon (mpg). Currently, none of these new cars makes the 80-mpg target that Vice President Al Gore hoped would be forthcoming from the program. The accompanying table shows the fuel economy for the currently available hybrids, all of which fall well below the 80-mpg benchmark. Many scientists, including those at the National Academy of Sciences, believe the 80-mpg hybrid isn't "economically viable" at current gasoline prices and costs for producing gas-electric cars. In other words, not enough consumers will find it optimal to switch from conventional cars to hybrids to achieve the large-scale efficiencies needed to make production profitable at prices low enough to justify switching from gasoline to hybrid technologies.

Marginal Analysis of Switching to Various Hybrid Cars

	(1) Toyota Echo	(2) Toyota Prius	(3) Honda Insight	(4) Honda Civic/Hybrid
Type	Gasoline	Hybrid	Hybrid	Hybrid
Price	$13,000	$20,000	$21,000	$21,000
Fuel economy[a]	38 mpg	41 mpg	51 mpg	48 mpg
Gallons to drive 15,000 miles	395 gallons	366 gallons	294 gallons	312 gallons
Gallons saved		29 gallons	101 gallons	83 gallons
MB[b]		$43.50	$151.50	$123
MC[c]		$350	$400	$400

[a]As reported in "Profiles: 2003 Autos," in the April 2003 issue of *Consumer Reports* (in miles per gallon [mpg]).

[b]Marginal benefit measured as the dollar value of fuel savings by switching from the Echo economy sedan to a hybrid, based on 15,000 miles and gasoline priced at $1.50 per gallon.

[c]Marginal cost of switching from Echo to hybrid is annual increase in opportunity cost of capital for purchasing the higher-priced vehicle, based on 5 percent opportunity cost.

continued

In this illustration, we apply marginal analysis to the decision car buyers make when they consider whether to switch from conventional cars to gas-electric hybrids. Our analysis makes some rather important simplifying assumptions to focus on the analytical process of making this decision but, in so doing, we can collect the key data required for computing marginal benefits and costs of making the switch and can show what makes switching technologies optimal.

To set a benchmark for decision making, let's suppose a hypothetical car buyer would choose a Toyota Echo, costing $13,000 and getting 38 miles per gallon, if he or she decides to buy a conventional gasoline-powered economy sedan capable of carrying five passengers. Of course, the buyer could choose from a number of small, economy sedans, but, to make the comparison reasonable, the benchmark car should have driving features similar to the hybrids—specifically, it should be small, carry five passengers, and have only modest ability to accelerate.

To decide whether switching from an Echo to a hybrid car is optimal, you know from our discussion of optimization theory in this chapter that car buyers will compare the marginal benefit and marginal cost of switching. The benefit of reduced fuel usage must be weighed against the higher cost of hybrid technology. To illustrate how these benefits and costs could be computed, let's consider a car buyer who plans to pay cash for a new car (instead of leasing or getting a car loan from a bank), then drive the new car 15,000 miles and sell it at the end of one year. By limiting the ownership period to one year, we avoid the modest complexities of multiperiod analysis, such as discounting future benefits and costs to get present values, while maintaining our focus on the key factors influencing marginal benefit and marginal cost. Since there is no particular reason to believe marginal benefits and costs will vary in a predictable way from year to year, it follows that the best decision for a one-year ownership period will be the same one for multiple years of ownership.[d]

First consider a Toyota Prius. The marginal benefit of switching to a Prius can be measured by the dollar value of the fuel savings. To make this computation, car buyers must consider how many miles they plan to drive and what they expect to pay for gasoline. Switching from the Echo to the Prius requires about 29 fewer gallons of gasoline to go 15,000 miles—the Prius needs 366 gallons (= 15,000 miles/41 mpg) and the Echo needs 395 gallons (= 15,000 miles/38 mpg). Suppose the expected price of gasoline is $1.50 per gallon; then the marginal benefit of higher fuel economy achieved by switching from an Echo to a Prius is $43.50 (= $1.50 × 29 gallons). Under our simplifying assumptions, the

[d]One cost item that could be higher for the more expensive hybrids than the cheaper Echo is the amount of depreciation in the value of the car. To the extent that hybrids suffer greater first-year depreciation than the benchmark Echo, the computed marginal costs of the hybrids shown in the table will understate the true marginal costs. In this example, including accurate figures for first-year depreciation, which are unavailable given the short time these cars have been on the market, would only widen the gap between marginal benefits and marginal costs of the hybrid cars and does not change the conclusions.

case, the number of adjustments made to reach A^* does not, of course, alter the optimal decision or the value of net benefit at its maximum point.

Now let's start from a position of too much activity instead of beginning with too little activity. Suppose the decision maker begins at 600 units of activity, which you can tell is too much activity by looking at the NB curve (in either Figure 3.1 or 3.3). Subtracting the 600th unit of activity will cause both total benefit and total cost to fall. As you can tell from points d and d' in Panel B of Figure 3.2, TC decreases by more than TB decreases ($8.20 is a larger decrease than $3.20). Consequently, reducing activity from 600 to 599 units will cause net benefit to rise by $5 (= $8.20 − $3.20). You can now verify in Figure 3.3 that at 600 units of activity (point d'') net benefit is rising at a rate of $5 per unit *decrease* in activity. Since MC

marginal cost of making the switch equals the additional opportunity cost of capital attributable to purchasing a more expensive hybrid. For the Prius, $7,000 more must be spent to purchase the hybrid. Assuming the buyer could have earned a 5 percent return on money (or must pay 5 percent to get a car loan from a bank), the marginal cost of purchasing a Prius that is $7,000 more expensive than an Echo is $350 (= $7,000 × 0.05) for one year of ownership. Following this same procedure, the marginal benefits and marginal costs are computed for switching from an Echo to a Honda Insight and to a Honda Civic/Hybrid. The table shows the results of these computations.

As you can see by comparing marginal benefits and marginal costs in columns 2, 3, and 4 of the table, the hypothetical car buyer used for this analysis would not find it optimal to switch from a conventional gasoline-powered Echo to any of the gas-electric hybrid cars shown in the table. Even for the Honda Insight, which offers the best fuel economy of the three, it is not optimal to spend $400 extra to get hybrid technology only to save $152 on fuel costs. Thus car buyers facing the conditions described in this example—15,000 miles of driving, gasoline prices of $1.50 per gallon, 5 percent opportunity cost of funds, and the car prices and fuel economies given in the table—will not find it optimal to switch to the gas-electric hybrid technology as it is currently offered in the Prius, Insight, and Civic/Hybrid.

It is useful and interesting to see how sensitive this decision is to changes in some of the factors that determine marginal benefits and marginal costs. For example, if expected gasoline prices are $4 per gallon

instead of $1.50 per gallon, all others factors remaining the same, switching to the Honda Insight is then just optimal. Gasoline prices need to exceed $12 per gallon for the hypothetical car buyer in this Illustration to purchase a Prius. At gasoline prices of $1.50 per gallon, the Prius would become an optimal purchase if its fuel economy could be boosted to 95 miles per gallon, which is better than the more expensive Insight and Civic/Hybrid that both need to get 120 mpg to be "optimal (best) buys" relative to the Echo. Some auto-industry analysts believe producing more hybrids will bring down production costs and prices. To succeed for car buyers in this example, the Insight's price needs to fall to below $16,000.

This illustration shows why many car buyers who want an economy sedan that carries five passengers choose conventional gasoline autos such as the Echo rather than the more fuel-efficient, environmentally friendly hybrids now available. Economists and policymakers know that a more complete measure of the marginal benefit of buying a hybrid car must add the benefits to society from reduced pollution, which are frequently referred to as "spillover benefits" because people other than hybrid car buyers benefit from their decision to drive hybrids. It is likely that many current buyers of hybrid cars are people who derive substantial satisfaction (benefit) from driving cars that do not pollute. These hybrid car buyers apparently place a sufficiently high value on driving "green" cars to make their marginal benefits exceed the marginal costs. So driving hybrids is optimal for them and beneficial for those who don't yet find it optimal to drive hybrids.

is still greater than *MB* at 599 units, the decision maker would continue reducing activity until *MB* exactly equals *MC* at 350 units (point *M*).

Table 3.1 summarizes the logic of marginal analysis by presenting the relation between marginal benefit, marginal cost, and net benefit set forth in the previous discussion and shown in Figure 3.3. We now summarize in the following principle

TABLE 3.1
Marginal Analysis Decision Rules

	$MB > MC$	$MB < MC$
Increase activity	NB rises	NB falls
Decrease activity	NB falls	NB rises

the logic of marginal analysis for unconstrained maximization problems in which the choice variable is continuous:

▢   **Principle**   If, at a given level of activity, a small increase or decrease in activity causes net benefit to increase, then this level of the activity is not optimal. The activity must then be increased (if marginal benefit exceeds marginal cost) or decreased (if marginal cost exceeds marginal benefit) to reach the highest net benefit. The optimal level of the activity—the level that maximizes net benefit—is attained when no further increases in net benefit are possible for any changes in the activity, which occurs at the activity level for which marginal benefit equals marginal cost: $MB = MC$.

While the preceding discussion of unconstrained optimization has allowed only one activity or choice variable to influence net benefit, sometimes managers will need to choose the levels of two or more variables. As it turns out, when decision makers wish to maximize the net benefit from several activities, precisely the same principle applies: The firm maximizes net benefit when the marginal benefit from each activity equals the marginal cost of that activity. The problem is somewhat more complicated mathematically because the manager will have to equate marginal benefits and marginal costs for all of the activities *simultaneously*. For example, if the decision maker chooses the levels of two activities A and B to maximize net benefit, then the values for A and B must satisfy two conditions at once: $MB_A = MC_A$ and $MB_B = MC_B$. As it happens in this text, all the unconstrained maximization problems involve just one choice variable or activity.

Maximization with Discrete Choice Variables

In the preceding analysis of unconstrained maximization, the choice variable or activity level was a continuous variable. When a choice variable can vary only discretely, the logic of marginal analysis applies in exactly the same manner as when the choice variable is continuous. However, when choice variables are discrete, incremental adjustments in activity cannot be extremely small, and decision makers will not usually be able to adjust the level of activity to the point where marginal benefit exactly equals marginal cost. To make optimal decisions under these circumstances, decision makers must increase activity until the *last* level of activity is reached for which marginal benefit exceeds marginal cost. We can explain this rule for discrete choice variables by referring to Table 3.2, which shows a schedule of total benefits and total costs for various levels of some activity, A, expressed in integers between 0 and 8.

Let's suppose the decision maker is currently doing none of the activity and wants to decide whether to undertake the first unit of activity. The marginal benefit of the first unit of the activity is $16, and the marginal cost is $2. Undertaking the first unit of activity adds $16 to total benefit and only $2 to total cost, so net benefit rises by $14 (from $0 to $14). The decision maker would choose to undertake the first unit of activity to gain a higher net benefit. Applying this reasoning to the second and third units of activity leads again to a decision to undertake more activity. Beyond the third unit, however, marginal cost exceeds marginal benefit for additional units of activity, so no further increase beyond three units of activity will add

TABLE 3.2

Optimization with a Discrete Choice Variable

(1) Level of activity (A)	(2) Total benefit of activity (TB)	(3) Total cost of activity (TC)	(4) Net benefit of activity (NB)	(5) Marginal benefit (MB)	(6) Marginal cost (MC)
0	$ 0	$ 0	$ 0	—	—
1	16	2	14	16	2
2	30	6	24	14	4
3	40	11	29	10	5
4	48	20	28	8	9
5	54	30	24	6	10
6	58	45	13	4	15
7	61	61	0	3	16
8	63	80	−17	2	19

to net benefit. As you can see, the optimal level of the activity is three units because the net benefit associated with three units ($29) is higher than for any other level of activity. These results are summarized in the following principle:

▣ **Principle**   When a decision maker faces an unconstrained maximization problem and must choose among discrete levels of an activity, the activity should be increased if *MB* > *MC* and decreased if *MB* < *MC*. The optimal level of activity is reached—net benefit is maximized—when the level of activity is the last level for which marginal benefit exceeds marginal cost.

Before moving ahead, we would like to point out that this principle *cannot* be interpreted to mean "choose the activity level where *MB* and *MC* are as close to equal as possible." To see why this interpretation can lead to the wrong decision, consider the fourth unit of activity in Table 3.2. At four units of activity, *MB* (= $8) is much closer to equality with *MC* (= $9) than at the optimal level of activity, where *MB* (= $10) is $5 larger than *MC* (= $5). Now you can see why the rule for discrete choice variables cannot be interpreted to mean "get *MB* as close to *MC* as possible."

Sunk Costs, Fixed Costs, and Average Costs Are Irrelevant

In our discussion of optimization problems, we never mentioned sunk costs or fixed costs. **Sunk costs** are costs that have previously been paid and cannot be recovered. **Fixed costs** are costs that are constant and must be paid no matter what level of an activity is chosen. Such costs are totally irrelevant in decision making. They either have already been paid and cannot be recovered, as in the case of sunk costs, or must be paid no matter what a manager or any other decision maker decides to do, as in the case of fixed costs.

Suppose you head your company's advertising department and you have just paid $2 million to an advertising firm for developing and producing a 30-second television ad, which you plan to air next quarter on broadcast television networks

sunk costs
Costs that have previously been paid and cannot be recovered.

fixed costs
Costs are constant and must be paid no matter what level of the activity is chosen.

nationwide. The $2 million one-time payment gives your company full ownership of the 30-second ad, and your company can run the ad as many times as it wishes without making any further payments to the advertising firm for its use. Under these circumstances, the $2 million payment is a sunk cost because it has already been paid and cannot be recovered, even if your firm decides not to use the ad after all.

To decide how many times to run the ad next quarter, you call a meeting of your company's advertising department. At the meeting, the company's media buyer informs you that 30-second television spots during *American Idol* will cost $250,000 per spot. The marketing research experts at the meeting predict that the 24th time the ad runs it will generate $270,000 of additional sales, while running it a 25th time will increase sales by $210,000. Using the logic of marginal analysis, the marketing team decides running the new ad 24 times next quarter is optimal because the 24th showing of the ad is the last showing for which the marginal benefit exceeds the marginal cost of showing the ad:

$$MB = \$270{,}000 > 250{,}000 = MC$$

It would be a mistake to go beyond 24 showings because the 25th showing would decrease net benefit; the change in net benefit would be $-\$40{,}000$ (= $\$210{,}000 - \$250{,}000$).

Two days after this meeting, you learn about a serious accounting error: Your company actually paid $3 million to the advertising firm for developing and producing your company's new television ad, not $2 million as originally reported. As you consider how to handle this new information, you realize that you don't need to call another meeting of the marketing department to reconsider its decision about running the ad 24 times next quarter. Because the amount paid to the advertising firm is a sunk cost, it doesn't affect either the marginal benefit or the marginal cost of running the ad one more time. The optimal number of times to run the ad is 24 times no matter how much the company paid in the past to obtain the ad.

Converting this example to a fixed cost, suppose that two days after your meeting you find out that, instead of making a sunk payment to buy the ad, your company instead decided to sign a 30-month contract leasing the rights to use the television ad for a monthly lease payment of $10,000 per month. This amount is a fixed payment in each of the 30 months and must be paid no matter how many times your company decides to run the ad, even if it chooses never to run the ad. Do you need to call another meeting of the market department to recalculate the optimal number of times to run the ad during *American Idol*? As before, no new decision needs to be made. Since the fixed monthly loan payment does not change the predicted gain in sales (*MB*) or the extra cost of running the ad (*MC*), the optimal number of times to run the ad remains 24 times.

While you should now understand that things over which you have no control should not affect decisions, some economic experiments do, however, find that many people do not ignore fixed or sunk costs when making decisions. They say things such as, "I've already got so much invested in this project, I have to go on with it." As you are aware, they should weigh the costs and benefits of going on before going on. Then, if the benefits are greater than the *additional* costs, they should go on; if the *additional* costs are greater than the benefits, they should not go on. As Illustration 3.1 shows, failing to ignore fixed or sunk costs is a bad policy even in everyday decision making.

average (unit) cost
Cost per unit of activity computed by dividing total cost by the number of units of activity.

Another type of cost that should be ignored in finding the optimal level of activity is the *average or unit cost* of an activity. **Average (or unit) cost** is the cost per unit of activity, which is computed by dividing total cost by the number of units of activity. In order to make optimal decisions, decision makers should not be concerned about whether the decision will push average costs up or down. The reason for ignoring average cost is quite straightforward: The impact on net benefit of making an incremental change in activity depends only on *marginal* benefit and *marginal* cost ($\Delta NB = MB - MC$), not on average benefit or average cost. In other words, optimal decisions are made at the margin, not "on the average."

To illustrate this point, consider the decision in Table 3.2 once again. The average cost of two units of activity is \$3 (= \$6/2) and average cost for three units of activity is \$3.67 (= \$11/3). Recall from our earlier discussion, the decision to undertake the third unit of activity is made because the marginal benefit exceeds the marginal cost (\$10 > \$5), and net benefit rises. It is completely irrelevant that the average cost of three units of activity is higher than the average cost of two units of activity. Alternatively, a decision maker should not decrease activity from three units to two units just to achieve a reduction in average cost from \$3.67 to \$3 per unit of activity; such a decision would cause net benefit to fall from \$29 to \$24. The following principle summarizes the role of sunk, fixed, and average costs in making optimal decisions:

▣ **Principle**   Decision makers wishing to maximize the net benefit of an activity should ignore any sunk costs, any fixed costs, and the average costs associated with the activity because none of these costs affect the marginal cost of the activity and so are irrelevant for making optimal decisions.

3.3 CONSTRAINED OPTIMIZATION

While many of the decisions facing a manager involve unconstrained choice of an activity in order to maximize net benefit, on many occasions a manager will face situations in which the choice of activity levels is constrained by the circumstances surrounding the maximization or minimization problem. These constrained optimization problems can be solved, as in the case of unconstrained maximization, using the logic of marginal analysis. As noted in Section 3.1, even though constrained optimization problems can be either maximization or minimization problems, the optimization rule is the same for both types.

A crucial concept for solving constrained optimization problems is the concept of marginal benefit per dollar spent on an activity. Before you can understand how to solve constrained optimization problems, you must first understand how to interpret the ratio of the marginal benefit of an activity divided by the price of the activity. We turn now to a discussion of marginal benefit per dollar and then show

how to use this concept to find the optimal levels of the activities in constrained optimization problems.

Marginal Benefit per Dollar Spent on an Activity

Retailers frequently advertise that their products give "more value for your money." People don't usually interpret this as meaning the best product in its class or the one with the highest value. Neither do they interpret it as meaning the cheapest. The advertiser wants to get across the message that customers will get more for their money or more value for each dollar spent on the product. When product rating services (such as *Consumer Reports*) rate a product a "best buy," they don't mean it is the best product or the cheapest; they mean that consumers will get more value per dollar spent on that product. When firms want to fill a position, they don't necessarily hire the person who would be the most productive in the job—that person may cost too much. Neither do they necessarily hire the person who would work for the lowest wages—that person may not be very productive. They want the employee who can do the job and give the highest productivity for the wages paid.

In these examples, phrases such as "most value for your money" and "best buy" mean that a particular activity yields the highest marginal benefit per dollar spent. To illustrate this concept, suppose you are the office manager for an expanding law firm and you find that you need an extra copy machine in the office—the one copier you have is being overworked. You shop around and find three brands of office copy machines (brands A, B, and C) that have virtually identical features. The three brands do differ, however, in price and in the number of copies the machines will make before they wear out. Brand A's copy machine costs $2,500 and will produce about 500,000 copies before it wears out. The marginal benefit of this machine is 500,000 ($MB_A = 500,000$) since the machine provides the law office with the ability to produce 500,000 additional copies. To find the marginal benefit *per dollar spent* on copy machine A, marginal benefit is divided by price ($P_A = 2,500$):

$$MB_A/P_A = 500,000 \text{ copies}/2,500 \text{ dollars}$$

$$= 200 \text{ copies}/\text{dollar}$$

You get 200 copies for each of the dollars spent to purchase copy machine A.

Now compare machine A with machine B, which will produce 600,000 copies and costs $4,000. The marginal benefit is greater, but so is the price. To determine how "good a deal" you get with machine B, compute the marginal benefit per dollar spent on machine B:

$$MB_B/P_B = 600,000 \text{ copies}/4,000 \text{ dollars}$$

$$= 150 \text{ copies}/\text{dollar}$$

Even though machine B provides a higher marginal benefit, its marginal benefit per dollar spent is lower than that for machine A. Machine A is a better deal than machine B because it yields higher marginal benefit per dollar. The third copy machine produces 580,000 copies over its useful life and costs $2,600. Machine C is neither the best machine (580,000 < 600,000 copies) nor is it the cheapest machine ($2,600 > $2,500), but of the three machines, machine C provides the greatest marginal benefit per dollar spent:

$$MB_C/P_C = 580,000 \text{ copies}/2,600 \text{ dollars}$$
$$= 223 \text{ copies/dollar}$$

You would rank machine C first, machine A second, and machine B third.

When choosing among different activities, a decision maker compares the marginal benefits per dollar spent on each of the activities, *not* the marginal benefits of the activities. Marginal benefit, by itself, does not provide sufficient information for decision-making purposes. It is marginal benefit per dollar spent that matters in decision making.

Constrained Maximization

In the general constrained maximization problem, a manager or decision maker must choose the levels of two or more activities in order to maximize a total benefit (objective) function subject to a constraint in the form of a budget that restricts the amount that can be spent.[7] To illustrate how marginal analysis can be employed to find the optimal levels of activities for a constrained maximization problem, consider a situation in which there are two activities, A and B. Each unit of activity A costs $4 to undertake, and each unit of activity B costs $2 to undertake. The manager faces a constraint that allows a total expenditure of only $100 on activities A and B combined. The manager wishes to allocate the $100 between activities A and B so that the total benefit from both activities combined is maximized.

The manager is currently choosing to employ 20 units of activity A and 10 units of activity B. The constraint is met for the combination 20A and 10B since ($4 × 20) + ($2 × 10) = $100. For this combination of activities, suppose that the marginal benefit of the last unit of activity A is 40 units of additional benefit and the marginal benefit of the last unit of B is 10 units of additional benefit. In this situation, the marginal benefit per dollar spent on activity A exceeds the marginal benefit per dollar spent on activity B:

$$\frac{MB_A}{P_A} = \frac{40}{4} = 10 > 5 = \frac{10}{2} = \frac{MB_B}{P_B}$$

---

[7]It may look like constrained maximization problems no longer use net benefit as the objective function to be maximized. Note, however, that maximizing total benefit while total cost must remain constant in order to meet a budget constraint does indeed result in the maximum possible amount of net benefit for a given level of total cost. A similar observation can be made for constrained minimization problems, which seek to minimize total cost for a given level of total benefit, which is given by the constraint. Net benefit is maximized for a given level of benefit by minimizing total cost. Thus for either constrained maximization or constrained minimization problems, net benefit is maximized given the level of total cost or total benefit set by the constraint.

Spending an additional dollar on activity A increases total benefit by 10 units, while spending an additional dollar on activity B increases total benefit by 5 units. Since the marginal benefit per dollar spent is greater for activity A, it provides "more for the money" or is a better deal at this combination of activities.

To take advantage of this fact, the manager can increase activity A by one unit and decrease activity B by two units (now, $A = 21$ and $B = 8$). This combination of activities still costs \$100 [(\$4 $\times$ 21) + (\$2 $\times$ 8) = \$100]. Purchasing one more unit of activity A causes total benefit to rise by 40 units, while purchasing two less units of activity B causes total benefit to fall by 20 units. The combined total benefit from activities A and B *rises* by 20 units (= 40 − 20) *and* the new combination of activities ($A = 21$ and $B = 8$) costs the same amount, \$100, as the old combination ($A = 20$ and $B = 10$). The decision maker has succeeded in increasing total benefit without spending any more than \$100 on the activities.

Naturally, the manager will continue to increase spending on activity A and reduce spending on activity B as long as MB_A/P_A exceeds MB_B/P_B. In most situations, the marginal benefit of an activity declines as the activity increases.[8] Consequently, as activity A is increased, MB_A gets smaller. As activity B is decreased, MB_B gets larger. Thus as spending on A rises and spending on B falls, MB_A/P_A falls and MB_B/P_B rises. As the manager increases activity A and decreases activity B, a point is eventually reached at which activity A is no longer a better deal than activity B; that is, MB_A/P_A equals MB_B/P_B. At this point, total benefit is maximized subject to the constraint that only \$100 is spent on the two activities.

If the original allocation of spending on activities A and B had been such that

$$\frac{MB_A}{P_A} < \frac{MB_B}{P_B}$$

the manager would recognize that activity B is the better deal. In this case, total benefit could be increased by spending more on activity B and less on activity A while maintaining the \$100 budget. Activity B would be increased by two units for every one-unit decrease in activity A (in order to satisfy the \$100 spending constraint) until the marginal benefit per dollar spent is equal for both activities:

$$\frac{MB_A}{P_A} = \frac{MB_B}{P_B}$$

If there are more than two activities in the objective function, the condition is expanded to require that the marginal benefit per dollar spent be equal for all activities. We have developed the following rule for finding the optimal activity levels for constrained maximization problems:

---

[8]Decreasing marginal benefit is quite common. As you drink several cans of Coke in succession, you get ever smaller amounts of additional satisfaction from successive cans. As you continue studying for an exam, each additional hour of study increases your expected exam grade by ever smaller amounts. In such cases, marginal benefit is inversely related to the level of the activity. Increasing the activity causes marginal benefit to fall, and decreasing the activity level causes marginal benefit to rise.

▣ **Principle** To maximize total benefits subject to a constraint on the levels of activities, choose the level of each activity so that the marginal benefit per dollar spent is equal for all activities

$$\frac{MB_A}{P_A} = \frac{MB_B}{P_B} = \frac{MB_C}{P_C} = \cdots = \frac{MB_Z}{P_Z}$$

T ▶ 9 10   and at the same time, the chosen level of activities must also satisfy the constraint.

Optimal Advertising Expenditures: An Example of Constrained Maximization

To illustrate how a firm can use the technique of constrained maximization to allocate its advertising budget, suppose a manager of a small retail firm wants to maximize the effectiveness (in total sales) of the firm's weekly advertising budget of $2,000. The manager has the option of advertising on the local television station or on the local AM radio station. As a class project, a marketing class at a nearby college estimated the impact on the retailer's sales of varying levels of advertising in the two different media. The manager wants to maximize the number of units sold; thus the total benefit is measured by the total number of units sold. The estimates of the *increases* in weekly sales (the marginal benefits) from increasing the levels of advertising on television and radio are as follows:

| | Increase in units sold | |
Number of ads	MB_{TV}	MB_{radio}
1	400	360
2	300	270
3	280	240
4	260	225
5	240	150
6	200	120

Television ads are more "powerful" than radio ads in the sense that the marginal benefits from additional TV ads tend to be larger than those for more radio ads. However, since the manager is constrained by the limited advertising budget, the relevant measure is not simply marginal benefit but, rather, marginal benefit per dollar spent on advertising. The price of television ads is $400 per ad, and the price of radio ads is $300 per ad. Although the first TV ad dominates the first radio ad in terms of its marginal benefit (increased sales), the marginal benefit per dollar's worth of expenditure for the first radio ad is greater than that for the first television ad:

| | Marginal benefit/price | |
	Television	Radio
Ad 1	400/400 = 1.00	360/300 = 1.2

This indicates that sales rise by 1 unit per dollar spent on the first television ad and 1.2 units on the first radio ad. Therefore, when the manager is allocating the budget, the first ad she selects will be a radio ad—the activity with the larger marginal benefit per dollar spent. Following the same rule, the $2,000 advertising budget would be allocated as follows:

Decision	MB/P	Ranking of MB/P	Cumulative expenditures
Buy radio ad 1	360/300 = 1.20	1	$ 300
Buy TV ad 1	400/400 = 1.00	2	700
Buy radio ad 2	270/300 = 0.90	3	1,000
Buy radio ad 3	240/300 = 0.80	4	1,300
Buy TV ad 2	300/400 = 0.75		1,700
Buy radio ad 4	225/300 = 0.75	5 (tie)	2,000

By selecting two television ads and four radio ads, the manager of the firm has maximized sales subject to the constraint that only $2,000 can be spent on advertising activity. Note that for the optimal levels of television and radio ads (two TV and four radio):

$$\frac{MB_{TV}}{P_{TV}} = \frac{MB_{radio}}{P_{radio}} = 0.75$$

The fact that the preceding application used artificially simplistic numbers shouldn't make you think that the problem is artificial. If we add a few zeros to the prices of TV and radio ads, we have the real-world situation faced by advertisers.

Constrained Minimization

Constrained minimization problems involve minimizing a total cost function (the objective function) subject to a constraint that the levels of activities be chosen such that a given level of total benefit is achieved. To illustrate how marginal analysis is applied to constrained minimization problems, consider a manager who must minimize the total cost of two activities, A and B, subject to the constraint that 3,000 units of benefit are to be generated by those activities. The price of activity A is $5 per unit and the price of activity B is $20 per unit. Suppose the manager is currently using 100 units of activity A and 60 units of activity B and this combination of activity generates total benefit equal to 3,000. At this combination of activities, the marginal benefit of the last unit of activity A is 30 and the marginal benefit of the last unit of activity B is 60. In this situation, the marginal benefit per dollar spent on activity A exceeds the marginal benefit per dollar spent on activity B:

$$\frac{MB_A}{P_A} = \frac{30}{5} = 6 < 3 = \frac{60}{20} = \frac{MB_B}{P_B}$$

Since the marginal benefit per dollar spent is greater for activity A than for activity B, activity A gives "more for the money."

To take advantage of activity A, the manager can reduce activity B by one unit, causing total benefit to fall by 60 units and reducing cost by $20. To hold total benefit constant, the 60 units of lost benefit can be made up by increasing activity A by two units with a marginal benefit of 30 each. The two additional units of activity A

cause total cost to rise by $10. By reducing activity B by one unit and increasing activity A by two units, the manager *reduces* total cost by $10 (= \$20 - \$10)$ without reducing total benefit.

As long as $MB_A/P_A > MB_B/P_B$, the manager will continue to increase activity A and decrease activity B at the rate that holds TB constant until

$$\frac{MB_A}{P_A} = \frac{MB_B}{P_B}$$

If there are more than two activities in the objective function, the condition is expanded to require that the marginal benefit per dollar spent be equal for all activities. We have developed the following rule for finding the optimal activity levels for constrained minimization problems:

◻ **Principle** In order to minimize total costs subject to a constraint on the levels of activities, choose the level of each activity so that the marginal benefit per dollar spent is equal for all activities

$$\frac{MB_A}{P_A} = \frac{MB_B}{P_B} = \frac{MB_C}{P_C} = \cdots = \frac{MB_Z}{P_Z}$$

and at the same time, the chosen level of activities must also satisfy the constraint.

As you can see, this is the same condition that must be met in the case of constrained maximization.

3.4 SUMMARY

In this chapter we have given you the key to the kingdom of economic decision making: marginal analysis. Virtually all of microeconomics involves solutions to optimization problems. The most interesting and challenging problems facing a manager involve trying either to maximize or to minimize particular objective functions. Regardless of whether the optimization involves maximization or minimization, or constrained or unconstrained choice variables, all optimization problems are solved by using marginal analysis. No other tool in managerial economics is more powerful than the ability to attack problems by using the logic of marginal analysis.

The results of this chapter fall neatly into two categories: the solution to unconstrained and the solution to constrained optimization problems. When the values of the choice variables are *not* restricted by constraints such as limited income, limited expenditures, or limited time, the optimization problem is said to be unconstrained. Unconstrained maximization problems can be solved by following this simple rule: To maximize net

benefit, increase or decrease the level of activity until the marginal benefit from the activity equals the marginal cost of the activity:

$$MB = MC$$

When the choice variable is not continuous but discrete, it may not be possible to precisely equate benefit and cost at the margin. For discrete choice variables, the decision maker simply carries out the activity up to the point where *any further* increases in the activity result in marginal cost exceeding marginal benefit.

Marginal analysis shows clearly why decision makers should ignore average costs, fixed costs, and sunk costs when making decisions about the optimal level of activities. Since it is *marginal* cost that must equal marginal benefit to reach the optimal level of activity, any other cost is irrelevant for making decisions about how much of an activity to undertake.

In many instances, managers face limitations on the range of values that the choice variables can take. For example, budgets may limit the amount of labor and capital managers may purchase. Time constraints may limit the number of hours managers can allocate to certain activities. Such constraints are common and require modifying the solution to optimization problems. To maximize or minimize an objective function subject to a constraint, the ratios of the marginal benefit to price must be equal for all activities,

and the values of the choice variables must meet the constraint.

The two decision rules presented in this chapter will be used throughout this text. If you remember these rules, economic analysis will be clear and straightforward. These two rules, although simple, are the essential tools for making economic decisions. And, as the rules emphasize, *marginal changes* are the keys to optimization decisions.

$$\frac{MB_A}{P_A} = \frac{MB_B}{P_B} = \cdots = \frac{MB_Z}{P_Z}$$

TECHNICAL PROBLEMS

1. For each of the following decision-making problems, determine whether the problem involves constrained or unconstrained optimization; what the objective function is and, for each constrained problem, what the constraint is; and what the choice variables are.

   a. We have received a foundation grant to purchase new PCs for the staff. You decide what PCs to buy.

   b. We aren't earning enough profits. Your job is to redesign our advertising program and decide how much TV, direct-mail, and magazine advertising to use. Whatever we are doing now isn't working very well.

   c. We have to meet a production quota but think we are going to spend too much doing so. Your job is to reallocate the machinery, the number of workers, and the raw materials needed to meet the quota.

2. Refer to Figure 3.2 and answer the following questions:

   a. At 600 units of activity, marginal benefit is _____ (rising, constant, positive, negative) because the tangent line at D is sloping _____ (downward, upward).

   b. The marginal benefit of the 600th unit of activity is $_____. Explain how this value of marginal benefit can be computed.

   c. At 600 units of activity, decreasing the activity by one unit causes total benefit to _____ (increase, decrease) by $_____. At point D, total benefit changes at a rate _____ times as much as activity changes, and TB and A are moving in the _____ (same, opposite) direction, which means TB and A are _____ (directly, inversely) related.

   d. At 1,000 units of activity, marginal benefit is _____. Why?

   e. The marginal cost of the 600th unit of activity is $_____. Explain how this value of marginal cost can be computed.

   f. At 600 units of activity, decreasing the activity by one unit causes total cost to _____ (increase, decrease) by $_____. At point D', total cost changes at a rate _____ times as much as activity changes, and TC and A are moving in the _____ (same, opposite) direction, which means TC and A are _____ (directly, inversely) related.

   g. Visually, the tangent line at point D appears to be _____ (flatter, steeper) than the tangent line at point D', which means that _____ (NB, TB, TC, MB, MC) is larger than _____ (NB, TB, TC, MB, MC).

h. Since point D lies above point D', _____ (NB, TB, TC, MB, MC) is larger than _____ (NB, TB, TC, MB, MC), which means that _____ (NB, TB, TC, MB, MC) is _____ (rising, falling, constant, positive, negative, zero).

3. Fill in the blanks below. In an unconstrained maximization problem:

    a. An activity should be increased if _____ exceeds _____.

    b. An activity should be decreased if _____ exceeds _____.

    c. The optimal level of activity occurs at the activity level for which _____ equals _____.

    d. At the optimal level of activity, _____ is maximized, and the slope of _____ equals the slope of _____.

    e. If total cost is falling faster than total benefit is falling, the activity should be _____.

    f. If total benefit is rising at the same rate that total cost is rising, the decision maker should _____.

    g. If net benefit is rising, then total benefit must be rising at a rate _____ (greater than, less than, equal to) the rate at which total cost is _____ (rising, falling).

4. Use the graph below to answer the following questions:

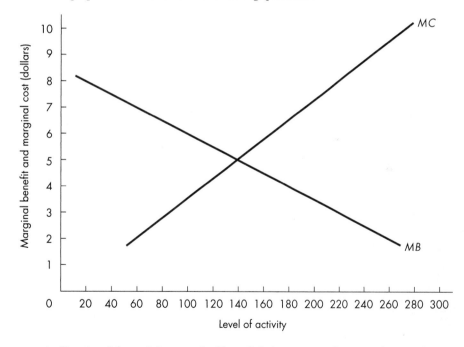

a. At 60 units of the activity, marginal benefit is $_____ and marginal cost is $_____.

b. Adding the 60th unit of the activity causes net benefit to _____ (increase, decrease) by $_____.

c. At 220 units of the activity, marginal benefit is $_____ and marginal cost is $_____.

d. Subtracting the 220th unit of the activity causes net benefit to _____ (increase, decrease) by $_____.

e. The optimal level of the activity is _____ units. At the optimal level of the activity, marginal benefit is $_____ and marginal cost is $_____.

5. Fill in the blanks in the following statement:

If marginal benefit exceeds marginal cost, then increasing the level of activity by one unit _____ (increases, decreases) _____ (total, marginal, net) benefit by more than it _____ (increases, decreases) _____ (total, marginal) cost. Therefore, _____ (increasing, decreasing) the level of activity by one unit must increase net benefit. The manager should continue to _____ (increase, decrease) the level of activity until marginal benefit and marginal cost are _____ (zero, equal).

6. Fill in the blanks in the following table to answer the questions below.

A	TB	TC	NB	MB	MC
0	$ 0	$___	$ 0		
1	___	___	27	$35	$___
2	65	___	___	___	10
3	85	30	___	___	___
4	___	___	51	___	14
5	___	60	___	8	___
6	___	___	___	5	20

a. What is the optimal level of activity in the table above?

b. What is the value of net benefit at the optimal level of activity? Can net benefit be increased by moving to any other level of A? Explain.

c. Using the numerical values in the table, comment on the statement, "The optimal level of activity occurs where marginal benefit is closest to marginal cost."

7. Now suppose the decision maker in Technical Problem 6 faces a fixed cost of $24. Fill in the blanks in the following table to answer the questions below. AC is the average cost per unit of activity.

A	TB	TC	NB	MB	MC	AC
0	$ 0	___	−$24			
1	___	___	3	$35	$___	$32
2	65	___	___	___	10	___
3	85	54	___	___	___	___
4	___	___	27	___	14	___
5	___	___	___	8	___	16.80
6	___	___	___	5	20	___

a. How does adding $24 of fixed costs affect total cost? Net benefit?

b. How does adding $24 of fixed cost affect marginal cost?

c. Compared to A* in Technical Problem 6, does adding $24 of fixed cost change the optimal level of activity? Why or why not?

d. What advice can you give decision makers about the role of fixed costs in finding A*?

e. What level of activity minimizes average cost per unit of activity? Is this level also the optimal level of activity? Should it be? Explain.

f. Suppose a government agency requires payment of a one-time, nonrefundable license fee of $100 to engage in activity A, and this license fee was paid last month. What kind of cost is this? How does this cost affect the decision maker's choice of activity level now? Explain.

8. You are interviewing three people for one sales job. On the basis of your experience and insight, you believe Jane can sell 600 units a day, Joe can sell 450 units a day, and Joan can sell 400 units a day. The daily salary each person is asking is as follows: Jane, $200; Joe, $150; and Joan, $100. How would you rank the three applicants?

9. Fill in the blanks. When choosing the levels of two activities, A and B, in order to maximize total benefits within a given budget:

  a. If at the given levels of A and B, MB/P of A is _____ MB/P of B, increasing A and decreasing B while holding expenditure constant will increase total benefits.

  b. If at the given levels of A and B, MB/P of A is _____ MB/P of B, increasing B and decreasing A while holding expenditure constant will increase total benefits.

  c. The optimal levels of A and B are the levels at which _____ equals _____.

10. A decision maker is choosing the levels of two activities, A and B, so as to maximize total benefits under a given budget. The prices and marginal benefits of the last units of A and B are denoted P_A, P_B, MB_A, and MB_B.

  a. If $P_A = \$20$, $P_B = \$15$, $MB_A = 400$, and $MB_B = 600$, what should the decision maker do?

  b. If $P_A = \$20$, $P_B = \$30$, $MB_A = 200$, and $MB_B = 300$, what should the decision maker do?

  c. If $P_A = \$20$, $P_B = \$40$, $MB_A = 300$, and $MB_B = 400$, how many units of A can be obtained if B is reduced by one unit? How much will benefits increase if this exchange is made?

  d. If the substitution in part c continues to equilibrium and MB_A falls to 250, what will MB_B be?

11. A decision maker wishes to maximize the total benefit associated with three activities, X, Y, and Z. The price per unit of activities X, Y, and Z is $1, $2, and $3, respectively. The following table gives the ratio of the marginal benefit to the price of the activities for various levels of each activity:

Level of activity	$\dfrac{MB_X}{P_X}$	$\dfrac{MB_Y}{P_Y}$	$\dfrac{MB_Z}{P_Z}$
1	10	22	14
2	9	18	12
3	8	12	10
4	7	10	9
5	6	6	8
6	5	4	6
7	4	2	4
8	3	1	2

  a. If the decision maker chooses to use one unit of X, one unit of Y, and one unit of Z, the total benefit that results is $_____.

  b. For the fourth unit of activity Y, each dollar spent increases total benefit by $_____. The fourth unit of activity Y increases total benefit by $_____.

c. Suppose the decision maker can spend a total of only $18 on the three activities. What is the optimal level of X, Y, and Z? Why is this combination optimal? Why is the combination 2X, 2Y, and 4Z not optimal?

d. Now suppose the decision maker has $33 to spend on the three activities. What is the optimal level of X, Y, and Z? If the decision maker has $35 to spend, what is the optimal combination? Explain.

12. Suppose a firm is considering two different activities, X and Y, which yield the total benefits presented in the schedule below. The price of X is $2 per unit, and the price of Y is $10 per unit.

Level of activity	Total benefit of activity X (TB_X)	Total benefit of activity Y (TB_Y)
0	$ 0	$ 0
1	30	100
2	54	190
3	72	270
4	84	340
5	92	400
6	98	450

a. The firm places a budget constraint of $26 on expenditures on activities X and Y. What are the levels of X and Y that maximize total benefit subject to the budget constraint?

b. What is the total benefit associated with the optimal levels of X and Y in part a?

c. Now let the budget constraint increase to $58. What are the optimal levels of X and Y now? What is the total benefit when the budget constraint is $58?

13. a. If, in a constrained minimization problem, $P_A = \$10$, $P_B = \$10$, $MB_A = 600$, and $MB_B = 300$ and one unit of B is taken away, how many units of A must be added to keep benefits constant?

b. If the substitution in part a continues to equilibrium, what will be the equilibrium relation between MB_A and MB_B?

APPLIED PROBLEMS

1. Using optimization theory, analyze the following quotations:

a. "The optimal number of traffic deaths in the United States is zero."

b. "Any pollution is too much pollution."

c. "We cannot pull U.S. troops out of Afghanistan. We have committed so much already."

d. "If Congress cuts out the NASA space station, we will have wasted all the resources that we have already spent on it. Therefore, we must continue funding it."

e. "Since JetGreen Airways has experienced a 25 percent increase in its insurance premiums, the airline should increase the number passengers it serves next quarter in order to spread the increase in premiums over a larger number of tickets."

2. Appalachian Coal Mining believes that it can increase labor productivity and, therefore, net revenue by reducing air pollution in its mines. It estimates that the marginal cost function for reducing pollution by installing additional capital equipment is

$$MC = 40P$$

where P represents a reduction of one unit of pollution in the mines. It also feels that for every unit of pollution reduction the marginal increase in revenue (MR) is

$$MR = 1,000 - 10P$$

How much pollution reduction should Appalachian Coal Mining undertake?

3. Two partners who own Progressive Business Solutions, which currently operates out of an office in a small town near Boston, just discovered a vacancy in an office building in downtown Boston. One of the partners favors moving downtown because she believes the additional business gained by moving downtown will exceed the higher rent at the downtown location plus the cost of making the move. The other partner at PBS opposes moving downtown. He argues, "We have already paid for office stationery, business cards, and a large sign that cannot be moved or sold. We have spent so much on our current office that we can't afford to waste this money by moving now." Evaluate the second partner's advice not to move downtown.

4. Twentyfirst Century Electronics has discovered a theft problem at its warehouse and has decided to hire security guards. The firm wants to hire the optimal number of security guards. The following table shows how the number of security guards affects the number of radios stolen per week.

Number of security guards	Number of radios stolen per week
0	50
1	30
2	20
3	14
4	8
5	6

a. If each security guard is paid $200 a week and the cost of a stolen radio is $25, how many security guards should the firm hire?

b. If the cost of a stolen radio is $25, what is the most the firm would be willing to pay to hire the first security guard?

c. If each security guard is paid $200 a week and the cost of a stolen radio is $50, how many security guards should the firm hire?

5. U.S. Supreme Court Justice Stephen Breyer's book *Breaking the Vicious Circle: Toward Effective Risk Regulation* (1993) examines government's role in controlling and managing the health risks society faces from exposure to environmental pollution. One major problem examined in the book is the cleanup of hazardous waste sites. Justice Breyer was extremely critical of policymakers who wish to see waste sites 100 percent clean.

a. Explain, using the theory of optimization and a graph, the circumstances under which a waste site could be made "too clean." (Good answers are dispassionate and employ economic analysis.)

b. Justice Breyer believes that society can enjoy virtually all the health benefits of cleaning up a waste site for only a "small fraction" of the total cost of completely cleaning a site. Using graphical analysis, illustrate this situation. (*Hint:* Draw *MB* and *MC* curves with shapes that specifically illustrate this situation.)

6. In Illustration 3.1 we noted that the rule for maximization set forth in the text contradicts some honored traditional principles such as "Never give up," "Anything worth doing is worth doing well," or "Waste not, want not." Explain the contradiction for each of these rules.

7. Janice Waller, the manager of the customer service department at First Bank of Jefferson County, can hire employees with a high school diploma for $20,000 annually and employees with a bachelor's degree for $30,000. She wants to maximize the number of customers served, given a fixed payroll. The following table shows how the total number of customers served varies with the number of employees:

Number of employees	Total number of customers served	
	High school diploma	Bachelor's degree
1	120	100
2	220	190
3	300	270
4	370	330
5	430	380
6	470	410

a. If Ms. Waller has a payroll of $160,000, how should she allocate this budget in order to maximize the number of customers served?

b. If she has a budget of $150,000 and currently hires three people with high school diplomas and three with bachelor's degrees, is she making the correct decision? Why or why not? If not, what should she do? (Assume she can hire part-time workers.)

c. If her budget is increased to $240,000, how should she allocate this budget?

8. Bavarian Crystal Works designs and produces lead crystal wine decanters for export to international markets. The production manager of Bavarian Crystal Works estimates total and marginal production costs to be

$$TC = 10,000 + 40Q + 0.0025Q^2$$

and

$$MC = 40 + 0.005Q$$

where costs are measured in U.S. dollars and Q is the number of wine decanters produced annually. Because Bavarian Crystal Works is only one of many crystal producers in the world market, it can sell as many of the decanters as it wishes for $70 apiece. Total and marginal revenue are

$$TR = 70Q \quad \text{and} \quad MR = 70$$

where revenues are measured in U.S. dollars and Q is annual decanter production.

a. What is the optimal level of production of wine decanters? What is the marginal revenue from the last wine decanter sold?

b. What are the total revenue, total cost, and net benefit (profit) from selling the optimal number of wine decanters?

c. At the optimal level of production of decanters, an extra decanter can be sold for $70, thereby increasing total revenue by $70. Why does the manager of this firm *not* produce and sell one more unit?

9. Joy Land Toys, a toy manufacturer, is experiencing quality problems on its assembly line. The marketing division estimates that each defective toy that leaves the plant costs the firm $10, on average, for replacement or repair. The engineering department recommends hiring quality inspectors to sample for defective toys. In this way many quality problems can be caught and prevented before shipping. After visiting other companies, a management team derives the following schedule showing the approximate number of defective toys that would be produced for several levels of inspection:

Number of inspectors	Average number of defective toys (per day)
0	92
1	62
2	42
3	27
4	17
5	10
6	5

The daily wage of inspectors is $70.

a. How many inspectors should the firm hire?

b. What would your answer to *a* be if the wage rate is $90?

c. What if the average cost of a defective toy is $5 and the wage rate of inspectors is $70?

☐   **MATHEMATICAL APPENDIX**   **A Brief Presentation of Optimization Theory**

Theory of Unconstrained Maximization

This section sets forth a mathematical analysis of unconstrained maximization. We begin with a single-variable problem in its most general form. An activity, the level of which is denoted as x, generates both benefits and costs. The total benefit function is $B(x)$ and the total cost function is $C(x)$. The objective is to maximize net benefit, NB, defined as the difference between total benefit and total cost. Net benefit is itself a function of the level of activity and can be expressed as

(1) $$NB = NB(x) = B(x) - C(x)$$

The necessary condition for maximization of net benefit is that the derivative of NB with respect to x equal zero:

(2) $$\frac{dNB(x)}{dx} = \frac{dB(x)}{dx} - \frac{dC(x)}{dx} = 0$$

Equation (2) can then be solved for the optimal level of x, denoted x^*. Net benefit is maximized when

(3) $$\frac{dB(x)}{dx} = \frac{dC(x)}{dx}$$

Since dB/dx is the change in total benefit with respect to the level of activity, this term is marginal benefit. Similarly for cost, dC/dx is the change in total cost with respect to the level of activity, and this term is marginal cost. Thus net benefit is maximized at the level of activity where marginal benefit equals marginal cost.

This unconstrained optimization problem can be easily expanded to more than one choice variable or kind of activity. To this end, let total benefit and total cost be functions of two different activities, denoted by x and y. The net benefit function with two activities is expressed as

(4) $\qquad NB = NB(x, y) = B(x, y) - C(x, y)$

Maximization of net benefit when there are two activities affecting benefit and cost requires both of the partial derivatives of NB with respect to each of the activities to be equal to zero:

(5a) $\qquad \dfrac{\partial NB(x,y)}{\partial x} = \dfrac{\partial B(x,y)}{\partial x} - \dfrac{\partial C(x,y)}{\partial x} = 0$

(5b) $\qquad \dfrac{\partial NB(x,y)}{\partial y} = \dfrac{\partial B(x,y)}{\partial y} - \dfrac{\partial C(x,y)}{\partial y} = 0$

Equations (5a) and (5b) can be solved simultaneously for the optimal levels of the variables, x^* and y^*. Maximization of net benefit thus requires

(6a) $\qquad \dfrac{\partial B}{\partial x} = \dfrac{\partial C}{\partial x}$

and

(6b) $\qquad \dfrac{\partial B}{\partial y} = \dfrac{\partial C}{\partial y}$

For each activity, the marginal benefit of the activity equals the marginal cost of the activity. The problem can be expanded to any number of choice variables with the same results.

Turning now to a mathematical example, consider the following specific form of the total benefit and total cost functions:

(7) $\qquad B(x) = ax - bx^2$

and

(8) $\qquad C(x) = cx - dx^2 + ex^3$

where the parameters, a, b, c, d, and e are all positive.

Now the net benefit function can be expressed as

(9) $\qquad NB = NB(x) = B(x) - C(x)$
$\qquad\qquad = ax - bx^2 - cx + dx^2 - ex^3$

To find the optimal value of x, take the derivative of the net benefit function with respect to x and set it equal to zero:

(10) $\qquad \dfrac{dNB}{dx} = a - 2bx - c + 2dx - 3ex^2$
$\qquad\qquad = (a - c) - 2(b - d)x - 3ex^2 = 0$

This quadratic equation can be solved using the quadratic formula or by factoring.[a]

Suppose the values of the parameters are $a = 60$, $b = 0.5$, $c = 24$, $d = 2$, and $e = 1$. The net benefit function is

(11) $\qquad NB = NB(x) = 60x - 0.5x^2 - 24x + 2x^2 - x^3$

Now take the derivative of NB [or substitute parameter values into equation (10)] to find the condition for optimization:

(12) $(60 - 24) - 2(0.5 - 2)x - 3(1)x^2 = 36 + 3x - 3x^2 = 0$

This equation can be factored: $(12 - 3x)(3 + x) = 0$. The solutions are $x = 4$, $x = -3$. (*Note:* The quadratic equation can also be used to find the solutions.) The value of x that maximizes net benefit is $x^* = 4$.[b] To find the optimal, or maximum, value of net benefit, substitute $x^* = 4$ into equation (11) to obtain

$\qquad NB^* = 60(4) - 0.5(4)^2 - 24(4) + 2(4)^2 - (4)^3 = 104$

Theory of Constrained Maximization

In a constrained maximization problem, a decision maker determines the level of the activities, or choice variables, in order to obtain the most benefit under a given cost constraint. In a constrained minimization problem, a decision maker determines the levels of the choice variables in order to obtain the lowest cost of achieving a given level of benefit. As we showed in the text, the solutions to the two types of problems are the same. We first consider constrained maximization.

––––––––

[a]The solution to a quadratic equation yields two values for x. The maximization, rather than minimization, solution is the value of x at which the second-order condition is met:

$$\dfrac{d^2NB}{dx^2} = -2(b - d) - 6ex < 0$$

[b]This value of x is the one that satisfies the second-order condition for a maximum in the preceding footnote:

$$\dfrac{d^2NB}{dx^2} = -2(-1.5) - 6(1)(4) = -21 < 0$$

Constrained maximization

We first assume a general total benefit function with two choice variables, the levels of which are denoted x and y: $B(x, y)$. The partial derivatives of this function represent the marginal benefit for each activity:

$$MB_x = \frac{\partial B(x,y)}{\partial x} \quad \text{and} \quad MB_y = \frac{\partial B(x,y)}{\partial y}$$

The constraint is that the total cost function must equal a specified level of cost, denoted as $\overline{C}$:

(13) $$C(x, y) = P_x x + P_y y = \overline{C}$$

where P_x and P_y are the prices of x and y. Now the Lagrangian function to be maximized can be written as

(14) $$\mathcal{L} = B(x, y) + \lambda(\overline{C} - P_x x - P_y y)$$

where λ is the Lagrangian multiplier. The first-order condition for a maximum requires the partial derivatives of the Lagrangian with respect to the variables x, y, and λ to be zero:

(14a) $$\frac{\partial \mathcal{L}}{\partial x} = \frac{\partial B}{\partial x} - \lambda P_x = 0$$

(14b) $$\frac{\partial \mathcal{L}}{\partial y} = \frac{\partial B}{\partial y} - \lambda P_y = 0$$

(14c) $$\frac{\partial \mathcal{L}}{\partial \lambda} = \overline{C} - P_x x - P_y y = 0$$

Notice that satisfaction of the first-order condition (14c) requires that the cost constraint be met.

Rearranging the first two equations (14a) and (14b):

$$\frac{\partial B}{\partial x} = \lambda P_x \quad \text{or} \quad \frac{MB_x}{P_x} = \lambda$$

$$\frac{\partial B}{\partial y} = \lambda P_y \quad \text{or} \quad \frac{MB_y}{P_y} = \lambda$$

It therefore follows that the levels of x and y must be chosen so that

(15) $$\frac{MB_x}{P_x} = \frac{MB_y}{P_y}$$

The marginal benefits per dollar spent on the last units of x and y must be equal.

The three equations in (14) can be solved for the equilibrium values x^*, y^*, and λ^* by substitution or by Cramer's rule. Therefore, x^* and y^* give the values of the choice variables that yield the maximum benefit possible at the given level of cost.

Constrained minimization

For the constrained minimization problem, we want to choose the levels of two activities, x and y, to obtain a given level of benefit at the lowest possible cost. Therefore, the problem is to minimize $C = P_x x + P_y y$, subject to $B = B(x, y)$, where $\overline{B}$ is the specified level of benefit. The Lagrangian function is

(16) $$\mathcal{L} = P_x x + P_y y + \lambda[\overline{B} - B(x, y)]$$

The first-order conditions are

$$\frac{\partial \mathcal{L}}{\partial x} = P_x - \lambda \frac{\partial B}{\partial x} = 0$$

(17) $$\frac{\partial \mathcal{L}}{\partial y} = P_y - \lambda \frac{\partial B}{\partial y} = 0$$

$$\frac{\partial \mathcal{L}}{\partial \lambda} = [\overline{B} - B(x, y)] = 0$$

As in the constrained maximization problem, the first two equations can be rearranged to obtain

(18) $$\frac{\partial B}{\partial x} = \frac{1}{\lambda} P_x \quad \text{or} \quad \frac{MB_x}{P_x} = \frac{1}{\lambda}$$

$$\frac{\partial B}{\partial y} = \frac{1}{\lambda} P_y \quad \text{or} \quad \frac{MB_y}{P_y} = \frac{1}{\lambda}$$

Once again the marginal benefits per dollar spent on the last units of x and y must be the same, because, from (18),

$$\frac{MB_x}{P_x} = \frac{MB_y}{P_y}$$

The three equations in (17) can be solved for the equilibrium values x^*, y^*, and λ^* by substitution or by Cramer's rule. These are the values of the choice variables that attain the lowest cost of reaching the given level of benefit.

MATHEMATICAL EXERCISES

1. Assume the only choice variable is x. The total benefit function is $B(x) = 170x - x^2$, and the cost function is $C(x) = 100 - 10x + 2x^2$.

   a. What are the marginal benefit and marginal cost functions?

   b. Set up the net benefit function and then determine the level of x that maximizes net benefit.

   c. What is the maximum level of net benefit?

2. The only choice variable is x. The total benefit function is $B(x) = 100x - 2x^2$, and the total cost function is $C(x) = \frac{1}{3}x^3 - 6x^2 + 52x + 80$.

   a. What are the marginal benefit and marginal cost functions?

   b. Set up the net benefit function and then determine the level of x that maximizes net benefit. (Use the positive value of x.)

   c. What is the maximum level of net benefit?

3. A decision maker wishes to maximize total benefit, $B = 3x + xy + y$, subject to the cost constraint, $\bar{C} = 4x + 2y = 70$. Set up the Lagrangian and then determine the values of x and y at the maximum level of benefit, given the constraint. What are the maximum benefits?

4. A decision maker wishes to minimize the cost of producing a given level of total benefit, $B = 288$. The cost function is $C = 6x + 3y$ and the total benefit function is $B = xy$. Set up the Lagrangian and then determine levels of x and y at the minimum level of cost. What is the minimum value of cost?

5. In Figure 3.1, the total benefit and total cost curves are represented by the following mathematical functions:

   $$TB = TB(A) = 8A - 0.004A^2$$

   and

   $$TC = TC(A) = A + 0.006A^2$$

   a. Find the marginal benefit function. Verify that points c, b, and d in Figure 3.2 lie on the marginal benefit curve.

   b. Find the marginal cost function. Verify that points c', b, and d' in Figure 3.2 lie on the marginal cost curve.

   c. Derive the net benefit function. Verify the slopes of net benefit at points M, c'', and d'' in Figure 3.3.

   d. Find the optimal level of activity and the maximum value of net benefit. Does your answer match Figure 3.3?

CHAPTER

4

Basic Estimation Techniques

In order to implement the various techniques discussed in this text, managers must be able to determine the mathematical relation between the economic variables that make up the various functions used in managerial economics: demand functions, production functions, cost functions, and others. For example, managers often must determine the total cost of producing various levels of output. As you will see in Chapter 10, the relation between total cost (C) and quantity (Q) can be specified as

$$C = a + bQ + cQ^2 + dQ^3$$

parameters
The coefficients in an equation that determine the exact mathematical relation among the variables.

where a, b, c, and d are the *parameters* of the cost equation. **Parameters** are coefficients in an equation that determine the exact mathematical relation among the variables in the equation. Once the numerical values of the parameters are determined, the manager then knows the quantitative relation between output and total cost. For example, suppose the values of the parameters of the cost equation are determined to be $a = 1,262$, $b = 1.0$, $c = -0.03$, and $d = 0.005$. The cost equation can now be expressed as

$$C = 1,262 + 1.0Q - 0.03Q^2 + 0.005Q^3$$

This equation can be used to compute the total cost of producing various levels of output. If, for example, the manager wishes to produce 30 units of output, the total cost can be calculated as

$$C = 1,262 + 30 - 0.03(30)^2 + 0.005(30)^3 = \$1,400$$

Thus in order for the cost function to be useful for decision making, the manager must know the numerical values of the parameters.

121

The process of finding estimates of the numerical values of the parameters of an equation is called **parameter estimation.** Although there are several techniques for estimating parameters, the values of the parameters are often obtained by using a technique called **regression analysis.** Regression analysis uses data on economic variables to determine a mathematical equation that describes the relation between the economic variables. Regression analysis involves both the estimation of parameter values and testing for statistical significance.

In this chapter, we will set forth the *basics* of regression analysis. We want to stress that throughout the discussion of regression analysis, in this chapter and the chapters that follow, we are not as much interested in your knowing the ways the various statistics are calculated as we are in your knowing how these statistics can be interpreted and used. We will often rely on intuitive explanations, leaving formal derivations for the appendixes at the end of the chapter.

parameter estimation
The process of finding estimates of the numerical values of the parameters of an equation.

regression analysis
A statistical technique for estimating the parameters of an equation and testing for statistical significance.

4.1 THE SIMPLE LINEAR REGRESSION MODEL

Regression analysis is a technique used to determine the mathematical relation between a **dependent variable** and one or more **explanatory variables.** The explanatory variables are the economic variables that are thought to affect the value of the dependent variable. In the *simple linear regression model*, the dependent variable Y is related to only *one* explanatory variable X, and the relation between Y and X is linear:

$$Y = a + bX$$

This is the equation for a straight line, with X plotted along the horizontal axis and Y along the vertical axis. The parameter a is called the **intercept parameter** because it gives the value of Y at the point where the regression line crosses the Y-axis. (X is equal to 0 at this point.) The parameter b is called the **slope parameter** because it gives the slope of the regression line. The slope of a line measures the rate of change in Y as X changes ($\Delta Y / \Delta X$); it is therefore the change in Y per unit change in X.

Note that Y and X are linearly related in the regression model; that is, the effect of a change in X on the value of Y is constant. More specifically, a one-unit change in X causes Y to change by a constant b units. The simple regression model is based on a linear relation between Y and X, in large part because estimating the parameters of a linear model is relatively simple statistically. As it turns out, assuming a linear relation is not overly restrictive. For one thing, many variables are actually linearly related or very nearly linearly related. For those cases where Y and X are instead related in a curvilinear fashion, you will see that a simple transformation of the variables often makes it possible to model nonlinear relations within the framework of the linear regression model. You will see how to make these simple transformations later in this chapter.

dependent variable
The variable whose variation is to be explained.

explanatory variables
The variables that are thought to cause the dependent variable to take on different values.

intercept parameter
The parameter that gives the value of Y at the point where the regression line crosses the Y-axis.

slope parameter
The slope of the regression line, $b = \Delta Y / \Delta X$, or the change in Y associated with a one-unit change in X.

A Hypothetical Regression Model

To illustrate the simple regression model, consider a statistical problem facing the Tampa Bay Travel Agents' Association. The association wishes to determine the

FIGURE 4.1

The True Regression Line: Relating Sales and Advertising Expenditures

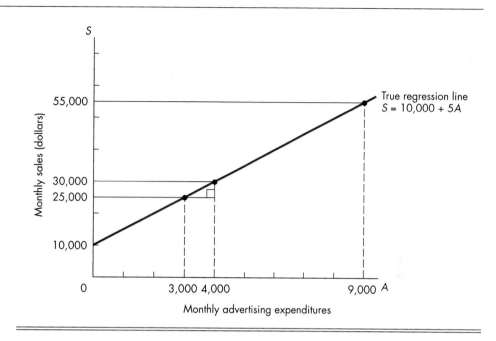

true (or actual) relation

The true or actual underlying relation between Y and X that is unknown to the researcher but is to be discovered by analyzing the sample data.

mathematical relation between the dollar volume of sales of travel packages (S) and the level of expenditures on newspaper advertising (A) for travel agents located in the Tampa–St. Petersburg metropolitan area. Suppose that the **true (or actual) relation** between sales and advertising expenditures is

$$S = 10,000 + 5A$$

where S measures monthly sales in dollars and A measures monthly advertising expenditures in dollars. The true relation between sales and advertising is unknown to the analyst; it must be "discovered" by analyzing data on sales and advertising. Researchers are never able to know with certainty the exact nature of the underlying mathematical relation between the dependent variable and the explanatory variable, but regression analysis does provide a method for estimating the true relation.

Figure 4.1 shows the true or actual relation between sales and advertising expenditures. If an agency chooses to spend nothing on newspaper advertising, its sales are expected to be $10,000 per month. If an agency spends $3,000 monthly on ads, it can expect sales of $25,000 (= 10,000 + 5 × 3,000). Because $\Delta S/\Delta A = 5$, for every $1 of additional expenditure on advertising, the travel agency can expect a $5 increase in sales. For example, increasing outlays from $3,000 to $4,000 per month causes expected monthly sales to rise from $25,000 to $30,000, as shown in the figure.

The Random Error Term

The regression equation (or line) shows the level of expected sales for each level of advertising expenditure. As noted, if a travel agency spends $3,000 monthly on

TABLE 4.1

The Impact of Random Effects on January Sales

Firm	Advertising expenditure	Actual sales	Expected sales	Random effect
Tampa Travel Agency	$3,000	$30,000	$25,000	$5,000
Buccaneer Travel Service	3,000	21,000	25,000	−4,000
Happy Getaway Tours	3,000	25,000	25,000	0

ads, it can expect on average to have sales of $25,000. We should stress that $25,000 should be interpreted not as the exact level of sales that a firm will experience when advertising expenditures are $3,000 but only as an average level. To illustrate this point, suppose that three travel agencies in the Tampa–St. Petersburg area each spends exactly $3,000 on advertising. Will all three of these firms experience sales of precisely $25,000? This is *not* likely. While each of these three firms spends exactly the same amount on advertising, each firm experiences certain *random* effects that are peculiar to that firm. These random effects cause the sales of the various firms to deviate from the expected $25,000 level of sales.

Table 4.1 illustrates the impact of random effects on the actual level of sales achieved. Each of the three firms in Table 4.1 spent $3,000 on advertising in the month of January. According to the true regression equation, each of these travel agencies would be expected to have sales of $25,000 in January. As it turns out, the manager of the Tampa Travel Agency used the advertising agency owned and managed by her brother, who gave better than usual service. This travel agency actually sold $30,000 worth of travel packages in January—$5,000 more than the expected or average level of sales. The manager of Buccaneer Travel Service was on a ski vacation in early January and did not start spending money on advertising until the middle of January. Buccaneer Travel Service's sales were only $21,000—$4,000 less than the regression line predicted. In January nothing unusual happened to Happy Getaway Tours, and its sales of $25,000 exactly matched what the average travel agency in Tampa would be expected to sell when it spends $3,000 on advertising.

Because of these random effects, the level of sales for a firm cannot be *exactly* predicted. The regression equation shows only the *average* or *expected* level of sales when a firm spends a given amount on advertising. The exact level of sales for any particular travel agency (such as the *i*th agency) can be expressed as

$$S_i = 10,000 + 5A_i + e_i$$

random error term
An unobservable term added to a regression model to capture the effects of all the minor, unpredictable factors that affect Y but cannot reasonably be included as explanatory variables.

where S_i and A_i are, respectively, the sales and advertising levels of the *i*th agency and e_i is the random effect experienced by the *i*th travel agency. Since e_i measures the amount by which the *actual* level of sales differs from the average level of sales, e_i is called an *error term*, or a *random error*. The **random error term** captures the effects of all the minor, unpredictable factors that cannot reasonably be included in the model as explanatory variables.

Because the *true* regression line is unknown, the first task of regression analysis is to obtain estimates of *a* and *b*. To do this, data on monthly sales and advertising

TABLE 4.2

Sales and Advertising Expenditures for a Sample of Seven Travel Agencies

Firm	Sales	Advertising expenditure
A	$15,000	$2,000
B	30,000	2,000
C	30,000	5,000
D	25,000	3,000
E	55,000	9,000
F	45,000	8,000
G	60,000	7,000

expenditures must be collected from Tampa Bay–area travel agents. Using these data, a regression line is then fitted. Before turning to the task of fitting a regression line to the data points in a sample, we summarize the simple regression model in the following statistical relation:

▣ **Relation**   The simple linear regression model relates a dependent variable Y to a single independent explanatory variable X in a linear equation called the true regression line:

$$Y = a + bX$$

where a is the Y-intercept, and b is the slope of the regression line $(\Delta Y/\Delta X)$. The regression line shows the average or expected value of Y for each level of the explanatory variable X.

4.2 FITTING A REGRESSION LINE

The purpose of regression analysis is twofold: (1) to estimate the parameters (a and b) of the true regression line and (2) to test whether the estimated values of the parameters are statistically significant. (We will discuss the meaning of statistical significance later.) We turn now to the first task—the estimation of a and b. You will see that estimating a and b is equivalent to fitting a straight line through a scatter of data points plotted on a graph. Regression analysis provides a way of finding the line that "best fits" the scatter of data points.

To estimate the parameters of the regression equation, an analyst first collects data on the dependent and explanatory variables. The data can be collected over time for a specific firm (or a specific industry); this type of data set is called a **time-series**. Alternatively, the data can be collected from several different firms or industries at a given time; this type of data set is called a **cross-sectional** data set. No matter how the data are collected, the result is a scatter of data points (called a **scatter diagram**) through which a regression line can be fitted.

To show how the parameters are estimated, we refer once again to the Tampa Bay Travel Agents' Association. Suppose the association asks seven agencies (out of the total 475 agencies located in the Tampa–St. Petersburg area) for data on their sales and advertising expenditures during the month of January. These data (a cross-sectional data set) are presented in Table 4.2 and are plotted in a scatter diagram in Figure 4.2. Each dot in the figure refers to a specific sales–expenditure combination

time-series
A data set in which the data for the dependent and explanatory variables are collected over time for a specific firm.

cross-sectional
A data set in which the data on the dependent and explanatory variables are collected from many different firms or industries at a given point in time.

scatter diagram
A graph of the data points in a sample.

FIGURE 4.2

The Sample Regression Line: Relating Sales and Advertising Expenditures

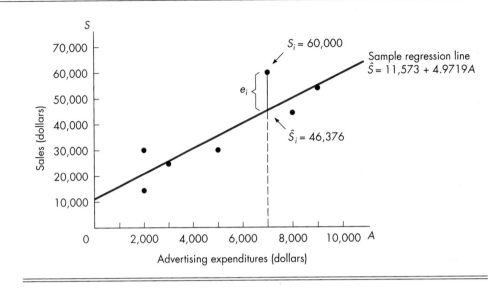

population regression line
The equation or line representing the true (or actual) underlying relation between the dependent variable and the explanatory variable(s).

sample regression line
The line that best fits the scatter of data points in the sample and provides an estimate of the population regression line.

method of least-squares
A method of estimating the parameters of a linear regression equation by finding the line that minimizes the sum of the squared distances from each sample data point to the sample regression line.

in the table. The data seem to indicate that a positive relation exists between sales and advertising: The higher the level of advertising, the higher (on average) the level of sales. The objective of regression analysis is to find the straight line that best fits the scatter of data points. Since fitting a line through a scatter of data points simply involves choosing values of the parameters a and b, fitting a regression line and estimation of parameters are conceptually the same thing.

The association wants to use the data in the sample to estimate the true regression line, also called the **population regression line.** The line that best fits the data in the sample is called the **sample regression line.** Since the sample contains information on only seven out of the total 475 travel agencies, it is highly unlikely that the sample regression line will be exactly the same as the true regression line. The sample regression line is only an estimate of the true regression line. Naturally, the larger the size of the sample, the more accurately the sample regression line will estimate the true regression line.

In Figure 4.2, the sample regression line that best fits the seven sample data points presented in Table 4.2 is given by

$$\hat{S} = 11{,}573 + 4.9719A$$

where $\hat{S}$ is called the fitted or predicted value of S. Regression analysis uses the **method of least-squares** to find the sample regression line that best fits the data in the sample. The principle of least-squares is based on the idea that the sample regression line that is most likely to match the *true* regression line is the line that minimizes the sum of the squared distances from each sample data point to the *sample* regression line.

fitted or predicted value

The predicted value of Y (denoted Ŷ) associated with a particular value of X, which is obtained by substituting that value of X into the sample regression equation.

residual

The difference between the actual value of Y and the fitted (or predicted) value of Y: $Y_i - \hat{Y}_i$.

estimators

The formulas by which the estimates of parameters are computed.

estimates

The estimated values of parameters obtained by substituting sample data into estimators.

Look at the sample data point for advertising expenditures of $7,000 and sales of $60,000 in Figure 4.2. The sample regression equation indicates that advertising expenditures of $7,000 will result in $46,376 (= 11,573 + 4.9719 × 7,000) of sales. The value $46,376 is called the **fitted** or **predicted value** of sales, which we denote as $\hat{S}_i$. The difference between the actual value of sales and the fitted (predicted) value, $S_i - \hat{S}_i$, is called the **residual** and is equal to the vertical distance between the data point and the fitted regression line (denoted e_i in Figure 4.2). The residual for the data point at ($7,000, $60,000) is $13,624 (= $60,000 − $46,376). Regression analysis selects the straight line (i.e., chooses a and b) in order to minimize the sum of the squared residuals ($\sum e_i^2$), which is why it is often referred to as least-squares analysis.

We are not concerned with teaching you the details involved in computing the least-squares estimates of a and b since computers are almost always used in regression analysis for this purpose. Nevertheless, it might be informative for you to see how the computer can calculate estimates of a and b. The formulas by which the estimates of a and b are computed are frequently called **estimators.** The formulas the computer uses for computing the least-squares estimates of a and b (denoted $\hat{a}$ and $\hat{b}$ to indicate that these are **estimates** and not the true values) are

$$\hat{b} = \frac{\sum(X_i - \overline{X})(Y_i - \overline{Y})}{\sum(X_i - \overline{X})^2}$$

and

$$\hat{a} = Y - b\overline{X}$$

where $\overline{Y}$ and $\overline{X}$ are, respectively, the sample means of the dependent variable and independent variable, and X_i and Y_i are the observed values for the ith observation. While our central concern is that you understand how to interpret regression analysis, we have provided the mathematical derivation of the least-squares formulas for $\hat{a}$ and $\hat{b}$ in the appendix at the end of this chapter for those who wish to see a formal derivation. So you can appreciate the tedious nature of the arithmetic involved in computing least-squares estimates, this chapter's appendix illustrates the computations that will be done for you by a computer. We can now summarize least-squares estimation with the following statistical relation:

▢ **Relation** Estimating the parameters of the true regression line is equivalent to fitting a line through a scatter diagram of the sample data points. The sample regression line, which is found using the method of least-squares, is the line that best fits the sample:

$$\hat{Y} = \hat{a} + \hat{b}X$$

where $\hat{a}$ and $\hat{b}$ are the least-squares estimates of the true (population) parameters a and b. The sample regression line estimates the true regression line.

Many computer software programs can compute the least-squares estimates for linear regression analysis, along with a variety of associated statistics for assessing the performance of the regression model, some of which we will explain to you in this chapter. Table 4.3 shows several versions of computer regression printouts for the regression analysis of the seven travel agencies presented in Table 4.2. In each panel, the parameter estimates for a and b are highlighted in color. Panel A shows a typical or "generic" regression printout, and we will use this simplified format throughout this book. Panel B shows the same regression analysis, as it looks when performed using the Student Edition of *Statistix* 8 software, which accompanies some versions of this textbook. Many business decision makers use Microsoft's *Excel* software to perform regression analysis. Panel C shows the *Excel* output. As you can see, cells B17 and B18 give $\hat{a}$ and $\hat{b}$, respectively. We want to emphasize that we do *not* intend to teach you how to use *all* of the statistics provided by these regression software packages. You must take one or two statistics courses to become proficient in regression analysis. In this textbook, we are attempting only to introduce you to basic estimation techniques and procedures.

We now turn to the task of testing hypotheses about the true values of a and b—which are unknown to the researcher—using the information contained in the sample. These tests involve determining whether the dependent variable is truly related to the independent variable or whether the relation as estimated from the sample data is due only to the randomness of the sample.

4.3 TESTING FOR STATISTICAL SIGNIFICANCE

statistically significant
There is sufficient evidence from the sample to indicate that the true value of the coefficient is not 0.

Once the parameters of an equation are estimated, the analyst must address the question of whether or not the parameter estimates ($\hat{a}$ and $\hat{b}$) are significantly different from 0. If the estimated coefficient is far enough away from 0—either sufficiently greater than 0 (a positive estimate) or sufficiently less than 0 (a negative estimate)—the estimated coefficient is said to be **statistically significant.** The question of statistical significance arises because the estimates are themselves random variables. The parameter estimates are random because they are calculated using values of Y and X that are collected in a random fashion (remember, the sample is a random sample). Since the values of the parameters are *estimates* of the true parameter values, the estimates are rarely equal to the true parameter values. In other words, the estimates calculated by the computer are almost always going to be either too large or too small.

hypothesis testing
A statistical technique for making a probabilistic statement about the true value of a parameter.

Because the estimated values of the parameters ($\hat{a}$ and $\hat{b}$) are unlikely to be the true values (a and b), it is possible that a parameter could truly be equal to 0 even though the computer calculates a parameter estimate that is not equal to 0. Fortunately, statistical techniques exist that provide a tool for making probabilistic statements about the true values of the parameters. This tool is called **hypothesis testing.**

To understand fully the concept of hypothesis testing, you would need to take at least one course, and probably two, in statistics. In this text we intend only to motivate through intuition the *necessity* and *process* of performing a test of statistical significance. Our primary emphasis will be to show you how to test the hypothesis that Y is truly related to X. If Y is indeed related to X, the true value of the

TABLE 4.3
Examples of Several Printouts for Regression Analysis

```
DEPENDENT VARIABLE: S      R-SQUARE     F-RATIO     P-VALUE ON F
        OBSERVATIONS: 7     0.7652       16.30       0.0100

                      PARAMETER      STANDARD
          VARIABLE    ESTIMATE       ERROR        T-RATIO      P-VALUE

          INTERCEPT   11573.0        7150.83      1.62         0.1665
          A           4.97191        1.23154      4.04         0.0100
```

Panel A—"Generic" style

```
UNWEIGHTED LEAST SQUARES LINEAR REGRESSION OF S

PREDICTOR
VARIABLES            COEFFICIENT    STD ERROR     STUDENT'S T      P
---------            -----------    ---------     -----------    ------

CONSTANT             11573.0        7150.83          1.62        0.1665
A                    4.97191        1.23154          4.04        0.0100

R-SQUARED            0.7652      RESID. MEAN SQUARE (MSE)    7.713E+07
ADJUSTED R-SQUARED   0.7183      STANDARD DEVIATION             8782.64

SOURCE          DF     SS               MS            F       P
---------       ---    ----------       ----------    -----   ------

REGRESSION       1     1.257E+09        1.257E+09     16.30   0.0100
RESIDUAL         5     3.857E+08        7.713E+07
TOTAL            6     1.643E+09

CASES INCLUDED   7        MISSING CASES    0
```

Panel B—*Statistix* 8

	A	B	C	D	E	F	G
1	SUMMARY OUTPUT						
2							
3	*Regression Statistics*						
4	Multiple R	0.8748					
5	R Square	0.7652					
6	Adjusted R Square	0.7183					
7	Standard Error	8782.6438					
8	Observations	7					
9							
10	ANOVA						
11		*df*	*SS*	*MS*	*F*	*Significance F*	
12	Regression	1	1257182986	1257182986	16.30	0.0100	
13	Residual	5	385674157.3	77134831.46			
14	Total	6	1642857143				
15							
16		*Coefficients*	*Standard Error*	*t Stat*	*P-value*	*Lower 95%*	*Upper 95%*
17	Intercept	11573.0	7150.83	1.62	0.1665	-6808.7222	29954.7896
18	A	4.97191	1.23154	4.04	0.0100	1.8061	8.1377

Panel C—Microsoft *Excel*

slope parameter b will be either a positive or a negative number. (Remember, if $b = \Delta Y / \Delta X = 0$, no change in Y occurs when X changes.) Thus the explanatory variable X has a statistically significant effect on the dependent variable Y when $b \neq 0$.[1]

We will now discuss the procedure for testing for statistical significance by describing how to measure the accuracy, or precision, of an estimate. Then we will introduce and explain a statistical test (called a t-test) that can be used to make a probabilistic statement about whether or not Y is truly related to the explanatory variable X—that is, whether or not the true value of the parameter b is zero.

The Relative Frequency Distribution for $\hat{b}$

As noted, the necessity of testing for statistical significance arises because the analyst does not know the true values of a and b—they are estimated from a random sample of observations on Y and X. Consider again the relation between sales of travel packages and advertising expenditures estimated in the previous section. The least-squares estimate of the slope parameter b from the sample of seven travel agencies shown in Table 4.2 is 4.9719. Suppose you collected a new sample by randomly selecting seven other travel agencies and use their sales and advertising expenditures to estimate b. The estimate for b will probably not equal 4.9719 for the second sample. Remember, $\hat{b}$ is computed using the values of S and A in the sample. Because of randomness in sampling, different samples generally result in different values of S and A, and thus different estimates of b. Therefore, $\hat{b}$ is a random variable—its value varies in repeated samples.

The relative frequency with which $\hat{b}$ takes on different values provides information about the *accuracy* of the parameter estimates. Even though researchers seldom have the luxury of taking repeated samples, statisticians have been able to determine theoretically the **relative frequency distribution** of values that $\hat{b}$ would take in repeated samples. Figure 4.3 shows the relative frequency, or likelihood, that $\hat{b}$ takes on different values in repeated samples, *when the true value of* b *is equal to 5.*

Notice that the distribution of values that $\hat{b}$ might take in various samples is centered around the true value of 5. Even though the probability of drawing a sample for which $\hat{b}$ exactly equals 5 is extremely small, the average (mean or expected) value of all possible values of $\hat{b}$ is 5. The estimator $\hat{b}$ is said to be an **unbiased estimator** if the average (mean or expected) value of the estimator is equal to the true value of the parameter. Statisticians have demonstrated that the least-squares estimators of a and b ($\hat{a}$ and $\hat{b}$) are unbiased estimators in a wide variety of statistical circumstances. Unbiasedness does not mean that any one estimate equals the true parameter value. Unbiasedness means only that, in repeated samples, the estimates tend to be centered around the true value.

relative frequency distribution
The distribution (and relative frequency) of values $\hat{b}$ can take because observations on Y and X come from a random sample.

unbiased estimator
An estimator that produces estimates of a parameter that are on average equal to the true value of the parameter.

---

[1]Testing for statistical significance of the intercept parameter a is typically of secondary importance to testing for significance of the slope parameters. As you will see, it is the slope parameters rather than the intercept parameter that provide the most essential information for managerial decision making. Nevertheless, it is customary to test the intercept parameter for statistical significance in exactly the same manner as the slope parameter is tested.

FIGURE 4.3
Relative Frequency Distribution for $\hat{b}$ When $b = 5$

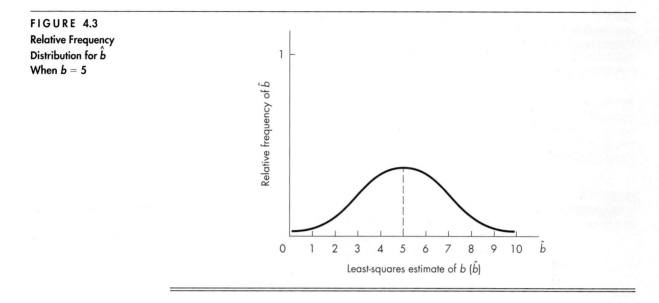

The smaller the dispersion of $\hat{b}$ around the true value, the more likely it is that an estimate of $\hat{b}$ is close to the true value. In other words, the smaller the variance of the distribution of $\hat{b}$, the more accurate estimates are likely to be. Not surprisingly, the variance of the estimate of b plays an important role in the determination of statistical significance. The square root of the variance of $\hat{b}$ is called the *standard error of the estimate,* which we will denote $S_{\hat{b}}$.[2] All computer regression routines compute standard errors for the parameter estimates.

The Concept of a *t*-Ratio

When we regressed sales on advertising expenditures for the seven travel agencies in Table 4.2, we obtained an estimate of b equal to 4.9719. Since 4.9719 is not equal to 0, this seems to suggest that the level of advertising does indeed affect sales. (Remember that if $b = 0$, there is no relation between sales and advertising.) As explained earlier, the estimate of b calculated using a random sample may take on a range of values. Even though 4.9719 is greater than 0, it is possible that the true value of b is 0. In other words, the analyst runs some risk that the true value of b is 0 even when $\hat{b}$ is not calculated to be 0.

The probability of drawing a sample for which the estimate of b is much larger than 0 is very small when the true value of b is actually 0. How large does $\hat{b}$ have to be for an analyst to be quite sure that b is not really 0 (i.e., advertising does play a significant role in determining sales)? The answer to this question is obtained by performing a hypothesis test. The hypothesis that one normally tests is that $b = 0$.

---

[2]More correctly, the standard error of the estimate is the square root of the *estimated* variance of $\hat{b}$.

t-test
A statistical test used to test the hypothesis that the true value of a parameter is equal to 0 (b = 0).

Statisticians use a **t-test** to make a probabilistic statement about the likelihood that the true parameter value b is not equal to 0. Using the t-test, it is possible to determine statistically how large $\hat{b}$ must be in order to conclude that b is not equal to 0.

In order to perform a t-test for statistical significance, we form what statisticians call a **t-ratio**:

$$t = \frac{\hat{b}}{S_{\hat{b}}}$$

t-ratio
The ratio of an estimated regression parameter divided by the standard error of the estimate.

where $\hat{b}$ is the least-squares estimate of b and $S_{\hat{b}}$ is the standard error of the estimate, both of which are calculated by the computer. The numerical value of the t-ratio is called a **t-statistic.**

t-statistic
The numerical value of the t-ratio.

By combining information about the size of $\hat{b}$ (in the numerator) and the accuracy or precision of the estimate (in the denominator), the t-ratio indicates how much confidence one can have that the true value of b is actually larger than (significantly different from) 0. The larger the absolute value of the t-ratio, the more confident one can be that the true value of b is not 0. To show why this is true, we must examine both the numerator and the denominator of the t-ratio. Consider the numerator when the estimate $\hat{b}$ is positive. When b actually is 0, drawing a random sample that will produce an estimate of b that is much larger than 0 is unlikely. Thus the larger the numerator of the t-ratio, the less likely it is that b really does equal 0. Turning now to the denominator of the t-ratio, recall that $S_{\hat{b}}$, the standard error of the estimate, measures the accuracy of the estimate of b. The smaller the standard error of $\hat{b}$ (and thus the more accurate $\hat{b}$ is), the smaller the error in estimation is likely to be. Consequently, the farther from 0 $\hat{b}$ is (i.e., the larger the numerator) and the smaller the standard error of the estimate (i.e., the smaller the denominator), the larger the t-ratio, and the more sure we are that the true value of b is greater than 0.

Now consider the situation when the estimate $\hat{b}$ is negative (e.g., if we had estimated the relation between profits and shoplifting). In this case we would be more certain that b was really negative if the t-ratio had a more negative magnitude. Regardless of whether $\hat{b}$ is positive or negative, the following important statistical relation is established:

Relation The larger the absolute value of $\hat{b}/S_{\hat{b}}$ (the t-ratio), the more probable it is that the true value of b is not equal to 0.

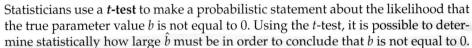

Performing a t-Test for Statistical Significance

critical value of t
The value that the t-statistic must exceed in order to reject the hypothesis that b = 0.

The t-statistic is used to test the hypothesis that the true value of b equals 0. If the calculated t-statistic or t-ratio is greater than the **critical value of t** (to be explained later), then the hypothesis that $b = 0$ is rejected in favor of the alternative hypothesis that $b \neq 0$. When the calculated t-statistic exceeds the critical value of t, b is significantly different from 0, or, equivalently, b is statistically significant. If the hypothesis that $b = 0$ cannot be rejected, then the sample data are indicating that X, the explanatory variable for which b is the coefficient, is not related to the dependent variable Y ($\Delta Y / \Delta X = 0$). Only when a parameter estimate is statistically significant should the associated explanatory variable be included in the regression equation.

Although performing a t-test is the correct way to assess the statistical significance of a parameter estimate, there is always some risk that the t-test will indicate $b \neq 0$ when in fact $b = 0$. Statisticians refer to this kind of mistake as a **Type I error**—finding a parameter estimate to be significant when it is not.[3] The probability of making a Type I error when performing a t-test is referred to as the **level of significance** of the t-test. The level of significance associated with a t-test is the probability that the test will indicate $b \neq 0$ when in fact $b = 0$. Stated differently, the significance level is the probability of finding the parameter to be statistically significant when in fact it is not. As we are about to show you, an analyst can control or select the level of significance for a t-test. Traditionally, either a 0.01, 0.02, 0.05, or 0.10 level of significance is selected, which reflects the analyst's willingness to tolerate at most a 1, 2, 5, or 10 percent probability of finding a parameter to be significant when it is not. In practice, however, the significance level tends to be chosen arbitrarily. We will return to the problem of selecting the appropriate level of significance later in this discussion of t-tests.

A concept closely related to the level of significance is the level of confidence. The **level of confidence** equals one minus the level of significance, and thus gives the probability that you will *not* make a Type I error. The confidence level is the probability a t-test will *correctly* find no relation between Y and X (i.e., $b = 0$). The lower the level of significance, the greater the level of confidence. If the level of significance chosen for conducting a t-test is 0.05 (5 percent), then the level of confidence for the test is 0.95 (95 percent), and you can be 95 percent confident that the t-test will correctly indicate lack of significance. The levels of significance and confidence provide the same information, only in slightly different ways: The significance level gives the probability of making a Type I error, while the confidence level gives the probability of *not* making a Type I error. A 5 percent level of significance and a 95 percent level of confidence mean the same thing.

Type I error
Error in which a parameter estimate is found to be statistically significant when it is not.

level of significance
The probability of finding the parameter to be statistically significant when in fact it is not.

level of confidence
The probability of correctly failing to reject the true hypothesis that $b = 0$; equals one minus the level of significance.

□ **Relation** In testing for statistical significance, the level of significance chosen for the test determines the probability of committing a Type I error, which is the mistake of finding a parameter to be significant when it is not truly significant. The level of confidence for a test is the probability of not committing a Type I error. The lower (higher) the significance level of a test, the higher (lower) the level of confidence for the test.

The t-test is simple to perform. First, calculate the t-statistic (t-ratio) from the parameter estimate and its standard error, both of which are calculated by the computer. (In most statistical software, the t-ratio is also calculated by the computer.)

---

[3]Statisticians also recognize the possibility of committing a Type II error, which occurs when an analyst *fails* to find a parameter estimate to be statistically significant when it *truly* is significant. In your statistics class you will study both types of errors, Type I and Type II. Because it is usually impossible to determine the probability of committing a Type II error, tests for statistical significance typically consider only the possibility of committing a Type I error.

Next, find the appropriate critical value of t for the chosen level of significance. (Critical values of t are provided in a t-table at the end of this book, along with explanatory text.) The critical value of t is defined by the level of significance and the appropriate degrees of freedom. The **degrees of freedom** for a t-test are equal to $n - k$, where n is the number of observations in the sample and k is the number of parameters estimated.[4] (In the advertising example, there are $7 - 2 = 5$ degrees of freedom, since we have seven observations and estimated two parameters, a and b.)

degrees of freedom
The number of observations in the sample minus the number of parameters being estimated by the regression analysis $(n - k)$.

Once the critical value of t is found for, say, the 5 percent level of significance or 95 percent level of confidence, the absolute value of the calculated t-statistic is compared with the critical value of t. If the absolute value of the t-statistic is greater than the critical value of t, we say that, at the 95 percent confidence level, the estimated parameter is (statistically) significantly different from zero. If the absolute value of the calculated t-statistic is less than the critical value of t, the estimated value of b cannot be treated as being significantly different from 0 and X plays no statistically significant role in determining the value of Y.

Returning to the advertising example, we now test to see if 4.9719, the estimated value of b, is significantly different from 0. The standard error of $\hat{b}$, which is calculated by the computer, is equal to 1.23. Thus the t-statistic is equal to 4.04 ($=$ 4.9719/1.23). Next we compare 4.04 to the critical value of t, using a 5 percent significance level (a 95 percent confidence level). As noted, there are 5 degrees of freedom. If you turn to the table of critical t-values at the end of the text, you will find that the critical value of t for 5 degrees of freedom and a 0.05 level of significance is 2.571. Since 4.04 is larger than 2.571, we reject the hypothesis that b is 0 and can now say that 4.9719 ($\hat{b}$) is significantly different from 0. This means that advertising expenditure is a statistically significant variable in determining the level of sales. If 4.04 had been less than the critical value, we would not have been able to reject the hypothesis that b is 0 and we would not have been able to conclude that advertising plays a significant role in determining the level of sales.

The procedure for testing for statistical significance of a parameter estimate is summarized in the following statistical principle:

▣ **Principle** In order to test for statistical significance of a parameter estimate $\hat{b}$, compute the *t*-ratio

$$t = \frac{\hat{b}}{S_{\hat{b}}}$$

where $S_{\hat{b}}$ is the standard error of the estimate $\hat{b}$. Next, for the chosen level of significance, find the critical *t*-value in the *t*-table at the end of the text. Choose the critical *t*-value with $n - k$ degrees of freedom for the chosen level of significance. If the absolute value of the *t*-ratio is greater (less) than the critical *t*-value, then $\hat{b}$ is (is not) statistically significant.

---

[4]Occasionally you may find other statistics books (or t-tables in other books) that define k as the "number of explanatory variables" rather than the "number of parameters estimated," as we have done in this text. When k is not defined to include the estimated intercept parameter, then the number of degrees of freedom must be calculated as $n - (k + 1)$. No matter how k is defined, the degrees of freedom for the t-test are always equal to the number of observations minus the number of parameters estimated.

Using *p*-Values to Determine Statistical Significance

Using a *t*-test to determine whether a parameter estimate is statistically significant requires that you select a level of significance at which to perform the test. In most of the situations facing a manager, choosing the significance level for the test involves making an arbitrary decision. We will now show you an alternative method of assessing the statistical significance of parameter estimates that does not require that you "preselect" a level of significance (or, equivalently, the level of confidence) or use a *t*-table to find a critical *t*-value. With this alternative method, the *exact degree* of statistical significance is determined by answering the question, "Given the *t*-ratio calculated for $\hat{b}$, what would be the lowest level of significance—or the highest level of confidence—that would allow the hypothesis $b = 0$ to be rejected in favor of the alternative hypothesis $b \neq 0$?"

Consider the *t*-test for the parameter estimate 4.9719. In the previous section, the effect of advertising (*A*) on sales (*S*) was found to be statistically significant because the calculated *t*-ratio 4.04 exceeded 2.571, the critical *t*-value for a 5 percent level of significance (a 95 percent level of confidence). A *t*-ratio *only* as large as 2.571 would be sufficient to achieve a 5 percent level of significance that $b \neq 0$. The calculated *t*-ratio 4.04 is much larger than the critical *t* for the 5 percent significance level. This means a significance level *lower* than 5 percent (or a confidence level *higher* than 95 percent) would still allow one to reject the hypothesis of no significance ($b = 0$). What is the lowest level of significance or, equivalently, the greatest level of confidence that permits rejecting the hypothesis that $b = 0$ when the computer calculates a *t*-ratio of 4.04? The answer is given by the *p-value* for 4.04, which most statistical software, and even spreadsheets, can calculate.

The **p-value** associated with a calculated *t*-ratio gives the *exact* level of significance for a *t*-ratio associated with a parameter estimate.[5] In other words, the *p*-value gives the exact probability of committing a Type I error—finding significance when none exists—if you conclude that $b \neq 0$ on the basis of the *t*-ratio calculated by the computer. One minus the *p*-value is the exact degree of confidence that can be assigned to a particular parameter estimate.

The *p*-value for the calculated *t*-ratio 4.04 (= 4.9719/1.23) is 0.010. A *p*-value of 0.010 means that the exact level of significance for a *t*-ratio of 4.04 is 1 percent and the exact level of confidence is 99 percent. Rather than saying *b* is statistically significant at the 5 percent level of significance (or the 95 percent level of confidence), using the *p*-value we can make a more precise, and stronger, statement: $\hat{b}$ is statistically significant at exactly the 1 percent level of significance. In other words, at the 99 percent confidence level advertising affects sales ($b \neq 0$); that is, there is only a 1 percent chance that advertising does *not* affect sales.

p-value
The exact level of significance for a test statistic, which is the probability of finding significance when none exists.

[5]Although this section discusses *t*-statistics, a *p*-value can be computed for any test statistic, and it gives the exact significance level for the associated test statistic.

While *t*-tests are the traditional means of assessing statistical significance, most computer software packages now routinely print the *p*-values associated with *t*-ratios. Rather than preselecting a level of significance (or level of confidence) for *t*-tests, it is now customary to report the *p*-values associated with the estimated parameters—usually along with standard errors and *t*-ratios—and let the users of the statistical estimations decide whether the level of significance is acceptably low or the level of confidence is acceptably high.

☐ **Relation** The exact level of significance associated with a *t*-statistic, its *p*-value, gives the exact (or minimum) probability of committing a Type I error—finding significance when none exists—if you conclude that $b \neq 0$ on the basis of the *t*-ratio calculated by the computer. One minus the *p*-value is the exact degree of confidence that can be assigned to a particular parameter estimate.

4.4 EVALUATION OF THE REGRESSION EQUATION

Once the individual parameter estimates $\hat{a}$ and $\hat{b}$ have been tested for statistical significance using *t*-tests, researchers often wish to evaluate the *complete* estimated regression equation, $Y = \hat{a} + \hat{b}X$. Evaluation of the regression equation involves determining how well the estimated regression equation "explains" the variation in Y. Two statistics are frequently employed to evaluate the overall acceptability of a regression equation. The first is called the *coefficient of determination*, normally denoted as "R^2" and pronounced "R-square." The second is the *F-statistic*, which is used to test whether the *overall* equation is statistically significant.

The Coefficient of Determination (R^2)

coefficient of determination (R^2)
The fraction of total variation in the dependent variable explained by the regression equation.

The **coefficient of determination (R^2)** measures the fraction of the total variation in the dependent variable that is explained by the regression equation. In terms of the example used earlier, it is the fraction of the variation in sales that is explained by variation in advertising expenditures. Therefore, the value of R^2 can range from 0 (the regression equation explains none of the variation in Y) to 1 (the regression equation explains all the variation in Y). While the R^2 is printed out as a decimal value by most computers, the R^2 is often spoken of in terms of a percentage. For example, if the calculated R^2 is 0.7542, we could say that approximately 75 percent of the variation in Y is explained by the model.

If the value of R^2 is high, there is high correlation between the dependent and independent variables; if it is low, there is low correlation. For example, in Figure 4.4, Panel A (page 138), the observations in the scatter diagram all lie rather close to the regression line. Because the deviations from the line are small, the correlation between X and Y is high and the value of R^2 will be high. In the extreme case when all of the observations lie on a straight line, R^2 will be equal to 1. In Panel B, the observations are scattered widely around the regression line. The correlation between X and Y in this case is much less than that in Panel A, so the value of R^2 is rather small.

We must caution you that high correlation between two variables (or even a statistically significant regression coefficient) does not necessarily mean the variation in the dependent variable Y is *caused by* the variation in the independent variable X.

ILLUSTRATION 4.1

How Confident Is "Confident Enough"?

When a hypothesis is true, the level of significance expresses the probability of making the wrong decision (rejection), and the level of confidence expresses the probability of making the correct decision (fail to reject). We have emphasized that the choice of significance level in a statistical analysis depends on the judgment of the analyst and the perceived consequences of making an error. While the choice of significance level also determines the confidence level—the two probabilities must sum to one—decision makers tend to focus their attention on choosing a sufficiently high level of confidence, rather than thinking of choosing a sufficiently low level of significance. We want to tell you a fictional story to better illustrate how the consequences of a wrong decision can affect the choice of confidence or significance levels.

During the first days of the Persian Gulf war, the world was stunned by the success rate of the bombing attacks against military targets in Iraq. In his first news briefing at the outbreak of the war, General Norman Schwarzkopf reported that 80 percent of the nearly 15,000 sorties flown had successfully hit their intended targets. Many of the correspondents in attendance were highly suspicious about such an extraordinary success rate, but two reporters, Barbara Smith and Heraldo Jones, decided to test the general's assertion that the true success rate was 80 percent. They obtained a list of the locations of 100 of the 15,000 targets, then enlisted the help of a pilot of a three-seater Stealth fighter to fly them over each of the 100 targets to see how many were damaged by bombs. Smith and Jones counted 65 bomb-damaged targets, indicating only a 65 percent success rate, as opposed to the reported 80 percent.

Each reporter had to decide whether 65 percent was far enough away from 80 percent to refute the Schwarzkopf assertion. Both realized the inherent randomness of sampling and that the 100 targets may not have exactly reflected the population of 15,000 targets, known only to the general and his staff.

Smith was tempted to report to her news director that she had discovered compelling evidence that General Schwarzkopf incorrectly reported the success rate of the air war. If correct, she would probably become famous and win a Pulitzer Prize; but if wrong, she would be ruined professionally. Smith was not willing to take more than a 5 percent chance of committing a Type I error: publicly rejecting the Schwarzkopf assertion of an 80 percent success rate when the assertion was correct. In other words, she had to be 95 percent confident that, if Schwarzkopf was correct, her "test" would not reject Schwarzkopf's assertion. Smith decided that 65 percent was not far enough below 80 percent to make her feel 95 percent confident that 80 percent was an exaggeration. Therefore, she did not report her findings.

Jones, in contrast to Smith, badly wanted to be an anchor. He was willing to bet his career by taking a 75 percent risk that he was wrong and the general was right; that is, he was comfortable with only a 25 percent level of confidence. At the 25 percent level of confidence, Jones viewed a 65 percent success rate as being far enough away from the asserted 80 percent success rate that he rejected the general's assertion. Jones called his news anchor with startling evidence that General Schwarzkopf had misinformed the public about the success of the air war. Jones's network reported his story on national news, and upon hearing this news report, General Schwarzkopf decided to reveal the list of the initial 15,000 sorties. Using the entire population of 15,000 targets, the Middle East press corps verified that 80 percent of the targets were indeed damaged by bombs. As it turned out, Barbara Smith was later promoted to anchor at her network. Heraldo Jones was fired and now hosts a talk show at an obscure radio station in College Station, Texas.

FIGURE 4.4
High and Low Correlation

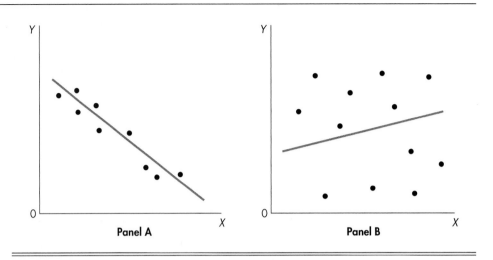

Panel A Panel B

It might be the case that variation in Y is caused by variation in Z, but X happens to be correlated to Z. Thus Y and X will be correlated even though variation in X does not cause Y to vary. A high R^2 does not prove that Y and X are causally related, only that Y and X are correlated. We summarize this discussion with a statistical relation:

▫ **Relation** The coefficient of determination (R^2) measures the fraction of the total variation in Y that is explained by the variation in X. R^2 ranges in value from 0 (the regression explains none of the variation in Y) to 1 (the regression explains all the variation in Y). A high R^2 indicates Y and X are highly correlated and the scatter diagram tightly fits the sample regression line.

The *F*-Statistic

F-statistic
A statistic used to test whether the overall regression equation is statistically significant.

Although the R^2 is a widely used statistic, it is subjective in the sense of how much explained variation—explained by the regression equation—is enough to view the equation as being statistically significant. An alternative is the **F-statistic.** In very general terms, this statistic provides a measure of the ratio of explained variation (in the dependent variable) to unexplained variation. To test whether the overall equation is significant, this statistic is compared with a critical F-value obtained from an F-table (at the end of this text). The critical F-value is identified by two separate degrees of freedom and the significance level. The first of the degrees of freedom is $k - 1$ (i.e., the number of independent variables) and the second is $n - k$. If the value for the calculated F-statistic exceeds the critical F-value, the regression equation is statistically significant at the specified significance level. The discussion of the F-statistic is summarized in a statistical relation:

▫ **Relation** The F-statistic is used to test whether the regression equation as a whole explains a significant amount of the variation in Y. The test involves comparing the F-statistic to the critical F-value with $k - 1$ and $n - k$ degrees of freedom and the chosen level of significance. If the F-statistic exceeds the critical F-value, the regression equation is statistically significant.

Rather than performing an *F*-test, which requires that you select arbitrarily a significance or confidence level, you may wish to report the exact level of significance for the *F*-statistic. The *p*-value for the *F*-statistic gives the exact level of significance for the regression equation as a whole. One minus the *p*-value is the exact level of confidence associated with the computed *F*-statistic.

All the statistics you will need in order to analyze a regression—the coefficient estimates, the standard errors, the *t*-ratios, R^2, the *F*-statistic, and the *p*-value—are automatically calculated and printed by most available regression programs. As mentioned before, our objective is not that you understand how these statistics are calculated. Rather, we want you to know how to set up a regression and interpret the results. We now provide you with a hypothetical example of a regression analysis that might be performed by a manager of a firm.

Controlling Product Quality at SLM: A Regression Example

Specialty Lens Manufacturing (SLM) produces contact lenses for patients who are unable to wear standard contact lenses. These specialty contact lenses must meet extraordinarily strict standards. The production process is not perfect, however, and some lenses have slight flaws. Patients receiving flawed lenses almost always detect the flaws, and the lenses are returned to SLM for replacement. Returned lenses are costly, in terms of both redundant production costs and diminished corporate reputation for SLM. Every week SLM produces 2,400 lenses, and inspectors using high-powered microscopes have time to examine only a fraction of the lenses before they are shipped to doctors.

Management at SLM decided to measure the effectiveness of its inspection process using regression analysis. During a 22-week time period, SLM collected data each week on the number of lenses produced that week that were later returned by doctors because of flaws (*F*) and the number of hours spent that week examining lenses (*H*). The manager estimated the regression equation

$$F = a + bH$$

using the 22 weekly observations on *F* and *H*. The computer printed out the following output:

DEPENDENT VARIABLE: F		R-SQUARE	F-RATIO	P-VALUE ON F
OBSERVATIONS: 22		0.4527	16.54	0.021
	PARAMETER	STANDARD		
VARIABLE	ESTIMATE	ERROR	T-RATIO	P-VALUE
INTERCEPT	90.0	28.13	3.20	0.004
H	−0.80	0.32	−2.50	0.021

ILLUSTRATION 4.2

R&D Expenditures and the Value of the Firm

To determine how much to spend on research and development (R&D) activities, a manager may wish to know how R&D expenditures affect the value of the firm. To investigate the relation between the value of a firm and the amount the firm spends on R&D, Wallin and Gilman[a] used simple regression analysis to estimate the model

$$V = a + bR$$

where the value of the firm (V) is measured by the price-to-earnings ratio, and the level of expenditures on R&D (R) is measured by R&D expenditures as a percentage of the firm's total sales.

Wallin and Gilman collected a cross-sectional data set on the 20 firms with the largest R&D expenditures in the 1981–1982 time period. The computer output from a regression program and a scatter diagram showing the 20 data points with the sample regression line are presented here:

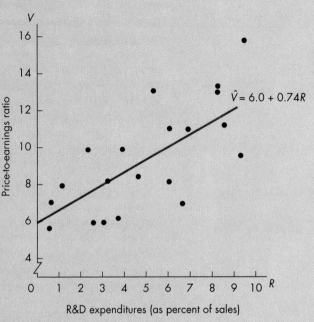

$\hat{V} = 6.0 + 0.74R$

Price-to-earnings ratio

R&D expenditures (as percent of sales)

DEPENDENT VARIABLE: V	R-SQUARE	F-RATIO	P-VALUE ON F
OBSERVATIONS: 20	0.5274	20.090	0.0003

VARIABLE	PARAMETER ESTIMATE	STANDARD ERROR	T-RATIO	P-VALUE
INTERCEPT	6.00	0.917	6.54	0.0001
R	0.74	0.165	4.48	0.0003

As expected, $\hat{a}$ is positive and $\hat{b}$ is negative. If no inspection is done $(H = 0)$, SLM's management expects 90 lenses from each week's production to be returned as defective. The estimate of b $(\hat{b} = \Delta F/\Delta H = -0.80)$ indicates that each additional hour per week spent inspecting lenses will decrease the number of flawed lenses by 0.8. Thus it takes 10 extra hours of inspection to find eight more flawed lenses.

In order to determine if the parameter estimates $\hat{a}$ and $\hat{b}$ are significantly different from zero, the manager can conduct a t-test on each estimated parameter. The t-ratios for $\hat{a}$ and $\hat{b}$ are 3.20 and -2.50, respectively:

$$t_{\hat{a}} = 90.0/28.13 = 3.20 \quad \text{and} \quad t_{\hat{b}} = -0.80/0.32 = -2.50$$

First, we test to see if the estimate of *a* is statistically significant. To test for statistical significance, use the *t*-ratio for *â*, which the computer has calculated for you as the ratio of the parameter estimate to its standard error:

$$t_{\hat{a}} = \frac{6.00}{0.917} = 6.54$$

and compare this value with the critical value of *t*. We use a 5 percent significance level (a 95 percent confidence level). Since there are 20 observations and two parameters are estimated, there are $20 - 2 = 18$ degrees of freedom. The table at the end of the text (critical *t*-values) gives us a critical value of 2.101. The calculated *t*-value for *â* is larger than 2.101, so we conclude that *â* is significantly different from 0. The *p*-value for *â* is so small (0.0001) that the probability of finding significance when none exists is virtually 0. In this case, the selection of a 5 percent significance level greatly underestimates the exact degree of significance associated with the estimate of *a*. The estimated value of *a* suggests that firms that spend nothing on R&D, on average, have price-to-earnings ratios of 6.

The estimate of *b* (0.74) is positive, which suggests *V* and *R* are directly related. The calculated *t*-ratio is 4.48, which is greater than the critical value of *t*. The *p*-value for *b̂* indicates the significance level of the *t*-test could have been set as low as 0.0003, or 0.03 percent, and the hypothesis that $b = 0$ could be rejected. In other words, with a *t*-statistic equal to 4.48, the probability of incorrectly concluding that R&D expenditures significantly affect the value of a firm is just 0.03 percent. Or stated equivalently in terms of a confidence level, we can be 99.97 percent confident that the *t*-test

would *not* indicate statistical significance if none existed. The value of *b̂* implies that if a firm increases R&D expenditures by 1 percent (of sales), the firm can expect its value (as measured by the P/E ratio) to rise by 0.74.

The R^2 for the regression equation indicates that about 53 percent of the total variation in the value of a firm is explained by the regression equation; that is, 53 percent of the variation in *V* is explained by the variation in *R*. The regression equation leaves 47 percent of the variation in the value of the firm unexplained.

The *F*-ratio is used to test for significance of the entire equation. To determine the critical value of *F* (with a 5 percent significance level), it is necessary to determine the degrees of freedom. In this case, $k - 1 = 2 - 1 = 1$ and $n - k = 20 - 2 = 18$ degrees of freedom. In the table of values of the *F*-statistic at the end of the text, you can look down the $k - 1 = 1$ column until you get to the 18th row ($n - k = 18$) and read the value 4.41. Since the calculated *F*-value (20.090) exceeds 4.41, the regression equation is significant at the 5 percent significance level. In fact, the *F*-value of 20.090 is much larger than the critical *F*-value for a 5 percent level of significance, suggesting that the exact level of significance will be much lower than 0.05. The *p*-value for the *F*-statistic, 0.0003, confirms that the exact significance level is much smaller than 0.05.

[a]C. Wallin and J. Gilman, "Determining the Optimal Level for R&D Spending," *Research Management* 14, no. 5 (Sep./Oct. 1986), pp. 19–24.

Source: Adapted from a regression problem presented in Terry Sincich, *A Course in Modern Business Statistics* (Dellen/Macmillan, 1994), p. 432.

The critical *t*-value is found in the table at the end of the book. There are 22 observations and two parameters, so the degrees of freedom are $n - k = 22 - 2 = 20$. Choosing the 5 percent level of significance (a 95 percent level of confidence), the critical *t*-value is 2.086. Since the absolute values of $t_{\hat{a}}$ and $t_{\hat{b}}$ both exceed 2.086, both *â* and *b̂* are statistically significant at the 5 percent significance level.

Instead of performing a *t*-test at a fixed level of significance, the manager could assess the significance of the parameter estimates by examining the *p*-values for *â* and *b̂*. The exact level of significance for *â* is 0.004, or 0.4 percent, which indicates that the *t*-statistic of 3.20 is just large enough to reject the hypothesis that *â* is 0 at a significance level of 0.004 (or a confidence level of 0.996). The *p*-value for $\hat{a}$ is so small that the manager almost certainly has avoided committing a Type I error (finding statistical significance where there is none). The exact level of significance for $\hat{b}$ is 0.021, or 2.1 percent. For both parameter estimates, the *p*-values provide a stronger assessment of statistical significance than could be established by satisfying the requirements of a *t*-test performed at a 5 percent level of significance.

Overall, because $R^2 = 0.4527$, the equation explains about 45 percent of the total variation in the dependent variable (F), with 55 percent of the variation in F remaining unexplained. To test for significance of the entire equation, the manager could use an *F*-test. The critical *F*-value is obtained from the table at the end of the book. Since $k - 1 = 2 - 1 = 1$, and $n - k = 22 - 2 = 20$, the critical *F*-value at the 5 percent significance level is 4.35. The *F*-statistic calculated by the computer, 16.54, exceeds 4.35, and the entire equation is statistically significant. The *p*-value for the *F*-statistic shows that the exact level of significance for the entire equation is 0.001, or 0.1 percent (a 99.9 percent level of confidence).

Using the estimated equation, $\hat{F} = 90.0 - 0.80H$, the manager can estimate the number of flawed lenses that will be shipped for various hours of weekly inspection. For example, if inspectors spend 60 hours per week examining lenses, SLM can expect 42 (= $90 - 0.8 \times 60$) of the lenses shipped to be flawed.

T ➤ 6 7

4.5 MULTIPLE REGRESSION

Thus far we have discussed simple regressions involving a linear relation between the dependent variable Y and a *single* explanatory variable X. In many problems, however, the variation in Y depends on more than one explanatory variable. There may be quite a few variables needed to explain adequately the variation in the dependent variable. **Multiple regression models** use two or more explanatory variables to explain the variation in the dependent variable. In this section we will show how to use and interpret multiple regression models.

multiple regression models
Regression models that use more than one explanatory variable to explain the variation in the dependent variable.

The Multiple Regression Model

A typical multiple regression equation might take the form

$$Y = a + bX + cW + dZ$$

In this equation, Y is the dependent variable; a is the intercept parameter; X, W, and Z are the explanatory variables; and b, c, and d are the slope parameters for each of these explanatory variables.

As in simple regression, the slope parameters b, c, and d measure the change in Y associated with a one-unit change in one of the explanatory variables, holding the rest of the explanatory variables constant. If, for example, $c = 3$, then a one-unit increase in W results in a three-unit increase in Y, holding X and Z constant.

Estimation of the parameters of a multiple regression equation is accomplished by finding a linear equation that best fits the data. As in simple regression, a computer is used to obtain the parameter estimates, their individual standard errors, the *F*-statistic, the R^2, and the *p*-values. The statistical significance of the individual parameters and of the equation as a whole can be determined by *t*-tests and an *F*-test, respectively.[6] The R^2 is interpreted as the fraction of the variation in *Y* explained by the *entire set* of explanatory variables taken together. Indeed, the only real complication introduced by multiple regression is that there are more *t*-tests to perform. Although (as you may know from courses in statistics) the *calculation* of the parameter estimates becomes much more difficult as additional independent variables are added, the manner in which they are *interpreted* does not change. Illustration 4.3 provides an example of multiple regression.

4.6 NONLINEAR REGRESSION ANALYSIS

While linear regression models can be applied to a wide variety of economic relations, there are also many economic relations that are nonlinear in nature. Nonlinear regression models are used when the underlying relation between *Y* and *X* plots as a curve, rather than a straight line. An analyst generally chooses a nonlinear regression model when the scatter diagram shows a curvilinear pattern. In some cases, economic theory will strongly suggest that *Y* and *X* are related in a nonlinear fashion, and the analyst can expect to see a curvilinear pattern in the scatter of data points. Later in this text, we will introduce you to several important economic relations that are nonlinear in nature. You will need to know how to estimate the parameters of a nonlinear economic relation using the techniques of regression analysis.

In this section, we will show you two forms of nonlinear regression models for which the parameters can be estimated using *linear* regression analysis. The trick to using *linear* regression to estimate the parameters in *nonlinear* models is to transform the nonlinear relation into one that is linear and can be estimated by the techniques of least-squares. Two extremely useful forms of nonlinear models that you will encounter later in the text are (1) quadratic regression models and (2) log-linear regression models. As you will see, using either one of these two nonlinear models does not complicate the analysis much at all.

Quadratic Regression Models

quadratic regression model
A nonlinear regression model of the form $Y = a + bX + cX^2$.

One of the most useful nonlinear forms for managerial economics is the **quadratic regression model,** which can be expressed as

$$Y = a + bX + cX^2$$

In a number of situations involving production and cost relations examined later in this book, the theoretical relations between economic variables will graph as either a U-shaped or an inverted-U-shaped curve. You may recall from your high school algebra class that quadratic functions have graphs that are either U- or ∩-shaped,

---

[6]When the *p*-value for a parameter estimate is not small enough to meet the researcher's tolerance for risk of committing a Type I error, the associated explanatory variable is typically dropped from the regression equation. A new equation is estimated with only the explanatory variables that have sufficiently small *p*-values.

ILLUSTRATION 4.3

Do Auto Insurance Premiums Really Vary with Costs?

In an article examining the effect of Proposition 103 on auto insurance rates in California, Benjamin Zycher noted that in 1988 an adult male with no citations or at-fault accidents who lived in Hollywood could expect to pay an annual insurance premium of $1,817. The same adult male driver would have to pay only $862 if he lived in Monrovia, only $697 in San Diego, and only $581 in San Jose. Zycher explains that this variability in premiums exists because insurers obviously determine premiums by considering the individual's driving record, type of car, sex, age, and various other factors that are "statistically significant predictors of an individual driver's future losses."

Also important in the determination of insurance premiums is the geographic location of the driver's residence. Future losses are likely to be smaller in rural areas compared with urban areas because of lower vehicle densities, reduced theft, smaller repair costs, and so on. Using data on bodily injury premiums for 20 California counties, we investigated the relation between insurance premiums and two explanatory variables: the number of claims and the average dollar cost of a claim in the various counties. Specifically, we wanted to determine if the variation in premiums across counties can be adequately explained by cost differences across the counties.

Using the data shown in the accompanying table, we estimated the following multiple regression equation:

$$P = a + b_1 N + b_2 C$$

Bodily Injury in California: Claims, Costs, and Premiums

County	Claims[a] (N)	Cost[b] (C)	Annual premium[c] (P)
Los Angeles	23.9	$10,197	$319.04
Orange	19.5	9,270	255.00
Ventura	16.7	9,665	225.51
San Francisco	16.3	8,705	208.95
Riverside	15.2	8,888	200.13
San Bernardino	15.6	8,631	196.22
San Diego	16.0	8,330	191.80
Alameda	14.4	8,654	191.46
Marin	13.0	8,516	190.78
San Mateo	14.1	7,738	189.01
Sacramento	15.3	7,881	181.42
Santa Clara	14.4	7,723	179.74
Contra Costa	13.2	8,702	177.92
Santa Barbara	10.7	9,077	176.65
Sonoma	10.6	9,873	171.38
Fresno	14.7	7,842	168.11
Kern	11.9	7,717	160.97
Humboldt	12.2	7,798	151.02
Butte	11.1	8,783	129.84
Shasta	9.7	9,803	126.34

[a]Per thousand insured vehicles.
[b]Average per claim.
[c]Average premium income per insured auto.
Source: Western Insurance information service.

where P is the average bodily insurance premium paid per auto, N is the number of claims per thousand

depending on the signs of b and c. If b is negative and c is positive, the quadratic function is U-shaped. If b is positive and c is negative, the quadratic function is ∩-shaped. Thus a U-shaped quadratic equation ($b < 0$ and $c > 0$) is appropriate when as X increases, Y first falls, eventually reaches a minimum, and then rises thereafter. Alternatively, an inverted-U-shaped quadratic equation ($b > 0$ and $c < 0$) is appropriate if as X increases, Y first rises, eventually reaches a peak, and then falls thereafter.

In order to estimate the three parameters of the quadratic relation (a, b, and c), the equation must be transformed into a linear form that can be estimated using

insured vehicles, and C is the average dollar amount of each bodily injury claim. The computer output for this multiple regression equation is the following:

```
DEPENDENT VARIABLE: P      R-SQUARE      F-RATIO      P-VALUE ON F

      OBSERVATIONS: 20       0.9116       87.659       0.0001


                    PARAMETER       STANDARD
VARIABLE            ESTIMATE        ERROR          T-RATIO      P-VALUE

INTERCEPT           -74.139         34.612         -2.14        0.0470
N                    11.320          0.953         11.88        0.0001
C                     0.01155        0.004          2.87        0.0107
```

There is evidence from these parameter estimates that bodily injury premiums in a particular county are positively related to both the number of claims in that county and the average cost of those claims. Specifically, an additional claim per thousand vehicles in a county ($\Delta N = 1$) tends to increase yearly premiums by $11.32. A $1,000 increase in the average cost of claims in a county ($\Delta C = 1,000$) tends to increase premiums by about $11 annually. The intercept in this regression has no meaningful interpretation.

The p-values for the individual parameter estimates indicate that all estimates are significant at less than the 0.05 level. You can confirm this by performing t-tests at the 5 percent significance level on each of the three estimated parameters.

Notice also that the R^2 is 0.9116, indicating that 91 percent of the variation in premiums is explained by

variables N and C. The p-value on the F-ratio also provides more statistical evidence that the relation between the dependent variable P and the explanatory variables N and C is quite strong. The critical F-value for $F_{2,\,17}$ at a 5 percent level of significance is 3.59. Since the F-statistic exceeds this value by a large amount, the regression equation is statistically significant at a level below 0.01 percent.

It is interesting to note how well the level of premiums can be explained using only two explanatory variables. Indeed, this regression analysis supports Benjamin Zycher's claim that the substantial statewide variation in California auto insurance premiums can be attributed to geographic differences in the costs incurred by insurers.

Source: See Benjamin Zycher, "Automobile Insurance Regulation, Direct Democracy, and the Interests of Consumers," *Regulation*, Summer 1990.

linear regression analysis. This task is accomplished by creating a new variable Z, defined as $Z = X^2$, then substituting Z for X^2 to transform the quadratic model into a linear model:

$$Y = a + bX + cX^2$$
$$= a + bX + cZ$$

The slope parameter for Z (c) is identical to the slope parameter for X^2 (c).

This simple transformation is accomplished by having the computer create a new variable Z by squaring the values of X for each observation. You then regress

FIGURE 4.5
A Quadratic Regression Equation

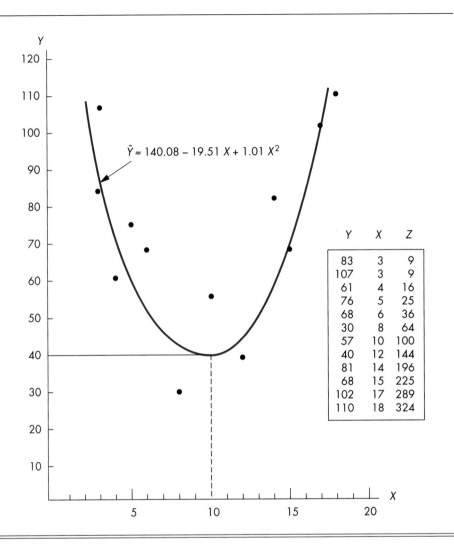

$$\hat{Y} = 140.08 - 19.51\,X + 1.01\,X^2$$

Y	X	Z
83	3	9
107	3	9
61	4	16
76	5	25
68	6	36
30	8	64
57	10	100
40	12	144
81	14	196
68	15	225
102	17	289
110	18	324

Y on X and Z. The computer will generate an intercept parameter estimate ($\hat{a}$), a slope parameter estimate for X ($\hat{b}$), and a slope parameter estimate for Z (c). The estimated slope parameter for Z is $\hat{c}$, which, of course, is the slope parameter on X^2. We illustrate this procedure with an example.

Figure 4.5 shows a scatter diagram for 12 observations on Y and X (shown by the table in the figure). When we look at the scatter of data points, it is clear that fitting a straight line through the data points would produce a "poor" fit but fitting a U-shaped curve will produce a much better fit. To estimate the parameters of a quadratic regression equation, a new variable Z ($= X^2$) is generated on the computer. The actual data used in the regression are presented in Figure 4.5. The computer printout from the regression of Y on X and Z is shown here:

DEPENDENT VARIABLE: Y		R-SQUARE	F-RATIO		P-VALUE ON F
OBSERVATIONS: 12		0.7542	13.80		0.0018
VARIABLE	PARAMETER ESTIMATE	STANDARD ERROR		T-RATIO	P-VALUE
INTERCEPT	140.08	16.80		8.34	0.0001
X	−19.51	4.05		−4.82	0.0010
Z	1.01	0.20		5.05	0.0006

Thus the estimated quadratic regression equation is

$$\hat{Y} = 140.08 - 19.51X + 1.01X^2$$

The estimated slope parameter for Z is 1.01. As explained above, 1.01 is also the slope parameter estimate for X^2. The estimated equation can be used to estimate the value of Y for any particular value of X. For example, if X is equal to 10, the quadratic regression equation predicts that Y will be equal to 45.98 (= 140.08 − 19.51 × 10 + 1.01 × 10^2). In any multiple regression equation, the estimated parameters are tested for statistical significance by performing the usual t-tests as discussed above.

Log-Linear Regression Models

log-linear regression model
A nonlinear regression model of the form $Y = aX^bZ^c$.

Another kind of nonlinear equation that can be estimated by transforming the equation into a linear form is a **log-linear regression model** in which Y is related to one or more explanatory variables in a multiplicative fashion:

$$Y = aX^bZ^c$$

This nonlinear functional form, which we employ in Chapter 7 to estimate demand functions and in the appendix to Chapter 10 to estimate production functions, is particularly useful because the parameters b and c are elasticities:

$$b = \frac{\text{Percentage change in } Y}{\text{Percentage change in } X}$$

$$c = \frac{\text{Percentage change in } Y}{\text{Percentage change in } Z}$$

Using this form of nonlinear regression, the elasticities are estimated directly: The parameter estimates associated with each explanatory variable are elasticities. (The parameter a, however, is not an elasticity.)

In order to estimate the parameters of this nonlinear equation, it must be transformed into a linear form. This is accomplished by taking *natural logarithms* of both sides of the equation. Taking the logarithm of the function $Y = aX^bZ^c$ results in

$$\ln Y = (\ln a) + b(\ln X) + c(\ln Z)$$

So, if we define

$$Y' = \ln Y$$
$$X' = \ln X$$
$$Z' = \ln Z$$
$$a' = \ln a$$

the regression equation is linear:

$$Y' = a' + bX' + cZ'$$

Once estimates have been obtained, tests for statistical significance and evaluation of the equation are done precisely as we described earlier. The only difference is that the intercept parameter estimate provided by the computer is not a; rather it is equal to $\ln a$. To obtain the parameter estimate for a, we must take the antilog of the parameter estimate $\hat{a}'$:

$$\text{antilog}\,(\hat{a}') = e^{a'}$$

The antilog of a number can be found using the "e^x" key on most hand calculators. We illustrate the log-linear regression model with an example.

Panel A of Figure 4.6 shows a scatter diagram of 12 observations on Y and X. The scatter diagram in Panel A suggests that a curvilinear model will fit these data better than a linear model. Suppose we use a log-linear model with one explanatory variable: $Y = aX^b$. Since Y is positive at all points in the sample, the parameter a is expected to be positive. Since Y is decreasing as X increases, the parameter on $\overline{X}$ (b) is expected to be negative. The actual values of Y and X plotted in the scatter diagram in Panel A are shown in the box in Panel A.

To estimate the parameters a and b in the nonlinear equation, we transform the equation by taking logarithms:

$$\ln Y = \ln a + b \ln X$$

Thus the curvilinear model in Panel A is transformed into an equivalent model that is linear when the variables are expressed in logarithms. In Panel B, the transformed variables, $\ln Y$ and $\ln X$, are obtained by instructing the computer to take logarithms of Y and X, respectively. The 12 observations, in terms of logarithms, are displayed in Panel B. Regressing $\ln Y$ on $\ln X$ results in the following computer printout:

DEPENDENT VARIABLE: LNY	R-SQUARE	F-RATIO	P-VALUE ON F
OBSERVATIONS: 12	0.8750	70.0	0.0001

VARIABLE	PARAMETER ESTIMATE	STANDARD ERROR	T-RATIO	P-VALUE
INTERCEPT	11.06	0.48	23.04	0.0001
LNX	−0.96	0.11	−8.73	0.0001

FIGURE 4.6

A Log-Linear Regression Equation

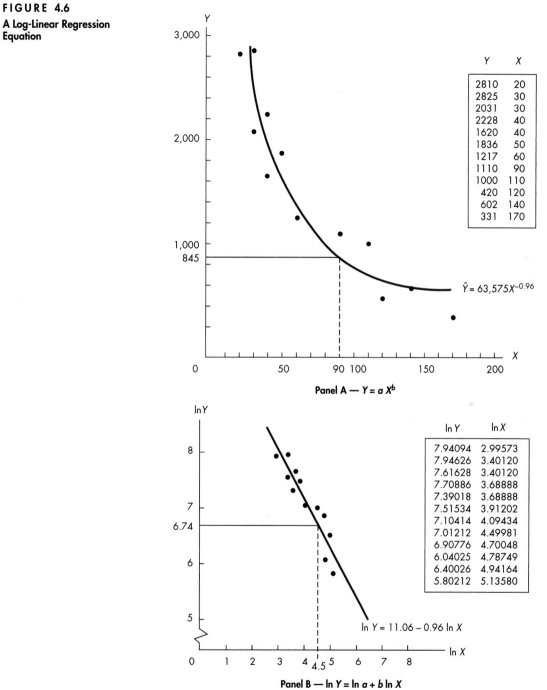

Y	X
2810	20
2825	30
2031	30
2228	40
1620	40
1836	50
1217	60
1110	90
1000	110
420	120
602	140
331	170

$\hat{Y} = 63,575X^{-0.96}$

Panel A — $Y = a X^b$

ln Y	ln X
7.94094	2.99573
7.94626	3.40120
7.61628	3.40120
7.70886	3.68888
7.39018	3.68888
7.51534	3.91202
7.10414	4.09434
7.01212	4.49981
6.90776	4.70048
6.04025	4.78749
6.40026	4.94164
5.80212	5.13580

$\ln Y = 11.06 - 0.96 \ln X$

Panel B — $\ln Y = \ln a + b \ln X$

As the F-ratio and R^2 indicate, a log-linear model does a quite reasonable job of explaining the variation in Y. The t-ratios for the intercept and slope parameters are 23.04 and -8.73, respectively. Both parameter estimates are statistically significant at the 1 percent level because both t-statistics exceed the critical t-value of 3.169. You can see by the p-values that the parameter estimates are significant at levels less than 0.0001.

Panel B of Figure 4.6 illustrates why this model is called a log-linear model. Notice that when the data points in Panel A are converted to logarithms (ln Y and ln X), the *natural logarithms* of Y and X exhibit a linear relation, as indicated by the scatter diagram shown in Panel B. The estimated log-linear regression equation is plotted in Panel B to show you how a straight line fits the natural logarithms of Y and X.

To obtain the parameter estimates in the nonlinear equation $Y = aX^b$, note that the slope parameter on ln X is also the exponent on X in the nonlinear equation ($\hat{b} = -0.96$). Because b is an elasticity, the estimated elasticity is -0.96. Thus a 10 percent increase in X results in a 9.6 percent decrease in Y. To obtain an estimate of a, we take the antilog of the estimated value of the intercept parameter:

$$\hat{a} = \text{antilog } (11.06) = e^{11.06} = 63,575$$

To show that the two models are mathematically equivalent, we have calculated the predicted value of ln Y when ln X is equal to 4.5. Using the estimated log-linear regression equation, we find that when ln $X = 4.5$, ln $Y = 6.74$ [$= 11.06 - 0.96(4.5)$]. Taking antilogs of ln Y and ln X, we get the point $X = 90$ and $Y = 845$ [$= 63,575(90)^{-0.96}$]. Thus the two equations are equivalent representations of the mathematical relation between Y and X.

4.7 REGRESSION ANALYSIS IN MANAGERIAL DECISION MAKING

We hope you have seen from this brief overview that regression analysis is extremely useful because it offers managers a way of estimating the functions they need for managerial decision making. While we say much more about specific applications of regression analysis in later chapters, at this point we want you simply to understand that regression techniques are actually used in managerial decision making.

As Robert F. Soergel (general marketing manager, E. L. Weingard Division, Emerson Electric Company) put it, "Regression analysis can be extremely helpful, and it's not as difficult as its name suggests."[7] Regression analysis is simply a tool to provide the information necessary for a manager to make decisions that maximize profits, or as Soergel observed, "The computer is a tool, not a master." We will use this tool to find estimates of the various functions we will describe later in the text. It's not that hard, and we agree with Soergel's conclusion of "the best part: it's not expensive."

---

[7]"Probing the Past for the Future," *Sales & Marketing Management*, Mar. 14, 1983.

The statistical analyses (or, if you wish, econometrics) that we are going to use in this text are really rather simple. Our two major objectives are also simple:

1. We want you to be able to set up a regression equation that could subsequently be estimated by using one of the readily available regression packages.
2. We want you to be able to use the output of a regression to examine those economic issues that are of interest to the manager of an enterprise.

Hence, in terms of the field of study known as econometrics, we will concentrate our attention on helping you avoid what are called *specification errors*. In simple terms, this means that we will show you how to set up an estimation equation that is appropriate for the use to which it is to be put. Specification errors—such as excluding important explanatory variables or using an inappropriate form for the equation—are serious; they can result in the estimates being *biased*.

In addition to specification errors, there are other problems that can be encountered in regression analysis. These problems, which are more difficult than the material we want to cover in this text, are reviewed briefly in the appendix to this chapter.

4.8 SUMMARY

This chapter set forth the basic principles of regression analysis: estimation and testing for statistical significance. The emphasis of the chapter was on explaining how to interpret the results of regression analysis, rather than on the mathematics of regression analysis. A mathematical derivation of the statistical techniques is presented in the appendix at the end of the chapter.

The simple linear regression model relates a dependent variable to a single explanatory variable in a linear fashion: $Y = a + bX$. The parameter a is the Y-intercept: the value of Y when X is 0. The parameter b is the slope of the regression line; it measures the rate of change in Y as X changes ($\Delta Y / \Delta X$). Because the variation in Y is affected not only by variation in X but also by various random effects, we cannot predict exactly the actual value of Y. Thus you should interpret the regression equation as giving the average or expected value of Y for any particular value of X.

Parameter estimates are obtained by choosing values of a and b that minimize the sum of the squared residuals. The residual is the difference between the actual value of Y and the fitted value of Y ($Y_i - \hat{Y}_i$). This method of estimating a and b is called the method of least-squares. The estimated regression line, $Y = \hat{a} + \hat{b}X$, is called the *sample regression line*. The sample regression line is an estimate of the true regression line.

The estimates $\hat{a}$ and $\hat{b}$ do not, in general, equal the true values of a and b. Because $\hat{a}$ and $\hat{b}$ are computed from the data in the random sample, the estimates themselves are random variables. Statisticians have shown that the distribution of values that the estimates might take is centered around the true value of the parameter. An estimator is *unbiased* if the mean value of the estimator is equal to the true value of the parameter. The method of least-squares produces unbiased estimates of a and b.

It is the randomness of the parameter estimates that necessitates testing for statistical significance. Just because the estimate $\hat{b}$ is not equal to 0 does *not* mean the true value of b is not actually equal to 0. Even when b *does* equal 0, it is still possible that the sample of Y and X values will produce a least-squares estimate $\hat{b}$ that is different from 0. It is necessary to determine statistically if there is sufficient evidence in the sample to indicate that Y is truly related to X (i.e., $b \neq 0$). This is called testing for statistical significance.

A t-test can be used to test for statistical significance of parameter estimates. To test for statistical significance of an individual parameter estimate, the researcher must first determine the level of significance for the test. The significance level of a test is the probability of finding a parameter estimate to be significantly different from 0 when, in fact, b is 0 (a Type I error). One minus the significance level is the level of confidence of the test. The choice of a significance or confidence level is in most cases rather arbitrary; lower (higher) levels of significance (confidence), other things equal, are more desirable. Traditionally, either a 0.01, 0.02, 0.05, or 0.10 level of significance is selected, which reflects the analyst's willingness to tolerate, at most, a 1, 2, 5, or 10 percent probability of finding a parameter to be significant when it is not truly significant. The appropriate significance level is determined by the analyst on the basis of the cost of making an error.

Once the level of significance (or confidence) is chosen, performing a t-test is straightforward. A t-test is based on the fact that the larger the absolute value of the t-ratio, $t = \hat{b}/S_{\hat{b}}$, the more probable it is that the true value of b is not equal to 0 ($S_{\hat{b}}$ is the standard error of the parameter estimate). So first compute the t-ratio as defined. Then find the critical t-value in the t-table. Locate the critical t-value with $n - k$ degrees of freedom for the chosen level of significance. If the absolute value of the t-ratio is greater than the critical t-value, $\hat{b}$ is statistically significant at the chosen level of significance. If the absolute value is less than the critical t-value, $\hat{b}$ is not statistically significant. If $\hat{b}$ is significant at the 0.05 level of significance, either of two equivalent statements can be made: (1) The probability of incorrectly finding $\hat{b}$ to be significant is less than 5 percent or (2) you can be at least 95 percent confident that the t-test will *not* find statistical significance when there is none ($b = 0$).

An alternative method of assessing the statistical significance of parameter estimates is to treat as statistically significant only those parameter estimates whose p-values are smaller than the maximum acceptable significance level. Most regression software now calculates a p-value for each parameter estimate. The p-value gives the exact (or minimum) level of significance for a parameter estimate.

To measure how well the sample regression line fits the data, the R^2 statistic (also called the coefficient of determination) is computed. The R^2 measures the fraction of the total variation in Y that is explained by the variation in X. The value of R^2 ranges from 0 (the regression equation explains none of the variation in Y) to 1 (the regression equation explains all the variation in Y). A high R^2 indicates Y and X are highly correlated, and the scatter diagram tightly fits the sample regression line.

The F-statistic is used to test whether the equation as a whole explains a significant amount of the variation in Y.

To test whether the overall equation is significant, the F-statistic is compared with the critical F-value with $k - 1$ and $n - k$ degrees of freedom and the chosen level of significance. If the value for the calculated F-statistic exceeds the critical F-value, the regression equation is statistically significant. Alternatively, if the p-value for the F-statistic is smaller than the acceptable level of significance, then the equation as a whole is statistically significant.

Multiple regression models use two or more explanatory variables to explain the variation in the dependent variable. The coefficient on each of the explanatory variables measures the degree of variation in Y associated with variation in that explanatory variable, holding all other explanatory variables constant. As in the case of simple regression, each coefficient is tested for significance by using the t-test. The degree of significance for each coefficient is given by its p-value. The F-statistic is used to test the overall equation for significance. The R^2 measures the fit of the equation.

Many economic relations of interest to managers are *nonlinear* in nature. Two types of nonlinear models are presented in this chapter: (1) quadratic regression models and (2) log-linear regression models. The quadratic regression model is appropriate when the curve fitting the scatter diagram is either U-shaped or inverted-U-shaped. The quadratic equation, $Y = a + bX + cX^2$, is transformed into a linear form by computing a new variable, $Z = X^2$, and substituting for X^2 to get a linear form: $Y = a + bX + cZ$. A second type of nonlinear model presented in this chapter is the log-linear model. In this nonlinear model, the dependent variable is related to one or more explanatory variables in a multiplicative fashion. The log-linear model for two explanatory variables takes the form $Y = aX^bZ^c$. A particularly useful feature of this specification is that the parameters b and c are elasticities. For example, b measures the percent change in Y that results when X changes by 1 percent. By taking natural logarithms, the logarithm of Y can be expressed as a linear function of the logarithms of the explanatory variables: $\ln Y = \ln a + b \ln X + c \ln Z$. Once this transformation is made, estimation and tests of statistical significance proceed as usual.

We must emphasize again that all the statistics needed for regression analysis are automatically computed when using a computerized regression routine. The purpose of this chapter was to show you how to interpret and use the regression statistics produced by the computer.

TECHNICAL PROBLEMS

1. A simple linear regression equation relates R and W as follows:

$$R = a + bW$$

   a. The explanatory variable is _____ , and the dependent variable is _____ .
   b. The slope parameter is _____ , and the intercept parameter is _____ .
   c. When W is zero, R equals _____ .
   d. For each one unit increase in W, the change in R is _____ units.

2. Regression analysis is often referred to as least-squares regression. Why is this name appropriate?

3. Regression analysis involves estimating the values of parameters and testing the estimated parameters for significance. Why must parameter estimates be tested for statistical significance?

4. Evaluate the following statements:
   a. "The smaller the standard error of the estimate, $S_{\hat{b}}$, the more accurate the parameter estimate."
   b. "If $\hat{b}$ is an unbiased estimate of b, then $\hat{b}$ equals b."
   c. "The more precise the estimate of $\hat{b}$ (i.e., the smaller the standard error of $\hat{b}$), the higher the t-ratio."

5. The linear regression in problem 1 is estimated using 26 observations on R and W. The least-squares estimate of b is 40.495, and the standard error of the estimate is 16.250. Perform a t-test for statistical significance at the 5 percent level of significance.
   a. There are _____ degrees of freedom for the t-test.
   b. The value of the t-statistic is _____ . The critical t-value for the test is _____ .
   c. Is $\hat{b}$ statistically significant? Explain.
   d. The p-value for the t-statistic is _____ . (*Hint:* In this problem, the t-table provides the answer.) The p-value gives the probability of rejecting the hypothesis that _____ ($b = 0$, $b \neq 0$) when b is truly equal to _____ . The confidence level for the test is _____ percent.
   e. What does it mean to say an estimated parameter is statistically significant at the 5 percent significance level?
   f. What does it mean to say an estimated parameter is statistically significant at the 95 percent confidence level?
   g. How does the level of significance differ from the level of confidence?

6. Ten data points on Y and X are employed to estimate the parameters in the linear relation $Y = a + bX$. The computer output from the regression analysis is the following:

DEPENDENT VARIABLE: Y		R-SQUARE	F-RATIO	P-VALUE ON F
OBSERVATIONS: 10		0.5223	8.747	0.0187
VARIABLE	PARAMETER ESTIMATE	STANDARD ERROR	T-RATIO	P-VALUE
INTERCEPT	800.0	189.125	4.23	0.0029
X	−2.50	0.850	−2.94	0.0187

    a. What is the equation of the sample regression line?

    b. Test the intercept and slope estimates for statistical significance at the 1 percent significance level. Explain how you performed this test, and present your results.

    c. Interpret the *p*-values for the parameter estimates.

    d. Test the overall equation for statistical significance at the 1 percent significance level. Explain how you performed this test, and present your results. Interpret the *p*-value for the *F*-statistic.

    e. If *X* equals 140, what is the fitted (or predicted) value of *Y*?

    f. What fraction of the total variation in *Y* is explained by the regression?

7. A simple linear regression equation, $Y = a + bX$, is estimated by a computer program, which produces the following output:

DEPENDENT VARIABLE: Y		R-SQUARE	F-RATIO	P-VALUE ON F
OBSERVATIONS: 25		0.7482	68.351	0.0106
VARIABLE	PARAMETER ESTIMATE	STANDARD ERROR	T-RATIO	P-VALUE
INTERCEPT	325.24	125.09	2.60	0.0160
X	0.8057	0.2898	2.78	0.0106

    a. How many degrees of freedom does this regression analysis have?

    b. What is the critical value of *t* at the 5 percent level of significance?

    c. Test to see if the estimates of *a* and *b* are statistically significant.

    d. Discuss the *p*-values for the estimates of *a* and *b*.

    e. How much of the total variation in *Y* is explained by this regression equation? How much of the total variation in *Y* is unexplained by this regression equation?

    f. What is the critical value of the *F*-statistic at a 5 percent level of significance? Is the overall regression equation statistically significant?

    g. If *X* equals 100, what value do you expect *Y* will take? If *X* equals 0?

8. Evaluate each of the following statements:

    a. "In a multiple regression model, the coefficients on the explanatory variables measure the percent of the total variation in the dependent variable *Y* explained by that explanatory variable."

    b. "The more degrees of freedom in the regression, the more likely it is that a given *t*-ratio exceeds the critical *t*-value."

    c. "The coefficient of determination (R^2) can be exactly equal to one only when the sample regression line passes through each and every data point."

9. A multiple regression model, $R = a + bW + cX + dZ$, is estimated by a computer package, which produces the following output:

DEPENDENT VARIABLE: R		R-SQUARE	F-RATIO	P-VALUE ON F
OBSERVATIONS: 34		0.3179	4.660	0.00865
VARIABLE	PARAMETER ESTIMATE	STANDARD ERROR	T-RATIO	P-VALUE
INTERCEPT	12.6	8.34	1.51	0.1413
W	22.0	3.61	6.09	0.0001
X	−4.1	1.65	−2.48	0.0188
Z	16.3	4.45	3.66	0.0010

a. How many degrees of freedom does this regression analysis have?

b. What is the critical value of t at the 2 percent level of significance?

c. Test to see if the estimates of a, b, c, and d are statistically significant at the 2 percent significance level. What are the exact levels of significance for each of the parameter estimates?

d. How much of the total variation in R is explained by this regression equation? How much of the total variation in R is unexplained by this regression equation?

e. What is the critical value of the F-statistic at the 1 percent level of significance? Is the overall regression equation statistically significant at the 1 percent level of significance? What is the exact level of significance for the F-statistic?

f. If W equals 10, X equals 5, and Z equals 30, what value do you predict R will take? If W, X, and Z are all equal to 0?

10. Eighteen data points on M and X are used to estimate the quadratic regression model $M = a + bX + cX^2$. A new variable, Z, is created to transform the regression into a linear form. The computer output from this regression is

DEPENDENT VARIABLE: M		R-SQUARE	F-RATIO	P-VALUE ON F
OBSERVATIONS: 18		0.6713	15.32	0.0002
VARIABLE	PARAMETER ESTIMATE	STANDARD ERROR	T-RATIO	P-VALUE
INTERCEPT	290.0630	53.991	5.37	0.0001
X	−5.8401	2.1973	−2.66	0.0179
Z	0.07126	0.01967	3.62	0.0025

a. What is the variable Z equal to?

b. Write the estimated quadratic relation between M and X.

c. Test each of the three estimated parameters for statistical significance at the 2 percent level of significance. Show how you performed these tests and present the results.

d. Interpret the p-value for $\hat{c}$.

e. What is the predicted value of M when X is 300?

11. Suppose Y is related to R and S in the following nonlinear way:

$$Y = aR^bS^c$$

a. How can this nonlinear equation be transformed into a linear form that can be analyzed by using multiple regression analysis?

Sixty-three observations are used to obtain the following regression results:

DEPENDENT VARIABLE: LNY	R-SQUARE	F-RATIO	P-VALUE ON F		
OBSERVATIONS: 63	0.8151	132.22	0.0001		
VARIABLE	PARAMETER ESTIMATE	STANDARD ERROR	T-RATIO	P-VALUE
INTERCEPT	−1.386	0.83	−1.67	0.1002
LNR	0.452	0.175	2.58	0.0123
LNS	0.30	0.098	3.06	0.0033

b. Test each estimated coefficient for statistical significance at the 5 percent level of significance. What are the exact significance levels for each of the estimated coefficients?

c. Test the overall equation for statistical significance at the 5 percent level of significance. Interpret the p-value on the F-statistic.

d. How well does this nonlinear model fit the data?

e. Using the estimated value of the intercept, compute an estimate of a.

f. If $R = 200$ and $S = 1,500$, compute the expected value of Y.

g. What is the estimated elasticity of R? Of S?

APPLIED PROBLEMS

1. The director of marketing at Vanguard Corporation believes that sales of the company's Bright Side laundry detergent (S) are related to Vanguard's own advertising expenditure (A), as well as the combined advertising expenditures of its three biggest rival detergents (R). The marketing director collects 36 weekly observations on S, A, and R to estimate the following multiple regression equation:

$$S = a + bA + cR$$

where S, A, and R are measured in dollars per week. Vanguard's marketing director is comfortable using parameter estimates that are statistically significant at the 10 percent level or better.

a. What sign does the marketing director expect a, b, and c to have?

b. Interpret the coefficients a, b, and c.

The regression output from the computer is as follows:

DEPENDENT VARIABLE: S		R-SQUARE	F-RATIO	P-VALUE ON F
OBSERVATIONS: 36		0.2247	4.781	0.0150

VARIABLE	PARAMETER ESTIMATE	STANDARD ERROR	T-RATIO	P-VALUE
INTERCEPT	175086.0	63821.0	2.74	0.0098
A	0.8550	0.3250	2.63	0.0128
R	−0.284	0.164	−1.73	0.0927

   c. Does Vanguard's advertising expenditure have a statistically significant effect on the sales of Bright Side detergent? Explain, using the appropriate p-value.

   d. Does advertising by its three largest rivals affect sales of Bright Side detergent in a statistically significant way? Explain, using the appropriate p-value.

   e. What fraction of the total variation in sales of Bright Side remains unexplained? What can the marketing director do to increase the explanatory power of the sales equation? What other explanatory variables might be added to this equation?

   f. What is the expected level of sales each week when Vanguard spends $40,000 per week and the combined advertising expenditures for the three rivals are $100,000 per week?

2. In his analysis of California's Proposition 103 (see Illustration 4.3), Benjamin Zycher notes that one of the most important provisions of this proposition is eliminating the practice by insurance companies of basing premiums (in part) on the geographic location of drivers. Prohibiting the use of geographic location to assess the risk of a driver creates a substantial implicit subsidy from low-loss counties to high-loss counties, such as Los Angeles, Orange, and San Francisco counties. Zycher hypothesizes that the percent of voters favoring Proposition 103 in a given county (V) is inversely related to the (average) percentage change in auto premiums (P) that the proposition confers upon the drivers of that county.

   The data in the table below were presented by Zycher to support his contention that V and P are inversely related:

County	Percent for Proposition 103 (V)	Change in average premium (P)
Los Angeles	62.8	−21.4
Orange	51.7	−8.2
San Francisco	65.2	−0.9
Alameda	58.9	+8.0
Marin	53.5	+9.1
Santa Clara	51.0	+11.8
San Mateo	52.8	+12.6
Santa Cruz	54.2	+13.0
Ventura	44.8	+1.4
San Diego	44.1	+10.7
Monterey	41.6	+15.3
Sacramento	39.3	+16.0
Tulare	28.7	+23.3
Sutter	32.3	+37.1
Lassen	29.9	+46.5
Siskiyou	29.9	+49.8
Modoc	23.2	+57.6

Sources: California Department of Insurance and Office of the California Secretary of State.

Using the data in the table, we estimated the regression equation

$$V = a + bP$$

to see if voting behavior is related to the change in auto insurance premiums in a statistically significant way. Here is the regression output from the computer:

```
DEPENDENT VARIABLE: V      R-SQUARE     F-RATIO      P-VALUE ON F
        OBSERVATIONS: 17    0.7399       42.674       0.0001

                 PARAMETER      STANDARD
VARIABLE         ESTIMATE       ERROR        T-RATIO      P-VALUE

INTERCEPT        53.682         2.112        25.42        0.0001
P                −0.528         0.081        −6.52        0.0001
```

a. Does this regression equation provide evidence of a statistically significant relation between voter support for Proposition 103 in a county and changes in average auto premiums affected by Proposition 103 in that county? Perform an F-test at the 95 percent level of confidence.

b. Test the intercept estimate for significance at the 95 percent confidence level. If Proposition 103 has no impact on auto insurance premiums in any given county, what percent of voters do you expect will vote for the proposition?

c. Test the slope estimate for significance at the 95 percent confidence level. If P increases by 10 percent, by what percent does the vote for Proposition 103 decline?

3. A security analyst specializing in the stocks of the motion picture industry wishes to examine the relation between the number of movie theater tickets sold in December and the annual level of earnings in the motion picture industry. Time-series data for the last 15 years are used to estimate the regression model

$$E = a + bN$$

where E is total earnings of the motion picture industry measured in dollars per year and N is the number of tickets sold in December. The regression output is as follows:

DEPENDENT VARIABLE: E		R-SQUARE	F-RATIO	P-VALUE ON F
OBSERVATIONS: 15		0.8311	63.96	0.0001
VARIABLE	PARAMETER ESTIMATE	STANDARD ERROR	T-RATIO	P-VALUE
INTERCEPT	25042000.0	20131000.0	1.24	0.2369
N	32.31	8.54	3.78	0.0023

a. How well do movie ticket sales in December explain the level of earnings for the entire year? Present statistical evidence to support your answer.

b. On average, what effect does a 100,000-ticket increase in December sales have on the annual earnings in the movie industry?

c. Sales of movie tickets in December are expected to be approximately 950,000. According to this regression analysis, what do you expect earnings for the year to be?

4. The manager of Collins Import Autos believes the number of cars sold in a day (Q) depends on two factors: (1) the number of hours the dealership is open (H) and (2) the number of salespersons working that day (S). After collecting data for two months (53 days), the manager estimates the following log-linear model:

$$Q = aH^bS^c$$

a. Explain how to transform this log-linear model into a linear form that can be estimated using multiple regression analysis.

The computer output for the multiple regression analysis is shown below:

DEPENDENT VARIABLE: LNQ		R-SQUARE	F-RATIO	P-VALUE ON F
OBSERVATIONS: 53		0.5452	29.97	0.0001
VARIABLE	PARAMETER ESTIMATE	STANDARD ERROR	T-RATIO	P-VALUE
INTERCEPT	0.9162	0.2413	3.80	0.0004
LNH	0.3517	0.1021	3.44	0.0012
LNS	0.2550	0.0785	3.25	0.0021

b. How do you interpret coefficients b and c? If the dealership increases the number of salespersons by 20 percent, what will be the percentage increase in daily sales?

c. Test the overall model for statistical significance at the 5 percent significance level.

d. What percent of the total variation in daily auto sales is explained by this equation? What could you suggest to increase this percentage?

e. Test the intercept for statistical significance at the 5 percent level of significance. If H and S both equal 0, are sales expected to be 0? Explain why or why not.

f. Test the estimated coefficient b for statistical significance. If the dealership decreases its hours of operation by 10 percent, what is the expected impact on daily sales?

◻ **STATISTICAL APPENDIX Further Development**

Least-Squares Parameter Estimation

Consider the sample regression line

$$(1) \qquad \hat{Y}_i = \hat{a} + \hat{b} X_i$$

where $\hat{a}$ and $\hat{b}$ are estimates of the population parameters a and b. The goal of least-squares regression is to find estimates of $\hat{a}$ and $\hat{b}$ that minimize the sum of the squared residuals (denoted ESS) for the sample of n observations on Y and X:

$$(2) \qquad ESS = \sum_{i=1}^{n} e_i^2 = \sum_{i=1}^{n} (Y_i - \hat{Y}_i)^2$$

$$= \sum_{i=1}^{n} (Y_i - \hat{a} - \hat{b} X_i)^2$$

Notice that ESS is a function of the estimates $\hat{a}$ and $\hat{b}$. To find the values of the estimates that minimize ESS, partially differentiate equation (2) with respect to $\hat{a}$ and $\hat{b}$, and then set the two partial derivatives equal to 0:

$$(3) \qquad \frac{\partial ESS}{\partial \hat{a}} = -2 \sum (Y_i - \hat{a} - \hat{b} X_i) = 0$$

$$(4) \qquad \frac{\partial ESS}{\partial \hat{b}} = -2 \sum X_i (Y_i - \hat{a} - \hat{b} X_i) = 0$$

Multiplying and rearranging terms:

$$(3a) \qquad \Sigma Y_i = n\hat{a} + \hat{b} \Sigma X_i$$

$$(4a) \qquad \Sigma Y_i X_i = \hat{a} \Sigma X_i + \hat{b} \Sigma X_i^2$$

Now solve (3a) and (4a) simultaneously for $\hat{a}$ and $\hat{b}$. To do this, multiply (3a) by ΣX_i and (4a) by n:

$$(3b) \qquad \Sigma X_i \Sigma Y_i = n\hat{a} \Sigma X_i + \hat{b} (\Sigma X_i)^2$$

$$(4b) \qquad n \Sigma Y_i \Sigma X_i = n\hat{a} \Sigma X_i + \hat{b} n \Sigma X_i^2$$

Next, subtract (3b) from (4b):

$$(5) \qquad n \Sigma Y_i X_i - \Sigma X_i \Sigma Y_i = \hat{b}[n \Sigma X^2 - (\Sigma X_i)^2]$$

and it follows that

$$(6) \qquad \hat{b} = \frac{n\Sigma X_i Y_i - \Sigma X_i \Sigma Y_i}{n\Sigma X_i^2 - (\Sigma X_i)^2}$$

where X and Y are the sample means of X and Y. After finding $\hat{b}$, $\hat{a}$ is calculated as

$$(7) \qquad \hat{a} = Y - \hat{b} X$$

To illustrate how the computer uses equations (6) and (7) to estimate a and b, Table 4A.1 shows the computations that will be done for you by a computer. Table 4A.1 calculates the parameter estimates for the sample regression line that best fits the data in Table 4.2.

Derivation of the Coefficient of Determination (R^2)

The coefficient of determination, denoted R^2, measures how well the overall equation explains the variation in the dependent variable Y. The total variation in Y can be attributed to one of two things: variation due to changes in the explanatory variable(s) or variation due to random influences. R^2 is derived by decomposing the variation in Y into these two component parts.

Statisticians measure the variation in the dependent variable as $Y_i - \overline{Y}$, the variation in Y about the sample mean ($\overline{Y}$). To motivate why the sample mean is used, recall that if Y_i does not vary at all in the sample (i.e., Y_i is constant for all observations), Y_i equals $\overline{Y}$ for every observation in the sample. The sample mean, then, provides a point of reference about which the variation in Y_i can be measured. The amount by which the value of Y predicted by the regression ($\hat{Y}_i$) deviates from the sample mean ($\overline{Y}$) is referred to as the explained variation and is denoted

TABLE 4A.1

Computing the Least-Squares Estimates $\hat{a}$ and $\hat{b}$ for the Sample of Seven Travel Agencies

Sales (Y_i)	Advertising expenditure (X_i)	$(X_i - \bar{X})$	$(X_i - \bar{X})^2$	$(Y_i - \bar{Y})$	$(X_i - \bar{X})(Y_i - \bar{Y})$
15,000	2,000	−3,143	9,878,551	−22,143	69,591,837
30,000	2,000	−3,143	9,878,551	−7,143	22,448,980
30,000	5,000	−143	20,408	−7,143	1,020,408
25,000	3,000	−2,143	4,591,837	−12,143	26,020,408
55,000	9,000	3,857	14,877,551	17,857	68,877,551
45,000	8,000	2,857	8,163,265	7,857	22,448,980
60,000	7,000	1,857	3,448,980	22,857	42,448,980
Σ 260,000	36,000		50,857,143		252,857,144

$\bar{Y} = 260,000/7 = 37,143.$
$\bar{X} = 36,000/7 = 5,143.$
$\hat{b} = \Sigma(X_i - \bar{X})(Y_i - \bar{Y})/\Sigma(X_i - \bar{X})^2 = 252,857,144/50,857,143 = 4.9719.$
$\hat{a} = \bar{Y} - \hat{b}\bar{X} = 37,143 - (4.9719 \times 5,143) = 11,573.$

$\hat{Y}_i - \bar{Y}$. The unexplained variation in Y_i is the residual amount, $Y_i - \hat{Y}_i$. Figure 4A.1 shows how the variation in Y_i is decomposed for one particular observation in the sample.

The total variation in Y_i in the sample is computed by squaring the total variation in Y_i and summing across all observations in the sample:

$$\text{Total variation} = \Sigma(Y_i - \bar{Y})^2$$

Given the decomposition discussed above, the total variation in Y can also be expressed as the sum of the explained and unexplained variation in Y:

$$\begin{array}{ccc} \text{Total} & \text{Total} & \text{Total} \\ \text{variation} & = \text{explained} & + \text{unexplained} \\ \text{in } Y & \text{variation} & \text{variation} \end{array}$$

$$\Sigma(Y_i - \bar{Y})^2 = \Sigma(\hat{Y}_i - \bar{Y})^2 + \Sigma(Y_i - \hat{Y}_i)^2$$

The coefficient of determination measures the fraction of total variation explained by the regression:

$$R^2 = \frac{\text{Total explained variation}}{\text{Total variation in } Y}$$

$$= \frac{\Sigma(\hat{Y}_i - \bar{Y})^2}{\Sigma(Y_i - \bar{Y}_i)^2}$$

Thus it follows that R^2 can vary from 0 to 1 in value.

Some Additional Problems in Regression Analysis

Multicollinearity

When using regression analysis, we assume that the explanatory (right-hand side) variables are linearly independent of one another. If this assumption is violated, we have the problem of *multicollinearity.* Under normal circumstances, multicollinearity will result in the estimated standard errors being larger than their true values. This means, then, that if multicollinearity exists, finding statistical significance will be more difficult. More specifically, if moderate multicollinearity is present, the estimate of the coefficient, $\hat{b}$, will be unbiased but the estimated standard error, $S_{\hat{b}}$, will be increased. Thus the t-coefficient, $t = \hat{b}/S_{\hat{b}}$, will be reduced, and it will be more difficult to find statistical significance.

Multicollinearity is not unusual. The question is what to do about it. As a general rule, the answer is *nothing*. To illustrate, consider the following function that denotes some true relation:

$$Y = a + bX + cZ$$

If X and Z are not linearly independent—if X and Z are collinear—the standard errors of the estimates for b and c will be increased. Shouldn't we just drop one? Not in the normal instance. If Z is an important explanatory variable, the exclusion of Z would be a *specification error* and would result in biased estimates of the coefficients—a much more severe problem.

FIGURE 4A.1

Decomposition of Total Variation in Y

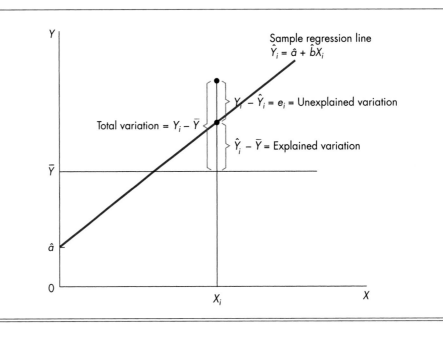

Heteroscedasticity

The problem of *heteroscedasticity* is encountered when the variance of the error term is not constant. It can be encountered when there exists some relation between the error term and one or more of the explanatory variables—for example, when there exists a positive relation between X and the errors (i.e., large errors are associated with large values of X).

In such a case, the estimated parameters are still unbiased, but the standard errors of the coefficients are biased, so the calculated *t*-ratios are unreliable. This problem, most normally encountered in cross-section studies, sometimes can be corrected by performing a transformation on the data or equation. Otherwise, it becomes necessary to employ a technique called weighted least-squares estimation.

Autocorrelation

The problem of *autocorrelation,* associated with time-series data, occurs when the errors are not independent over time. For example, it could be the case that a high error in one period tends to promote a high error in the following period.

With autocorrelation (sometimes referred to as *serial correlation*) the estimated parameters are unbiased, but the standard errors are again biased, resulting in unreliability of the calculated *t*-ratios. Tests for determining if autocorrelation is present (most notably the Durbin-Watson test) are included in most of the available regression packages. Furthermore, most packages also include techniques for estimating an equation in the presence of autocorrelation.

CHAPTER
5

Theory of Consumer Behavior

The willingness of consumers to purchase a product or service is the fundamental source of profit for any business. No matter how efficiently production is accomplished, a firm cannot earn a profit unless buyers believe they can benefit by consuming the firm's product rather than buying a rival's product or even saving their money for future consumption. Understanding consumer behavior, then, is the first step in making profitable pricing, advertising, product design, and production decisions.

Firms spend a great deal of time and money trying to estimate and forecast the demand for their products. Obtaining accurate estimates of demand requires more than a superficial understanding of the underpinnings of demand functions. While we are sympathetic to students who find the level of abstraction in this chapter somewhat daunting, we nevertheless encourage you to meet the challenge of learning these fundamental concepts of consumer behavior. A manager's need for practical analysis of demand—both estimation of demand and demand forecasting—requires an economic model of consumer behavior to guide the analysis.

This chapter presents only the most important aspects of the theory of consumer behavior. The theory follows directly from the theory of constrained maximization described in Chapter 3. (As you read this chapter, you may want to look back at Chapter 3 to see how closely the analysis here follows that general framework.)

Few, if any, people have incomes sufficient to buy as much as they desire of every good or service. Because consumers are constrained by the amount of their incomes, they attempt to maximize their satisfaction from the goods and services they purchase, given this constraint.

When you finish this chapter, you will have a good understanding of why consumers choose to purchase one bundle of products rather than some other bundle. You will also discover that the theory of consumer behavior, as presented in this chapter, is an important tool in other business courses you take, particularly in marketing and finance. Even though a full appreciation of the value of this chapter may not come with a single course in managerial economics, you will begin to see its value in the next two chapters when we examine demand elasticities in Chapter 6 and when we show you how to estimate and forecast consumer demand in Chapter 7.

5.1 CONSUMER PREFERENCES AND UTILITY

As with all economic models, the theory of consumer behavior employs some simplifying assumptions. These assumptions permit us to go directly to the fundamental determinants of consumer behavior and to abstract away from the less important aspects of the consumer's decision process. Let us briefly describe these assumptions.

Complete Information

We assume for now that consumers have complete information pertaining to their consumption decisions. They know the full range of goods and services available and the capacity of each to provide utility. Further, the price of each good is known exactly, as is each consumer's income during the time period in question. Admittedly, to assume perfect knowledge is an abstraction from reality, but the assumption of complete information does not distort the relevant aspects of real-world consumer decisions. It allows us to concentrate on how real consumption choices are made without becoming bogged down with extraneous details.

Preference Ordering

The second assumption is that consumers are able to rank all conceivable bundles of commodities. When confronted with two or more bundles of goods, consumers can determine their order of preference among them. As an example, suppose a consumer is confronted with two bundles consisting of different combinations of two goods. Bundle *A* consists of five candy bars and one soft drink. Bundle *B* consists of three candy bars and three soft drinks. Ranking the two bundles, the person can make one of three possible responses: (1) I prefer bundle *A* to bundle *B*, (2) I prefer bundle *B* to bundle *A*, or (3) I would be equally satisfied with either.

The same is true when ranking any two bundles of goods and services. The consumer either prefers one bundle to the other or is indifferent between the two. A consumer who is indifferent between two bundles clearly feels that either bundle would yield the same level of satisfaction. A preferred bundle would yield more satisfaction than the other, less-preferred bundle. We should also note that price has nothing to do with preferences. Preference is a theoretical concept about how people can rank bundles of goods.

We also assume that the consumer is rational in the following sense: If there are three bundles of goods, *A, B,* and *C,* and if the consumer prefers *A* to *B* and *B* to *C,* then bundle *A* must be preferred to bundle *C.* Or if the consumer is indifferent between *A* and *B* and prefers *B* to *C,* then *A* must be preferred to *C.* We can extend this assumption to any number of combinations; if consumers can rank any two bundles of goods, they can rank all conceivable combinations of goods and services.

Finally, we assume consumers always prefer to have more of a good rather than less of the good. We do recognize that people may consume so much of something that they become satiated with it and do not want any more; however, no one would purchase so much of a good that they would be happier to have less of it. We summarize this discussion with a principle:

Principle   Consumers have a preference pattern that (1) establishes a rank ordering of all bundles of goods and (2) compares all pairs of bundles, indicating that Bundle *A* is preferred to Bundle *B*, *B* is preferred to *A*, or the consumer is indifferent between *A* and *B*. In a three- (or more) way comparison, if *A* is preferred (indifferent) to *B*, and *B* is preferred (indifferent) to *C*, *A* must be preferred (indifferent) to *C*. Consumers prefer more of a good to less of that good.

$T \Rightarrow \boxed{1}$

The Utility Function

Economists name the benefits consumers obtain from the goods and services they consume **utility.** This is not completely descriptive. Utility implies usefulness, and many of the products most of us consume may not be particularly useful. Many people are willing to pay a lot more for a Mercedes or BMW than they would pay for a Geo, which may well be just as useful. And people can differ drastically over what is and is not useful. A child would probably consider a Nintendo game more useful than new clothes, while the parents would have the opposite opinion. Most people probably buy a lot of things that others would not consider particularly useful. Nonetheless, we will follow tradition and refer to the benefits obtained from goods and services as utility.

utility
Benefits consumers obtain from the goods and services they consume.

Settling on a name for the benefits does not solve the problem of how to measure these benefits from consumption. Who could say how many units of benefit, or how much utility, they receive from consuming an ice cream cone or a pizza or from going to the dentist? After all, it is not possible to plug a "utility meter" into a consumer's ear and measure the amount of utility generated by consuming some good or service. And even if we could measure utility, what units or denomination would we use? In class, we have used terms such as "utils," which is too serious; "globs," which is too frivolous; "bushels," which is too precise; and others we need not mention. Over time, we have settled on the phrase "units of utility," which is certainly pedestrian and dull, but it seems as good a name as any.

utility function
An equation that shows an individual's perception of the level of utility that would be attained from consuming each conceivable bundle of goods: $U = f(X, Y)$.

Consumer preferences can be represented as a **utility function.** A utility function shows an individual's perception of the level of utility that would be attained from consuming each conceivable bundle or combination of goods and services. A simple form of a utility function for a person who consumes only two goods, *X* and *Y,* might be

$$U = f(X, Y)$$

where X and Y are, respectively, the amounts of goods X and Y consumed, f means "a function of" or "depends on," and U is the amount of utility the person receives from each combination of X and Y. Thus utility depends on the quantities consumed of X and Y.

The actual numbers assigned to the levels of utility are arbitrary. It is inconceivable that anyone could actually assign specific numbers for the amount of utility received from consuming every possible combination of goods. Therefore, a utility function is a theoretical concept that proves useful in analysis. We need only say that if a consumer prefers one combination of goods, say, $20X$ and $30Y$, to some other combination, say, $15X$ and $32Y$, the amount of utility derived from the first bundle is greater than the amount from the second. It makes no difference if the amount of utility assigned to the first bundle is 150 and the amount to the second is 100 or if the first number is 90 and the second is 80. The only thing that matters is that

$$U = f(20,30) > U = f(15,32)$$

For analytical simplicity and graphical convenience we will analyze the case of a consumer choosing between only two goods or services. The utility function will therefore be as specified earlier. We could express a utility function with any number of goods and services. Such a utility function would be

$$U = f(X_1, X_2, X_3, \ldots, X_n)$$

where X_1 is the amount of the ith good or service, and U is an index of utility depending on the quantities consumed of goods $X_1, X_2, X_3, \ldots, X_n$. We should emphasize, however, that the two-good approach enables us to derive every important theoretical concept that can be derived from the n-good model and is far less complex analytically.

5.2 INDIFFERENCE CURVES

indifference curve
A locus of points representing different bundles of goods and services, each of which yields the same level of total utility.

Consumers are willing to make trade-offs or substitute among different goods. This willingness to substitute is determined by the form of that person's utility function. A fundamental tool for analyzing consumer behavior is an **indifference curve,** which is a locus of points representing different combinations of goods and services, each of which provides an individual with the same level of utility. Therefore the consumer is indifferent among all combinations of goods shown on an indifference curve—hence the name. The above assumption that a consumer chooses among bundles consisting of only *two* goods enables us to analyze consumer behavior using two-dimensional graphs of indifference curves without any loss of explanatory capability.

Properties

Figure 5.1 shows a representative indifference curve with the typically assumed shape. The quantity of good X is plotted along the horizontal axis; the quantity of good Y is plotted along the vertical axis.

FIGURE 5.1

A Typical Indifference Curve

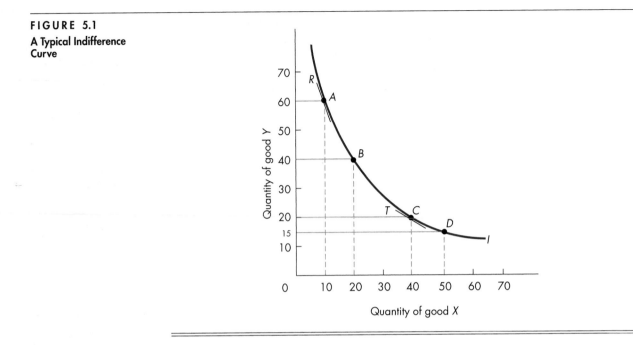

All combinations of goods X and Y along indifference curve I yield the consumer the same level of utility. In other words, the consumer is indifferent among all points, such as point A, with 10 units of X and 60 units of Y; point B, with $20X$ and $40Y$; point C, with $40X$ and $20Y$; and so on. At any point on I, it is possible to take away some amount of X and add some amount of Y (though not necessarily the same amount) and leave the consumer with the same level of utility. Conversely, we can add X and take away just enough Y to make the consumer indifferent between the two combinations.

An indifference curve is downward-sloping. This assumption reflects the fact that the consumer obtains utility from both goods. Thus if more X is added, some Y must be taken away in order to maintain the same level of utility. If the curve in Figure 5.1 were to begin sloping upward at, say, 60 units of X, this would mean that the consumer has so much X that any additional X would reduce utility if the quantity of Y remains constant. In such a case, to keep the consumer at the same level of utility when X is added, more Y would have to be added to compensate for the lost utility from having more X. Likewise, if the curve were to begin bending backward at, say, 75 units of Y, this would mean that the consumer experiences reduced levels of utility with increases in Y.

Indifference curves are convex. This shape requires that as the consumption of X is increased relative to consumption of Y, the consumer is willing to accept a smaller reduction in Y for an equal increase in X in order to stay at the same level of utility. This property is apparent in Figure 5.1. Begin at point A, with 10 units of X and 60 units of Y. In order to increase the consumption of X by 10 units, to 20, the consumer is willing to reduce the consumption of Y by 20 units, to 40. Given indifference curve I, the consumer will be indifferent between the two combinations represented by A and B. Next begin at C, with $40X$ and $20Y$. From this point, to gain an additional 10 units of X (move to point D), the consumer is willing to give up only 5 units of Y, much less than the 20 units willingly given up to obtain 10 more units at point A. The convexity of indifference curves implies a diminishing marginal rate of substitution, to which we now turn.

Marginal Rate of Substitution

marginal rate of substitution (MRS)
A measure of the number of units of Y that must be given up per unit of X added so as to maintain a constant level of utility.

An important concept in indifference curve analysis is the marginal rate of substitution. The **marginal rate of substitution (MRS)** measures the number of units of Y that must be given up per unit of X added so as to maintain a constant level of utility. Returning to Figure 5.1, you can see that the consumer is indifferent between combinations A ($10X$ and $60Y$) and B ($20X$ and $40Y$). Thus the rate at which the consumer is willing to substitute is

$$\frac{\Delta Y}{\Delta X} = \frac{60 - 40}{10 - 20} = -\frac{20}{10} = -2$$

The marginal rate of substitution is 2, meaning that the consumer is willing to give up two units of Y for each unit of X added. Since it would be cumbersome to have the minus sign on the right side of the equation, the marginal rate of substitution is defined as

$$MRS = -\frac{\Delta Y}{\Delta X} = 2$$

For the movement from C to D along I, the marginal rate of substitution is

$$MRS = -\frac{\Delta Y}{\Delta X} = -\frac{(20 - 15)}{(40 - 50)} = \frac{5}{10} = \frac{1}{2}$$

In this case the consumer is willing to give up only ½ unit of Y per additional unit of X added.

Therefore, the marginal rate of substitution diminishes along an indifference curve. When consumers have a small amount of X relative to Y, they are willing to give up a lot of Y to gain another unit of X. When they have less Y relative to X, they are willing to give up less Y in order to gain another unit of X.

We have, thus far, calculated the marginal rate of substitution for relatively large changes in the quantities of the two goods: that is, over *intervals* along an indifference curve. In Figure 5.1 the MRS over the interval from A to B is 2, and the MRS over the interval from C to D is $1/2$. Now consider measuring the MRS at a *point* on an indifference curve; that is, let the changes in X and Y along the indifference curve be extremely small. The marginal rate of substitution at a point can be closely approximated by (the absolute value of) the slope of a line tangent to the indifference curve at the point. For example, consider point C in Figure 5.2 A line tangent to indifference curve I at point C, TT', has a slope of -0.75 ($\Delta Y/\Delta X = -600/800$). The (absolute value of the) slope of the tangent line gives a good

FIGURE 5.2
The Slope of an
Indifference Curve
and the MRS

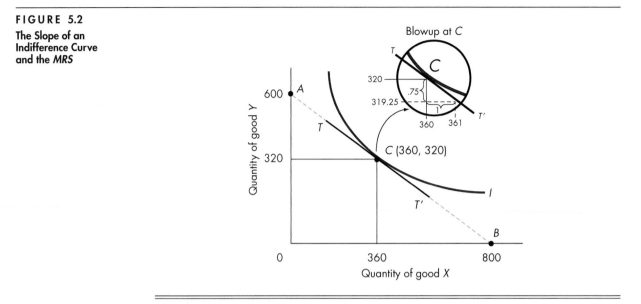

estimate of the amount of Y that must be given up to keep utility constant when one more unit of X is consumed. Suppose the consumer moves along the indifference curve by adding one more unit of X, from 360 to 361 units. Using the slope of the tangent line as an approximation, the change in Y needed to keep utility constant is −0.75; in other words, a one-unit increase in X requires a 0.75-unit decrease in Y to remain indifferent. But as the blowup in Figure 5.2 shows, if the movement is along the indifference curve, only a little *less* than 0.75 unit of Y must be sacrificed to remain indifferent. Nevertheless, the (absolute value of the) slope of the tangent line is a fairly close approximation of the exact *MRS*. As the changes in X and Y become smaller and smaller, the (absolute value of the) tangent line becomes a better and better approximation of the *MRS* at that point.

In Figure 5.1 the (absolute values of the) slopes of tangent lines R and T give the marginal rates of substitution at points A and C, respectively. When we look at these tangents, it is easy to see that the (absolute value of the) slope of the indifference curve, and hence the *MRS*, decreases as X increases and Y decreases along the indifference curve. This results from the assumption that indifference curves are convex.

▣ **Relation** Indifference curves are negatively sloped and convex. Moving along an indifference curve, when the consumption of one good is increased, consumption of the other good is necessarily reduced by the amount required to maintain a constant level of utility. For a unit increase (decrease) in X, the marginal rate of substitution measures the decrease (increase) in Y needed to keep utility constant ($MRS = -\Delta Y/\Delta X$). For very small changes in X, the marginal rate of substitution is the negative of the slope of the indifference curve at a point. The marginal rate of substitution decreases as the consumer moves down an indifference curve.

FIGURE 5.3
Indifference Map

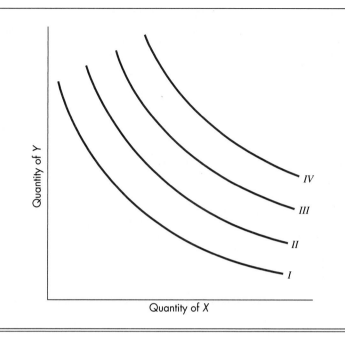

Indifference Maps

An indifference map is made up of two or more indifference curves. Figure 5.3 shows a typical indifference map, with four indifference curves, *I, II, III,* and *IV.* Any indifference curve lying above and to the right of another represents a higher level of utility. Thus any combination of *X* and *Y* on *IV* is preferred to any combination on *III*, any combination on *III* is preferred to any on *II*, and so on. All bundles of goods on the same indifference curve are equivalent; all combinations lying on a higher curve are preferred.

The indifference map in Figure 5.3 consists of only four indifference curves. We could have drawn many, many more. In fact, the *X–Y* space actually contains an infinite number of indifference curves. Each point in the space lies on one and only one indifference curve. That is, the same combination of goods cannot give two levels of utility. Thus indifference curves cannot intersect.

Relation   An indifference map consists of several indifference curves. The higher (or further to the right) an indifference curve, the greater the level of utility associated with the curve. Combinations of goods on higher indifference curves are preferred to combinations on lower curves.

A Marginal Utility Interpretation of *MRS*

The concept of *marginal utility* can give additional insight into the properties of indifference curves, particularly the slope of indifference curves. **Marginal utility** is the addition to total utility that is attributable to consuming one more unit of a

marginal utility
The addition to total utility that is attributable to the addition of one unit of a good to the current rate of consumption, holding constant the amounts of all other goods consumed.

good, holding constant the amounts of all other goods consumed. Thus marginal utility (*MU*) of some good equals $\Delta U / \Delta Q$, where Q is the quantity of the good. Economists typically assume that as the consumption of a good increases, the marginal utility from an additional unit of the good diminishes. While diminishing marginal utility cannot be proved theoretically, falling marginal utility appears to characterize the pattern of consumption for most people with most goods.

Just imagine how you feel about the soft drinks you consume at a football game on a hot day. The first soft drink boosts your utility by a substantial amount. The second soft drink does taste good, and it increases your utility, but the increase in utility is not as great as it was for the first soft drink. So while the marginal utility of the second soft drink is positive, it is smaller than the marginal utility of the first soft drink. Similarly, the third and fourth soft drinks also make you feel better (i.e., increase your utility), but by successively smaller amounts. This demonstrates the concept of diminishing marginal utility.

While some economists object to the concept of marginal utility on the grounds that utility is not measurable, many other economists find it useful to relate marginal utility to the marginal rate of substitution along an indifference curve. The change in total utility that results when both X and Y change by small amounts is related to the marginal utilities of X and Y as

$$\Delta U = (MU_x \times \Delta X) + (MU_y \times Y)$$

where MU_x and MU_y are the marginal utilities of X and Y, respectively.[1] To illustrate this relation, suppose a consumer increases consumption of X by 2 units ($\Delta X = 2$) and decreases consumption of Y by 1 unit ($\Delta Y = -1$). Further suppose the marginal utility of X is 25 for each additional unit of X, and the marginal utility of Y is 10. The amount by which utility changes is computed as

$$\Delta U = (25 \times 2) + (10 \times -1) = 40$$

Consuming 2 more X and 1 less Y causes total utility to rise by 40 units of utility.

For points on a given indifference curve, all combinations of goods yield the same level of utility, so ΔU is 0 for all changes in X and Y that would keep the consumer on the same indifference curve. From the above equation, if $\Delta U = 0$, it follows that

$$\Delta U = 0 = (MU_x \times \Delta X) + (MU_y \times \Delta Y)$$

Therefore, solving for $-\Delta Y / \Delta X$,

$$-\frac{\Delta Y}{\Delta X} = \frac{MU_x}{MU_y}$$

---

[1]Note that we have stretched one of the assumptions in this analysis. Recall that marginal utility is the increase in utility from a one-unit increase in the rate of consumption of a good, holding the consumption of all other goods constant. In this example, we speak of marginal utility while letting the consumption of both goods change at the same time. However, if the change in each is small, this presents little or no problem.

ILLUSTRATION 5.1

To Fly Fast or to Fly Far:
Trade-offs in the Market

When Cessna Aircraft Corp. and Gulfstream Aircraft, Inc., each introduced new business jets—the Cessna Citation X and the Gulfstream V—analysts predicted that the success of the two different aircraft would reveal the relative importance to business buyers of speed and range. The Citation X, with a speed up to 600 miles per hour, was the fastest civilian plane short of the Concord. The Gulfstream V, with a range up to 7,500 miles, was the longest-range business jet. Cessna boasted that its jet could fly moguls from New York to California for breakfast, then back to New Jersey in time for cocktails. Gulfstream cited its jet's ability to fly 14 hours nonstop, from California to Spain or India.

Industry analysts differed in their predictions about the success in the market of the two planes. Some predicted consumers would value the range of Gulfstream more; others said that Cessna's speed would prevail. Obviously the Gulfstream also flies pretty fast, and the Cessna also flies pretty far, but the two manufacturers chose to emphasize different features. In terms of indifference curves, Cessna viewed the indifference map of corporate jet buyers as being something like the curves shown in Panel A of the graph in the next column. It believed that consumers would be willing to trade off a lot of range for more speed. In this case, the marginal rate of substitution between range and speed is high. Gulfstream viewed the indifference map as being like the curves shown in Panel B. That is, consumers would not be willing to trade off as much range for more speed. In this view, the marginal rate of substitution between range and speed is low.

A great deal of money rode on these decisions, since the startup cost of a new airplane is very high and it often takes the market a long time to render a verdict. A Canadian firm planning to introduce a competitor to the Gulfstream estimated that its startup costs would be about $1 billion (U.S.).

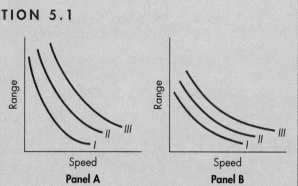

This situation illustrates the importance of predicting trade-offs in business decision making. Products have many different characteristics. Managers making long-range decisions often try to determine the relative values that consumers place on these different characteristics, and one product generally cannot incorporate all the desirable characteristics.

For example, an ice cream manufacturer must decide how much fat to put into a new product. Fat makes ice cream taste good, but for dietary reasons many consumers value low-fat, low-cholesterol food. The manufacturer must evaluate consumer trade-offs between taste and health. Automobile manufacturers must predict the willingness of consumers to trade off performance, styling, and reliability in their cars. According to some observers, U.S. auto manufacturers made the wrong decision several years ago when they emphasized size and style over reliability. As it turned out, consumers valued reliability more than the U.S. automakers had predicted, and the firms subsequently lost considerable sales to foreign producers.

It is not the actual estimation and graphing of indifference curves that is useful to decision makers. It is the *concept* of these curves that is useful. All products have some substitutes, and consumers are willing to trade one product for another at some rate. The important thing is estimating the rate at which they are willing to make the trade-off.

where $-\Delta Y / \Delta X$ is the negative of the slope of the indifference curve, or the marginal rate of substitution. Thus the marginal rate of substitution can be interpreted as the ratio of the marginal utility of X divided by the marginal utility of Y:

$$MRS = \frac{MU_x}{MU_y}$$

5.3 THE CONSUMER'S BUDGET CONSTRAINT

Recall from Chapter 2 that demand functions indicate what consumers are both *willing and able* to do. Because indifference curves are derived from the preference patterns of consumers, they show what consumers are willing to do. They indicate the rate at which consumers are willing to substitute among different goods. They give no indication of the consumer's income or the prices that must be paid for the goods. Consumers are, however, constrained as to what they are able to do—what bundles of goods they can purchase—by the market-determined prices of the goods and by their incomes. We now turn to an analysis of the income constraint faced by consumers.

Budget Lines

If consumers had unlimited money incomes or if goods were free, there would be no problem of economizing. People could buy whatever they wanted and would have no problem of choice. But this is not generally the case.

Consumers normally have limited incomes and goods are not free. Their problem is how to spend the limited income in a way that gives the maximum possible utility. The constraint faced by consumers can be illustrated graphically.

Continue to assume the consumer buys only two goods, bought in quantities X and Y. The consumer has a fixed money income of $1,000, which is the maximum amount that can be spent on the two goods in a given period.[2] For simplicity, assume the entire income is spent on X and Y. If the price of X is $5 per unit and the price of Y is $10 per unit, the amount spent on X ($5 \times X$) plus the amount spent on Y ($10 \times Y$) must equal the $1,000 income:

$$\$5X + \$10Y = \$1,000$$

Alternatively, solving for Y in terms of X,

$$Y = \frac{\$1,000}{\$10} - \frac{\$5}{\$10} X = 100 - \frac{1}{2} X$$

The graph of this equation, shown in Figure 5.4, is a straight line called the *budget line*. A **budget line** is the locus of all combinations or bundles of goods that can be purchased at given prices if the entire money income is spent.

To purchase any one of the bundles of X and Y on the budget line AB in Figure 5.4, the consumer spends exactly $1,000. If the consumer decides to spend all $1,000 on good Y and spend nothing on good X, 100 (= $1,000/$10) units of Y can

budget line
The locus of all bundles of goods that can be purchased at given prices if the entire money income is spent.

---

[2]More advanced theories permit consumers to save and borrow between periods.

FIGURE 5.4

A Consumer's Budget Constraint

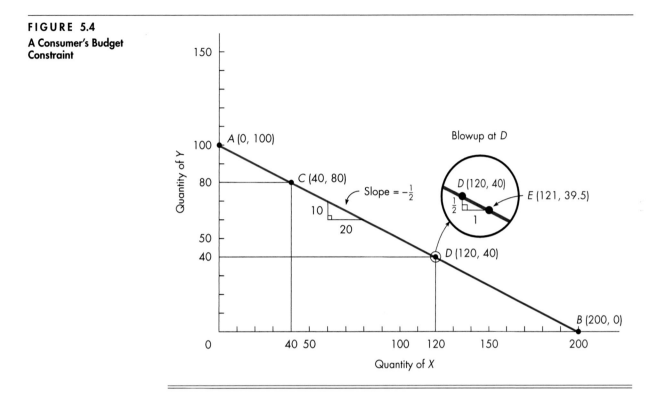

be purchased (point A in Figure 5.4). If the consumer spends all $1,000 on X and buys no Y, 200 (= $1,000/$5) units of X can be purchased (point B). In Figure 5.4, consumption bundles C, with $40X$ and $80Y$, and D, with $120X$ and $40Y$, represent two other combinations of goods X and Y that can be purchased by spending exactly $1,000, because $(80 \times \$10) + (40 \times \$5) = \$1,000$ and $(40 \times \$10) + (120 \times \$5) = \$1,000$.

The slope of the budget line, $-1/2$ (= $\Delta Y / \Delta X$), indicates the amount of Y that must be given up if one more unit of X is purchased. For every additional unit of X purchased, the consumer must spend $5 more on good X. To continue meeting the budget constraint, $5 less must be spent on good Y; thus the consumer must give up $1/2$ unit of Y. To illustrate this point, suppose the consumer is currently purchasing bundle D but wishes to move to bundle E, which is composed of 1 more unit of X and $1/2$ unit less of Y (see the blowup in Figure 5.4). Bundles D and E both cost $1,000 to purchase, but the consumer must trade off $1/2$ unit of good Y for the extra unit of good X in bundle E. Note also that if the consumer buys 1 less unit of X, then an *additional* $1/2$ unit of Y can be purchased with the same money income.

The rate at which the consumer can trade off Y for one more unit of X is equal to the price of good X (here $5) divided by the price of good Y (here $10); that is,

$$\text{Slope of the budget line} = -P_x/P_y$$

FIGURE 5.5

A Typical Budget Line

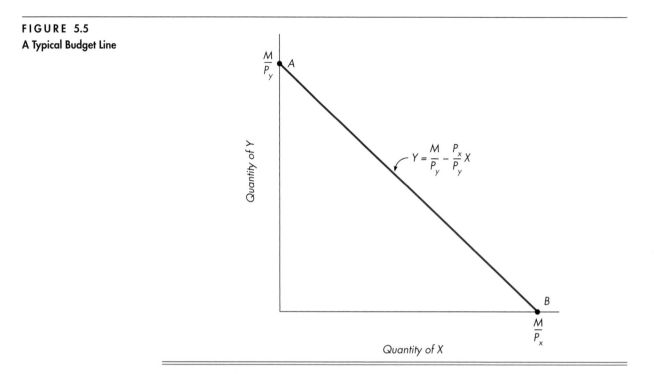

where P_x and P_y are the prices of goods X and Y, respectively. In Figure 5.4, the slope of the budget line is $-1/2$, which equals $-\$5/\$10$.

The relation between money income (M) and the amount of goods X and Y that can be purchased can be expressed in general as

$$M = P_x X + P_y Y$$

This equation can be rewritten in the form of a straight line:

$$Y = \frac{M}{P_y} - \frac{P_x}{P_y} X$$

The first term, M/P_y, gives the amount of Y the consumer can buy if no X is purchased. As noted, $-P_x/P_y$ is the slope of the budget line and indicates how much Y must be given up for an additional unit of X.

The general form of a typical budget line is shown in Figure 5.5. The line AB shows all combinations of X and Y that can be purchased with the given money income (M) and given prices of the goods (P_x and P_y). The intercept on the Y axis, A, is M/P_y; the horizontal intercept, B, is M/P_x. The slope of the budget line is $-P_x/P_y$. Note that this slope can be derived by the typical "rise-over-run" formula $[(M/P_y \div M/P_x) = -P_x/P_y]$.

FIGURE 5.6
Shifting Budget Lines

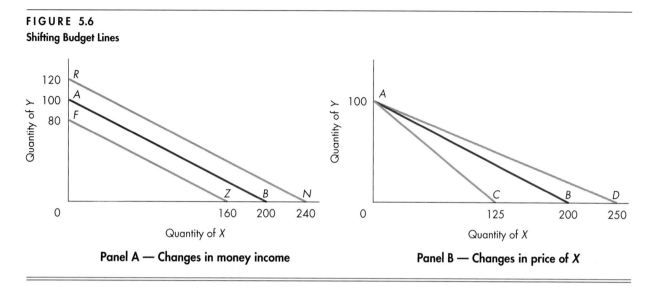

Panel A — Changes in money income

Panel B — Changes in price of X

Shifting the Budget Line

If money income (M) or the price ratio (P_x/P_y) changes, the budget line must change. Panel A of Figure 5.6 shows the effect of changes in income. Begin with the original budget line shown in Figure 5.4, AB, which corresponds to $1,000 money income and prices of X and Y of $5 and $10, respectively. Next let money income increase to $1,200, holding the prices of X and Y constant. Since the prices do not change, the slope of the budget line remains the same ($-1/2$). But since money income increases, the vertical intercept (M/P_y) increases (shifts upward) to 120 (= $1,200/$10). That is, if the consumer now spends the entire income on good Y, 20 more units of Y can be purchased than was previously the case. The horizontal intercept (M/P_x) also increases, to 240 (= $1,200/$5). The result of an increase in income is, therefore, a parallel shift in the budget line from AB to RN. The increase in income increases the set of combinations of the goods that can be purchased.

Alternatively, begin once more with budget line AB and then let money income decrease to $800. In this case the set of possible combinations of goods decreases. The vertical and horizontal intercepts decrease to 80 (= $800/$10) and 160 (= $800/$5), respectively, causing a parallel shift in the budget line to FZ, with intercepts of 80 and 160.

Panel B shows the effect of changes in the price of good X. Begin as before with the original budget line AB and then let the price of X fall from $5 to $4 per unit. Since M/P_y does not change, the vertical intercept remains at B (100 units of Y). However, when P_x decreases, the absolute value of the slope (P_x/P_y) falls to 4/10 (= $4/$10). In this case, the budget line becomes less steep. After the price of X falls, more X can be purchased if the entire money income is spent on X. Thus the horizontal intercept increases from 200 to 250 units of X (= $1,000/$4). In Panel B the budget line pivots (or rotates) from AB to AD.

An increase in the price of good X to $8 causes the budget line to pivot backward, from AB to AC. The intercept on the horizontal axis decreases to 125 (= $1,000/$8). When P_x increases to $8, the absolute value of the slope of the line, P_x/P_y, increases to 8/10 (= $8/$10). The budget line becomes steeper when P_x rises, while the vertical intercept remains constant.

□ **Relation** An increase (decrease) in money income causes a parallel outward (backward) shift in the budget line. An increase (decrease) in the price of X causes the budget line to pivot backward (outward) around the original vertical intercept.

5.4 UTILITY MAXIMIZATION

To this point we have set forth the tools needed to analyze consumer choice. The budget line shows all bundles of commodities that are available to the consumer, given the limited income and market-determined prices. The indifference map shows the preference ordering of all conceivable bundles of goods. In order to make marketing decisions, managers need to know how consumers choose the bundle of goods and services they actually purchase from all the possible bundles that they could purchase. Managers should be aware of the consumer-choice process when estimating the demand for their firms' products, forecasting future demand, and making advertising decisions. We now use these tools to show how consumers choose, from all possible combinations of goods, the combination that yields the highest level of utility.

Maximizing Utility Subject to a Limited Money Income[3]

We will illustrate the maximization process graphically with the use of a rather far-fetched example. Joan Johnson is a young, overworked, underpaid management trainee working for a large corporation. Johnson's monthly food budget is $400, which, because she works such long hours, is spent only on pizzas and burgers. The price of a pizza is $8, and the price of a burger is $4. The water with which she washes down the burgers and pizzas is free. Johnson's task is to determine the combination of pizzas and burgers that yields the highest level of utility possible from the $400 food budget at the given prices.

The maximization process is shown graphically in Figure 5.7. Indifference curves I through IV represent a portion of Johnson's indifference map between pizzas, plotted along the vertical axis, and burgers, plotted along the horizontal axis. Her budget line, from 50 pizzas to 100 burgers, shows all combinations of the two fast foods that Johnson can consume during a month. If she spends the entire $400 on pizzas at $8 each, she can consume 50 pizzas. If she spends the entire $400 on burgers at $4 each, she can consume 100 burgers. Or she can consume any other

---

[3]A mathematical approach to constrained utility maximization is provided in the appendix to this chapter.

FIGURE 5.7

**Constrained Utility
Maximization**

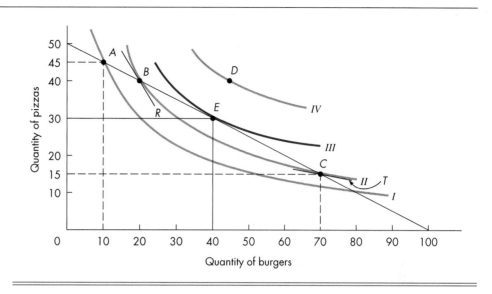

combination on the line. The absolute value of the slope of the budget line is the price of burgers divided by the price of pizzas, or $P_B/P_P = \$4/\$8 = 1/2$. This indicates that to consume one additional $4 burger, Johnson must give up half of an $8 pizza. Alternatively, 1 more pizza can be bought at a cost of 2 burgers.

As is clear from the graph, the highest possible level of utility is reached when Johnson purchases 30 pizzas and 40 burgers a month. This combination is represented by point E, at which the budget line is tangent to indifference curve III. Many other combinations of the two fast foods, such as 40 pizzas and 45 burgers at point D on indifference curve IV, are preferable to the combination at E, but these other combinations cannot be purchased at the given prices and the $400 income. For example, 40 pizzas and 45 burgers would cost $500. All such bundles lie outside Johnson's budget constraint.

Johnson can purchase many combinations along her budget line other than the one at point E. These other combinations all lie on lower indifference curves and are therefore less preferred. Consider the combination at point A, consisting of 45 pizzas and 10 burgers. This combination can be purchased with the $400 income but, because it is on indifference curve I, it clearly gives a lower level of utility than combination E on indifference curve III. If Johnson is consuming the combination at point A, she can increase the number of burgers, decrease the number of pizzas at the rate of 1 more burger for 1/2 less pizza, and move down the budget line. This substitution leads to higher and higher levels of utility—for example, 40 pizzas and 20 burgers (combination B) are on indifference curve II and therefore provide more utility than combination A on curve I. Johnson should not stop at B. She should continue substituting pizzas for burgers until point E on curve III is attained. Thus every combination on the budget line above point E represents a lower level of utility than can be attained by consuming 30 pizzas and 40 burgers.

Alternatively, suppose Johnson is consuming 15 pizzas and 70 burgers—combination C. This combination is on indifference curve *II*, which is below *III* and therefore represents a lower level of utility than combination E. Johnson can increase the number of pizzas and decrease the number of burgers at the rate of 1/2 of a pizza for every burger given up and can move to higher indifference curves. She should continue substituting pizzas for burgers until combination E is reached. Thus every combination on the budget line below E represents a lower level of utility than is attainable with 30 pizzas and 40 burgers.

By elimination, we have shown that every other combination on the budget line yields less utility than combination E. Thus utility is maximized with the given income and prices when Johnson consumes at point E, the point at which the budget line is tangent to indifference curve *III*, the highest attainable indifference curve. It therefore follows that the highest attainable level of utility is reached by consuming the combination at which the marginal rate of substitution (the absolute value of the slope of the indifference curve) equals the price ratio (the absolute value of the slope of the budget line).

We can use this relation between the *MRS* and the price ratio to provide more insight into why every other combination on the budget line yields less utility than the combination at point E. Consider again the combination at B, with 40 pizzas and 20 burgers. At this combination, the *MRS* (the absolute value of the slope of indifference curve *II*) is greater than the absolute value of the slope of the budget line, $P_B/P_P = 1/2$. Suppose the *MRS* at B is 2 (the slope of tangent R equals 2). This means that Johnson, in order to obtain 1 more burger, is *just willing* to exchange 2 pizzas. Exchanging 2 pizzas for 1 more burger leaves Johnson at the same level of utility—she is made no better and no worse off by this exchange. If Johnson could get 1 burger and give up *less* than 2 pizzas, she would be better off. Since burgers cost only half as much as pizzas, the market allows Johnson to obtain 1 more burger while only giving up half a pizza. Giving up half a pizza to get 1 more burger is a much more favorable exchange rate than the exchange rate she is just willing to make (giving up 2 pizzas for one burger). Thus Johnson moves to a higher indifference curve by trading only half a pizza for an additional burger.

As you can see, at every other combination on the budget line above E, the absolute value of the slope of the indifference curve—the *MRS*—must be greater than the absolute value of the slope of the budget line. Therefore, at each of these combinations, Johnson, by the same argument, can raise her utility by adding a burger and giving up less pizza than she would be willing to give up in order to gain the additional burger. Thus all combinations above E, at which the *MRS* is greater than 1/2, leads to less utility than combination E.

At any combination on the budget line below E, the *MRS* is obviously less than the price ratio. Suppose the *MRS* at combination C is 1/10 (the absolute value of the slope of tangent T equals 1/10), meaning that Johnson is just willing to give up 10 burgers in order to obtain an additional pizza. Since the absolute value of the slope of the budget line is 1/2, she can obtain the additional pizza by giving up only 2 burgers. She clearly becomes better off by sacrificing the 2 burgers for the additional pizza.

At every point on the budget line below E, the MRS is less than 1/2, and Johnson can obtain the additional pizza by giving up fewer burgers than the amount she is just willing to give up. Thus she should continue reducing the number of burgers and increasing the number of pizzas until utility is maximized at E with 30 pizzas and 40 burgers. Again we have shown that all combinations other than E yield less utility from the given income.

The marginal rate of substitution is the rate at which the consumer is *willing* to substitute one good for another. The price ratio is the rate at which the consumer is *able* to substitute one good for another in the market. Thus the optimal combination of goods occurs where the rate at which the consumer is willing to substitute equals the rate at which he or she is able to substitute. We can summarize the concept of consumer utility maximization with the following:

Principle   A consumer maximizes utility subject to a limited money income at the combination of goods for which the indifference curve is just tangent to the budget line. At this combination, the marginal rate of substitution (the absolute value of the slope of the indifference curve) is equal to the price ratio (the absolute value of the slope of the budget line):

$$- \frac{\Delta Y}{\Delta X} = MRS = \frac{P_x}{P_y}$$

Marginal Utility Interpretation of Consumer Optimization

As noted in the beginning of this chapter, the theory of constrained utility maximization is a straightforward application of the theory of constrained maximization developed in Chapter 3. Recall from Chapter 3 that a decision maker attains the highest level of benefits possible within a given cost constraint when the marginal benefit per dollar spent on each activity is the same and the cost constraint is met.

As shown earlier, a consumer attains the highest level of utility from a given income when the marginal rate of substitution for any two goods, say, goods X and Y, is equal to the ratio of the prices of the two goods: that is, $-\Delta Y / \Delta X = MRS = P_x/P_y$. Recall that the marginal rate of substitution is equal to the ratio of the marginal utilities of the two goods. Therefore, utility-maximization occurs when the entire income is spent and

$$MRS = - \frac{\Delta Y}{\Delta X} = \frac{MU_x}{MU_y} = \frac{P_x}{P_y}$$

or, by rearranging this equation,

$$\frac{MU_x}{P_x} = \frac{MU_y}{P_y}$$

This second expression means that the marginal utility per dollar spent on the last unit of good X equals the marginal utility per dollar spent on the last unit of good Y. For example, if $MU_x = 10$ and $P_x = \$2$, $MU_x/P_x = 5$, meaning that 1 additional dollar spent on X (which buys 1/2 of a \$2 unit of X) increases utility by five units, or 1 less dollar spent on X decreases utility by five units.

ILLUSTRATION 5.2

"We're Number One" (in *MU/P*) and That's Not Bad

In 1990, Buick advertised extensively that a survey of over 26,000 new-car buyers had revealed that Buick was the only American car line ranked in the top 10 in initial quality—according to owner-reported problems during the first 90 days. Buick featured in its ads a list of the top-10 automobiles in the survey, in which it was ranked fifth: behind Lexus, Mercedes-Benz, Toyota, and Infiniti and ahead of Honda, Nissan, Acura, BMW, and Mazda. All nine of these other car lines are Japanese or German.

In his nationally syndicated column, "High Five Is Goodbye Wave, Not the Symbol of Quality," August 23, 1990, columnist George Will somewhat berated Buick for bragging about *only* being fifth. He stated that the "We're Number One" boasts of winning college football players and their fans may be "mistaken, and the passion may be disproportionate to the achievement, but at least it is better than chanting 'We're Number Five.'"

Mr. Will noted that such ads imply, "Don't expect us to measure up to the big boys—the ones overseas." He wanted Americans to become "impatient and censorious about lax standards (We're Number 5) that are producing pandemic shoddiness in everything rom cars to art to second graders' homework." Mr. Will ended his column: "Americans would feel better, and might be more inclined to buy Buick, if they saw an ad reprinting the list above, but with a text that says: 'Fifth place is not nearly good enough for Americans to brag about. And until we do better, we apologize!'"

Mr. Will may well have been correct that many U.S. firms were not producing products up to the quality standards of many foreign firms. We want to point out, however, that his criticism of Buick's boast of being number five as indicative of shoddy American quality may not have been quite valid. In fact, it may be great to be "Number Five."

The annual auto issue of *Consumer Reports*, April 1990, gave the following list prices of the top-10 automobile lines for their medium-size models, the category of most Buick models:

1. Lexus $35,000
2. Mercedes-Benz $48,000 (avg.)
3. Toyota $21,500
4. Infiniti $38,000

To see why marginal utilities per dollar spent must be equal for the last unit consumed of both goods, suppose the condition did not hold and

$$\frac{MU_x}{P_x} < \frac{MU_y}{P_y}$$

The marginal utility per dollar spent on good X is less than the marginal utility per dollar spent on Y. The consumer can take dollars away from X and spend them on Y. As long as the inequality holds, the lost utility from each dollar taken away from X is less than the added utility from each additional dollar spent on Y, and the consumer continues to substitute Y for X. As the consumption of X decreases, we would expect the marginal utility of X to rise. As Y increases, its marginal utility would decline. The consumer continues substituting until MU_x/P_x equals MU_y/P_y.

A simple numerical example should make this concept more concrete: Suppose a customer with an income of $140 is spending it all on 20 units of X priced at $4 each and 30 units of Y priced at $2 each: ($4 \times 20) + ($2 \times 30) = $140. Further suppose

5. Buick $15,000 (avg.)
6. Honda $14,500 (compact)
7. Nissan $18,000
8. Acura $26,000
9. BMW $37,000 (avg.)
10. Mazda $25,000

Buick was priced lower than all the other cars except the Honda Accord, a compact car listed because Honda did not produce a medium-size car. This Honda, which was ranked below Buick, was only $500 less than Buick despite being a smaller car. All the other models were priced higher, some more than double. Of the cars ranked above Buick, Toyota's price was 40 percent higher, and the prices of the other three were two to three times Buick's price.

Following the approach used in the theory of consumer behavior, consider the quality-per-dollar cost of a car:

$$\frac{\text{Quality of the brand}}{\text{Price of the brand}}$$

For the top-ranked automobile, Lexus, to have more quality per dollar, that is,

$$\frac{\text{Quality of Lexus}}{\text{Price of Lexus}} > \frac{\text{Quality of Buick}}{\text{Price of Buick}}$$

Lexus would have to have 2 1/3 more or better quality than Buick, because its price was 2 1/3 higher. Mercedes-Benz would have to have 3.2 times the quality of Buick; Infiniti, 2.5 times the quality; and Toyota, 1.4 times Buick's quality. Because the cars ranked 7 through 10 were higher priced and ranked lower in quality, they could not have more quality per dollar. Since Buick's price was only 3 percent higher than Honda's, Buick would have to have only a bit more than 3 percent more quality to be ranked higher in quality per dollar.

Based on a measure of quality per dollar of cost, Buick could easily have been ranked higher than fifth. Quite possibly, it was really number one, and should not have been disparaged. Perhaps Buick should not have apologized in its ads as suggested but, instead, should have said, "We're Number One (or maybe Number Two) in quality per dollar."

Source: George Will, "High Five Is Goodbye Wave, Not the Symbol of Quality," *The San Diego Tribune*, Aug. 23, 1990, p. B-11.

that the marginal utility of the last unit of X is 20 and the marginal utility of the last unit of Y is 16. The ratio of marginal utilities per dollar spent on X and Y is

$$\frac{MU_x}{P_x} = \frac{20}{4} = 5 < 8 = \frac{16}{2} = \frac{MU_y}{P_y}$$

The consumer should reallocate spending on X and Y because it is possible to increase utility while still spending only $140. To see how this can be done, let the consumer spend one more dollar on Y. Buying another dollar's worth of good Y causes utility to increase by 8 units.[4] In order to stay within the $140 budget, the

---

[4]Even though one extra dollar of expenditure on Y allows the consumer to purchase only half a unit of Y, and producers may be willing to sell only integer amounts (i.e., you can't buy half a burger at most fast-food restaurants), Y is in fact measuring the *rate* of consumption of good Y per unit of time and can include fractional units. If, for example, 12 burgers are consumed weekly, the number of burgers consumed daily is a fraction—1.71 (= 12/7) burgers per day.

consumer must also reduce spending on good X by one dollar. Spending $1 less on good X causes utility to fall by 5 units. Since the consumer loses 5 units of utility from reduced consumption of good X but gains 8 units of utility from the increased consumption of good Y, the consumer experiences a net gain in utility of 3 units while still spending only $140. Note that it is not marginal utility per se that matters; it is marginal utility per dollar. In this example, the marginal utility of X was higher than that of Y. But the consumer is made better off by giving up some X and buying more Y.

The consumer should continue transferring dollars from X to Y as long as $MU_x/P_x < MU_y/P_y$. Because MU_x increases as less X is purchased and MU_y decreases as more Y is purchased, the consumer will achieve utility maximization when $MU_x/P_x = MU_y/P_y$, and no further changes should be made.

Alternatively, if

$$\frac{MU_x}{P_x} > \frac{MU_y}{P_y}$$

the marginal utility per dollar spent on X is greater than the marginal utility per dollar spent on Y. The consumer takes dollars away from Y and buys additional X, continuing to substitute until the equality holds.

□ **Principle** To obtain maximum satisfaction from a limited money income, a consumer allocates money income so that the marginal utility per dollar spent on each good is the same for all commodities purchased, and all income is spent.

Thus far, for graphical purposes, we have assumed that the consumer purchases only two goods. The analysis is easily extended, although not graphically, to any number of goods. Since the above equilibrium conditions must apply to *any* two goods in a consumer's consumption bundle, they must apply to all goods in the bundle. Therefore, if a consumer purchases N goods, $X_1, X_2, X_3, \ldots, X_N$ with prices $P_1, P_2, P_3, \ldots, P_N$ from a given income M, utility maximization requires

$$P_1X_1 + P_2X_2 + P_3X_3 + \cdots + P_NX_N = M$$

and

$$-\frac{\Delta X_i}{\Delta X_j} = MRS = \frac{P_j}{P_i}$$

for any two goods, X_i and X_j. Alternatively, in terms of marginal utilities per dollar spent,

$$\frac{MU_1}{P_1} = \frac{MU_2}{P_2} = \frac{MU_3}{P_3} = \cdots = \frac{MU_N}{P_N}$$

In this way the maximization principle is expanded to cover any number of goods.

Before ending this section, we should note that we have assumed thus far that a consumer purchases some positive amount of each good considered. We have not analyzed why someone chooses not to buy any amount of some goods. This can be easily shown within the framework of the theory. Suppose that in the previous discussion all income is spent on goods 1 through N but the consumer chooses to purchase zero units of some good, Z. Then it must be the case that the marginal utility per dollar that would have been spent on the *first* unit of Z is less than the marginal utility per dollar spent on the last unit of all the other goods purchased:

$$\frac{MU_Z}{P_Z} < \frac{MU_1}{P_1} = \frac{MU_2}{P_2} = \cdots = \frac{MU_N}{P_N}$$

The first unit of good Z was not worth taking dollars away from the goods that are purchased. Perhaps if the price of Z goes down, this person might choose to buy some.

Finding the Optimal Bundle of Hot Dogs and Cokes

The following numerical example will illustrate the points made in this section. Suppose your boss decides that you have been working too hard and gives you the rest of the day off and a ticket to the afternoon baseball game. After getting seated at the stadium, you discover that you have only $40, and the concessionaire won't take American Express (or Visa, for that matter). Hot dogs and Cokes are the only snack items you plan to consume while at the game, but it's a hot day, you missed lunch, and $40 is not going to be enough money to buy all the Cokes and hot dogs you would want to consume. The only rational thing to do is to maximize your utility subject to your $40 budget constraint.

On the back of your baseball program you make a list of the marginal utility you expect to receive from various levels of hot dog and Coke consumption. You then divide the marginal utilities by the prices of hot dogs and Cokes, $5 and $4, respectively. The back of your baseball program looks like the table below.

Units per game	Marginal utility of hot dogs (MU_H)	$\dfrac{MU_H}{P_H}$	Marginal utility of Cokes (MU_C)	$\dfrac{MU_C}{P_C}$
1	40	8	120	30
2	30	6	80	20
3	25	5	40	10
4	20	4	32	8
5	15	3	16	4
6	10	2	8	2

Using this information, you can now figure out how to get the most satisfaction from consuming hot dogs and Cokes, given your budget constraint. Should you buy a Coke or a hot dog first? The first unit of Coke increases total utility by 30 units for each dollar spent (on the first Coke), while the first hot dog increases total utility by only 8 units per dollar spent (on the first hot dog). You buy the first Coke and have $36 left. After finishing the first Coke, you consider whether to buy the first hot dog or the second Coke. Since 8 (= MU_H/P_H) < 20 (= MU_C/P_C), you buy the second Coke and have $32 left. Using similar reasoning, you buy the third Coke.

The fourth Coke and the first hot dog both increase total utility by 8 units per dollar spent. You buy both of them and note that the marginal utilities per dollar spent both equal 8. This is not yet optimal, however, because you have spent only $21 (1 hot dog and 4 Cokes). You continue using marginal analysis until you end up buying 4 hot dogs and 5 Cokes, at which $MU_H/P_H = 4 = MU_C/P_C$. You have spent the entire $40 on the 4 hot dogs and 5 Cokes. No other combination of Cokes and hot dogs that you could have purchased for $40 would have yielded more total utility.

5.5 INDIVIDUAL CONSUMER AND MARKET DEMAND CURVES

Of major interest to a manager is how consumer choice or consumer behavior relates to the demand for a product. We can now use the theory of consumer utility maximization to derive a demand curve for an individual consumer and, by aggregating individual demand curves, we can derive market demand curves. In this way we will provide a complete analysis of the underpinnings of demand, which were briefly discussed in Chapter 2. Recall from Chapter 2 that demand was defined as the quantity of a good the consumer is willing and able to purchase at each price in a list of prices, holding other things constant. You have just seen that consumers maximize utility when the rate at which they are *willing* to substitute one good for another just equals the rate at which they are *able* to substitute. It would seem, therefore, that the two theories are closely related, and they are. The theory of demand can be easily developed from the theory of consumer behavior.

An Individual Consumer's Demand Curve

We can use Figure 5.8 to show how an individual consumer's demand curve is obtained. Begin with a money income of $1,000 and prices of good X and good Y both equal to $10. The corresponding budget line is given by budget line 1, from 100Y to 100X, in the upper panel of the figure. From the previous analysis, you know the consumer maximizes utility where budget line 1 is tangent to indifference curve I, consuming 50 units of X. Thus when income is $1,000, one point on this consumer's demand for X is $10 and 50 units of X. This point is illustrated on the price–quantity graph in the lower panel of Figure 5.8.

Following the definition of demand, we hold money income and the price of the other good Y constant, while letting the price of X fall from $10 to $8. The new budget line is the less steep budget line 2. Since money income and the price of Y remain constant, the vertical intercept does not change, but because the price of X has fallen, the budget line must pivot outward along the X-axis. The new X-intercept for budget line 2 is 125 (= $1,000/$8). With this new budget line, the consumer now maximizes utility where budget line 2 is tangent to indifference curve

FIGURE 5.8

Deriving a Demand Curve

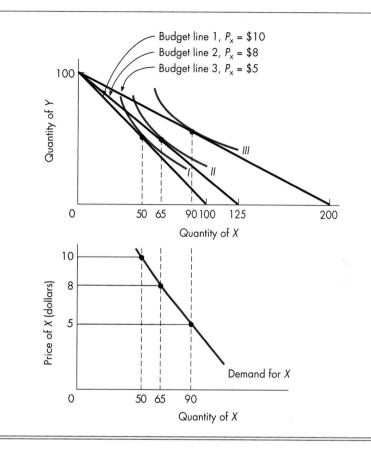

II, consuming 65 units of X. Thus another point on the demand schedule in the lower panel must be $8 and 65 units of X.

Next, letting the price of X fall again, this time to $5, the new budget line is budget line 3, from 100 to 200. Again the price of Y and money income are held constant. The new utility-maximizing combination of X and Y is on indifference curve III. At the price $5, the consumer chooses 90 units of X, another point on this consumer's demand curve.

Thus we have derived the following demand schedule for good X:

Price	Quantity demanded
$10	50
8	65
5	90

This schedule, with other points so generated, is graphed as a demand curve in price–quantity space in the lower part of Figure 5.8. This demand curve is downward-sloping. As the price of X falls, the quantity of X the consumer is willing and able to purchase increases, following the rule of demand. Furthermore, we followed the definition of demand, holding money income and the price of the other good (goods) constant. Thus an individual's demand for a good is derived from a series of utility-maximizing points. We used only three such points, but we could easily have used more in order to obtain more points on the demand curve. We can summarize this section with the following:

Principle The demand curve of an individual for a specific commodity relates utility-maximizing quantities purchased to market prices, holding constant money income and the prices of all other goods. The slope of the demand curve illustrates the law of demand: Quantity demanded varies inversely with price.

Market Demand Curves

market demand
A list of prices and the quantities consumers are willing and able to purchase at each price in the list, other things being held constant.

Managerial decision makers are typically more interested in the market demand for a product than in the demand of an individual consumer. Nonetheless, the behavior of individual consumers in the market determines market demand. Recall that in Chapter 2 we defined **market demand** as a list of prices and the corresponding quantity consumers are willing and able to purchase at each price in the list, holding constant money income, the prices of other goods, tastes, price expectations, and the number of consumers. When deriving individual demand in this chapter, we pivoted the budget line around the vertical intercept, therefore holding income and the prices of other goods constant. Since the indifference curves remained constant, tastes were unchanged.

Thus the discussion here conforms to the conditions of market demand. To obtain the market demand function, we need only to aggregate the individual demand functions of all potential customers in the market. We now demonstrate this aggregation.

Suppose there are only three individuals in the market for a particular commodity. In Table 5.1, the quantities demanded by each consumer at each price in column 1 are shown in columns 2, 3, and 4. Column 5 shows the sum of these quantities demanded at each price and is therefore the market demand. Since the demand for each consumer is negatively sloped, market demand is negatively sloped also. Quantity demanded is inversely related to price.

TABLE 5.1
Aggregating Individual Demands

| Price | Quantity demanded | | | Market demand |
	Consumer 1	Consumer 2	Consumer 3	
$6	3	0	0	3
5	5	1	0	6
4	8	3	1	12
3	10	5	4	19
2	12	7	6	25
1	13	10	8	31

FIGURE 5.9

Derivation of Market Demand

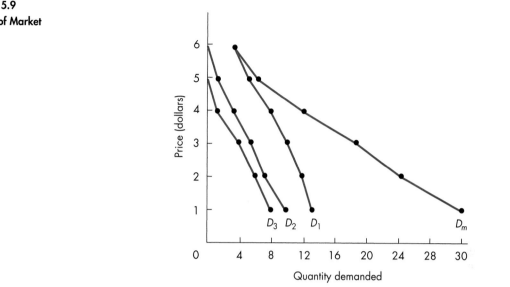

Figure 5.9 shows graphically how a market demand curve can be derived from the individual demand curves. The individual demands of consumers 1, 2, and 3 from Table 5.1 are shown graphically as D_1, D_2, and D_3, respectively. The market demand curve D_m is simply the sum of the quantities demanded at each price. At $6, consumer 1 demands 3 units. Since the others demand nothing, 3 is the quantity demanded by the market. At every other price, D_m is the horizontal summation of the quantities demanded by the 3 consumers. And if other consumers came into the market, their demand curves would be added to D_m to obtain the new market demand.

□ **Relation**   The market demand curve is the horizontal summation of the demand curves of all consumers in the market. It therefore shows how much all consumers demand at each price over the relevant range of prices.

5.6 SUBSTITUTION AND INCOME EFFECTS

As emphasized in Chapter 2, when the price of a good decreases, consumers tend to substitute more of that good for other goods, since the good in question has become cheaper relative to other goods. Conversely, when the price of a good rises, it becomes more expensive relative to other goods, and consumers tend to substitute some additional amounts of the other goods for some of the good with the now higher price. This is called the *substitution effect*.

There is also another effect, called the *income effect*. If a good becomes cheaper, people who are consuming that good are made better off. Since the price of that good has fallen, people can consume the same amount as before, but because of

FIGURE 5.10
The Substitution Effect

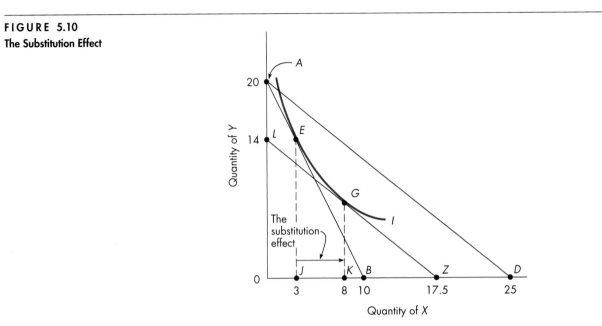

the reduced price, they have some income left over that can be spent on the good with the now lower price and on other goods as well. The opposite happens when the price of a good increases. Consumers are worse off in the sense that they now cannot afford the bundle they originally chose. They must consume less of the now more expensive good, less of the other good, or less of both.

Substitution Effect

substitution effect
The change in the consumption of a good that would result if the consumer remained on the same indifference curve after the price of the good changed.

We begin the analysis of the substitution effect with a precise definition. The **substitution effect** is the change in the consumption of a good that would result if the consumer remained on the original indifference curve after the price of the good changes.

We develop the substitution effect formally in Figure 5.10. Begin with the original budget line *AB*, which corresponds to money income of $150, $P_y = \$7.50$, and $P_x = \$15$. The consumer is originally in equilibrium where budget line *AB* is tangent to indifference curve *I* at 3 units of *X* (point *E*). Now let the price of *X* decrease to $6 so that the new budget line pivots outward to *AD*, because $150/$6 = 25.

The consumer, being better off because more choices are now available, can move to an indifference curve higher than *I*. But the substitution effect concerns changes along the *same* indifference curve. To this end, we theoretically take away just enough of the consumer's income to force a new budget line, with the same slope as *AD* to reflect the lower price of *X*, to become tangent to the original indifference curve *I*. This is shown as the parallel shift of the budget line *AD* to the adjusted budget line LZ. It is important to note that the slope of LZ, 4/5 (= \$6/\$7.50), reflects the new, lower price of X, but is associated with a lower money income than is the original budget line AB. Since budget line LZ is tangent to indifference curve I at point G, the consumer now chooses to purchase 8 units of X. Note that the consumer's adjustment from point E to point G, which takes place along the original indifference curve I, is a theoretically conceived (or hypothetical) adjustment in consumption. It is the change in the optimal consumption that would occur when the price of X relative to the price of Y falls from 2 (= 15/7.50) to 0.8 (= 6/7.50) *and* the consumer is forced by a *hypothetical* reduction in income to remain on the same indifference curve.

The substitution effect is shown as the distance JK (5 additional units of X), resulting from the movement along I from E to G. It is clear that this effect is negative—a decrease in price must result in an increase in consumption of the good when utility is held constant. This must always be the case, given the shape of indifference curves. When the price of X falls from \$15 to \$6, the budget line becomes flatter; so the budget line, after taking away some income, must be tangent to the original indifference curve at a point with a less steep slope (MRS) than was the case at the original equilibrium. This can occur only with increased consumption of X.

▣ **Principle**   The substitution effect is the change in the consumption of a good after a change in its price, when the consumer is forced by a change in money income to consume at some point on the original indifference curve. Considering the substitution effect only, the amount of the good consumed must vary inversely with its price.

Income Effect

income effect
The change in the consumption of a good resulting strictly from a change in purchasing power after the price of a good changes.

The direction of the income effect is not unambiguous, as was the case for the substitution effect. Before we analyze the income effect, let us define it. The **income effect** from a price change is the change in the consumption of a good resulting strictly from the change in purchasing power.

We noted earlier that a decrease in the price of a good makes a consumer of that good better off in the sense of being able to purchase the same bundle of goods and have income left over; that is, the consumer can move to a higher indifference curve. An increase in the price of a good makes a consumer worse off because he or she is unable to purchase the original bundle; that is, the consumer must move to a lower indifference curve. Since the consumer moves to a higher or lower indifference curve, depending upon the direction of the price change, and the substitution effect takes place along the original indifference curve, the income effect is simply the difference between the total effect of the price change—the movement from one indifference curve to another—and the substitution effect.

Figure 5.11 illustrates how to isolate the substitution and income effects for a decrease in the price of X. First consider (in Panel A) the case of a normal good. The consumer initially faces the budget line AB (M = \$150, P_x = \$15, and P_y = \$7.50), and maximizes utility subject to budget line AB at point E on indifference curve I. Let the price of X fall from \$15 to \$6, so that the budget line pivots to AD.

FIGURE 5.11

Income and Substitution Effects: A Decrease in P_x

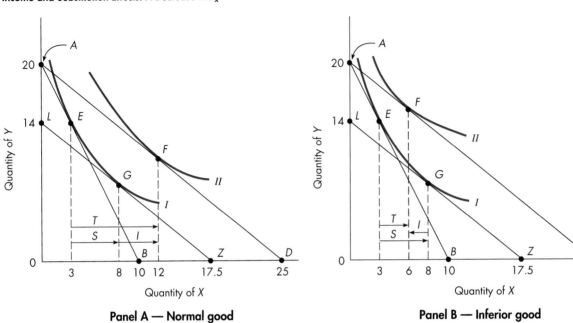

Panel A — Normal good

Panel B — Inferior good

The new equilibrium is at point F on indifference curve II. The total effect of the price decrease is an increase in the consumption of X from 3 units to 12.

As explained earlier, the substitution effect is the change in consumption of X that would result if the consumer remained on the same indifference curve after the change in price. At the new price ratio $P_x/P_y = \$6/\$7.50 = 0.8$, we again temporarily take away just enough income to keep the consumer on the original indifference curve. This reduction in income causes the budget line to shift downward to LZ. In this example, income must be reduced to $105 (= \$7.50 \times 14 = \$6 \times 17.5$) to isolate the substitution effect. On the adjusted budget line LZ, $MRS = P_x/P_y$ at point G. The substitution effect of the price *reduction* is an *increase* in consumption of X by 5 units. For the substitution effect alone, the price and consumption of X move in opposite directions.

Recall from Chapter 2 that consumption of a normal good increases when income increases, prices held constant. This is exactly what happens when the hypothetical reduction in income is restored and the budget line shifts from LZ back to AD. When the income that was hypothetically taken away to isolate the substitution effect is returned, the consumer increases the consumption of X by 4 units. You can see in Panel A that good X is a normal good because the increase in income from $105 to $150 ($LZ$ to AD) causes consumption of X to increase from 8 to 12.

When the price of X *falls*, both the substitution effect and the income effect cause the consumer to purchase *more* of the good: The income effect reinforces the substitution effect. Both of these effects cause consumption of X to move in the opposite direction of the change in price. The **total effect** of the decrease in price is equal to the sum of the substitution and income effects:

total effect
The sum of the substitution and income effects.

$$\text{Total effect of} \atop \text{price decrease} = \text{Substitution} \atop \text{effect} + \text{Income} \atop \text{effect}$$
$$9 = 5 \qquad + 4$$

The situation is different for an inferior good. Recall from Chapter 2 that if a good is inferior, an increase in income (holding prices constant) causes less of the good to be consumed. The case of an inferior good is illustrated in Panel B of Figure 5.11. Begin, as before, with budget line AB. Equilibrium is at E on indifference curve I with 3 units of X being consumed. Let the price of X fall from $15 to $6, which causes the budget line to pivot outward to AD. The new equilibrium is at F on indifference curve II, with 6 units of X being consumed. The total effect of the price decrease is an increase of 3 units in the consumption of X.

In Panel B, the substitution effect is isolated in exactly the same way as in Panel A and is again equal to 5 units of X. Note that the substitution effect is greater than the total effect. It is apparent that the income effect has partially offset the substitution effect. This will always be true for inferior goods because the income effect for inferior goods moves in the opposite direction from the substitution effect. When the budget line moves back to AD from LZ, the increase in income causes the consumption of X to *fall* from 8 to 6 units of X, and thus the income effect is −2 units of X. The total effect of the decrease in the price of X is

$$\text{Total effect of} \atop \text{price decrease} = \text{Substitution} \atop \text{effect} + \text{Income} \atop \text{effect}$$
$$3 = 5 \qquad + (-2)$$

Figure 5.12 shows the substitution, income, and total effects for an increase in the price of good X. Panel A illustrates the case of a normal good. The initial budget line is AR (M = $60, P_x = $2.40, and P_y = $4), and the consumer initially maximizes utility at point E on indifference curve II. When the price of X increases from $2.40 to $6, the budget line pivots to AS and the new equilibrium is at point F on indifference curve I. The substitution effect is isolated by temporarily increasing income to $84 (the adjusted budget line is LZ). The substitution effect of the price *increase* is a *reduction* in the consumption of X by 5 units. When income is returned to $60, the adjusted budget line shifts back to AS, and the consumer reduces consumption by 2 more units of X. The total effect of the increase in price is

$$\text{Total effect of} \atop \text{price increase} = \text{Substitution} \atop \text{effect} + \text{Income} \atop \text{effect}$$
$$-7 = -5 \qquad + (-2)$$

FIGURE 5.12
Income and Substitution Effects: An Increase in P_x

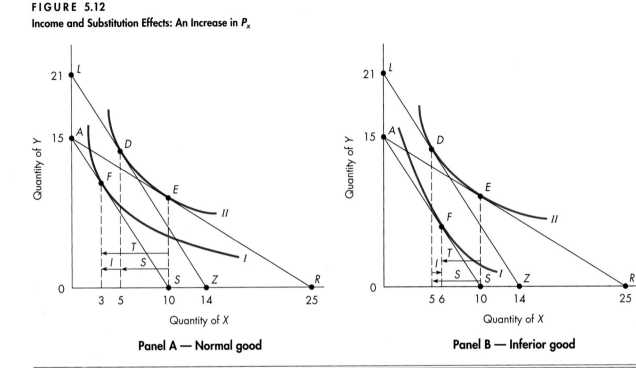

Panel A — Normal good

Panel B — Inferior good

Note that the income and substitution effects reinforce each other since X is a normal good.

In Panel B, good X is inferior. The substitution effect is the same as in Panel A, but now the income effect partially offsets the substitution effect. When the budget line shifts backward from LZ to AS, income falls from \$84 to \$60, and consumption of the inferior good X increases from 5 to 6 units. The total effect of the increase in price is

$$\begin{matrix} \text{Total effect of} \\ \text{price increase} \end{matrix} = \begin{matrix} \text{Substitution} \\ \text{effect} \end{matrix} + \begin{matrix} \text{Income} \\ \text{effect} \end{matrix}$$

$$-4 = -5 \qquad +1$$

Because X is inferior in Panel B, the substitution and income effects move in opposite directions. These effects are summarized in Table 5.2 and the following relation:

□ **Relation** Considering the substitution effect alone, an increase (decrease) in the price of a good causes less (more) of the good to be demanded. For a normal good, the income effect—from the consumer's being made better or worse off by the price change—adds to or reinforces the substitution effect. The income effect in the case of an inferior good offsets or takes away from the substitution effect.

TABLE 5.2

Summary of Substitution and Income Effects for a Change in the Price of X

	Substitution effect	Income effect
Price of X decreases:		
Normal good	X rises	X rises
Inferior good	X rises	X falls
Price of X increases:		
Normal good	X falls	X falls
Inferior good	X falls	X rises

Why Demand Slopes Downward

In the case of a normal good, it is clear why price and quantity demanded are negatively related along demand. From the substitution effect alone, a decrease in price is accompanied by an increase in quantity demanded. (An increase in price decreases quantity demanded.) For a normal good, the income effect must add to the substitution effect. Since both effects move quantity demanded in the same direction, demand must be negatively sloped.

In the case of an inferior good, the income effect does not move in the same direction, and to some extent it offsets the substitution effect. However, looking at Panel B in Figures 5.11 and 5.12 again, you can see that the income effect only *partially* offsets the substitution effect, so quantity demanded still varies inversely with price. This is generally the case: Even if the commodity is inferior, the substitution effect almost always dominates the income effect and the demand curve still slopes downward.

It is *theoretically* possible that the income effect for an inferior good could dominate the substitution effect. In this case—the case of a so-called **Giffen good**—quantity demanded would vary directly with price and the demand curve would be upward-sloping. However, in this text, we will ignore Giffen goods. While experimental economists have suggested that a Giffen good may exist for an individual, we have as yet seen no convincing evidence of the existence of a Giffen good for a group of consumers.

Giffen good
A good for which the demand curve is upward-sloping.

5.7 SUMMARY

This chapter has provided the theoretical underpinnings for demand analysis. We began with the assumption that consumers can rank various bundles of goods as to whether they prefer one bundle to another or are indifferent between the two. We then constructed an indifference curve showing all combinations of two commodities among which a consumer is indifferent. The collection of all indifference curves—the consumer's indifference map—shows what the consumer is willing to purchase.

On a more technical level, we discussed why the marginal rate of substitution diminishes as more of good X is consumed and why the slope of the indifference curve—the marginal rate of substitution—is equal to the ratio of the marginal utilities of the two commodities:

$$MRS = MU_x/MU_y$$

The consumers' budget line determines what the consumer is able to consume. The budget line is a straight line with a slope equal to the ratio of the prices of the two commodities:

$$Y = (M/P_y) - (P_x/P_y)X$$

As income changes, the budget line shifts. As price changes, the budget line rotates.

The consumer maximizes utility subject to the constraint of a limited income by consuming that combination of the two commodities at which the budget line is tangent to an indifference curve. At that point, the slope of the budget line is equal to the slope of the highest attainable indifference curve, so the maximization condition can be expressed as

$$MRS = MU_x/MU_y = P_x/P_y$$

or

$$\frac{MU_x}{P_x} = \frac{MU_y}{P_y}$$

An individual consumer's demand curve can be derived by holding income and the prices of all other commodities constant and then altering the price of one commodity and observing how the constrained utility-maximizing consumption of that commodity changes. Price changes have two effects: a substitution effect and an income effect. The substitution effect of a price change upon the consumption of a good is always negative; that is, quantity demanded varies inversely with price, holding utility constant and considering the substitution effect only. If the good is normal, the income effect reinforces the substitution effect. If the good is inferior, the income effect offsets to some extent the substitution effect.

The market demand curve is the horizontal summation of the demand curves of all consumers in the market. It shows how much all consumers demand at each price in the relevant range of prices.

TECHNICAL PROBLEMS

1. Answer the following questions about consumer preferences:

   a. If Julie prefers Diet Coke to Diet Pepsi and Diet Pepsi to regular Pepsi but is indifferent between Diet Coke and Classic Coke, what are her preferences between Classic Coke and regular Pepsi?

   b. If James purchases a Ford Mustang rather than a Ferrari, what are his preferences between the two cars?

   c. If Julie purchases a Ferrari rather than a Ford Mustang, what are her preferences between the two cars?

   d. James and Jane are having a soft drink together. Coke and Pepsi are the same price. If James orders a Pepsi and Jane orders a Coke, what are the preferences of each between the two colas?

2. Suppose that two units of X and eight units of Y give a consumer the same utility as four units of X and two units of Y. Over this range:

   a. If the consumer obtains one more unit of X, how many units of Y must be given up in order to keep utility constant?

   b. If the consumer obtains one more unit of Y, how many units of X must be given up in order to keep utility constant?

   c. What is the marginal rate of substitution?

3. Use the graph (page 197) of a consumer's indifference curve to answer the questions:

   a. What is the MRS between A and B?

   b. What is the MRS between B and C?

   c. What is the MRS at B?

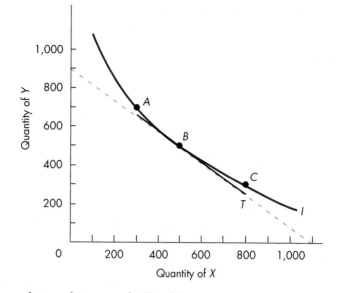

4. A consumer buys only two goods, X and Y.
   a. If the MRS between X and Y is 2 and the marginal utility of X is 20, what is the marginal utility of Y?
   b. If the MRS between X and Y is 3 and the marginal utility of Y is 3, what is the marginal utility of X?
   c. If a consumer moves downward along an indifference curve, what happens to the marginal utilities of X and Y? What happens to the MRS?

5. Use the figure below to answer the following questions:

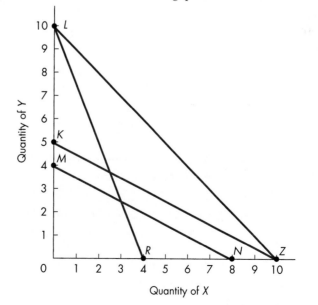

a. The equation of budget line LZ is $Y = $ _____ $-$ _____ X.
b. The equation of budget line LR is $Y = $ _____ $-$ _____ X.
c. The equation of budget line KZ is $Y = $ _____ $-$ _____ X.
d. The equation of budget line MN is $Y = $ _____ $-$ _____ X.
e. If the relevant budget line is LR and the consumer's income is $200, what are the prices of X and Y? At the same income, if the budget line is LZ, what are the prices of X and Y?
f. If the budget line is MN, $P_y = 40, and $P_x = 20, what is income? At the same prices, if the budget line is KZ, what is income?

6. Suppose a consumer has the indifference map shown below. The relevant budget line is LZ. The price of good Y is $10.

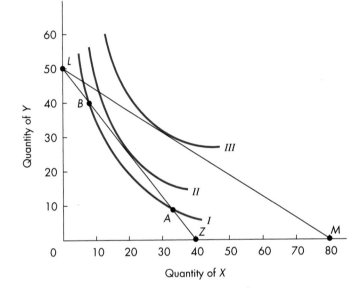

a. What is the consumer's income?
b. What is the price of X?
c. Write the equation for the budget line LZ.
d. What combination of X and Y will the consumer choose? Why?
e. What is the marginal rate of substitution at this combination?
f. Explain in terms of the MRS why the consumer would not choose combinations designated by A or B.
g. Suppose the budget line pivots to LM, money income remaining constant. What is the new price of X? What combination of X and Y is now chosen?
h. What is the new MRS?

7. Suppose that the marginal rate of substitution is 2, the price of X is $3, and the price of Y is $1.
a. If the consumer obtains 1 more unit of X, how many units of Y must be given up in order to keep utility constant?

b. If the consumer obtains 1 more unit of *Y*, how many units of *X* must be given up in order to keep utility constant?

c. What is the rate at which the consumer is *willing* to substitute *X* for *Y*?

d. What is the rate at which the consumer is *able* to substitute *X* for *Y*?

e. Is the consumer making the utility-maximizing choice? Why or why not? If not, what should the consumer do? Explain.

8. The following graph shows a portion of a consumer's indifference map. The consumer faces the budget line *LZ*, and the price of *X* is $20.

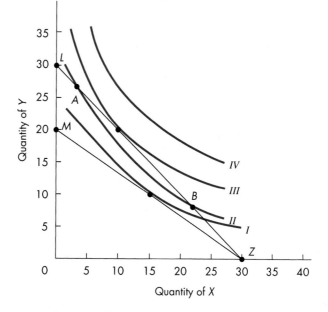

a. The consumer's income = $_____.

b. The price of *Y* is $_____.

c. The equation for the budget line *LZ* is _____.

d. What combination of *X* and *Y* does the consumer choose? Why?

e. The marginal rate of substitution for this combination is _____.

f. Explain in terms of *MRS* why the consumer does not choose either combination *A* or *B*.

g. What combination is chosen if the budget line is *MZ*?

h. What is the price of *Y*?

i. What is the price of *X*?

j. What is the *MRS* in equilibrium?

9. Sally purchases only pasta and salad with her income of $160 a month. Each month she buys 10 pasta dinners at $6 each and 20 salads at $5 each. The marginal utility of the last unit of each is 30. What should Sally do? Explain.

10. Assume that an individual consumes three goods, X, Y, and Z. The marginal utility (assumed measurable) of each good is independent of the rate of consumption of other goods. The prices of X, Y, and Z are, respectively, $1, $3, and $5. The total income of the consumer is $65, and the marginal utility schedule is as follows:

Units of good	Marginal utility of X (units)	Marginal utility of Y (units)	Marginal utility of Z (units)
1	12	60	70
2	11	55	60
3	10	48	50
4	9	40	40
5	8	32	30
6	7	24	25
7	6	21	18
8	5	18	10
9	4	15	3
10	3	12	1

a. Given a $65 income, how much of each good should the consumer purchase to maximize utility?

b. Suppose income falls to $43 with the same set of prices; what combination will the consumer choose?

c. Let income fall to $38; let the price of X rise to $5 while the prices of Y and Z remain at $3 and $5. How does the consumer allocate income now? What would you say if the consumer maintained that X is not purchased because he or she could no longer afford it?

11. The following graph shows a portion of a consumer's indifference map and three budget lines. The consumer has an income of $1,000.

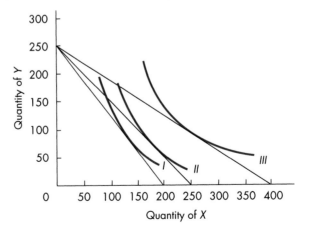

What is the price of Y? What are three price–quantity combinations on this consumer's demand curve?

12. Suppose there are only 3 consumers in the market for good X. The quantities demanded by each consumer at each price between $1 and $9 are shown in the following table:

Price of X	Quantity demanded			Market demand
	Consumer 1	Consumer 2	Consumer 3	
$9	0	5	10	_____
8	0	10	20	_____
7	10	15	30	_____
6	20	20	40	_____
5	30	25	50	_____
4	40	30	60	_____
3	50	35	70	_____
2	60	40	80	_____
1	70	45	90	_____

a. Using the following axes, draw the demand curve for each of the 3 consumers. Label the three curves D_1, D_2, and D_3, respectively.

b. Fill in the blanks in the table for the market quantity demanded at each price.

c. Construct the market demand curve in the graph, and label it D_m.

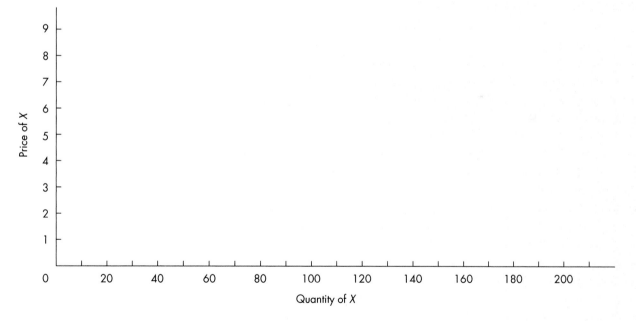

13. In the following graph the consumer begins in equilibrium with an income of $2,000, facing prices of $P_x = \$5$ and $P_y = \$10$.

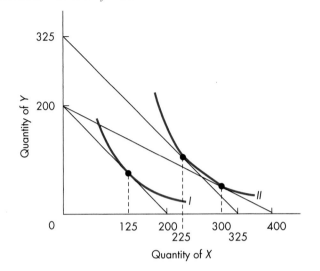

a. In equilibrium, _____ units of X are consumed.

Now let the price of X rise to $10.

b. In the new equilibrium, _____ units of X are consumed.

c. In order to isolate the substitution effect, $_____ must be given to the consumer.

d. The total effect of the price increase is _____. The substitution effect is _____. The income effect is _____.

e. Good X is a _____ good.

14. In the following graph the consumer begins in equilibrium with an income of $5,000, facing the prices $P_x = \$50$ and $P_y = \$25$.

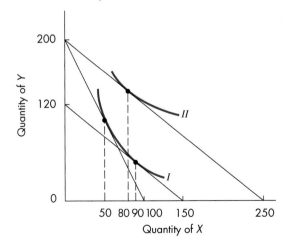

a. In equilibrium, _____ units of X are consumed.

Now let the price of X fall to $20, income and the price of Y remaining constant.

b. In the new equilibrium, _____ units of X are consumed.

c. In order to isolate the substitution effect, $_____ must be taken away from the consumer.

d. The total effect of the price decrease is _____. The substitution effect is _____. The income effect is _____.

APPLIED PROBLEMS

1. Gigi has a limited income and consumes only wine and cheese; her current consumption choice is four bottles of wine and 10 pounds of cheese. The price of wine is $10 per bottle, and the price of cheese is $4 per pound. The last bottle of wine added 50 units to Gigi's utility, while the last pound of cheese added 40 units.

   a. Is Gigi making the utility-maximizing choice? Why or why not?

   b. If not, what should she do instead? Why?

2. Suppose Bill is on a low-carbohydrate diet. He can eat only three foods: Rice Krispies, cottage cheese, and popcorn. The marginal utilities for each food are tabulated below. Bill is allowed only 167 grams of carbohydrates daily. Rice Krispies, cottage cheese, and popcorn provide 25, 6, and 10 grams of carbohydrates per cup, respectively. Referring to the accompanying table, respond to the following questions:

Units of food (cups/day)	Marginal utility of Rice Krispies	Marginal utility of cottage cheese	Marginal utility of popcorn
1	175	72	90
2	150	66	80
3	125	60	70
4	100	54	60
5	75	48	50
6	50	36	40
7	25	30	30
8	25	18	20

   a. Given that Bill can consume only 167 grams of carbohydrates daily, how many cups of each food will he consume daily? Show your work.

   b. Suppose Bill's doctor tells him to further reduce his carbohydrate intake to 126 grams per day. What combination will he consume?

3. Increasingly, employees are being allowed to choose benefit packages from a menu of items. For instance, workers may be given a package of benefits that includes basic and optional items. Basics might include modest medical coverage, life insurance equal to a year's salary, vacation time based on length of service, and some retirement pay. But then employees can use credits to choose among such additional benefits as full medical coverage, dental and eye care, more vacation time, additional disability income, and higher company payments to the retirement fund. How do you think flexible benefit packages would affect an employee's choice between higher wages and more benefits?

4. Have you ever made mistakes such as the following: studying too long for a test that turned out to be easy, not studying long enough for a test that turned out to be extremely hard, agreeing to go on a blind date that turned out to be miserable, buying a package of cookies that were so bad you threw most of them away, and not buying enough potato chips and soft drinks for a party? Does the possibility that people make mistakes necessarily contradict or negate the theory of consumer behavior? Discuss.

5. The owner–manager of Good Guys Enterprises obtains utility from income (profit) and from having the firm behave in a socially conscious manner, such as making charitable contributions or civic expenditures. Can you set up the problem and derive the optimization conditions if the owner–manager wishes to obtain a specific level of utility at the lowest possible cost? Do these conditions differ from the utility-maximizing conditions?

6. After Iraq invaded Kuwait, gasoline prices rose dramatically—up to 50 percent. There were many effects of the increased price of gasoline. Explain the following effects in terms of the income effect, or the substitution effect, or both effects:

   a. People drove less and purchased less gas.

   b. People ate out less often.

   c. People had more tune-ups done on their cars.

   d. Bike sales went up.

   e. The sale of lottery tickets fell.

   f. People took vacations closer to home.

7. In terms of the consumer theory set forth in this chapter, can you explain the meaning of the following statements?

   a. "I think you get more for your money from Nike than from Reebok."

   b. "I wanted to buy an RX-7 rather than a Mazda 626, but it just wasn't worth it."

   c. "I'd like to go to Mexico over spring break, but I just can't afford it," said Don. Jill asked, "Don't you have enough money in your account?" Don replied, "Yeah, but I can't afford to go."

   d. "I'll have to flip a coin to decide whether to buy chocolate chip or vanilla fudge ice cream."

8. On April 23, 1991, the Air Force awarded a $93 billion (or more) contract to a group led by Lockheed, Boeing, and General Dynamics to build the new fighter plane for the 21st century, the YF-22 Lightning 2. A group headed by Northrop and McDonnell Douglas, which had spent more than $1 billion on development for their alternative YF-23, lost out on the contract. That evening on CNN's *Crossfire*, the Secretary of Defense explained that the Lockheed group got the contract because their "quality for the price per plane was higher." He didn't elaborate. In terms of the theory set forth in this chapter, did he mean

   a. The Lockheed quality was higher?

   b. The Lockheed price was lower?

   If neither, what did he mean?

☐ **MATHEMATICAL APPENDIX**   **A Brief Presentation of Consumer Theory**

This appendix provides a mathematical analysis of the theory of consumer behavior and the derivation of demand functions from a consumer's utility-maximization conditions. The analytical tools required are the fundamentals of constrained maximization.

The Relation between the Marginal Rate of Substitution and Marginal Utility

A consumer has a general utility function with two goods of

$$U = U(X, Y)$$

The marginal utilities are defined as

$$MU_x = \partial U/\partial X \quad \text{and} \quad MU_y = \partial U/\partial Y$$

The marginal rate of substitution (*MRS*), showing the rate at which the consumer is willing to substitute one good for the other while holding utility constant, is

$$MRS = -dY/dX$$

The minus sign is included to keep *MRS* positive since $dY/dX < 0$ along an indifference curve.

To derive the relation between *MRS* and marginal utilities, take the total differential of the utility function and set $dU = 0$ to hold utility constant along a given indifference curve:

(1) $$dU = \frac{\partial U}{\partial X} + \frac{\partial U}{\partial Y} dY = 0$$

Solving equation (1) for $MRS = -dY/dX$,

$$MRS = -\frac{\partial Y}{\partial X} = \frac{\partial U/\partial X}{\partial U/\partial Y} = \frac{MU_x}{MU_y}$$

Since MU_x decreases and MU_y increases as X increases and Y decreases when moving downward along an indifference curve, the indifference curve is convex; that is, $-d^2Y/dX^2 < 0$.

Utility Maximization Subject to an Income Constraint: The General Case

We now derive mathematically the consumer's utility-maximizing conditions, set forth graphically and algebraically in the text, using the tools of differential calculus.

The consumer maximizes utility

$$U = U(X, Y)$$

subject to an income (budget) constraint

$$M = P_x X + P_y Y$$

The Lagrangian function to be maximized is

$$\mathcal{L} = U(X, Y) + \lambda(M - P_x X - P_y Y)$$

where P_x and P_y are the prices of goods X and Y, M is income, and λ is the Lagrangian multiplier. Maximization of the function with respect to the levels of X and Y requires the following first-order conditions:

(2a) $$\frac{\partial \mathcal{L}}{\partial X} = \frac{\partial U}{\partial X} - \lambda P_x = 0$$

(2b) $$\frac{\partial \mathcal{L}}{\partial Y} = \frac{\partial U}{\partial Y} - \lambda P_y = 0$$

Setting $\partial \mathcal{L}/\partial \lambda$ equal to zero forces the budget constraint to be met:

(3) $$M - P_x X - P_y Y = 0$$

Combining equations (2a) and (2b), the necessary conditions for maximizing utility subject to the budget constraint are

(4) $$\frac{\partial U/\partial X}{\partial U/\partial Y} = P_x/P_y$$

Note that $\partial U/\partial X$ and $\partial U/\partial Y$ are the marginal utilities of the two goods; their ratio is the marginal rate of substitution. The ratio P_x/P_y is the absolute value of the slope of the budget line. Hence, the necessary condition for income-constrained utility maximization is that the marginal rate of substitution between the two commodities be equal to the ratio of their prices. That is, from equation (4),

$$\frac{\partial U/\partial X}{\partial U/\partial Y} = \frac{MU_x}{MU_y} = \frac{P_x}{P_y}$$

or

(5) $$\frac{MU_x}{P_x} = \frac{MU_y}{P_y}$$

The marginal utilities per dollar spent on the last units of X and Y are equal.

Derivation of the Consumer's Demand Function

The optimization conditions shown in equations (2) and (3) form a system of three equations that can be solved for the optimal values of λ^*, X^*, and Y^* in terms of the parameters M, P_x, and P_y. The demand functions from this solution are

$$X^* = X^*(M, P_x, P_y)$$

(6)   and

$$Y^* = Y^*(M, P_x, P_y)$$

These demands are functions of the good's own price, the price of the related good, and income, as discussed in this chapter and in Chapter 2. To conform to the law of demand,

$$\frac{\partial X^*}{\partial P_x} < 0 \quad \text{and} \quad \frac{\partial Y^*}{\partial P_y} < 0$$

The derivatives $\dfrac{\partial X^*}{\partial P_x}$, $\dfrac{\partial X^*}{\partial M}$, $\dfrac{\partial Y^*}{\partial P_y}$, and $\dfrac{\partial Y^*}{\partial M}$ can be of any sign, although $\dfrac{\partial X^*}{\partial M}$ and $\dfrac{\partial Y^*}{\partial M}$ cannot both be negative. That is, both goods cannot be inferior because more income would lead to less expenditure, which violates the assumptions of consumer theory.

The price elasticities of demand in equilibrium are

$$E_x = \frac{\partial X^*}{\partial P_x} \times \frac{P_x}{X^*} \quad \text{and} \quad E_y = \frac{\partial Y^*}{\partial P_y} \times \frac{P_y}{Y^*}$$

Derivation of Demand from a Specific Utility Function

We now assume a consumer with the simple utility function

$$U = U(X, Y) = XY$$

As above, the income constraint is

$$M = P_x X + P_y Y$$

so that the Lagrangian to be maximized is

$$\mathcal{L} = U(X, Y) + \lambda(M - P_x X - P_y Y)$$

The first-order maximization conditions are

(7a)
$$\frac{\partial \mathcal{L}}{\partial X} = Y - \lambda P_x = 0$$

(7b)
$$\frac{\partial \mathcal{L}}{\partial Y} = X - \lambda P_y = 0$$

and

(8)
$$M - P_x X - P_y Y = 0$$

Thus from equations (7a) and (7b):

(9)
$$\frac{MU_x}{MU_y} = \frac{Y}{X} = \frac{P_x}{P_y}$$

Solving (9) for Y,

(10)
$$Y = \left(\frac{P_x}{P_y}\right) X$$

then, using (8) to solve for X in terms of Y, equation (10) is

$$Y = \frac{P_x}{P_y}\left(\frac{M}{P_x} - \frac{P_y}{P_x} Y\right) = \frac{M}{P_x} - Y$$

or

(11)
$$Y^* = \frac{M}{2P_y}$$

Similarly, using (10) and substituting into the budget constraint,

$$X = \frac{P_y}{P_x} Y = \frac{P_y}{P_x}\left(\frac{M}{P_y} - \frac{P_x}{P_y} X\right)$$

Thus

(12)
$$X^* = \frac{M}{2P_x}$$

Equations (11) and (12) are the demand functions for goods Y and X. These demands are both negatively sloped because

$$\frac{\partial Y^*}{\partial P_y} = -\frac{M}{2P_y^2} \quad \text{and} \quad \frac{\partial X^*}{\partial P_x} = -\frac{M}{2P_x^2}$$

The two goods are normal because

$$\frac{\partial Y^*}{\partial M} = \frac{1}{2P_y} \quad \text{and} \quad \frac{\partial X^*}{\partial M} = \frac{1}{2P_x}$$

Both $\partial Y^*/P_x$ and $\partial X^*/P_y$ equal zero, so the two goods are independent. With this specific form of the utility function, the consumer spends half of the income on good X [$P_x X^* = (1/2)M$] and half on Y [$P_y Y^* = (1/2)M$] regardless of the level of income and the price of the other good.

Since the same amount is spent on each good at any price of that good, the price elasticity of each is unitary. This can be verified as follows:

$$E_x = \frac{\partial X^*}{\partial P_x} \frac{P_x}{X^*} = -\frac{M}{2P_x^2} \frac{P_x}{X^*} = -\frac{M}{2P_x^2} \frac{P_x}{(M/2P_x)} = -1$$

and

$$E_y = \frac{\partial Y^*}{\partial P_y} \frac{P_x}{Y^*} = -\frac{M}{2P_y^2} \frac{P_y}{Y^*} = -\frac{M}{2P_y^2} \frac{P_y}{(M/2P_y)} = -1$$

MATHEMATICAL EXERCISES

1. Assume a consumer with the utility function

$$U = U(X, Y) = X^2 Y^2$$

and the typical budget constraint

$$M = P_x X + P_y Y$$

   a. Set up the constrained maximization problem and derive the first-order conditions.
   b. Derive the consumer's demand for X and Y in terms of the parameters.
   c. Derive the own-price elasticities of demand. Do the demand functions obey the law of demand?

2. To demonstrate that a utility function that is a monotonic transformation of another utility function gives the same first-order conditions and hence the same demand functions, multiply the utility function $U = U(X, Y)$ by a constant term, k, and show that the two yield the same first-order conditions.

3. Assume a consumer with the utility function

$$U = U(X, Y) = (X + 2)(Y + 1)$$

and the budget constraint

$$M = P_x X + P_y Y$$

   a. Set up the constrained maximization problem, and derive the first-order conditions.
   b. Derive the demand for X and Y.
   c. Derive the price elasticities of demand. Do the demands obey the law of demand?
   d. Are the products substitutes or complements?

4. Demonstrate that if income and both prices change by exactly the same proportions, this does not change the optimization conditions and therefore the equilibrium quantities of the two goods do not change.

CHAPTER
6

Elasticity and Demand

Most managers agree that the toughest decision they face is the decision to raise or lower the price of their firms' products. When Walt Disney Company decided to raise ticket prices at its theme parks in Anaheim, California, and Orlando, Florida, the price hike caused attendance at the Disney parks to fall. The price increase was a success, however, because it boosted Disney's revenue: the price of a ticket multiplied by the number of tickets sold.[1] For Disney, the higher ticket price more than offset the smaller number of tickets purchased, and revenue increased. You might be surprised to learn that price increases do not always increase a firm's revenue. For example, suppose just one gasoline producer, ExxonMobil, were to increase the price of its brand of gasoline while rival gasoline producers left their gasoline prices unchanged. ExxonMobil would likely experience falling revenue, even though it increased its price, because many ExxonMobil customers would switch to one of the many other brands of gasoline. In this situation, the reduced amount of gasoline sold would more than offset the higher price of gasoline, and ExxonMobil would find its revenue falling.

When managers *lower* price to attract more buyers, revenues may either rise or fall, again depending upon how responsive consumers are to a price reduction. For example, in an unsuccessful marketing strategy, called "Campaign 55," McDonald's Corporation lowered the price of its Big Mac and Quarter Pounders to 55 cents in an effort to increase revenue. The price reduction resulted in *lower* revenue, and

---

[1]See Stacy Kravetz, "Disney's Earnings, Boosted by Park, Top Expectations," *The Wall Street Journal*, July 23, 1997, p. B5.

McDonald's abandoned the low-price strategy for all but its breakfast meals—lower prices did increase breakfast revenues.[2] Obviously, managers need to know how a price increase or decrease is going to affect the quantity sold and the revenue of the firm. In this chapter you will learn how to use the concept of price elasticity to predict how revenue will be affected by a change in the price of the product. You can easily understand why managers of price-setting firms find this chapter to be particularly useful; they can use knowledge about demand elasticities to help them make better decisions about raising or lowering prices. And, even for managers of price-taking firms (i.e., firms in competitive markets where prices are determined by the intersection of market demand and supply), knowledge of price elasticity of industry demand can help managers predict the effect of changes in market price on total industry sales and total consumer expenditures in the industry.

Managers recognize that quantity demanded and price are inversely related. When they are making pricing decisions, as you saw in the examples of Disney, ExxonMobil, and McDonald's, it is even more important for managers to know *by how much* sales will change for a given change in price. A 10 percent decrease in price that leads to a 2 percent increase in quantity demanded differs greatly in effect from a 10 percent decrease in price that causes a 50 percent increase in quantity demanded. There is a substantial difference in the effect on total revenue to the firm between these two responses to a change in price. Certainly, when making pricing decisions, managers should have a good idea about how responsive consumers will be to any price changes and whether revenues will rise or fall.

The majority of this chapter is devoted to the concept of *price elasticity of demand*, a measure of the responsiveness of quantity demanded to a change in price along a demand curve and an indicator of the effect of a price change on total consumer expenditure on a product. The concept of price elasticity provides managers, economists, and policymakers with a framework for understanding why consumers in some markets are extremely responsive to changes in price while consumers in other markets are not. This understanding is useful in many types of managerial decisions. As noted, demand elasticity is so crucial to managerial decision making that we have devoted most of this chapter to examining this concept.

We will begin by defining the price elasticity of demand and then show how to use price elasticities to find the percentage changes in price or quantity that result from movements along a demand curve. Next, the relation between elasticity and the total revenue received by firms from the sale of a product is examined in detail. Then we discuss three factors that determine the degree of responsiveness of consumers, and hence the price elasticity of demand. We also show how to compute the elasticity of demand either over an interval or at a point on demand. Then we examine the concept of marginal revenue and demonstrate the relation among demand, marginal revenue, and elasticity. The last section of this chapter introduces two other important elasticities: income and cross-price elasticities.

---

[2]See Richard Gibson, "With Egg on Its Face, McDonald's Cuts the 55-Cent Specials to Breakfast Only," *The Wall Street Journal,* June 4, 1997, p. B7.

6.1 THE PRICE ELASTICITY OF DEMAND

As noted above, price elasticity of demand measures the responsiveness or sensitivity of consumers to changes in the price of a good or service. We will begin this section by presenting a formal (mathematical) definition of price elasticity and then show how price elasticity can be used to predict the change in sales when price rises or falls or to predict the percentage reduction in price needed to stimulate sales by a given percentage amount.

Consumer responsiveness to a price change is measured by the **price elasticity of demand (E)**, defined as

price elasticity of demand (E)
The percentage change in quantity demanded, divided by the percentage change in price. E is always a negative number because P and Q are inversely related.

$$E = \frac{\%\Delta Q}{\%\Delta P} = \frac{\text{Percentage change in quantity demanded}}{\text{Percentage change in price}}$$

Since price and quantity demanded are inversely related by the law of demand, the numerator and denominator always have opposite algebraic signs, and the price elasticity is always negative. The price elasticity is calculated for movements along a given demand curve (or function) as price changes and all other factors affecting quantity demanded are held constant. Suppose a 10 percent price decrease ($\%\Delta P = -10\%$) causes consumers to increase their purchases by 30 percent ($\%\Delta Q = +30\%$). The price elasticity is equal to -3 ($= +30\%/-10\%$) in this case. In contrast, if the 10 percent decrease in price causes only a 5 percent increase in sales, the price elasticity would equal -0.5 ($= +5\%/-10\%$). Clearly, the smaller (absolute) value of E indicates less sensitivity on the part of consumers to a change in price.

When a change in price causes consumers to respond so strongly that the percentage by which they adjust their consumption (in absolute value) *exceeds* the percentage change in price (in absolute value), demand is said to be **elastic** over that price interval. In mathematical terms, demand is elastic when $|\%\Delta Q|$ exceeds $|\%\Delta P|$, and thus $|E|$ is greater than 1. When a change in price causes consumers to respond so weakly that the percentage by which they adjust their consumption (in absolute value) is *less than* the percentage change in price (in absolute value), demand is said to be **inelastic** over that price interval. In other words, demand is inelastic when the numerator (in absolute value) is smaller than the denominator (in absolute value), and thus $|E|$ is less than 1. In the special instance in which the percentage change in quantity (in absolute value) *just equals* the percentage change in price (in absolute value), demand is said to be **unitary elastic,** and $|E|$ is equal to 1. Table 6.1 summarizes this discussion.

elastic
Segment of demand for which $|E| > 1$.

inelastic
Segment of demand for which $|E| < 1$.

unitary elastic
Segment of demand for which $|E| = 1$.

TABLE 6.1

Price Elasticity of Demand (E)

$$E = \frac{\%\Delta Q}{\%\Delta P}$$

Elasticity	Responsiveness	$|E|$
Elastic	$|\%\Delta Q| > |\%\Delta P|$	$|E| > 1$
Unitary elastic	$|\%\Delta Q| = |\%\Delta P|$	$|E| = 1$
Inelastic	$|\%\Delta Q| < |\%\Delta P|$	$|E| < 1$

Note: The symbol "| |" denotes the absolute value.

Predicting the Percentage Change in Quantity Demanded

Suppose a manager knows the price elasticity of demand for a company's product is equal to -2.5 over the range of prices currently being considered by the firm's marketing department. The manager is considering decreasing price by 8 percent and wishes to predict the percentage by which quantity demanded will increase. From the definition of price elasticity, it follows that

$$-2.5 = \frac{\%\Delta Q}{-8\%}$$

so, with a bit of algebraic manipulation, $\%\Delta Q = +20\%$ ($= -2.5 \times -8\%$). Thus the manager can increase sales by 20 percent by lowering price 8 percent. As we mentioned in the introduction, price elasticity information about industry demand can also help price-taking managers make predictions about industry- or market-level changes. For example, suppose an increase in industry supply is expected to cause market price to fall by 8 percent, and the price elasticity of *industry* demand is equal to -2.5 for the segment of demand over which supply shifts. Using the same algebraic steps just shown, total industry output is predicted to increase by 20 percent in this case.

Predicting the Percentage Change in Price

Suppose a manager of a different firm faces a price elasticity equal to -0.5 over the range of prices the firm would consider charging for its product. This manager wishes to stimulate sales by 15 percent. The manager is willing to lower price to accomplish the increase in sales but needs to know the percentage amount by which price must be lowered to obtain the 15 percent increase in sales. Again using the definition of price elasticity of demand, it follows that

$$-0.5 = \frac{+15\%}{\%\Delta P}$$

so, after some algebraic manipulation, $\%\Delta P = -30\%$ ($= 15\%/-0.5$). Thus this manager must lower price by 30 percent in order to increase sales by 15 percent. As we explained in the case of predicting percentage changes in quantity demanded, elasticity of industry demand can also be used to make predictions about changes in market-determined prices. For example, suppose an increase in industry supply is expected to cause market output to rise by 15 percent, and the price elasticity of *industry* demand is equal to -0.5 for the portion of demand over which supply shifts. Following the algebraic steps shown above, market price is predicted to fall by 30 percent. As you can see, the techniques for predicting percentage changes in quantity demanded and price can be applied to both individual firm demand curves or industry demand curves.

As you can see, the concept of elasticity is rather simple. Price elasticity is nothing more than a mathematical measure of how sensitive quantity demanded is to changes in price. We will now apply the concept of price elasticity to a crucial question facing managers. How does a change in the price of the firm's product affect the total revenue received?

6.2 PRICE ELASTICITY AND TOTAL REVENUE

total revenue (TR)
The total amount paid to producers for a good or service (TR = P × Q).

Managers of firms, as well as industry analysts, government policymakers, and academic researchers, are frequently interested in how total revenue changes when there is a movement along the demand curve. **Total revenue (TR),** which also equals the total expenditure by consumers on the commodity, is simply the price of the commodity times quantity demanded, or

$$TR = P \times Q$$

As we have emphasized, price and quantity demanded move in opposite directions along a demand curve: If price rises, quantity falls; if price falls, quantity rises. The change in price and the change in quantity have opposite effects on total revenue. The relative strengths of these two effects will determine the overall effect on *TR*. We will now examine these two effects, called the price effect and the quantity effect, along with the price elasticity of demand to establish the relation between changes in price and total revenue.

Price Elasticity and Changes in Total Revenue

price effect
The effect on total revenue of changing price, holding output constant.

When a manager raises the price of a product, the increase in price, by itself, would increase total revenue if the quantity sold remained constant. Conversely, when a manager lowers price, the decrease in price would decrease total revenue if the quantity sold remained constant. This effect on total revenue of changing price, for a given level of output, is called the **price effect.** When price changes, the quantity sold does not remain constant; it moves in the opposite direction of price. When quantity increases in response to a decrease in price, the increase in quantity, by itself, would increase total revenue if the price of the product remained constant. Alternatively, when quantity falls after a price increase, the reduction in quantity, by itself, would decrease total revenue if product price remained constant. The effect on total revenue of changing the quantity sold, for a given price level, is called the **quantity effect.** The price and quantity effects always push total revenue in opposite directions. Total revenue moves in the direction of the stronger of the two effects. If the two effects are equally strong, no change in total revenue can occur.

quantity effect
The effect on total revenue of changing output, holding price constant.

Suppose a manager increases price, causing quantity to decrease. The price effect, represented below by an upward arrow above *P*, and the quantity effect, represented by a downward arrow above *Q*, show how the change in *TR* is affected by opposing forces:

$$\overset{\uparrow}{TR} = \overset{\uparrow}{P} \times \overset{\downarrow}{Q}$$

To determine the direction of movement in *TR*, information about the relative strengths of the price effect and output effect must be known. The elasticity of demand tells a manager which effect, if either, is dominant.

If demand is elastic, $|E|$ is greater than one, the percentage change in Q (in absolute value) is greater than the percentage change in P (in absolute value), and the quantity effect dominates the price effect. To better see how the dominance of the quantity effect determines the direction in which TR moves, you can represent the dominance of the quantity effect by drawing the arrow above Q longer than the arrow above P. The direction of the dominant effect—the quantity effect here—tells a manager that TR will fall when price rises and demand is elastic:

$$\downarrow \quad \uparrow \quad \downarrow$$
$$TR = P \times Q$$

If a manager *decreases* price when demand is elastic, the arrows in this diagram reverse directions. The arrow above Q is still the longer arrow since the quantity effect always dominates the price effect when demand is elastic.

Now consider a price increase when demand is *inelastic*. When demand is inelastic, $|E|$ is less than one, the percentage change in Q (in absolute value) is less than the percentage change in P (in absolute value), and the price effect dominates the quantity effect. The dominant price effect can be represented by an upward arrow above P that is longer than the downward arrow above Q. The direction of the dominant effect tells the manager that TR will rise when price rises and demand is inelastic:

$$\uparrow \quad \uparrow \quad \downarrow$$
$$TR = P \times Q$$

When a manager decreases price and demand is inelastic, the arrows in this diagram would reverse directions. A downward arrow above P would be a long arrow since the price effect always dominates the quantity effect when demand is inelastic.

When demand is unitary elastic, $|E|$ is equal to one, and neither the price effect nor the quantity effect dominates. The two effects exactly offset each other, so price changes have no effect on total revenue when demand is unitary elastic.

☐ **Relation**   The effect of a change in price on total revenue ($TR = P \times Q$) is determined by the price elasticity of demand. When demand is elastic (inelastic), the quantity (price) effect dominates. Total revenue always moves in the same direction as the variable (P or Q) having the dominant effect. When demand is unitary elastic, neither effect dominates, and changes in price leave total revenue unchanged.

Table 6.2 on the following page summarizes the relation between price changes and revenue changes under the three price elasticity conditions.

Changing Price at Borderline Music Emporium: A Numerical Example

The manager at Borderline Music Emporium faces the demand curve for compact discs shown in Figure 6.1 on page 215. At the current price of $18 per compact disc, Borderline can sell 600 CDs each week. The manager can lower price to $16 per compact disc and increase sales to 800 CDs per week. In Panel A of Figure 6.1, over

TABLE 6.2		Elastic $\lvert \%\Delta Q \rvert > \lvert \%\Delta P \rvert$ Q-effect dominates	Unitary elastic $\lvert \%\Delta Q \rvert = \lvert \%\Delta P \rvert$ No dominant effect	Inelastic $\lvert \%\Delta Q \rvert < \lvert \%\Delta P \rvert$ P-effect dominates
Relations between Price Elasticity and Total Revenue (TR)	Price rises	TR falls	No change in TR	TR rises
	Price falls	TR rises	No change in TR	TR falls

the interval a to b on demand curve D the price elasticity is equal to -2.43. (You will learn how to make this calculation in Section 6.4 of this chapter.) Since the demand for compact discs is elastic over this range of prices ($\lvert -2.43 \rvert > 1$), the manager knows the quantity effect dominates the price effect. Lowering price from \$18 to \$16 results in an increase in the quantity of CDs sold, so the manager knows that total revenue, which always moves in the direction of the dominant effect, must increase.

To verify that revenue indeed rises when the manager at Borderline lowers the price over an elastic region of demand, you can calculate total revenue at the two prices, \$18 and \$16:

$$\text{Point } a: TR = \$18 \times 600 = \$10{,}800$$

$$\text{Point } b: TR = \$16 \times 800 = \$12{,}800$$

Total revenue rises by \$2,000 (= 12,800 − 10,800) when price is reduced over this elastic region of demand. While Borderline earns less revenue on each CD sold, the number of CDs sold each week rises enough to more than offset the downward price effect, causing total revenue to rise.

Now suppose the manager at Borderline is charging just \$9 per compact disc and sells 1,500 CDs per week (see Panel B). The manager can lower price to \$7 per disc and increase sales to 1,700 CDs per week. Over the interval c to d on demand curve D, the elasticity of demand equals -0.50. Over this range of prices for CDs, the demand is inelastic ($\lvert -0.50 \rvert < 1$), and Borderline's manager knows the price effect dominates the quantity effect. If the manager lowers price from \$9 to \$7, total revenue, which always moves in the direction of the dominant effect, must decrease.

To verify that revenue falls when the manager at Borderline lowers price over an inelastic region of demand, you can calculate total revenue at the two prices, \$9 and \$7:

$$\text{Point } c: TR = \$9 \times 1{,}500 = \$13{,}500$$

$$\text{Point } d: TR = \$7 \times 1{,}700 = \$11{,}900$$

Total revenue falls by \$1,600 ($\Delta TR = \$11{,}900 - \$13{,}500 = -\$1{,}600$). Total revenue always falls when price is reduced over an inelastic region of demand. Borderline again earns less revenue on each CD sold, but the number of CDs sold each week does not increase enough to offset the downward price effect and total revenue falls.

If the manager decreases (or increases) the price of compact discs over a unitary-elastic region of demand, total revenue does not change. You should verify that demand is unitary elastic over the interval f to g in Panel A of Figure 6.1.

FIGURE 6.1
Changes in Total Revenue of Borderline Music Emporium

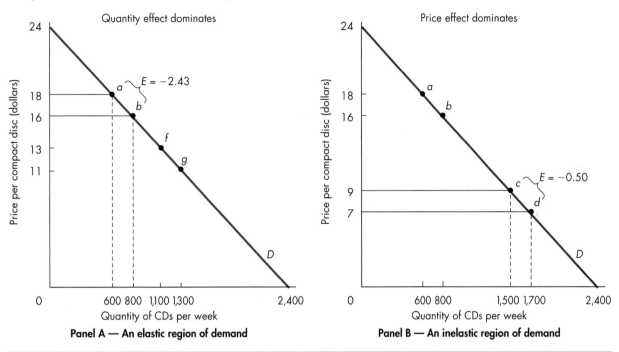

Panel A — An elastic region of demand

Panel B — An inelastic region of demand

Note in Figure 6.1 that demand is elastic over the $16 to $18 price range but inelastic over the $7 to $9 price range. In general, the elasticity of demand varies along any particular demand curve, even one that is linear. It is usually incorrect to say a demand curve is either elastic or inelastic. You can say only that a demand curve is elastic or inelastic over a particular price range. For example, it is correct to say that demand curve D in Figure 6.1 is elastic over the $16 to $18 price range and inelastic over the $7 to $9 price range.

6.3 FACTORS AFFECTING PRICE ELASTICITY OF DEMAND

Price elasticity of demand plays such an important role in business decision making that managers should understand not only how to use the concept to obtain information about the demand for the products they sell but also how to recognize the factors that affect price elasticity. We will now discuss the three factors that make the demand for some products more elastic than the demand for other products.

Availability of Substitutes

The availability of substitutes is by far the most important determinant of price elasticity of demand. The better the substitutes for a given good or service, the more elastic the demand for that good or service. When the price of a good rises, consumers will substantially reduce consumption of that good if they perceive that close substitutes are readily available. Naturally, consumers will be less responsive to a price increase if they perceive that only poor substitutes are available.

Some goods for which demand is rather elastic include fruit, corporate jets, and life insurance. Alternatively, goods for which consumers perceive few or no good substitutes have low price elasticities of demand. Wheat, salt, and gasoline tend to have low price elasticities because there are only poor substitutes available—for instance, corn, pepper, and diesel fuel, respectively.

The definition of the market for a good greatly affects the number of substitutes and thus the good's price elasticity of demand. For example, if all the grocery stores in a city raised the price of milk by 50 cents per gallon, total sales of milk would undoubtedly fall—but probably not by much. If, on the other hand, only the Food King chain of stores raised price by 50 cents, the sales of Food King milk would probably fall substantially. There are many good substitutes for Food King milk, but there are not nearly as many substitutes for milk in general.

Percentage of Consumer's Budget

The percentage of the consumer's budget that is spent on the commodity is also important in the determination of price elasticity. All other things equal, we would expect the price elasticity to be directly related to the percentage of consumers' budgets spent on the good. For example, the demand for refrigerators is probably more price elastic than the demand for toasters, because the expenditure required to purchase a refrigerator would make up a larger percentage of the budget of a "typical" consumer.

Time Period of Adjustment

The length of the time period used in measuring the price elasticity affects the magnitude of price elasticity. In general, the longer the time period of measurement, the larger (the more elastic) the price elasticity will be (in absolute value). This relation is the result of consumers' having more time to adjust to the price change.

Consider, again, the way consumers would adjust to an increase in the price of milk. Suppose the dairy farmers' association is able to convince all producers of milk nationwide to raise their milk prices by 15 percent. During the first week the price increase takes effect, consumers come to the stores with their grocery lists already made up. Shoppers notice the higher price of milk but have already planned their meals for the week. While a few of the shoppers will react immediately to the higher milk prices and reduce the amount of milk they purchase, many shoppers will go ahead and buy the same amount of milk as they purchased the week before. If the dairy association collects sales data and measures the price elasticity of demand for milk after the first week of the price hike, they will be happy to see that the 15 percent increase in the price of milk caused only a modest reduction in milk sales.

Over the coming weeks, however, consumers begin looking for ways to consume less milk. They substitute foods that have similar nutritional composition to milk; consumption of cheese, eggs, and yogurt all increase. Some consumers will even switch to powdered milk for some of their less urgent milk needs—perhaps to feed the cat or to use in cooking. Six months after the price increase, the dairy association again measures the price elasticity of milk. Now the price elasticity of demand is probably much larger in absolute value (more elastic) because it is measured over a six-month time period instead of a one-week time period.

For most goods and services, given a longer time period to adjust, the demand for the commodity exhibits more responsiveness to changes in price—the demand becomes more elastic. Of course, we can treat the effect of time on elasticity within the framework of the effect of available substitutes. The greater the time period available for consumer adjustment, the more substitutes become available and economically feasible. As we stressed earlier, the more available are substitutes, the more elastic is demand.

6.4 CALCULATING PRICE ELASTICITY OF DEMAND

As noted at the beginning of the chapter, the price elasticity of demand is equal to the ratio of the percentage change in quantity demanded divided by the percentage change in price. When calculating the value of E, it is convenient to avoid computing percentage changes by using a simpler formula for computing elasticity that can be obtained through the following algebraic operations:

$$E = \frac{\%\Delta Q}{\%\Delta P} = \frac{\frac{\Delta Q}{Q} \times 100}{\frac{\Delta P}{P} \times 100}$$

$$= \frac{\Delta Q}{\Delta P} \times \frac{P}{Q}$$

Thus price elasticity can be calculated by multiplying the slope of demand ($\Delta Q/\Delta P$) times the ratio of price divided by quantity (P/Q), which avoids making tedious percentage change computations. The computation of E, while involving the rather simple mathematical formula derived here, is complicated somewhat by the fact that elasticity can be measured either (1) over an interval (or arc) along demand or (2) at a specific point on the demand curve. In either case, E still measures the sensitivity of consumers to changes in the price of the commodity.

The choice of whether to measure demand elasticity at a point or over an interval of demand depends on the length of demand over which E is measured. If the change in price is relatively small, a point measure is generally suitable. Alternatively, when the price change spans a sizable arc along the demand curve, the interval measurement of elasticity provides a better measure of consumer responsiveness than the point measure. As you will see shortly, point elasticities are more easily computed than interval elasticities. We begin with a discussion of how to calculate elasticity of demand over an interval.

Computation of Elasticity over an Interval

interval (or arc) elasticity
Price elasticity calculated over an interval of a demand curve:

$$E = \frac{\Delta Q}{\Delta P} \times \frac{\text{Average } P}{\text{Average } Q}$$

When elasticity is calculated over an interval of a demand curve (either a linear or a curvilinear demand), the elasticity is called an **interval (or arc) elasticity.** To measure E over an arc or interval of demand, the simplified formula presented earlier—slope of demand multiplied times the ratio of P divided by Q—needs to be modified slightly. The modification only requires that $\Delta Q/\Delta P$ be calculated *over the interval* and that the *average values* of P and Q over the interval be used:

$$E = \frac{\Delta Q}{\Delta P} \times \frac{\text{Average } P}{\text{Average } Q}$$

Recall from our previous discussion of Figure 6.1 that we did not show you how to compute the two values of the interval elasticities given in Figure 6.1. You can now make these computations for the intervals of demand ab and cd using the above formula for interval price elasticities:

$$E_{ab} = \frac{+200}{-2} \times \frac{17}{700} = -2.43$$

$$E_{cd} = \frac{+200}{-2} \times \frac{8}{1600} = -0.5$$

T ▷ 7 ▫ **Relation** When calculating the price elasticity of demand over an interval of demand, use the interval or arc elasticity formula:

$$E = \frac{\Delta Q}{\Delta P} \cdot \frac{\text{Average } P}{\text{Average } Q}$$

Computation of Elasticity at a Point

point elasticity
A measurement of demand elasticity calculated at a point on a demand curve rather than over an interval.

As we explained previously, it is appropriate to measure elasticity at a point on a demand curve rather than over an interval when the price change covers only a small interval of demand. Elasticity computed at a point on demand is called **point elasticity** of demand. Computing the price elasticity at a point on demand is accomplished by multiplying the slope of demand ($\Delta Q/\Delta P$), computed *at the point of measure*, times the ratio P/Q, computed using the values of P and Q *at the point of measure*. To show you how this is done, we can compute the *point* elasticities in Figure 6.1 when Borderline Music Emporium charges $18 and $16 per compact disc at points a and b, respectively. Notice that the value of $\Delta Q/\Delta P$ for the linear demand in Figure 6.1 is -100 ($= +2400/-24$) at every point along D, so the two point elasticities are computed as

$$E_a = -100 \times \frac{18}{600} = -3$$

$$E_b = -100 \times \frac{16}{800} = -2$$

ILLUSTRATION 6.1

Texas Calculates Price Elasticity

In addition to its regular license plates, the state of Texas, as do other states, sells personalized or "vanity" license plates. To raise additional revenue, the state will sell a vehicle owner a license plate saying whatever the owner wants as long as it uses six letters (or numbers), no one else has the same license as the one requested, and it isn't obscene. For this service, the state charges a higher price than the price for standard licenses. Many people are willing to pay the higher price rather than display a license of the standard form such as 387 BRC.

For example, an ophthalmologist announces his practice with the license MYOPIA. Others tell their personalities with COZY-1 and ALL MAN. A rabid *Star Trek* fan has BM ME UP.

In 1986, Texas increased the price for such plates from $25 to $75. The *Houston Post* (October 19, 1986) reported that before the price increase about 150,000 cars in Texas had personalized licenses. After the increase in price, only 60,000 people ordered the vanity plates. As it turned out, demand was rather inelastic over this range. As you can calculate, the price elasticity is −0.86. Thus revenue rose after the price increase, from $3,750,000 to $4,500,000.

But the *Houston Post* article quoted the assistant director of the Texas Division of Motor Vehicles as saying, "Since the demand dropped[a] the state didn't make money from the higher fees, so the price for next year's personalized plates will be $40." If the objective of the state is to make money from these licenses and if the numbers in the article are correct, this is the wrong thing to do. It's hard to see how the state lost money by increasing the price from $25 to $75—the revenue increased and the cost of producing plates must have decreased since fewer were produced. So the move from $25 to $75 was the right move.

Moreover, let's suppose that the price elasticity between $75 and $40 is essentially the same as that calculated for the movement from $25 to $75 (−0.86). We can use this estimate to calculate what happens to revenue if the state drops the price to $40. We must first find what the new quantity demanded will be at $40. Using the arc elasticity formula and the price elasticity of −0.86,

$$E = \frac{\Delta Q}{\Delta P} \times \frac{\text{Average } P}{\text{Average } Q}$$

$$= \frac{60,000 - Q}{75 - 40} \times \frac{(75 + 40)/2}{(60,000 + Q)/2} = -0.86$$

where Q is the new quantity demanded. Solving this equation for Q, the estimated sales are 102,000 (rounded) at a price of $40. With this quantity demanded and price, total revenue would be $4,080,000, representing a decrease of $420,000 from the revenue at $75 a plate. If the state's objective is to raise revenue by selling vanity plates, it should increase rather than decrease price.

This application actually makes two points. First, even decision makers in organizations that are not run for profit, such as government agencies, should be able to use economic analysis. Second, managers whose firms are in business to make a profit should make an effort to know (or at least have a good approximation for) the elasticity of demand for the products they sell. Only with this information will they know what price to charge.

[a]It was, of course, quantity demanded that decreased, not demand.

Source: Barbara Boughton, "A License for Vanity," *Houston Post*, Oct. 19, 1986, pp. 1G, 10G.

▫ **Relation** When calculating the price elasticity of demand at a point on demand, multiply the slope of demand ($\Delta Q/\Delta P$), computed at the point of measure, times the ratio P/Q, computed using the values of P and Q at the point of measure.

We will now discuss in more detail how to calculate point price elasticities for both linear and curvilinear demand functions.

Point elasticity when demand is linear

Consider a linear demand function of three variables—price (P), income (M), and the price of a related good (P_R):

$$Q = a + bP + cM + dP_R$$

Suppose income and the price of the related good take on specific values of $\hat{M}$ and $\hat{P}_R$, respectively. Recall from Chapter 2 when values of the demand determinants (M and P_R in this case) are held constant, they become part of the constant term in demand:

$$Q = a' + bP$$

where $a' = a + c\hat{M} + d\hat{P}_R$. The slope parameter b, of course, measures the rate of change in quantity demanded per unit change in price: $b = \Delta Q / \Delta P$. Thus price elasticity at a point on a linear demand curve can be calculated as

$$E = b\frac{P}{Q}$$

where P and Q are the values of price and quantity at the point of measure.

Even though multiplying b times the ratio P/Q is rather simple, there happens to be an even easier formula for computing point price elasticities of demand. This alternative point elasticity formula equals the ratio of price at the point on demand where elasticity is to be measured (P) divided by the difference between this price and the price-intercept of demand (A):[3]

$$E = \frac{P}{P - A}$$

Note that, for the linear demand equation $Q = a' + bP$, the price intercept A is $-a'/b$. In Figure 6.1, let us apply this alternative formula to calculate again the elasticities at points a and b. In this case, the price-intercept A is \$24, so the elasticities are

$$E_a = \frac{18}{18 - 24} = -3$$

---

[3]For the case of linear demand functions, this alternative formula for computing price elasticity can be derived algebraically as follows. Let the linear demand be expressed as $Q = a' + bP$, where $a' = a + c\hat{M} + d\hat{P}_R$. The inverse of the linear demand is $P = -\dfrac{a'}{b} + \dfrac{1}{b}Q$. Now, substitute the appropriate terms into the general formula for demand elasticity:

$$E = \frac{\Delta Q}{\Delta P} \times \frac{P}{Q} = b\frac{P}{a' + bP} = \frac{b}{b}\left(\frac{bP}{a' + bP}\right) = \frac{P}{\dfrac{a'}{b} + P}$$

Now let A denote the price-intercept of demand, $A = -\dfrac{a'}{b}$, and substitute $-A = a'/b$ into the above expression to get $E = P/(P - A)$.

$$E_b = \frac{16}{16 - 24} = -2$$

The values -3 and -2 are exactly equal to the values obtained previously by multiplying the slope of demand times the ratio P/Q. We must stress that, because the two formulas $b\dfrac{P}{Q}$ and $\dfrac{P}{P - A}$ are mathematically equivalent, they always yield identical values for point price elasticities.

 Relation For linear demand functions $Q = a' + bP$, the price elasticity of demand can be computed using either of two equivalent formulas:

$$E = b\frac{P}{Q} = \frac{P}{P - A}$$

where P and Q are the values of price and quantity demanded at the point of measure on demand, and $A\ (= -a'/b)$ is the price-intercept of demand.

Point elasticity when demand is curvilinear

When demand is curvilinear, the formula $E = \dfrac{\Delta Q}{\Delta P} \times \dfrac{P}{Q}$ can be used for computing point elasticity simply by substituting the slope of the *curved* demand at the point of measure for the value of $\Delta Q/\Delta P$ in the formula. This can be accomplished by measuring the slope of the tangent line at the point of measure. Figure 6.2 illustrates this procedure.

In Figure 6.2, let us measure elasticity at a price of \$100 on demand curve D. We first construct the tangent line T at point R. By the "rise over run" method, the

---

FIGURE 6.2
Calculating Point Elasticity for Curvilinear Demand

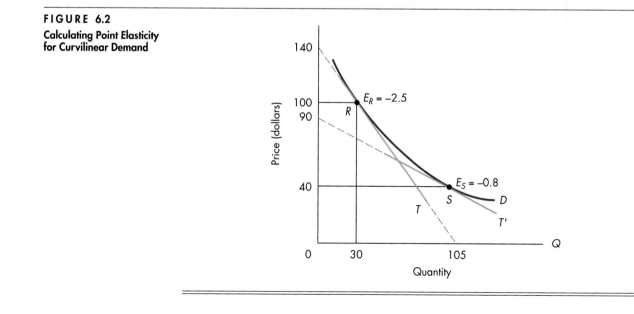

slope of T equals $-4/3$ $(= -140/105)$. Of course, because P is on the vertical axis and Q is on the horizontal axis, the slope of tangent line T gives $\Delta P/\Delta Q$ not $\Delta Q/\Delta P$. This is easily fixed by taking the inverse of the slope of tangent line T to get $\Delta Q/\Delta P = -3/4$. At point R price elasticity is calculated using $-3/4$ for the slope of demand and using $\$100$ and 30 for P and Q, respectively:

$$E_R = \frac{\Delta Q}{\Delta P} \times \frac{P}{Q} = -\frac{3}{4} \times \frac{100}{30} = -2.5$$

As it turns out, the alternative formula $E = P/(P - A)$ for computing point elasticity on *linear* demands can also be used for computing point elasticities on *curvilinear* demands. To do so, the price-intercept of the tangent line T serves as the value of A in the formula.[4] As an example, we can recalculate elasticity at point R in Figure 6.2 using the formula $E = P/(P - A)$. The price-intercept of tangent line T is $\$140$:

$$E_R = \frac{P}{P - A} = \frac{100}{100 - 140} = -2.5$$

As expected, -2.5 is the same value for E_R obtained earlier.

Because the formula $E = P/(P - A)$ doesn't require the slope of demand or the value of Q, it can be used to compute E in situations like point S in Figure 6.2 where the available information is insufficient be able to multiply slope times the P/Q ratio. Just substitute the price-intercept of T' $(= \$90)$ into the formula $E = P/(P - A)$ to get the elasticity at point S:

$$E_S = \frac{P}{P - A} = \frac{40}{40 - 90} = -0.8$$

□ **Relation** For curvilinear demand functions, the price elasticity at a point can be computed using either of two equivalent formulas:

$$E = \frac{\Delta Q}{\Delta P} \times \frac{P}{Q} = \frac{P}{P - A}$$

where $\Delta Q/\Delta P$ is the slope of the curved demand at the point of measure (which is the inverse of the slope of the tangent line at the point of measure), P and Q are the values of price and quantity demanded at the point of measure, and A is the price-intercept of the tangent line extended to cross the price-axis.

------

[4]Since P, Q, and the slope are identical at point R for the curvilinear demand D and a linear demand formed by extending tangent line T to both axes, their elasticities are identical at R. Thus it is correct to substitute the price-intercept of T for A in the formula $E = P/(P - A)$. For a formal proof of this result, as well as detailed discussion of comparing demand elasticities, see Michael Nieswiadomy, "A Note on Comparing Elasticities of Demand Curves," *Journal of Economic Education* 17 (Spring 1986), pp. 125–28.

We have now established that both formulas for computing point elasticities will give the same value for the price elasticity of demand whether demand is linear or curvilinear. Nonetheless, students frequently ask which formula is the "best" one. Because the two formulas give identical values for E, neither one is better or more accurate than the other. We should remind you, however, that you may not always have the required information to compute E both ways, so you should make sure you know both methods. (Recall the situation in Figure 6.2 at point S.) Of course, when it is possible to do so, we recommend computing the elasticity using *both* formulas to make sure your price elasticity calculation is correct!

Elasticity (Generally) Varies along a Demand Curve

In general, different intervals or points along the same demand curve have differing elasticities of demand, even when the demand curve is linear. When demand is linear, the slope of the demand curve is constant. Even though the *absolute* rate at which quantity demanded changes as price changes ($\Delta Q/\Delta P$) remains constant, the *proportional* rate of change in Q as P changes ($\%\Delta Q/\%\Delta P$) varies along a linear demand curve. To see why, we can examine the basic formula for elasticity, $E = \dfrac{\Delta Q}{\Delta P} \times \dfrac{P}{Q}$. Moving along a linear demand does not cause the term $\Delta Q/\Delta P$ to change, but elasticity does vary because the ratio P/Q changes. Moving down demand, by reducing price and selling more output, causes the term P/Q to decrease which reduces the absolute value of E. And, of course, moving up a linear demand, by increasing price and selling less output, causes P/Q and $|E|$ to increase. Thus P and $|E|$ vary directly along a *linear* demand curve.

For movements along a *curved* demand, both the slope and the ratio P/Q vary continuously along demand. For this reason, elasticity generally varies along curvilinear demands, but there is no general rule about the relation between price and elasticity as there is for linear demand.

As it turns out, there is an exception to the general rule that elasticity varies along curvilinear demands. A special kind of curvilinear demand function exists for which the demand elasticity is constant for all points on demand. When demand takes the form $Q = aP^b$, the elasticity is constant along the demand curve and equal to b.[5] Consequently, no calculation of elasticity is required, and the price elasticity is simply the value of the exponent on price, b. The absolute value of b can be greater than, less than, or equal to one, so that this form of demand can be elastic, inelastic, or unitary elastic at all points on the demand curve. As we will show you in the next chapter, this kind of demand function can be useful in statistical demand estimation and forecasting.

Figure 6.3 shows a constant elasticity of demand function, $Q = aP^b$, with the values of a and b equal to 100,000 and -1.5, respectively. Notice that price elasticity equals -1.5 at both points U and V where prices are \$20 and \$40, respectively:

---

[5]See the appendix at the end of this chapter for a mathematical proof of this result.

FIGURE 6.3
Constant Elasticity of Demand

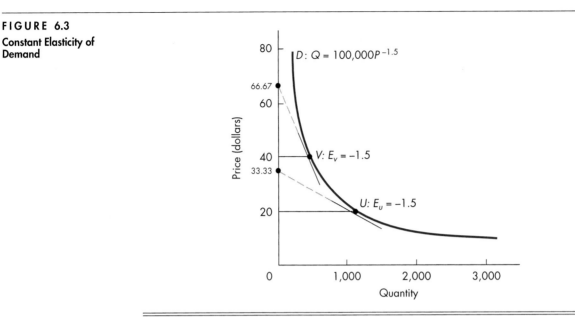

$$E_U = \frac{P}{P - A} = \frac{20}{20 - 33.33} = -1.5$$

$$E_V = \frac{P}{P - A} = \frac{40}{40 - 66.67} = -1.5$$

Clearly, you never need to compute the price elasticity of demand for this kind of demand curve since E *is* the value of the exponent on price (*b*).

▣ **Relation** In general, the price elasticity of demand varies along a demand curve. For linear demand curves, price and $|E|$ vary directly: The higher (lower) the price, the more (less) elastic is demand. For a curvilinear demand, there is no general rule about the relation between price and elasticity, except for the special case of $Q = aP^b$, which has a constant price elasticity (equal to *b*) for all prices.

T ⟩ 11

6.5 MARGINAL REVENUE, DEMAND, AND PRICE ELASTICITY

marginal revenue (MR)
The addition to total revenue attributable to selling one additional unit of output; the slope of total revenue.

The responsiveness of consumers to changes in the price of a good must be considered by managers of price-setting firms when making pricing and output decisions. The price elasticity of demand gives managers essential information about how total revenue will be affected by a change in price. As it turns out, an equally important concept for pricing and output decisions is *marginal revenue*. **Marginal revenue (MR)** is the addition to total revenue attributable to selling one additional unit of output:

$$MR = \Delta TR / \Delta Q$$

TABLE 6.3
Demand and Marginal Revenue

(1) Unit sales	(2) Price	(3) Total revenue	(4) Marginal revenue $(\Delta TR/\Delta Q)$
0	$4.50	$ 0	—
1	4.00	4.00	$4.00
2	3.50	7.00	3.00
3	3.10	9.30	2.30
4	2.80	11.20	1.90
5	2.40	12.00	0.80
6	2.00	12.00	0
7	1.50	10.50	−1.50

Because marginal revenue measures the rate of change in total revenue as quantity changes, *MR* is the slope of the *TR* curve. Marginal revenue is related to price elasticity because marginal revenue, like price elasticity, involves changes in total revenue caused by movements along a demand curve.

Marginal Revenue and Demand

As noted, marginal revenue is related to the way changes in price and output affect total revenue along a demand curve. To see the relation between marginal revenue and price, consider the following numerical example. The demand schedule for a product is presented in columns 1 and 2 of Table 6.3. Price times quantity gives the total revenue obtainable at each level of sales, shown in column 3.

Marginal revenue, shown in column 4, indicates the change in total revenue from an additional unit of sales. Note that marginal revenue equals price only for the first unit sold. For the first unit sold, total revenue is the demand price for 1 unit. The first unit sold adds $4—the price of the first unit—to total revenue, and the marginal revenue of the first unit sold equals $4; that is, *MR* = *P* for the first unit. If 2 units are sold, the second unit should contribute $3.50 (the price of the second unit) to total revenue. But total revenue for 2 units is only $7, indicating that the second unit adds only $3 (= $7 − $4) to total revenue. Thus the marginal revenue of the second unit is not equal to price, as it was for the first unit. Indeed, examining columns 2 and 4 in Table 6.3 indicates that *MR* < *P* for all but the first unit sold.

Marginal revenue is less than price (*MR* < *P*) for all but the first unit sold because price must be lowered in order to sell more units. Not only is price lowered on the marginal (additional) unit sold, but price is also lowered for all the *inframarginal units* sold. The **inframarginal units** are those units that could have been sold at a higher price had the firm not lowered price to sell the marginal unit. Marginal revenue for any output level can be expressed as

inframarginal units
Units of output that could have been sold at a higher price had a firm not lowered its price to sell the marginal unit.

$$MR = \text{Price} - \frac{\text{Revenue lost by lowering price}}{\text{on the inframarginal units}}$$

The second unit of output sells for $3.50. By itself, the second unit contributes $3.50 to total revenue. But marginal revenue is not equal to $3.50 for the second unit because in order to sell the second unit, price on the first unit is lowered from $4 to $3.50. In other words, the first unit is an inframarginal unit, and the $0.50 lost on the first unit must be subtracted from the price. The net effect on total revenue of selling the second unit is $3 (= $3.50 − $0.50), the same value as shown in column 4 of Table 6.3.

If the firm is currently selling 2 units and wishes to sell 3 units, it must lower price from $3.50 to $3.10. The third unit increases total revenue by its price, $3.10. In order to sell the third unit, the firm must lower price on the 2 units that could have been sold for $3.50 if only 2 units were offered for sale. The revenue lost on the 2 inframarginal units is $0.80 (= $0.40 × 2). Thus the marginal revenue of the third unit is $2.30 (= $3.10 − $0.80), and marginal revenue is less than the price of the third unit.

It is now easy to see why $P = MR$ for the first unit sold. For the first unit sold, price is not lowered on any inframarginal units. Since price must fall in order to sell additional units, marginal revenue must be less than price at every other level of sales (output).

As shown in column 4, marginal revenue declines for each additional unit sold. Notice that it is positive for each of the first 5 units sold. However, marginal revenue is 0 for the sixth unit sold, and it becomes negative thereafter. That is, the seventh unit sold actually causes total revenue to decline. Marginal revenue is positive when the effect of lowering price on the inframarginal units is less than the revenue contributed by the added sales at the lower price. Marginal revenue is negative when the effect of lowering price on the inframarginal units is greater than the revenue contributed by the added sales at the lower price.

Relation   Marginal revenue must be less than price for all units sold after the first, because the price must be lowered in order to sell more units. When marginal revenue is positive, total revenue increases when quantity increases. When marginal revenue is negative, total revenue decreases when quantity increases. Marginal revenue is zero when total revenue is maximized.

Figure 6.4 shows graphically the relations among demand, marginal revenue, and total revenue for the demand schedule in Table 6.3. As noted, MR is below price (in Panel A) at every level of output except the first. When total revenue (in Panel B) begins to decrease, marginal revenue becomes negative. Demand and marginal revenue are both negatively sloped.

Sometimes the interval over which marginal revenue is measured is greater than one unit of output. After all, managers don't necessarily increase output by just one unit at a time. Suppose in Table 6.3 that we want to compute marginal revenue when output increases from 2 units to 5 units. Over the interval, the change in total revenue is $5 (= $12 − $7), and the change in output is 3 units. Marginal revenue is $1.67 (= $\Delta TR / \Delta Q$ = $5/3) per unit change in output; that is, each of the 3 units contributes (on average) $1.67 to total revenue. As a general rule, whenever the interval over which marginal revenue is being measured is more than a single

FIGURE 6.4
Demand, Marginal Revenue, and Total Revenue

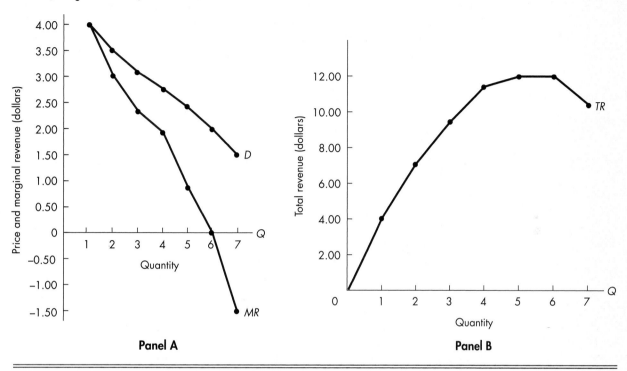

| Panel A | Panel B |

unit, divide ΔTR by ΔQ to obtain the marginal revenue for each of the units of output in the interval.

As mentioned in Chapter 2 and as you will see in Chapter 7, *linear* demand equations are frequently employed for purposes of empirical demand estimation and demand forecasting. The relation between a linear demand equation and its marginal revenue function is no different from that set forth in the preceding relation. The case of a linear demand is special because the relation between demand and marginal revenue has some additional properties that do not hold for nonlinear demand curves.

When demand is linear, marginal revenue is linear and lies halfway between demand and the vertical (price) axis. This implies that marginal revenue must be twice as steep as demand, and demand and marginal revenue share the same intercept on the vertical axis.[6] We can explain these additional properties and show how to apply them by returning to the simplified linear demand function

---

[6]The mathematical relation between demand and marginal revenue in the case of a linear demand is derived in the appendix to this chapter.

$(Q = a + bP + cM + dP_R)$ examined earlier in this chapter (and in Chapter 2). Again we hold the values of income and the price of the related good R constant at the specific values $\hat{M}$ and $\hat{P}_R$, respectively. This produces the linear demand equation $Q = a' + bP$, where $a' = a + c\hat{M} + d\hat{P}_R$. Next, we find the inverse demand equation by solving for $P = f(Q)$ as explained in Chapter 2 (you may wish to review Technical Problem 2 in Chapter 2):

$$P = -\frac{a'}{b} + \frac{1}{b}Q$$

$$= A + BQ$$

where $A = -a'/b$ and $B = 1/b$. Using the values of A and B from inverse demand, the equation for marginal revenue is $MR = A + 2BQ$. Thus marginal revenue is linear, has the same vertical intercept as inverse demand (A), and is twice as steep as inverse demand ($\Delta MR/\Delta Q = 2B$).

□ **Relation** When inverse demand is linear, $P = A + BQ$, marginal revenue is also linear, intersects the vertical (price) axis at the same point demand does, and is twice as steep as the inverse demand function. The equation of the linear marginal revenue curve is $MR = A + 2BQ$.

Figure 6.5 (on page 229) shows the linear inverse demand curve $P = 6 - 0.05Q$. (Remember that B is negative because P and Q are inversely related.) The associated marginal revenue curve is also linear, intersects the price axis at \$6, and is twice as steep as the demand curve. Because it is twice as steep, marginal revenue intersects the quantity axis at 60 units, which is half the output level for which demand intersects the quantity axis. The equation for marginal revenue has the same vertical intercept but twice the slope: $MR = 6 - 0.10Q$.

Marginal Revenue and Price Elasticity

Using Figure 6.5, we now examine the relation of price elasticity to demand and marginal revenue. Recall that if total revenue increases when price falls and quantity rises, demand is elastic; if total revenue decreases when price falls and quantity rises, demand is inelastic. When marginal revenue is positive in Panel A, from a quantity of 0 to 60, total revenue increases as price declines in Panel B; thus demand is elastic over this range. Conversely, when marginal revenue is negative, at any quantity greater than 60, total revenue declines when price falls; thus demand must be inelastic over this range. Finally, if marginal revenue is 0, at a quantity of 60, total revenue does not change when quantity changes, so the price elasticity of demand is unitary at 60.

Except for marginal revenue being linear and twice as steep as demand, all the preceding relations hold for nonlinear demands. Thus the following relation (also summarized in Table 6.4) holds for all demand curves:

□ **Relation** When MR is positive (negative), total revenue increases (decreases) as quantity increases, and demand is elastic (inelastic). When MR is 0, the price elasticity of demand is unitary.

FIGURE 6.5

Linear Demand, Marginal Revenue, and Elasticity ($Q = 120 - 20P$)

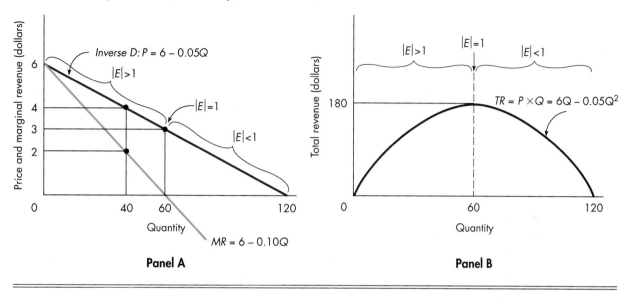

Panel A   **Panel B**

TABLE 6.4	(1) Marginal revenue	(2) Total revenue	(3) Price elasticity of demand
Marginal Revenue, Total Revenue, and Price Elasticity of Demand	$MR > 0$	TR increases as Q increases	Elastic ($|E| > 1$)
	$MR = 0$	TR is maximized	Unit elastic ($|E| = 1$)
	$MR < 0$	TR decreases as Q increases	Inelastic ($|E| < 1$)

The relation among marginal revenue, price elasticity of demand, and price at any quantity can be expressed still more precisely. As shown in this chapter's appendix, the relation between marginal revenue, price, and price elasticity, *for linear or curvilinear demands*, is

$$MR = P\left(1 + \frac{1}{E}\right)$$

where E is the price elasticity of demand and P is product price. When demand is elastic ($|E| > 1$), $|1/E|$ is less than 1, $1 + (1/E)$ is positive, and marginal revenue is positive. When demand is inelastic ($|E| < 1$), $|1/E|$ is greater than 1, $1 + (1/E)$ is negative, and marginal revenue is negative. In the case of unitary price elasticity ($E = -1$), $1 + (1/E)$ is 0, and marginal revenue is 0.

To illustrate the relation between MR, P, and E numerically, we calculate marginal revenue at 40 units of output for the demand curve shown in Panel A of

Figure 6.5. At 40 units of output, the point elasticity of demand is equal to -2 [$= P/(P - A) = 4/(4 - 6)$]. Using the formula presented on page 229, MR is equal to 2 [$= 4(1 - 1/2)$]. This is the same value for marginal revenue that is obtained by substituting $Q = 40$ into the equation for marginal revenue: $MR = 6 - 0.1(40) = 2$.

▣ **Relation** For any demand curve, when demand is elastic ($|E| > 1$), marginal revenue is positive. When demand is inelastic ($|E| < 1$), marginal revenue is negative. When demand is unitary elastic ($|E| = 1$), marginal revenue is zero. For all demand and marginal revenue curves:

$$MR = P\left(1 + \frac{1}{E}\right)$$

T ▷ 12 13 14 where E is the price elasticity of demand.

6.6 OTHER DEMAND ELASTICITIES

Sometimes economists and business decision makers are interested in measuring the sensitivity of consumers to changes in either income or the price of a related good. **Income elasticity** measures the responsiveness of quantity demanded to changes in income, holding all other variables in the generalized demand function constant. **Cross-price elasticity** measures the responsiveness of quantity demanded to changes in the price of a related good, when all the other variables in the generalized demand function remain constant. In this section we show how to calculate and interpret these two elasticities.

income elasticity (E_M)
A measure of the responsiveness of quantity demanded to changes in income, holding all other variables in the generalized demand function constant.

cross-price elasticity (E_{XR})
A measure of the responsiveness of quantity demanded to changes in the price of a related good, when all the other variables in the generalized demand function remain constant.

Income Elasticity (E_M)

As noted, income elasticity measures the responsiveness of quantity purchased when income changes, all else constant. Income elasticity, E_M, is the percentage change in quantity demanded divided by the percentage change in income, holding all other variables in the generalized demand function constant, including the good's own price:

$$E_M = \frac{\% \Delta Q}{\% \Delta M} = \frac{\Delta Q/Q}{\Delta M/M} = \frac{\Delta Q}{\Delta M} \times \frac{M}{Q}$$

As you can see, the sign of E_M depends on the sign of $\Delta Q/\Delta M$, which may be positive (if the good is normal) or negative (if the good is inferior). Thus if the good is normal, the income elasticity is positive. If the good is inferior, the income elasticity is negative.

Income elasticity, like price elasticity of demand, can be measured either over an interval or at a point on the generalized demand. For the interval measure of income elasticity, compute $\Delta Q/\Delta M$ over the interval and multiply this slope times the ratio of average income divided by average quantity:

$$E_M = \frac{\Delta Q}{\Delta M} \times \frac{\text{Average } M}{\text{Average } Q}$$

When the change in income is relatively small, the point measure of income elasticity is calculated by multiplying the slope $\Delta Q/\Delta M$ times the ratio M/Q. For the linear demand function, $Q = a + bP + cM + dP_R$, the point measure of income elasticity is

$$E_M = c \frac{M}{Q}$$

because slope parameter c measures $\Delta Q/\Delta M$, as you learned in Chapter 2.

To illustrate the use of income elasticity, consider Metro Ford, a new-car dealership in Atlanta. The manager of Metro Ford expects average household income in Fulton County to increase from $45,000 to $50,000 annually when the current recession ends, causing an increase in the demand for new cars. At a constant average price of $30,000 per car, the increase in income will cause sales to rise from 800 to 1,400 units per month. Panel A in Figure 6.6 illustrates this situation. The increase in income shifts the demand for new cars rightward—a new car is a normal good. To calculate the income elasticity of demand, we use the arc elasticity method of computing percentage changes over an interval. The income elasticity of demand in Panel A is

$$E_M = \frac{\Delta Q}{\Delta M} \times \frac{\text{Average } M}{\text{Average } Q} = \frac{600}{5,000} \times \frac{47,500}{1,100} = 5.18$$

We should mention that the choice of $30,000 as the price at which to measure income elasticity is arbitrary. The manager at Metro Ford probably chose a price of $30,000 as a typical new-car price. Also notice that averages for Q and M are used since the income elasticity is computed for the interval A to B.

FIGURE 6.6
Calculating Income Elasticity of Demand

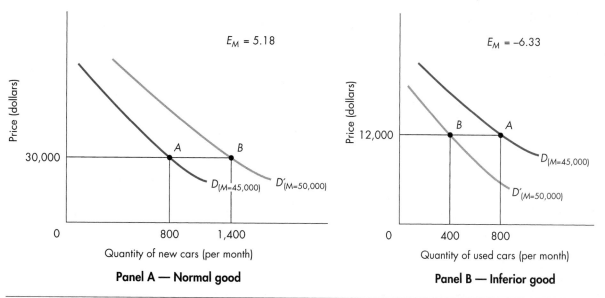

Panel A — Normal good

Panel B — Inferior good

Now consider Lemon Motors, a used-car dealership in Atlanta. Panel B in Figure 6.6 depicts the demand for used cars at Lemon Motors. The increase in household income in Fulton County causes a decrease in demand for used cars from D to D'—used cars are assumed to be inferior goods in this example. If used-car prices hold at $12,000, sales at the used-car dealership fall from 800 to 400 units per month. Again using the arc method of computing percentage changes, the income elasticity of demand is

$$E_M = \frac{\Delta Q}{\Delta M} \times \frac{\text{Average } M}{\text{Average } Q} = \frac{-400}{5,000} \times \frac{47,500}{600} = -6.33$$

As expected, the income elasticity is negative for an inferior good.

□ **Relation** The income elasticity measures the responsiveness of consumers to changes in income when the price of the good and all other determinants of demand are held constant. The income elasticity is positive (negative) for normal (inferior) goods.

Cross-Price Elasticity (E_{XR})

The cross-price elasticity of a good, as already noted, measures the responsiveness of quantity demanded of one good to changes in the price of a related good R, when all the other variables in the generalized demand function remain constant. The cross-price elasticity between the good in question (X) and another good (R)—denoted E_{XR}—is calculated by taking the ratio of the percentage change in the quantity demanded of good X ($\%\Delta Q_X$) and dividing by the percentage change in the price of the other good R ($\%\Delta P_R$):

$$E_{XR} = \frac{\%\Delta Q_X}{\%\Delta P_R} = \frac{\Delta Q_X/Q_X}{\Delta P_R/P_R} = \frac{\Delta Q_X}{\Delta P_R} \times \frac{P_R}{Q_X}$$

Note that the sign of E_{XR} depends on the sign of $\Delta Q_X/\Delta P_R$, which can be positive or negative. Recall from Chapter 2 that if an increase in the price of one good causes the quantity purchased of another good to increase, the goods are substitutes (i.e., $\Delta Q_X/\Delta P_R > 0$). If the rise in the price of one good causes the quantity purchased of another good to fall, the goods are complements (i.e., $\Delta Q_X/\Delta P_R < 0$). If there is no change in the quantity purchased of the other good, the two goods are independent (i.e., $\Delta Q_X/\Delta P_R = 0$). Thus E_{XR} is positive when X and R are substitutes; E_{XR} is negative when X and R are complements.[7]

Cross-price elasticity, like price and income elasticities of demand, can be measured over intervals or at points on the generalized demand. As before, to obtain the interval measure of elasticity, compute $\Delta Q/\Delta P_R$ over the interval and multiply this slope times the ratio of average price of the related good divided by average quantity:

$$E_{XR} = \frac{\Delta Q}{\Delta P_R} \times \frac{\text{Average } P_R}{\text{Average } Q}$$

---

[7]We should note that the cross-price elasticity of X for R need not equal the cross-price elasticity of R for X, although the two will generally have the same signs.

When the change in the price of the related good is relatively small, the point measure of E_{XR} is calculated by multiplying the slope $\Delta Q / \Delta P_R$ times the ratio P_R / Q. For the linear demand function, $Q = a + bP + cM + dP_R$, the point measure of E_{XR} is

$$E_{XR} = d\,\frac{P_R}{Q}$$

because, as explained in Chapter 2, d measures $\Delta Q / \Delta P_R$.

Suppose the general manager of the Tampa Bay Buccaneers is studying the demand for Buccaneer football tickets. Of particular concern is the sensitivity of Buccaneer fans to the price of Tampa Bay Lightning tickets (P_L)—Tampa's hockey team—and the price of parking for football games at Raymond James Stadium (P_P), a substitute good and a complementary good, respectively, for Buccaneer football fans. The Bucs' general manager has learned that the owner of the Lightning plans to cut its already "low" ticket price of $45 per hockey game by 5 percent. After the Buccaneers became Super Bowl champions in 2003, general seating ticket prices (P) were raised to $75 per game. Since the Super Bowl victory, average household income has stagnated at $50,000 ($M$). So, rather than raise ticket prices any further at this time, the general manager plans to increase parking fees by 10 percent (currently $15 per vehicle), unless, of course, ticket demand turns out to be quite sensitive to parking fees.

The Buccaneer general manager obtains from a consulting firm the following statistically estimated demand for tickets in the general seating areas, which excludes club and luxury seating:

$$Q = 49{,}800 - 750P + 0.85M + 400P_L - 625P_P$$

The general manager decides to calculate the cross-price elasticities for hockey tickets and parking fees, E_{XL} and E_{XP}, respectively, at the point on demand corresponding to the current values of the demand variables: $P = \$75$, $M = \$50{,}000$, $P_L = \$45$, and $P_P = \$15$. The estimated quantity demanded of Buccaneer football tickets in the general seating areas is $44{,}675\,[= 49{,}800 - (750 \times 75) + (0.85 \times 50{,}000) + (400 \times 45) - (625 \times 15)]$. The cross-price elasticity of Buccaneer ticket demand with respect to Lightning ticket prices (E_{XL}) can be calculated as follows:

$$E_{XL} = \frac{\Delta Q}{\Delta P_L} \times \frac{P_L}{Q} = 400\,\frac{45}{44{,}675} = 0.40$$

Note that the cross-price elasticity between Buccaneer and Lightning tickets is positive (for substitutes) but rather small, indicating football and hockey are rather weak substitutes in Tampa. Similarly, the cross-price elasticity of Buccaneer ticket demand with respect to parking fees (E_{XP}) is computed as

$$E_{XP} = \frac{\Delta Q}{\Delta P_P} \times \frac{P_P}{Q} = -625\,\frac{15}{44{,}675} = -0.21$$

The cross-price elasticity between football and parking is negative (as expected for complements) but small, indicating that Buccaneer fans are not particularly responsive to changes in the price of parking.

ILLUSTRATION 6.2

Empirical Elasticities of Demand

When we use the appropriate data and statistical techniques, it is possible to estimate price, income, and cross-price elasticities from actual demand schedules. We have collected a sample of estimated demand elasticities from a variety of sources and present them in the accompanying table. In the chapter on empirical demand functions, we will show how to estimate actual demand elasticities.

Looking at the price elasticities presented in the table, note that the demand for some basic agricultural products such as butter, chicken, pork, and eggs is inelastic. Fruit, for which consumers can find many substitutes, has a much more elastic demand than chicken, pork, or eggs. Whether ground into hamburger or cut into steaks, beef is usually more expensive than the other two basic meats, chicken and pork. Since beef represents a larger fraction of households' grocery bill, consumers are more sensitive to change in beef prices than to changes in chicken prices. And, because steaks are more expensive than ground beef, consumers will be more sensitive to steak prices. Apparently consumers of beer, wine, and cigarettes can find few substitutes for these items since the demand elasticities are quite inelastic for all three. Demand for clothing, something most of us are unwilling to go without, is inelastic. A recent study found that buyers of dynamic random access memory (DRAM) chips are so insensitive to price changes that it estimated demand to be perfectly inelastic for DRAM chips! We do not wish to dispute the results of this study, but we suspect the demand for DRAM chips is perfectly inelastic only for a very narrow range of prices. As prices for bandwidth decline, Internet service providers (ISPs) apparently gobble up bandwidth to transmit data between different countries on fiber-optic cables. For any particular make and model of automobile, consumers can find plenty of readily available substitutes. Consequently, the demand elasticity for General Motors' Pontiac Catalina is very large. Another factor affecting price elasticity is the length of time consumers have to adjust to a price change. For example, electricity demand is more price-responsive in the long run than in the short run. It is interesting that gasoline demand is inelastic in the short run but elastic in the long run.

Normal goods have positive income elasticities of demand (E_M), and inferior goods have negative income elasticities. Ground beef and potatoes are inferior goods since E_M is negative. Steaks are more strongly normal than chicken or pork, indicating that a given percentage increase in income causes over a fourfold (fivefold) greater increase in steak consumption than chicken (pork) consumption. Wine is more strongly normal than beer. The high income elasticity of demand for foreign travel indicates that consumer demand for foreign travel is quite responsive to changes in income. Life insurance is a normal good for both Japanese and Americans, but Japanese demand for life insurance is nearly twice as sensitive to changes in income as U.S. demand for life insurance.

We explained in the text that cross-price elasticities are positive for substitutes and negative for complements. All four pairs of goods in the table are substitutes ($E_{XY} > 0$). Steaks and chicken are weak substitutes, while margarine and butter seem to be rather strong substitutes. Beer and wine drinkers substitute between the two alcoholic beverages but apparently not with much enthusiasm. The extremely high cross-price elasticity of demand between Pontiac Catalinas and Chevrolet Impalas suggests that these two cars were virtually identical in the eyes of consumers.

Table of Empirical Elasticities of Demand

Price elasticities of demand (E):

Butter	−0.24
Chicken	−0.30
Pork	−0.77
Eggs	−0.26
Beef (ground)	−1.01
Beef (steaks)	−1.15
Fruit	−3.02
Beer	−0.20
Wine	−0.67
Cigarettes	−0.51
Clothing	−0.62
Dynamic Random Access Memory (DRAM) chips	−0.0
Transnational fiber optic bandwidth	−2.0
GM Pontiac Catalina	−16.99
Electricity (short run)	−0.28
Electricity (long run)	−0.90
Gasoline (short run)	−0.43
Gasoline (long run)	−1.50

Income elasticities of demand (E_M):

Beef (ground)	−0.19
Beef (steaks)	1.87
Chicken	0.42
Pork	0.34
Potatoes	−0.81
Beer	0.76
Wine	1.72
Life insurance in Japan	2.99
Life insurance in United States	1.65

Cross-price elasticities of demand (E_{XR}):

Beef (steaks) and chicken	0.24
Margarine and butter	1.53
Beer and wine	0.56
Catalinas and Impalas	19.3

Sources: For price, cross-price, and income elasticities for agricultural products, see Dale Heien, "The Structure of Food Demand: Interrelatedness and Duality," *American Journal of Agricultural Economics*, May 1982; and K. S. Huang, "A Complete System of U.S. Demand for Food," *Technical Bulletin* No. 1821, Economic Research Service, U.S. Department of Agriculture, Sept. 1993. For cigarettes price elasticity, see Frank Chaloupka, "Rational Addictive Behavior and Cigarette Smoking," *Journal of Political Economy*, Aug. 1991. For clothing price elasticities, see Richard Blundell, Panos Pashardes, and Guglielmo Weber, "What Do We Learn about Consumer Demand Patterns from Micro Data," *American Economic Review*, June 1993. For alcohol elasticities, see Jon Nelson, "Broadcast Advertising and U.S. Demand for Alcoholic Beverages," *Southern Economic Journal*, Apr. 1999. For automobile price and cross-price elasticities, see F. Owen Irvine, Jr., "Demand Equations for Individual New Car Models Estimated Using Transaction Prices with Implications for Regulatory Issues," *Southern Economic Journal*, Jan. 1983. For short-run and long-run gasoline and electricity elasticities, see Robert Archibald and Robert Gillingham, "An Analysis of Short-Run Consumer Demand for Gasoline Using Household Survey Data," *Review of Economics and Statistics*, Nov. 1980; and Chris King and Sanjoy Chatterjee, "Predicting California Demand Response: How Do Customers React to Hourly Prices?" *Public Utilities Fortnightly* 141, no. 13 (July 1, 2003). For income elasticity of demand for electricity, see Cheng Hsiao and Dean Mountain, "Estimating the Short-Run Income Elasticity of Demand for Electricity by Using Cross-Sectional Categorized Data," *Journal of the American Statistical Association*, June 1985. For the price elasticity of fiber-optic bandwidth, see the editorial "Fear of Fiber-Optic Glut May be Misguided," *Lightwave* 17, no. 9 (Aug. 2000). Life insurance elasticities can be found in Dai I. Chi, "Japan: Life, But Not as We Know It," *Euromoney*, Oct. 1998. For the price elasticity of DRAM chips, see Jim Handy, "Has the Market Perked Up Yet?" *Electronics Times*, June 5, 2000.

With such small absolute values of the cross-price elasticities, the Buccaneers' general manager can reasonably conclude that falling hockey ticket prices and rising parking fees are not likely to have much effect on demand for general seating football tickets. More precisely, the 5 percent drop in Lightning ticket prices is likely to cause only a 2 percent ($= 5\% \times 0.40$) decrease in the quantity of Bucs tickets sold, and the 10 percent increase in parking fees is predicted to decrease ticket sales by just 2.1 percent ($= 10\% \times -0.21$).

> ▣ **Relation** The cross-price elasticity measures the responsiveness of the quantity demanded of one good when the price of another good changes, holding the price of the good and all other determinants of demand constant. Cross-price elasticity is positive (negative) when the two goods are substitutes (complements).

6.7 SUMMARY

The price elasticity of demand measures the responsiveness or sensitivity of consumers to changes in the price of a good. Price elasticity is the ratio of the percentage change in quantity demanded to the percentage change in the price of the good. Over a specified price range, demand is said to be either elastic, unitary elastic, or inelastic according to whether the absolute value of the price elasticity is greater than, equal to, or less than one, respectively.

An extremely important relation in economic analysis relates the change in total revenue (due to a change in price) and the price elasticity of demand. If demand is elastic for a given change in price, an increase in price causes total revenue to fall. A decrease in price causes total revenue to rise if demand is elastic over the price range. If demand is inelastic for a given price change, an increase in price causes total revenue to rise, while a decrease in price causes total revenue to fall.

Several factors affect the price elasticity of demand. The most important of these is the availability of close substitutes. The better and more numerous the substitutes for a good, the more elastic the demand for the good. Demand elasticity is directly related to the percentage of the consumers' budgets spent on the good. Also, the longer the time period that consumers have to adjust to price changes, the more responsive they will be, and the more elastic is demand.

Calculating price elasticity of demand can be accomplished by multiplying the slope of demand ($\Delta Q/\Delta P$) times the ratio of price divided by quantity (P/Q):

$$E = \frac{\%\Delta Q}{\%\Delta P} = \frac{\Delta Q}{\Delta P} \times \frac{P}{Q}$$

Elasticity can be measured either (1) over an interval (or arc) along demand or (2) at a specific point on the demand curve depending on the length of demand over which E is measured. If the change in price is relatively small (large), then a point (interval) measure is usually chosen.

When calculating the price elasticity of demand over an *interval* of demand, the interval or arc elasticity formula is applied

$$E = \frac{\Delta Q}{\Delta P} \times \frac{\text{Average } P}{\text{Average } Q}$$

When calculating price elasticity at a *point* on demand, either of two mathematically equivalent formulas can be used to compute point elasticities:

$$E = \frac{\Delta Q}{\Delta P} \times \frac{P}{Q} \quad \text{and} \quad E = \frac{P}{P - A}$$

For linear demand functions, $Q = a' + bP$, the slope parameter b can be substituted for $\Delta Q/\Delta P$ in the first formula and A ($= -a'/b$) is the price-intercept of linear demand in the second formula. For curvilinear demand functions, $\Delta Q/\Delta P$ is the slope of the curved demand calculated at the point of measure (which is the inverse of the slope of the tangent line constructed at the point of measure), and A is the price-intercept of the tangent line extended to cross the price axis.

In general, the price elasticity of demand varies along a demand curve. For linear demand curves, price and |E| vary directly: The higher (lower) the price, the more (less) elastic is demand. For a curvilinear demand, there is no general rule about the relation between price and elasticity, except for the special case of $Q = aP^b$, which has a constant price elasticity (equal to b) for all prices.

Marginal revenue is the change in total revenue resulting from the sale of an additional unit of output. Marginal revenue declines as output increases and is less than price for every quantity except the first unit, in which case marginal revenue equals price. When MR is positive, TR is rising as price falls and quantity demanded increases. When MR is negative, TR is falling. When MR is 0, TR is neither rising nor falling; it is at its maximum value. In the case of linear demand, $Q = a' + bP$, inverse demand is $P = A + BQ$, where $A (= -a'/b)$ is the price-intercept and B equals $1/b$. Marginal revenue is also linear and takes the mathematical form $MR = A + 2BQ$. In other words, marginal revenue is linear, intersects the price axis at the same point as demand, and is twice as steep as the inverse demand function.

For any demand (linear or curvilinear) marginal revenue can be expressed as $MR = P[1 + (1/E)]$, where E is the price elasticity of demand. Hence, if demand is elastic, marginal revenue is positive. If demand is inelastic, marginal revenue is negative. When demand is unitary elastic, marginal revenue is equal to 0.

Two other important elasticities are income elasticity (E_M), which measures the responsiveness of quantity purchased to changes in income, and cross-price elasticity (E_{XR}), which measures the responsiveness of quantity purchased to changes in the price of related goods (substitutes or complements). In the case of income elasticity, the elasticity measure is positive if the good is normal; negative if the good is inferior. In the case of cross-price elasticity, the elasticity measure is positive if the two goods are substitutes; negative if they are complements. To calculate interval measures of income and cross-price elasticities, the following formulas can be employed:

$$E_M = \frac{\Delta Q}{\Delta M} \times \frac{\text{Average } M}{\text{Average } Q} \quad \text{and} \quad E_{XR} = \frac{\Delta Q}{\Delta P_R} \times \frac{\text{Average } P_R}{\text{Average } Q}$$

For the linear demand function, $Q = a + bP + cM + dP_R$, point measures of income and cross-price elasticities can be calculated as

$$E_M = c\frac{M}{Q} \quad \text{and} \quad E_{XR} = d\frac{P_R}{Q}$$

Now that we have presented the theory of consumer demand, we will show you in the next chapter how to use real-world data to estimate demand functions and forecast future demand conditions. You will use the techniques of regression analysis to estimate empirical demand equations that can be used in managerial decision making.

TECHNICAL PROBLEMS

1. Moving along a demand curve, quantity demanded decreases 8 percent when price increases 10 percent.
   a. The price elasticity of demand is calculated to be _____.
   b. Given the price elasticity calculated in part a, demand is _____ (elastic, inelastic, unitary elastic) along this portion of the demand curve.
   c. For this interval of demand, the percentage change in quantity in absolute value is _____ (greater than, less than, equal to) the percentage change in price in absolute value.

2. Fill in the blanks:
   a. The price elasticity of demand for a firm's product is equal to -1.5 over the range of prices being considered by the firm's manager. If the manager decreases the price of the product by 6 percent, the manager predicts the quantity demanded will _____ (increase, decrease) by _____ percent.
   b. The price elasticity of demand for an industry's demand curve is equal to -1.5 for the range of prices over which supply increases. If total industry output is expected to increase by 30 percent as a result of the supply increase, managers in this industry should expect the market price of the good to _____ (increase, decrease) by _____ percent.

3. Fill in the blanks:

   a. When demand is elastic, the _____ effect dominates the _____ effect.

   b. When demand is inelastic, the _____ effect dominates the _____ effect.

   c. When demand is unitary elastic, _____ effect dominates.

   d. When a change in price causes a change in quantity demanded, total revenue always moves in the _____ direction as the variable (P or Q) having the _____ effect.

4. Fill in the blanks:

   a. When demand is elastic, an increase in price causes quantity demanded to _____ and total revenue to _____.

   b. When demand is inelastic, a decrease in price causes quantity demanded to _____ and total revenue to _____.

   c. When demand is unitary elastic, an increase in price causes quantity demanded to _____ and total revenue to _____.

   d. If price falls and total revenue falls, demand must be _____.

   e. If price rises and total revenue stays the same, demand must be _____.

   f. If price rises and total revenue rises, demand must be _____.

5. In Panel A of Figure 6.1, verify that demand is unitary elastic over the price range of $11 to $13 without calculating the price elasticity of demand.

6. For each pair of price elasticities, which elasticity (in absolute value) is larger? Why?

   a. The price elasticity for carbonated soft drinks or the price elasticity for Coca-Cola.

   b. The price elasticity for socks (men's or women's) or the price elasticity for business suits (men's or women's).

   c. The price elasticity for electricity in the short run or the price elasticity for electricity in the long run.

7. Use the graph below to answer the following questions:

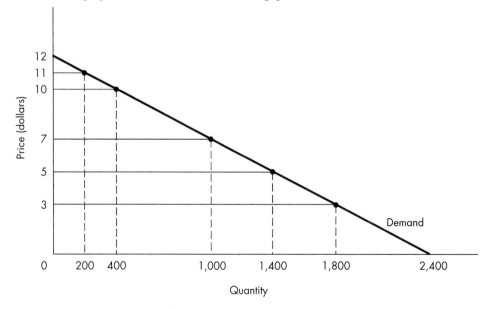

    a. The interval elasticity of demand over the price range $3 to $5 is _____.

    b. The interval elasticity of demand over the price range $10 to $11 is _____.

    c. The interval elasticity of demand over the price range $5 to $7 is _____.

8. *a.* For the linear demand curve in problem 7, compute the price elasticity at each of the price points given in the following table. Make the elasticity calculations using the two alternative formulas, $E = (\Delta Q / \Delta P) \times (P/Q)$ and $E = P/(P - A)$.

Price point	$E = \dfrac{\Delta Q}{\Delta P} \times \dfrac{P}{Q}$	$E = \dfrac{P}{P - A}$
$ 3	_____	_____
5	_____	_____
7	_____	_____
10	_____	_____
11	_____	_____

    b. Which formula is more accurate for computing price elasticities? Explain.

9. Use the linear demand curve shown below to answer the following questions:

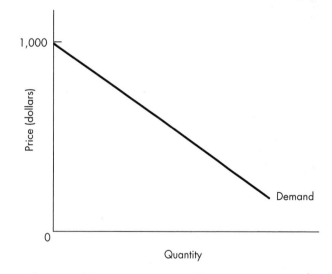

    a. The point elasticity of demand at a price of $800 is _____.

    b. The point elasticity of demand at a price of $200 is _____.

    c. Demand is unitary elastic at a price of $ _____.

    d. As price rises, $|E|$ _____ (gets larger, gets smaller, stays the same) for a linear demand curve.

10. Use the figure on the next page to answer the following questions:

    a. Calculate price elasticity at point S using the method $E = \dfrac{\Delta Q}{\Delta P} \times \dfrac{P}{Q}$.

    b. Calculate price elasticity at point S using the method $E = \dfrac{P}{P - A}$.

    c. Compare the elasticities in parts *a* and *b*. Are they equal? Should they be equal?

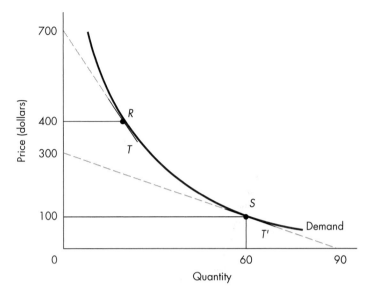

d. Calculate price elasticity at point R.

e. Which method did you use to compute E in part d, $E = \dfrac{\Delta Q}{\Delta P} \times \dfrac{P}{Q}$ or $E = \dfrac{P}{P - A}$? Why?

11. Suppose the demand for good X is $Q = 20P^{-1}$.

   a. When $P = \$1$, total revenue is _____.

   b. When $P = \$2$, total revenue is _____.

   c. When $P = \$4$, total revenue is _____.

   d. The price elasticity of demand is equal to _____. Why?

12. The figure on the next page shows a linear demand curve. Fill in the blanks a through l as indicated in the figure.

13. For the linear demand curve in problem 12 (on the next page):

   a. Write the equation for the demand curve.

   b. Write the equation for the inverse demand curve.

   c. Write the equation for the total revenue curve.

   d. Write the equation for the marginal revenue curve.

   e. Check your answers for problem 12 using the equations for demand, inverse demand, and marginal revenue, and total revenue.

14. Write the equation for the demand curve in the graph for problem 7. What is the equation for marginal revenue? At what price is demand unitary elastic? At what output is marginal revenue equal to 0?

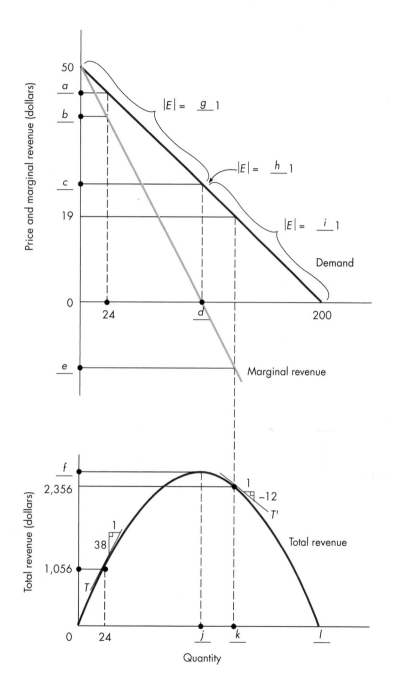

15. In the following two panels, the demand for good X shifts due to a change in income (Panel A) and a change in the price of a related good Y (Panel B). Holding the price of good X constant at $50, calculate the following elasticities:

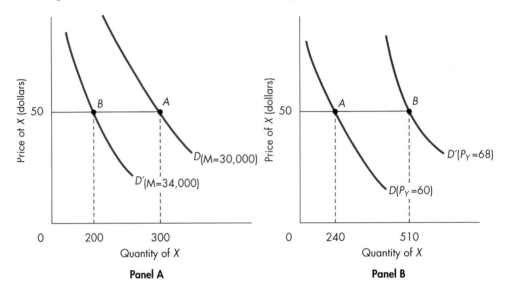

Panel A

Panel B

a. Panel A shows how the demand for X shifts when income increases from $30,000 to $34,000. Use the information in Panel A to calculate the income elasticity of demand for X. Is good X normal or inferior?

b. Panel B shows how the demand for X shifts when the price of related good Y increases from $60 to $68. Use the information in Panel B to calculate the cross-price elasticity. Are goods X and Y substitutes or complements?

16. The generalized linear demand for good X is estimated to be

$$Q = 250{,}000 - 500P - 1.50M - 240P_R$$

where P is the price of good X, M is average income of consumers who buy good X, and P_R is the price of related good R. The values of P, M, and P_R are expected to be $200, $60,000, and $100, respectively. Use these values at this point on demand to make the following computations.

a. Compute the quantity of good X demanded for the given values of P, M, and P_R.

b. Calculate the price elasticity of demand E. At this point on the demand for X, is demand elastic, inelastic, or unitary elastic? How would increasing the price of X affect total revenue? Explain.

c. Calculate the income elasticity of demand E_M. Is good X normal or inferior? Explain how a 4 percent increase in income would affect demand for X, all other factors affecting the demand for X remaining the same.

d. Calculate the cross-price elasticity E_{XR}. Are the goods X and R substitutes or complements? Explain how a 5 percent decrease in the price of related good R would affect demand for X, all other factors affecting the demand for X remaining the same.

APPLIED PROBLEMS

1. In an article about the financial problems of *USA Today*, *Newsweek* reported that the paper was losing about $20 million a year. A Wall Street analyst said that the paper should raise its price from 50 cents to 75 cents, which he estimated would bring in an additional $65 million a year. The paper's publisher rejected the idea, saying that circulation could drop sharply after a price increase, citing *The Wall Street Journal*'s experience after it increased its price to 75 cents. What implicit assumptions are the publisher and the analyst making about price elasticity?

2. Assume that the demand for plastic surgery is price inelastic. Are the following statements true or false? Explain.
   a. When the price of plastic surgery increases, the number of operations decreases.
   b. The percentage change in the price of plastic surgery is less than the percentage change in quantity demanded.
   c. Changes in the price of plastic surgery do not affect the number of operations.
   d. Quantity demanded is quite responsive to changes in price.
   e. If more plastic surgery is performed, expenditures on plastic surgery will decrease.
   f. The marginal revenue of another operation is negative.

3. What effect, if any, does each of the following events have on the price elasticity of demand for corporate-owned jets?
   a. Reduced corporate earnings lead to cuts in travel budgets and increase the share of expenditures on corporate jet travel.
   b. Further deregulation of the commercial airlines industry substantially increases the variety of departure times and destinations offered by commercial airlines.
   c. The cost of manufacturing corporate jets rises.
   d. A new, much more fuel-efficient corporate jet is introduced.

4. Aztec Enterprises depends heavily on advertising to sell its products. Management at Aztec is allowed to spend $2 million monthly on advertising, but no more than this amount. Each month, Aztec spends exactly $2 million on advertising. What is Aztec's elasticity of demand for advertising? Can you write the equation for Aztec's demand for advertising?

5. U.S. cigarette makers face enormous punitive damage penalties after losing a series of class-action lawsuits that heaped penalties amounting to several hundred billion dollars on the tobacco industry. In spite of the huge penalties, *The Wall Street Journal* reported, "The damage (to cigarette makers) is generally under control." What action do you suppose the cigarette companies took to avoid bankruptcy? Why did this action succeed?

6. The price elasticity of demand for imported whiskey is estimated to be −0.20 over a wide interval of prices. The federal government decides to raise the import tariff on foreign whiskey, causing its price to rise by 20 percent. Will sales of whiskey rise or fall, and by what percentage amount?

7. As manager of Citywide Racquet Club, you must determine the best price to charge for locker rentals. Assume that the (marginal) cost of providing lockers is zero. The monthly demand for lockers is estimated to be

$$Q = 100 - 2P$$

where P is the monthly rental price and Q is the number of lockers rented per month.

  a. What price would you charge?

  b. How many lockers are rented monthly at this price?

  c. Explain why you chose this price.

8. The demand curve for haircuts at Terry Bernard's Hair Design is

$$P = 15 - 0.15Q$$

where Q is the number of cuts per week and P is the price of a haircut. Terry is considering raising her price above the current price of $9. Terry is unwilling to raise price if the price hike will cause revenues to fall.

  a. Should Terry raise the price of haircuts above $9? Why or why not?

  b. Suppose demand for Terry's haircuts increases to $P = 22 - 0.22Q$. At a price of $9, should Terry raise the price of her haircuts? Why or why not?

9. Movie attendance dropped 8 percent as ticket prices rose a little more than 5 percent. What is the price elasticity of demand for movie tickets? Could price elasticity be somewhat overestimated from these figures? That is, could other things have changed, accounting for some of the decline in attendance?

10. *The Dallas Morning News* reported the findings of a study by the Department of Transportation that examined the effect on average airfares when new, low-priced carriers, such as Southwest Airlines or Vanguard Airlines, entered one of three city-pair markets: Baltimore–Cleveland, Kansas City–San Francisco, or Baltimore–Providence. Use the following excerpts from the newspaper article to calculate the arc elasticity of demand for each of the three city-pairs. How do the three computed elasticities compare? Based on the computed elasticities, describe travelers' responsiveness to the reductions in airfares.

  a. "(In) Baltimore and Cleveland, for example, . . . just 12,790 people flew between those cities in the last three months of 1992, at an average fare of $233. Then Dallas-based Southwest Airlines entered the market. In the last three months of 1996, 115,040 people flew between the cities at an average fare of $66."

  b. "(On) the Kansas City–San Francisco connection . . . (during) the last quarter of 1994 some 35,690 people made the trip at an average fare of $165. Two years later, after the arrival of Vanguard Airlines, fares had dropped to an average of $107 and traffic had nearly doubled to 68,100."

  c. "On the Baltimore–Providence, R.I., route, where the average fare fell from $196 to $57, . . . the number of passengers carried jumped from 11,960 to 94,116."

◻   **MATHEMATICAL APPENDIX**   **Demand Elasticity**

The Price Elasticity of Demand

Let the demand function be expressed as $Q = Q(P)$, where the law of demand requires that quantity demanded and price be inversely related: $dQ/dP = Q'(P) < 0$, so the demand curve is downward-sloping. The slope of the demand curve measures the *absolute* rate of change in Q as P changes. The value of the absolute rate of change depends upon the units of measure of both P and Q. A measure of the *proportional* rate of change is invariant to the units of measure of P and Q. The price elasticity, E, measures the proportional rate of change in quantity demanded as price changes:

$$(1) \qquad E = \dfrac{\dfrac{dQ}{Q}}{\dfrac{dP}{P}} = \dfrac{dQ}{dP}\dfrac{P}{Q} = Q'(P)\dfrac{P}{Q}$$

As shown here, the price elasticity can also be expressed as the slope of demand, $Q'(P)$, times a proportionality factor, P/Q. Because the slope of demand is negative and the proportionality factor is always positive, E is always a negative number.

When demand is linear, $Q'(P)$ is constant. E, however, is *not* constant as changes in price cause movements along a linear demand function. Moving down a linear demand, P falls and Q increases, causing the proportionality factor to decrease. Thus as P decreases, E diminishes in absolute value; that is, $|E|$ decreases.

Price Elasticity and Changes in Total Revenue

In this section it will be useful to employ the inverse demand function, $P = P(Q)$, so that total revenue can be conveniently expressed as a function of Q. Total revenue for a firm is the price of the product times the number of units sold:

$$(2) \qquad \text{Total revenue} = TR = R(Q) = P(Q)Q$$

In order to examine how total revenue changes as sales increase with lower prices, the derivative of total revenue, known as marginal revenue, is defined as

$$(3) \ \text{Marginal revenue} = MR = R'(Q) = P(Q) + P'(Q)Q$$

where $P'(Q) = dP/dQ < 0$. Marginal revenue is positive, negative, or zero as total revenue is rising, falling, or at its maximum value, respectively.

To derive the relation between price elasticity and changes in total revenue (i.e., marginal revenue), marginal revenue can be expressed as a function of E as follows: First, factor P out of the expression for MR in (3):

$$(4) \qquad MR = R'(Q) = P\left(1 + P'(Q)\dfrac{Q}{P}\right)$$

Notice that $P'(Q)(Q/P)$ is the inverse of E. Substituting $1/E$ into expression (4) results in a useful relation between MR, P, and E:

$$(5) \qquad MR = R'(Q) = P\left(1 + \dfrac{1}{E}\right)$$

Several important relations can be derived from equation (5):

1. When Q is continuous and $Q > 0$, MR is less than P.[a] In the special case of a horizontal demand curve, $E = -\infty$, $MR = P$. You see this special case in a later chapter.
2. When demand is unitary elastic ($E = -1$), $MR = 0$ and an infinitesimally small change in Q causes no change in TR. Therefore, TR is at its maximum value when demand is unitary elastic and $MR = 0$.
3. When demand is elastic (inelastic), MR is positive (negative), a decrease in P causes an increase in Q, and total revenue rises (falls).

Linear Demand, Marginal Revenue, and Point Elasticity

Let the straight-line demand be expressed as an inverse demand function:

$$(6) \qquad P = P(Q) = A + BQ$$

where A is the positive price intercept and $B = dP/dQ$ is the negative slope of the inverse demand line. The total revenue received by the firm for a given level of sales Q is

$$(7) \quad TR = R(Q) = P(Q)Q = (A + BQ)Q = AQ + BQ^2$$

Notice that a linear demand function has a quadratic total revenue function that graphs as a ∩-shaped curve.

Marginal revenue associated with a linear demand function can be found by taking the derivative of total revenue:

$$(8) \qquad MR = R'(Q) = A + 2BQ$$

In absolute value, the slope of MR, $2B$, is twice as great as the slope of inverse demand, B. Both curves have the same vertical intercept A. This relation is shown in Figure 6A.1.

To derive the point price elasticity for a linear demand, it is convenient to employ the demand function expressed as $Q = Q(P)$, rather than the inverse demand in equation (6). The demand function associated with the inverse demand in equation (6) is

$$(9) \qquad Q = Q(P) = -\dfrac{A}{B} + \dfrac{1}{B}P = \dfrac{1}{B}(-A + P)$$

---

[a]When quantity is a discrete variable, rather than a continuous variable, $P = MR$ for the first unit sold. For the first unit sold, there are no inframarginal units, so no revenue is lost by lowering price to sell the first unit. After the first unit sold, $P > MR$.

FIGURE 6A.1

Linear Demand and Marginal Revenue

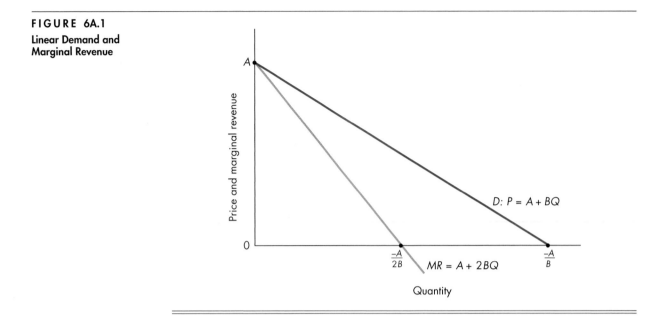

The slope of the demand function, dQ/dP, is $1/B$. Substituting $1/B$ for dQ/dP and expression (9) for Q in the elasticity equation (1) provides a rather simple algebraic expression for the point elasticity of demand when demand is linear:

(10)
$$E = \frac{1}{B}\frac{P}{\frac{1}{B}(-A + P)} = \frac{P}{(P - A)}$$

Equation (10) makes it clear that E is not constant for linear demands. The elasticity of demand varies inversely with price along a linear demand curve:

(11)
$$\frac{dE}{dP} = \frac{-A}{(P - A)^2} < 0$$

As price falls along a linear demand, E gets larger algebraically (i.e., less negative), $|E|$ gets smaller, and demand becomes less elastic. Similarly, as price rises, $|E|$ gets larger and demand becomes more elastic.

The Special Case of Constant Elasticity of Demand: $Q = aP^b$

When demand takes the form $Q = aP^b$, the elasticity of demand is constant and equal to b:

(12)
$$E = \frac{dQ}{dP}\frac{P}{Q} = baP^{b-1}\left(\frac{P}{aP^b}\right) = b$$

For example, when $Q = aP^{-1}$, demand is unitary elastic for all prices.

MATHEMATICAL EXERCISES

1. Consider the linear demand function $Q = 20 - 0.5P$.
   a. Write the inverse demand function.
   b. Write the total revenue function.
   c. Using calculus, find the level of output, Q_{rmax}, where total revenue reaches its maximum value. What price P_{rmax} maximizes total revenue? What is the value of TR at its maximum point?

    d. Write the equation for marginal revenue. Using *MR*, verify that Q_{rmax} derived in part *c* maximizes total revenue.

    e. Calculate the point elasticity of demand at P_{rmax}. Does *E* have the expected value? Explain briefly.

2. Let a linear demand function be expressed as $Q = a + bP$, where $b < 0$.

    a. Express the point elasticity of demand as a function of Q and a only.

    b. Take the derivative dE/dQ and verify that demand becomes less elastic moving down the demand curve.

3. Suppose demand takes the form $Q = 36P^{-1}$.

    a. Show that the price elasticity of demand is constant and equal to -1.

    b. Write the total and marginal revenue functions.

CHAPTER
7

Demand Estimation and Forecasting

Information about demand is essential for making pricing and production decisions. General Motors, Ford, DaimlerChrysler, Nissan, and other large automobile manufacturers all use empirical estimates of demand in making decisions about how many units of each model to produce and what prices to charge for different car models. Managers at the national headquarters of Domino's Pizza need to estimate how pizza demand in the United States is affected by a downturn in the economy: Take-out food businesses tend to prosper during recessions. At HCA, Inc., one of the largest hospital operators in the United States, short-run and long-run estimates of patient load (demand) in its various geographic markets are crucial for making expansion plans. Virtually all large electric utilities employ economists and statisticians to estimate current demand for electricity. A knowledge of *future* demand conditions can also be extremely useful to managers of both price-taking and price-setting firms when they are planning production schedules, inventory control, advertising campaigns, output in future periods, and investment, among other things. Many medium- and large-size firms rely on their own forecasting departments to provide forecasts of industry or firm-level demand.

Large business enterprises pioneered the use of empirical demand functions and econometric price forecasts in business pricing decisions. When thousands, even millions, of units are to be priced, managers are understandably uncomfortable making "seat-of-the-pants" guesses about the optimal price to charge. Furthermore, businesses, large and small, know that changing prices is a costly practice. New-price lists must be disseminated both to the salesforce and to customers. Changing prices may give loyal buyers a reason to shop around again.

Most managers wish to avoid, or at least reduce, the substantial anxiety that accompanies pricing decisions. Indeed, many managers admit that they avoid, as much as they possibly can, making pricing decisions for fear of making enormously costly mistakes. As a general rule, managers intensely dislike "throwing darts" until they find the right price (the bull's eye); they covet any information or technique of analysis that can help them make profitable pricing decisions. We cannot, in fairness, tell you that econometric analysis and forecasting of demand solves all of management's pricing problems. It can, however, provide managers with valuable information about demand, which should improve any manager's price-setting skills.

Like all tools used in decision making, statistical demand analysis and forecasting has some important limits, which we discuss at the end of this chapter. Profitable pricing decisions require skillful use of both judgment and quantitative analysis. While large firms generally have been more willing to employ statistical demand analysis, significant improvement in the sophistication, availability, and ease of use of econometric software—coupled with falling prices on powerful desktop computers—is now luring more medium- and small-size firms into using statistical demand analysis and forecasting. Some of the latest methods for pricing—known by such buzz-words as demand-based management (DBM), revenue management (RM), yield management, and market segmentation—all require highly accurate statistical estimates of the demand equations for every product and market served by the firm wishing to implement these techniques. Point-of-sale data, which are generated at checkout by laser scans of specially coded price tags, create large-scale data sets that make it possible to estimate and forecast demand much more accurately.

empirical demand functions
Demand equations derived from actual market data.

The fundamental building block of statistical demand analysis is the *empirical demand function*. **Empirical demand functions** are demand equations derived from actual market data. From empirical demand functions, managers can get quantitative estimates of the effect on sales of changes in the price of the product, changes in the level of consumer income, and changes in the price of competing products and products that are complements in consumption. As you will see in later chapters, empirical demand functions can be extremely useful in making pricing and production decisions.

We begin our discussion of empirical demand analysis and forecasting by showing you how to use regression analysis to estimate demand functions and associated demand elasticities: price, income, and cross-price elasticities (Sections 7.1 through 7.4). The important difference between estimating demand for a price-taking industry and demand for a single price-setting firm is carefully examined because the best regression technique for estimating industry demand differs from the technique for estimating a firm's demand. We will provide examples, some with real data, to show how demand functions are estimated and interpreted.

In the second part of this chapter (Sections 7.5 through 7.8), we examine methods for forecasting future prices and sales levels for both firms and industries. The range of forecasting techniques is so wide that a complete discussion is quite beyond the scope of this text. Therefore, we confine ourselves to a brief description of some of the more widely used techniques. Specifically, our examination of forecasting is limited to linear trend forecasting techniques and the more challenging econometric forecasting method.

This chapter about demand estimation and forecasting is intended to provide you with an introductory treatment of empirical demand analysis. While our discussion of statistical demand estimation and statistical demand forecasting is limited to the simpler methods, these methods are widely used in business to analyze and forecast market demand. Almost all of the more advanced techniques of empirical demand analysis that you will encounter in your marketing research, business forecasting, advanced statistics, and econometrics courses are extensions of, or related to, the methods we present in this chapter.

7.1 SPECIFICATION OF THE EMPIRICAL DEMAND FUNCTION

Managers can use the techniques of regression analysis outlined in Chapter 4 to obtain estimates of the demand for their firms' products. The theoretical foundation for specifying and analyzing empirical demand functions is provided by the theory of consumer behavior, which was presented in Chapter 5. In this section, we will show you two possible specifications of the demand function to be estimated. Again, we do not intend to teach you statistics or econometrics. Instead, we want to give you an idea of how these techniques of demand estimation can provide useful information for managerial decision making.

As we will discuss later in this chapter (Section 7.2), the statistical method used to estimate the parameters of an empirical demand function differs depending on whether the price of the product is determined by the simultaneous forces of demand and supply or is set directly by the manager. Despite the differences in the way the parameters are estimated, the way that empirical demand functions are specified and interpreted is essentially the same.

A General Empirical Demand Specification

In order to estimate a demand function for a product, it is necessary to use a specific functional form. Here we will consider both linear and nonlinear forms. Before proceeding, however, we must simplify the general demand relation. Recall that quantity demanded depends on the price of the product, consumer income, the price of related goods, consumer tastes or preferences, expected price, and the number of buyers. Given the difficulties inherent in quantifying taste and price expectations, we will ignore these variables—as is commonly done in many empirical demand studies—and write the general demand function as

$$Q = f(P, M, P_R, N)$$

where

Q = quantity purchased of a good or service

P = price of the good or service

M = consumers' income

P_R = price(s) of related good(s)

N = number of buyers

While this general demand specification seems rather simple and straight-forward, the task of defining and collecting the data for demand estimation re-quires careful consideration of numerous factors. For example, it is important to recognize the geographic boundaries of the product market. Suppose a firm sells its product only in California. In this case, the consumer income variable (M) should measure the buyers' incomes in the state of California. Using average household income in the United States would be a mistake unless California's household income level matches nationwide income levels and trends. It is also crucial to include the prices of all substitute and complement goods that affect sales of the firm's product in California. While we will illustrate empirical demand functions using just one related good (either a substitute or a complement), there are often numerous related goods whose prices should be included in the speci-fication of an empirical demand function. Whether the market is growing (or shrinking) in size is another consideration. Researchers frequently include a mea-sure of population in the demand specification as a proxy variable for the number of buyers. As you can see from this brief discussion, defining and collecting data to estimate even a simple general demand function requires careful consideration.

A Linear Empirical Demand Specification

The simplest demand function is one that specifies a linear relation. In linear form, the empirical demand function is specified as

$$Q = a + bP + cM + dP_R + eN$$

In this equation, the parameter b measures the change in quantity demanded that would result from a one-unit change in price. That is, $b = \Delta Q/\Delta P$, which is as-sumed to be negative. Also,

$$c = \Delta Q/\Delta M \gtrless 0 \text{ if the good is } \begin{cases} \text{normal} \\ \text{inferior} \end{cases}$$

and

$$d = \Delta Q/\Delta P_R \gtrless 0 \text{ if commodity } R \text{ is a } \begin{cases} \text{substitute} \\ \text{complement} \end{cases}$$

The parameter e measures the change in quantity demanded per one-unit change in the number of buyers; that is, $e = \Delta Q/\Delta N$, which is assumed to be positive. Us-ing the techniques of regression analysis, this linear demand function can be esti-mated to provide estimates of the parameters a, b, c, d, and e. Then t-tests are performed, or p-values examined, to determine if these parameters are statistically significant.

As stressed in Chapter 6, elasticities of demand are an important aspect of de-mand analysis. The elasticities of demand—with respect to price, income, and the prices of related commodities—can be calculated from a linear demand function without much difficulty. From our discussion in Chapter 6, it follows that, for a linear specification, the *estimated* price elasticity of demand is

$$\hat{E} = \hat{b} \times \frac{P}{Q}$$

As you know from the discussion of demand elasticity in Chapter 6, the price elasticity depends on where it is measured along the demand curve (note the P/Q term in the formula). The elasticity should be evaluated at the price and quantity values that correspond to the point on the demand curve being analyzed. In similar manner, the income elasticity may be estimated as

$$\hat{E}_M = \hat{c} \times \frac{M}{Q}$$

Likewise, the estimated cross-price elasticity is

$$\hat{E}_{XR} = \hat{d} \times \frac{P_R}{Q}$$

where the X in the subscript refers to the good for which demand is being estimated. Note that we denote values of variables and parameters that are statistically estimated (i.e., empirically determined) by placing a "hat" over the variable or parameter. In this discussion, for example, the empirical elasticities are designated as $\hat{E}$, $\hat{E}_M$, and $\hat{E}_{XR}$, while the empirically estimated parameter values are designated by $\hat{a}$, $\hat{b}$, $\hat{c}$, $\hat{d}$, and $\hat{e}$.

A Nonlinear Empirical Demand Specification

The most commonly employed nonlinear demand specification is the log-linear (or constant elasticity) form. A log-linear demand function is written as

$$Q = aP^b M^c P_R^d N^e$$

The obvious potential advantage of this form is that it provides a better estimate if the true demand function is indeed nonlinear. Furthermore, as you may recall from Chapter 4, this specification allows for the direct estimation of the elasticities. Specifically, the value of parameter b measures the price elasticity of demand. Likewise, c and d, respectively, measure the income elasticity and cross-price elasticity of demand.[1]

As you learned in Chapter 4, to obtain estimates from a log-linear demand function, you must convert it to natural logarithms. Thus the function to be estimated is linear in the logarithms:

$$\ln Q = \ln a + b \ln P + c \ln M + d \ln P_R + e \ln N$$

---

[1]The appendix to this chapter shows the derivation of the elasticities associated with the log-linear demand specification.

Choosing a Demand Specification

Although we have presented only two functional forms (linear and log-linear) as possible choices for specifying the empirical demand equation, there are many possible functional forms from which to choose. Unfortunately, the exact functional form of the demand equation generally is not known to the researcher. As noted in Chapter 4, choosing an incorrect functional form of the equation to be estimated results in biased estimates of the parameters of the equation. Selecting the appropriate functional form for the empirical demand equation warrants more than a toss of a coin on the part of the researcher.

In practice, choosing the functional form to use is, to a large degree, a matter of judgment and experience. Nevertheless, there are some things a manager can do to suggest the best choice of functional form. When possible, a manager should consider the functional form used in similar empirical studies of demand. If a linear specification has worked well in the past or has worked well for other products that are similar, specifying a linear demand function may be justified. In some cases a manager may have information or experience that indicates whether the demand function is either linear or curvilinear, and this functional form is then used to estimate the demand equation.

Sometimes researchers employ a series of regressions to settle on a suitable specification of demand. If the estimated coefficients of the first regression specification have the wrong signs, or if they are not statistically significant, the specification of the model may be wrong. Researchers may then estimate some new specifications, using the same data, to search for a specification that gives significant coefficients with the expected signs.[2]

For the two specifications we have discussed here, a choice between them should consider whether the sample data to be used for estimating demand are best represented by a demand function with varying elasticities (linear demand) or by one with constant elasticity (log-linear demand). When price and quantity observations are spread over a wide range of values, elasticities are more likely to vary, and a linear specification with its varying elasticities is usually a more appropriate specification of demand. Alternatively, if the sample data are clustered over a narrow price (and quantity) range, a constant-elasticity specification of demand, such as a log-linear model, may be a better choice than a linear model. Again we stress that experience in estimating demand functions and additional training in econometric techniques are needed in order to become skilled at specifying the empirical demand function.

We now discuss how to estimate the parameters of the empirical demand function. As it turns out, not only must you choose the proper functional form for the empirical demand equation, but you must also choose the correct method of estimation.

---

[2]In a strict statistical sense, it is incorrect to estimate more than one model specification with the same set of data. This practice is common, however, given the high costs often associated with collecting sample data.

ILLUSTRATION 7.1

Demand for Imported Goods in Trinidad and Tobago:
A Log-Linear Estimation

Trinidad and Tobago, two small developing countries in the Caribbean, rely heavily on imports from other nations to provide their citizens with consumer and capital goods. Policymakers in these two countries need estimates of the demand for various imported goods to aid them in their trade-related negotiations and to make forecasts of trade balances in Trinidad and Tobago. The price elasticities and income elasticities of demand are of particular interest.

In a recent empirical study, John S. Gafar estimated the demand for imported goods in the two countries, using a log-linear specification of demand.[a] According to Gafar, the two most common functional forms used to estimate import demand are the linear and log-linear forms. As we noted, the choice of functional form is often based on the past experience of experts in a particular area of empirical research. Gafar chose to use the log-linear specification because a number of other import studies "have shown that the log-linear specification is preferable to the linear specification."[b] Gafar noted that he experimented with both the linear and log-linear forms and found the log-linear model had the higher R^2.

In his study, Gafar estimated the demand for imports of eight groups of commodities. The demand for any particular group of imported goods is specified as

$$Q_d = aP^bM^c$$

where Q_d is the quantity of the imported good demanded by Trinidad and Tobago, P is the price of the imported good (relative to the price of a bundle of domestically produced goods), and M is an income variable. Taking natural logarithms of the demand equation results in the following demand equation to be estimated:

$$\ln Q_d = \ln a + b \ln P + c \ln M$$

Recall from the discussion in the text that b is the price elasticity of demand and c is the income elasticity of demand. The sign of $\hat{b}$ is expected to be negative and the sign of $\hat{c}$ can be either positive or negative. The results of estimation are presented in the accompanying table.

Estimated Price and Income Elasticities in Trinidad and Tobago

Product group	Price elasticity estimates ($\hat{b}$)	Income elasticity estimates ($\hat{c}$)
Food	−0.6553	1.6411
Beverages and tobacco	−0.0537[n]	1.8718
Crude materials (except fuel)	−1.3879	4.9619
Animal and vegetable oils and fats	−0.3992	1.8688
Chemicals	−0.7211	2.2711
Manufactured goods	−0.2774[n]	3.2085
Machinery and transport equipment	−0.6159	2.9452
Miscellaneous manufactured articles	−1.4585	4.1997

Only two of the estimated parameters are *not* statistically significant at the 5 percent level of significance (denoted by "n" in the table). Note that all the product groups have the expected sign for $\hat{b}$, except manufactured goods, for which the parameter estimate is not statistically significant. The estimates of $\hat{c}$ suggest that all eight product groups are normal goods ($\hat{c} > 0$). As you can see, with the log-linear specification, it is much easier to estimate demand elasticities than it is with a linear specification.

[a]This illustration is based on John S. Gafar, "The Determinants of Import Demand in Trinidad and Tobago: 1967–84," *Applied Economics* 20 (1988).
[b]Ibid.

7.2 MARKET-DETERMINED VERSUS MANAGER-DETERMINED PRICES

As noted earlier, estimating the parameters of the empirical demand function can be accomplished using regression analysis, and the method of estimating the parameters depends on whether the price of the product is determined by the intersection of demand and supply curves (a *market-determined* price) or is set by the manager of a firm (a *manager-determined* price). As we have stressed throughout the text, our goal is to show you how to *use* estimated values of parameters in decision making, rather than to show you the statistical details involved in computing the estimates. In this section, we will briefly discuss *why* the parameters of a demand function in which price is market-determined cannot be correctly estimated using the same estimation method that is appropriate for estimating parameters of a demand function in which price is manager-determined. While it is not important for the purposes of managerial decision making to understand the computational procedure required to estimate correctly demand curves with market-determined prices, it is quite important that you know which statistical estimation procedure is the appropriate one for your firm. As you will see, the statistical problems that sometimes arise in demand estimation can be routinely handled by "asking" the computer to use the correct estimation procedure.

For some firms, a manager does not set the price of the firm's product; rather, as you saw in Chapter 2, price is determined by the point where the industry's supply curve crosses its demand curve. Recall from Chapter 1 that firms in this situation are called *price-taking* firms. For example, firms producing agricultural commodities must generally accept market-determined prices for their products. When price is determined by the simultaneous interaction of demand and supply, price is being "set" within a system of demand and supply equations. When a variable is determined by a system of equations, it is said to be an **endogenous variable** in that system. For price-taking firms, managers must accept the price of the product as it is determined by market forces in a system of demand and supply equations.

endogenous variable
A variable whose value is determined by a system of equations.

When a firm produces a differentiated product or competes with a relatively small number of rivals, the firm can choose the price of its product and the associated quantity along the firm's downward-sloping demand curve. Recall from our discussion in Chapter 1 that firms such as these are called *price-setting* firms and possess market power. For price-setting firms, price is not determined by a system of demand and supply equations. Price, in this situation, is an **exogenous variable** because it is *not* determined within a system of demand and supply equations. A force outside the system, the manager of the firm, determines price.[3] We can summarize our discussion with a relation:

exogenous variable
A variable in a system of equations that is determined outside the system.

---

[3]Another situation in which price is exogenous occurs when a government agency determines the price a firm can charge, as when public service commissions set the price utilities can charge for electricity.

▢ **Relation** Managers of price-taking firms do not set the price of the product they sell; rather, prices are endogenous or market-determined by the intersection of demand and supply. Managers of price-setting firms set the price of the product they sell by producing the quantity associated with the chosen price on the downward-sloping demand curve facing the firm. Because price is manager-determined rather than market-determined, price is exogenous for price-setting firms.

The distinction between price-taking firms and price-setting firms plays an important role in determining how the parameters of an empirical demand function must be estimated in order to obtain estimates that are not biased. In order for the least-squares method of estimating the parameters of a regression equation to yield unbiased estimates of the regression parameters, the explanatory variables cannot be correlated with the random error term of the equation. We did not mention this fact in our discussion of regression analysis in Chapter 4 because virtually all the applications covered in this book involve explanatory variables that are not likely to be correlated with the random error term in the equation. There is one important exception, however, and it involves the estimation of demand when the price of the product or service—an explanatory variable in all demand functions— is endogenously determined by demand and supply. In the next section, we discuss estimation of demand when price is endogenous and show how to use a method of estimation called *two-stage least-squares* that is appropriate for estimating the industry demand for price-taking firms. Then in Section 7.4 we show how to use the standard regression procedure discussed in Chapter 4—frequently called **ordinary least-squares (OLS)** by econometricians to differentiate it from other regression procedures such as two-stage least-squares—to estimate empirical demand functions for price-setting firms.

ordinary least-squares (OLS)
Another name for standard regression analysis.

7.3 ESTIMATING INDUSTRY DEMAND FOR PRICE-TAKING FIRMS

As we discussed in the last section, a fundamental difficulty arises in estimating industry demand for price-taking firms because the observed quantity and price data used in a regression analysis of demand are determined simultaneously by the intersection of demand and supply. Consequently, the observed variation in equilibrium quantity and price is caused by all the factors that can shift either demand or supply, and estimation of industry demand for price-taking firms involves a bit more of a challenge than estimation of demand curves for price-setting firms (discussed in Section 7.4). The problem of estimating demand when price is market-determined is frequently referred to as the **simultaneity problem.**

simultaneity problem
The problem in estimating industry demand that arises because variation in observed values of market quantity and price is simultaneously determined by changes in both demand and supply.

To understand the nature of the simultaneity problem, consider the following simple model of industry demand and supply curves for gasoline (say, unleaded 89 octane grade):

$$\text{Demand:} \quad Q = a + bP + cM + \varepsilon_d$$
$$\text{Supply:} \quad Q = h + kP + lP_I + \varepsilon_s$$

where Q is the number of gallons of gasoline sold in a month (i.e., equilibrium Q), P is the average price of gasoline (before taxes are added), M is consumer income,

FIGURE 7.1
The Nature of Simultaneity

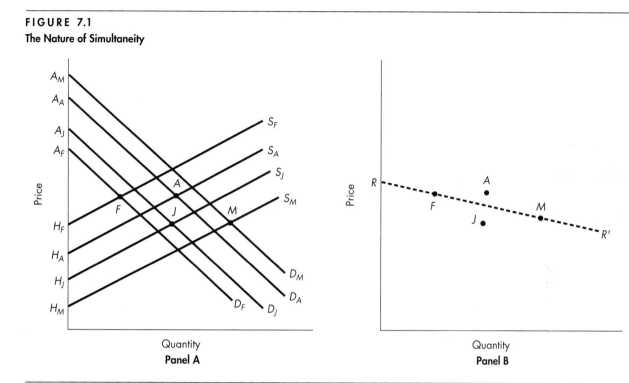

P_I is the average price of crude oil (a key ingredient input for gasoline production), and ε_d and ε_s are the random error terms representing random influences on demand and supply, respectively. These two equations make up a system of two simultaneous equations with two *endogenous* variables: Q and P. The values of the other economic variables in the system, M and P_I, are determined outside this system of equations and are exogenous variables.

Panel A of Figure 7.1 shows how four monthly observations, from January through April, on P and Q are generated by the demand and supply curves for gasoline. The demand and supply equations in Panel A can be represented as

$$\text{Demand:}\quad Q = A + bP, \quad \text{where } A = a + cM + \varepsilon_d$$
$$\text{Supply:}\quad Q = H + kP, \quad \text{where } H = h + lP_I + \varepsilon_s$$

The location of the demand curve in any one of the four months is determined by the value of the demand intercept, A, for that month. The demand intercept is itself determined by the value of the exogenous variable M and the random error term ε_d, which accounts for random variation in monthly gasoline demand. Similarly, the location of monthly supply is determined by the values of P_I and ε_s. The four monthly values of the demand and supply intercepts are shown as A_J, A_F, A_M, A_A, and H_J, H_F, H_M, H_A, respectively. The observed values of price and quantity at points J, F, M, and A in Panel A of Figure 7.1 are determined solely by the values of the exogenous variables of the system and the random errors in both demand and supply. Consequently, the equilibrium values of price and quantity, P_E and Q_E, can be expressed as functions of M, P_I, ε_d, and ε_s:

$$P_E = f(M, P_I, \varepsilon_d, \varepsilon_s) \quad \text{and} \quad Q_E = g(M, P_I, \varepsilon_d, \varepsilon_s)$$

reduced-form equations

Equations expressing each endogenous variable as functions of all exogenous variables and random errors in the system.

These equations, which express the endogenous variables as functions of the exogenous variables and the random error terms, are called the **reduced-form equations** of the system. The reduced-form equations show two things clearly: (1) The observed values of P and Q are each determined by *all* the exogenous variables and random errors in both the demand *and* the supply equations, and (2) the observed values of price are correlated with the random errors in both demand and supply. The first point shows why, in estimating industry demand, information about variation in supply-shifting variables is required to properly explain the observed variation in quantity demanded (which is Q_E). The second point explains why price is correlated with the random errors. As we mentioned, when explanatory variables are correlated with the random error term of the equation to be estimated, the ordinary method of least-squares estimation will produce biased estimates of the parameters of a demand equation. Because price must always be one of the explanatory variables in demand estimation, the ordinary least-squares method (OLS) presented in Chapter 4 is not the best way to estimate an industry demand equation when price is market-determined.

Panel B of Figure 7.1 illustrates the challenge of estimating the true demand equation that is generating the observed price-quantity combinations J, F, M, and A. Fitting a regression line through the scatter of data points at J, F, M, and A produces a regression line RR' that does not accurately reflect the true demand function. The slope of RR' is too flat, and the intercept of RR' is smaller than it should be for any of the four monthly values of M.

identification of demand

The process of making sure the sample data will trace out the true demand curve.

two-stage least-squares (2SLS)

A method of estimating parameters of demand when price is endogenous or market-determined.

To properly estimate industry demand when price is endogenously determined by the intersection of demand and supply, two steps must be followed. The first step, called **identification of demand,** involves determining whether it is possible to trace out the true demand curve from the sample data generated by the underlying system of equations. If the demand curve can be identified from sample data—as it can be in most cases—then the second step involves using the method of **two-stage least-squares (2SLS)** to estimate the parameters of the industry demand equation. A complete discussion of the identification of demand and the use of two-stage least-squares is quite complex and unnecessary for our purpose, which, throughout the book, is to show you how to use and interpret the parameters estimated using regression analysis. We turn now to a brief intuitive discussion of identification and then to the use of two-stage least-squares regression.

Identification of Industry Demand

The observed quantities sold and the observed prices are not simply points on a specific demand curve but, rather, points of market equilibrium that occur at the

FIGURE 7.2
Identification of Industry
Demand

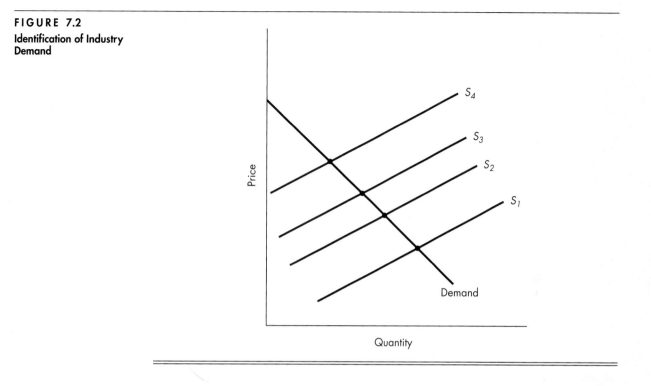

intersection of the demand and supply curves. As you saw in Panel B of Figure 7.1, the observed price-quantity combinations (J, F, M, A) may not trace out a picture of the underlying industry demand curve. Before a researcher runs a regression analysis to estimate an industry demand equation, the researcher must be sure that the data generated by the underlying system of demand and supply equations will trace out the true demand equation.

There are several ways to identify an industry demand equation, but we will show you only the most widely used method here. Figure 7.2 illustrates this method of identifying demand. When the supply equation contains an exogenous supply-shifting variable that does not also cause the demand curve to shift, then changes in this exogenous variable shift the supply curve along a stationary demand curve. The resulting points of intersection along the demand curve generate observable points of equilibrium that trace out the true underlying demand curve; demand is identified.

Typically, the identification problem is solved when, in addition to the price of the product, quantity supplied is a function of at least one of the supply-shifting variables discussed in Chapter 2 (technology, input prices, prices of goods related in production, price expectations, or the number of sellers). Since a supply-shifting variable will not generally also be a demand-shifting variable, the industry demand function is identified in most commonly occurring situations. We can summarize this method of identifying demand in a relation:

□ **Relation** An industry demand equation is identified when it is possible to estimate the true demand function from a sample of observations of equilibrium output and price. Industry demand is identified when supply includes at least one exogenous variable that is not also in the demand equation.

Estimation of Industry Demand Using Two-Stage Least-Squares (2SLS)

In order for the ordinary least-square method of estimating the parameters of a regression equation to yield unbiased estimates of the regression parameters, the right-hand-side explanatory variables cannot be correlated with the random error term of the equation. Since all demand functions will have price as one of the explanatory variables, OLS estimation is not a suitable method of estimating industry demand when price is an endogenous variable. As can be seen by examining the reduced-form equations, random variations in either the demand or the supply equations will cause variation in price, and, consequently, price will be correlated with the random error term in the demand (and supply) equation(s). Thus when price is market-determined—as it will be for price-taking firms—price will be correlated with the random error term in the demand equation, and the least-squares estimates of the parameter of the demand equation will be biased. Recall that a parameter estimate is biased if the average (or expected) value of the estimate does not equal the true value of the parameter. The bias that occurs when the OLS estimation method is employed to estimate parameters of an equation for which one, or more, of the right-hand-side variables (price in this case) is an endogenous variable is called a **simultaneous equations bias.**

simultaneous equations bias
Bias in estimation that occurs when the ordinary least-squares estimation method is used to estimate the parameters of an equation for which one, or more, of the explanatory variables is an endogenous variable.

Econometricians employ the two-stage least-squares (2SLS) estimation technique to address the problem of simultaneous equations bias. As its name suggests, the estimation proceeds in two steps. In the first stage, a proxy variable for the endogenous variable (price in this case) is created in such a way that the proxy variable is correlated with market price but uncorrelated with the random error term in the demand equation. In the second stage, price is replaced with the proxy variable created in the first stage, and the usual least-squares procedure is then employed to estimate the parameters of the demand equation.[4] Two-stage least-squares can be applied only to demand equations that are identified. If industry demand is not identified, there is no estimation technique that will correctly estimate the parameters of the demand equation. We summarize this discussion in a principle:

□ **Principle** When market price is an endogenous variable, price will be correlated with the random error term in the demand equation, causing a simultaneous equations bias if the ordinary least-squares (OLS) method of estimation is applied. To avoid simultaneous equations bias, the two-stage least-squares method of estimation (2SLS) can be employed if the industry demand equation is identified.

---

[4]A more complete presentation of 2SLS estimation is given in the appendix to this chapter.

Before we illustrate in the next section how to estimate an industry demand function using 2SLS, we will summarize the previous theoretical discussion with a step-by-step guide to estimating an industry demand function:[5]

Step 1: Specify the industry demand and supply equations

Since price is determined by the intersection of industry demand and supply curves, *both* a demand and a supply equation must be specified in order to estimate the demand function. For example, a rather typical specification of demand and supply functions can be written as

$$\text{Demand:} \quad Q = a + bP + cM + dP_R$$
$$\text{Supply:} \quad Q = h + kP + P_I$$

where Q is market quantity, P is price, M is income, P_R is price of a good related in consumption, and P_I is price of a production input. Other exogenous demand-shifting or supply-shifting variables, could, of course, be utilized when needed, and nonlinear functional forms also can be estimated.

Step 2: Check for identification of industry demand

As explained earlier, estimation of demand cannot proceed unless the industry demand is identified. You cannot successfully estimate parameters of an industry demand function, even using the two-stage least-squares procedure, if demand is not identified.[6] As you can verify, the demand equation specified in Step 1 is identified because the specification of *supply* includes at least one exogenous variable—P_I in this instance—that is not also in the demand equation.

Step 3: Collect data for the variables in demand and supply

Data must be collected for the endogenous and exogenous variables in *both* the demand and the supply equations, even if only one of the equations is to be estimated. The 2SLS procedure requires data for the exogenous variables in both functions in order to correct for simultaneous equations bias in estimating either *one* of the equations.

Step 4: Estimate industry demand using 2SLS

Many regression programs are available, even for personal computers, that have a two-stage least-squares routine, and these 2SLS packages perform the two stages of estimation automatically. It is normally necessary for the user to specify which variables are endogenous and which are exogenous in the system equations. Once the estimates for the parameters of a demand (or supply) equation have been

---

[5]Industry supply can be estimated by following the same steps as for estimating industry demand. As we will show you later in this chapter, forecasting future industry prices and quantities requires estimation of *both* the demand and the supply equations in the system.

[6]Should you accidentally attempt to use 2SLS to estimate a function that is not identified, the 2SLS procedure will not be able to calculate parameter estimates, and the computer software will generate an error message.

obtained from the second stage of the regression, their significance can be evaluated using either a t-test or the p-values in precisely the same manner as for any other regression equation.[7] Demand elasticities can then be computed as explained at the beginning of this chapter.

To illustrate how to implement these steps to estimate the industry demand when price is market-determined and to illustrate how to calculate and interpret estimates of the associated demand elasticities, we will now estimate the worldwide demand for copper using data from the world copper market.

The World Demand for Copper: Estimating Industry Demand Using 2SLS

To illustrate how an industry demand function is estimated using two-stage least-squares, we estimate the world demand for copper (i.e., the market demand for all countries buying copper). In its simplest form, the world demand for copper is a function of the price of copper, income, and the price of any related commodities. Using aluminum as the related commodity, because it is the primary substitute for copper in manufacturing, the demand function can be written in linear form as

$$Q_{copper} = a + bP_{copper} + cM + dP_{aluminum}$$

It is tempting to simply regress copper consumption on the price of copper, income, and the price of aluminum. Because the price of copper and the quantity of copper consumed are determined simultaneously by the intersection of industry demand and supply, it is necessary first to determine if copper demand is identified; then, if it is, the empirical demand function for copper can be estimated using 2SLS. The copper demand function is identified if it is reasonable to believe that the copper supply equation includes at least one exogenous variable not found in the copper demand function. We turn now to the specification of copper supply.

Begin by letting the quantity supplied of copper depend on the price of copper and the level of available technology. Next consider inventories, which play a particularly important role in the market for copper. When inventories rise, current production usually falls. To measure *changes* in copper inventory, define a variable denoted by X to be the ratio of consumption to production in the preceding period. As consumption declines relative to production, X will fall, and current production is expected to decline. Thus the supply function can be reasonably specified in linear form as

$$Q_{copper} = e + fP_{copper} + gT + hX$$

Since the supply function includes two exogenous variables that are excluded from the demand equation (T and X), the demand function is identified and may be estimated using 2SLS.

The data needed to estimate demand are (1) the world consumption (sales) of copper in 1,000 metric tons; (2) the price of copper and aluminum in cents per

---

[7]Due to the manner in which 2SLS estimates are calculated, the R^2 and F-statistics are not particularly meaningful and are not reported in many instances.

pound, deflated by a price index to obtain the real (i.e., constant-dollar) prices; (3) an index of real per capita income; and (4) the world production of copper (to calculate the inventory variable, X). Time serves as a proxy for available technology (this assumes that the level of technology increased steadily over time). The resulting data set is presented in Table A of the appendix at the end of this chapter.

Using these data, the demand function is estimated using 2SLS. The results of these estimations are presented here:

```
             Two-Stage Least-Squares Estimation

DEPENDENT VARIABLE:

    OBSERVATIONS:

                 PARAMETER      STANDARD
  VARIABLE       ESTIMATE       ERROR        T-RATIO     P-VALUE

  INTERCEPT      -6837.800      1264.500     -5.408      0.0001
  PC             -66.495        31.534       -2.109      0.0472
  M              13997.7        1306.300     10.715      0.0001
  PA             107.662        44.510       2.419       0.0247
```

Before estimating the industry demand equation, we determined whether the estimated coefficients $\hat{b}$, $\hat{c}$, and $\hat{d}$ should be positive or negative based on theoretical considerations. We expected that (1) due to a downward-sloping demand curve for copper, $b < 0$; (2) because copper is a normal good, $c > 0$; and (3) because copper and aluminum are substitutes, $d > 0$. The estimated coefficients do conform to this sign pattern. Examining the p-values for the parameter estimates shows that all parameter estimates are statistically significant at the 5 percent level, or better.

Now, we calculate estimates of the demand elasticities. While the elasticity can be evaluated at any point on the demand curve, we choose to estimate the elasticities for the values of P_c, M, and P_A in the last year of the sample. From Table A in the appendix, we obtain, for the 25th observation in the sample, the values $P_c = 36.33$, $M = 1.07$, and $P_A = 22.75$. At the point associated with the 25th observation on the estimated demand curve, the estimated quantity of copper demanded is calculated to be 8,172.49 ($= -6,837.8 - 66.495 \times 36.33 + 13,997 \times 1.07 + 107.66 \times 22.75$). The price elasticity of demand is estimated to be

$$\hat{E} = \hat{b}\,\frac{P_c}{Q_c} = -66.495 \times \frac{36.33}{8,172.49} = -0.296$$

Similarly, the estimated income elasticity of demand is

$$\hat{E}_M = \hat{c}\,\frac{M_c}{Q_c} = 13,997 \times \frac{1.07}{8,172.49} = 1.833$$

and the estimated cross-price elasticity of demand is

$$\hat{E}_{CA} = \hat{d}\,\frac{P_A}{Q_c} = 107.66 \times \frac{22.75}{8{,}172.49} = 0.300$$

Thus the demand for copper—when evaluated at the point associated with the 25th observation in the sample—is inelastic ($|E| < 1$), copper is a normal good ($E_M > 0$), and copper is a substitute for aluminum ($E_{CA} > 0$). Note that copper is a rather poor substitute for aluminum since a 10 percent increase in the price of aluminum increases the quantity demanded of copper by only 3 percent.

We have stressed throughout this and the previous sections that estimation of demand for a price-taking industry must be carried out using the technique of two-stage least-squares (2SLS) rather than with the somewhat easier method of ordinary least-squares (OLS), which can be used to estimate the demand facing a price-setting firm. Unfortunately, business statisticians and forecasters sometimes ignore this important principle, perhaps because they don't know better or they think it really doesn't matter all that much. As stated previously, a simultaneous equations bias results when OLS is used when 2SLS should be used. In Technical Problem 6 at the end of this chapter, you will see that estimating the copper demand equation using OLS instead of 2SLS does indeed cause problems for estimating copper demand. Having established this most important distinction, we now turn to estimating demand when the price on a firm's demand curve is chosen by the manager.

T ▷ 5 6 7

7.4 ESTIMATING DEMAND FOR A PRICE-SETTING FIRM

When a manager sets the price of a product, price is an *exogenous* variable because its value is determined by forces other than those of demand and supply—namely, by the "force" of the manager. When price is set by a manager, no simultaneity problem exists. Demand is identified because the manager's price changes can trace out the firm's demand function. Ordinary least-squares (OLS) estimation is appropriate since price is not correlated with the random error terms, because it is exogenously determined by the manager. We summarize this important point with a principle:

□ **Principle** When a firm is a price-setting firm, the problem of simultaneity vanishes, and the demand curve for the firm can be estimated using the ordinary least-squares method of estimation.

Before discussing an example of how to estimate the demand function for a price-setting firm using OLS, we give you the following step-by-step guide.

Step 1: Specify the price-setting firm's demand function
As discussed in Section 7.1, the demand function for the firm is specified by choosing a linear or curvilinear functional form and by deciding which demand-shifting variables to include in the empirical demand equation along with the price of the good or service.

Step 2: Collect data on the variables in the firm's demand function

Data must be collected for quantity and price as well as for the demand-shifting variables specified in Step 1.

Step 3: Estimate the price-setting firm's demand using OLS

Since there is no simultaneity problem when estimating demand for a price-setting firm, the parameters of the firm's demand function can be estimated using the OLS procedure. Demand elasticities can then be computed as discussed earlier in Section 7.1.

As you can see by comparing these steps with the ones presented in the previous section, demand for a price-setting firm is generally easier to estimate than industry demand for a price-taking firm.

Estimating the Demand for a Pizza Firm: An Example

We will now illustrate how a firm with price-setting power can estimate the demand equation for its output. Consider Checkers Pizza, one of only two home delivery pizza firms serving the Westbury neighborhood of Houston. The manager and owner of Checkers Pizza, Ann Chovie, knows that her customers are rather price-conscious. Pizza buyers in Westbury pay close attention to the price she charges for a home-delivered pizza and the price her competitor, Al's Pizza Oven, charges for a similar home-delivered pizza.

Ann decides to estimate the empirical demand function for her firm's pizza. She collects data on the last 24 months of pizza sales from her own company records. She knows the price she charged for her pizza during that time period, and she also has kept a record of the prices charged at Al's Pizza Oven. Ann is able to obtain average household income figures from the Westbury Small Business Development Center. The only other competitor in the neighborhood is the local branch of McDonald's. Ann is able to find the price of a Big Mac for the last 24 months from advertisements in old newspapers. She adjusts her price and income data for the effects of inflation by deflating the dollar figures, using a deflator she obtained from the *Survey of Current Business*.[8] To measure the number of buyers in the market area (N), Ann collected data on the number of residents in Westbury. As it turned out, the number of residents had not changed during the last 24 months, so Ann dropped N from her specification of demand. The data she collected are presented in Table B in the appendix at the end of this chapter.

Since the price of pizza at Checkers Pizza is set by Ann, and therefore is an exogenous variable, she can estimate the empirical demand equation using the OLS procedure—2SLS is not required. Ann first estimates the following linear specification of demand using the 24 monthly observations she collected:

$$Q = a + bP + cM + dP_{Al} + eP_{BMac}$$

---

[8]The *Survey of Current Business* can be found at the website for the U.S. Department of Commerce, Bureau of Economic Analysis: *www.bea.doc.gov*. Implicit price deflators are presented quarterly from 1959 to the present in Table C.1, "GDP and Other Major NIPA Aggregates."

ILLUSTRATION 7.2

Estimating the Demand for Corporate Jets

Given the success that many of our former students have experienced in their careers and the success we predict for you, we thought it might be valuable for you to examine the market for corporate aircraft. Rather than dwell on the lackluster piston-driven and turboprop aircraft, we instead focus this illustration on the demand for corporate jets. In a recent empirical study of general aviation aircraft, McDougall and Cho estimated the demand using techniques that are similar to the ones in this chapter.[a] Let's now look at how regression analysis can be used to estimate the demand for corporate jets.

To estimate the demand for corporate jets, Mc-Dougall and Cho specified the variables that affect jet aircraft sales and the general demand relation as follows:

$$Q_J = f(P, P_R, M, D)$$

when

Q_J = number of new corporate jets purchased

P = price of a new corporate jet

P_R = price of a used corporate jet

M = income of the buyers

D = so-called dummy variable to account for seasonality of jet sales

Since the market for used jets is extensively used by corporations, the price of used jets (a substitute) is included in the demand equation. We should note that P and P_R are not the actual prices paid for the aircraft but are instead the user costs of an aircraft. A jet aircraft provides many miles of transportation, not all of which are consumed during the first period of ownership. The user cost of a jet measures the cost per mile (or per hour) of operating the jet by spreading the initial

purchase price over the lifetime of jet transportation services and adjusting for depreciation in the value of the aircraft.

The income of the buyers (M) is approximated by corporate profit since most buyers of small jet aircraft are corporations. The data used to estimate the demand equation are quarterly observations (1981I–1985III). Many corporations purchase jets at year-end for tax purposes. Consequently, jet sales tend to be higher in the fourth quarter, all else constant, than in the other three quarters of any given year. Adjusting for this pattern of seasonality is accomplished by adding a variable called a "dummy variable," which takes on values of 1 for observations in the fourth quarter and 0 for observations in the other three quarters. In effect, the dummy variable shifts the estimated demand equation rightward during the fourth quarter. A complete explanation of the use of dummy variables to adjust for seasonality in data is presented later in this chapter (Section 7.6).

The following linear model of demand for corporate jets is estimated:

$$Q_J = a + bP + cP_R + dM + eD_4$$

McDougall and Cho estimated this demand equation using least-squares estimation rather than two-stage least-squares because they noted that the supply curve for aircraft is almost perfectly elastic or horizontal. If the supply of jets is horizontal, the supply price of new jets is constant no matter what the level of output. Because the market price of jets is determined by the position of the (horizontal) jet supply curve, and the position of supply is fixed by the exogenous determinants of supply, the price of jets is itself exogenous. If jet price (P) is exogenous, least-squares regression is appropriate. The computer output obtained by McDougall and Cho from estimating this equation follows:

DEPENDENT VARIABLE: QJ	R-SQUARE	F-RATIO	P-VALUE ON F		
OBSERVATIONS: 18	0.8623	20.35	0.0001		
VARIABLE	PARAMETER ESTIMATE	STANDARD ERROR	T-RATIO	P-VALUE
INTERCEPT	17.33	43.3250	0.40	0.6956
P	−0.00016	0.000041	−3.90	0.0018
PR	0.00050	0.000104	4.81	0.0003
M	−0.85010	0.7266	−1.17	0.2630
D4	31.99	8.7428	3.66	0.0030

Theoretically, the predicted signs of the estimated coefficients are (1) $\hat{b} < 0$, because demand for corporate jets is expected to be downward-sloping; (2) $\hat{c} > 0$, because new and used jets are substitutes; (3) $\hat{d} > 0$, because corporate jets are expected to be normal goods; and (4) $\hat{e} > 0$, because the tax effect at year-end should cause jet demand to increase (shift rightward) during the fourth quarter. All the estimates, except $\hat{d}$, match the expected signs.

The p-values for the individual parameter estimates indicate that all the variables in the model play a statistically significant role in determining sales of jet aircraft, except corporate profits. The model as a whole does a good job of explaining the variation in sales of corporate jets: 86 percent of this variation is explained by the model ($R^2 = 0.8623$). The F-ratio indicates that the model as a whole is significant at the 0.01 percent level.

McDougall and Cho estimated the price and cross-price elasticities of demand using the values of Q_J, P, and P_R in the third quarter of 1985:

$$E = \hat{b}\, \frac{P_{1985III}}{Q_{1985III}} = -3.95$$

$$E_{NU} = \hat{c}\, \frac{P_{R'1985III}}{Q_{1985III}} = 6.41$$

where E_{NU} is the cross-price elasticity between new-jet sales and the price of used jets. The price elasticity estimate suggests that the quantity demanded of new corporate jets is quite responsive to changes in the price of new jets ($|E| > 1$). Furthermore, a 10 percent decrease in the price of used jets is estimated to cause a 64.1 percent decrease in sales of new corporate jets. Given this rather large cross-price elasticity, used jets appear to be viewed by corporations as extremely close substitutes for new jets, and for this reason, we advise all of our managerial economics students to look closely at the used-jet market before buying a new corporate jet.

[a]The empirical results in this illustration are taken from Gerald S. McDougall and Dong W. Cho, "Demand Estimates for New General Aviation Aircraft: A User-Cost Approach," *Applied Economics* 20 (1988).

where

Q = sales of pizza at Checkers Pizza

P = price of a pizza at Checkers Pizza

M = average annual household income in Westbury

P_{Al} = price of a pizza at Al's Pizza Oven

P_{BMac} = price of a Big Mac at McDonald's

The following computer printout shows the results of her least-squares regression:

DEPENDENT VARIABLE: Q		R-SQUARE	F-RATIO	P-VALUE ON F
OBSERVATIONS: 24		0.9555	101.90	0.0001

VARIABLE	PARAMETER ESTIMATE	STANDARD ERROR	T-RATIO	P-VALUE
INTERCEPT	1183.80	506.298	2.34	0.0305
P	−213.422	13.4863	−15.83	0.0001
M	0.09109	0.01241	7.34	0.0001
PAL	101.303	38.7478	2.61	0.0171
PBMAC	71.8448	27.0997	2.65	0.0158

Ann tests the four estimated slope parameters ($\hat{b}$, $\hat{c}$, $\hat{d}$, and $\hat{e}$) for statistical significance at the 2 percent level of significance. The critical t-value for 19 degrees of freedom ($n - k = 24 - 5$) at the 2 percent significance level is 2.539. The t-ratios for all four slope parameters exceed 2.539, and thus the coefficients are all statistically significant. She is pleased to see that the model explains about 95.5 percent of the variation in her pizza sales ($R^2 = 0.9555$) and that the model as a whole is highly significant, as indicated by the p-value on the F-statistic of 0.0001.

Ann decides to calculate estimated demand elasticities at values of P, M, P_{Al}, and P_{BMac} that she feels "typify" the pizza market in Westbury for the past 24 months. These values are $P = 9.05$, $M = 26,614$, $P_{Al} = 10.12$, and $P_{BMac} = 1.15$. At this "typical" point on the estimated demand curve, the quantity of pizza demanded is

$$Q = 1,183.80 - 213.422(9.05) + 0.09109(26,614) + 101.303(10.12) + 71.8448(1.15)$$
$$= 2,784.4$$

The elasticities for the linear demand specification are estimated in the now familiar fashion:

$$\hat{E} = \hat{b}(P/Q) = -213.422(9.05/2,784.4) = -0.694$$
$$\hat{E}_M = \hat{c}(M/Q) = 0.09109(26,614/2,784.4) = 0.871$$
$$\hat{E}_{XAl} = \hat{d}(P_{Al}/Q) = 101.303(10.12/2,784.4) = 0.368$$
$$\hat{E}_{XBMac} = \hat{e}(P_{BMac}/Q) = 71.8448(1.15/2,784.4) = 0.030$$

Ann's estimated elasticities show that she prices her pizzas at a price where demand is inelastic ($|\hat{E}| < 1$). A 10 percent increase in average household income will cause sales to rise by 8.71 percent—pizzas are a normal good in Westbury. The estimated cross-price elasticity $\hat{E}_{XA1}$ suggests that if Al's Pizza Oven raises its pizza price by 10 percent, sales of Checkers' pizzas will increase by 3.68 percent. While the price of a Big Mac does play a statistically significant role in determining sales of Checkers' pizzas, the effect is estimated to be quite small. Indeed, a 10 percent decrease in the price of a Big Mac will decrease sales of Checkers' pizzas only by about one-third of 1 percent (0.30 percent). Apparently families in Westbury aren't very willing to substitute a Big Mac for a home-delivered pizza from Checkers Pizza.

While Ann is satisfied that a linear specification of demand for her firm's pizza does an outstanding job of explaining the variation in her pizza sales, she decides to estimate a nonlinear model just for comparison. Ann chooses a log-linear demand specification of the form

$$Q = aP^b M^c P_{A1}^d P_{BMac}^e$$

which can be transformed (by taking natural logarithms) into the following estimable form:

$$\ln Q = \ln a + b \ln P + c \ln M + d \ln P_{A1} + e \ln P_{BMac}$$

The regression results from the computer are presented here:

DEPENDENT VARIABLE: LNQ	R-SQUARE	F-RATIO	P-VALUE ON F
OBSERVATIONS: 24	0.9492	88.72	0.0001

VARIABLE	PARAMETER ESTIMATE	STANDARD ERROR	T-RATIO	P-VALUE
INTERCEPT	−0.72517	1.31437	−0.55	0.5876
LNP	−0.66269	0.04477	−14.80	0.0001
LNM	0.87705	0.12943	6.78	0.0001
LNPAL	0.50676	0.14901	3.40	0.0030
LNPBMAC	0.02843	0.01073	2.65	0.0158

While the F-ratio and R^2 for the log-linear model are just slightly smaller than those for the linear specification and the intercept estimate is not statistically significant at any generally used level of significance, the log-linear specification certainly performs well. Recall that the slope parameter estimates in a log-linear model are elasticities. While the elasticity estimates from the log-linear model come close to the elasticity estimates from the linear model, linear and log-linear specifications may not always produce such similar elasticity estimates. In general, the linear demand is appropriate when elasticities are likely to vary, and a log-linear specification is appropriate when elasticities are constant. In this case, Ann could use either one of the empirical demand functions for business decision making.

7.5 TIME-SERIES FORECASTS OF SALES AND PRICE

As explained in the introduction to this chapter, we will confine our discussion of statistical forecasting methods to the two most widely used categories: time-series models and econometric models. This section begins the discussion of forecasting by examining time-series models. The next section develops the econometric forecasting method.

A *time-series* is simply a time-ordered sequence of observations on a variable. In general, a **time-series model** uses only the time-series history of the variable of interest to predict future values. Time-series models describe the process by which these historical data were generated. Thus to forecast using time-series analysis, it is necessary to specify a mathematical model that represents the generating process. We will first discuss a general forecasting model and then give examples of price and sales forecasts.

time-series model
A statistical model that shows how a time-ordered sequence of observations on a variable is generated.

Linear Trend Forecasting

A linear trend is the simplest time-series forecasting method. Using this type of model, one could posit that sales or price increases or decreases linearly over time. For example, a firm's sales for the period 1994–2003 are shown by the 10 data points in Figure 7.3. The straight line that best fits the data scatter, calculated using simple regression analysis, is illustrated by the solid line in the figure. The fitted line indicates a positive trend in sales. Assuming that sales in the future will continue to follow the same trend, sales in any future period can be forecast by extending this line and picking the forecast values from this *extrapolated* dashed line for the desired future period. We have illustrated sales forecasts for 2004 and 2009 ($\hat{Q}_{2004}$ and $\hat{Q}_{2009}$) in Figure 7.3.

FIGURE 7.3
A Linear Trend Forecast

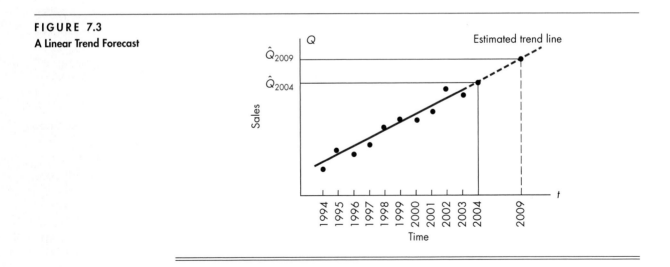

Summarizing this procedure, we assumed a linear relation between sales and time:

$$\hat{Q}_t = a + bt$$

Using the 10 observations for 1994–2003, we regressed time (t = 1994, 1995, ..., 2003), the independent variable expressed in years, on sales, the dependent variable expressed in dollars, to obtain the estimated trend line:

$$\hat{Q}_t = \hat{a} + \hat{b}t$$

This line best fits the historical data. It is important to test whether there is a statistically significant positive or negative trend in sales. As shown in Chapter 4, it is easy to determine if $\hat{b}$ is significantly different from zero either by using a t-test for statistical significance or by examining the p-value for $\hat{b}$. If $\hat{b}$ is positive and statistically significant, sales are trending upward over time. If $\hat{b}$ is negative and statistically significant, sales are trending downward over time. However, if $\hat{b}$ is not statistically significant, one would assume that $b = 0$, and sales are constant over time. That is, there is no relation between sales and time, and any variation in sales is due to random fluctuations.

If the estimation indicates a statistically significant trend, you can then use the estimated trend line to obtain forecasts of future sales. For example, if a manager wanted a forecast for sales in 2004, the manager would simply insert 2004 into the estimated trend line:

$$\hat{Q}_{2004} = \hat{a} + \hat{b} \times (2004)$$

A Sales Forecast for Terminator Pest Control

In January 2004, Arnold Schwartz started Terminator Pest Control, a small pest-control company in Atlanta. Terminator Pest Control serves mainly residential customers citywide. At the end of March 2005, after 15 months of operation, Arnold decides to apply for a business loan from his bank to buy another pest-control truck. The bank is somewhat reluctant to make the loan, citing concern that sales at Terminator Pest Control did not grow significantly over its first 15 months of business. In addition, the bank asks Arnold to provide a forecast of sales for the next three months (April, May, and June).

Arnold decides to do the forecast himself using a time-series model based on past sales figures. He collects the data on sales for the last 15 months—sales are measured as the number of homes serviced during a given month. Since data are collected monthly, Arnold creates a continuous time variable by numbering the months consecutively as January 2004 = 1, February 2004 = 2, and so on. The data for Terminator and a scatter diagram are shown in Figure 7.4. Arnold estimates the linear trend model

$$Q_t = a + bt$$

and gets the following printout from the computer:

FIGURE 7.4

Forecasting Sales for Terminator Pest Control

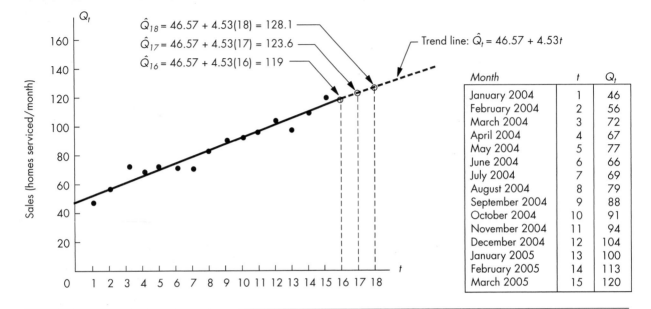

The t-ratio for the time variable, 12.49, exceeds the critical t of 3.012 for 13 degrees of freedom ($= 15 - 2$) at the 1 percent level of significance. The exact level of significance for the estimate 4.53 is less than 0.0001, as indicated by the p-value. Thus the sales figures for Terminator suggest a statistically significant upward trend in sales. The sales forecasts for April, May, and June of 2005 are

$$\text{April 2005: } \hat{Q}_{16} = 46.57 + (4.53 \times 16) = 119$$
$$\text{May 2005: } \hat{Q}_{17} = 46.57 + (4.53 \times 17) = 123.6$$
$$\text{June 2005: } \hat{Q}_{18} = 46.57 + (4.53 \times 18) = 128.1$$

The bank decided to make the loan to Terminator Pest Control in light of the statistically significant upward trend in sales and the forecast of higher sales in the three upcoming months.

A Price Forecast for Georgia Lumber Products

Suppose you work for Georgia Lumber Products, a large lumber producer in south Georgia, and your manager wants you to forecast the price of lumber for the next two quarters. Information about the price of a ton of lumber is readily available. Using eight quarterly observations on lumber prices since 2001 (III), you estimate a linear trend line for lumber prices through the 2003 (II) time period. Your computer output for the linear time trend model on lumber price looks like the following printout:

VARIABLE	DEPENDENT VARIABLE: P	R-SQUARE	F-RATIO	P-VALUE ON F
	OBSERVATIONS: 8	0.7673	19.79	0.0043

VARIABLE	PARAMETER ESTIMATE	STANDARD ERROR	T-RATIO	P-VALUE
INTERCEPT	2066.0	794.62	2.60	0.0407
T	25.00	5.62	4.45	0.0043

Both parameter estimates $\hat{a}$ and $\hat{b}$ are significant at the 5 percent significance level since both t-ratios exceed 2.447, the critical t for the 5 percent significance level. (Notice also that both p-values are less than 0.05.) Thus the real (inflation-adjusted) price for a ton of lumber exhibited a statistically significant trend upward since the third quarter of 2001. Lumber prices have risen, on average, $25 per ton each quarter over the range of this sample period (2001 III through 2003 II).

To forecast the price of lumber for the next two quarters, you make the following computations:

$$\hat{P}_{2003\ (III)} = 2066 + (25 \times 9) = \$2,291 \text{ per ton}$$
$$\hat{P}_{2003\ (IV)} = 2066 + (25 \times 10) = \$2,316 \text{ per ton}$$

As you can see by the last two hypothetical examples, the linear trend method of forecasting is a simple procedure for generating forecasts for either sales or price. Indeed, this method can be applied to forecast any economic variable for which a time-series of observations is available.

7.6 SEASONAL (OR CYCLICAL) VARIATION

Time-series data may frequently exhibit regular, **seasonal,** or **cyclical variation** over time, and the failure to take such regular variations into account when estimating a forecasting equation would bias the forecast. Frequently, when quarterly

seasonal or cyclical variation
The regular variation that time-series data frequently exhibit.

or monthly sales are being used to forecast sales, seasonal variation may occur—the sales of many products vary systematically by month or by quarter. For example, in the retail clothing business, sales are generally higher before Easter and Christmas. Thus sales would be higher during the second and fourth quarters of the year. Likewise, the sales of hunting equipment would peak during early fall, the third quarter. In such cases, you would definitely wish to incorporate these systematic variations when estimating the equation and forecasting future sales. We now describe the technique most commonly employed to handle cyclical variation.

Correcting for Seasonal Variation by Using Dummy Variables

Consider the simplified example of a firm producing and selling a product for which sales are consistently higher in the fourth quarter than in any other quarter. A hypothetical data scatter is presented in Figure 7.5. In each of the four years, the data point in the fourth quarter is much higher than in the other three. While a time trend clearly exists, if the analyst simply regressed sales against time, without accounting for the higher sales in the fourth quarter, too large a trend would be estimated (i.e., the slope would be too large). In essence, there is an upward shift of the trend line in the fourth quarter. Such a relation is presented in Figure 7.6. In the fourth quarter, the intercept is higher than in the other quarters. In other words, a', the intercept of the trend line for the fourth-quarter data points, exceeds a, the intercept of the trend line for the data points in the other quarters. One way of specifying this relation is to define a' as $a' = a + c$, where c is some positive number. Therefore, the regression line we want to estimate will take the form

$$\hat{Q}_t = a + bt + c$$

where $c = 0$ in the first three quarters.

dummy variable
A variable that takes only values of 0 and 1.

To estimate the preceding equation, statisticians use what is commonly referred to as a *dummy variable* in the estimating equation. A **dummy variable** is a variable

---

FIGURE 7.5

Sales with Seasonal Variation

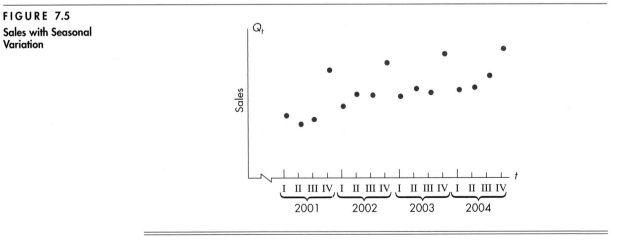

that can take on only the values of *zero* or *one*. In this case, we would assign the dummy variable (*D*) a value of 1 if the sales observation is from the fourth quarter and zero in the other three quarters. The data are shown in Table 7.1, where Q_t represents the sales figure in the tth period and $D = 1$ for quarter IV and zero otherwise. Since quarterly data are being used, time is converted into integers to obtain a continuous time variable. Using these data, the following equation is estimated:

$$Q_t = a + bt + cD$$

This specification produces two equations like those shown in Figure 7.6. The estimated slope of the two equations would be the same. For quarters I, II, and III

FIGURE 7.6
The Effect of Seasonal Variation

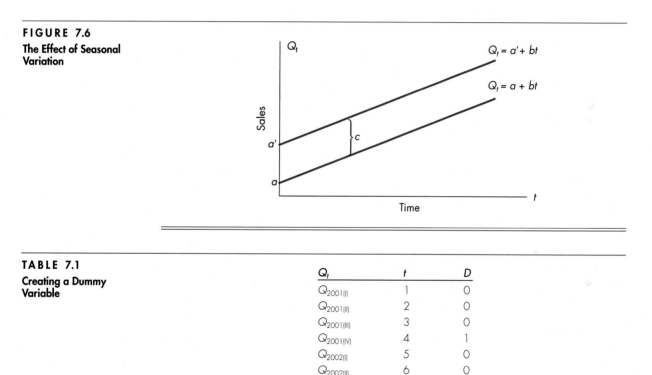

TABLE 7.1
Creating a Dummy Variable

Q_t	t	D
$Q_{2001(I)}$	1	0
$Q_{2001(II)}$	2	0
$Q_{2001(III)}$	3	0
$Q_{2001(IV)}$	4	1
$Q_{2002(I)}$	5	0
$Q_{2002(II)}$	6	0
$Q_{2002(III)}$	7	0
$Q_{2002(IV)}$	8	1
$Q_{2003(I)}$	9	0
$Q_{2003(II)}$	10	0
$Q_{2003(III)}$	11	0
$Q_{2003(IV)}$	12	1
$Q_{2004(I)}$	13	0
$Q_{2004(II)}$	14	0
$Q_{2004(III)}$	15	0
$Q_{2004(IV)}$	16	1

the estimated intercept is $\hat{a}$, while for the fourth quarter the estimated intercept is $\hat{a} + \hat{c}$. This estimation really means that for any future period t, the sales forecast would be

$$\hat{Q}_t = \hat{a} + \hat{b}t$$

unless period t occurs in the fourth quarter, in which case the sales forecast would be

$$\hat{Q}_t = \hat{a} + \hat{b}t + \hat{c} = (\hat{a} + \hat{c}) + \hat{b}t$$

For example, referring to the data in Table 7.1, when a manager wishes to forecast sales in the third quarter of 2005, the manager uses the equation

$$\hat{Q}_{2005(III)} = \hat{a} + \hat{b}\,(19)$$

If a manager wishes to forecast sales in the fourth quarter of 2005, the forecast is

$$\hat{Q}_{2005(IV)} = (\hat{a} + \hat{c}) + \hat{b}(20)$$

In other words, when the forecast is for quarter IV, the forecast equation adds the amount $\hat{c}$ to the sales that would otherwise be forecast.[9]

Going a step further, it could be the case that there exist quarter-to-quarter differences in sales (i.e., in Figure 7.6 there would be four trend lines). In this case, three dummy variables are used: D_1 (equal to 1 in the first quarter and 0 otherwise), D_2 (equal to 1 in the second quarter and 0 otherwise), and D_3 (equal to 1 in the third quarter and 0 otherwise).[10] Then, the manager estimates the equation

$$Q_t = a + bt + c_1 D_1 + c_2 D_2 + c_3 D_3$$

In quarter I the intercept is $a + c_1$, in quarter II it is $a + c_2$, in quarter III it is $a + c_3$, and in quarter IV it is a only.

To obtain a forecast for some future quarter, it is necessary to include the coefficient for the dummy variable for that particular quarter. For example, predictions for the third quarter of a particular year would take the form

$$\hat{Q}_t = \hat{a} + \hat{b}t + \hat{c}_3$$

Perhaps the best way to explain how dummy variables can be used to account for cyclical variation is to provide an example.

---

[9]Throughout this discussion, we have assumed that trend lines differ only with respect to the intercepts—the slope is the same for all the trend lines. Dummy variables can also be used to reflect differences in slopes. This technique is beyond the scope of this text, and we refer the interested reader to Damodar Gujarati, *Basic Econometrics*, 4/e. (New York: McGraw-Hill, 2002).

[10]Likewise, if there were month-to-month differences, 11 dummy variables would be used to account for the monthly change in the intercept. When using dummy variables, you must always use one less dummy variable than the number of periods being considered.

TABLE 7.2

Quarterly Sales Data for Statewide Trucking Company (2001–2004)

(1) Year	(2) Quarter	(3) Sales	(4) t	(5) D_1	(6) D_2	(7) D_3
	I	$ 72,000	1	1	0	0
	II	87,000	2	0	1	0
2001	III	87,000	3	0	0	1
	IV	150,000	4	0	0	0
	I	82,000	5	1	0	0
	II	98,000	6	0	1	0
2002	III	94,000	7	0	0	1
	IV	162,000	8	0	0	0
	I	97,000	9	1	0	0
	II	105,000	10	0	1	0
2003	III	109,000	11	0	0	1
	IV	176,000	12	0	0	0
	I	105,000	13	1	0	0
	II	121,000	14	0	1	0
2004	III	119,000	15	0	0	1
	IV	180,000	16	0	0	0

The Dummy-Variable Technique: An Example

Jean Reynolds, the sales manager of Statewide Trucking Company, wishes to predict sales for all four quarters of 2005. The sales of Statewide Trucking are subject to seasonal variation and also have a trend over time. Reynolds obtains sales data for 2001–2004 by quarter. The data collected are presented in Table 7.2. Note that since quarterly data are used, time is converted into a continuous variable by numbering quarters consecutively in column 4 of the table.

Reynolds knows, from a college course in managerial economics, that obtaining the desired sales forecast requires that she estimate an equation containing three dummy variables—one less than the number of time periods in the annual cycle. She chooses to estimate the following equation:

$$Q_t = a + bt + c_1 D_1 + c_2 D_2 + c_3 D_3$$

where D_1, D_2, and D_3 are, respectively, dummy variables for quarters I, II, and III.[11] Using the data in Table 7.2, she estimates the preceding equation, and the results of this estimation are shown here:

---

[11]This is only one of the specifications that is appropriate. Other equally appropriate specifications are

$$Q_t = a + bt + c_2 D_2 + c_3 D_3 + c_4 D_4$$
$$Q_t = a + bt + c_1 D_1 + c_3 D_3 + c_4 D_4$$

or

$$Q_t = a + bt + c_1 D_1 + c_2 D_2 + c_4 D_4$$

It is necessary only to have *any three* of the quarters represented by the dummy variables.

```
DEPENDENT VARIABLE: QT      R-SQUARE     F-RATIO       P-VALUE ON F

        OBSERVATIONS: 16     0.9965      794.126       0.0001

                     PARAMETER      STANDARD
    VARIABLE         ESTIMATE       ERROR        T-RATIO      P-VALUE

    INTERCEPT        139625.0       1743.6       80.08        0.0001
    T                2737.5         129.96       21.06        0.0001
    D1               -69788.0       1689.5       -41.31       0.0001
    D2               -58775.0       1664.3       -35.32       0.0001
    D3               -62013.0       1649.0       -37.61       0.0001
```

Upon examining the estimation results, Reynolds notes that a positive trend in sales is indicated ($\hat{b} > 0$). To determine whether the trend is statistically significant, either a t-test can be performed on $\hat{b}$ or the p-value for $\hat{b}$ can be assessed for significance. The calculated t-value for $\hat{b}$ is $t_{\hat{b}} = 21.06$. With $16 - 5 = 11$ degrees of freedom, the critical value of t (using a 5 percent significance level) is 2.201. Since $21.06 > 2.201$, $\hat{b}$ is statistically significant. The p-value for b is so small (0.01 percent) that the chance of making a Type I error—incorrectly finding significance—is virtually 0. Thus Reynolds has strong evidence suggesting a positive trend in sales.

Next, Reynolds calculates the estimated intercepts of the trend line for each of the four quarters. In the first quarter,

$$\hat{a} + \hat{c}_1 = 139{,}625 - 69{,}788$$
$$= 69{,}837$$

in the second quarter

$$\hat{a} + \hat{c}_2 = 139{,}625 - 58{,}775$$
$$= 80{,}850$$

in the third quarter

$$\hat{a} + \hat{c}_3 = 139{,}625 - 62{,}013$$
$$= 77{,}612$$

and in the fourth quarter

$$\hat{a} = 139{,}625$$

These estimates indicate that the intercepts, and thus sales, are lower in quarters I, II, and III than in quarter IV. The question that always must be asked is: Are these intercepts *significantly* lower?

To answer this question, Reynolds decides to compare quarters I and IV. In quarter I, the intercept is $\hat{a} + \hat{c}_1$; in quarter IV, it is $\hat{a}$. Hence, if $\hat{a} + \hat{c}$ is significantly lower than $\hat{a}$, it is necessary that $\hat{c}_1$ be significantly less than 0. That is, if

$$\hat{a} + \hat{c}_1 < \hat{a}$$

it follows that $\hat{c}_1 < 0$. Reynolds already knows that $\hat{c}_1$ is negative; to determine if it is significantly negative, she can perform a t-test. The calculated value of t for $\hat{c}_1$ is -41.31. Since $|-41.31| > 2.201$, $\hat{c}_1$ is significantly less than 0. This indicates that the intercept—and the sales—in the first quarter are less than that in the fourth. The t-values for $\hat{c}_2$ and $\hat{c}_3$, -35.32 and -37.61, respectively, are both greater (in absolute value) than 2.201 and are significantly negative. Thus the intercepts in the second and third quarters are also significantly less than the intercept in the fourth quarter. Hence, Reynolds has evidence that there is a significant increase in sales in the fourth quarter.

She can now proceed to forecast sales by quarters for 2005. In the first quarter of 2005, $t = 17$, $D_1 = 1$, $D_2 = 0$, and $D_3 = 0$. Therefore, the forecast for sales in the first quarter of 2005 would be

$$
\begin{aligned}
\hat{Q}_{2005(I)} &= \hat{a} + \hat{b} \times 17 + \hat{c}_1 \times 1 + \hat{c}_2 \times 0 + \hat{c}_3 \times 0 \\
&= \hat{a} + \hat{b} \times 17 + \hat{c}_1 \\
&= 139{,}625 + 2{,}737.5 \times 17 - 69{,}788 \\
&= 116{,}374.5
\end{aligned}
$$

Using precisely the same method, the forecasts for sales in the other three quarters of 2005 are as follows:

$$
\begin{aligned}
2005(II){:}\ \hat{Q}_{2005(II)} &= \hat{a} + \hat{b} \times 18 + \hat{c}_2 \\
&= 139{,}625 + 2{,}737.5 \times 18 - 58{,}775 \\
&= 130{,}125 \\
2005(III){:}\ \hat{Q}_{2005(III)} &= \hat{a} + \hat{b} \times 19 + \hat{c}_3 \\
&= 139{,}625 + 2{,}737.5 \times 19 - 62{,}013 \\
&= 129{,}624.5 \\
2005(IV){:}\ \hat{Q}_{2005(IV)} &= \hat{a} + \hat{b} \times 20 \\
&= 139{,}625 + 2{,}737.5 \times 20 \\
&= 194{,}375
\end{aligned}
$$

In this example, we have confined our attention to quarterly variation. However, exactly the same techniques can be used for monthly data or any other type of seasonal or cyclical variation. In addition to its application to situations involving seasonal or cyclical variation, the dummy-variable technique can be used to account for changes in sales (or any other economic variable that is being forecast) due to forces such as wars, bad weather, or even strikes at a competitor's production facility. We summarize the dummy-variable technique with the following:

▣ **Relation** When seasonal variation causes the intercept of the demand equation to vary systematically from season to season, dummy variables can be added to the estimated forecasting equation to account for the cyclical variation. If there are N seasonal time periods to be accounted for, $N - 1$ dummy variables are added to the demand equation. Each of these dummy variables accounts for one of the seasonal time periods by taking a value of 1 for those observations that occur during that season, and a value of 0 otherwise. Used in this way, dummy variables allow the intercept of the demand equation to vary across seasons.

Before leaving the discussion of time-series models, we should mention that the linear trend model is just one—and probably the simplest—of many different types of time-series models that can be used to forecast economic variables. More advanced time-series models fit cyclical patterns, rather than straight lines, to the scatter of data over time. These techniques, which involve moving-average models, exponential smoothing models, and Box-Jenkins models, go well beyond the scope of a managerial textbook. In fact, you can take entire courses in business forecasting that will teach how to implement some of these more sophisticated time-series forecasting techniques.

7.7 ECONOMETRIC MODELS

econometric model
A statistical model that employs an explicit structural model to explain the underlying economic relations.

Another method used in statistical forecasting and decision making is econometric modeling. The primary characteristic of **econometric models,** which differentiates this approach from the preceding approaches, is the use of an explicit structural model that attempts to *explain* the underlying economic relations. More specifically, if we wish to employ an econometric model to forecast future sales, we must develop a model that incorporates the variables that actually determine the level of sales (e.g., income, the price of substitutes, and so on).

The use of econometric models has several advantages. First, econometric models require analysts to define explicit causal relations. This specification of an explicit model helps eliminate problems such as spurious (false) correlation between normally unrelated variables and may make the model more logically consistent and reliable.

Second, this approach allows analysts to consider the sensitivity of the variable to be forecasted to changes in the exogenous explanatory variables. Using estimated elasticities, forecasters can determine which of the variables are most important in determining changes in the variable to be forecasted. Therefore, the analyst can examine the behavior of these variables more closely.

Econometric forecasting can be utilized to forecast either future industry price and quantity for price-taking firms or future demand for a price-setting firm. We begin our discussion of econometric models by showing you, in a step-by-step fashion, how to forecast future industry price and sales for price-taking firms. We then apply this procedure using data from the world copper market to forecast future copper price and sales. Next, we show you the steps for forecasting future demand for a price-setting firm and then illustrate this process by forecasting future demand for the pizza restaurant introduced previously in this chapter.

Forecasting Future Industry Price and Sales

Using econometric models to forecast future price and sales in an industry is slightly more complicated and requires more information than forecasting future demand for a price-setting firm. To forecast industry price and sales, an analyst must estimate not only demand but also supply. You will see, in the following step-by-step discussion, that the process of making forecasts using simultaneous demand and supply equations is not particularly difficult.

Step 1: Estimate the industry demand and supply equations

The process begins with the specification of industry demand and supply equations. As we explained earlier (Section 7.3), the parameters of a demand or a supply equation in a simultaneous system cannot be estimated unless the equation is identified. Because both equations in a system must be estimated in order to forecast future price and sales, demand and supply must be specified in such a way that they are *both* identified. Recall that demand is identified when supply includes at least one exogenous explanatory variable that is not also in the demand equation. In the same fashion, supply is identified when demand includes at least one exogenous explanatory variable that is not also in the supply equation. The two-stage least-squares (2SLS) estimation procedure can now be employed to estimate the parameters of the identified demand and supply equations. For example, the forecasting department of a firm can use 2SLS to estimate the industry demand function:

$$Q = a + bP + cM + dP_R$$

and the industry supply function

$$Q = e + fP + gP_I$$

where Q is industry sales, P is the market-determined price, M is income, P_R is the price of a good related in consumption, and P_I is the price of an input used in production. Notice that both demand and supply are identified: Each equation contains an exogenous variable not contained in the other equation.

Step 2: Locate industry demand and supply in the forecast period

To forecast price and sales in a future period, a forecaster must know where demand and supply will be located in the future period of the forecast. The process of locating demand and supply in a future period is straightforward. The forecaster obtains future values of *all* of the exogenous explanatory variables in the system of demand and supply equations and then substitutes these values into the *estimated* demand and supply equations. As already mentioned, forecasted values of exogenous variables can be acquired either by using time-series techniques to generate predicted values of the exogenous explanatory variables or by purchasing forecasts of the exogenous explanatory variables from forecasting firms.

ILLUSTRATION 7.3

Forecasting New-Home Sales
A Time-Series Forecast

Suppose that in January 1999, the market analyst of a national real estate firm wanted to forecast the total number of new homes that would be sold in the United States in March 1999. Let's examine how this analyst could have used time-series techniques to forecast sales of new homes. The data for the number of new homes sold monthly during the years 1996–1998 are presented in the accompanying table (columns 1–3) and are shown by the solid line (Q_t) in the accompanying graph. These data can be found at the Internet site for the U.S. Department of Housing and Urban Development: *http://www.census.gov/newhomesales*.

Suppose the market analyst forecasts sales using a linear trend, and the following linear specification is estimated:

$$Q_t = a + bt$$

where Q_t is the number of new homes sold in the tth month, and $t = 1, 2, \ldots, 36$. Note that because these are monthly data, the analyst must convert time into integers, as shown in column 4 of the table (ignore column 5 for now). When the analyst runs a regression analysis on the 36 time-series observations on new-home sales, the following computer output results:

DEPENDENT VARIABLE: QT	R-SQUARE	F-RATIO	P-VALUE ON F
OBSERVATIONS: 36	0.1196	4.62	0.0389

VARIABLE	PARAMETER ESTIMATE	STANDARD ERROR	T-RATIO	P-VALUE
INTERCEPT	62823.8	2762.88	22.74	0.0001
T	279.794	130.219	2.15	0.0389

To locate the industry demand and supply equations in the future period 2006, for example, a forecaster must obtain forecasts of all exogenous variables for that year: M_{2006}, $P_{R,2006}$, and $P_{I,2006}$. Then the forecasted future demand equation for 2006 is

$$
\begin{aligned}
Q_{2006} &= \hat{a} + \hat{b}P_{2006} + \hat{c}M_{2006} + \hat{d}P_{R,2006} \\
&= (\hat{a} + \hat{c}M_{2006} + \hat{d}P_{R,2006}) + \hat{b}P_{2006} \\
&= \hat{a}_{2006} + \hat{b}P_{2006}
\end{aligned}
$$

Monthly Sales of New Homes in the United States (1996–1998)

(1) Year	(2) Month	(3) Sales	(4) t	(5) D_t
1996	1	$54,000	1	0
	2	68,000	2	0
	3	70,000	3	1
	4	70,000	4	1
	5	69,000	5	1
	6	65,000	6	1
	7	66,000	7	1
	8	73,000	8	1
	9	62,000	9	0
	10	56,000	10	0
	11	54,000	11	0
	12	51,000	12	0
1997	1	61,000	13	0
	2	69,000	14	0
	3	81,000	15	1
	4	70,000	16	1
	5	71,000	17	1
	6	71,000	18	1
1997	7	69,000	19	1
	8	72,000	20	1
	9	67,000	21	0
	10	62,000	22	0
	11	61,000	23	0
	12	51,000	24	0
1998	1	64,000	25	0
	2	75,000	26	0
	3	81,000	27	1
	4	82,000	28	1
	5	82,000	29	1
	6	83,000	30	1
	7	75,000	31	1
	8	75,000	32	1
	9	68,000	33	0
	10	69,000	34	0
	11	70,000	35	0
	12	61,000	36	0

Source: U.S. Department of Housing and Urban Development. Internet site: http://www.census.gov/newhomesales.

The estimated trend line, $\hat{Q}_t = 62{,}823.8 + 279.794t$, is labeled $\hat{Q}_t$ in the figure.

The estimate of b is positive ($\hat{b} = 279.794$), indicating sales were increasing over the time period 1996–1998. The analyst needs to assess the statistical significance of $\hat{b}$. The p-value for $\hat{b}$ is less than 0.05, which indicates the upward trend in new-home sales over the period 1996–1998 is statistically significant at better than the 5 percent level of significance (to be precise, the 3.89 percent level). Note also that the R^2 indicates the trend line poorly fits the sales data, as can be seen in the figure as well. Only about 12 percent of the total variation in home sales can be explained by the passage of time (t), even though the time trend is statistically significant at better than the 5 percent level. About 88 percent of the variation in sales remains unexplained, which suggests that something more than just the time trend (t) may be needed to explain satisfactorily the variation in new-home sales. In a moment, we show that adding seasonality to the trend model can improve matters substantially.

Using the estimated linear trend line, the market analyst can forecast sales for March 1999 ($t = 39$) by substituting the value 39 for t:

$$\hat{Q}_{\text{March1999}} = 62{,}823.8 + 279.794 \times 39 = 73{,}736$$

Thus, using linear trend analysis, the number of new homes sold in March 1999 is forecast to be 73,736. The number of homes actually sold in March 1999 turned out to be 86,000. You can verify this figure at the Internet site mentioned earlier and in the table. The analyst's forecast, using a trend-line technique, underestimates the actual number of homes sold by 14.3 per-

(continued)

and the forecasted future supply equation for 2006 is

$$Q_{2006} = \hat{e} + \hat{f}P_{2006} + \hat{g}P_{I,2006}$$
$$= (\hat{e} + \hat{g}P_{I,2006}) + \hat{f}P_{2006}$$
$$= \hat{e}_{2006} + \hat{f}P_{2006}$$

These future demand and supply equations are illustrated in Figure 7.7.

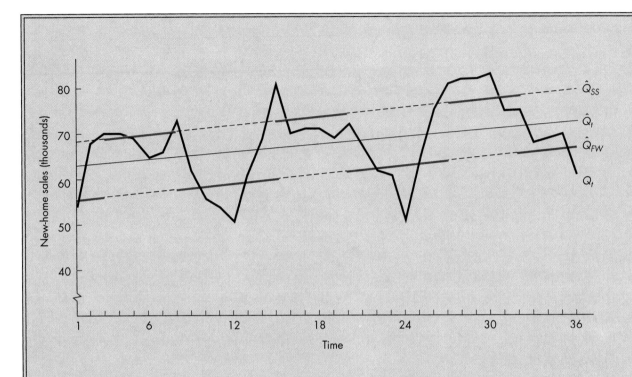

cent [= (73,736 − 86,000) × 100/86,000)], a rather sizable error.

The market analyst could improve the forecast by modifying the forecast equation to reflect the seasonality of new-home sales: In the spring and summer months, new-home sales tend to be higher than in other months as families try to relocate while school is out of session. Let's examine how adding a dummy variable to account for this seasonality can substantially improve the market analyst's sale forecast.

To account for the seasonal increase in new-home sales during the spring and summer months (March through August), the analyst can define a dummy variable, D_t, to be equal to 1 when $t = 3, \ldots, 8, 15, \ldots, 20,$ and $27, \ldots, 32$. The dummy variable is equal to zero for all other months. The values of the dummy variable are shown in column 5 of the table. Adding this dummy variable to the trend line results in the following equation to be estimated:

$$Q_t = a + bt + cD_t$$

Again using the sales data for 1996–1998, a regression analysis results in the following computer output:

As in the first regression when no adjustment was made for seasonality, a statistically significant upward trend in sales is present. The p-value for each of the parameter estimates in the model with a dummy variable is so small that there is less than a 0.01 percent chance of making a Type I error (mistakenly finding significance). Note that after accounting for seasonal variation, the trend line becomes steeper (334.892 > 279.794).

The estimated intercept for the trend line is 55,858.5 for fall and winter months ($D_t = 0$). During the spring

DEPENDENT VARIABLE: QT	R-SQUARE	F-RATIO	P-VALUE ON F
OBSERVATIONS: 36	0.6152	26.38	0.0001

VARIABLE	PARAMETER ESTIMATE	STANDARD ERROR	T-RATIO	P-VALUE
INTERCEPT	55858.5	2139.72	26.11	0.0001
T	334.892	87.7877	3.81	0.0006
D	11892.0	1823.93	6.52	0.0001

and summer buying season, the estimated intercept of the trend line is

$$\hat{a} + \hat{c} = 55{,}858.5 + 11{,}892.0 = 67{,}750.5$$

To check for statistical significance of $\hat{c}$, we note that the p-value for $\hat{c}$ indicates less than a 0.01 percent chance that $c = 0$. Thus the statistical evidence suggests that there is a significant increase in sales of new homes during the spring and summer months. The increase in the average number of new homes sold in March through August compared with September through February is about 11,892 more homes per month. In other words, entering the selling season (March–August) causes sales to spike upward by 11,892 homes per month while continuing to trend upward by 334.892 units per month.

The estimated trend lines representing the spring and summer months ($\hat{Q}_{SS}$) and the fall and winter months ($\hat{Q}_{FW}$) are shown in the figure. Note that the spring and summer trend line is parallel to the fall and winter line, but the sales intercept is higher during spring and summer months. The estimated trend line for the fall and winter months is the solid portion of the lower trend line. For the spring and summer months, the estimated trend line is the solid portion of

the upper trend line. Note how much better the line fits when it is seasonally adjusted. Indeed, the R^2 increased from 0.1196 to 0.6152.

We now determine whether adding the dummy variable improves the accuracy of the market analyst's forecast of sales in March 1999. Using the estimated trend line accounting for seasonal variation in sales, the sales forecast for March 1999 ($t = 39$) is now

$$\hat{Q}_{\text{March1999}} = 55{,}858.5 + 334.892 \times 39 + 11{,}892.0 \times 1$$
$$= 80{,}811.3$$

Clearly, this forecast is an improvement over the unadjusted forecast. The sales forecast that accounts for seasonality underestimates the actual level of sales by 5,189 homes, or 6.0 percent [$= (80{,}811.3 - 86{,}000) \times 100/86{,}000$]. Compare this with the previous forecast of 73,736, which underestimated actual sales by 14.3 percent. Accounting for seasonality of new-home sales reduces the forecast error by more than half. To further improve the accuracy of the forecast, the analyst might try using one of the more complicated time-series techniques that fit cyclical curves to the data, thereby improving the fit (R^2) and the forecast. As already noted, these techniques are well beyond the scope of this text.

FIGURE 7.7
Locating Future Industry
Demand and Supply

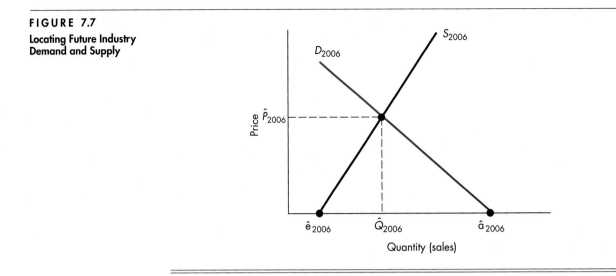

Step 3: Calculate the intersection of future demand and supply

The intersection of the forecasted industry demand and supply equations provides the forecasted industry price and sales in the future period. In Figure 7.7, the forecasted price $\hat{P}_{2006}$, and the forecasted level of sales, $\hat{Q}_{2006}$, are found by solving for the intersection of demand and supply equations in precisely the same way that you found equilibrium price and quantity in Chapter 2.

To illustrate the implementation of these steps, we turn now to the world copper market to forecast the industry price and quantity of copper. We continue here to use the data from the copper market that were presented and discussed previously in this chapter.

The World Market for Copper: A Simultaneous Equations Forecast

Recall that the copper data consist of 25 annual observations on world consumption of copper, copper price, and the exogenous variables required to estimate industry demand and supply equations. Using these data, we now follow the steps set forth above to forecast industry price and sales of copper in year 26.

Step 1: Estimate the copper industry demand and supply equations

Recall from our earlier discussion that world demand for copper was specified as

$$Q_{copper} = a + bP_{copper} + cM + dP_{aluminum}$$

and world supply as

$$Q_{copper} = e + fP_{copper} + gT + hX$$

where time (T) is a proxy for the level of available technology and X is the ratio of consumption of copper to production of copper in the previous period to reflect inventory changes. Both of these equations are identified and can be estimated using two-stage least-squares (2SLS). Recall that the estimated demand for copper is

$$\hat{Q}_{copper} = -6{,}837.8 - 66.495P_{copper} + 13{,}997.9M + 107.662P_{aluminum}$$

The estimated supply function, using the 2SLS procedure, is

$$\hat{Q}_{copper} = 149.104 + 18.154P_{copper} + 213.88T + 1{,}819.7X$$

Step 2: Locate copper demand and supply in year 26

To locate demand and supply in year 26, we must obtain forecast values for the exogenous variables in year 26. Because time is a proxy for technology, the period-26 value of T is simply $T_{26} = 26$. As previously mentioned, the value of X in any period is the ratio of consumption to production in the preceding period. Since both of these values are known (consumption was 7,157.2 and production was 8,058.0), $\hat{X}_{26} = 0.88821 \ (= 7{,}157.2/8{,}058.0)$. For the other two exogenous explanatory variables, M and P_R, values must be obtained using time-series forecasting.

To obtain values for M_{26} and $\hat{P}_{R,26}$, a linear trend method of forecasting was used to obtain

$$\hat{M}_{26} = 1.13 \quad \text{and} \quad \hat{P}_{R,26} = 23.79$$

Using $\hat{M}_{26}$ and $\hat{P}_{R,\,26}$, the demand function in time period 26 is

$$\hat{Q}_{copper,\,26} = -6{,}837.8 - 66.495\,P_{copper,\,26} + 13{,}997(1.13) + 107.662(23.79)$$
$$= 11{,}540.09 - 66.495\,P_{copper,\,26}$$

Likewise, using $\hat{T}_{26} = 26$ and $\hat{X}_{26} = 0.88821$, the supply function in time period 26 is

$$\hat{Q}_{copper,\,26} = 149.104 + 18.154\,P_{copper,\,26} + 213.88(26) + 1{,}819.7(0.88821)$$
$$= 7{,}326.26 + 18.154\,P_{copper,\,26}$$

Step 3: Calculate the intersection of the demand and supply functions.

We set quantity demanded equal to quantity supplied and solve for equilibrium price:

$$11{,}540.09 - 66.495\,P_{copper,\,26} = 7{,}326.26 + 18.154\,P_{copper,\,26}$$
$$P_{copper,\,26} = 49.78$$

The sales forecast is then found by substituting $P_{copper,\,26}$ into either the demand or the supply equation. Using the demand function,

$$Q_{copper,\,26} = 11{,}540.09 - 66.495(49.78) = 7{,}326.26 + 18.154(49.78)$$
$$= 8{,}230.0$$

Thus we forecast that sales of copper in year 26 will be 8,230.0 (thousand) metric tons.[12] The price of copper in year 26 is forecast to be 49.8 cents per pound.

---

[12]As we noted, the data we used for this copper market illustration are the actual data for the period 1951–1975. Hence, our forecast for year 26 can be interpreted as the forecast for 1976. The actual value for copper consumption in 1976 was 8,174.0, so the forecast error in this example was 0.54 percent—about one-half of 1 percent.

We now turn our attention to forecasting future demand for a price-setting firm. As we previously explained, when prices are manager-determined for price-setting firms, it is not necessary to estimate supply functions, check for identification, or utilize the two-stage least-squares (2SLS) estimation technique.

Forecasting Future Demand for Price-Setting Firms

In addition to wanting to know the current demand for their firm's products or services, managers of price-setting firms frequently want to forecast what demand will be during some future period. The process of forecasting future demand for price-setting firms is a three-step procedure.

Step 1: Estimate the firm's demand function

The forecaster begins by estimating the current demand equation for the firm. After specifying the generalized demand relation for a firm's product, ordinary least-squares (OLS) can be used to estimate the empirical demand function. Let's suppose the estimated demand function takes the following rather typical form:

$$Q = a + bP + cM + dP_R$$

Step 2: Forecast the future values of the demand-shifting variables

Recall from our discussion in Chapter 2 that demand shifts when one or more of the five demand-shifting variables (M, P_R, $\mathcal{T}$, P_e, and N) change in value. The future location of demand, then, is determined by shifts in demand caused by changes in the values of the demand-shifting variables. Thus a forecaster must predict future values of M and P_R in order to predict the location of future demand.[13]

Forecasted values of the demand-shifting variables are generally obtained from one of two sources: (1) the firm's own time-series forecasts of the demand-shifting variables or (2) commercial vendors' forecasts from macroeconomic (econometric) models that forecast the values of many aggregate economic variables.[14]

Step 3: Calculate the location of future demand

Once forecasts for the demand-shifting variables are obtained, the "location" of the future demand curve can be determined by substituting the values of the

---

[13]Generally forecasters assume the parameters of demand a, b, c, and d do not change over the forecast period. In other words, future forecasted demand differs from current demand only because the demand-shifting variables (M and P_R, in this example) change in value over time. More sophisticated forecasting techniques can be employed to allow parameter values to change over time, but these methods are more complex than we wish to discuss here and they are not warranted when parameter values remain stable over the period of the forecast.

[14]Numerous private firms are in the business of selling macroeconomic forecasts of dozens of economic variables to businesses. While businesses wish to forecast the price and sales of their own products, they do not wish to undertake the formidable task of building a large, simultaneous equations model of the U.S. or world economy in order to forecast for the next four quarters such variables as the rate of inflation, interest rates, or the level of household income.

forecasted demand-shifting variables into the estimated demand relation. The resulting equation is the firm's forecasted demand function.

Forecasting Demand for Checkers Pizza

To illustrate the process of forecasting future demand for a price-setting firm, we return to the example of Checkers Pizza. Recall that the pizza market data consist of 24 monthly observations. Using these data, we can follow the preceding procedure to forecast the demand for Checkers Pizza six months in the future, which is month 30.

Step 1: Estimate the demand function for Checkers Pizza
Previously in this chapter, the demand function for Checkers Pizza was estimated in linear functional form to be:

$$\hat{Q} = 1{,}183.8 - 213.422P + 0.09109M + 101.303P_{Al} + 71.8448P_{BMac}$$

where Q is the sales of pizza at Checkers, P is the price of a pizza at Checkers, M is average annual household income in the neighborhood, P_{Al} is the price of a pizza at Al's Pizza Oven, and P_{BMAC} is the price of a Big Mac at McDonald's.

Step 2: Forecast the values of M, P_{Al}, and P_{BMac}
The manager of Checkers Pizza believes that Al's Pizza Oven and McDonald's do not intend to raise their prices for at least the next six months. Thus the prices of Al's pizza and the price of a Big Mac are forecasted to be the same as they were in month 24:

$$P_{Al,\,30} = P_{Al,\,24} = \$10.25$$
$$P_{BMac,\,30} = P_{BMac,\,24} = \$1.20$$

The manager employs a linear trend regression model to forecast income in month 30:

$$\hat{M}_{30} = \hat{a} + \hat{b}t = 25{,}004.1 + 128.727(30) = \$28{,}866$$

where $\hat{a}$ and $\hat{b}$ are the parameter estimates obtained when the income data (M), found in Table B of the appendix, are regressed against time ($t = 1, \ldots, 24$).

Step 3: Calculate the location of Checkers' future demand
The forecasted demand for Checkers Pizza in month 30 is obtained by substituting the forecasted values of the demand-shifting variables into the estimated demand function:

$$\hat{Q} = [1{,}183.8 + 0.09109(28{,}866) + 101.303(10.25) + 71.8448(1.20)] - 213.422P$$
$$= 4{,}937.77 - 213.422P$$

Again, let us emphasize that changes in the future values of the demand-shifting variables cause the demand function in the future to be different from the demand function of the current period. The parameters of the demand function are assumed to be constant. In the case of Checkers Pizza, a, b, c, and d do not change value; rather, M and P_R change demand.

7.8 SOME FINAL WARNINGS

We have often heard it said about forecasting that "he who lives by the crystal ball ends up eating ground glass." While we do not make nearly so dire a judgment, we do feel that you should be aware of the major limitations of and problems inherent in forecasting. Basically, our warnings are concerned with three issues: confidence intervals, specification, and change of structure.

To illustrate the issue of confidence intervals in forecasting, consider once again the simple linear trend model,

$$Q_t = a + bt$$

To obtain the prediction model, we must estimate two coefficients a and b. Obviously, we cannot estimate these coefficients with certainty. Indeed, the estimated standard errors reflect the magnitude of uncertainty (i.e., potential error) about the values of the parameters.

In Figure 7.8, we have illustrated a situation in which there are observations on sales for periods t_1 through t_n. Due to the manner in which it was calculated, the regression line will pass through the sample mean of the data points $(\overline{Q}, \overline{t})$. In Panel A, we have illustrated as the shaded area our confidence region if there exist errors only in the estimation of the slope b. In Panel B, the shaded area represents the confidence region if an error exists only in the estimation of the intercept a. These two shaded areas are combined in Panel C. As you can see, the further the value of t is from the mean value of t, the wider the zone of uncertainty becomes.

Now consider what happens when we use the estimated regression line to predict future sales. At a future time period t_{n+k}, the prediction for sales will be a point on the extrapolated regression line (i.e., $\hat{Q}$). However, note what happens to the region of uncertainty about this estimate. The further one forecasts into the future, the wider is this region of uncertainty, and this region increases geometrically rather than arithmetically.

This warning applies not just to time-series models. It applies to all statistical techniques. The further the variables used in the forecasts are from the mean values used in the regression, the wider will be the region of uncertainty and, therefore, the less precise the forecast will be. For example, consider the econometric forecasting model for copper. If we attempt to forecast copper sales using a value of per capita income that is much higher than the mean in the data set, the confidence interval for the forecast will be much wider than would be the case if the value of income used in the forecast was close to the mean value in the data set.

We mentioned the problem of incorrect specification in our discussion of demand estimation, but we feel that it is important enough to deserve another mention here. In order to generate reliable forecasts, the model used must incorporate the appropriate variables. The quality of the forecast can be severely reduced if important explanatory variables are excluded or if an improper functional form is employed (e.g., using a linear form when a nonlinear form is appropriate).

We have saved what we feel to be the most important problem for last. This problem stems from potential changes in structure. Forecasts are widely, and often

FIGURE 7.8
Confidence Intervals

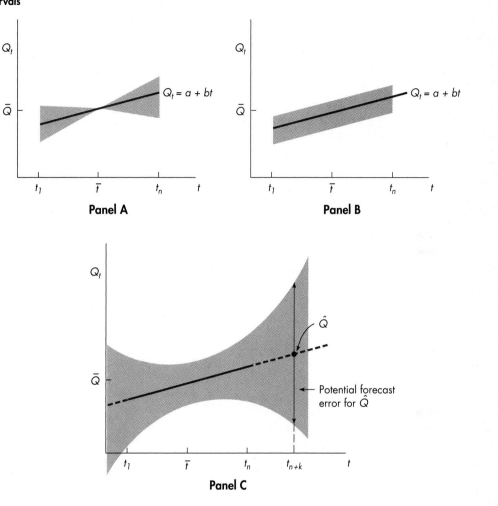

correctly, criticized for failing to predict turning points—sharp changes in the variable under consideration. If it were the case that these changes were only the result of radical changes in the exogenous variables, the simulation approach should be able to handle the problem. However, it is often the case that such changes are the result of changes in the structure of the market itself.

For example, in our consideration of the copper market, there exists the potential for a major change in structure. A major consumer of copper is the telecommunications industry. This industry has been replacing copper transmitting cables with glass fibers. As this change occurs, the demand for copper will be affected

ILLUSTRATION 7.4

Econometric Forecasters Profit by Watching the Weather

Economic forecasting is frequently compared, sometimes derisively so, to weather forecasting. Both economic and meteorological forecasts share the reputation of being stubbornly difficult to perform accurately, even though both types of forecasting often employ rather complex mathematical models and statistical methods. You might be surprised to learn, however, that econometric forecasters of some types of commodities find it quite profitable to include weather forecast information in their demand and supply forecasting models. Commodity trading firms—financial service companies that specialize in buying and selling legal contracts for future delivery of commodities such as electricity, natural gas, heating oil, crude oil, coal, wheat, corn, and some precious metals—have long recognized that large profits can be made by correctly forecasting changes in the prices of commodities that other market forecasters failed to predict. In the high-stakes business of commodity price forecasting, weather forecasts can play a crucial role in two important categories of weather-sensitive commodities: agricultural and energy products. For this reason, meteorologists are now indispensable members of econometric forecasting teams for agricultural and energy commodities.

Recall from our discussion of econometric forecasting that price and quantity forecasts are made by finding the intersection of empirical demand and supply equations at future points in time. Meteorological forecasts of rainfall, temperature, and destructive weather phenomena (such as flooding, drought, tornado, and hurricane activity) can greatly improve the accuracy of supply equations in agricultural forecasting models. For energy commodities such as electricity, natural gas, and home heating oil, econometric forecasters know that they cannot accurately forecast energy demand (and hence energy prices) without including in demand equations weather forecasts of average temperatures in upcoming months. Of course, the accuracy of econometric forecasts improves only when the weather forecasts turn out to be correct. Unfortunately, weather forecasting remains an inexact science. While short-term weather forecasts are pretty accurate, forecasts beyond the next two weeks are still considered to be quite risky. As you know from our discussion of econometric forecasting, the accuracy of future price and quantity forecasts crucially depends on accurately determining the future values of the exogenous variables—weather is an exogenous variable, of course—which are substituted into estimated demand and supply equations to compute future prices and quantities.

Despite the criticism and jokes, meteorologists' forecasts are good enough to generate a high demand for weather forecasters by commodity trading firms and electric utilities. A recent article in *The Wall Street Journal* reported that "deep-pocketed trading companies are offering many meteorologists with graduate degrees salaries ranging from $60,000 to $90,000 (and) performance and trading bonuses can double or even triple the figure."[a] In 1985, Salomon Smith Barney hired its first meteorologist to begin providing its agricultural traders with weather forecasts. Energy trading firms and electric utilities have also discovered the value of weathermen and -women. Before it collapsed, the giant energy-trading firm Enron Corp. employed nine weather forecasters. Other trading firms and utilities, such as Duke Energy Corp. and Aquila, Inc. (a trading subsidiary of a big midwestern utility), are continuing to add meteorologists to their forecasting teams.

Apparently then, if you want to know whether a hard freeze is going to occur in Florida next week, you do not need to wait for the Weather Channel to televise its forecast; just watch what happens to the prices of orange juice concentrate or electricity in the commodity futures markets! With some of the best and brightest meteorologists working for them, commodity forecasting firms will act immediately on their own forecasts of a freeze and begin buying orange juice and electricity contracts at prices lower than will exist once other commodity and energy traders discover a hard freeze is about to hit Florida.

[a]Chip Cummins, "Meteorologists Find Job Offers Coming from Unlikely Places," *The Wall Street Journal*, March 8, 2001, p. 1.

significantly. More specifically, any temporal or econometric relation estimated using data before such a change occurred would be incapable of correctly forecasting quantity demanded after the change. In the context of a demand function, the coefficients would be different before and after the change.

Unfortunately, we know of no satisfactory method of handling this problem of "change in structure." Instead, we must simply leave you with the warning that changes in structure are likely. The further you forecast into the future, the more likely it is that you will encounter such a change.

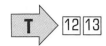

7.9 SUMMARY

This chapter presented the basic techniques of estimating demand functions and forecasting future sales and prices. Estimation of demand functions is most often accomplished using the technique of regression analysis. Two specifications for demand, linear and log-linear, are presented in this chapter. When demand is specified to be linear in form, the coefficients on each of the explanatory variables measure the rate of change in quantity demanded as that explanatory variable changes, holding all other explanatory variables constant. In linear form, the empirical demand specification is

$$Q = a + bP + cM + dP_R$$

where Q is the quantity demanded, P is the price of the good or service, M is consumer income, and P_R is the price of some related good R. The estimated demand elasticities are computed as

$$\hat{E} = \hat{b} \times \frac{P}{Q} \quad E_M = \hat{c} \times \frac{M}{Q} \quad \text{and} \quad \hat{E}_{XR} = \hat{d} \times \frac{P_R}{Q}$$

As in any regression analysis, the statistical significance of the parameter estimates can be assessed by performing t-tests or examining p-values.

When demand is specified as log-linear, the demand function is written as

$$Q = aP^bM^cP_R^d$$

In order to estimate the log-linear demand function, it is converted to natural logarithms:

$$\ln Q = \ln a + b \ln P + c \ln M + d \ln P_R$$

In log-linear form, the elasticities of demand are constant, and the estimated elasticities are

$$\hat{E} = \hat{b}, \quad \hat{E}_M = \hat{c}, \quad \text{and} \quad \hat{E}_{XR} = \hat{d}$$

To choose between these two specifications of demand, a researcher should consider whether the sample data to be used for estimating demand are best represented by a demand function with varying elasticities (linear demand) or by one with constant elasticity (log-linear demand). When price and quantity observations are spread over a wide range of values, elasticities are likely to vary, and a linear specification with its varying elasticities is usually a more appropriate specification of demand. Alternatively, if the sample data are clustered over a narrow price (and quantity) range, a constant-elasticity specification of demand, such as a log-linear model, may be a better choice than a linear model.

The method of estimating the parameters of an empirical demand function depends on whether the price of the product is market-determined or manager-determined. Managers of price-taking firms do not set the price of the product they sell; rather, prices are endogenous or "market-determined" by the intersection of demand and supply. Managers of price-setting firms set the price of the product they sell by producing the quantity associated with the chosen price on the downward-sloping demand curve facing the firm. Since price is manager-determined rather than market-determined, price is exogenous for price-setting firms.

When estimating industry demand for price-taking firms, complications arise because of the problem of simultaneity. The simultaneity problem refers to the fact that the observed variation in equilibrium output and price is the result of changes in the determinants of both demand and supply. Because output and price are determined jointly by the forces of supply and demand, two econometric problems arise when a researcher tries to estimate the coefficients of industry demand: the identification problem and the simultaneous equations bias problem.

The identification problem involves determining whether it is possible to trace out the true demand curve from the sample data. Industry demand is identified when supply includes at least one exogenous variable that is not also in the demand equation. The problem of simultaneous equations bias arises when price is an endogenous variable, as it is when price is market-determined for price-taking firms. In order for the standard or ordinary least-squares (OLS) regression procedure to yield unbiased parameter estimates, all explanatory variables must be uncorrelated with the random error term in the demand equation. An endogenous variable is always correlated with the error term in both the demand and supply equations. (This can be verified by examining the reduced form equation for Q, which shows how Q is related to all the exogenous variables and error terms in the system.) Because price is an explanatory variable in the demand equation, and an endogenous variable in the case of price-taking firms, a simultaneous equations bias will result when the OLS procedure is used to estimate demand. The simultaneous equations bias is eliminated by estimating the parameters of the industry demand equation using 2SLS.

When estimating the demand curve facing a price-setting firm—a firm that can control or set the price of its product by varying its own level of production—the problem of simultaneity does not arise. The demand curve for price-setting firms is estimated using the ordinary least-squares (OLS) method of estimation.

Statistical forecasting models can be subdivided into two categories: time-series models and econometric models. Time-series forecasts use the time-ordered sequence of historical observations on a variable to develop a model for predicting future values of that variable. Time-series models specify a mathematical model representing the generating process, then use statistical techniques to fit the historical data to the mathematical model.

The simplest time-series forecast is a linear trend forecast where the generating process is assumed to be the linear model $Q_t = a + bt$. Using time-series data on Q, regression analysis is used to estimate the trend line that best fits the data. If b is greater (less) than 0, sales are increasing (decreasing) over time. If b equals 0, sales are constant over time.

When data exhibit cyclical variation, such as seasonal patterns, dummy variables can be added to the time-series model to account for the seasonality. If there are N seasonal time periods to be accounted for, $N - 1$ dummy variables are added to the demand equation. Each dummy variable accounts for one of the seasonal time periods. The dummy variable takes a value of 1 for those observations that occur during the season assigned to that dummy variable and a value of 0 otherwise. This type of dummy variable allows the intercept of the demand equation to take on different values for each season—the demand curve can shift up and down from season to season.

In contrast to time-series models, econometric models use an explicit structural model to explain the underlying economic relations. Econometric forecasting can be employed to forecast future industry price and sales or to forecast future demand for price-setting firms. The three steps for forecasting industry price and sales are

1. Estimate the industry demand and supply equations.
2. Locate industry demand and supply in the forecast period.
3. Calculate the intersection of future demand and supply.

We illustrated this process by forecasting future copper price and consumption. The three steps for forecasting the future demand for a price-setting firm are

1. Estimate the firm's demand function.
2. Forecast the future values of the demand-shifting variables.
3. Calculate the location of future demand.

We illustrated this process by forecasting the future demand facing a pizza restaurant.

When making forecasts, analysts must be careful to recognize that the further into the future the forecast is made, the wider the confidence interval or region of uncertainty. Incorrect specification of the demand equation (as well as supply in the case of simultaneous equations forecasts) can seriously undermine the quality of a forecast. An even greater problem for accurate forecasting is posed by the occurrence of structural changes that cause turning points in the variable being forecast. Forecasts often fail to predict turning points. While there is no satisfactory way to account for unexpected structural changes, forecasters should note that the further into the future you forecast, the more likely it is that a structural change will occur.

This chapter concludes Part II of the text on demand analysis. In Part III of the text, we will present the theory of production and cost. We also will describe the empirical techniques used to estimate production functions and the various cost equations used by managers to make output and investment decisions.

TECHNICAL PROBLEMS

1. The estimated market demand for good X is

$$\hat{Q} = 70 - 3.5P - 0.6M + 4P_Z$$

where $\hat{Q}$ is the estimated number of units of good X demanded, P is the price of the good, M is income, and P_Z is the price of related good Z. (All parameter estimates are statistically significant at the 1 percent level.)

   a. Is X a normal or an inferior good? Explain.

   b. Are X and Z substitutes or complements? Explain.

   c. At $P = 10$, $M = 30$, and $P_Z = 6$, compute estimates for the price ($\hat{E}$), income ($\hat{E}_M$), and cross-price elasticities ($\hat{E}_{XZ}$).

2. The empirical demand function for good X is estimated in log-linear form as

$$\ln \hat{Q} = 11.74209 - 1.65 \ln P + 0.8 \ln M - 2.5 \ln P_Y$$

where $\hat{Q}$ is the estimated number of units of good X demanded, P is the price of X, M is income, and P_Y is the price of related good Y. (All parameter estimates are significantly different from 0 at the 5 percent level.)

   a. Is X a normal or an inferior good? Explain.

   b. Are X and Y substitutes or complements? Explain.

   c. Express the empirical demand function in the alternative (nonlogarithmic) form:
   $\hat{Q} = $ _____.

   d. At $P = 50$, $M = 36,000$, and $P_Y = 25$, what are the estimated price ($\hat{E}$), income ($\hat{E}_M$), and cross-price elasticities ($\hat{E}_{XY}$)? What is the predicted number of units of good X demanded?

3. For each of the following sets of industry demand and supply functions, determine if the demand function is identified and explain why or why not:

   a. Demand: $Q = a + bP$
   Supply: $Q = e + fP$

   b. Demand: $Q = a + bP + cM$
   Supply: $Q = e + fP$

   c. Demand: $Q = a + bP + cW$
   Supply: $Q = e + fP + gW$

   d. Demand: $Q = a + bP + cM$
   Supply: $Q = e + fP + gT + hP_I$

4. Evaluate the following statement: "If industry demand is not identified, then two-stage least-squares (2SLS) must be used to estimate the demand equation."

5. With the data in Table A of the appendix, the world demand for copper can be estimated by using ordinary least-squares, rather than by using 2SLS, as done in the text example. The estimation results using OLS are as follows:

DEPENDENT VARIABLE: QC		R-SQUARE	F-RATIO	P-VALUE ON F
OBSERVATIONS: 25		0.9648	191.71	0.0001

VARIABLE	PARAMETER ESTIMATE	STANDARD ERROR	T-RATIO	P-VALUE
INTERCEPT	−6245.43	961.291	−6.50	0.0001
PC	−13.4205	14.4504	−0.93	0.3636
M	12073.0	719.326	16.78	0.0001
PA	70.7161	31.8441	2.22	0.0375

Compare the OLS parameter estimates to the 2SLS estimates presented in this chapter. Do you see any problems with using OLS to estimate the parameters of world copper demand? Explain.

6. In the text example dealing with the world demand for copper, we estimated the demand elasticities. Using these estimates, evaluate the impact on the world consumption of copper of

   a. The formation of a worldwide cartel in copper that increases the price of copper by 10 percent.

   b. The onset of a recession that reduces world income by 5 percent.

   c. A technical breakthrough that is expected to reduce the price of copper by 6 percent.

   d. A 10 percent reduction in the price of aluminum.

7. A linear industry demand function of the form

$$Q = a + bP + cM + dP_R$$

was estimated using 2SLS. (Industry demand was first identified by specifying the supply function.) The results of this estimation are as follows:

Two-Stage Least-Squares Estimation				
DEPENDENT VARIABLE: Q				
OBSERVATIONS: 24				

VARIABLE	PARAMETER ESTIMATE	STANDARD ERROR	T-RATIO	P-VALUE
INTERCEPT	68.38	12.65	5.41	0.0001
P	−6.50	3.15	−2.06	0.0492
M	0.13926	0.0131	10.63	0.0001
PR	−10.77	2.45	−4.40	0.0002

    a. Is the sign of $\hat{b}$ as would be predicted theoretically? Why?

    b. What does the sign of $\hat{c}$ imply about the good?

    c. What does the sign of $\hat{d}$ imply about the relation between the commodity and the related good R?

    d. Are the parameter estimates $\hat{a}$, $\hat{b}$, $\hat{c}$, and $\hat{d}$ statistically significant at the 5 percent level of significance?

    e. Using the values $P = 225$, $M = 24{,}000$, and $P_R = 60$, calculate estimates of

        (1) The price elasticity of demand ($\hat{E}$).

        (2) The income elasticity of demand ($\hat{E}_M$).

        (3) The cross-price elasticity ($\hat{E}_{XR}$).

8. The following log-linear demand curve for a price-setting firm is estimated using the ordinary least-squares method:

$$Q = aP^b M^c P_R^d$$

Following are the results of this estimation:

DEPENDENT VARIABLE: LNQ	R-SQUARE	F-RATIO	P-VALUE ON F
OBSERVATIONS: 25	0.8587	89.165	0.0001

VARIABLE	PARAMETER ESTIMATE	STANDARD ERROR	T-RATIO	P-VALUE
INTERCEPT	6.77	4.01	1.69	0.0984
LNP	−1.68	0.70	−2.40	0.0207
LNM	−0.82	0.22	−3.73	0.0005
LNPR	1.35	0.75	1.80	0.0787

    a. The estimated demand equation can be expressed in natural logarithms as ln $Q =$ _____.

    b. Does the parameter estimate for b have the expected sign? Explain.

    c. Given these parameter estimates, is the good a normal or an inferior good? Explain. Is good R a substitute or a complement? Explain.

    d. Which of the parameter estimates are statistically significant at the 5 percent level of significance?

    e. Find the following estimated elasticities:

        (1) The price elasticity of demand ($\hat{E}$).

        (2) The cross-price elasticity of demand ($\hat{E}_{XR}$).

        (3) The income elasticity of demand ($\hat{E}_M$).

    f. A 10 percent decrease in household income, holding all other things constant, will cause quantity demanded to _____ (increase, decrease) by _____ percent.

    g. All else constant, a 10 percent increase in price causes quantity demanded to _____ (increase, decrease) by _____ percent.

    h. A 5 percent decrease in the price of R, holding all other variables constant, causes quantity demanded to _____ (increase, decrease) by _____ percent.

9. A linear trend equation for sales of the form

$$Q_t = a + bt$$

was estimated for the period 1990–2004 (i.e., $t = 1990, 1991, \ldots, 2004$). The results of the regression are as follows:

DEPENDENT VARIABLE: QT	R-SQUARE	F-RATIO	P-VALUE ON F
OBSERVATIONS: 15	0.6602	25.262	0.0002

VARIABLE	PARAMETER ESTIMATE	STANDARD ERROR	T-RATIO	P-VALUE
INTERCEPT	73.71460	34.08	2.16	0.0498
T	3.7621	0.7490	5.02	0.0002

a. Evaluate the statistical significance of the estimated coefficients. (Use 5 percent for the significance level.) Does this estimation indicate a significant trend?

b. Using this equation, forecast sales in 2005 and 2006.

c. Comment on the precision of these two forecasts.

10. Consider a firm subject to quarter-to-quarter variation in its sales. Suppose that the following equation was estimated using quarterly data for the period 1997–2004 (the time variable goes from 1 to 32). The variables D_1, D_2, and D_3 are, respectively, dummy variables for the first, second, and third quarters (e.g., D_1 is equal to 1 in the first quarter and zero otherwise).

$$Q_t = a + bt + c_1 D_1 + c_2 D_2 + c_3 D_3$$

The results of the estimation are presented here:

DEPENDENT VARIABLE: QT	R-SQUARE	F-RATIO	P-VALUE ON F
OBSERVATIONS: 32	0.9817	361.133	0.0001

VARIABLE	PARAMETER ESTIMATE	STANDARD ERROR	T-RATIO	P-VALUE
INTERCEPT	51.234	7.16	7.15	0.0001
T	3.127	0.524	5.97	0.0001
D1	−11.716	2.717	−4.31	0.0002
D2	−1.424	0.636	−2.24	0.0985
D3	−17.367	2.112	−8.22	0.0001

a. At the 5 percent level of significance, perform t- and F-tests to check for statistical significance of the coefficients and the equation. Discuss also the significance of the coefficients and equation in terms of p-values.

b. Calculate the intercept in each of the four quarters. What do these values imply?

c. Use this estimated equation to forecast sales in the four quarters of 2005.

11. Supply and demand functions were specified for commodity X:

$$\text{Demand: } Q = a + bP + cM + dP_R$$
$$\text{Supply: } Q = e + fP + gP_I$$

Using quarterly data for the period 1997(I) through 2004(IV), these functions were estimated via 2SLS. The resulting parameter estimates are presented in the following estimated equations. (All estimated coefficients are statistically significant.)

$$\text{Demand: } Q = 500 - 300P + 1.0M - 200P_R$$
$$\text{Supply: } Q = -400 + 200P - 100P_I$$

The predicted values for the exogenous variables (M, P_R, and P_I) for the first quarter of 2006 were obtained from a macroeconomic forecasting model. These predicted values are:

Income (M) = 10,000
The price of the commodity related in consumption (P_R) = 20
The price of inputs (P_I) = 6.

a. Are the signs of the estimated coefficients as would be predicted theoretically? Explain.

b. Predict the sales of commodity X in the first quarter of 2006.

c. Perform a simulation analysis to determine the sales of commodity X in 2006(I) if income were $9,000 and $12,000.

12. Describe the major shortcomings of time-series models.

13. In the final section of this chapter we provided warnings about three problems that frequently arise. List, explain, and provide an example of each.

APPLIED PROBLEMS

1. Wilpen Company, a price-setting firm, produces nearly 80 percent of all tennis balls purchased in the United States. Wilpen estimates the U.S. demand for its tennis balls by using the following linear specification:

$$Q = a + bP + cM + dP_R$$

where Q is the number of cans of tennis balls sold quarterly, P is the wholesale price Wilpen charges for a can of tennis balls, M is the consumers' average household income, and P_R is the average price of tennis rackets. The regression results are as follows:

```
DEPENDENT VARIABLE: Q      R-SQUARE    F-RATIO     P-VALUE ON F

      OBSERVATIONS: 20      0.8435      28.75        0.001


                 PARAMETER     STANDARD
VARIABLE         ESTIMATE      ERROR        T-RATIO     P-VALUE

INTERCEPT        425120.0      220300.0     1.93        0.0716
P                -37260.6      12587        -22.96      0.0093
M                1.49          0.3651       4.08        0.0009
PR               -1456.0       460.75       -3.16       0.0060
```

a. Discuss the statistical significance of the parameter estimates $\hat{a}$, $\hat{b}$, $\hat{c}$, and $\hat{d}$ using the p-values. Are the signs of $\hat{b}$, $\hat{c}$, and $\hat{d}$ consistent with the theory of demand?

Wilpen plans to charge a wholesale price of $1.65 per can. The average price of a tennis racket is $110, and consumers' average household income is $24,600.

b. What is the estimated number of cans of tennis balls demanded?

c. At the values of P, M, and P_R given, what are the estimated values of the price ($\hat{E}$), income ($\hat{E}_M$), and cross-price elasticities ($\hat{E}_{XR}$) of demand?

d. What will happen, in percentage terms, to the number of cans of tennis balls demanded if the price of tennis balls decreases 15 percent?

e. What will happen, in percentage terms, to the number of cans of tennis balls demanded if average household income increases by 20 percent?

f. What will happen, in percentage terms, to the number of cans of tennis balls demanded if the average price of tennis rackets increases 25 percent?

2. In the examination of world demand for copper, we used a linear specification. However, we could have estimated a log-linear specification. That is, we could have specified the copper demand function as

$$Q_c = aP_c^b M^c P_A^d$$

or

$$\ln Q_c = \ln a + b \ln P_c + c \ln M + d \ln P_A$$

The results of such an estimation, using the data in Table A of the appendix, are presented here:

```
                Two-Stage Least-Squares Estimation

DEPENDENT VARIABLE: LNQC

      OBSERVATIONS: 25

                 PARAMETER     STANDARD
VARIABLE         ESTIMATE      ERROR        T-RATIO     P-VALUE

INTERCEPT        9.49265       1.56146      6.08        0.0001
LNPC             -0.88307      0.56457      -1.56       0.1327
LNM              2.69818       0.50542      5.34        0.0001
LNPA             0.83530       0.33400      2.50        0.0207
```

a. Using the p-values, discuss the statistical significance of the parameter estimates $\hat{a}$, $\hat{b}$, $\hat{c}$, and $\hat{d}$. Are the signs of $\hat{b}$, $\hat{c}$, and $\hat{d}$ consistent with the theory of demand?

b. What are the estimated values of the price ($\hat{E}$), income ($\hat{E}_M$), and cross-price ($\hat{E}_{CA}$) elasticities of demand? Compare these elasticity estimates with the estimated elasticities for the linear specification of copper demand (estimated in this chapter).

c. Which specification of copper demand, the linear or log-linear, appears to be more appropriate?

3. Cypress River Landscape Supply is a large wholesale supplier of landscaping materials in Georgia. Cypress River's sales vary seasonally; sales tend to be higher in the spring months than in other months.

a. Suppose Cypress River estimates a linear trend *without* accounting for this seasonal variation. What effect would this omission have on the estimated sales trend?

b. Alternatively, suppose there is, in fact, no seasonal pattern to sales, and the trend line is estimated using dummy variables to account for seasonality. What effect would this have on the estimation?

4. Rubax, a U.S. manufacturer of athletic shoes, estimates the following linear trend model for shoe sales:

$$Q_t = a + bt + c_1 D_1 + c_2 D_2 + c_3 D_3$$

where

Q_t = sales of athletic shoes in the t-th quarter

$t = 1, 2, \ldots, 28[1998(I), 1998(II), \ldots, 2004(IV)]$

$D_1 = 1$ if t is quarter I (winter); 0 otherwise

$D_2 = 1$ if t is quarter II (spring); 0 otherwise

$D_3 = 1$ if t is quarter III (summer); 0 otherwise

The regression analysis produces the following results:

DEPENDENT VARIABLE: QT	R-SQUARE	F-RATIO	P-VALUE ON F
OBSERVATIONS: 28	0.9651	159.01	0.0001

VARIABLE	PARAMETER ESTIMATE	STANDARD ERROR	T-RATIO	P-VALUE
INTERCEPT	184500	10310	17.90	0.0001
T	2100	340	6.18	0.0001
D1	3280	1510	2.17	0.0404
D2	6250	2220	2.82	0.0098
D3	7010	1580	4.44	0.0002

a. Is there sufficient statistical evidence of an upward trend in shoe sales?

b. Do these data indicate a statistically significant seasonal pattern of sales for Rubax shoes? If so, what is the seasonal pattern exhibited by the data?

    c. Using the estimated forecast equation, forecast sales of Rubax shoes for 2005(III) and 2006(II).

    d. How might you improve this forecast equation?

5. Suppose you are the market analyst for a major U.S. bank and the bank president asks you to forecast the median price of new homes and the number of new homes that will be sold in the first quarter of 2006. You specify the following demand and supply functions for the U.S. housing market:

$$\text{Demand: } Q_H = a + bP_H + cM + dP_A + eR$$
$$\text{Supply: } Q_H = f + gP_H + hP_M$$

where the endogenous variables are measured in the following way:

$$Q_H = \text{thousands of units sold quarterly}$$
$$P_H = \text{median price of a new home in thousands of dollars}$$

The exogenous variables are median income in dollars (M), average price of apartments (P_A), mortgage interest rate as a percent (R), and the price of building materials as an index (P_M).

    a. Is the demand equation identified? Explain.

    b. What signs do you expect each of the estimated coefficients to have? Explain.

Using quarterly data for the period 1993(I) through 2005(IV), you estimate these equations using two-stage least-squares. All the coefficients are statistically significant and the estimated equations are

$$\text{Demand: } Q_H = 504.5 - 10.0P_H + 0.01M + 0.5P_A - 11.75R$$
$$\text{Supply: } Q_H = 326.0 + 15P_H - 1.8P_M$$

The predicted values for the exogenous variables for the first quarter of 2006 are obtained from a private econometrics firm. The predicted values are:

Median income (M) = 26,000
Average price of apartments (P_A) = 400
Mortgage interest rate (R) = 14
Price of building materials (P_M) = 320 (an index)

    c. Using these predicted values of the exogenous variables, forecast the median price and sales of new homes in the first quarter of 2006.

    d. Suppose you feel that the predicted mortgage interest rate for the first quarter of 2006, 14 percent, is much too high. Determine how changing the forecast interest rate to 10 percent affects the forecast price and sales for the first quarter of 2006.

□ **MATHEMATICAL APPENDIX**

Derivation of Elasticity Estimates for Linear and Log-Linear Demands

As demonstrated in Chapter 6, the price elasticity of demand is

$$E = \frac{\partial Q}{\partial P} \times \frac{Q}{P}$$

With the linear specification of the demand function,

$$Q = a + bP + cM + dP_R$$

the parameter b is an estimate of the partial derivative of quantity demanded with respect to the price of the product,

$$\hat{b} = \text{Estimate of} \left(\frac{\partial Q}{\partial P} \right)$$

Hence for any price–quantity demanded combination (P, Q), the estimated price elasticity of that point on the demand function is

$$\hat{E} = \hat{b} \times \frac{P}{Q}$$

With the log-linear specification of the demand function,

$$Q = aP^b M^c P_R^d$$

the partial derivative of quantity demanded with respect to price is

$$\frac{\partial Q}{\partial P} = baP^{b-1} M^c P_R^d = \frac{bQ}{P}$$

Hence, $\hat{b}$ is an estimate of price elasticity

$$\hat{E} = \frac{\hat{b}Q}{P} \times \frac{P}{Q} = \hat{b}$$

Using the same methodology, estimates of income and cross-price elasticities can be obtained. The estimates are summarized in the following table:

Empirical Elasticities and Two-Stage Least-Squares Estimation

Elasticity	Definition	Estimate from linear specification	Estimate from log-linear specification
Price	$E = \frac{\partial Q}{\partial P} \times \frac{P}{Q}$	$\hat{b} \times \frac{P}{Q}$	$\hat{b}$
Income	$E_M = \frac{\partial Q}{\partial M} \times \frac{M}{Q}$	$\hat{c} \times \frac{M}{Q}$	$\hat{c}$
Cross-price	$E_{XR} = \frac{\partial Q}{\partial P_R} \times \frac{P_R}{Q}$	$\hat{d} \times \frac{P_R}{Q}$	$\hat{d}$

Note that the elasticity estimates from the linear specification depend on the point on the demand curve at which the elasticity estimate is evaluated. In contrast, the log-linear demand curve exhibits constant elasticity estimates.

Simultaneous Equations Bias and Two-Stage Least-Squares Estimation

Simultaneous equations bias

Consider the following system of demand and supply equations

$$\text{Demand: } Q = a + bP + cM + \varepsilon_d$$

$$\text{Supply: } Q = d + eP + fP_I + \varepsilon_s$$

where P and Q are the endogenous variables, M and P_I are the exogenous variables, and ε_d and ε_s are the random error terms for demand and supply. We now solve for the *reduced-form equations*, which show how the values of the endogenous variables are determined by the exogenous variables and the random error terms. First we set $Q_d = Q_s$ and solve for P^*:

$$a + bP + cM + \varepsilon_d = d + eP + fP_I + \varepsilon_s$$

$$P(b - e) = d - a + fP_I - cM + \varepsilon_s - \varepsilon_d$$

$$P^* = \frac{d - a}{b - e} + \frac{f}{b - e} P_I + \frac{-c}{b - e} M + \frac{\varepsilon_s - \varepsilon_d}{b - e}$$

Next, we substitute P^* into either demand or supply and solve for Q^*:

$$Q^* = \frac{bd - ae}{b - e} + \frac{bf}{b - e} P_I + \frac{-ce}{b - e} M + \frac{b\varepsilon_s - e\varepsilon_d}{b - e}$$

The reduced-form equations for P^* and Q^* can be expressed in a simpler, more general form as follows:

$$P^* = f(P_I, M, \varepsilon_d, \varepsilon_s)$$

$$Q^* = g(P_I, M, \varepsilon_d, \varepsilon_s)$$

The reduced-form equations show

1. *The problem of simultaneity:* Each one of the endogenous variables, P^* and Q^* in this case, is clearly determined by all the exogenous variables in the system and by all the random error terms in the system. Thus the observed variations in both P and Q are reflecting variations in both demand- and supply-side determinants.

2. *The simultaneous equations bias:* If the ordinary least-squares estimation procedure is to produce unbiased estimates of a, b, and c in the demand equation, the explanatory variables (P and M) must *not* be correlated with the error term in the demand equation, ε_d (for a proof of this statement, see Gujarati[a]). The reduced-form equations show us clearly that all endogenous variables are functions of all random error terms in the system. P is an endogenous variable, and we have seen that P is a function of ε_d. Thus P will be correlated with the error term in the demand equation, and the estimates of a, b, and c will be biased if the ordinary least-squares procedure is employed. The bias that results because P is an endogenous explanatory variable is called simultaneous equations bias.

Two-stage least-squares estimation

If an industry demand equation is identified, it can be estimated using any number of available techniques. Perhaps the most widely used of these techniques—and the one that is most likely to be preprogrammed into the available regression packages—is two-stage least-squares (2SLS).

As shown earlier, the estimates of the parameters of the demand equation will be biased if ordinary least-squares is employed because price is an endogenous variable that is on the right-hand side of the demand equation. Because price is endogenous, it will be correlated with the error term in the demand equation, causing simultaneous equations bias.

Conceptually, the endogenous right-hand-side variable (in this case, price) must be made to behave as if it is exogenous; traditional regression techniques are used to obtain estimates of the parameters. In the linear example

we have been using, we have a system of two simultaneous equations:

Demand: $Q = a + bP + cM + \varepsilon_d$

Supply: $Q = d + eP + fP_I + \varepsilon_s$

In these equations, P is an endogenous variable. To obtain unbiased estimates of a, b, and c, the estimation of the demand function proceeds in two steps or stages, which is why the technique is called two-stage least-squares:

Stage 1: The endogenous right-hand-side variable is regressed on all the exogenous variables in the system:

$$P = \alpha + \beta M + \gamma P_I$$

From this estimation, we obtain estimates of the parameters, that is, $\hat{\alpha}$, $\hat{\beta}$, and $\hat{\gamma}$. Using these estimates and the *actual values* of the exogenous variables, we generate a *new* price series—predicted price—as follows:

$$\hat{P} = \hat{\alpha} + \hat{\beta}M + \hat{\gamma}P_I$$

Note how the predicted price, $\hat{P}$, is obtained. $\hat{P}$ is simply a linear combination of the exogenous variables, so it follows that $\hat{P}$ is now also exogenous. However, given the way that the predicted price series is obtained, the values of $\hat{P}$ will correspond closely to the original values of P. In essence, this first stage forces price to behave as if it were exogenous.

Stage 2: We then use the predicted price variable (P) in the demand function we wish to estimate. That is, in the second stage, we estimate the regression equation:

$$Q = a + b\hat{P} + cM$$

Note that this estimation uses the exogenous variable constructed in the first stage. We use predicted price, P, rather than the actual price variable, $\hat{P}$, in the final regression.

----

[a]Damodar N. Gujarati, *Basic Econometrics* (New York: McGraw-Hill, 2002).

MATHEMATICAL EXERCISES

1. Let demand be specified as

$$Q = 200\, P^{-1.5}\, M^{0.8}\, P_R^{-1.2}$$

where Q is quantity demanded of the good, P is the price, M is disposable income, and P_R is the price of good R.

a. Using partial derivatives, find the price ($\hat{E}$), income ($\hat{E}_M$), and cross-price ($\hat{E}_{XR}$) elasticities. Verify that the price, income, and cross-price elasticities are constant and equal to the exponents of P, M, and P_R, respectively.

b. Calculate quantity demanded when $P = \$10$, $M = \$15{,}000$, and $P_R = \$4$.

c. Write the log-linear specification of demand: $\ln Q = $ _____.

d. Using logarithms and the expression in part c, find the value of Q when $P = \$10$, $M = \$15{,}000$, and $P_R = \$4$. Does your answer using logarithms match your answer in part b?

2. Consider the following system of industry demand and supply equations:

$$\text{Demand: } Q = 400 - 3P + 0.1M + \varepsilon_d$$

$$\text{Supply: } Q = 20 + 2P + 4P_I + \varepsilon_s$$

where P and Q are endogenous variables, M and P_I are exogenous variables, and ε_d and ε_s are the random error terms for demand and supply, respectively.

a. Solve algebraically for the reduced-form equations for price and quantity.

b. Using the reduced-form equations, explain why ordinary least-squares is not the appropriate method for estimating the parameters of *either* the demand or the supply function.

c. Demonstrate that the structural parameters for the slopes of demand and supply (-3 and 2, respectively) can be identified from the coefficients in the two reduced-form equations. (*Hint:* Examine the algebraic expressions for the reduced-form equations in this appendix to find a way to solve for the coefficients on P in the demand and supply equations by using some of the coefficients in the reduced-form equations.)

◻ **DATA APPENDIX** Data Used in Chapter 7 Examples

TABLE A
The World Copper Market[a]

Year	World consumption (Q_C)	Real price, copper (P_C)	Index of real income (M)	Real price, aluminum (P_A)	World production (Q_P)	X (Q_C/Q_P)	T
	3,056.5				3,129.1		
1	3,173.0	26.56	0.70	19.76	3,052.8	0.97679	1
2	3,281.1	27.31	0.71	20.78	3,120.3	1.03937	2
3	3,135.7	32.95	0.72	22.55	3,222.3	1.05153	3
4	3,359.1	33.90	0.70	23.06	3,282.0	0.97312	4
5	3,755.1	42.70	0.74	24.93	3,606.0	1.02349	5
6	3,875.9	46.11	0.74	26.50	3,967.7	1.04135	6
7	3,905.7	31.70	0.74	27.24	3,982.6	0.97686	7
8	3,957.6	27.23	0.72	26.21	3,846.5	0.98069	8
9	4,279.1	32.89	0.75	26.09	4,138.7	1.02888	9
10	4,627.9	33.78	0.77	27.40	4,726.1	1.03392	10
11	4,910.2	31.66	0.76	26.94	4,926.0	0.97922	11
12	4,908.4	32.28	0.79	25.18	5,079.6	0.99679	12
13	5,327.9	32.38	0.83	23.94	5,177.0	0.96630	13
14	5,878.4	33.75	0.85	25.07	5,445.5	1.02915	14
15	6,075.2	36.25	0.89	25.37	5,781.9	1.07950	15
16	6,312.7	36.24	0.93	24.55	6,141.5	1.05073	16
17	6,056.8	38.23	0.95	24.98	5,891.9	1.02788	17
18	6,375.9	40.83	0.99	24.96	6,430.5	1.02799	18
19	6,974.3	44.62	1.00	25.52	6,961.0	0.99151	19
20	7,101.6	52.27	1.00	26.01	7,425.0	1.00191	20
21	7,071.7	45.16	1.02	25.46	7,294.4	0.95644	21
22	7,754.8	42.50	1.07	22.17	7,895.3	0.96947	22
23	8,480.3	43.70	1.12	18.56	8,413.6	0.98220	23
24	8,105.2	47.88	1.10	21.32	8,640.0	1.00793	24
25	7,157.2	36.33	1.07	22.75	8,054.1	0.93810	25

[a]The data presented are actual values for 1950–1975.
Q_c = world consumption (sales) of copper in 1000s of metric tons,
P_c = price of copper in cents per pound (inflation adjusted),
M = index of real per capita income (1970 = 1.00),
P_A = price of aluminum in cents per pound (inflation adjusted),
X = ratio of consumption in the previous year to production in the previous year (= Q_c/Q_P), and
T = technology (time period is a proxy).

TABLE B
Data for Checkers Pizza

Observation	Q	P	M	P_{Al}	P_{BMac}
1	2,659	8.65	25,500	10.55	1.25
2	2,870	8.65	25,600	10.45	1.35
3	2,875	8.65	25,700	10.35	1.55
4	2,849	8.65	25,970	10.30	1.05
5	2,842	8.65	25,970	10.30	0.95
6	2,816	8.65	25,750	10.25	0.95
7	3,039	7.50	25,750	10.25	0.85
8	3,059	7.50	25,950	10.15	1.15
9	3,040	7.50	25,950	10.00	1.25
10	3,090	7.50	26,120	10.00	1.75
11	2,934	8.50	26,120	10.25	1.75
12	2,942	8.50	26,120	10.25	1.85
13	2,834	8.50	26,200	9.75	1.50
14	2,517	9.99	26,350	9.75	1.10
15	2,503	9.99	26,450	9.65	1.05
16	2,502	9.99	26,350	9.60	1.25
17	2,557	9.99	26,850	10.00	0.55
18	2,586	10.25	27,350	10.25	0.55
19	2,623	10.25	27,350	10.20	1.15
20	2,633	10.25	27,950	10.00	1.15
21	2,721	9.75	28,159	10.10	0.55
22	2,729	9.75	28,264	10.10	0.55
23	2,791	9.75	28,444	10.10	1.20
24	2,821	9.75	28,500	10.25	1.20

PART III

Production and Cost Analysis

CHAPTER

8

Production and Cost in the Short Run

No doubt almost all managers know that profit is determined not only by the revenue a firm generates but also by the costs associated with production of the firm's good or service. Many managers, however, find managing the revenue portion of the profit equation more interesting and exciting than dealing with issues concerning the costs of production. After all, revenue-oriented decisions may involve such tasks as choosing the optimal level and mix of advertising media, determining the price of the product, and making decisions to expand into new geographic markets or new product lines. Even the decision to buy or merge with other firms may be largely motivated by the desire to increase revenues. When revenue-oriented tasks are compared with those involved in production issues—spending time with production engineers discussing productivity levels of workers or the need for more and better capital equipment, searching for lower-cost suppliers of production inputs, adopting new technologies to reduce production costs, and perhaps even engaging in a downsizing plan—it is not surprising that managers may enjoy time spent on revenue decisions more than time spent on production and cost decisions.

As barriers to trade weakened or vanished in the 1990s, the resulting globalization of markets and heightened competition made it much more difficult to increase profits by simply selling more units or charging higher prices. Global competition has intensified the need for managers to increase productivity and reduce costs in order to satisfy stockholders' desire for greater profitability. As one management consultant recently interviewed in *The Wall Street Journal* put it, "Cost-cutting has become the holy-grail of corporate management." As we will discuss further in Chapter 9, managers must understand the theory of production and cost in order to reduce costs successfully. Many costly errors have been made by managers seeking to "reengineer" or "restructure" production. Most of these errors could have been avoided by managers possessing an understanding of the fundamentals of production and cost that we will now set forth. This chapter and Chapter 9 show how the structure of a firm's costs is determined by the nature of the production process that transforms inputs into goods and services and by the prices of the inputs used in producing the goods or services. In Chapter 10, we show you how to employ regression analysis to estimate the parameters of the production and cost functions for a firm.

Managers make production decisions in two different decision-making time frames: short-run production decisions and long-run production decisions. In short-run decision-making situations, a manager must produce with at least some inputs that are fixed in quantity. In a typical short-run situation, the manager has a fixed amount of plant and equipment with which to produce the firm's output. The manager can change production levels by hiring more or less labor and purchasing more or less raw materials, but the size of the plant is viewed by the manager as essentially unchangeable or fixed for the purposes of making production decisions in the short run.

Long-run decision making concerns the same types of decisions as the short run with one important distinction: The usage of all inputs can be either increased or decreased. In the long run, a manager can choose to operate in any size plant with any amount of capital equipment. Once a firm builds a new plant or changes the size of an existing plant, the manager is once more in a short-run decision-making framework. Sometimes economists think of the short run as the time period during which production actually takes place and the long run as the planning horizon during which future production will take place. As it turns out, the structure of costs differs in rather crucial ways depending on whether production is taking place in the short run or whether the manager is planning for a particular level of production in the long run.

This chapter presents the fundamentals of the theory of production and the theory of cost in the short run. We will show how the theory of short-run cost is based on the theory of short-run production. Using production theory, managers determine how much of the variable input(s) to use in combination with the fixed input(s) to produce a particular level of output. After we set forth the theory of production in the short run, we derive the structure of the firm's costs in the short run. By applying the concepts of production theory, the manager can determine the combination of inputs to use to produce a given amount of output at the lowest total cost. Given input prices and the amount of each input that will be purchased, it is a straightforward task to determine the total cost of production.

8.1 SOME BASIC CONCEPTS OF PRODUCTION THEORY

production
The creation of goods and services from inputs or resources.

Production is the creation of goods and services from inputs or resources, such as labor, machinery and other capital equipment, land, raw materials, and so on. Obviously, when a company such as Ford makes a truck or car or when Exxon refines a gallon of gasoline, the activity is production. But production goes much further than that. A doctor produces medical services, a teacher produces education, and a singer produces entertainment. So production involves services as well as making the goods people buy. Production is also undertaken by governments and non-profit organizations. A city police department produces protection, a public school produces education, and a hospital produces health care.

In the following chapters, as in most of this text, we will analyze production within the framework of business firms using inputs to produce goods, rather than services. Such an approach is more simple and straightforward than the study of the production of services or production by agencies of the government. It is conceptually easier to visualize the production of cars, trucks, or refrigerators than the production of education, health, or security, which are hard to measure and even harder to define. Nonetheless, throughout the discussion, remember that the concepts developed here apply to services as well as goods and to government production as well as firm production.

Production Functions

production function
A schedule (or table or mathematical equation) showing the maximum amount of output that can be produced from any specified set of inputs, given the existing technology.

A production function is the link between levels of input usage and attainable levels of output. That is, the production function formally describes the relation between physical rates of output and physical rates of input usage. With a given state of technology, the attainable quantity of output depends on the quantities of the various inputs employed in production. A **production function** is a schedule (or table or mathematical equation) showing the maximum amount of output that can be produced from any specified set of inputs, given the existing technology or state of the art of production.

Many different inputs are used in production. So, in the most general case, we can define maximum output Q to be a function of the level of usage of the various inputs X. That is,

$$Q = f(X_1, X_2, \ldots, X_n)$$

But in our discussion we will generally restrict attention to the simpler case of a product whose production entails only one or two inputs. We will normally use capital and labor as the two inputs. Hence, the production function we will usually be concerned with is

$$Q = f(L, K)$$

where L and K represent, respectively, the amounts of labor and capital used in production. However, we must stress that the principles to be developed apply to situations with more than two inputs and, as well, to inputs other than capital and labor.

technical efficiency
Production of the maximum level of output that can be obtained from a given combination of inputs.

Technical Efficiency and Economic Efficiency

Before proceeding, we want to distinguish between *technical efficiency* and *economic efficiency*. **Technical efficiency** is achieved when the maximum possible amount of output is being produced with a given combination of inputs. The definition of a production function assumes that technical efficiency is being achieved because the production function gives the *maximum* output level that can be achieved for any particular combination of inputs. Thus technical efficiency is implied by the production function.

To illustrate the concept of technical efficiency, consider Amergen, Inc., a firm that manufactures electric generators. Amergen builds its generators using an assembly-line process that begins with workers manually performing five steps before the generator reaches a computer-controlled drill press. At this stage, the computer-controlled drill press makes 36 holes, which are required for final assembly. In the process of drilling 36 holes, almost two pounds of iron are removed. Using this production process, Amergen employs 10 assembly-line workers and one computer-controlled drill press and produces 140 generators each day. An industrial engineer studying this process discovers that moving the computer-controlled drill press to the beginning of the assembly line, ahead of five steps that are performed manually, will save laborers energy each day—the generators weigh two pounds less when they get to the workers on the assembly line. By moving the drilling to the beginning of the production process, the same 10 workers and one drill press can produce 150 generators per day. The industrial engineer is unable to find any other change in the production process that would further increase output. Now Amergen is operating in a technically efficient manner; 150 generators are the maximum number of generators that can be produced daily using 10 laborers and one drill press.

Economic efficiency is achieved when the firm is producing a given amount of output at the lowest possible cost. As you will recall from Chapter 3, this is a constrained optimization problem. The optimization rules discussed there and those to be developed in Chapter 9 lead a producer to an economically efficient method of production.

One should be careful about labeling a particular production process inefficient. Certainly a process would be technically inefficient if another process can produce the same amount of output using less of one or more inputs and the same amounts of all others. If, however, the second process uses less of some inputs but more of others, the economically efficient method of producing a given level of output depends on the prices of the inputs. Even when both are technically efficient, one process might cost less—be economically efficient—under one set of input prices while the other may be economically efficient at other input prices.

economic efficiency
Production of a given amount of output at the lowest possible cost.

Short Run and Long Run

When analyzing the process of production, it is convenient to introduce the classification of inputs as *fixed* or *variable*. A **fixed input** is one for which the level of usage cannot readily be changed. To be sure, no input is ever absolutely fixed, no matter how short the period of time under consideration. However, the cost of immediately varying the use of an input may be so great that, for all practical purposes, the input is fixed. For example, buildings, major pieces of machinery, and managerial personnel are inputs that generally cannot be rapidly augmented or

fixed input
An input for which the level of usage cannot readily be changed.

variable input
An input for which the level of usage may be changed quite readily.

short run
That period of time in which the level of usage of one or more of the inputs is fixed.

diminished. A **variable input,** on the other hand, is one for which the level of usage may be changed quite readily in response to desired changes in output. Many types of labor services as well as certain raw and processed materials would be in this category.

As mentioned in the introduction, economists distinguish between the *short run* and the *long run*. The **short run** refers to that period of time in which the level of usage of one or more of the inputs is fixed. Therefore, in the short run, changes in output must be accomplished exclusively by changes in the use of the variable inputs. Thus, if producers wish to expand output in the short run, they must do so by using more hours of labor (a variable service) and other variable inputs, with the existing plant and equipment. Similarly, if they wish to reduce output in the short run, they may discharge only certain inputs. They cannot immediately "discharge" a building or a blast furnace (even though its use may fall to zero). In the context of our simplified production function, we might consider capital to be the fixed input and write the resulting short-run production function as

$$Q = f(L, \overline{K})$$

where the bar over capital means that it is fixed. Furthermore, since capital is fixed, output depends only on the level of usage of labor, so we could write the short-run production function as simply

$$Q = f(L)$$

long run
The production period when all inputs are variable and $Q = f(L, K)$

The **long run** refers to that time in the future when all inputs are variable inputs. Thus, in the long run, output can be varied by changing the levels of both labor and capital, and the long-run production function is expressed as

$$Q = f(L,K)$$

Once a firm purchases and installs a particular amount of capital, however, it then operates in a short-run situation with the now fixed amount of capital. Thus, in a sense, the long run consists of all possible short-run situations (i.e., all possible choices of capital usage) from which a firm may choose. For this reason, the long-run production period is also called the firm's *planning horizon*. A firm's long-run **planning horizon** is the collection of all possible short-run situations the firm may face, one short-run situation for each level of capital that can be chosen in the long run. Naturally, in the long run a manager will choose the most advantageous amount of capital for its intended output, but as the changes in production levels occur in the short run, the firm may find itself with too much or too little capital. We will have much more to say in Chapter 9 about the cost advantages of adjusting capital usage in the long run.

planning horizon
The collection of all possible short-run situations a firm may face, one for every level of capital.

Fixed or Variable Proportions

Most of the discussion in this chapter and Chapter 9 refers to production functions that allow at least some substitution of one input for another in reaching an output

target. When substitution is possible, we say inputs may be used in *variable propor-*
tions. As a consequence, producers must determine not only the optimal level of
output to produce but also the optimal combination of inputs. **Variable propor-**
tions production means that output can be changed in the short run by changing
the variable inputs without changing the fixed inputs. And it means that the same
output can be produced using different combinations of inputs.

**variable proportions
production**
Production in which a given
level of output can be
produced with more than
one combination of inputs.

Most economists regard production under conditions of variable proportions as
typical of both the short and the long run. There is certainly no doubt that proportions are variable in the long run. When making an investment decision, for instance, a producer may choose among a wide variety of different production
processes. As an example of polar-opposite processes, an automobile can be practically handmade or it can be made by assembly-line techniques. In the short run,
however, there may be some cases where there is little opportunity for substitution
among inputs.

**fixed proportions
production**
Production in which one,
and only one, ratio or mix
of inputs can be used to
produce a good.

Fixed proportions production means that there is one, and only one, ratio or
mix of inputs that can be used to produce a good. If output is expanded or contracted, all inputs must be expanded or contracted at the same rate to maintain the
fixed input ratio. At first glance, this might seem the usual condition: One worker
and one shovel produce a ditch; two parts hydrogen and one part oxygen produce
water. Adding a second shovel or a second part of oxygen will not augment the
rate of production. In such cases, the producer has little discretion about what
combination of inputs to employ. The only decision is how much to produce.

In actuality, examples of fixed proportions production are hard to come by. Certainly some "ingredient" inputs are often used in relatively fixed proportions to
output. Otherwise, the quality of the product would change. There is so much
leather in a pair of shoes of a particular size and style. Use less leather, and we
have a different type of shoe. There is so much tobacco in a cigarette. And so on. In
these cases, the producer has little choice over the quantity of input per unit of output. But fixed-ingredient inputs are really only a short-run problem. Historically,
when these necessary ingredients have become very expensive, businesses have
invented new processes, discovered new ingredients, or somehow overcome the
problem of a given production function and increasingly scarce ingredients. As a
consequence, we will direct attention here to production in which the producer has
some control over the mix of inputs and will concentrate on production with variable proportions.

8.2 PRODUCTION IN THE SHORT RUN

We begin the analysis of production in the short run with the simplest kind of
short-run situation: only *one* variable input and *one* fixed input:

$$Q = f(L, \overline{K})$$

The firm has chosen the level of capital (made its investment decision), so capital
is fixed in amount. Once the level of capital is fixed, the only way the firm can
change its output is by changing the amount of labor it employs.

Total Product

Suppose a firm with a production function of the form $Q = f(L, K)$ can, in the long run, choose levels of both labor and capital between 0 and 10 units. A production function giving the maximum amount of output that can be produced from every possible combination of labor and capital is shown in Table 8.1. For example, from the table, 4 units of labor combined with 3 units of capital can produce a maximum of 325 units of output; 6 labor and 6 capital can produce a maximum of 655 units of output; and so on. Note that with 0 capital, no output can be produced regardless of the level of labor usage. Likewise, with 0 labor, there can be no output.

Once the level of capital is fixed, the firm is in the short run, and output can be changed only by varying the amount of labor employed. Assume now that the capital stock is fixed at 2 units of capital. The firm is in the short run and can vary output only by varying the usage of labor (the variable input). The column in Table 8.1 under 2 units of capital gives the total output, or total product of labor, for 0 through 10 workers. This column, for which $K = 2$, represents the short-run production function when capital is fixed at 2 units.

These total products are reproduced in column 2 of Table 8.2 for each level of labor usage in column 1. Thus columns 1 and 2 in Table 8.2 define a production function of the form $Q = f(L, \overline{K})$, where $\overline{K} = 2$. In this example, total product (Q) rises with increases in labor up to a point (9 workers) and then declines. While total product does eventually *fall* as more workers are employed, managers would not (knowingly) hire additional workers if they knew output would fall. In Table 8.2, for example, a manager can hire either 8 workers or 10 workers to produce 314 units of output. Obviously, the economically efficient amount of labor to hire to produce 314 units is eight workers.

Average and Marginal Products

Average and marginal products are obtained from the production function and may be viewed merely as different ways of looking at the same information. The **average product of labor (AP)** is the total product divided by the number of workers:

average product of labor (AP)
Total product (output) divided by the number of workers ($AP = Q/L$).

$$AP = Q/L$$

In our example, average product, shown in column 3, first rises, reaches a maximum at 56.7, then declines thereafter.

The **marginal product of labor (MP)** is the additional output attributable to using one additional worker with the use of all other inputs fixed (in this case, at 2 units of capital). That is,

marginal product of labor (MP)
The additional output attributable to using one additional worker with the use of all other inputs fixed ($MP = \Delta Q/\Delta L$).

$$MP = \Delta Q/\Delta L$$

where Δ means "the change in." The marginal product schedule associated with the production function in Table 8.2 is shown in column 4 of the table. Because no output can be produced with 0 workers, the first worker adds 52 units of output; the

TABLE 8.1
A Production Function

					Units of capital (K)						
		0	1	2	3	4	5	6	7	8	9	10
	0	0	0	0	0	0	0	0	0	0	0	0
	1	0	25	52	74	90	100	108	114	118	120	121
	2	0	55	112	162	198	224	242	252	258	262	264
Units of labor (L)	3	0	83	170	247	303	342	369	384	394	400	403
	4	0	108	220	325	400	453	488	511	527	535	540
	5	0	125	258	390	478	543	590	631	653	663	670
	6	0	137	286	425	523	598	655	704	732	744	753
	7	0	141	304	453	559	643	708	766	800	814	825
	8	0	143	314	474	587	679	753	818	857	873	885
	9	0	141	318	488	609	708	789	861	905	922	935
	10	0	137	314	492	617	722	809	887	935	953	967

TABLE 8.2
Total, Average, and Marginal Products of Labor (with capital fixed at 2 units)

(1) Number of workers (L)	(2) Total product (Q)	(3) Average product (AP = Q/L)	(4) Marginal product (MP = ΔQ/ΔL)
0	0	—	—
1	52	52	52
2	112	56	60
3	170	56.7	58
4	220	55	50
5	258	51.6	38
6	286	47.7	28
7	304	43.4	18
8	314	39.3	10
9	318	35.3	4
10	314	31.4	−4

second adds 60 units (i.e., increases output from 52 to 112); and so on. Note that increasing the amount of labor from 9 to 10 actually decreases output from 318 to 314. Thus the marginal product of the 10th worker is negative. In this example, marginal product first increases as the amount of labor increases, then decreases, and finally becomes negative. This is a pattern frequently assumed in economic analysis.

In this example, the production function assumes that labor, the variable input, is increased one worker at a time. But we can think of the marginal product of an input when more than 1 unit is added. At a fixed level of capital, suppose that 20 units of labor can produce 100 units of output and that 30 units of labor can produce 200 units of output. In this case, output increases by 100 units as labor increases by 10. Thus

$$MP = \frac{\Delta Q}{\Delta L} = \frac{100}{10} = 10$$

Output increases by 10 units for each additional worker hired.

We might emphasize that we speak of the marginal product of labor, not the marginal product of a particular laborer. We assume that all workers are the same, in the sense that if we reduce the number of workers from 8 to 7 in Table 8.2, total product falls from 314 to 304 regardless of which of the 8 workers is released. Thus the order of hiring makes no difference; a third worker adds 58 units of output no matter who is hired.

Figure 8.1 shows graphically the relations among the total, average, and marginal products set forth in Table 8.2. In Panel A, total product increases up to 9 workers, then decreases. Panel B incorporates a common assumption made in production theory: Average product first rises then falls. When average product is increasing, marginal product is greater than average product (after the first worker, at which they are equal). When average product is decreasing, marginal product is less than average product.[1] This result is not peculiar to this particular production function; it occurs for any production function for which average product first increases then decreases.

An example might help demonstrate that for any average and marginal schedule, the average must increase when the marginal is above the average and decrease when the marginal is below the average. If you have taken two tests and made grades of 70 and 80, your average grade is 75. If your third test grade is higher than 75, the marginal grade is above the average, so your average grade increases. Conversely, if your third grade is less than 75—the marginal grade is below the average—your average falls. In production theory, if each additional worker adds more than the average, average product rises; if each additional worker adds less than the average, average product falls.

As shown in Figure 8.1, marginal product first increases then decreases, becoming negative after 9 workers. The maximum marginal product occurs before the maximum average product is attained. When marginal product is *increasing*, total product increases at an *increasing* rate. When marginal product begins to *decrease* (after 2 workers), total product begins to increase at a *decreasing* rate. When marginal product becomes negative (10 workers), total product declines.

We should note another important relation between average and marginal product that is not obvious from the table or the graph but does follow directly from the discussion. If labor is allowed to vary continuously rather than in discrete units of one, as in the example, marginal product equals average product when average is at its maximum. This follows because average product must increase when marginal is above average and decrease when marginal is below average. The two, therefore, must be equal when average is at its maximum.

---

[1]This relation is demonstrated in the appendix to this chapter.

FIGURE 8.1

Total, Average, and
Marginal Products ($\overline{K} = 2$)

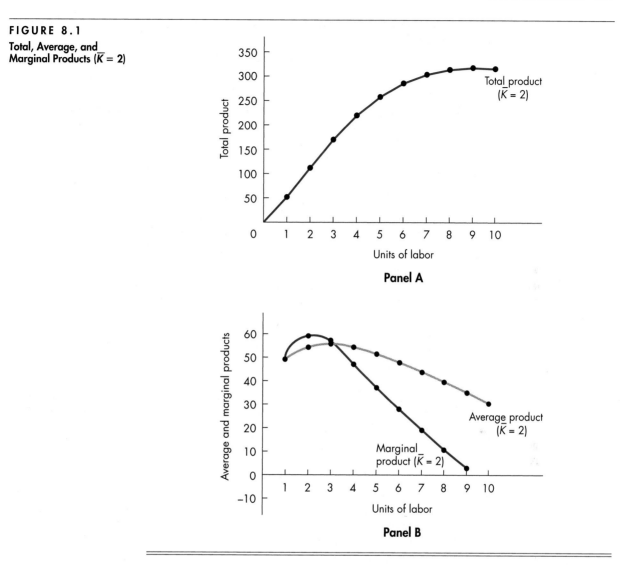

Panel A

Panel B

Law of Diminishing Marginal Product

law of diminishing
marginal product
The principle that as the
number of units of the
variable input increases,
other inputs held constant, a
point will be reached
beyond which the marginal
product decreases.

The slope of the marginal product curve in Panel B of Figure 8.1 illustrates an important principle, the **law of diminishing marginal product.** As the number of units of the variable input increases, other inputs held constant, there exists a point beyond which the marginal product of the variable input declines. When the amount of the variable input is small relative to the fixed inputs, more intensive utilization of fixed inputs by variable inputs may initially increase the marginal product of the variable input as this input is increased. Nonetheless, a point is reached beyond which an increase in the use of the variable input yields progressively less additional output. Each additional unit has, on average, fewer units of the fixed inputs with which to work.

To illustrate the concept of diminishing marginal returns, consider the kitchen at Mel's Hot Dogs, a restaurant that sells hot dogs, french fries, and soft drinks. Mel's kitchen has one gas range for cooking the hot dogs, one deep-fryer for cooking french fries, and one soft-drink dispenser. One cook in the kitchen can prepare 15 meals (consisting of a hot dog, fries, and soft drink) per hour. Two cooks can prepare 35 meals per hour. The marginal product of the second cook is 20 meals per hour, 5 more than the marginal product of the first cook. One cook possibly concentrates on making fries and soft drinks while the other cook prepares hot dogs. Adding a third cook results in 50 meals per hour being produced, so the marginal product of the third worker is 15 (= 50 − 35) additional meals per hour.

Therefore, after the second cook, the marginal product of additional cooks begins to decline. The fourth cook, for example, can increase the total number of meals prepared to 60 meals per hour—a marginal product of just 10 additional meals. A fifth cook adds only 5 extra meals per hour, an increase to 65 meals. While the third, fourth, and fifth cooks increase the total number of meals prepared each hour, their marginal contribution is diminishing because the amount of space and equipment in the kitchen is fixed (i.e., capital is fixed). Mel could increase the size of the kitchen or add more cooking equipment to increase the productivity of all workers. The point at which diminishing returns set in would then possibly occur at a higher level of employment.

The marginal product of additional cooks can even become negative. For example, adding a sixth cook reduces the number of meals from 65 to 60. The marginal product of the sixth cook is –5. Do not confuse *negative* marginal product with *diminishing* marginal product. Diminishing marginal product sets in with the third cook, but marginal product does not become negative until the sixth cook is hired. Obviously, the manager would not want to hire a sixth cook, since output would fall. The manager would hire the third, or fourth, or fifth cook, even though marginal product is decreasing, if more than 35, 50, or 60 meals must be prepared. As we will demonstrate, managers do in fact employ variable inputs beyond the point of diminishing returns but not to the point of negative marginal product.

The law of diminishing marginal product is a simple statement concerning the relation between marginal product and the rate of production that comes from observing real-world production processes. While the eventual diminishing of marginal product cannot be proved or refuted mathematically, it is worth noting that a contrary observation has never been recorded. That is why the relation is called a law.

Changes in Fixed Inputs

The production function shown in Figure 8.1 and also in Table 8.2 was derived from the production function shown in Table 8.1 by holding the capital stock fixed at 2 units ($\overline{K} = 2$). As can be seen in Table 8.1, when different amounts of capital are used, total product changes for each level of labor usage. Indeed, each column in

Table 8.1 represents a different short-run production function, each corresponding to the particular level at which capital stock is fixed. Because the output associated with every level of labor usage changes when capital stock changes, a change in the level of capital causes a *shift* in the total product curve for labor. Since total product changes for every level of labor usage, average product and marginal product of labor also must change at every level of labor usage.

Referring once more to Table 8.1, notice what happens when the capital stock is increased from 2 to 3 units. The total product of 3 workers increases from 170 to 247, as shown in column 3. The average product of three workers increases from 56.7 to 82.3 ($= 247/3$). The marginal product of the third worker increases from 58 to 85 [$\Delta Q/\Delta L = (247 - 162)/1 = 85$]. Table 8.3 shows the total, average, and marginal product schedules for two levels of capital stock, $\overline{K} = 2$ and $\overline{K} = 3$. As you can see, *TP, AP,* and *MP* all increase at each level of labor usage as K increases from 2 to 3 units. Figure 8.2 shows how a change in the fixed amount of capital shifts the product curves. In Panel A, increasing $\overline{K}$ causes the total product curve to shift upward, and in Panel B, the increase in $\overline{K}$ causes both *AP* and *MP* to shift upward. Note that the two capital levels in Figure 8.2 represent two of the 10 possible short-run situations (see Table 8.1) comprising the firm's long-run planning horizon.

We are now ready to derive the cost structure of the firm in the short run. For any level of output the manager wishes to produce, the economically efficient amount of labor to combine with the fixed amount of capital is found from the total product curve. In Figure 8.1, if the manager wishes to produce 220 units of output, the amount of labor that will produce 220 units at the lowest total cost is 4 units. The total cost of producing 220 units of output is found by multiplying the price of labor per unit times 4 to get the total expenditure on labor; this amount is then added to the cost of the fixed input. This computation can be done for every level of output to get the short-run total cost of production. We turn now to the costs of production in the short run.

T ⟹ 7

TABLE 8.3
The Effect of Changes in Capital Stock

L	Q	AP	MP	Q	AP	MP
		$\overline{K} = 2$			$\overline{K} = 3$	
0	0	—	—	0	—	—
1	52	52	52	74	74	74
2	112	56	60	162	81	88
3	170	56.7	58	247	82.3	85
4	220	55	50	325	81.3	78
5	258	51.6	38	390	78	65
6	286	47.7	28	425	70.8	35
7	304	43.4	18	453	64.7	28
8	314	39.3	10	474	59.3	21
9	318	35.3	4	488	54.2	14
10	314	31.4	−4	492	49.2	4

FIGURE 8.2

Shifts in Total, Average, and Marginal Product Curves

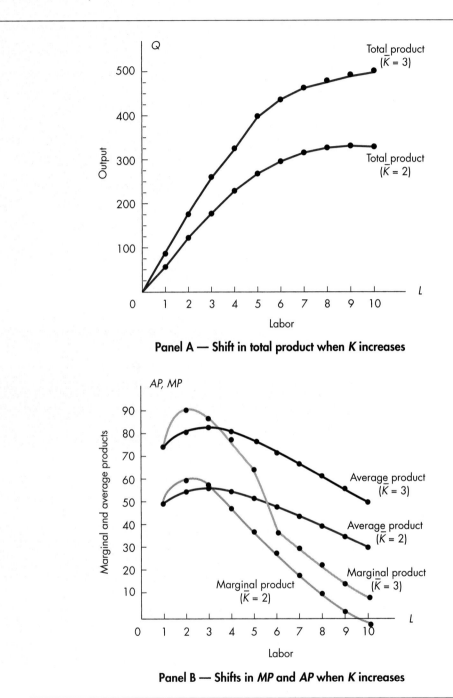

Panel A — Shift in total product when *K* increases

Panel B — Shifts in *MP* and *AP* when *K* increases

8.3 SHORT-RUN COSTS OF PRODUCTION

Recall from the discussion of total economic cost of using resources in Chapter 1 that the opportunity cost to the owners of a firm of using resources to produce goods and services is the amount the owners give up by using these resources. We recommend that you take a few minutes before continuing with this section to review Figure 1.1 and the associated principle for measuring the total economic cost of using inputs or resources in the production of goods or services.

As noted in Chapter 1, the opportunity costs of using productive inputs can be either explicit costs or implicit costs. As we explained in Chapter 1, explicit costs arise when a firm uses resources that it does not own and must therefore purchase in the markets for these resources. Thus the monetary payments to hire, rent, or lease resources owned by others represent the explicit opportunity costs of using market-supplied inputs. Implicit costs are the costs of using any resources the firm owns. The opportunity costs of using owner-supplied resources are the greatest earnings forgone from using resources owned by the firm in the firm's own production process. As we stressed in Chapter 1, even though no explicit monetary payment is made for the use of owner-supplied resources, $1 of implicit costs are no less (and no more) of an opportunity cost of using resources than $1 of explicit costs. Including implicit costs in both personal and business decision making is so important that we offer Illustration 8.2 to reinforce this point.

As explained in Chapter 1 and illustrated in Figure 1.1, total economic cost of using inputs in the production process is the sum of all explicit and implicit costs. Throughout the remainder of this chapter and in later chapters, when we refer to a firm's costs, we include both explicit and implicit costs, even though we will not explicitly divide them into two separate categories. In all cases, "cost" will mean the entire opportunity cost of using resources.

Fixed and Variable Costs

In the short run some inputs are fixed. Since these inputs have to be paid for regardless of the level of output produced, payments for fixed inputs remain constant no matter what level of output is produced. Such payments are called *fixed costs*. An example of a fixed cost is a machine that is leased for one year at a cost of $500 per month. The cost of the machine is $500 every month for one year regardless of how many units of output are produced using the machine. Even if the firm shuts down for a month and does not use the machine, the firm still must pay $500 for the machine that month.

Payments for variable inputs are called *variable costs*. Producing more output requires more variable inputs. Thus variable costs increase as the level of output increases. Examples of variable costs are payments for many types of labor, ingredient inputs or raw materials, or the energy used in production.

Short-Run Total Costs

As noted earlier, in the short run the levels of use of some inputs are fixed, and the costs associated with these fixed inputs must be paid regardless of the level of

ILLUSTRATION 8.1

Employing More and Better Capital Boosts Productivity in U.S. Petroleum and Chemical Industries

One of the important relations of production theory established in this chapter holds that increasing the amount of capital employed by a firm increases the productivity of the *other* inputs employed by the firm. Recall in Panel A of Figure 8.2, an increase in capital from 2 to 3 units resulted in higher total output at every level of labor usage, because using more capital causes the total product curve to shift upward. With 3 units of capital, each level of output can be produced with less labor than if the firm employs only 2 units of capital. While increasing the quantity of capital boosts labor productivity and output at every level of labor usage, the productivity gained will be even greater if the additional capital input embodies advanced, state-of-the-art technology. Technological progress makes newly acquired capital equipment more productive than the firm's existing stock of capital since the older, currently employed capital is designed around less advanced technology. Thus purchasing *better* capital magnifies the increase in productivity that results from having *more* capital. This strategy of combining more and better capital to sharply increase productivity is exactly what has

happened in two very important industries: crude oil production and petrochemical refining.

Petroleum-producing firms in the United States are experiencing a period of high productivity in exploration operations (the process of finding underground and undersea oil deposits) and development and production operations (the process of getting the oil to the earth's surface). The amount of new crude oil discovered and produced is increasing rapidly, even as the amount of time, labor, energy, and number of wells drilled have decreased. To achieve the impressive gains in productivity, oil-producing firms in the United States invested heavily during the 1990s in new technologies that promised to lower both the cost of finding oil deposits and the cost of getting oil out of the ground. These new technologies involve adding new and better types of capital to the exploration and production process. Three of the most important new and better technologies are three-dimensional seismology, horizontal drilling, and new deepwater drilling technologies.

Three-dimensional (3D) views of underground rock formations provide a tremendous advantage over two-dimensional (2D) seismology techniques. Even though 3D seismological analysis costs twice as much as 2D analysis, the success rate in exploration is more than

---

total fixed cost (TFC)
The total amount paid for fixed inputs. Total fixed cost does not vary with output.

total variable cost (TVC)
The amount paid for variable inputs. Total variable cost increases with increases in output.

total cost (TC)
The sum of total fixed cost and total variable cost. Total cost increases with increases in output ($TC = TFC + TVC$).

output produced. Other costs vary with the level of output. **Total fixed cost (TFC)** is the sum of the short-run fixed costs that must be paid regardless of the level of output produced. **Total variable cost (TVC)** is the sum of the amounts spent for each of the variable inputs used. Total variable cost increases as output increases. Short-run **total cost (TC)**, which also increases as output increases, is the sum of total variable and total fixed cost:

$$TC = TVC + TFC$$

To show the relation between output (Q) and total cost in the short run, we present the simplest case. A firm uses two inputs, capital and labor, to produce output. The total fixed cost paid for capital is $6,000 per period. In Table 8.4 on page 326, column 2, the total fixed cost (TFC) for each of 7 possible levels of output is $6,000, including 0 units of output. Column 3 shows the total variable cost (TVC) for each level of output. Total variable cost is 0 when output is 0 because the firm

doubled and average costs of exploration decrease more than 20 percent. The 3D seismology method, coupled with horizontal drilling techniques and so-called geosteering drill bits, makes it possible to recover more of the oil in the newly discovered deposits. Deepwater drilling, which on average yields five times as much crude oil as onshore drilling does, is booming now. Advances in deepwater drilling platform technology—such as computer-controlled thrusters using coordinate readings from satellites to keep floating platforms in place—have made deep deposits in the Gulf of Mexico accessible. Some deep deposits in the Gulf of Mexico are as large as some of the oil fields in the Middle East. According to *The Wall Street Journal*, "Reserves at depths approaching a mile or more now represent the biggest single new old resource since the Middle East came on line in the 1930s."[a]

In the petrochemical industry, equally impressive advancements in technology are changing the methods and processes for obtaining fuels and valuable chemicals from crude oil. An article in *Fortune* magazine explains how this is being accomplished: "Instead of highly trained technicians manually monitoring hundreds of complex processes, the work is now done faster, smarter, and more precisely by computer . . . The result: greater efficiency . . . and significant savings."[b]

In one such project, BP (formerly British Petroleum), purchased $75 million of new capital to renovate an old petrochemical plant in Texas City. By adding computer-controlled digital automation to the old plant and equipment, the old plant was transformed into a leading producer of specialty chemicals. Adding more (and better) capital increased the productivity of the other refinery resources, making it possible to decrease the usage of some of these inputs. According to the article in *Fortune*, overall productivity increased a "steep 55 percent," which allowed BP to relocate 10 percent of the workers at the Texas City plant to other BP refineries, and "the plant now uses 3 percent less electricity and 10 percent less natural gas."

As we explain in this chapter, productivity and costs are inversely related. All of this new and better capital makes the oil patch much more productive, which in turn makes it less costly to secure future energy supplies.

[a]See Steve Liesman, "Big Oil Starts to Tap the Vast Reserves That Are Buried Far Below the Waves," *The Wall Street Journal*, July 3, 2000, p. 1.
[b]Gene Bylinsky, "Elite Factories: Two of American's Best Have Found New Life Using Digital Technology," *Fortune*, August 11, 2003.

hires none of the variable input, labor, if it decides not to produce. As the level of production rises, more labor must be hired, and total variable cost rises, as shown in column 3. Total cost (*TC*) is obtained by adding total fixed cost and total variable cost. Column 4 in Table 8.4, which shows the total cost of production for various levels of output, is the sum of columns 2 and 3.

Figure 8.3 on page 327 shows the total cost curves associated with the total cost schedules in Table 8.4. The total-fixed-cost curve is horizontal at $6,000, indicating that *TFC* is constant for all levels of output. Total variable cost starts at the origin, since the firm incurs no variable costs if production is zero; *TVC* rises thereafter as output increases, because to produce more the firm must use more resources, thereby increasing cost. Because total cost is the sum of *TFC* and *TVC*, the *TC* curve lies above the *TVC* curve by an amount exactly equal to $6,000 (*TFC*) at each output level. Consequently, *TC* and *TVC* are parallel and have identical shapes.

ILLUSTRATION 8.2

Implicit Costs and Household Decision Making

As we explain in the text, the implicit opportunity cost to the firm of using a resource owned by the firm equals the best possible forgone payment the firm could have received if it had rented or leased the resource to another firm or had chosen to sell the resource in the market and invest the returns from the sale rather than retain the input for its own use. Producers decide how much of a resource to use on the basis of the opportunity cost of the resource, regardless of whether that opportunity cost is an explicit cost or an implicit cost. You should not get the impression that opportunity costs, particularly implicit costs, are relevant only to decisions about production. All decision makers, including household decision makers, must consider both explicit and implicit costs in order to get the most from their limited resources.

Consider homeowners who pay off their mortgages early. Suppose a homeowner wins the state lottery and decides to pay off a $100,000 balance on a home mortgage. After "burning the mortgage," the homeowner no longer must make monthly mortgage payments, an explicit cost of homeownership. Ignoring maintenance costs and changes in the market value of the home, is the cost of owning the home now zero? Certainly not. By using his or her own financial resources to pay off the mortgage, the homeowner must forgo the income that could have been earned if the $100,000 had been invested elsewhere. If the homeowner could earn 7.5 percent on a certificate of deposit, the implicit cost (opportunity cost) of paying off the mortgage is $7,500 per year. Smart lottery winners do not pay off their mortgages if the interest rate on the mortgage is less than the rate of interest they can earn by putting their money into investments no more risky than homeownership. They do pay off their mortgages if the rate on the mortgage is higher than the rate they can earn by making investments no more risky than homeownership.

Another example of how implicit costs affect decisions made by households involves the story of Jamie Lashbrook, an 11-year-old boy from Brooksville, Florida. Jamie won two tickets to Super Bowl XXV by kicking a field goal before a Tampa Bay Buccaneers game. Jamie quickly discovered that using the two "free" tickets does in fact involve an opportunity cost. Less than one day after winning the tickets, Jamie's father had received more than a dozen requests from people who were willing to pay as much as $1,200 for each ticket. While the boy *obtained* the tickets at little or no cost, *using* these tickets involved an implicit cost—the payment Jamie could have received if he had sold the tickets in the marketplace rather than using them himself. We don't know if Jamie actually went to the Super Bowl or not, but even this 11-year-old decision maker knew better than to ignore the implicit cost of using a resource.

TABLE 8.4
Short-Run Total Cost Schedules

(1) Output (Q)	(2) Total fixed cost (TFC)	(3) Total variable cost (TVC)	(4) Total Cost (TC) $TC = TFC + TVC$
0	$6,000	$ 0	$ 6,000
100	6,000	4,000	10,000
200	6,000	6,000	12,000
300	6,000	9,000	15,000
400	6,000	14,000	20,000
500	6,000	22,000	28,000
600	6,000	34,000	40,000

FIGURE 8.3
Total Cost Curves

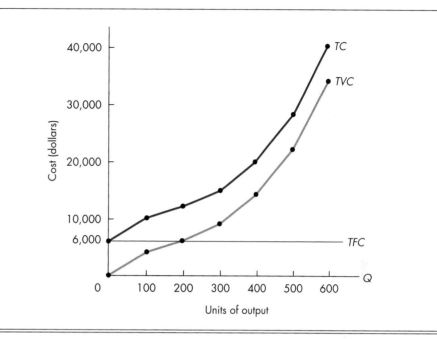

Average and Marginal Costs

A more useful way of depicting the firm's cost structure is through the behavior of short-run average and marginal costs. Table 8.5 presents the average and marginal costs derived from the total cost schedules in Table 8.4. First, consider average fixed cost, given in column 2. **Average fixed cost (AFC)** is total fixed cost divided by output:

average fixed cost (AFC)
Total fixed cost divided by output ($AFC = TFC/Q$).

$$AFC = TFC/Q$$

Average fixed cost is obtained by dividing the fixed cost (in this case $6,000) by output. Thus AFC is high at relatively low levels of output; since the denominator increases as output increases, AFC decreases over the entire range of output. If output were to continue increasing, AFC would approach 0 as output became extremely large.

average variable cost (AVC)
Total variable cost divided by output ($AVC = TVC/Q$).

Average variable cost (AVC) is total variable cost divided by output:

$$AVC = TVC/Q$$

The average variable cost of producing each level of output in Table 8.5 is shown in column 3. AVC at first falls to $30, then increases thereafter.

average total cost (ATC)
Total cost divided by output or the sum of average fixed cost plus average variable cost ($ATC = TC/Q = AVC + AFC$).

Average total cost (ATC) is short-run total cost divided by output:

$$ATC = TC/Q$$

TABLE 8.5
Average and Marginal Cost Schedules

(1) Output (Q)	(2) Average fixed cost (AFC) AFC = TFC/Q	(3) Average variable cost (AVC) AVC = TVC/Q	(4) Average total cost (ATC) ATC = TC/Q	(5) Short-run marginal cost (SMC) SMC = ΔTC/ΔQ
0	—	—	—	
				$ 40
100	$60	$40	$100	
				20
200	30	30	60	
				30
300	20	30	50	
				50
400	15	35	50	
				80
500	12	44	56	
				120
600	10	56.7	66.7	

The average total cost of producing each level of output is given in column 4 of Table 8.5. Since total cost is total variable cost plus total fixed cost,

$$ATC = \frac{TC}{Q} = \frac{TVC + TFC}{Q} = AVC + AFC$$

The average total cost in the table has the same general structure as average variable cost. It first declines, reaches a minimum at $50, then increases thereafter. The minimum ATC is attained at a larger output (between 300 and 400) than that at which AVC attains its minimum (between 200 and 300). This result is not peculiar to the cost schedules in Table 8.5; as we will show later, it follows for all average cost schedules of the general type shown here.

short-run marginal cost (SMC)
The change in either total variable cost or total cost per unit change in output (ΔTVC/ΔQ = ΔTC/ΔQ).

Finally, **short-run marginal cost (SMC)** is defined as the change in either total variable cost or total cost per unit change in output:

$$SMC = \frac{\Delta TVC}{\Delta Q} = \frac{\Delta TC}{\Delta Q}$$

The two definitions are the same because when output increases, total cost increases by the same amount as the increase in total variable cost. Thus since TC = TFC + TVC,

$$SMC = \frac{\Delta TC}{\Delta Q} = \frac{\Delta TFC}{\Delta Q} + \frac{\Delta TVC}{\Delta Q} = 0 + \frac{\Delta TVC}{\Delta Q} = \frac{\Delta TVC}{\Delta Q}$$

The short-run marginal cost is given in column 5 of Table 8.5. It is the per-unit change in cost resulting from a change in output when the use of the variable input changes. For example, when output increases from 0 to 100, both total and variable costs increase by $4,000. The change in cost per unit of output is, therefore,

FIGURE 8.4
Average and Marginal Cost
Curves

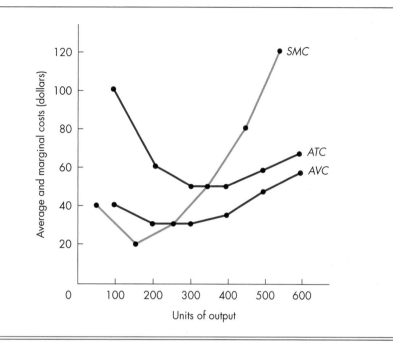

FIGURE 8.4
Average and Marginal Cost Curves

$4,000 divided by the increase in output, 100, or $40. Thus the marginal cost over this range is $40. It can be seen that *MC* first declines, reaches a minimum of $20, then rises. Note that minimum marginal cost is attained at an output (between 100 and 200) below that at which either *AVC* or *ATC* attains its minimum. Marginal cost equals *AVC* and *ATC* at their respective minimum levels. We will return to the reason for this result later.

The average and marginal cost schedules in columns 3, 4, and 5 are shown graphically in Figure 8.4. Average fixed cost is not graphed because it is a curve that simply declines over the entire range of output and because, as you will see, it is irrelevant for decision making. The curves in Figure 8.4 depict the properties of the cost schedules we have discussed. All three curves decline at first and then rise. Marginal cost equals *AVC* and *ATC* at each of their minimum levels. Marginal cost is below *AVC* and *ATC* when they are declining and above them when they are increasing. Since *AFC* decreases over the entire range of output and since *ATC* = *AVC* + *AFC*, *ATC* becomes increasingly close to *AVC* as output increases. As we show later, these are the general properties of typically assumed average and marginal cost curves.

General Short-Run Average and Marginal Cost Curves

Most of the properties of cost curves set forth thus far in this section were derived by using the specific cost schedules in Tables 8.4 and 8.5. These properties also hold for general cost curves when output and therefore cost vary continuously

FIGURE 8.5
Short-Run Average and
Marginal Cost Curves

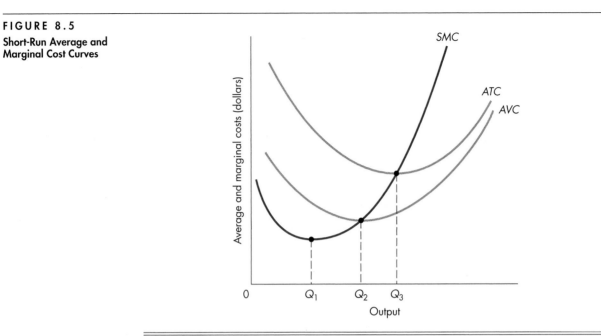

rather than discretely. These typical average and marginal cost curves are shown in Figure 8.5. These curves show the following:

▢ **Relations** (1) *AFC* declines continuously, approaching both axes asymptotically (as shown by the decreasing distance between *ATC* and *AVC*). (2) *AVC* first declines, reaches a minimum at Q_2, and rises thereafter. When *AVC* is at its minimum, *SMC* equals *AVC*. (3) *ATC* first declines, reaches a minimum at Q_3, and rises thereafter. When *ATC* is at its minimum, *SMC* equals *ATC*. (4) *SMC* first declines, reaches a minimum at Q_1, and rises thereafter. *SMC* equals both *AVC* and *ATC* when these curves are at their minimum values. Furthermore, *SMC* lies below both *AVC* and *ATC* over the range for which these curves decline; *SMC* lies above them when they are rising.

In general, the reason marginal cost crosses *AVC* and *ATC* at their respective minimum points follows from the definitions of the cost curves. If marginal cost is below average variable cost, each additional unit of output adds less to cost than the average variable cost of that unit. Thus average variable cost must decline over this range. When *SMC* is above *AVC*, each additional unit of output adds more to cost than *AVC*. In this case, *AVC* must rise.

So when *SMC* is less than *AVC*, average variable cost is falling; when *SMC* is greater than *AVC*, average variable cost is rising. Thus *SMC* must equal *AVC* at the minimum point on AVC. Exactly the same reasoning can be used to show that *SMC* crosses *ATC* at the minimum point on the latter curve.[2]

---

[2]This relation is derived in the appendix to this chapter.

TABLE 8.6
Short-Run Production and
Short-Run Total Costs

		Short-run total costs		
Short-run production				
(1) Labor (L)	(2) Output (Q)	(3) Total variable cost (TVC = wL)	(4) Total fixed cost (TFC = rK)	(5) Total cost (TC = wL + rK)
0	0	0	$6,000	$ 6,000
4	100	$ 4,000	6,000	10,000
6	200	6,000	6,000	12,000
9	300	9,000	6,000	15,000
14	400	14,000	6,000	20,000
22	500	22,000	6,000	28,000
34	600	34,000	6,000	40,000

8.4 RELATIONS BETWEEN SHORT-RUN COSTS AND PRODUCTION

We will now describe, in some detail, exactly how the short-run cost curves set forth in the preceding section are derived. As you will recall, once the total variable cost (*TVC*) and the total fixed cost (*TFC*) are developed, all the other costs—*TC*, *ATC*, *AVC*, *AFC*, and *SMC*—can be derived directly from the simple formulas that define these costs. Total fixed cost is simply the sum of the payments for the fixed inputs. As we will now show, total variable cost is derived directly from the short-run production function. In addition to deriving *TVC* from the total product curve, we also show how average variable cost can be derived from average product and how marginal cost can be derived from marginal product.

Total Costs and the Short-Run Production Function

We begin with the short-run production function shown in columns 1 and 2 in Table 8.6. If 4 units of labor are employed, the firm can produce (a maximum of) 100 units; if 6 units of labor are employed, the firm's maximum output is 200 units; and so on. (Remember, the production function assumes technical efficiency.) For this example, we assume the wage rate—the price of a unit of labor services (w)—is $1,000. Total variable cost for any given level of output is simply the amount of labor employed multiplied by the wage rate:

$$TVC = w \times L$$

Column 3 shows the total variable costs associated with the various levels of output. Obviously, *TVC* is derived directly from the short-run production function. Note that *TVC* is derived for a particular wage rate. If the wage rate increases, *TVC* must increase at each level of output.

To see how total fixed cost is determined, assume that the short-run production function in columns 1 and 2 is derived for a firm using 3 units of capital in the short run ($\overline{K} = 3$) and that capital costs $2,000 per unit to employ. Thus the total fixed cost is

$$TFC = r \times K = \$2,000 \times 3 = \$6,000$$

where r is the price of a unit of capital services. Column 4 shows the total fixed cost for each level of output.

Short-run total cost (TC) is the sum of the total variable cost and total fixed costs of production:

$$TC = wL + rK$$

Column 5 in Table 8.6 shows the total cost of producing each level of output in the short run when the firm's level of capital is fixed at three units. Note that these total cost schedules are the same as the ones in Table 8.4. Using the formulas set forth earlier in this chapter, we could easily derive AVC and SMC from the TVC schedule and ATC from the TC schedule. However, we can give you more of an understanding of the reasons for the typical shape of these curves by showing the relation between AVC and AP and SMC and MP, which we discuss next.

Average Variable Cost and Average Product

Table 8.7 reproduces the production function in columns 1 and 2 of Table 8.6. The average product of labor ($AP = Q/L$) is calculated in column 3 of Table 8.7. The relation between AVC and AP can be seen as follows: Consider the 100 units of output that can be produced by 4 workers. The total variable cost of using 4 workers is found by multiplying $1,000—the wage rate—by the 4 workers employed:

$$TVC = \$1,000 \times 4$$

The 100 units of output produced by the 4 workers can be found by multiplying 25—the average product—by the 4 workers employed:

$$Q = 25 \times 4$$

TABLE 8.7 **Average and Marginal Relations between Cost and Production**	Short-run production				Short-run costs	
	(1) Labor	(2) Q	(3) AP (Q/L)	(4) MP (ΔQ/ΔL)	(5) AVC (w/AP)	(6) SMC (w/MP)
	0	0	—		—	
				25		$ 40
	4	100	25		$40	
				50		20
	6	200	33.33		30	
				33.33		30
	9	300	33.33		30	
				20		50
	14	400	28.57		35	
				12.50		80
	22	500	22.73		44	
				8.33		120
	34	600	17.65		56.67	

Since *AVC* is *TVC* divided by *Q*,

$$AVC = \frac{TVC}{Q} = \frac{\$1,000 \times 4}{25 \times 4} = \frac{\$1,000}{25} = \frac{w}{AP} = \$40$$

From this numerical illustration, you can see that *AVC* can be calculated as either *TVC/Q* or *w/AP*. It is easy to show that this relation holds in general for any production function with one variable input. In general,

$$AVC = \frac{TVC}{Q} = \frac{w \times L}{AP \times L} = \frac{w}{AP}$$

In Table 8.7, column 5 shows the value of average variable cost calculated by dividing $1,000 by average product at each level of output. You should verify that the computation of *AVC* in Table 8.7 (*AVC = w/AP*) yields the same values for *AVC* as the values obtained for *AVC* in Table 8.5 (*AVC = TVC/Q*).

Marginal Cost and Marginal Product

The relation between marginal cost and marginal product is also illustrated in Table 8.7. Column 4 shows the marginal product associated with the additional labor employed to increase production in 100-unit intervals. For example, to increase production from 100 to 200 units, two additional workers are required (an increase from 4 to 6 units of labor), so the marginal product is 50 units per additional worker. The change in total variable cost associated with going from 100 to 200 units of output is $2,000—$1,000 for each of the two extra workers. So,

$$SMC = \frac{\Delta TVC}{\Delta Q} = \frac{\$1,000 \times 2}{50 \times 2} = \frac{w}{MP} = \$20$$

Repeating this calculation for each of the 100-unit increments to output, you can see that the marginal cost at each level of output is the wage rate divided by the marginal product, and this will be true for any production function with one variable input, since

$$SMC = \frac{\Delta TVC}{\Delta Q} = \frac{\Delta(w \times L)}{\Delta Q} = w \frac{\Delta L}{\Delta Q} = \frac{w}{MP}$$

 You can verify that the values for marginal cost calculated as *w/MP* in Table 8.7 are identical to the values for marginal cost calculated as $\Delta TC/\Delta Q$ in Table 8.5.

The Graphical Relation between AVC, MC, AP, and MP

Figure 8.6 illustrates the relation between cost curves and product curves. We have constructed a typical set of product and cost curves in Panels A and B, respectively. Assume the wage rate is $21, and consider first the product and cost curves over the range of labor usage from 0 to 500 units of labor. In Panel A, marginal product lies above average product over this range, so average product is rising. Because marginal cost is inversely related to marginal product (*SMC = w/MP*) and average variable cost is inversely related to average product (*AVC = w/AP*), and

FIGURE 8.6
Short-Run Production and Cost Relations

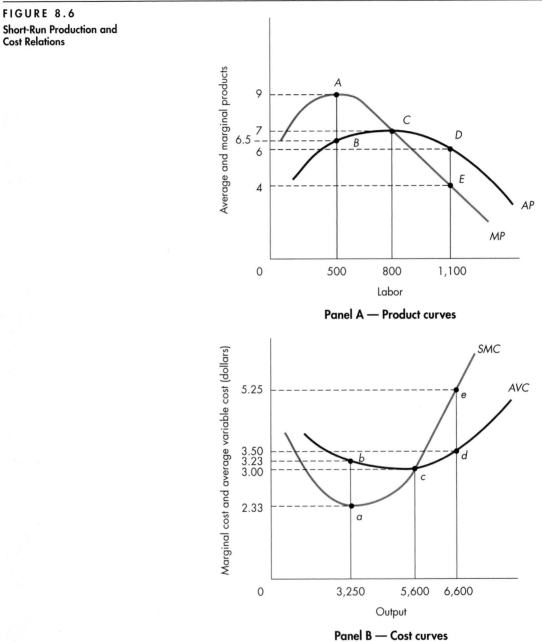

Panel A — Product curves

Panel B — Cost curves

because both MP and AP are rising, both SMC and AVC are falling as output rises when labor usage increases (up to points A and B in Panel A). Marginal product reaches a maximum value of 9 at 500 units of labor usage (point A). The level of output that corresponds to using 500 units of labor is found by using the relation $AP = Q/L$. Since $AP = 6.5$ and $L = 500$, Q must be 3,250 (= 6.5 × 500). Thus marginal product reaches its *maximum* value at 3,250 units of output, and, consequently, marginal cost must reach its *minimum* value at 3,250 units of output. At 3,250 units, marginal cost is equal to $2.33 (= w/MP = $21/9$), and average variable cost is equal to $3.23 (= w/AP = $21/6.5$). Points A and B in Panel A correspond to points *a* and *b* in Panel B of Figure 8.6.

One of the most important relations between production and cost curves in the short run involves the effect of the law of diminishing marginal product on the marginal cost of production. While marginal product generally rises at first, the law of diminishing marginal product states that when capital is fixed, a point will eventually be reached beyond which marginal product must begin to fall. As marginal product begins to fall, marginal cost begins to rise. In Figure 8.6, marginal product begins to fall beyond 500 units of labor (beyond point A in Panel A). Marginal cost begins to rise beyond 3,250 units of output (beyond point *a* in Panel B).

Consider the range of labor usage between 500 and 800 units of labor. Marginal product is falling, but while marginal product still lies above average product, average product continues to rise up to point C, where $MP = AP$. At point C, average product reaches its maximum value at 800 units of labor. When 800 units of labor are employed, 5,600 units of output are produced (5,600 = $AP × L$ = 7 × 800). Thus, at 5,600 units of output, marginal cost and average variable cost are both equal to $3:

$$SMC = w/MP = \$21/7 = \$3$$
$$AVC = w/AP = \$21/7 = \$3$$

So, at 5,600 units of output, average variable cost reaches its minimum and is equal to marginal cost.

Finally, consider the cost and product relations as labor usage increases beyond 800 units. Marginal product is below average product, and average product continues to decrease but never becomes negative. Marginal product will eventually become negative, but a manager who wishes to minimize costs would never hire an amount of labor that would have a negative marginal product. If marginal product is negative, the manager could *increase* output by *decreasing* labor usage, and this would also decrease the firm's expenditure on labor. Points D and E in Panel A correspond to points *d* and *e* in Panel B. At 1,100 units of labor, average product is 6, and output is 6,600 units (= $AP × L$ = 6 × 1,100). You should verify for yourself that marginal cost is $5.25 and average variable cost is $3.50 when 6,600 units are produced.

We now can summarize the discussion of the relation between production and cost by restating the two fundamental relations between product and cost variables:

$$SMC = w/MP \quad \text{and} \quad AVC = w/AP$$

Thus the following relations must hold:

▣ **Relations** When marginal product (average product) is increasing, marginal cost (average variable cost) is decreasing. When marginal product (average product) is decreasing, marginal cost (average variable cost) is increasing. When marginal product equals average product at maximum AP, marginal cost equals average variable cost at minimum AVC.

As we explained in Section 8.2, when the fixed inputs are allowed to change, all the product curves, TP, AP, and MP, shift. This, of course, will shift the short-run cost curves.

8.5 SUMMARY

The production function gives the maximum amount of output that can be produced from any given combination of inputs, given the state of technology. The production function assumes technological efficiency in production, because technological efficiency occurs when the firm is producing the maximum possible output with a given combination of inputs. Economic efficiency occurs when a given output is being produced at the lowest possible total cost.

In the short run, at least one input is fixed. In the long run, all inputs are variable. This chapter examines the short-run situation when only one input is variable, labor (L), and one fixed, capital (K). In the short run, the total product curve, which is a graph of the short-run production relation $Q = f(L, \overline{K})$ with Q on the vertical axis and L on the horizontal axis, gives the economically efficient amount of labor for any output level when capital is fixed at $\overline{K}$ units. The average product of labor is the total product divided by the number of workers: $AP = Q/L$. The marginal product of labor is the additional output attributable to using one additional worker with the use of capital fixed: $MP = \Delta Q/\Delta L$. The law of diminishing marginal product states that as the number of units of the variable input increases, other inputs held constant, there exists a point beyond which the marginal product of the variable input declines. When marginal product is greater (less) than average product, average product is increasing (decreasing). When average product is at its maximum—that is, neither rising nor falling—marginal product equals average product.

In the short run when some inputs are fixed, short-run total cost (TC) is the sum of total variable cost (TVC) and total fixed cost (TFC):

$$TC = TVC + TFC$$

Average fixed cost is total fixed cost divided by output:

$$AFC = TFC/Q$$

Average variable cost is total variable cost divided by output:

$$AVC = TVC/Q$$

Average total cost is total cost divided by output:

$$ATC = TC/Q = AVC + AFC$$

Short-run marginal cost (SMC) is the change in either total variable cost or total cost per unit change in output:

$$SMC = \Delta TVC/\Delta Q = \Delta TC/\Delta Q$$

A typical set of short-run cost curves is characterized by the following features: (1) AFC decreases continuously as output increases, (2) AVC is U-shaped, (3) ATC is U-shaped, (4) SMC is U-shaped and crosses both AVC and ATC at their minimum points, and (5) SMC lies below (above) both AVC and ATC over the output range for which these curves fall (rise).

The link between product curves and cost curves in the short run when one input is variable is reflected in the following relations:

$$SMC = w/MP \quad \text{and} \quad AVC = w/AP$$

When MP (AP) is increasing, SMC (AVC) is decreasing. When MP (AP) is decreasing, SMC (AVC) is increasing. When MP equals AP at AP's maximum value, SMC equals AVC at AVC's minimum value. Similar but not identical relations hold when more than one input is variable.

TECHNICAL PROBLEMS

1. "When a manager is using a technically efficient input combination, the firm is also producing in an economically efficient manner." Evaluate this statement.

2. Firms A and B both produce good X, and each firm plans to produce 1,000 units per day of good X. The firms can choose either of the two following production processes (i.e., input combinations) to produce 1,000 units daily:

	Process 1	Process 2
Labor	10	8
Capital	20	25

   a. Is it possible for both process 1 and process 2 to be technically efficient? Explain why or why not.

   b. Firm A must pay $200 per day for a unit of labor and $100 per day for a unit of capital. For Firm A, process _____ is economically efficient.

   c. Firm B must pay $250 per day for a unit of labor and $75 per day for a unit of capital. For Firm B, process _____ is economically efficient.

3. Economists frequently say that the firm plans in the long run and operates in the short run. Explain.

4. For each of the following situations, determine whether the manager is concerned with a short-run or a long-run production decision. Explain briefly in each case.

   a. A petroleum drilling supervisor on an offshore drilling platform decides to add an extra six-hour shift each day in order to keep the drill rig running 24 hours per day.

   b. The vice president of offshore petroleum drilling operations in the Gulf of Mexico chooses to deploy three more offshore drilling platforms in the Gulf.

   c. A manufacturing engineer plans the production schedule for the month.

   d. After studying a demographic report on future increases in birthrates, a hospital administrator decides to add a new pediatric wing to the hospital.

5. Fill in the blanks in the following table:

Units of labor	Total product	Average product	Marginal product
1	_____	40	_____
2	_____	_____	48
3	138	_____	_____
4	_____	44	_____
5	_____	_____	24
6	210	_____	_____
7	_____	29	_____
8	_____	_____	−27

6. Refer to Table 8.2 and explain precisely why using 10 units of labor and 2 units of capital is not economically efficient.

7. The following table shows the amount of total output produced from various combinations of labor and capital:

Units of labor	Units of capital			
	1	2	3	4
1	50	120	160	180
2	110	260	360	390
3	150	360	510	560
4	170	430	630	690
5	160	480	710	790

a. Calculate the marginal product and average product of labor when capital is held constant at 2 units. When the average product of labor is increasing, what is the relation between the average product and the marginal product? What about when the average product of labor is decreasing?

b. Calculate the marginal product of labor for each level of the capital stock. How does the marginal product of the second unit of labor change as the capital stock increases? Why?

8. Fill in the blanks in the following table:

Output	Total cost	Total fixed cost	Total variable cost	Average fixed cost	Average variable cost	Average total cost	Marginal cost
100	260	___	60	___	___	___	___
200	___	___	___	___	___	___	0.30
300	___	___	___	___	0.50	___	___
400	___	___	___	___	___	1.05	___
500	___	___	360	___	___	___	___
600	___	___	___	___	___	___	3.00
700	___	___	___	___	1.60	___	___
800	2,040	___	___	___	___	___	___

9. Assume average variable cost is constant over a range of output. What is marginal cost over this range? What is happening to average total cost over this range?

10. Suppose that a firm is currently employing 20 workers, the only variable input, at a wage rate of $60. The average product of labor is 30, the last worker added 12 units to total output, and total fixed cost is $3,600.

a. What is marginal cost?

b. What is average variable cost?

c. How much output is being produced?

d. What is average total cost?

e. Is average variable cost increasing, constant, or decreasing? What about average total cost?

11. The first two columns in the following table give a firm's short-run production function when the only variable input is labor, and capital (the fixed input) is held constant at 5 units. The price of capital is $2,000 per unit, and the price of labor is $500 per unit.

Units of labor	Units of output	Average product	Marginal product	Cost			Average cost			Marginal cost
				Fixed	Variable	Total	Fixed	Variable	Total	
0	0	xx	xx	——	——	——	xx	xx	xx	xx
20	4,000	——	——	——	——	——	——	——	——	——
40	10,000	——	——	——	——	——	——	——	——	——
60	15,000	——	——	——	——	——	——	——	——	——
80	19,400	——	——	——	——	——	——	——	——	——
100	23,000	——	——	——	——	——	——	——	——	——

a. Complete the table.

b. What is the relation between average variable cost and marginal cost? Between average total cost and marginal cost?

c. What is the relation between average product and average variable cost? Between marginal product and marginal cost?

12. Assume that labor—the only variable input of a firm—has the average and marginal product curves shown in the following graph. Labor's wage is $2 per unit.

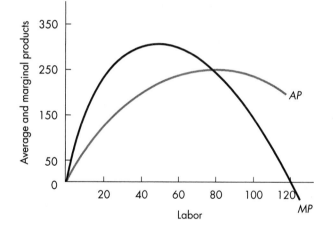

a. When the firm attains minimum average variable cost, how many units of labor is it using?

b. What level of output is associated with minimum average variable cost?

c. What is the average variable cost of producing this output?

d. Suppose the firm is using 100 units of labor. What is output? What is marginal cost? What is average variable cost?

APPLIED PROBLEMS

1. At a management luncheon, two managers were overheard arguing about the following statement: "A manager should never hire another worker if the new person causes diminishing returns." Is this statement correct? If so, why? If not, explain why not.

2. Engineers at a national research laboratory built a prototype automobile that could be driven 180 miles on a single gallon of unleaded gasoline. They estimated that in mass production the car would cost $40,000 per unit to build. The engineers argued that Congress should force U.S. automakers to build this energy-efficient car.

   a. Is energy efficiency the same thing as economic efficiency? Explain.

   b. Under what circumstances would the energy-efficient automobile described here be economically efficient?

   c. If the goal of society is to get the most benefit from its limited resources, then why not ignore economic efficiency and build the energy-saving automobile?

3. After two quarters of increasing levels of production, the CEO of Canadian Fabrication & Design was upset to learn that, during this time of expansion, productivity of the newly hired sheet metal workers declined with each new worker hired. Believing that the new workers were either lazy or ineffectively supervised (or possibly both), the CEO instructed the shop foreman to "crack down" on the new workers to bring their productivity levels up.

   a. Explain carefully in terms of production theory why it might be that no amount of "cracking down" can increase worker productivity at CF&D.

   b. Provide an alternative to cracking down as a means of increasing the productivity of the sheet metal workers.

4. An article in *Business Week* warned of the dangers of deflation as the collapse of numerous Asian economies was creating worries that Asia might try to "export its way out of trouble" by oversupplying everything from automobiles to semiconductors. Evidence that deflation had become a genuine concern for managers was provided by a statement in the article by John Smith, chairman and CEO of General Motors Corporation: "Fundamentally, something has changed in the economy. In today's age, you cannot get price increases." The article offers the following advice to managers: "Productivity growth lets companies boost profits even as prices fall." Using short-run production and cost theory, comment on this advice.

5. *Business Week,* in an article dealing with management, wrote, "When he took over the furniture factory three years ago . . . [the manager] realized almost immediately that it was throwing away at least $100,000 a year worth of wood scrap. Within a few weeks, he set up a task force of managers and workers to deal with the problem. And within a few months, they reduced the amount of scrap to $7,000 worth [per year]." Was this necessarily an *economically efficient* move?

▣   **MATHEMATICAL APPENDIX**   Short-Run Production and Cost Relations

This appendix uses calculus to derive several useful relations in short-run production and cost analysis. We consider only the two-input case; however, all results hold for any number of inputs in production. Define the production function as

$$(1) \qquad Q = f(L, K)$$

where Q is the maximum possible output attainable when L units of labor and K units of capital are employed to produce a good or service. Thus the production function is characterized by technical efficiency. Assume that production requires positive amounts of both inputs:

$$(2) \qquad Q = f(0, K) = f(L, 0) = 0$$

If the usage of either input is zero, output is zero. In the short run, at least one input is fixed. Assume capital is the fixed input. By holding capital constant at $\overline{K}$ units, the short-run production function can be expressed as

(3) $$Q = f(L, \overline{K}) = g(L)$$

Thus $g(L)$ is the short-run production function when capital is fixed at $\overline{K}$ units.

Average Product and Marginal Product

The relation between average and marginal product plays an important role in understanding the nature of production and the shape of short-run cost curves. Average product is defined as

(4) $$AP = AP(L) = Q/L$$

and marginal product is defined as the rate of change in output as the variable input labor changes:

(5) $$MP = MP(L) = \frac{dQ}{dL} = \frac{dg(L)}{dL} = g'(L)$$

Recall from this chapter that *when AP is increasing (decreasing), MP is greater (less) than AP. When AP reaches its maximum value, MP = AP.* This relation can be demonstrated by differentiating AP with respect to L to find the condition under which AP increases or decreases:

(6) $$\frac{d(AP)}{dL} = \frac{d(Q/L)}{dL} = \frac{(dQ/dL)L - Q}{L^2}$$
$$= \frac{1}{L}(MP - AP)$$

Thus the sign of $d(AP)/dL$ is positive (negative) when MP is greater (less) than AP. So AP rises (falls) when MP is greater (less) than AP. The peak of AP occurs where the slope of AP is zero; that is, $d(AP)/dL$ is zero. Thus the maximum point on AP is reached where $MP = AP$.

The Cost Relations: ATC, AVC, and SMC

Begin by defining short-run total cost TC to be a function of the level of production, Q:

$$TC = TC(Q) = TVC(Q) + TFC$$

where $TVC(Q)$ is total variable cost and TFC is total fixed cost. Since $dTFC/dQ = 0$, short-run marginal cost is the rate of change in either TC or TVC as output changes:

(7) $$SMC = \frac{dTC}{dQ} = \frac{dTVC}{dQ}$$

Recall that TC and TVC are parallel, so their slopes are identical at any level of production. Average total cost, ATC, can be expressed as

(8) $$ATC = ATC(Q) = \frac{TC(Q)}{Q} = \frac{TVC(Q)}{Q} + \frac{TFC}{Q}$$
$$= AVC(Q) + AFC(Q)$$

Note that *average* fixed cost is a function of Q, while *total* fixed cost is not a function of Q.

Recall from this chapter that *when ATC is increasing (decreasing), MC is greater (less) than ATC. When ATC reaches its minimum value, SMC = ATC.* This relation can be demonstrated by differentiating ATC with respect to Q to find the condition under which ATC increases or decreases:

$$\frac{dATC}{dQ} = \frac{d[TVC(Q)/Q + TFC/Q]}{dQ}$$

$$= \frac{\frac{dTVC(Q)}{dQ}Q - TVC \times 1 + 0 \times Q - TFC \times 1}{Q^2}$$

Factoring the term $1/Q$ simplifies the expression:

(9) $$\frac{dATC}{dQ} = \frac{1}{Q}\left(\frac{dTVC}{dQ} - \frac{TVC}{Q} - \frac{TFC}{Q}\right)$$
$$= \frac{1}{Q}(SMC - AVC - AFC)$$
$$= \frac{1}{Q}(SMC - ATC)$$

Thus the sign of $dATC/dQ$ is positive (negative) when SMC is greater (less) than ATC. The minimum point on ATC occurs where its slope is zero, which is where $SMC = ATC$.

Relations between Production and Cost

The structure of a firm's cost curves is determined by the production function. To show that the shapes of the cost curves are determined by the production function, we now derive the relations between (1) MP and SMC and (2) AP and AVC.

Relation between MP and SMC

Recall that $SMC = dTVC/dQ$. If $TVC = wL$ and w is a constant, SMC can be expressed as

(10) $$SMC = \frac{d(wL)}{dQ} = w\frac{dL}{dQ} = w\frac{1}{MP} = \frac{w}{MP}$$

SMC and MP are inversely related. As labor productivity rises (falls) in the short run, SMC falls (rises). Over the range of input usage characterized by diminishing returns (*MP* is falling), marginal cost is rising in the short run.

Relation between AP and AVC

Recall also that $AVC = TVC/Q$. Again substituting wL for TVC:

(11)
$$AVC = \frac{wL}{Q} = w\frac{L}{Q} = w\frac{1}{AP} = \frac{w}{AP}$$

From expression (11), it is clear that when average product is rising (falling), average variable cost is falling (rising). Average variable cost reaches its minimum value where average product reaches its maximum value, which, as we demonstrated above, is where $MP = AP$.

MATHEMATICAL EXERCISES

1. Consider the production function $Q = 20K^{1/2}L^{1/2}$. The firm operates in the short run with 16 units of capital.
   a. The firm's short-run production function is $Q = $ _____.
   b. The average product of labor function is $AP = $ _____.
   c. The marginal product of labor function is $MP = $ _____.
   d. Show that marginal product diminishes for all levels of labor usage.
2. Total cost (*TC*) and total variable cost (*TVC*) are parallel, yet average total cost (*ATC*) and average variable cost (*AVC*) are not parallel.
   a. Demonstrate mathematically that *ATC* and *AVC* are not parallel.
   b. Show mathematically that when both *ATC* and *AVC* are falling, *ATC* falls faster than *AVC*, and when both are rising, *AVC* rises faster than *ATC*.
3. For the short-run production function in exercise 1, let the wage be $20.
   a. Derive $AVC(Q)$.
   b. When 160 units are produced, _____ units of labor are employed, and the average product is _____. Average variable cost is $ _____.
   c. Derive $SMC(Q)$.
   d. Using the marginal product (*MP*) function derived in part *c*, the marginal product is _____ when 160 units are produced. *SMC* is $ _____. Verify that $SMC(Q)$ evaluated at $Q = 4$ is identical to calculating *SMC* by using the ratio w/MP.

CHAPTER
9

Production and Cost in the Long Run

Long-run production decisions involve changing the level of employment of inputs that are fixed in the short run. A firm may wish to increase its scale of operation by building a larger production facility, which typically requires a substantial lead time for planning the new facility; getting various government permits, licenses, and environmental approvals; building the facility; and testing the new equipment before production begins. Managers involved in the planning of a new plant are engaged in long-run decision making and will be interested in knowing something about the long-run cost of production: the cost of producing in the future when any scale of production facility can be employed. In many cases, the desirability of increasing the size of operations in the long run is driven by a need to achieve economies of scale in production. As you will see in this chapter, it may be possible to reduce unit costs by expanding the production levels in the long run.

Other interesting managerial decisions involve long-run analysis of costs. For example, when economies of scope exist, it may be possible to reduce the cost of producing one good by becoming a producer of other goods related in production. Adding new products generally involves changing the types and amounts of various inputs and, consequently, is a long-run decision. Restructuring by either upsizing or downsizing a firm may be a long-run decision if it requires changing the amount of fixed inputs employed in the short run. Restructuring at a hospital could involve adding a new wing to the building; at an electric utility, a new coal-fired generator may be needed. Restructuring production may also involve moving

343

production facilities to new geographic locations, perhaps overseas to reduce labor costs.

During the 1990s, a historically unprecedented amount of merger and acquisition activity transformed numerous industries. Some corporate strategists attempted to achieve economies of scale by merging with other companies producing similar products. In other cases, acquisitions were designed to take advantage of cost savings associated with multiproduct production—economies of scope. And in some cases, such as the surprising divestiture by AT&T of its computer and electronic equipment divisions, divestitures and spin-offs were undertaken to avoid diseconomies of scope or scale. The analysis of cost in the long run is essential in making these decisions.

In all the examples mentioned above, managers are trying to find and exploit opportunities to reduce costs in the long run by changing the employment of inputs that are fixed in the short run. In this chapter, we analyze the situation in which there are two or more variable inputs, a situation that is both more complex and more interesting than production with only one variable input. The analysis of production set forth here can be considered long run if capital and labor are the only inputs the firm employs—no inputs are fixed. In the short run, however, when two or more inputs are variable, the economically efficient choice of variable inputs is also determined using the same analytical techniques presented in this chapter. It is crucial for you to keep in mind that while we typically will refer to production in this chapter as "long-run" production, the material also applies to the short-run situation when a firm combines more than one variable input with its fixed inputs to produce a good or service.[1]

We first develop some tools to be used later in the analysis; then we derive and set forth the principles of cost minimization at a given level of output. As will become apparent, these principles follow directly from the principles of constrained minimization and constrained maximization set forth in Chapter 3. Once we show how the economically efficient (optimal) input combination is found for producing various levels of output, it is a straightforward task to derive the long-run total cost schedule or curve. We then analyze several important concepts concerning costs of production in the long run. We will discuss in Chapters 11 and 12 how managers of profit-maximizing firms choose, in an *unconstrained* setting, the profit-maximizing employment levels of the variable inputs. In this chapter, however, managers make *constrained* input choices subject to either output or cost considerations, which force them to find the economically efficient input combination for each possible level of output. As you will see shortly, managers must know the economically efficient amount of all inputs to employ for each output level in order to determine long-run costs of production for the various output levels.

---

[1]The appendix to this chapter demonstrates mathematically that the efficient combination of inputs, when two or more inputs are variable, is chosen in the same way in both the short run and the long run.

9.1 PRODUCTION ISOQUANTS

isoquant
A curve showing all possible combinations of inputs physically capable of producing a given fixed level of output.

An important tool of analysis when two inputs are variable is the *production iso-quant* or simply *isoquant*. An **isoquant** is a curve (or locus of points) showing all possible combinations of the inputs physically capable of producing a given (fixed) level of output. Each point on an isoquant is technically efficient; that is, for each combination on the isoquant, the maximum possible output is that associated with the given isoquant. The concept of an isoquant implies that it is possible to substitute some amount of one input for some of the other, say, labor for capital, while keeping output constant. Therefore, if the two inputs are continuously divisible, as we will assume, there are an infinite number of input combinations capable of producing each level of output.

To understand the concept of an isoquant, return for a moment to Table 8.1 in the preceding chapter. This table shows the maximum output that can be produced by combining different levels of labor and capital. Now note that several levels of output in this table can be produced in two ways. For example, 108 units of output can be produced using either 6 units of capital and 1 worker or 1 unit of capital and 4 workers. Thus these two combinations of labor and capital are two points on the isoquant associated with 108 units of output. And if we assumed that labor and capital were continuously divisible, there would be many more combinations on this isoquant.

Other input combinations in Table 8.1 that can produce the same level of output are:

$$Q = 258: \text{using } K = 2, \quad L = 5 \text{ or } K = 8, L = 2$$
$$Q = 400: \text{using } K = 9, \quad L = 3 \text{ or } K = 4, L = 4$$
$$Q = 453: \text{using } K = 5, \quad L = 4 \text{ or } K = 3, L = 7$$
$$Q = 708: \text{using } K = 6, \quad L = 7 \text{ or } K = 5, L = 9$$
$$Q = 753: \text{using } K = 10, L = 6 \text{ or } K = 6, L = 8$$

Each pair of combinations of K and L is two of the many combinations associated with each specific level of output. Each demonstrates that it is possible to increase capital and decrease labor (or increase labor and decrease capital) while keeping the level of output constant. For example, if the firm is producing 400 units of output with 9 units of capital and 3 units of labor, it can increase labor by 1, decrease capital by 5, and keep output at 400. Or if it is producing 453 units of output with $K = 3$ and $L = 7$, it can increase K by 2, decrease L by 3, and keep output at 453. Thus an isoquant shows how one input can be substituted for another while keeping the level of output constant.

Characteristics of Isoquants

We now set forth the typically assumed characteristics of isoquants when labor, capital, and output are continuously divisible. Figure 9.1 illustrates three such isoquants. Isoquant Q_1 shows all the combinations of capital and labor that yield 100

FIGURE 9.1

Typical Isoquants

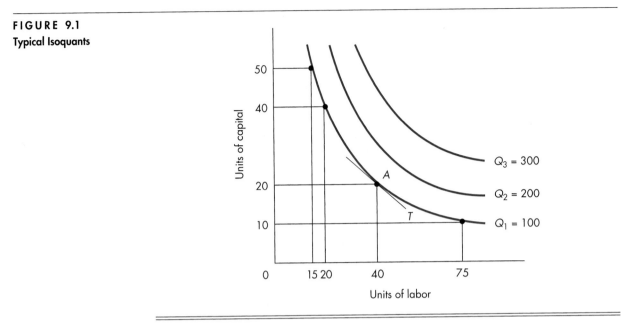

units of output. As shown, the firm can produce 100 units of output by using 10 units of capital and 75 of labor, or 50 units of capital and 15 of labor, or any other combination of capital and labor on isoquant Q_1. Similarly, isoquant Q_2 shows the various combinations of capital and labor that can be used to produce 200 units of output. And isoquant Q_3 shows all combinations that can produce 300 units of output. Each capital-labor combination can be on only one isoquant. That is, isoquants cannot intersect.

Isoquants Q_1, Q_2, and Q_3 are only three of an infinite number of isoquants that could be drawn. A group of isoquants is called an isoquant map. In an *isoquant map*, all isoquants lying above and to the right of a given isoquant indicate higher levels of output. Thus in Figure 9.1 isoquant Q_2 indicates a higher level of output than isoquant Q_1, and Q_3 indicates a higher level than Q_2.

We should also note that combinations other than those on a given isoquant can be used to produce the given level of output, but such combinations would not reflect the "maximum-amount-of-output" concept we introduced in the definition of a production function. Clearly, 100 units of output *could* be produced using *more than* 10 units of capital and *more than* 75 units of labor, but such production would involve wasting some inputs. In contrast, it is impossible to produce 100 units of output using less than 10 units of capital with 75 units of labor, or vice versa. For any combination along an isoquant, if the usage level of either input is reduced and the other is held constant, output must decline.

Marginal Rate of Technical Substitution

As depicted in Figure 9.1, isoquants slope downward over the relevant range of production. This negative slope indicates that if the firm decreases the amount of capital employed, more labor must be added in order to keep the rate of output constant. Or if labor use is decreased, capital usage must be increased to keep output constant. Thus the two inputs can be substituted for one another to maintain a constant level of output.

Great theoretical and practical importance is attached to the rate at which one input must be substituted for another to keep output constant. This rate at which one input is substituted for another along an isoquant is called the **marginal rate of technical substitution (MRTS)** and is defined as

$$MRTS = -\frac{\Delta K}{\Delta L}$$

The minus sign is added to make *MRTS* a positive number, since $\Delta K/\Delta L$, the slope of the isoquant, is negative.

Over the relevant range of production, the marginal rate of technical substitution diminishes. That is, as more and more labor is substituted for capital while holding output constant, the absolute value of $\Delta K/\Delta L$ decreases. This can be seen in Figure 9.1. If capital is reduced from 50 to 40 (a decrease of 10 units), labor must be increased by 5 units (from 15 to 20) in order to keep the level of output at 100 units. That is, when capital is plentiful relative to labor, the firm can discharge 10 units of capital but must substitute only 5 units of labor in order to keep output at 100. The marginal rate of technical substitution in this case is $-\Delta K/\Delta L = -(-10)/5 = 2$, meaning that for every unit of labor added, 2 units of capital can be discharged in order to keep the level of output constant. However, consider a combination where capital is more scarce and labor more plentiful. For example, if capital is decreased from 20 to 10 (again a decrease of 10 units), labor must be increased by 35 units (from 40 to 75) to keep output at 100 units. In this case the *MRTS* is 10/35, indicating that for each unit of labor added, capital can be reduced by slightly more than one-quarter of a unit.

Thus as capital decreases and labor increases along an isoquant, the amount of capital that can be discharged for each unit of labor added declines. Or, put another way, the amount of labor that must be added for each unit of capital eliminated, holding output constant, must increase. This relation is seen in Figure 9.1. As the change in labor and the change in capital become extremely small around a point on an isoquant, the absolute value of the slope of a tangent to the isoquant at that point is the *MRTS* $(-\Delta K/\Delta L)$ in the neighborhood of that point. For example, in Figure 9.1, the absolute value of the slope of tangent T to isoquant Q_1 at point A shows the marginal rate of technical substitution at that point. Thus the slope of the isoquant reflects the rate at which labor can be substituted for capital. It is easy to see that the isoquant becomes less and less steep with movements downward along the isoquant. Thus *MRTS* declines along an isoquant as labor increases and capital decreases.

marginal rate of technical substitution (MRTS)

The rate at which one input is substituted for another along an isoquant

Relation of *MRTS* to Marginal Products

For very small movements along an isoquant, the marginal rate of technical substitution equals the ratio of the marginal products of the two inputs. We will now demonstrate why this comes about.

The level of output, Q, depends on the use of the two inputs, L and K. Because Q is constant along an isoquant, ΔQ must equal zero for any change in L and K that would remain on a given isoquant. Suppose that, at a point on the isoquant, the marginal product of capital (MP_K) is 3 and the marginal product of labor (MP_L) is 6. If we add 1 unit of labor, output would increase by 6 units. To keep Q at the original level, capital must decrease just enough to offset the 6-unit increase in output generated by the increase in labor. Because the marginal product of capital is 3, 2 units of capital must be discharged in order to reduce output by 6 units. In this case the $MRTS = -\Delta K/\Delta L = -(-2)/1 = 2$, which is exactly equal to $MP_L/MP_K = 6/3 = 2$.

Or if we were to increase capital by 1 unit, output would rise by 3. Labor must decrease by one-half a unit to offset the increase of 3 units of output and keep output constant, since $MP_L = 6$. In this case, the $MRTS = -\Delta K/\Delta L = -(1)/(-1/2) = 2$, which is again equal to MP_L/MP_K.

In more general terms, we can say that when L and K are allowed to vary slightly, the change in Q resulting from the change in the two inputs is the marginal product of L times the amount of change in L plus the marginal product of K times its change. Put in equation form,

$$\Delta Q = (MP_L)(\Delta L) + (MP_K)(\Delta K)$$

In order to remain on a given isoquant, it is necessary to set ΔQ equal to 0. Then, solving for the marginal rate of technical substitution yields[2]

$$MRTS = -\frac{\Delta K}{\Delta L} = \frac{MP_L}{MP_K}$$

Using this relation, the reason for diminishing *MRTS* is easily explained. As additional units of labor are substituted for capital, the marginal product of labor diminishes. Two forces are working to diminish labor's marginal product: (1) Less capital causes a downward shift of the marginal product of labor curve, and (2) more units of the variable input (labor) cause a downward movement along the marginal product curve. Thus, as labor is substituted for capital, the marginal product of labor must decline. For analogous reasons the marginal product of capital increases as less capital and more labor are used. The same two forces are present in this case: a movement along a marginal product curve and a shift in the location of the curve. In this situation, however, both forces work to increase the

---

[2]This relation is demonstrated mathematically in the appendix to this chapter.

marginal product of capital. Thus, as labor is substituted for capital, the marginal product of capital increases. Combining these two conditions, as labor is substituted for capital, MP_L decreases and MP_K increases, so MP_L/MP_K will decrease.[3]

9.2 ISOCOST CURVES

isocost curve
Line that shows the various combinations of inputs that may be purchased for a given level of expenditure at given input prices.

Producers must consider relative input prices in order to find the least-cost combination of inputs to produce a given level of output. An extremely useful tool for analyzing the cost of purchasing inputs is an *isocost curve*. An **isocost curve** shows all combinations of inputs that may be purchased for a given level of total expenditure at given input prices. As you will see in the next section, isocost curves play a key role in finding the combination of inputs that produce a given output level at the lowest possible total cost.

Before we develop the concept of isocost curves, we need to discuss briefly how input prices are determined. For most managers, the price of each input is determined in the market for that input by the intersection of the demand for the input and the supply of the input. In such cases, the manager simply takes the market-determined price of the input as given when deciding how much of the input to purchase for production. In some cases, however, managers may be large enough buyers of resources that they can bargain with sellers of the resource to get a better price. They may, for example, get a lower price on an input if they buy a greater quantity of that input. In this case, the price of the input is not constant but, rather, declines as more of the input is purchased. While some managers may have the ability to negotiate lower prices for their inputs, we concentrate upon producers who are relatively small purchasers, so we treat input prices as constant.

Characteristics of Isocost Curves

Suppose a manager must pay $25 for each unit of labor services and $50 for each unit of capital services employed. The manager wishes to know what combinations of labor and capital can be purchased for $400 total expenditure on inputs. Figure 9.2 shows the isocost curve for $400 when the price of labor is $25 and the price of capital is $50. Each combination of inputs on this isocost curve costs $400 to purchase. Point A on the isocost curve shows how much capital could be purchased if no labor is employed. Since the price of capital is $50, the manager can spend all $400 on capital alone and purchase 8 units of capital and 0 units of labor. Similarly, point D on the isocost curve gives the maximum amount of labor—16 units—that can be purchased if labor costs $25 per unit and $400 is spent on

---

[3]Note that we have violated our assumption about marginal product somewhat. The marginal product of an input is defined as the change in output per unit change in the input, the use of other inputs held constant. In this case we allow the usage of both inputs to change; thus the marginal product is really an approximation. But we are speaking only of slight or very small changes in use. Thus violation of the assumption is small and the approximation approaches the true variation for small changes.

FIGURE 9.2

An Isocost Curve
(w = $25 and r = $50)

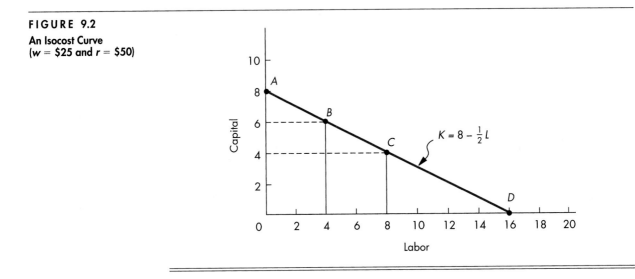

labor alone. Points B and C also represent input combinations that cost $400. At point B, for example, $300 (= 50×6) is spent on capital and $100 = 25×4) is spent on labor, which represents a total cost of $400.

If we continue to denote the quantities of capital and labor by K and L, and denote their respective prices by r and w, total cost, C, is $C = wL + rK$. Total cost is simply the sum of the cost of L units of labor at w dollars per unit and of K units of capital at r dollars per unit:

$$C = wL + rK$$

In this example, the total cost function is $400 = 25L + 50K$. Solving this equation for K, you can see the combinations of K and L that can be chosen: $K = \dfrac{400}{50} - \dfrac{25}{50}L = 8 - \dfrac{1}{2}L$. More generally, if a fixed amount $\overline{C}$ is to be spent, the firm can choose among the combinations given by

$$K = \frac{\overline{C}}{r} - \frac{w}{r}L$$

If $\overline{C}$ is the total amount to be spent on inputs, the most capital that can be purchased (if no labor is purchased) is $\overline{C}/r$ units of capital, and the most labor that can be purchased (if no capital is purchased) is $\overline{C}/w$ units of labor.

The slope of the isocost curve is equal to the negative of the relative input price ratio, $-w/r$. This ratio is important because it tells the manager how much capital

FIGURE 9.3

Shift in an Isocost Curve

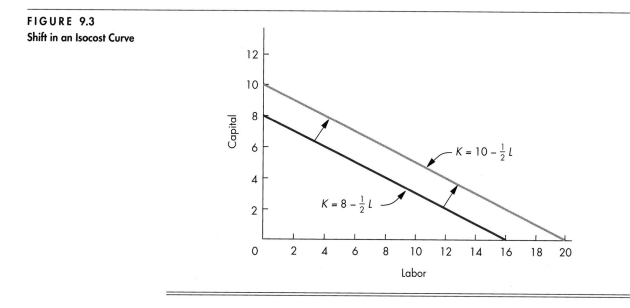

must be given up if one more unit of labor is purchased. In the example just given and illustrated in Figure 9.2, $-w/r = -\$25/\$50 = -1/2$. If the manager wishes to purchase 1 more unit of labor at $25, 1/2 unit of capital, which costs $50, must be given up to keep the total cost of the input combination constant. If the price of labor happens to rise to $50 per unit, r remaining constant, the slope of the isocost curve is $-\$50/\$50 = -1$, which means the manager must give up 1 unit of capital for each additional unit of labor purchased in order to keep total cost constant.

Shifts in Isocost Curves

If the constant level of total cost associated with a particular isocost curve changes, the isocost curve shifts parallel. Figure 9.3 shows how the isocost curve shifts when the total expenditure on resources ($\overline{C}$) increases from $400 to $500. The isocost curve shifts out parallel, and the equation for the new isocost curve is

$$K = 10 - \frac{1}{2}L$$

The slope is still $-1/2$ because $-w/r$ does not change. The K-intercept is now 10, indicating that a maximum of 10 units of capital can be purchased if no labor is purchased and $500 is spent.

In general, an increase in cost, holding input prices constant, leads to a parallel upward shift in the isocost curve. A decrease in cost, holding input prices constant, leads to a parallel downward shift in the isocost curve. An infinite number of isocost curves exist, one for each level of total cost.

▣   **Relation**   At constant input prices, w and r for labor and capital, a given expenditure on inputs ($\overline{C}$) will purchase any combination of labor and capital given by the following equation, called an isocost curve:

$$K = \frac{\overline{C}}{r} - \frac{w}{r} L$$

9.3 FINDING THE OPTIMAL COMBINATION OF INPUTS

A manager who wishes to maximize profit must first decide how much output to produce and then how to produce that amount at the lowest possible total cost. We have shown that any given level of output can be produced by many combinations of inputs—as illustrated by isoquants. When a manager wishes to produce a given level of output at the lowest possible total cost, the manager chooses the combination on the desired isoquant that costs the least. This is a constrained minimization problem that a manager can solve by following the rule for constrained optimization set forth in Chapter 3. The ability to find the optimal or cost-minimizing combination of inputs is a fundamental skill a manager must master if profit is to be maximized.

While managers whose goal is profit maximization are generally and primarily concerned with searching for the least-cost combination of inputs to produce a given (profit-maximizing) output, managers of nonprofit organizations may face an alternative situation. In a nonprofit situation, a manager may have a budget or fixed amount of money available for production and wish to maximize the amount of output that can be produced. As we have shown using isocost curves, there are many different input combinations that can be purchased for a given (or fixed) amount of expenditure on inputs. When a manager wishes to maximize output for a given level of total cost, the manager must choose the input combination on the isocost curve that lies on the highest isoquant. This is a constrained maximization problem; the rule for solving it was set forth in Chapter 3.

Whether the manager is searching for the input combination that minimizes cost for a given level of production or maximizes total production for a given level of expenditure on resources, the optimal combination of inputs to employ is found using the same rule. We first illustrate the fundamental principles of cost minimization with an output constraint; then we will turn to the case of output maximization given a cost constraint.

Production of a Given Output at Minimum Cost

The principle of minimizing the total cost of producing a given level of output is illustrated in Figure 9.4.[4] The manager wants to produce 10,000 units of output at the lowest possible total cost. All combinations of labor and capital capable of producing this level of output are shown by isoquant Q_1. The price of labor (w) is $40 per unit, and the price of capital (r) is $60 per unit.

---

[4]Conditions for minimizing total cost subject to an output constraint are derived mathematically in the appendix to this chapter.

FIGURE 9.4

Optimal Input Combination to Minimize Cost for a Given Output

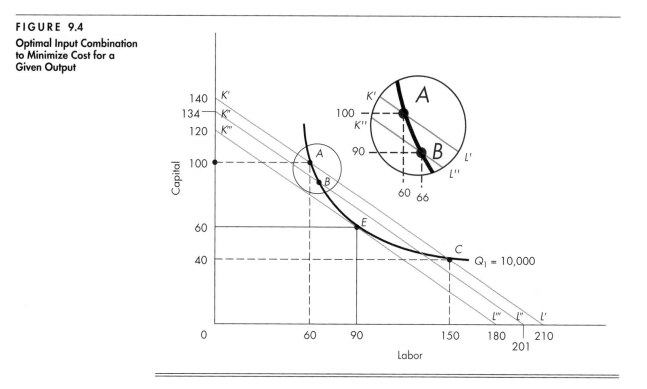

Consider the combination of inputs 60L and 100K, represented by point A on isoquant Q_1. At point A, 10,000 units can be produced at a total cost of $8,400, where the total cost is calculated by adding the total expenditure on labor and the total expenditure on capital:[5]

$$C = wL + rK = (\$40 \times 60) + (\$60 \times 100) = \$8,400$$

The manager can lower the total cost of producing 10,000 units by moving down along the isoquant and purchasing input combination B, because this combination of labor and capital lies on a lower isocost curve ($K''L''$) than input combination A, which lies on $K'L'$. The blowup in Figure 9.4 shows that combination B uses 66L and 90K. Combination B costs $8,040 [= ($40 × 66) + ($60 × 90)]. Thus the manager can decrease the total cost of producing 10,000 units by $360 (= $8,400 − $8,040) by moving from input combination A to input combination B on isoquant Q_1.

Since the manager's objective is to choose the combination of labor and capital on the 10,000-unit isoquant that can be purchased at the lowest possible cost, the

---

[5]Alternatively, you can calculate the cost associated with an isocost curve as the maximum amount of labor that could be hired at $40 per unit if no capital is used. For $K'L'$, 210 units of labor could be hired (if K = 0) for a cost of $8,400. Or 140 units of capital can be hired at $60 (if L = 0) for a cost of $8,400.

manager will continue to move downward along the isoquant until the lowest possible *isocost* curve is reached. Examining Figure 9.4 reveals that the lowest cost of producing 10,000 units of output is attained at point E by using 90 units of labor and 60 units of capital on isocost curve $K'''L'''$, which shows all input combinations that can be purchased for $7,200. Note that at this cost-minimizing input combination:

$$C = wL + rK = (\$40 \times 90) + (\$60 \times 60) = \$7,200$$

No input combination on an isocost curve below the one going through point E is capable of producing 10,000 units of output. The total cost associated with input combination E is the lowest possible total cost for producing 10,000 units when w = $40 and r = $60.

Suppose the manager chooses to produce using 40 units of capital and 150 units of labor—point C on the isoquant. The manager could now increase capital and reduce labor along isoquant Q_1, keeping output constant and moving to lower and lower isocost curves, and hence lower costs, until point E is reached. Regardless of whether a manager starts with too much capital and too little labor (such as point A) or too little capital and too much labor (such as point C), the manager can move to the optimal input combination by moving along the isoquant to lower and lower isocost curves until input combination E is reached.

At point E, the isoquant is tangent to the isocost curve. Recall that the slope (in absolute value) of the isoquant is the *MRTS*, and the slope of the isocost curve (in absolute value) is equal to the relative input price ratio, w/r. Thus, at point E, *MRTS* equals the ratio of input prices. At the cost-minimizing input combination,

$$MRTS = \frac{w}{r}$$

T ▷ ③ To minimize the cost of producing a given level of output, the manager employs the input combination for which $MRTS = w/r$.

The Marginal Product Approach to Cost Minimization

Recall from the discussion in Chapter 3 that finding the optimal levels of two activities A and B in a constrained optimization problem involved equating the marginal benefit per dollar spent on each of the activities (MB/P). A manager compares the marginal benefit per dollar spent on each activity to determine which activity is the "better deal": that is, which activity gives the higher marginal benefit per dollar spent. At their optimal levels, both activities are equally good deals ($MB_A/P_A = MB_B/P_B$) and the constraint is met.

The tangency condition for cost minimization, $MRTS = w/r$, is equivalent to the condition of equal marginal benefit per dollar spent set forth in Chapter 3. Recall that $MRTS = MP_L/MP_K$; thus the cost-minimizing condition can be expressed in terms of marginal products:

$$MRTS = \frac{MP_L}{MP_K} = \frac{w}{r}$$

After a bit of algebraic manipulation, the optimization condition may be expressed as

$$\frac{MP_L}{w} = \frac{MP_K}{r}$$

The marginal benefits of hiring extra units of labor and capital are the marginal products of labor and capital. Dividing each marginal product by its respective input price tells the manager the additional output that will be forthcoming if one more dollar is spent on that input. Thus, at point E in Figure 9.4, the marginal product per dollar spent on labor is equal to the marginal product per dollar spent on capital, and the constraint is met ($Q = 10,000$ units).

To illustrate how a manager uses information about marginal products and input prices to find the least-cost input combination, we return to point A in Figure 9.4, where $MRTS$ is greater than w/r. Assume that at point A, $MP_L = 160$ and $MP_K = 80$; thus $MRTS = 2$ ($= MP_L/MP_K = 160/80$). Since the slope of the isocost curve is 2/3 ($= w/r = 40/60$), $MRTS$ is greater than w/r, and

$$\frac{MP_L}{w} = \frac{160}{40} = 4 > 1.33 = \frac{80}{60} = \frac{MP_K}{r}$$

The firm should substitute labor, which has the higher marginal product per dollar, for capital, which has the lower marginal product per dollar. For example, an additional unit of labor would increase output by approximately 160 units while increasing labor cost by $40.[6] To keep output constant, 2 units of capital must be released, causing output to fall 160 units (the marginal product of each unit of capital released is approximately 80), but the cost of capital would fall by $120, which is $60 for each of the 2 units of capital released. Output remains constant at 10,000 because the higher output from 1 more unit of labor is just offset by the lower output from 2 fewer units of capital. However, because labor cost rises by only $40 while capital cost falls by $120, the total cost of producing 10,000 units of output falls by $80 ($= $120 − $40).

This example shows that when MP_L/w is greater than MP_K/r, the manager can reduce cost by increasing labor usage while decreasing capital usage just enough to keep output constant. Since $MP_L/w > MP_K/r$ for every input combination along Q_1 from point A to point E, the firm should continue to substitute labor for capital until it reaches point E. As more labor is used, MP_L falls because of diminishing marginal product. As less capital is used, MP_K rises for the same reason. As the manager substitutes labor for capital, $MRTS$ falls until equilibrium is reached.

Now consider point C, where $MRTS$ is less than w/r, and consequently MP_L/w is less than MP_K/r. The marginal product per dollar spent on the last unit of labor is less than the marginal product per dollar spent on the last unit of capital. In this case, the manager can reduce cost by increasing capital usage and decreasing labor

---

[6]Note that we use "approximately" because we have ignored the possibility of diminishing marginal product.

usage in such a way as to keep output constant. To see this, assume that at point C, $MP_L = 40$ and $MP_K = 240$, and thus $MRTS = 40/240 = 1/6$, which is less than w/r ($= 2/3$). If the manager uses 1 more unit of capital and 6 fewer units of labor, output stays constant while total cost falls by $180. (You should verify this yourself.) The manager can continue moving upward along isoquant Q_1, keeping output constant but reducing cost until point E is reached. As capital is increased and labor decreased, MP_L rises and MP_K falls until, at point E, MP_L/w equals MP_K/r. We have now derived the following:

▣ **Principle**   To produce a given level of output at the lowest possible cost when two inputs (L and K) are variable and the prices of the inputs are, respectively, w and r, a manager chooses the combination of inputs for which

$$MRTS = \frac{MP_L}{MP_K} = \frac{w}{r}$$

which implies that

$$\frac{MP_L}{w} = \frac{MP_K}{r}$$

The isoquant associated with the desired level of output (the slope of which is the $MRTS$) is tangent to the isocost curve (the slope of which is w/r) at the optimal combination of inputs. This optimization condition also means that the marginal product per dollar spent on the last unit of each input is the same.

Production of Maximum Output with a Given Level of Cost

As discussed earlier, in most cases managers choose the firm's level of production, then choose the input combination that permits production of that output at least cost. There may be times, however, when managers can spend only a fixed amount on production and wish to attain the highest level of production consistent with that amount of expenditure. This is a constrained maximization problem, and as we showed in Chapter 3, the optimization condition for constrained maximization is the same as that for constrained minimization.[7] In other words, the input combination that maximizes the level of output for a given level of total cost of inputs is that combination for which

$$MRTS = \frac{w}{r} \quad \text{or} \quad \frac{MP_L}{w} = \frac{MP_K}{r}$$

This is the same condition that must be satisfied by the input combination that minimizes the total cost of producing a given output level.

This situation is illustrated in Figure 9.5 on page 357. The isocost line KL shows all possible combinations of the two inputs that can be purchased for the level of total cost (and input prices) associated with this isocost curve. Suppose the manager chooses point R on the isocost curve and is thus meeting the cost constraint.

---

[7]Conditions for output maximization subject to a cost constraint are derived mathematically in the appendix.

FIGURE 9.5

Output Maximization for a Given Level of Cost

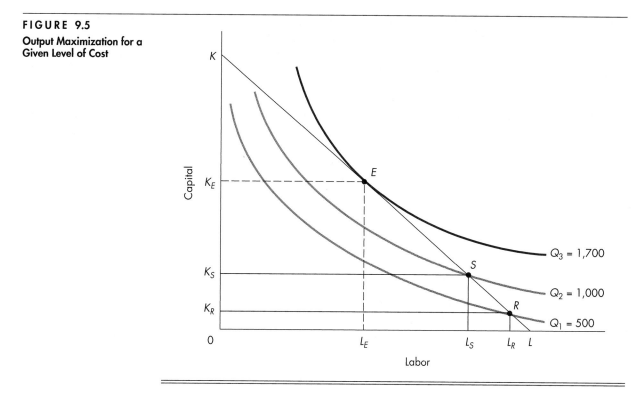

While 500 units of output are produced using L_R units of labor and K_R units of capital, the manager could produce more output at no additional cost by using less labor and more capital.

This can be accomplished, for example, by moving up the isocost curve to point S. Point S and point R lie on the same isocost curve and consequently cost the same amount. Point S lies on a higher isoquant, Q_2, allowing the manager to produce 1,000 units without spending any more than the given amount on inputs (represented by isocost curve KL). The highest level of output attainable with the given level of cost is 1,700 units (point E), which is produced by using L_E labor and K_E capital. At point E, the highest attainable isoquant, isoquant Q_3, is just tangent to the given isocost, and $MRTS = w/r$ or $MP_L/w = MP_K/r$, the same conditions that must be met to minimize the cost of producing a given output level.

To see why MP_L/w must equal MP_K/r in order to maximize output for a given level of expenditures on inputs, suppose that this optimizing condition does not hold. Specifically, assume that $w = \$2$, $r = \$3$, $MP_L = 6$, and $MP_K = 12$, so that

$$\frac{MP_L}{w} = \frac{6}{2} = 3 < 4 = \frac{12}{3} = \frac{MP_K}{r}$$

The last unit of labor adds 3 units of output per dollar spent; the last unit of capital adds 4 units of output per dollar. If the firm wants to produce the maximum output possible with a given level of cost, it could spend $1 less on labor, thereby reducing labor by half a unit and hence output by 3 units. It could spend this dollar on capital, thereby increasing output by 4 units. Cost would be unchanged, and total output would rise by 1 unit. And the firm would continue taking dollars out of labor and adding them to capital as long as the inequality holds. But as labor is reduced, its marginal product will increase, and as capital is increased, its marginal product will decline. Eventually the marginal product per dollar spent on each input will be equal. We have established the following:

Principle In the case of two variable inputs, labor and capital, the manager of a firm maximizes output for a given level of cost by using the amounts of labor and capital such that the marginal rate of technical substitution (MRTS) equals the input price ratio (w/r). In terms of a graph, this condition is equivalent to choosing the input combination where the slope of the given isocost curve equals the slope of the highest attainable isoquant. This output-maximizing condition implies that the marginal product per dollar spent on the last unit of each input is the same.

9.4 OPTIMIZATION AND COST

Using Figure 9.4 we showed how a manager can choose the optimal (least-cost) combination of inputs to produce a given level of output. We also showed how the total cost of producing that level of output is calculated. When the optimal input combination for each possible output level is determined and total cost is calculated for each one of these input combinations, a total cost curve (or schedule) is generated. In this section, we illustrate how any number of optimizing points can be combined into a single graph and how these points are related to the firm's cost structure.

An Expansion Path

In Figure 9.4 we illustrated one optimizing point for a firm. This point shows the optimal (least-cost) combination of inputs for a given level of output. However, as you would expect, there exists an optimal combination of inputs for every level of output the firm might choose to produce. And the proportions in which the inputs are used need not be the same for all levels of output. To examine several optimizing points at once, we use the *expansion path*.

expansion path
The curve or locus of points that shows the cost-minimizing input combination for each level of output with the input/price ratio held constant.

The **expansion path** shows the cost-minimizing input combination for each level of output with the input price ratio held constant. It therefore shows how input usage changes as output changes. Figure 9.6 illustrates the derivation of an expansion path. Isoquants Q_1, Q_2, and Q_3 show, respectively, the input combinations of labor and capital that are capable of producing 500, 700, and 900 units of output. The price of capital (r) is $20 and the price of labor (w) is $10. Thus any isocost curve would have a slope of $10/20 = 1/2$.

The three isocost curves KL, $K'L'$, and $K''L''$, each of which has a slope of $1/2$, represent the minimum costs of producing the three levels of output, 500, 700, and 900, because they are tangent to the respective isoquants. That is, at optimal input combinations A, B, and C, MRTS $= w/r = 1/2$. In the figure, the expansion path connects these optimal points and all other points so generated.

FIGURE 9.6

An Expansion Path

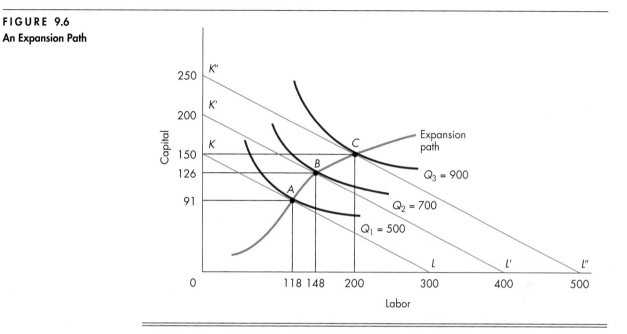

Note that points *A*, *B*, and *C* are also points indicating the combinations of inputs that can produce the maximum output possible at each level of cost given by isocost curves *KL*, *K′L′*, and *K′′L′′*. The optimizing condition, as emphasized, is the same for cost minimization with an output constraint and output maximization with a cost constraint. For example, to produce 500 units of output at the lowest possible cost, the firm would use 91 units of capital and 118 units of labor. The lowest cost of producing this output is therefore $3,000 (from the vertical intercept, $20 × 150 = $3,000). Likewise, 91 units of capital and 118 units of labor are the input combination that can produce the maximum possible output (500 units) under the cost constraint given by $3,000 (isocost curve *KL*). Each of the other optimal points along the expansion path also shows an input combination that is the cost-minimizing combination for the given output or the output-maximizing combination for the given cost. At every point along the expansion path,

$$MRTS = \frac{MP_L}{MP_K} = \frac{w}{r}$$

and

$$\frac{MP_L}{w} = \frac{MP_k}{r}$$

Therefore, the expansion path is the curve or locus of points along which the marginal rate of technical substitution is constant and equal to the input price ratio. It is a curve with a special feature: It is the curve or locus along which the firm will expand output when input prices are constant.

ILLUSTRATION 9.1

Downsizing or Dumbsizing
Optimal Input Choice Should Guide
Restructuring Decisions

As we stress in the introduction to this chapter and in the previous chapter, successful managers know how to manage costs. Increased competition, both domestically (as a result of deregulation in many industries) and globally (as trade barriers fall and free markets emerge in many parts of the world), is pressuring managers to reduce costs to remain profitable. One of the most disparaged strategies for cost cutting in the 1990s has been corporate "downsizing" or, synonymously, corporate "restructuring." Managers downsize or restructure a firm by permanently laying off a sizable fraction of their workforce. In many cases, managers achieve the targeted level of reduction in workforce using across-the-board layoffs.

If a firm employs more than the efficient amount of labor, reducing the amount of labor employed can lead to lower costs for producing the same amount of output. The value of a firm, measured by the market value of its common stock, often rises when corporate executives announce plans for downsizing or restructuring the firm. Sometimes the enthusiasm of investors over a downsizing plan fades once managers begin to implement the labor cuts. During the 1990s, business publications documented dozens of restructuring plans that

failed to realize the promised cost savings. Apparently, a successful restructuring requires more than "meat-ax," across-the-board cutting of labor. *The Wall Street Journal* reported that "despite warnings about downsizing becoming dumbsizing, many companies continue to make flawed decisions—hasty, across-the-board cuts —that come back to haunt them."[a]

The reason that across-the-board cuts in labor do not generally deliver the desired lower costs can be seen by applying the efficiency rule for choosing inputs that we have developed in this chapter. In order to either minimize the total cost of producing a given level of output or to maximize the output for a given level of cost, a manager must base employment decisions on the marginal product per dollar spent on labor, MP/w. Across-the-board downsizing, when no consideration is given to productivity or wages, cannot lead to an efficient reduction in the amount of labor employed by the firm. Workers with the lowest MP/w ratios must be cut first if the manager is to realize the greatest possible cost savings.

Consider this example: A manager is ordered to cut the firm's labor force by as many workers as it takes to lower its labor costs by $10,000 per month. The manager wishes to meet the lower level of labor costs with as little loss of output as possible. The manager examines the employment performance of six workers: workers A and B are senior employees, and workers $C, D, E,$ and F

Relation The expansion path is the curve along which a firm expands (or contracts) output when input prices remain constant. Each point on the expansion path represents an efficient (least-cost) input combination. Along the expansion path, the marginal rate of technical substitution equals the constant input price ratio. The expansion path indicates how input usage changes when output or cost changes.

The Expansion Path and the Structure of Cost

An important aspect of the expansion path that was implied in this discussion and will be emphasized in the remainder of this chapter is that the expansion path gives the firm its cost structure. The lowest cost of producing any given level of output can be determined from the expansion path. Thus the structure of the relation between output and cost is determined by the expansion path.

Recall from the discussion of Figure 9.6 that the lowest cost of producing 500 units of output is $3,000, which was calculated as the price of capital, $20, times the

are junior employees. The accompanying table shows the productivity and wages paid monthly to each of these six workers. The senior workers (*A* and *B*) are paid more per month than the junior workers (*C*, *D*, *E*, and *F*), but the senior workers are more productive than the junior workers. Per dollar spent on wages, each senior worker contributes 0.50 unit of output per month, while each dollar spent on junior workers contributes 0.40 unit per month. Consequently, the senior workers provide the firm with more "bang per buck," even though their wages are higher. The manager, taking an across-the-board approach to cutting workers, could choose to lay off $5,000 worth of labor in each category: lay off worker *A* and workers *C* and *D*. This across-the-board strategy saves the required $10,000, but output falls by 4,500 units per month (= 2,500 + 2 × 1,000). Alternatively, the manager could rank the workers according to the marginal product per dollar spent on each worker. Then, the manager could start by sequentially laying off the workers with the smallest marginal product per dollar spent. This alternative approach would lead the manager to lay off four junior workers. Laying off workers *C*, *D*, *E*, and *F* saves the required $10,000 but reduces output by 4,000 units per month (= 4 × 1,000). Sequentially laying off the workers that give the least bang for the buck results in a smaller reduction in output while achieving the required labor savings of $10,000.

Worker	Marginal product (MP)	Wage (w)	MP/w
A	1,500	$5,000	0.50
B	2,500	$5,000	0.50
C	1,000	$2,500	0.40
D	1,000	$2,500	0.40
E	1,000	$2,500	0.40
F	1,000	$2,500	0.40

This illustration shows that restructuring decisions should be made on the basis of the production theory presented in this chapter. Input employment decisions cannot be made efficiently without using information about both the productivity of an input *and* the price of the input. A manager must consider marginal product per dollar spent. Across-the-board approaches to restructuring cannot, in general, lead to efficient reorganizations because these approaches do not consider information about worker productivity per dollar spent when making the layoff decision. Reducing the amount of labor employed is not "dumbsizing" if a firm is employing more than the efficient amount of labor. *Dumbsizing* occurs only when a manager lays off the wrong workers or too many workers.

[a]Alex Markels and Matt Murray, "Call It Dumbsizing: Why Some Companies Regret Cost-Cutting," *The Wall Street Journal*, May 14, 1996.

vertical intercept of the isocost curve, 150. Alternatively, the cost of producing 500 units can be calculated by multiplying the price of labor by the amount of labor used plus the price of capital by the amount of capital used:

$$wL + rK = (\$10 \times 118) + (\$20 \times 91) = \$3,000$$

Using the same method, we calculate the lowest cost of producing 700 and 900 units of output, respectively, as

$$(\$10 \times 148) + (\$20 \times 126) = \$4,000$$

and

$$(\$10 \times 200) + (\$20 \times 150) = \$5,000[8]$$

_____

[8]As you can verify, these are the same costs that would be obtained by multiplying the price of capital (labor) times the vertical (horizontal) intercept of the relevant isocost curve.

Similarly, the sum of the quantities of each input used times the respective input prices gives the minimum cost of producing every level of output along the expansion path. As you will see later in this chapter, this allows the firm to relate its cost to the level of output used.

9.5 RETURNS TO SCALE

We will now describe the effect of a proportional increase in all inputs on the level of output produced. For example, if the firm's usage of all inputs doubles, output would increase. The question is: By how much? The answer to this question depends upon the concept of returns to scale.

constant returns to scale
Condition in which all inputs are increased by the same proportion and output also increases by that exact proportion.

increasing returns to scale
Condition in which all inputs are increased by the same proportion and output increases by more than that proportion.

decreasing returns to scale
Condition in which all inputs are increased by the same proportion and output increases by less than that proportion.

Assume the usage of all inputs increases by 25 percent. If output increases by exactly 25 percent, the production function exhibits **constant returns to scale.** If, however, output increases by more than 25 percent, the production function exhibits **increasing returns to scale.** Alternatively, if output increases by less than 25 percent, the production function is characterized by **decreasing returns to scale.**

These relations can be illustrated using Figure 9.7. Begin with an arbitrary level of capital and labor at K_0 and L_0. This combination of capital and labor produces some level of output, Q_0. For purposes of illustration, we define Q_0 to be 100 units. Now, double the level of input usage to $2K_0$ and $2L_0$. Output increases to Q_1. The question is the magnitude of the increase. Input usage has increased by 100 percent. If Q_1 is equal to 200, output would have exactly doubled (increased by 100 percent) in response to the doubling of input usage, so constant returns to scale are indicated. If Q_1 is greater than 200 units (e.g., 215), increasing returns to scale are indicated. If Q_1 is less than 200 units (e.g., 180), the production function exhibits decreasing returns to scale.

Returns to scale are defined more analytically by writing the production function in functional form:

$$Q = f(L,K)$$

If input usage increases by a constant proportion (e.g., c) and the proportionate change in output is z,

$$f(cL,cK) = zQ$$

Again remember that c and z represent proportionate increases in the level of input usage and level of output, respectively.

We have noted, in the case of constant returns to scale, that if inputs are increased by a given percentage, output rises by the same percentage, that is, $z = c$. More generally, if all inputs increase by a factor of c and output goes up by a factor of z, then a firm experiences:

1. Increasing returns to scale if $z > c$ (output goes up proportionately more than the increase in input usage).
2. Constant returns to scale if $z = c$ (output goes up by the same proportion as the increase in input usage).

FIGURE 9.7
Returns to Scale

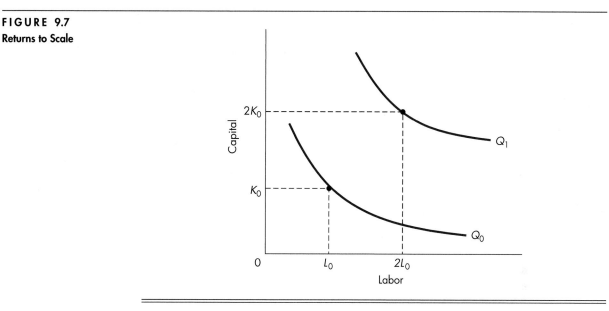

3. Decreasing returns to scale if $z < c$ (output goes up proportionately less than the increase in input usage).

Do not deduce from this discussion of returns to scale that firms with variable proportions production functions actually expand output by increasing their usage of every input in exactly the same proportion. As you have seen, the very concept of variable proportions means that the firms do not necessarily expand inputs in the same proportions. The expansion path may twist and turn in many directions. However, the concept of returns to scale does enter into some aspects of production and cost theory, and you should be familiar with this term.

Now that we have demonstrated how a manager can find the cost-minimizing input combination when more than one input is variable, we can derive the cost curves facing a manager in the long run. The structure of long-run cost curves is determined by the structure of long-run production, as reflected in the expansion path.

T ▷ 8

9.6 LONG-RUN COSTS

Recall from Chapter 8 that the long run is not some particular date in the future. The long run simply means that all inputs are variable to the firm. One of the first decisions to be made by the firm is to determine the scale of operations: that is, the size of the firm. To make this decision, a manager must know the cost of producing each relevant level of output. As emphasized above, just as short-run cost is derived from the short-run production function, long-run cost is derived from the long-run expansion path, to which we now turn.

FIGURE 9.8
Long-Run Expansion Path

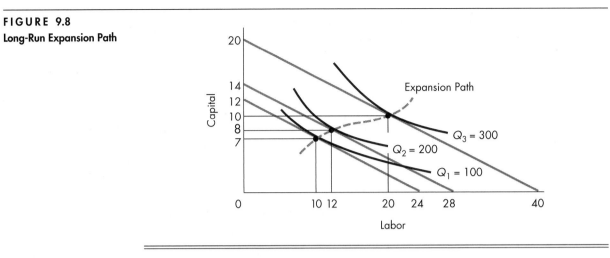

Derivation of Cost Schedules from a Production Function

As we have throughout this chapter, we assume that the firm's levels of usage of the inputs do not affect the prices that must be paid for the inputs—the manager takes input prices as given. We also continue to assume that the only two inputs used in production are labor and capital. We begin the discussion with a situation in which the price of labor (w) is $5 per unit and the price of capital (r) is $10 per unit. Figure 9.8 shows a portion of the firm's expansion path. Isoquants Q_1, Q_2, and Q_3 are associated, respectively, with 100, 200, and 300 units of output.

For the given set of input prices, the isocost curve with intercepts of 12 units of capital and 24 units of labor, which clearly has a slope of $-5/10$ ($= -w/r$), shows the least-cost method of producing 100 units of output: Use 10 units of labor and seven units of capital. If the firm wants to produce 100 units, it spends $50 ($5 × 10) on labor and $70 ($10 × 7) on capital, giving it a total cost of $120.

long-run average cost (LAC)
Long-run total cost divided by output ($LAC = LTC/Q$).

Similar to the short run, we define **long-run average cost (LAC)** as

$$LAC = \frac{\text{Long–run total cost } (LTC)}{\text{Output } (Q)}$$

long-run marginal cost (LMC)
The change in long-run total cost per unit change in output ($LMC = \Delta LTC/\Delta Q$).

and **long-run marginal cost (LMC)** as

$$LMC = \frac{\Delta LTC}{\Delta Q}$$

Therefore at an output of 100,

$$LAC = \frac{LTC}{Q} = \frac{\$120}{100} = \$1.20$$

Since there are no fixed inputs in the long run, there is no fixed cost when output is 0. Thus the long-run marginal cost of producing the first 100 units is

TABLE 9.1
Derivation of a Long-Run Cost Schedule

(1) Output	(2) Least-cost combination of Labor (units)	(3) Capital (units)	(4) Total cost ($w = \$5, r = \$10$)	(5) Long-run average cost (LAC)	(6) Long-run marginal cost (LMC)
100	10	7	$120	$1.20	$1.20
200	12	8	140	0.70	0.20
300	20	10	200	0.67	0.60
400	30	15	300	0.75	1.00
500	40	22	420	0.84	1.20
600	52	30	560	0.93	1.40
700	60	42	720	1.03	1.60

$$LMC = \frac{\Delta LTC}{\Delta Q} = \frac{\$120 - 0}{100 - 0} = \$1.20$$

The first row of Table 9.1 gives the level of output (100), the least-cost combination of labor and capital that can produce that output, and the long-run total, average, and marginal costs when output is 100 units.

Returning to Figure 9.8, you can see that the least-cost method of producing 200 units of output is to use 12 units of labor and 8 units of capital. Thus producing 200 units of output costs $140 (= $5 × 12 + $10 × 8). The average cost is $0.70 (= $140/200) and, since producing the additional 100 units increases total cost from $120 to $140, the marginal cost is $0.20 (= $20/100). These figures are shown in the second row of Table 9.1, and they give additional points on the firm's long-run total, average, and marginal cost curves.

Figure 9.8 shows that the firm will use 20 units of labor and 10 units of capital to produce 300 units of output. Using the same method as before, we calculate total, average, and marginal costs, which are given in row 3 of Table 9.1.

Figure 9.8 shows only three of the possible cost-minimizing choices. But, if we were to go on, we could obtain additional least-cost combinations, and in the same way, we could calculate the total, average, and marginal costs of these other outputs. This information is shown in the last four rows of Table 9.1 for output levels from 400 through 700.

Thus, at the given set of input prices and with the given technology, column 4 shows the long-run total cost schedule, column 5 the long-run average cost schedule, and column 6 the long-run marginal cost schedule. The corresponding long-run total cost curve is given in Panel A, Figure 9.9. This curve shows the least cost at which each quantity of output in Table 9.1 can be produced when no input is fixed. Its shape depends exclusively on the production function and the input prices.

This curve reflects three of the commonly assumed characteristics of long-run total cost. First, because there are no fixed costs, LTC is 0 when output is 0. Second, cost and output are directly related; that is, LTC has a positive slope. It costs more

FIGURE 9.9
Long-Run Total, Average, and Marginal Cost

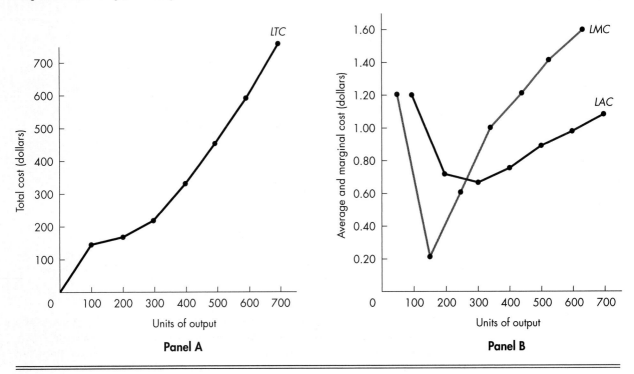

Panel A

Panel B

to produce more, which is to say that resources are scarce or that one never gets something for nothing. Third, *LTC* first increases at a decreasing rate, then increases at an increasing rate. This implies that marginal cost first decreases, then increases.

Turn now to the long-run average and marginal cost curves derived from Table 9.1 and shown in Panel B of Figure 9.9. These curves reflect the characteristics of typical *LAC* and *LMC* curves. They have essentially the same shape as they do in the short run—but, as we shall show below, for different reasons. Long-run average cost first decreases, reaches a minimum (at 300 units of output), then increases. Long-run marginal cost first declines, reaches its minimum at a lower output than that associated with minimum *LAC* (between 100 and 200 units), and then increases thereafter.

In Figure 9.9, marginal cost crosses the average cost curve at approximately the minimum of average cost. As we will show next, when output and cost are allowed to vary continuously, *LMC* crosses *LAC* at exactly the minimum point on the latter. (It is only approximate in Figure 9.9 because output varies discretely by 100 units in the table.)

FIGURE 9.10

Long-Run Average and Marginal Cost Curves

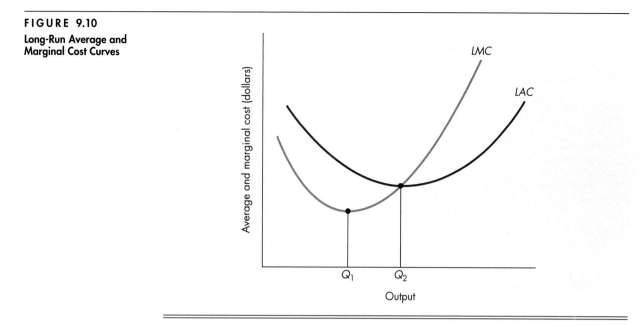

The reasoning is the same as that given for short-run average and marginal cost curves. When marginal cost is less than average cost, each additional unit produced adds less than average cost to total cost, so average cost must decrease. When marginal cost is greater than average cost, each additional unit of the good produced adds more than average cost to total cost, so average cost must be increasing over this range of output. Thus marginal cost must be equal to average cost when average cost is at its minimum.

Figure 9.10 shows long-run marginal and average cost curves that reflect the typically assumed characteristics when output and cost can vary continuously.

▣ **Relations** As illustrated in Figure 9.10, (1) long-run average cost, defined as

$$LAC = \frac{LTC}{Q}$$

first declines, reaches a minimum (here at Q_2 units of output), and then increases. (2) When LAC is at its minimum, long-run marginal cost, defined as

$$LMC = \frac{\Delta LTC}{\Delta Q}$$

equals LAC. (3) LMC first declines, reaches a minimum (here at Q_1, less than Q_2), and then increases. LMC lies below LAC over the range in which LAC declines; it lies above LAC when LAC is rising.

Economies and Diseconomies of Scale

economies of scale
The range of output over which long-run average cost (*LAC*) falls as output increases.

diseconomies of scale
The range of output over which long-run average cost (*LAC*) rises as output increases.

The economic forces that explain the shape of long-run cost curves are economies and diseconomies of scale. **Economies of scale** occur when long-run average cost falls as output increases. In Figure 9.10, economies of scale exist over the range of output from 0 units up to Q_2 units of output. **Diseconomies of scale** occur when long-run average cost rises as output increases. Diseconomies of scale set in beyond Q_2 units of output in Figure 9.10. We first discuss why economists believe economies of scale exist, and then we present some reasons why firms may eventually experience diseconomies of scale.

Probably the most fundamental reason for economies of scale is that larger-scale firms are able to take greater advantage of opportunities for specialization and division of labor. Consider, for example, a small-scale automobile brake and muffler shop. With only a few mechanics and a small number of customers each day, each mechanic must be able to perform *both* brake and muffler repairs. As the number of customers grows larger, the shop can have some mechanics specialize in brake repair and other mechanics specialize in muffler repair. Thus, in the long run, when workers and equipment are expanded together to create larger-scale operations, very substantial gains may be reaped by division of jobs and the specialization of workers in one job or another.

Technological factors constitute a second force contributing to economies of scale. We now discuss three important ways in which they can do so. First, if several different machines, each with a different rate of output, are required in a production process, the operation may have to be quite sizable to permit proper meshing of equipment. Suppose only two types of machines are required, one that produces the product and one that packages it. If the first machine can produce 30,000 units per day and the second can package 45,000 units per day, output will have to be 90,000 units per day in order to utilize fully the capacity of each type of machine.

A second technological source of scale economies is the fact that the cost of purchasing and installing larger machines is usually proportionately less than the cost of smaller machines. For example, a printing press that can run 200,000 papers per day does not cost 10 times as much as one that can run 20,000 per day—nor does it require 10 times as much building space, 10 times as many people to operate it, and so forth. Again, expanding size tends to reduce the unit cost of production.

The final technological element is perhaps the most important technological factor of all: As the scale of operation expands, there is usually a qualitative, as well as a quantitative, change in equipment. Consider ditchdigging: The smallest scale of operation is one worker and one shovel. But as the scale expands beyond a certain point, the firm does not simply continue to add workers and shovels. Shovels and most workers are replaced by a modern ditchdigging machine. In like manner, expansion of scale normally permits the introduction of various types of automation devices, all of which tend to reduce the unit cost of production.

Thus two broad forces, (1) specialization and division of labor and (2) technological factors, enable producers to reduce unit cost by expanding the scale of operation.[9] These forces give rise to the negatively sloped portion of the long-run average cost curve.

You may wonder why the long-run average cost curve would ever rise. After all possible economies of scale have been realized, why doesn't the curve become horizontal?

The rising portion of *LAC*, or diseconomies of scale, is generally attributed to limitations to efficient management. Managing any business entails controlling and coordinating a wide variety of activities: production, transportation, finance, sales, and so on. To perform these managerial functions efficiently, a manager must have accurate information; otherwise, the essential decision making is done in ignorance.

As the scale of plant expands beyond a certain point, top management necessarily has to delegate responsibility and authority to lower-echelon employees. Contact with the daily routine of operation tends to be lost, and efficiency of operation declines. Red tape and paperwork expand; management is generally not as efficient. Thus the cost of the managerial function increases, as does the unit cost of production.

It is difficult to determine just when diseconomies of scale set in and when they become strong enough to outweigh the economies of scale. In businesses where economies of scale are negligible, diseconomies may soon become of paramount importance, causing *LAC* to turn up at a relatively small volume of output. Panel A of Figure 9.11 shows a long-run average cost curve for a firm of this type. In other cases, economies of scale are extremely important. Even after the efficiency of management begins to decline, technological economies of scale may offset the diseconomies over a wide range of output. Thus the *LAC* curve may not turn upward until a very large volume of output is attained. This case is illustrated in Panel B of Figure 9.11.

In many actual situations, however, neither of these extremes describes the behavior of *LAC*. A very modest scale of operation may enable a firm to capture all the economies of scale, and diseconomies may not be incurred until the volume of output is very great. In this case, *LAC* would have a long horizontal section, as shown in Panel C of Figure 9.11. Some economists and business executives feel this type of *LAC* curve describes many production processes in the global economy.

On occasion, it is convenient and realistic to assume that constant returns to scale occur over the entire range of output for a firm. In this special case, the firm experiences constant costs in the long run, and its *LAC* curve is flat and equal to *LMC* at all output levels. Figure 9.12 illustrates a firm with constant unit and

---

[9]This discussion of economies of scale has concentrated on physical and technological forces. There are financial reasons for economies of scale as well. Large-scale purchasing of raw and processed materials may enable the buyer to obtain more favorable prices (quantity discounts). The same is frequently true of advertising. As another example, financing large-scale businesses is normally easier and less expensive: A nationally known business has access to organized security markets, so it may place its bonds and stocks on a more favorable basis. Bank loans also usually come easier and at lower interest rates to large, well-known corporations.

FIGURE 9.11
Various Shapes of LAC

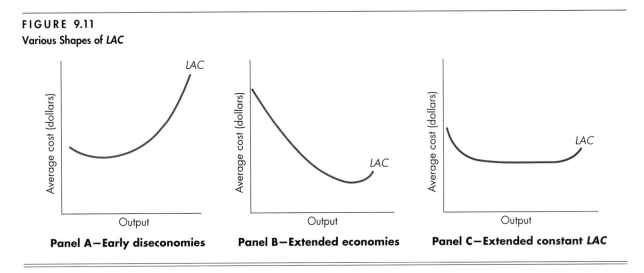

| Panel A—Early diseconomies | Panel B—Extended economies | Panel C—Extended constant LAC |

FIGURE 9.12
Constant Long-Run Costs

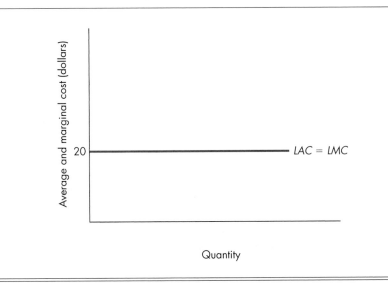

marginal costs of $20. The firm experiences neither economies nor diseconomies of scale and is said to experience **constant costs.** In most cases, we assume a representative *LAC*, such as that illustrated earlier in Figure 9.10.

constant costs
LAC is flat and equal to *LMC* at all output levels.

Economies of Scope

Many firms produce a number of different products. These multiproduct firms use inputs that contribute simultaneously to the production of two or more goods: A citrus orchard produces both oranges and grapefruit, an oil well produces both crude oil and natural gas, an automotive plant produces both cars and trucks, and commercial banks use the same assets to provide a variety of different financial services. Whenever it is less costly for a single firm to produce two or more products together than for separate firms to produce the same level of output for each product, **economies of scope** are said to exist.

economies of scope
The situation in which the joint cost of producing two or more goods is less than the sum of the separate costs of producing the goods.

For example, consider Precision Mufflers, a firm that installs replacement mufflers and also repairs brakes. This firm uses inputs that simultaneously contribute to the production of two different services. Precision Mufflers can replace 25 mufflers and perform 10 brake jobs a day for a total cost of $1,400. A firm that specializes in muffler replacement can install only 25 replacement mufflers at a total cost of $1,000. Another firm that specializes in brake repair can perform 10 brake jobs for a total cost of $600. Since the joint cost of replacing 25 mufflers and fixing the brakes on 10 cars ($1,400) is less than the total cost of two separate firms producing the same level of outputs ($1,600 = $1,000 + $600), economies of scope exist.

Let $C(X)$ be the total cost of producing a given level of some good X by a single-product firm and $C(Y)$ be the total cost of producing a given level of another good Y by a single-product firm. If $C(X, Y)$ represents the cost of a single firm's jointly producing the same levels of X and Y, economies of scope exist when

$$C(X, Y) < C(X) + C(Y)$$

The degree to which economies of scope exist (SC) can be measured by the fraction

$$SC = \frac{C(X) + C(Y) - C(X,Y)}{C(X,Y)}$$

When production involves economies of scope, the sum of the separate costs of producing X and Y by separate firms exceeds the cost of producing X and Y jointly by the same firm, and SC is positive. If diseconomies of scope exist, the sum of producing X and Y by separate firms is less than producing X and Y jointly by the same firm, and SC is negative. The greater the economies of scope, the larger the value of SC.

The reasons for the existence of economies of scope are varied. Economies of scope frequently arise when inputs can be jointly used to produce more than one product. The shared resources that lead to economies of scope may be the inputs used in the manufacture of the product, whereas in some cases it may involve only the administrative and marketing resources of the firm. In other cases, the production process may involve joint products for which the production of one good results in the production of another good at little or no extra cost. Examples of joint products are beef and leather, wool and mutton, chickens and fertilizer, and sometimes crude oil and natural gas.

▣   **Relation**   Economies of scope exist when the joint cost of producing two or more goods is less than the sum of the separate costs of producing the goods. In the case of two goods X and Y, economies of scope are measured by

$$SC = \frac{C(X) + C(Y) - C(X,Y)}{C(X,Y)}$$

T ▷ 12   where SC is greater (less) than 0 when (dis)economies of scope exist.

Managing Economies and Diseconomies of Scale

Our discussion of why economies and diseconomies of scale exist may have given you the impression that economies and diseconomies are unavoidable and beyond the control of a firm's management. To some extent this is correct: The production function and the state of technology determine the range of economies and diseconomies of scale. The manager of a firm, however, does choose the size of the firm that, in turn, determines where the firm will operate on the long-run average cost curve. The manager's choice of firm size is often subject to a great deal of uncertainty, since the precise shape of *LAC* is not known with certainty. Management sometimes makes decisions about firm size that turn out to be incorrect, choosing a size or scale that is either too small or too large. Two business articles in *The Wall Street Journal* illustrate how firms have been affected by past decisions about firm size. Some of these decisions turned out well; others did not.

What can firms too small to compete effectively with larger firms in the market do to enhance their competitive position? For two personal computer manufacturers the answer was to merge their businesses. In May 1993, AST Research, the eighth-largest U.S. PC producer, agreed to acquire the personal computer business of Tandy Corporation, the seventh-largest U.S. producer. This merger would move AST into fourth place in the industry. Recent price wars had hurt the two firms, and according to one industry analyst, "Computer makers like AST have been forced to look to high volume sales for profit [with the] focus on turning out [units] more efficiently and at lower cost."

According to the *WSJ*, the acquisition of Tandy's business would provide some innovative new products and better economies of scale for AST. The economies would come from AST's acquired ability to expand into new markets and increase its market share. The merger would help it establish a direct consumer sales channel through Tandy's 6,600 Radio Shack stores and other chains of computer stores. In essence, AST wanted Tandy's sales capacity in order to achieve previously unattainable economies of scale, thereby leading to lower costs and enhanced ability to compete by reducing prices.

Sometimes firms are actually too big to compete successfully with smaller rivals that have lower per-unit costs. *The Wall Street Journal* reported that many of Japan's biggest steel producers had become too large and were being outperformed by smaller, more efficient firms. Nippon Steel Corporation, the biggest

9.7 RELATIONS BETWEEN SHORT-RUN AND LONG-RUN COSTS

Now that you understand how long-run production decisions determine the structure of long-run costs, we can demonstrate more clearly the important relations between short-run and long-run costs. As we explained at the beginning of Chapter 8, the long run or planning horizon is the collection of all possible short-run situations, one for every amount of fixed input that may be chosen in the long-run planning period. For example, in Table 8.1 on page 317, the columns associated with the 10 levels of capital employment each represent a different short-run production function, and, as a group of short-run situations, they comprise the firm's planning horizon. In the first part of this section we will show you how to construct a firm's long-run planning horizon—in the form of its long-run average cost curve (*LAC*)—from the short-run average total cost (*ATC*) curves associated with each possible level of capital the firm might choose. Then, in the next part of this section, we will explain how managers can exploit the flexibility of input choice available in long-run decision making to alter the structure of short-run costs in order to reduce production costs (and increase profit).

steelmaker in the world's number-one steel-producing country, symbolizes the problem facing firms that grow too large. Close to Nippon's largest mill, the little Tokyo Steel Company opened a plant that was 1/20th the size of traditional Japanese steel mills but five times as efficient. The new mill undercut the prices of Nippon and other big steelmakers by 39 percent. According to the *WSJ*, Tokyo Steel planned to build two more "minimills." Other small Japanese steel producers were following suit with more small mills. "Big Steel" in Japan was beginning to look like Big Steel in the United States had a decade before. Net profits for Japan's largest three steel producers were down between 77 and 92 percent. And, according to a study by Paine-Webber, Nippon's largest mill did not even rank among the 40 lowest-cost steel producers in the world.

The trend was worldwide: "Large, high-volume 'integrated' plants with disjointed production lines are giving way to small plants with faster, cheaper production methods that can adjust quickly to demand variations." The president of the world's second-largest steelmaker said, "It's quite sure that in the future the largest part of steel will be produced in smaller mills." The chairman of another large steel firm observed, "If the integrated [plants] take this chance to restructure, they can keep their position. If not,

newcomers will take it." But the *WSJ* was less optimistic for the huge firms: "Unlike nimbler minimill operators, however, many old-line makers remain saddled with slow-moving corporate cultures, bloated staffs, and huge investments in increasingly outdated mills." It appears then that the largest steelmakers had become too large and inflexible because of, among other things, serious managerial diseconomies of scale.

These two examples are intended to show the crucial role played by the shape of the long-run average cost curve in promoting or hindering a firm's ability to compete. As we mentioned in the introduction to this chapter, successful managers must recognize and exploit opportunities to reduce unit costs either by increasing the scale of operation when economies of scale exist or by decreasing scale in the presence of diseconomies of scale. In the appendix to the next chapter, we will show you how to estimate empirically the long-run average cost curve for your firm.

Sources: Ken Yamada and Kyle Pope, "AST to Acquire PC Business of Tandy Corporation," *The Wall Street Journal,* May 27, 1993; Dana Milbank, "Big Steel Is Threatened by Low-Cost Rivals, Even in Japan, Korea," *The Wall Street Journal,* Feb. 2, 1993.

Long-Run Average Cost as the Planning Horizon

To keep matters simple, we will continue to discuss a firm that employs only two inputs, labor and capital, and capital is the plant size that becomes fixed in the short run (labor is the variable input in the short run). Since the long run is the set of all possible short-run situations, you can think of the long run as a catalog, and each page of the catalog shows a set of short-run cost curves for one of the possible plant sizes. For example, suppose a manager can choose from only three plant sizes, say plants with 10, 30, and 60 units of capital. In this case, the firm's long-run planning horizon is a catalog with three pages: page 1 shows the short-run cost curves when 10 units of capital are employed, page 2 shows the short-run cost curves when 30 units of capital are employed, and page 3 the cost curves for 60 units of capital.

The long-run planning horizon can be constructed by overlaying the cost curves from the three pages of the catalog to form a "group shot" showing all three short-run cost structures in one figure. Figure 9.13 shows the three short-run average total cost (*ATC*) curves for the three plant sizes that make up the planning horizon in

ILLUSTRATION 9.3

Economies of Scale and Scope in Banking

During the 1980s, the banking industry in the United States experienced an unprecedented period of deregulation. One of the key results of this deregulation has been widespread legislative changes by state legislatures allowing interstate banking activities. By 1990, only three states completely prohibited interstate banking. One of the most controversial effects of interstate banking was the consolidation that took place through mergers and acquisitions of local banks by large out-of-state banks. According to Robert Goudreau and Larry Wall, the primary incentives for interstate expansion appear to be to gain market power, to diversify earnings, and to exploit economies of scale and scope.[a] To the extent that significant economies of scale exist in banking, large banks will have a cost advantage over small banks. If there are economies of scope in banking, then banks offering more banking services (products) will have lower costs than banks that provide a small number of services.

Two empirical studies attempted to measure economies of both scale and scope in the financial services industry. John Murray and Robert White studied 61 credit unions in British Columbia.[b] They found significant economies of scale in the credit union industry. Larger credit unions had lower long-run average costs than smaller ones. They also found evidence of economies of scope for credit unions offering a full line of consumer loans and mortgage loans. Thus credit unions that offered automobile loans as well as home mortgage loans could provide mortgage loans and automobile loans at a lower cost than credit unions specializing only in home mortgages or only in automobile loans.

In another study, Thomas Gilligan, Michael Smirlock, and William Marshall examined 714 commercial banks to determine the extent of economies of scale and scope in commercial banking.[c] They concluded that economies of scale in banking are exhausted at relatively low output levels. In other words, the long-run average cost curve (LAC) for commercial banks is shaped like LAC in Panel C of Figure 9.12. When LAC reaches its minimum value at relatively low levels of output, small banks are not necessarily at a cost disadvantage when they compete with large banks. Economies of scope also appear to be present for banks producing the traditional set of bank products (various types of loans and deposits). Given their empirical evidence that economies of scale do not extend over a wide range of output, Gilligan, Smirlock, and Marshall argued that public policymakers should not encourage bank mergers on the basis of cost savings. They also pointed out that government regulations restricting the types of loans and deposits that a bank may offer can lead to higher costs, given their evidence of economies of scope in banking.

[a]Robert Goudreau and Larry Wall, "Southeastern Interstate Banking and Consolidation: 1984–90," *Economic Review* (Federal Reserve Bank of Atlanta), Nov./Dec. 1990, pp. 32–41.

[b]John Murray and Robert White, "Economies of Scale and Economies of Scope in Multiproduct Financial Institutions: A Study of British Columbia Credit Unions," *Journal of Finance*, June 1983, pp. 302–21.

[c]Thomas Gilligan, Michael Smirlock, and William Marshall, "Scale and Scope Economies in the Multi-Product Banking Firm," *Journal of Monetary Economics* 13 (1984), pp. 393–405.

this example: $ATC_{K=10}$, $ATC_{K=30}$, and $ATC_{\bar{K}=60}$. Note that we have omitted the associated AVC and SMC curves to keep the figure as simple as possible.

When the firm wishes to produce any output from 0 to 4,000 units, the manager will choose the small plant size with the cost structure given by $ATC_{K=10}$ because the average cost, and hence the total cost, of producing each output over this range is lower in a plant with 10 units of capital than in a plant with either 30 units or 60 units of capital. For example, when 3,000 units are produced in the plant with 10 units of capital, average cost is $0.50 and total cost is $1,500, which is better than

FIGURE 9.13

Long-Run Average Cost
(*LAC*) as the Planning
Horizon

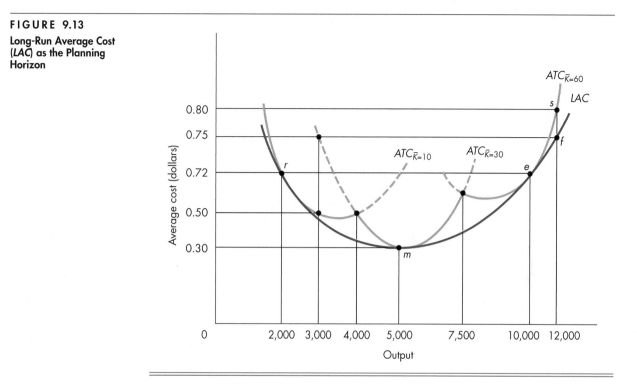

spending $2,250 (= $0.75 × 3,000) to produce 3,000 units in the medium plant with 30 units of capital. (Note that if the *ATC* curve for the large plant in Figure 9.13 is extended leftward to 3,000 units of production, the average and total cost of producing 3,000 units in a plant with 60 units of capital is higher than both of the other two plant sizes.)

When the firm wishes to produce output levels between 4,000 and 7,500 units, the manager would choose the medium plant size (30 units of capital) because $ATC_{\bar{K}=30}$ lies below both of the other two *ATC* curves for all outputs over this range. Following this same reasoning, the manager would choose the large plant size (60 units of capital) with the cost structure shown by $ATC_{\bar{K}=60}$ for any output greater than 7,500 units of production. In this example, the planning horizon, which is precisely the firm's long-run average cost (*LAC*) curve, is formed by the light-colored, solid portions of the three *ATC* curves shown in Figure 9.13.

Firms can generally choose from many more than three plant sizes. When a very large number of plant sizes can be chosen, the *LAC* curve smoothes out and typically takes a ∪-shape as shown by the dark-colored *LAC* curve in Figure 9.13. The set of all tangency points, such as *r*, *m*, and *e* in Figure 9.13, form a *lower envelope* of average costs. For this reason, long-run average cost is called an "envelope" curve.

While we chose to present the firm's planning horizon as the envelope of short-run average cost curves, the same relation holds between the short-run and long-run total or marginal cost curves: Long-run cost curves are always comprised of all possible short-run curves (i.e., they are the envelope curves of their short-run counterparts). Now that we have established the relation between short- and long-run costs, we can demonstrate why short-run costs are generally higher than long-run costs.

Restructuring Short-Run Costs

In the long run, a manager can choose any input combination to produce the desired output level. As we demonstrated earlier in this chapter, the optimal amount of labor and capital for any specific output level is the combination that minimizes the long-run total cost of producing that amount of output. When the firm builds the optimal plant size and employs the optimal amount of labor, the total (and average) cost of producing the intended or planned output will be the same in both the long run and the short run. In other words, long-run and short-run costs are identical when the firm produces the output in the short run for which the fixed plant size (capital input) is optimal. However, if demand or cost conditions change and the manager decides to increase or decrease output in the short run, then the current plant size is no longer optimal. Now the manager will wish to restructure its short-run costs by adjusting plant size to the level that is optimal for the new output level, as soon as the next opportunity for a long-run adjustment arises.[10]

We can demonstrate the gains from restructuring short-run costs by returning to the situation presented in Figure 9.4, which is shown again in Figure 9.14. Recall that the manager wishes to minimize the total cost of producing 10,000 units when the price of labor (w) is $40 per unit and the price of capital (r) is $6 per unit. As explained previously, the manager finds the optimal (cost-minimizing) input combination at point E: $L^* = 90$ and $K^* = 60$. As you also know from our previous discussion, point E lies on the expansion path, which we will now refer to as the "long-run" expansion path in this discussion.

We can most easily demonstrate the gains from adjusting plant size (or capital levels) by employing the concept of a *short-run expansion path*. A **short-run expansion path** gives the cost-minimizing (or output-maximizing) input combination for each level of output when capital is fixed at $\overline{K}$ units in the short run. To avoid any confusion in terminology, we must emphasize that the term "expansion path" always refers to a *long-run* expansion path, while an expansion path for the short run, to distinguish it from its long-run counterpart, is always called a *short-run* expansion path.

short-run expansion path
Horizontal line showing the cost-minimizing input combinations for various output levels when capital is fixed in the short run.

---

[10]A number of things can cause a firm to change output from the intended level used for long-run planning purposes. For example, fluctuations in demand for the firm's product will require a change in output. Alternatively, production costs may change if the expansion path is altered by either a change in the input price ratio (w/r) or a change in technology that reshapes isoquants. While any of these changes can create an opportunity to reduce costs by adjusting input levels, the discussion in this section focuses only on cost savings that arise in response to changes in output along the original long-run expansion path.

FIGURE 9.14

Gains from Restructuring Short-Run Costs

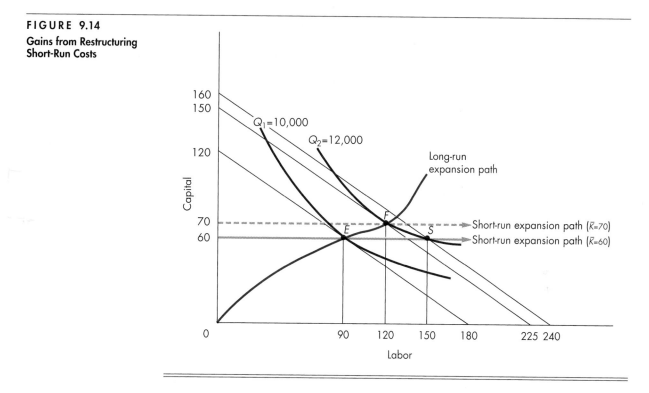

Suppose the manager wishes to produce 10,000 units. From the planning hori-zon in Figure 9.13, the manager determines that a plant size of 60 units of capital is the optimal plant to build for short-run production. As explained previously, once the manager builds the production facility with 60 units of capital, the firm oper-ates with the short-run cost structure given by $ATC_{\bar{K}=60}$. This cost structure corre-sponds to the firm's short-run expansion path in Figure 9.14, which is a horizontal line at 60 units of capital passing through point E on the long-run expansion path. As long as the firm produces 10,000 units in the short run, all of the firm's inputs are optimally adjusted and its long- and short-run costs are identical: Total cost is $7,200 (= $40 × 90 + $60 × 60) and average cost is $0.72 (= $7,200/10,000). In gen-eral, when the firm is producing the output level in the short run using the long-run optimal plant size, ATC and LAC are tangent at that output level. For example, when the firm produces 10,000 units in the short run using 60 units of capital, $ATC_{\bar{K}=60}$ is tangent to LAC at point e.

If the manager decides to increase or decrease output in the short run, short-run production costs will then exceed long-run production costs because input levels will not be at the optimal levels given by the long-run expansion path. For example, if the manager increases output to 12,000 units in the short run, the manager must employ the input combination at point S on the short-run expansion path in

Figure 9.14. The short-run total cost of producing 12,000 units is $9,600 (= $40 × 150 + $60 × 60) and average total cost is $0.80 (= $9,600/12,000) at point *s* in Figure 9.13. Of course, the manager realizes that point *F* is a less costly input combination for producing 12,000 units, since input combination *F* lies on a lower isocost line than *S*. In fact, with input combination *F*, the total cost of producing 12,000 units is $9,000 (= $40 × 120 + $60 × 70), and average cost is $0.75 (= $9,000/12,000), as shown at point *f* in Figure 9.13. Short-run costs exceed long-run costs for output levels below 10,000 units as well, because a plant size of 60 units of capital is too big (i.e., larger than the optimal plant size) for every output below point *E* on the long-run expansion path.

At the next opportunity to adjust plant size, the manager will increase plant size to 70 units, as long as the firm plans to continue producing 12,000 units. Increasing capital to 70 units causes the short-run expansion path to shift upward as shown by the broken horizontal line in Figure 9.14. By restructuring short-run production, the manager reduces the short-run total costs of producing 12,000 units by $600 (= $9,600 − $9,000). As you will see in Part IV, firms can increase their profits—sometimes even convert losses to profits—by adjusting their fixed inputs to create a lower cost structure for short-run production operations. We can now summarize this discussion with following principle.

Principle Since managers have the greatest flexibility to choose inputs in the long run, costs are lower in the long run than in the short run for all output levels except the output level for which the fixed input is at its optimal level. Thus the firm's short-run costs can generally be reduced by adjusting the fixed inputs to their optimal long-run levels when the long-run opportunity to adjust fixed inputs arises.

T ⟩ 14

9.8 SUMMARY

In the long run all inputs are variable. Isoquants show all possible combinations of labor and capital capable of producing a given level of output. Isoquants are downward-sloping to reflect the fact that if larger amounts of labor are used, less capital is required to produce the same output level. The marginal rate of technical substitution (*MRTS*) is the absolute value of the slope of an isoquant and measures the rate at which the two inputs can be substituted for one another while maintaining a constant level of output: $MRTS = -\Delta K/\Delta L$. The marginal rate of technical substitution can be expressed as the ratio of the two marginal products:

$$-\frac{\Delta K}{\Delta L} = MRTS = \frac{MP_L}{MP_K}$$

As labor is substituted for capital, MP_L declines and MP_K rises, causing *MRTS* to diminish along the isoquant.

The isocost curves show the various combinations of inputs that may be purchased for a given dollar outlay. The equation of an isocost curve is given by

$$K = \frac{\overline{C}}{r} - \frac{w}{r}L$$

where $\overline{C}$ is the cost of any of the input combinations on this isocost curve and *w* and *r* are the prices of labor and capital, respectively. The slope of an isocost curve is the negative of the input price ratio $(-w/r)$.

A manager minimizes the total cost of producing a given level of output or maximizes output for a given level of cost (expenditure on inputs) by choosing an input combination at the point of tangency between the relevant isoquant and isocost curves. The point of tangency indicates the *lowest* isocost curve that includes an input combination that is capable of producing the desired output level. Alternatively, the point of tangency indicates the largest output (the highest isoquant) that is attainable from any combination on the given isocost curve.

Since the cost-minimizing or output-maximizing input combination occurs at the point of tangency between the isoquant and the isocost curve, the slopes of the two curves are equal at the optimal input combination. The optimization condition may be expressed as

$$MRTS = \frac{MP_L}{MP_K} = \frac{w}{r}$$

or

$$\frac{MP_L}{w} = \frac{MP_K}{r}$$

Thus the marginal product per dollar spent on the last unit of each input is the same. Equating marginal product per dollar spent on all variable inputs is the rule managers should follow both in the long run when all inputs are variable and in the short run when two or more inputs are variable.

The expansion path shows the equilibrium (or optimal) input combination for every level of output. An expansion path shows how input usage changes when output changes, input prices remaining constant. Along the expansion path the marginal rate of technical substitution is constant, because the ratio of input prices (w/r) is constant. All points on the expansion path are both cost-minimizing and output-maximizing combinations of labor and capital.

Returns to scale, a long-run concept, involve the effect on output of changing all inputs by equiproportionate amounts. If all inputs are increased by a factor of c and output goes up by a factor of z, then a firm experiences increasing returns to scale if $z > c$, constant returns to scale if $z = c$, and decreasing returns to scale if $z < c$.

The long-run cost curves are derived from the expansion path. Since the expansion path gives the efficient combination of labor and capital used to produce any particular level of output, the long-run total cost of producing that output level is the sum of the optimal amounts of labor and capital times their prices. Long-run average cost (*LAC*) is defined as

$$LAC = LTC/Q$$

and is U-shaped. Long-run marginal cost (*LMC*) is defined as

$$LMC = \Delta LTC/\Delta Q$$

and is also U-shaped. *LMC* lies below (above) *LAC* over the output range for which *LAC* is decreasing (increasing). *LMC* crosses *LAC* at the minimum point on *LAC*. When *LAC* is decreasing, economies of scale are present. When *LAC* is increasing, diseconomies are present.

When a firm produces more than one good or service, economies of scope may be present. Economies of scope exist when the joint cost of producing two or more goods is less than the sum of the separate costs of producing the goods. In the case of two goods X and Y, economies of scope are measured by

$$SC = \frac{C(X) + C(Y) - C(X,Y)}{C(X,Y)}$$

where SC is greater (less) than 0 when (dis)economies of scope exist.

The long-run average cost curve gives the lowest possible unit costs of producing various output levels because in the long run all inputs are adjusted optimally and the firm operates on the (long-run) expansion path. Once the firm installs the optimal input combination for its planned production level, the firm then operates in the short run, facing the set of short-run cost curves determined by the amount of the fixed input selected from the long-run planning horizon. Because managers have the greatest flexibility in choosing inputs in the long run, long-run costs are lower than short-run costs for all output levels except the output level for which the fixed input is at its optimal level. Unless the firm is operating at the point of intersection between the long-run expansion path and its current short-run expansion path, a firm's short-run costs can be reduced by adjusting the fixed inputs to their optimal long-run levels when the opportunity to adjust fixed inputs arises in the long run.

TECHNICAL PROBLEMS

1. The accompanying figure shows the isoquant for producing 1,000 units.

   a. At point A in the figure, the marginal rate of technical substitution (MRTS) is _____.

   b. At point A in the figure, increasing labor usage by 1 unit requires that the manager _____ (increase, decrease) capital usage by (approximately) _____ units to keep the level of production at exactly 1,000 units.

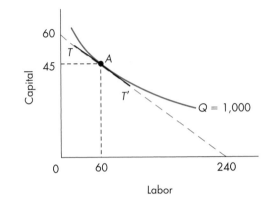

   c. If the marginal product of the 45th unit of capital is 80, then the marginal product of the 60th unit of labor is _____.

2. The price of capital is $50 per unit. Use the accompanying figure, which shows an isocost curve, to answer the questions that follow:

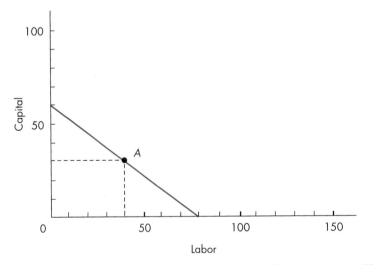

   a. The equation for the isocost curve shown in the figure is K = _____. The price of labor is $_____ per unit. The total cost associated with this isocost curve is $_____.

b. Input combination A is _____ units of labor and _____ units of capital. The total cost of input combination A is $_____. Verify that point A satisfies the isocost equation in part a.

c. For the input prices used in parts a and b, construct the isocost curve for input combinations costing $4,500. For the $4,500 isocost curve, the capital intercept is _____ and the labor intercept is _____. The equation of the isocost curve is K = _____. If 40 units of labor are employed, then _____ units of capital can be employed for a total cost of $4,500.

3. In the accompanying figure, labor costs $100 per unit. The manager wants to produce 2,500 units of output. Answer the following questions:

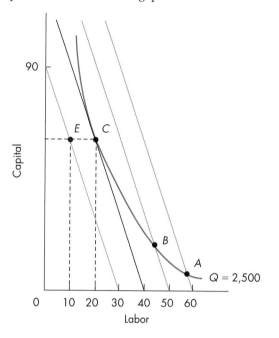

a. At point A, the MRTS is _____ (less than, greater than, equal to) the input price ratio w/r. The total cost of producing 2,500 units with input combination A is $_____. The price of capital is $_____ per unit.

b. By moving from A to B, the manager _____ (decreases, increases) labor usage and _____ (decreases, increases) capital usage. The move from A to B decreases _____ but leaves _____ unchanged. At B, MRTS is _____ (less than, greater than, equal to) the input price ratio w/r. The total cost of producing at B is $_____.

c. At point C, the manager _____ the _____ cost of producing 2,500 units of output. MRTS is _____ (less than, greater than, equal to) the input price ratio w/r.

d. The optimal input combination is _____ units of labor and _____ units of capital. The minimum total cost for which 2,500 units can be produced is $_____.

e. Input combination E costs $_____. Explain why the manager does not choose input combination E.

4. Suppose a firm is currently using 500 laborers and 325 units of capital to produce its product. The wage rate is $25, and the price of capital is $130. The last laborer adds 25 units to total output, while the last unit of capital adds 65 units to total output. Is the manager of this firm making the optimal input choice? Why or why not? If not, what should the manager do?

5. In the following graph, LZ is the isocost curve and Q_1 is an isoquant.

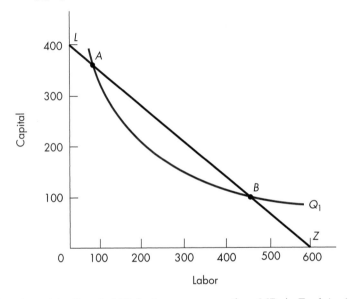

a. For input combination A, MP_L/w is _____ than MP_K/r. Explain, in terms of MP_L/w and MP_K/r, why combination A is not efficient.

b. For input combination B, MP_L/w is _____ than MP_K/r. Explain, in terms of MP_L/w and MP_K/r, why combination B is not efficient.

c. In the graph, find and label the optimal input combination for producing the output designated by isoquant Q_1. (*Hint:* You need to use the straight edge of a ruler.)

6. An expansion path can be derived under the assumption either that the manager attempts to produce each output at minimum cost or that the manager attempts to produce the maximum output at each level of cost. The paths are identical in both cases. Explain.

7. In the following graph, the price of capital is $100 per unit.

a. The price of labor is $_____.

b. To produce 500 units efficiently, a manager would use _____ units of labor and _____ units of capital. The minimum cost of producing 500 units is $_____.

c. To produce 1,000 units efficiently, a manager would use _____ units of labor and _____ units of capital. The minimum cost of producing 1,000 units is $_____.

d. To produce 1,500 units efficiently, a manager would use _____ units of labor and _____ units of capital. The minimum cost of producing 1,500 units is $_____.

e. In the graph, construct the expansion path.

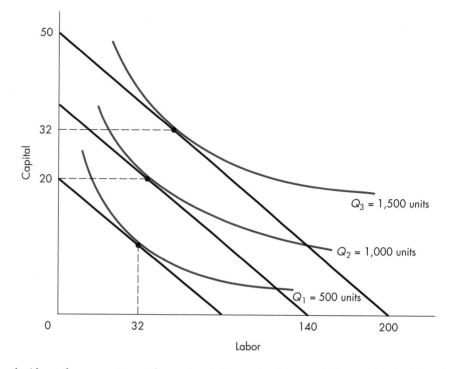

f. Along the expansion path constructed in part *e*, the marginal rate of technical substitution is equal to _____.

8. The following figure shows two points of production, *A* and *B*, and the levels of output for each input combination. Assume a manager moves from *A* to *B*.

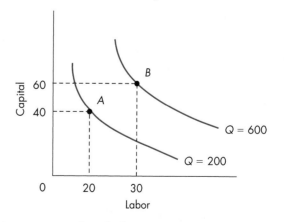

a. The proportionate amount by which input usage increases, *c*, is _____.

b. The proportionate amount by which output increases, *z*, is _____.

c. Since *c* is _____ (less than, equal to, greater than) *z*, _____ returns to scale are present when the manager adjusts input usage from point *A* to point *B*.

9. The accompanying graph shows five points on a firm's expansion path when the price of labor is $25 per unit and the price of capital is $100 per unit. From this graph, fill in the blanks in the following table:

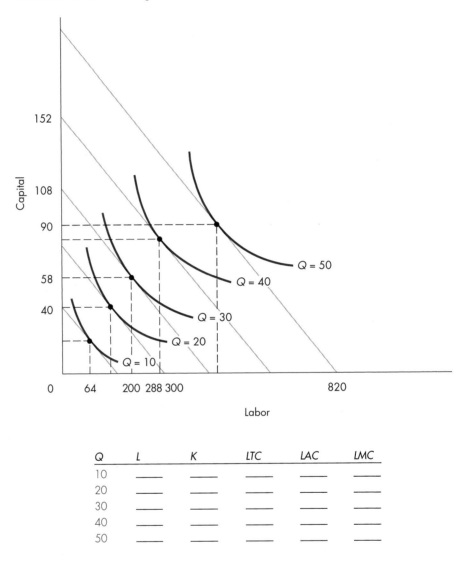

Q	L	K	LTC	LAC	LMC
10	____	____	____	____	____
20	____	____	____	____	____
30	____	____	____	____	____
40	____	____	____	____	____
50	____	____	____	____	____

10. In problem 9, economies of scale exist over the range of output _____ to _____ units. Diseconomies of scale exist over the range of output _____ to _____ units.

11. For the firm in Figure 9.12 that experiences constant long-run costs, calculate the following costs:

    a. At 200 units of output, long-run average cost is $_____, long-run marginal cost is $_____, and long-run total cost is $_____.

b. At 500 units of output, long-run average cost is $_____, long-run marginal cost is $_____, and long-run total cost is $_____.

c. Under what circumstances of production can a firm experience constant long-run costs as shown in Figure 9.12?

12. Using the example in the text concerning Precision Muffler, calculate the degree to which economies of scope exist (*SC*) when the firm is producing 25 muffler replacements and 10 brake jobs. Are there economies or diseconomies of scope?

13. Use Figure 9.13 to answer the following questions.

a. If the firm produces 5,000 units of output with a plant using 10 units of capital, the average cost is $_____ and total cost is $_____.

b. If the firm produces 5,000 units of output with a plant using 30 units of capital, the average cost is $_____ and total cost is $_____.

c. In the long-run planning horizon, which plant should the manager choose to produce 5,000 units of output? Why?

14. The following figure shows the long-run and short-run expansion paths illustrated in Figure 9.14. Continue to assume that the price of labor is $40 per unit and the price of capital is $60 per unit. The manager is operating in the short run with 60 units of capital. Suppose the manager wants to produce 8,000 units of output.

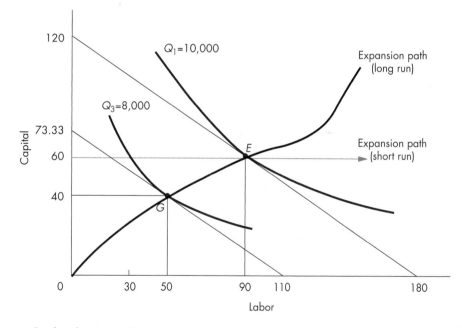

a. In the short run, the cost-minimizing input combination is _____ units of labor and _____ units of capital.

b. The short-run total cost of producing 8,000 units is $_____ and average total cost (*ATC*) is $_____ per unit.

c. If the manager plans to continue producing 8,000 units in the long run, the manager could lower the total cost of producing 8,000 units by $_____ by employing _____ units of labor and _____ units of capital.

d. Construct the new short-run expansion path once the long-run adjustment in part *c* has been completed.

APPLIED PROBLEMS

1. A study by the Computer Manufacturers Association of America analyzed the significant increase in the usage of computers by business firms in the United States over the last two decades. In terms of production theory, one might say the computer-labor ratio has risen.

   a. Using production theory, provide a rationale for this trend.

   b. Given the falling prices of business computers, what types of changes in business offices would you expect to have occurred?

2. The Largo Publishing House uses 400 printers and 200 printing presses to produce books. A printer's wage rate is $20, and the price of a printing press is $5,000. The last printer added 20 books to total output, while the last press added 1,000 books to total output. Is the publishing house making the optimal input choice? Why or why not? If not, how should the manager of Largo Publishing House adjust input usage?

3. How does the theory of efficient production apply to managers of government bureaus or departments that are not run for profit? How about nonprofit clubs that collect just enough dues from their members to cover the cost of operation?

4. The MorTex Company assembles garments entirely by hand even though a textile machine exists that can assemble garments faster than a human can. Workers cost $50 per day, and each additional laborer can produce 200 more units per day (i.e., marginal product is constant and equal to 200). Installation of the first textile machine on the assembly line will increase output by 1,800 units daily. Currently the firm assembles 5,400 units per day.

   a. The financial analysis department at MorTex estimates that the price of a textile machine is $600 per day. Can management reduce the cost of assembling 5,400 units per day by purchasing a textile machine and using less labor? Why or why not?

   b. The Textile Workers of America is planning to strike for higher wages. Management predicts that if the strike is successful, the cost of labor will increase to $100 per day. If the strike is successful, how would this affect the decision in part *a* to purchase a textile machine? Explain.

5. Gamma Corporation, one of the firms that retains you as a financial analyst, is considering buying out Beta Corporation, a small manufacturing firm that is now barely operating at a profit. You recommend the buyout because you believe that new management could substantially reduce production costs, and thereby increase profit to a quite attractive level. You collect the following product information in order to convince the CEO at Gamma Corporation that Beta is indeed operating inefficiently:

$$MP_L = 10 \qquad P_L = \$20$$
$$MP_K = 15 \qquad P_K = \$15$$

Explain how these data provide evidence of inefficiency. How could the new manager of Beta Corporation improve efficiency?

6. Government at all levels sometimes imposes regulations on business firms, such as pollution controls on the amount of emissions, safety regulations for workers, and requirements on access for workers or customers with disabilities.

    a. How might such regulations be thought of as being negative technological change—that is, technological deterioration rather than technological improvement?

    b. What effect would such regulations be expected to have?

    c. Given your answer to part *b* of this question, is it still possible for such regulations to be efficient from the point of view of society? Explain.

7. We frequently hear the following terms used by businesspersons. What does each mean in economic terminology?

    a. Spreading the overhead.

    b. A break-even level of production.

    c. The efficiency of mass production.

8. The production engineers at Impact Industries have derived the expansion path shown in the following figure. The price of labor is $100 per unit.

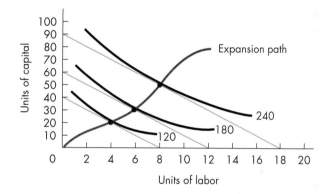

    a. What price does Impact Industries pay for capital?

    b. If the manager at Impact decides to produce 180 units of output, how much labor and capital should be used in order to minimize total cost?

    c. What is the total cost of producing 120, 180, and 240 units of output in the long run?

    d. Impact Industries originally built the plant (i.e., purchased the amount of capital) designed to produce 180 units optimally. *In the short run with capital fixed,* if the manager decides to expand production to 240 units, what is the amount of labor and capital that will be used? (*Hint:* How must the firm expand output in the short run when capital is fixed?)

    e. Given your answer to part *d,* calculate average variable, average fixed, and average total cost in the short run.

9. Commercial bakeries typically sell a variety of products (breads, rolls, muffins, cakes, etc.) to local grocery stores. There are substantial economies of scale in the production of each one of the bakery products, which makes it cost-effective for bakeries to specialize in the production of just one product. Grocery stores, however, prefer to buy from multiproduct bakeries that sell a full line of bakery products. How might managers organize production to take advantage of the economies of scale and scope in production and marketing that exist in the baking industry?

10. The Qwik Serve Walk-In Clinic always has three M.D.s and eight R.N.s working at its 24-hour clinic, which serves customers with minor emergencies and ailments. The clinic has hired an efficiency expert to examine its operations and make suggestions for reducing costs.

    For some of the medical procedures done at the clinic, experienced nurses can perform the medical tasks approximately as well as the physicians can, as long as the nurses are supervised by M.D.s. Since M.D.s are more highly trained than nurses, the marginal product of M.D.s is higher than the marginal product of R.N.s.

    The manager of the clinic is confused by the efficiency consultant's report because the report recommends using more R.N.s and fewer M.D.s to lower the cost of providing a given level of medical services. Under what circumstances would it be economically efficient for this clinic to use more R.N.s and fewer M.D.s (given $MP_{MD} > MP_{RN}$)? Explain.

11. The speed at which data are transmitted in a computer chip can be dramatically increased by deep-freezing the "interconnects"—wires that connect computer chips—to temperatures in the range of 75 to 125 degrees below zero centigrade. *The Wall Street Journal* reported that "such cooling (technology) was considered 10 years ago, but was rejected as too costly and cumbersome in light of easier chip advancements." Now, according to the *WSJ*, improvements in cooling technology have created widespread interest. A vice president of research at IBM says, "The technology may [now be able to] as much as double processor performance," while the cost of the technology has "less-than-doubled." Explain in terms of the marginal product per dollar spent on this cooling technology:

    a. Why the cooling technology was *not* adopted by computer manufacturers 10 years ago.

    b. Why "the whole industry is looking at it again" 10 years later.

12. Ross Perot added his memorable "insight" to the debate over the North American Free Trade Agreement (NAFTA) when he warned that passage of NAFTA would create a "giant sucking sound" as U.S. employers shipped jobs to Mexico, where wages are lower than wages in the United States. As it turned out, many U.S. firms chose *not* to produce in Mexico despite the much lower wages there. Explain why it may not be economically efficient to move production to foreign countries, even ones with substantially lower wages.

☐   **MATHEMATICAL APPENDIX**   **Production and Cost Relations with Two Variable Inputs**

Production with Two Variable Inputs

This appendix examines the manager's choice of the optimal input combination for variable proportions production, and it relates this choice of inputs to the costs of production. Two situations are examined. In the first, a long-run decision framework is developed. We specify the production function as $Q = f(L, K)$ and assume both L and K are variable inputs. Since all inputs in the production function are variable, this is a long-run production decision. We derive mathematically the rules for cost

minimization given an output constraint and for output maximization given a cost constraint. We then show how to derive the input demand functions for L and K and how to derive the expansion path in the long run. We also demonstrate the relation between the long-run average and marginal costs. We end our discussion of the long run with a derivation of long-run costs for the specific production function $Q = AL^aK^{1-a}$.

In the second situation, we briefly show how the optimization rules are identical for short-run decisions in which three inputs are employed, $Q = f(L, M, K)$. Two of these inputs, labor (L) and raw materials (M), are variable inputs, while the third input, capital (K), is fixed in the short run. In this short-run situation, we examine only the optimal choice for minimizing the cost of producing a given output.

Cost Minimization When All Inputs Are Variable

Define a two-input production function as

$$(1) \qquad Q = f(L, K)$$

The marginal products of the two inputs are the partial derivatives

$$MP_L = \frac{\partial Q}{\partial L} \quad \text{and} \quad MP_K = \frac{\partial Q}{\partial K}$$

Before we begin discussing optimization, we will establish that the slope of an isoquant (in absolute value) can be expressed as the ratio of the marginal products. Begin by taking the total differential of the production function in equation (1) above:

$$dQ = \frac{\partial f}{\partial L} dL + \frac{\partial f}{\partial K} dK = MP_L dL + MP_K dK$$

Along an isoquant dL and dK must be such that dQ is 0. Thus we set $dQ = 0$ and solve for the *MRTS*:

$$MP_L dL + MP_K dK = 0$$

$$MP_K dK = - MP_L dL$$

$$MRTS \equiv -\frac{dK}{dL} = \frac{MP_L}{MP_K}$$

Now consider a manager who plans to produce a specific level of output, denoted as $\overline{Q}$. The manager's optimization problem is to choose L and K to minimize the long-run total cost (C) of producing $\overline{Q}$ units of output. Given input prices for L and K, denoted as w and r, respectively, the long-run total cost of employing any input combination (L, K) is $C = wL + rK$. The constrained minimization problem is solved by minimizing the following Lagrangian function:

$$\mathcal{L} = wL + rK + \lambda[\overline{Q} - f(L, K)]$$

where λ is the Lagrangian multiplier. Minimization of the Lagrangian equation, which is a function of three variables L, K, and λ, requires that L, K, and λ be chosen such

that the first-order necessary conditions in the following system are simultaneously satisfied:

$$(2a) \qquad \frac{\partial \mathcal{L}}{\partial L} = w - \frac{\partial Q}{\partial L} = 0$$

$$(2b) \qquad \frac{\partial \mathcal{L}}{\partial K} = r - \frac{\partial Q}{\partial K} = 0$$

$$(2c) \qquad \frac{\partial \mathcal{L}}{\partial \lambda} = \overline{Q} - f(L, K) = 0$$

Combining conditions (2a) and (2b) in ratio form, it follows that the necessary condition for minimizing the cost of producing $\overline{Q}$ units of output is

$$(3) \quad \frac{w}{r} = \frac{\partial Q/\partial L}{\partial Q/\partial K} = \frac{MP_L}{MP_K} = MRTS \quad \text{or} \quad \frac{MP_L}{w} = \frac{MP_K}{r}$$

Necessary condition (3) for minimization requires that the manager choose an input combination such that the slope of the isocost line is equal to the slope of the isoquant, which is the tangency solution derived in this chapter. Thus conditions (2a) and (2b) require that the manager select input combinations that lie on the expansion path. Alternatively, the conditions for minimization require that the marginal products per dollar spent on each input be equal. Finally, to ensure that $\overline{Q}$ units of output are produced, the manager must not only be on the expansion path but also be on the $\overline{Q}$ isoquant. Necessary condition (2c) forces the manager to be on the $\overline{Q}$ isoquant.

Output Maximization When All Inputs Are Variable

Now let the manager choose L and K to maximize output for a given level of total cost, C. This constrained maximization problem is solved by maximizing the following Lagrangian function:

$$\mathcal{L} = f(L, K) + \lambda(\overline{C} - wL - rK)$$

Maximization of the Lagrangian equation, which is a function of three variables, L, K, and λ, requires that L, K, and λ be chosen so that the following partial derivatives simultaneously equal 0:

$$(4a) \qquad \frac{\partial \mathcal{L}}{\partial L} = \frac{\partial Q}{\partial L} - \lambda w = 0$$

$$(4b) \qquad \frac{\partial \mathcal{L}}{\partial K} = \frac{\partial Q}{\partial K} - \lambda r = 0$$

$$(4c) \qquad \frac{\partial \mathcal{L}}{\partial \lambda} = \overline{C} - wL - rK = 0$$

Combining conditions (4a) and (4b) in ratio form, it follows that the necessary condition for maximizing output for a given level of cost is the same as that in expression (3), the conditions for cost minimization.

Thus, as we showed in this chapter, both cost minimization or output maximization require that the manager choose the input combination where the isoquant is tangent to the isocost line. The tangency requirement can also be interpreted as requiring the marginal product per dollar spent on the last unit of each input to be the same. [*Note:* Maximization condition (4c) forces the manager to select L and K from the $\overline{C}$ isocost line.]

The Expansion Path and Efficient Input-Usage Functions

We now derive the expansion line when L and K are both variable inputs. Then, using the expansion path, the efficient levels of L and K can be expressed as functions of Q, w, and r. Recall from the chapter that the expansion path is the locus of L and K combinations for which the marginal rate of technical substitution equals the (constant) input price ratio. Thus the expansion path can be expressed as

(5) $$K^* = K^*(L^*; w, r)$$

where K^* and L^* are the efficient levels of input usage for producing various levels of output, *given* fixed input prices w and r. The expansion path in expression (5) is obtained from expression (3) by solving algebraically for K^* in terms of L^*, w, and r. For each value of L^* in (5), there is a single value of K^*.

From the expansion path, it is possible to express the optimal levels of input usage as functions of $\overline{Q}$ given the fixed input prices w and r:

(6a) $$L^* = L^*(\overline{Q}; w, r)$$

(6b) $$K^* = K^*(\overline{Q}; w, r)$$

To derive the efficient input-usage functions (6a) and (6b), substitute the values of labor and capital (L^*, K^*) that solve the system of first-order necessary conditions (2a to 2c) for the cost-minimization problem in expression (2c):

(7) $$\overline{Q} - f(L^*, K^*) = 0$$

To find $L^*(\overline{Q}; w, r)$, substitute the expansion path equation (5) into (7) and solve for L^* in terms of $\overline{Q}$, w, and r. To find $K^*(\overline{Q}; w, r)$, substitute the expression $L^*(Q; w, r)$ into the expansion path equation (5) to get $K^*(\overline{Q}; w, r)$. The efficient

input functions, which are derived from the expansion path, are used to derive the long-run cost functions for a firm. Later in this appendix, we show how this is done for the production function $Q = AL^aK^{1-a}$.

Cost Relations in the Long Run

As noted, the efficient input-usage functions are employed to derive the cost functions for a firm in the long run. Long-run total cost LTC for each level of output can be expressed as

(8) $$LTC = LTC(Q; w, r) = wL^*(Q; w, r) + rK^*(Q; w, r)$$

Because LTC is expressed as a function of *efficient* input usage, the LTC function embodies economic efficiency. That is, for any level of output, and a given set of input prices w and r, LTC is the lowest possible cost for producing that output level when a manager is able to vary the levels of input usage for all inputs in the long run.

Long-run average cost (LAC) and long-run marginal cost (LMC) are defined as

(9) $$LAC = \frac{LTC(Q; w, r)}{Q}$$

and

(10) $$LMC = \frac{\partial LTC(Q; w, r)}{\partial Q}$$

The relation between LAC and LMC is identical to the relation between ATC (and AVC) and SMC in the short-run situation. *When LAC is decreasing (increasing), LMC is less (greater) than LAC. When LAC reaches its minimum value, $LMC = LAC$.* The mathematical derivation of these results follows precisely the procedure set forth for the short-run situation in the appendix to Chapter 8.

The Expansion Path and Long-Run Costs: $Q = AL^aK^{1-a}$

Let the production function be defined as $Q = AL^aK^{1-a}$, where a is restricted by $0 < a < 1$. Begin by finding the two marginal product functions:

(11a) $$MP_L = \frac{\partial Q}{\partial L} = aAL^{a-1}K^{1-a}$$

(11b) $$MP_K = \frac{\partial Q}{\partial K} = (1 - a)AL^aK^{-a}$$

The *MRTS* can be expressed as the ratio of the marginal products:

$$(12) \quad MRTS = \frac{MP_L}{MP_K} = \frac{aAL^{a-1}K^{1-a}}{(1-a)AL^aK^{-a}} = \frac{a}{(1-a)}\frac{K}{L}$$

Since the *MRTS* is a function of the capital-labor ratio (*K/L*), the *MRTS* will be constant along a straight line out of the origin in *K-L* space. Thus the expansion path must be linear in this case. (Why?) The expansion path, given fixed input prices *w* and *r*, is derived from the tangency condition:

$$(13) \qquad \frac{aK^*}{(1-a)L^*} = \frac{w}{r}$$

Substituting for *K**, the expansion path is expressed as

$$(14) \qquad K^* = K^*(L^*; w, r) = \frac{w}{r}\frac{(1-a)}{a}L^*$$

As noted, the expansion path for this production function is a straight line out of the origin: $K^* = mL^*$, where $m = w(1-a)/ra > 0$.

Now we derive the efficient input-usage functions. For *L**, substitute (14) into (2c):

$$(15) \quad \overline{Q} - f(L^*, K^*) = \overline{Q} - A(L^*)^a\left(\frac{w}{r}\frac{1-a}{a}L^*\right)^{1-a} = 0$$

Solving implicit function (15) for *L** yields the following efficient usage function for labor:

$$(16) \qquad L^* = L^*(\overline{Q}; w, r) = \frac{\overline{Q}}{A}\left[\frac{w(1-a)}{ra}\right]^{-(1-a)}$$

To find the efficient usage function for capital, substitute (16) into (14):

$$(17) \quad K^* = K^*(\overline{Q}; w, r) = \frac{w}{r}\frac{1-a}{a}\left[\frac{\overline{Q}}{A}\left(\frac{w(1-a)}{ra}\right)^{-(1-a)}\right]$$

$$= \left(\frac{w}{r}\frac{1-a}{a}\right)^{1-(1-a)}\frac{\overline{Q}}{A}$$

$$= \left(\frac{w}{r}\frac{1-a}{a}\right)^a\frac{\overline{Q}}{A}$$

The efficient input-usage functions (16) and (17) are single-valued functions; that is, for any $\overline{Q}$, there is a single

*L** and a single *K**. The long-run cost functions are derived using the efficient input-usage functions for *L** and *K**:

$$(18) \quad LTC(Q; w, r) = wL^* + rK^*$$

$$= \frac{Q}{A}w^ar^{1-a}\left[\left(\frac{a}{1-a}\right)^{1-a} + \left(\frac{1-a}{a}\right)^a\right]$$

$$(19) \quad LAC(Q; w, r) = \frac{LTC}{Q}$$

$$= \frac{1}{A}w^ar^{1-a}\left[\left(\frac{a}{1-a}\right)^{1-a} + \left(\frac{1-a}{a}\right)^a\right]$$

$$(20) \quad LMC(Q; w, r) = \frac{\partial LTC}{\partial Q}$$

$$= \frac{1}{A}w^ar^{1-a}\left[\left(\frac{a}{1-a}\right)^{1-a} + \left(\frac{1-a}{a}\right)^a\right]$$

Notice that, for this production function, *LAC* and *LMC* are constant (i.e., not functions of *Q*) and are the same (*LAC* = *LMC*).

Short-Run Production and Costs with Two Variable Inputs

Let the firm produce in the short run with two variable inputs, labor (*L*) and raw materials (*M*), and one fixed input, capital (*K*). The short-run production function in this situation can be expressed as

$$(21) \qquad Q = f(L, M, \overline{K}) = g(L, M)$$

With fixed input prices, *w*, *i*, and *r*, the short-run total cost of production is *TC* = *TVC* + *TFC*, where *wL* + *iM* is *TVC* and $r\overline{K}$ is *TFC*. The short-run constrained minimization problem is solved by minimizing the following Lagrangian function:

$$\mathscr{L} = wL + iM + r\overline{K} + \lambda[\overline{Q} - g(L, M)]$$

Minimization of the Lagrangian equation, which is a function of three variables *L*, *M*, and λ, requires that *L*, *M*, and λ be chosen such that the first-order necessary conditions in the following system are simultaneously satisfied:

$$(22a) \qquad \frac{\partial \mathscr{L}}{\partial L} = w - \lambda\frac{\partial g(L, M)}{\partial L} = 0$$

$$(22b) \qquad \frac{\partial \mathscr{L}}{\partial M} = i - \lambda\frac{\partial g(L, M)}{\partial M} = 0$$

$$(22c) \qquad \frac{\partial \mathscr{L}}{\partial \lambda} = \overline{Q} - g(L, M) = 0$$

Combining conditions (22a) and (22b) in ratio form, it follows that the necessary condition for minimizing the cost of producing $\overline{Q}$ units of output is

Necessary condition (23) shows that the manager chooses *variable* inputs in exactly the same way regardless of whether it is the short run or the long run.

(23) $$\frac{w}{i} = \frac{\partial Q/\partial L}{\partial Q/\partial M} = \frac{MP_L}{MP_M} \quad \text{or} \quad \frac{MP_L}{w} = \frac{MP_M}{i}$$

MATHEMATICAL EXERCISES

1. The production function is $Q = AL^aK^b$, where $a > 0$ and $b > 0$.
    a. The marginal product of labor is $MP_L = $ _____.
    b. The marginal product of capital is $MP_K = $ _____.
    c. The marginal rate of technical substitution is $MRTS = $ _____.
    d. Show that the isoquants for this production function are convex. [*Hint:* Show that $MRTS$ diminishes as L increases. (Why?)]
    e. Derive the equation for the long-run expansion path.
2. For the production function in exercise 1, let the price of labor be w and the price of capital be r.
    a. The efficient usage function for labor is $L^* = $ _____.
    b. The efficient usage function for capital is $K^* = $ _____.
    c. Find the long-run cost functions: LTC, LAC, and LMC.
    d. Show that both LAC and LMC increase at any Q when either w or r increases.
3. The production function for a firm is $Q = 24L^{.5}K^{.5}$. In the short run, the firm has a fixed amount of capital, $\overline{K} = 121$. The price of labor is $10 per unit, and the price of capital is $20 per unit.
    a. The short-run production function is $Q = $ _____.
    b. The marginal product of labor is $MP_L = $ _____. Show that the marginal product of labor diminishes for all levels of labor usage.
    c. Write the equation for the short-run expansion path.
    d. Derive the short-run TVC, TFC, and TC functions.
    e. Derive SMC, AVC, ATC, and AFC.
4. For the production function in exercise 3:
    a. Find the long-run expansion path.
    b. Derive the efficient input-usage functions for labor and capital.
    c. Derive the long-run cost functions: LTC, LAC, and LMC.
    d. Show that neither economies nor diseconomies of scale exist at any level of production.

CHAPTER
10

Production and Cost Estimation

empirical production function
The mathematical form of the production function to be estimated.

M anagers use estimates of production and cost functions to make output, pricing, hiring, and investment decisions. Chapters 8 and 9 set forth the basic theories of production and cost. We will now show you some statistical techniques that can be used to estimate production and cost functions. The focus will be on estimating short-run production functions and short-run cost functions. These are the functions that managers need to make a firm's pricing, output, and hiring decisions. Although long-run production and cost functions can help managers make long-run decisions about investments in plant and equipment, most of the analysis in this text concerns short-run operational decisions. Application of regression analysis to the estimation of short-run production and cost functions is a rather straightforward task. However, because of difficult problems with the data that are required to estimate long-run production and cost functions—as well as the more complex regression equations required—managers typically restrict their use of regression analysis to estimation of short-run production and cost functions.

We begin by showing how to use regression analysis to estimate short-run production functions. The first step in estimating a production function and the associated product curves (such as average product and marginal product) is to specify the **empirical production function,** which is the exact mathematical form of the equation to be estimated. We discuss how to specify a cubic equation to estimate short-run production functions when only one input, labor, is variable. As we see, the cubic equation has the properties of the theoretical short-run production function discussed in Chapter 8. Next, we explain how to estimate the parameters of the short-run production function and test for statistical significance.

After developing the techniques of empirical production analysis, we turn to estimation of short-run cost equations. The cubic specification is also employed to estimate the short-run cost functions. The analysis of empirical cost functions begins with a brief discussion of some general issues concerning the nature of estimating cost functions, such as adjusting for inflation and measurement of economic cost. We then explain how to estimate the various short-run cost functions derived in Chapter 8: the average variable cost (*AVC*), marginal cost (*SMC*), and total variable cost (*TVC*) curves. Then we demonstrate how to estimate and test the parameters of these cost functions.

We must stress at the outset that the purpose here is not so much to teach you how to do the actual estimations of the functions but, rather, to show how to use and interpret the estimates of production and cost equations. As emphasized in Chapter 4, the computer will do the tedious calculations involved with estimation. However, you must tell it what to estimate. Therefore, you should learn how to choose the particular function that is best suited for the purpose at hand.

As already noted, this chapter focuses primarily on short-run production and cost estimation. However, we have set forth the techniques used to estimate long-run production and cost functions in the appendix at the end of this chapter. Once you see that application of regression analysis to short-run functions is rather easy, you may wish to tackle this more difficult appendix treating long-run empirical analysis.

10.1 SPECIFICATION OF THE SHORT-RUN PRODUCTION FUNCTION

Before describing how to estimate short-run production functions, we will first specify an appropriate functional form for the long-run production function. Recall from Chapter 8 that the short-run production function is derived from the long-run production function when holding the levels of some inputs constant. Once the fixed inputs are held constant at some predetermined levels and only one input is allowed to vary, the production equation to be estimated should have the theoretical characteristics set forth in Chapter 8.

In this chapter, we will continue to consider the case of two variable inputs, labor and capital. The most general form of such a production function is

$$Q = f(L, K)$$

long-run production function
A production function in which all inputs are variable.

In this form, the production function can be viewed as a **long-run production function** because both labor (*L*) and capital (*K*) are variable inputs. In the short run, when the level of capital usage is fixed at *K*, the **short-run production function** is expressed in general form as

$$Q = f(L, \overline{K}) = g(L)$$

short-run production function
A production function in which at least one input is fixed.

The exact mathematical form of this production function is frequently referred to as the *estimable form* of the production function. In general, an *estimable form* of an equation—whether it is a production equation, cost equation, or any other type of equation—is the exact mathematical form of the equation that can be estimated using regression analysis.

cubic production function
A production function of the form $Q = aK^3L^3 + bK^2L^2$.

A suitable functional form for estimating either a long-run or a short-run production function is the **cubic production function:**

$$Q = aK^3L^3 + bK^2L^2$$

For this form of the production function, both inputs are required to produce output. If either capital or labor usage equals zero, no output is produced. Furthermore, the cubic production function has convex isoquants, so the marginal rate of technical substitution diminishes as required by the theory of production. (All the mathematical properties of cubic production functions set forth in this chapter are mathematically derived in this chapter's appendix.)

short-run cubic production function
A production function of the form $Q = AL^3 + BL^2$.

Holding capital constant at $\overline{K}$ units ($K = \overline{K}$), the **short-run cubic production function** is

$$Q = a\overline{K}^3L^3 + b\overline{K}^2L^2$$

$$= AL^3 + BL^2$$

where $A = a\overline{K}^3$ and $B = b\overline{K}^2$, and both A and B are constant when $\overline{K}$ is constant. The average and marginal products for the cubic short-run production function are, respectively,

$$AP = \frac{Q}{L} = AL^2 + BL$$

and

$$MP = \frac{\Delta Q}{\Delta L} = 3AL^2 + 2BL$$

As shown in the appendix, for the average and marginal products to first rise, reach a maximum, and then fall (as illustrated in Chapter 8), A must be negative and B must be positive. This requires that, in the above production function, $a < 0$ and $b > 0$. It is also shown in the appendix that the level of labor usage beyond which marginal product begins to fall, and diminishing returns set in, is

$$L_m = -\frac{B}{3A}$$

When marginal product equals average product and average product is at its maximum (as discussed in Chapter 8),[1]

$$L_a = -\frac{B}{2A}$$

---

[1]The level of labor usage at which AP reaches its maximum value, L_a, can be found algebraically. First, set AP equal to MP:

$$AL^2 + BL = 3AL^2 + 2BL$$

or

$$0 = 2AL^2 + BL$$

Solving for L, the level of labor usage at which average product is maximized is $L_a = -B/2A$.

FIGURE 10.1

Marginal and Average Product Curves for the Short-Run Cubic Production Function: $Q = AL^3 + BL^2$

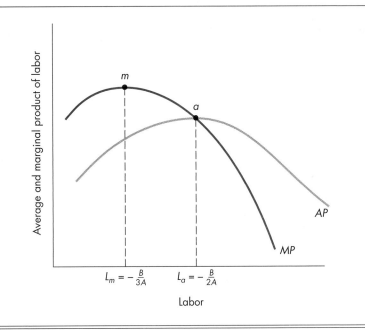

Recall that A is negative ($A < 0$) and B is positive ($B > 0$), so both L_m and L_a are positive. These relations are shown in Figure 10.1.

Note that when the fixed level of capital changes, both A ($= a\overline{K}^3$) and B ($= b\overline{K}^2$) change in value and all three product curves (*TP, AP,* and *MP*) shift.[2] Also note that once estimates of A and B are obtained for any one of the three product equations (*TP, AP,* and *MP*), the other two have also been estimated; that is, A and B are the only two parameters that need to be estimated to get all three equations.

The short-run cubic production function exhibits all the theoretical properties discussed in Chapter 8. Table 10.1 summarizes the cubic specification of the short-run production function.

10.2 ESTIMATION OF A SHORT-RUN PRODUCTION FUNCTION

Now that we have specified a cubic form for the short-run production function, we can discuss how to estimate this production function. As we see, only the simple techniques of regression analysis presented in Chapter 4 are needed to estimate the cubic production function in the short run when capital is fixed. We illustrate the process of estimating the production function with an example.

---

[2]Recall from Tables 8.1 and 8.3 in Chapter 8 that capital is held constant in any given column. The entire marginal and average product schedules change when capital usage changes.

TABLE 10.1
Summary of the Short-Run Cubic Production Function

	Short-run cubic production function
Total product	$Q = Al^3 + Bl^2$
	where $A = a\overline{K}^3$
	$B = b\overline{K}^2$
Average product	$AP = Al^2 + Bl$
Marginal product	$MP = 3Al^2 + 2Bl$
Diminishing marginal returns	Beginning at $L_m = -\dfrac{B}{3A}$
Diminishing average product	Beginning at $L_a = -\dfrac{B}{2A}$
Restrictions on parameters	$A < 0$
	$B > 0$

FIGURE 10.2
Scatter Diagram for a Cubic Production Function

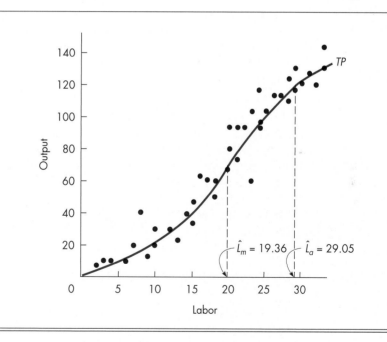

Suppose a small plant uses labor with a fixed amount of capital to assemble a product. There are 40 observations on labor usage (hours per day) and output (number of units assembled per day). The manager wishes to estimate the production function and the marginal product of labor. Figure 10.2 presents a scatter diagram of the 40 observations.

The scatter diagram suggests that a cubic specification of short-run production is appropriate because the scatter of data points appears to have an S-shape, similar to the theoretical total product curve set forth in Chapter 8. For such a curve, the slope first increases and then decreases, indicating that the marginal product of labor first increases, reaches a maximum, and then decreases. Both the marginal product and average product curves should take on the inverted-U-shape described in Chapter 8 and shown in Figure 8.3.

Since it seems appropriate to estimate a cubic production function in this case, we specify the following estimable form:

$$Q = AL^3 + BL^2$$

regression through the origin
A regression in which the intercept term is forced to equal zero.

Following the procedure discussed in Chapter 4, we transform the cubic equation into a linear form for estimation:

$$Q = AX + BW$$

where $X = L^3$ and $W = L^2$. To correctly estimate the cubic equation, we must account for the fact that the cubic equation does not include an intercept term. In other words, the estimated regression line must pass through the origin; that is, when $L = 0$, $Q = 0$. **Regression through the origin** simply requires that the analyst specify in the computer routine that the intercept term be "suppressed." Most computer programs for regression analysis provide the user with a simple way to suppress the intercept term. After we use a regression routine to estimate a cubic equation for the 40 observations on output and labor usage (and suppressing the intercept), the following computer output is forthcoming:

DEPENDENT VARIABLE: Q	R-SQUARE	F-RATIO	P-VALUE ON F
OBSERVATIONS: 40	0.9837	1148.83	0.0001

VARIABLE	PARAMETER ESTIMATE	STANDARD ERROR	T-RATIO	P-VALUE
L3	−0.0047	0.0006	−7.833	0.0001
L2	0.2731	0.0182	15.005	0.0001

The F-ratio and the R^2 for the cubic specification are quite good.[3] The critical value of F with $k - 1 = 1$ and $n - k = 38$ degrees of freedom is 4.1 at the 5 percent significance level. The p-values for both estimates $\hat{A}$ and $\hat{B}$ are so small that there is

---

[3]For purposes of illustration, the hypothetical data used in this example were chosen to fit closely an S-shaped cubic equation. In most real-world applications, you will probably get smaller values for the F-ratio, R^2, and t-statistics.

less than a 0.01 percent chance of making a Type I error (mistakenly concluding that $A \neq 0$ and $B \neq 0$). The following parameter estimates are obtained from the printout:

$$\hat{A} = -0.0047 \quad \text{and} \quad \hat{B} = 0.2731$$

The estimated short-run cubic production function is

$$\hat{Q} = -0.0047L^3 + 0.2731L^2$$

The parameters theoretically have the correct signs: $\hat{A} < 0$ and $\hat{B} > 0$. We must test to see if $\hat{A}$ and $\hat{B}$ are significantly negative and positive, respectively. The computed t-ratios allow us to test for statistical significance:

$$t_{\hat{a}} = -7.83 \quad \text{and} \quad t_{\hat{b}} = 15.00$$

The absolute values of both t-statistics exceed the critical t-value for 38 degrees of freedom at a 5 percent level of significance (2.021). Hence, $\hat{A}$ is significantly negative and $\hat{B}$ is significantly positive. Both estimates satisfy the theoretical characteristics of a cubic production function.

The estimated marginal product of labor is

$$\widehat{MP} = 3\hat{A}L^2 + 2\hat{B}L$$

$$= 3(-0.0047)L^2 + 2(0.2731)L$$

$$= -0.0141L^2 + 0.5462L$$

The level of labor usage beyond which diminishing returns set in (after MP_L reaches its maximum) is estimated as

$$\hat{L}_m = -\frac{\hat{B}}{3\hat{A}} = -\frac{0.2731}{3(-0.0047)} = 19.36$$

Note in Figure 10.2 that $\hat{L}_m$ is at the point where total product no longer increases at an increasing rate but begins increasing at a decreasing rate. The estimated average product of labor is

$$\widehat{AP} = \hat{A}L^2 + \hat{B}L$$

$$= (-0.0047)L^2 + (0.2731)L$$

The maximum average product is attained when $AP = MP$ at the estimated level of labor usage:

$$\hat{L}_a = -\frac{\hat{B}}{2\hat{A}} = -\frac{0.2731}{2(-0.0047)} = 29.05$$

Maximum AP, as expected, occurs at a higher level of labor usage than maximum MP (see Figure 10.2). The evidence indicates that the cubic estimation of the production function from the data points in Figure 10.2 provides a good fit and has all the desired theoretical properties.

10.3 SHORT-RUN COST ESTIMATION: SOME PROBLEMS WITH MEASURING COST

The techniques of regression analysis can also be used to estimate cost functions. Cost depends on the level of output being produced, as well as the prices of the inputs used in production. This relation can be expressed mathematically as

$$TC = TC(Q; w, r)$$

where we continue to let w denote the price of a unit of labor services and r the price of a unit of capital services. Before describing procedures used in estimating short-run cost functions, we must discuss two important considerations that arise when measuring the cost of production: the problem of inflation and that of measuring economic cost.

When short-run cost functions are being estimated, the data will necessarily be such that the level of usage of one (or more) of the inputs is fixed. In the context of the two-input production function employed in Chapter 8, this restriction could be interpreted to mean that the firm's capital stock is fixed while labor usage is allowed to vary. In most cases, a manager will be using a time-series set of observations on cost, output, and input prices to estimate the short-run cost function. The time period over which the data are collected should be short enough so that at least one input remains fixed. For instance, an analyst might collect monthly observations over a two-year period in which the firm did not change its basic plant (i.e., capital stock). Thus the analyst could obtain 24 observations on cost, output, and input prices. When using a time-series data set of this type, an analyst should be careful to adjust the cost and input price data (which are measured in dollars) for inflation and to make sure the cost data measure economic cost. We now discuss these two possible problems.

Correcting Data for the Effects of Inflation

nominal cost data

Data that have not been corrected for the effects of inflation.

While output is expressed in physical units, cost and input prices are expressed in nominal dollars. Hence, the **nominal cost data** would include the effect of inflation. That is, over time, inflation could cause reported costs to rise, even if output remained constant. Such a situation is depicted in Figure 10.3. As you can see in this figure, estimation based on a data set affected by inflation indicates that cost rises more steeply than it would if inflation did not exist in the data. To accurately measure the real increase in cost caused by increases in output, it is necessary to eliminate the effects of inflation.

deflating

Correcting for the influence of inflation by dividing nominal cost data by an implicit price deflator.

Correcting for the effects of inflation is easily accomplished by **deflating** nominal cost data into constant (or real) dollars using an *implicit price deflator.* To convert nominal cost into a constant-dollar amount, the nominal cost data are divided by the appropriate price deflator for the period under consideration. Implicit price deflators can be obtained from the *Survey of Current Business*, published by the Bureau of Economic Analysis at the U.S. Department of Commerce (www.bea.doc.gov). We will illustrate the process of deflating nominal cost data later in this chapter.

Inflation also can affect input prices, but for short-run cost estimation this is seldom a problem. As long as inflation affects all input prices and cost equally—that is,

FIGURE 10.3
The Problem of Inflation

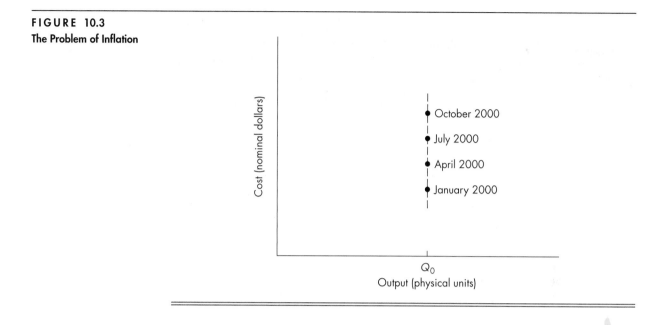

all input prices and cost rise equiproportionately—the effect of inflation on cost estimation is fully corrected for by deflating nominal cost. For example, if there is a 4 percent increase in cost and in the prices of both labor and capital, deflating cost by 4 percent will remove the effect of inflation, even when the prices of the inputs are not included in the cost equation. Therefore, it is a fairly common practice to omit input prices in short-run cost estimation because the span of the time-series data set is generally short enough that changes in the real input prices do not occur or are quite small. Thus we will concentrate on showing how to adjust for inflation in the cost data and not be concerned with the effects of inflation on input prices.

Problems Measuring Economic Cost

Another potentially troublesome problem can result from the difference between the accounting definition of cost and the economic definition of cost. As stressed in Chapter 8, the cost of using resources in production is the opportunity cost of using the resources. Since accounting data are of necessity based on expenditures, opportunity cost may not be reflected in the firm's accounting records. To illustrate this problem, suppose a firm owns its own machinery. The opportunity cost of this equipment is the income that could be derived if the machinery were leased to another firm, but this cost would not be reflected in the accounting data.

In a two-input setting, total cost at a given level of outputs is

$$C = wL + rK$$

The wage rate should reflect the opportunity cost of labor to the firm; so expenditures on labor, wL (including any additional compensation not paid as wages), would reflect opportunity cost. The problem is the calculation of the firm's opportunity cost of capital. The cost of capital, r, must be calculated in such a way that it reflects the **user cost of capital.** User cost includes not only the acquisition cost of a unit of capital but also (1) the return forgone by using the capital rather than renting it, (2) the depreciation charges resulting from the use of the capital, and (3) any capital gains or losses associated with holding the particular type of capital. Likewise, the measurement of the capital stock K must be such that it reflects the stock actually owned by the firm. For example, you might want the capital variable to reflect the fact that a given piece of capital has depreciated physically or embodies a lower technology than a new piece of capital. While these problems are difficult, they are not insurmountable. The main thing to remember is that such opportunity-cost data would be expected to differ greatly from the reported cost figures in accounting data.

user cost of capital
The firm's opportunity cost of using capital.

10.4 ESTIMATION OF A SHORT-RUN COST FUNCTION

As is the case when estimating a production function, specification of an appropriate equation for a cost function must necessarily precede the estimation of the parameters using regression analysis. The specification of an empirical cost equation must ensure that the mathematical properties of the equation reflect the properties and relations described in Chapter 8. Figure 10.4 illustrates again the typically assumed total variable cost, average variable cost, and marginal cost curves.

Estimation of Typical Short-Run Costs

Since the shape of any one of the three cost curves determines the shape of the other two, we begin with the average variable cost curve. Because this curve is U-shaped, we use the following quadratic specification:

$$AVC = a + bQ + cQ^2$$

As explained earlier, input prices are not included as explanatory variables in the cost equation because the input prices (adjusted for inflation) are assumed to be constant over the relatively short time span of the time-series data set. In order for the AVC curve to be U-shaped, a must be positive, b must be negative, and c must be positive; that is, $a > 0$, $b < 0$, and $c > 0$.[4]

Given the specification for average variable cost, the specifications for total variable cost and marginal cost are straightforward. If $AVC = TVC/Q$, it follows that

$$TVC = AVC \times Q = (a + bQ + cQ^2)Q = aQ + bQ^2 + cQ^3$$

---

[4]The appendix to this chapter derives the mathematical properties of a cubic cost function.

FIGURE 10.4
Typical Short-Run Cost Curves

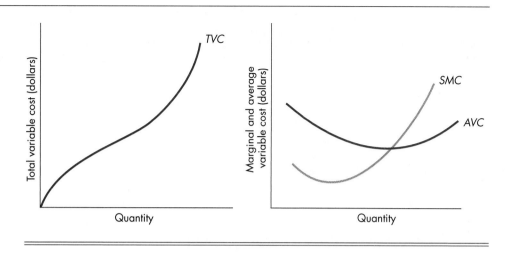

Note that this equation is a cubic specification of *TVC*, which conforms to the S-shaped *TVC* curve in Figure 10.4.

The equation for marginal cost is somewhat more difficult to derive. It can be shown, however, that the marginal cost equation associated with the above *TVC* equation is

$$SMC = a + 2bQ + 3cQ^2$$

If, as specified for *AVC*, $a > 0$, $b < 0$, and $c > 0$, the marginal cost curve will also be U-shaped.

Because all three of the cost curves, *TVC*, *AVC*, and *SMC*, employ the same parameters, it is necessary to estimate only one of these functions in order to obtain estimates of all three. For example, estimation of *AVC* provides estimates of a, b, and c, which can then be used to generate the marginal and total variable cost functions. The total cost curve is trivial to estimate; simply add the constant fixed cost to total variable cost.

As for the estimation itself, ordinary least-squares estimation of the total (or average) variable cost function is usually sufficient. Once the estimates of a, b, and c are obtained, it is necessary to determine whether the parameter estimates are of the hypothesized signs and statistically significant. The tests for significance are again accomplished using either t-tests or p-values.

Using the estimates of a total or average variable cost function, we can also obtain an estimate of the output at which average cost is a minimum. Remember that when average variable cost is at its minimum, average variable cost and marginal cost are equal. Thus we can define the minimum of average variable cost as the output at which

$$AVC = SMC$$

TABLE 10.2

Summary of a Cubic Specification for Total Variable Cost

	Cubic total variable cost function
Total variable cost	$TVC = aQ + bQ^2 + cQ^3$
Average variable cost	$AVC = a + bQ + cQ^2$
Marginal cost	$SMC = a + 2bQ + 3cQ^2$
AVC reaches minimum point	$Q_m = -b/2c$
Restrictions on parameters	$a > 0$
	$b < 0$
	$c > 0$

FIGURE 10.5

A Potential Data Problem

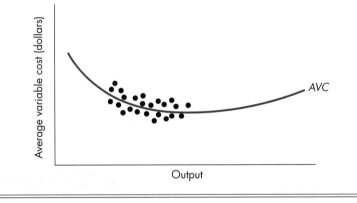

Using the specifications of average variable cost and marginal cost presented earlier, we can write this condition as

$$a + bQ + cQ^2 = a + 2bQ + 3cQ^2$$

or

$$bQ + 2cQ^2 = 0$$

Solving for Q, the level of output at which average variable cost is minimized is

$$Q_m = -b/2c$$

Table 10.2 summarizes the mathematical properties of a cubic specification for total variable cost.

Before estimating a short-run cost function, we want to mention a potential problem that can arise when the data for average variable cost are clustered around the minimum point of the average cost curve, as shown in Figure 10.5. If the average variable cost function is estimated using data points clustered as shown in the figure, the result is that while $\hat{a}$ is positive and $\hat{b}$ is negative, a t-test or a p-value would indicate that $\hat{c}$ is not statistically different from 0. This result does not mean that the average cost curve is not U-shaped. The problem is that because there are no observations for the larger levels of output, the estimation simply cannot determine whether or not average cost is rising over that range of output.

Estimation of Short-Run Costs at Rockford Enterprises: An Example

In October 2003, the manager at Rockford Enterprises decided to estimate the total variable, average variable, and marginal cost functions for the firm. The capital stock at Rockford has remained unchanged since the third quarter of 2001. The manager collected quarterly observations on cost and output over this period and the resulting data were as follows:

Quarter	Output	Average variable cost ($)
2001 (III)	300	$39.86
2001 (IV)	100	40.98
2002 (I)	150	29.85
2002 (II)	250	29.71
2002 (III)	400	49.95
2002 (IV)	200	34.87
2003 (I)	350	47.27
2003 (II)	450	61.84
2003 (III)	500	69.53

Average variable cost was measured in nominal (i.e., current) dollars, and the cost data were subject to the effects of inflation. Over the period for which cost was to be estimated, costs had increased due to the effects of inflation. The manager's analyst decided to eliminate the influence of inflation by deflating the nominal costs. Recall that such a deflation involves converting nominal cost into constant-dollar cost by dividing the nominal cost by an appropriate price index. The analyst used the implicit price deflator for GDP published in the *Survey of Current Business,* which can be found at the website for the Bureau of Economic Analysis (www.bea.doc.gov). The following values for the price deflator were used to deflate the nominal cost data:

Quarter	Implicit Price Deflator (1996 = 1.00)
2001 (III)	109.92
2001 (IV)	109.78
2002 (I)	110.14
2002 (II)	110.48
2002 (III)	110.76
2002 (IV)	111.25
2003 (I)	111.90
2003 (II)	112.17
2003 (III)	112.63

To obtain the average variable cost, measured in constant (1996) dollars, for the 300 units produced in the third quarter of 2001, $39.86 is divided by the implicit price deflator 109.92 (divided by 100), which gives $36.26:

$$\$36.26 = \frac{\$39.86}{109.92 \div 100}$$

Note that it is necessary to divide the implicit price deflator by 100 because the price deflators in the *Survey of Current Business* are expressed as percentages. Repeating this computation for each of the average variable cost figures, the manager obtained the following inflation-adjusted cost data:

Quarter	Output	Deflated average variable cost ($)
2001 (III)	300	$36.26
2001 (IV)	100	37.33
2002 (I)	150	27.10
2002 (II)	250	26.89
2002 (III)	400	45.10
2002 (IV)	200	31.34
2003 (I)	350	42.24
2003 (II)	450	55.13
2003 (III)	500	61.73

Given these inflation-adjusted data, the manager estimated the cost functions. As shown above, it is sufficient to estimate any one of the three cost curves in order to obtain the other two because each cost equation is a function of the same three parameters: a, b, and c. The manager decided to estimate the average variable cost function:

$$AVC = a + bQ + cQ^2$$

and obtained the following printout from the estimation of this equation:

DEPENDENT VARIABLE: AVC	R-SQUARE	F-RATIO	P-VALUE ON F
OBSERVATIONS: 9	0.9382	45.527	0.0002

VARIABLE	PARAMETER ESTIMATE	STANDARD ERROR	T-RATIO	P-VALUE
INTERCEPT	44.473	6.487	6.856	0.0005
Q	−0.143	0.0482	−2.967	0.0254
Q2	0.000362	0.000079	4.582	0.0037

After the estimates were obtained, the manager determined that the estimated coefficients had the theoretically required signs: $\hat{a} > 0$, $\hat{b} < 0$, and $\hat{c} > 0$. To determine whether these coefficients are statistically significant, the p-values were examined, and the exact level of significance for each of the estimated coefficients was acceptably low (all the t-ratios are significant at better than the 5 percent level of significance).

The estimated average variable cost function for Rockford Enterprises is, therefore,

$$\widehat{AVC} = 44.473 - 0.143Q + 0.000362Q^2$$

which conforms to the shape of the average variable cost curve in Figure 10.4. As emphasized above, the marginal cost and total variable cost equations are easily determined from the estimated parameters of AVC, and no further regression analysis is necessary. In this case,

$$\widehat{SMC} = \hat{a} + 2\hat{b}Q + 3\hat{c}Q^2$$
$$= 44.473 - 0.286Q + 0.0011Q^2$$

and

$$\widehat{TVC} = \hat{a}Q + \hat{b}Q^2 + \hat{c}Q^3$$
$$= 44.473Q - 0.143Q^2 + 0.000362Q^3$$

To illustrate the use of the estimated cost equations, suppose the manager wishes to calculate the marginal cost, average variable cost, and total variable cost when Rockford is producing 350 units of output. Using the estimated marginal cost equation, the marginal cost associated with 350 units is

$$SMC = 44.473 - 0.286(350) + 0.0011(350)^2$$
$$= 44.473 - 100.10 + 134.75$$
$$= \$79.12$$

Average variable cost for this level of output is

$$AVC = 44.473 - 0.143(350) + 0.000362(350)^2$$
$$= 44.473 - 50.05 + 44.345$$
$$= \$38.77$$

and total variable cost for 350 units of output is

$$TVC = AVC \times Q$$
$$= 38.77 \times 350$$
$$= \$13,569$$

The total cost of 350 units of output would, of course, be $13,569 plus fixed cost.

Finally, the output level at which average variable cost is minimized can be computed as

$$Q_m = -b/2c$$

In this example,

$$Q_m = \frac{0.143}{2 \times 0.000362} = 197$$

At Rockford Enterprises, average variable cost reaches its minimum at an output level of 197 units, when

$$AVC = 44.473 - 0.143(197) + 0.000362(197)^2$$
$$= 44.473 - 28.17 + 14.05$$
$$= \$30.35$$

As you can see from this example, estimation of short-run cost curves is just a straightforward application of cost theory and regression analysis. Many firms do, in fact, use regression analysis to estimate their costs of production.

10.5 SUMMARY

This chapter showed how to specify and estimate a popular form of production and cost functions: the cubic specification. We discussed how to use the results of the estimations to investigate a variety of production and cost issues that are relevant to managerial decision making, such as finding the point of diminishing returns and estimating the values of marginal products and marginal costs.

Estimation of the short-run cubic production function involves estimating the two parameters A and B. This is accomplished by regressing output on L^3 and L^2 using the technique of regression through the origin. Once A and B are estimated, the estimated t-ratios or p-values are examined to test that A is significantly negative and B is significantly positive. Once estimates of A and B are obtained for any one of the three product equations (TP, AP, and MP), the other two product equations will also have been estimated, since A and B are the only two parameters in all three equations. The cubic production function exhibits all the theoretical properties discussed in Chapter 8.

When estimating cost equations, researchers must be careful to adjust for the effects of inflation. The effects of inflation are removed from the data by "deflating" using price indexes, which can be obtained from a variety of sources including the *Survey of Current Business*, published by the Bureau of Economic Analysis at the U.S. Department of Commerce. Researchers must also be careful to use economic costs, rather than accounting costs, to measure the cost of production.

A suitable specification for estimating a set of short-run cost curves (TVC, AVC, and SMC) is a cubic TVC equation with the associated AVC and SMC equations summarized in Table 10.3. If $a > 0$, $b < 0$, and $c > 0$, the total variable cost curve has the typical S-shape and average variable cost and marginal cost are U-shaped. Average variable cost reaches its minimum value at an output level of $Q_m = -b/2c$.

This chapter concludes Part III of this text, which discussed production and cost. Now that both revenue and cost relations have been presented, we are ready to proceed with the analysis of managerial decision making in the context of a profit-maximizing firm.

TABLE 10.3

Summary of the Short-Run Cubic Production and Cost Specification

	Short-run cubic production equations
Total product	$Q = AL^3 + BL^2$
Average product of labor	$AP = AL^2 + BL$
Marginal product of labor	$MP = 3AL^2 + 2BL$
Diminishing marginal returns	Beginning at $L_m = -B/3A$
Restrictions on parameters	$A < 0$
	$B > 0$

	Short-run cubic cost equations
Total variable cost	$TVC = aQ + bQ^2 + cQ^3$
Average variable cost	$AVC = a + bQ + cQ^2$
Marginal cost	$SMC = a + 2bQ + 3cQ^2$
Average variable cost reaches minimum at	$Q_m = -\dfrac{b}{2c}$
Restrictions on parameters	$a > 0, b < 0, c > 0$

TECHNICAL PROBLEMS

1. The following cubic equation is a long-run production function for a firm:

$$Q = -0.002K^3L^3 + 6K^2L^2$$

Suppose the firm employs 10 units of capital.

a. What are the equations for the total product, average product, and marginal product of labor curves?

b. At what level of labor usage does the marginal product of labor begin to diminish?

c. Calculate the marginal product and average product of labor when 10 units of labor are being employed.

Now suppose the firm doubles capital usage to 20 units.

d. What are the equations for the total product, average product, and marginal product of labor curves?

e. What happened to the marginal and average product of labor curves when capital usage increased from 10 to 20 units? Calculate the marginal and average products of labor for 10 units of labor now that capital usage is 20 units. Compare your answer to part c. Did the increase in capital usage affect marginal and average product as you expected?

2. A firm estimates its cubic production function of the following form

$$Q = AL^3 + BL^2$$

and obtains the following estimation results:

DEPENDENT VARIABLE: Q	R-SQUARE	F-RATIO	P-VALUE ON F
OBSERVATIONS: 25	0.8457	126.10	0.0001

VARIABLE	PARAMETER ESTIMATE	STANDARD ERROR	T-RATIO	P-VALUE
L3	−0.002	0.0005	−4.00	0.0005
L2	0.400	0.080	5.00	0.0001

a. What are the estimated total, average, and marginal product functions?

b. Are the parameters of the correct sign, and are they significant at the 1 percent level?

c. At what level of labor usage is average product at its maximum?

Now recall the following formulas derived in Chapter 8: $AP = Q/L$, $AVC = w/AP$, and $SMC = w/MP$. Assume that the wage rate for labor (w) is $200.

d. What is output when average product is at its maximum?

e. At the output level for part d, what are average variable cost and marginal cost?

f. When the rate of labor usage is 120, what is output? What are AVC and SMC at that output?

g. Conceptually, how could you derive the relevant cost curves from this estimate of the production functions?

3. Consider estimation of a short-run average variable cost function of the form

$$AVC = a + bQ + cQ^2$$

Using time-series data, the estimation procedure produces the following computer output:

DEPENDENT VARIABLE: AVC	R-SQUARE	F-RATIO	P-VALUE ON F
OBSERVATIONS: 15	0.4135	4.230	0.0407

VARIABLE	PARAMETER ESTIMATE	STANDARD ERROR	T-RATIO	P-VALUE
INTERCEPT	30.420202	6.465900	4.70	0.0005
Q	−0.079952	0.030780	−2.60	0.0232
Q2	0.000088	0.000032	2.75	0.0176

a. Do the parameter estimates have the correct signs? Are they statistically significant at the 5 percent level of significance?

b. At what level of output do you estimate average variable cost reaches its minimum value?

c. What is the estimated marginal cost curve?

d. What is the estimated marginal cost when output is 700 units?

  e. What is the estimated average variable cost curve?

  f. What is the estimated average variable cost when output is 700 units?

APPLIED PROBLEMS

1. You are planning to estimate a short-run production function for your firm, and you have collected the following data on labor usage and output:

Labor usage	Output
3	1
7	2
9	3
11	5
17	8
17	10
20	15
24	18
26	22
28	21
30	23

  a. Does a cubic equation appear to be a suitable specification, given these data? You may wish to construct a scatter diagram to help you answer this question.

  b. Using a computer and software for regression analysis, estimate your firm's short-run production function using the data given here. Do the parameter estimates have the appropriate algebraic signs? Are they statistically significant at the 5 percent level?

  c. At what point do you estimate marginal product begins to fall?

  d. Calculate estimates of total, average, and marginal products when the firm employs 23 workers.

  e. When the firm employs 23 workers, is short-run marginal cost (*SMC*) rising or falling? How can you tell?

2. Dimex Fabrication Co., a small manufacturer of sheet-metal body parts for a major U.S. automaker, estimates its long-run production function to be

$$Q = -0.015625K^3L^3 + 10K^2L^2$$

where Q is the number of body parts produced daily, K is the number of sheet-metal presses in its manufacturing plant, and L is the number of labor-hours per day of sheet-metal workers employed by Dimex. Dimex is currently operating with eight sheet-metal presses.

  a. What is the total product function for Dimex? The average product function? The marginal product function?

  b. Managers at Dimex can expect the marginal product of additional workers to fall beyond what level of labor employment?

    c. Dimex plans to employ 50 workers. Calculate total product, average product, and marginal product.

3. The chief economist for Argus Corporation, a large appliance manufacturer, estimated the firm's short-run cost function for vacuum cleaners using an average variable cost function of the form

$$AVC = a + bQ + cQ^2$$

where AVC = dollars per vacuum cleaner and Q = number of vacuum cleaners produced each month. Total fixed cost each month is $180,000. The following results were obtained:

DEPENDENT VARIABLE: AVC	R-SQUARE	F-RATIO	P-VALUE ON F
OBSERVATIONS: 19	0.7360	39.428	0.0001

VARIABLE	PARAMETER ESTIMATE	STANDARD ERROR	T-RATIO	P-VALUE
INTERCEPT	191.93	54.65	3.512	0.0029
Q	−0.0305	0.00789	23.866	0.0014
Q2	0.0000024	0.00000098	2.449	0.0262

    a. Are the estimates $\hat{a}$, $\hat{b}$, and $\hat{c}$ statistically significant at the 2 percent level of significance?

    b. Do the results indicate that the average variable cost curve is U-shaped? How do you know?

    c. If Argus Corporation produces 8,000 vacuum cleaners per month, what is the estimated average variable cost? Marginal cost? Total variable cost? Total cost?

    d. Answer part *c*, assuming that Argus produces 10,000 vacuum cleaners monthly.

    e. At what level of output will average variable cost be at a minimum? What is minimum average variable cost?

▣ **MATHEMATICAL APPENDIX**   Empirical Production and Cost Relations

The Cubic Production Function

In this chapter, the cubic production function was introduced:

$$Q = aK^3L^3 + bK^2L^2$$

This functional form is best suited for short-run applications, rather than long-run applications. When capital is fixed ($K = \overline{K}$), the short-run cubic production function is

$$Q = a\overline{K}^3L^3 + b\overline{K}^2L^2$$

$$= AL^3 + BL^2$$

where $A = a\overline{K}^3$ and $B = b\overline{K}^2$. This section of the appendix presents the mathematical properties of the short-run cubic production function.

Input usage

To produce output, some positive amount of labor is required:

$$Q(0) = A(0)^3 + B(0)^2 = 0$$

Marginal product

The marginal product function for labor is

$$\frac{dQ}{dL} = Q_L = 3AL^2 + 2BL$$

The slope of marginal product is

$$\frac{d^2Q}{dL^2} = Q_{LL} = 6AL + 2B$$

For marginal product of labor to first rise, then fall, Q_{LL} must first be positive and then negative. Q_{LL} will be positive, then negative (as more labor is used) when A is negative and B is positive. These are the only restrictions on the short-run cubic production function:

$$A < 0 \quad \text{and} \quad B > 0$$

Marginal product of labor reaches its maximum value at L_m units of labor usage. This occurs when $Q_{LL} = 0$. Setting $Q_{LL} = 0$ and solving for L_m,

$$L_m = -\frac{B}{3A}$$

Average product

The average product function for labor is

$$AP = \frac{Q}{L} = AL^2 + BL$$

Average product reaches its maximum value at L_a units of labor usage. This occurs when $dAP/dL = 2AL + B = 0$. Solving for L_a,

$$L_a = -\frac{B}{2A}$$

The Cubic Cost Function

The cubic cost function,

$$TVC = aQ + bQ^2 + cQ^3$$

generates average and marginal cost curves that have the typical U-shapes set forth in Chapter 8. If $AVC = TVC/Q$,

$$AVC = a + bQ + cQ^2$$

The slope of the average variable cost function is

$$\frac{dAVC}{dQ} = b + 2cQ$$

Average variable cost is at its minimum value when $dAVC/dQ = 0$, which occurs when $Q = -b/2c$. To guarantee a minimum, the second derivative,

$$\frac{d^2AVC}{dQ^2} = 2c$$

must be positive, which requires c to be positive. When $Q = 0$, $AVC = a$, which must be positive. For average variable cost to have a downward-sloping region, b must be negative. Thus the parameter restrictions for a short-run cubic cost function are

$$a > 0, \quad b < 0, \quad \text{and} \quad c > 0$$

The marginal cost function is

$$SMC = \frac{dTVC}{dQ} = a + 2bQ + 3cQ^2$$

The Cobb-Douglas Production Function

In this chapter, we used a cubic specification for estimating the production function. In this appendix, we show you another nonlinear specification of the production function that has been widely used in business economics applications. We will describe the mathematical properties of both the long-run and the short-run Cobb-Douglas production function and explain how to estimate the parameters using regression analysis. To help you distinguish between the Cobb-Douglas form and the cubic form, we will use Greek letters to represent the parameters of the Cobb-Douglas functions.

The long-run Cobb-Douglas production function:
$Q = \gamma K^\alpha L^\beta$

Input Usage
To produce output, both inputs are required:

$$Q(0, L) = \gamma 0^\alpha L^\beta = Q(K, 0) = \gamma K^\alpha 0^\beta = 0$$

Marginal Products
The marginal product functions for capital and labor are

$$\frac{\partial Q}{\partial K} = Q_K = \alpha\gamma K^{\alpha-1}L^\beta = \alpha\frac{Q}{K}$$

and

$$\frac{\partial Q}{\partial L} = Q_L = \beta\gamma K^\alpha L^{\beta-1} = \beta\frac{Q}{L}$$

For the marginal products to be positive, α and β must be positive. The second derivatives,

$$\frac{\partial^2 Q}{\partial K^2} = Q_{KK} = \alpha(\alpha - 1)\gamma K^{\alpha-2}L^\beta$$

and

$$\frac{\partial^2 Q}{\partial L^2} = Q_{LL} = \beta(\beta - 1)\gamma K^\alpha L^{\beta-2}$$

demonstrate that, if the marginal products are diminishing (i.e., Q_{KK} and $Q_{LL} < 0$), α and β must be less than one.

Marginal Rate of Technical Substitution

From Chapter 9, the MRTS of L for K is Q_L/Q_K. In the context of the Cobb-Douglas function,

$$MRTS = \frac{Q_L}{Q_K} = \frac{\beta}{\alpha} \times \frac{K}{L}$$

Note first that the MRTS is invariant to output,

$$\frac{\partial MRTS}{\partial Q} = 0$$

Hence, the Cobb-Douglas production is *homothetic*—the production function has a straight-line expansion path and changes in the output level have no effect on relative input usage. Moreover, the MRTS demonstrates that the Cobb-Douglas production function is characterized by convex isoquants. Taking the derivative of the MRTS with respect to L,

$$\frac{\partial MRTS}{\partial L} = -\frac{\beta}{\alpha} \times \frac{K}{L^2}$$

Hence, the MRTS diminishes as capital is replaced with labor: The isoquants are convex.

Output Elasticities

Output elasticities are defined as

$$E_K = \frac{\partial Q}{\partial K} \times \frac{K}{Q} = Q_K \times \frac{K}{Q}$$

and

$$E_L = \frac{\partial Q}{\partial L} \times \frac{L}{Q} = Q_L \times \frac{L}{Q}$$

Using the Cobb-Douglas specification,

$$E_K = \left(\alpha\frac{Q}{K}\right) \times \frac{K}{Q} = \alpha$$

and

$$E_L = \left(\beta\frac{Q}{L}\right) \times \frac{L}{Q} = \beta$$

The Function Coefficient

Begin with a production function, $Q = Q(K, L)$. Suppose that the levels of usage of both inputs are increased by the same proportion (λ); that is, $Q = Q(\lambda K, \lambda L)$. The definition of the function coefficient ($\mathscr{E}$) is

$$\mathscr{E} = \frac{dQ/Q}{d\lambda/\lambda}$$

Take the total differential of the production function

$$dQ = Q_K dK + Q_L dL$$

and rewrite this as

$$dQ = Q_K K \frac{dK}{K} + Q_L L \frac{dL}{L}$$

Because K and L were increased by the same proportion, $dK/K = dL/L = d\lambda/\lambda$. Thus

$$dQ = \frac{d\lambda}{\lambda}(Q_K K + Q_L L)$$

When we use this expression, the function coefficient is

$$\mathscr{E} = Q_K \times \frac{K}{Q} + Q_L \times \frac{L}{Q} = E_K + E_L$$

In the context of the Cobb-Douglas production function, it follows that

$$\mathscr{E} = \alpha + \beta$$

Estimating the long-run Cobb-Douglas production function

The mathematical properties of the Cobb-Douglas production function make it a popular specification for estimating long-run production functions. After converting to natural logarithms, the estimable form of the Cobb-Douglas function ($Q = \gamma K^\alpha L^\beta$) is

$$\ln Q = \ln \gamma + \alpha\ln K + \beta\ln L$$

Recall from the previous discussion that $\hat{\alpha}$ and $\hat{\beta}$ are estimates of the output elasticities of capital and labor, respectively. Recall also that the estimated marginal products,

$$MP_K = \hat{\alpha}\frac{Q}{K} \quad \text{and} \quad MP_L = \hat{\beta}\frac{Q}{L}$$

are significantly positive and decreasing (the desired theoretical property) if the t-tests or p-values on $\hat{\alpha}$ and $\hat{\beta}$ indicate that these coefficients are significantly positive but less than 1 in value.

The function coefficient is estimated as

$$\hat{\xi} = \hat{\alpha} + \hat{\beta}$$

and provides a measure of returns to scale. To determine whether $(\hat{\alpha} + \hat{\beta})$ is significantly greater (less) than 1, a t-test is performed. If $(\hat{\alpha} + \hat{\beta})$ is not significantly greater (less) than 1, we cannot reject the existence of constant returns to scale. To determine whether the sum, $(\hat{\alpha} + \hat{\beta})$, is significantly different from 1, we use the following t-statistic:

$$t_{\hat{\alpha}+\hat{\beta}} = \frac{(\hat{\alpha} + \hat{\beta}) - 1}{S_{\hat{\alpha}+\hat{\beta}}}$$

where the value 1 indicates that we are testing "different from" and $S_{\hat{\alpha}+\hat{\beta}}$ is the estimated standard error of the sum of the estimated coefficients $(\hat{\alpha} + \hat{\beta})$. After calculating this t-statistic, it is compared to the critical t-value from the table. Again note that since the calculated t-statistic can be negative (when $\hat{\alpha} + \hat{\beta}$ is less than 1), it is the absolute value of the t-statistic that is compared with the critical t-value. Some statistical software can give p-values for this test.

The only problem in performing this test involves obtaining the estimated standard error of $(\hat{\alpha} + \hat{\beta})$. All regression packages can provide the analyst, upon request, with variances and covariances of the regression coefficients, $\hat{\alpha}$ and $\hat{\beta}$, in a variance–covariance matrix.[a] Traditionally, variances of $\hat{\alpha}$ and $\hat{\beta}$ are denoted as $\text{Var}(\hat{\alpha})$ and $\text{Var}(\hat{\beta})$ and the covariance between $\hat{\alpha}$ and $\hat{\beta}$ as $\text{Cov}(\hat{\alpha}, \hat{\beta})$. As you may remember from a statistics course,

$$\text{Var}(\hat{\alpha} + \hat{\beta}) = \text{Var}(\hat{\alpha}) + \text{Var}(\hat{\beta}) + 2\,\text{Cov}(\hat{\alpha}, \hat{\beta})$$

The estimated standard error of $(\hat{\alpha} + \hat{\beta})$ is

$$S_{\hat{\alpha}+\hat{\beta}} = \sqrt{\text{Var}(\hat{\alpha}) + \text{Var}(\hat{\beta}) + 2\text{Cov}(\hat{\alpha}, \hat{\beta})}$$

The short-run Cobb-Douglas production function

When capital is fixed in the short run at K, the short-run Cobb-Douglas production function is

$$Q = \gamma \overline{K}^{\alpha} L^{\beta} = \delta L^{\beta}$$

where $\delta = \gamma K^{\alpha}$. Note that if L is 0, no output is forthcoming. For output to be positive, δ must be positive. The marginal product of labor is

$$Q_L = \delta \beta L^{\beta-1}$$

For marginal product to be positive, β must be positive. The second derivative

$$Q_{LL} = \beta(\beta - 1)\delta L^{\beta-2}$$

reveals that if the marginal product of labor is diminishing, β must be less than 1. Thus the restrictions for the Cobb-Douglas production in the short run are

$$\delta > 0 \quad \text{and} \quad 0 < \beta < 1$$

Estimating the short-run Cobb-Douglas production function

As in the case of the long-run Cobb-Douglas production function, the short-run Cobb-Douglas production function must also be transformed into a linear form by converting it to natural logarithms. The equation actually estimated is

$$\ln Q = \tau + \beta \ln L$$

where $\tau = \ln \delta$. Recall that β must be positive for the marginal product of labor to be positive and less than 1 for the marginal product to be decreasing (i.e., $0 < \beta < 1$). It is common practice to test that $\beta > 0$ and $\beta < 1$ using a t-test.

Estimation of a Long-Run Cost Function

Because the general form for the long-run cost function with two inputs is

$$LTC = f(Q, w, r)$$

and because cross-sectional data are generally used for long-run estimation, the empirical specification of a long-run cost function must, as emphasized earlier, include the prices of inputs as explanatory variables. At first glance, it would appear that the solution would be simply to add

---

[a]The variance–covariance matrix is a listing (in the form of a matrix on the computer printout) of the estimated variances and covariances of all the estimated coefficients. For example, in the regression of $Y = \hat{\alpha} + \hat{\beta}X$, the variance–covariance matrix provides estimates of $\text{Var}(\hat{\alpha})$, $\text{Var}(\hat{\beta})$, and $\text{Cov}(\hat{\alpha}, \hat{\beta})$. As noted in Chapter 4, the variance of a regression coefficient provides a measure of the dispersion of the variable about its mean. The covariance of the regression coefficients provides information about the joint distribution: that is, the relation between the two regression coefficients.

the input prices as additional explanatory variables in the cost function developed above and express total cost as

$$LTC = aQ + bQ^2 + cQ^3 + dw + er$$

This function, however, fails to satisfy a basic characteristic of cost functions. A total cost function can be written as $LTC = wL + rK$. If both input prices double, holding output constant, input usage will not change but total cost will double. Letting LTC' denote total cost after input prices double,

$$LTC' = (2w)L + (2r)K$$
$$= 2(wL + rK)$$
$$= 2LTC$$

The long-run cost function suggested here does not satisfy this requirement. For a given output, if input prices double,

$$LTC' = aQ + bQ^2 + cQ^3 + d(2w) + e(2r)$$
$$= aQ + bQ^2 + cQ^3 + dw + er + (dw + er)$$
$$= LTC + dw + er$$

and LTC' is not equal to $2LTC$.

Therefore, an alternative form for estimating a long-run cost function must be found. The most commonly employed form is a log-linear specification such as the Cobb-Douglas specifications. With this type of specification, the total cost function is expressed as

$$LTC = \alpha Q^\beta w^\gamma r^\delta$$

Using this functional form, when input prices double while holding output constant:

$$LTC' = \alpha Q^\beta (2w)^\gamma (2r)^\delta$$
$$= 2^{(\gamma+\delta)} (\alpha Q^\beta w^\gamma r^\delta)$$
$$= 2^{(\gamma+\delta)} LTC$$

If $\gamma + \delta = 1$, doubling input prices indeed doubles the total cost of producing a given level of output—the required characteristic of a cost function. Hence, it is necessary to *impose* this condition on the proposed log-linear cost function by defining δ as $1 - \gamma$; so

$$LTC = \alpha Q^\beta w^\gamma r^{1-\gamma}$$
$$= \alpha Q^\beta w^\gamma r^{-\gamma} r$$
$$= \alpha Q^\beta (w/r)^\gamma r$$

The parameter restrictions are $\alpha > 0$, $\beta > 0$, and $0 < \gamma < 1$, which ensure that total cost is positive and increases when output and input prices increase.

To estimate the above total cost equation, it must be converted to natural logarithms:

$$\ln LTC = \ln \alpha + \beta \ln Q + \gamma \ln\left(\frac{w}{r}\right) + 1 \ln r$$

While we can estimate the parameters α, β, and γ, this formulation requires that the coefficient for $\ln r$ be *precisely* equal to 1. If we were to estimate this equation, such a value cannot be guaranteed. To impose this condition on the empirical cost function, we simply move $\ln r$ to the left-hand side of the equation to obtain

$$\ln LTC - \ln r = \ln \alpha + \beta \ln Q + \gamma \ln(w/r)$$

which, using the rules of logarithms, can be rewritten as

$$\ln\left(\frac{LTC}{r}\right) = \ln \alpha + \beta \ln Q + \gamma \ln(w/r)$$

This equation is then estimated to obtain an estimate of the long-run cost function.

As noted earlier, the primary use of the long-run cost function is in the firm's investment decision. Therefore, once the previous cost equation is estimated, its most important use is determining the extent of economies of scale. From the discussion of log-linear functions in Chapter 4, the coefficient β indicates the *elasticity of total cost* with respect to output; that is,

$$\beta = \frac{\text{Percentage change in total cost}}{\text{Percentage change in output}}$$

When $\beta > 1$, cost is increasing more than proportionately to output (e.g., if the percentage change in output is 25 percent and the percentage change in cost is 50 percent, β would be equal to 2); therefore long-run average cost would be increasing. Hence if $\beta > 1$, the estimates indicate diseconomies of scale. If $\beta < 1$, total cost increases proportionately less than the increase in output and economies of scale would be indicated. Furthermore, note that the magnitude of the estimate of β indicates the "strength" of the economies or diseconomies of scale. Finally, if $\beta = 1$, there are constant returns to scale. The statistical significance of β is tested in the manner outlined earlier. Table 10A.1 summarizes the mathematical properties of the Cobb-Douglas specification for long-run total cost.

TABLE 10A.1

Summary of the Cobb-Douglas Specification for Long-Run Total Cost

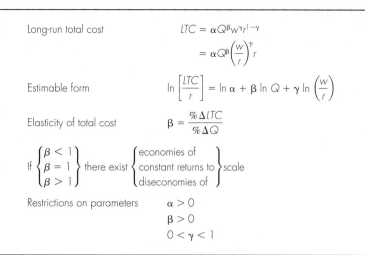

Long-run total cost	$LTC = \alpha Q^{\beta} w^{\gamma} r^{1-\gamma}$
	$= \alpha Q^{\beta} \left(\dfrac{w}{r}\right)^{\gamma} r$
Estimable form	$\ln\left[\dfrac{LTC}{r}\right] = \ln \alpha + \beta \ln Q + \gamma \ln\left(\dfrac{w}{r}\right)$
Elasticity of total cost	$\beta = \dfrac{\%\,\Delta LTC}{\%\,\Delta Q}$

If $\begin{cases} \beta < 1 \\ \beta = 1 \\ \beta > 1 \end{cases}$ there exist $\begin{cases} \text{economies of} \\ \text{constant returns to} \\ \text{diseconomies of} \end{cases}$ scale

Restrictions on parameters	$\alpha > 0$
	$\beta > 0$
	$0 < \gamma < 1$

MATHEMATICAL EXERCISES

1. Why would the restrictions $A > 0$ and $B < 0$ be inappropriate for a short-run cubic production function?

2. For the short-run cubic production function, show that increasing $\overline{K}$ always results in an increase in the level of labor usage at which diminishing returns begin.

3. Consider the Cobb-Douglas production function $Q = 36K^{0.5}L^{1.0}$.

   a. Find the marginal product functions.

   b. Write equations for the *MRTS* and the output elasticities.

   c. The function coefficient is equal to _____, so the production function is characterized by _____ returns to scale.

4. Let the long-run total cost function be $LTC = (1/12)Qw^{0.5}r^{0.5}$.

   a. Demonstrate that a doubling of input prices causes *LTC* to double.

   b. Find the elasticity of total cost. This long-run total cost function is characterized by _____ scale.

   c. Let $w = \$16$ and $r = \$25$, and find *LMC* and *LAC*. Graph the *LMC* and *LAC* curves. Are these curves consistent with part *b*?

   d. Is your answer to part *b* consistent with your answer to part *d* in mathematical exercise 4 in Chapter 9?

CHAPTER
11

Managerial Decisions in Competitive Markets

N ow we are ready to get to the bottom line. Literally. Up to this point in the text, we have developed several tools—optimization theory, demand analysis and forecasting, and production and cost analysis—that you may have found interesting enough as single topics. But now, and for the rest of the text, we bring these tools together to build a framework for making the most important decisions affecting the profitability of the firm: how much to produce and what price to charge. We are going to analyze how managers make price and output decisions to maximize the profit of the firm.

As it turns out, the nature of the price and output decision is strongly influenced by the structure of the market in which the firm sells its product. Recall from Chapter 1 that we discussed the characteristics of several market structures. Market structure determines whether a manager will be a price-setter or a price-taker. The theoretical market structure in which firms take the market price as given is called perfect competition. We begin our discussion of pricing and output decisions by examining how managers of price-taking, perfectly competitive firms should make production decisions in order to maximize profit. We will develop a number of important ideas that will carry over and apply to managers who are price-setters. For example, we will demonstrate that output decisions should never be based on considerations of fixed costs, that a firm may find it desirable to continue producing even though the firm is losing money, that a manager should not stop hiring labor just because labor productivity begins to fall, and that in the absence of entry barriers a firm can be expected to earn zero economic profit in the long run.

As we begin our discussion of profit maximization for price-taking firms, you may wonder how many managers are really price-takers, rather than price-setters. In a recent survey of one of our executive M.B.A. classes, even we were surprised to find that 34 of the 38 manager-students felt that their firms had little or no control over the price they could charge for their products; their prices were determined by market forces beyond their control. Although the assumptions of perfect competition, to be set forth in the next section, may seem quite narrowly focused, many managers face market conditions that closely approximate the model of perfect competition. And even if you are a manager of a price-setting firm, you will find the analysis of profit maximization under competitive conditions to be a valuable framework for making profitable decisions.

We assume in this chapter and the following four chapters that the goal of the manager is to maximize the firm's profit. It has been suggested that a manager may have other goals: to maximize the firm's sales, or rate of growth of sales; to maximize the manager's own utility by using the firm's resources for personal benefit; to promote the manager's favorite social causes. As we discussed in Chapter 1, such goals can lead to conflicts between owners and managers. It is our goal in this book to show how to make decisions that will make you a more effective manager, which generally means maximizing the profit of the firm. If you choose a different goal, you do so at your own risk.

As Chapter 1 discussed in some detail, when we assume that a firm maximizes its profit, we refer to its economic profit. Economic profit (π) is the firm's total revenue minus its total economic cost. Recall from Figure 1.1 that total economic cost is the sum of the explicit costs of using market-supplied resources (monetary payments to outside suppliers of inputs) plus the implicit costs of using owner-supplied resources (best returns forgone by using owners' resources). Thus

$$\text{Economic profit} = \pi = \text{Total revenue} - \text{Total economic cost}$$

$$= \text{Total revenue} - \text{Explicit costs} - \text{Implicit costs}$$

As you might expect, the manager's profit-maximizing decision is a direct application of the theory of unconstrained maximization, set forth in Chapter 3. Managers of firms that are price-takers look at price and cost conditions to answer three fundamental questions: (1) Should the firm produce or shut down? (2) If the firm produces, what is the optimal level of production? (3) What are the optimal levels of inputs to employ? Since the manager of a perfectly competitive firm takes product price as given, there is obviously no pricing decision.

After briefly setting forth all the characteristics of perfect competition, we first analyze how a manager determines the firm's output or level of production that maximizes profit. We address the short-run decision, when some inputs are fixed, and then the long-run decision, when all inputs are variable. Finally, we discuss how a manager chooses the levels of input usage that maximize profit. We will show that the output and the input decisions each leads to the same results.

11.1 CHARACTERISTICS OF PERFECT COMPETITION

The most important characteristic of perfectly competitive markets is that each firm in a competitive market behaves as a price-taker: Competitive firms take the market price of the product, which is determined by the intersection of supply and demand, as given. This price-taking behavior is the hallmark of a competitive market. In all other market structures—monopoly, monopolistic competition, and oligopoly—firms enjoy some degree of price-setting power. Three characteristics define **perfect competition:**

perfect competition
A market structure that exists when (1) firms are price-takers, (2) all firms produce a homogeneous product, and (3) entry and exit are unrestricted.

1. Perfectly competitive firms are price-takers because each individual firm in the market is so small relative to the total market that it cannot affect the market price of the good or service it produces by changing its output. Of course, if *all* producers act together, changes in quantity will definitely affect market price. But if perfect competition prevails, each producer is so small that individual changes will go unnoticed.

2. All firms produce a homogeneous or perfectly standardized commodity. The product of each firm in a perfectly competitive market is identical to the product of every other firm. This condition ensures that buyers are indifferent as to the firm from which they purchase. Product differences, whether real or imaginary, are precluded under perfect competition.

3. Entry into and exit from perfectly competitive markets are unrestricted. There are no barriers preventing new firms from entering the market, and nothing prevents existing firms from leaving a market.

In spite of the term "competitive," perfectly competitive firms do not recognize any competitiveness among themselves; that is, no direct competition among firms exists. The theoretical concept of perfect competition is diametrically opposed to the generally accepted concept of competition. Because firms in perfectly competitive markets produce identical products and face a market-determined price, managers of competitive firms have no incentive to "beat their rivals" out of sales since each firm can sell all it wants. And, of course, price-taking firms cannot compete through any kind of pricing tactics.

Markets that do not precisely meet the three conditions set forth for perfect competition frequently come close enough that the firms nonetheless behave as if they are perfect competitors. The managers in the executive M.B.A. class surveyed in the introduction to this chapter do not operate in perfectly competitive markets, but they do face a sufficient number of firms producing nearly identical goods in markets with only weak restrictions on entry, and so view themselves as price-takers. As we will show you in the next section and in the next chapter, the degree of competition faced by managers is reflected in the elasticity of the *firm's* demand. The profit-maximizing decisions developed in this chapter apply even to firms that are not exactly or perfectly competitive.

11.2 DEMAND FACING A PRICE-TAKING FIRM

Suppose you are the owner–manager of a small citrus orchard that specializes in the production of oranges, which your firm then processes to be sold as frozen concentrate. You wish to determine the maximum price you can charge for various levels of output of frozen concentrate; that is, you wish to find the demand schedule facing your firm. After consulting *The Wall Street Journal,* you find that the market-determined price of orange juice concentrate is $1.20 per pound. You have 50,000 pounds of concentrate to sell, which makes your output minuscule compared with the tens of millions of pounds of orange juice concentrate sold in the market as a whole. On top of that, you realize that buyers of orange juice concentrate don't care from whom they buy since all orange juice concentrate is virtually identical (homogeneous).

All at once it hits you like a ton of oranges: You can sell virtually all the orange juice concentrate you wish at the going market price of $1.20 per pound. Even if you increased your output tenfold to 500,000 pounds, you could still find buyers willing to pay you $1.20 per pound for the entire 500,000 pounds because your output, by itself, is not going to affect (shift) market supply in any perceptible way. Indeed, if you lowered the price to sell more oranges, you would be needlessly sacrificing revenue. You also realize that you cannot charge a price higher than $1.20 per pound because buyers will simply buy from one of the thousands of other citrus producers that sell orange juice concentrate identical to your own.

By this reasoning, you realize that the demand curve facing your citrus grove can be drawn as shown in Figure 11.1. The demand for your firm's product is horizontal at a price of $1.20 per pound of orange juice concentrate. The demand

FIGURE 11.1

Demand and Marginal Revenue Facing a Citrus Producer

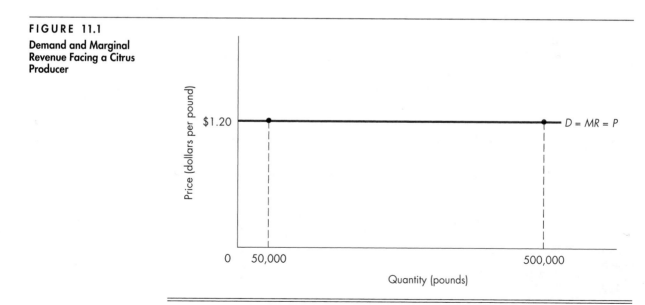

FIGURE 11.2

Derivation of Demand for a Price-Taking Firm

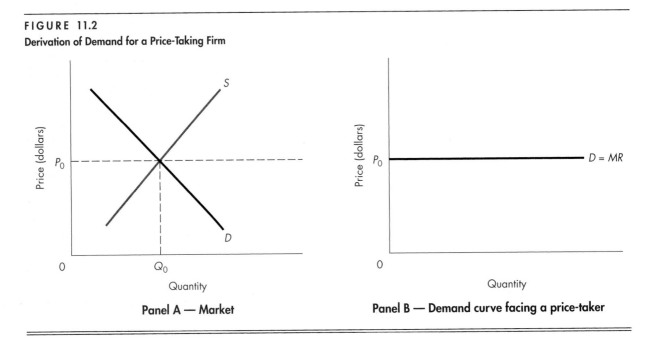

Panel A — Market   Panel B — Demand curve facing a price-taker

price for any level of orange juice concentrate is $1.20, no matter how many pounds you produce. This means that every extra pound sold contributes $1.20 to total revenue, and hence the market price of $1.20 is also the marginal revenue for every pound of orange juice concentrate sold. The demand curve facing the citrus producer is also its marginal revenue curve.

We can generalize this discussion to apply to *any* firm that operates as a price-taker in a competitive market. When a market is characterized by a large number of (relatively) small producers, each producing a homogeneous product, the demand curve facing the manager of each individual firm is horizontal at the price determined by the intersection of the *market* demand and supply curves. In addition, the horizontal demand curve is also the marginal revenue curve facing the manager.

Figure 11.2 illustrates the derivation of demand for a price-taking firm. Note, in the figure, that the *market* demand curve D in Panel A is downward-sloping, which the law of demand always requires of a demand curve. It is the demand curve faced by a single price-taking firm that is horizontal, as shown in Panel B of Figure 11.2. Recall from Chapter 2 that demand price is the maximum price buyers can be charged for a given amount of the good. The demand price is constant, and equal to P_0, for any level of output produced by the firm. Since each additional unit sold adds exactly P_0 to total revenue, marginal revenue equals P_0 for all output levels for the firm, as shown in Panel B in Figure 11.2.

The horizontal demand curve facing a price-taking firm is frequently called a **perfectly** (or infinitely) **elastic demand.** Recall from Chapter 6 that the point

perfectly elastic demand
Horizontal demand facing a single, price-taking firm in a competitive market $(|E| = \infty)$.

elasticity of demand is measured by $E = P/(P - A)$, where A is the price intercept of the demand curve. Measured at any given price, as demand becomes flatter, $|P - A|$ becomes smaller and $|E|$ becomes larger. In the limit when demand is horizontal, $P - A = 0$, and $|E| = \infty$. Thus, for a horizontal demand, demand is said to be infinitely elastic or perfectly elastic.

Looked at another way, the product sold by a competitive firm has a large number of *perfect* substitutes: the identical (homogeneous) products sold by the other firms in the industry. As we stressed in Chapter 6, the better the substitutes for a product, the more elastic the demand for the product. It follows from this relation that a perfectly competitive firm, facing many perfect substitutes, will have a perfectly elastic demand.

Again, we emphasize that the fact that perfectly competitive firms face a perfectly elastic or horizontal demand does not mean that the law of demand does not apply to perfectly competitive markets. It does. The *market demand* for the product is downward-sloping.

Relation The demand curve facing a competitive price-taking firm is horizontal or perfectly elastic at the price determined by the intersection of the *market* demand and supply curves. Since marginal revenue equals price for a competitive firm, the demand curve is also simultaneously the marginal revenue curve (i.e., $D = MR$). Price-taking firms can sell all they want at the market price. Each additional unit of sales adds to total revenue an amount equal to price.

11.3 PROFIT MAXIMIZATION IN THE SHORT RUN

We now turn to the output decision facing the manager of a price-taking firm in a competitive industry in the short run. Recall that the short run is that time period of decision making during which the firm has at least one of its inputs fixed in quantity. In the short-run period of analysis, the manager has fixed costs that must be paid regardless of the level of output and variable costs that vary with the level of output.

In the short run, a manager must make two decisions. The first decision is whether to produce or shut down during the period. By **shut down,** we mean the manager decides to produce zero output and to hire none of the variable inputs. When production is zero, the only costs incurred by the firm are the fixed costs. If the first decision is to produce (rather than shut down), the second decision is the choice of the optimal level of output.

> **shut down**
> Condition in which a firm produces zero output but must still pay for fixed inputs.

Using the terminology presented in Chapter 3, the optimal level of output is the level of output that maximizes the firm's net benefit function, which is economic profit (π):

$$\pi = TR - TC$$

where TR is total revenue and TC is total economic cost. Under some circumstances, which we discuss later, a manager will choose to incur losses (i.e., profit is negative) yet continue to produce rather than shut down. In such a situation, the manager chooses the level of output that *minimizes* the loss of the firm. Because minimizing a loss is equivalent to maximizing a (negative) profit, the decision rule for finding the optimal level of output is exactly the same regardless of whether profit is positive or negative. For this reason, we will speak of profit maximization even though the rule applies to a firm that is minimizing a loss.

In this section, we first discuss the firm's output decision when the firm can earn positive economic profit. We apply marginal analysis to find the profit-maximizing output, which allows us to demonstrate why cost per unit and profit per unit (profit margin) should be ignored when choosing the optimal level of output. We then give the conditions under which the manager should choose to shut down rather than produce. Next, a numerical example is presented to emphasize, as we stressed in Chapter 3, that fixed costs are completely irrelevant for managerial decision making. After briefly summarizing the firm's output decision in the short run, we derive the supply curve for a competitive firm.

The Output Decision: Positive Economic Profit

Figure 11.3 shows a typical set of short-run cost curves: marginal (SMC), average total cost (ATC), and average variable cost (AVC). Average fixed cost is omitted for convenience and because, as we demonstrated in Chapter 3 and show you again in this section, fixed costs are irrelevant for decision-making purposes. Let's suppose the market-determined price, and therefore marginal revenue, is $36 per unit. What level of output should the firm produce to maximize profit?

profit margin (or average profit)
The difference between price and average total cost: $P - ATC$. Profit margin is irrelevant for making optimal output decisions.

Before we show you the correct output decision, we want to explain why managers should not choose the output level that maximizes *average profit* or *profit margin*. **Average profit,** which is total profit divided by output (π/Q), is equal to **profit margin,** which is the difference between price and unit cost ($P - ATC$):

$$\text{Average profit} = \frac{\pi}{Q} = \frac{(P - ATC)Q}{Q}$$
$$= P - ATC = \text{Profit margin}$$

Suppose the manager mistakenly chooses to produce 400 units of output because the difference between price and average total cost, profit margin, is maximized. At 400 units of output, profit margin or average profit is maximized at a value of $20 (= $36 − 16) because price is constant at $36 and ATC reaches its minimum value of $16 at 400 units (Point N). The mistake in producing 400 units is that *total* profit (π) is not maximized. As we will show you shortly, the maximum profit that can be earned when price is $36 occurs at 600 units. At 400 units, total revenue is $14,400, which is price times quantity ($36 × 400), and total cost of production is $6,400, which is average total cost times quantity ($16 × 400). Thus total profit at the point that maximizes profit *margin* is only $8,000 (= $14,400 − $6,400), which can also be calculated by multiplying profit margin (average profit) times quantity: $8,000 = $20 × 400.

Now let us apply marginal analysis to see why 400 units do not maximize profit and to find the output level that does so. At 400 units, suppose the firm increases production by 1 unit, which, of course, it can sell for $36. The marginal cost of the

FIGURE 11.3
Profit Maximization: $P = \$36$

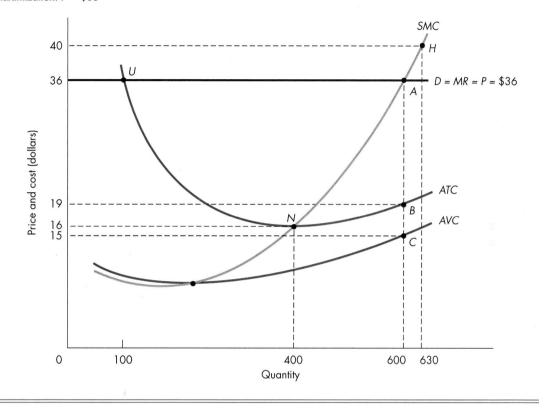

401st unit is (approximately) $16 (see point N in Figure 11.3). By choosing to produce and sell the 401st unit, the manager adds $36 to revenue and only $16 to cost, thereby adding $20 to the firm's profit. By this same reasoning, the manager would continue to increase production as long as $MR\ (= P)$ is greater than SMC. In Figure 11.3, output would be increased to 600 units, the output level for which $MR = SMC = \$36$ (point A in Figure 11.3). At 600 units, total revenue is $21,600 (= $36 × 600). Total cost is $11,400, which is average total cost times quantity ($19 × 600). The maximum possible profit is $10,200 (= $21,600 − $11,400), which is $2,200 more profit than the firm would earn if it produced 400 units to maximize profit margin. As long as the firm can earn positive profit, the profit-maximizing output level occurs at a higher output than the output that maximizes profit margin (average profit). For this reason, profit margin should be ignored when finding the optimal level of output. This principle holds not just for competitive markets but for all market structures.

▢ **Principle** Average profit, which is total profit divided by output (π/Q), is equal to profit margin, which is the difference between price and unit cost $(P - ATC)$. The level of output that maximizes total profit occurs at a higher level of output than the output that maximizes profit margin (and average profit). Managers should ignore profit margin (average profit) when making optimal decisions.

Suppose, on the other hand, the manager makes the mistake of producing too much output by producing 630 units. Note that for 630 units marginal revenue (price) is less than marginal cost: Price is $36 and the marginal cost of producing the 630th unit of output is $40 (see point *H* in Figure 11.3). The manager could decrease output by 1 unit and reduce the firm's cost by $40 (the cost of the extra resources needed to produce the 630th unit). The lost sale of that unit would reduce revenue by only $36, so the firm's profit would increase by $4. By the same reasoning, the manager would continue to decrease production as long as *MR* (= *P*) is less than *SMC* (up to point *A* in Figure 11.3). It follows then that the manager maximizes profit by choosing that level of output where *MR* (= *P*) = *SMC*. This rule is, of course, the rule for unconstrained maximization set forth in Chapter 3 (*MB* = *MC*).

Figure 11.4 shows the total revenue, total cost, and profit curves for the situation presented in Figure 11.3. Notice in Panel A that *TR* is linear with slope equal to $36 (= *P* = *MR*) since each additional unit sold adds $36 to total revenue. Also note that in Panel B, at 401 units, the slope of the profit curve is $20, which follows from the preceding discussion about producing the 401st unit. At 600 units, profit is maximized at $10,200, which occurs at the peak of the profit curve (point *A'*) where the slope of the profit curve is 0. The points *U* and *V* in Figure 11.4 (100 units and 950 units) are sometimes referred to as *break-even points* because total revenue equals total cost and the firm earns zero profit.

Since total cost of producing 600 units, $11,400, includes the opportunity cost of the resources provided by the firm's owners (the implicit costs), the owners, by producing 600 units, earn $10,200 more than they could if they had employed their resources in their best alternative use. The $10,200 economic profit is a return to the owners *in excess* of what they could have earned in their best alternative.

T ▷ ②

The Output Decision: Operating at a Loss

In the short run, when the price of a firm's product is less than average total cost $(P < ATC)$ for all output levels, total revenue $(P \times Q)$ will fall short of total cost $(ATC \times Q)$ and the firm will suffer a loss no matter what output it produces—even if it shuts down and produces nothing. In this situation, the manager must choose an output level—either 0 output or a positive output—that will minimize the unavoidable loss in the short run. Obviously, if a firm shuts down and produces no output, it generates no revenue and incurs no variable costs but must still pay for its fixed inputs. Thus a firm that shuts down in the short run loses an amount equal to its fixed costs:

$$\pi = TR - TVC - TFC$$
$$= 0 - 0 - TFC$$
$$= -TFC$$

FIGURE 11.4
Profit Maximization When $P = \$36$

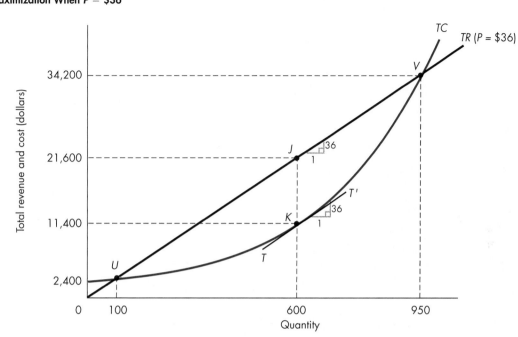

Panel A — Total revenue and total cost

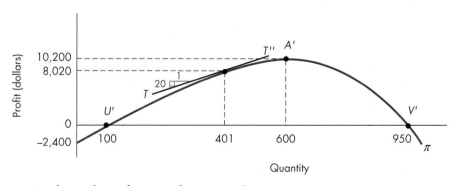

Panel B — The profit curve when price is $36

Clearly, a manager should only produce a positive output, instead of shutting down, if producing a positive output results in a smaller loss than total fixed cost.

Whenever a firm faces a loss in the short run (i.e., $P < ATC$), the firm's loss is minimized by producing the positive level of output where $P = SMC$—rather than producing nothing at all—as long as price exceeds average variable cost ($P > AVC$). When $P > AVC$, total revenue exceeds total variable cost ($TR > TVC$). The firm generates enough revenue to pay all its variable costs and has some revenue left over to apply toward its fixed costs. Consequently, the loss incurred from production must be less than total fixed cost, which, as we just explained, is the amount lost if nothing is produced. In the alternative situation when $P < AVC$, total revenue will not be enough even to cover all fixed costs, so the firm would lose *more* than its fixed costs: It loses the portion of variable costs it cannot cover plus all of its fixed costs. Because it will lose more than TFC by producing, the firm should shut down and produce nothing when price falls below average variable cost.

When price exactly equals average variable cost ($P = AVC$), short-run profit is, of course, the same for either decision, and the manager is indifferent between producing the output where $P = SMC$ or producing no output at all. To resolve any confusion over this point of indifference, we will assume managers choose to produce rather than shut down when P exactly equals AVC. We can summarize the manager's decision to produce or not to produce with a principle:

☐ **Principle**   In the short run, the manager of a firm will choose to produce the output where $P = SMC$, rather than shut down, as long as total revenue is greater than or equal to total variable cost ($TR \geq TVC$) or, equivalently, price is greater than or equal to average variable cost ($P \geq AVC$). If price is less than average variable cost ($P < AVC$), the manager will shut down and produce nothing, losing an amount equal to total fixed cost.

Figure 11.5 illustrates the manager's decision to produce or shut down. Suppose the manager faces a price of $10.50. The firm suffers an unavoidable loss in the short run because $10.50 is less than average total cost ($P < ATC$) at every level of output. If the manager does decide to produce, rather than shut down, the firm should produce 300 units where $MR (= P) = SMC = \$10.50$. At 300 units of output, total revenue is $3,150 (= $10.50 × 300), total cost is $5,100 (= $17 ×300), and the firm earns a (negative) profit equal to −$1,950 (= $3,150 − $5,100). The manager should choose to produce 300 units at a loss of $1,950 only if the firm would lose more than $1,950 by producing nothing.

To compute the total fixed cost (the loss when $Q = 0$), recall that $TFC = AFC \times Q$. Also recall that $AFC = ATC - AVC$. You can see in Figure 11.5 that at 300 units of output $AFC = \$8$ (the distance from G to F, or $17 − $9), so $TFC = \$8 \times \$300 = \$2,400$. Clearly, the manager should produce 300 units at a loss of $1,950 rather than produce 0 units (shut down) and lose $2,400.

Notice also that, at 300 units, price ($10.50) exceeds average variable cost ($9) by $1.50. Thus, on 300 units of output, the total revenue of $3,150 exceeds the total variable cost of $2,700 (= $9 × 300) by $450 (= $3,150 − $2,700). The $450 revenue left over after paying variable costs can then be applied toward paying a part of

FIGURE 11.5

Loss Minimization in the Short Run: $P = \$10.50$

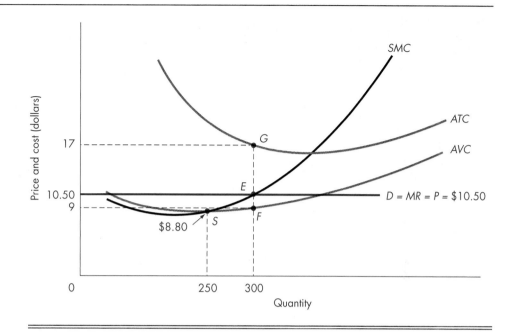

the $2,400 fixed cost. The remainder of the fixed costs that are not covered represent the loss to the firm ($1,950 = $2,400 − $450).

As you can now see, when price falls below *minimum* average variable cost, the firm will shut down in the short run. For this reason, minimum average variable cost is called the **shutdown price.** In Figure 11.5, the firm's shutdown price is $8.80 at point S. If price is greater than or equal to $8.80, the firm should produce the output where $P = SMC$. If price falls below $8.80, the firm should shut down.

shutdown price
The price below which a firm shuts down in the short run (minimum *AVC*).

The Irrelevance of Fixed Costs

When managers make production decisions, they decide how much to produce (if they do produce) by choosing the level of output where price equals marginal cost. They decide whether or not to produce that output by comparing price with average variable cost. If $P > AVC$, the firm should produce (even at a loss) the output level at which $P = SMC$. Thus fixed costs or sunk costs play absolutely no role in the manager's output decision.

To provide you with more insight into why fixed costs do not matter in decision making, we remind you that the marginal cost curve is unaffected by changes in fixed cost. Recall from Chapter 8 that the U-shape of the marginal cost curve is determined by the S-shape of the total variable cost curve or the shape of the marginal product curve. In Figure 11.5, for example, any change whatsoever in fixed cost has no effect on the marginal cost curve. If total fixed costs double, SMC does not shift or change shape, and marginal revenue still intersects marginal cost at the

TABLE 11.1
The Irrelevance of Fixed Costs

(1)	(2)	(3)	(4)	(5)	(6)	(7)	(8)
					Revenue		
				Total	remaining	Profit	Profit
Total			Total	variable	after paying	(loss) if	(loss) if
fixed costs	Price	Output	revenue	costs	variable costs	Q = 300	Q = 0
$ 200	$10.50	300	$3,150	$2,700	$450	$ 250	$ −200
2,400	10.50	300	3,150	2,700	450	−1,950	−2,400
3,000	10.50	300	3,150	2,700	450	−2,550	−3,000
10,000	10.50	300	3,150	2,700	450	−9,550	−10,000
100,000	10.50	300	3,150	2,700	450	−99,550	−100,000

same level of output. No matter what the level of fixed costs, 300 units is the profit-maximizing (loss-minimizing) level of output when price is $10.50.

To illustrate that fixed costs do not affect the decision to produce or not to produce, we chose five different levels of total fixed costs and examined the shutdown decision for a firm with the SMC and AVC curves shown in Figure 11.5. Keeping market price at $10.50, Table 11.1 shows all the relevant revenue, cost, and profit information for each of the five levels of fixed cost. First note that the optimal level of production for any of the five levels of fixed cost is 300 units because SMC equals $10.50 at 300 units, no matter what the level of fixed costs. In all cases shown in Table 11.1, total revenue is $3,150, total variable cost is $2,700, and, after all variable costs are paid, $450 remains to apply toward the fixed costs.

When fixed cost is only $200, economic profit is positive because revenue exceeds all costs. Obviously the manager chooses to produce and earn a profit, rather than produce nothing and lose the fixed cost. For each of the other four cases, the revenue remaining after paying variable cost is not enough to pay all the fixed cost, and profit is negative. Columns 7 and 8, respectively, show the loss if the firm produces 450 units (where $P = SMC$) and the loss if the firm produces nothing and loses its fixed cost.

Note that in all cases when the firm makes a loss, the loss from producing 300 units is $450 less than the loss if the firm shuts down. No matter how high the total fixed cost, the firm loses $450 less by producing a positive amount of output than by producing nothing (shutting down). The level of fixed cost has no effect on the firm's decision to produce.

We can now summarize the short-run output decision for price-taking firms with a principle:

☐ **Principle** (1) Average variable cost tells whether to produce; the firm ceases to produce—shuts down—if price falls below minimum AVC. (2) Marginal cost tells how much to produce; if $P \geq$ minimum AVC, the firm produces the output at which SMC = P. (3) Average total cost tells how much profit or loss is made if the firm decides to produce; profit equals the difference between P and ATC (average profit or profit margin) multiplied by the quantity produced and sold.

ILLUSTRATION 11.1

Do R&D Expenditures Affect Drug Prices?

In August 1997, the Clinton administration announced that drug companies would be required to test whether the medicines they sell for adults are also safe and effective for children and to put the pediatric dosages on the labels. It was estimated that the new requirement would increase the cost of drug development by more than $200 million annually. A former official with the Food and Drug Administration (FDA), in an editorial in *The Wall Street Journal*, noted that this regulation would delay the introduction of new drugs and that "government regulation imposes enormous costs on drug development that must be passed along to consumers in higher prices."[a]

A well-known economist, in a follow-up letter to the *WSJ*, agreed that more stringent requirements would increase expected research costs per product introduction.[b] However, he disagreed that increased costs of drug development would be passed along to consumers in higher prices. He pointed out, "Nearly all pharmaceutical research and development costs are borne prior to FDA approval and before the first dose is ever sold." Such costs would be fixed or sunk costs

and would not affect a firm's price or output decisions: "The value of a product depends on its acceptance in the marketplace and the costs of producing another unit of output, but not at all on whether it was discovered either after a long and arduous effort or fortuitously at the first attempt."

According to the letter, price setting depends on anticipated future conditions and not on those in the past, even though expected research costs may affect research budgets and thereby the number of new products in the future. These costs would not influence prices charged for products already discovered.

This response reinforces our emphasis in this text that sunk costs, already borne, and fixed costs, which must be paid no matter what decision is made, should not be taken into account in price and output decisions. There is, however, more to this story, which we will continue in Illustration 11.2 after we set forth the theory of the firm in the long run.

[a]Henry I. Miller, "FDA Loves Kids So Much, It'll Make You Sick," *The Wall Street Journal*, Aug. 18, 1997.
[b]William S. Comanor, "Higher Price Means Better Medicine," *The Wall Street Journal*, Sept. 9, 1997.

11.4 SHORT-RUN SUPPLY FOR THE FIRM AND INDUSTRY

Using the concepts developed in the preceding discussion, it is possible to derive the short-run supply curve for an individual firm in a competitive market. Figure 11.6 illustrates the process. In Panel A, points a, b, and c are the profit-maximizing equilibrium points for the firm at prices of $5, $9, and $17, respectively. That is, the marginal cost curve above average variable cost indicates the quantity the firm would be willing and able to supply at each price, which is the definition of supply. Panel B shows 80, 110, and 150 units of output as the quantities supplied from Panel A when market price is $5, $9, and $17, respectively. For a market price lower than minimum average variable cost, quantity supplied is 0.

▫ **Relation** The short-run supply curve for an individual price-taking firm is the portion of the firm's marginal cost curve above minimum average variable cost. For market prices less than minimum average variable cost, quantity supplied is zero.

Just as we described in Chapter 5 for market demand curves, the industry supply curve can be obtained by summing (horizontally) the marginal cost curves of each producer. If, for example, the industry has 100 firms identical to the one

FIGURE 11.6
Derivation of a Short-Run Supply Curve for an Individual Firm

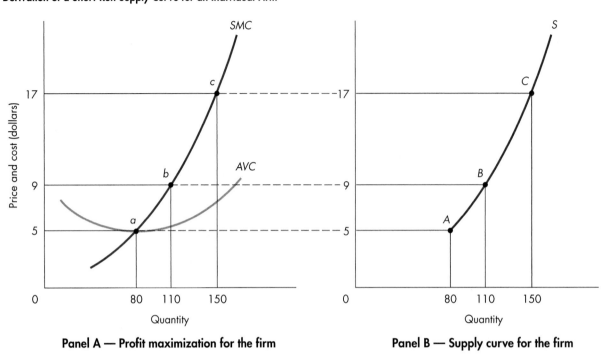

Panel A — Profit maximization for the firm

Panel B — Supply curve for the firm

shown in Panel B, the industry quantity supplied is 8,000 units at a price of $5, 11,000 units at a price of $9, and 15,000 at a price of $17. The firm's short-run supply is upward-sloping, so supply for a competitive industry must also be upward-sloping. We should note that any change that shifts the firm's marginal cost curve shifts each firm's supply curve and hence the industry's supply curve. For example, an increase in wage rates would increase (shift upward) each firm's marginal cost curve, since labor is usually a variable input. With higher wages, the marginal cost of producing each additional unit of output would rise, so each firm would supply less at each price of the product.

▣ **Relation**   The short-run supply curve for a competitive industry can be obtained by horizontally summing the supply curves of all the individual firms in the industry. Short-run supply for a competitive industry is always upward-sloping.

This concludes our analysis of a competitive price-taking firm's short-run profit-maximizing output decision. As you saw, the firm can make an economic profit or a loss in the short run, depending on market price. Certainly a firm would not go on indefinitely suffering a loss in each period. In the long run, a firm would exit from the industry if it could not cover its total cost with its revenue. Or even if the firm is making a profit in the short run, it may wish to change its plant size or capacity in the long run in order to earn even more profit. We will now analyze the profit-maximizing output decision of price-taking firms in the long run when all inputs, and therefore all costs, are variable.

11.5 PROFIT MAXIMIZATION IN THE LONG RUN

In the short run, the manager's production decisions are limited because some of the inputs used by the firm are fixed for the short-run period of production. Typically, the key input that a manager views as fixed in the short run is the amount of capital available to the firm in the form of plant or equipment. In the long run, all inputs are variable, and a manager can choose to employ any size plant—amount of capital—required to produce most efficiently the level of output that will maximize profit. The choice of plant size is often referred to as the "scale of operation." The scale of operation may be fixed in the short run, but in the long run it can be altered as economic conditions warrant.

The long run can also be viewed as the planning stage, prior to a firm's entry into an industry. In this stage the firm is trying to decide how large a production facility to construct: that is, the optimal scale of operation. Once the plans have congealed (a particular-size plant is built), the firm operates in a short-run situation. Recall that a fundamental characteristic of perfect competition is unrestricted entry and exit of firms into and out of the industry. As you will see in this section, the entry of new firms, which is possible only in the long run, plays a crucial role in long-run analysis of competitive industries.

In the long run, just as in the short run, the firm attempts to maximize profits. Exactly the same approach is used, except in this case there are no fixed costs; all costs are variable. As before, the firm takes a market-determined price as given. This market price is again the firm's marginal revenue. As in the preceding section, the firm would increase output as long as the marginal revenue from each additional unit is greater than the marginal cost of that unit. It would decrease output when marginal cost exceeds marginal revenue. The firm maximizes profit by equating marginal cost and marginal revenue.

Profit-Maximizing Equilibrium for the Firm in the Long Run

Suppose that an entrepreneur is considering entering a competitive industry in which the firms already in the industry are making economic profits. The prospective entrant, knowing the long-run costs and the product price, expects to make an economic profit also. Since all inputs are variable, the entrant can choose the scale or the plant size for the new firm. We examine the decision graphically.

In Figure 11.7, *LAC* and *LMC* are the long-run average and marginal cost curves. The firm's perfectly elastic demand *D* indicates the equilibrium price ($17) and is the same as marginal revenue. As long as price is greater than long-run average

FIGURE 11.7

**Profit-Maximizing
Equilibrium in the Long Run**

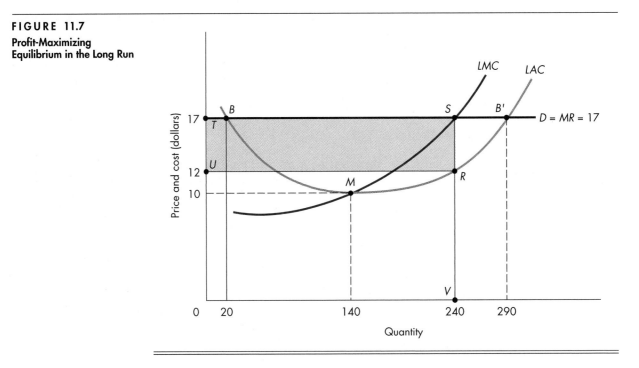

cost, the firm can make a profit. Thus, in Figure 11.7, any output between 20 and 290 units yields some economic profit. As mentioned earlier, the points of output B and B' are sometimes called the break-even points. At these two points, price equals long-run average cost and economic profit is 0.

Maximum profit occurs at 240 units of output (point S), where marginal revenue equals long-run marginal cost. The firm would want to select the plant size to produce 240 units of output. Note that the firm, under these circumstances, would not want to produce 140 units of output at point M, the minimum point of long-run average cost. At M, marginal revenue exceeds marginal cost, so the firm can gain by producing more output. As shown in Figure 11.7, at point S total revenue (price times quantity) at 240 units of output is equal to $4,080 (= 17×240), which is the area of the rectangle $0TSV$. The total cost (average cost times quantity) is equal to $2,880 (= 12×240), which is the area of the rectangle $0URV$. The total profit is $1,200 [= ($17 - $12) \times 240$], which is the area of the rectangle $UTSR$.

Thus the firm would plan to operate at a scale (or plant size) such that long-run marginal cost equals price. This would be the most profitable situation under the circumstances. But, as we shall show, these circumstances will change. If the firm illustrated in Figure 11.7 is free to enter the industry, so are other prospective entrants. And this entry will drive down the market price. We will now show how this occurs.

ILLUSTRATION 11.2

Do R&D Expenditures Affect Drug Prices?
The Rest of the Story

Recall from Illustration 11.1 a *Wall Street Journal* editorial that argued that new regulations on drugs would raise the cost of drug development, thus causing delays in drug introduction and higher drug prices to consumers. In a letter to the editor, an economist pointed out that the research and development costs are sunk or fixed costs and therefore would have *no effect on prices for drugs already discovered.* This is correct. But because the previous illustration was in the context of our discussion of the firm's short-run decision making, we did not focus there on the long-run implications of the analysis. Now that we have discussed the long run, we can address these long-run implications here.

Note that this statement that R&D costs would have no effect on the prices of drugs already discovered is short-run analysis. Although we cannot know for certain, it appears that the editorial writer was analyzing possible long-run effects of drug regulation. Obviously, research and development expenses are a sunk cost once they have been made. However, if a firm is in the planning stage of developing a new drug or modifying a drug to comply with new regulations, these potential development costs would be variable. As such, they would affect a firm's decision about how much to spend on development or whether to spend at all.

Suppose, for example, that a drug manufacturer is considering developing a new drug and, if the decision is made to do it, is determining how much to spend. In making this decision, the manager would weigh the expected additional costs of research and development plus the expected costs of production and sales along with the expected additional revenues to be generated. This is a long-run marginal cost–marginal benefit decision. The manager would have some idea about the price that could be charged for the new drug if it is introduced. Suppose new FDA regulations are expected to increase these expected R&D costs. That could tip the balance against development of the new drug if expected additional costs are now greater than expected additional revenues. If such is the case, there would be a little less competition among related drugs than would have been the case with the new drug, possibly resulting in higher prices of similar drugs.

We do not mean to imply that such a scenario would occur in all cases. Certainly some new drugs would be profitable even after the increased development costs necessary to comply with new regulations. But some probably would not. Depending on how many would not, the supply of new drugs on the market would decrease, prices would rise, and fewer drugs would be available.

In the long run all costs are variable. To undertake any new investment project, including R&D expenditure, managers must expect that these costs will be covered by revenue. Anything that raises these costs is likely to raise prices.

So in the case of drug regulations' raising drug prices, both writers were correct. In the short run, additional development costs would not increase the price of drugs already on the market. In the long run, additional development costs would be likely to raise drug prices.

Long-Run Competitive Equilibrium for the Industry

While the individual firm is in long-run profit-maximizing equilibrium when $MR = LMC$ (as shown in Figure 11.7), the *industry* will not be in long-run equilibrium until there is no incentive for new firms to enter or incumbent firms to exit. The economic force that induces firms to enter into an industry or that drives firms out of an industry is the existence of economic profits or economic losses, respectively.

Economic profits attract new firms into the industry, and entry of these new firms increases industry supply. This increased supply drives down price. As price falls, all firms in the industry adjust their output levels in order to remain in profit-maximizing equilibrium. New firms continue to enter the industry, price continues to fall, and existing firms continue to adjust their outputs until all economic profits are eliminated. There is no longer an incentive for new firms to enter, and the owners of all firms in the industry earn only what they could make in their best alternatives.

Economic losses motivate some existing firms to exit, or leave, the industry. The exit of these firms decreases industry supply. The reduction in supply drives up market price. As price is driven up, all firms in the industry must adjust their output levels in order to continue maximizing profit. Firms continue to exit until economic losses are eliminated, and economic profit is zero.

long-run competitive equilibrium
Condition in which all firms are producing where $P = LMC$ and economic profits are zero $(P = LAC)$.

Long-run competitive equilibrium, then, requires not only that all firms be maximizing profits, but also that economic profits be zero.[1] These two conditions are satisfied when price equals marginal cost $(P = LMC)$, so that firms are maximizing profit, and price also equals average cost $(P = LAC)$, so that no entry or exit occurs. These two conditions for equilibrium can be satisfied simultaneously only when price equals minimum LAC, at which point $LMC = LAC$.

Figure 11.8 shows a typical firm in long-run competitive equilibrium.[2] The long-run cost curves in Figure 11.8 are similar to those in Figure 11.7. The difference between the two figures is that in Figure 11.7 the *firm* is maximizing profit, but the industry is not yet in 0-profit equilibrium. In Figure 11.8, the firm is maximizing profit (P equals LMC), and the industry is also in long-run competitive equilibrium because economic profit is 0 $(P = LAC)$.

Long-run equilibrium occurs at a price of $10 and output of 140, at point M. Each (identical) firm in the industry makes neither economic profit nor loss. There is no incentive for further entry because the rate of return in this industry is the normal rate of return, which is equal to the firm's best alternative. For the same reason, there is no incentive for a firm to leave the industry. The number of firms stabilizes, and each firm operates with a plant size represented by short-run marginal and average cost, SMC and ATC, respectively. We can now summarize long-run competitive equilibrium with a principle:

---

[1]Economists, regulators, and policy analysts sometimes refer to the implicit cost of owner-supplied resources as "normal profit." Total economic costs of production equal explicit costs plus normal profit. Thus when economic profit is zero, the owners are making just enough accounting profit (total revenue minus explicit costs) to pay themselves an amount equal to what they could have earned by using their resources in their best alternative use. When economic profit is zero, we can say the firm is earning just a normal profit or normal rate of return.

[2]We will assume that all firms in the industry have identical cost curves. For example, Figures 11.7 and 11.8 show the cost curves of a typical firm. While it is not necessary to assume identical costs for all firms, this assumption substantially simplifies the theoretical analysis without affecting the conclusions.

FIGURE 11.8
Long-Run Equilibrium for a
Firm in a Competitive
Industry

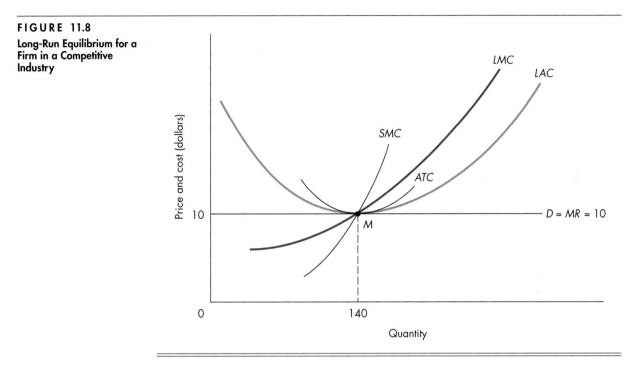

□ **Principle**   In long-run competitive equilibrium, all firms are maximizing profit ($P = LMC$), and there
is no incentive for firms to enter or exit the industry because economic profit is zero ($P = LAC$).
Long-run competitive equilibrium occurs because of the entry of new firms into the industry or the
exit of existing firms from the industry. The market adjusts so that $P = LMC = LAC$, which is at the
minimum point on LAC.

Long-Run Supply for a Perfectly Competitive Industry

In the short run when the amount of capital in an industry is fixed, as well as the
number of firms, an increase in price causes industry output to increase. This increase is accomplished by each firm's using its fixed capital more intensively; that
is, each firm hires more of the variable inputs to increase output. As we discussed
previously, the short-run industry supply curve is always upward-sloping.

In the long run, when entry of new firms is possible, the industry's response to
an increase in price takes on a new dimension: The industry's supply adjustment
to a change in price is not complete until entry or exit results in zero economic
profit. This means that for all points on the long-run industry supply curve, economic profit must be zero.

To derive the industry supply curve in the long run, we must differentiate between two types of industries: (1) an increasing-cost industry and (2) a constant-
cost industry. An industry is an **increasing-cost industry** if, as all firms in the
industry expand output and thus input usage, the prices of some inputs used
in the industry rise. For example, if the personal computer industry expands

**increasing-cost
industry**
An industry in which input
prices rise as all firms in the
industry expand output.

FIGURE 11.9
Long-Run Industry Supply for a Constant-Cost Industry

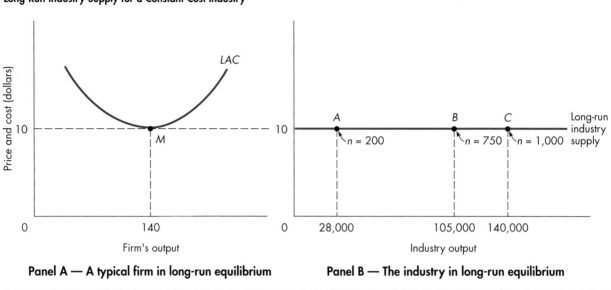

Panel A — A typical firm in long-run equilibrium   Panel B — The industry in long-run equilibrium

constant-cost industry
An industry in which input prices remain constant as all firms in the industry expand output.

production by 15 percent, the price of many specialized inputs (such as microprocessor chips, RAM boards, disk drives, and so on) will increase, causing marginal and average cost for all firms to shift upward. An industry is a **constant-cost industry** if, as industry output and input usage increase, all prices of inputs used in the industry remain constant.[3] For example, the rutabaga industry is probably so small that its usage of inputs such as fertilizer, farm labor, and machinery have no effect on the prices of these inputs. This industry is therefore probably a constant-cost industry.

Figure 11.9 shows the relation between a typical firm (Panel A) in a constant-cost industry and the long-run industry supply curve (Panel B) for a constant-cost industry. Note that the supply price in the long run is constant and equal to $10 for all levels of industry output. This result follows from the long-run equilibrium condition that economic profit must be 0. The long-run supply price, $10, is equal to minimum long-run average cost for every level of output produced by the industry because the entry of new firms always bids price down to the point of 0 economic profit (point M in Figure 11.9). Because the industry is a constant-cost industry, expansion of industry output does not cause minimum LAC (point M) to rise. Therefore, long-run supply price (= minimum LAC) is constant.

---

[3]Theoretically it is possible that input prices might fall as industry output rises, in which case there is a decreasing-cost industry. Decreasing-cost industries are so extremely rare that we will not consider them in this text.

FIGURE 11.10

Long-Run Industry Supply for an Increasing-Cost Industry

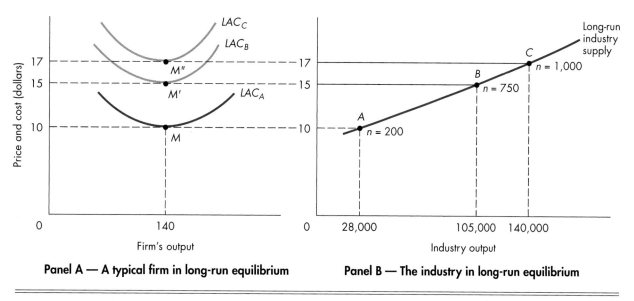

Panel A — A typical firm in long-run equilibrium

Panel B — The industry in long-run equilibrium

For example, if industry output expands from 28,000 units to 105,000 units through the entry of new firms, each firm (old and new) ends up producing 140 units of output at the minimum LAC of $10. No single firm expands output in the long run; output expands because there are more firms, each producing 140 units. When the industry produces 28,000, 105,000, and 140,000 units, the industry is in long-run equilibrium with 200, 750, and 1,000 firms, respectively. Finally, note that at all points on long-run industry supply (A, B, and C, for example), economic profit is 0. For a constant-cost industry, long-run industry supply is perfectly elastic.

Next consider an increasing-cost industry. Figure 11.10 illustrates the relation between a typical firm (Panel A) in an increasing-cost industry and the long-run industry supply curve (Panel B). In contrast to the constant-cost case, the supply price for an increasing-cost industry rises as industry output increases.

Since the industry is an increasing-cost industry, as the industry expands output, resource prices rise, causing the long-run average cost in Panel A to shift upward. LAC_A, LAC_B, and LAC_C represent the increasingly higher long-run average costs associated with industry output levels of 28,000, 105,000, and 140,000 units, respectively. For example, when the industry output increases from 28,000 units, produced by 200 firms, to 105,000 units, input prices rise, causing minimum LAC to rise to M' (in Panel A). Each firm in the industry still produces 140 units, but there are now 750 firms producing a total industry output of 105,000 units at an

ILLUSTRATION 11.3

Asian Chipmakers Headed for Trouble (Again)?

Looking for a way to invest in the new, high-tech economy? For only a couple *billion* dollars you can buy a state-of-the-art fabrication plant for making semiconductor chips. You could be the first person on your block to own a "foundry"—a semiconductor manufacturer that makes chips for sale to third parties. Should you decide to make such an investment, you would then need to decide whether to produce generic *memory* chips (chips that store programs and data) or specialty *logic* chips (the "thinking" chips in various consumer products). For either kind of semiconductor chip, investing in a foundry sounds like a sure thing to you. After all, demand for chips should be strong for years to come and, at $2 billion to enter the business, how much competition can there be anyway? Apparently plenty, as it turns out.

A recent article in *BusinessWeek* reported that Asian chipmakers have embarked on a spending spree, adding billions of dollars of new fabrication plants in just the last year. "The last time Asian chipmakers went on such a binge was in the mid-1990s. The results were tragic: huge overcapacity, a crash in exports, and

the financial ruin of hard-charging new entrants." Well, that's hardly the kind of news you were looking for, so you decide to give your investment advisor a call to see what she thinks about investing in a chip foundry. She tells you not to worry; the disastrous meltdown in semiconductor prices happened back in the "old" days when everyone was producing memory chips. With no means of differentiating their generic DRAM memory chips, the Asian chipmakers were selling a high-tech commodity in a perfectly competitive market. She tells you, "The Asian chipmakers might as well have been selling orange juice concentrate or pork bellies. With a homogeneous product and no barriers to entry, Asian foundries were on their way to becoming another (textbook) example of perfect competitors making economic losses on their way to earning no profit at all in long-run equilibrium."

Maybe things will be different this time around. According to *BusinessWeek*, "Now, the overwhelming majority of spending is for the logic chips used in wireless phones, set-top boxes, and countless other digital appliances that are in hot demand as Internet use explodes." Indeed, the foundries producing specialty chips have experienced sharp increases in profits.

average cost of $15.[4] Just as in the case of a constant-cost industry, economic profit is 0 at all points along the long-run supply curve. And similarly, when industry output increases from 105,000 to 140,000 units, input prices rise further, causing minimum LAC to rise to M''. At point C, 1,000 firms each produces 140 units at an average cost of $17 per unit and earns 0 economic profit.

☐ **Relations** For a constant-cost industry, as industry output expands, input prices remain constant, and the minimum point on long-run average cost (LAC) is unchanged. Since long-run supply price equals minimum LAC, the long-run industry supply curve is perfectly elastic (horizontal) for a constant-cost industry. For an increasing-cost industry, as industry output expands, input prices are bid up, causing minimum LAC to rise and long-run supply price to rise. The long-run industry supply curve for an increasing-cost industry is upward-sloping. Economic profit is zero at all points on the long-run industry supply curve for both constant- and increasing-cost industries.

---

[4]In Figure 11.10 we have assumed that the minimum points on the higher LAC curves, LAC_B and LAC_C, remain at 140 units of output. Actually, M' and M'' could also be at output levels either larger or smaller than 140 units; in this case, we would simply have to adjust the number of firms associated with points B and C in Panel B.

Many chipmakers have abandoned memory chips for the currently more profitable specialty logic chips. "We are now virtually out of the commodity memory business," said the CEO of Chartered Semiconductor, a large, state-controlled chipmaker in Singapore. The article also reported that "even though Chartered is opening three new fabs [chip fabrication plants] this year and has another on the way, [Chartered's CEO] believes there is plenty of demand for its foundry services to stay in the black. [And financial] analysts agree [with the CEO]."

Although your investment advisor seems ready to invest your money in an Asian chip manufacturing plant, you are starting to get cold feet after reading the *Business Week* article. You know that high profits in logic chips will continue to attract more new production capacity. Given the number of new fabs being built, billion dollar price tags on fabrication plants apparently present little or no barrier to entry. And, even though logic chips are more easily differentiated than ordinary memory chips, you worry that engineers designing consumer products at Lucent Technologies, Motorola, Micron, and Broadcom Corp. might look for ways to use generic, "off-the-shelf" logic chips rather than custom chips. Eventually, perhaps logic chips could become commodities just like memory chips did. You also recognize that, in the absence of entry barriers, even product differentiation cannot protect profits if enough firms enter the market for logic chips. (You recognize this situation as the kind of long-run equilibrium occurring under monopolistic competition, which we will examine in the next chapter.)

As the article warns, "There still is a danger that in their desperation to pursue the profitable market niches of the next decade (i.e., custom-made logic chips), Asian manufacturers will repeat the mistakes of the 1990s. Too many producers could pile into the foundry business and multimedia chips, killing prices for everyone." So, all things considered, it looks like investing in a state-of-the-art fabrication plant will be risky indeed. Too bad, you had hoped that investing in the New Economy would allow you to ignore the "old economics" of competitive markets. Perhaps the New Economy isn't so "new" after all.

Source: Bruce Einhorn, Moon Ihlwan, Michael Shari, and Sebastian Moffett, "Fat City for Asia's Chipmakers," *Business Week*, Mar. 20, 2000, pp. 131–34.

Managers of firms in industries that have the characteristics of perfect competition (in particular, low barriers to entry and homogenous product) should expect to see economic profit competed away in the long run by the entry of new firms, regardless of whether constant or increasing costs characterize the industry. Likewise, managers should expect that losses in the short run will be eliminated in the long run as firms exit the industry and the price of the product rises. Managers can also expect to see entry of new firms driving up the prices they pay for inputs if they are operating in an increasing-cost industry that is expanding.

We should note that in our discussion of long-run competitive equilibrium we have assumed that the adjustment process goes smoothly. That is, when economic profits are being earned, expansion takes place just as long as it takes to drive price down to minimum long-run average cost and to reduce economic profits to zero. Industry expansion ceases when this point is reached. In reality this process may not be so smooth. The industry can overexpand and drive price below minimum average cost. In this case the losses would cause firms to exit until price is driven back up to where the losses are eliminated. Sometimes this process may not be completed until a long period of time has elapsed. Illustration 11.3 describes one such situation.

Rent and Long-Run Competitive Equilibrium

The fact that economic profit is zero in long-run competitive equilibrium does not mean that "nobody gets rich" in a competitive industry. Obviously, those with skills or talent that are greatly in demand can make a lot of money if the market salary or wage for people with those skills is high. Resource owners can earn a substantial return over and above owners of similar types of resources if their resources are highly demanded because they are more productive than the others employed in the industry.

We can best illustrate the concept of more productive, scarce resources with an example. Suppose that you are an experienced construction supervisor for a builder of medium-priced homes and you are exceptionally talented at organizing subcontractors: concrete workers, carpenters, bricklayers, plumbers, painters, and so forth. You can build a house in 10 percent less time than the typical experienced construction supervisor in the industry, and this saving of time reduces the average costs of constructing a house by $2,500.

The home construction industry in your market is in long-run equilibrium. Each firm in the market, including yours, is selling homes at the going market price of $175,000, which is the minimum long-run average cost for every other firm but your employer. Each of the other firms builds 30 houses a year and earns 0 economic profit at the $175,000 price. Panel A of Figure 11.11 illustrates the situation for every other contractor in the market. Each of these produces at point A in the

FIGURE 11.11

Economic Rent in Long-Run Competitive Equilibrium

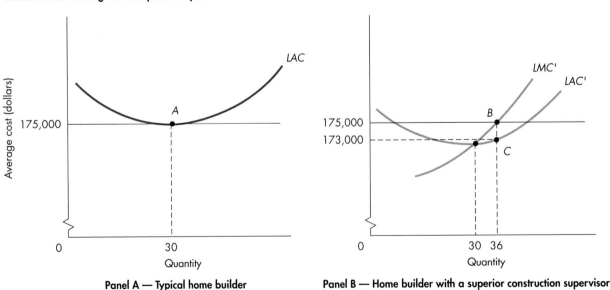

Panel A — Typical home builder

Panel B — Home builder with a superior construction supervisor

figure. Assume that an experienced construction contractor is typically paid $95,000 a year, which is what you are paid.

The situation for the firm that employs you is illustrated in Panel B. *LAC'* and *LMC'* are your firm's long-run average and marginal cost curves. At each level of output, *LAC'* is $2,500 below the long-run average cost for every other firm (*LAC* in Panel A) because you can construct a house for $2,500 less than any other contractor. Your firm produces where *LMC'* equals price ($175,000), building 36 houses per year, as shown by point *B* in Panel B. Your firm makes an economic profit of $2,000 per house, or $72,000 (= $2,000 × 36). You are solely responsible for the $72,000 economic profit. Your firm is identical in every way to every other firm except for your superior skills. (As the famous football coach and philosopher Bum Phillips said about Don Shula, the brilliant coach of the Miami Dolphins, "He can take his'n and beat your'n, and take your'n and beat his'n.") You could be the supervisor for any other firm in the market and earn $72,000 economic profit for that firm. You know it, and presumably the other firms know it also, as does the owner of the firm that employs you.

You know now, and probably would have known anyway, that you should ask for a raise of around $72,000, to a salary of $167,000. You could get a raise of about $72,000 from other firms in the market because, presumably, you could lower their costs as well. Even if you didn't ask your employer for the raise, other firms, aware of your ability to lower costs, would try to lure you away by bidding up your salary.

Your employer, and any other employer in the market, really has little choice. A firm could pay you the additional $72,000 and then just break even because all economic profit would go toward your salary. Or your firm could refuse to pay the additional $72,000, causing you to move to another firm or perhaps start your own. Your original employer would find that its costs had shifted back to *LAC* after you left and would consequently earn 0 profit because it would be in the situation shown in Panel A. Thus each firm in the market would earn 0 profit whether it hires you at $167,000 or not. But you would earn a premium because of your superior skills.

economic rent (or rent)
A payment in excess of a resource's opportunity cost (the highest payment a resource could earn in alternative employment).

The additional payment you receive above the typical salary of $95,000 is called **economic rent** or simply **rent.** Rent is the payment to a superior or more productive resource over and above its opportunity cost (what the resource could earn in its best alternative occupation). The opportunity cost for experienced supervisors is what they could earn in their best alternative occupation—such as selling insurance or supervising a factory. If this opportunity cost is around $95,000, the other supervisors are earning zero rent and you are earning $72,000 rent after your salary increase.

This same type of analysis holds for any resource that, if compensated at only its opportunity cost, would result in the firm's earning economic profit in long-run competitive equilibrium. The return to that resource will be bid up as in the above example. Therefore, even in a competitive industry, owners of particularly productive resources can earn substantial premiums even though economic profit is zero. While this example examined rents to superior skills of a manager, resources such as superior land, superior location, superior craftsmanship, or superior capital (that cannot be easily duplicated) can also earn economic rent for their owners.

▢ **Relation** Economic rent is a payment to the owner of a resource in excess of the resource's opportunity cost. Firms that employ such exceptionally productive resources earn zero economic profit in long-run competitive equilibrium because the potential economic profit from employing a superior resource is paid to the resource as rent.

11.6 PROFIT-MAXIMIZING INPUT USAGE

Thus far we have analyzed the firm's profit-maximizing decision in terms of the output decision. But we can also consider profit maximization from the input side. When we determine the profit-maximizing level of output, we implicitly have determined the economically efficient level of input usage of the firm. Recall from Chapters 8 and 9 that the cost function is directly related to the production function. Thus when we determine a unique profit-maximizing level of output, we also determine the cost-minimizing quantity of each input that is used in the production process. It is possible, then, to determine a profit-maximizing output level directly from the input decision.

Marginal Revenue Product and the Hiring Decision

The principle of choosing input usage to maximize profits is simple and follows directly from the theory of unconstrained maximization set forth in Chapter 3. The firm should expand its usage of any input or resource as long as additional units of the input add more to the firm's revenue than to its cost. The firm would not increase the usage of any input if hiring more units increases the firm's cost more than its revenue.

marginal revenue product (MRP)
($MRP = \Delta TR / \Delta I$)
The additional revenue earned when the firm hires one more unit of the input.

The additional revenue added by another unit of the input is called the **marginal revenue product (MRP)** of that input and is equal to the marginal revenue from selling the output produced times the marginal product of the input:[5]

$$MRP = \frac{\Delta TR}{\Delta I} = MR \times MP$$

where I is the level of usage of a particular input.

For a competitive firm, the marginal revenue from the additional production of an input is equal to the price of the product, which *is* marginal revenue for a perfectly competitive firm, times the marginal product of the input:

$$MRP = P \times MP$$

For example, if 1 additional unit of an input, say, labor, has a marginal product of 10 and the price at which the product can be sold is $5, the marginal revenue product

---

[5]The appendix at the end of this chapter demonstrates mathematically that $MRP = MR \times MP$.

FIGURE 11.12
Profit-Maximizing Labor Usage

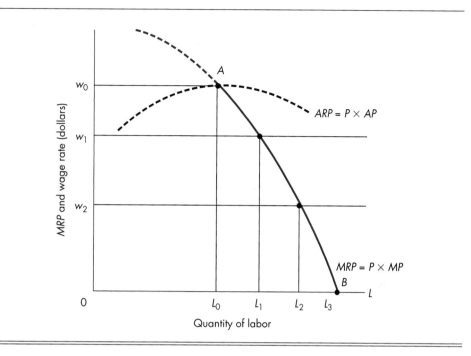

for that unit of the input is $50 (= $P \times MP$ = 5×10). In other words, hiring the extra unit of labor adds 10 extra units of output that can be sold for $5 each, and thus the addition to total revenue attributable to hiring this extra unit of labor is $50.

As shown in Chapter 8, the "typical" marginal product curve first increases, reaches a maximum, then declines thereafter. Therefore, the MRP curve, which is simply price times marginal product, also rises then declines. At the level of input usage at which marginal product becomes negative, the marginal revenue product becomes negative also.

The quantity of an input a manager chooses to hire depends on the marginal revenue product and the price of the input. Assume that a manager can hire as much of an input as is desired at a constant price—that is, the price that must be paid for the input is the same no matter how much or how little is hired.

A general rule for a continuously variable input is illustrated graphically in Figure 11.12. In this example, labor is the only variable input, and only the decreasing portion of MRP is shown. The MRP curve is simply the MP curve multiplied by the market price of the product produced at each level of labor usage over the relevant range. Therefore, if at a labor usage of $\overline{L}$ the marginal product is $\overline{MP}$, $\overline{MRP} = \overline{P} \times \overline{MP}$, where $\overline{P}$ is product price. This means that the $\overline{L}$th worker adds $\overline{MRP}$ to total revenue. If the wage rate is w_1, the manager would wish to hire L_1 units of labor. The manager would not stop short of L_1, because up to employment level L_1 an additional unit of labor adds more to revenue than to cost. The manager would not hire more than L_1, because beyond L_1 the added cost would exceed the added revenue. If the wage rate falls to w_2, the manager would increase labor usage to L_2 units. Hence, if labor is the firm's only variable input, the manager maximizes profits or minimizes loss by employing the amount of labor for which the marginal revenue product of labor equals the wage rate:

$$MRP = w$$

This result holds for any variable input.[6]

□ **Principle**   If the MRP of an additional unit of a variable input is greater than the price of that input, that unit should be hired. If the MRP of an additional unit adds less than its price, that unit should not be hired. If the usage of the variable input varies continuously, the manager should employ the amount of the input at which

$$MRP = \text{Input price}$$

This principle is equivalent to the condition that the profit-maximizing, competitive firm will produce the level of output at which $P = SMC$. Recall from Chapter 8 that cost minimization at any level of output requires that

$$SMC = \frac{w}{MP}$$

Recall also that the profit-maximizing level of output is where

$$P = SMC$$

But, from the cost-minimization condition, when one input is variable,

$$P = SMC = \frac{w}{MP}$$

or

$$P \times MP = w$$

which gives the profit-maximizing level of input usage. Thus the profit-maximizing, output-choice condition, $P = SMC$, is equivalent to the profit-maximizing, input-choice condition, $MRP = w$. Each leads to the same level of output and the same level of input usage.

Average Revenue Product and the Shutdown Decision

We now want to be more precise about the range of MRP over which a manager would actually operate. Clearly, a manager never hires labor beyond the point at which MRP becomes negative: When MRP is negative, hiring more labor *decreases*

---

[6]As noted, we did not include the upward-sloping portion of the MRP curve because this segment is not relevant to the hiring decision. If the wage equals MRP and MRP is increasing, the manager could hire additional units, and the marginal revenue product of these inputs would be greater than the wage. Therefore, this level of input use would not be profit-maximizing.

total revenue. Furthermore, we will now demonstrate that a manager shuts down operations (i.e., hires no labor) if the wage rate rises above the *average revenue product* of labor. The **average revenue product (ARP)** of labor is the average revenue per worker, $ARP = TR/L$, and it is easy to see that ARP can be calculated as price times average product:

average revenue product (ARP)
The average revenue per worker ($ARP = TR/L$).

$$ARP = \frac{TR}{L} = \frac{PQ}{L} = P\frac{Q}{L} = P \times AP$$

To see why a manager shuts down when $w > ARP$, suppose $MRP = w$—as necessary for profit maximization—at a level of labor usage where ARP is less than the wage rate:

$$w > ARP$$

Substituting TR/L for ARP into this inequality results in the following expression:

$$w > TR/L$$

Now multiply both sides of the inequality by L, and you can see that

$$wL > TR \quad \text{or} \quad TVC > TR$$

Thus total variable cost exceeds total revenue when $w > ARP$. From previous analysis, you know that the manager should shut down when total revenue does not cover total variable costs.[7] Therefore, no labor would be hired if the average revenue product is less than the wage rate. In Figure 11.12, the competitive firm shuts down if the wage rate rises above w_0 at point A.

In Figure 11.12, the firm's demand for labor is the MRP curve over the range of labor usage L_0 to L_3 (between points A and B). To maximize profit, the manager chooses the level of labor usage for which $MRP = w$. When wages rise above w_0 in Figure 11.12 at the level of labor usage for which $MRP = w$, the wage rate exceeds the average revenue product ($w > ARP$) and the manager will shut the firm down and hire no labor at all. At all wage rates above point A, the firm shuts down. Below point B, MRP is negative, and the manager would never hire more than L_3 units of labor. We now summarize the discussion in a principle:

Principle   If the price of a single variable input employed by a competitive firm rises above the point of maximum ARP ($= P \times AP$), then the firm minimizes its loss by shutting down and hiring none of the variable input.

Before concluding the discussion of the hiring decision, we should explain that when there is more than one variable input, the firm's hiring decision remains essentially the same as for a single variable input, even though it is more complicated mathematically. For every variable input, the manager maximizes profit by hiring the quantity of the input at which its MRP equals its price. If, for example,

---

[7]This result is demonstrated mathematically in the appendix to this chapter.

the firm uses two variable inputs, labor and capital, the manager maximizes profits by using both inputs at such levels that

$$MRP_L = w$$

$$MRP_K = r$$

Since the marginal product of either input shifts according to the level of usage of the other, these conditions must hold *simultaneously*.[8]

11.7 IMPLEMENTING THE PROFIT-MAXIMIZING OUTPUT DECISION

Although it is useful for managers to know the fundamentals of the theory of profit maximization, it is even more useful for them to know how to implement and use the theory to maximize their firms' profits. A manager should be able to use empirical estimates or forecasts of the relevant variables and equations to determine the actual values of the decision variables that maximize the firm's profit. You have spent a lot of time learning the techniques of estimating the various demand, production, and cost functions. Now you will learn how to use these empirical skills to answer an important question facing a manager: How can the theory of profit maximization be used in practice to make profit-maximizing decisions about production?

We will first outline how managers can, in general, determine the optimizing conditions. This outline gives a pattern for situations in which numerical estimates of the variables and equations are available. Then we present an example of how a firm can use this approach to determine the optimal level of output.

General Rules for Implementation

We emphasized that a manager must answer two questions when choosing the level of output that maximizes profit. These two questions and the answers forthcoming from the theoretical analysis are summarized as follows:

1. Should the firm produce or shut down? *Produce as long as the market price is greater than or equal to minimum average variable cost: $P \geq AVC_{min}$. Shut down otherwise.*

2. If production occurs, how much should the firm produce? *Produce the output at which market price (which is marginal revenue) equals marginal cost: $P = SMC$.*

---

[8]With a bit of algebra, after substituting the relations $MRP_L = P \times MP_L$ and $MRP_K = P \times MP_K$ into these conditions for profit maximization, it can be shown that the amounts of labor and capital that maximize profit are also economically efficient (lie on the expansion path) because they also meet the condition $w/r = MP_L/MP_K$. While all input combinations that maximize profit lie on the expansion path, only one input combination on the expansion path maximizes profit—the input combination on the isoquant corresponding the profit-maximizing output.

It follows from these rules that to determine the optimal level of output, a manager must obtain estimates or forecasts of the market price of the good produced by the firm, the firm's average variable cost function, and the firm's marginal cost function. The steps explained next can be followed to find the profit-maximizing rate of production and the level of profit the firm will earn.

Step 1: Forecast the price of the product

To decide whether or not to produce and how much to produce, a manager must obtain a forecast of the price at which the completed product can be sold. Remember that a perfectly competitive firm does not face a downward-sloping demand curve but simply takes the market price as given. We showed in Chapter 7 how to use two statistical techniques—time-series forecasting and econometric forecasting—to forecast the price of the product.

Step 2: Estimate average variable cost (AVC) and marginal cost (SMC)

As emphasized in Chapter 10, the cubic specification is the appropriate form for estimating a family of short-run cost curves. Thus the manager could estimate the following average variable cost function:

$$AVC = a + bQ + cQ^2$$

As demonstrated in Chapter 10, the marginal cost function associated with this average variable cost function is

$$SMC = a + 2bQ + 3cQ^2$$

Step 3: Check the shutdown rule

When P is less than AVC, the firm loses less money by shutting down than it would lose if it produced where $P = SMC$. A manager can determine the price below which a firm should shut down by finding the *minimum* point on the AVC curve, AVC_{min}. As long as price is greater than (or equal to) AVC_{min}, the firm will produce rather than shut down. Recall from Chapter 10 that the average variable cost curve reaches its minimum value at $Q_m = -b/2c$. The minimum value of average variable cost is then determined by substituting Q_m into the AVC function:

$$AVC_{min} = a + bQ_m + c(Q_m)^2$$

The firm should produce as long as $P \geq AVC_{min}$. If the forecasted price is greater than (or equal to) minimum average variable cost ($P \geq AVC_{min}$), the firm should produce the output level where $P = SMC$. If the forecasted price is less than the minimum average variable cost ($P < AVC_{min}$), the firm should shut down in the short run, and it loses an amount equal to its total fixed costs.

Step 4: If $P \geq AVC_{min}$, find the output level where $P = SMC$

A perfectly competitive firm should produce the level of output for which $P = SMC$—if $P \geq AVC_{min}$. Thus if the manager decides to produce in the short run, the manager maximizes profit by finding the output level for which $P = SMC$. In the case of a cubic specification for cost, profit maximization or loss minimization requires that

$$P = SMC = a + 2bQ + 3cQ^2$$

Solving this equation for Q^* gives the optimal output level for the firm—unless P is less than AVC, and then the optimal output level is 0.

Step 5: Computation of profit or loss

Once a manager determines how much to produce, the calculation of total profit or loss is straightforward. Profit or loss is equal to total revenue minus total cost. Total revenue for a competitive firm is price times quantity sold. Total cost is the sum of total variable cost and total fixed cost, where total variable cost is average variable cost times the number of units sold. Hence, total profit, denoted as π is

$$\begin{aligned}\pi &= TR - TC\\ &= (P \times Q^*) - [(AVC \times Q^*) + TFC]\\ &= (P - AVC)Q^* - TFC\end{aligned}$$

If $P < AVC_{min}$, the firm shuts down, and $\pi = -TFC$.

To illustrate how to implement these steps to find the profit-maximizing level of output and to forecast the profit of the firm, we now turn to a hypothetical firm that operates in a perfectly competitive market.

Profit Maximization at Beau Apparel: An Illustration

As an example, we use the output decision facing the manager of Beau Apparel, Inc., a clothing manufacturer that produces moderately priced men's shirts. Beau Apparel is only one of many firms that produce a fairly homogeneous product, and none of the firms in this moderate-price shirt market engages in any significant advertising.

Price forecasts

In mid-December 2004, the manager of Beau Apparel was preparing the firm's production plan for the first quarter of 2005. The manager wanted to obtain a forecast of the wholesale price of shirts for the first quarter of 2005. This price forecast would subsequently be used in making the production decision for Beau Apparel. The manager requests price forecasts from Beau Apparel's Marketing/Forecasting Division. The market researchers, using forecasting techniques similar to those described in Chapter 7, provided the manager with three wholesale price forecasts based on three different assumptions about economic conditions in the first quarter of 2005:

High:	$20
Medium:	$15
Low:	$10

Estimation of average variable cost and marginal cost

The manager of Beau Apparel chose a cubic specification of short-run cost for estimating the average variable cost and the marginal cost curves. Using time-series data over the seven-year time period 1999(I) through 2004(IV), during which Beau Apparel had the same-size plant, the following average variable cost function was estimated:

$$AVC = 20 - 0.003Q + 0.00000025Q^2$$

All the estimated coefficients (20, −0.003, and 0.00000025) had the required signs and were statistically significant. The estimated average cost function provided the information needed for making the decision to produce or shut down. We will return to this decision after we discuss how the manager of Beau Apparel estimated the marginal cost function.

As explained in Chapter 10, the parameter estimates for the average variable cost function can be used to obtain the estimated marginal cost function:

$$SMC = a + 2bQ + 3cQ^2$$

where a, b, and c are the estimated parameters (coefficients) for the AVC function. The manager used the estimated coefficients of the average variable cost equation to obtain the corresponding marginal cost function. For the estimate of the average variable cost function given above, the corresponding marginal cost function for shirts was

$$SMC = 20 + 2(-0.003)Q + 3(0.00000025)Q^2$$
$$= 20 - 0.006Q + 0.00000075Q^2$$

After obtaining forecasts of price and estimates of the average variable cost and marginal cost curves, the manager was able to answer the two production questions: (1) Should the firm produce or shut down? And (2) if production is warranted, how much should the firm produce? We now can show how the manager of Beau Apparel made these two decisions and calculated the firm's forecasted profit.

The shutdown decision

Since the estimated average variable cost function for shirts was

$$AVC = 20 - 0.003Q + 0.00000025Q^2$$

AVC reaches its minimum value at

$$Q_m = \frac{-(-0.003)}{2(0.00000025)} = 6,000$$

Substituting this output level into the estimated average variable cost function, the value of average variable cost at its minimum point is

$$AVC_{min} = 20 - 0.003(6,000) + 0.00000025(6,000)^2 = \$11$$

Thus average variable cost reaches its minimum value of $11 at 6,000 units of output.

The manager of Beau Apparel then compared this minimum average variable cost with the three price forecasts for the first quarter of 2005. For the high forecast, $20,

$$\hat{P}_{2005(I)} = \$20 > \$11 = AVC_{min}$$

so the firm should produce in order to maximize profit or minimize loss. Likewise, with the medium forecast, $15,

$$\hat{P}_{2005(I)} = \$15 > \$11 = AVC_{min}$$

and the firm also should produce. However, if the market-determined price of shirts turned out to be equal to the low forecast, $10, the firm should shut down (produce zero output) since

$$\hat{P}_{2005(I)} = \$10 < \$11 = AVC_{min}$$

In this case, total revenue would not cover all variable costs of production, and the firm would be better off shutting down and losing only its fixed costs. The manager, therefore, must determine only how much output to produce when price is either $20 or $15.

The output decision

Given the estimated marginal cost equation for Beau Apparel, profit maximization or loss minimization requires that

$$P = SMC = 20 - 0.006Q + 0.00000075Q^2$$

The manager first considered the high forecast of wholesale shirt prices. After setting the $20 forecasted price equal to estimated marginal cost, the optimal production of shirts when price is $20 was found by solving

$$20 = 20 - 0.006Q + 0.00000075Q^2$$

Subtracting 20 from both sides of the equation and factoring out a Q term results in the following expression:

$$0 = Q(-0.006 + 0.00000075Q)$$

There are two solutions to this equation, since the right-hand side of the equation is 0 if either $Q = 0$ or $Q = 8,000$. Because the manager of Beau Apparel had already determined that price was greater than AVC_{min} and production was warranted, the manager concluded that the profit-maximizing output level was 8,000 units.

Using the medium price forecast of $15, the manager again determined the optimal output by equating the forecasted price to estimated marginal cost:

$$15 = 20 - 0.006Q + 0.00000075Q^2$$

or

$$0 = 5 - 0.006Q + 0.00000075Q^2$$

The solution to this equation is not as simple as was the preceding case, because the left-hand side of the equation cannot be factored. To solve a quadratic equation that cannot be factored, the quadratic formula must be used:[9]

$$Q = \frac{-(-0.006) \pm \sqrt{(0.006)^2 - 4(5)(0.00000075)}}{2(0.00000075)} = \frac{0.006 \pm 0.004583}{0.0000015}$$

The two solutions for this quadratic equation are $Q = 945$ and $Q = 7,055$.

To determine which solution is optimal, the manager computed the average variable cost for each level of output:

$$AVC_{Q = 945} = 20 - 0.003(945) + 0.00000025(945)^2 = \$17.39$$

$$AVC_{Q = 7,055} = 20 - 0.003(7,055) + 0.00000025(7,055)^2 = \$11.28$$

Since the price forecast of $15 is less than $17.39, the manager would not produce the output level $Q = 945$. If the wholesale price is expected to be $15, the manager would produce 7,055 units, at which AVC is $11.28. We now consider the amount of profit or loss that Beau Apparel would earn at each of the optimal levels of output.

Computation of total profit or loss

Total revenue is price times quantity sold. Total cost is the sum of total variable cost and total fixed cost, where total variable cost is average variable cost times the number of units sold. Hence, total profit (loss) is

$$\pi = TR - TC$$

$$= (P \times Q) - [(AVC \times Q) + TFC]$$

The manager expects total fixed costs for the shirt division for 2005(I) to be $30,000. The values for total revenue and total variable cost depend on the price forecast and corresponding optimal output. We now show how the manager of Beau Apparel computed profit or loss for each of the three forecasts of the wholesale price of shirts.

High-price forecast (P = $20)   In this case, Beau Apparel's manager determined that the optimal level of production would be 8,000 units. The average variable cost when 8,000 units are produced is

$$AVC_{Q = 8,000} = 20 - 0.003(8,000) + 0.00000025(8,000)^2 = \$12$$

Economic profit when price is $20 would be

$$\pi = (\$20 \times 8,000) - [(\$12 \times 8,000) + \$30,000] = \$34,000$$

---

[9]For an equation of the form $A + BX + CX^2 = 0$, the two solutions, X_1 and X_2, are

$$X_1, X_2 = \frac{-B \pm \sqrt{B^2 - 4AC}}{2C}$$

If you are accustomed to the alternative expression of the equation, $AX^2 + BX + C = 0$, then the denominator for the solution is $2A$ (instead of $2C$).

If the price of shirts is $20 per unit in the first quarter of 2005, Beau Apparel should produce 8,000 units to earn a profit of $34,000, which is the maximum profit possible, given this price.

Middle-price forecast ($P = \$15$) If the price of shirts is $15 in the first quarter of 2005, the optimal level of output is 7,055 units. The average variable cost is

$$AVC_{Q = 7,055} = 20 - 0.003(7,055) + 0.00000025(7,055)^2 = \$11.28$$

Economic profit when price is $15 would be

$$\pi = (\$15 \times 7,055) - [(\$11.28 \times 7,055) + \$30,000] = -\$3,755$$

When the price of shirts is $15, the shirt division of Beau Apparel would be expected to suffer a *loss* of $3,755 in the first quarter of 2005. Note that the firm should continue to produce since this is the minimum loss possible when price is $15. If Beau Apparel shut down production when price is $15, the firm would lose an amount equal to the total fixed cost of $30,000—considerably more than the $3,755 the firm loses by producing 7,055 units.

Low-price forecast ($P = \$10$) At a price of $10 per shirt, the firm would shut down and produce 0 output ($Q = 0$). In this case, economic profit would be equal to $-TFC$:

$$\pi = (\$10 \times 0) - (0 + \$30,000) = -\$30,000$$

Beau Apparel would minimize loss in this situation by producing nothing and losing only its fixed costs of $30,000.

This extended example about Beau Apparel's production decision illustrates how the manager of a firm that sells in a perfectly competitive market can find the optimal level of output. Our purpose in using the three different price forecasts was to illustrate the decision-making rules developed earlier in the chapter, where we showed that a firm makes one of the following choices in the short run:

1. Produce a positive level of output and earn an economic profit (if $P \geq AVC$ and $P > ATC$).
2. Produce a positive level of output and suffer an economic loss less than the amount of total fixed cost (if $AVC \leq P < ATC$).
3. Produce 0 output and suffer an economic loss equal to total fixed cost (if $P < AVC$).

The profit-maximizing and loss-minimizing decisions of Beau Apparel are shown graphically in Figure 11.13. The marginal, average variable, and average total cost curves are a graphical representation of those estimated previously. In Panel A, the product price is $20 ($= MR$). As you can see in the graph, $SMC = \$20$ at 8,000 units of output. At 8,000 units, $AVC = \$12$, as shown, and $AFC = \$30,000/8,000 = \$3.75$. Therefore $ATC = \$12 + \$3.75 = \$15.75$. Profit is $(P - ATC)Q = (\$20 - \$15.75)8,000 = \$34,000$, as derived earlier.

FIGURE 11.13
Profit and Loss at Beau Apparel

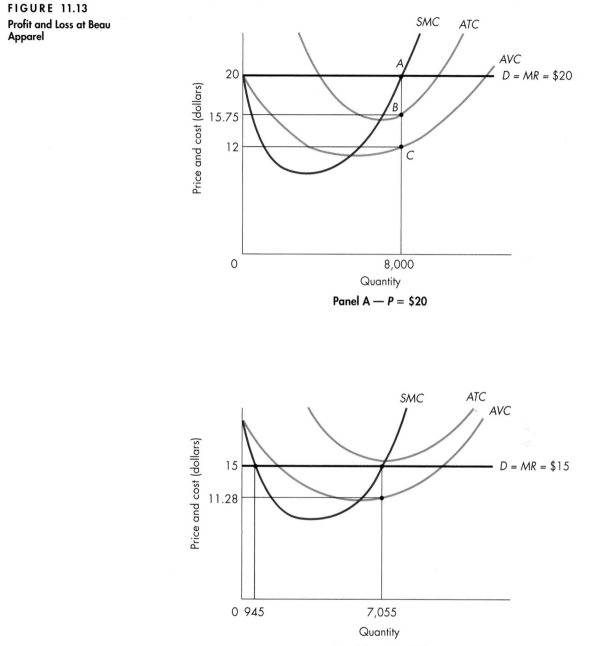

Panel A — P = $20

Panel B — P = $15

Panel B illustrates the loss-minimizing situation when $P = MR = \$15$. As shown, $SMC = \$15$ at 945 and 7,055 units of output. The lower output would not be chosen because price is less than average variable cost at this output. Thus the firm produces 7,055 units of output, where AVC is less than \$15. As shown in the graph, average total cost is greater than \$15 at every level of output, so Beau Apparel cannot make an economic profit. In the figure, at an output of 7,055, average variable cost is \$11.28, so total variable cost is \$79,580 (= \$11.28 × 7,055). The firm can use its total revenue of \$105,825 (= \$15 × 7,055) to pay all its variable cost and use the remainder, \$26,245, to pay part of its fixed cost. Therefore, Beau Apparel loses \$3,755 (= \$30,000 − \$26,245), the portion of total fixed cost not covered by revenue.

As the figure shows, average variable cost reaches its minimum at 6,000 units of output, where $AVC = \$11$. The firm would shut down and produce 0 output if price falls below \$11.

11.8 SUMMARY

Price-taking behavior, which is the hallmark of competitive markets, arises because each individual firm in the market is so small relative to the total market that it cannot affect the market price of the good or service it produces by changing its output. Furthermore, all firms produce a homogeneous or perfectly standardized commodity, and thus no buyer would be willing to pay more than the going market price for any firm's output. For this reason, firms in competitive markets face perfectly elastic demand curves and possess no market power to change price. Managers of competitive firms can only choose output (or inputs) to make the most of market-determined prices over which they have no control. While the conditions of perfect competition do not precisely describe real-world markets, many markets come so close to the situation that firms face nearly horizontal demand curves and behave as price-takers. This chapter provides the profit-maximizing rules for managers who operate as price-takers.

A competitive firm's demand curve is a horizontal line at the market-determined price. The horizontal demand curve is also the firm's marginal revenue curve because price equals marginal ($P = MR$) revenue for a competitive firm. In the short run, if the firm chooses to produce, profit is maximized by producing the output where price equals marginal cost ($P = SMC$). If price falls below average total cost ($P < ATC$), the manager cannot avoid making a loss in the short run, no matter what output level is chosen. The loss in this situation is minimized—the negative profit is maximized—by producing the output where price equals marginal cost ($P = SMC$) as long as price does not fall below average variable cost (i.e., as long as $P \geq AVC$). If price is less than AVC at the output where $P = SMC$, then the manager should shut the firm down and produce no output. When the firm shuts down, it loses its fixed costs ($\pi = -TFC$), but this is the minimum possible loss when price is less than average variable cost. Because firms shut down when price falls below AVC, the minimum point on the AVC curve is the firm's shutdown price.

When choosing the profit-maximizing level of output, managers should not attempt to maximize profit margin or average profit (profit per unit), two terms that both equal the difference between price and average total cost ($P - ATC$). The output level that maximizes profit margin and average profit does not result in maximization of total profit (unless price happens to equal minimum average total cost). Since maximization of total profit is the objective that a firm's owners expect the manager to pursue (as we explained in Chapter 1), measures of profit margin and average profit should be ignored for decision-making purposes.

Fixed costs should also be ignored when making profit-maximizing decisions. Fixed costs play no role in determining the profit-maximizing level of output. The shutdown rule involves comparing total revenue and total variable cost (or, equivalently, price and average variable cost). The optimal level of production is found by equating marginal revenue and marginal cost. Fixed costs have nothing to do with determining how much to produce or with the decision to shut down.

In the long run, competitive firms earn zero economic profit because entry into and exit from competitive markets is unrestricted. If price exceeds average cost in the long run ($P > LAC$), new firms are attracted to enter the market by the positive economic profit. The entry of new firms causes industry supply to increase and market price to fall until price equals minimum long-run average cost and economic profit is bid away. If price is less than long-run average cost ($P < LAC$), some of the incumbent or existing firms choose to exit by moving their resources to their best alternative uses. The resulting decrease in industry supply continues until price equals minimum long-run average cost and economic losses are bid away.

The long-run industry supply curve for a competitive industry can be either upward-sloping in the case of an increasing-cost industry or horizontal in the case of a constant-cost industry. When industry output expands, the prices of inputs may be bid up, causing the minimum point on LAC to rise. Since long-run supply price equals minimum LAC, an upward shift in LAC due to rising input prices causes supply price to increase. This is why the industry supply curve is upward-sloping in the long run

for an increasing-cost industry. If input prices are constant as industry output and input usage increase, minimum LAC remains constant and the long-run supply curve is perfectly elastic for the constant-cost industry.

When choosing the profit-maximizing level of labor usage to maximize the profit of the firm, the manager hires labor up to the point where the marginal revenue product of labor ($MRP = P \times MP$) equals the wage rate. When average revenue product ($ARP = P \times AP$) is less than the wage rate, the manager should shut down and hire no labor.

As you can see, managers that operate in competitive markets are likely to feel somewhat helpless in their efforts to deliver profits to the firm's owners. Managers in competitive markets possess little or no market power because there are so many firms producing goods or services that buyers view as essentially identical. As price-takers, the managers can only react to market-determined prices by adjusting output to maximize any profits or minimize any losses that may occur in the short run. In the long run, the prospects for earning profit are slim because entry into competitive markets is unrestricted and any short-run profits will be competed away by entry of new firms. Possibly the best news managers can provide owners of firms in competitive industries is that any period of negative profits in the short run will likely disappear in the long run as some of the incumbent firms will exit the industry, driving prices up and eventually eliminating the losses. Over a long enough period, the owners are likely to earn, on average, just enough revenue to cover all the explicit costs of production and have just enough revenue left to pay themselves what they could have earned by putting their resources to the best alternative use.

In the next two chapters we will examine markets in which price-setting firms facing downward-sloping demand curves (instead of horizontal demand curves) can earn economic profit in the long run as well as in the short run. These firms can earn long-run profits because barriers exist to block partially or completely the entry of new firms.

TECHNICAL PROBLEMS

1. The left-hand side of the following graph shows market demand and supply curves in a competitive market. Draw the demand facing a competitive firm selling in this market on the right-hand graph.

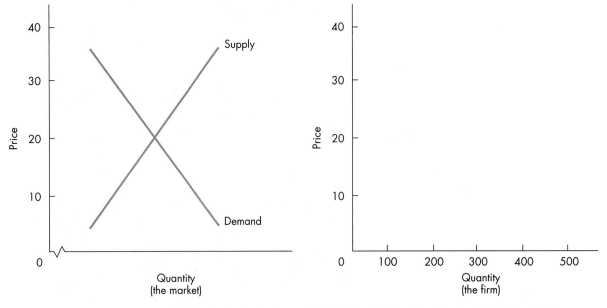

   a. What is the firm's demand elasticity at 200 units of output? At 400 units?
   b. What is the firm's marginal revenue from selling the 200th unit of output? From the 400th unit?

2. The following figure shows the marginal cost for a price-taking firm and its demand and marginal revenue ($D = MR = P$).

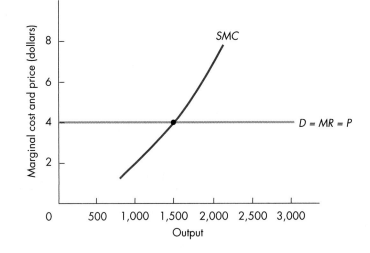

a. What output should the firm produce?

b. If the firm is producing 1,000 units of output, adding another unit of output would increase cost by $_____ and revenue by $_____. The firm's profit would _____ by $_____.

c. If the firm is producing 2,000 units of output, taking away one unit of output would reduce cost by $_____ and revenue by $_____. The firm's profit would _____ by $_____.

3. Answer the questions below using the cost curves for the price-taking firm shown in the following graph:

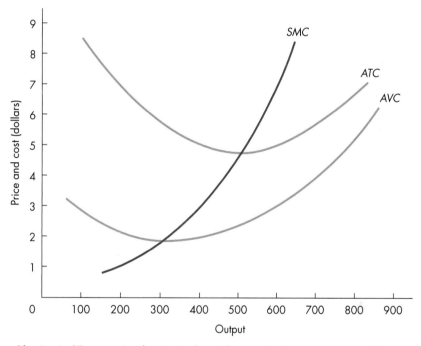

a. If price is $7 per unit of output, draw the marginal revenue curve. The manager should produce _____ units in order to maximize profit.

b. Since average total cost is $_____ for this output, total cost is $_____.

c. The firm makes a profit of $_____.

d. At _____ units, profit margin (or average profit) is maximized. Why is this output level *different from* the answer to part a?

e. Let price fall to $3, and draw the new marginal revenue curve. The manager should now produce _____ units in order to maximize profit.

f. Total revenue is now $_____ and total cost is $_____. The firm makes a loss of $_____.

g. Total variable cost is $_____, leaving $_____ to apply to fixed cost.

h. If price falls below $_____, the firm will produce 0 output. Explain why.

4. In a competitive industry the market-determined price is $12. A firm is currently producing 50 units of output; average total cost is $10, marginal cost is $15, and average variable cost is $7.

   a. Is the firm making the profit-maximizing decision? Why or why not? If not, what should the firm do?

   b. Consider another firm in a competitive industry that faces a market-determined price of $25. This firm is producing 10,000 units of output, and average total cost, which at its minimum value, is $25. Answer part a for this firm.

5. The following figure shows the cost and profit curves for a price-taking firm facing a market-determined price of $225. Fill in the blanks a through e as indicated in the figure.

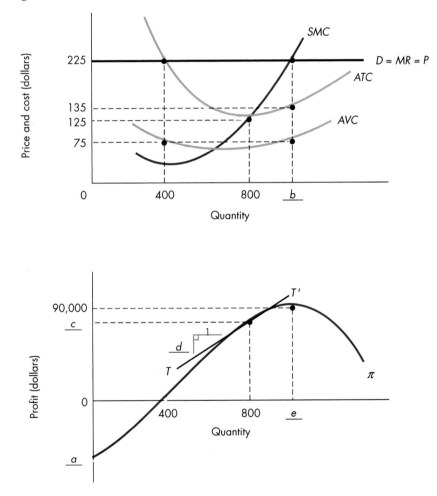

6. The following figure shows long-run average and marginal cost curves for a competitive firm. The price of the product is $40.

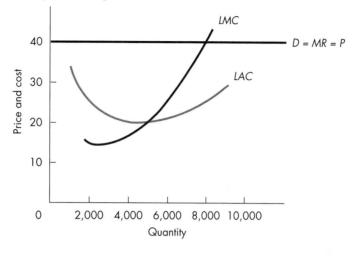

a. How much will the firm produce? What will be its economic profit?

b. When the industry attains long-run competitive equilibrium, what will be the price and the firm's output? What will be the firm's economic profit?

7. Suppose that a competitive industry is in long-run competitive equilibrium. Then the price of a substitute good (in consumption) decreases. What will happen in the short run to

a. The market demand curve.

b. The market supply curve.

c. Market price.

d. Market output.

e. The firm's output.

f. The firm's profit.

What will happen in the long run?

8. The supply curve for an industry shows the relation between supply price and industry output.

a. The long-run competitive supply curve for a constant-cost industry is horizontal. Why is supply price constant?

b. The long-run competitive supply curve for an increasing-cost industry is upward-sloping. Why does supply price increase as industry production rises?

9. A manufacturing firm employs a superior plant manager to manage production at its plant. This plant manager is much more efficient than the typical plant manager employed at the rest of the firms in the industry, which is perfectly competitive. Typical plant managers make $5,000 per month in salary. By employing the superior plant manager, the firm faces the LAC and LMC curves shown in the following figure. In long-run equilibrium, the price of the product is $10.

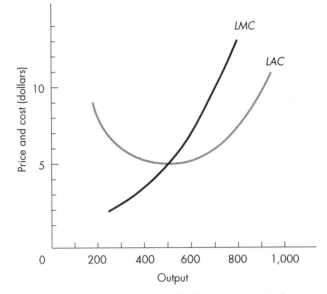

a. Minimum *LAC* for a firm with a typical plant manager is $_____. The typical firm earns economic profit of $_____.

b. The firm with the superior plant manager earns economic profit of $_____.

c. The superior plant manager earns a salary of $_____ per month, $_____ of which is economic rent.

10. Consider a price-taking firm that has total fixed cost of $50 and faces a market-determined price of $2 per unit for its output. The wage rate is $10 per unit of labor, the only variable input. Using the following table, answer the questions below.

(1) Units of labor	(2) Output	(3) Marginal product	(4) Marginal revenue product	(5) Marginal cost	(6) Profit
1	5	_____	_____	_____	_____
2	15	_____	_____	_____	_____
3	30	_____	_____	_____	_____
4	50	_____	_____	_____	_____
5	65	_____	_____	_____	_____
6	77	_____	_____	_____	_____
7	86	_____	_____	_____	_____
8	94	_____	_____	_____	_____
9	98	_____	_____	_____	_____
10	96	_____	_____	_____	_____

a. Fill in the blanks in column 3 of the table by computing the marginal product of labor for each level of labor usage.

b. Fill in the blanks in column 4 of the table by computing the marginal revenue product for each level of labor usage.

    c. How much labor should the manager hire in order to maximize profit? Why?

    d. Fill in the blanks in column 5 of the table by computing marginal cost.

    e. How many units of output should the manager produce in order to maximize profit? Why?

    f. Fill in the blanks in column 6 with the profit earned at each level of labor usage.

    g. Do your answers to parts *c* and *e* maximize profit? Does it matter whether the manager chooses labor usage or chooses output in order to maximize profit? Why?

    h. How much labor should the manager hire when the wage rate is $20? How much profit is earned? Is marginal product greater or less than average product at this level of labor usage? Why does it matter?

11. Suppose that the manager of a firm operating in a competitive market has estimated the firm's average variable cost function to be

$$AVC = 10 - 0.03Q + 0.00005Q^2$$

Total fixed cost is $600.

    a. What is the corresponding marginal cost function?

    b. At what output is *AVC* at its minimum?

    c. What is the minimum value for *AVC*?

If the forecasted price of the firm's output is $10 per unit:

    d. How much output will the firm produce in the short run?

    e. How much profit (loss) will the firm earn?

If the forecasted price is $7 per unit:

    f. How much output will the firm produce in the short run?

    g. How much profit (loss) will the firm earn?

If the forecasted price is $5 per unit:

    h. How much output will the firm produce in the short run?

    i. How much profit (loss) will the firm earn?

12. Suppose the marginal cost function is estimated to be

$$SMC = 80 - 0.1Q + 0.0001Q^2$$

The price of the product is forecasted to be $75.

    a. The average variable cost equation is $AVC =$ _____.

    b. At what two levels of output does price equal marginal cost?

    c. What is average variable cost at the two levels of output in part *b*? Which of the two output levels is optimal? Explain.

APPLIED PROBLEMS

1. The MidNight Hour, a local nightclub, earned $100,000 in accounting profit last year. This year the owner, who had invested $1 million in the club, decided to close the club. What can you say about economic profit (and the rate of return) in the nightclub business?

2. In an article on the steel industry, *The Wall Street Journal* noted that as steel prices were falling, steelmakers were not cutting production since "steelmakers can't afford to lose any sales because their costs, especially their fixed costs, are so high." What does this statement mean? Explain.

3. The manager of All City Realtors wants to hire some real estate agents to specialize in selling housing units acquired by the Resolution Trust Corporation (RTC) in its attempt to bail out the savings and loan industry. The commission paid by the RTC to the company to sell these homes is a flat rate of $2,000 per unit sold, rather than the customary commission that is based on the sale price of a home. The manager estimates the following marginal product schedule for real estate agents dealing in government-owned housing:

Number of real estate agents	Marginal product (number of additional units sold per year)	Marginal revenue product
1	20	_____
2	17	_____
3	15	_____
4	12	_____
5	8	_____
6	4	_____

   a. Construct the marginal revenue product schedule by filling in the blanks in the table.

   b. If the manager of All City Realtors must pay a wage rate of $32,000 per year to get agents who will specialize in selling RTC housing, how many agents should the manager hire? Why?

   c. If the wage rate falls to $18,000 per year, how many agents should the manager hire?

   d. Suppose the RTC raises its commission to $3,000 per unit sold. Now what is the marginal revenue product for each real estate agent employed?

   e. Now that the RTC is paying $3,000 per unit sold, how many agents should the manager hire if the wage rate is $30,000?

4. HoneyBee Farms, a medium-size producer of honey, operates in a market that fits the competitive market definition relatively well. However, honey farmers are assisted by support prices above the price that would prevail in the absence of controls. The owner of HoneyBee Farms, as well as some other honey producers, complain that they can't make a profit even with these support prices. Explain why. Explain why even higher support prices would not help honey farmers in the long run.

5. Insurance agents receive a commission on the policies they sell. Many states regulate the rates that can be charged for insurance. Would higher or lower rates increase the incomes of agents? Explain, distinguishing between the short run and the long run.

6. If all the assumptions of perfect competition hold, why would firms in such an industry have little incentive to carry out technological change or much research and development? What conditions would encourage research and development in competitive industries?

7. At a recent board meeting, the president and CEO got into a heated argument about whether or not to shut down the firm's plant in Miami. The Miami plant currently loses $60,000 monthly. The president of the firm argued that the Miami plant should continue

to operate, at least until a buyer is found for the production facility. The president's argument was based on the fact that the Miami plant's fixed costs are $68,000 per month. The CEO exploded over this point, castigating the president for considering fixed costs in making the shutdown decision. According to the CEO, "Everyone knows fixed costs don't matter!"

a. Should the Miami plant be closed or continue to operate at a loss in the short run?

b. How would you explain to the incorrect party that he or she is wrong?

8. Suppose you own a home remodeling company. You are currently earning short-run profits. The home remodeling industry is an increasing-cost industry. In the long run, what do you expect will happen to

a. Your firm's costs of production? Explain.

b. The price you can charge for your remodeling services? Why?

c. Profits in home remodeling? Why?

9. The New York City Parks Department doubled the annual fee for the hot-dog pushcart that had the exclusive license for the spot just south of the Metropolitan Museum of Art to $288,000. Why would anyone pay almost $300,000 for a pushcart license? Who is obtaining the economic rent for the obviously lucrative pushcart location? How much economic profit is the pushcart owner probably earning?

10. Grocery stores and gasoline stations in a large city would appear to be examples of competitive markets: There are numerous relatively small sellers, each seller is a price-taker, and the products are quite similar.

a. How could we argue that these markets are *not* competitive?

b. Could each firm face a demand curve that is *not* perfectly elastic?

c. How profitable do you expect grocery stores and gasoline stations to be in the long run?

11. During a coffee-room debate among several young M.B.A.s who had recently graduated, one of the young executives flatly stated, "The most this company can lose on its Brazilian division is the amount it has invested (its fixed costs)." Not everyone agreed with this statement. In what sense is this statement correct? Under what circumstances could it be false? Explain.

12. EverKleen Pool Services provides weekly swimming pool maintenance in Atlanta. Dozens of firms provide this service. The service is standardized; each company cleans the pool and maintains the proper levels of chemicals in the water. The service is typically sold as a four-month summer contract. The market price for the four-month service contract is $115.

EverKleen Pool Services has fixed costs of $3,500. The manager of EverKleen has estimated the following marginal cost function for EverKleen, using data for the last two years:

$$SMC = 125 - 0.42Q + 0.0021Q^2$$

where SMC is measured in dollars and Q is the number of pools serviced each summer. Each of the estimated coefficients is statistically significant at the 5 percent level.

a. Given the estimated marginal cost function, what is the average variable cost function for EverKleen?

b. At what output level does AVC reach its minimum value? What is the value of AVC at its minimum point?

c. Should the manager of EverKleen continue to operate, or should the firm shut down? Explain.

d. The manager of EverKleen finds two output levels that appear to be optimal. What are these levels of output and which one is actually optimal?

e. How much profit (or loss) can the manager of EverKleen Pool Services expect to earn?

f. Suppose EverKleen's fixed costs rise to $4,000. How does this affect the optimal level of output? Explain.

▢ MATHEMATICAL APPENDIX Profit Maximization for Price-Taking Firms

This appendix describes a manager's choice of output and input usage in order to maximize profit for a perfectly competitive firm facing a market-determined price for the product it sells. We examine the decision about the profit-maximizing output level first using the most general cost function and then using a quadratic cost function. Next we derive the profit-maximizing conditions when the manager chooses the level of usage of first one variable input and then two variable inputs.

The Firm Chooses the Level of Output

Assume that the firm is in the short run, so some costs are fixed. Let the market-determined price be $\bar{P}$. The firm's total revenue is

$$R(Q) = \bar{P}Q$$

The firm's profit function is

$$(1) \qquad \pi = \bar{P}Q - TVC(Q) - TFC$$

where $TVC(Q)$ is total variable cost and TFC is total fixed cost.

The first-order condition for a maximum requires

$$(2) \qquad \frac{d\pi}{dQ} = \bar{P} - \frac{dTVC}{dQ} = 0$$

The second-order condition for a maximum is that at the equilibrium quantity

$$(3) \qquad \frac{d^2\pi}{dQ^2} = -\frac{d^2TVC}{dQ^2} < 0$$

Since, in equation (2), $dTVC/dQ$ is marginal cost (SMC), choosing the quantity of output that maximizes profit requires that price equal marginal cost: $\bar{P} = SMC$. The second-order condition shows that in profit-maximizing equilibrium, marginal cost must be upward-sloping: $d^2TVC/dQ^2 > 0$. Equation (2) can be solved for the profit-maximizing output, Q^*.

If, at Q^*,

$$\pi = \bar{P}Q^* - TVC(Q^*) - TFC > 0$$

the firm makes an economic profit. If

$$\pi = \bar{P}Q^* - TVC(Q^*) - TFC < 0$$

the firm makes a loss. In this case the firm should produce Q^* rather than shutting down when

$$|\bar{P}Q^* - TVC(Q^*) - TFC| < TFC$$

which occurs if, at Q^*, price is greater than average variable cost:

$$(4) \qquad \bar{P} > \frac{TVC(Q^*)}{Q^*}$$

The firm loses less than its fixed cost, which is the amount it would lose if it shuts down and produces nothing. If at Q^* price is less than average variable cost, the firm should shut down and produce nothing. It loses all its fixed cost rather than its fixed cost plus the amount of variable cost not covered by revenue.

Since the second-order condition in equation (3) requires that marginal cost be upward-sloping, the firm's short-run supply must be upward-sloping. The higher the price, the greater the equilibrium output at which price equals marginal cost. Since, from equation (4), the firm produces nothing if price falls below minimum average variable cost, the supply is 0 at prices below minimum AVC.

For a less general approach, let the total variable cost function be the cubic function

$$TVC(Q) = aQ - bQ^2 + cQ^3$$

where a, b, and c are positive. We continue to assume that the market-determined price is $\bar{P}$. The profit function is

$$(5) \qquad \pi = \bar{P}Q - TVC(Q) - TFC$$
$$= \bar{P}Q - aQ + bQ^2 - cQ^3 - TFC$$

For profit maximization, differentiate equation (5) and set the derivative equal to zero:

(6) $$\frac{d\pi}{dQ} = \overline{P} - (a - 2bQ + 3cQ^2) = 0$$

Since $SMC = dTVC(Q)/dQ = a - 2bQ + 3cQ^2$, price equals marginal cost in profit-maximizing equilibrium. The second-order condition for a maximum is

(7) $$\frac{d^2\pi}{dQ^2} = 2b - 6cQ < 0$$

or, solving equation (7) for Q, for a maximum it must be the case that

(8) $$Q > \frac{b}{3c}$$

To obtain the profit-maximizing level of output Q^*, solve the quadratic equation formed from equation (6):

$$(\overline{P} - a) - 2bQ + 3cQ^2 = 0$$

After solving such a quadratic equation, you will get two values for Q^*. The profit-maximizing Q^* will be the one at which the second-order condition in (8) holds, ensuring that this is the value of Q^* at which marginal cost is upward-sloping. This will be the larger of the two solutions. If total revenue exceeds total variable cost, that is, if

$$\overline{P} > AVC(Q^*) = TVC(Q^*)/Q^* = a - bQ^* + cQ^{*2}$$

the firm produces Q^* and profit or loss is

$$\pi = \overline{P}Q^* - aQ^* + bQ^{*2} - cQ^{*3} - TFC$$

If $P < AVC(Q^*) = a - bQ^* + cQ^{*2}$ the firm shuts down, produces nothing, and loses its total fixed cost.

The Firm Chooses Input Usage

First we assume the firm chooses the level of usage of a single variable input, labor (L), in order to maximize profit. All other inputs ($\overline{K}$) are fixed in amount. The price of the product is $\overline{P}$. Let the production function be as derived for the short run in the Mathematical Appendix to Chapter 8:

$$Q = f(L, \overline{K}) = g(L)$$

The firm chooses L, so the following profit function is maximized:

(9) $$\pi = \overline{P}g(L) - wL - TFC$$

where w is the wage paid to labor and TFC is the fixed payment to the fixed input. Profit maximization requires

(10) $$\frac{d\pi}{dL} = \overline{P}\left(\frac{dQ}{dL}\right) - w = 0$$

Since $dQ/dL = MP_L$ is the marginal product of labor, equation (10) can be expressed as

$$MP_L \times \overline{P} = \text{Marginal revenue product} = w$$

Equation (10) can be solved for L^*, then $Q^* = g(L^*)$.

If, at L^*, $MRP < ARP = \overline{P}g(L^*)/L^*$, total revenue will be greater than total variable cost ($PQ^* > wL^*$) and the firm will produce. Its profit or loss will be

$$\pi = \overline{P}g(L^*) - w - TFC$$

If, however, $MRP = w > \overline{P}Q^*/L^*$, total revenue will be less than total variable cost ($\overline{P}Q^* < wL^*$). In this case the firm would shut down and lose only its total fixed cost, rather than its total fixed cost plus the portion of total variable cost not covered by revenue.

Now assume that the firm uses two variable inputs, L and K, to produce Q and no inputs are fixed. The prices of L and K are, respectively, w and r. The production function is

$$Q = f(L, K)$$

The product price remains $\overline{P}$. The profit function is

$$\pi = \overline{P}f(L, K) - wL - rK$$

Since the firm chooses the levels of L and K to maximize profit, the first-order equilibrium conditions are

(11a) $$\overline{P}\frac{dQ}{dL} - w = 0$$

(11b) $$\overline{P}\frac{dQ}{dK} - r = 0$$

Equations (11a) and (11b) can be solved for the profit-maximizing levels of L^* and K^*; then the optimal level of output is $Q^* = f(L^*, K^*)$. This value of Q^* can be substituted into the profit equation to find the maximum level of profit.

Equations (11a) and (11b) can be rewritten as

(12a) $$\overline{P}MP_L = MRP_L = w$$

(12b) $$\overline{P}MP_K = MRP_K = r$$

Thus, in equilibrium, the marginal revenue product of each input equals its price.

CHAPTER 12

Managerial Decisions for Firms with Market Power

For many years, most "premium" brands of coffee carried by grocery stores sold for prices very close to the prices of generic "value brands." Even substantial advertising expenditures by the makers of Folgers and Maxwell House premium brands failed to create strong brand loyalties among coffee drinkers. The coffee industry seemed to be locked in the kind of competitive structure described in Chapter 11: Buyers viewed coffee as essentially a standardized commodity with little product differentiation, sellers viewed themselves as price-takers, and investors saw little prospect for long-run profit in the retail coffee business. All of this changed, however, when Starbucks succeeded in giving coffee a new cachet. Not only did Starbucks cafés reap impressive profits, but many other coffee companies also earned much higher profits as they followed Starbucks' innovative lead and developed new, more creative flavors.[1] For example, Maxwell House sells Master Blend, Columbian Supreme, Rich French Roast, and Italian Espresso Roast. Now, instead of being price-takers, makers of premium coffee brands enjoy considerable price-setting power as a result of their successful investment in product differentiation. Instead of facing flat, perfectly elastic demand curves, premium brand coffee makers now face downward-sloping demand curves that give them market power to set prices above the generic "value brands."

---

[1]See Vijay Vishwanath and David Harding, "The Starbucks Effect," *Harvard Business Review,* Mar.–Apr. 2000.

market power
The ability of all price-setting firms to raise price without losing all sales, which causes the price-setting firm's demand to be downward-sloping.

Market power—something competitive firms don't have—makes long-run profit possible. As we explained in Chapter 1, **market power** is the ability possessed by all price-setting firms to raise their prices without losing all their sales.[2] In contrast to the competitive price-taking firms discussed in Chapter 11, price-setting firms do not sell standardized commodities in markets with many other sellers of nearly identical products, and so price-setting firms do not face perfectly elastic (horizontal) demand curves. Because the product is somehow differentiated from rivals' products or perhaps because the geographic market area has only one (or just a few) sellers of the product, firms with market power face a downward-sloping demand for the products they sell. All firms except price-taking competitors—monopolies, monopolistic competitors, and oligopolies—have some market power.

When firms with market power raise price, even though sales do not fall to zero, sales do, of course, decrease because of the law of demand. The effect of the change in price on the firm's sales depends to a large extent on the amount of its market power, which can differ greatly among firms. Firms with market power range in scope from virtual monopolies with a great deal of latitude over the prices they charge, such as Pfizer's Celebrex drug for arthritis treatment, to firms with a great deal of competition and only a small amount of market power, such as shoe stores or clothing stores in a large mall. In oligopoly markets, which we will examine carefully in Chapter 13, a firm with large market share may nonetheless possess only a small degree of market power if the other large rivals choose not to match the firm's price increases.

The primary focus of this chapter is to show how managers of price-setting firms with downward-sloping demands can choose price, output, and input usage so as to maximize the firm's profit. No matter how much market power a firm has, the primary objective of the manager is to maximize profit. As you would expect, the profit-maximization rule is to choose price and output so that the revenue from the last unit sold is equal to the marginal cost of producing and selling that unit. As we will discuss in the next chapter on oligopoly firms, complications can arise for oligopoly managers when their demand and marginal revenue conditions depend critically on the decisions of rival firms. For the types of firms discussed in this chapter—firms with some degree of market power (i.e., with downward-sloping demands) that can set price without worrying too much about a retaliatory response by any rival—the profit-maximizing decision is a straightforward application of the $MR = MC$ rule. Understanding the complexities of decision making when rivals can undermine a planned price change will require the tools of strategic decision making presented in the next chapter.

---

[2]Economists frequently use the terms "monopoly power" and "market power" interchangeably, both terms meaning the firm has the ability to raise price without losing all sales. In this text we will always use the term "market power" instead of "monopoly power" because we do not want you to have the mistaken impression that only monopoly firms have market power. Monopolies, monopolistic competitors, and oligopolies all face downward-sloping demand curves and consequently have market power.

The first part of this chapter describes some ways of measuring market power that are more precise and concrete than terms such as "great deal" or "limited amount." We then discuss some of the determinants of the market power possessed by a firm and reasons why some firms have much more market power than others.

The major portion of the chapter is devoted to the theory of monopoly. A **monopoly** exists when a firm produces and sells a good or service for which there are no close substitutes and other firms are prevented by some type of entry barrier from entering the market. A monopoly, consequently, has more market power than any other type of firm. Although there are few true monopolies in real-world markets—and most of these are subject to some form of government regulation—many large and small firms possess a considerable amount of market power in the sense of having few close substitutes for the products they sell. The theory of monopoly provides the basic analytical framework for the analysis of how managers of all price-setting firms with market power can make decisions to maximize their profit (except, as mentioned, oligopolistic firms that face a high degree of interdependence).

We end this chapter with a fairly brief analysis of firms selling in markets under conditions of **monopolistic competition.** Under monopolistic competition, the market consists of a large number of relatively small firms that produce similar but slightly differentiated products and therefore have some, but not much, market power. Monopolistic competition is characterized by easy entry into and exit from the market. Most retail and wholesale firms and many small manufacturers are examples of monopolistic competition.

Certainly, monopoly and monopolistic competition are very different market structures, but firms in both of these market structures possess some degree of market power. In both cases, managers employ precisely the same analysis to choose the profit-maximizing point on a downward-sloping demand curve. As we will show you in this chapter, there is virtually no difference between monopoly and monopolistic competition in the short run. And even though the outcomes are somewhat different in the long run for the two structures, it is convenient to examine decision making in both of these kinds of market structures in a single chapter.

monopoly
A firm that produces a good for which there are no close substitutes in a market that other firms are prevented from entering because of a barrier to entry.

monopolistic competition
A market consisting of a large number of firms selling a differentiated product with low barriers to entry.

12.1 MEASUREMENT OF MARKET POWER

Even though we have not set forth a precise way to measure a firm's market power, you have probably figured out that the amount of market power is related to the availability of substitutes. The better the substitutes for the product sold by a firm, the less market power the firm possesses. However, there is no single measurement of market power that is totally acceptable to economists, policymakers, and the courts. Economists have come to rely on several measures of market power. These methods are widely used, frequently in antitrust cases that require objective measurement of market power.

Any of the methods of measuring the market power of a firm will fail to provide an accurate measure of market power if the scope of the market in which the firm competes has not been carefully defined. This section begins by discussing how to determine the proper market definition: identifying the products that compete with one another and the geographic area in which the competition occurs. Then we discuss some measures of market power.

Market Definition

market definition
The identification of the producers and products that compete for consumers in a particular geographic area.

A **market definition** identifies the producers and products or service types that compete in a particular geographic area, which is just large enough to include all competing sellers. As you can see by this definition of a market, properly defining a market requires considering the level of competition in both the product dimension and the geographic dimension of a market. Although the methodology of appropriately defining a market is primarily of interest to firms engaged in federal or state antitrust litigation—specifically cases involving illegal monopolization of a market or the impact of a proposed merger on the merged firm's market power—managers should know how to properly define the firm's market in order to measure correctly the firm's market power. We will now discuss some guidelines for determining the proper product and geographic dimensions of a market.

A properly defined market should include all the products or services that consumers perceive to be substitutes. A manager who fails to identify all the products that consumers see as substitutes for the firm's product will likely overestimate the firm's market power. The CEO of Coca-Cola would be foolish to view the company as a monopolist in the production of cola soft drinks and expect it to enjoy substantial market power. No doubt Coca-Cola's syrup formula is a closely guarded secret, but most soft-drink consumers consider rival brands of soft drinks, as well as a variety of noncarbonated drinks such as iced tea and Gatorade, as reasonable substitutes for Coca-Cola.

The geographic boundaries of a market should be just large enough to include all firms whose presence limits the ability of other firms to raise price without a substantial loss of sales. Two statistics provide guidelines for delineating the geographic dimensions of a market: (1) the percentage of sales to *buyers* outside the market and (2) the percentage of sales from *sellers* outside the market. Both percentages will be small if the geographic boundary includes all active buyers and sellers. These two guidelines for determining the geographic dimensions of a market are sometimes referred to as LIFO and LOFI: little in from outside and little out from inside.

As mentioned earlier, economists have developed several measures of market power. We will discuss briefly only a few of the more important measures.

Elasticity of Demand

One approach to measuring how much market power a firm possesses is to measure the elasticity of the firm's demand curve. Recall from Chapter 6 that a firm's ability to raise price without suffering a substantial reduction in unit sales is inversely related to the price elasticity of demand. The less elastic is demand, the smaller the percentage reduction in quantity demanded associated with any particular price increase. The more elastic is demand, the larger the percentage decrease in unit sales associated with a given increase in price. Also recall from Chapter 6 that the elasticity of demand is greater (i.e., more elastic) the larger the number of substitutes available for a firm's product. As demand becomes less elastic, consumers view the product as having fewer good substitutes.

Although a firm's market power is greater the less elastic its demand, this does not mean a firm with market power chooses to produce on the inelastic portion of its demand. In other words, market power does not imply that a manager produces where $|E| < 1$; rather, the less elastic is demand, the greater the degree of market power. We will demonstrate later in this chapter that a monopolist always chooses to produce and sell on the elastic portion of its demand.

▣   **Relation**   The degree to which a firm possesses market power is inversely related to the elasticity of demand. The less (more) elastic the firm's demand, the greater (less) its degree of market power. The fewer the number of close substitutes consumers can find for a firm's product, the smaller the elasticity of demand and the greater the firm's market power. When demand is perfectly elastic (demand is horizontal), the firm possesses no market power.

The Lerner Index

Lerner index
A ratio that measures the proportionate amount by which price exceeds marginal cost: $\dfrac{P - MC}{P}$.

A closely related method of measuring the degree of market power is to measure the extent to which price deviates from the price that would exist under competition. The **Lerner index,** named for Abba Lerner, who popularized this measure, is a ratio that measures the proportionate amount by which price exceeds marginal cost:

$$\text{Lerner index} = \frac{P - MC}{P}$$

Price equals marginal cost when firms are price-takers, so the Lerner index equals zero under competition. The higher the value of the Lerner index, the greater the degree of market power.

The Lerner index can be related to the price elasticity of demand. In profit-maximizing equilibrium, marginal cost equals marginal revenue. Also recall from Chapter 6 that $MR = P(1 + 1/E)$. Thus the Lerner index can be expressed as

$$\text{Lerner index} = \frac{P - MR}{P} = \frac{P - P(1 + 1/E)}{P} = 1 - (1 + 1/E) = -\frac{1}{E}$$

In this form, it is easy to see that the less elastic is demand, the higher the Lerner index and the higher the degree of market power. The Lerner index is consistent with this discussion, showing that market power is inversely related to the elasticity of demand.

▣   **Relation**   The Lerner index, $\dfrac{P - MC}{P}$, measures the proportionate amount by which price exceeds marginal cost. Under perfect competition, the index is equal to zero, and the index increases in magnitude as market power increases. The Lerner index can be expressed as $-1/E$, which shows that the index, and market power, vary inversely with the elasticity of demand. The lower (higher) the elasticity of demand, the greater (smaller) the Lerner index and the degree of market power.

Cross-Price Elasticity of Demand

An indicator, though not strictly a measure, of market power is the cross-price elasticity of demand. Recall from Chapter 6 that cross-price elasticity measures the sensitivity of the quantity purchased of one good to a change in the price of another good. It indicates whether two goods are viewed by consumers as substitutes. A large, positive cross-price elasticity means that consumers consider the goods to be readily substitutable. Market power in this case is likely to be weak. If a firm produces a product for which there are no other products with a high (positive) cross-price elasticity, the firm is likely to possess a high degree of market power.

The cross-price elasticity of demand is often used in antitrust cases to help determine whether consumers of a particular firm's product perceive other products to be substitutes for that product. Using cross-price elasticities, antitrust officials try to determine which products compete with one another. For example, antitrust officials might wish to determine the degree of market power enjoyed by Nike brand athletic shoes. Nike Corporation has spent a great deal of money advertising to establish a prominent position in the market for athletic shoes. To determine which other products compete with Nike, the cross-price elasticity of the quantity demanded of Nike shoes with respect to a change in the price of a rival's product can be calculated. Using such cross-price elasticities, antitrust officials can determine whether consumers view Nike as having any real competitors in the market for athletic shoes.

Relation   If consumers view two goods to be substitutes, the cross-price elasticity of demand (E_{XY}) is positive. The higher the cross-price elasticity, the greater the perceived substitutability and the smaller the degree of market power possessed by the firms producing the two goods.

These are only a few of the measures of market power. The courts in antitrust cases and the Justice Department in merger and acquisition hearings sometimes use a combination of measures, including concentration ratios and share of the market. It is also not always clear just how high a cross elasticity or how low an elasticity constitutes "too much" market power. If you are ever involved in such a hearing, you should be aware of the problems in measuring market power. Illustration 12.1 shows the difficulty of determining what constitutes a market and what determines the amount of market power.

12.2 DETERMINANTS OF MARKET POWER

strong barrier to entry
A condition that makes it difficult for new firms to enter a market in which economic profits are being earned.

Entry or potential entry of new firms into a market can erode the market power of existing firms by increasing the number of substitutes. Therefore, as a general case, a firm can possess a high degree of market power only when strong barriers to the entry of new firms exist. A **strong barrier to entry** exists when it is difficult for new firms to enter a market where existing firms are making an economic profit. Strong barriers to entry hinder the introduction of new, substitute products and protect the profits of firms already in the market.

ILLUSTRATION 12.1

Is Microsoft a Monopoly?

Some of the most contentious issues in the recent antitrust case against Microsoft stemmed from the question of whether or not Microsoft had a monopoly in the market for PC operating systems. And, even if Microsoft did have a monopoly in its Windows operating system, did it have sufficient market power to harm consumers? And, even if Microsoft possessed sufficient market power to harm consumers, would consumers benefit by breaking Microsoft up into two smaller companies? Don't think for a moment that we can answer these questions definitively in a short illustration, or even in a long one for that matter. We can't. But we can illustrate the rich complexities of these interesting questions by surveying the opinions of a number of economists as reported by various business news publications.

Alan Reynolds (Director of Economic Research at the Hudson Institute)

It was routinely reported that Microsoft's Windows software "runs on more than 90 percent of the world's PCs." This fraction would be worrisome if it meant that Microsoft had captured all but 10 percent of the *total market* for operating systems. To evaluate the usefulness of the reported market share, we must consider the market definition employed to make the calculation. As we emphasized in the text, a properly defined market should include all the products that consumers perceive to be substitutes. Reynolds argued that the Department of Justice defined the market for operating systems far too narrowly, and so inflated Windows' share of the operating system market.

The Justice Department defined the market in the Microsoft case to be "single-user computers with Intel microprocessors." Reynolds noted that this narrow definition of the market in which Microsoft competes excludes such competitors as Apple computers, since they don't use Intel microprocessors; Sun Microsystems workstations; any operating system used as part of a business network (e.g., Solaris and UNIX); and operating systems used in handheld and subnotebook computers. In short, Reynolds believed the Justice Department stacked the deck against Microsoft by excluding many genuine competitors of Microsoft's Windows operating system. Reynolds also noted that, in high-tech industries, dominant firms are normal: Quicken has 80 percent of the home-finance software market, Netscape once had 90 percent of the browser market, and Intel has 76 percent of the microprocessor chip market.

Richard Schmalensee (MIT Economist and Expert Witness for Microsoft)

During his testimony as an expert witness for Microsoft, Schmalensee made a particularly insightful point: Microsoft may indeed have owned most of the market for operating systems, but it did not have a high degree of market power and was not a harmful monopoly. Schmalensee calculated that, if Microsoft was indeed a monopolist wielding great market power because it faced little or no competition, the profit-maximizing price for Windows 98 would have been somewhere between $900 and $2,000. The Justice Department's attorney expressed his astonishment over this calculation by asking Schmalensee if he thought a price of $2,000 made sense as the profit-maximizing

An example of a strong barrier to entry is a cable TV franchise granted by a city government to only one cable company. This fortunate company is protected from other firms' competing away any economic profits and is close to being a monopoly. Note that we said "close" to being a monopoly because the cable company has some outside competition even though it is the only cable company in town. Possible substitutes, though certainly not perfect ones, might be regular broadcast television, satellite dishes, radio, books and magazines, rental movies, and so on. Thus the firm would be a monopoly if the cable TV market is the relevant market

price for Microsoft to actually charge for Windows. "Of course not, because Microsoft faces significant long-run competition. That's precisely the point." As we explained in the text, the degree of market power a monopolist possesses depends on the availability of close substitutes. Schmalensee explained that not only did Windows 98 face potential competition from new entrants in the future, it also had to compete with two highly successful and widely available rival products: Windows 3.1 and Windows 95. Perhaps a consumer's best protection from the alleged Microsoft monopoly was to own an early version of Windows.

Franklin Fisher (MIT Economist and Expert Witness for Department of Justice)

"Microsoft has engaged in anticompetitive conduct that has no compelling economic justification but for its effect of restricting competition," according to testimony in the case by Franklin Fisher, an expert in antitrust matters pertaining to monopoly practices. The government introduced into evidence numerous internal Microsoft memos and strategy documents. The language in these documents painted a picture of a firm obsessed with beating its rivals in every way possible. In one e-mail circulated among the top executives at Microsoft on the topic of subverting rival Java software language: "Subversion has always been our best tactic . . . Subversion is almost always a better tactic than a frontal assault. It leaves the competition confused; they don't know what to shoot at anymore." While the tactics employed by Microsoft to beat its rivals do seem ruthless to us, we suspect the same kind of memos would surface if the trial involved Pfizer, Toyota, Bank of America, or any other profit-maximizing firm.

The Economist (Editorial Opinion in the British Business News Magazine)

In an editorial opinion, The Economist expressed its concern that many of the high-tech markets in the New Economy experience network externalities, which increase the likelihood that a single firm may dominate a market. Once a dominant firm establishes a large, "installed" base of customers who use its brand of high technology, consumers may become locked in, creating a monopoly by blocking the entry of new firms and new technologies. For antitrust enforcement agencies charged with the duty of preventing new monopolies and breaking up old ones, the continual product improvement and falling computer product prices make it difficult to demonstrate that consumers are harmed by "monopoly abuse" in high-tech markets. Consequently, The Economist worried that Microsoft could stifle innovation and inflict serious harm to high-tech consumers and the New Economy.

The Economist, like Franklin Fisher, viewed Microsoft's business behavior as evidence of its intent to use its market power to maintain its market dominance. "An amazing trail of e-mails and management papers has depicted a company ready, it seems, to do almost anything to protect its Windows monopoly . . . When, as in the Microsoft case, a monopolist's conduct seems to be chilling innovation in markets in which the competition is largely defined by innovation, the argument for antitrust intervention is compelling."

Gary Becker (Nobel Prize–Winning Economist at University of Chicago)

The Department of Justice proposed breaking Microsoft into two independent firms: an operating-system

but not if the entertainment market is the relevant market. We should note that in cases in which a government body protects a firm from entry by other firms into a market, it typically regulates the protected firm.

Weak barriers to entry generally exist in most retail markets. Retail stores typically do not have much market power because entry by other firms into the market is easy and there are good substitutes for the products of firms selling in the market. The products are not perfect substitutes, as is the case for perfect competition, because other firms cannot sell identical products or sell in the same location.

company (Windows) and an applications company (MS Office, Internet Explorer, and other Microsoft applications). DOJ believed a breakup was needed to encourage faster technological innovation. Becker saw two problems with the Justice Department's arguments. First, economists are not sure that competition fosters greater rates of innovation than monopoly. Becker referred to the original thinking on this issue by Joseph Schumpeter (1883–1950), who believed that monopoly markets experience higher rates of innovation than competitive ones. Monopolies stimulate more technological innovation, according to Schumpeter, because they don't have to worry about competitors (quickly) imitating their innovations, driving down their profits.

Becker also argued that the Department of Justice has not provided any quantitative evidence that the dominant position held by Microsoft in operating systems had slowed technical progress in the computer-Internet industry:

> The government and its experts cite a few potential innovations that were supposedly discouraged by Microsoft's aggressive behavior. Even if these examples are valid, the government does not consider whether there have been other innovations stimulated by a large market for new software applications made possible by the dominant Windows platform.

Over the last 40 years, enormous technological progress has occurred in the computer-Internet industry. That progress, Becker pointed out, did not slow down as Microsoft built its powerful position in operating systems during the last 20 years of this period. Maybe Microsoft's rivals who complained in court were hoping the Justice Department would *protect* them from competition rather than *promote* competition?

As we told you at the beginning of this illustration, we wish we could give you the answer to all of these questions, but we can't. Indeed, the answers proved difficult for all involved in this case. Eventually, the trial judge, Judge Thomas Penfield Jackson, found Microsoft guilty of illegal monopolization and ordered Microsoft to be split into two firms. On appeal, the U.S. Appeals Court reversed the breakup order and removed Judge Jackson from the case. In November 2001, Microsoft and the Justice Department reached a settlement on penalties and remedies that received final approval in November 2002 by the new judge in the case, Judge Colleen Kollar-Kotelly. Clearly, the question of illegal monopolization proved to be quite challenging for all concerned. You should try to reach your own conclusion and discuss your reasoning with classmates and your professor. This case will likely be debated for many years.

Sources: Alan Reynolds, "U.S. v. Microsoft: The Monopoly Myth," *The Wall Street Journal*, April 4, 1999; "Big Friendly Giant," *The Economist*, Jan. 30, 1999; John R. Wilke and Keithe Perine, "Final Government Witness Testifies Against Microsoft in Antitrust Trial," *The Wall Street Journal*, Jan. 6, 1999; "Lessons from Microsoft," *The Economist*, Mar. 6, 1999; Gary S. Becker, "Uncle Sam Has No Business Busting Up Microsoft," *BusinessWeek*, June 19, 2000; Don Clark, Mark Wigfield, Nick Wingfield, and Rebecca Buckman, "Judge Approves Most of Pact, in Legal Victory for Microsoft," *The Wall Street Journal*, Nov. 1, 2002.

However, firms can produce close substitutes. Therefore, even though perfect competition would not exist in such markets because products are not perfect substitutes, no firm has much market power since it cannot raise its price much above its rivals' without a substantial loss of sales. Many types of barriers to entry exist, but we will discuss here only a few of the most common types.

Economies of Scale

An important barrier to entry is created when the long-run average cost curve of a firm decreases over a wide range of output, relative to the demand for the product.

Consequently, a new firm that wishes to enter this type of market must enter on a large scale in order to keep its costs as low as the large-scale firm or firms already operating in the market. The necessity of entering on a large scale is usually not a barrier to entry by itself, but when it is coupled with relatively small product demand, a strong barrier to entry can be created.

Consider an industry where four existing firms each produces about 200,000 units annually to take advantage of substantial economies of scale. At the current price of the product, annual sales are running at about 800,000 units per year. While many entrepreneurs could obtain the financial backing to enter this industry with a large-scale plant capable of producing 200,000 units, there is no room in the industry for a fifth large-scale producer without a significant decline in the price of the product. Even though a fifth firm could enter the industry producing perhaps 50,000 units annually, the per-unit production costs would be much higher than competitors' costs because of the substantial economies of scale. There just isn't room for a new firm to enter this industry on a scale big enough to enjoy costs as low as those of rivals. In such situations, economies of scale create a barrier to entry.

Barriers Created by Government

An obvious entry barrier is government. Licensing and franchises are ways monopolies are created by government decree. For example, licenses are granted to radio and television stations by the Federal Communications Commission (FCC), and only those stations possessing a license are allowed to operate. Governments also grant exclusive franchises for city, county, and state services. For example, local telephone and cable television utilities have a great deal of market power in that they are the only regional producers of the products. By law, no other producer can exist.

Another legal barrier to competition lies in the patent laws. These laws make it possible for a person to apply for and obtain the exclusive right to produce a certain commodity, or to produce a commodity by means of a specified process that provides an absolute cost advantage. Despite examples to the contrary, however, holding a patent on a product or production process may not be quite what it seems in many instances. A patent does not preclude the development of closely related substitute goods or closely allied production processes. International Business Machines (IBM) has the exclusive right to produce its patented computers, but many other computers are available and there is competition in the computer market.

Input Barriers

Historically, an important reason for market power has been the control of raw-material supplies. If one firm (or perhaps a few firms) controls all the known supply of a necessary ingredient for a particular product, the firm (or firms) can refuse to sell that ingredient to other firms at a price low enough for them to compete. When no others can produce the product, monopoly results. For many years the

ILLUSTRATION 12.2

Terminating Discounts: Rise of the Machines

There's a war going on in stores across America, and it's no Hollywood film. Steely-eyed consumers are staring down store clerks demanding something that sellers wish to avoid: discounts. The battle over discounts is raging, according to *The Wall Street Journal*, as buyers and sellers arm themselves with ever more powerful weapons of the computer age.[a] Consumers are attempting to vanquish the market power of retailers, who use this power to set prices well above costs and earn large profits on items sold at full prices. Consumers are fighting back by learning the secret discount strategies of retailers.

Lately, consumers have been winning the battle, partly because they have discovered a new weapon on the Internet: price-search "engines." These engines not only let buyers compare prices across many stores to find the best prices, but they also send out notices when prices drop. Consumers have been so successful in learning how to use new information technologies for price searching that many of them just won't buy anything without a significant discount. For example, the *WSJ* reports that "in the past year alone, the amount of clothing sold on sale jumped 4 percent to 63 percent of all clothing sold."

Some of the nation's most sophisticated retailers—JCPenney, Best Buy, Brooks Brothers, Saks Fifth Avenue, and Circuit City—are counterattacking to protect their market power by developing their own high-tech weapons. Many of the nation's top retailers of clothing, electronics, furniture, and even wedding gifts are now employing computers—even supercomputers in some cases—armed with sophisticated pricing software designed along the lines of the tremendously successful software used by airlines to set ticket prices. Stores, of course, deny that they are using such weapons, but they are! They have adopted several strategies to protect (and even increase) their revenues against discount-thirsty shoppers:

- Offer discounts at more unexpected times, rather than at the usual, predictable times, such as right after Christmas. Best Buy and J&R Music, for example, have adopted a counterintuitive discount pattern for new CDs and DVDs. They offer deep discounts immediately after new CDs

and DVDs are released; then they raise prices over time "to capitalize on the excitement created by new releases [after they] launch deep discounts at the outset to drive demand even higher."

- "Bundle" discounted items with steeply marked-up complement goods. Electronics retailers might discount prices on home-theater components while raising prices on strongly recommended, gold-plated connecting cables or other related components.

- Separate buyers, for pricing purposes, into groups with different price sensitivities. The group of buyers who are quite price sensitive will be targeted to receive lower prices for the same merchandise that the less-price-sensitive group pays the higher full price. For example, Dell Computer Co. offers on its website discounts and specially priced bundles of computer components called "Hot Deals" that are available only to online buyers. Because Hot Deals are not published in printed catalogs, they can be offered spontaneously and ended unexpectedly. This pattern favors the group of buyers who will only buy when they find "bargains." Another group of buyers who only buy when they need a new computer are likely to miss any Hot Deal that might match their needs, and so they end up paying higher prices on average. This pricing technique, sometimes called market segmentation or price discrimination, is a widely used method for increasing revenues, and one that we will discuss in some detail in Chapter 14.

As you can see, each one of these methods seeks to preserve or extend market power. Much of the recent advancement in pricing methodology involves using powerful computers and statistical software to analyze the vast amounts of sales data that can be cheaply collected and stored in the digital age. If you plan to become an expert in product pricing, you must be prepared to learn how to apply these new methods. As noted, we will show you some of the pricing models these techniques employ, as well as some applications, in Chapter 14.

[a]Jane Spencer, "How to Beat Retailers at the Discount Game," *The Wall Street Journal*, Nov. 27, 2002.

Aluminum Company of America (Alcoa) owned almost every source of bauxite, a necessary ingredient in the production of aluminum, in North America. The control of resource supply, coupled with certain patent rights, provided Alcoa with an absolute monopoly in aluminum production. It was only after World War II that the federal courts effectively broke Alcoa's monopoly in the aluminum industry. There have been other such historical examples, but at the present time there are few cases of firms with considerable market power because of exclusive control of a raw material.

Brand Loyalties

On the demand side, older firms may have, over time, built up the allegiance of their customers. New firms can find this loyalty difficult to overcome. For example, no one knows what the service or repair policy of a new firm may be. The preference of buyers can also be influenced by a long successful advertising campaign; established brands, for instance, allow customers recourse if the product should be defective or fall short of its advertised promises. Although technical economies of scale may be insignificant, new firms might have considerable difficulty establishing a market organization and overcoming buyer preference for the products of older firms. A classic example of how loyalty preserves monopoly power can be found in the concentrated-lemon-juice market. ReaLemon lemon juice successfully developed such strong brand loyalties among consumers that rival brands evidently could not survive in the market. The situation was so serious that the courts forced ReaLemon to license its name to would-be competitors.

The role of advertising as a barrier to entry has long been a source of controversy. Some argue that advertising acts as a barrier to entry by strengthening buyer preferences for the products of established firms. On the other hand, consider the great difficulty of entering an established industry without access to advertising. A good way for an entrenched monopoly to discourage entry would be to get the government to prohibit advertising. The reputation of the old firm would enable it to continue its dominance. A new firm would have difficulty informing the public about the availability of a new product unless it was able to advertise. Thus advertising may be a way for a new firm to overcome the advantages of established firms. The effect of advertising on entry remains a point of disagreement among economists.

Consumer Lock-In

switching costs
Costs consumers incur when they switch to new or different products or services.

For some products or services, consumers may find it costly to switch to another brand—either an existing rival's brand or a new entrant's brand of product or service. Some of the kinds of **switching costs** incurred by consumers include things such as installation or initiation fees, search costs to learn about availability and prices of substitutes, and costs of learning how to use a new or different product or service. When high switching costs make previous consumption decisions so costly to alter that rivals do not believe they can induce many, if any, consumers to change their consumption decisions, then a situation known as **consumer lock-in** results.

consumer lock-in
High switching costs make previous consumption decisions very costly to change.

Consumer lock-in, of course, discourages new firms from entering a profitable market, and thus protects incumbent firms from new competition. High switching costs may arise naturally, or firms may strategically design products and services to have high switching costs in order to create a consumer lock-in barrier to entry.

While consumer lock-in can certainly create a strong barrier to entry, high monopoly profits nonetheless create a strong incentive for potential entrants to find ways to overcome a lock-in barrier. For example, when Microsoft decided to enter the market for household financial software with its Money program, Quicken had already established a virtual monopoly, and satisfied consumers seemed unwilling to incur the costs of switching from Quicken to Money. Microsoft, however, overcame this consumer lock-in barrier by designing its Money program to accept financial data files stored in Quicken's proprietary format so that switchers would not need to reenter their financial data. Microsoft also employed similar commands for its software and provided specialized help menus for users making the switch from Quicken. Thus, by lowering the switching costs facing consumers, Microsoft overcame a consumer lock-in barrier to entry and successfully ended Quicken's monopoly.

Network Externalities

network externalities
A product's value rises as more consumers use it.

Network externalities can make it difficult for new firms to enter markets where incumbent firms have established a large base or network of buyers. **Network externalities** occur when the value of a product to consumers increases as more consumers buy and use the product. As more people buy the good, even more people will find the good worth buying, and a snowball effect can propel the product into a monopoly position, making new entry extremely difficult, if not impossible.

Some examples of goods believed to experience network externalities include cellular phones, Internet access services, computer operating systems (such as Microsoft Windows), e-mail, and so on. The value to you of having a cellular phone increases the greater the number of cell phones in the network. Network externalities can create *first-mover advantages* for firms that first establish a base of users. We will discuss the concept of first- (and second-) mover advantages in the next chapter.

The purpose of this discussion is to expose you to several of the most common types of entry barriers and to illustrate the diversity of factors that hinder entry into a market and, consequently, foster market power. It is noteworthy that several of the barriers mentioned are somewhat influenced by the firm with market power. The control of inputs, the development of consumer loyalties, and the exploitation of switching costs and network externalities are effective barriers essentially erected by firms already producing in the market. We will discuss other strategic barriers to entry, erected by existing firms, in the next chapter.

Despite the existence of barriers to entry, firms can lose and have lost their positions of extensive market power. Even quite strong barriers to entry can be overcome. A monopolist can become complacent in its protected position and allow inefficiencies to enter the production process. This raises the cost, and hence the price, and allows new, more efficient firms to enter the market. Some potential entrants are ingenious enough to find ways to lower cost, or (as noted earlier) get around patent protection, or overcome brand loyalty to the established firm. Thus barriers to entry cannot completely protect the established firm with great market power.

12.3 PROFIT MAXIMIZATION UNDER MONOPOLY: OUTPUT AND PRICING DECISIONS

We will now analyze the profit-maximizing decision of firms that are pure monopolies. Keep in mind that the fundamentals of this monopoly decision apply to a large extent to all firms with market power. The manager of a monopoly treats the market demand curve as the firm's demand curve. As was the case for perfect competition, we assume that the manager wishes to maximize profit. Thus the manager of a monopoly firm chooses the point on the market demand curve that maximizes the profit of the firm. While the manager of a monopoly does, in fact, determine the price of the good, price cannot be chosen independent of output. The manager must choose price and output combinations that lie on the market demand curve.

In Figure 12.1, for example, if the manager wishes to charge a price of $14 per unit, the monopoly firm can sell (consumers will buy) only 900 units of the product. Alternatively, if the manager decides to sell 900 units, the highest price that

FIGURE 12.1
Demand and Marginal Revenue Facing a Monopolist

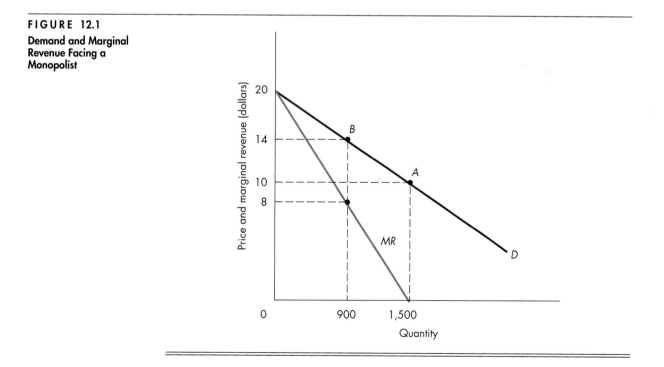

can be charged for this output is $14. So, while the monopolist can choose both price and output, the two choices are not independent of one another.

In practice, some monopolists choose price and let market demand determine how many units will be sold, whereas other monopolists choose the level of output to produce and then sell that output at the highest price market demand allows. Consider your electric utility company. Electric utilities set the price of a unit of electricity, say, 8 cents per kilowatt-hour, and then stand ready to supply as many kilowatt-hours as consumers wish to buy at that price. You can be sure that your electric company has estimated its demand function and knows approximately how much electricity will be demanded at various prices.

Alternatively, an automobile manufacturer might decide to produce 300,000 cars of a particular model in a given year. The manufacturer sells these cars at the highest possible price given the existing market demand. Again, you can be sure that the automobile manufacturer has estimated the demand for its cars and knows approximately the average price at which each car can be sold.

Given the demand curve facing a monopolist, choosing price to maximize profit is equivalent to choosing output to maximize profit. To be consistent with our discussion of profit maximization under perfect competition, we will view the monopolist as choosing *output* to maximize profit.

The basic principle of profit maximization—profit is maximized by producing and selling the output at which marginal cost equals marginal revenue—is the same for the monopoly as for the competitive firm. A manager can increase profit by expanding output as long as the marginal revenue from the expansion exceeds the marginal cost of expanding output. A manager would reduce output if marginal revenue is less than marginal cost. The fundamental difference for a monopolist is that marginal revenue is not equal to price.

☐   **Principle**   A monopolist chooses the point on the market demand curve that maximizes profit. If marginal revenue exceeds marginal cost, a profit-maximizing monopolist increases output. If marginal revenue is less than marginal cost, the monopolist does not produce these additional units.

Demand and Marginal Revenue for a Monopolist

A monopoly, facing a downward-sloping demand, must lower the price in order to sell more. As shown in Figure 12.1 and discussed in Chapter 6, marginal revenue is less than price for every unit sold except the first. You will recall that marginal revenue is the change in the firm's total revenue from an additional unit of sales; symbolically, $MR = \triangle TR/\triangle Q$. In Figure 12.1, if the firm sells 900 units at $14 each, you can see from the marginal revenue curve that the marginal or additional revenue from selling the 900th unit is $8. This means that reducing the price just enough to increase sales from 899 to 900 adds $8 to the firm's revenue, rather than the $14 price at which the 900th unit is sold. The reason is that in order to sell the 900th unit, the firm must reduce the price on the 899 units it could have sold at the slightly higher price.

Although we set forth a technical analysis of the relation between MR and P in Chapter 6, we can perhaps give you a bit more understanding of why MR is less than P with a hypothetical example. Suppose you manage a small appliance store that has been selling 20 radios a day at $50 apiece. You want to increase your sales of radios, so one day you reduce the price to $49. Sure enough, you sell 21 radios that day at the reduced price. So you sold one more at $49. You check the cash register and compare the receipts with those from previous days. You had been receiving $1,000 (= $50 × 20). Now you see that you have taken in $1029 (= $49 × 21) from selling radios. Your revenue increased by $29, but what happened to the $49 at which the additional radio was sold? Did someone steal $20 from the register? What happened was that, in order to sell the 21st radio, you had to take a $1 price reduction on the 20 you could have sold at $50. This $1 price reduction accounts for the "missing" $20.

Figure 12.1 illustrates the relation between demand and marginal revenue for a linear demand curve, as set forth in Chapter 6. When demand is linear, marginal revenue is twice as steep as demand and consequently lies halfway between demand and the vertical axis. When MR is positive, between 0 and 1,500 units, demand is elastic. When MR is negative, above 1,500 units, demand is inelastic. When MR equals 0, at 1,500 units, demand is unitary elastic.

Relation   The market demand curve is the demand curve for the monopolist. Because the monopolist must lower price in order to sell additional units of output, marginal revenue is less than price for all but the first unit of output sold. When marginal revenue is positive (negative), demand is elastic (inelastic). For a linear market demand, the monopolist's marginal revenue is also linear, with the same vertical intercept as demand, and is twice as steep.

Maximizing Profit at Southwest Leather Designs: An Example

Southwest Leather Designs specializes in the production of fashionable leather belts for women. Southwest's original designs are sometimes imitated by rival leather goods manufacturers, but the Southwest logo is a registered trademark that affords the company some protection from outright counterfeiting of its products. Consequently, Southwest Leather enjoys a degree of market power that would not be present if imitators could make identical copies of its belts, trademark and all.

Table 12.1 presents the demand and cost conditions faced by the manager of Southwest Leather Designs. Columns 1 and 2 give the demand schedule for 1,000 through 9,000 units of output (leather belts) in discrete intervals of 1,000. Column 3 shows the associated total revenue schedule (price times quantity). The total cost of producing each level of output is given in column 4. The manager computes profit or loss from producing and selling each level of output by subtracting total cost from total revenue. Profit is presented in column 7. Examination of the profit column indicates that the maximum profit ($56,020) occurs when Southwest Leather Designs sells 6,000 belts at a price of $18.92.

The manager of Southwest Leather Designs can reach the same conclusion using the marginal revenue–marginal cost approach. Marginal revenue and marginal cost are shown, respectively, in columns 5 and 6. The marginal revenue from selling additional leather belts exceeds the marginal cost of producing the additional belts until 6,000 units are sold. After 6,000 units the marginal revenue for each of

	(1)	(2)	(3)	(4)	(5) Marginal revenue	(6) Marginal cost	(7)
TABLE 12.1 **Profit Maximization for Southwest Leather Designs**	Output (Q)	Price (P)	Total revenue (TR = PQ)	Total cost (TC)	$\left(MR = \dfrac{\Delta TR}{\Delta Q}\right)$	$\left(SMC = \dfrac{\Delta TC}{\Delta Q}\right)$	Profit (π)
	0	$40.00	$ 0	$40,000	—	—	$−40,000
	1,000	35.00	35,000	42,000	$35.00	$ 2.00	−7,000
	2,000	32.50	65,000	43,500	30.00	1.50	21,500
	3,000	28.00	84,000	45,500	19.00	2.00	38,500
	4,000	25.00	100,000	48,500	16.00	3.00	51,500
	5,000	21.50	107,500	52,500	7.50	4.00	55,000
	6,000	18.92	113,520	57,500	6.02	5.00	56,020
	7,000	17.00	119,000	63,750	5.48	6.25	55,250
	8,000	15.35	122,800	73,750	3.80	10.00	49,050
	9,000	14.00	126,000	86,250	3.20	12.50	39,750

the next 1,000 belts is $5.48 per belt while the marginal cost for each of the next 1,000 belts is $6.25 per belt. Clearly, increasing output and sales from 6,000 to 7,000 belts would lower profit. Thus profit must increase until 6,000 units are produced; then profit decreases thereafter. This is the same solution that was obtained by subtracting total cost from total revenue: An output of 6,000 belts maximizes profit.

The example in Table 12.1 is shown graphically in Figure 12.2. Since marginal revenue and marginal cost are per-unit changes in revenue and cost over discrete changes in output of 1,000 units, we plot these values in the middle of the 1,000-unit interval. For example, marginal revenue for the first 1,000 units sold is $35 per unit for each of these 1,000 units. We plot this value of marginal revenue ($35) at 500 units of output. We do this at all levels of output for both marginal revenue and marginal cost.

In Figure 12.2, marginal revenue equals marginal cost at 6,000 units of output, which, as you saw from the table, is the profit-maximizing level of output. The demand curve shows that the price that Southwest Leather Designs will charge for the 6,000 belts is $18.92.

We turn now from a specific numerical example of profit maximization for a monopolist to a more general graphical analysis of a monopolist in the short run. In this case, we will assume for analytical convenience that output and price are continuously divisible.

Short-Run Equilibrium: Profit Maximization or Loss Minimization

A monopolist, just as a perfect competitor, attains maximum profit by producing and selling the rate of output for which the positive difference between total revenue and total cost is greatest; or it attains a minimum loss by producing the rate of output for which the negative difference between total revenue and total cost is least. When price exceeds average variable cost, this condition occurs when

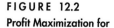

FIGURE 12.2

Profit Maximization for Southwest Leather Designs: Choosing Output

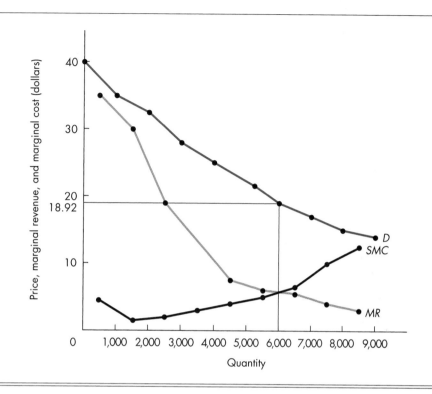

marginal revenue equals marginal cost.[3] As was the case for the perfectly competitive firm, when price is less than average variable cost, the manager shuts down production in the short run. We will first discuss profit maximization and then loss minimization.

The position of short-run equilibrium is easily described graphically. Figure 12.3 shows the relevant cost and revenue curves for a monopolist. Because *AVC* and *AFC* are not necessary for exposition, they are omitted. Note that demand is the downward-sloping market demand curve. Marginal revenue is also downward-sloping and lies below the demand curve everywhere except at the vertical intercept. The short-run cost curves confronting a monopolist are derived in exactly the fashion described in Chapter 8 and have the typically assumed shapes. Figure 12.3 shows a situation in which price exceeds average total cost, and thus the monopolist earns an economic profit.

The monopolist maximizes profit by producing 200 units of output where *MR* = *SMC*. From the demand curve, the monopolist can (and will) charge $7 per unit. Total revenue is $1,400 (= $7 × 200), or the area of the rectangle 0*ABE*. The average total cost of producing 200 units of output is $5. Total cost of producing

---

[3]This result is derived mathematically in the appendix to this chapter.

FIGURE 12.3

Short-Run Profit-Maximizing Equilibrium under Monopoly

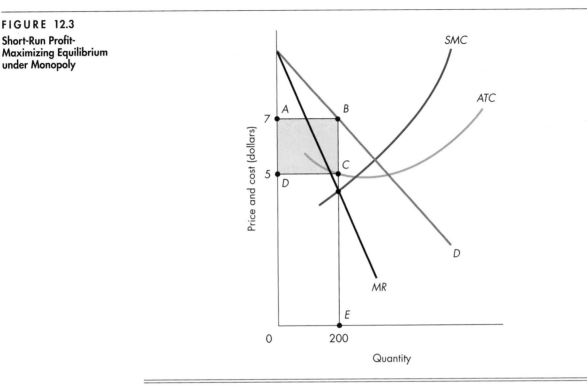

200 units is $1,000 (= $5 × 200), or the area of the rectangle 0*DCE*. Economic profit is *TR* minus *TC*, $400 (= $1,400 − $1,000), or the shaded area *ABCD*. Since price is greater than average total cost at the equilibrium output of 200 units, the monopolist earns an economic profit. This need not be the case, however.

  People often have the idea that monopoly firms can always make a profit; if the firm is making losses, it can simply raise price until it makes a profit. It is, however, a misconception that all monopolies are ensured a profit. Figure 12.4 illustrates a monopolist that makes losses in the short run. Marginal cost equals marginal revenue at 50 units of output, which, from the demand curve, can be sold for $75 each. Total revenue, then, is $3,750 (= $75 × 50), or the area 0*DCE*. Since average total cost is $80 per unit, total cost is $4,000 (= $80 × 50), or the area 0*ABE*. Since total cost exceeds total revenue, the firm experiences a loss of $250 (= $4,000 − $3,750), which is the shaded area *ABCD*.

  Note that in Figure 12.4 the monopolist would produce rather than shut down in the short run since total revenue (area 0*DCE*) exceeds the total variable cost of $3,250 (= $65 × 50), or area 0*GFE*. After all variable costs have been covered, there is still some revenue, $500 (area *GDCF*), left over to apply to fixed cost. Since total fixed cost in this example is $750 (= $15 × 50), or area *ABFG*, the firm loses less by producing 50 units than by shutting down. If the monopolist shuts down, it would, of course, lose its entire fixed cost of $750.

FIGURE 12.4

Short-Run Loss Minimization under Monopoly

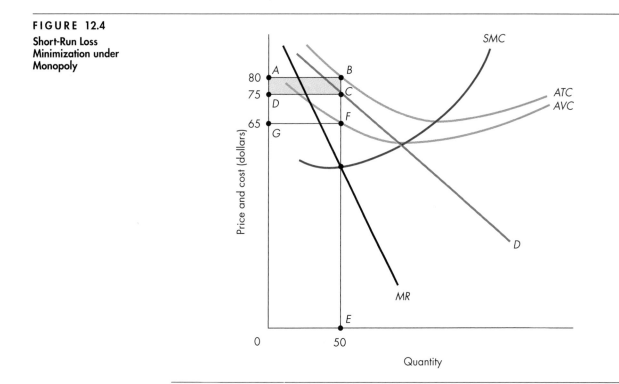

If demand decreases so that it lies below *AVC* at every level of output and the monopolist could not cover all its variable cost at any price, the firm would shut down and lose only fixed cost. This is exactly the same shutdown rule as that of the perfect competitor.

We should note that a monopolist would never choose a situation in which it was producing and selling an output on the inelastic portion of its demand. When demand is inelastic, marginal revenue is negative. Since marginal cost is always positive, it must equal marginal revenue when the latter is also positive. Thus the monopolist will always be on the elastic portion of demand.

In the short run, the primary difference between a monopoly and a perfect competitor lies in the slope of the demand curve. Either may earn a pure profit; either may incur a loss.

□   **Relations**   In the short run a monopoly will produce a positive output if some price on the demand curve exceeds average variable cost. It maximizes profit or minimizes loss by producing the quantity for which *MR* = *SMC*. The price for that output is given by the demand curve. If the price exceeds average total cost, the firm makes a pure economic profit. If price is less than average total cost but exceeds average variable cost, the firm suffers an economic loss but continues to produce in the short run. If demand falls below average variable cost at every output, the firm shuts down in the short run and loses only its fixed cost.

Long-Run Equilibrium

A monopoly exists if there is only one firm in the market. Among other things, this statement implies that entry into the market is closed. Thus, if a monopolist earns an economic profit in the short run, no new producer can enter the market in the hope of sharing whatever profit potential exists. Therefore, economic profit is not eliminated in the long run, as was the case under perfect competition. The monopolist, however, will make adjustments in plant size as demand conditions warrant, in order to maximize profit in the long run.

Clearly, in the long run, a monopolist would choose the plant size designed to produce the quantity at which long-run marginal cost equals marginal revenue. Profit would be equal to the product of output times the difference between price and long-run average cost:

$$\pi = P \times Q - LAC \times Q = Q\,(P - LAC)$$

New entrants cannot come into the industry and compete away profits—entry will not shift the demand curve facing the monopolist.

Demand conditions may change for reasons other than the entry of new firms, and any such change in demand and marginal revenue causes a change in the optimal level of output in both the short run and the long run. Suppose demand does change, due perhaps to a change in consumer income. In the short run, the manager will adjust output to the level where the new marginal revenue curve intersects the short-run marginal cost curve (or it will shut down if $P < AVC$). This short-run adjustment in output is accomplished without the benefit of being able to adjust the size of the plant to its optimal size. Recall from Chapter 9 that the plant size that minimizes the cost of production varies with the level of output. Hence, in the long run, the manager would adjust plant size to the level that minimizes the cost of producing the optimal level of output. If there is no plant size for which long-run average cost is less than price, the monopolist would not operate in the long run and would exit the industry.

▣ **Principle** The manager of a monopoly firm maximizes profit in the long run by choosing to produce the level of output where marginal revenue equals long-run marginal cost ($MR = LMC$), unless price is less than long-run average cost ($P < LAC$), in which case the firm exits the industry. In the long run, the manager will adjust plant size to the optimal level; that is, the optimal plant is the one with the short-run average cost curve tangent to the long-run average cost at the profit-maximizing output level.

This principle is illustrated in Figure 12.5. The level of output that maximizes profit in the long run is 350 units, the point at which $MR = LMC$. In the long run, the manager adjusts plant size so that 350 units are produced at the lowest possible total cost. In Figure 12.5, the optimal plant size is the one with short-run average total cost and marginal cost curves labeled ATC_1 and SMC_1, respectively. Thus the average cost of producing 350 units is $50 per unit. The manager will sell the 350 units at a price of $55 to maximize profit. Long-run profit is $1,750 [$= Q \times (P - LAC) = 350 \times (\$55 - \$50)$], or the area $ABCD$. By the now familiar argument, this is the maximum profit possible under the given revenue and cost conditions.

FIGURE 12.5
Long-Run Profit
Maximization under
Monopoly

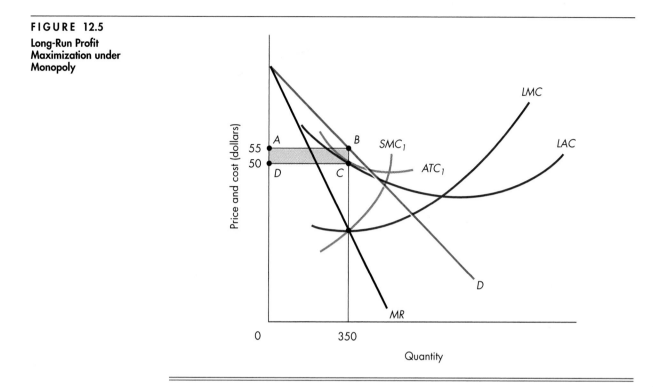

12.4 PROFIT-MAXIMIZING INPUT USAGE

Thus far we have analyzed monopoly profit maximization in terms of the output decision. As was the case for competition, the manager can also maximize profit by choosing the optimal level of input usage. Choosing the optimal level of input usage results in exactly the same output, price, and profit level as choosing the optimal level of output would. We now discuss the monopoly firm's input decision assuming that there is only one variable input.

The analytical principles underlying the input decision for the manager of a monopoly are the same as those for managers of perfectly competitive firms. But since price does not equal marginal revenue for a monopoly, $P \times MP$ is not the correct measure of the **marginal revenue product (MRP)**—the increase in revenue attributable to hiring an additional unit of the variable input. Suppose a monopolist employs an additional unit of labor, which causes output to increase by the amount of the marginal product of labor. To sell this larger output, the manager must reduce the price of the good. Each additional unit adds marginal revenue (*MR*) to total revenue. Thus the additional unit of labor adds to total revenue an amount equal to marginal revenue times the marginal product of labor:

$$MRP = \triangle TR/\triangle L = MR \times MP$$

marginal revenue
product (MRP)
The additional revenue
attributable to hiring one
additional unit of the input,
which is also equal to the
product of marginal revenue
times marginal product,
$MRP = MR \times MP$.

For example, suppose hiring the 10th unit of labor increases output by 20 units ($MP = 20$). To sell these 20 additional units of output, the monopolist must lower price. Further suppose that marginal revenue is $5 per additional unit. Thus the additional revenue attributable to hiring the 10th unit of labor is the $5 additional revenue received on each of the 20 additional units of output produced and sold, or $100 ($= \$5 \times 20$). The marginal revenue product of the 10th unit of labor is $100.

Recall that in the case of perfect competition, marginal revenue product is measured by multiplying price ($= MR$) by the marginal product of labor. Also recall that MRP for a perfect competitor declines because marginal product declines. For a monopolist, marginal revenue product declines with increases in input usage not only because marginal product declines but also because marginal revenue declines as output is increased.

Figure 12.6 shows the positive portion of MRP below ARP, which is the relevant portion of the MRP curve for a monopolist employing labor as its only variable input. Just as for a perfectly competitive firm, a monopolist shuts down and hires no labor when the wage rate exceeds average revenue product ($w > ARP$) at the level of input usage where $MRP = w$. Suppose the wage rate is $45. To maximize profit, the manager should hire 400 units of labor at a wage rate of $45. To see why this is the optimal level of labor usage, suppose the manager hires only 300 units of labor. Hiring the 301st unit of labor adds slightly less than $58 to total revenue while adding only $45 to total cost. Clearly, hiring the 301st unit increases profit, in this case, $13 ($= \$58 - \$45$). The manager should continue to hire additional units of labor until $MRP = w_1 = \$45$ at point A in Figure 12.6. If the manager mistakenly hired more than 400 units, say, 500 units of labor, the additional revenue from hiring the last unit of labor ($30 for the 500th unit) is less than the additional cost, $45, and profit falls if the 500th worker is hired. Getting rid of the 500th worker lowers cost by $45 but revenue falls by only $30; thus, reducing labor by 1 unit increases profit by $15. And each additional 1 unit reduction in labor similarly increases profit until labor usage is reduced down to the 400th worker.

If the wage rate falls to $30 per unit (shown by the horizontal line w_2), the manager should hire 500 units of labor (point B) to maximize monopoly profit. Similarly, at a wage of $58, the manager would hire 300 workers (point C). Thus you can see that, over the relevant range, the MRP curve is the monopolist's demand curve for a single variable input.

We now show that a monopolist would never choose a level of variable input usage at which the average revenue product is less than the marginal revenue product ($ARP < MRP$). If, at the level of input usage where $MRP = w$,

$$MRP > ARP$$

then

$$w > PQ/L$$

and

$$wL > PQ$$

FIGURE 12.6
A Monopoly Firm's Demand for Labor

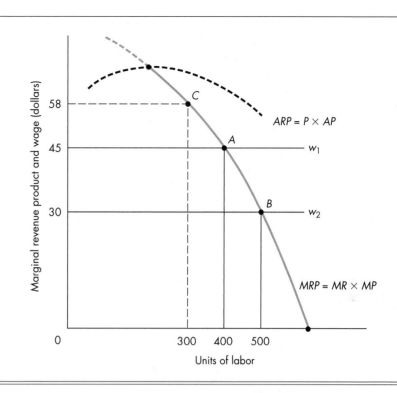

which implies that total variable cost exceeds total revenue, and the profit-maximizing monopolist would hire 0 units of the variable input and shut down.[4]

▣ **Principle** When producing with a single variable input, a monopolist will maximize profit by employing that amount of the input for which marginal revenue product (*MRP*) equals the price of the input when input price is given. Consequently, the *MRP* curve, over the relevant range, is the monopolist's demand curve for the variable input when only one variable input is employed. The relevant range of the *MRP* curve is the downward-sloping, positive portion of *MRP* for which *ARP* > *MRP*.

As for the case of a competitive firm, the manager of a firm with market power that employs two or more variable inputs maximizes profits by choosing input levels so that the marginal revenue product equals the input price for all inputs simultaneously.

Recall that, for a price-taking firm, the profit-maximizing condition that the marginal revenue product of labor equals the wage rate ($MRP = w$) is equivalent to the profit-maximizing condition that product price equals marginal cost ($P = SMC$). By "equivalent" we mean that regardless of whether the manager chooses

---

[4]This result is demonstrated mathematically in the appendix at the end of this chapter.

Q or L to maximize profit, the resulting levels of output, labor usage, and profit are identical. We will now demonstrate that, for a monopolist, the profit-maximizing condition $MRP = w$ is equivalent to the profit-maximizing condition $MR = SMC$.

Suppose the manager of a monopoly firm chooses the level of output to maximize profit. The optimal output for the monopolist is where

$$MR = MC$$

Recall from Chapter 8 that

$$SMC = \frac{w}{MP}$$

where MP is the marginal product of labor and w is its price. Substituting this equation for marginal cost, the profit-maximizing condition $MR = SMC$ can be expressed as

$$MR = \frac{w}{MP}$$

or

$$MR \times MP = w$$
$$MRP = w$$

Thus you can see that the two profit-maximizing rules are equivalent: $MR = MC$ implies $MRP = w$, and vice versa.[5]

☐ **Relation** For a monopolist, the profit-maximizing condition that the marginal revenue product of the variable input must equal the price of the input ($MRP = w$) is equivalent to the profit-maximizing condition that marginal revenue must equal marginal cost ($MR = MC$). Thus, regardless of whether the manager chooses Q or L to maximize profit, the resulting levels of input usage, output, price, and profit are the same in either case.

12.5 MONOPOLISTIC COMPETITION

As we pointed out at the beginning of this chapter, the general model of monopoly is useful in the analysis of firm behavior in other types of markets in which firms have some degree of market power but are not pure monopolies. Firms in such markets, facing downward-sloping demands, attempt to maximize profit in the same way a monopoly does: by setting $MR = MC$. In these intermediate markets, between firms with the most market power (monopoly) and firms with the least (perfect competition), certain complications arise for the profit-maximizing decision. In this section, we analyze intermediate market structure in which firms have the least market power of all firms that are not perfect competitors: monopolistic competition.

Monopolistically competitive markets are characterized by (1) a large number of relatively small firms; (2) products that are similar to, but somewhat different

---

[5]This result is demonstrated mathematically in the appendix at the end of this chapter.

from, one another; and (3) unrestricted entry and exit of firms into and out of the market. The only difference between monopolistic competition and perfect competition is that under monopolistic competition firms produce a differentiated product. The major difference between monopolistic competition and monopoly is that under monopolistic competition firms can easily enter into and exit out of the market. Thus, as the name implies, monopolistic competition has characteristics of both monopoly and perfect competition.

Product differentiation under monopolistic competition prevents a firm's demand from becoming horizontal. Real or perceived differences between goods, though slight, will make them less than perfect substitutes. For example, gasoline stations in a particular city are good, but not perfect, substitutes for one another. Your car would run on gasoline from any gasoline station, but stations differ in location, and people's tastes differ: Some people prefer BP, some prefer ExxonMobil, some prefer the service at Joe's, others prefer Julie's service. And the differentiating characteristics go on and on. The most important point is that although the products are similar, they are differentiated, causing each firm to have a small amount of market power.

We will first set forth the theory of monopolistic competition in its original form, as developed by Edward Chamberlin in the 1930s.[6] Because each firm in the market sells a slightly differentiated product, it faces a downward-sloping demand curve, which is relatively elastic but not horizontal. Any firm could raise its price slightly without losing all its sales, or it could lower its price slightly without gaining the entire market. Under the original set of assumptions employed by Chamberlin, each firm's output is so small relative to the total sales in the market that the firm believes that its price and output decisions will go unnoticed by other firms in the market. It therefore acts independently.

As you will see, the theory of monopolistic competition is essentially a long-run theory; in the short run, there is virtually no difference between monopolistic competition and monopoly. In the long run, because of unrestricted entry into the market, the theory of monopolistic competition closely resembles the theory of perfect competition.

Short-Run Equilibrium

With the given demand, marginal revenue, and cost curves, a monopolistic competitor maximizes profit or minimizes loss by equating marginal revenue and marginal cost. Figure 12.7 illustrates the short-run, profit-maximizing equilibrium for a firm in a monopolistically competitive market. Profit is maximized by producing an output of Q and selling at price P.

In the situation illustrated, the firm will earn an economic profit, shown as the shaded area $PABC$. However, as was the case for perfect competition and monopoly, in the short run the firm could operate with a loss, if the demand curves lies

_____

[6]E. H. Chamberlin, *The Theory of Monopolistic Competition* (Cambridge, MA: Harvard University Press, 1933).

FIGURE 12.7
**Short-Run Profit
Maximization under
Monopolistic Competition**

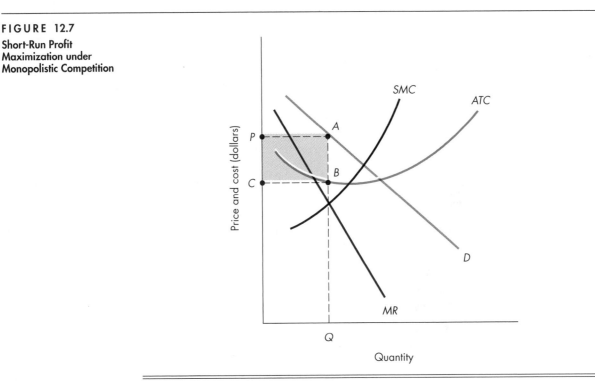

below *ATC* but above *AVC*. If the demand curve falls below *AVC*, the firm would shut down.

In its original form, there appears to be little competition in monopolistic competition as far as the short run is concerned. Indeed Figure 12.7 is identical to one illustrating short-run equilibrium for a monopoly. In the long run, however, a monopoly cannot be maintained if there is unrestricted entry into the market. If firms are earning economic profit in the short run, other firms will enter and produce the product, and they will continue to enter until all economic profits are eliminated.

Long-Run Equilibrium

While the short-run equilibrium for a firm under monopolistic competition is similar to that under monopoly, the long-run equilibrium is more closely related to the equilibrium position under competition. Because of unrestricted entry, all economic profit must be eliminated in the long run, which occurs at an output at which price equals long-run average cost. This occurs when the firm's demand is tangent to long-run average cost. The only difference between this equilibrium and that for perfect competition is that, for a firm in a monopolistically competitive market, the tangency cannot occur at minimum average cost. Since the demand curve facing the firm is downward-sloping under monopolistic competition,

FIGURE 12.8
Long-Run Equilibrium under
Monopolistic Competition

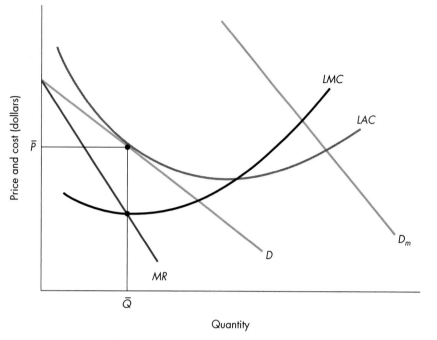

FIGURE 12.8

Long-Run Equilibrium under Monopolistic Competition

the point of tangency must be on the downward-sloping range of long-run average cost. Thus the long-run equilibrium output under monopolistic competition is less than that forthcoming under perfect competition in the long run.

This long-run result is shown in Figure 12.8. LAC and LMC are the long-run average and marginal cost curves for a typical monopolistically competitive firm. Suppose that the original demand curve is given by D_m. In this case the firm would be making substantial economic profits because demand lies above LAC over a wide range of output, and if this firm is making profits, potential new entrants would expect that other firms in the market are also earning economic profits. These profits would then attract new firms into the market. While the new firms would not sell exactly the same products as existing firms, their products would be very similar. So as new firms enter, the number of substitutes would increase and the demand facing the typical firm would shift backward and probably become more elastic (though not perfectly elastic). Entry will continue as long as there is some economic profit being earned. Thus entry causes each firm's demand curve to shift backward until a demand curve such as D in Figure 12.8 is reached. This long-run demand curve, D, is tangent to LAC at a price of $\overline{P}$ and output of $\overline{Q}$.

In such an equilibrium either an increase or a decrease in price by the firm would lead to losses. No further entry would occur since there are no economic profits to be earned in this market.

If too many firms enter the market, each firm's demand curve would be pushed so far back that demand falls below *LAC*. Firms would be suffering losses and exit would take place. As this happened, the demand curve would be pushed back up to tangency with *LAC*. Free entry and exit under monopolistic competition must lead to a situation where demand is tangent to *LAC*—where price equals average cost—and no economic profit is earned, but the firms do earn a normal profit.

The equilibrium in Figure 12.8 must also be characterized by the intersection of *LMC* and *MR*. Only at output $\overline{Q}$ can the firm avoid a loss, so this output must be optimal. But the optimal output requires that marginal cost equal marginal revenue. Thus at $\overline{Q}$, it must be the case that $MR = LMC$.

Relation Long-run equilibrium in a monopolistically competitive market is attained when the demand curve for each producer is tangent to the long-run average cost curve. Unrestricted entry and exit lead to this equilibrium. At the equilibrium output, price equals long-run average cost and marginal revenue equals long-run marginal cost.

In closing our discussion of monopolistic competition, we briefly mention two points. First, according to the original model as set forth here, firms act independently when making decisions, ignoring the actions of other firms in the market. In reality firms may not act independently when faced with competition from closely related firms, possibly because of proximity; in fact, they may exhibit a great deal of interdependence and intense personal rivalry. We will address this possibility at more length in the next chapter. This change in assumptions will not alter the long-run, zero-profit conclusions of the theory, however.

Short of getting the government to prevent entry, there is nothing firms in a monopolistically competitive market can do about having their profits competed away. Even if the firms were to conspire to fix a price, new firms would enter. Each firm would find its demand decreased and its sales reduced until price equaled average cost and economic profits were zero, although possibly at a higher price than would occur in the absence of the price-fixing agreement.

Second, we have emphasized that, under monopolistic competition, profits are competed away in the long run. This is correct in general. But we do not mean to imply that there is no opportunity for astute managers to postpone this situation to the future by innovative decision making. Firms selling in monopolistically competitive markets can and do advertise and change product quality in an effort to lengthen the time period over which they earn economic profit. Those managers who are successful in their marketing strategy can sometimes earn profit for a long time. Some firms can reduce their cost. However, successful strategies can be imitated by competitors' selling a product that is rather similar. Therefore, under monopolistic competition there is always a strong tendency for economic profit to be eliminated in the long run, no matter what strategies managers undertake.

12.6 IMPLEMENTING THE PROFIT–MAXIMIZING OUTPUT AND PRICING DECISION

Managers of firms that have some control over the price they charge should know the fundamentals of the theory of profit maximization by firms with market

ILLUSTRATION 12.3

Can Monopolistic Competitors Protect Their Profits?
Only Time Will Tell

In May 1996, a *Wall Street Journal* article on apparel pricing began this way: "Remember all the nifty bargains you found shopping for clothes last year? So do retailers. And they vow never again. For two years, stores have countered slowing demand for apparel—from sweats to cocktail dresses—with constant discounting, trying to spur demand by giving up profits. Now, after one of their least profitable years, big apparel merchants are ruling out another avalanche of sales and markdowns . . . They are deploying an array of merchandising gimmicks to wean shoppers off their addiction to deep discounts."[a]

Laura Bird, the author of the article, was not optimistic for the merchants: "There's just one catch: Shoppers' addiction to the steal lingers on." A customer of Marshall Field's said, "I know everyone has to make their money, but I just feel taken somehow when I pay full price." Another shopper agreed, "There are certain stores where I would feel horribly guilty buying anything at full price because everything eventually goes on sale." Said another shopper, "I'm more embarrassed when I pay full price."

To counter such feelings, the large fashion merchants were "conducting what amounts to a mass effort at behavior modification." One huge merchandiser was cutting the number of sales events by half at its department stores. Many retailers were trying to encourage full-price purchases by displaying fewer clothes. They believed that if there were only a few of something on the rack, people would be more likely to pay full price. One retailer was planning to abandon high-low pricing and switch to everyday low prices, also called "value pricing," despite the fact that other large chains, such as Sears, had previously tried such a strategy with little success. According to the *WSJ*, "Retailers are dressing up modest discounts in other ways." For example, sales racks displayed signs with the sale price rather than "40% Off." Some were selling one item at full price with 50 percent off the second item. The result would be a fairly low 25 percent off for the two.

Nevertheless, as Bird stated, there was a lot of resistance on the part of consumers. But profits had been terrible for two years. And changing consumers' perception of what is and what isn't a bargain is a long-term process. Fashion retailers do have to reduce prices to clear out old merchandise and make room for the new. Otherwise, their inventories would be so small that they would lose sales by not having the goods on hand.

Did the new policy work? Possibly not as well as the retailers would have liked, but also a little better than customers would have preferred. As the 1996 Christmas shopping season got well under way with the huge post-Thanksgiving shopping weekend, *USA Today* ran a story entitled "Retailers Slow to Slash Prices in Robust Season."[b] The article began, "In spite of a wealth of sale items in stores, the holiday season is starting without the heavy discounts of a year ago. While merchants responded to last year's sluggish sales with deep markdowns, increased consumer spending and tighter retail inventories are expected to keep heavy price slashing in check." Retail sales were good, but many shoppers were still waiting for the big discounts.

One research analyst gave a reason for the general absence of large price decreases: "People are feeling that they don't have to buy at the lowest possible prices because there are a few more bucks in their pockets." It would appear that the rise in consumer income increased sales and slowed the return to extensive discounting.

There were some exceptions. The article mentioned big sales at some stores: Circuit City, Mervyn's, and Sears. However, two of the large chains noted as wanting to reduce the number of sales events had scheduled 13 fewer promotion days for December than they had the year before and still expected a strong fourth quarter. One reason given was leaner inventories. As a whole most merchants were optimistic. By the 1997 Christmas shopping season most stores had returned to heavy discounting.

So sometimes good planning can help monopolistic competitors. But so does a little luck and a lot of economic prosperity.

[a]Laura Bird, "Apparel Stores Seek to Cure Shoppers Addicted to Discounts," *The Wall Street Journal*, May 29, 1996.
[b]"Retailers Slow to Slash Prices in Robust Season," *USA Today*, Dec. 4, 1996.

power. They should also know how to use empirical estimates of the demand for the firm's product and the cost equations for determining the price and level of output that maximize the firm's profit. This section describes how to use empirical analysis to find that optimal price and output. We devote most of this section to examining the price and output decision for a monopoly. However, as we stressed previously, the decision-making process for a monopoly is applicable to any firm with market power, with perhaps a few modifications for changes in the form of the demand and marginal revenue functions to account for differences in the market structure.

We will first outline how managers can, in general, determine the optimizing conditions. This outline gives a pattern for situations in which numerical estimates of the variables and equations are available. Then we present an example of how a firm can use this approach to determine the optimal level of output.

General Rules for Implementation

A manager must answer two questions when finding the price and output that maximizes profit. These two questions and the answers forthcoming from the theoretical analysis are summarized as follows:

1. Should the firm produce or shut down? *Produce as long as the market price equals or exceeds minimum average variable cost: $P \geq AVC_{min}$. Shut down otherwise.*
2. If production occurs, how much should the firm produce and what price should it charge? *Produce the output at which marginal revenue equals marginal cost—MR = SMC—and charge the price from the demand curve for the profit-maximizing output.*

It follows from these rules that to determine the optimal price and output, a manager will need estimates or forecasts of the market demand of the good produced by the firm, the inverse demand function, the associated marginal revenue function, the firm's average variable cost function, and the firm's marginal cost function. We now set forth the steps that can be followed to find the profit-maximizing price and output for a firm with market power.

Step 1: Estimate the demand equation
To determine the optimal level of output, the manager must estimate the marginal revenue function. Marginal revenue is derived from the demand equation; thus the manager begins by estimating demand. In the case of a linear demand specification, the empirical demand function facing the monopolist can be written as

$$Q = a + bP + cM + dP_R$$

where Q is output, P is price, M is income, and P_R is the price of a good related in consumption. As discussed in Chapter 7, to obtain the estimated demand curve for the relevant time period, the manager must have forecasts for the values of the exogenous variables, M and P_R, for that time period. Once the empirical demand equation has been estimated, the forecasts of M and P_R (denoted $_a\hat{M}$ and $_a\hat{P}_R$) are substituted into the estimated demand equation, and the demand function is expressed as

$$Q = a' + bP$$

where $a' = a + c\hat{M} + d\hat{P}_R$.

Step 2: Find the inverse demand equation

Before we can derive the marginal revenue function from the demand function, the demand function must be expressed so that price is a function of quantity: $P = f(Q)$. This is accomplished by solving for P in the estimated demand equation in step 1:

$$P = \frac{-a'}{b} + \frac{1}{b}Q$$

$$= A + BQ$$

inverse demand function
The demand function with demand price expressed as a function of output, $P = f(Q)$.

where $A = \dfrac{-a'}{b}$ and $B = \dfrac{1}{b}$. This form of the demand equation is called the **inverse demand function.** Now the demand equation is expressed in a form that makes it possible to solve for marginal revenue in a straightforward manner.

Step 3: Solve for marginal revenue

Now recall from Chapter 6 that when demand is expressed as $P = A + BQ$, marginal revenue is $MR = A + 2BQ$. Using the inverse demand function, we can write the marginal revenue function as

$$MR = A + 2BQ$$

$$= \frac{-a'}{b} + \frac{2}{b}Q$$

Step 4: Estimate average variable cost (AVC) and marginal cost (SMC)

In Chapter 10 we discussed in detail the empirical techniques for estimating cubic cost functions. There is nothing new or different about estimating SMC and AVC for a monopoly firm. The usual forms for the AVC and SMC functions, when TVC is specified as a cubic equation, are

$$AVC = a + bQ + cQ^2$$

$$SMC = a + 2bQ + 3cQ^2$$

You may wish to review this step by returning to Chapter 10 or to Chapter 11.

Step 5: Find the output level where MR = SMC

To find the level of output that maximizes profit or minimizes losses, the manager sets marginal revenue equal to marginal cost and solves for Q:

$$MR = A + 2BQ = a + 2bQ + 3cQ^2 = SMC$$

Solving this equation for Q^* gives the optimal level of output for the firm—unless P is less than AVC, and then the optimal level of output is zero.

Step 6: Find the optimal price

Once the optimal quantity, Q^*, has been found in step 5, the profit-maximizing price is found by substituting Q^* into the inverse demand equation to obtain the optimal price, P^*:

$$P^* = A + BQ^*$$

This price and output will be optimal only if price exceeds average variable cost.

Step 7: Check the shutdown rule

For any firm, with or without market power, if price is less than average variable cost, the firm will shut down ($Q^* = 0$) because it makes a smaller loss producing nothing than it would lose if it produced any positive amount of output. The manager calculates the average variable cost at Q^* units:

$$AVC^* = a + bQ^* + cQ^{*2}$$

If $P^* \geq AVC^*$, then the monopolist produces Q^* units of output and sells each unit of output for P^* dollars. If $P^* < AVC^*$, then the monopolist shuts down in the short run.

Step 8: Computation of profit or loss

To compute the profit or loss, the manager makes the same calculation regardless of whether the firm is a monopolist, oligopolist, or perfect competitor. Total profit or loss is

$$\pi^* = TR - TC$$
$$= (P^* \times Q^*) - [(AVC^* \times Q^*) + TFC]$$

If $P < AVC$, the firm shuts down, and $\pi = -TFC$.

To illustrate how to implement these steps to find the profit-maximizing price and output level and to forecast profit, we now turn to a hypothetical firm that possesses a degree of market power.

Maximizing Profit at Aztec Electronics: An Example

By virtue of several patents, Aztec Electronics possesses substantial market power in the market for advanced wireless stereo headphones. In December 2004, the manager of Aztec wished to determine the profit-maximizing price and output for its wireless stereo headphones for 2005.

Estimation of demand and marginal revenue

The demand for wireless headphones was specified as a linear function of the price of wireless headphones, the income of the buyers, and the price of stereo tuners (a complementary good):

$$Q = f(P, M, P_R)$$

Using data available for the period 1994–2004, a linear form of the demand function was estimated. The resulting estimated demand function was

$$Q = 41,000 - 500P + 0.6M - 22.5P_R$$

where output (Q) is measured in units of sales and average annual family income (M) and the two prices (P and P_R) are measured in dollars. Each estimated parameter has the expected sign and is statistically significant at the 5 percent level. The R^2 and F-statistics were both quite high, indicating the linear model specification does an excellent job of explaining the variation in quantity demanded.[7]

From an economic consulting firm, the manager obtained 2002 forecasts for income and the price of the complementary good (stereo tuners) as, respectively, \$45,000 and \$800. Using these values—$M = 45,000$ and $P_R = 800$—the estimated (forecasted) demand function in 2001 was

$$Q = 41,000 - 500P + 0.6(45,000) - 22.5(800) = 50,000 - 500P$$

The inverse demand function for the estimated (empirical) demand function was obtained by solving for P:

$$P = 100 - 0.002Q$$

From the inverse demand function, the manager of Aztec Electronics obtained the estimated marginal revenue function:

$$MR = 100 - 0.004Q$$

We should note that if the parameters of the demand equation are statistically significant, so are the parameters of the marginal revenue equation.

Figure 12.9 illustrates the estimated linear demand and marginal revenue curves for Aztec Electronics.

Estimation of average variable cost and marginal cost

The manager of Aztec Electronics obtained an estimate of the firm's average variable cost function using a short-run quadratic specification (as described in Chapter 10). The estimated average variable cost function was

$$AVC = 28 - 0.005Q + 0.000001Q^2$$

For this estimation, AVC was measured in dollar units and Q was measured in units of sales. Given the estimated average variable cost function, the marginal cost function is

$$SMC = 28 - 0.01Q + 0.000003Q^2$$

As you can see, the specification and estimation of cost functions are the same regardless of whether a firm is a price-taker or a price-setter.

The output decision

Once the manager of Aztec obtained estimates of the marginal revenue function and the marginal cost function, the determination of the optimal level of output was accomplished by equating the estimated marginal revenue equation with the

---

[7]Recall from Chapter 7 that when a firm is a price-setting firm (i.e., possesses some degree of market power), the problem of simultaneity vanishes. Thus the demand for a monopolist can be estimated using the standard method of least-squares estimation—two-stage least-squares is not necessary.

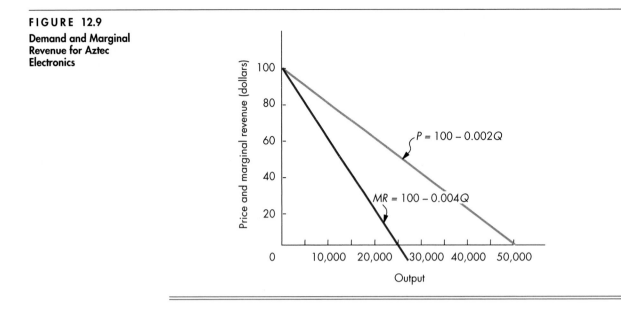

estimated marginal cost equation and solving for Q^*. Setting MR equal to SMC results in the following expression:

$$100 - 0.004Q = 28 - 0.01Q + 0.000003Q^2$$

Solving this equation for Q, the manager of Aztec finds two solutions: $Q = 6{,}000$ and $Q = -4{,}000$. Since $Q = -4{,}000$ is an irrelevant solution—negative outputs are impossible—the optimal level of output is $Q^* = 6{,}000$. That is, the profit-maximizing (or loss-minimizing) number of wireless stereo headphones to produce and sell in 2005 is 6,000 units—if the firm chooses to produce rather than shut down.

The pricing decision

Once the manager of Aztec Electronics has found the optimal level of output, determining the profit-maximizing price is really nothing more than finding the price on the firm's demand curve that corresponds to the profit-maximizing level of output. The optimal output level Q^* is substituted into the inverse demand equation to obtain the optimal price. Substituting $Q^* = 6{,}000$ into the inverse demand function, the optimal price P^* is

$$P^* = 100 - 0.002(6{,}000) = \$88$$

Thus Aztec will charge $88 for a set of headphones in 2005.

The shutdown decision

To see if Aztec Electronics should shut down production in 2005, the manager compared the optimal price of $88 with the average variable cost of producing 6,000 units. Average variable cost for 6,000 units was computed as

$$AVC^* = 28 - 0.005(6{,}000) + 0.000001(6{,}000)^2 = \$34$$

Obviously, $88 is greater than $34; so if these forecasts prove to be correct in 2005, all the variable costs will be covered and the manager should operate the plant rather than shut it down. Note that Aztec's expected total revenue in 2002 is $528,000 (= $88 × 6,000) and estimated total variable cost was $204,000 (= $34 × 6,000). Since total revenue exceeds total variable cost ($TR > TVC$), the manager would produce rather than shut down.

Computation of total profit or loss

Computation of profit is a straightforward process once the manager has estimated total revenue and all costs. The manager of Aztec has already estimated price and average variable cost for 2005, but total fixed cost is needed to calculate total profit or loss. On the basis of 2004 data, the manager of Aztec Electronics estimated that fixed costs would be $270,000 in 2005. The profit for 2005 was calculated to be

$$\pi = TR - TVC - TFC$$
$$= \$528,000 - \$204,000 - \$270,000$$
$$= \$54,000$$

Figure 12.10 shows the estimated equations for 2005 and the profit-maximizing price and output. At point A, $MR = SMC$, and the profit-maximizing level of output is 6,000 units ($Q^* = 6,000$). At point B, the profit-maximizing price is $88, the price at which 6,000 units can be sold. At point C, ATC is $79, which was calculated as

$$ATC = TC/Q = (\$204,000 + \$270,000)/6,000$$
$$= \$79$$

The total profit earned by Aztec is represented by the area of the shaded rectangle.

The firm makes a loss

Now suppose that per capita income falls, causing the demand facing Aztec to fall to

$$P = 80 - 0.002Q$$

so marginal revenue is now

$$MR = 80 - 0.004Q$$

Average variable and marginal costs remain constant.

To determine the new level of output under the new estimated demand conditions, the manager equates the new estimated marginal revenue equation with the marginal cost equation and solves for Q^*:

$$80 - 0.004Q = 28 - 0.01Q + 0.000003Q^2$$

Again there are two solutions: $Q = -3,167$ and $Q = 5,283$. Ignoring the negative level of output, the optimal level is $Q^* = 5,283$. Substituting this value into the inverse demand function, the optimal price is

$$P^* = 80 - 0.002(5,283) = \$69.43$$

FIGURE 12.10

Profit Maximization at Aztec Electronics

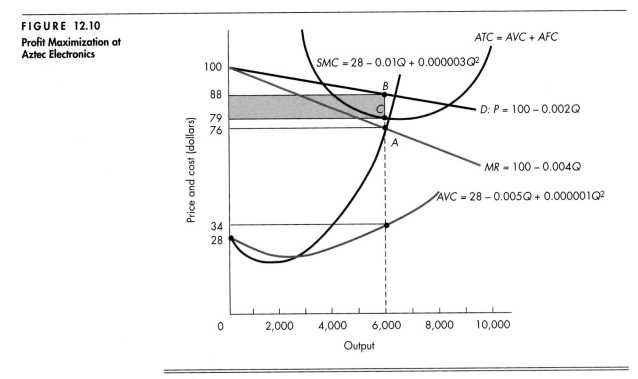

To determine whether to produce or shut down under the reduced-demand situation, the manager calculated the average variable cost at the new level of output and compared it with price:

$$AVC = 28 - 0.005(5{,}283) + 0.000001(5{,}283)^2 = \$29.49$$

Clearly if Aztec produces in 2005, total revenue will cover all of total variable cost since

$$P = \$69.43 > \$29.49 = AVC$$

Aztec's profit or loss is

$$\pi = TR - TVC - TFC$$
$$= \$69.43(5{,}283) - \$29.49(5{,}283) - \$270{,}000$$
$$= \$366{,}799 - \$155{,}796 - \$270{,}000$$
$$= -\$58{,}997$$

 Despite the predicted loss of $58,997 in 2005, Aztec should continue producing. Losing $58,997 is obviously better than shutting down and losing the entire fixed cost of $270,000.

12.7 SUMMARY

A monopoly exists if a single firm produces and sells a good or service for which there are no close substitutes and new firms are prevented from entering the market in the long run. While these conditions are seldom met in the real world, many firms do have the power to make price and output decisions in essentially the same way that a monopolist chooses price and output to maximize profit. For this reason, managers can use the theory of monopoly as a guide to making pricing decisions when their firms face downward-sloping demand curves: that is, when their firms possess market power.

Market power is the ability of a firm to raise price without losing all its sales. Any firm that faces a downward-sloping demand curve has market power. Market power gives a firm the ability to raise price above average cost and earn economic profit, demand and cost conditions permitting. In the long run, a firm with market power may be able to earn economic profit because entry of new firms is difficult. In order to be a true monopolist, there must be some barriers to entry to prevent rival firms from entering and competing away the monopolist's profit. Barriers to entry, therefore, must exist in order for a firm to be a monopoly in the long run. Barriers to entry include economies of scale, barriers created by government, input barriers, barriers resulting from brand loyalties, consumer lock-in, and network externalities.

Market power is possessed not absolutely but, rather, to varying degrees. The degree to which a firm possesses market power is inversely related to the availability of close substitutes for the firm's product and thus can be measured (approximately) by the price and cross-price elasticities of demand.

The less elastic the demand for the monopolist's product, the less available are good substitutes and the greater its degree of market power. The higher the (positive) cross-price elasticity, the greater the perceived substitutability and the smaller the degree of market power enjoyed by the monopolist. The Lerner index, $(P - MC)/P$, measures the proportionate amount by which monopoly price exceeds marginal cost (i.e., the competitive price

level). The higher the Lerner index, the greater the degree of market power.

As in the case of competition, the profit-maximizing decision for a monopoly can take either of two equivalent forms. The manager can choose either output or input usage to maximize profit using the rule $MR = MC$ or $MRP = w$, respectively. The two rules lead to identical prices, outputs, input usage, and profits.

In the short run, the manager of a firm with market power maximizes profit by producing and selling that level of output for which $MR = SMC$, as long as $P \geq AVC$ for this output level. If $P < AVC$ for all output levels, the manager should shut down in the short run. Alternatively, the manager of a monopoly that produces using a single variable input can maximize profit by hiring the amount of labor for which $MRP = w$, as long as average revenue product exceeds marginal revenue product. If ARP is less than MRP, the manager should shut down.

In the long run, the manager should produce the output level for which $MR = LMC$ and adjust plant size so that the optimal plant is used to produce the profit-maximizing output. The optimal plant is the one associated with the short-run average cost curve that is tangent to long-run average cost at the profit-maximizing output. If $P < LAC$ for all levels of output, the monopolist exits the industry.

In this chapter, we also briefly developed the theory of monopolistic competition. Of all firms with market power, a monopolistically competitive firm has the least. The barriers to entry are so low that it is easy for new firms to enter the market when economic profits are made by existing firms. As we showed, the key feature of monopolistic competition is that, in the long run, the firm's economic profit is competed away even though each firm has some market power. The firm's demand curve is downward-sloping because each firm sells a product that is somewhat differentiated from that of every other firm in the market. In the short run, a monopolistic competitor simply acts like a monopoly. In the long run, the entry of new firms causes each firm's demand to become tangent to long-run average cost.

TECHNICAL PROBLEMS

1. Compare the market power of the following pairs of firms. Explain.
   a. Chase Manhattan Bank and the First National Bank of Pecos, Texas.
   b. The "Big Three" U.S. auto manufacturers prior to the early 1970s and the same firms after the early 1970s.
   c. A regional phone company and a regional electric company in the same area.

2. Explain why input barriers to entry have probably declined in importance with the recent expansion of international markets.

3. For each of the following products, could consumer lock-in or network externalities (or both) create a barrier to entry? Explain why or why not.
   a. Toothpaste.
   b. Long-play (LP) record albums.

4. Assume a monopoly has the following demand schedule:

Price	Quantity
$20	200
15	300
10	500
5	700

   a. Calculate total revenue at each P and Q combination.
   b. Calculate marginal revenue per unit for each decrease in price.
   c. For the change in price from $20 to $15, is demand elastic or inelastic? How much revenue does the firm lose from reducing the price on the 200 units it could have sold for $20? How much revenue does the firm gain from selling 100 more units at $15? Compare the two changes; then compare these changes with MR.
   d. Answer part c for the price change from $15 to $10.

5. The following graph shows demand and MR for a monopoly:

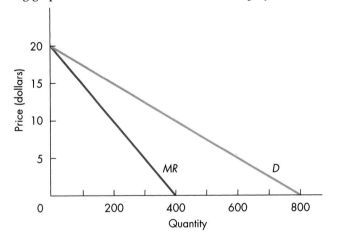

   a. If the firm wants to sell 200 units, what price does it charge?
   b. If the firm charges a price of $15, how much will it sell?

   c. What is *MR* for parts *a* and *b*? Is demand elastic or inelastic?

   d. If the firm charges $10, how much will it sell? What is demand elasticity?

6. A monopolist faces the following demand and cost schedules:

Price	Quantity	Total cost
$20	7	$36
19	8	45
18	9	54
17	10	63
16	11	72
15	12	81

   a. How much output should the monopolist produce?

   b. What price should the firm charge?

   c. What is the maximum amount of profit that this firm can earn?

7. The following graph shows demand, *MR*, and cost curves for a monopoly in the short run:

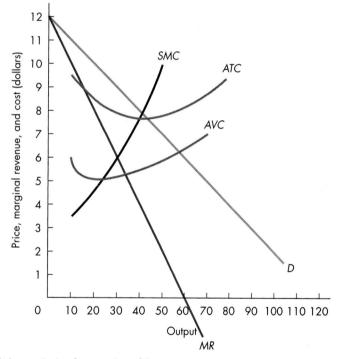

   a. Profit is maximized at a price of $_____.

   b. The profit-maximizing level of output is _____.

   c. At the optimal level of output, total revenue is $_____, total cost is $_____, and profit is $_____.

8. Explain why the manager of a profit-maximizing monopoly always produces and sells on the elastic portion of the demand curve. If costs are 0, what output will the manager produce? Explain.

9. The figure below shows demand, marginal revenue, and short-run cost curves for a monopoly:

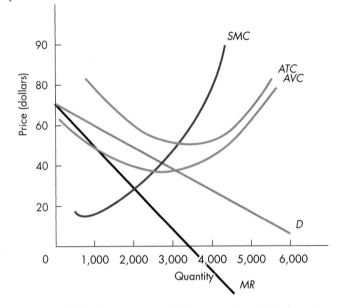

a. How much should the firm produce? What price should it charge?
b. What is the firm's profit (loss)?
c. What is total revenue? What is total variable cost?
d. If the firm shuts down in the short run, how much will it lose?

10. Consider a monopoly firm with the demand and cost curves below. Assume that the firm is operating in the short run with the plant designed to produce 400 units of output optimally.

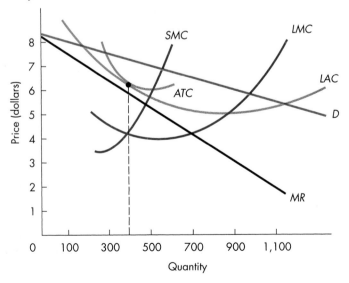

a. What output should be produced?

b. What will be the price?

c. How much profit is made?

d. If the firm can change plant size and move into the long run, what will be output and price?

e. Will profit increase? How do you know?

f. Draw in the new short-run average and marginal cost curves associated with the new plant size.

11. In the following table, columns 1 and 2 make up a portion of the production function of a monopolist using a single variable input, labor. Columns 2 and 3 make up the demand function facing the monopolist over this range of output.

(1) Labor	(2) Quantity	(3) Price
9	50	$21
10	100	20
11	140	19
12	170	18
13	190	17
14	205	16
15	215	15

a. Derive MP, MR, and MRP over this range.

b. If the wage rate is $60, how much labor would the manager hire? Why? What if the wage falls to $40?

12. The following figure shows the average revenue product and the marginal revenue product of labor for a monopoly:

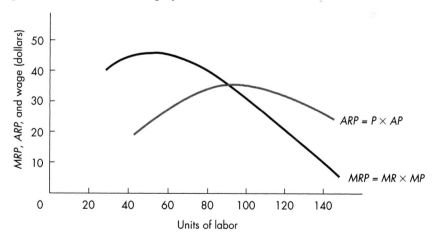

a. If the wage is $20, how much labor would the firm hire?

b. If the wage is $10, how much labor would the firm hire?

c. If the wage is $40, how much labor would the firm hire?

13. Describe the features of monopolistic competition:
    a. How is it similar to monopoly?
    b. How is it similar to perfect competition?
    c. What are the characteristics of short-run equilibrium?
    d. What are the characteristics of long-run equilibrium?
    e. How is long-run equilibrium attained?

14. The following graph shows the long-run average and marginal cost curves for a monopolistically competitive firm:

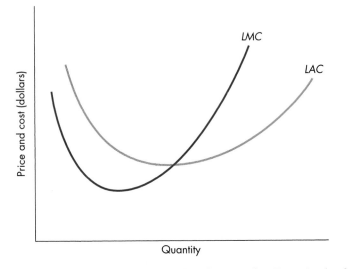

a. Assume the firm is in the short run and making profits. Draw in the demand and marginal revenue curves. Show output and price.
b. Now let the firm reach long-run equilibrium. Draw in precisely the new demand and marginal revenue curves. Show output and price.
c. Why must $MR = LMC$ at *exactly* the same output at which LAC is tangent to demand?
d. Contrast this firm's output and price in long-run equilibrium with the price and output if this firm was a perfect competitor.

15. The manager of a monopoly firm obtained the following estimate of the demand function for its output:

$$Q = 2,600 - 100P + 0.2M - 500P_R$$

From an econometric forecasting firm, the manager obtained forecasts for the 2005 values of M and P_R as, respectively, $20,000 and $2. For 2005 what is:
a. The forecasted demand function?
b. The inverse demand function?
c. The marginal revenue function?

16. For the firm in problem 15, the manager estimated the average variable cost function as

$$AVC = 20 - 0.07Q + 0.0001Q^2$$

where *AVC* was measured in dollars per unit and *Q* is the number of units sold.

a. What is the estimated marginal cost function?

b. What is the optimal level of production in 2005?

c. What is the optimal price in 2005?

d. Check to make sure that the firm should actually produce in the short run rather than shut down.

In addition, the manager expects fixed costs in 2005 to be $22,500.

e. What is the firm's expected profit or loss in 2005?

APPLIED PROBLEMS

1. QuadPlex Cinema is the only movie theater in Idaho Falls. The nearest rival movie theater, the Cedar Bluff Twin, is 35 miles away in Pocatello. Thus QuadPlex Cinema possesses a degree of market power. Despite having market power, QuadPlex Cinema is currently suffering losses. In a conversation with the owners of QuadPlex, the manager of the movie theater made the following suggestions: "Since QuadPlex is a local monopoly, we should just increase ticket prices until we make enough profit."

a. Comment on this strategy.

b. How might the market power of QuadPlex Cinema be measured?

c. What options should QuadPlex consider in the long run?

2. The *El Dorado Star* is the only newspaper in El Dorado, New Mexico. Certainly, the *Star* competes with *The Wall Street Journal*, *USA Today*, and *The New York Times* for national news reporting, but the *Star* offers readers stories of local interest, such as local news, weather, sporting events, and so on. The *El Dorado Star* faces the revenue and cost schedules shown in the table that follows:

Number of newspapers per day (Q)	Total revenue (including advertising revenues) per day (TR)	Total cost per day (TC)
0	$ 0	$2,000
1,000	1,500	2,100
2,000	2,500	2,200
3,000	3,000	2,360
4,000	3,250	2,520
5,000	3,450	2,700
6,000	3,625	2,890
7,000	3,725	3,090
8,000	3,625	3,310
9,000	3,475	3,550

a. How many papers should the manager of the *El Dorado Star* print and sell daily?

b. How much profit (or loss) will the *Star* earn?

c. Graph the marginal revenue and marginal cost curves. Do these curves support your answer to part *a*? (*Hint:* Be sure to plot the values of *MR* and *SMC* in the middle of the intervals over which they are computed.)

d. What is total fixed cost for the *El Dorado Star?* If total fixed cost increases to $5,000, how many papers should be printed and sold in the short run? What should the owners of the *Star* do in the long run?

3. Tots-R-Us operates the only day-care center in an exclusive neighborhood just outside of Washington, D.C. Tots-R-Us is making substantial economic profit, but the owners know that new day-care centers will soon learn of this highly profitable market and attempt to enter the market. The owners decide to begin spending immediately a rather large sum on advertising designed to decrease elasticity. Should they wait until new firms actually enter? Explain how advertising can be employed to allow Tots-R-Us to keep price above average cost without encouraging entry.

4. Antitrust authorities at the Federal Trade Commission are reviewing your company's recent merger with a rival firm. The FTC is concerned that the merger of two rival firms in the same market will increase market power. A hearing is scheduled for your company to present arguments that your firm has not increased its market power through this merger. Can you do this? How? What evidence might you bring to the hearing?

5. You own a small bank in a state that is now considering allowing interstate banking. You oppose interstate banking because it will be possible for the very large money center banks in New York, Chicago, and San Francisco to open branches in your bank's geographic market area. While proponents of interstate banking point to the benefits to consumers of increased competition, you worry that economies of scale might ultimately force your now profitable bank out of business. Explain how economies of scale (if significant economies of scale in fact do exist) could result in your bank being forced out of business in the long run.

6. The Harley-Davidson motorcycle company, which had a copyright on the word "hog," applied for exclusive rights to its engine sound. Why would a company want copyrights on two such mundane things?

7. An industry said to be characterized by monopolistic competition is the apparel industry. Suppose you were hired as a consultant by a firm in this industry. How would you advise the firm as to the levels of output, price, input usage, and advertising? What problems might the firm encounter?

8. Even if the firms in a monopolistically competitive market collude successfully and fix price, economic profit will still be competed away if there is unrestricted entry. Explain. Will price be higher or lower under such an agreement in long-run equilibrium than would be the case if firms didn't collude? Explain.

9. The Ali Baba Co. is the only supplier of a particular type of Oriental carpet. The estimated demand for its carpets is

$$Q = 112,000 - 500P + 5M$$

where Q = number of carpets, P = price of carpets (dollars per unit), and M = consumers' income per capita.

The estimated average variable cost function for Ali Baba's carpets is

$$AVC = 200 - 0.012Q + 0.000002Q^2$$

Consumers' income per capita is expected to be $20,000 and total fixed cost is $100,000.

a. How many carpets should the firm produce in order to maximize profit?

b. What is the profit-maximizing price of carpets?

c. What is the maximum amount of profit that the firm can earn selling carpets?

d. Answer parts *a* through *c* if consumers' income per capita is expected to be $30,000 instead.

10. Dr. Leona Williams, a well-known plastic surgeon, has a reputation for being one of the best surgeons for reconstructive nose surgery. Dr. Williams enjoys a rather substantial degree of market power in this market. She has estimated demand for her work to be

$$Q = 480 - 0.2P$$

where Q is the number of nose operations performed monthly and P is the price of a nose operation.

a. What is the inverse demand function for Dr. Williams's services?

b. What is the marginal revenue function?

The average variable cost function for reconstructive nose surgery is estimated to be

$$AVC = 2Q^2 - 15Q + 400$$

where AVC is average variable cost (measured in dollars), and Q is the number of operations per month. The doctor's fixed costs each month are $8,000.

c. If the doctor wishes to maximize her profit, how many nose operations should she perform each month?

d. What price should Dr. Williams charge to perform a nose operation?

e. How much profit does she earn each month?

▣   MATHEMATICAL APPENDIX   Profit Maximization for a Monopoly

This appendix describes a manager's choice of output and price or input usage in order to maximize profit for a monopoly. First, we examine the decision about the profit-maximizing price and output using the most general demand and cost functions, then using a linear demand and cubic cost function. We also demonstrate that the profit-maximizing price and output are always on the elastic portion of demand. Next, we derive the profit-maximizing conditions when the manager chooses the level of usage of one variable input and then two variable inputs.

The Monopolist Chooses Output and Price

Assume that the firm is in the short run, so some costs are fixed. Let the inverse demand for a monopoly be

$$P = P(Q)$$

so total revenue is

$$R(Q) = P(Q)Q$$

The monopoly profit function is

$$(1) \qquad \pi = R(Q) - TVC(Q) - TFC$$

where $TVC(Q)$ is total variable cost and TFC is total fixed cost.

The first-order condition for profit maximization requires

$$(2) \qquad d\pi/dQ = dR/dQ - dTVC/dQ = 0$$

The second-order condition for a maximum is that at the equilibrium quantity

$$d^2\pi/dQ^2 = d^2R/dQ^2 - d^2TVC/dQ^2 < 0$$

Since in equation (2) dR/dQ is marginal revenue and dC/dQ is marginal cost, choosing the quantity of output that maximizes profit requires that marginal revenue equal marginal cost: $MR = SMC$. Solve equation (2) for the equilibrium output Q^* so the equilibrium price is $P^* = P(Q^*)$.

If

$$\pi = P(Q^*)Q^* - TVC(Q^*) - TFC > 0$$

the firm makes an economic profit. If

$$\pi = P(Q^*)Q^* - TVC(Q^*) - TFC < 0$$

the firm makes a loss. In this case the firm should produce Q^* rather than shutting down when

$$|P(Q^*)Q^* - TVC(Q^*) - TFC| \leq TFC$$

which occurs if, at Q^*, price is greater than or equal to average variable cost:

$$P(Q^*) \geq TVC(Q^*)/Q^*$$

The firm loses less than its total fixed cost, which is the amount it would lose if it shuts down and produces nothing. If at Q^* price is less than average variable cost, the firm should shut down and produce nothing. It loses all its fixed cost rather than its fixed cost plus the amount of variable cost not covered by revenue.

We next demonstrate that the profit-maximizing price and quantity must lie on the elastic portion of demand. Since

$$MR = dR/dQ = P(Q) + Q(dP/dQ)$$
$$= P[1 + (Q/P)(dP/dQ)] = P[1 + (1/E)]$$

where E is the elasticity of demand, in equilibrium

(3) $$MR = P[1 + 1/E] = MC$$

Since MC and P must be positive, $(1 + 1/E) > 0$, which, because $E < 0$, requires that E be greater than one in absolute value: $|E| > 1$. Thus in equilibrium P^* and Q^* must lie on the elastic portion of demand.

For a less general approach, assume that the inverse demand function is the linear function:

$$P(Q) = a - bQ$$

where a and b are positive. Let the total variable cost function be the cubic function,

$$TVC(Q) = dQ - eQ^2 + fQ^3$$

where d, e, and f are positive. The profit function is therefore

(4) $$\pi = PQ - TVC(Q) - TFC$$
$$= aQ - bQ^2 - dQ + eQ^2 - fQ^3 - TFC$$

For profit maximization, differentiate (4) and set it equal to 0:

(5) $$d\pi/dQ = (a - 2bQ) - (d - 2eQ + 3fQ^2) = 0$$

Since $MR = a - 2bq$, and $SMC = d - 2eQ + 3fQ^2$, $MR = SMC$ in profit-maximizing equilibrium. The second-order condition for a maximum is

(6) $$d^2\pi/dQ^2 = -2b + 2e - 6fQ < 0$$

or, solving equation (6) for Q, for a maximum, it must be the case that

(7) $$Q > (e - b)/3f$$

To obtain the profit-maximizing level of Q^*, solve the quadratic equation formed from equation (5):

$$(a - d) - (2b + 2e)Q - 3fQ^2 = 0$$

After solving such a quadratic equation, you will obtain two values for Q^*. The profit-maximizing Q^* will be the value at which the second-order condition in (7) holds, ensuring that this is the value of Q^* at which marginal cost crosses marginal revenue from below. This will be the larger of the two solutions in such problems. To obtain the equilibrium price, substitute Q^* into the inverse demand function:

$$P^* = a - bQ^*$$

If the total revenue equals or exceeds total variable cost, that is, if $P(Q^*) \geq TVC(Q^*)/Q^*$, then profit or loss is

$$\pi = aQ^* - bQ^{*2} - dQ^* + eQ^{*2} - fQ^{*3} - TFC$$

The Monopolist Chooses Input Usage

Now we assume that the manager chooses the level of usage of a single variable input, L, in order to maximize profit. All other inputs are fixed in amount. Let the production function be as derived for the short run in the Mathematical Appendix to Chapter 8:

$$Q = f(L, K) = g(L)$$

The inverse demand function is

$$P = P(Q) = P[g(L)]$$

The firm chooses L so that the following profit function is maximized:

(8) $$\pi = P[g(L)]g(L) - wL - TFC$$

where w is the wage paid to labor and TFC is the fixed payment for the fixed inputs. Profit maximization requires

(9a) $d\pi/dL = (dP/dQ)(dQ/dL)g(L) + P(dQ/dL) - w$

$= 0$

or

(9b) $(dQ/dL)[(dP/dQ)Q + P] = w$

Since dQ/dL is marginal product and $[(dP/dQ)Q + P]$ is marginal revenue, equation (9b) can be expressed as

$MP \times MR =$ Marginal revenue product $= w$

Equation (9a) or (9b) can be solved for L^*; then $Q^* = g(L^*)$ and $P^* = P(Q^*)$.

If, at L^*, $MRP \leq ARP = P[g(L^*)]/L^*$, the firm will produce and its profit or loss will be

$\pi = P[g(L^*)]g(L^*) - wL^* - TFC$

If, however, $MRP = w > P^*Q^*/L^*$, total revenue will be less than total variable cost; that is, $wL^* > P^*Q^*$. In this case the firm would shut down and lose only its total fixed cost, rather than its total fixed cost plus the portion of total variable cost not covered by revenue.

Now assume that the firm uses two variable inputs, L and K, and no inputs are fixed. The prices of L and K are, respectively, w and r. The production function is

$Q = f(L, K)$

and the inverse demand function is

$P = P(Q) = P[f(L, K)]$

The profit function is now

$\pi = f(L, K)P[f(L, K)] - wL - rK$

Since the firm chooses the levels of L and K to maximize profit, the first-order equilibrium conditions are

(10a) $P[f(L, K)](\partial Q/\partial L) + Q(dP/dQ)(\partial Q/\partial L) - w = 0$

(10b) $P[f(L, K)](\partial Q/\partial K) + Q(dP/dQ)(\partial Q/\partial K) - r = 0$

Equations (10a) and (10b) can be solved for the optimal levels of L^* and K^*; then the optimal levels of output and price are $Q^* = f(L^*, K^*)$ and $P^* = P[f(L^*, K^*)]$. These values can be substituted into the above profit equation to find the maximum level of profit.

Equations (10a) and (10b) can be rewritten as

(11a) $\partial Q/\partial L(P + QdP/dQ) = MP_L \times MR = MRP_L = w$

(11b) $\partial Q/\partial K(P + QdP/dQ) = MP_K \times MR = MRP_K = r$

Thus in equilibrium the marginal revenue product of each input equals its price.

CHAPTER 13

Strategic Decision Making in Oligopoly Markets

We are now going to address some new types of business-decision-making problems that arise when just a few firms produce most or all of the total market output. When the number of firms competing in a market is small, any one firm's pricing policy will have a significant effect on sales of other firms in the market. Indeed, in markets where a relatively small number of firms compete, *every* kind of decision affecting any one firm's profit—such as decisions about pricing, output, and advertising as well as decisions about expanding production facilities or increasing spending on research and development—also affects profits of every other firm in the market. The profit earned by each firm in a market having only a few sellers depends on decisions made by every other firm competing in the same market, and so profits of all firms are interdependent. Consider these examples of rival firms whose sales, and consequently profits, are interdependent:

- American Airlines might be debating whether or not to reduce fares on all its European flights this summer. The reductions could substantially increase its profitable vacation-travel business. But if Delta, United, and other large overseas carriers match the reductions, a costly fare war could result, causing losses for all.

- Coca-Cola may be preparing an expensive new advertising campaign. Its advertising agency says the new campaign should be extremely effective. But how will Pepsi react? Will it respond with an even-more-expensive advertising campaign of its own, or will it continue as is? Pepsi's response will have a huge effect on the profitability of Coca-Cola's decision.

- At a much smaller marketing level, Joe's Pizza Express, a successful local restaurant in the downtown business district, wants to open a new restaurant in a recently developed suburban area. But will Pizza Hut or Domino's also come into the new suburb, which, for the next several years, will probably not be large enough to support more than one pizza place? During this period, Joe could lose a lot of money.

These types of business decisions differ substantially from the decision-making processes developed in previous chapters in which managers took price or demand as given and did not need to consider the reactions of rival managers when making decisions. In these examples, managers must make decisions knowing that their decisions will affect the sales and profitability of their rivals and that their rivals will then react to their decisions. Depending on how their rivals react, their own sales and profitability will then be affected. But these managers do not know what their rivals will actually do. To make the best decisions, even though they almost never know for sure what their competitors' reactions will be, these managers must "get into the heads" of their rival managers in order to make predictions or conjectures about their reactions.

strategic behavior
Actions taken by firms to plan for and react to competition from rival firms.

Successful managers must learn how to anticipate the actions and reactions of other firms in their markets. In this chapter we will show you how successfully predicting a rival's reaction requires managers to assume their rivals will always make those decisions that are likely to be the most profitable ones for them given the decisions they expect *their* rivals to make. Interdependence, then, requires *strategic behavior*. **Strategic behavior** consists of the actions taken by firms and any actions that firms can convincingly threaten to take, in order to plan for, and react to, the actions of competitors. Knowing about and anticipating potential moves and countermoves of other firms is of critical importance to managers in markets where firms' sales and profits are interdependent.

oligopoly
A market consisting of a few relatively large firms, each with a substantial share of the market and all recognize their interdependence.

As we discussed in Chapter 1, economists generally use the term **oligopoly** in reference to a market in which a few relatively large firms have moderate to substantial market power and, what is more important, they recognize their interdependence. Each firm knows that its actions or changes will have an effect on other firms and that the other firms will, in response, take actions or make changes that will affect its sales. But no firm is really sure how the other firms will react.

This scenario applies to the previous examples in which American Airlines considered how its rivals would react before it decided to reduce fares. Coca-Cola didn't know what Pepsi would do if it introduced a new advertising campaign or what the effect of Pepsi's reaction would be. The owner of Joe's Pizza Express considered what the large pizza chains would do if Pizza Express entered the new suburb. We will devote this chapter to analyzing how managers of firms operating in oligopoly markets can make decisions when they are uncertain about the reaction of rivals; yet these reactions affect their own sales and profits and so must be considered in reaching decisions. We can now summarize in a principle the problem of interdependence in oligopoly.

☐ **Principle** Interdependence of firms' profits, the distinguishing characteristic of oligopoly markets, arises when the number of firms in a market is small enough that every firm's price and output decision affects the demand and marginal revenue conditions of every other firm in the market.

The discussion of oligopoly in this chapter is designed to introduce you to and give you some insight into the way managers of firms in oligopoly markets make decisions. As you will see, the study of strategic behavior is similar to the study of players participating in a game of strategy, such as chess, poker, bridge, or checkers. This is why this important area of economic analysis is called "game theory." In this chapter, we will use models of game theory to show how managers of oligopoly firms can try to get into the heads of their rivals to make the most profitable decisions for themselves. You will see that strategic decision making in oligopoly markets frequently results in a situation in which each firm makes the best decision for itself given the decisions it expects its rivals will make, but this kind of "noncooperative" decision making leads to lower profits for all firms. Noncooperative oligopoly outcomes are generally good for consumers but bad for the firms that earn lower profits as a consequence.

In the last section of this chapter, we examine some ways in which cooperative oligopoly decisions may arise. When you finish this chapter, you will understand why oligopoly firms may wish to make decisions cooperatively and how they can sometimes, but certainly not always, achieve cooperation in making decisions. We must warn you at the outset of this chapter that many forms of overt or explicit cooperation, also called "collusion" or "price-fixing" by legal authorities, are illegal in the United States and in many other countries. For example, the CEO of American Airlines could call the CEO of Delta and work out a pricing agreement between the two firms. But such price fixing is illegal in the United States, and business executives have been fined or even sent to prison for doing just that. We will show you how cooperative outcomes can sometimes be achieved in oligopoly markets without resorting to illegal practices and why price-fixing agreements generally do not last very long in any case.

13.1 DECISION MAKING WHEN RIVALS MAKE SIMULTANEOUS DECISIONS

As emphasized in the introduction, the "fewness of firms" in oligopoly markets causes each firm's demand and marginal revenue conditions, and hence each firm's profits, to depend on the pricing decisions, output decisions, expansion decisions, and so forth, of every rival firm in an oligopoly market. The resulting interdependence and strategic behavior make decisions much more complicated and uncertain. To make the best decisions they can when every firm is trying to anticipate the decisions of every other firm, managers must learn to think strategically.

Perhaps you are thinking, "Sure, interdependence complicates decision making and makes it messy. So what do I as a manager do in such situations? How do I go about making strategic decisions?" We can't give you a set of rules to follow. The art of making strategic decisions is learned from experience.

game theory
An analytical guide or tool for making decisions in situations involving interdependence.

We can, however, introduce you to a tool for thinking about strategic decision making: *game theory*. **Game theory** provides a useful guideline on how to behave in strategic situations involving interdependence. This theory was developed more than 50 years ago to provide a systematic approach to strategic decision making. During the past 25 years, it has become increasingly important to economists for analyzing oligopoly behavior. And it is also becoming more useful to managers in making business decisions. Unfortunately, learning the principles of game theory will not guarantee that you will always "win" or make greater profit than your rivals. In the real world of business decision making, your rival managers will also be strategic thinkers who will try to predict your actions, and they will try to counteract your strategic decisions. And, to make winning even less certain, many unpredictable, and even unknown, events are frequently just as important as strategic thinking in determining final outcomes in business. Game theory can only provide you with some general principles or guidelines to follow in strategic situations like those that oligopoly managers face.

You might think of the word "game" as meaning something fun or entertaining to do, but managers may or may not find it fun to play the strategic games that arise in oligopoly. To game theorists—economists who specialize in the study of strategic behavior—a **game** is any decision-making situation in which people compete with each other for the purpose of gaining the greatest individual payoff, rather than group payoff, from playing the game. In the game of oligopoly, the people in the game, often called "players," are the managers of the oligopoly firms. Payoffs in the oligopoly game are the individual profits earned by each firm.

In this section, we will introduce you to strategic thinking by illustrating some of the fundamental principles of strategic decision making that can help you make better decisions in one of the more common kinds of strategic situations managers face: making *simultaneous decisions* about prices, production, advertising levels, product styles, quality, and so on. **Simultaneous decision games** occur in oligopoly markets when managers must make their individual decisions without knowing the decisions of their rivals. Simultaneous decision games can arise when managers make decisions at precisely the same time without knowledge of their rivals' decisions. However, decisions don't have to take place at the same time in order to be "simultaneous"; it is only necessary for managers not to know what their rivals have decided to do when they make their own decisions. If you have information about what your rival has chosen to do *before* you make your decision, then you are in a *sequential* decision-making game, which we will discuss in the next section of this chapter.

Making decisions without the benefit of knowing what their rivals have decided is, as you might suspect, a rather common, and unpleasant, situation for managers. For example, to meet publishers' deadlines, two competing clothing retailers must decide by Friday, July 1, whether or not to run expensive full-page ads in local papers for the purpose of notifying buyers of their Fourth of July sales that begin on Monday. Both managers would rather save the expense of advertising because they know buyers expect both stores to have holiday sales and will shop at both stores on the Fourth of July even if no ads are run by either store.

Unless they tell each other—or receive a tipoff from someone working at the newspaper—neither manager will know whether the other has placed an ad until Monday morning, long after they have made their "simultaneous" decisions. As we mentioned earlier, making decisions without knowing what rivals are going to do is quite a common situation for managers. Any of the strategic decisions described at the beginning of this chapter could be a simultaneous decision game.

game
Any decision-making situation in which people compete with each other for the purpose of gaining the greatest individual payoff.

simultaneous decision games
A situation in which competing firms must make their individual decisions without knowing the decisions of their rivals.

ILLUSTRATION 13.1

How Can Game Theory Be Used in Business Decision Making?
Answers from a Manager

"Game theory is hot . . . it's been used to analyze everything from the baseball strike to auctions at the FCC . . . Why are 50-year-old ideas being used by companies to answer basic questions about pricing, investments in capacity, purchasing, and other matters?" So began an article in *The Wall Street Journal* by F. William Barnett.[a]

Barnett points out that game theory helps managers pay attention to interactions with competitors, customers, and suppliers and focus on how near-term actions promote long-term interests by influencing what the players do. After describing a version of the prisoners' dilemma game, he notes that an equilibrium (such as the one we showed in cell D of Table 13.1) is unattractive to all players. He warns, "But you have to know your industry inside-out before game theory is truly valuable . . . you will need to understand entry costs, demand functions, revenue structures, cost curves, etc. Without that understanding, the answer you get [from game theory] may be wrong."

Some rules of the road: Examine the number, concentration, and size distribution of the players. For example, industries with four or fewer players have the greatest potential for game theory, because (1) the competitors are large enough to benefit more from an improvement in general industry conditions than they would from improving their position at the expense of others (making the pie bigger rather than getting a bigger share of a smaller pie) and (2) with fewer competitors it is possible to think through the different combination of moves and countermoves.

Keep an eye out for strategies inherent in your market share. Small players can take advantage of larger companies, which are more concerned with maintaining the status quo. Barnett's example: Kiwi Airlines, with a small share of the market, was able to cut fares by up to 75 percent between Atlanta and Newark without a significant response from Delta and Continental. But, he notes, large players can create economies of scale or scope, such as frequent-flier programs, that are unattractive to small airlines.

Understand the nature of the buying decision. For example, if there are only a few deals in an industry each year, it is very hard to avoid aggressive competition. Scrutinize your competitors' cost and revenue structures. If competitors have a high proportion of fixed-to-variable cost, they will probably behave more aggressively than those whose production costs are more variable.

Examine the similarity of firms. When competitors have similar cost and revenue structures, they often behave similarly. The challenge is to find prices that create the largest markets, then use nonprice competition—distribution and service. Finally, analyze the nature of demand. The best chances to create value with less aggressive strategies are in markets with stable or moderately growing demand.

Barnett concludes, "Sometimes [game theory] can increase the size of the pie; on other occasions it can make your slice of the pie bigger; and sometimes it may even help you do both. But for those who misunderstand [the] fundamentals of their industry, game theory is better left to the theorists." As we said earlier, strategic decision making is best learned from experience.

[a]F. William Barnett, "Making Game Theory Work in Practice," *The Wall Street Journal*, Feb. 13, 1995.

To introduce you to the concept of oligopoly games, we begin with the grandfather of most economic games. While it doesn't involve oligopoly behavior at all, it is a widely known and widely studied game of simultaneous decision making that captures many of the essential elements of oligopoly decision making. This famous game is known as the *prisoners' dilemma*.

TABLE 13.1
The Prisoners' Dilemma: A Dominant Strategy Equilibrium

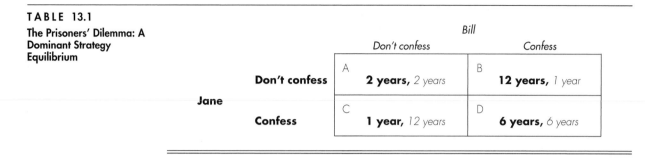

		Bill	
		Don't confess	*Confess*
Jane	**Don't confess**	A **2 years,** *2 years*	B **12 years,** *1 year*
	Confess	C **1 year,** *12 years*	D **6 years,** *6 years*

The Prisoners' Dilemma

payoff table
A table showing, for every possible combination of decisions players can make, the outcomes or "payoffs" for each of the players in each decision combination.

common knowledge
A situation in which all decision makers know the payoff table, and they believe all other decision makers also know the payoff table.

The model of the prisoners' dilemma is best illustrated by the story for which it is named. Suppose that a serious crime—say, grand-theft auto—is committed and two suspects, Bill and Jane, are apprehended and questioned by the police. The suspects know that the police do not have enough evidence to make the charges stick unless one of them confesses. If neither suspect confesses to the serious charges, then the police can only convict the suspects on much less serious charges—perhaps, felony vandalism. So the police separate Bill and Jane and make each one an offer that is known to the other. The offer is this: If one suspect confesses to the crime and testifies in court against the other, the one who confesses will receive only a 1-year sentence, while the other (who does not confess) will get 12 years. If both prisoners confess, each receives a 6-year sentence. If neither confesses, both receive 2-year sentences on the minor charges. Thus Bill and Jane each could receive 1 year, 2 years, 6 years, or 12 years, depending on what the other does.

Table 13.1 shows the four possibilities in a table called a *payoff table*. A **payoff table** is a table showing, for every possible combination of actions that players can make, the outcomes or "payoffs" for each player. Each of the four cells in Table 13.1 represents the outcome of one of the four possible combinations of actions that could be taken by Bill and Jane. For example, cells A and D in the payoff table show the payoffs for Bill and Jane if both do not confess or do confess, respectively. Cells B and C show the consequences if one confesses and the other does not. In each cell, the years spent in prison for each one of the two suspects is listed as a pair of numbers separated by a comma. The first number, shown in bold face, gives Jane's prison sentence, and the second number, shown in italics gives Bill's prison sentence.[1] Both suspects know the payoff table in Table 13.1, and they both know that the other one knows the payoff table. This **common knowledge** of the payoff table plays a crucial role in determining the outcome of a simultaneous decision game. What the suspects don't know, since their decisions are made simultaneously, is what the other has decided to do.

---

[1] Throughout this chapter, we will follow the convention of listing payoffs to players in each cell of a payoff table as **payoff to row player,** *payoff to column player.*

The police have designed the situation so that both Bill and Jane will be induced to confess and both will end up in cell D (excuse the pun). To see this, put yourself into Bill's head and imagine what he must be thinking. Bill knows that Jane must decide between the two actions "confess" and "don't confess." If Jane does not confess ("bless her heart"), Bill receives a lighter sentence by confessing ("sorry Jane, I promise I'll visit you often"). If Jane confesses ("Jane, you dirty rat"), Bill still receives a lighter sentence by confessing: 6 years compared with 12. Therefore, confessing is always better than not confessing for Bill ("Sorry Jane, what did you expect me to do?")—it gives Bill a lighter sentence no matter what Jane does. The only rational thing for Bill to do is confess. The police, of course, counted on Bill thinking rationally, so they are not surprised when he confesses. And they also expect Jane to confess for precisely the same reason: Confessing is the best action Jane can take, no matter what action she predicts Bill will take. So both Bill and Jane will probably confess and end up with sentences of 6 years each.

The prisoners' dilemma illustrates a way of predicting the likely outcome of a strategic game using the concept of a *dominant strategy*. In game theory a **dominant strategy** is a strategy or action that provides the best outcome no matter what decisions rivals decide to make. In the prisoner's dilemma, confessing is a dominant strategy for each suspect. Naturally, rational decision makers should always take the action associated with a dominant strategy, if they have one. This establishes the following principle for strategic decision making.

dominant strategy
A strategy or action that always provides the best outcome no matter what decisions rivals make.

▢ **Principle** When a dominant strategy exists—an action that always provides a manager with the best outcome no matter what action the manager's rivals choose to take—a rational decision maker always chooses to follow its own dominant strategy and predicts that if its rivals have dominant strategies, they also will choose to follow their dominant strategies.

Finding dominant strategies, especially in larger payoff tables, can sometimes be difficult. A useful method for finding dominant strategies can be easily illustrated using the payoff table for the prisoners' dilemma in Table 13.1. Let's begin with Jane: For each *column* (i.e., for each decision Bill could make), find the cell that gives Jane her best payoff and pencil a "*J*" in that cell. Following this procedure for this game, you will mark two *J*'s: one in cell C and one in cell D. Now repeat this process for Bill: For each *row* (i.e., for each decision Jane could make), find the cell that gives Bill's best payoff and pencil a "*B*" in that cell. Following this procedure, you will mark two *B*'s: one in cell B and one in cell D. Since *all J*'s line up in *one* row, that row (**Confess**) is a dominant strategy for Jane. Similarly, Bill possesses a dominant strategy because *all B*'s line up in *one* column (*Confess*).

As you can now see, it is easy, once dominant strategies are discovered, to predict the likely outcome of games in which both players have dominant strategies. Game theorists call such an outcome a **dominant-strategy equilibrium.** When both players have dominant strategies, the outcome of the game can be predicted with a high degree of confidence. The compelling nature of a dominant-strategy equilibrium results from the fact that, when all decision makers have dominant strategies (and know their dominant strategies), managers will be able to predict the actions of their rivals with a great deal of certainty.

dominant-strategy equilibrium
Both players have dominant strategies and play them.

An important characteristic of the prisoners' dilemma, and one that makes it valuable for understanding oligopoly outcomes, is that cooperation is unlikely to occur because there is an incentive to cheat. To see this, suppose that, before committing their crime, Bill and Jane make a promise to each other that they will never confess to their crime. Once again let's get into Bill's head to see what he is thinking. Suppose Bill predicts that Jane will keep her promise not to confess ("Jane loves me; she would never break her promise to me."). He then has an incentive to cheat on his promise because he can get out of jail in just one year instead of two years by confessing ("Oh Jane, come on; I promise I'll wait for you."). Alternatively, if you think that it's farfetched for Bill to trust Jane ("Jane *never* loved me the way I loved her."), then suppose Bill predicts Jane will confess. Now his best decision, when he predicts Jane will cheat by confessing, is also to cheat and confess. Without some method of forcing each other to keep their promises not to confess, Bill and Jane will probably both cheat by confessing.

Despite the fact that both suspects choose dominant strategies that are best for them no matter what the other suspect chooses to do, they end up in a cell (cell D) where they are both worse off than if they had cooperated by not confessing. This paradoxical outcome has made the prisoners' dilemma one of the most studied games in economics because it captures the difficult nature of cooperation in oligopoly markets. We now summarize the nature of a prisoners' dilemma.

▣   **Relation**   A prisoners' dilemma arises when all rivals possess dominant strategies, and, in dominant-strategy equilibrium, they are all worse off than if they had cooperated in making their decisions.

As we will explain later in this chapter, managers facing prisoners' dilemma situations may be able to reach cooperative outcomes if, instead of having only one opportunity to make their decisions, they get to repeat their decisions many times in the future. We will save our examination of repeated decisions, as well as a more precise discussion of "cooperation" and "cheating," for Section 13.3. Until then, our discussion will continue examining situations in which managers have only a single opportunity to make their decisions.

Most strategic situations, in contrast to the prisoners' dilemma game, do not have a dominant-strategy equilibrium. We will now examine some other ways oligopoly managers can make simultaneous decisions when some, or even all, of the firms do not have dominant strategies.

Decisions with One Dominant Strategy

In a prisoners' dilemma situation, all firms have dominant strategies to follow and managers rationally decide to follow their dominant strategies, even though the outcome is not as good as it could be if the firms cooperated in making their decisions. If just one firm possesses a dominant strategy, rival managers know that particular firm will choose its dominant strategy. Knowing what your rival is going to do can tell you much about what you should do. We illustrate the value of knowing what your rival is going to do with the following example.

TABLE 13.2
Pizza Pricing: A Single
Dominant Strategy

		Palace's price	
		High ($10)	Low ($6)
Castle's price	**High ($10)**	A **$1,000,** $1,000	B **$500,** $1,200
	Low ($6)	C **$1,200,** $300	D **$400,** $400

Payoffs in dollars of profit per week.

Pizza Castle and Pizza Palace are located almost side by side across the street from a major university. The products of Castle and Palace are somewhat differentiated, yet their primary means of competition is pricing. For illustrative purposes, suppose each restaurant can choose between only two prices for its pizza: a high price of $10 and a low price of $6. Clearly the profit for each firm at each of the prices depends greatly on the price charged by the other firm. Once again, you see that profits of oligopolists are interdependent.

Table 13.2 shows the payoff table facing Castle and Palace. If both charge $10, each does quite well, making $1,000 a week profit, as shown in cell A. If both lower their prices to $6, sales increase some; each restaurant will probably maintain its market share; and, because of the lower price, the profit of each falls to $400 a week, as shown in cell D. However, if either firm lowers its price to $6 while the other maintains its price at $10, the firm with the lower price will capture most of the other's business. Comparing cells B and C shows that the loss of market share is less serious for Castle when it is underpriced by Palace than the loss of market share for Palace when it is underpriced by Castle: Castle, when underpriced makes $500 a week, but Palace, when underpriced makes only $300. The reason for this difference is Castle's policy, which Palace does not believe in, of offering free soft drinks whenever it is underpriced by its rival.

As you can determine from the payoff table in Table 13.2, Castle does *not* have a dominant strategy. However, the manager at Castle sees (as does the manager at Palace) that Palace does have a dominant strategy: price low at $6. Knowing that Palace's manager will rationally choose to set price low at $6, Castle's manager will likely decide to price high at $10 (and give away soft drinks). Thus cell B is the outcome of the simultaneous decision game. We have established another important principle for making simultaneous decisions.

Principle   When a firm does not have a dominant strategy, but at least one of its rivals *does* have a dominant strategy, the firm's manager can predict with confidence that its rivals will follow their dominant strategies. Then, the manager can choose its own best strategy, knowing the actions that will almost certainly be taken by those rivals possessing dominant strategies.

Successive Elimination of Dominated Strategies

dominated strategies
Strategies that would never be chosen because at least one other strategy provides a higher payoff no matter what rivals choose to do.

successive elimination of dominated strategies
An iterative decision-making process in which dominated strategies are eliminated to create a reduced payoff table with fewer decisions for managers to consider.

When deciding what to do in a simultaneous decision situation, managers should eliminate from consideration **dominated strategies:** (i.e., strategies that would never be chosen because there is always a better strategy); at least one other strategy) provides a higher payoff no matter what rivals choose to do. The full strategic benefit of using dominated strategies to simplify decision making requires that managers eliminate all dominated strategies (those that can be identified on a "first-round" of searching and then any other dominated strategies that reveal themselves after one or more rounds of elimination). **Successive elimination of dominated strategies** is an iterative decision-making process in which managers first eliminate all dominated strategies in the original payoff table. The first round of elimination creates a new payoff table, known as a *reduced* payoff table, that has fewer decisions for the manager to consider. Then, any strategies that become dominated after the first round of elimination are likewise eliminated to create yet another reduced payoff table, which, of course, has still fewer decisions to consider. The process of elimination continues until no dominated strategies remain in the final payoff table.

We can illustrate this elimination procedure by making the pizza pricing problem facing Castle and Palace somewhat more complex. Consider the new, larger payoff table in Table 13.3. Managers at Castle and Palace can now choose high ($10), medium ($8), or low ($6) pizza prices. In the beginning payoff table, shown in a Panel A of Table 13.3, no dominant strategy exists for either Castle or Palace. Both managers, however, have dominated strategies in the beginning payoff table that they will never choose. Palace will never choose to price high, since no matter what price it believes Castle might set, a high price is never the best decision for Palace. Similarly, Castle will never believe setting a medium price is its best solution. Both dominated strategies—high for Palace and medium for Castle—should be removed from the beginning payoff table in Panel A.[2]

After the managers remove the two dominated strategies, the reduced payoff table, shown in Panel B of Table 13.3, has only two rows and two columns. Notice that now, after eliminating dominated strategies, both firms have dominant strategies. Castles' dominant strategy is to price high, and Palace's dominant strategy is to price low. Both pizza firms will want to follow their newly discovered dominant strategies, and they end up in the payoff table in cell C with Castle earning $500 of profit a week and Palace earning $1,200 of profit a week. Notice that cell C can also be found by a *second* round of elimination of dominated strategies. In Panel B, Castle's low price and Palace's medium price are both dominated strategies, which, when eliminated, produce the unique solution in Panel C.

---

[2]The procedure we discussed earlier for finding dominant strategies by marking each player's best decision for each decision the rival player might make also identifies *dominated* strategies. For the player whose decisions are listed by rows in the payoff table—call this player "Rowe"—a dominated strategy exists for Rowe if there is a row with no *R*'s marked in that row. Similarly, for the player whose decisions are listed by columns in the payoff table—call this player "Collum"—a dominated strategy exists for Collum if there is a column with no *C*'s marked in that column.

TABLE 13.3
Pizza Pricing: Successive Elimination of Dominated Strategies

| | | Palace's price | | |
		High ($10)	Medium ($8)	Low ($6)
	High ($10)	A **$1,000,** $1,000	B **$900,** $1,100	C **$500,** $1,200
Castle's price	**Medium ($8)**	D **$1,100,** $400	E **$800,** $800	F **$450,** $500
	Low ($6)	G **$1,200,** $300	H **$500,** $350	I **$400,** $400

Payoffs in dollars of profit per week.

Panel A—Beginning Payoff Table

| | | Palace's price | |
		Medium ($8)	Low ($6)
	High ($10)	B **$900,** $1,100	C **$500,** $1,200
Castle's price	**Low ($6)**	H **$500,** $350	I **$400,** $400

Panel B—Reduced Payoff Table

| | | Palace's price |
		Low ($6)
Castle's price	**High ($10)**	C **$500,** $1,200

Panel C—Unique Solution

We wish we could tell you that every time you can apply successive elimination of dominated strategies, you will discover a pair of dominant strategies. We can, however, tell you that eliminating dominated strategies *always* simplifies a decision-making problem, even when it doesn't completely solve the decision problem as it did for Castle and Palace in Panel C of Table 13.3. We summarize this discussion with the following principle for decision making:

▣   **Principle**   In a simultaneous decision having no dominant strategy equilibrium, managers can simplify their decisions by eliminating all dominated strategies that may exist. The process of elimination should be repeated until no more dominated strategies turn up.

When it occurs, strategic dominance, whether it takes the form of dominant strategies or dominated strategies, delivers a powerful tool to managers for making simultaneous decisions. Strategically astute managers always search first for dominant strategies, and, if no dominant strategies can be discovered, they next look for dominated strategies. Unfortunately, simultaneous decisions frequently fail to provide managers with either dominant or dominated strategies. In the absence of any form of strategic dominance, managers must use a different, but related, guiding concept for making simultaneous decisions. This concept, known as *Nash equilibrium,* can sometimes, but not always, guide managers in making simultaneous decisions.

Nash Equilibrium: Making Mutually Best Decisions

When simultaneous decisions cannot be made using the clear and powerful rules of strategic dominance, decision makers must find some other guide for making strategic decisions. We will now discuss an approach frequently employed by game theorists to explain how decision makers can make the best decisions in simultaneous decision situations. This solution to making simultaneous decisions is known as a *Nash equilibrium,* named for the game theorist John F. Nash, who first proposed the solution in the 1940s and whose lifework provided the basis for the movie *A Beautiful Mind.*

The fundamental idea guiding managers to a Nash equilibrium is that managers will choose the strategy that gives them the highest payoff, given what they believe will be the actions of their rivals. To achieve this end, managers must correctly anticipate the actions of rivals. Unless managers correctly predict what their rivals will do, they will make the wrong decisions. So managers will not believe they are making best decisions for themselves unless they also believe they are correctly predicting the actions of their rivals. How, then, can managers correctly predict what their rivals will do so that they can choose the best response to their rivals?

As we just mentioned, every rival is trying to accomplish precisely the same thing: Each tries to make the best decision for itself given its beliefs about what the rest of its rivals will do. To accomplish this end, they must believe they are correctly predicting each other's actions; otherwise they will not believe they are making the best decisions for themselves. Strategically thinking managers, however, will not be satisfied that their predictions are correct unless the predicted action for each and every rival would be the best decision for that rival to take based on the rival's own predictions about the actions its rivals will take. This discussion establishes the following relation:

Relation In order for all firms in an oligopoly market to be predicting correctly each others' decisions—managers cannot make *best* decisions without *correct* predictions—all firms must be choosing individually best actions given the predicted actions of their rivals, which they can then believe are correctly predicted.

It follows, then, that strategically astute managers will search the payoff table for *mutually best decisions:* cells in the payoff table in which all managers are doing the best they can given their beliefs about the other managers' actions. Strategic thinkers realize that only mutually best decisions can result in mutually correct predictions about rival decisions, which, in turn, ensure that the decisions are indeed the best ones to make. This is the subtle and complex nature of a **Nash equilibrium,** which we can now define formally as a set of actions or decisions for which all managers are choosing their best actions given the actions chosen by their rivals. Payoff tables may contain more than one Nash equilibrium cell, and some payoff tables may have no Nash cells. As you will see shortly, the concept of Nash equilibrium is only helpful when payoff tables have exactly one Nash equilibrium cell.

While Nash equilibrium allows all managers to do best for themselves given other managers' own best decisions, we must stress that the managers are not cooperating with each other when they choose a Nash set of actions. The reason they choose a Nash equilibrium is not because they are trying to help each other do their best. They make Nash decisions only because they know they cannot make the best decisions for themselves unless they *correctly* predict the decisions their rivals will make. And, as we explained, unless managers correctly predict what their rivals will do, they will not, individually, make the best decisions for themselves.

We wish to be extremely clear about how you interpret each decision or action associated with a Nash equilibrium cell. In a Nash cell, managers view their own decisions as the actions they should take to achieve their own best outcomes based on the actions they believe or anticipate the others will take to reach their best outcomes. Since the rivals' actions have not yet been taken, they must be regarded as the actions a manager *believes* they will take, *anticipates* they will take, *predicts* they will take, or *expects* them to take. The words "believe," "anticipate," "predict," and "expect" all reflect the fundamental problem of simultaneous decisions: Managers cannot know ahead of time what actions rivals will actually take. While this interpretation of decisions in a Nash equilibrium cell is, as we mentioned earlier, a subtle one, you will need to remind yourself of this interpretation throughout most of the rest of this chapter.

Because all decisions are mutually best decisions in Nash equilibrium, no single firm can *unilaterally* (by itself) make a different decision and do better. This property or condition of Nash equilibrium is known as **strategic stability,** and it provides the fundamental reason for believing that strategic decision makers will likely decide on a Nash pair of decisions. If they do not choose a Nash equilibrium set of decisions, then at least one of the managers could choose a different action, without any change in other managers' actions, and do better. When a unilateral change in one firm's decision can make that firm better off, strategically thinking managers cannot reasonably believe or predict the actions of a non-Nash cell will be chosen. In a game with two players, for example, only a Nash equilibrium pair of decisions makes strategic sense for *both* managers. As you can now appreciate, the reason strategically astute managers will likely make Nash decisions is a rather subtle line of reasoning. We can now summarize the case for choosing a Nash equilibrium set of actions in a principle.

Nash equilibrium
A set of actions for which all managers are choosing their best actions given the actions chosen by their rivals.

strategic stability
In a Nash equilibrium cell, no decision maker can unilaterally change its decision and improve its individual payoff.

□   **Principle**   Nash decisions are likely to be chosen because Nash sets of decisions are mutually best and, thus, "strategically stable." No firm can do better unilaterally changing its decision. Non-Nash decisions are unlikely to be chosen because at least one firm can do better by unilaterally changing its action.

Even though strategic stability provides a compelling reason for choosing a Nash equilibrium set of decisions, reaching a Nash equilibrium outcome in practice can be difficult and uncertain. In many strategic decisions, there may be two or more mutually best cells in the payoff table. Managers then must choose from a number of different Nash equilibrium decision sets.[3] Generally, it is so difficult to predict how decision makers choose a single Nash equilibrium cell from multiple Nash equilibria that we cannot give you a guideline, or any kind of rule, for making best decisions when you find multiple sets of mutually best decisions. Once again, we must stress that, in many strategic situations, game theory cannot tell you how to make the best decisions. And, even when game theory can provide rules for making best decisions, the rules only tell you the best decision assuming that your rival views the payoff table exactly as you do and that your rival thinks strategically.

Actual decision outcomes can, and often do, differ from the decisions that would seem to be mutually best for firms because managers may calculate payoffs differently or they may not know with certainty the payoffs in every cell of the payoff table. And, of course, one or more of the decision makers may not recognize the subtle strategic logic of making Nash decisions. Unfortunately, we cannot assure you that every manager making strategic decisions has read and understood this chapter. Strategic errors happen.

Super Bowl Advertising: An Example of Nash Equilibrium

To illustrate the "mutually best" nature of a Nash equilibrium outcome, we will now consider Coke and Pepsi's advertising decision for an upcoming Super Bowl game. As you can see from studying the payoff table in Table 13.4, Coke has found a more effective advertising agency than Pepsi: In every cell, Coke's payoff is greater than Pepsi's payoff. The effect on sales and profit of Super Bowl ads lasts about six months, so payoffs in Table 13.4 reflect profits (in millions of dollars) for the first half of the year, since the Super Bowl game will be played in January.

Even with a better advertising agency, however, Coke does not have a dominant strategy: If Pepsi chooses a low budget, Coke's best choice is a low budget; if Pepsi chooses a medium budget, Coke's best choice is a medium budget; and if Pepsi chooses a high budget, Coke's best choice is a high budget. Also notice that each and every one of Coke's budget actions will be the best action for one of Pepsi's decisions, so Coke does not have any *dominated* strategies either.

---

[3]Game theorists have shown that, under rather common circumstances and with a modified concept of equilibrium, all simultaneous decision games have at least one Nash equilibrium strategy set. The nature of these circumstances and the extended definition of Nash equilibrium require more discussion than we wish to undertake in this introductory discussion of strategic decision making.

TABLE 13.4
Super Bowl Advertising: A Unique Nash Equilibrium

		Pepsi's budget		
		Low	Medium	High
Coke's budget	**Low**	A **$60,** *$45*	B **$57.5,** *$50*	C **$45,** *$35*
	Medium	D **$50,** *$35*	E **$65,** *$30*	F **$30,** *$25*
	High	G **$45,** *$10*	H **$60,** *$20*	I **$50,** *$40*

Payoffs in millions of dollars of semiannual profit.

Searching across each row in the payoff table, you can verify that Pepsi's best action for each of Coke's actions is *Medium, Low,* or *High* respectively, as Coke chooses **Low, Medium,** or **High** levels of Super Bowl advertising. Since Pepsi does not have one action that is best no matter what Coke does, Pepsi has no dominant strategy. And, since each and every one of Pepsi's three budget choices will be the best action for one of the decisions Coke can make, Pepsi, like Coke, has no *dominated* strategies. Thus there are no dominant or dominated strategies for either Coke or Pepsi.

After examining each cell in the payoff table in Table 13.4, you can confirm that the only Nash equilibrium pair of actions is cell I (**High,** *High*), where Coke earns $50 million and Pepsi earns $40 million in semiannual profits.[4] Even though this is a mutually best decision for Coke and Pepsi, this unique Nash equilibrium does not provide Coke and Pepsi with the highest possible payoffs. They could both do better than the Nash outcome if they cooperated in making their advertising decisions. In Table 13.4, you can see that Coke and Pepsi could both do better by agreeing to choose low advertising budgets for the Super Bowl. In cell A (**Low,** *Low*), Coke's semiannual profit is $60 million and Pepsi's semiannual profit is $45 million, and both firms are better off than in Nash equilibrium.

Why don't Coke and Pepsi agree to cooperate and choose the decision pair in cell A (**Low,** *Low*), which increases both of their individual profits? You can answer this question quite convincingly by considering the strategic stability property of

[4]Once again, the procedure we discussed earlier for finding dominant and dominated strategies by marking each player's best decisions also identifies Nash equilibrium pairs of actions. For each column in Table 13.4, find the cell that gives Coke's best payoff and pencil a *C* in that cell. For each row, find the cell that gives Pepsi's best payoff and pencil a *P* in that cell. Following this procedure for Table 13.4 results in *C*'s in cells A, E, and I, and *P*'s in cells B, D, and I. Any cell, such as cell I, with *both* a *C* and a *P* in it will be a Nash equilibrium.

Nash equilibrium. In cell A, as in every other cell except the Nash cell (**High,** *High*), either Coke or Pepsi, or in some cells, both firms, could increase their profits by changing advertising levels, *even with no change in the other's level of advertising.* In cell A (**Low,** *Low*), both managers know that if Coke decides to go with **Low,** Pepsi can unilaterally improve its profit by increasing its ad budget from *Low* to *Medium* in cell B. So it would be foolish for Coke to believe that Pepsi will decide on a low budget if Pepsi believes Coke will choose a low budget.

As we explained earlier, neither manager can believe that its prediction about a rival's decision will be correct unless the predicted action is the best action the rival can take given the decision of *its* rival. Only decision pairs that are mutually best decisions result in both managers correctly anticipating their rival's decision. Mutually best decisions will also be mutually correct or believable decisions, and mutually correct or believable decisions will also be mutually best decisions.

The strategic stability of a Nash equilibrium pair of decisions is sufficiently compelling as a means of predicting the decisions that managers will make when faced with simultaneous decisions that game theorists expect most managers will choose the Nash decision cell when there is only *one* Nash cell in the payoff table. When payoff tables contain more than one Nash equilibrium cell, no prediction is possible in general.

Principle   When managers face a simultaneous decision-making situation possessing a unique Nash equilibrium set of decisions, rivals can be expected to make the decisions leading to the Nash equilibrium. If there are multiple Nash equilibria, there is generally no way to predict the likely outcome.

Before leaving our discussion of Nash equilibrium, we need to explain the relation between dominant strategy equilibrium and a Nash equilibrium. In a dominant-strategy equilibrium, both firms are making best decisions *no matter what the rival does.* In a Nash equilibrium, both firms are making the best decisions *given the decision they believe their rivals will make.* Managers believe rivals choose dominant strategies when they have them, and a dominant strategy equilibrium is also a Nash equilibrium: Managers believe rivals will choose their dominant strategies. So all dominant strategy equilibria are also Nash equilibria, but Nash equilibria can, and often do, occur without either dominant or dominated strategies, as we just showed you in the Super Bowl advertising game. You should now be able to show that the dominant strategy equilibrium in the prisoners' dilemma, cell D in Table 13.1, is a Nash equilibrium by verifying that (**Confess,** *Confess*) allows both suspects to do the best they can given the action they predict the other will take.

Relation   All dominant strategy equilibria are also Nash equilibria, but Nash equilibria can occur without either dominant or dominated strategies.

Best-Response Curves and Continuous Decision Choices

Thus far we have assumed that managers face only two or three discrete decision alternatives, with each one represented by a row or column in a payoff table. In

ILLUSTRATION 13.2

Mr. Nash Goes to Hollywood[a]

There's trouble in Hollywood, and big trouble it is. Too many movie stars are becoming members of an elite club that film producers detest. The troublesome club, which some producers have reportedly named the "$25 Million per Movie Club," had just two members in 2000: Mel Gibson and Adam Sandler. The two film producers that paid Gibson and Sandler record-breaking $25 million salaries for single movies, Columbia Pictures and New Line Cinema, wanted to keep this news a secret because, once other producers and actors learn of these deals, many more actors will likely demand and receive entry into "the club." The new benchmark salary for top stars comes at a time when Hollywood's profits are falling sharply. According to market analysts, the primary cause for falling profits in the motion picture industry is soaring costs of production—and actors' salaries make up a large chunk of total production costs. Joe Roth, chairman of Walt Disney Studios, worries that the lack of cooperation in holding the line on salaries "could send the whole thing into chaos," and every big star would gain membership to the $25 Million per Movie Club. And even more worrisome, some producers think a $30 Million per Movie Club might soon open and begin a membership drive.

You might wonder, then, why the four or five largest film studios don't cooperate with one another by holding the line on actors' salaries. After all, film producers don't need to worry that big-name stars will turn down movie roles at the old benchmark of $20 million per film if all producers can agree to pay the same amount for top stars ($20 million per film). Why, then, are all of the Hollywood film producers hiking salaries?

We can answer this question by applying the concept of a prisoners' dilemma to the film makers' salary decision to "hold the line" at $20 million per film or to "hike salaries" to $25 million per film. To keep things simple, suppose that there are only two major film producers in Hollywood, New Line Cinema and Columbia Pictures. The two film producers compete to hire the big-name stars in Hollywood whose names can almost guarantee a film will be hugely profitable. Assume Hollywood has only six such big-name stars. Each studio plans to make six films this year, and each film could use one top star who would be paid either $20 million or $25 million, depending on the salary decision made by each studio. Furthermore, assume producers can make their films and earn their entire theater and video revenues in the same year. New Line and Columbia make their salary decisions without knowing the other's decision at the time they make their own decision, so that the situation represents a simultaneous strategic decision.

The payoff table on the next page shows the profit outcomes for each studio for the various decision situations. In cell A, both film producers stick to a $20 million benchmark and end up splitting the talent pool of six top stars: Columbia and New Line each lands three of the six big-name stars. They do not plan to cooperate in splitting the stars equally; they just *expect* to get equal shares of the total number when they both pay the same salary. By keeping costs "low" and sharing equally the biggest stars, each studio expects to make $100 million of total profit on its six films this year. In cell D, the producers each decide to hike salaries to $25 million per film and expect to share equally the big stars. Annual profits are just $85 million each because production costs rise by $15 million (= 3 top stars × $5 million salary hike) for each filmmaker.

best-response curve
A curve indicating the best decision (usually the profit-maximizing one) given the decision the manager believes a rival will make.

many decisions, actions or strategies are continuous decision variables. (Recall the discussion in Chapter 3 of continuous and discrete decision variables.) When managers make pricing decisions, they seldom view the choices as being either "low" or "high" prices. Instead they choose the best price from a continuous range of prices. Economists have developed a tool, called *best-response curves*, to analyze and explain simultaneous decisions when decision choices are continuous rather than discrete. A firm's **best-response curve** indicates the best decision to make

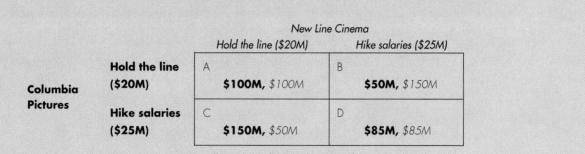

Payoffs in millions of dollars of annual profit.

Cells B and C show payoffs when one studio "holds the line" and the other "hikes salaries." The studio hiking salaries expects to attract all six of the top stars, while the studio that holds the line at $20 million per film cannot expect to attract any of the six top stars and will have to hire less-profitable actors. The payoffs in cells B and C reflect the advantage to one studio of getting all the stars ($150 million annual profit) and the disadvantage to the other studio of getting none of the stars ($50 million annual profit).

As we explained in our discussion of prisoners' dilemma games, both Columbia and New Line have dominant strategies: hike salaries. Dominant strategy equilibrium occurs in cell D, which is also strategically stable and is the only Nash equilibrium cell in this strategic game. Notice that when both studios choose their dominant strategies in cell D, they both do worse than they could if they both would decide to hold the line on salaries in cell A. Cell A, however, is not strategically stable because both film studios can unilaterally increase their profits by hiking salaries *if they believe the other studio will hold the line on salaries.* And, as we have stressed throughout this chapter, rational decision makers do not believe it is correct to predict rivals will do anything other than what is best for themselves. Since, in cell A, both film studios are not doing best for themselves given the expected choice of the other studios, cell A would not be chosen by rational decision makers.

The prisoners' dilemma model of making salary decisions provides a rather convincing explanation of what might otherwise seem like an irrational situation in Hollywood: Filmmakers are losing money because of rising production costs, but the film producers continue to hike salaries of top stars. While we cannot confirm the truth of this rumor, we have heard from reliable sources that the secret toast of Hollywood's most highly paid stars is "All hail to Mr. Nash." Film producers have been overheard using a slight variation of this salute.

[a]This illustration is based on Tom King, "Hollywood Raises Salaries Past the $20-Million Mark," *The Wall Street Journal*, Jan. 7, 2000.

(usually the profit-maximizing one) based on, or accounting for, the decision the firm expects its rival will make.

To illustrate the concept of best-response curves, we use an example of two oligopoly airlines that compete with each other through pricing, although we could have chosen an example of output, advertising, product quality, or any other form of nonprice competition. The two airlines, Arrow Airlines and Bravo Airways, are the only airlines offering service to customers traveling between Lincoln,

Nebraska, and Colorado Springs, Colorado. Managers at Arrow and Bravo are planning to set their round-trip coach ticket prices for travel during an upcoming four-day period of peak travel demand around Christmas. When prices are set, neither manager will know the price set by the other, so the decision is a simultaneous one.

Product differentiation exists between the two airlines because Arrow has newer, more comfortable jets than Bravo. The following demand functions for Arrow and Bravo are both known to both airline managers (airline demand, then, is common knowledge):

$$Q_A = 4,000 - 25P_A + 12P_B$$
$$Q_B = 3,000 - 20P_B + 10P_A$$

where Q_A and Q_B are the total number of round-trip tickets sold and P_A and P_B are the prices charged, respectively, by Arrow and Bravo airlines over the four-day Christmas holiday travel period.

As it turns out, the managers make their pricing decisions several months before Christmas—but they won't be able to change their prices once they are chosen—and thus all of their costs during the Christmas season are variable costs at the time of the pricing decision. To keep matters simple, we will assume long-run costs are constant for airlines—so that marginal costs and average costs are equal—even though we know that airlines don't really experience constant costs.[5] Because Arrow uses newer, more fuel-efficient planes than Bravo, Arrow has lower costs than Bravo:

$$LAC_A = LMC_A = \$160$$
$$LAC_B = LMC_B = \$180$$

Arrow incurs, on average, a cost of $160 per round-trip passenger, which is also Arrow's marginal cost of an extra round-trip passenger. Bravo, with its older planes, faces higher average and marginal costs of $180 per round-trip passenger.

To facilitate making simultaneous pricing decisions, each airline needs to know the best price for it to charge for any price it might expect its rival to charge. To fully account for their interdependence when making simultaneous pricing decisions, both managers need to know *both* their own best-response curve as well as the best-response curve of their rival. Managers must have knowledge of both their own and their rival's demand and cost conditions in order to construct their best-response curves. We will now show you how Arrow can construct its best-response curve, which is a straight line in this example.

---

[5]Carrying one more passenger on a plane requires very little extra fuel and peanuts, so marginal cost is much lower than average cost; indeed marginal cost is virtually zero for additional passengers sitting in otherwise empty seats. Since *LMC* is less than *LAC,* long-run average cost for airlines falls as the number of passengers increases. While allowing average costs to decrease would be more realistic in this airline example, it would only complicate the graphical analysis yet add nothing to your understanding of response curve analysis.

Suppose Arrow believes Bravo will set a price of $100. The demand facing Arrow is found by substituting Bravo's price of $100 into Arrow's demand:

$$Q_A = 4,000 - 25P_A + 12 \times \$100 = 5,200 - 25P_A$$

Following the steps set forth in Chapter 12 (Section 12.7), Arrow's manager can derive the following inverse demand and marginal revenue functions for Arrow:

$$P_A = 208 - 0.04Q_A$$

and

$$MR_A = 208 - 0.08Q_A$$

Then, setting $MR_A = LMC_A$, the manager finds that Arrow's profit-maximizing output when Bravo charges $100 is 600 round-trip tickets:

$$208 - 0.08Q_A = 160$$

and

$$Q_A^* = 600$$

The best price for Arrow to charge when it thinks Bravo is going to charge $100 is found by substituting $Q^*_A = 600$ into the inverse demand, and this price is $184 (= 208 − 0.04 × 600).

This process for finding Arrow's best price when Bravo charges $100, which is illustrated by point r in Panel A of Figure 13.1, locates only *one* point (point R) on the best-response curve for Arrow Airlines shown in Panel B. By repeating the process for all other prices that Bravo might be expected to charge, Arrow can construct a complete best-response curve. For any price that Bravo might set, Arrow's best-response curve, shown as BR_A in Panel B, gives the price that Arrow should set to maximize Arrow's profit.

You might be concerned, and quite reasonably so, that constructing a best-response curve requires far too much computational effort since the process just discussed, and illustrated in Panel A, must be repeated for *every* price Bravo might choose. Best-response curves, however, are rather easily constructed when demand and marginal cost curves are both linear, as they are in this example, because the best-response curves will be straight lines.[6] Arrow's manager only needs to find best prices for *two* of the prices Bravo might set. A straight line passing through these two points will then produce Arrow's entire best-response curve.

To see how this works, suppose now that Bravo is expected to set a price of $200 instead of $100. You can verify for yourself that Arrow's best-response is to set a price of $208. After plotting this best-response point in Panel B, shown there as point S, a straight line passing through points R and S produces Arrow's best-response curve BR_A.

Figure 13.2 shows the best-response curves for both Arrow Airlines and Bravo Airways. Managers at both airlines are likely to set prices at the intersection of the

---

[6]When demand or marginal cost curves, or both, are not linear, calculus can be used to derive mathematical equations for best-response curves. In the appendix to this chapter, we show you how to derive best-response curves using calculus.

FIGURE 13.1

Deriving the Best-Response
Curve for Arrow Airlines

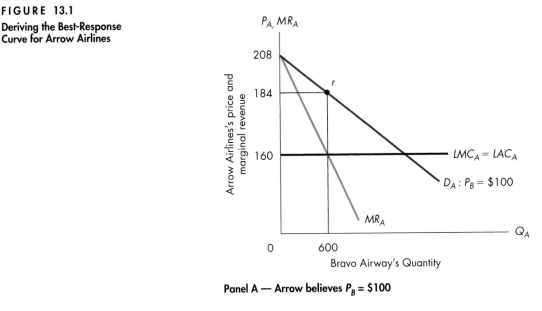

Panel A — Arrow believes P_B = $100

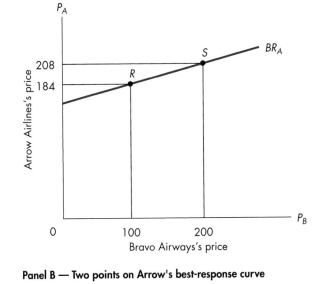

Panel B — Two points on Arrow's best-response curve

best-response curves because, at the point of intersection, mutually best prices result. At point N, Arrow's price of $212 maximizes Arrow's profit if Bravo sets its price at $218. Bravo's price of $218 maximizes Bravo's profit if Arrow sets its price at $212. At point N, neither airline can increase its individual profit by unilaterally changing its own price. Point N is strategically stable, and the pair of prices is a Nash equilibrium.

FIGURE 13.2

Best-Response Curves and Nash Equilibrium

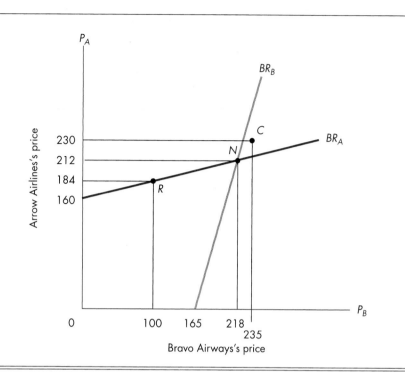

When both airlines price at the Nash point for the Christmas holiday, Arrow sells 1,316 round-trip tickets, and Bravo sells 760 tickets:

$$Q_A = 4{,}000 - (25 \times 212) + (12 \times 218) = 1{,}316$$
$$Q_B = 3{,}000 - (20 \times 218) + (10 \times 212) = 760$$

At the Nash prices, Arrow Airlines earns profit of $68,432 [= (212 − 160) × 1,316], and Bravo can expect to earn profit of $28,880 [= (218 − 180) × 760].

Once again, we want to emphasize that the Nash equilibrium at point *N* is not chosen because the managers are coordinating their pricing in a cooperative way. The prices at point *N* are chosen because both managers, keenly aware of their interdependence, know that they cannot do the best for themselves individually unless they correctly anticipate the price the other will set. Beliefs about what rivals will charge can only be correct if rivals are also setting their best prices.

While the prices at point *N* allow each one of the airlines to do the best it can given the price set by its rival, this does *not* mean that no other price pair is better for both airlines. Actually, point *N* in Figure 13.2 may well be similar to cell D in the prisoners' dilemma. Neither firm is making as much profit as would be possible if both firms *cooperated* and both set higher prices.

To confirm that Arrow and Bravo could both make more profit if they cooperated in setting higher prices, we will let you verify that point *C* in Figure 13.2, where Arrow's price is $230 and Bravo's price is $235, is a more profitable pair of prices for *both* airlines. Point *C* is not unique. There are many other price pairs that can increase both firms' profits. The airlines don't end up with one of these better combinations of prices because such price pairs are not strategically stable when firms behave noncooperatively. Neither airline can prevent the other from cheating on a cooperative agreement to set prices at point *C*. Both airlines have an incentive to cheat on an agreement to set their prices at point *C* because both airlines can increase their individual profits by unilaterally lowering their own prices.

As we will show you later in this chapter, this is exactly why managers seldom succeed at colluding to set high prices. Unilateral cheating by either firm's secretly lowering its price will increase the profit of the cheating firm—unless, as you will see later, all firms cheat. Once again, you can see the crucial role that interdependence plays in making pricing decisions in oligopoly markets. We can now summarize this section with a principle.

Principle When decision choices are continuous, best-response curves give managers the profit-maximizing price to set given the price they anticipate their rival will set. A Nash equilibrium occurs at the price pair where the firms' best-response curves intersect.

13.2 STRATEGY WHEN RIVALS MAKE SEQUENTIAL DECISIONS

sequential decisions
A decision in which one firm makes its decision first, then a rival firm makes its decision.

In contrast to simultaneous decisions, the natural process of some decisions requires one firm to make a decision, and then a rival firm, *knowing the action taken by the first firm*, makes its decision. Such decisions are called **sequential decisions.** For example, a potential entrant into a market will make its decision to enter or stay out of a market first, and then the incumbent firm or firms respond to the entry decision by adjusting prices and outputs to maximize profit given the decision of the potential entrant. In another common kind of sequential decision, one firm makes its pricing, output, or advertising decision ahead of another. The firm making its decision second knows the decision of the first firm. As we will show you in this section, the order of decision making can sometimes, but not always, create an advantage to going first or going second when making sequential decisions.

Even though they are made at different times, sequential decisions nonetheless involve strategic interdependence. Sequential decisions are linked over time: The best decision a manager can make today depends on how rivals will respond tomorrow. Strategically astute managers, then, must think ahead to anticipate their rivals' future decisions. Current decisions are based on what managers believe rivals will likely do in the future. You might say a manager jumps ahead in time and then thinks backward to the present. Making sequential decisions, like making simultaneous decisions, involves getting into the heads of rivals to predict their decisions so that you can make better decisions for yourself. Once again, oligopoly decisions involve strategic interdependence.

game tree
A diagram showing the structure and payoff of a sequential decision situation.

Making Sequential Decisions

Sequential decisions can be analyzed using payoff tables, but an easier method, which we will employ here, involves the use of *game trees.* A **game tree** is a diagram

decision nodes
Points in a game tree, represented by boxes, where decisions are made.

showing firms' decisions as **decision nodes** with branches extending from the nodes, one for each action that can be taken at the node. The sequence of decisions usually proceeds from left to right along branches until final payoffs associated with each decision path are reached. Game trees are fairly easy to understand when you have one to look at, so let's look at an example now. Suppose that the pizza pricing decision in Table 13.2 is now a sequential decision. Castle Pizza makes its pricing decision first at decision node 1, and then Palace Pizza makes its pricing decision second at one of the two decision nodes labeled with 2's. Panel A in Figure 13.3 shows the game tree representing the sequential decision.

Castle goes first in this example, as indicated by the leftmost position of decision node 1. Castle can choose either a high price along the top branch or a low price along the bottom branch. Next, Palace makes its decision to go high or low. Since Palace goes second, it knows the pricing decision of Castle. Castle's decision, then, requires two decision nodes, each one labeled 2: one for Palace's decision if Castle prices high and one for Palace's decision if Castle prices low. Payoffs for the four possible decision outcomes are shown at the end of Palace's decision branches. Notice that the payoffs match those shown in the payoff table of Table 13.2.

Castle decides first, so it doesn't know Palace's price when it makes its pricing decision. How should the manager of Castle pizza make its pricing decision? As in simultaneous decisions, the manager of Castle tries to anticipate Palace's decision by assuming Palace will take the action giving Palace the highest payoff. So Castle's manager looks ahead and puts itself in Palace's place: "If I price high, Palace receives its best payoff by pricing low: $1,200 is better than $1,000 for Palace. If I price low, Palace receives its best payoff by pricing low: $400 is better than $300." In this situation, since Palace chooses low no matter what Castle chooses, Palace has a dominant strategy: price low. Panel B in Figure 13.3 shows Palace's best decisions as light-colored branches.

Knowing that Palace's dominant strategy is low, Castle predicts Palace will price low for either decision Castle might make. Castle's manager, then, should choose to price high and earn $500 because $500 is better than pricing low and earning $400. This process of looking ahead to future decisions to make the best current decision is called the *backward induction technique* or, more simply, the **roll-back method** of making sequential decisions.

roll-back method
Method of finding a Nash solution to a sequential decision by looking ahead to future decisions to reason back to the best current decision. (Also known as backward induction.)

Notice that the roll-back solution to a sequential decision is a Nash equilibrium: Castle earns the highest payoff, given the (best) decision it predicts Palace will make, and Palace is making its best decision given the (best) decision Castle makes. We must stress, however, that Palace, by making its decision last, does not need to *anticipate* or *predict* Castle's decision; Castle's decision is known with certainty when Palace chooses its price. The complete roll-back solution to the pizza pricing decision, also referred to as the *equilibrium decision path,* is indicated in Panel B by the unbroken sequence of light-colored branches on which arrowheads have been attached: Castle **High,** Palace *Low.* Furthermore, the roll-back equilibrium decision path is unique—a game tree contains only one such path—because in moving backward through the game, roll back requires that the *single* best

FIGURE 13.3
Sequential Pizza Pricing

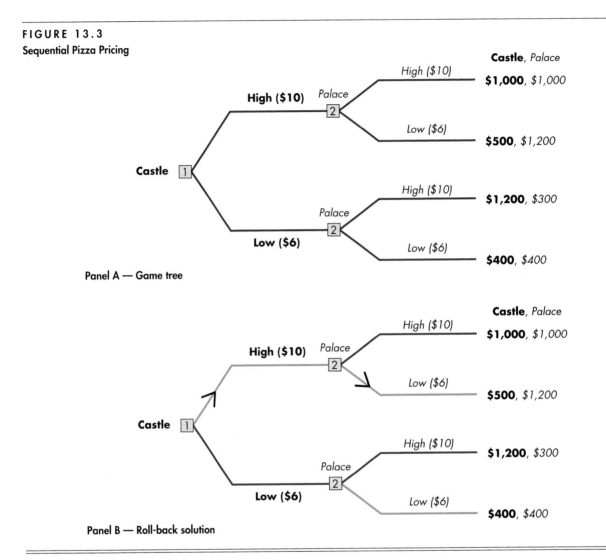

Panel A — Game tree

Panel B — Roll-back solution

decision be chosen at each node of the game.[7] We summarize our discussion of this important concept with a principle.

▣   **Principle**   When firms make sequential decisions, managers make best decisions for themselves by working backward through the game tree using the roll-back method. The roll-back method results in a unique path that is also a Nash decision path: Each firm does the best for itself given the best decisions made by its rivals.

---

[7]Game theorists refer to the Nash equilibrium path found by implementing the roll-back method as a *subgame–perfect equilibrium path* because best decisions are made at every node or "subgame" in the game tree.

First-Mover and Second-Mover Advantages

As you might have already guessed, the outcome of sequential decisions may depend on which firm makes its decision first and which firm goes second. Sometimes you can increase your payoff by making your decision first in order to influence later decisions made by rivals. Letting rivals know with certainty what you are doing—going first usually, but not always, does this—increases your payoff if rivals then choose actions more favorable to you. In such situations, a **first-mover advantage** can be secured by making the first move or taking the first action in a sequential decision situation.

In other situations, firms may earn higher payoffs by letting rivals make the first move, committing themselves to a course of action and making that action known to firms making later decisions. When higher payoffs can be earned by reacting to earlier decisions made by rivals, the firm going second in a sequential decision enjoys a **second-mover advantage.**

How can you tell whether a sequential decision has a first-mover advantage, a second-mover advantage, or neither type of advantage (the order of decision making doesn't matter either way)? The simplest way, and frequently the only way, is to find the roll-back solution for both sequences. If the payoff increases by being the first-mover, a first-mover advantage exists. If the payoff increases by being the second-mover, a second-mover advantage exists. If the payoffs are unchanged by reversing the order of moves, then, of course, the order doesn't matter. We now illustrate a decision for which a first-mover advantage exists.

Suppose the Brazilian government awards two firms, Motorola and Sony, the exclusive rights to share the market for cellular phone service in Brazil. Motorola and Sony are allowed to service as many customers in Brazil as they wish, but the government sets a ceiling price for cellular service at $800 annually per customer. The two companies know that each plans to charge the maximum price allowed, $800.

Motorola and Sony can both provide either *analog* or *digital* cellular phones. Motorola, however, has a cost advantage in analog technology, and Sony has a cost advantage in digital technology. Their annual costs per customer, which remain constant for any number of customers served, are as follows:

	Motorola	Sony
Annual cost of analog service	$250	$400
Annual cost of digital service	$350	$325

Demand forecasters at Motorola and Sony work together to estimate the total demand for cellular phone service in Brazil. They discover that Brazilians do not care which technology they buy, but total sales will suffer if Motorola and Sony do not agree to offer the *same* technology. The desire to have a single technology arises because the two technologies will probably not be compatible: Analog customers and digital customers will not be able to communicate. (Motorola and Sony can solve the compatibility problem, but it will take several years to solve the problem.) Demand estimates show that, at a price of $800 per year, a total of 50,000

first-mover advantage
A firm can increase its payoff by making its decision first.

second-mover advantage
A firm can increase its payoff by making its decision second.

FIGURE 13.4
First-Mover Advantage in Technology Choice

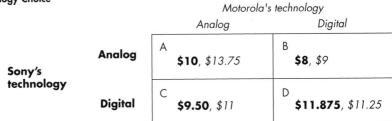

		Motorola's technology	
		Analog	Digital
Sony's technology	**Analog**	A $10, $13.75	B $8, $9
	Digital	C $9.50, $11	D $11.875, $11.25

Payoffs in millions of dollars of profit annually

Panel A — Simultaneous technology decision

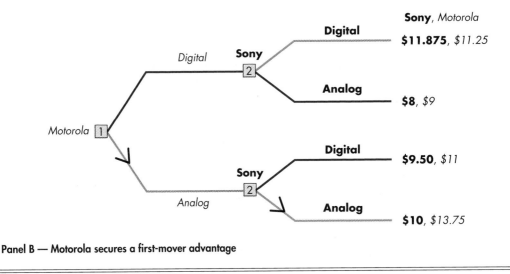

Panel B — Motorola secures a first-mover advantage

Brazilians will sign up for cell phone service if Motorola and Sony provide the same technology, but only 40,000 will sign up at $800 per year if the two firms offer different technologies. Motorola and Sony expect that sales will be evenly divided between them: 25,000 customers each if the same technologies are chosen or 20,000 customers each if they choose different technologies.

You can see from the payoff table in Figure 13.4 that Motorola and Sony both make greater profit if they choose the same technologies than if they choose opposite technologies: Cells A and D are both better than either cell C or B. If the technology decision is made simultaneously, *both* cells A and D are Nash equilibrium cells, and game theory provides no clear way to predict the outcome. Motorola, of course, would like to end up in cell A since it has a cost advantage in analog technology and will sell more analog phone service if Sony also chooses analog. How can Motorola entice Sony to choose analog technology so that the outcome is cell A?

The clever manager at Motorola sees that, if Motorola chooses its (analog) technology first, cell A is the predicted outcome. To see why cell A is the likely outcome, we turn to Panel B, which shows the game tree when Motorola goes first. To find the solution to this sequential game, Motorola's manager applies the roll-back method. First, the manager finds Sony's best decisions at Sony's two decision nodes. At the decision node where Motorola chooses *Digital,* Sony's best decision is **Digital,** which is the outcome in cell D. At the decision node where Motorola chooses *Analog,* Sony's best decision is **Analog,** which is the outcome in cell A. Then, rolling back to Motorola's decision, Motorola knows that if it chooses *Digital,* then it will end up with $11.25 million when Sony makes its best decision, which is to go **Digital.** If Motorola chooses *analog,* then it will end up with $13.75 million when Sony makes its best decision, which is to go **Analog.** Roll-back analysis indicates Motorola does best, given the choice Sony will later make, by choosing *Analog.* This Nash equilibrium path is shown in Panel B as the light-colored branches with arrows.

To have a first-mover advantage, Motorola must receive a higher payoff when it goes first compared with its payoff when it goes second. In this game, Motorola does indeed experience a first-mover advantage because roll-back analysis shows that Motorola earns only $11.25 million when Sony goes first. (You will verify this in Technical Problem 13.) Thus Motorola gains a first-mover advantage in this game of choosing cellular phone technology. We summarize our discussion of first-mover and second-mover advantage with a relation.

Relation   To determine whether the order of decision making can confer an advantage when firms make sequential decisions, the roll-back method can be applied to the game trees for each possible sequence of decisions. If the payoff increases by being the first (second) to move, then a first-mover (second-mover) advantage exists. If the payoffs are identical, then order of play confers no advantage.

As you probably noticed, we did not discuss here *how* Motorola gains the first-mover position in this game of choosing cellular phone technology. Determining which firm goes first (or second) can be quite complex, and difficult to predict, when both firms recognize that going first (or second) confers a first-mover (or second-mover) advantage. We will now examine several strategic moves that firms might employ to alter the structure of a game to their advantage.

Strategic Moves: Commitments, Threats, and Promises

As we have emphasized, strategic decision making requires you to get into the heads of your rivals to anticipate their reactions to your decisions. We now want to take you a step beyond *anticipating* your rivals' reactions to taking actions to *manipulate* your rivals' reactions. We will now examine three kinds of actions managers can take to achieve better outcomes for themselves, usually to the detriment of their rivals. These strategic actions, which game theorists refer to as **strategic moves,** are called *commitments, threats,* and *promises.*

These three strategic moves, which, in most cases, must be made before rivals have made their decisions, may be utilized separately or in combination with each

strategic moves
Three kinds of actions that can be used to put rivals at a disadvantage: commitments, threats, or promises.

credible
A strategic move that will be carried out because it is in the best interest of the firm making the move to carry it out.

commitments
Unconditional actions taken for the purpose of increasing payoffs to the committing firms.

other. Strategic moves will achieve their desired effects only if rivals think the firms making the moves will actually carry out their commitments, threats, or promises. Rivals will ignore strategic moves that are not *credible*. A strategic move is **credible** if, when a firm is called upon to act on the strategic move, it is in the best interest of the firm making the move to carry it out. Making strategic moves credible is not easy, and we cannot give you any specific rules that will work in every situation. We will, however, provide you with the basic ideas for making credible strategic moves in the discussions that follow.[8] We first discuss commitments, which are unconditional strategic moves, and then we turn to threats and promises, which are conditional moves.

Managers make **commitments** by announcing, or demonstrating to rivals in some other way, that they will bind themselves to take a particular action or make a specific decision *no matter what action or decision is taken by its rivals*. Commitments, then, are unconditional actions the committing firms undertake for the purpose of increasing their payoffs. A commitment only works if rivals believe the committing firm has genuinely locked itself into a specific decision or course of action. In other words, commitments, like all strategic moves, must be credible in order to have strategic value.

Generally, a firm's commitment will not be credible unless it is *irreversible*. If some other decision later becomes the best decision for the committing firm, rivals will expect the committing firm to abandon its commitment if it can. Rivals will believe a commitment is irreversible only if it would be prohibitively costly, or even impossible, for the committing firm to reverse its action. In short, only *credible* commitments—those that are irreversible—successfully alter rivals' beliefs about the actions the committing firm will take.

To illustrate how credible commitments can improve profitability, suppose that Motorola and Sony make their choices between analog and digital technologies *simultaneously* according to the payoff table shown in Panel A of Figure 13.4. The outcome of the simultaneous game is difficult for either firm to predict since there are *two* Nash equilibrium cells, A and D. The manager of Motorola, however, decides to make a commitment to analog technology *before* the simultaneous decision takes place by building a facility in Brazil specifically designed for manufacturing and servicing *only* analog phones. Both firms know that the cost of converting Motorola's new plant to production of digital cellular phones is enormous. Consequently, Motorola is unlikely to incur the huge costs of converting to digital technology, so Sony views Motorola's action as irreversible. Thus Motorola's strategic move is a *credible* commitment because Sony believes Motorola's action is irreversible.

---

[8]To get a more thorough and richer development of the practical application of strategic moves to business decision making than is possible in one or two chapters of a textbook, we recommend you read two of our favorite books on the subject: Avinash Dixit and Barry Nalebuff, *Thinking Strategically: The Competitive Edge in Business, Politics, and Everyday Life* (New York: W. W. Norton, 1991); and John MacMillan, *Games, Strategies, and Managers* (New York: Oxford University Press, 1992).

Notice that Motorola's commitment transforms the *simultaneous* decision situation in Panel A into the *sequential* decision situation shown in Panel B. Motorola, through its use of credible commitment, seizes the first-mover advantage and ensures itself the outcome in cell A. We have now established the following principle.

▣ **Principle** Firms make credible commitments by taking unconditional, irreversible actions. Credible commitments give committing firms the first moves in sequential games, and by taking the first actions, committing firms manipulate later decisions their rivals will make in a way that improves their own profitability.

threats
Conditional strategic moves that take the form: "If you do A, I will do B, which is costly to you."

In contrast to commitments, which are unconditional in nature, threats and promises are *conditional* decisions or actions. **Threats,** whether they are made explicitly or tacitly, take the form of a conditional statement, "If you take action *A*, I will take action *B*, which is undesirable or costly to you." The purpose of making threats is to manipulate rivals' beliefs about the likely behavior of the threatening firms in a way that increases payoffs to the threatening firms. For example, firms that are already producing a product or service in a market and earning profits there may try to deter new firms from entering the profitable market by threatening, "If you enter this market, I will then lower my price to make the market unprofitable for you."

Threats do not always succeed in altering the decisions of rivals. In order for threats to be successful in changing rivals' behavior, rivals must believe the threat will actually be carried out. Following our discussion about credible strategic moves, a threat is credible if, when the firm is called upon to act on the threat, it is in the best interest of the firm making the threat to carry it out.

Consider again the simultaneous technology decision in Panel A of Figure 13.4. Suppose, before the simultaneous decisions are made, Motorola threatens Sony by saying to Sony, "If you choose digital technology for your cellular phones, we will choose analog." In making this threat, Motorola wants Sony to think, "Since Motorola is going to go analog if we choose digital, then we might as well choose analog since cell A is better for us than cell C." Motorola's threat, however, will fail to produce this thinking by Sony. Instead of this reasoning, it is much more likely that Sony will think, "Motorola's threat is not credible: if we choose digital, Motorola's best decision is to choose digital, and so Motorola will not carry out its threat." As you can see, Motorola's threat is ignored and, consequently, has no strategic value. Once again, only credible strategic moves matter.

promises
Conditional strategic moves that take the form: "If you do A, I will do B, which is desirable to you."

Promises, like threats, are also conditional statements that must be credible to affect strategic decisions. Promises take the form of a conditional statement, "If you take action *A*, I will take action *B*, which is desirable or rewarding to you." For example, one rival may promise other rivals that if they do not add to their product some costly improvement that consumers desire, it will not add the costly improvement to its product either. Promises, just like commitments and threats, must be credible in order to affect the decisions of rivals. We summarize our discussion of strategic moves—commitments, threats, and promises—in a principle.

⊡   **Principle**   *Managers make strategic moves to manipulate their rivals' decisions for the purpose of increasing their own profits by putting rivals at a strategic disadvantage. Only credible strategic moves matter; rivals ignore any commitments, threats, or promises that will not be carried out should the opportunity to do so arise.*

We cannot overstate the value of learning to utilize strategic moves in decision making. Stories in the business press about "smart" or "successful" managers quite often are stories about how managers have utilized credible commitments, threats, or promises to secure more profitable outcomes. We will now discuss one of the most important types of strategic moves: moves that deter new rivals from entering markets where economic profits are being earned.

13.3 COOPERATION IN REPEATED STRATEGIC DECISIONS

cooperation
When firms make decisions that make every firm better off than in a noncooperative Nash equilibrium.

As you know, oligopolists pursuing their individual gains can, and often do, end up worse off than if they were to cooperate. The situation is analogous to dividing a pie. People are struggling to get a larger share of a pie, but in the struggle some of the pie gets knocked off the table and onto the floor, and they end up sharing a smaller pie. A solution preferred by all participants exists but is difficult to achieve. And, even if the preferred situation is somehow reached, such as the results in cell A in the prisoners' dilemma (Table 13.1) or point C in the airline example (Figure 13.2), rivals have a strong incentive to change their actions, which leads back to the noncooperative Nash equilibrium: cell D in the prisoners' dilemma or point N in the airline example. **Cooperation** occurs, then, when oligopoly firms make individual decisions that make every firm better off than they would be in a noncooperative Nash equilibrium outcome.

repeated decisions
Decisions made over and over again by the same firms.

As we have now established, when prisoners' dilemma decisions are made just one time, managers have almost no chance of achieving cooperative outcomes. In many instances, however, decisions concerning pricing, output, advertising, entry, and other such strategic decisions are made repeatedly. Decisions made over and over again by the same firms are called **repeated decisions**. Repeating a strategic decision provides managers with something they do not get in one-time decisions: a chance to punish cheaters. The opportunity to punish cheating in repeated decisions can completely change the outcome of strategic decisions.

One-Time Prisoners' Dilemma Decisions

Prisoners' dilemma scenarios, as we explained previously, always possess a set of decisions for which every firm earns a higher payoff than they can when they each choose to follow their dominant strategies and end up in the noncooperative Nash equilibrium.[9] Cooperation is possible, then, in all prisoners' dilemma decisions.

---

[9]To keep things simple, we continue to restrict our discussion to decisions having only one Nash equilibrium. Game theorists so far have been unable to provide much useful guidance for decisions possessing multiple Nash equilibria.

TABLE 13.5
A Pricing Dilemma for AMD and Intel

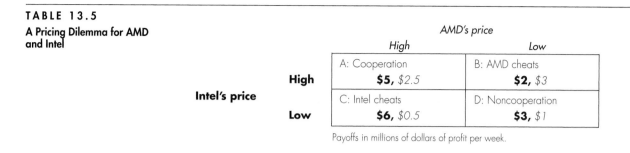

		AMD's price	
		High	Low
Intel's price	**High**	A: Cooperation **$5,** $2.5	B: AMD cheats **$2,** $3
	Low	C: Intel cheats **$6,** $0.5	D: Noncooperation **$3,** $1

Payoffs in millions of dollars of profit per week.

cheating
When a manager makes a noncooperative decision.

Cooperation does not happen in one-time prisoners' dilemma situations because cooperative decisions are strategically unstable. If a firm believes its rivals are going to choose the cooperative decision in a simultaneous decision, then the firm can increase its profit by choosing the noncooperative decision. For convenience in discussions concerning cooperation, game theorists call making noncooperative decisions **cheating.** We must stress, however, that "cheating" does not imply that the oligopoly firms have made any kind of explicit, or even tacit, agreement to cooperate. If a firm's rivals expect that firm to make a cooperative decision, they will have an incentive to cheat by making a noncooperative decision. All oligopoly managers know this and so choose not to cooperate. While the incentive to cheat makes cooperation a strategically unstable outcome in a one-time simultaneous decision, cooperation may arise when decisions are repeated.

We can best illustrate the possibility of cooperation, as well as the profit incentive for cheating, with an example of a pricing dilemma. Suppose two firms, Intel and Advanced Micro Devices (AMD), dominate the wholesale market for high-speed microprocessor chips for personal computers. Intel and AMD simultaneously set their chip prices. For now, let us consider this a one-time simultaneous pricing decision, and the prices set by the firms will be valid for a period of one week. (In the next section, we will reconsider this decision when it is repeated every week.) Table 13.5 shows the profit payoffs from setting either high or low prices for high-speed computer chips. You can verify from the payoff table that a prisoners' dilemma situation exists.

When the semiconductor chip prices are set noncooperatively, as they will be when the pricing decision is made only once, both firms will choose to set low prices and end up in cell D. Setting a low price for computer chips is the dominant strategy for both firms and this leads to the noncooperative Nash equilibrium outcome (cell D). As in every prisoners' dilemma game, both firms can do better by cooperating rather than by choosing their dominant strategy–Nash equilibrium actions. Intel and AMD both can choose high prices for their chips and both can then earn greater profits in cell *A* than in the noncooperative cell D: Intel earns an additional $2 million ($5 million − $3 million) and AMD earns an additional $1.5 million ($2.5 million − $1 million) through cooperation.

The problem with cooperation, as we have stressed previously, is that the decisions Intel and AMD must make to get to cell A are not strategically stable. Both firms worry that the other will cheat if one of them decides to cooperate and price high. For example, if AMD expects Intel is going to cooperate and set a high price, AMD does better by cheating and setting a low price in cell B: AMD earns $0.5 million more ($3 million − $2.5 million) by cheating than by making the cooperative decision to price high. Similarly, Intel can cheat on AMD in cell C and earn $1 million more ($6 million − $5 million) by cheating than by cooperating.

Suppose the managers at AMD and Intel tell each other that they will set high prices. This is, of course, farfetched since such a conversation is illegal. We are only trying to explain here why such an agreement would not work to achieve cooperation, so we can go ahead with our examination of this hypothetical scenario anyway. If the simultaneous pricing decision is to be made just once, neither firm can believe the other will live up to the agreement. Let us get into the head of AMD's manager to see what she thinks about setting AMD's price high. If AMD cooperates and prices high, it dawns on her that Intel has a good reason to cheat: Intel does better by cheating ($1 million better in cell C than in cell A) when Intel believes AMD will honor the agreement. And furthermore, she thinks, "What's the cost to Intel for cheating?" She won't know if Intel cheated until after they have both set their prices (the prices are set simultaneously). At that point, Intel's manager could care less if he ruins his reputation with her; it's a one-time decision and the game is over. Any hope of reaching a cooperative outcome vanishes when she realizes that Intel's manager must be thinking precisely the same things about her incentive to cheat. There is no way he is going to trust her not to cheat, so she *expects* him to cheat. The best she can do when he cheats is to cheat as well. And so an opportunity to achieve cooperation collapses over worries about cheating.

Even though cooperation is possible in all prisoners' dilemma situations, oligopoly firms have compelling reasons to believe rivals will cheat when the decision is to be made only one time. In these one-time decisions, there is no practical way for firms to make their rivals believe they will not cheat. When there is no tomorrow in decision making, rivals know they have only one chance to get the most for themselves. A decision to cheat seems to be costless to the cheating firm because it expects its rival to cheat no matter what it decides to do. Furthermore, firms don't have to worry about any future costs from their decisions to cheat since they are making one-time decisions. Our discussion of decision making in one-time prisoners' dilemmas establishes the following principle.

Principle Cooperation is possible in every prisoners' dilemma decision, but cooperation is not strategically stable when the decision is made only once. In one-time prisoners' dilemmas, there can be no future consequences from cheating, so both firms *expect* the other to cheat, which then makes cheating the best response for each firm.

Punishment for Cheating in Repeated Decisions

Punishment for cheating, which cannot be done in a one-time decision, makes cheating costly in repeated decisions. Legal sanctions or monetary fines for cheating

punishment for cheating
Making a retaliatory decision that forces rivals to return to a noncooperative Nash outcome.

are generally illegal in most countries; **punishment for cheating** usually takes the form of a retaliatory decision by the firm doing the punishment that returns the game to a noncooperative Nash decision—the decision everyone wanted to avoid through cooperation.

To illustrate how retaliatory decisions can punish rivals for noncooperative behavior, suppose that AMD and Intel make their pricing decisions repeatedly. AMD and Intel list their wholesale computer chip prices on the Internet every Monday morning, and the managers expect this to go on forever.[10] Table 13.5 shows the weekly payoffs for the repeated pricing decisions, and these payoffs are not expected to change from week to week in this hypothetical example. Further suppose that AMD and Intel have been making, up until now, cooperative weekly pricing decisions in cell A. Now, in the current week—call this week 1—AMD's manager decides to cheat by setting a low price. Thus during week 1, Intel and AMD receive the profit payoffs in cell B of Table 13.5. Intel's manager can punish AMD in the next weekly repetition, which would be week 2, by lowering its price. Notice that AMD cannot avoid getting punished in week 2 should Intel decide to retaliate by pricing low. In week 2, AMD can either price low and end up in cell D or price high and end up in cell C; either decision punishes AMD. Of course we predict AMD would choose to price low in week 2, because cell D minimizes AMD's cost of punishment from Intel's retaliatory price cut.

It follows from the discussion above that Intel can make a *credible* threat in week 1 to punish cheating with a retaliatory price cut in week 2 because cutting price is Intel's best response in week 2 to cheating in week 1. You can see from the payoff table (Table 13.5) that Intel's profit increases by making the retaliatory cut from $2 million per week to either $3 million per week or to $6 million per week, depending on AMD's pricing decision in week 2. You can also verify for yourself that AMD can similarly make a credible threat to cut price in retaliation for an episode of cheating by Intel.

In repeated decisions, unlike one-time decisions, cheating can be punished in later rounds of decision making. By making credible threats of punishment, strategically astute managers can sometimes, but not always, achieve cooperation in prisoners' dilemmas. We are now ready to examine how punishment can be used to achieve cooperation in repeated decisions.

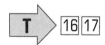 16 17

Deciding to Cooperate

Recall from Chapter 1 that managers should make decisions that maximize the (present) value of a firm, which is the sum of the discounted expected profits in current and future periods. The decision to cooperate, which is equivalent to

---

[10]Game theorists have studied a variety of repeated games: games repeated forever and games repeated a fixed or finite number of times. They even distinguish the finite games according to whether players do or do not know when the games will end. These subtle differences are important because they can dramatically affect the possibility of cooperation, and hence, the outcome of repeated games. To keep our discussion as simple and meaningful as possible, we will limit our analysis to situations in which managers believe the decisions will be repeated forever.

FIGURE 13.5
A Firm's Benefits and Costs of Cheating

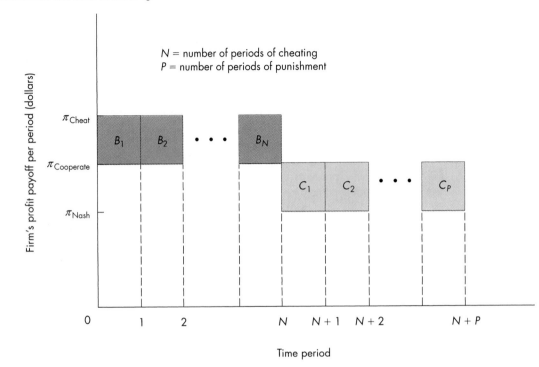

N = number of periods of cheating
P = number of periods of punishment

deciding not to cheat, affects a firm's future stream of profits. Consequently, managers must gauge the effect of cheating on the present value of their firm. Cooperation will increase a firm's value if the present value of the costs of cheating exceeds the present value of the benefits from cheating. Alternatively, cheating will increase a firm's value if the present value of the benefits from cheating outweigh the present value of the costs of cheating. When all firms in an oligopoly market choose not to cheat, then cooperation is achieved in the market.

Figure 13.5 shows the stream of future benefits and costs for a firm that cheats for N periods of time before getting caught, after which it is punished by a retaliatory price cut for P periods of time.[11] The benefits from cheating received in each

---

[11]The pattern of benefits and costs shown in Figure 13.5 assumes that the firm making the decision to cheat in period 1 can receive the cooperative profit payoff in period 1 if it makes the cooperative decision rather than the cheating decision. The pattern also assumes that there are no further costs for cheating after the punishment ends in period $(N + P)$. The figure also depicts equal benefits and costs of cheating in each time period. Other patterns of benefits and costs are certainly possible. Figure 13.5 provides a general approach to modeling the benefits and costs of cheating.

of the N time periods $(B_1, B_2, \ldots, B_N)$ are the gains in profit each period from cheating rather than cooperating: $\pi_{\text{Cheat}} - \pi_{\text{Cooperate}}$. For simplicity, we assume the payoffs, and hence the benefits and costs of cheating, are constant in all repetitions of the decision. Of course, the benefits and costs from cheating occur in the future and so must be discounted using the appropriate discount rate for the cheating firm. The present value of the benefits from cheating when the discount rate per period is r can be calculated as

$$PV_{\text{Benefits of cheating}} = \frac{B_1}{(1+r)^1} + \frac{B_2}{(1+r)^2} + \cdots + \frac{B_N}{(1+r)^N}$$

where $B_i = \pi_{\text{Cheat}} - \pi_{\text{Cooperate}}$ for $i = 1, \ldots, N$. The cost of cheating in each period, after cheating is discovered and continuing for P periods, is the loss in profit caused by the retaliatory price cut that results in a noncooperative Nash equilibrium: $\pi_{\text{Cooperate}} - \pi_{\text{Nash}}$. The costs of cheating, like the benefits from cheating, occur in the future and must be discounted. The present value of the costs of punishment for P periods (when the discount rate per period is r) can be calculated as

$$PV_{\text{Costs of cheating}} = \frac{C_1}{(1+r)^{N+1}} + \frac{C_2}{(1+r)^{N+2}} + \cdots + \frac{C_P}{(1+r)^{N+P}}$$

where $C_j = \pi_{\text{Cooperate}} - \pi_{\text{Nash}}$ for $j = 1, \ldots, P$. We have now established the following principle.

Principle   Cooperation (deciding not to cheat) maximizes the value of a firm when the present value of the costs of cheating is greater than the present value of the benefits from cheating. Cooperation is achieved in an oligopoly market when all firms decide not to cheat.

Trigger Strategies for Punishing Cheating

In repeated decisions, punishment itself becomes a strategy. We will now discuss a widely studied category of punishment strategies known in game theory as *trigger strategies*. Managers implement **trigger strategies** by initially choosing the cooperative action and continuing to choose the cooperative action in successive repetitions of the decision until a rival cheats. The act of cheating then "triggers" a punishment phase in the next repetition of the game that may last one or more repetitions, depending on the nature of the trigger scheme. The firm initiating the trigger strategy can announce openly to its rivals that it plans to follow a trigger strategy. Or, where attempts to facilitate cooperation might bring legal action, firms can secretly begin following a trigger strategy and hope that rivals will recognize what they are doing and choose to cooperate.

Two trigger strategies that have received much attention by game theorists are *tit-for-tat* and *grim strategies*. In a **tit-for-tat strategy,** cheating triggers punishment in the next decision period, and the punishment continues unless the cheating stops, which triggers a return to cooperation in the following decision period. In other words, if firm B cheated in the last decision period, firm A will cheat in this decision period. If firm B cooperated last time, then firm A will cooperate this time.

trigger strategies
Punishment strategies that choose cooperative actions until an episode of cheating triggers a period of punishment.

tit-for-tat strategy
A trigger strategy that punishes after an episode of cheating and returns to cooperation if cheating ends.

grim strategy
A trigger strategy that punishes forever after an episode of cheating.

Hence the name "tit-for-tat." Tit-for-tat is both simple to implement and simple for rivals to understand. A tit-for-tat strategy imposes a less severe punishment for cheating than a grim strategy. In a **grim strategy,** cheating triggers punishment in the next decision period, and the punishment continues forever, even if cheaters make cooperative decisions in subsequent periods. This is "grim" indeed!

Many experimental studies of repeated games have been undertaken to see how decision makers actually behave and also to determine which punishment strategies make cooperation most likely. In a famous "tournament" of strategies, Robert Axelrod at the University of Michigan invited game theorists to devise strategies for competition in repeated prisoners' dilemma games.[12] Numerous strategies were submitted, and computers were used to pit the strategies against each other in prisoners' dilemma decisions repeated hundreds of times. The strategies winning most of the time tended to be simple strategies rather than complicated or clever strategies. In a surprise to many game theorists, tit-for-tat emerged as the most profitable strategy because of its ability to initiate and sustain cooperation among oligopoly rivals. Other experimental studies and subsequent strategy tournaments have confirmed tit-for-tat to be the most profitable strategy to follow in repeated games. Eventually, game theorists, or perhaps oligopoly managers, may discover a better strategy for making repeated decisions, but for now, tit-for-tat is the winner.

Pricing Practices That Facilitate Cooperation

facilitating practices
Generally lawful methods of encouraging cooperative pricing behavior.

Cooperation usually increases profits, as well as the value of oligopoly firms; thus managers of firms in oligopoly markets frequently adopt tactics or methods of doing business that make cooperation among rivals more likely. Such tactics, called **facilitating practices** by antitrust officials, encourage cooperation either by reducing the benefits of cheating or by increasing the costs of cheating. And, sometimes, both of these things can be accomplished at the same time. You should know about some of these practices because they are generally legal and they can increase the likelihood of achieving cooperation and earning higher profits.[13] While numerous business practices and tactics can assist or encourage cooperative behavior in oligopoly markets, we will limit our discussion here to four pricing practices that discourage or limit noncooperative price-cutting: price matching, sale-price guarantees, public pricing, and price leadership.

Price matching
From our discussion in the previous section, you know that any action a manager takes reducing the benefit of cheating will make cooperation more likely. Perhaps

---

[12]See Robert Axelrod, *The Evolution of Competition* (New York: Basic Books, 1984).

[13]While the facilitating practices discussed here are not prohibited under U.S. antitrust law, antitrust officials can, nonetheless, take legal action against firms engaged in any of these practices—or any other business practice for that matter—if they believe such practices "substantially lessen competition."

ILLUSTRATION 13.3

How to Avoid Price Wars and Stay Out of Jail Too

When a rival firm cuts its price, a manager's best strategic response, in many cases, is to retaliate with a price cut of its own. Successive repetitions of price cutting, frequently referred to as "price wars," can result in all firms doing worse than if they had not entered a price war. As we showed you in this chapter, if managers can find a way to cooperate in setting their prices, they can avoid getting into a low-price, low-profit situation and instead reach a higher-price, higher-profit situation. As the forces of globalization and deregulation of markets have made markets more competitive, price wars have become more common. Indeed, price wars are so common now that most managers will face a price war some time in their careers.

Price wars leave oligopoly firms in situations like the noncooperative Nash cell D in the prisoners' dilemmas we have discussed in this chapter and the last chapter. Price wars can be avoided, just as cell D can be avoided, if firms can find ways to cooperate. As we have stressed several times, explicit arrangements to coordinate prices, called "collusion" and "price-fixing," are per se (categorically) illegal in the United States, and many other countries, especially in Europe, are outlawing price-fixing. Tacit collusion—agreement without explicit communication—is also illegal but is more difficult to discover and prove. As we mentioned in the text, penalties for price-fixing in the United States can be quite severe. In addition to facing steep fines, business executives can and do go to prison for the crime of price fixing.

So there is the problem of price wars: Retaliatory price-cutting can lead to costly price wars, but attempts at setting prices cooperatively are generally illegal. What can managers do, that won't land them in jail for attempted price-fixing, to avoid being drawn into price wars? In a recent article in *Harvard Business Review*, Akshay Rao, Mark Bergen, and Scott Davis provide business executives with some practical advice on how to avoid price wars and, when they cannot be avoided, how to fight them successfully.[a] We will briefly discuss several of their tactics for avoiding price wars:

- Adopt a policy of price matching and advertise it so that your rivals believe your commitment to matching price cuts cannot (easily) be reversed. If rivals expect you to match price cuts, they are less likely to start a price war. And, if they expect you to match price hikes, they are more likely to expect you to cooperate by following their price increases.

- Make sure your competitors know you have low variable costs. Recall that firms only stop selling and shut down when price falls below average variable costs. Rivals will be wary of a price war if they believe you have low variable costs. In practice, it can be difficult to convince rivals that your variable costs are low, since rivals may believe you are providing them with false information about your costs to keep them from cutting price.

- Don't retaliate with a price cut of your own if you can maintain sales by increasing product or service quality. In those market segments where customers are particularly quality conscious, you may be able to hold on to customers, even though rivals' prices are lower, if consumers strongly demand quality products or services. When consumers view price as a measure of product quality, price cutting may do permanent damage to a firm's reputation for high quality.

- Generally try to communicate to rivals that you prefer to compete in nonprice ways. Nonprice competition involves differentiating your product from rivals' products primarily through advertising and product quality.

These are a few of the practical (and legal) methods for avoiding price wars that are discussed in the article by Rao, Bergen, and Davis. While we agree with these authors that avoiding a price war is generally the most profitable policy, we must admit that, as consumers, we rather like price wars. Our advice to you, nonetheless, is to avoid price wars but don't go to jail trying!

[a]Akshay R. Rao, Mark E. Bergen, and Scott Davis, "How to Fight a Price War," *Harvard Business Review,* Mar.–Apr. 2000, pp. 107–16.

price matching
A commitment to match any rival's lower price.

one of the most effective ways for reducing benefits of noncooperative price-cutting involves making a strategic commitment to *price matching*. A firm commits to a **price matching** strategy by publicly announcing, usually in an advertisement, that it will match any lower prices offered by its rivals. Price matching represents a strategic commitment since legal costs and loss of goodwill would be substantial for any firm reneging on its public offer to match its rivals' lower prices. Thus the benefit of cutting prices to steal rivals' customers largely vanishes when rivals force themselves to match immediately any other firm's price cuts.

Sale-price guarantees

sale-price guarantee
A firm's promise to give its buyers today any sale price it might offer during a stipulated future period.

Another way oligopoly firms can discourage price-cutting behavior is for most, and better still, all rival firms to agree to give buyers *sale-price guarantees*. Your firm offers a **sale-price guarantee** by promising customers who buy an item from you today that they are entitled to receive any sale price your firm might offer for some stipulated future period, say, for 30 days after purchase. While this kind of insurance against lower future prices may increase current demand as some buyers decide to buy now rather than wait for a sale, the primary purpose of sale-price guarantees is to make it costly for firms to cut their prices. With a 30-day sale-price guarantee policy, for example, a manager who cuts price today not only loses revenue on today's sales but also loses revenue on *all* units sold for the past 30 days. Sale-price guarantees, then, discourage price-cutting by making the price cuts apply to more customers.

Public pricing

public pricing
Informing buyers about prices in a way that makes pricing information public knowledge.

Noncooperative price-cutters expect to be discovered quickly, and so gain very little profit, when rival managers can monitor each other's pricing decisions easily and cheaply. For this reason, oligopoly managers frequently make pricing information available to their buyers using **public pricing** methods that give everyone access to their prices—not just potential buyers, but, more importantly, rival sellers. To be effective, publicly available prices must be timely and authentic. Prices that are not up-to-date or that do not reflect actual transaction prices (i.e., list prices minus any negotiated discounts) offer little or no help for facilitating quick detection of noncooperative price cuts. As you can see in Figure 13.5, quick detection of a unilateral price-cut shortens the period during which a price-cutter benefits (N decreases in Figure 13.5), and early detection also speeds up delivery of retaliatory price cuts. Both of these effects reduce the likelihood that unilateral price cuts will increase the value of price-cutting firms.

Managers of oligopoly firms have found many simple, as well as ingenious, methods for making information about prices more openly available. Oligopoly managers, for example, may post their prices on the Internet, not so much as a convenience to buyers but to facilitate quick detection and punishment of unilateral price cuts. Oligopoly firms sometimes form trade associations or other similar types of organizations to monitor prices or even to publish member firms' prices in trade association publications or websites.

Price leadership

The final method we wish to mention for facilitating cooperative pricing involves behavior known as *price leadership*. **Price leadership** occurs when one oligopoly firm (the leader) sets its price at a level it believes will maximize total industry profit, and then the rest of the firms (the followers) cooperate by setting the same price. Once the price leader sets a price, all firms in the industry compete for sales through advertising and other types of marketing. The price remains constant until the price leader changes the price or one or more other firms break away. This arrangement does not require an explicit agreement among firms to follow the pricing behavior of the leader; the follower firms in the market just implicitly agree to the arrangement. For this reason, price leadership is not generally an unlawful means of achieving cooperative pricing.

Price leadership has been quite common in certain industries. It was characteristic of the steel industry some time ago. At times it has characterized the tire, oil, cigarette, and banking industries. Any firm in an oligopoly market can be the price leader. While it is frequently the dominant firm in the market, it may be simply the firm with a reputation for good judgment. There could exist a situation in which the most efficient—the least-cost—firm is the price leader, even though this firm is not the largest. In any case, the rival firms will follow the price leader only as long as they believe that the price leader's behavior accurately and promptly reflects changes in market conditions. We now turn our attention to the use of explicit price-fixing agreements to achieve cooperative pricing, which, in sharp contrast to price leadership, is always illegal.

Explicit Price-Fixing Agreements and Cartels

While various facilitating practices can provide effective means of achieving cooperation, managers of oligopoly firms sometimes resort to explicit pricing agreements that seek to drive up prices by restricting competition. A group of firms or nations entering such an agreement is called a price-fixing **cartel**. Cartel agreements may take the form of open collusion with members entering into contracts about price and other market variables, or the cartel may involve secret collusion among members. One of the most famous cartels is OPEC (the Organization of Petroleum Exporting Countries), an association of some of the world's major oil-producing nations. Numerous other cartels over the past century, often international in scope, have attempted to hike prices of agricultural products (such as rubber, tea, citric acid, lysine, cocoa, and coffee) and mineral resources (such as bauxite, tin, copper, uranium, and diamonds).[14] We now want to explain two reasons joining a cartel agreement to raise prices probably is not on this year's list of "Smartest Management Decisions."

---

[14]For a fascinating and detailed study of international price-fixing cartels, see John M. Connor, *Global Price Fixing: Our Customers Are the Enemy* (Boston: Kluwer Academic Publishers, 2001).

price leadership
A leader firm sets the industry profit-maximizing price and the follower firms cooperate by all setting the same price.

cartel
A group of firms or nations entering an explicit agreement to restrict competition for the purpose of driving up prices.

We will begin with the clearest reason for avoiding cartels: Participating in cartels is illegal in most countries, and, if convicted, you will face personal fines and possibly prison time. All explicit agreements among industry rivals that actually do, or potentially could, lead to higher prices are illegal and actively prosecuted in the United States, Canada, Mexico, Germany, and the European Union. No manager or executive is above the law. Consider the sentence for Alfred Taubman, former chairman of Sotheby's art auction house, who was convicted in 2002 of conspiring with rival auction house Christie's International to fix sales commissions for art auctions. Federal Judge George Daniels sentenced the wealthy 78-year-old business tycoon—his personal wealth when incarcerated was estimated at $700 million—to serve one year and a day in federal prison. The judge also fined Taubman personally $7.5 million in addition to $186 million Taubman paid from his personal fortune to settle numerous civil lawsuits spawned by his criminal conviction. We could tell you quite a few more stories about pricing conspiracies, but, as you might guess, they all end painfully for convicted business executives.

Even if you think you can avoid getting caught conspiring to fix prices, you should know about another, even more compelling, reason to shun cartels: Historically, most cartels fail to raise prices much or for long. The tendency for cartels to fail can be explained using concepts developed in this chapter. As emphasized in our discussions of prisoners' dilemma situations, the opportunity for any one firm to increase its profit by unilaterally cutting price leads inevitably to a noncooperative Nash equilibrium with lower profits. The high prices desired by all firms in the industry are strategically unstable. Any one firm, if it is the only firm to do so, can cut its price and enjoy higher profit. When all firms do this, however, prices drop sharply, and every cartel member ends up making less profit.

Consider again in Table 13.5 the microprocessor pricing problem facing Intel and AMD. Suppose now both computer chip manufacturers reach a secret price-fixing agreement to set high prices for their computer chips. Cell A, then, is where the cartel conspires to operate. As you know from our previous discussions, cell A is not strategically stable. Either cartel member can, if it is the only firm doing so, cut its price and increase its own profit (see cells B and C) while reducing the profit of the other member. All cartel members have an incentive to cheat, so one or both of them will likely do so eventually. Once Intel and AMD discover each other's cheating behavior, they are likely to do what most cartels do: collapse. By abandoning all pretense of cooperation, widespread price-cutting breaks out, possibly even leading to a costly price war—a noncooperative pricing situation represented in cell D in Table 13.5.

Before we leave this discussion of cartel cheating, we should explain a bit more carefully why cartels face payoff tables structured like the one in Table 13.5, which forms the basis for believing cartels will fail. After all, the payoff matrix of Table 13.5 appears contrived to make Intel and AMD want to cheat. Why, exactly, do cartels face payoff structures that are strategically unstable? We can answer this question with the help of Figure 13.6, which illustrates why Intel is likely to cheat without resorting to specific numerical values for prices or quantities. Although Figure 13.6 shows why Intel wants to cheat, a similar figure also applies to AMD's incentive to cheat.

FIGURE 13.6
Intel's Incentive to Cheat

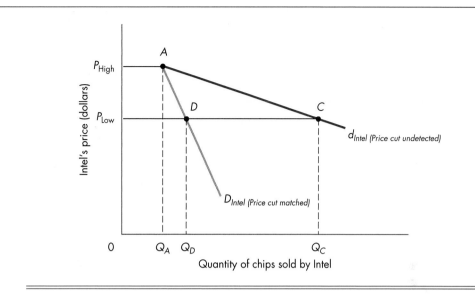

In Figure 13.6, which shows only Intel's pricing decisions, point A represents the situation when Intel and AMD are both pricing high in support of the cartel agreement (also cell A in Table 13.5). When both firms price high, Intel sells Q_A microprocessing chips. At this point, Intel believes that if it secretly cheats on the cartel agreement by cutting its price to P_{Low}, it can increase its sales tremendously as long as AMD does not detect the cheating and match Intel's price cut. Under these conditions, Intel believes its unmatched price cut will greatly increase its sales to Q_C (cell C in Table 13.5). In other words, Intel believes its price cut, if undetected by AMD, will move Intel down along a rather elastic demand from point A to point C. Of course, such price reductions are unlikely to go unnoticed for very long, because other members are likely to notice their own sales falling off.

Once AMD discovers Intel has been cheating on the cartel agreement to set high prices, AMD's best response is to lower its price as well, perhaps matching the amount of Intel's price cut. Notice, however, that when AMD matches Intel's price cut, Intel's demand is much less elastic since few, if any, AMD buyers will switch to Intel. Intel, then, ends up moving down along the less elastic demand segment in Figure 13.6 from point A to point D. At point D, both firms have abandoned their price fixing agreement and the cartel no longer works to increase profits for either firm. As you can see from this discussion, which does not rely on numerical payoff values, cartel members do indeed have incentives to cheat on price-fixing agreements, and they usually do.

Tacit Collusion

tacit collusion
Cooperation among rival firms that does not involve any explicit agreement.

A far less extreme form of cooperation than explicit price-fixing cartels arises when firms engage in **tacit collusion**, which refers to cooperative behavior that arises without any explicit communication. Recall that we mentioned this type of cooperation in our earlier discussion of price leadership, a pricing practice sometimes facilitating cooperation, which may arise without any explicit agreement to designate a price leader. There are many other types of tacit collusion that firms have tried. For instance, the producers in a market may restrict their sales to specific geographical regions or countries without meeting and explicitly designating marketing areas on a map. One firm's market area is understood from the ongoing relations it has had with its rivals. As opposed to forming a cartel to monopolize a market, tacit collusion is not categorically illegal. However, specific evidence of any attempt by rival firms to reach agreement would quickly tip the legal balance against accused participants.

Tacit collusion arises because all or most of the firms in an oligopoly market recognize their mutual interdependence and understand the consequences of noncooperation. The managers of these firms may wish to avoid the legal risks and penalties of getting caught making explicit agreements to cooperate (recall again the fate of Alfred Taubman). Or it may simply be too difficult to organize and coordinate behavior when there are numerous firms operating in the industry. In either case, tacit cooperation provides an alternative method of achieving cooperation, one that is generally less likely to result in charges of unlawful collusion. Tacit collusion might even be the end result of many repeated decisions in which oligopoly managers eventually learn that noncooperative decisions will be met with retaliatory noncooperative decisions from rivals, and everyone gives up cheating—at least until one of the firms hires a new manager!

13.4 SUMMARY

When the number of firms competing in a market is small, any decision one firm makes about pricing, output, expansion, advertising, and so forth will affect the demand, marginal revenue, and profit conditions of every other firm in the market. Consequently, the profits of oligopoly firms are interdependent, and managers must engage in strategic decision making in order to make the most profitable decisions. Strategic decision making means that managers must get into the heads of their rivals to make predictions about how rivals will react to any decision they make. The resulting interdependence and strategic behavior make decisions much more complicated and uncertain. The consequent uncertainty about marginal revenue makes it difficult for managers in oligopoly markets to make profit-maximizing decisions by equating marginal revenue and marginal cost, even though $MR = MC$ is the profit-maximizing rule for oligopoly firms (as it is for firms operating in any market structure).

This chapter introduced you to game theory, an indispensable tool for thinking about strategic decision making. We focused on three types of strategic decision situations:

(1) *simultaneous decisions*, in which managers make their individual decisions without knowing the decisions of their rivals; (2) *sequential decisions*, in which one manager makes a decision before the other; and (3) *repeated decisions*, in which strategic decisions are made repeatedly over time by the same firms. We covered a huge amount of territory in this chapter, and yet, you may have noticed, we were not able to provide you with a simple profit-maximizing rule of the type described in Chapters 11 and 12. Our purpose in this chapter was to provide a framework for strategic analysis of how oligopolists have tried to cope with the problem of interdependence and why they have succeeded or why they have failed. We believe game theory offers a promising guide for decision making when interdependence makes it impossible to ignore rivals' reactions to managerial decisions. However, even several courses in game theory cannot teach you how to make such decisions; this type of decision making is best learned from experience. But a good economics foundation will make it easier for you to learn from experience.

TECHNICAL PROBLEMS

1. For each of the following statements concerning the role of strategic thinking in management decisions, explain whether the statement is true or false.

   a. "Managers of firms operating in perfectly competitive markets need to 'get into the heads' of rival managers in order to make more profitable decisions."

   b. "Strategic thinking by managers in oligopolistic industries promotes rational decision making, which will increase total industry profit."

   c. "Despite the interdependent nature of profits, oligopoly managers have the same goal as perfect competitors, monopolists, and monopolistic competitors."

2. Evaluate the following statement: "In simultaneous decision games, all players know the payoffs from making various decisions, but the players still do not have all the information they would like to have in order to decide which action to take."

3. In each of the following three payoff tables, two decision makers, Gates and Dell, must make simultaneous decisions to either cooperate or not cooperate with each other. Explain, for each payoff table, why it does or does not represent a prisoners' dilemma situation for Dell and Gates.

   a.

		Gates	
		Don't cooperate	Cooperate
Dell	Don't cooperate	$75, $75	$600, $50
	Cooperate	$100, $300	$400, $400

   b.

		Gates	
		Don't cooperate	Cooperate
Dell	Don't cooperate	$100, $100	$300, $200
	Cooperate	$200, $300	$500, $500

   c.

		Gates	
		Don't cooperate	Cooperate
Dell	Don't cooperate	$100, $100	$600, $50
	Cooperate	$50, $600	$500, $500

4. Two firms, Small and Large, compete by price. Each can choose either a low price or a high price. The following payoff table shows the profit (in thousands of dollars) each firm would earn in each of the four possible decision situations:

		Large	
		Low price	High price
Small	Low price	$200, $500	$600, $600
	High price	$0, $1,500	$400, $1,000

a. Is there a dominant strategy for Small? If so, what is it? Why?

b. Is there a dominant strategy for Large? If so, what is it? Why?

c. What is the likely pair of decisions? What payoff will each receive?

5. Verify the following statement: "The solution to the prisoners' dilemma in Table 13.2 is equivalent to the solution found by elimination of dominated strategies."

6. Find the solution to the following advertising decision game between Coke and Pepsi by using the method of successive elimination of dominated strategies.

| | | Pepsi's budget | | |
		Low	Medium	High
	Low	A $400, $400	B $320, $720	C $560, $600
Coke's budget	Medium	D $500, $300	E $450, $525	F $540, $500
	High	G $375, $420	H $300, $378	I $525, $750

Payoffs in millions of dollars of annual profit.

a. Does Coke have a dominated strategy in the original payoff table? If so, what is it and why is it dominated? If not, why not?

b. Does Pepsi have a dominated strategy in the original payoff table? If so, what is it and why is it dominated? If not, why not?

c. After the first round of eliminating any dominated strategies that can be found in the original payoff table, describe the strategic situation facing Coke and Pepsi in the reduced payoff table.

d. What is the likely outcome of this advertising decision problem?

e. Pepsi's highest payoff occurs when Coke and Pepsi both choose high ad budgets. Explain why Pepsi will not likely choose a high ad budget.

7. Verify that each of the following decision pairs is a Nash equilibrium by explaining why each decision pair is strategically stable:

a. Cell D of the prisoners' dilemma in Table 13.1

b. The decision pair for firms Large and Small in part c of Technical Problem 4.

c. The decision pair for Coke and Pepsi in part d of Technical Problem 6.

8. Following the procedure illustrated in Panel A of Figure 13.1, show that when Arrow Airlines believes Bravo Airways is going to charge $200 per round-trip ticket, Arrow's best response is to charge $208.

9. Carefully explain why Arrow Airlines and Bravo Airways are not likely to choose the pair of prices at point R in Figure 13.2. Do not simply state that point R is not at the intersection of the best-response curves.

10. In Figure 13.2, point C makes both Arrow and Bravo more profitable. Getting to point C requires the airlines to cooperate: Arrow agrees to charge $230 per round-trip ticket and Bravo agrees to charge $235 per round-trip ticket.

a. At these prices, how much profit does each airline earn? Does the higher price increase Arrow's profit? Does the higher price increase Bravo's profit?

b. Suppose Arrow cheats by unilaterally lowering its price to $229, while Bravo honors the agreement and continues to charge $235. Calculate Arrow's profit when it cheats. Does cheating increase Arrow's profit?

c. Suppose Bravo cheats by unilaterally lowering its price to $234, while Arrow honors the agreement and continues to charge $230. Calculate Bravo's profit when it cheats. Does cheating increase Bravo's profit?

11. Managers at Firm A and Firm B must make pricing decisions simultaneously. The following demand and long-run cost conditions are common knowledge to the managers:

$$Q_A = 72 - 4P_A + 4P_B \qquad \text{and} \qquad LAC_A = LMC_A = 2$$

$$Q_B = 100 - 3P_B + 4P_A \qquad \text{and} \qquad LAC_B = LMC_B = 6.67$$

The accompanying figure shows Firm B's best-response curve, BR_B. Only one point on Firm A's best-response curve, point G, is shown in the figure.

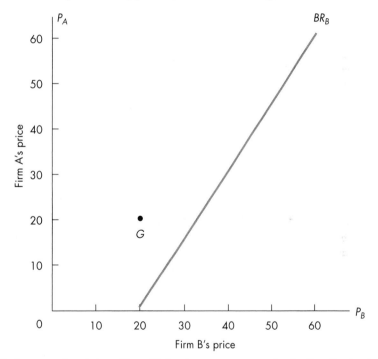

a. Find a second point on Firm A's best-response curve by finding the best response when Firm A believes Firm B will set a price of $60. Plot this price pair on the graph, label it H, draw the best-response curve for Firm A, and label it BR_A.

b. What prices do you expect the managers of Firm A and B to set? Why? Label this point on the graph N.

c. Compute each firm's profit at point N.

d. Explain carefully why the pair of prices at point H in the figure is not likely to be chosen by the managers.

e. Suppose that the managers of the two firms decide to cooperate with each other by both agreeing to set prices $P_A = \$45$ and $P_B = \$60$. Label this point C in the figure.

Compute each firm's profit at point *C*. Which firm(s) make(s) more profit at point *C* than at point *N*? Why didn't you give point *C* as your answer to part *b*?

12. Using the payoff table for Castle Pizza and Palace Pizza in Table 13.2, draw the game tree for a sequential decision situation in which Palace makes its pricing decision first.

    a. Find the equilibrium decision path using the roll-back method. Show the decision path on your game tree.

    b. Is the decision outcome in part *a* a Nash equilibrium? Explain why or why not.

13. In the technology choice game presented in Figure 13.4, draw the game tree when Sony makes its technology decision first. Find the outcome of the game using the roll-back method. Does Sony experience a first-mover advantage? Explain.

14. Consider again the sequential technology choice game in Technical Problem 13 in which Sony chooses its cell phone technology before Motorola. Motorola makes the most profit for itself if both firms choose analog technology for their cell phones. Motorola considers the following strategic moves:

    a. Motorola makes the following threat *before* Sony makes its decision: "If you (Sony) choose **Digital,** then we will choose *Analog.*" Does this threat accomplish Motorola's objective of getting both firms to adopt analog technology? Explain.

    b. Motorola makes the following statement *before* Sony makes its decision: "If you (Sony) choose **Analog,** then we promise to choose *Analog.*" Is this a strategic promise? Why or why not? Does the statement accomplish Motorola's objective of getting both firms to adopt analog technology? Explain.

15. Alpha and Beta, two oligopoly rivals in a duopoly market, choose prices of their products on the first day of the month. The following payoff table shows their monthly payoffs resulting from the pricing decisions they can make.

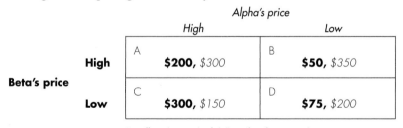

Alpha's price

Beta's price		High	Low
High		A $200, $300	B $50, $350
Low		C $300, $150	D $75, $200

Payoffs in thousands of dollars of profit per month.

    a. Is the pricing decision facing Alpha and Beta a prisoners' dilemma? Why or why not?

    b. What is the cooperative outcome? What is the noncooperative outcome?

    c. Which cell(s) represents cheating in the pricing decision? Explain.

    d. If Alpha and Beta make their pricing decision just one time, will they choose the cooperative outcome? Why or why not?

16. For the weekly decision by AMD and Intel to set the prices of their semiconductor chips, verify in Table 13.5 that AMD can credibly threaten to make a retaliatory price cut if Intel cheats.

17. In the pricing decision in Technical Problem 15, can Alpha make a credible threat to punish Beta with a retaliatory price cut? Can Beta make a credible threat of a retaliatory price cut?

18. Alpha and Beta in Technical Problem 15 repeat their pricing decision on the first day of every month. Suppose they have been cooperating for the past few months, but now the manager at Beta is trying to decide whether to cheat or to continue cooperating. Beta's manager believes Beta can get away with cheating for two months, but would be punished for the next two months after cheating. After punishment, Beta's manager expects the two firms would return to cooperation. Beta's manager uses a discount rate of 2 percent per month for computing present values.

   a. What is the monthly (undiscounted) gain to Beta from cheating? What is the present value of the benefit from cheating?

   b. What is the monthly (undiscounted) cost of punishment to Beta? What is the present value of the cost of cheating?

   c. Will Beta cooperate or cheat? Explain.

   d. Suppose Beta discounts future benefits and costs at a rate of 30 percent per week. Will Beta choose cooperation or cheating?

19. For each of the following events, explain whether Beta in the previous question would be more or less likely to cooperate?

   a. Beta expects to be able to cheat for more than two months before getting caught by Alpha.

   b. Alpha announces that it will match any price cut by Beta, and it will do so immediately following any price cut by Beta.

   c. Alpha hires a new CEO who has a reputation for relentlessly matching price cuts by rivals, even after rivals are ready to resume cooperative pricing.

   d. Alpha alters the design of its product to make it more desirable to some consumers than Beta's product.

APPLIED PROBLEMS

1. When McDonald's Corp. reduced the price of its Big Mac by 75 percent if customers also purchased french fries and a soft drink, *The Wall Street Journal* reported that the company was hoping the novel promotion would revive its U.S. sales growth. It didn't. Within two weeks sales had fallen. Using your knowledge of game theory, what do you think disrupted McDonald's plans?

2. The well-known nationally syndicated columnist David Broder reported the recent findings of two academic political scientists. These scholars found that voters are quite turned off by "negative campaigns" of politicians. Many people went as far as not voting because of this. Nevertheless, the political scientists noted it is futile to urge candidates to stay positive. The damage from staying positive is heaviest when the opponent is attacking. Explain the dilemma in terms of strategic behavior.

3. Dell Computer Corp., the world's largest personal-computer maker, is keenly aware of everything its rival PC manufacturers decide to do. Explain why Dell usually reacts more quickly and more substantially to pricing, product design, and advertising decisions made by Hewlett-Packard and Gateway than when these same types of decisions are made by Apple Computer.

4. Some states have had laws restricting the sale of most goods on Sunday. Consumers, by and large, oppose such laws because they find Sunday afternoon a convenient time to

shop. Paradoxically, retail trade associations frequently support the laws. Discuss the reasons for merchants' supporting these laws.

5. Thomas Schelling, an expert on nuclear strategy and arms control, observed in his book *The Strategy of Conflict* (Cambridge, MA: Harvard University Press, 1960), "The power to constrain an adversary depends upon the power to bind oneself." Explain this statement using the concept of strategic commitment.

6. Many economists argue that more research, development, and innovation occur in the oligopolistic market structure than in any other. Why might this conclusion be true?

7. In the 2000 U.S. presidential contest, Al Gore was advised by his strategists to wait for George W. Bush to announce his vice-presidential running mate before making his own decision on a running mate. Under what circumstances would Gore be better off giving Bush a head start on putting together his presidential ticket? What kind of strategic situation is this?

8. When he retired as CEO of American Airlines, a position he held for 18 years, Robert Crandall was described in a *Newsweek* article (June 1, 1998) as "one tough [expletive]." Other nicknames Crandall garnered during his career included Fang, Bob the Butcher, and Wretched Robert. *Newsweek* noted that Crandall's "salty language and brass-knuckle, in-your-face" style of dealing with employees and rival airlines is now out of style in the executive suites of U.S. corporations. In strategic decision-making situations, why might Crandall's style of management have been advantageous to American Airlines?

9. The secretary-general of OPEC, Ali Rodriquez, stated that it would be easier for OPEC nations to make future supply adjustments to fix oil prices that are too high than it would be to rescue prices that are too low. Evaluate this statement.

10. A church signboard offers the following advice: "Live every day as if it were your last." Taken literally, could this advice encourage "bad" behavior? Explain.

11. In 1999 Mercedes-Benz USA adopted a new pricing policy, which it called NFP (negotiation-free process), that sought to eliminate price negotiations between customers and new-car dealers. An article in the *New York Times* (August 29, 1999) reported that a New Jersey Mercedes dealer who had his franchise revoked is suing Mercedes, claiming that he was fired for refusing to go along with Mercedes' no-haggling pricing policy. The New Jersey dealer said he thought the NFP policy was illegal. Why might Mercedes' NFP policy be illegal? Can you offer another reason why the New Jersey dealer might not have wished to follow a no-haggling policy?

12. Suppose the two rival office supply companies Office Depot and Staples both adopt price-matching policies. If consumers can find lower advertised prices on any items they sell, then Office Depot and Staples guarantee they will match the lower prices. Explain why this pricing policy may not be good news for consumers.

13. Recently one of the nation's largest consumer electronics retailers began a nationwide television advertising campaign kicking off its "Take It Home Today" program, which is designed to encourage electronics consumers to buy today rather than continue postponing a purchase hoping for a lower price. For example, the "Take It Home Today" promotion guarantees buyers of new plasma TVs that they are entitled to get any sale price the company might offer for the next 30 days.

   a. Do you think such a policy will increase demand for electronic appliances? Explain.

   b. What other reason could explain why this program is offered? Would you expect the other large electronics stores to match this program with one of their own? Why or why not?

14. When Advanta Corp. decided that it wished to begin charging a fee to holders of its credit cards for periods during which the card is not used and for closing the account, it first "signaled" its intentions to hike fees by publicly announcing its plans in advance. The company notified its cardholders that it wouldn't begin charging the fees right away but would reserve the right to do so. One worried cardholder told *The Wall Street Journal*, "I hope the other credit card companies don't follow suit." Apparently, cardholders had good reason to worry, according to one credit card industry analyst: "Everyone is considering (raising fees), but everyone's afraid. The question is, who'll be daring and be second? If there's a second, then you'll see a flood of people doing it."

   a. If Advanta believes raising fees is a profitable move, then why would it delay implementing the higher fees, which could reduce the amount of profit generated by higher fees?

   b. Are rivals waiting for Advanta to implement its fee hikes before they do in order to secure a second-mover advantage? Explain. Is there any other reason rivals might wait to raise their prices?

   c. Could Advanta Corp. be trying to establish itself as the price leader in the consumer credit card industry?

15. Economists believe terrorists behave rationally: If country *A* (America) increases security efforts while country *B* (Britain) remains complacent, terrorists will focus their attacks on targets in the relatively less well-protected country *B*. Suppose the following payoff table shows the net benefits for the United States and Great Britain according to their decisions either to maintain their annual spending levels at the optimal levels (when both countries spend proportionately equal amounts) or to increase annual spending by 10 percent. The payoffs in the table measure net benefits (in dollars) from antiterrorism activities, that is, the value of property not destroyed and lives not lost due to reduced terrorism minus spending on antiterrorism.

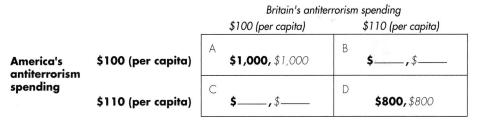

Payoffs in millions of dollars of net benefit annually.

   a. Antiterrorism policy analysts believe allies in the war against terror face a prisoners' dilemma concerning how much each country chooses to spend on activities that reduce the incidence of terrorist attacks on their own nation's people and property. In the payoff table, make up your own values for payoffs in cells B and C that will create a prisoners' dilemma situation.

   b. "When all nations spend more and more preventing terrorist acts, they may actually all end up worse off for their efforts." Evaluate this statement using the payoff table you created in part *a*.

16. The two largest diner chains in Kansas compete for weekday breakfast customers. The two chains, Golden Inn and Village Diner, each offer weekday breakfast customers a "breakfast club" membership that entitles customers to a breakfast buffet between 6:00 A.M. and 8:30 A.M. Club memberships are sold as "passes" good for 20 weekday breakfast visits.

Golden Inn offers a modest but tasty buffet, while Village Diner provides a wider variety of breakfast items that are also said to be quite tasty. The demand functions for breakfast club memberships are

$$Q_G = 5{,}000 - 25P_G + 10P_V$$

$$Q_V = 4{,}200 - 24P_V + 15P_G$$

where Q_G and Q_V are the number of club memberships sold monthly and P_G and P_V are the prices of club memberships, both respectively, at Golden Inn and Village Diner chains. Both diners experience long-run constant costs of production, which are

$$LAC_G = LMC_G = \$50 \text{ per membership}$$

$$LAC_V = LMC_V = \$75 \text{ per membership}$$

The best-response curves for Golden Inn and Village Diner are, respectively,

$$P_G = BR_G(P_V) = 125 + 0.2P_V$$

$$P_V = BR_V(P_G) = 125 + 0.3125P_G$$

a. If Village Diner charges $200 for its breakfast club membership, find the demand, inverse demand, and marginal revenue functions for Golden Inn. What is the profit-maximizing price for Golden Inn given Village Diner charges a price of $200? Verify mathematically that this price can be obtained from the appropriate best-response curve given above.

b. Find the Nash equilibrium prices for the two diners. How many breakfast club memberships will each diner sell in Nash equilibrium? How much profit will each diner make?

c. How much profit would Golden Inn and Village Diner earn if they charged prices of $165 and $180, respectively? Compare these profits to the profits in Nash equilibrium (part c). Why would you *not* expect the managers of Golden Inn and Village Diner to choose prices of $165 and $180, respectively?

□ **Mathematical Appendix** **Derivation of Best-Response Curves for Continuous Simultaneous Decisions**

For simultaneous decisions in which managers choose actions or strategies that are continuous rather than discrete decision variables, best-response curve analysis can be employed to analyze and explain strategic decision making. In this appendix, we show how to derive the equations for best-response curves when two firms make simultaneous decisions. We examine first the situation in which the two managers choose *outputs* to achieve mutually best outcomes, and so the corresponding best-response curves give each firm's best output given its rival's output. Then we derive the best-response curves when managers choose their best *prices*, given the price they expect their rival to charge.

Best-Response Curves When Firms Choose Quantities

Assume two firms, 1 and 2, produce a homogeneous product, and the linear inverse demand for the product is

$$(1) \qquad P = a + bQ$$

$$= a + bq_1 + bq_2$$

where P is the price of the good, Q is total output of the good, q_1 is firm 1's output, q_2 is firm 2's output, and $Q = q_1 + q_2$. The price intercept a is positive, and the slope parameter for inverse demand, b, is negative.

Constant returns to scale characterize long-run costs, so costs are assumed to be constant and equal for both firms. Let c denote long-run marginal and average cost for both firms; thus each firm's total cost can be expressed as

(2) $\qquad C_1(q_1) = cq_1 \quad$ and $\quad C_2(q_2) = cq_2$

To ensure that a positive quantity of the good is produced (i.e., marginal cost is below the vertical intercept of demand), c is restricted to be less than a ($c < a$). Common knowledge prevails: Both firms know market demand for the product, and they know their own cost and their rival's cost (and they both know they know).

The profit functions for the two firms are

(3a) $\quad \pi_1 = Pq_1 - C_1(q_1) = [a + b(q_1 + q_2)]q_1 - cq_1$

(3b) $\quad \pi_2 = Pq_2 - C_2(q_2) = [a + b(q_1 + q_2)]q_2 - cq_2$

Both firms choose their individual quantities to maximize their individual profits, taking the output of their rival as given. Profit maximization requires, respectively, for firm 1 and firm 2

(4a) $\qquad \dfrac{\partial \pi_1}{\partial q_1} = a + 2bq_1 + bq_2 - c = 0$

(4b) $\qquad \dfrac{\partial \pi_2}{\partial q_2} = a + 2bq_2 + bq_1 - c = 0$

The equations for best-response curves, which show the optimal output for a firm given the output of a rival firm, are obtained from each firm's first-order conditions for profit maximization. Solve equations (4a) and (4b) to get the following best-response functions for firms 1 and 2, respectively:

(5a) $\qquad q_1 = BR_1(q_2) = \dfrac{c - a}{2b} - \dfrac{1}{2}q_2$

(5b) $\qquad q_2 = BR_2(q_1) = \dfrac{c - a}{2b} - \dfrac{1}{2}q_1$

Firm 1's best-response function, $BR_1(q_2)$, gives the profit-maximizing level of output for firm 1, given the level of output produced by firm 2. Firm 2's best-response curve, $BR_2(q_1)$, gives firm 2's optimal output response to any given level of output produced by firm 1. For convenience in graphing the two firms' best-response functions, we find the inverse of firm 2's best-response function, which is $q_1 = BR_2^{-1}(q_2) = \dfrac{c - a}{b} - 2q_2$. Figure 13.A1 shows both firms' best-response curves.

Nash equilibrium occurs where the two best-response curves intersect: point N in Figure 13.A1. The Nash duopoly equilibrium can be found by substituting each best-response function into the other to obtain

(6) $\qquad q_1^* = \dfrac{c - a}{3b} \quad$ and $\quad q_2^* = \dfrac{c - a}{3b}$

Thus total duopoly output is

(7) $\qquad Q^*{}_{\text{Duopoly}} = q_1^* + q_2^* = \dfrac{2(c - a)}{3b}$

and the duopoly price of the product is

(8) $\qquad P^* = a + b(Q^*) = \dfrac{2(c + a)}{3}$

For the demand and cost conditions set forth in equations (1) and (2), the output if the market is perfectly competitive is $Q_C = \dfrac{c - a}{b}$ and the output if the market is a monopoly is $Q_M = \dfrac{c - a}{2b}$. (Problem 1 in the Mathematical Exercises asks you to derive competitive output and monopoly output.) Thus competitive output is greater than *total* duopoly output, and total duopoly output is greater than monopoly output:

(9) $\qquad Q_C > Q_{\text{Duopoly}} > Q_M$

Prices of the good, consequently, are related as follows:

(10) $\qquad P_M < P_{\text{Duopoly}} < P_C$

Best-Response Curves When Firms Choose Prices

Now we examine a simultaneous decision in which duopoly firms A and B, producing goods A and B, respectively, choose their prices rather than their outputs. Assume goods A and B are fairly close substitutes for each other. The linear demand functions for the two products are

(11a) $\qquad Q_A = a + bP_A + cP_B$

(11b) $\qquad Q_B = d + eP_B + fP_A$

where parameters a and d are positive, b and e are negative (by the law of demand), and c and f are positive (for substitutes).

Again let constant returns to scale characterize long-run costs, so costs are assumed to be constant. In this example, however, we let costs differ between the two firms. Let c_A and c_B denote long-run marginal and average costs for firms A and B, respectively:

(12) $\quad C_A(Q_A) = c_A Q_A \quad$ and $\quad C_B(Q_B) = c_B Q_B$

FIGURE 13.A1

**Best-Response Curves:
Firms Choose Quantities**

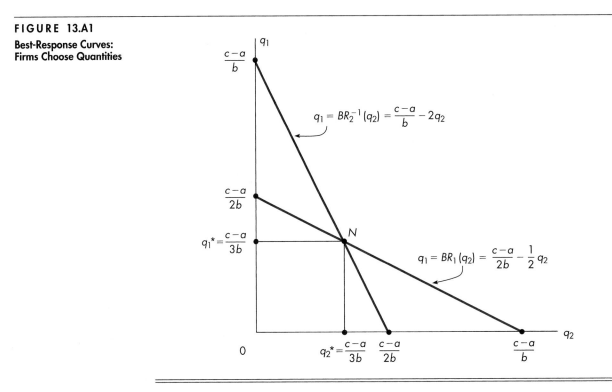

The profit functions for firms A and B are

(13a) $\pi_A = P_A Q_A - C_A(Q_A) = (P_A - c_A)(a + bP_A + cP_B)$

(13b) $\pi_B = P_B Q_B - C_B(Q_B) = (P_B - c_B)(d + eP_B + fP_A)$

Each firm's first-order condition for profit-maximization is

(14a) $\dfrac{\partial \pi_A}{\partial P_A} = a + 2bP_A + cP_B - bc_A = 0$

(14b) $\dfrac{\partial \pi_B}{\partial P_B} = d + 2eP_B + fP_A - ec_B = 0$

Solving equation (14a) for firm A's best-response curve:

(15a) $P_A = BR_A(P_B) = \dfrac{bc_A - a}{2b} - \dfrac{c}{2b}P_B$

Solving equation (14b) for firm B's best-response curve:

(15b) $P_B = BR_B(P_A) = \dfrac{ec_B - d}{2e} - \dfrac{f}{2e}P_A$

Firm A's best-response function, $BR_A(P_B)$, gives the profit-maximizing price for firm A, given the price firm A

predicts firm B will set. Firm A's best-response function is shown in Figure 13.A2 as $BR_A(P_B)$. Firm B's best-response curve, $BR_B(P_A)$, gives firm B's optimal price response to any given price set by firm A. The inverse of firm B's best-response function, $P_A = BR_B^{-1}(P_B) = \dfrac{ec_B - d}{f} - \dfrac{2e}{f}P_B$ is shown in Figure 13.A2.

The intersection of the best-response functions is found by substituting each best-response function into the other best-response function to obtain the Nash equilibrium prices:

(16a) $P_A^N = \dfrac{2e(bc_A - a) + c(d - ec_B)}{4be - cf}$

(16b) $P_B^N = \dfrac{2e(ec_B - d) + f(a - bc_A)}{4be - cf}$

At point N in Figure 13.A2, where the two best-response functions cross, is the Nash equilibrium. Each firm is doing the best it can, given what the other is doing.

FIGURE 13.A2

Best-Response Curves: Firms Choose Prices

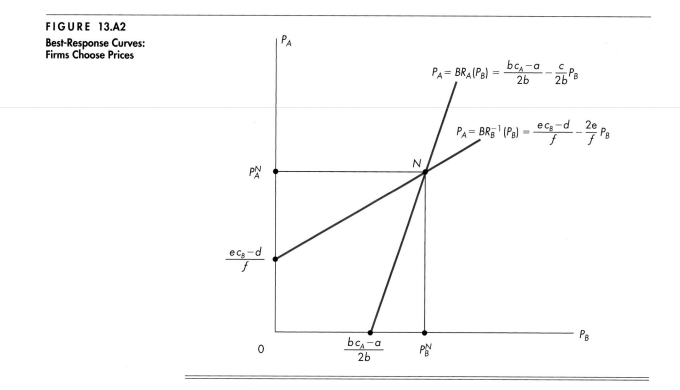

$$P_A = BR_A(P_B) = \frac{bc_A - a}{2b} - \frac{c}{2b}P_B$$

$$P_A = BR_B^{-1}(P_B) = \frac{ec_B - d}{f} - \frac{2e}{f}P_B$$

MATHEMATICAL EXERCISES

1. For the demand and cost conditions in equations (1) and (2), respectively, of the appendix, derive the output and prices under perfect competition and under monopoly and verify the output and price relations in equations (9) and (10), respectively.

2. Doctors Smith and Jones, two rival ophthalmologists, plan to enter the market for laser corrective eye surgery in a medium-size community in Illinois. Smith and Jones both utilize the same laser technology and face constant long-run costs of $1,000 per patient ($LMC = LAC = \$1{,}000$). For planning purposes, the doctors assume that all patients have both eyes corrected, so the $1,000 cost is for correcting both eyes of each patient. The doctors know about each other's plans to enter the market, and they both believe the (inverse) market demand for laser eye surgery is

$$P = 7{,}000 - 2Q$$

where $Q = q_S + q_J$ and q_S and q_J are the number of patients Drs. Smith and Jones, respectively, treat annually. Each of the doctors will choose the size of their clinic, and thus the number of patients they intend to treat each year, without knowledge of their rival's decision. Demand and cost conditions are common knowledge.

a. Using calculus, derive the equations for the best-response curves.

b. Sketch a graph of the two best-response curves. Be sure to label both axes and both response curves.

    c. If Dr. Smith expects Dr. Jones to treat 500 patients annually, what is Dr. Smith's best response? If Dr. Jones predicts Dr. Smith will treat 750 patients annually, what is Dr. Jones's best response?

    d. Find Nash equilibrium. How much profit does each doctor earn annually in Nash equilibrium?

    e. If Drs. Smith and Jones agree to serve annually only 750 patients *each* (1,500 patients in total in one year), how much annual profit does each doctor earn? Why don't they do this?

    f. If Drs. Smith and Jones merge into a single company forming a monopoly in the community, how many patients will they serve each year? What price will they charge? How much profit will they earn?

    g. Instead of the monopoly in part *f*, suppose perfect competition characterizes the market in the long run. How many patients will be treated? What price will they pay in a competitive market? How much profit will the doctors earn?

3. Two firms, *A* and *B*, produce goods *A* and *B*, respectively. The linear demands for the two goods are, respectively,

$$Q_A = 100 - 4P_A + 1.5P_B$$
$$Q_B = 120 - 2P_B + 0.5P_A$$

Production costs are constant but not equal:

$$LAC_A = LMC_A = \$2$$
$$LAC_B = LMC_B = \$3$$

    a. Using calculus, derive the equations for the best-response curves.

    b. Sketch a graph of the two best-response curves. Be sure to label both axes and both response curves.

    c. If firm *A* expects firm *B* to set its price at $20, what is firm *A*'s best response? If firm *B* predicts firm *A* will price good *A* at $36, what is firm *B*'s best response?

    d. What is the Nash equilibrium price and quantity for each firm?

    e. How much profit does each firm earn in Nash equilibrium?

    f. If firm *A* and firm *B* set prices of $22 and $35, respectively, how much profit does each firm earn? Why don't they choose these prices then?

CHAPTER
14

Advanced Techniques for Profit Maximization

After your completing the first four parts of this textbook, we can understand that you might be a bit apprehensive about tackling "advanced"
techniques in managerial decision making. In many instances, semesters
end before managerial economics courses can reach or complete this final part. For
this reason, you may only cover portions of these last two chapters on advanced
decision-making areas, and it is certainly possible that some of the topics in Part V
will show up in other business courses, such as finance, marketing, and production management.

This chapter examines a number of issues concerning production and pricing
decisions for more complicated situations than we have so far encountered in this
text. Specifically, until now we have considered only a rather simple firm. This
firm has a single plant in which it produces a single product that is sold in a single
market at a single price set by equating marginal revenue to marginal cost with no
means of discouraging the entry of new rivals. Although the simpler models provide great insight into a firm's decision process, this is frequently not the type of
situation faced by real-world firms or corporations. In this chapter, we show how
managers can deal with some of the real-world complexities that frequently arise
in production and pricing decisions by applying the concepts and principles set
forth in Parts I through IV of this text.

As you will see, interesting and challenging complications arise when the firm
(1) produces its product in multiple plants, (2) adopts cost-plus pricing to simplify
pricing decisions, (3) charges different prices (rather than a single uniform price)
for the same product sold to different groups of buyers, (4) produces multiple
products that are related in consumption or production, and (5) makes strategic

pricing and production decisions to prevent the entry of new firms into its established markets. The discussion of each of these five advanced topics, of necessity, will be brief. It is not our intention to provide an exhaustive discussion of these five techniques for increasing profits. Furthermore, there are many additional extensions of the basic models developed in this book that are beyond the scope of a single course in managerial economics. Indeed, you may wish to take several more courses, such as industrial organization, international trade, and econometrics, to expand your knowledge of areas of economics that can be quite valuable in business decision making.

In the first four topic areas covered in this chapter, we limit our attention to price-setting firms with market power—specifically including monopoly and monopolistic competition, with only limited application to oligopoly markets. Since the first four techniques do not employ game-theoretic analysis, the analysis of these four topics applies primarily to oligopoly markets in which the oligopoly firms produce sufficiently differentiated products to eliminate—or reduce substantially—the interdependence that gives rise to strategic decision making in the first place. For all but the last technique of this chapter, we will normally consider a monopoly firm, but the conclusions also apply, with perhaps a few modifications, to monopolistic competition and to oligopoly with weak interdependence. The last topic of the chapter, strategic entry deterrence, applies to oligopoly markets and to monopoly markets that would become oligopoly markets with successful entry of new rivals.

We begin with a discussion of multiplant firms. This will be followed by a discussion of the problems that arise when firms attempt to simplify their pricing decisions by using cost-plus pricing. Then we examine firms that sell in multiple markets, and this is followed by a discussion of firms that produce multiple products. We end the chapter by analyzing two strategic moves that established firms can sometimes make to prevent entry of new firms: a pricing decision to discourage entry (limit pricing) and a production decision to create a barrier to entry (capacity expansion).

14.1 MULTIPLANT FIRMS

A firm often produces output in more than one plant. In this situation, it is likely that the various plants will have different cost conditions. The problem facing the firm is how to allocate the firm's desired level of total production among these plants so that the total cost is minimized.

For simplicity, suppose there are only two plants, A and B, producing the desired total output level (Q_T) of 450 units, but at different marginal costs such that

$$MC_A > MC_B$$

where plant A produces 160 units (Q_A) and plant B produces 290 units (Q_B). In this situation, the manager should transfer output from the higher-cost plant A to the lower-cost plant B. As long as the marginal cost of producing in plant B is lower, total cost of producing Q_T units can be lowered by transferring production. For example, suppose MC_A equals \$25 (for the 160th unit at plant A) and MC_B equals \$10 (for the 290th unit at plant B). One unit of output taken away from plant A lowers the firm's total cost by \$25. Making up the lost unit by producing it at plant B increases total cost only by \$10, and 450 units are still produced. As you can see, however, the total cost of producing 450 units falls by \$15. The firm would continue taking output away from plant A and increasing the output of plant B, thus lowering total cost, until $MC_A = MC_B$. This equality would result because MC_A falls as the output of plant A decreases and MC_B rises as the output of plant B increases. Thus we can conclude that marginal costs must be equal for both plants in order to minimize the total cost of producing 450 units.

□ **Principle** For a firm that produces using two plants, A and B, with marginal costs MC_A and MC_B, respectively, the total cost of producing any given level of total output $Q_T (= Q_A + Q_B)$ is minimized when the manager allocates production between the two plants so that the marginal costs are equal: $MC_A = MC_B$.

total marginal cost curve (MC_T)
Horizontal summation of all plants' marginal cost curves, which gives the addition to total cost attributable to increasing total output (Q_T) by one unit.

The total output decision is easily determined. The horizontal summation of all plants' marginal cost curves is the firm's **total marginal cost curve.** This total marginal cost curve is equated to marginal revenue in order to determine the profit-maximizing output and price. This output is divided among the plants so that the marginal cost is equal for all plants.[1]

The two-plant case is illustrated in Figure 14.1. Demand facing the firm is D, and marginal revenue is MR. The marginal cost curves for plants A and B are, respectively, MC_A and MC_B. The total marginal cost curve for the firm is the *horizontal summation* of MC_A and MC_B, labeled MC_T. Profit is maximized at that output level where MC_T equals marginal revenue, at an output of 175 units and a price of \$45. Marginal cost at this output is \$20. Equalization of marginal cost requires that plant A produce 50 units and plant B produce 125 units, which of course sums to 175 since MC_T is the horizontal summation of MC_A and MC_B. This allocation equalizes marginal cost and consequently minimizes the total cost of producing 175 units.

To further illustrate the principle of optimally allocating output in a multiplant situation, we turn now to a numerical illustration. As you will see, the algebra is somewhat more complex than it is for the single-plant case, but the principle is the same: The manager maximizes profit by producing the output level for which marginal revenue equals marginal cost.

Multiplant Production at Mercantile Enterprises

Mercantile Enterprises—a firm with some degree of market power—produces its product in two plants. Hence, when making production decisions, the manager of Mercantile must decide not only how much to produce but also how to allocate the desired production between the two plants.

---

[1]For a mathematical demonstration, see the appendix to this chapter.

FIGURE 14.1
A Multiplant Firm

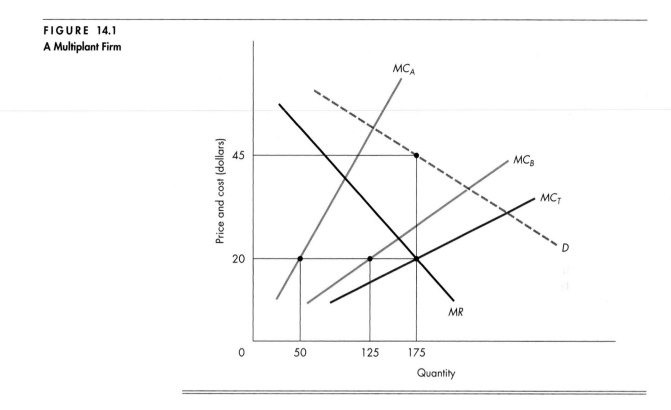

The production engineering department at Mercantile was able to provide the manager with simple, linear estimates of the incremental (marginal) cost functions for the two plants:

$$MC_A = 28 + 0.04Q_A \quad \text{and} \quad MC_B = 16 + 0.02Q_B$$

Note that the estimated marginal cost function for plant A (a plant built in 1978) is higher for every output than that for plant B (a plant built in 1995); plant B is more efficient.

The equation for the total marginal cost function (the horizontal sum of MC_A and MC_B) can be derived algebraically using the following procedure. First, solve for both inverse marginal cost functions:

$$Q_A = 25MC_A - 700$$

and

$$Q_B = 50MC_B - 800$$

Next, $Q_T (= Q_A + Q_B)$ is found by summing the two inverse marginal cost functions. Recall, however, that the horizontal summing process requires that $MC_A = MC_B = MC_T$ for all levels of total output Q_T. Thus it follows that

$$Q_A = 25MC_T - 700$$

and

$$Q_B = 50MC_T - 800$$

Summing the two inverse marginal cost functions results in the inverse *total* marginal cost function:

$$Q_T = Q_A + Q_B = 75MC_T - 1{,}500$$

which, after taking the inverse to express marginal cost once again as a function of output, results in the total marginal cost function:

$$MC_T = 20 + 0.0133Q_T$$

The marginal cost functions for plants A and B and the associated total marginal cost function are shown in Panel A of Figure 14.2. The process of horizontal summation can be seen by noting that when $MC = \$40$, $Q_A = 300$ units (point A), $Q_B = 1{,}200$ units (point B), and $Q_T = Q_A + Q_B = 1{,}500$ units (point C). Thus, if 1,500 units are to be produced, the manager should allocate production so that 300 units are produced in plant A and 1,200 units are produced in plant B. This allocation of production between the two plants minimizes the total cost of producing a total of 1,500 units.

Note that when Q_T is less than 600 units, plant A is shut down and only plant B is operated. Until Mercantile increases total production to 600 units or more (point K), the marginal cost of producing any output at all in plant A is greater than the marginal cost of producing additional units in plant B. For output levels in the 0 to 600-unit range, MC_B is the relevant total marginal cost curve since $Q_A = 0$. For total output levels greater than 600 units, Mercantile Enterprises will operate *both* plants and MC_T is the total marginal cost function.

Suppose that the estimated demand curve for Mercantile's output is

$$Q_T = 5{,}000 - 100P$$

The inverse demand function is

$$P = 50 - 0.01Q_T$$

and marginal revenue is

$$MR = 50 - 0.02Q_T$$

Equating marginal revenue and total marginal cost,

$$50 - 0.02Q_T = 20 + 0.0133Q_T$$

and solving for Q_T, the profit-maximizing level of output for Mercantile Enterprises is $Q_T^* = 900$. At this output level, marginal revenue and total marginal cost are both $32 at point E in Panel B of Figure 14.2. To minimize the cost of producing 900 units, the production of the 900 units should be allocated between plants A and B so that the marginal cost of the last unit produced in either plant is $32:

$$MC_A = 28 + 0.04Q_A = 32 \qquad \text{and} \qquad MC_B = 16 + 0.02Q_B = 32$$

FIGURE 14.2

Multiplant Production at Mercantile Enterprises

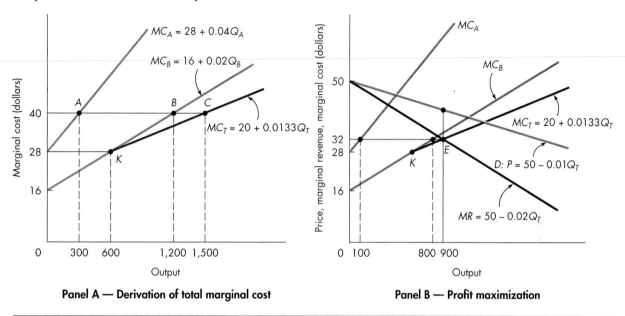

Panel A — Derivation of total marginal cost

Panel B — Profit maximization

Hence, for plant A, $Q_A^* = 100$, so 100 units will be produced in plant A. For plant B, $Q_B^* = 800$, so 800 units will be produced in plant B.

Now suppose that forecasted demand decreases and a new forecast of the demand for Mercantile's output is

$$Q_T = 4,000 - 100P$$

Given that the corresponding marginal revenue function is

$$MR = 40 - 0.02Q_T$$

the firm's profit-maximizing output (where $MR = MC_T$) declines to 600 units. At this output, marginal revenue and marginal cost are both $28. Equating MC_A and MC_B to $28, the manager found that for plant A, $Q_A^* = 0$, and for plant B, $Q_B^* = 600$. With the new (lower) forecast of demand, plant A will be shut down and all the output will be produced in plant B. As you can verify, if demand declines further, Mercantile would still produce, using only plant B. So for output levels of 600 or fewer units, the total marginal cost function is MC_B.

In effect, the total marginal cost function has a "kink" at point K in the figure. The kink at point K represents the total output level below which the high-cost plant is shut down. A kink occurs when marginal cost in the low-cost plant equals the minimum level of marginal cost in the high-cost plant, thereby making it optimal to begin producing with an additional plant.[2] The output at which the kink occurs is found by setting marginal cost in the *low*-cost plant equal to the minimum value of marginal cost in the *high*-cost plant:

$$MC_B = 28 = 16 + 0.02Q$$

so the high-cost plant begins operating when Q exceeds 600 units.

The preceding discussion and example show how a manager should allocate production between two plants to minimize the cost of producing the level of output that maximizes profit. The principle of equating marginal costs applies in exactly the same fashion to the case of three or more plants: Marginal cost is the same in all plants that produce. The only complication arises in the derivation of total marginal cost.

Once the total marginal cost function is derived, either by summing the individual plants' marginal cost curves graphically or by solving algebraically, the manager uses the total marginal cost function to find the profit-maximizing level of total output.

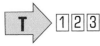

▣ **Principle**   A manager who has n plants that can produce output will maximize profit when the firm produces the level of total output and allocates that output among the n plants so that

$$MR = MC_T = MC_1 = \cdots = MC_n$$

14.2 COST-PLUS PRICING

It should be clear by now that for firms with market power, the short-run pricing decision based on the equality of marginal revenue and marginal cost yields the maximum profit for a firm. Why, then, do some firms use other techniques and rules of thumb to set the prices of their products? Surveys of managers report several reasons managers choose alternative pricing techniques. Some managers believe it is too difficult, or even impossible, for their firms to obtain reliable estimates of the demand and marginal cost functions. Other firms have long-established traditions of assigning responsibility for pricing (and production) decisions to senior executives with extensive industry experience. Their knowledge and feel for market conditions presumably give them the ability to make optimal pricing decisions using their judgment, perhaps coupled with one or more marketing rules of thumb.

One popular alternative technique for pricing is called *cost-plus pricing*. Firms using **cost-plus pricing** determine their price by setting price equal to the projected average total cost (*ATC*) plus a percentage of this average total cost as a markup:

cost-plus pricing
A method of determining price by setting price equal to average total cost plus a portion (*m*) of *ATC* as a markup.

$$P = ATC + (m \times ATC)$$
$$= (1 + m)ATC$$

---

[2]The low-cost (high-cost) plant is the plant with lowest (highest) marginal cost at $Q = 0$.

where m is the markup on unit cost. Note that profit margin, which equals $P - ATC$ as we discussed in Section 11.3, can be calculated by multiplying the markup times average total cost: $P - ATC = m \times ATC$. For example, if the markup m is 0.2 and average total cost is \$40, the percentage markup on average total cost is 20 percent, and price would be \$48 ($= 1.2 \times ATC$).[3] The profit margin, or profit per unit, is \$8 ($= 0.2 \times \$40$). As we stressed in our discussion of profit margin in Chapter 11, managers should ignore profit margin when making profit-maximizing decisions. We will return to this important point shortly.

Practical and Conceptual Shortcomings

The basic concept of cost-plus pricing is deceptively simple, and some managers choose to use the technique without recognizing or understanding its shortcomings. The problems with cost-plus pricing are both *practical* and *theoretical* in nature. After we discuss these problems, we will then show you that, when the variable costs of production are constant, the conceptual problems with cost-plus pricing can be overcome by estimating the firm's empirical demand function. In this situation, however, cost-plus pricing is probably no easier to implement than estimating demand and following the $MR = MC$ rule.

Practical problems using cost-plus pricing

Two important practical problems, which are frequently glossed over in marketing courses, complicate implementation of the cost-plus pricing formula. The first problem with using the formula involves choosing the value of average total cost (ATC), and the second problem concerns selecting the appropriate markup (m).

Because costs vary with the level of output produced, determining the value of ATC to multiply by $1 + m$ requires that a firm first specify the level of output that will be produced, which in turn determines the value of ATC for calculating price. Firms typically specify some standard or average level of production, based on the manager's *assumption* about how intensively the firm's fixed plant capacity will be utilized. However, without a consideration of prevailing demand conditions—a feature not incorporated in cost-plus pricing—the computed cost-plus price (absent extremely good fortune) will not equal the demand price for the output corresponding to the value of ATC. Consequently, the actual (or realized) profit margin will miss the target.

The nature of this critical problem is illustrated in Figure 14.3, which shows the firm's average total cost curve (ATC) and the prevailing demand and marginal revenue conditions facing the firm (D and MR), which are ignored when choosing ATC. Suppose the manager assumes the firm will operate at 5,000 units, which means that average total cost is expected to be \$20 per unit (point A). Further suppose the firm historically employs a 50 percent markup on average total cost

---

[3]Firms typically utilize cost-plus pricing for short-run pricing decisions. Of course, the formula can be applied to long-run pricing by substituting long-run average cost (LAC) for average total cost (ATC) in the formula. We will concentrate in this section on short-run pricing decisions.

FIGURE 14.3
Practical Problems with
Cost-Plus Pricing

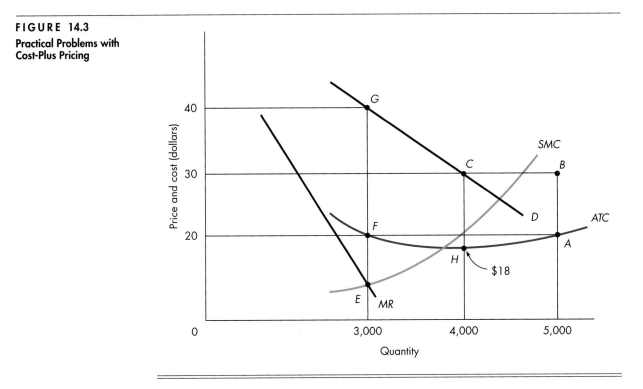

(*m* = 0.5), so the manager charges $30 (= 1.5 × $20) per unit and expects a profit margin of $10 (= $30 − $20) per unit. If things were to go as planned, the firm would earn $50,000 (= $10 × 5,000) of profit. However, because the price was set without considering existing demand conditions (*D* and *MR* in Figure 14.3), there is no reason to believe 5,000 units can be sold for $30 apiece. Given actual demand *D*, only 4,000 units are sold at $30 (point *C*). While the manager might be pleasantly surprised by the higher than expected profit margin of $12 (= $30 − 18), the firm's actual profit is only $48,000 (= $12 × 4,000) instead of the expected $50,000.

Notwithstanding the difficulties involved in determining average cost, a potentially more troublesome problem is the selection of the markup. Recent studies suggest that firms select markups to achieve target profit margins that generate "fair" returns on invested capital. Of course, as we stressed in Chapter 1, owners do not want to earn just a "fair" profit: they want to earn the *maximum* profit possible, which maximizes the value of the firm. Profit margin (or average profit) plays no role in making profit-maximizing decisions (see the discussion in Section 11.3), so it is unlikely that following arbitrary rules or historical precedent to choose the markup will produce the maximum profit. For example, in Figure 14.3, a marketing expert using cost-plus methodology to reach point G must guess the required markup is precisely 1.0, after first guessing that the firm will produce exactly 3,000 units (to set *ATC* equal to $20). These two practical problems are actually closely related to the theoretical problems with cost-plus methodology.

Theoretical problems with cost-plus pricing

Any method of pricing, whether it is cost-plus pricing or some other rule for setting price, will be generally unreliable for finding the profit-maximizing price and output if the technique is *not* mathematically equivalent to setting marginal revenue equal to marginal cost. In other words, a decision-making rule or technique that does not work in *theory* cannot generally provide optimal decisions in *practice*. Cost-plus pricing suffers from two conceptual problems that restrict the conditions under which cost-plus pricing is equivalent to the $MR = MC$ rule.

As you know from Chapter 3, marginal cost must be used for making optimizing decisions. Because cost-plus pricing employs *average* rather than *marginal* cost, it does not generally give the profit-maximizing price. This problem can be overcome in the special case when production conditions that are characterized by constant costs; that is, average variable cost is constant and equal to short-run marginal cost ($AVC = SMC$). We will discuss this special case shortly.

Another conceptual problem arises because cost-plus pricing does not incorporate a consideration of prevailing demand conditions, which, as explained earlier, also creates practical problems for implementing the cost-plus technique. With the $MR = MC$ pricing rule, demand conditions enter explicitly through the marginal revenue function, but cost-plus pricing does not utilize this information. While neglecting demand conditions does simplify the pricing decision, the lack of information about demand makes it impossible, except by sheer luck, to find the optimal or profit-maximizing price using the cost-plus pricing method. According to some studies of product pricing, it appears that the markups for different products do, in practice, differ according to such factors as the degree of competitiveness in the market and the price elasticity of demand. These findings suggest that marketing managers may indeed employ knowledge, gained through years of experience, about market demand conditions to determine the markup that maximizes profits. In any case, it is clear that knowledge of demand conditions must be part of any pricing technique in order to yield pricing decisions that are profit maximizing (i.e., equivalent to setting MR equal to MC).

Optimal Cost-Plus Pricing When Costs Are Constant

As mentioned earlier, under conditions of constant-cost production, cost-plus pricing can result in $MR = MC$ pricing. However, even when costs are constant, the manager must choose the optimal markup, which cannot be determined without information about the price elasticity of demand. We now show you how this can occur. As we saw in Chapter 3, marginal revenue may be written as

$$MR = P\left(1 + \frac{1}{E}\right)$$

where E is the price elasticity of demand. Setting marginal revenue equal to marginal cost, the condition for profit maximization may be written as

$$P\left(1 + \frac{1}{E}\right) = SMC$$

and thus

$$P = \left(\frac{E}{1 + E}\right) SMC$$

As previously noted, if the firm's average variable cost of production (AVC) is constant, then marginal cost (SMC) is constant and equal to (the constant) average variable cost ($SMC = AVC$).[4] Under conditions of constant costs, the profit-maximizing price can be expressed as

$$P = \left(\frac{E}{1 + E}\right) AVC$$

Note the similarity between this expression for profit-maximizing price and the equation for cost-plus pricing, $P = (1 + m)ATC$. In the former, price is a multiple of AVC and, in the latter, price is a multiple of ATC. The difference between ATC and AVC is, of course, average fixed cost (AFC). Since fixed costs are irrelevant for optimal decision making, AFC should be ignored, and the markup should be applied only to average variable cost. In order for multiplying $(1 + m)$ times AVC to yield the profit-maximizing price, m must be chosen so that

$$(1 + m^*) = \left(\frac{E^*}{1 + E^*}\right)$$

where m^* is the profit-maximizing markup, and E^* is the price elasticity computed at the profit-maximizing point on demand. Solving this equality for m^* shows precisely how the optimal markup is related to price elasticity at the profit-maximizing point on demand:

$$m^* = -\frac{1}{1 + E^*}$$

This formulation shows that, as the demand curve becomes more elastic at the profit-maximizing point (i.e., as $|E^*|$ increases), the profit-maximizing markup decreases. For example, if $E^* = -2$, the profit-maximizing markup would be 100 percent. However, if the demand curve were more elastic, say, $E^* = -5$, the profit-maximizing markup would fall to 25 percent. We have now established the following principle.

☐ **Principle** When costs are constant, cost-plus pricing yields the profit-maximizing price when the optimal markup, m^*, is applied to average variable costs as follows:

$$P = (1 + m^*)AVC$$

---

[4]Even when costs are not perfectly constant, basing the markup on average variable cost may nonetheless come close to the profit-maximizing price if the AVC curve has only a slight or gradual U-shape (so that SMC is almost equal to AVC over a range of output).

and the optimal markup is chosen according to the following relation with price elasticity of demand:

$$m^* = -\frac{1}{1 + E^*}$$

where E^* is price elasticity at the profit-maximizing point on the firm's demand.

Even when costs are constant, the previous principle does not solve the problem of finding the optimal markup (m^*), since managers must have knowledge of the firm's demand function in order to find the profit-maximizing value of price elasticity (E^*). In other words, without E^* the value of m^* cannot be calculated. For managers who are unable (or unwilling) to undertake statistical estimation of their firms' demand functions, the previous principle can, nonetheless, provide some practical guidance for choosing markup levels. As we explained previously, the less price elastic demand is expected to be at the assumed level of production, the larger the optimal markup will be. Furthermore, if the firm's pricing experts can accurately judge or guess the value of the product's price elasticity based on "intuitive feel" gained through experience, then m can be calculated using the formula presented in the above principle. Obviously, the better the guess about E^*, the closer the computed markup will be to m^*.

While cost-plus pricing is a commonly used alternative to direct application of the $MR = MC$ rule, cost-plus pricing may become less popular as managers gain a better understand of its shortcomings and as more firms take advantage of the detailed data on consumer transactions made possible by point-of-sale technology. In most cases, firms do not rely exclusively on either empirical demand techniques or on the experienced judgment of senior marketing experts. Sometimes both approaches are employed together to "cross-validate" pricing decisions. We will now discuss an example of how statistical demand estimation can be applied to the cost-plus pricing technique (when costs are constant) to achieve optimal pricing.

Markast Foundry: Empirical Validation of Markup Decisions

Markast Foundry produces titanium bearings used for manufacturing ultra-reliable electric motors. Markast faces constant production costs at its Chicago plant: Marginal and average variable costs are constant and equal to $6 per bearing. Total fixed costs are $31,250 per month. The president of marketing at Markast, who is in charge of pricing, has 20 years of experience in the industry and a reputation for understanding demand conditions in the industry.

For a number of years, the marketing president has followed a cost-plus pricing approach, marking up average variable cost by 100 percent ($m = 1$) to insure that the owners of Markast earn a "fair" return on their investment.[5] Currently,

---

[5]In practice, firms sometimes add an additional amount to AVC to cover average fixed costs, a variation of cost-plus pricing known as "full-cost pricing." Of course, since fixed costs are irrelevant in optimal decision making, the optimal markup can be determined without considering fixed costs, and thus the full-cost methodology in no way improves the pricing decision.

Markast sells 30,000 bearings per month at a price of $12 each, which is determined according to the cost-plus formula:

$$P = (1 + m)AVC = (1 + 1)\$6$$
$$= \$12$$

Markast's monthly profit is $148,750 [= $(P - AVC) \times Q - TFC = (\$12 - \$6) \times$ 30,000 $- \$31,250$].

The vice-president of marketing at Markast Foundry recently completed an executive MBA program and knows that cost-plus pricing will not typically maximize Markast's profits. The VP would like to replace cost-plus pricing with the $MR = SMC$ approach, but the president will overrule such a change on the grounds that cost-plus pricing can be utilized for pricing decisions at Markast Foundry because it produces under conditions of constant costs. Even so, the VP realizes that price cannot be optimally set unless the optimal markup is employed in the cost-plus formula. The VP decides to estimate Markast's demand function to see whether the marketing president is on target with his 100 percent markup. To ensure the president does not view his effort as hostile, the VP promises to share his findings with the president for the purpose of empirically validating pricing decisions at Markast.

The VP estimates Markast's monthly demand for its titanium bearings using a linear demand specification. After substituting values for the demand determinants, the estimated linear demand function is

$$Q = 45,000 - 1,250P$$

where Q is the number of titanium bearings demanded each month, and P is the price of a bearing in dollars. To determine the optimal value for elasticity, E^*, the VP applies a bit of algebra to discover that when costs are constant and demand is linear:

$$E^* = 1 + \frac{A}{0.5(AVC - A)}$$

where A is the price-intercept of the linear demand and E^* is the value of the price elasticity of demand at the profit-maximizing price.[6] To find A, the VP obtains the following inverse demand by the usual method (described in Chapters 2 and 12):

$$P = 36 - 0.0008Q$$

Substituting the values for AVC (= 6) and A (= 36) into the expression for E^* reveals that -1.4 is the value of E at the profit-maximizing point on Markast's demand:

$$E^* = 1 + \frac{\$36}{0.5(\$6 - \$36)} = 1 + (-2.4) = -1.4$$

---

[6]Begin with the expressions $MR = A + 2BQ$ and $SMC = AVC$; then set MR equal to AVC and solve for Q^* to get the profit-maximizing output, $Q^* = (AVC - A)/2B$. Next, substitute $P^* = A + BQ^*$ in $E^* = P^*/(P^* - A)$ to get $E^* = (A + BQ^*)/BQ^*$. Finally, substitute the previous expression for Q^* into E^* and apply a bit of algebra to get the formula for the optimal elasticity.

Now the VP calculates the optimal markup to be 2.5 or 250 percent:

$$m^* = -\frac{1}{1 + E^*} = -\frac{1}{1 + (-1.4)} = 2.5$$

Clearly, the president of marketing is not choosing a large enough markup and the price of Markast's bearings is currently below the profit-maximizing price, which is $21 [= (1 + 2.5) × $6]. In this example, the error is quite costly. By selling 18,750 (= 45,000 − 1,250 × 21) bearings per month at $21 per unit, Markast can earn monthly profit of $250,000 [= ($21 − 6) × 18,750 − 31,250] by pricing at $21 instead of $12.

The purpose of this example is to show that making optimal pricing decisions using cost-plus pricing under conditions of constant costs—without constant costs, cost-plus pricing cannot provide P^*—requires empirical demand information to find the optimal elasticity. As you will verify in Technical Problem 5, this procedure is mathematically equivalent to setting MR equal to SMC. While we see no reason to use cost-plus pricing, even when costs are constant, we understand that old habits die hard.

14.3 FIRMS WITH MULTIPLE MARKETS—PRICE DISCRIMINATION

price discrimination
Method in which firms charge different groups of customers different prices for the same good or service.

Thus far we have treated demand as simply the horizontal summation of the demands of all consumers, and every consumer is charged the same price for the product. But because consumers are different, their demands differ. At times, firms can take advantage of these differences in demand to increase their profit. Price discrimination is the method by which this is accomplished. **Price discrimination** means that the firm charges different consumers different prices for the same good (when there are no corresponding differences in costs). For example, price discrimination can occur when a firm charges different prices in its domestic and foreign markets or when a movie theater charges adults a higher price to see a movie than it charges children.

Certain conditions are necessary for the firm to be *able* to price-discriminate. First, the firm obviously must possess some market power. Economists normally think of price discrimination in the context of a monopoly firm, but since they have market power, monopolistic competitors and oligopolists may also be able to price-discriminate. Second, the demand functions for the individual consumers or groups of consumers must differ. As we will demonstrate later, this statement can be made more specific to require that the price elasticities must be different. Third, the different markets must be separable. The firm must be able to identify the individuals or groups of individuals and effectively separate them into submarkets. Finally, purchasers of the product must not be able to resell it to other customers. If consumers could buy and sell the product among themselves, there is no way that the firm could keep the submarkets separated. (A firm doesn't want the low-price buyers to sell its product to the high-price buyers.)

Normally, economists speak of three degrees of price discrimination. However, because we want to provide only a brief overview of price discrimination, we will

TABLE 14.1
Allocation of Sales between Two Markets

Quantity	Marginal revenue in market 1	Order of sales	Marginal revenue in market 2	Order of sales
1	$45	(1)	$34	(3)
2	36	(2)	28	(5)
3	30	(4)	22	(7)
4	22	(6)	13	(10)
5	17	(8)	10	(12)
6	15	(9)	8	
7	10	(11)	7	
8	7		4	
9	4		2	
10	0		1	

limit our discussion to what is referred to as third-degree price discrimination. This is the form most commonly observed and is the form that best illustrates our primary concern in this section: profit maximization with multiple markets.

Allocation of Sales in Two Markets to Maximize Revenue

The analysis of price discrimination is a straightforward application of the $MR = MC$ rule. As a first step in that analysis, assume that a firm has two separate markets for its product. Demand conditions in each market are such that the marginal revenues from selling specified quantities are as given in Table 14.1. Assume also that the manager has decided to produce 12 units. How should the manager allocate sales between the two markets in order to maximize the total revenue from the sale of 12 units? Clearly, revenue from selling the chosen level of output must be maximized if profit is to be maximized.

Consider the first unit; the firm can increase revenue by $45 by selling it in market 1 or by $34 by selling in market 2. Obviously, the firm will sell the first unit in market 1. The second unit also is sold in market 1 since its sale there increases revenue by $36, whereas it would increase revenue by only $34 in market 2. If $34 can be gained in market 2 but only $30 in market 1, unit 3 is sold in market 2. Similar reasoning shows that the fourth unit goes to market 1 and the fifth to market 2. Since unit 6 adds $22 to revenue in either market, it makes no difference where it is sold; 6 and 7 go one to each market. Units 8 and 9 are sold in market 1 because they yield higher marginal revenue there; 10 goes to market 2 for the same reason. Unit 11 can go to either market, because the additional revenues are the same, and unit 12 goes to the other. Thus the 12 units will be divided so that the marginal revenue is the same for the last unit sold in each market; the firm sells 7 units in market 1 and 5 in market 2. Thus the price-discriminating firm allocates a given output in such a way that the marginal revenues in each market are equal.[7]

_____

[7] For a mathematical demonstration, see the appendix to this chapter.

The results from Table 14.1 indicate that a manager will maximize profit at a given level of output when that output is allocated in such a way that

$$MR_1 = MR_2$$

This condition should not be surprising since it is just another application of the principle of constrained optimization presented in Chapter 3. If a manager wants to maximize total revenue subject to the constraint that there is only a limited number of units to sell, the manager should allocate sales so that the marginal revenues (marginal benefits) per unit are equal in the two markets. The marginal cost of selling 1 unit in market 1 is the 1 unit not available for sale in market 2 ($MC_1 = MC_2 = 1$ unit).

▣ **Principle** A manager who wishes to maximize the total revenue from selling a given amount of output in two separate markets (A and B) should allocate sales between the two markets so that

$$MR_A = MR_B$$

and all units are sold.

Although the marginal revenues in the two markets are equal, the prices charged are not. The higher price will be charged in the market with the less elastic demand; the lower price will be charged in the market having the more elastic demand. In the more elastic market, price could be raised only at the expense of a large decrease in sales. In the less elastic market, higher prices bring less reduction in sales.

This assertion can be demonstrated as follows: Let the prices in the two markets be P_1 and P_2. Likewise, let E_1 and E_2 denote the respective price elasticities. As shown in Chapter 6, marginal revenue can be expressed as

$$MR = P\left(1 + \frac{1}{E}\right)$$

As shown, managers will maximize revenue if they allocate output so that $MR_1 = MR_2$. That is,

$$MR_1 = P_1\left(1 + \frac{1}{E_1}\right) = P_2\left(1 + \frac{1}{E_2}\right) = MR_2$$

Since MR_1 and MR_2 must both be positive, E_1 and E_2 must both be greater (in absolute value) than 1 (i.e., demand must be elastic in each market). Assume that

$$P_1 < P_2$$

when $MR_1 = MR_2$. By manipulating the equation above,

$$\frac{P_1}{P_2} = \frac{\left(1 + \dfrac{1}{E_2}\right)}{\left(1 + \dfrac{1}{E_1}\right)} < 1$$

Therefore, since

$$\left(1 + \frac{1}{E_2}\right) < \left(1 + \frac{1}{E_1}\right)$$

it must be the case that

$$\left|\frac{1}{E_2}\right| > \left|\frac{1}{E_1}\right|$$

so that

$$|E_1| > |E_2|$$

The market with the lower price must have the higher elasticity at that price. Therefore, if a firm price-discriminates, it will always charge the lower price in the market having the more elastic demand curve.

▢ **Principle** A manager who price-discriminates in two separate markets, A and B, will maximize total revenue for a given level of output by charging the lower price in the more elastic market and the higher price in the less elastic market. If $|E_A| > |E_B|$, then $P_A < P_B$.

Profit Maximization with Price Discrimination

Thus far we have assumed that the price-discriminating firm wishes to allocate a *given level of output* among its markets in order to maximize the revenue from selling that output. Now we discuss how a manager determines the profit-maximizing level of output and the prices to charge in the different markets.

As you probably expected, the manager maximizes profit by equating marginal revenue with marginal cost. The firm's marginal cost curve is no different from that of a nondiscriminating firm with market power. So the problem is to derive the marginal revenue curve.

With discrete data such as those in Table 14.1, we would simply increase sales as discussed above, then determine the total marginal revenue from the allocation of each unit of output to the market with the higher marginal revenue. Thus total marginal revenue from Table 14.1 would be $45 for the first unit sold, $36 for the second (both in market 1), $34 for the third (in market 2), $30 for the fourth, and so on.

For continuous demand and marginal revenue curves in each submarket, the total marginal revenue curve for a price-discriminating firm is simply the horizontal summation of the marginal revenues in each market. Assume that the firm sells in two markets, 1 and 2. The demand and marginal revenue curves in markets 1 and 2 are shown, respectively, as D_1 and MR_1 in Panel A of Figure 14.4 and as D_2 and MR_2 in Panel B. In Panel C of the figure, the total marginal revenue, MR_T, is the horizontal summation of MR_1 and MR_2.

From the preceding discussion, a manager will allocate any given output between the two markets so that MR_1 equals MR_2. For example, if the firm produces 300 units of output at which MR equals $30, it will sell 100 units in market 1 and

FIGURE 14.4
Deriving Total Marginal Revenue

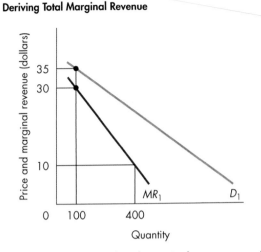

Panel A — Demand and marginal revenue: market 1

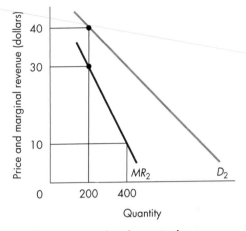

Panel B — Demand and marginal revenue: market 2

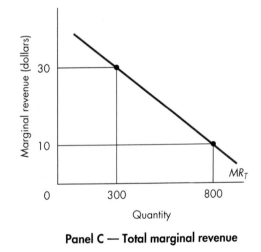

Panel C — Total marginal revenue

200 in market 2. At 100 units of output (from Panel A), MR_1 equals \$30. At 200 units of output (from Panel B), MR_2 also equals \$30. Thus, no matter in which market unit 300 is sold, the firm's marginal revenue is \$30, as shown in Panel C. And this is the only allocation of 300 total units that equates the marginal revenues in the two markets. Likewise, if the firm wants to sell 800 units, it will sell 400 in market 1 and 400 in market 2; as shown in the figure, the marginal revenue is \$10 in each market. Thus for 800 units of output, the total marginal revenue is \$10.

At every other output, the marginal revenue in Panel C (MR_T) is obtained in the same way.

For each level of output, the price in each market is given by the demand in that market. For example, if 300 units are sold, from D_1 the price of the 100 units sold in market 1 is $35; from D_2 the price of the 200 units sold in market 2 is $40. (The horizontal sum of D_1 and D_2 was not graphed because this curve is irrelevant for the price-discriminating firm.)

The only decision remaining is how much total output the firm should produce to maximize its profits. To see how this decision is made, consider Figure 14.5, in which all the relations are generalized graphically. Again the firm is selling a product in two markets: D_1 and MR_1 are demand and marginal revenue in market 1; D_2 and MR_2 are demand and marginal revenue in market 2. MR_T is the horizontal summation of the two marginal revenue curves. For convenience, all these curves are shown on the same graph, along with the firm's average cost (ATC) and marginal cost (MC) curves.

As always, the firm maximizes profit by producing the output at which total marginal revenue equals marginal cost. In this case, Q_T, where MC equals MR_T, is the total output. The marginal revenue and marginal cost are both equal to the dollar amount M in Figure 14.5.

The market allocation rule, previously determined, requires that marginal revenue be the same in each submarket. Since the total market marginal revenue is the added revenue from selling the last unit in either submarket, $MR_1 = MR_2 = M$. At a marginal revenue of M, the quantity sold in market 1 is Q_1; in market 2, Q_2. Since MR_T is the horizontal summation of MR_1 and MR_2, $Q_1 + Q_2 = Q_T$, the total output. Furthermore, from the relevant demand curves, the price associated with output Q_1 in market 1 is P_1, and the price associated with Q_2 in market 2 is P_2.

Summarizing these results, if the aggregate market for a firm's product can be divided into submarkets with different price elasticities, the firm can profitably practice price discrimination. Total output is determined by equating marginal cost with total marginal revenue. The output is allocated among the submarkets so as to equate marginal revenue in each submarket with total marginal revenue at the profit-maximizing level of output. With two markets, the profit-maximization rule for the price-discriminating firm is

$$MR_T = MC = MR_1 = MR_2$$

Price in each submarket is determined from the submarket demand curve.

Examples of price discrimination are not hard to find. Many drugstores offer discounts on drugs to persons 65 and over. Thus the drugstores price-discriminate. Retired persons probably have a more elastic demand for drugs, because the market value of their time is lower. Retired persons would tend to shop around more for lower prices, and differences in price among different age groups can be explained by different price elasticities, resulting from different evaluations of time.

Movies, plays, concerts, and similar forms of entertainment practice price discrimination according to age. Generally, younger people pay lower prices. Supposedly, in such cases, younger people have more elastic demands for tickets,

FIGURE 14.5
Profit Maximization with Two Markets

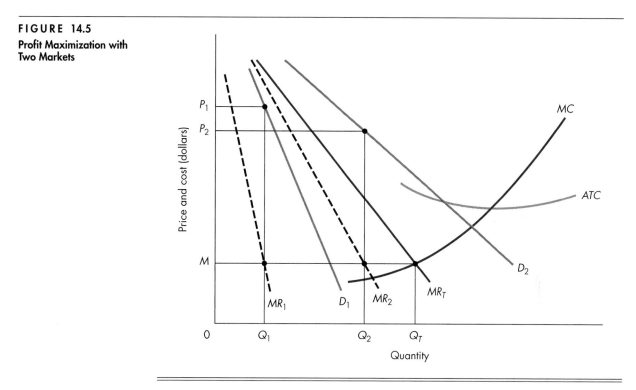

possibly because of the availability of more substitute forms of entertainment. (It is not correct to say that different ticket prices for afternoon and evening performances are evidence of price discrimination. These are different products in the eye of the consumer.)

Airlines frequently discriminate between vacation and business travel. Vacation travelers would have a more elastic demand than business travelers, probably because the value of time in business travel is greater. Other examples of price discrimination are electric companies that charge lower rates to industrial users than to households (although this may be, in part, due to differences in costs), and university bookstores that charge lower prices to faculty than to students. On the other hand, students frequently are charged a lower price for subscriptions to newspapers and magazines.

Manufacturers and sellers of durable goods, such as automobiles and large appliances, sometimes practice price discrimination also. Automobiles with exactly the same characteristics all have the same window or sticker price (excluding the shipping charge). But as you probably know, dealers generally discount these prices on many models. Except for extremely hot sellers, people seldom pay the listed price. However, everyone does not pay the same price for the same vehicle. Ms. Jones may pay a lower price than Mr. Smith because Ms. Jones is willing to bargain longer or possibly the dealer recognized that Mr. Smith is already sold on the car. Perhaps Mr. Smith came into the showroom, saw the list price, and said, "Wow, is that all you're charging for that great car?" In any case, Mr. Smith probably has the less elastic demand. We should note, however, that this is a slightly different form of price discrimination than that discussed earlier. In this case the dealer treats each potential consumer as a separate market, and charges as much as the consumer is willing to pay, if possible.

To implement profit maximization with multiple markets, it would be necessary for the manager to estimate demand and marginal revenue functions for each of the markets. After summing to obtain a total marginal revenue function, total output would be that at which total marginal revenue is equal to marginal cost. Then, this output will be allocated to the various markets so that the marginal revenues are all equal to total marginal revenue at the profit-maximizing output. We illustrate this procedure with a simple algebraic example.

Multiple Market Pricing at Galactic Manufacturing

The manager of Galactic Manufacturing—a firm with substantial monopoly power—knows that the firm faces two distinct markets. Using the techniques described earlier in this text, the demand curves for these two markets were forecasted to be

$$\text{Mkt 1: } Q_1 = 1,000 - 20P_1 \quad \text{and} \quad \text{Mkt 2: } Q_2 = 500 - 5P_2$$

Solving for the inverse demand functions in the two markets,

$$\text{Mkt 1: } P_1 = 50 - 0.05Q_1 \quad \text{and} \quad \text{Mkt 2: } P_2 = 100 - 0.2Q_2$$

The marginal revenue functions associated with these inverse demand functions are

$$\text{Mkt 1: } MR_1 = 50 - 0.1Q_1 \quad \text{and} \quad \text{Mkt 2: } MR_2 = 100 - 0.4Q_2$$

To obtain the total marginal revenue function, $MR_T = f(Q_T)$, we follow steps identical to those employed in the algebraic derivation of the total marginal cost function. First, the inverse marginal revenue functions are obtained for both markets in which Galactic Manufacturing sells its product:

$$\text{Mkt 1: } Q_1 = 500 - 10MR_1 \quad \text{and} \quad \text{Mkt 2: } Q_2 = 250 - 2.5MR_2$$

For any given level of total output, $MR_1 = MR_2 = MR_T$; thus

$$\text{Mkt 1: } Q_1 = 500 - 10MR_T \quad \text{and} \quad \text{Mkt 2: } Q_2 = 250 - 2.5MR_T$$

Since $Q_T = Q_1 + Q_2$, the inverse of total marginal revenue is obtained by summing the two inverse marginal revenue curves to get

$$Q_T = Q_1 + Q_2 = 500 - 10MR_T + 250 - 2.5MR_T = 750 - 12.5MR_T$$

Taking the inverse, we obtain the total marginal revenue function facing Galactic Manufacturing:

$$MR_T = 60 - 0.08Q_T$$

FIGURE 14.6
Multiple Market Pricing at Galactic Manufacturing

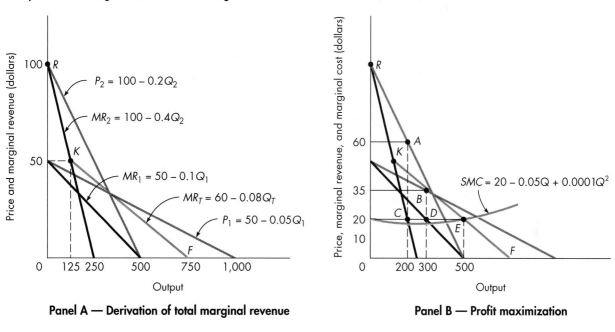

Panel A — Derivation of total marginal revenue

Panel B — Profit maximization

Panel A of Figure 14.6 illustrates graphically the derivation of total marginal revenue for Galactic Manufacturing. Panel A shows graphs of the demand and marginal revenue functions in markets 1 and 2. The total marginal revenue function is the line RKF. If total output is less than 125, every unit produced should be sold in market 2 in order to maximize revenue (for that output level) because MR_2 exceeds MR_1 until Galactic chooses to sell more than 125 units. Thus total marginal revenue has a kink at 125 (point K), and MR_2 is the total marginal revenue function since $Q_1 = 0$ when total output is 125 units or less.

The manager of Galactic Manufacturing obtained from the engineering department an estimate of the firm's marginal cost function:

$$MC = 20 - 0.05Q + 0.0001Q^2$$

Equating estimated total marginal revenue and marginal cost,

$$60 - 0.08Q = 20 - 0.05Q + 0.0001Q^2$$

the manager of Galactic solved for Q using the quadratic formula and determined the profit-maximizing level of output to be 500. As you can see in Panel B of Figure 14.6, MR_T intersects MC at 500 units (point E). At 500 units of output, total marginal revenue and marginal cost both equal $20. To find the optimal allocation of 500 units between the two markets, the manager allocates sales so that marginal revenues are equated across the two markets at a value of $20. The manager must solve the following two equations:

$$\text{Mkt 1: } 20 = 50 - 0.1Q_1 \qquad \text{and} \qquad \text{Mkt 2: } 20 = 100 - 0.4Q_2$$

The solution is to sell 300 units in market 1 and 200 units in market 2. These points, where $MR_1 = MR_2 = MR_T$ are shown in Panel B by points C, D, and E.

The manager determines the price to charge in the two markets by substituting the optimal quantities into the demand equations in each of the markets. The manager finds that profit is maximized by selling the 300 units of output in market 1 at a price of $35 and the 200 units of output in market 2 at a price of $60. Points A and B in Panel B show the optimal pricing solution for Galactic Manufacturing. By charging different prices in the separate markets, Galactic Manufacturing collects total revenues of $10,500 (= $35 × 300) in market 1 and $12,000 (= $60 × 200) in market 2, for a combined market total revenue of $22,500 (= $10,500 + $12,000).

To verify that charging two (different) prices generates more revenue than charging a single price in both markets, we now calculate the total revenue Galactic could collect if it instead charged a single price to sell 500 units.[8] The price Galactic can charge to sell a total of 500 units is $40, which is the price for 500 units obtained from the horizontally summed demand curves in markets 1 and 2. Mathematically, this price can be obtained from the price equation associated with MR_T:

$$P_T = 60 - 0.04Q_T = 60 - 0.04(500) = \$40$$

If Galactic charged all customers a single price of $40, it would sell 500 units and generate just $20,000 (= $40 × 500) in total revenue—a reduction in revenue of $2,500 compared with the revenue from charging different prices in the two market segments. We now summarize this discussion of pricing in multiple markets with a principle.

Principle   A manager who wishes to sell output in *n* separate markets will maximize profit if the firm produces the level of total output and allocates that output among the *n* separate markets so that

$$MR_T = MR_1 = \cdots = MR_n = MC$$

The optimal prices to charge in each market are determined from the demand functions in each of the *n* markets.

14.4 FIRMS SELLING MULTIPLE PRODUCTS

Even the most cursory survey of firms operating in the United States shows that many firms produce several different products or at least several different models in their product lines. While in some cases a firm's products are unrelated, in most

---

[8]Notice that 500 units are also the profit-maximizing output level when Galactic chooses to charge all buyers a single price. This is true because MR_T is the monopolist's marginal revenue curve when the two market demand curves are horizontally summed to construct the total demand facing the monopolist. In this example, the horizontal summation of the two demand equations is $P_T = 60 - 0.04Q_T$ and the associated marginal revenue is $MR_T = 60 - 0.08Q_T$.

cases the products are related either in consumption or in production. When the products that a firm produces are related, the firm's output and pricing decision must incorporate the interrelations in order to maximize total profit.

Multiple Products Related in Consumption

Recall that the demand for a particular commodity depends not only on the price of the product itself but also on the prices of related commodities, incomes, tastes, and so on. For simplicity, we ignore the other factors and write one demand function as

$$Q_X = f(P_X, P_Y)$$

where Q_X is the quantity demanded of commodity X, P_X is the price of X, and P_Y is the price of a related commodity Y—either a substitute or complement.

In the discussion so far in the text, we have treated P_Y as if it were given to the firm. That is, we assumed P_Y to be a parameter determined outside the firm. Thus the firm would maximize its profits by selecting the appropriate level of production and price for X. If, however, the firm in question produces *both* commodities X and Y, the price of the related commodity Y is no longer beyond the control of the manager.

To maximize profit, the levels of output and prices for the related commodities must be determined *jointly*. For a two-product firm, the profit-maximizing conditions remain the same:

$$MR_X = MC_X \qquad \text{and} \qquad MR_Y = MC_Y$$

However, the marginal revenue of X will depend on the quantities sold of both X and Y, as will the marginal revenue of Y. The interdependence of the two marginal revenues, MR_X and MR_Y, requires that the marginal conditions set forth earlier must be satisfied *simultaneously*. (Note that in this case the products are not related in production, so MC_X and MC_Y depend only on, respectively, the output of X and the output of Y.) When products are used together, consumers typically buy them together, and these kinds of goods are **complements in consumption.** A different situation, **substitutes in consumption,** arises when a firm sells multiple products that are substitutes. Then buyers would purchase only one of the firm's products. In both cases, marginal revenues are interdependent.

complements in consumption
Products that are used together and purchased together.

substitutes in consumption
Products are substitutes and buyers purchase only one of the firm's products.

Principle   When a firm produces two products, X and Y, that are related in consumption either as substitutes or complements, the manager of the multiple-product firm maximizes profit by producing and selling the amounts of X and Y for which

$$MR_X = MC_X$$

and

$$MR_Y = MC_Y$$

are *simultaneously* satisfied. The profit-maximizing prices, P_X and P_Y, are determined by substituting the optimal levels of X and Y into the demand functions and solving for P_X and P_Y.

To show how a manager would maximize profit under these circumstances, we will use another hypothetical example. In this example we will look at a firm that

ILLUSTRATION 14.1

Sometimes It's Hard to Price-Discriminate

In the theoretical discussion of price discrimination, we made two important points: (1) Firms must separate the markets according to demand elasticity, and (2) firms must be able to separate markets so as to keep buyers in the higher-price market from buying in the lower-price market. In some of the market examples we used, it was relatively easy to separate the markets. For example, at movie theaters it is fairly simple, and relatively inexpensive, to prevent an adult from entering the theater with a lower-priced child's ticket. In other cases of price discrimination, it is rather difficult or costly to separate the markets. If it is impossible or expensive to separate markets, price discrimination will not be profitable, and the monopolist will charge a single price to all customers.

One of the most frequently cited examples of a market in which separation is difficult is the airline market. It is no secret that airlines attempt to charge leisure fliers lower fares than business travelers. The story of such an attempt by Northwest Airlines illustrates the difficulty of separating markets.

The Wall Street Journal reported: "Northwest Airlines, seeking to entice families and groups of leisure travelers who often wait for deep fare cuts before flying, has introduced a permanent discount fare. The new supersaver fare will offer savings of 20 percent to 40 percent anytime *groups of two or more people* travel together." According to a Northwest vice president, "We're trying to decouple the leisure fares from the rest of the fare market by offering fares low enough so that it won't pay for them to wait for a special fare sale."

The *WSJ* noted that this change would be likely to stimulate family travel but would also eliminate the use of supersaver fares by business travelers. Previously, many business travelers purchased round-trip supersaver tickets when fares dropped below 50 percent, then threw away the return portion of the ticket or used it later. Northwest was planning to raise or do away with its other supersaver fares designed to attract leisure travelers. Most business travelers fly alone and would not be able to take advantage of the new, lower fares requiring groups of two or more. The Northwest executive also predicted that businesspeople would not abuse these tickets. Should the plan stick and spread, he said, it will allow airlines to maintain an attractive offering for the most price-sensitive travelers, while allowing the basic supersaver fares to continue rising along with business rates.

This reasoning was a bit optimistic on the part of the airline. The *WSJ* noted that groups of business travelers could work around the restrictions that currently applied to supersavers. The president of one travel agency said, "Groups of businesspeople going to company meetings or conventions might be able to save thousands." One airline official expressed concern that travel agents would match travelers who did not know each other who were going to the same destination. Clearly there were many ways to defeat the airline's attempts to price-discriminate effectively.

But Northwest knew about the problems and tried to make the practice of cross-buying difficult. Travelers were required to book their flights together, check in together, and follow identical itineraries in order to qualify for the group discounts. The fares were nonrefundable, required a Saturday night stay, and had to be booked 14 days in advance—practices that business travelers typically would find difficult to accomplish. Of course, some of these restrictions designed to weed out business travelers could discourage many leisure travelers, the very people the new discounts were designed to attract. And obviously single leisure travelers would be left out.

As you can see, the problem of separating markets—preventing customers in the higher-price market from buying in the lower-price market—can be an extremely challenging task for the would-be price discriminator. For airlines, it would be much easier if passengers came with signs saying "business traveler" or "leisure traveler." As previously noted, in markets where separating the higher-price buyers from the lower-price buyers is too difficult or too expensive, price discrimination will not be profitable.

Source: Brett Pulley, "Northwest Cuts Fares to Boost Leisure Travel," *The Wall Street Journal*, Jan. 12, 1993.

produces products that are substitutes in consumption, but exactly the same technique applies for products that are complements in consumption.

Producing Multiple Products at Zicon Manufacturing

Zicon Manufacturing produces two types of automobile vacuum cleaners. One, which we denote as product X, plugs into the cigarette lighter receptacle; the other, product Y, has rechargeable batteries. Assuming that there is no relation between the two products other than the apparent substitutability in consumption, the manager of Zicon wanted to determine the profit-maximizing levels of production and price for the two products.

Using the techniques described in Chapter 7, the demand functions for the two products were forecasted to be

$$Q_X = 80{,}000 - 8{,}000P_X + 6{,}000P_Y \quad \text{and} \quad Q_Y = 40{,}000 - 4{,}000P_Y + 4{,}000P_X$$

Solving these two forecasted demand functions simultaneously for P_X and P_Y, the manager obtained the following inverse demand functions in which each price is a function of both quantities:[9]

$$P_X = 70 - 0.0005Q_X - 0.00075Q_Y \quad \text{and} \quad P_Y = 80 - 0.001Q_Y - 0.0005Q_X$$

The total revenue functions for each product are

$$TR_X = P_X Q_X = 70Q_X - 0.0005Q_X^2 - 0.00075Q_Y Q_X \quad \text{and}$$
$$TR_Y = P_Y Q_Y = 80Q_Y - 0.001Q_Y^2 - 0.0005Q_X Q_Y$$

The (grand) total revenue from both products is obtained by adding the revenues from both products: $TR = TR_X + TR_Y$. The associated marginal revenue functions for each product are[10]

$$MR_X = 70 - 0.001Q_X - 0.00125Q_Y \quad \text{and} \quad MR_Y = 80 - 0.002Q_Y - 0.00125Q_X$$

---

[9]One way to solve these two equations simultaneously is to use the method of substitution. First, solve one demand function for P_X in terms of Q_X and P_Y and the other demand function for P_Y in terms of Q_Y and P_X. Then substitute the equation for P_Y into the equation for P_X, and vice versa. These two equations can then be solved for P_X and P_Y in terms of Q_X and Q_Y. The mathematical appendix at the end of this chapter shows how to use matrix algebra to find equations for linear inverse demand curves.

[10]As noted several times, the marginal revenue curve associated with a linear demand curve has the same intercept and is twice as steep as linear demand. In this case of interdependent demand curves, an additional term must be included in each marginal revenue function to reflect the effect of selling another unit of one good on the *price* of the other good. The intercepts for MR_X and MR_Y are, respectively, $(70 - 0.00075Q_Y)$ and $(80 - 0.0005Q_X)$. The additional terms reflecting the interdependence of MR_X and MR_Y are, respectively, $-0.0005Q_Y$ and $-0.00075Q_X$. Thus

$$MR_X = (70 - 0.00075Q_Y) - 2(0.0005)Q_X - 0.0005Q_Y = 70 - 0.001Q_X - 0.00125Q_Y$$
and
$$MR_Y = (80 - 0.005Q_X) - 2(0.001)Q_Y - 0.00075Q_X = 80 - 0.002Q_Y - 0.00125Q_X$$

The mathematical appendix at the end of this chapter provides the general algebraic solution for linear demands and marginal revenues for the case of two goods.

The production manager obtained estimates of the total cost functions:

$$TC_X = 7.5Q_X + 0.00025Q_X^2 \quad \text{and} \quad TC_Y = 11Q_Y + 0.000125Q_Y^2$$

The marginal cost functions associated with these total costs are

$$MC_X = 7.5 + 0.0005Q_X \quad \text{and} \quad MC_Y = 11 + 0.00025Q_Y$$

To determine the outputs of each product that will maximize profit, the manager of Zicon equated MR and MC for the two products:

$$70 - 0.001Q_X - 0.00125Q_Y = 7.5 + 0.0005Q_X$$
$$80 - 0.002Q_Y - 0.00125Q_X = 11 + 0.00025Q_Y$$

Solving these equations simultaneously for Q_X and Q_Y (following the approach in footnote 9), the profit-maximizing outputs were found to be $Q_X^* = 30,000$ and $Q_Y^* = 14,000$. Using these outputs in the price functions, the manager of Zicon found that the profit-maximizing prices for X and Y were

$$P_X^* = 70 - 0.0005(30,000) - 0.00075(14,000) = \$44.50$$

and

$$P_Y^* = 80 - 0.001(14,000) - 0.0005(30,000) = \$51$$

The total revenue from selling the optimal amounts of X and Y was $2,049,000, which was the sum of TR_X and TR_Y:

$$TR_X + TR_Y = \$44.50(30,000) + \$51(14,000)$$
$$= \$2,049,000$$

The total cost of producing the optimal amounts of X and Y was $628,500, which equals the sum of TC_X and TC_Y:

$$TC_X + TC_Y = 7.5(30,000) + 0.00025(30,000)^2 + 11(14,000) + 0.000125(14,000)^2$$
$$= \$628,500$$

The manager expected Zicon Manufacturing to earn profit of $1,420,500 (= $2,049,000 - $628,500).

Multiple Products That Are Substitutes in Production

substitutes in production
Goods, produced by the same firm, that compete for limited production facilities.

It is not uncommon for multiproduct firms to produce goods that are **substitutes in production.** This situation is often encountered when a firm produces several models of the same basic product. These different models compete for the limited production facilities of the firm and are therefore substitutes in the firm's production process. In the long run, the firm can adjust its production facility in order to produce the profit-maximizing level of each product. We will now demonstrate how a manager could determine the profit-maximizing number of total hours to operate a production facility (H_T^*) and the optimal allocation of hours between the production of good X (H_X^*) and good Y (H_Y^*).

The optimization condition for the allocation of the production facility between the production of X and Y is easy to demonstrate. A manager first must determine, for each of the two products X and Y, the additional revenue that can be generated by allocating to a good one more hour of the production facility. Consider production of good X. The amount of additional output of X that can be produced by using the facility one more hour in the production of X can be expressed as $\Delta X / \Delta H_X$, which is the marginal product for good X of one more hour of time spent producing X. The same relation holds for good Y. The marginal products of X and Y for extra hours of production time can be expressed as

$$\frac{\Delta X}{\Delta H_X} = MP_{H_X} \quad \text{and} \quad \frac{\Delta Y}{\Delta H_Y} = MP_{H_Y}$$

To determine the value to the firm of one more hour of time spent producing either good X or good Y, the manager must have estimates of marginal revenue for each good, MR_X and MR_Y. As shown in Chapter 12 for firms with market power, the marginal revenue product of an input measures the additional revenue the firm can earn by using one more unit of an input. For goods X and Y, the marginal revenue products are

$$MRP_X = \frac{\Delta TR}{\Delta H_X} = MR_X \times MP_{H_X} \quad \text{and} \quad MRP_Y = \frac{\Delta TR}{\Delta H_Y} = MR_Y \times MP_{H_Y}$$

For a given number of total hours of production facility time, the firm will maximize total revenue and profit by allocating the facility so that its marginal revenue product in producing each good is the same:

$$MRP_X = MRP_Y$$

If the allocation of total hours were such that $MRP_X > MRP_Y$, total revenue could be increased by reallocating hours away from the production of Y to the production of X—increase H_X and decrease H_Y. This reallocation would reduce MRP_X and increase MRP_Y. Reallocation should continue until the marginal revenue products are equal, $MRP_X = MRP_Y$.

To find the optimal number of total hours to operate a facility (H_T^*), the *total marginal revenue product curve* (MPR_T) must be constructed by horizontally summing MRP_X and MRP_Y, as shown in Figure 14.7. The profit-maximizing condition is

$$MRP_T = MC = MRP_X = MRP_Y$$

Profits will be maximized when total marginal revenue product equals marginal cost and this production is allocated so that the marginal additions to revenue are the same for the two products. H_X^* is devoted to the production of X, H_Y^* is devoted to the production of Y, and $H_X^* + H_Y^* = H_T^*$. To see how this condition can be utilized, let's look at a simplified example.

FIGURE 14.7

Profit-Maximizing Allocation of Production Facilities

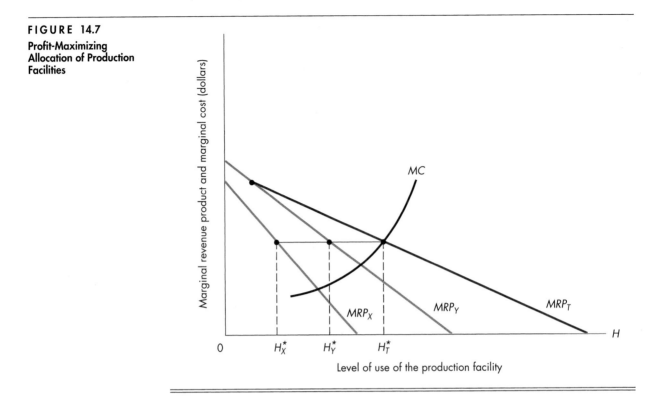

Multiple-Product Production at Surefire Products

Surefire Products, Inc., manufactures two products, X and Y, that are unrelated in consumption but are substitutes in production. The manager can increase or decrease the total number of hours that the firm can use its production facilities. The manager wants to know the answer to two questions: (1) What is the optimal level of usage (hours of operation) of the plant? (2) How should the level of usage be allocated between the production of the two products?

The demand functions for the two products were forecasted to be

$$Q_X = 60 - 0.5P_X \quad \text{and} \quad Q_Y = 40 - 0.67P_Y$$

where the quantities were the number of units demanded per day and the prices were expressed in dollars per unit. The inverse demand functions were

$$P_X = 120 - 2Q_X \quad \text{and} \quad P_Y = 60 - 1.5Q_Y$$

From these inverse demand functions, the marginal revenue functions were

$$MR_X = 120 - 4Q_X \quad \text{and} \quad MR_Y = 60 - 3Q_Y$$

Discussions with the plant supervisor indicated that in one hour of production time either 2 units of X or 4 units of Y could be produced. In a sense, the production functions for the two products are

$$Q_X = 2H_X \quad \text{and} \quad Q_Y = 4H_Y$$

where H_X and H_Y denote, respectively, hours of assembly-line time in the production of X and Y. From the production functions, the marginal products are $MP_{H_X} = 2$ and $MP_{H_Y} = 4$.

Using the demand forecasts and the estimates of the production functions provided by the plant supervisor, estimates of the marginal revenue product of the production facility in the production of X and Y were

$$MP_{H_X} = MR_X \times MP_{H_X} = [120 - 4(2H_X)] \times (2)$$
$$= 240 - 16H_X$$

and

$$MP_{H_Y} = MR_Y \times MP_{H_Y} = [60 - 3(4H_Y)] \times (4)$$
$$= 240 - 48H_Y$$

To obtain the total marginal revenue product function, these two curves were summed horizontally; that is, these functions were inverted to find H_X and H_Y, the hours were summed ($H_T = H_X + H_Y$), then the inverse was taken once again. The resulting total MRP was

$$MRP_T = 240 - 12H_T$$

Working with the engineers for Surefire, the plant supervisor was able to come up with an estimate of the additional cost of operating the plant an additional hour—an incremental (marginal) cost for usage of the plant. This estimate was

$$MC = 72 + 2H_T$$

Figure 14.8 shows MRP_X, MRP_Y, MRP_T, and MC for this example.

Equating the total marginal revenue product of an hour's usage of the plant with the marginal cost of an additional hour's usage,

$$240 - 12H_T = 72 + 2H_T$$

the manager then solved for H_T and found that the optimal level of usage of the plant was 12 hours per day. At this level of usage, $MRP_T = MC = \$96$. To allocate these hours between the production of X and Y, the marginal revenue products for the production facility in the production of X and Y must both be equal to \$96:

$$240 - 16H_X = 96 \quad \text{and} \quad 240 - 48H_Y = 96$$

Since $H_X^* = 9$ and $H_Y^* = 3$, the optimal allocation would be 9 hours in the production of X and 3 hours in the production of Y. Figure 14.8 shows the profit-maximizing solution for Surefire Products.

FIGURE 14.8
Substitutes in Production at Surefire Products, Inc.

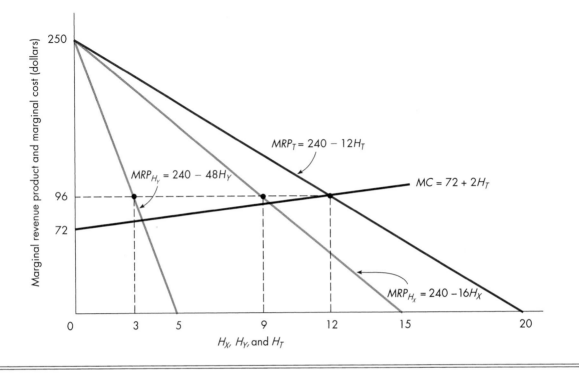

From the production functions, the quantity of X produced is 18 $(= 2 \times 9)$ units, and the quantity of Y produced is 12 $(= 4 \times 3)$. The prices are $P_X^* = \$84$ [$= 120 - 2(18)$] and $P_Y^* = \$42$ [$= 60 - 1.5(12)$].

Multiple Products That Are Complements in Production

complements in production
Two or more goods that are produced using a common input.

Complements in production typically occur when an ingredient input is used to produce two or more products. One of the classic examples is that of beef carcasses and hides. The food products produced with the beef carcasses and the leather products produced with the hides are complement goods in production. Furthermore, the joint production of the two products is characterized by fixed proportions: For each additional beef carcass produced, one additional hide is produced also.

Petroleum refining has similar characteristics. With an existing refinery and a given mix of input crude oils, production of an additional barrel of one of the lighter distillates, such as gasoline, requires that the refinery produce some additional amount of the heavy distillates, such as fuel oil. Complementarity in production can also be observed in mineral extraction. Frequently, two or more metals are found together in the same ore deposit. When the ore goes into the smelter, more than one metal is produced. For example, nickel and zinc frequently are in the same deposit, so the smelters are designed to produce both metals from the same ore.

Since complements in production frequently result when one raw material is used to produce two or more products, this type of joint production results in the products being produced in fixed proportions from the ingredient. When a firm produces products that are complements in production, the manager maximizes profit by choosing to produce the level of output of the joint product at which the joint marginal revenue (MR_J) equals the marginal cost:

$$MR_J = MC$$

The joint marginal revenue gives the additional revenue attributable to producing one more unit of the joint product—say, one more beef carcass or one more ton of mineral ore—from which two (or more) products will be forthcoming. In the case of complements in production, the relevant marginal revenue for decision making is the joint or combined additional revenue from selling the additional units of *both* products that come from one extra unit of the joint product. Once the profit-maximizing production level is determined, the prices for the individual products are taken from the individual demand curves.

While this decision-making procedure is just another application of the optimization theory developed in Chapter 3, it differs a bit from the other cases in this chapter, which involved horizontally summing either marginal cost curves or marginal revenues. To derive the joint marginal revenue, we sum the individual marginal revenue curves *vertically* over the range of production for which both individual marginal revenues are positive. Because the firm earns additional revenue from the sale of two products, for a given level of output of the joint product, the total or joint marginal revenue is the sum of the marginal revenues from the two goods, MR_X and MR_Y. Thus joint marginal revenue, MR_J, is obtained by vertically summing the individual marginal revenues over the range of outputs for which both MR_X and MR_Y are positive. When the marginal revenue of one of the goods becomes zero, as all marginal revenue curves will do at sufficiently high sales levels, that marginal revenue is set equal to zero and the vertical summation continues until all (or both in this case) marginal revenues are zero. At each point where one of the marginal revenue curves being vertically summed is equal to zero, a kink in the joint marginal revenue curve is created.

Figure 14.9 illustrates this vertical summation process for the case of two complement goods in production. In the figure, MR_Y becomes 0 at an output denoted as Q_Y. For sales of commodity Y in excess of Q_Y, the marginal revenue for Y would be negative. Because no manager would wish to sell a unit of a product for which the marginal revenue is negative, the maximum amount of Y the firm will *sell* is Q_Y. Therefore, the marginal revenue curve for the joint product is the vertical sum of MR_X and MR_Y until MR_Y equals 0. For outputs in excess of Q_Y, the excess units of Y would be discarded, and only commodity X would be sold. Beyond Q_Y the joint marginal revenue curve corresponds to MR_X. The result is the kinked MR_J curve shown in the figure.

FIGURE 14.9

**Profit Maximization with
Joint Products**

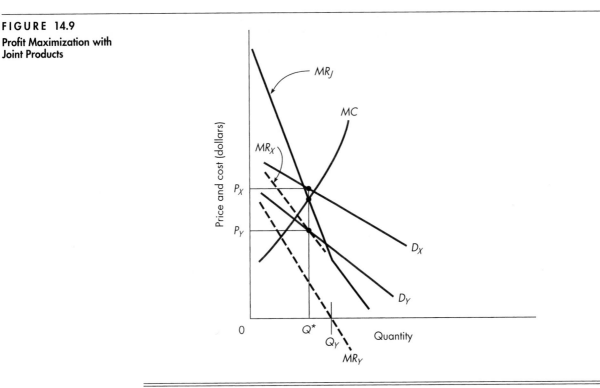

Figure 14.9 shows the profit-maximizing equilibrium situation for a firm producing joint products. The profit-maximizing condition stated above, $MR_J = MC$, determines the optimal level of production of the joint good, Q^* ($= Q_X^* = Q_Y^*$). The profit-maximizing prices P_X^* and P_Y^* are found on the individual demand curves. To see how the firm can implement profit maximization with joint products, we turn to a stylized example.

Joint Products at ChemTech Corporation

ChemTech Corporation produces refined chemicals, and two of these chemicals are complements in production. As it refines the raw chemical input, the processes yield equal amounts of xylene and ylene, denoted, of course, as X and Y.[11] The manager of ChemTech must determine the profit-maximizing amounts of xylene and ylene to produce and the prices to charge.

The manager has forecasts of the demand functions for the two products:

$$Q_X = 285{,}000 - 1{,}000P_X \quad \text{and} \quad Q_Y = 150{,}000 - 2{,}000P_Y$$

---

[11]In other words, to keep this example simple, one drum of raw chemical input yields one drum of xylene and one drum of ylene.

where quantities are measured in 55-gallon drums and prices are in dollars per drum. The marginal revenue curves associated with these demand functions (derived from the inverse demand functions) are

$$MR_X = 285 - 0.002Q_X \quad \text{and} \quad MR_Y = 75 - 0.001Q_Y$$

Note that MR_Y is equal to 0 at an output of 75,000 drums. Over the range of output from 0 to 75,000 units, the joint marginal revenue function is the vertical summation of the two marginal revenue curves:

$$MR_J = 285 - 0.002Q + 75 - 0.001Q = 360 - 0.003Q$$

where Q represents both Q_X and Q_Y ($Q = Q_X = Q_Y$). For output levels greater than 75,000, the joint marginal revenue is the same as MR_X. The joint marginal revenue function for ChemTech is shown in Figure 14.10 as the line between A and C, with the kink at point B, where MR_Y becomes negative. If production of the joint product exceeds 75,000 drums, the production of ylene in excess of 75,000 drums will be destroyed, discarded, or disposed of somehow rather than sold.

The marginal cost function for refining the raw chemical input is estimated to be

$$MC = 10 + 0.002Q$$

where Q is the number of drums of joint product, $Q = Q_X = Q_Y$. Equating marginal revenue and marginal cost for the joint product,

$$MR_J = MC$$
$$360 - 0.003Q = 10 + 0.002Q$$

Solving for the production level of the joint product, the profit-maximizing level of output is 70,000 drums. From the demand functions, the profit-maximizing prices for xylene and ylene are $215 per drum of xylene and $40 per drum of ylene.[12] Using the profit-maximizing pricing decisions results in total revenue of $17,850,000 [$= (215 + 40) \times 70,000$].

14.5 WHY MULTIPLE PRODUCTS?

The preceding discussion simply assumed that firms produce not one but several products; then it described the conditions of production under several sets of product characteristics. No attempt was made to answer why firms would want to produce multiple products. In some cases the answer is obvious; in others it is not so obvious. Certainly firms produce multiple products for a multitude of reasons. We can summarize only a few of the most common reasons.

---

[12]The two demand functions, which can be derived from the marginal revenue functions, are $P_X^* = 285 - 0.001Q_X$ and $P_Y^* = 75 - 0.0005Q_Y$. Substituting 70,000 for Q_X and Q_Y in the two functions provides the profit-maximizing prices $P_X^* = \$215$ and $P_Y^* = \$40$.

FIGURE 14.10

**Complements in Production
at ChemTech Corporation**

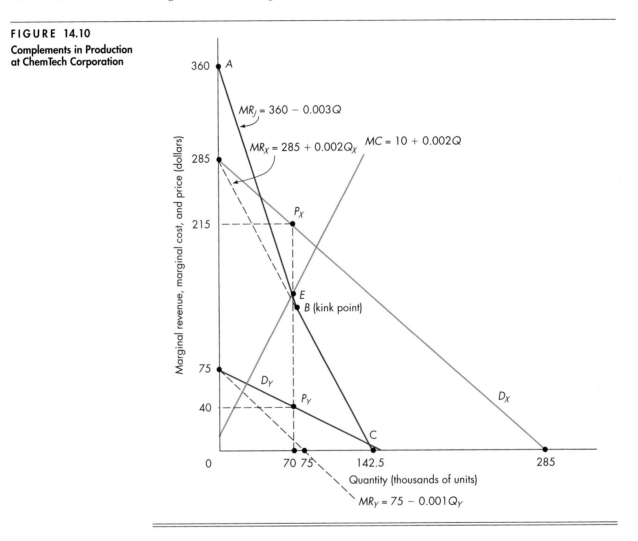

Complements in Consumption

It is rather easy to see why a firm would produce and sell two or more products that are complements in consumption. These products are used together and are frequently purchased together. The firm would be able to set prices and quantities that maximize the total profit from the products.

As noted in Illustration 14.2, single firms manufacture razors and the blades that fit the razors. The firm has control over both design and prices. It may well want to set a very low price for the razor to increase sales and extend the future market for its blades. It can also advertise the two together.

Another example is a firm such as Coleman, which produces several commodities that are complementary: tents, lanterns, stoves, ice chests, and so forth.

ILLUSTRATION 14.2

Computer Printers and Replacement Cartridges: Pricing Multiple Products That Are Complements

When a firm sells two (or more) products that are related in consumption, as either substitutes or complements, the price of each good affects the demand for the other good. Therefore, a manager must account for this interdependence by choosing prices that result in equalization of marginal revenue and marginal cost for both goods *simultaneously*. While you may have found our discussion of this rule a bit tedious because of the messy algebra required to solve marginal conditions simultaneously, we want you to see that, messy or not, the rule can offer a manager a way to make sizable profits. Gillette, the manufacturer of razors and blades, understood this pricing relation and made a fortune nearly a half-century ago by setting a low price for razors to stimulate demand for its high-profit-margin blades.[a] Today, many multiproduct firms still can increase profits by making pricing decisions that account for product complementarities.

The Wall Street Journal recently reported that manufacturers of computer printers are enjoying exceptional profitability despite dramatically falling prices for computer printers.[b] Managers at companies such as Hewlett-Packard, Seiko-Epson, and Canon have exploited the multiproduct pricing rule for complements, discussed in this chapter, to make huge profits in the market for replacement printer cartridges—both ink-jet cartridges and laser toner cartridges. Computer printers enjoy nearly the same popularity as personal computers: More than 100 million of them are in use worldwide. In the *WSJ* article John B. Jones, Jr., an analyst at Salomon Brothers, estimated that H-P, which has about half of the entire printer market, earned an astonishing $3.4 billion worldwide on sales of ink-jet and laser replacement cartridges.

The strategy for making the replacement cartridge market enormously profitable is a straightforward application of some of the tools developed in managerial economics. First, since the two goods, printers and replacement cartridges, are complements produced by the multiproduct firms, the printer firms lower prices on the printers and raise prices on replacement cartridges. The *WSJ* reported that the profit margin on printers is just 30 percent while the profit margin on replacement cartridges is a whopping 70 percent. One H-P official, commenting on the firm's pricing policy for replacement cartridges, was quoted as saying, "We just charge what the market will bear." Of course this is true of any firm with market power, but H-P has cleverly boosted "what the market will bear" by lowering prices of its printers, the complement good.

A second part of the strategy for exploiting profits in the printer–replacement cartridge business involves securing profits over the long run by slowing or blocking entry of rivals into the replacement cartridge market. The large printer manufacturers now design their printer cartridges so that they are not simply plastic boxes with ink or toner in them. Purposely, engineers design the cartridges to include some or all of the printer-head technology required to make the printer work. In so doing, the printer cartridge can be covered by patents to prevent other companies from producing "clone" replacement cartridges. Clearly, this second part of the strategy is just as important as the first part, at least if long-run profitability is the manager's objective.

It is interesting to note that H-P, Canon, and Seiko-Epson are all suing Nu-Kote Holding, a Dallas supplier of generic replacement cartridges, for patent infringement. Nu-Kote, in turn, is suing the three manufacturers for allegedly colluding to keep replacement cartridge prices artificially high. It seems to us that Nu-Kote would be smart to spend its litigation resources winning the patent infringement case and let any alleged pricing conspiracy continue to prop up prices of its product.

[a]King Gillette invented the disposable razor blade but did not make much profit selling it. He sold the patent and the name, and it was the new owner who devised the strategy of setting a low price for razors and a high price for the blades. Using this now widely used pricing strategy, the new owner of Gillette was enormously successful.

[b]Lee Gomez, "Industry Focus: Computer-Printer Price Drop Isn't Starving Makers," *The Wall Street Journal*, Aug. 16, 1996.

Consumers of outdoor recreational equipment frequently wish to purchase this bundle of commodities. Therefore, we would expect the sales of, say, lanterns to depend to some extent on the price charged for goods that are used in conjunction, for example, tents. It follows that the price charged for tents would affect the profits of the division producing lanterns and those of the firm as a whole. Even if the goods were not purchased at the same time, buyer loyalty can carry over for the next purchase. A family that was well satisfied with a Coleman tent would be likely to choose a Coleman product when it purchased a stove.

Similar examples of complementary goods produced and sold by the same firm are golf clubs and golf balls, tennis rackets and tennis balls, and baseball equipment. In all such cases, the firm will set output and price to maximize total profits rather than the profit from a single item. Therefore, as stressed in Section 14.4, the firm must determine output and price for all the products simultaneously.

Complements in Production

The discussion of complements in production in Section 14.4 deals specifically with the fixed-proportions production of two or more products from the same ingredient input. We mentioned as examples the production of beef carcasses and hides, a refinery that produces several final products from crude oil, and a smelter that obtains different minerals from the same ore. But there are more subtle examples of complementarity in production for which the final products need not be produced in fixed proportions.

Less obvious examples arise from capital expenditures that contribute to the production of more than one product. Railroads, for instance, offer both freight and passenger transportation over the same tracks and between the same depots. These inputs are shared. The postal service shares its capital in sorting and delivering parcels and letters. In these instances, a single investment contributes to the production of more than one product. This is a common phenomenon among multiproduct firms.

Whenever it is less costly to produce products together than to produce them separately, economies of scope exist. Recall from the discussion of economies of scope in Chapter 9 that multiproduct firms enjoy a cost advantage over single-product rivals when there are economies of scope in production. With economies of scope, not only does a multiproduct firm benefit from higher profits due to lower costs, but the economies of scope can provide a barrier to entry that enhances market power and profit.

There are other examples of the production of goods that are complementary in production. But we can summarize the majority of such cases simply by saying that when such complementarity exists, it is less costly to produce the goods together than to produce them separately.

Substitution in Consumption and Production

One reason that many firms produce products that are good substitutes for other products they sell is to block entry or gain a competitive advantage by introducing substitutes for its own product in the market. Such a maneuver is frequently preferred to seeing new entrants or old rivals introduce them. Producing related products crowds the market with choices. As the demand for each individual product decreases and becomes more elastic, a new firm finds it more difficult to enter that segment of the market because it would face a smaller demand.

Certainly not all firms that produce multiple products that are substitutes in consumption do so to strengthen their market power. Many oligopolists are caught in a product-quality dilemma, similar to the advertiser's dilemma discussed in Chapter 13. If they don't enter a particular segment of the market, they will lose a considerable market share to their rivals. It is possible that each of the oligopolists would be better off if each offered fewer products. In spite of this possible problem, producing a variety of differentiated yet similar products that are substitutes is simply another way that firms, particularly oligopolists, compete among themselves.

14.6 STRATEGIC ENTRY DETERRENCE

strategic entry deterrence
Strategic moves taken by established firms to prevent entry of new firms.

Managers of firms in oligopoly markets sometimes use different types of strategic pricing and production behavior to prevent new rival firms from competing with them. **Strategic entry deterrence** occurs when an established firm (or firms) makes strategic moves designed to discourage or even prevent the entry of a new firm or firms into a market. Entry barriers arising from strategic behavior differ somewhat from the *structural* barriers to entry discussed previously in Chapter 12—economies of scale and scope, input barriers, government barriers, brand loyalty, consumer lock-in, and network externalities—as those barriers block entry of new firms by altering a market's underlying cost or revenue conditions so that a new firm cannot be profitable. Strategic entry deterrence is the result of actions taken by established firms to alter the *beliefs* potential entrants hold about the behavior of established firms—primarily pricing and output behavior—*after* they enter.

A firm selling in a particular market may be making positive economic profit. The firm's manager realizes that entry of new firms into the market will probably reduce, or possibly eliminate, its profit in the future. Sometimes the manager can take measures to reduce the probability of new firms entering. These actions are *strategic moves*—commitments, threats, or promises—designed to alter beliefs of potential entrants about the level of profits they are likely to earn should they decide to enter the market. Like all strategic moves, entry-deterring strategies only succeed if they are credible. This section discusses two types of strategic moves designed to manipulate the beliefs of potential entrants about the profitability of entering: lowering prices prior to entry of new firms (limit pricing) and increasing production capacity prior to entry of new firms.

Limit Pricing

limit pricing
An established firm commits to setting price below the profit-maximizing level to prevent entry.

Under certain circumstances, an oligopolist, or possibly a monopolist, may be able to make a credible commitment to charge a price lower than the profit-maximizing price to discourage new firms from entering the market. Such a strategic move is called **limit pricing.** To practice limit pricing, an established or incumbent firm must be able to make a credible commitment that it will continue to price below the profit-maximizing level even *after* new firms enter. If potential entrants think the incumbent is pricing low just to scare off new firms and the incumbent is likely to raise its price should new firms decide to enter anyway, then potential entrants see no credible commitment and will go ahead and enter.

We can best illustrate the use of limit pricing with an example. At the beginning of the year, Star Coffee is the only coffee shop in a fashionable San Francisco shopping mall. As a monopolist, it maximizes its profit by charging an average price of $4 ($P^*$) for each cup of coffee it sells. (Coffee shops sell many different kinds of coffees in numerous sizes, so we must consider the *average* price of each cup sold.) Burned Bean, attracted by the economic profit earned by Star Coffee, wants to open its own shop in the mall and compete with Star.

The manager at Star Coffee is aware of the potential new entrant and, as you would expect, she wants to discourage Burned Bean from entering. She is willing to consider lowering her average coffee price to $3 per cup ($P_L$) and commit to keeping it low for the rest of the year if she thinks this limit pricing strategy will prevent Burned Bean from entering the mall this year. To make a commitment to the low price, she cleverly asks the owners of the mall to make her sign an irreversible contract that requires Star Coffee to leave its coffee prices unchanged for the entire year, in effect fixing Star's prices at the level she chooses on January 1. She then tapes the signed contract to the front window of her shop for customers to see and, much more importantly, for the manager of Burned Bean to see. The manager of Bean Burned will make his decision to enter or to stay out of the mall after observing the contract on the door of the shop and after observing Star's coffee prices on January 1.

Figure 14.11 presents the sequential decision situation facing Star Coffee at the beginning of the year. On January 1 (decision node *a*), Star Coffee makes its

FIGURE 14.11
Limit Pricing: Entry Deterred

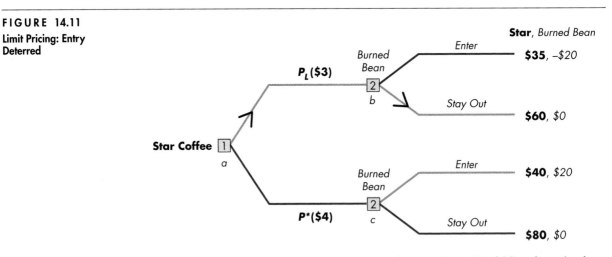

Payoffs measured in 1,000s of dollars of annual profits.

pricing decision, and then Burned Bean makes a one-time decision either to enter or to stay out of the mall. Burned Bean's decision is represented by either node *b* or node *c* depending on the price Star Coffee commits to for the rest of the year: either profit-maximizing price, P^*, or limit price, P_L.

The payoffs shown in Figure 14.11 are the annual profits for the various combinations of decisions. The best outcome for Star, $80,000 of profit, happens when it sets its profit-maximizing price of $4 per cup and Burned Bean decides to stay out. Compare this with the outcome when Star implements the entry limit price of $3 per cup and Burned Bean decides to stay out: Star makes only $60,000 of profit at the lower price. In both situations for which Burned Bean chooses to stay out of the mall, Burned Bean makes no profit.

When Burned Bean chooses to enter, the profit outcomes depend on whether Star is committed to price at $3 or $4. At the entry limit price of $3, Burned Bean cannot compete successfully with Star and loses $20,000 for the year, while Star makes $35,000 for the year.[13] If, however, Star prices at $4, Burned Bean makes a profit of $20,000 for the year, while Star makes $40,000 for the year.

The manager at Star Coffee is no fool when it comes to strategic thinking. And, while she does not know the manager of Burned Bean, she assumes he is no fool either. At decision node *a* in Figure 14.11, Star's manager decides whether to make a commitment to price low at P_L or to price high at P^*. Using the roll-back method, she determines that Burned Bean will choose to stay out at decision node *b* and choose to enter at decision node *c*. In Figure 14.11, Burned Bean's decisions at nodes *b* and *c* are shaded in light-color. Rolling back to decision node *a*, Star's manager chooses the limit pricing strategy (setting a price of $3) because, given Burned Bean's best actions at *b* and *c*, she predicts she will make $60,000 of profit by setting P_L instead of only $40,000 of profit by setting P^*.

Limit pricing succeeds in deterring entry in this example because Star's manager found a way to make a credible commitment to price at $3. Credibly committing to a limit price tends to be difficult in practice, however. Generally, incumbent firms do better after entry occurs by abandoning limit prices for Nash equilibrium prices, which are mutually best prices when the two firms make their pricing decisions simultaneously. In other words, when entry does occur, the best price for the established firm is found at the intersection of the two firms' best-response curves, and both firms earn more profit than if the incumbent continues at P_L. Thus, in the absence of an irreversible decision to price at P_L, the incumbent does best for itself, if entry occurs, by abandoning its limit price and setting a Nash equilibrium price instead. Suppose that, in this example, the best-response curves of Star Coffee and Burned Bean intersect at the Nash price P_N of $3.50.

---

[13]If Burned Bean is to suffer a loss when the price of coffee is $3 while Star Coffee makes a profit at the same price, Star Coffee must have a cost advantage over Burned Bean, perhaps due to economies of scale or access to cheaper inputs or better technology. In general, limit pricing cannot succeed unless the incumbent firm has a cost advantage over potential new entrants.

FIGURE 14.12
Limit Pricing: Entry Occurs

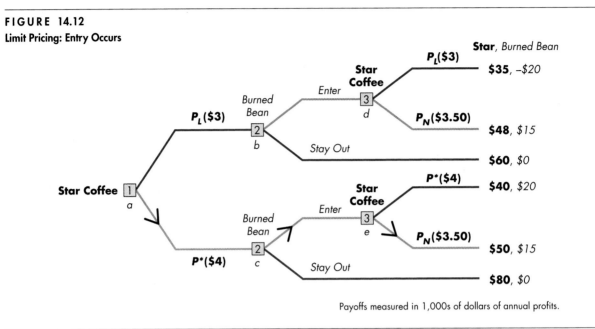

Payoffs measured in 1,000s of dollars of annual profits.

To illustrate this argument, let us modify our coffee shop example by removing Star Coffee's ability to make an irreversible commitment to P_L. (Star Coffee discovers from its legal team that malls in California cannot legally control retail prices.) Now, without a credible commitment to maintain the price it chooses at decision node a, Star's initial pricing decision is reversible: Star can change its price after Burned Bean makes its entry decision. Figure 14.12 shows the new game tree now that Star cannot irreversibly choose its limit price of $3 per cup. Two additional decision nodes (d and e) represent Star's ability to change its price, which it would do in the event of entry by Burned Bean. Note also that, because Burned Bean spends several days contemplating its entry decision (nodes b and c), Star makes just a little less profit ($2,000 less to be precise) at P_N if it begins pricing at $3 instead of $4.

At decision node d, Star can either continue pricing at the limit price ($P_L = $3) or raise its price to the more profitable Nash price ($P_N = $3.50). Now, as we discussed previously, Burned Bean believes Star will abandon its limit price if Burned Bean enters because P_N is more profitable for Star than P_L. The limit price in this situation fails to deter entry. Burned Bean predicts Star will choose its best price, P_N, when it enters, and thus Burned Bean makes the most profit by choosing to enter. Finishing the roll-back analysis, you can see that Star chooses to price at the profit-maximizing level, P^*, at the beginning of the year.

Many economists, game theorists, and government antitrust officials believe that limit pricing can seldom be practiced successfully because it is difficult for incumbents to make credible commitments to limit prices. No doubt you realize that our example of successful limit pricing utilized a rather unlikely, although not entirely farfetched, method of creating a credible commitment. Another method of making credible commitments (or credible threats and promises) is to create a reputation for yourself of being a "tough guy" or a "tough gal" who never reverses a decision (or backs down on threats or reneges on promises). Game theorists have suggested that developing an image of being irrational, or even crazy, may also serve to make strategic moves credible. Of course, we are not suggesting that craziness will advance your career as a manager, but rather that "crazy" people may be more clever than they appear.

Capacity Expansion as a Barrier to Entry

Under some circumstances, it is possible for an established firm to discourage entry of new firms by threatening to cut price to an unprofitable level should any new firm decide to enter its market. If the threat of a retaliatory price cut is to be credible, the threatened price cut must be the best decision for the established firm should a new firm decide to enter. In most cases, however, the best response to entry is for the established firm to accommodate the new firm's entry by reducing its own output so that price does not fall sharply after the new firm enters. This makes it difficult for established firms to issue credible threats that will successfully deter entry.

Sometimes, but not always, an established firm can make its threat of a retaliatory price cut in the event of entry credible by irreversibly increasing its plant capacity. When increasing production capacity results in lower marginal costs of production for an established firm, the established firm's best response to entry of a new firm may then be to increase its own level of production, which requires the established firm to cut its price to sell the extra output. If potential entrants believe the threatened price cut will make entry unprofitable *and* if they believe the capacity expansion cannot be reversed to accommodate their entry, then established firms may be able to utilize **capacity expansion as a barrier to entry.**

capacity expansion as a barrier to entry
Strategy in which an established firm irreversibly expands capacity to make credible its threat to decrease price if entry occurs.

We can use our previous example of Star Coffee to illustrate the nature of capacity expansion as a barrier to entry. Suppose that Star Coffee, the established coffee shop in the mall, is charging the monopoly price of $4 per cup and making $80,000 profit annually as the only coffee shop in the mall. Naturally, Star Coffee would like to deter Burned Bean from entering this profitable market. Suppose Star attempts to deter Burned Bean from entering by threatening to lower its price from $4 to $3 per cup if Burned Bean enters. Can Star's threat to lower price deter Burned Bean from entering?

Consider Panel A in Figure 14.13, which shows the strategic decision-making situation when Burned Bean decides first whether to enter or stay out of the market, and then Star Coffee chooses its best price, either $3 or $4. As you can see from the payoffs in Panel A, Star's threat to charge $3 per cup is not credible: If Burned Bean enters, Star's best response is to charge $4 per cup and earn annual profit of $40,000.

As a way of making credible its threat to lower price if Burned Bean enters, the manager of Star Coffee decides to invest in greater capacity to serve coffee. Star's manager gets permission from the owners of the mall to remodel its store at its

FIGURE 14.13
**Excess Capacity Barrier to
Entry**

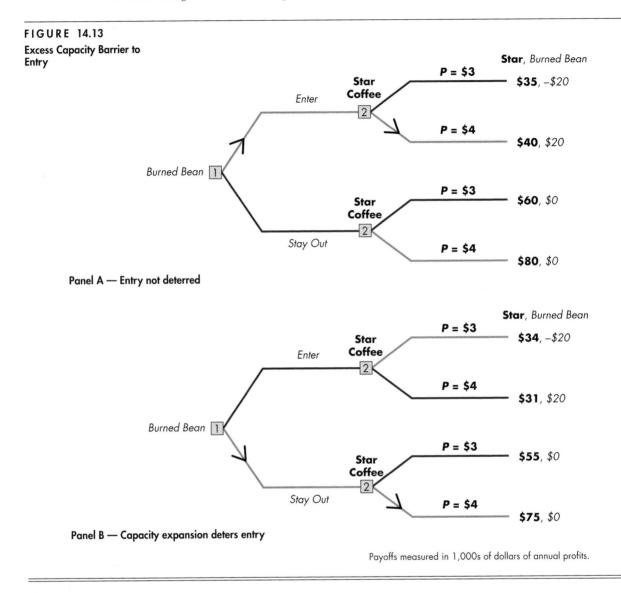

Panel A — Entry not deterred

Panel B — Capacity expansion deters entry

Payoffs measured in 1,000s of dollars of annual profits.

own expense. None of the remodeling costs will be paid for by the mall nor will
Star be reimbursed for any of the remodeling costs should it decide to leave the
mall. The remodeling project adds a sidewalk seating area in front of the store that
increases seating capacity by 25 percent. Two additional brewing machines are
also added to the store. This investment in greater capacity to serve coffee represents more seating and more brewing capacity than Star would find optimal if its
monopoly were not being threatened. In fact, this extra capacity probably won't
even be used if Burned Bean doesn't enter the market.

We must emphasize, again, that the cost of the extra capacity must be sunk so that there is no chance for Star to reverse its commitment to the higher capacity that causes Star's marginal costs to fall. In this example, the costs of expanding capacity are largely sunk costs. While the cost of the two extra brewing machines is not a sunk cost, adding the sidewalk seating area is, of course, a sunk cost and this accounts for most of the cost of expanding capacity.

The profit payoffs after the investment in extra capacity are shown in Panel B of Figure 14.13. As you can see, Star makes lower profit in every outcome because it pays for more seating capacity and brewing capacity than in Panel A. Notice, however, that with the extra capacity and lower marginal costs, Star finds it best when Burned Bean enters to lower its price to $3 and sell more coffee: Annual profit of $34,000 is better than annual profit of $31,000.

The investment in greater capacity has strategic value because, with the expansion in capacity, Star's best response to entry by Burned Bean is to cut price to $3 and increase the number of customers it serves. While it might seem like a better idea for Star to reverse its investment in extra capacity and continue pricing at $4 per cup once Star sees that Burned Bean is not going to enter, Star cannot do this: Most of its investment in extra capacity is sunk and cannot be reversed. In fact, it is precisely this inability to reverse its investment in capacity that makes Star's threatened price cut a credible threat and so deters entry by Burned Bean.

Once the manager at Star Coffee sees that investing in extra production capacity makes its threat of a retaliatory price cut credible, the manager will seize the first move of the game by making its decision to increase capacity *before* Burned Bean makes its decision to enter or stay out of the market. By committing to expand capacity, Star effectively alters the payoffs in a way that makes credible the threat of lowering price in the event of entry. Thus Burned Bean will face the strategic situation shown in Panel B, and entry is deterred.

Once again, we must emphasize that, even though entry is deterred, Star is stuck with extra capacity that reduces the amount of profit it earns as a monopolist. Certainly holding idle capacity would add to a firm's costs, thereby reducing profits somewhat. However, compared with a limit pricing strategy, carrying idle capacity may be a less expensive (more profitable) way for a firm to hold its market share in the face of potential entry. The choice would depend on the expected relative stream of profit from extra capacity compared with the stream from limit pricing. If demand is not particularly elastic, a small increase in output would cause price to fall a great deal. In this case the required amount of idle capacity would be small, and capacity expansion may be a less costly way to block entry.

14.7 SUMMARY

In this chapter we have looked at a lot of special situations for which production and pricing decisions are more complicated than for the simple firm that we studied in the first four parts of this text. While it might seem that we have introduced a lot of new conditions, we really have not. Essentially, all we have done is apply the basic principles of profit maximization to instances in which the firm has more than one plant or more than one product or more than one market, perhaps trying to simplify pricing decisions or even discourage the entry of new rivals through pricing and production decisions. We now summarize the analysis of the five advanced topics in production and pricing decisions covered in this chapter.

1. Multiple Plants

If a firm produces in two plants, A and B, it should allocate production between the two plants so that $MC_A = MC_B$. The optimal total output for the firm is that at which $MR = MC_T$. Hence, for profit maximization, the firm should produce the level of output and allocate the production of this output between the two plants so that

$$MR = MC_T = MC_A = MC_B$$

2. Cost-Plus Pricing

Cost-plus pricing is a popular technique for pricing when firms cannot or do not wish to estimate demand conditions and apply the $MR = MC$ rule to find the profit-maximizing price and output. The price charged represents a markup (margin) over average cost and is determined as follows:

$$P = (1 + m)ATC$$

This pricing approach does not generally produce the profit-maximizing price because it fails to incorporate information about demand and marginal revenue, and it utilizes average, not marginal, cost. While it is possible to determine a markup that will maximize profit when costs are constant, this procedure requires statistical demand estimation and is actually no simpler than using the $MR = MC$ rule in the first place.

3. Multiple Markets

If a firm sells in two distinct markets, 1 and 2, it should allocate output (sales) between the two markets such that $MR_1 = MR_2$. The optimal level of total output for the firm is that at which $MR_T = MC$. Hence, for profit maximization, the firm should produce the level of output and allocate the sales of this output between the two markets so that

$$MR_T = MC = MR_1 = MR_2$$

4a. Multiple Products/Related in Consumption

Defining the two products to be X and Y, the firm will produce and sell those levels of output for which

$$MR_X = MC_X \quad \text{and} \quad MR_Y = MC_Y$$

Since the products are related in consumption, MR_X is a function not only of Q_X but also of Q_Y, as is MR_Y. Therefore, the marginal conditions for the two products must be satisfied simultaneously.

4b. Multiple Products/Substitutes in Production

If a firm produces two products, X and Y, that compete for the firm's limited production facilities, the firm should allocate the production facility so that the marginal revenue product of the production facility is equal for the two products, $MRP_X = MRP_Y$. If in the long run the firm can vary its usage of or size of the production facility, the optimal level of usage of the facility is that at which $MRP_T = MC$. Hence, for profit maximization, the firm should select the level of usage of its production facility and allocate this level of usage between the production of the two products so that

$$MRP_T = MC = MRP_X = MRP_Y$$

4c. Multiple Products/Complements in Production

When a firm produces goods that are complements in production and the two goods are produced in fixed proportions from the common input, the joint marginal revenue curve MR_J is the vertical summation of the two individual marginal revenue functions MR_X and MR_Y over the range of output for which both marginal revenues are positive. Beyond the output level where one of the marginal revenues becomes negative, the joint marginal revenue MR_J is the same as the marginal revenue for the other good.

To maximize profit, the manager produces the level of joint product where the joint marginal revenue equals marginal cost: $MR_J = MC$. If the profit-maximizing level of joint production exceeds the output where the MR_J kinks, then, for the good with negative marginal revenue, the units beyond the point of zero marginal revenue are disposed of rather than sold in the market. The profit-maximizing prices are found using the demand functions for the two goods.

5. Strategic Entry Deterrence

Firms that are successful in making decisions that create profit will attract new firms to enter their markets. Absent any of the structural barriers to entry discussed in Chapter 12, firms may be able to alter the perceptions of potential entrants by making strategic pricing or capacity decisions. The same rules for successful strategic decision making developed in Chapter 13 hold. Decisions must be Nash solutions arrived at through the roll-back technique for sequential decisions, and the threat of lowering price if new firms enter must be credible. As it turns out, limit pricing and capacity expansion are usually difficult methods for blocking entry.

The pricing and output decisions presented in this chapter represent some of the most challenging decisions facing managers in the "real world." By employing the powerful logic of marginal analysis and game theory, we showed how managers can make these decisions in a way that maximizes the profit, and value, of a firm.

TECHNICAL PROBLEMS

1. In the following graph, D represents the demand for dishwashers facing the Allclean Company. The firm manufactures dishwashers in two plants; MC_1 and MC_2 are their marginal cost curves.

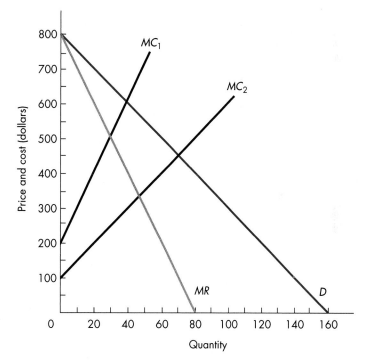

a. How many dishwashers should the firm produce?
b. What price should the firm set?
c. How should the output be allocated between the two plants so as to maximize profit?

2. Consider a firm that is using two plants, A and B, with these MC functions:

$$MC_A = 10 + 0.01Q_A \quad \text{and} \quad MC_B = 4 + 0.03Q_B$$

a. Find the inverse marginal cost functions.
b. Set $MC_A = MC_T$ and $MC_B = MC_T$, and find the algebraic sum $Q_A + Q_B = Q_T$.

c. Take the inverse of the horizontal sum in part *b* to get the total marginal cost (MC_T) expressed as a function of total output (Q_T).

d. Beyond what level of output will the firm use both plants in production? (*Hint:* Find the output level where MC_T kinks.)

e. If the manager of this firm wished to produce 1,400 units at the least possible total cost, should 700 units be produced in each plant? Why or why not? If not, what should the allocation be?

f. Draw a graph of MC_A, MC_B, and MC_T. Check your algebraic derivation of total marginal cost with your graph. Check your answer to part *e*.

3. Suppose the firm in Technical Problem 2 faces the following demand function:

$$Q = 4{,}000 - 125P$$

a. Write the equation for the inverse demand function.

b. Find the marginal revenue function.

c. How much output should the manager produce to maximize profit? What price should be charged for the output?

d. How should the manager allocate production between plants A and B?

Now suppose demand decreases to $Q = 800 - 80P$.

e. How many units should the manager produce in order to maximize profit?

f. How should the manager allocate production between plants *A* and *B*?

4. Cost-plus pricing does not generally result in profit-maximization.

a. Under what condition(s) would cost-plus pricing be equivalent to profit-maximizing pricing, that is, $MR = MC$ pricing?

b. If the condition(s) in part *a* are satisfied and if the price elasticity of demand facing the firm is -1.5, what is the profit-maximizing markup?

c. What is the profit-maximizing markup if the price elasticity is equal to -3?

5. Return to the example of cost-plus pricing at Markast Foundry.

a. Demonstrate that $21 is the profit-maximizing price by using the $MR = MC$ rule.

Now suppose that average variable cost at Markast rises to $8.

b. What price would the vice-president of marketing set? How many units will Markast likely sell at this price? How much profit will it earn?

c. What is the elasticity of demand at the profit-maximizing price (E^*)? What is the optimal markup (m^*)? What are the profit-maximizing price and output?

d. How much profit does Markast earn using the optimal markup in part *c*? Is this more profit than in part *b*? Why?

6. A hotel serves both business and vacation travelers. In the following figure, D_B is the demand for business travelers and D_V is the demand for vacation travelers. The firm wishes to price-discriminate.

a. What is the profit-maximizing number of business travelers to serve? Vacationers?

b. What price should be charged to each? How much revenue is collected from each market?

c. If the hotel charged just one price to all travelers, what price would it be? How much revenue would the firm collect? Compare this revenue with that in part *b*.

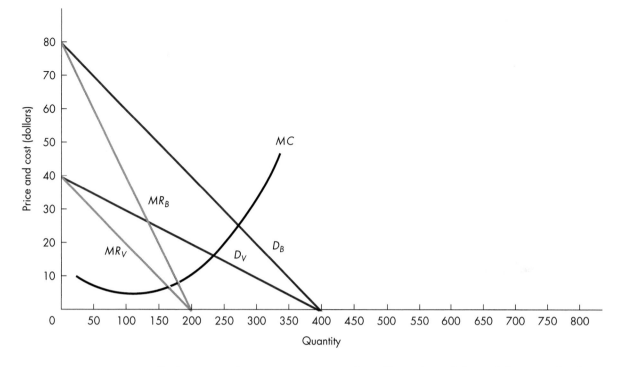

7. A manager faces two separate markets. The estimated demand functions for the two markets are

$$Q_A = 1{,}600 - 80P_A \quad \text{and} \quad Q_B = 2{,}400 - 100P_B$$

a. Find the inverse marginal revenue functions.
b. Find the total marginal revenue functions.
c. Draw a graph of MR_A, MR_B, and MR_T. Check your algebraic derivation of total marginal revenue.
d. If the manager has a total of 650 units to sell, how should the 650 units be allocated to maximize total revenue?

8. Suppose the manager in Technical Problem 7 decides to price-discriminate. The long-run marginal cost is estimated to be

$$LMC = 4.5 + 0.005Q$$

a. How many units should the manager produce and sell?
b. How should the manager allocate the profit-maximizing output between the two markets?
c. What prices should the manager charge in the two markets?
d. Measured at the prices found in part c, which market has the more elastic demand?

9. How would the profit-maximizing decision for a firm that produces two products that are related in consumption differ from that for a firm whose two products are unrelated?

10. Look again at Zicon Manufacturing—a firm that produces products that are substitutes in consumption. Suppose that the production manager changed the estimates of the total and marginal cost functions to

$$TC_X = 27Q_X + 0.00025Q_X^2 \quad \text{and} \quad TC_Y = 20Q_Y + 0.000125Q_Y^2$$

$$MC_X = 27 + 0.0005Q_X \quad \text{and} \quad MC_Y = 20 + 0.00025Q_Y$$

   a. Calculate the new profit-maximizing levels of output and price for the two products.
   b. How much profit does Zicon earn?

11. In the example dealing with the optimal usage of a production facility (Surefire Products, Inc.), suppose that the plant supervisor changes the estimate of the marginal cost for usage of the plant to

$$MC = 150 + 3H_T$$

   a. What is the optimal level of usage for the plant (hours per day)?
   b. How will this level of usage be allocated between the production of the two products?
   c. What will be the daily outputs?
   d. What prices will be charged?

12. Consider again the pricing and output decision facing the manager at ChemTech Corporation. New estimates for the demand for xylene and ylene are

$$Q_X = 200,000 - 1,000P_X \quad \text{and} \quad Q_Y = 180,000 - 2,000P_Y$$

   The manager also reestimates marginal cost and finds the new marginal cost function to be

$$MC = 50 + 0.001Q$$

   a. Find the equation for the joint marginal revenue function.
   b. What is the profit-maximizing level of production for the joint product?
   c. What prices should the manager charge for xylene and ylene to maximize profit?

   A technological innovation in chemical processing reduces the marginal cost of production to

$$MC = 3.3 + 0.00005Q$$

   d. What is the profit-maximizing level of production of xylene? Of ylene?
   e. What are the profit-maximizing prices to charge for xylene and ylene?

APPLIED PROBLEMS

1. *The Financial Herald,* a weekly newspaper specializing in corporate financial news, is purchased by both businesspeople and students. A marketing research firm has estimated the two linear demand and marginal revenue functions shown in the following figure. MR_B is the estimated marginal revenue for the business readers, and MR_S is the estimated marginal revenue for the student readers. The production department at *The Financial Herald* estimates a linear marginal cost function for newspaper production, which also is graphed in the following figure. All quantities are in units of 1,000 per week.

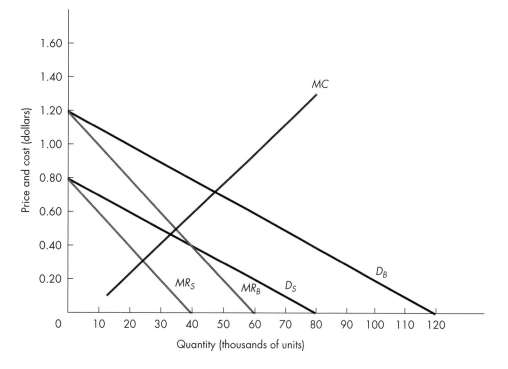

a. How many total copies should *The Financial Herald* print each week?

b. How many copies should be sold to business readers? How many copies should be sold to students?

c. What price should business readers be charged? What price should students be charged?

2. The board of directors of R & B Root Beer Corporation recently called a meeting of the managers of the five regional bottling companies. The reason for calling the meeting was to consider closing the Milwaukee bottling plant. Over the past decade, the Milwaukee facility's marginal costs of production have increased to the point where its marginal cost of production now exceeds that of each of the other four bottling companies at every level of output. Several members of the board of directors and two of the managers favored closing the Milwaukee plant. The manager of the Milwaukee bottling plant pointed out that, while the Milwaukee plant is the oldest of the five, with the oldest capital equipment, it would be inefficient to close it given the current growth rate in sales. Only if sales fell by a rather substantial amount would it be profit-maximizing to shut the Milwaukee plant. Draw a graph and defend the manager of the Milwaukee plant.

3. EZ Sharp Industries, Inc., manufactures the Keen Edge™ line of diamond-abrasive cutlery sharpeners for home use. EZ Sharp holds a patent on its unique design and can earn substantial economic profit if it prices its Keen Edge™ products wisely. EZ Sharp sells two models of its Keen Edge™ sharpeners: the Classic, which is the entry-level model, and the Professional, which has a sonic sensor that controls the speed of the sharpening wheels.

Short-run production of sharpeners is subject to constant costs: $AVC = SMC$ for both models. The constant costs of production at EZ Sharp Industries are estimated to be

$$\$20 = AVC_C = SMC_C$$
$$\$30 = AVC_P = SMC_P$$

where AVC_C and SMC_C are the constant costs for the Classic model and AVC_P and SMC_P are the constant costs for the Professional model. Total fixed costs each month are $10,000 per month. The sole owner of EZ Sharp also manages the firm and makes all pricing decisions. The owner–manager believes in assuring himself a 200 percent profit margin by using the cost-plus pricing methodology to set prices for his two product lines. At these prices, EZ Sharp is selling 3,750 units of the Classic model per month and 2,000 units of the Supreme model per month.

a. Using the cost-plus technique, compute the prices the owner-manager charges for the Classic and the Supreme models, based on his required 200 percent profit margin.

b. How much profit is EZ Sharp earning each month using the cost-plus prices in part a?

The owner–manager is ready to sell the firm, but he knows the value of the firm will increase if he can increase the monthly profit somehow. He decides to hire Andrews Consulting to recommend ways for EZ Sharp to increase its profits. Andrews reports that production is efficient, but pricing can be improved. Andrews argues that the cost-plus pricing technique is not working well for EZ Sharp and presents a new pricing plan based on optimal pricing techniques (i.e., the $MR = MC$ rule).

To implement the $MR = MC$ methodology, Andrews undertakes a statistical study to estimate the demands for two Keen Edge™ products. The estimated demands are

$$Q_C = 6,000 - 75P_C + 25P_P$$
$$Q_P = 5,000 - 50P_P + 25P_C$$

where Q_C and Q_P are the monthly quantities demanded of Classic and Professional models, respectively, and P_C and P_P are the prices of the Classic and Professional models, respectively. Andrews Consulting solved the demand equations simultaneously to get the following inverse demand functions, which is why Anderson gets paid the "big bucks":

$$P_C = 136 - 0.016Q_C - 0.008Q_P$$
$$P_S = 168 - 0.008Q_C - 0.024Q_P$$

c. Find the two marginal revenue functions for the Classic and Professional model sharpeners.

d. Set each marginal revenue function in part c equal to the appropriate cost and solve for the profit-maximizing quantities.

e. Using the results from part d, what prices will Andrews Consulting recommend for each of the models?

f. When the owner–manager sees the prices recommended by Andrews Consulting, he brags about how close his simple cost-plus pricing method had come to their suggested prices. Compute the profit EZ Sharp can earn using the consultants' prices in part d. Is there any reason for the owner–manager to brag about his cost-plus pricing skills?

4. Although there is relatively little difference in the cost of producing hardcover and paperback books, these books sell for very different prices. Explain this pricing behavior.

5. *The Wall Street Journal* once reported on dating services, noting that the fees were $300 for men and $250 for women. The owner of the service said that the difference in fees was to compensate for inequalities in pay scales for men and women. Can you suggest any alternative reasons for this difference?

6. Caytel Products manufactures two models of a particular product: the "good" model (G) and the "best" model (B). The two models are substitutes in production and must share Caytel's production facilities. Caytel has determined that the production functions for the two models are

$$\text{Good model: } Q_G = 4.0H_G$$

$$\text{Best model: } Q_B = 4.0H_B$$

where H_G and H_B measure the number of hours per month Caytel's plant spends producing the good and best models, respectively. The demand functions for the two models are forecasted to be

$$Q_G = 4{,}000 - 256P_G$$

and

$$Q_B = 600 - 4P_B$$

The marginal cost of using Caytel's plant is estimated to be

$$MC = 5.0 + 0.05H \qquad \text{where } H = H_G + H_B$$

   a. To maximize profit, how many hours per month should Caytel's plant operate?
   b. How should the manager allocate production time between the good model and the best model?
   c. How many units of the good model should be produced to maximize Caytel's profit? How many units of the best model?
   d. What prices should Caytel charge for the two models?

7. Airlines practice price discrimination by charging leisure travelers and business travelers different prices. Different customers pay varying prices for essentially the same coach seat because some passengers qualify for discounts and others do not. Since the discounts are substantial in many cases, the customer who qualifies for a discount pays a significantly lower airfare.

   a. Which group of customers tends to pay the higher price: business travelers or leisure travelers?
   b. Why would business travelers generally have a different elasticity of demand for air travel than leisure travelers? Is the more elastic market paying the lower or higher price? Is this consistent with profit maximization?

   Airlines rely on an assortment of restrictions that travelers must meet to qualify for the discounted fares. In effect, these restrictions roughly sort flyers into business travelers and leisure travelers.

   c. Explain how each of the following restrictions sometimes used by airlines tends to separate business and leisure travelers.
      (1) Advance purchase requirements, which require payment at least 14 days before departure.
      (2) Weekend stay requirements, which require travelers to stay over a Saturday night before returning.

(3) Time-of-day restrictions, which disallow discounts for travel during peak times of the day.

d. In each of these cases, which group of passengers effectively pays a higher price for air travel? Is this consistent with profit maximization?

8. Maytag wants to prevent Whirlpool from entering the market for high-priced, side-load washing machines. Side-load washing machines clean clothes better and use less water than conventional top-load machines. Even though side-load machines are more costly to manufacture than top-loaders, Maytag is nonetheless earning economic profit as the only firm making side-loaders for upscale consumers. The following payoff table shows the annual profits (in millions of dollars) for Maytag and Whirlpool for the pricing and entry decisions facing the two firms.

		Maytag	
		P = $500	P = $1,000
Whirlpool	Stay out	$0, $20	$0, $34
	Enter	−$5, $15	$17, $17

a. Can Maytag deter Whirlpool from entering the market for side-load washing machines by threatening to lower price to $500 if Whirlpool enters the market? Why or why not?

Suppose the manager of Maytag decides to make an investment in extra production capacity before Whirlpool makes its entry decision. The extra capacity raises Maytag's total costs of production but lowers its marginal costs of producing extra side-load machines. The payoff table after this investment in extra production capacity is shown here:

		Maytag	
		P = $500	P = $1,000
Whirlpool	Stay out	$0, $16	$0, $24
	Enter	−$6, $14	$12, $12

b. Can Maytag deter Whirlpool from entering the profitable market for side-load washing machines? What must be true about the investment in extra production capacity in order for the strategic move to be successful? Explain.

c. Construct the sequential game tree when Maytag makes the first move by deciding whether or not to invest in extra production capacity. Use the roll-back technique to find the Nash equilibrium path. How much profit does each firm earn? (*Hint:* The game tree will have three sequential decisions: Maytag decides first whether to invest in extra plant capacity, Whirlpool decides whether or not to enter, and Maytag makes its pricing decision.)

9. A woman complained to "Dear Abby" that a laundry charged $1.25 each to launder and press her husband's shirts, but for her shirts—the same description, only smaller—the laundry charted $3.50. When asked why, the owner said, "Women's blouses cost more." Abby suggested sending all the shirts in one bundle and enclosing a note saying, "There are no blouses here—these are all shirts."

a. Is the laundry practicing price discrimination, or is there really a $2.25 difference in cost?

b. Assuming the laundry is engaging in price discrimination, why do men pay the lower price and women the higher?

c. Could the laundry continue to separate markets if people followed Abby's advice? What about the policing costs associated with separating the markets?

10. A firm with two factories, one in Michigan and one in Texas, has decided that it should produce a total of 500 units to maximize profit. The firm is currently producing 200 units in the Michigan factory and 300 units in the Texas factory. At this allocation between plants, the last unit of output produced in Michigan added $5 to total cost, while the last unit of output produced in Texas added $3 to total cost.

a. Is the firm maximizing profit? If so, why? If not, what should it do?

b. If the firm produces 201 units in Michigan and 299 in Texas, what will be the increase (decrease) in the firm's total cost?

11. A bar offers female patrons a lower price for a drink than male patrons. The bar will maximize profit by selling a total of 200 drinks (a night). At the current prices, male customers buy 150 drinks, while female customers buy 50 drinks. At this allocation between markets, the marginal revenue from the last drink sold to a male customer is $1.50, while the marginal revenue from the last drink sold to a female customer is $0.50.

a. What should the bar do about its pricing?

b. If the bar sells 151 drinks to males and 49 to females, what will be the increase (decrease) in total revenue?

▣ MATHEMATICAL APPENDIX   Derivation of Decision Rules

The Multiplant Firm's Allocation Decision

To maximize profit, a multiplant firm will produce the level of output at which the horizontal sum of each plant's marginal cost equals marginal revenue. Each plant will produce the output at which the marginal costs of all plants are equal.

Assume the firm has two plants, A and B, whose total cost functions are, respectively, $C_A(Q_A)$ and $C_B(Q_B)$. The firm's total revenue function is $R(Q_A + Q_B) = R(Q)$. Thus the firm's profit function is

$$\pi = R(Q) - C_A(Q_A) - C_B(Q_B)$$

Maximizing profit with respect to Q_A and Q_B requires

$$\frac{\partial \pi}{\partial Q_A} = \frac{dR}{dQ} - \frac{dC_A(Q_A)}{dQ_A} = 0$$

$$\frac{\partial \pi}{\partial Q_B} = \frac{dR}{dQ} - \frac{dC_B(Q_B)}{dQ_B} = 0$$

Combining these conditions, profit is maximized when

$$MR = MC_A = MC_B$$

Thus MC must be the same in both plants and also equal to MR.

Price Discrimination in Multiple Markets

A price-discriminating manager maximizes profit at the level of output at which marginal revenue in each market equals marginal cost. The price in each market is given by the demand in that market.

Assume the firm sells its output in two markets. The demands in these markets are

$$P_1(Q_1) \quad \text{and} \quad P_2(Q_2)$$

Cost is a function of total output:

$$C = C(Q_1 + Q_2) = C(Q)$$

The firm maximizes profit,

$$\pi = P_1(Q_1)Q_1 + P_2(Q_2)Q_2 - C(Q)$$

with respect to the levels of output sold in the two markets.

Thus the first-order conditions for profit maximization are

$$\frac{dP_1}{dQ_1}Q_1 + P_1 - \frac{dC}{dQ} = MR_1 - MC = 0$$

$$\frac{dP_2}{dQ_2}Q_2 + P_2 - \frac{dC}{dQ} = MR_2 - MC = 0$$

Thus profit maximization requires that the marginal revenues in the two markets be equal and equal to marginal cost. Once Q_1^* and Q_2^* are determined, P_1^* and P_2^* are given by the demand functions.

Multiproduct Firms: Finding Inverse Demands and Marginal Revenue Functions

For a firm producing two goods that are either substitutes or complements in consumption, let the demand functions be linear:

$$Q_X = a + bP_X + cP_Y \quad \text{and} \quad Q_Y = d + eP_Y + fP_X$$

To facilitate simultaneously solving for P_x and P_Y, express the two demand equations as

$$bP_X + cP_Y = Q_X - a$$

$$fP_X + eP_Y = Q_Y - b$$

Now express the two-equation system in matrix form:

$$\begin{pmatrix} b & c \\ f & e \end{pmatrix}\begin{pmatrix} P_X \\ P_Y \end{pmatrix} = \begin{pmatrix} Q_X - a \\ Q_Y - d \end{pmatrix}$$

The solution is found using the usual tools of matrix algebra:

$$\begin{pmatrix} P_X \\ P_Y \end{pmatrix} = \begin{pmatrix} Q_X - a \\ Q_Y - d \end{pmatrix}\begin{pmatrix} b & c \\ f & e \end{pmatrix}^{-1} =$$

$$\begin{pmatrix} Q_X - a \\ Q_Y - d \end{pmatrix}\begin{pmatrix} \dfrac{e}{be - cf} & \dfrac{-c}{db - cf} \\ \dfrac{-f}{be - cf} & \dfrac{b}{be - cf} \end{pmatrix}$$

The inverse demand functions are

$$P_X = \frac{cd - ae}{be - cf} + \frac{e}{be - cf}Q_X + \frac{-c}{be - cf}Q_Y$$

$$P_Y = \frac{fa - bd}{be - cf} + \frac{-f}{be - cf}Q_X + \frac{b}{be - cf}Q_Y$$

The marginal revenue functions are derived by taking partial derivatives of total revenue with respect to Q_X to find MR_X and Q_Y to find MR_Y:

$$TR = TR(Q_X, Q_Y) = P_X(Q_X, Q_Y)Q_X + P_Y(Q_X, Q_Y)Q_Y$$

$$= \frac{cd - ae}{be - cf}Q_X + \frac{e}{be - cf}Q_X^2 + \frac{-c}{be - cf}Q_YQ_X +$$

$$\frac{fa - bd}{be - cf}Q_Y + \frac{-f}{be - cf}Q_XQ_Y + \frac{b}{be - cf}Q_Y^2$$

so

$$\frac{\partial TR}{\partial Q_X} = \frac{cd - ae}{be - cf} + \frac{2e}{be - cf}Q_X + \frac{-c - f}{be - cf}Q_Y$$

$$\frac{\partial TR}{\partial Q_Y} = \frac{fa - bd}{be - cf} + \frac{-c - f}{be - cf}Q_X + \frac{2b}{be - cf}Q_Y$$

CHAPTER 15

Decisions under Risk and Uncertainty

Allll the analysis of managerial decision making up to this point in the text has been developed under the assumption that the manager knows with certainty the marginal benefits and marginal costs associated with a decision. While managers do have considerable information about the outcome for many decisions, they must frequently make decisions in situations in which the outcome of a decision cannot be known in advance. A manager may decide, for example, to invest in a new production facility with the expectation that the new technology and equipment will reduce production costs. Even after studying hundreds of technical reports, a manager may still not know with certainty the cost savings of the new plant until the plant is built and operating. In other words, the outcome of the decision to build the new plant is random because the reduction in costs (the outcome) is not known with certainty at the time of the decision. Another risky decision involves choosing the profit-maximizing production level or the price to charge when the marginal benefit and marginal cost can take on a range of values with differing probabilities.

In this chapter we will present some basic rules that managers, and for that matter all decision makers, can and do use to help make decisions under conditions of risk and uncertainty. In the first section, we explain the difference between decision making under risk and decision making under uncertainty. The larger portion of this chapter is devoted to analyzing decisions under risk, rather than situations of uncertainty, because, as you will see, managers facing random benefits and costs are more often confronted with situations involving risk than uncertainty. As you will also see, the rules we present in this chapter for decision making under risk and uncertainty provide only guidelines for making decisions when outcomes are not certain, because no single rule for making such decisions is, or can be, universally employed by all managers at all times. Nevertheless, the rules presented give an overview of some of the helpful methods of analyzing risk and uncertainty.

Before plunging into our presentation of decision making under uncertainty and risk, we want to address a question that may be concerning you: Why do we devote such a large portion of this text to managerial decision making under certainty or complete information, knowing full well that a large proportion of managerial decisions are made with incomplete information—that is, under risk or uncertainty? There are two good reasons. First, the theory of optimization, weighing marginal benefits and marginal costs, as explained in Chapter 3 and applied throughout the text, provides the basic foundation for all decision making regardless of the amount of information available to a decision maker about the potential outcomes of various actions. In order to learn how to do something under less-than-ideal conditions, one must first learn how to do it under ideal conditions. Second, even though a decision maker does not have complete information about the marginal benefits and marginal costs of all levels of an activity or choice variable, the $MB = MC$ rule from Chapter 3 is the most productive approach to profit-maximization decisions under many, if not most, relevant circumstances.

15.1 DISTINCTIONS BETWEEN RISK AND UNCERTAINTY

risk
A decision-making condition under which a manager can list all outcomes and assign probabilities to each outcome.

When the outcome of a decision is not known with certainty, a manager faces a decision-making problem under either conditions of risk or conditions of uncertainty. A decision is made under **risk** when a manager can make a list of all possible outcomes associated with a decision and assign a probability of occurrence to each one of the outcomes. The process of assigning probabilities to outcomes sometimes involves rather sophisticated analysis based on the manager's extensive experience in similar situations or on other data. Probabilities assigned in this way are *objective probabilities*. In other circumstances, in which the manager has little experience with a particular decision situation and little or no relevant historical data, the probabilities assigned to the outcomes are derived in a subjective way and are called *subjective probabilities.* Subjective probabilities are based upon hunches, "gut feelings," or personal experiences rather than on scientific data.

An example of a decision made under risk might be the following: A manager decides to spend $1,000 on a magazine ad believing there are three possible outcomes for the ad: a 20 percent chance the ad will have only a small effect on sales, a 60 percent chance of a moderate effect, and a 20 percent chance of a very large effect. This decision is made under risk because the manager can list each potential outcome and determine the probability of each outcome occurring.

uncertainty
A decision-making condition under which a manager cannot list all possible outcomes and/or cannot assign probabilities to the various outcomes.

In contrast to risk, **uncertainty** exists when a decision maker cannot list all possible outcomes and/or cannot assign probabilities to the various outcomes. When faced with uncertainty, a manager would know only the different decision options available and the different possible *states of nature*. The states of nature are the future events or conditions that can influence the final outcome or payoff of a decision but cannot be controlled or affected by the manager. Even though both risk and uncertainty involve less than complete information, there is more information under risk than under uncertainty.

An example of a decision made under uncertainty would be, for a manager of a pharmaceutical company, the decision of whether or not to spend $3 million on the research and development of a new medication for high blood pressure. The payoff from the research and development spending will depend on whether or not the president's new health plan imposes price regulations on new drugs. The two states of nature facing the manager in this problem are (1) government does impose price regulations or (2) government does *not* impose price regulations. While the manager knows the payoff that will occur under either state of nature, the manager has no idea of the probability that price regulations will be imposed on drug companies. Under such conditions, a decision is made under uncertainty.

This important distinction between conditions of uncertainty and conditions of risk will be followed throughout this chapter. The decision rules employed by managers when outcomes are not certain differ under conditions of uncertainty and conditions of risk.

15.2 MEASURING RISK WITH PROBABILITY DISTRIBUTIONS

Before we can discuss rules for decision making under risk, we must first discuss how risk can be measured. The most direct method of measuring risk involves the characteristics of a probability distribution of outcomes associated with a particular decision. This section will describe these characteristics.

Probability Distributions

probability distribution
A table or graph showing all possible outcomes or payoffs of a decision and the probabilities that each outcome will occur.

A **probability distribution** is a table or graph showing all possible outcomes (payoffs) for a decision and the probability that each outcome will occur. The probabilities can take values between 0 and 1, or, alternatively, they can be expressed as percentages between 0 and 100 percent.[1] If *all possible* outcomes are assigned probabilities, the probabilities must sum to 1 (or 100 percent); that is, the probability that some other outcome will occur is 0 because there is no other possible outcome.

To illustrate a probability distribution, we assume that the director of advertising at a large corporation believes the firm's current advertising campaign may result in any one of five possible outcomes for corporate sales. The probability distribution for this advertising campaign is as follows:

---

[1]If the probability of an outcome is 1 (or 100 percent), the outcome is certain to occur and no risk exists. If the probability of an outcome is 0, then that particular outcome will not occur and need not be considered in decision making.

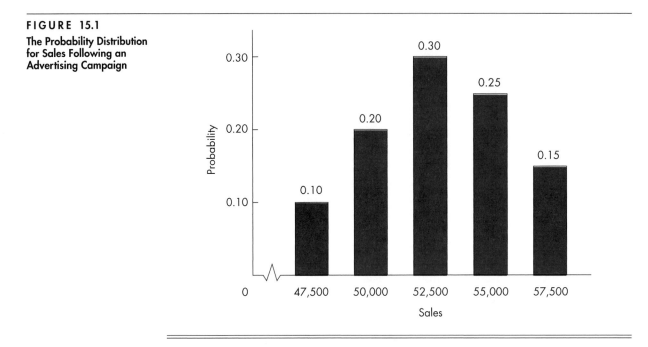

FIGURE 15.1

The Probability Distribution for Sales Following an Advertising Campaign

Outcome (sales)	Probability (percent)
47,500 units	10
50,000 units	20
52,500 units	30
55,000 units	25
57,500 units	15

Each outcome has a probability greater than 0 but less than 100 percent, and the sum of all probabilities is 100 percent (= 10 + 20 + 30 + 25 + 15). This probability distribution is represented graphically in Figure 15.1.

From a probability distribution (either in tabular or in graphical form), the riskiness of a decision is reflected by the variability of outcomes indicated by the different probabilities of occurrence. For decision-making purposes, managers often turn to mathematical properties of the probability distribution to facilitate a formal analysis of risk. The nature of risk can be summarized by examining the central tendency of the probability distribution, as measured by the expected value of the distribution, and by examining the dispersion of the distribution, as measured by the standard deviation and coefficient of variation. We discuss first the measure of central tendency of a probability distribution.

Expected Value of a Probability Distribution

expected value
The weighted average of the outcomes, with the probabilities of each outcome serving as the respective weights.

The **expected value** of a probability distribution of decision outcomes is the weighted average of the outcomes, with the probabilities of each outcome serving as the respective weights. The expected value of the various outcomes of a probability distribution is

$$E(X) = \text{Expected value of } X = \sum_{i=1}^{n} p_i X_i$$

where X_i is the ith outcome of a decision, p_i is the probability of the ith outcome, and n is the total number of possible outcomes in the probability distribution. Note that the computation of expected value requires the use of fractions or decimal values for the probabilities p_i, rather than percentages. The expected value of a probability distribution is often referred to as the **mean of the distribution.**

mean of the distribution
The expected value of the distribution.

The expected value of sales for the advertising campaign associated with the probability distribution shown in Figure 15.1 is

$$E(\text{sales}) = (0.10)(47{,}500) + (0.20)(50{,}000) + (0.30)(52{,}500)$$
$$+ (0.25)(55{,}000) + (0.15)(57{,}500)$$
$$= 4{,}750 + 10{,}000 + 15{,}750 + 13{,}750 + 8{,}625$$
$$= 52{,}875$$

While the amount of actual sales that occur as a result of the advertising campaign is a random variable possibly taking values of 47,500, 50,000, 52,500, 55,000, or 57,500 units, the expected level of sales is 52,875 units. If only one of the five levels of sales can occur, the level that actually occurs will not equal the expected value of 52,875, but expected value does indicate what the *average* value of the outcomes would be if the risky decision were to be repeated a large number of times.

Dispersion of a Probability Distribution

As you may recall from your statistics classes, probability distributions are generally characterized not only by the expected value (mean) but also by the variance. The **variance** of a probability distribution measures the dispersion of the distribution about its mean. Figure 15.2 shows the probability distributions for the profit outcomes of two different decisions, A and B. Both decisions, as illustrated in Figure 15.2, have identical expected profit levels but different variances. The larger variance associated with making decision B is reflected by a larger dispersion (a wider spread of values around the mean). Because distribution A is more compact (less spread out), A has a smaller variance.

variance
The dispersion of a distribution about its mean.

The variance of a probability distribution of the outcomes of a given decision is frequently used to indicate the level or degree of risk associated with that decision. If the expected values of two distributions are the same, the distribution with the higher variance is associated with the riskier decision. Thus in Figure 15.2, decision B has more risk than decision A. Furthermore, variance is often used to

FIGURE 15.2

Two Probability Distributions with Identical Means but Different Variances

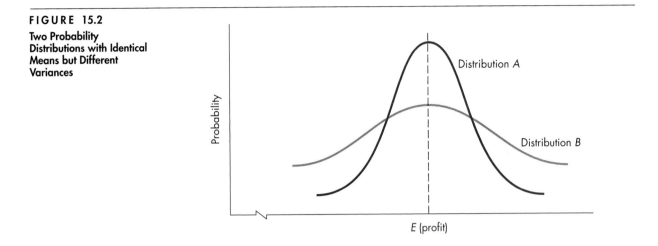

compare the riskiness of two decisions even though the expected values of the distributions differ.

Mathematically, the variance of a probability distribution of outcomes X_i, denoted by σ_x^2, is the probability-weighted sum of the squared deviations about the expected value of X:

$$\text{Variance } (X) = \sigma_x^2 = \sum_{i=1}^{n} p_i[X_i - E(X)]^2$$

As an example, consider the two distributions illustrated in Figure 15.3. As is evident from the graphs and demonstrated in the following table, the two distributions have the same mean, 50. Their variances differ, however. Decision A has a smaller variance than decision B, and it is therefore less risky. The calculation of the expected values and variance for each distribution are shown here:

Profit (X_i)	Decision A Probability (p_i)	p_iX_i	$[X_i - E(X)]^2 p_i$	Decision B Probability (p_i)	p_iX_i	$[X_i - E(X)]^2 p_i$
30	0.05	1.5	20	0.10	3	40
40	0.20	8	20	0.25	10	25
50	0.50	25	0	0.30	15	0
60	0.20	12	20	0.25	15	25
70	0.05	3.5	20	0.10	7	40
		$E(X) = 50$	$\sigma_A^2 = 80$		$E(X) = 50$	$\sigma_B^2 = 130$

Because variance is a squared term, it is usually much larger than the mean. To avoid this scaling problem, the standard deviation of the probability distribution

FIGURE 15.3
Probability Distributions with Different Variances

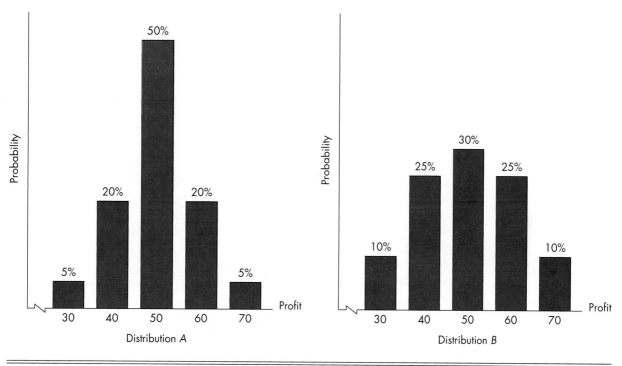

Distribution A

Distribution B

standard deviation
The square root of the variance.

is more commonly used to measure dispersion. The **standard deviation** of a probability distribution, denoted by σ_x, is the square root of the variance:

$$\sigma_x = \sqrt{\text{Variance}(X)}$$

The standard deviations of the distributions illustrated in Figure 15.3 and in the preceding table are $\sigma_A = 8.94$ and $\sigma_B = 11.40$. As in the case of the variance of a probability distribution, the higher the standard deviation, the more risky the decision.

Managers can compare the riskiness of various decisions by comparing their standard deviations, as long as the expected values are of similar magnitudes. For example, if decisions C and D both have standard deviations of 52.5, the two decisions can be viewed as equally risky if their expected values are close to one another. If, however, the expected values of the distributions differ substantially in magnitude, it can be misleading to examine only the standard deviations. Suppose decision C has a mean outcome of $400 and decision D has a mean outcome of $5,000 but the standard deviations remain 52.5. The dispersion of outcomes for decision D is much smaller *relative to its mean value of $5,000* than is the dispersion of outcomes for decision C *relative to its mean value of $400.*

coefficient of variation
The standard deviation divided by the expected value of the probability distribution.

When the expected values of outcomes differ substantially, managers should measure the riskiness of a decision *relative* to its expected value. One such measure of relative risk is the coefficient of variation for the decision's distribution. The **coefficient of variation,** denoted by v, is the standard deviation divided by the expected value of the probability distribution of decision outcomes:

$$v = \frac{\text{Standard deviation}}{\text{Expected value}} = \frac{\sigma}{E(X)}$$

The coefficient of variation measures the level of risk *relative* to the mean of the probability distribution. In the preceding example, the two coefficients of variation are $v_C = 52.5/400 = 0.131$ and $v_D = 52.5/5{,}000 = 0.0105$.

15.3 DECISIONS UNDER RISK

Now that we have shown how to measure the risk associated with making a particular managerial decision, we will discuss how these measures of risk can help managers make decisions under conditions of risk. We now set forth three rules to guide managers making risky decisions.

Maximization of Expected Value

Information about the likelihood of the various possible outcomes, while quite helpful in making decisions, does not solve the manager's decision-making problem. How should a manager choose among various decisions when each decision has a variety of possible outcomes? One rule or solution to this problem, called the **expected value rule,** is to choose the decision with the highest expected value. The expected value rule is easy to apply. Unfortunately, this rule uses information about only one characteristic of the distribution of outcomes, the mean. It fails to incorporate into the decision the riskiness (dispersion) associated with the probability distribution of outcomes. Therefore, the expected value rule is not particularly useful in situations where the level of risk differs very much across decisions—unless the decision maker does not care about the level of risk associated with a decision and is concerned only with expected value. (Such a decision maker is called *risk neutral*, a concept we will discuss later in this chapter.) Also, the expected value rule is only useful to a manager when the decisions have *different* expected values. Of course, if decisions happen to have identical expected values, the expected value rule offers no guidance for choosing between them, and, considering only the mean, the manager would be indifferent to a choice among them. The expected value rule *cannot* be applied when decisions have identical expected values and *should not* be applied when decisions have different levels of risk, except in the circumstance noted earlier: that is, when the decision maker is risk neutral.

To illustrate the expected value rule (and other rules to be discussed later), consider the owner and manager of Chicago Rotisserie Chicken, who wants to decide where to open one new restaurant. Figure 15.4 shows the probability distributions of possible weekly profits if the manager decides to locate the new restaurant in

expected value rule
Choosing the decision with the highest expected value.

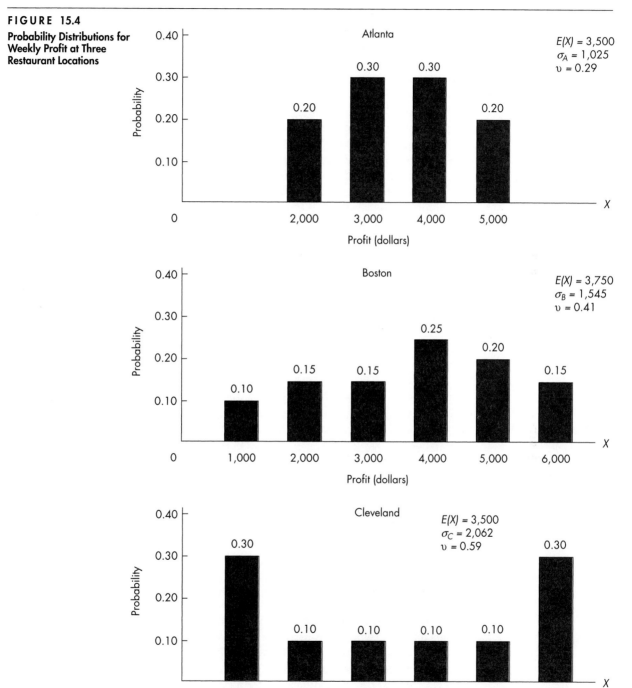

FIGURE 15.4

Probability Distributions for Weekly Profit at Three Restaurant Locations

either Atlanta (Panel A), Boston (Panel B), or Cleveland (Panel C). The expected values, standard deviations, and coefficients of variation for each distribution are displayed in each panel.

On the basis of past experience, the manager calculates that weekly profit in Atlanta will take one of four values: $3,000 or $4,000 per week each with a 30 percent chance of occurring, and $2,000 or $5,000 a week each with a 20 percent chance of occurring. The expected weekly profit in Atlanta is $3,500. If the manager decides to open a restaurant in Boston, the weekly profits may be any of six indicated values ranging from $1,000 to $6,000 weekly with the indicated probabilities and an expected value of $3,750. For Cleveland, the manager assigns a probability of 30 percent to weekly profits of $1,000 and $6,000 and a probability of 10 percent to each of the profits $2,000, $3,000, $4,000, and $5,000, with an expected value of $3,500 for the distribution. If the manager is not concerned with risk (is risk neutral) and follows the expected value rule, the new restaurant will be opened in Boston, with the highest expected profit of $3,750. Note that if the manager had been choosing between only the Atlanta and Cleveland locations, the expected value rule could not have been applied because each has an expected value of $3,500. In such cases some other rule may be used.

Mean–Variance Analysis

Managers who choose among risky alternatives using the expected value rule are, in effect, ignoring risk (dispersion) and focusing exclusively on the mean outcome. An alternative method of making decisions under risk uses both the mean *and* the variance of the probability distribution, which incorporates information about the level of risk into the decisions. This method of decision making, commonly known as **mean–variance analysis,** employs both the mean and the variance (or standard deviation) to make decisions according to the rules listed below.

Given two risky decisions (designated *A* and *B*), the *mean–variance rules* for decisions under risk are

mean–variance analysis
Method of decision making that employs both the mean and the variance to make decisions.

1. If decision *A* has a higher expected outcome *and* a lower variance than decision *B*, decision *A* should be made.
2. If both decisions *A* and *B* have identical *variances* (or standard deviations), the decision with the higher expected value should be made.
3. If both decisions *A* and *B* have identical *expected values,* the decision with the lower variance (standard deviation) should be made.

The mean–variance rules are based on the assumption that a decision maker prefers a higher expected return to a lower, other things equal, and a lower risk to a higher, other things equal. It therefore follows that the *higher* the expected outcome and the *lower* the variance (risk), the more desirable a decision will be. Under rule 1, a manager would always choose a particular decision if it has *both* a greater expected value *and* a lower variance than other decisions being considered. With the same level of risk, the second rule indicates managers should choose the decision with the higher expected value. Under rule 3, if the decisions have identical expected values, the manager chooses the less risky (lower standard deviation) decision.

Returning to the problem of Chicago Rotisserie Chicken, no location dominates both of the other locations in terms of any of the three rules of mean–variance analysis. Boston dominates Cleveland because it has both a higher expected value and a lower risk (rule 1). Atlanta also dominates Cleveland in terms of rule 3 because both locations have the same expected value ($3,500), but Atlanta has a lower standard deviation—less risk ($\sigma_A = 1,025 < 2,062 = \sigma_C$).

If the manager compares the Atlanta and Boston locations, the mean–variance rules cannot be applied. Boston has a higher weekly expected profit ($3,750 > $3,500), but Atlanta is less risky ($\sigma_A = 1,025 < 1,545 = \sigma_B$). Therefore, when making this choice, the manager must make a trade-off between risk and expected return, so the choice would depend on the manager's valuation of higher expected return versus lower risk. We will now set forth an additional decision rule that uses information on both the expected value and dispersion and can be used to make decisions involving trade-offs between expected return and risk.

Coefficient of Variation Analysis

As we noted in the discussion about measuring the riskiness of probability distributions, variance and standard deviation are measures of *absolute risk*. In contrast, the coefficient of variation [$\sigma/E(X)$] measures risk *relative* to the expected value of the distribution. The coefficient of variation, therefore, allows managers to make decisions based on relative risk instead of absolute risk. The **coefficient of variation rule** states: "When making decisions under risk, choose the decision with the smallest coefficient of variation [$\sigma/E(X)$]." This rule takes into account both the expected value and the standard deviation of the distribution. The lower the standard deviation and the higher the expected value, the smaller the coefficient of variation. Thus a desired movement in either characteristic of a probability distribution moves the coefficient of variation in the desired direction.

We return once more to the decision facing the manager of Chicago Rotisserie Chicken. The coefficients of variation for each of the possible location decisions are

$$v_{Atlanta} = 1,025/3,500 = 0.29$$

$$v_{Boston} = 1,545/3,750 = 0.41$$

$$v_{Cleveland} = 2,062/3,500 = 0.59$$

coefficient of variation rule
Decision-making rule that the decision to be chosen is the one with the smallest coefficient of variation.

The location with the smallest coefficient of variation is Atlanta, which has a coefficient of 0.29. Notice that the choice between locating in either Atlanta or Boston, which could not be made using mean–variance rules, is now resolved using the coefficient of variation to make the decision. Atlanta wins over Boston with the smaller coefficient of variation (0.29 < 0.41), while Cleveland comes in last.

Which Rule Is Best?

At this point, you may be wondering which one of the three rules for making decisions under risk is the "correct one. After all, the manager of Chicago Rotisserie Chicken either reached a different decision or reached no decision at all depending on which rule was used. Using the expected value rule, Boston was the choice. Using the coefficient of variation rule, Atlanta was chosen. According to mean–variance analysis, Cleveland was out, but the decision between Atlanta and Boston could not be resolved using mean–variance analysis. If the decision rules do not all lead to the same conclusion, a manager must decide which rule to follow.

When a decision is to be made repeatedly, with identical probabilities each time, the expected value rule provides managers with the most reliable rule for maximizing (expected) profit. The average return of a given risky course of action repeated many times will approach the expected value of that action. Therefore, the average return of the course of action with the highest expected value will tend to be higher than the average return of any course of action with a lower expected value, when carried out a large number of times. Situations involving repeated decisions can arise, for example, when a manager must make the same risky decision once a month or even once every week. Or a manager at corporate headquarters may make a decision that directs activities of dozens, maybe even hundreds, of corporate offices in the country or around the world. When the risky decision is repeated many times, the manager at corporate headquarters believes strongly that each of the alternative decision choices will probably result in an average profit level that is equal to the expected value of profit, even though any one corporate office might experience either higher or lower returns. In practice, then, the expected value rule is justifiable when a decision will be repeated many times under identical circumstances.

When a manager makes a one-time decision under risk, there will not be any follow-up repetitions of the decision to "average out" a bad outcome (or a good outcome). Unfortunately, there is no best rule to follow when decisions are not repetitive. The rules we present for risky decision making should be used by managers to help *analyze* and *guide* the decision-making process. Ultimately, making decisions under risk (or uncertainty) is as much an art as it is a science.

The "art" of decision making under risk or uncertainty is closely associated with a decision maker's preferences with respect to risk taking. Managers can differ greatly in their willingness to take on risk in decision making. Some managers are quite cautious, while others may actually seek out high-risk situations. In the next section, we present a theory, not a rule, of decision making under risk that formally accounts for a manager's attitude toward risk. This theory, usually referred to as *expected utility theory*, postulates that managers make risky decisions with the objective of maximizing the expected *utility* of profit. The theory can, in some situations, provide a more powerful tool for making risky decisions than the rules presented in this section.

ILLUSTRATION 15.1

Lowering Risk by Diversification

Although investors can't do much about the amount of risk associated with any specific project or investment, they do have some control over the amount of risk associated with their entire portfolio of investments. *The Wall Street Journal* (April 8, 1993) advised: "[F]or anyone who doesn't need . . . money right away, this may be a good time to broaden your investment horizon. The best strategy, investment advisors say, is to diversify by spreading your money among a wide variety of stocks, bonds, real estate, cash, and other holdings."

The *WSJ* pointed out that you will have to expect the value of your holdings to fluctuate with changes in the economy or market conditions. The returns should comfortably beat those from CDs, and the ups and downs should be a lot smaller than if you simply put all your money in the stock market. One investment adviser stated, "Diversified portfolios of stocks and bonds had much less risk while providing nearly as much return as an all-stock portfolio during the past 15, 20, and 25 years." During the period since 1968, stocks soared in five years but were losing investments in six years. Investors who put a third of their money in stocks, a third in Treasury bonds, and a third in "cash equivalent" investments would have lost money in only four years, with the largest annual loss being less than 5 percent. The annual compound return over the 25 years in that investment would have been 9 percent, compared with 10.56 percent in an all-stock portfolio, 8.26 percent in all bonds, and 9.89 percent in 60 percent stock and 40 percent bonds. But the more diversified investment would have been less risky.

The theoretical arguments in the *WSJ* article are based on portfolio theory. The core of portfolio theory is deceptively simple: As more securities are added to an investor's portfolio, the portfolio risk (the standard deviation of portfolio returns) declines. A particular se-

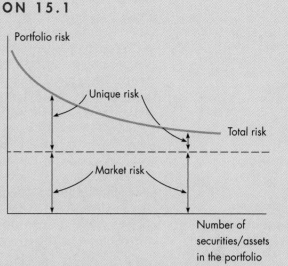

curity or investment is subject to two types of risk: market risk and unique risk. Market risk is the risk faced due to economywide changes, such as economic fluctuations and fluctuations in the market rate of interest. Unique risk is the risk associated with the particular security or investment, such as fluctuations in the sales of a particular firm or region relative to the entire economy.

As different securities are added to a portfolio, the unique risk associated with a specific security is diversified away. That is, as more securities are added, the entire portfolio is less subject to the unique risk associated with a given stock. As the number of securities or assets is increased, unique risk decreases and the total risk of the portfolio (the standard deviation) approaches the market risk.

Source: Tom Herman, "The First Rollovers of Spring Bring Advice on Diversification," *The Wall Street Journal,* Apr. 8, 1993.

15.4 EXPECTED UTILITY: A THEORY OF DECISION MAKING UNDER RISK

As we just mentioned, managers differ in their willingness to undertake risky decisions. Some managers avoid risk as much as possible, while other managers actually prefer more risk to less risk in decision making. To allow for different attitudes toward risk taking in decision making, modern decision theory treats managers as deriving utility or satisfaction from the profits earned by their firms. Just as consumers derived utility from the consumption of goods in Chapter 5, in **expected utility theory,** managers are assumed to derive utility from earning profits. Expected utility theory postulates that managers make risky decisions in a way that maximizes the expected utility of the profit outcomes. While expected utility theory does provide a tool for decisions under risk, the primary purpose of the theory, and the reason for presenting this theory here, is to explain why managers make the decisions they do make when risk is involved. We want to stress that expected utility theory is an economic model of how managers *actually* make decisions under risk, rather than a rule dictating how managers *should* make decisions under risk.

Suppose a manager is faced with a decision to undertake a risky project or, more generally, must make a decision to take an action that may generate a range of possible profit outcomes, $\pi_1, \pi_2, \ldots, \pi_n,$ that the manager believes will occur with probabilities $p_1, p_2, \ldots, p_n,$ respectively. The **expected utility** of this risky decision is the sum of the probability-weighted utilities of each possible profit outcome:

$$E[U(\pi)] = p_1 U(\pi_1) + p_2 U(\pi_2) + \cdots + p_n U(\pi_n)$$

where $U(\pi)$ is a utility function for profit that measures the utility associated with a particular level of profit. Notice that expected *utility* of profit is different from the concept of expected *profit,* which is the sum of the probability-weighted profits. To understand expected utility theory, you must understand how the manager's attitude toward risk is reflected in the manager's utility function for profit. We now discuss the concept of a manager's utility of profit and show how to derive a utility function for profit. Then we demonstrate how managers could employ expected utility of profit to make decisions under risk.

A Manager's Utility Function for Profit

Since expected utility theory is based on the idea that managers enjoy utility or satisfaction from earning profit, the nature of the relation between a manager's utility and the level of profit earned plays a crucial role in explaining how managers make decisions under risk. As we now show, the manager's attitude toward risk is determined by the manager's *marginal utility of profit.*

It would be extremely unusual for a manager *not* to experience a higher level of total utility as profit increases. Thus the relation between an index of utility and the level of profit earned by a firm is assumed to be an upward-sloping curve. The amount by which total utility increases when the firm earns an additional dollar of profit is the **marginal utility of profit:**

$$MU_{\text{profit}} = \Delta U(\pi)/\Delta \pi$$

where $U(\pi)$ is the manager's utility function for profit. The utility function for profit gives an index value to measure the level of utility experienced when a given amount of profit is earned. Suppose, for example, the marginal utility of

expected utility theory
A theory of decision making under risk that accounts for a manager's attitude toward risk.

expected utility
The sum of the probability-weighted utilities of each possible profit outcome.

marginal utility of profit
The amount by which total utility increases with an additional dollar of profit earned by a firm.

profit is 8. This means a $1 increase in profit earned by the firm causes the utility index of the manager to increase by eight units. Studies of attitudes toward risk have found most business decision makers experience *diminishing marginal utility of profit*. Even though additional dollars of profit increase the level of total satisfaction, the additional utility from extra dollars of profit typically falls for most managers.

The shape of the utility curve for profit plays a pivotal role in expected utility theory because the shape of $U(\pi)$ determines the manager's attitude toward risk, which determines which choices a manager makes. Attitudes toward risk may be categorized as *risk averse, risk neutral,* or *risk loving.* People are said to be **risk averse** if, facing two risky decisions with equal expected profits, they choose the less risky decision. In contrast, someone choosing the more risky decision, when the expected profits are identical, is said to be **risk loving.** The third type of attitude toward risk arises for someone who is indifferent between risky situations when the expected profits are identical. In this last case, a manager ignores risk in decision making and is said to be **risk neutral.**

Figure 15.5 shows the shapes of the utility functions associated with the three types of risk preferences. Panel A illustrates a utility function for a risk-averse manager. The utility function for profit is upward-sloping, but its slope diminishes as profit rises, which corresponds to the case of diminishing marginal utility. When profit increases by $50,000 from point *A* to point *B*, the manager experiences an increase in utility of 10 units. When profit falls by $50,000 from point *A* to point *C*, utility falls by 15 units. A $50,000 loss of profit creates a larger reduction in utility than a $50,000 gain would add to utility. Consequently, risk-averse managers are more sensitive to a dollar of lost profit than to a dollar of gained profit and will place an emphasis in decision making on avoiding the risk of loss.

In Panel B, the marginal utility of profit is constant ($\Delta U/\Delta \pi = 15/50 = 0.3$), and the loss of $50,000 reduces utility by the same amount that a gain of $50,000 increases it. In this case, a manager places the same emphasis on avoiding losses as on seeking gains. Managers are risk neutral when their utility functions for profit are linear or, equivalently, when the marginal utility of profit is constant.

Panel C shows a utility function for a manager who makes risky decisions in a risk-loving way. The extra utility from a $50,000 increase in profit (20 units) is greater than the loss in utility suffered when profit falls by $50,000 (10 units). Consequently, a risk-loving decision maker places a greater weight on the potential for gain than on the potential for loss. We have now developed the following relation.

risk averse
Term describing a decision maker who makes the less risky of two decisions that have the same expected value.

risk loving
Term describing a decision maker who makes the riskier of two decisions that have the same expected value.

risk neutral
Term describing a decision maker who ignores risk in decision making and considers only expected values of decisions.

□ **Relation** A manager's attitude toward risky decisions can be related to his or her marginal utility of profit. Someone who experiences diminishing (increasing) marginal utility for profit will be a risk-averse (risk-loving) decision maker. Someone whose marginal utility of profit is constant is risk neutral.

Deriving a Utility Function for Profit

As discussed earlier, when managers make decisions to maximize expected utility under risk, it is the utility function for profit that determines which decision a

FIGURE 15.5
A Manager's Attitude toward Risk

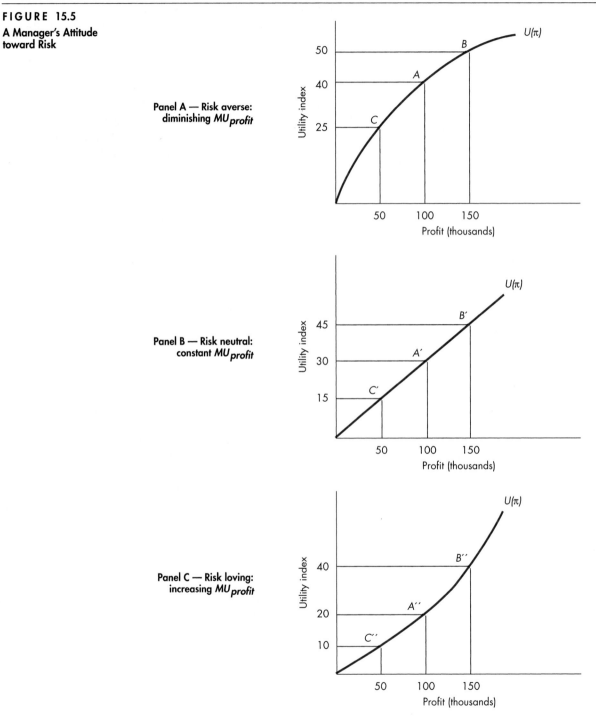

Panel A — Risk averse:
diminishing MU_{profit}

Panel B — Risk neutral:
constant MU_{profit}

Panel C — Risk loving:
increasing MU_{profit}

manager chooses. We now show the steps a manager can follow to derive his or her own utility function for profit, $U(\pi)$. Recall that the utility function does not directly measure utility but does provide a number, or index value, and that it is the magnitude of this index that reflects the desirability of a particular profit outcome.

The process of deriving a utility function for profit is conceptually straightforward. It does, however, involve a substantial amount of subjective evaluation. To illustrate the procedure, we return to the decision problem facing the manager of Chicago Rotisserie Chicken (CRC). Recall that CRC must decide where to locate the next restaurant. The profit outcomes for the three locations range from $1,000 to $6,000 per week. Before the expected utilities of each location can be calculated, the manager must derive her utility function for profits covering the range $1,000 to $6,000.

The manager of CRC begins the process of deriving $U(\pi)$ by assigning minimum and maximum values that the index will be allowed to take. For the lower bound on the index, suppose the manager assigns a utility index value of 0—although any number, positive or negative, will do—to the lowest profit outcome of $1,000. For the upper bound, suppose a utility index value of 1 is assigned—any value greater than the value of the lower bound will do—to the highest profit outcome of $6,000. Again, we emphasize, choosing 0 and 1 for the upper and lower bounds is completely arbitrary, just as long as the upper bound is greater algebraically than the lower bound. For example, lower and upper bounds of -12 and 50 would also work just fine. Two points on the manager's utility function for profit are

$$U(\$1,000) = 0 \quad \text{and} \quad U(\$6,000) = 1$$

Next, a value of the utility index for each of the remaining possible profit outcomes between $1,000 and $6,000 must be determined. In this case, examining profit in increments of $1,000 is convenient. To find the value of the utility index for $5,000, the manager employs the following subjective analysis: The manager begins by considering two decision choices, A and B, where decision A involves receiving a profit of $5,000 with certainty and risky decision B involves receiving either a $6,000 profit with probability p or a $1,000 profit with probability $1 - p$. Decisions A and B are illustrated in Figure 15.6. Now the probability p that will make the manager indifferent between the two decisions A and B must be determined. This is a subjective determination, and any two managers likely will find different values of p depending on their individual preferences for risk.

Suppose the manager of Chicago Rotisserie Chicken decides $p = 0.95$ makes decisions A and B equally desirable. In effect, the manager is saying that the expected utility of decision A equals the expected utility of decision B. If the expected utilities of decisions A and B are equal, $E(U_A) = E(U_B)$:

$$1 \times U(\$5,000) = 0.95 \times U(\$6,000) + 0.05 \times U(\$1,000)$$

Only $U(\$5,000)$ is unknown in this equation, so the manager can solve for the utility index for $5,000 of profit:

$$U(\$5,000) = (0.95 \times 1) + (0.05 \times 0) = 0.95$$

FIGURE 15.6
Finding a Certainty Equivalent for a Risky Decision

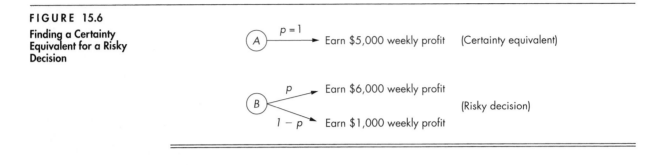

The utility index value of 0.95 is an indirect measure of the utility of $5,000 of profit. This procedure establishes another point on the utility function for profit. The sum of $5,000 is called the **certainty equivalent** of risky decision B because it is the dollar amount that the manager would be just willing to trade for the opportunity to engage in risky decision B. In other words, the manager is indifferent between having a profit of $5,000 for sure or making a risky decision having a 95 percent chance of earning $6,000 and a 5 percent chance of earning $1,000. The utility indexes for $4,000, $3,000, and $2,000 can be established in exactly the same way.

This procedure for finding a utility function for profit is called the *certainty equivalent method*. We now summarize the steps for finding a utility function for profit, $U(\pi)$, in a principle.

certainty equivalent
The dollar amount that a manager would be just willing to trade for the opportunity to engage in a risky decision.

🔲 **Principle** To implement the certainty equivalent method of deriving a utility of profit function, the following steps can be employed:

1. Set the utility index equal to 1 for the highest possible profit (π_H) and 0 for the lowest possible profit (π_L).
2. Define a risky decision to have probability p_0 of profit outcome π_H and probability $(1 - p_0)$ of profit outcome π_L. For *each* possible profit outcome π_0 $(\pi_H < \pi_0 < \pi_L)$, the manager determines subjectively the probability p_0 that gives that risky decision the same expected utility as receiving π_0 with certainty:

$$p_0 U(\pi_H) + (1 - p_0) U(\pi_L) = U(\pi_0)$$

The certain sum π_0 is called the certainty equivalent of the risky decision. Let the subjective probability p_0 serve as the utility index for measuring the level of satisfaction the manager enjoys when earning a profit of π_0.

Figure 15.7 illustrates the utility function for profit for the manager of Chicago Rotisserie Chicken. The marginal utility of profit diminishes over the entire range of possible profit outcomes ($1,000 to $6,000), and so this manager is a risk-averse decision maker.

Maximization of Expected Utility

When managers choose among risky decisions in accordance with expected utility theory, the decision with the greatest expected utility is chosen. Unlike maximiza-

FIGURE 15.7
A Manager's Utility Function for Profit

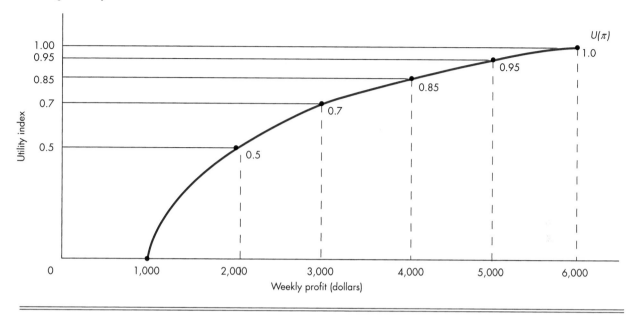

tion of expected profits, maximizing expected utility takes into consideration the manager's preferences for risk. As you will see in this example, maximizing expected utility can lead to a different decision than the one reached using the maximization of expected profit rule.

Return once more to the location decision facing Chicago Rotisserie Chicken. The manager calculates the expected utilities of the three risky location decisions using her own utility function for profit shown in Figure 15.7. The expected utilities for the three cities are calculated as follows:

$$\text{Atlanta } E(U_A) = 0U(\$1{,}000) + 0.2U(\$2{,}000) + 0.3U(\$3{,}000) + 0.3U(\$4{,}000)$$
$$+ 0.2U(\$5{,}000) + 0U(\$6{,}000)$$

$$= 0 + (0.2)(0.5) + (0.3)(0.7) + (0.3)(0.85) + (0.2)(0.95) + 0$$

$$= 0.755$$

$$\text{Boston } E(U_B) = 0.1U(\$1{,}000) + 0.15U(\$2{,}000) + 0.15U(\$3{,}000)$$
$$+ 0.25U(\$4{,}000) + 0.2U(\$5{,}000) + 0.15U(\$6{,}000)$$

$$= (0.1)(0) + (0.15)(0.50) + (0.15)(0.7) + (0.25)(0.85)$$
$$+ (0.2)(0.95) + (0.15)(1)$$

$$= 0.733$$

Cleveland $E(U_C) = 0.3U(\$1,000) + 0.1U(\$2,000) + 0.1U(\$3,000) + 0.1U(\$4,000)$
$+ 0.1U(\$5,000) + 0.3U(\$6,000)$

$= (0.3)(0) + (0.1)(0.5) + (0.1)(0.7) + (0.1)(0.85) + (0.1)(0.95)$
$+ (0.3)(1.0)$

$= 0.600$

To maximize the expected utility of profits, the manager of Chicago Rotisserie Chicken chooses to open its new restaurant in Atlanta. Even though Boston has the highest expected profit [$E(\pi) = \$3,750$], Boston also has the highest level of risk ($\sigma = 1,545$), and the risk-averse manager at CRC prefers to avoid the relatively high risk of locating the new restaurant in Boston. In this case of a risk-averse decision maker, the manager chooses the less risky Atlanta location over the more risky Cleveland location even though both locations have identical expected profit levels.

To show what a risk-neutral decision maker would do, we constructed a utility function for profit that exhibits constant marginal utility of profit, which, as we have explained, is the condition required for risk neutrality. This risk-neutral utility function is presented in columns 1 and 2 of Table 15.1. Marginal utility of profit, in column 3, is constant, as it must be for risk-neutral managers. From the table you can see that the expected utilities of profit for Atlanta, Boston, and Cleveland are 0.50, 0.55, and 0.50, respectively. For a risk-neutral decision maker, locating in Boston is the decision that maximizes expected utility. Recall that Boston also is the city with the maximum expected profit [$E(\pi) = \$3,750$]. This is not a coincidence. As we explained earlier, a risk-neutral decision maker ignores risk when making decisions and relies instead on expected profit to make decisions in risky situations. Under conditions of risk neutrality, a manager makes the same decision by maximizing either the expected value of profit, $E(\pi)$, or the expected utility of profit, $E[U(\pi)]$.[2]

Finally, consider how a manager who is risk loving decides on a location for CRC's new restaurant. In Table 15.2, columns 1 and 2 show a utility function for profit for which marginal utility of profit is increasing. Column 3 shows the marginal utility of profit, which, as it must for a risk-loving manager, increases as profit increases. The expected utilities of profit outcomes for Atlanta, Boston, and Cleveland are 0.32, 0.41, and 0.43, respectively. In the case of a risk-loving decision maker, Cleveland is the decision that maximizes expected utility. If Atlanta and Cleveland were the only two sites being considered, then the risk-loving manager would choose Cleveland over Atlanta, a decision that is consistent with the definition of risk loving. We now summarize our discussion in the following principle.

□ **Principle** If a manager behaves according to expected utility theory, decisions are made to maximize the manager's expected utility of profits. Decisions made by maximizing expected utility of profit reflect the manager's risk-taking attitude and generally differ from decisions reached by decision rules that do not consider risk. In the case of a risk-neutral manager, the decisions are identical under either maximization of expected utility or maximization of expected profit.

---

[2]The appendix to this chapter demonstrates the equivalence for risk-neutral decision makers of maximizing expected profit and maximizing expected utility of profit.

TABLE 15.1
Expected Utility of Profit: A Risk-Neutral Manager

(1)	(2)	(3)	(4)	(5)	(6)	(7)	(8)	(9)
			Probabilities			Probability-weighted utility		
Profit (π)	Utility $[U(\pi)]$	Marginal utility $[\Delta U(\pi)/\Delta\pi]$	Atlanta (P_A)	Boston (P_B)	Cleveland (P_C)	$P_A \times U$	$P_B \times U$	$P_C \times U$
$1,000	0	—	0	0.1	0.3	0	0	0
$2,000	0.2	0.0002	0.2	0.15	0.1	0.04	0.03	0.02
$3,000	0.4	0.0002	0.3	0.15	0.1	0.12	0.06	0.04
$4,000	0.6	0.0002	0.3	0.25	0.1	0.18	0.15	0.06
$5,000	0.8	0.0002	0.2	0.2	0.1	0.16	0.16	0.08
$6,000	1.0	0.0002	0	0.15	0.3	0	0.15	0.3
					Expected utility =	0.50	0.55	0.50

Table 15.2
Expected Utility of Profit: A Risk-Loving Manager

(1)	(2)	(3)	(4)	(5)	(6)	(7)	(8)	(9)
			Probabilities			Probability-weighted utility		
Profit (π)	Utility $[U(\pi)]$	Marginal utility $[\Delta U(\pi)/\Delta\pi]$	Atlanta (P_A)	Boston (P_B)	Cleveland (P_C)	$P_A \times U$	$P_B \times U$	$P_C \times U$
$1,000	0	—	0	0.1	0.3	0	0	0
$2,000	0.08	0.00008	0.2	0.15	0.1	0.016	0.012	0.008
$3,000	0.2	0.00012	0.3	0.15	0.1	0.06	0.03	0.02
$4,000	0.38	0.00018	0.3	0.25	0.1	0.114	0.095	0.038
$5,000	0.63	0.00025	0.2	0.2	0.1	0.126	0.126	0.036
$6,000	1.0	0.00037	0	0.15	0.3	0	0.15	0.3
					Expected utility =	0.32	0.41	0.43

15.5 DECISIONS UNDER UNCERTAINTY

maximax rule
Decision-making guide that calls for identifying the best outcome for each possible decision and choosing the decision with the maximum payoff of all the best outcomes.

Practically all economic theories about behavior in the absence of complete information deal with risk rather than uncertainty. Furthermore, decision science has little guidance to offer managers making decisions when they have no idea about the likelihood of various states of nature occurring. This should not be too surprising, given the nebulous nature of uncertainty. We will, however, present four rather simple decision rules that can help managers make decisions under uncertainty.

The Maximax Criterion

For managers who tend to have an optimistic outlook on life, the **maximax rule** provides a guide for making decisions when uncertainty prevails. Under the

ILLUSTRATION 15.2

Floating Power Plants Lower Risks and Energize Developing Nations

Two crucial industries in developing countries are agriculture and manufacturing. A third-world nation cannot emerge from poverty without achieving a significant ability to feed itself and to manufacture both durable goods for consumption and capital goods for production. Neither of these two crucial industries can develop without energy. Domestically generated electricity can provide a versatile source of energy capable of meeting many of the most fundamental energy demands of a developing country.

A serious roadblock to construction of electric power plants in developing countries has been the risk of default on the financing required to purchase power plants. With prices beginning in the hundreds of millions of dollars, investors are understandably reluctant to lend these enormous amounts when repossession of the asset is, for all practical purposes, impossible. Donald Smith, president of Smith Cogeneration, found a solution to the problem of default risk: Build floating power plants on huge barges that can be relocated in the event of a default.

The Wall Street Journal reported that Smith's idea of building power plants on barges spawned a niche industry that "could become a significant portion of the world's [electricity] generating capacity." Nations such as the Dominican Republic, Ghana, India, and Haiti have signed agreements with producers of floating power plants that would not have been financed without the risk reduction created by the mobility of a floating platform. Indeed, the *WSJ* estimated that the floating nature of the power plant not only makes financing possible but also probably "lower(s) the financing costs by two or three percentage points"—no small change on a half-a-billion-dollar loan.

This illustration highlights the importance of risk in decision making. If financial institutions were managed by risk-loving managers, land-based power plants would likely be common in developing nations. Apparently, developing nations can expect to generate most of their electricity on barges anchored in their harbors—evidence that large financial lenders are indeed risk-averse.

Source: William M. Bulkley, "Building Power Plants That Can Float," *The Wall Street Journal*, May 22, 1996.

---

maximax rule, a manager identifies for each possible decision the best outcome that could occur and then chooses the decision that would give the maximum payoff of all the best outcomes. Under this rule a manager ignores all possible outcomes except the best outcome from each decision.

To illustrate the application of this rule, suppose the management at Dura Plastic is considering changing the size (capacity) of its manufacturing plant. Management has narrowed the decision to three choices. The plant's capacity will be (1) expanded by 20 percent, (2) maintained at the current capacity, or (3) reduced by 20 percent. The outcome of this decision depends crucially on how the economy performs during the upcoming year. Thus the performance of the economy is the "state of nature" in this decision problem. Management envisions three possible states of nature occurring: (1) The economy enters a period of recovery, (2) economic stagnation sets in, or (3) the economy falls into a recession.

For each possible decision and state of nature, the managers determine the profit outcome, or payoff, shown in the *payoff matrix* in Table 15.3. A **payoff matrix** is a table with rows corresponding to the various decisions and columns corresponding to the various states of nature. Each cell in the payoff matrix in Table 15.3 gives the outcome (payoff) for each decision when a particular state of nature

payoff matrix
A table with rows corresponding to various decisions and columns corresponding to various states of nature, with each cell giving the outcome or payoff associated with that decision and state of nature.

TABLE 15.3
The Payoff Matrix for Dura Plastic, Inc.

Decisions	States of nature		
	Recovery	Stagnation	Recession
Expand plant capacity by 20%	$5 million	−$1 million	−$3.0 million
Maintain same plant capacity	3 million	2 million	0.5 million
Reduce plant capacity by 20%	2 million	1 million	0.75 million

occurs. For example, if management chooses to expand the manufacturing plant by 20 percent and the economy enters a period of recovery, Dura Plastic is projected to earn profits of $5 million. Alternatively, if Dura Plastic expands plant capacity but the economy falls into a recession, it is projected that the company will lose $3 million. The managers do not know which state of nature will actually occur, or the probabilities of occurrence, so the decision to alter plant capacity is made under conditions of uncertainty. To apply the maximax rule to this decision, management first identifies the best possible outcome for each of the three decisions. The best payoffs are

$5 million for expand plant size by 20 percent.

$3 million for maintain plant size.

$2 million for reduce plant size by 20 percent.

Each best payoff occurs if the economy recovers. Under the maximax rule, management would decide to expand its plant.

While the maximax rule is simple to apply, it fails to consider "bad" outcomes in the decision-making process. The fact that two out of three states of nature result in losses when management decides to expand plant capacity, and neither of the other decisions would result in a loss, is overlooked when using the maximax criteria. Only managers with optimistic natures are likely to find the maximax rule to be a useful decision-making tool.

The Maximin Criterion

For managers with a pessimistic outlook on business decisions, the *maximin rule* may be more suitable than the maximax rule. Under the **maximin rule,** the manager identifies the worst outcome for each decision and makes the decision associated with the maximum worst payoff. For Dura Plastic, the worst outcomes for each decision from Table 15.3 are

−$3 million for expand plant size by 20 percent.

$0.5 million for maintain plant size.

$0.75 million for reduce plant size by 20 percent.

Using the maximin criterion, Dura Plastic would choose to reduce plant capacity by 20 percent. The maximin rule is also simple to follow, but it fails to consider any of the "good" outcomes.

maximin rule
Decision-making guide that calls for identifying the worst outcome for each decision and choosing the decision with the maximum worst payoff.

TABLE 15.4
Potential Regret Matrix for Dura Plastic, Inc.

	States of nature		
Decisions	Recovery	Stagnation	Recession
Expand plant capacity by 20%	$0 million	$3 million	$3.75 million
Maintain same plant capacity	2 million	0 million	0.25 million
Reduce plant capacity by 20%	3 million	1 million	0 million

The Minimax Regret Criterion

potential regret
For a given decision and state of nature, the improvement in payoff the manager could have experienced had the decision been the best one when that state of nature actually occurs.

Managers concerned about their decisions not turning out to be the best *once the state of nature is known* (i.e., after the uncertainty is resolved) may make their decisions by minimizing the potential regret that may occur. The **potential regret** associated with a particular decision and state of nature is the improvement in payoff the manager could have experienced had the decision been the best one when that state of nature actually occurred. To illustrate, we calculate from Table 15.3 the potential regret associated with Dura Plastic's decision to maintain the same level of plant capacity if an economic recovery occurs. The best possible payoff when recovery occurs is $5 million, the payoff for expanding plant capacity. If a recovery does indeed happen and management chooses to maintain the same level of plant capacity, the payoff is only $3 million, and the manager experiences a regret of $2 million (= $5 − $3 million).

Table 15.4 shows the potential regret for each combination of decision and state of nature. Note that every state of nature has a decision for which there is no potential regret. This occurs when the correct decision is made for that particular state of nature. To apply the **minimax regret rule,** which requires that managers make a decision with the minimum worst potential regret, management identifies the maximum possible potential regret for each decision from the matrix:

minimax regret rule
Decision-making guide that calls for determining the worst potential regret associated with each decision, then choosing the decision with the minimum worst potential regret.

$3.75 million for expand plant size by 20 percent.

$2 million for maintain plant size.

$3 million for reduce plant size by 20 percent.

Management chooses the decision with the lowest worst potential regret: maintain current plant capacity. For Dura Plastic, the minimax regret rule results in management's choosing to maintain the current plant capacity.

equal probability rule
Decision-making guide that calls for assuming each state of nature is equally likely to occur, computing the average payoff for each equally likely possible state of nature, and choosing the decision with the highest average payoff.

The Equal Probability Criterion

In situations of uncertainty, managers have no information about the probable state of nature that will occur and sometimes simply assume that each state of nature is equally likely to occur. In terms of the Dura Plastic decision, management assumes each state of nature has a one-third probability of occurring. When managers assume each state of nature has an equal likelihood of occurring, the decision can be made by considering the *average* payoff for each equally possible state of nature. This approach to decision making is often referred to as the **equal probability rule.**

To illustrate, the manager of Dura Plastic calculates the average payoff for each decision as follows:

$0.33 million [= (5 + (−1) + (−3))/3] for expand plant size.

$1.83 million [= (3 + 2 + 0.5)/3] for maintain plant size.

$1.25 million [= (2 + 1 + 0.75)/3] for reduce plant size.

Under the equal probability rule, the manager's decision is to maintain the current plant capacity, since this decision has the maximum average return.

The four decision rules discussed here do not exhaust the possibilities for managers making decisions under uncertainty. We present these four rules primarily to give you a feel for decision making under uncertainty and to show the imprecise or "unscientific" nature of these rules. Recall that management could choose any of the courses of action depending upon which rule was chosen. These and other rules are meant only to be guidelines to decision making and are not substitutes for the experience and intuition of management.

15.6 SUMMARY

When managers make choices or decisions under risk or uncertainty, they must somehow incorporate this risk into their decision-making process. This chapter presented some basic rules for managers to help them make decisions under conditions of risk and uncertainty. Conditions of *risk* occur when a manager must make a decision for which the outcome is not known with certainty. Under conditions of risk, the manager can make a list of all possible outcomes and assign probabilities to the various outcomes. *Uncertainty* exists when a decision maker cannot list all possible outcomes and/or cannot assign probabilities to the various outcomes.

To measure the risk associated with a decision, the manager can examine several characteristics of the probability distribution of outcomes for the decision. A probability distribution is a table or graph showing all possible outcomes (payoffs) for a decision and the probability that each outcome will occur. The various rules for making decisions under risk require information about several different characteristics of the probability distribution of outcomes: (1) the expected value (or mean) of the distribution, (2) the variance and standard deviation, and (3) the coefficient of variation.

The expected value (or mean) of a probability distribution is

$$E(X) = \text{Expected value of } X = \sum_{i=1}^{n} p_i X_i$$

where X_i is the ith outcome of a decision, p_i is the probability of the ith outcome, and n is the total number of possible outcomes in the probability distribution. The variance of a probability distribution measures the dispersion of the outcomes about the mean outcome. The variance is calculated as

$$\text{Variance } (X) = \sigma_x^2 = \sum_{i=1}^{n} p_i (X_i - E(X))^2$$

Because the variance is a squared term and usually much larger than the mean, the standard deviation is often used to measure the dispersion of a probability distribution:

$$\sigma_x = \sqrt{\text{Variance } (X)}$$

When the expected values of outcomes differ substantially, managers should measure riskiness of a decision relative to its expected value using the coefficient of variation:

$$v = \frac{\text{Standard deviation}}{\text{Expected value}} = \frac{\sigma_x}{E(X)}$$

The coefficient of variation measures the level of risk relative to the mean of the probability distribution.

When managers make decisions under risk, they must incorporate the risk into their decision-making process. While there is no single decision rule that managers can follow to guarantee that profits are actually maximized,

TABLE 15.5

Summary of Decision Rules under Conditions of Risk

Expected value rule	Choose the decision with the highest expected value.
Mean–variance rules	Given two risky decisions A and B:
	If decision A has a higher expected outcome *and* a lower variance than decision B, decision A should be made.
	If both decisions A and B have identical *variances* (or standard deviations), the decision with the higher expected value should be made.
	If both decisions A and B have identical *expected* values, the decision with the lower variance (standard deviation) should be made.
Coefficient of variation rule	Choose the decision with the smallest coefficient of variation.

there are a number of decision rules that managers can use to help them make decisions under risk: (1) the expected value rule, (2) the mean–variance rules, and (3) the coefficient of variation rule. These three rules are summarized in Table 15.5. These rules can only guide managers in their analysis of risky decision making.

The actual decisions made by a manager will depend in large measure on the manager's willingness to take on risk. Managers' propensity to take on risk can be classified in one of three categories: risk averse, risk loving, or risk neutral. These categories of risk preference are defined according to how that manager would choose between the following two alternatives:

1. Take a risky course of action with a known expected value and variance.
2. Receive the expected value of that course of action with certainty.

A *risk-averse* person would choose to receive with certainty the expected value of the risky course of action (alternative 2). A *risk-loving* person would choose the risky course of action (alternative 1). A *risk-neutral* person would be indifferent between the two alternative decisions.

Expected utility theory explains how managers can make decisions in risky situations. The theory postulates that managers make risky decisions with the objective of maximizing the expected utility of profit. The manager's attitude for risk is captured by the shape of the utility function for profit. If a manager experiences diminishing (increasing) marginal utility for profit, the manager is risk averse (risk loving). If marginal utility for profit is constant, the manager is risk neutral.

If a manager maximizes expected utility for profit, the decisions can differ from decisions reached using the three decision rules discussed for making risky decisions. However, in the case of a risk-neutral manager, the decisions are the same under maximization of expected profit and maximization of expected utility of profit. Consequently, a risk-neutral decision maker can follow the simple rule of maximizing the expected value of profit and simultaneously also be maximizing utility of profit.

In the case of uncertainty, decision science can provide very little guidance to managers beyond offering them some simple decision rules to aid them in their analysis of uncertain situations. Four basic rules for decision making under uncertainty are presented in this chapter: (1) the maximax rule, (2) the maximin rule, (3) the minimax regret rule, and (4) the equal probability rule. Table 15.6 summarizes these rules.

TABLE 15.6
Summary of Decision Rules under Conditions of Uncertainty

Maximax rule	Identify the best outcome for each possible decision, and choose the decision with the maximum payoff.
Maximin rule	Identify the worst outcome for each decision, and choose the decision associated with the maximum worst payoff.
Minimax regret rule	Determine the worst potential regret associated with each decision, where the potential regret associated with any particular decision and state of nature is the improvement in payoff the manager could have experienced had the decision been the best one when that state of nature actually occurred. The manager chooses the decision with the minimum worst potential regret.
Equal probability rule	Assume each state of nature is equally likely to occur and compute the average payoff for each equally likely possible state of nature. Choose the decision with the highest average payoff.

TECHNICAL PROBLEMS

1. Consider the following two probability distributions for sales:

Sales (thousands of units)	Distribution 1 probability (percent)	Distribution 2 probability (percent)
50	10	10
60	20	15
70	40	20
80	20	30
90	10	25

   a. Graph the two distributions shown in the table. What are the expected sales for the two probability distributions?

   b. Calculate the variance and standard deviation for both distributions. Which distribution is more risky?

   c. Calculate the coefficient of variation for both distributions. Which distribution is more risky relative to its mean?

2. A firm is making its production plans for next quarter, but the manager of the firm does not know what the price of the product will be next month. He believes that there is a 40 percent probability the price will be $15 and a 60 percent probability the price will be $20. The manager must decide whether to produce 7,000 units or 8,000 units of output. The following table shows the four possible profit outcomes, depending on which output management chooses and which price actually occurs:

	Profit (loss) when price is	
	$15	$20
Option A: produce 7,100	−$3,750	+$31,770
Option B: produce 8,000	−8,000	+34,000

   a. If the manager chooses the option with the higher expected profits, which output is chosen?

b. Which option is more risky?

c. What is the decision if the manager uses the mean–variance rules to decide between the two options?

d. What is the decision using the coefficient of variation rule?

3. Suppose in Technical Problem 2 that the price probabilities are reversed: The manager expects a price of $15 with a probability of 60 percent and a price of $20 with a probability of 40 percent. Answer all parts of Technical Problem 2 under the assumption of these reversed probabilities. What would the probabilities have to be to make the expected values of the two options equal?

4. A manager's utility function for profit is $U(\pi) = 20\pi$, where π is the dollar amount of profit. The manager is considering a risky decision with the four possible profit outcomes shown here. The manager makes the following subjective assessments about the probability of each profit outcome:

Probability	Profit outcome
0.05	−$10,000
0.45	−2,000
0.45	4,000
0.05	20,000

a. Calculate the expected profit.

b. Calculate the expected utility of profit.

c. The marginal utility of an extra dollar of profit is _____.

d. The manager is risk _____ because the marginal utility of profit is _____.

5. Suppose the manager of a firm has a utility function for profit of $U(\pi) = 20 \ln(\pi)$, where π is the dollar amount of profit. The manager is considering a risky project with the following profit payoffs and probabilities:

Probability	Profit outcome	Marginal utility of profit
0.05	$1,000	—
0.15	2,000	_____
0.30	3,000	_____
0.50	4,000	_____

a. Calculate the expected profit.

b. Calculate the expected utility of profit.

c. Fill in the blanks in the table showing the marginal utility of an additional $1,000 of profit.

d. The manager is risk _____ because the marginal utility of profit is _____.

6. Derive your own utility function for profit for the range of profits shown in the following table:

Profit outcome	Utility index	Marginal utility of profit
$1,000	0.0	—
2,000	_____	_____
3,000	_____	_____
3,200	_____	_____
4,000	1.0	_____

    a. Find the probability *p* that would make you indifferent between (1) accepting a risky project with probability *p* of making $4,000 and probability $1 - p$ of making a profit of $1,000 or (2) making a profit of $2,000 with certainty. Write this probability in the correct blank in the table.

    b. Repeat part *a* for $3,000 and $3,200.

    c. Compute the marginal utility of profit. (*Hint:* $MU_{profit} = \Delta$utility index$/\Delta$profit, and the denominator, Δprofit, is not constant in this table.)

    d. Does your utility index indicate that you have a risk-averse, risk-neutral, or risk-loving attitude toward risk? Explain.

7. Suppose the manager in Technical Problem 4 can avoid the risky decision in that problem by choosing instead to receive with certainty a sum of money exactly equal to the expected profit of the risky decision in Technical Problem 4.

    a. The utility of the expected profit is _____.

    b. Compare the utility of the expected profit with the expected utility of the risky decision (which you calculated in part *b* of Technical Problem 4). Which decision yields the greatest expected utility for the manager?

    c. Is your decision in part *b* consistent with the manager's attitude toward risk, as it is reflected by the utility function for profit? Explain.

8. The manager in Technical Problem 5 receives an offer from another party to buy the rights to the risky project described in that problem. This party offers the manager $3,200, which the manager believes will be paid with certainty.

    a. The utility of $3,200 is _____.

    b. Comparing the utility of $3,200 with the expected utility of the risky project (you calculated this for part *b* of Technical Problem 5), what should the manager do if the manager wishes to maximize expected utility of profit? Explain.

    c. Is your decision in part *b* consistent with the manager's attitude toward risk as it is reflected by the utility function for profit? Explain.

    d. Is the decision consistent with the mean–variance rules for decision making under risk? Explain.

9. Suppose the manager in Technical Problem 2 has absolutely no idea about the probabilities of the two prices occurring. Which option would the manager choose under each of the following rules?

    a. Maximax rule

    b. Maximin rule

    c. Minimax regret rule

    d. Equal probability rule

APPLIED PROBLEMS

1. Consider a firm that is deciding whether to operate plants only in the United States or also in either Mexico or Canada or both. Congress is currently discussing an overseas investment in new capital (OINC) tax credit for U.S. firms that operate plants outside the country. If Congress passes OINC in 2005, management expects to do well if it is operating plants in Mexico and Canada. If OINC does not pass in 2005 and the firm does operate plants in Mexico and Canada, it will incur rather large losses. It is also possible that Congress will table OINC in 2006 and wait until 2003 to vote on it. The profit payoff matrix (profits in 2005) is shown here:

| | States of nature | | |
	OINC passes	OINC fails	OINC stalls
Operate plants in U.S. only	$10 million	−$1 million	$2 million
Operate plants in U.S. and Mexico	15 million	−4 million	1.5 million
Operate plants in U.S., Mexico, and Canada	20 million	−6 million	4 million

Assuming the managers of this firm have no idea about the likelihood of congressional action on OINC in 2005, what decision should the firm make using each of the following rules?

a. Maximax rule

b. Maximin rule

c. Minimax regret rule

d. Equal probability rule

2. Suppose your company's method of making decisions under risk is "making the best out of the worst possible outcome." What rule would you be forced to follow?

3. "A portfolio manager needs to pick winners—assets or securities with high expected returns and low risk." What is wrong with this statement?

4. Remox Corporation is a British firm that sells high-fashion sportswear in the United States. Congress is currently considering the imposition of a protective tariff on imported textiles. Remox is considering the possibility of moving 50 percent of its production to the United States to avoid the tariff. This would be accomplished by opening a plant in the United States. The following table lists the profit outcomes under various scenarios:

| | Profit in 2005 | |
	No tariff	Tariff
Option A: Produce all output in Britain	$1,200,000	$ 800,000
Option B: Produce 50% in the United States	875,000	1,000,000

Remox hires a consulting firm to assess the probability that a tariff on imported textiles will in fact pass a congressional vote and not be vetoed by the president. The consultants forecast the following probabilities:

	Probability
Tariff will pass	30%
Tariff will fail	70

a.   Compute the expected profits for both options.

b. Based on the expected profit only, which option should Remox choose?

c. Compute the probabilities that would make Remox indifferent between options *A* and *B* using that rule.

d. Compute the standard deviations for options A and B facing Remox Corporation.

e. What decision would Remox make using the mean–variance rule?

f. What decision would Remox make using the coefficient of variation rule?

5. Using the information in Applied Problem 4, what decision would Remox make using each of the following rules if it had no idea of the probability of a tariff?

a. Maximax

b. Maximin

c. Minimax regret

d. Equal probability criterion

6. Return to Applied Problem 1 and suppose the managers of the firm decide on the following subjective probabilities of congressional action on OINC:

	Probability
OINC passes	40%
OINC fails	10
OINC stalls	50

a. Compute the expected profits for all three decisions.

b. Using the expected value rule, which option should the managers choose?

c. Compute the standard deviations for all three decisions. Using the mean–variance rule, does any one of the decisions dominate? If so, which one?

d. What decision would the firm make using the coefficient of variation rule?

□ **MATHEMATICAL APPENDIX** Decisions under Risk

The Equivalence of Maximizing Expected Profit and Maximizing Expected Utility of Profit

As discussed, but not demonstrated, in this chapter, maximizing expected profit $E(\pi)$ is equivalent to maximizing the expected utility of profit $E[U(\pi)]$ when the manager or decision maker is risk neutral. We now demonstrate this result for a simple case where profit can take only two values: π_A, with probability p, and π_B, with probability $(1 - p)$. Thus the expected profit in this case is

(1) $$E(\pi) = p\,\pi_A + (1 - p)\,\pi_B$$

Recall that the utility function for profit is linear for risk-neutral decision makers. Thus the utility function for profit $U(\pi)$ can be expressed as

(2) $$U(\pi) = a + b\,\pi$$

where $a \geq 0$ and $b > 0$. Using this expression for utility of profit, the *expected* utility of profit in the risky situation described above can be expressed as

(3) $$E[U(\pi)] = pU(\pi_A) + (1 - p)U(\pi_B)$$

Using the linear utility function for profit (2), expected utility in equation (3) can be expressed as a linear function of $E(\pi)$:

(4) $$E[U(\pi)] = p[a + b\,\pi_A] + (1 - p)[a + b\,\pi_B]$$
$$= a + b[p\,\pi_A + (1 - p)\,\pi_B]$$
$$= a + bE(\pi)$$

From expression (4), it follows immediately that maximizing $E[U(\pi)]$ requires maximizing $E(\pi)$. Thus when the utility function for profit is linear—the decision maker is risk neutral—maximizing expected profit and maximizing expected *utility* of profit are equivalent.

APPENDIX

Statistical Tables

STUDENT'S *t*-DISTRIBUTION

The table on page 662 provides critical values of the *t*-distribution at four levels of significance: 0.10, 0.05, 0.02 and 0.01. It should be noted that these values are based on a two-tailed test for significance: a test to determine if an estimated coefficient is significantly different from zero. For a discussion of one-tailed hypothesis tests, a topic not covered in this text, the reader is referred to Terry Sincich, *A Course in Modern Business Statistics*, 2nd ed. (New York: Dellen/Macmillan College Publishing, 1994).

To illustrate the use of this table, consider a multiple regression that uses 30 observations to estimate three coefficients, *a*, *b*, and *c*. Therefore, there are $30 - 3 = 27$ degrees of freedom. If the level of significance is chosen to be 0.05 (the confidence level is $0.95 = 1 - 0.05$), the critical *t*-value for the test of significance is found in the table to be 2.052. If a lower level of significance (a higher confidence level) is required, a researcher can use the 0.01 level of significance (0.99 level of confidence) to obtain a critical value of 2.771. Conversely, if a higher significance level (lower level of confidence) is acceptable, the researcher can use the 0.10 significance level (0.90 confidence level) to obtain a critical value of 1.703.

THE *F*-DISTRIBUTION

The table on pages 663–664 provides critical values of the *F*-distribution at the 0.05 and 0.01 levels of significance (or the 0.95 and 0.99 levels of confidence, respectively). To illustrate how the table is used, consider a multiple regression that uses 30 observations to estimate three coefficients; that is, $n = 30$ and $k = 3$. The appropriate *F*-statistic has $k - 1$ degrees of freedom for the numerator and $n - k$ degrees of freedom for the denominator. Thus, in the example, there are 2 and 27 degrees of freedom. From the table, the critical *F*-value corresponding to a 0.05 level of significance (or 0.95 level of confidence) is 3.35. If a 0.01 significance level is desired, the critical *F*-value is 5.49.

Critical *t*-Values

Degrees of freedom	Significance level			
	0.10	0.05	0.02	0.01
1	6.314	12.706	31.821	63.657
2	2.920	4.303	6.965	9.925
3	2.353	3.182	4.541	5.841
4	2.132	2.776	3.747	4.604
5	2.015	2.571	3.365	4.032
6	1.943	2.447	3.143	3.707
7	1.895	2.365	2.998	3.499
8	1.860	2.306	2.896	3.355
9	1.833	2.262	2.821	3.250
10	1.812	2.228	2.764	3.169
11	1.796	2.201	2.718	3.106
12	1.782	2.179	2.681	3.055
13	1.771	2.160	2.650	3.012
14	1.761	2.145	2.624	2.977
15	1.753	2.131	2.602	2.947
16	1.746	2.120	2.583	2.921
17	1.740	2.110	2.567	2.898
18	1.734	2.101	2.552	2.878
19	1.729	2.093	2.539	2.861
20	1.725	2.086	2.528	2.845
21	1.721	2.080	2.518	2.831
22	1.717	2.074	2.508	2.819
23	1.714	2.069	2.500	2.807
24	1.711	2.064	2.492	2.797
25	1.708	2.060	2.485	2.787
26	1.706	2.056	2.479	2.779
27	1.703	2.052	2.473	2.771
28	1.701	2.048	2.467	2.763
29	1.699	2.045	2.462	2.756
30	1.697	2.042	2.457	2.750
40	1.684	2.021	2.423	2.704
60	1.671	2.000	2.390	2.660
120	1.658	1.980	2.358	2.617
∞	1.645	1.960	2.326	2.576

Source: Adapted with permission from R. J. Wonnacott and T. H. Wonnacott, *Econometrics*, 2nd ed. (New York: John Wiley & Sons, 1979).

Critical F-Values

Note: The values corresponding to a 0.05 significance level are printed in lightface type and the values corresponding to a 0.01 significance level are printed in boldface type.

Degrees of freedom for numerator $(k - 1)$

Degrees of freedom for denominator $(n - k)$	1	2	3	4	5	6	7	8	9	10	11	12	14	16	20	24	30	40	50	∞
1	161	200	216	225	230	234	237	239	241	242	243	244	245	246	248	249	250	251	252	254
	4052	**4999**	**5403**	**5625**	**5764**	**5859**	**5928**	**5981**	**6022**	**6056**	**6082**	**6106**	**6142**	**6169**	**6208**	**6234**	**6258**	**6286**	**6302**	**6366**
2	18.51	19.00	19.16	19.25	19.30	19.33	19.36	19.37	19.38	19.39	19.40	19.41	19.42	19.43	19.44	19.45	19.46	19.47	19.47	19.50
	98.49	**99.01**	**99.17**	**99.25**	**99.30**	**99.33**	**99.34**	**99.36**	**99.38**	**99.40**	**99.41**	**99.42**	**99.43**	**99.44**	**99.45**	**99.46**	**99.47**	**99.48**	**99.48**	**99.50**
3	10.13	9.55	9.28	9.12	9.01	8.94	8.88	8.84	8.81	8.78	8.76	8.74	8.71	8.69	8.66	8.64	8.62	8.60	8.58	8.53
	34.12	**30.81**	**29.46**	**28.71**	**28.24**	**27.91**	**27.67**	**27.49**	**27.34**	**27.23**	**27.13**	**27.05**	**26.92**	**26.83**	**26.69**	**26.60**	**26.50**	**26.41**	**26.30**	**26.12**
4	7.71	6.94	6.59	6.39	6.26	6.16	6.09	6.04	6.00	5.96	5.93	5.91	5.87	5.84	5.80	5.77	5.74	5.71	5.70	5.63
	21.20	**18.00**	**16.69**	**15.98**	**15.52**	**15.21**	**14.98**	**14.80**	**14.66**	**14.54**	**14.45**	**14.37**	**14.24**	**14.15**	**14.02**	**13.93**	**13.83**	**13.74**	**13.69**	**13.46**
5	6.61	5.79	5.41	5.19	5.05	4.95	4.88	4.82	4.78	4.74	4.70	4.68	4.64	4.60	4.56	4.53	4.50	4.46	4.44	4.36
	16.26	**13.27**	**12.06**	**11.39**	**10.97**	**10.67**	**10.45**	**10.27**	**10.15**	**10.05**	**9.96**	**9.89**	**9.77**	**9.68**	**9.55**	**9.47**	**9.38**	**9.29**	**9.24**	**9.02**
6	5.99	5.14	4.76	4.53	4.39	4.28	4.21	4.15	4.10	4.06	4.03	4.00	3.96	3.92	3.87	3.84	3.81	3.77	3.75	3.67
	13.74	**10.92**	**9.78**	**9.15**	**8.75**	**8.47**	**8.26**	**8.10**	**7.98**	**7.87**	**7.79**	**7.72**	**7.60**	**7.52**	**7.39**	**7.31**	**7.23**	**7.14**	**7.09**	**6.88**
7	5.59	4.74	4.35	4.12	3.97	3.87	3.79	3.73	3.68	3.63	3.60	3.57	3.52	3.49	3.44	3.41	3.38	3.34	3.32	3.23
	12.25	**9.55**	**8.45**	**7.85**	**7.46**	**7.19**	**7.00**	**6.84**	**6.71**	**6.62**	**6.54**	**6.47**	**6.35**	**6.27**	**6.15**	**6.07**	**5.98**	**5.90**	**5.85**	**5.65**
8	5.32	4.46	4.07	3.84	3.69	3.58	3.50	3.44	3.39	3.34	3.31	3.28	3.23	3.20	3.15	3.12	3.08	3.05	3.03	2.93
	11.26	**8.65**	**7.59**	**7.01**	**6.63**	**6.37**	**6.19**	**6.03**	**5.91**	**5.82**	**5.74**	**5.67**	**5.56**	**5.48**	**5.36**	**5.28**	**5.20**	**5.11**	**5.06**	**4.86**
9	5.12	4.26	3.86	3.63	3.48	3.37	3.29	3.23	3.18	3.13	3.10	3.07	3.02	2.98	2.93	2.90	2.86	2.82	2.80	2.71
	10.56	**8.02**	**6.99**	**6.42**	**6.06**	**5.80**	**5.62**	**5.47**	**5.35**	**5.26**	**5.18**	**5.11**	**5.00**	**4.92**	**4.80**	**4.73**	**4.64**	**4.56**	**4.51**	**4.31**
10	4.96	4.10	3.71	3.48	3.33	3.22	3.14	3.07	3.02	2.97	2.94	2.91	2.86	2.82	2.77	2.74	2.70	2.67	2.64	2.54
	10.04	**7.56**	**6.55**	**5.99**	**5.64**	**5.39**	**5.21**	**5.06**	**4.95**	**4.85**	**4.78**	**4.71**	**4.60**	**4.52**	**4.41**	**4.33**	**4.25**	**4.17**	**4.12**	**3.91**
11	4.84	3.98	3.59	3.36	3.20	3.09	3.01	2.95	2.90	2.86	2.82	2.79	2.74	2.70	2.65	2.61	2.57	2.53	2.50	2.40
	9.65	**7.20**	**6.22**	**5.67**	**5.32**	**5.07**	**4.88**	**4.74**	**4.63**	**4.54**	**4.46**	**4.40**	**4.29**	**4.21**	**4.10**	**4.02**	**3.94**	**3.86**	**3.80**	**3.60**
12	4.75	3.89	3.49	3.26	3.11	3.00	2.92	2.85	2.80	2.76	2.72	2.69	2.64	2.60	2.54	2.50	2.46	2.42	2.40	2.30
	9.33	**6.93**	**5.95**	**5.41**	**5.06**	**4.82**	**4.65**	**4.50**	**4.39**	**4.30**	**4.22**	**4.16**	**4.05**	**3.98**	**3.86**	**3.78**	**3.70**	**3.61**	**3.56**	**3.36**
13	4.67	3.80	3.41	3.18	3.02	2.92	2.84	2.77	2.72	2.67	2.63	2.60	2.55	2.51	2.46	2.42	2.38	2.34	2.32	2.21
	9.07	**6.70**	**5.74**	**5.20**	**4.86**	**4.62**	**4.44**	**4.30**	**4.19**	**4.10**	**4.02**	**3.96**	**3.85**	**3.78**	**3.67**	**3.59**	**3.51**	**3.42**	**3.37**	**3.16**
14	4.60	3.74	3.34	3.11	2.96	2.85	2.77	2.70	2.65	2.60	2.56	2.53	2.48	2.44	2.39	2.35	2.31	2.27	2.24	2.13
	8.86	**6.51**	**5.56**	**5.03**	**4.69**	**4.46**	**4.28**	**4.14**	**4.03**	**3.94**	**3.86**	**3.80**	**3.70**	**3.62**	**3.51**	**3.43**	**3.34**	**3.26**	**3.26**	**3.00**
15	4.54	3.68	3.29	3.06	2.90	2.79	2.70	2.64	2.59	2.55	2.51	2.48	2.43	2.39	2.33	2.29	2.25	2.21	2.18	2.07
	8.68	**6.36**	**5.42**	**4.89**	**4.56**	**4.32**	**4.14**	**4.00**	**3.89**	**3.80**	**3.73**	**3.67**	**3.56**	**3.48**	**3.36**	**3.29**	**3.20**	**3.12**	**3.07**	**2.87**
16	4.49	3.63	3.24	3.01	2.85	2.74	2.66	2.59	2.54	2.49	2.45	2.42	2.37	2.33	2.28	2.24	2.20	2.16	2.13	2.01
	8.53	**6.23**	**5.29**	**4.77**	**4.44**	**4.20**	**4.03**	**3.89**	**3.78**	**3.69**	**3.61**	**3.55**	**3.45**	**3.37**	**3.25**	**3.18**	**3.10**	**3.01**	**2.96**	**2.75**
17	4.45	3.59	3.20	2.96	2.81	2.70	2.62	2.55	2.50	2.45	2.41	2.38	2.33	2.29	2.23	2.19	2.15	2.11	2.08	1.96
	8.40	**6.11**	**5.18**	**4.67**	**4.34**	**4.10**	**3.93**	**3.79**	**3.68**	**3.59**	**3.52**	**3.45**	**3.35**	**3.27**	**3.16**	**3.08**	**3.00**	**2.92**	**2.86**	**2.65**

Critical F-Values (continued)

	Degrees of freedom for numerator $(k - 1)$																			
Degrees of freedom for denominator $(n - k)$	1	2	3	4	5	6	7	8	9	10	11	12	14	16	20	24	30	40	50	∞
18 . . .	4.41	3.55	3.16	2.93	2.77	2.66	2.58	2.51	2.46	2.41	2.37	2.34	2.29	2.25	2.19	2.15	2.11	2.07	2.04	1.92
	8.28	**6.01**	**5.09**	**4.58**	**4.25**	**4.01**	**3.85**	**3.71**	**3.60**	**3.51**	**3.44**	**3.37**	**3.27**	**3.19**	**3.07**	**3.00**	**2.91**	**2.83**	**2.78**	**2.57**
19 . . .	4.38	3.52	3.13	2.90	2.74	2.63	2.55	2.48	2.43	2.38	2.34	2.31	2.26	2.21	2.15	2.11	2.07	2.02	2.00	1.88
	8.18	**5.93**	**5.01**	**4.50**	**4.17**	**3.94**	**3.77**	**3.63**	**3.52**	**3.43**	**3.36**	**3.30**	**3.19**	**3.12**	**3.00**	**2.92**	**2.84**	**2.76**	**2.70**	**2.49**
20 . . .	4.35	3.49	3.10	2.87	2.71	2.60	2.52	2.45	2.40	2.35	2.31	2.28	2.23	2.18	2.12	2.08	2.04	1.99	1.96	1.84
	8.10	**5.85**	**4.94**	**4.43**	**4.10**	**3.87**	**3.71**	**3.56**	**3.45**	**3.37**	**3.30**	**3.23**	**3.13**	**3.05**	**2.94**	**2.86**	**2.77**	**2.69**	**2.63**	**2.42**
21 . . .	4.32	3.47	3.07	2.84	2.68	2.57	2.49	2.42	2.37	2.32	2.28	2.25	2.20	2.15	2.09	2.05	2.00	1.96	1.93	1.81
	8.02	**5.78**	**4.87**	**4.37**	**4.04**	**3.81**	**3.65**	**3.51**	**3.40**	**3.31**	**3.24**	**3.17**	**3.07**	**2.99**	**2.88**	**2.80**	**2.72**	**2.63**	**2.58**	**2.36**
22 . . .	4.30	3.44	3.05	2.82	2.66	2.55	2.47	2.40	2.35	2.30	2.26	2.23	2.18	2.13	2.07	2.03	1.98	1.93	1.91	1.78
	7.94	**5.72**	**4.82**	**4.41**	**3.99**	**3.76**	**3.59**	**3.45**	**3.35**	**3.26**	**3.18**	**3.12**	**3.02**	**2.94**	**2.83**	**2.75**	**2.67**	**2.58**	**2.53**	**2.31**
23 . . .	4.28	3.42	3.03	2.80	2.64	2.53	2.45	2.38	2.32	2.28	2.24	2.20	2.14	2.10	2.04	2.00	1.96	1.91	1.88	1.76
	7.88	**5.66**	**4.76**	**4.26**	**3.94**	**3.71**	**3.54**	**3.41**	**3.30**	**3.21**	**3.14**	**3.07**	**2.97**	**2.89**	**2.78**	**2.70**	**2.62**	**2.53**	**2.48**	**2.26**
24 . . .	4.26	3.40	3.01	2.78	2.62	2.51	2.43	2.36	2.30	2.26	2.22	2.18	2.13	2.09	2.02	1.98	1.94	1.89	1.86	1.73
	7.82	**5.61**	**4.72**	**4.22**	**3.90**	**3.67**	**3.50**	**3.36**	**3.25**	**3.17**	**3.09**	**3.03**	**2.93**	**2.85**	**2.74**	**2.66**	**2.58**	**2.49**	**2.44**	**2.21**
25 . . .	4.24	3.38	2.99	2.76	2.60	2.49	2.41	2.34	2.28	2.24	2.20	2.16	2.11	2.06	2.00	1.96	1.92	1.87	1.84	1.71
	7.77	**5.57**	**4.68**	**4.18**	**3.86**	**3.63**	**3.46**	**3.32**	**3.21**	**3.13**	**3.05**	**2.99**	**2.89**	**2.81**	**2.70**	**2.62**	**2.54**	**2.45**	**2.40**	**2.17**
26 . . .	4.22	3.37	2.89	2.74	2.59	2.47	2.39	2.32	2.27	2.22	2.18	2.15	2.10	2.05	1.99	1.95	1.90	1.85	1.82	1.69
	7.72	**5.53**	**4.64**	**4.14**	**3.82**	**3.59**	**3.42**	**3.29**	**3.17**	**3.09**	**3.02**	**2.96**	**2.86**	**2.77**	**2.66**	**2.58**	**2.50**	**2.41**	**2.36**	**2.13**
27 . . .	4.21	3.35	2.96	2.73	2.57	2.46	2.37	2.30	2.25	2.20	2.16	2.13	2.08	2.03	1.97	1.93	1.88	1.84	1.80	1.67
	7.68	**5.49**	**4.60**	**4.11**	**3.79**	**3.56**	**3.39**	**3.26**	**3.14**	**3.06**	**2.98**	**2.93**	**2.83**	**2.74**	**2.63**	**2.55**	**2.47**	**2.38**	**2.33**	**2.10**
28 . . .	4.20	3.34	2.95	2.71	2.56	2.44	2.36	2.29	2.24	2.19	2.15	2.12	2.06	2.02	1.96	1.91	1.87	1.81	1.78	1.65
	7.64	**5.45**	**4.57**	**4.07**	**3.76**	**3.53**	**3.36**	**3.23**	**3.11**	**3.03**	**2.95**	**2.90**	**2.80**	**2.71**	**2.60**	**2.52**	**2.44**	**2.35**	**2.30**	**2.06**
29 . . .	4.18	3.33	2.93	2.70	2.54	2.43	2.35	2.28	2.22	2.18	2.14	2.10	2.05	2.00	1.94	1.90	1.85	1.80	1.77	1.64
	7.60	**5.52**	**4.54**	**4.04**	**3.73**	**3.50**	**3.33**	**3.20**	**3.08**	**3.00**	**2.92**	**2.87**	**2.77**	**2.68**	**2.57**	**2.49**	**2.41**	**2.32**	**2.27**	**2.03**
30 . . .	4.17	3.32	2.92	2.69	2.53	2.43	2.34	2.27	2.21	2.16	2.12	2.09	2.04	1.99	1.93	1.89	1.84	1.79	1.76	1.62
	7.56	**5.39**	**4.51**	**4.02**	**3.70**	**3.47**	**3.30**	**3.17**	**3.06**	**2.98**	**2.90**	**2.84**	**2.74**	**2.66**	**2.55**	**2.47**	**2.38**	**2.29**	**2.24**	**2.01**
40 . . .	4.08	3.23	2.84	2.61	2.45	2.34	2.25	2.18	2.12	2.08	2.04	2.00	1.95	1.90	1.84	1.79	1.74	1.69	1.66	1.51
	7.31	**5.18**	**4.31**	**3.83**	**3.51**	**3.29**	**3.12**	**2.99**	**2.88**	**2.80**	**2.73**	**2.66**	**2.56**	**2.49**	**2.37**	**2.29**	**2.20**	**2.11**	**2.05**	**1.81**
50 . . .	4.03	3.18	2.79	2.56	2.40	2.29	2.20	2.13	2.07	2.02	1.98	1.95	1.90	1.85	1.78	1.74	1.69	1.63	1.60	1.44
	7.17	**5.06**	**4.20**	**3.72**	**3.41**	**3.18**	**3.02**	**2.88**	**2.78**	**2.70**	**2.62**	**2.56**	**2.46**	**2.39**	**2.26**	**2.18**	**2.10**	**2.00**	**1.94**	**1.68**
60 . . .	4.00	3.15	2.76	2.52	2.37	2.25	2.17	2.10	2.04	1.99	1.95	1.92	1.86	1.81	1.75	1.70	1.65	1.59	1.56	1.39
	7.08	**4.98**	**4.13**	**3.65**	**3.34**	**3.12**	**2.95**	**2.82**	**2.72**	**2.63**	**2.56**	**2.50**	**2.40**	**2.32**	**2.20**	**2.12**	**2.03**	**1.93**	**1.87**	**1.60**
125 . . .	3.92	3.07	2.68	2.44	2.29	2.17	2.08	2.01	1.95	1.90	1.86	1.83	1.77	1.72	1.65	1.60	1.55	1.49	1.45	1.25
	6.84	**4.78**	**3.94**	**3.47**	**3.17**	**2.95**	**2.79**	**2.65**	**2.56**	**2.47**	**2.40**	**2.33**	**2.23**	**2.15**	**2.03**	**1.94**	**1.85**	**1.75**	**1.68**	**1.37**
∞	3.84	2.99	2.60	2.37	2.21	2.09	2.01	1.94	1.88	1.83	1.79	1.75	1.69	1.64	1.57	1.52	1.46	1.40	1.35	1.00
	6.64	**4.60**	**3.78**	**3.32**	**3.02**	**2.80**	**2.64**	**2.51**	**2.41**	**2.32**	**2.24**	**2.18**	**2.07**	**1.99**	**1.87**	**1.79**	**1.69**	**1.59**	**1.52**	**1.00**

Source: Adapted with permission from R. J. Wonnacott and T. H. Wonnacott, *Econometrics* (New York: John Wiley & Sons, 1970).

ANSWERS TO TECHNICAL PROBLEMS

Chapter 1: Managers, Profits, and Markets

1. a. Explicit cost of $6,000 per year. The firm forgoes $6,000 per year to obtain the use of the computer server.

   b. Implicit cost of $5,000 per year. The owner forgoes earning $5,000 (= 0.10 × $50,000) annually by letting the firm use the money rather than investing it and earning a return.

   c. Implicit cost of $3 million per year. The owner could sell the building and invest the proceeds to earn 10 percent annually. The owner sacrifices $3 million (= 0.10 × $30 million) annually.

   d. Explicit cost of $6 million this year. The owner must pay the computer programmers $30 per hour for 200,000 hours. So the owner gives up $6 million (= $30 × 200,000) to hire the programmers.

   e. No cost. The incinerator has zero market value since no other firm pays anything to have it. So there is nothing given up by the owner to keep the incinerator and opportunity cost is zero—even the Smithsonian wouldn't give a nickel for it.

2. a. $80,000; $70,000; $150,000

   b. $25,000; $70,000

   c. $95,000

   d. −$5,000

3. a. $299,925; $299,925

   b. $310,522; $310,522

4. a. profit; independent of decisions in other time periods

   b. smaller

   c. larger

Chapter 2: Demand, Supply, and Market Equilibrium

1. a. 600 units of good A can be sold each month if $P, M, P_B, \mathcal{T}, P_e,$ and N are all simultaneously equal to zero.

   b. −4. The slope parameter for a good's own price must be negative because the law of demand stipulates that quantity demanded and price of a good are inversely related.

   c. The slope parameter on M (−0.03) indicates that a $1 increase in average household income, all else constant, will *decrease* sales of good A by 0.03 unit per month. (Or a $1,000 increase in M will decrease Q_d by 30 units per month.) Good A is an inferior good because the slope coefficient on M is negative.

   d. Complements. The slope parameter on P_B is negative. A $1 increase in the price of good B, all other factors constant, will cause the quantity demanded of good A to decrease by 12 units per month.

   e. These three slope parameters should all be positive, since each of the variables varies directly (rather than inversely) with quantity demanded. For tastes, note that the slope parameter e (= 15) is *not* restricted to the range 1 to 10 as is the value of the taste index $\mathcal{T}$.

   f. $Q_d = 600 - 4(5) - 0.03(25,000) - 12(40)$
   $\qquad + 15(6.5) + 6(5.25) + 1.5(2,000)$
   $\qquad = 2,479.0$ units of good A per month

2. a. $Q_d = 8,000 - 16P + 0.75(30,000) + 30(50) = 8,000 - 16P + 22,500 + 1,500 = 32,000 - 16P$

   b. Intercept parameter: If price were 0, consumers would take 32,000 units of the good for free. Slope parameter: A $1 increase in price, all else constant, will cause consumers to buy 16 fewer units per period.

   c. The following sketch plots price on the vertical axis and quantity demanded on the horizontal axis. Demand is a straight line that intersects the price axis at $2,000 and the quantity demanded axis at 32,000 units.

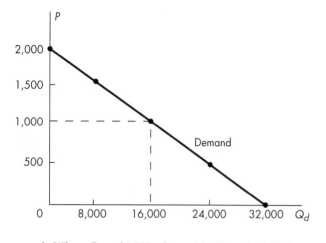

variables, is shown in the figure by the shift in D to D' or to D".

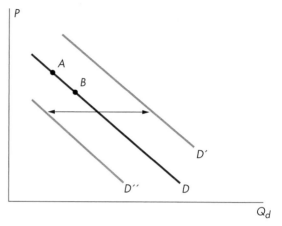

d. When $P = \$1{,}000$, $Q_d = 32{,}000 - 16(1{,}000) = 16{,}000$ units. When $P = \$1{,}500$, $Q_d = 8{,}000$.

e. $P = 2{,}000 - (1/16)Q_d$ or $P = 2{,}000 - 0.0625Q_d$. To calculate demand price: $P = 2{,}000 - 0.0625(24{,}000)$, and $P = \$500$. The maximum price consumers will pay to buy 24,000 units per period is $500.

3. (1) For a price of $2, the maximum amount of the good consumers are willing and able to buy is 35 units, or (2) the maximum price consumers will pay for 35 units of the good is $2.

4. a. $Q_d = 1{,}800 - 20P + 0.6(19{,}500) - 50(250)$
      $= 1{,}800 - 20P + 11{,}700 - 12{,}500$
      $= 1{,}000 - 20P$

   b. D_3 is a line parallel to D_2 with a quantity intercept 300 units less than the quantity intercept for D_2, i.e., $1{,}000 - 300 = 700$; D_3: $Q_d = 700 - 20P$; $0.6 \times \Delta M = -300$, so $\Delta M = -500$ (if income falls to $19,000, then D_3 is the demand function).

5. Whenever the price of a good (P) changes, *quantity demanded* (Q_d) changes in the opposite direction. This results in a movement along a given demand curve. A change in quantity demanded due to a change in P is shown in the figure by a movement from A to B. When any one of the five demand-shifting variables changes in value, the demand curve shifts either leftward or rightward. The five demand-shifting variables that cause demand to shift are (1) consumer income (M), (2) price of related goods (P_R), (3) price expectations (P_e), (4) consumer tastes ($\mathcal{T}$), and (5) the number of consumers (N). A *change in demand*, which can be caused only by a change in one of these five

6. a. No change in demand. A change in price causes a change in *quantity* demanded, which is a movement along the demand curve.

   b. Demand increases.

   c. Demand decreases.

   d. Demand increases.

   e. Demand decreases.

   f. Demand decreases.

   g. Demand increases.

7. a. For P: A $1 increase in the price of the commodity, all else constant, will increase quantity supplied by 5 units per period.

   For P_i: A $1 increase in the price of a key input, all other factors affecting producers held constant, will decrease quantity supplied by 12 units per period.

   For F: If one more firm begins producing the commodity, all other things held constant, the quantity supplied of the commodity will increase by 10 units each period.

   b. $Q_s = 60 + 5P - 12(90) + 10(20)$
       $= 60 + 5P - 1{,}080 + 200 = -820 + 5P$

   c. The sketch plots price on the vertical axis and quantity supplied on the horizontal axis. Supply is a straight line that intersects the price axis at $164 and the quantity supplied axis at -820 units. Only the segment of the supply line at and above $P = \$164$ is economically meaningful. The price intercept of the supply curve, $164, is found by setting

$Q_s = 0$ in the supply function and solving for P. Since the price intercept is $164, it follows that the price below which firms will quit producing the commodity is $164.

d. $Q_s = -820 + 5(300) = 680$, and

$Q_s = -820 + 5(500) = 1,680$

e. To derive the inverse supply function, take the supply equation in part b and solve algebraically for P as a function of Q_s. The inverse supply equation is $P = 164 + 0.20Q$. Supply price for 680 units: $P = 164 + 0.20(680) = 300$. The minimum price producers will accept to produce 680 units per period is $300.

8. (1) For a price of $25, the maximum amount producers are willing to supply is 500 units, or (2) the minimum price producers will accept to produce 500 units is $25.

9. a. $Q_s = -30 + 20P_x$

b. $Q_s' = -40 + 20P_x$

The graph is shown here as a dotted line.

c. Since the coefficient on P_r is negative (-32), an increase in the price of the related good results in a reduction in the quantity supplied, all other things held constant. Therefore the related good is a substitute in production.

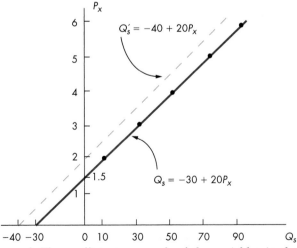

d. The coefficients on each of the variables in the supply relation are interpreted as follows:

P_x: A $1 increase in price results in 20 more units being supplied, *all other things remaining constant.*

P_l: A $1 increase in the price of labor results in 10 fewer units being supplied, *all other things remaining constant.*

T: A 1-unit increase in the technology index results in 6 more units being produced, *all other things remaining constant.*

P_r: A $1 increase in the price of related good R results in 32 fewer units being produced, *all other things remaining constant.*

P_e: A $1 increase in the expected future price of X results in 20 fewer units of X being produced in the current period, *all other things remaining constant.*

F: The addition of one more firm results in 5 more units being produced, *all other things remaining constant.*

10. Whenever the price of a good (P) changes, *quantity supplied* (Q_s) changes in the same direction. This results in a movement along a given supply curve. A change in quantity supplied due to a change in P is shown in the figure by a movement from A to B. When any one of the five supply-shifting variables changes value, the supply curve shifts either leftward or rightward. The five supply-shifting variables that cause supply to shift are (1) technology (T), (2) input prices (P_l), (3) price of goods related in production (P_r), (4) price expectations (P_e), and (5) the number of firms producing the good (F). A *change in supply,* which can be caused only by a change in one of these five variables, is shown in the figure by the shift in S to S' or to S''.

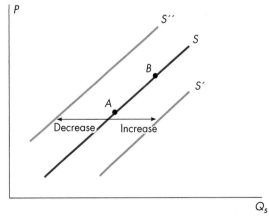

11. a. Supply is unchanged (quantity supplied decreases).

b. Supply increases.

c. Supply decreases.

d. Supply increases.

e. Supply decreases in the current period as managers hold back some current output for sale at the higher price expected in the future period.

f. Supply increases.

12. a. supply; 15,000; fall

b. demand; 78,000; rise

c. $550

d. 60,000

13. a. At equilibrium, $Q_d = Q_s$. So $50 - 8P = -17.5 + 10P$, and $P_E = \$3.75$ and $Q_E = 20$.

b. When $P = \$2.75$, $Q_d = 50 - 8(2.75) = 28$ and $Q_s = -17.5 + 10(2.75) = 10$; there is a shortage of 18 units. Due to the excess demand, consumers will bid up the price, decreasing quantity demanded and increasing quantity supplied. Consumers will bid up price until it reaches $3.75, the price at which quantity demanded equals quantity supplied.

c. When $P = \$4.25$, $Q_d = 16$ and $Q_s = 25$; there is a surplus of 9 units. Producers will lower price in order to avoid accumulating unwanted inventories. The price will fall (reducing the excess supply) until equilibrium is attained at a price of $3.75.

d. At equilibrium, $59 - 8P = -17.5 + 10P$; thus $P_E = \$4.25$ and $Q_E = 25$.

e. At equilibrium, $50 - 8P = -40 + 10P$; thus $P_E = \$5$ and $Q_E = 10$.

14. a. The increase in demand results in an increase in both P_E and Q_E.

b. The increase in demand results in an increase in both P_E and Q_E.

c. The decrease in supply results in an increase in P_E and a decrease in Q_E.

d. The decrease in demand results in a decrease in both P_E and Q_E.

e. The decrease in supply results in an increase in P_E and a decrease Q_E.

f. The increase in demand results in an increase in both P_E and Q_E.

g. The decrease in demand results in a decrease in both P_E and Q_E.

h. The increase in supply results in a decrease in P_E and an increase Q_E.

15. a. By itself, event a would cause an increase in P_E and an increase in Q_E. By itself, event h would cause a decrease in P_E and an increase in Q_E. Since both events occur simultaneously, only Q_E is "pushed" in the same direction by both events. Therefore, Q_E is predicted to rise, but change in P_E is indeterminate because the two events "push" in opposite directions. This is the situation presented in Panel A of Figure 2.9.

b. By itself, event d would cause a decrease in P_E and a decrease in Q_E. By itself, event e would cause an increase in P_E and a decrease in Q_E. Since both events occur simultaneously, only Q_E is "pushed" in the same direction by both events. Therefore, Q_E is predicted to fall, but change in P_E is indeterminate because the two events "push" in opposite directions. This is the situation presented in Panel D of Figure 2.9.

c. P_E falls and change in Q_E is indeterminate. See Panel B of Figure 2.9.

d. P_E rises and change in Q_E is indeterminate. See Panel C of Figure 2.9.

16. a. Good X is normal because when income (M) increases, *all other variables held constant,* quantity demanded (Q_d) increases (the coefficient on M is positive).

b. Goods X and R are substitutes because when the price of the related good (P_R) increases, *all other variables constant,* quantity demanded (Q_d) increases (the coefficient on P_R is positive).

c. $Q_d = 60 - 2P + 0.01(40,000) + 7(20) = 600 - 2P$

d. $600 - 2P = -600 + 10P \Rightarrow P_E = \$100$ and $Q_E = 400$ units

e. Now $Q_d = 60 - 2P + 0.01(52,000) + 7(20) = 720 - 2P$. $P_E = \$110$ and $Q_E = 500$ units.

f. Now $Q_d = 60 - 2P + 0.01(40,000) + 7(14) = 558 - 2P$. $P_E = \$96.50$ and $Q_E = 365$ units.

g. At equilibrium, $600 - 2P = -360 + 10P$, and thus $P_E = \$80$ and $Q_E = 440$ units.

17. a. shortage; 59,000

b. $19,000 = 60,000 - 41,000$

c. surplus; 15,000

18. a. $P_E = \$60$ and $Q_E = 400$ units.

b. A shortage of 400 ($= 600 - 200$) units occurs.

c. A price floor of $50 has no effect on market price and output since market price ($60) exceeds $50. A floor price of $70 results in a surplus of 200 (= 500 − 300) units.

d. $P_E = \$65$ and $Q_E = 450$ units.

e. $P_E = \$55$ and $Q_E = 550$ units.

Chapter 3: Marginal Analysis for Optimal Decisions

1. a. Constrained maximization subject to the cost constraint of the grant. The choice variables are the types of PCs. The objective is probably to maximize staff productivity.

b. An unconstrained maximization problem with the objective of getting the most profit from advertising. The choice variables are the amounts to spend on each of the media.

c. A constrained minimization problem with the objective of the lowest production cost subject to making the quota. The constraint is the quota. The choice variables are the levels of the three inputs.

2. a. positive; upward

b. $3.20. The slope of the tangent line at point D rises at a rate of $320 per 100 unit increase in activity A, so the slope of the tangent line at point D is $3.20 per unit change in A (= $\Delta TB/\Delta A$ = 320/100).

c. decrease; $3.20; 3.2; same; directly

d. 0. At the maximum or minimum point on a curve, the slope of a curve is zero. Since MB is the slope of TB, it follows that MB is zero at point G, the maximum point on TB.

e. $8.20. The slope of the tangent line at point D' rises at a rate of $820 per 100 unit increase in activity A, so the slope of the tangent line at point D' is $8.20 per unit change in A.

f. decrease; $8.20; 8.2; same; directly

g. flatter; MC; MB

h. $TB, TC; NB$; positive

3. a. $MB; MC$

b. $MC; MB$

c. $MB; MC$

d. $NB; TB; TC$

e. decreased

f. maintain this level of activity since it is the optimal level

g. greater than; rising

4. a. $7; $2

b. increase; $5 (= $7 − $2)

c. $3; $8

d. increase; $5

e. 140; $5; $5

5. increases; total; increases; total; increasing; increase; equal

6. Your table should look like this:

A	TB	TC	NB	MB	MC
0	$ 0	$ 0	$ 0		
1	35	8	27	$35	$ 8
2	65	18	47	30	10
3	85	30	55	20	12
4	95	44	51	10	14
5	103	60	43	8	16
6	108	80	28	5	20

a. $A^* = 3$

b. $NB^* = \$55$. The optimal level of activity, by definition, is the level with the greatest possible net benefit, so no other level of A can have higher net benefit than A^*.

c. For unconstrained optimization problems with discrete activity levels, it may not be possible to adjust A to precisely the level where $MB = MC$. However, adjusting A to the point where MB is closest to MC may fail to produce maximum net benefit, as in this example. At 4 units of activity MB is closer to MC, only $4 apart (= $10 − $14), than at the optimal level, where MB and MC are $8 apart (= $20 − $12). The correct rule to follow for discrete choice variables is to increase A until the last (or highest) level of activity is reached for which MB is greater than MC.

7. Your table should look like this:

A	TB	TC	NB	MB	MC	AC
0	$ 0	$ 24	−$24			
1	35	32	3	$35	$ 8	$32
2	65	42	23	30	10	21
3	85	54	31	20	12	18
4	95	68	27	10	14	17
5	103	84	19	8	16	16.80
6	108	104	4	5	20	17.33

a. Adding the $24 fixed cost causes total cost to *rise* by $24 *at every level of activity*. This also causes net benefit to *fall* by $24 *at every level of activity*.

b. Marginal cost is not affected in any way by adding a fixed cost of $24. The values of MC are precisely the same as in Technical Problem 6.

c. The optimal level of activity is 3, just as in Technical Problem 6. Since MB and MC are unchanged by adding fixed costs, the optimal activity level doesn't change.

d. Adding or changing the amount of fixed costs does not affect MC (or MB), so any change in fixed cost has no affect on the optimal level of activity, even though higher (lower) fixed costs cause net benefit to fall (rise).

e. AC is minimized at $A = 5$, which is not the optimal level of activity. In general, there is no reason to expect average costs to be minimized at the optimal level of activity because changes in average costs have no bearing on what is happening either to total costs or net benefits as the activity level changes. Average costs, like fixed costs, don't matter for finding A^*.

f. The $100 license fee is a sunk cost since it has already been paid and cannot be recovered no matter what decision is made now regarding the current level of activity. Sunk costs, like fixed costs and average costs, are irrelevant for finding A^*.

8. Compare the marginal benefit per dollar for each applicant: For Jane, $MB/P = 600/200 = 3$; for Joe, $MB/P = 450/150 = 3$; for Joan, $MB/P = 400/100 = 4$. Thus Joan ranks first, and Joe and Jane are tied for second.

9. a. greater than

b. less than

c. MB_A/P_A, MB_B/P_B

10. Always compare MB_A/P_A and MB_B/P_B.

a. $\dfrac{MB_A}{P_A} = \dfrac{400}{20} = 20 < \dfrac{MB_B}{P_B} = \dfrac{600}{15} = 40$

Use more B and less A, keeping expenditure constant.

b. $\dfrac{MB_A}{P_A} = \dfrac{200}{20} = 10 = \dfrac{MB_B}{P_B} = \dfrac{300}{30} = 10$

Make no changes.

c. $\dfrac{MB_A}{P_A} = 300/20 = 15 > \dfrac{MB_B}{P_B} = \dfrac{400}{40} = 10$

A 1-unit reduction in B reduces cost by $40, which can purchase 2 units of A at $20. Total benefits will

increase by 600 $(= \Delta A \times MB_A = 2 \times 300) - 400$ $(= \Delta B \times MB_B = 1 \times 400) = 200$.

d. In equilibrium $MB_A/P_A = MB_B/P_B$; then $250/20 = 12.5 = MB_B/40$, so MB_B must equal 500.

11. a. $10 + 2(22) + 3(14) = \$96$

b. 10; $20 $(= 2 \times 10)$

c. The combination $1X$, $4Y$, $3Z$ is optimal when income is $18. At this combination $MU_X/P_X = MU_Y/P_Y = MU_Z/P_Z$. The combination $2X$, $2Y$, $4Z$ is not optimal because $MU_Y/P_Y > MU_X/P_X = MU_Z/P_Z$. The decision maker should engage in more units of activity Y and fewer units of activities X and Z.

d. When income is $33, the optimal combination is $5X$, $5Y$, $6Z$. With two more dollars to spend (income $= \$35$), the decision maker can either increase activity X by 2 units or activity Y by 1 unit. Two more dollars spent on activity X increases benefit by $9 $(= \$5 + \$4)$, while two more dollars spent on activity Y increases benefit by only $4. The optimal combination of activities is $7X$, $5Y$, $6Z$.

12. a. The combination $3X$, $2Y$ maximizes total benefit subject to a budget constraint of $26.

b. Total benefit of $3X$, $2Y$ is $262 $(= \$72 + \$190)$.

c. The combination $4X$, $5Y$ is optimal when the budget constraint is $58. Total benefit of $4X$, $5Y$ is $484 $(= \$84 + \$400)$.

13. Compare MB_A/P_A and MB_B/P_B.

a. $MB_A/P_A = 600/10 = 60 > MB_B/P_B = 300/10 = 30$. One less B reduces benefits by 300. One-half unit of A adds $(1/2)600 = 300$. Cost falls by $10 - \$5 = \$5$.

b. Since $P_A = P_B$, in equilibrium, where $MB_A/P_A = MB_B/P_B$, MB_A must equal MB_B.

Chapter 4: Basic Estimation Techniques

1. a. W; R

b. b; a

c. a

d. b

2. Regression analysis chooses parameter values to fit a line to a particular data set. The best fit results when the parameter values minimize the sum of the squared errors: hence the name "least-squares."

3. Tests for statistical significance must follow estimation of parameters because the estimates themselves

are random variables that are not likely to be equal to the true value of the parameter. Testing for statistical significance allows a researcher to determine whether or not an estimate is far enough away from zero to conclude that the true value of the parameter is *not* equal to zero.

4. *a.* Correct; the smaller is S_b, the smaller the dispersion of the parameter estimate around its true value.

  b. Incorrect; when an estimate is unbiased, the parameter estimate tends to equal the true value only *on average*.

  c. Correct; the *t*-ratio ($= \hat{b}/S_{\hat{b}}$) is indeed larger the smaller the standard error of $\hat{b}$.

5. *a.* 24

  b. 2.492; 2.064

  c. Yes, 2.492 > 2.064, so the estimate is significant at the 0.05 level.

  d. 0.02 (2.492 is the critical *t* for a 0.02 significance level); $b = 0$; zero; 95

  e. The hypothesis that $b = 0$ can be rejected with only a 5 percent chance of being wrong (i.e., making a Type I error).

  f. You can be 95 percent sure that if *b* is actually zero, the *t*-test will not reject the hypothesis that $b = 0$ (i.e., will *not* make a Type I error).

  g. The significance level gives the probability of making a Type I error, while the confidence level gives the probability of *not* making a Type I error. They mean the same thing since knowing one gives the same information as knowing the other.

6. *a.* $Y = 800 - 2.50X$

  b. The critical *t* for $n - k = 10 - 2 = 8$ degrees of freedom at the 0.01 level of significance is 3.355. The *t*-tests are:

  For $\hat{a}$: $t = 4.23 > 3.355$; $\hat{a}$ is statistically significant.
  For $\hat{b}$: $t = -2.94$. Since *t* is negative, $|t| = |-2.94| < 3.355$; $\hat{b}$ is *not* statistically significant.

  c. For $\hat{a}$ the exact level of significance is 0.0029, which means there is only a 0.29 percent chance that $a = 0$ with a *t*-ratio as large as 4.23. For $\hat{b}$ the *exact* significance is 0.0187, which means there is only a 1.87 percent chance that $b = 0$ with a *t*-ratio as large as -2.94.

  d. The critical *F*-statistic with 1 ($= k - 1$) and 8 ($= n - k$) degrees of freedom at the 1 percent significance level is 11.26. Since the *F*-statistic 8.747 is

less than 11.26, the overall equation is *not* statistically significant at the 1 percent level of significance. The *p*-value for the *F*-statistic, 0.0182, shows that the equation is statistically significant at the 1.8 percent level.

  e. $\hat{Y} = 800 - 2.5(140) = 450$

  f. $R^2 = 0.5223$, so 52.23 percent of the total variation in *Y* is explained by the regression equation.

7. *a.* $n - k = 25 - 2 = 23$

  b. 2.069

  c. For $\hat{a}$: $t = 2.60 > 2.069$; statistically significant.
  For $\hat{b}$: $t = 2.78 > 2.069$; statistically significant.

  d. The exact significance level for $\hat{a}$ is 0.0160, and the exact significance level for $\hat{b}$ is 0.0106. The exact confidence levels are 0.984 (98.4 percent) and 0.989 (98.9 percent), respectively. A *t*-test at the 95 percent confidence level understates the degree of confidence associated with $\hat{a}$ and $\hat{b}$.

  e. $R^2 = 0.7482$ tells us that 74.82 percent of the total variation in *Y* is explained by the regression equation (i.e., by variation in *X*); and 25.18 percent of the variation in *Y* is unexplained.

  f. $k - 1 = 2 - 1 = 1$ and $n - k = 23$, so at a 95 percent confidence level, the critical value of *F* is 4.28. The regression equation is statistically significant because the *F*-ratio (68.351) is greater than the critical value of *F*. The *p*-value on the *F*-statistic is less than 0.0001, so there is virtually no chance that the *F*-test is mistakenly indicating significance for the equation as a whole.

  g. $325.24 + 0.8057(100) = 405.81$
  $325.24 + 0.8057(0) = 325.24$

8. *a.* In a multiple regression model, the coefficients on the explanatory variables do *not* measure the percent of the total variation in *Y* explained by that explanatory variable. The coefficients measure the rate of change in *Y* as that explanatory variable changes, all *other* explanatory variables remaining constant.

  b. This statement is correct because critical *t*-values get smaller as the number of degrees of freedom increases. See the *t*-table at the end of the textbook to verify this.

  c. This statement is correct because R^2 equals 1.0 when $Y = \hat{Y}$ for all observations.

9. *a.* $n - k = 34 - 4 = 30$

  b. 2.457

c. For $\hat{a}$: $t = 1.51 < 2.457$; *not* statistically significant at 2 percent level; exact significance = 14.13 percent.

For $\hat{b}$: $t = 6.09 > 2.457$; statistically significant at 2 percent level; exact significance < 0.01 percent.

For $\hat{c}$: $|t| = |-2.48| > 2.457$; statistically significant at 2 percent level; exact significance = 1.88 percent.

For $\hat{d}$: $t = 3.66 > 2.457$; statistically significant at 2 percent level; exact significance = 0.01 percent.

d. 31.79 percent of variation R is explained by the model. 68.21 percent of the variation is unexplained.

e. The critical F with $k - 1 = 4 - 1 = 3$ and $n - k = 30$ degrees of freedom and a significance level of 1 percent is 4.51. Since the F-ratio = $4.66 > 4.51$, the overall regression equation is statistically significant at the 1 percent level of significance. The exact significance level for the F-statistic is 0.865 percent.

f. $12.6 + 22.0(10) - 4.1(5) + 16.3(30) = 701.1$

$12.6 + 22.0(0) - 4.1(0) + 16.3(0) = 12.6$

10. a. $Z = X^2$

b. $\hat{M} = 290.0630 - 5.8401X + 0.07126X^2$

c. The critical t-value for 15 ($= n - k = 18 - 3$) degrees of freedom and a 2 percent level of significance is 2.602, which is found in the table of critical t-values at the end of the text. Since all three t-ratios, 5.37, -2.66, and 3.62, are greater in absolute value than the critical t-ratio ($= 2.602$), all three parameter estimates are statistically significant at the 2 percent level of significance.

d. The p-value for $\hat{c}$ is 0.0025. This means that there is a 0.25 percent ($= 0.0025 \times 100$) chance that the true value of c is 0 even though $\hat{c} = 0.07126$.

e. $4,951$ ($= 290.0630 - 5.8401X + 0.07126X^2$).

11. a. Take logarithms: $\ln Y = \ln a + b \ln R + c \ln S$.

b. The critical t for 60 ($= 63 - 3$) degrees of freedom and a 5 percent level of significance is 2.000.

For $\ln \hat{a}$: $t = |-1.67| < 2.000$; *not* statistically significant; exact significance = 10 percent.

For $\hat{b}$: $t = 2.58 > 2.000$; statistically significant; exact significance = 1.23 percent.

For $\hat{c}$: $t = 3.06 > 2.000$; statistically significant; exact significance = 0.33 percent.

c. The critical F for $k - 1 = 2$ and $n - k = 60$ degrees of freedom and a 5 percent level of significance is 3.15. The F-ratio of 132.22 is greater than 3.15, so the overall equation is statistically significant at

the 5 percent level. Since the p-value is less than 0.01 percent, the equation as a whole is extremely significant.

d. The model fits the data well, as 81.5 percent of the total variation in $\ln Y$ is explained by the model. Only 18.5 percent of the variation is not explained by the model.

e. Since $\ln a$ is estimated to be -1.386, a is equal to $e^{\hat{a}} = e^{-1.386} = 0.25$.

f. $\hat{Y} = 0.25(200)^{0.452}(1,500)^{0.30} = 24.6$ units per day

g. Estimated elasticity of $R = \%\Delta Y / \%\Delta R = \hat{b} = 0.452$. Estimated elasticity of $S = \%\Delta Y / \%\Delta S = \hat{c} = 0.30$.

Chapter 5: Theory of Consumer Behavior

1. a. Prefers Classic Coke to regular Pepsi.

b. Cannot say because the Ferrari obviously costs more. He might prefer the Ferrari but isn't willing or able to pay the higher price.

c. She clearly prefers the Ferrari because she is willing to pay the higher price.

d. Cannot say for sure. Can say, however, that James's and Jane's preferences are either (1) indifference between brands of colas—so they might flip a coin to choose a drink, or (2) they prefer the cola they chose.

2. a. Utility will be unchanged if the consumer exchanges 3 units of Y for 1 unit of X ($\Delta Y / \Delta X = -6/2 = -3$).

b. Utility will be unchanged if the consumer exchanges $1/3$ unit of X for 1 unit of Y ($\Delta X / \Delta Y = -1/3$).

c. $MRS = -\Delta Y / \Delta X = 3$.

3. a. $MRS = -\Delta Y / \Delta X = -(-200/200) = 1$

b. $MRS = -\Delta Y / \Delta X = -(-200/300) = 2/3$

c. Extend tangent T to the two axes to obtain $MRS = -(-900/1,100) = 9/11 = 0.82$.

4. a. $MRS = -\Delta Y / \Delta X = MU_x / MU_y = 2$. If $MU_x = 20$, $MU_y = 10$ since $20/10 = 2$.

b. $MU_x / MU_y = 3$. If $MU_y = 3$, $MU_x = 9$ since $9/3 = 3$.

c. As more X is added, MU_x decreases; as Y is reduced, MU_y increases, so MRS decreases.

5. a. $Y = 10 - 1X$

b. $Y = 10 - 2.5X$

c. $Y = 5 - 0.5X$

d. $Y = 4 - 0.5X$

e. Given the vertical and horizontal intercepts of budget line *LR*, it follows that $P_y \times 10 = \$200$ and $P_x \times 4 = \$200$. Thus $P_y = \$20$ and $P_x = \$50$. For budget line *LZ*, if income is \$200, then $P_y \times 10 = \$200$ and $P_x \times 10 = \$200$, which means $P_y = \$20$ and $P_x = \$20$.

f. Given the vertical and horizontal intercepts of budget line *MN*, it follows that income along *MN* can be calculated by either $4 \times P_y$ or $8 \times P_x$. Given $P_y = \$40$ and $P_x = \$20$, income can be calculated in either of two equivalent ways: $M = 4 \times \$40 = \$160$ or $M = 8 \times \$20 = \$160$. Similarly, for budget line *KZ*, $M = 5 \times P_y$ or $10 \times P_x$. Given $P_y = \$40$ and $P_x = \$20$, then income along *KZ* can be found either as $M = 5 \times \$40 = \$200$ or $M = 10 \times \$20 = \$200$.

6. a. $50 \times \$10 = \$500$

b. $40 \times P_x = \$500$; thus $P_x = \$12.50$.

c. For *LZ*: $12.50X + 10Y = 500$, or $Y = 50 - 1.25X$.

d. The consumer will choose 20 units of *X* and 25 units of *Y*, where indifference curve *II* is tangent to budget line *LZ*. No other combination costing \$500 provides more utility than $X = 20$, $Y = 25$.

e. At the optimal choice, $MRS = P_x/P_y = \$12.50/\$10 = 1.25$.

f. At combination *A:* By the definition of *MRS*, the consumer can give up 1 unit of *X* in return for *MRS* more units of *Y* and the consumer's utility will not change. With market prices P_x and P_y, the consumer can buy P_x/P_y $(= 1.25)$ more units of *Y* if 1 less unit of *X* is purchased and remain on the budget line. Visual inspection of the slopes of the indifference curve and budget line at point *A* shows that $P_x/P_y > MRS$ at combination *A*. The consumer can buy P_x/P_y more *Y* if 1 fewer unit of *X* is purchased, which is *more Y* than would be needed to remain indifferent. Therefore, giving up 1 unit of *X* to get *MRS* more units of *Y* must increase utility, and combination *A* would not be chosen by the consumer. At combination *B:* The consumer could trade (give up) *MRS* units of *Y* to get 1 more unit of *X* and the consumer's utility would be unchanged. The consumer must give up P_x/P_y units of *Y* to get 1 more unit of *X* and remain on the budget line. By visual inspection of slopes, $MRS > P_x/P_y$ at combination *B*. Thus the consumer can buy 1 more *X* and

give up only P_x/P_y units of *Y*, which is *less* than the loss of *Y* that would leave utility unchanged (i.e., *MRS* units of *Y*). Since the consumer gives up less *Y* than the amount that would leave the consumer indifferent, trading P_x/P_y units of *Y* for 1 more *X* must increase utility, and combination *B* would not be chosen by the consumer.

g. $80 \times P_x = \$500$; thus $P_x = \$6.25$. The consumer will now choose 30 units of *Y* and 32 units of *X* ($\$10 \times 30 + \$6.25 \times 32 = \$500$), where indifference curve *III* is tangent to budget line *LM*.

h. $MRS = P_x/P_y = \$6.25/\$10 = 0.625$.

7. a. $MRS = -\Delta Y/\Delta X = 2$. Utility will be unchanged if the consumer gives up 2 units of *Y* for 1 unit of *X*.

b. Utility will be unchanged if the consumer gives up 1/2 unit of *X* for 1 unit of *Y* $(-\Delta X/\Delta Y = 1/2)$.

c. $MRS = 2$

d. Market rate of exchange $= P_x/P_y = \$3/\$1 = 3$.

e. No, the consumer is not making the utility-maximizing choice. At the current choice, $MRS = MU_x/MU_y < P_x/P_y$, so $MU_x/P_x < MU_y/P_y$. By spending one more dollar on *Y* and one less dollar on *X*, total expenditures will be unchanged, and utility will increase by $(MU_y/P_y - MU_x/P_x)$. The consumer can increase utility by continuing to purchase more *Y* and less *X* (thus decreasing MU_y and increasing MU_x) until the marginal utility per dollar is equal for the two goods, and the consumer obtains the maximum possible utility given a limited income.

8. a. $30 \times \$20 = \$600$.

b. $P_y = \$20$.

c. For *LZ*: $20X + 20Y = 600$, or $Y = 30 - X$.

d. The consumer chooses $10X$ and $20Y$. This combination lies on the highest indifference curve that can be attained given the budget line *LZ*.

e. $MRS = 1 = P_x/P_y = \$20/\$20$

f. At point *A*, $MRS > 1$. The consumer is willing to give up *more* than 1 unit of *Y* for 1 more unit of *X* and remain indifferent. The consumer can obtain 1 more unit of *X* in the marketplace by giving up exactly 1 unit of *Y*. Since the consumer gives up fewer units of *Y* than necessary to remain indifferent, the consumer must be better off when trading 1 *Y* for 1 more *X* at point *A*. At point *B*, $MRS < 1$. The consumer is willing to give up 1 unit of *X* in return for *less* than 1 unit more of Y and remain indifferent. In the market, the consumer can purchase exactly 1 more Y by giving up 1 X. By giving up 1 X, the consumer gets more Y than the amount necessary to leave him or her just indifferent, so the consumer must be better off at point B when giving up X for more Y.

g. $15X, 10Y$

h. $P_y = \$30$

i. $P_x = \$20$

j. $MRS = 2/3 = P_x/P_y = \$20/\$30$

9. Since $MU_p/P_p < MU_s/P_s$, she should buy more salad and less pasta. The marginal utility per dollar is higher for salad.

10. a. $8X, 9Y, 6Z$

b. $5X, 6Y, 4Z$

c. $0X, 6Y, 4Z$. Since the price of X is $5 and income is $38, the consumer can indeed *afford* to buy X. The consumer chooses not to purchase X because MU_x/P_x is so small relative to MU_y/P_y and MU_z/P_z that zero consumption of X maximizes utility subject to the budget constraint.

11. $P_y = \$4$, since $\$4 \times 250 = \$1,000$. Three price-quality combinations are $P_x = \$5, Q_x = 125; P_x = \$4, Q_x = 175; P_x = \$2.50, Q_x = 250$.

12. a, b, c: see figure below.

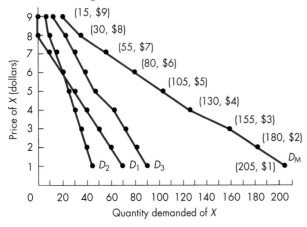

Chapter 6: Elasticity and Demand

1. a. $E = -8\%/10\% = -0.8$

b. inelastic (since $|-0.8| = 0.8 < 1$)

c. less than (When $|E| < 1$, the numerator of E is less than the denominator.)

2. a. increase; 9 ($\%\Delta Q/-6\% = -1.5 \Rightarrow \%\Delta P = 9\%$)

b. decrease; 20 ($+30\%/\%\Delta P = -1.5 \Rightarrow \%\Delta P = -20\%$)

3. a. quantity; price

b. price; quantity

c. neither

d. same; dominant

4. a. decrease; fall

b. increase; fall

c. decrease; stay the same

d. inelastic

e. unitary elastic

f. inelastic

5. To verify $E = -1$, show $TR_f = TR_g$. $\$13 \times 1,100 = \$14,300 = \$11 \times 1,300$

6. a. Coca-Cola. More substitutes are available for one brand than for the product group as a whole.

b. Business suits. Suits account for a larger share of a clothes shopper's budget than socks.

c. Long-run demand for electricity is more elastic than short-run demand because homeowners and businesses can buy energy-efficient appliances and improve insulation given a longer period of time to adjust to a price increase.

7. a. $-0.5 = (\Delta Q/\Delta P) \times (\text{Avg } P/\text{Avg } Q) = (-400/+2) \times (4/1,600)$

b. $-7 = (\Delta Q/\Delta P) \times (\text{Avg } P/\text{Avg } Q) = (-200/+1) \times (10.50/300)$

c. $-1 = (\Delta Q/\Delta P) \times (\text{Avg } P/\text{Avg } Q) = (-400/+2) \times (6/1,200)$

8. a. $3: $-0.\overline{33} = (-2,400/12) \times (3/1,800) = 3/(3 - 12)$

$5: $-0.71 = (-2,400/12) \times (5/1,400) = 5/(5 - 12)$

$7: $-1.40 = (-2,400/12) \times (7/1,000) = 7/(7 - 12)$

$10: $-5 = (-2,400/12) \times (10/400) = 10/(10 - 12)$

$11: $-11 = (-2,400/12) \times (11/200) = 11(11 - 12)$

b. Neither formula is "more accurate" since they give identical numerical values, as demonstrated in part a.

9. a. $E = P/(P - A) = 800/(800 - 1,000) = 800/-200 = -4$

b. $E = 200/(200 - 1,000) = 200/-800 = -1/4 = -0.25$

c. Demand will be unit elastic at a price of $500 since $E = 500/(500 - 1,000) = -1$.

d. gets larger

10. a. $E = \dfrac{\Delta Q}{\Delta P} \times \dfrac{P}{Q} = \dfrac{+90}{-300} \times \dfrac{100}{60} = -0.5$

b. $E = \dfrac{P}{P - A} = \dfrac{100}{100 - 300} = \dfrac{100}{-200} = -0.5$

c. The values of E in parts a and b are equal, as they should be, because the two methods are mathematically equivalent formulas for computing price elasticity.

d. $E = \dfrac{P}{P - A} = \dfrac{400}{400 - 700} = \dfrac{400}{-300} = -1.\overline{33}$

e. At point R, Q is not given, and $\Delta Q/\Delta P$ cannot be computed. Thus $E = \dfrac{P}{P - A}$ is the only method to use at point R.

11. a. $20

b. $20

c. $20

d. -1. This is a special case where demand has a constant elasticity, $Q = aP^b$, where $a = 20$ and $b = -1$. Since TR is constant at all prices, demand is unitary elastic.

12. Values for the blanks a through l in the figure:

a. $44. $TR = P \times Q \Rightarrow 1,056 = P \times 24 \Rightarrow P = \$44$.

b. $38. Slope of total revenue is $+\$38$ at $Q = 24$.

c. $25. Since $MR = 0$, demand is unitary elastic, which requires that P equal $25 [-1 = 25/(25 - 50)]$

d. 100. Since MR is twice as steep as demand, MR passes through the midpoint on the horizontal axis between 0 and 200.

e. $-\$12. The slope of total revenue at the corresponding output is -12.

f. $2,500. $TR = P \times Q = 25 \times 100 = \$2,500$

g. $>$; demand is elastic for output levels where MR is positive.

h. $=$; demand is unitary elastic at the output level where MR is zero.

i. $<$; demand is inelastic for output levels where MR is negative.

j. 100. Total revenue reaches its maximum value at the output level for which $MR = 0$.

k. 124. $TR = P \times Q \Rightarrow 2,350 = 19 \times Q \Rightarrow Q = 124$

l. 200. Total revenue is zero when demand price is zero (or quantity demanded is zero). Demand price is zero when $Q = 200$.

13. a. Demand: $Q = 200 - 4P$

b. Inverse demand: $P = 50 - 0.25Q$

c. Total revenue: $TR = P \times Q = 50Q - 0.25Q^2$

d. Marginal revenue: $MR = 50 - 0.5Q$

e. Substituting $Q = 24$ into the preceding equations: $P = \$44$; $TR = \$1,056$; $MR = \$38$. Substituting $Q = 100$ into these equations: $P = \$25$; $TR = \$2,500$; $MR = \$0$. Substituting $Q = 124$ into the equations: $P = \$19$; $TR = \$2,356$; $MR = -\$12$.

14. $Q_d = 2,400 - 200P$; $MR = 12 - 0.01Q$; $E = -1$ at $P = \$6$; $MR = 0$ at $Q_d = 1,200$ units.

15. a. $-3.20 = (\Delta Q/\Delta M) \times (\text{Avg } M/\text{Avg } Q) = (-100/+4,000) \times (32,000/250)$; inferior

b. $5.76 = (\Delta Q/\Delta P_Y) \times (\text{Avg } P_Y/\text{Avg } Q) = (270/8) \times (64/375)$; substitutes

16. a. $36,000 = 250,000 - 500(200) - 1.50(60,000) - 240(100)$

b. $E = -2.78 = -500 \times \dfrac{200}{36,000}$; elastic since $|E| > 1$. Increasing price at a point on demand where $|E| > 1$ causes total revenue to fall because the quantity effect dominates the price effect.

c. $E_M = -2.50 = -1.50 \times \dfrac{60,000}{36,000}$; inferior. A 4 percent increase in M, all else constant, would cause Q to decrease by 10 percent $(= 4\% \times -2.5)$.

d. $E_{XR} = -0.67 = -240 \times \dfrac{100}{36,000}$; complements. A 5 percent decrease in P_R, all else constant, would cause Q to increase by 3.35 percent $(= -5\% \times -0.67)$.

Chapter 7: Demand Estimation and Forecasting

1. a. X is an inferior good. A negative parameter estimate for income (-0.6) means the quantity of X demanded decreases (increases) when income increases (decreases).

b. X and Z are substitutes. A positive parameter estimate for the price of Z (4) means that the quantity of X demanded increases (decreases) when the price of Z increases (decreases).

c. $\hat{Q} = 70 - 3.5(10) - 0.6(30) + 4(6) = 41.0$
$\hat{E} = \hat{b}(P/Q) = -3.5(10/41) = -0.85$
$\hat{E}_M = \hat{c}(M/Q) = -0.6(30/41) = -0.44$
$\hat{E}_{XZ} = \hat{d}(P_z/Q) = 4(6/41) = 0.59$

2. a. X is a normal good since the estimated coefficient on ln M, the income elasticity, is positive (0.8).

 b. X and Y are complements since the estimated coefficient on ln P_y, the cross-price elasticity, is negative (-2.5).

 c. $\hat{Q} = 125{,}755P^{-1.65}M^{0.8}P_Y^{-2.5}$ (Note: $125{,}755 = e^{11.74209}$.)

 d. For all values of P, M, P_Y, the elasticity estimates are constant and equal to $\hat{E} = -1.65$; $E_M = 0.8$; $\hat{E}_{XY} = -2.5$. Estimated Q: $\hat{Q} = 279.52 = 125{,}755(50)^{-1.65}(36{,}000)^{0.8}(25)^{-2.5}$.

3. a. Demand is not identified because supply does not contain any exogenous variables.

 b. The supply equation contains no exogenous variables excluded from the demand equation, so the demand function is not identified.

 c. The demand function is not identified because the exogenous variable in supply is also an explanatory variable in the demand equation.

 d. Demand is identified because supply contains at least one (two in this case) exogenous variable that is not an explanatory variable in demand.

4. If a demand equation is not identified, there is no estimation technique (2SLS or otherwise) capable of estimating the parameters of the demand equation. 2SLS can be used only when the demand equation is identified.

5. Using OLS to estimate industry demand for price-taking firms when price is an endogenous variable results in a simultaneous equations bias for each of the estimated parameters of the demand equation. The most obvious problem with the OLS estimation results is the parameter estimate for copper price. The OLS estimate (-13.4205) is much smaller in absolute value than the 2SLS estimate. Further, price does not appear to have a statistically significant effect on the quantity demanded of copper (p-value $= 0.3636$).

6. a. The quantity of copper demanded will decrease 2.96 percent if the price of copper increases 10 percent.

$[\hat{E} = -0.296 = \%\Delta QC/10\% \Rightarrow \%\Delta QC = (-0.296)(10\%) = -2.96\%]$

 b. The quantity of copper demanded will decrease 9.165 percent if income decreases 5 percent.
$[\hat{E}_M = 1.833 = \%\Delta QC/-5\% \Rightarrow \%\Delta QC = (1.833)(-5\%) = -9.165\%]$

 c. The quantity of copper demanded will increase 1.776 percent if the price of copper decreases 6 percent.
$[\hat{E} = -0.296 = \%\Delta QC/-6\% \Rightarrow \%\Delta QC = (-0.296)(-6\%) = +1.776\%]$

 d. The quantity of copper demanded will decrease 3.0 percent if the price of aluminum decreases 10 percent.
$[\hat{E}_{CA} = 0.30 = \%\Delta QC/-10\% \Rightarrow \%\Delta QC = (0.30)(-10\%) = -3.0\%]$

7. a. The theory of demand predicts that price and quantity demanded will be inversely related. Since $\hat{b}$ is negative, the estimate of b is consistent with economic theory.

 b. Since $\hat{c}$ is positive, the good is a normal good.

 c. A negative coefficient of the price of related good R means that the price of R and the quantity of X demanded are inversely related. In other words, X and R are complements.

 d. The p-values show all parameter estimates are significant at the 5 percent level, or better.

 e. $\hat{Q} = 68.38 - 6.50(225) + 0.13926(24{,}000) - 10.77(60) = 1{,}302$
  (1) $\hat{E} = \hat{b}(P/Q) = -6.50(225/1{,}302) = -1.12$
  (2) $\hat{E}_M = \hat{c}(M/Q) = (0.13926)(24{,}000/1{,}302) = 2.57$
  (3) $\hat{E}_{XR} = \hat{d}(P_R/Q) = (-10.77)(60/1{,}302) = -0.50$

8. a. ln $Q = 6.77 - 1.68$ ln $P - 0.82$ ln $M + 1.35$ ln P_R

 b. Yes, the sign of $\hat{b}$ is negative, indicating demand is downward-sloping.

 c. Since the sign of c is negative, X is an inferior good. Goods X and R are substitutes since $\hat{d}$ is positive.

 d. The p-values show that $\hat{b}$ and $\hat{c}$ are significant at the 5 percent level, while $\hat{a}$ and $\hat{d}$ are significant at the 10 percent level.

 e. (1) $\hat{E} = -1.68$; (2) $\hat{E}_{XR} = 1.35$; (3) $\hat{E}_M = -0.82$

 f. increase; 8.2 percent

 g. decrease; 16.8 percent

 h. decrease; 6.75 percent ($= 5\% \times 1.35$)

9. *a.* $\hat{a}$: *p*-value is 0.0498, so $\hat{a}$ is just barely significant at the 5 percent level of significance.

$\hat{b}$: *p*-value is 0.0002, so $\hat{b}$ is highly significant. It is significant at the 0.02 percent level of significance which is much better than the 5 percent level. Conclusion: Sales exhibit a statistically significant positive trend over time (i.e., $\hat{b} > 0$ and *p*-value is very small).

The model as a whole, as indicated by the extremely small *p*-value on the *F*-statistic, explains a statistically significant amount of the variation in sales.

b. $Q_{2005} = 73.71460 + 3.7621(2005) = 7{,}617$

$Q_{2006} = 73.7146 + 3.7621(2006) = 7{,}620$

c. The farther the values of the variables in the forecast are from the mean values of the regression, the less precise the forecast will be. Thus the forecast for 2006 will be less precise than the forecast for 2005.

10. *a.* For a 5 percent significance level with 27 (32 − 5) degrees of freedom, the critical value of *t* is 2.052.

For $\hat{a}$: $t = 7.15 > 2.052$; statistically significant at the 5 percent level.

For $\hat{b}$: $t = 5.97 > 2.052$; statistically significant at the 5 percent level.

For $\hat{c}_1$: $|t| = |-4.31| > 2.052$; statistically significant at the 5 percent level.

For $\hat{c}_2$: $|t| = |-2.24| > 2.052$; statistically significant at the 5 percent level.

For $\hat{c}_3$: $|t| = |-8.22| > 2.052$; statistically significant at the 5 percent level.

For a 5 percent significance level with 4 (= 5 − 1) and 27 (= 32 − 5) degrees of freedom, the critical value of *F* is 2.73. The regression equation is statistically significant because the *F*-ratio (361.133) is greater than the critical value of *F*.

In terms of *p*-values, all estimated coefficients are significant at the 5 percent level of significance. The *p*-value for *F* shows the equation to be highly significant.

b. The intercepts are 51.234 − 11.716 = 39.518 for the first quarter, 51.234 − 1.424 = 49.81 for the second quarter, 51.234 − 17.367 = 33.867 for the third quarter, and 51.234 for the fourth quarter. These intercept values imply that, after accounting for trend, sales will be greatest in quarter 4, then quarter 2, then quarter 1, and smallest in quarter 3.

c. $\hat{Q}_{2005(I)} = 51.234 + 3.127 \times 33 - 11.716 = 142.709$

$\hat{Q}_{2005(II)} = 51.234 + 3.127 \times 34 - 1.424 = 156.128$

$\hat{Q}_{2005(III)} = 51.234 + 3.127 \times 35 - 17.367 = 143.312$

$\hat{Q}_{2005(IV)} = 51.234 + 3.127 \times 36 = 163.806$

11. *a.* Economic theory predicts that price and quantity demanded will be inversely related, income and quantity demanded will be positively related for a normal good, and the price of a complement and quantity demanded will be inversely related. The signs of the coefficients in the demand equation thus are consistent with economic theory and imply that *X* is a normal good and that *X* and *R* are complements. The signs of the coefficients in the supply equation are also consistent with economic theory because price and quantity supplied are positively related, while input prices and quantity supplied are inversely related.

b. Demand $Q_{2006(I)} = 500 - 300P + 1(10{,}000) - 200(20) = 6{,}500 - 300P$

Supply $Q_{2006(I)} = -400 + 200P - 100(6) = -1{,}000 + 200P$

In equilibrium, $6{,}500 - 300P = -1{,}000 + 200P$ $\Rightarrow P = \$15 \Rightarrow Q = 2{,}000.$

c. For $M = \$9{,}000$:

$Q_{2006(I)} = 500 - 300P + 1(9{,}000) - 200(20) = 5{,}500 - 300P$

In equilibrium, $5{,}500 - 300P = -1{,}000 + 200P$ $\Rightarrow P = \$13$ and $Q = 1{,}600.$

For $M = \$12{,}000$:

$Q_{2006(I)} = 500 - 300P + 1(12{,}000) - 200(20) = 8{,}500 - 300P$

In equilibrium, $8{,}500 - 300P = -1{,}000 + 200P$ $\Rightarrow P = \$19$ and $Q = 2{,}800.$

Thus increasing projected income in 2006(I) from \$9,000 to \$12,000 causes forecasted price to rise by \$6 (from \$13 to \$19) and forecasted sales to rise by 1,200 units (from 1,600 to 2,800).

12. The major shortcoming of time-series models is that they do not use a structural model that explains the economic determinants of a forecast. Instead, they assume that the future behavior of an economic variable can be predicted solely on the basis of past behavior.

13. First, the further in the future, the less reliable the forecast; parameter estimates become more uncertain as the variable values move further away from the

regression mean values. For example, a researcher can provide a more reliable forecast of pencil sales in 2005 than in 2050. (After all, some people claim that personal computers eventually will make paper and pencil obsolete.) Incorrect specification is another potential problem because the exclusion of important explanatory variables or the choice of an inappropriate functional form will result in biased estimates and incorrect forecasts. A forecast of rail freight, for instance, would be misspecified if it omitted the prices of alternative means of transportation, such as air, truck, and barge freight. Finally, structural changes will undermine a forecast's accuracy. Unforeseen events can alter the underlying assumptions of a forecast and thus invalidate predictions based on the model. Suppose, for example, a consultant predicted that tourist expenditures in Key West would be $100 million in 2006. A hurricane that devastated Key West in 2005 would make the forecast useless.

Chapter 8: Production and Cost in the Short Run

1. This statement is not true in general. All technically efficient input combinations are not economically efficient. It is true, however, that all economically efficient input combinations are technically efficient.

2. *a.* Yes, both processes can be technically efficient. With variable proportions production, many different technically efficient input combinations can be employed to produce 1,000 units daily.

   b. Process 1, since the total cost of using process 1 ($4,000) is less than the total cost of process 2 ($4,100).

   c. Process 2, since the total cost of using process 2 ($3,875) is less than the total cost of process 1 ($4,000).

3. A manager's "plans" often involve changes in future levels of inputs that are, for now, fixed. In this sense, a manager's "plans" involve long-run production decisions. The day-to-day operation of the firm requires that the manager make production decisions without being able to change the usage of certain fixed inputs. In this sense, "operation" decisions are short-run production decisions.

4. *a.* Short-run decision. The drilling supervisor has just one rig (a fixed input) but plans to use more variable input (rig hands) to increase output (number of feet drilled per day).

b. Long-run decision. Increasing the number of drill platforms involves changing the level of usage of an input that is fixed in the short-run period.

c. Short-run decision. Production operation decisions are generally made with the understanding that at least some inputs cannot be changed during the production period.

d. Long-run decision. Adding a new wing to a hospital represents a long-run increase in an input that is fixed in size in the short run.

5. Your table should look like this:

Labor	TP	AP	MP
0	0	—	—
1	40	40	40
2	88	44	48
3	138	46	50
4	176	44	38
5	200	40	24
6	210	35	10
7	203	29	−7
8	176	22	−27

6. The combination of $10L$ and $2K$ is not economically efficient because 314 units of output can be produced with just 8 units of labor (and $2K$), which would represent a lower total cost of producing 314 units.

7. *a.* When capital is held constant at 2 units:

L	Q	AP	MP
1	120	120	120
2	260	130	140
3	360	120	100
4	430	107.5	70
5	480	96	50

When marginal product is greater than average product, average product is increasing. When marginal product is less than average product, average product is decreasing.

b.

	Marginal product of labor			
L	K = 1	K = 2	K = 3	K = 4
1	50	120	160	180
2	60	140	200	210
3	40	100	150	170
4	20	70	120	130
5	−10	50	80	100

As the capital stock increases for each level of labor usage, the marginal product of labor increases. The additional unit of labor is more productive because it has more capital with which to work.

8.

Q	TC	TFC	TVC	AFC	AVC	ATC	SMC
100	260	200	60	2.00	0.60	2.60	0.60
200	290	200	90	1.00	0.45	1.45	0.30
300	350	200	150	0.67	0.50	1.17	0.60
400	420	200	220	0.50	0.55	1.05	0.70
500	560	200	360	0.40	0.72	1.12	1.40
600	860	200	660	0.33	1.10	1.43	3.00
700	1,320	200	1,120	0.29	1.60	1.89	4.60
800	2,040	200	1,840	0.25	2.30	2.55	7.20

9. If AVC is constant over a range of output, then MC is also constant and equal to AVC. ATC, however, would be decreasing over this range of output, since $ATC = AVC + AFC$, and AFC declines as output increases.

10. *a.* $SMC = w/MP = \$60/12 = \$5$
    b. $AVC = w/AP = \$60/30 = \$2$
    c. $AP = 30 = Q/L = Q/20$, so $Q = (30)(20) = 600$
    d. $AFC = TFC/Q = \$3,600/600 = \$6$; $ATC = AFC + AVC = \$6 + \$2 = \$8$
    e. $SMC = \$5 > AVC = \$2$; AVC is increasing.
       $SMC = \$5 < ATC = \$8$; ATC is decreasing.

11. *a.*

L	Q	AP	MP	TFC	TVC
0	0	—	—	10,000	0
20	4,000	200	200	10,000	10,000
40	10,000	250	300	10,000	20,000
60	15,000	250	250	10,000	30,000
80	19,400	242.5	220	10,000	40,000
100	23,000	230	180	10,000	50,000

TC	AFC	AVC	ATC	SMC
10,000	—	—	—	—
20,000	2.50	2.50	5.00	2.50
30,000	1.00	2.00	3.00	1.67
40,000	0.67	2.00	2.67	2.00
50,000	0.52	2.06	2.58	2.27
60,000	0.43	2.17	2.61	2.78

b. When SMC is less than (greater than) AVC, AVC is decreasing (increasing). When SMC is less than (greater than) ATC, ATC is decreasing (increasing).

c. When AP is increasing (decreasing), AVC is decreasing (increasing). When MP is increasing (decreasing), MC is decreasing (increasing).

12. *a.* $AVC (= w/AP)$ reaches its minimum value when AP reaches its maximum, i.e., when $L = 80$.
    b. When $L = 80$, $AP = Q/L = 250$, so $Q = (250)(80) = 20,000$.
    c. $AVC = w/AP = \$2/250 = \$0.008$ or $AVC = TVC/Q = wL/Q = \$2(80)/20,000 = \$0.008$
    d. When $L = 100$, AP appears to be approximately 240 and MP is 150. Output is $Q = AP \times L = 240(100) = 24,000$ units. $SMC = w/MP = \$2/150 = \$0.0133$. $AVC = w/AP = \$2/240 = \$0.00833$ or $AVC = TVC/Q = wL/Q = \$2(100)/24,000 = \$0.00833$.

Chapter 9: Production and Cost in the Long Run

1. *a.* $1/4$
   b. decrease; $1/4$
   c. 20
2. *a.* $K = 60 - 3/4L$; \$37.50; \$3,000
   b. 40; 30; \$3,000; $60 - 3/4(40) = 30\checkmark$
   c. 90; 120; $K = 90 - 3/4L$; 60
3. *a.* less than; \$6,000; \$33.33
   b. decreases; increases; total cost; output; less than; \$5,000
   c. minimizes; total; equal to
   d. 20; 60; \$4,000
   e. \$3,000. Although E costs less than C, E cannot produce the 2,500 units required by the manager.
4. Since $MP_L/w = (= 25/25 = 1)$ is greater than MP_K/r $(= 65/130 = 1/2)$, the manager is using too much capital and not enough labor. In order to produce efficiently, the manager should increase L and decrease K until $MP_L/w = MP_K/r$.
5. *a.* greater. The manager can increase spending on labor by \$1, which causes output to rise by MP_L/w units. Since $MP_K/r < MP_L/w$, spending on capital must be decreased by *more* than \$1 in order to keep output at the initial level of output represented by isoquant I. Hence it is possible to find another input combination that produces the level of output associated with isoquant I but costs less to obtain than combination A.

b. less. The manager can increase spending on capital by $1, which causes output to rise by MP_K/r units. Since $MP_L/w < MP_K/r$, spending on labor must be reduced by *more* than $1 to keep output at the level associated with isoquant I. Hence it is possible to find another input combination that produces the level of output associated with isoquant I but costs less to obtain than combination B.

c. When an isocost line parallel to LZ is constructed such that the new isocost curve is tangent to the Q_1 isoquant, the point of tangency occurs at approximately $200L$ and $200K$.

6. In either case, minimizing cost or maximizing output, the optimal input combinations must satisfy the same condition that $MRTS = w/r$, or equivalently, the slope of the isoquant must equal the slope of the isocost curve. Since an expansion path is the locus of tangency points, the expansion path looks the same regardless of whether the manager is trying to minimize cost for a given output or maximize output for a given cost.

7. a. $w = \$25 (= \$5,000/200)$

   b. 32; 12; $2,000

   c. 60; 20; $3,500

   d. 72; 32; $5,000

   e. The expansion path is the curve passing through each of the tangency points.

   f. $MRTS = 0.25$

8. a. 1.5

   b. 3

   c. less than; increasing

9.

Q	L	K	LTC	LAC	LMC
10	64	24	4,000	400	400
20	140	40	7,500	375	350
30	200	58	10,800	360	330
40	288	80	15,200	380	440
50	460	90	20,500	410	530

10. Economies of scale exist for 0 to 30 units of output; there are diseconomies of scale for 30 to 50 units of output.

11. a. $20; $20; $4,000 (= $20 × 200)

    b. $20; $20; $10,000 (= $20 × 500)

    c. When production is characterized by constant returns to scale, a firm faces constant costs.

12. $SC = [(\$1,000 + \$600) - 1,400]/1,400 = 0.143 > 0$. Since $SC > 0$, there are economies of scope.

13. a. $0.72; $3,600 = $0.72 × 5,000

    b. $0.30; $1,500 = $0.30 × 5,000

    c. A plant size of 30 units of capital should be chosen because this plant size allows the firm to operate on its long-run expansion path and produce 5,000 units at the lowest possible total cost.

14.

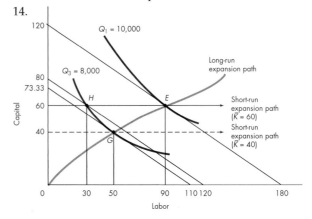

a. 30; 60. Point H in the accompanying figure gives the cost-minimizing point for producing 8,000 units in the short run. *Note:* Your answer for L^* may differ slightly from 30, but your answer for K^* must be 60.

   b. $4,800 = $40(30) + $60(60); $0.60 = $4,800/8,000

   c. $400, which is the difference between short-run and long-run total cost [$LTC = \$4,400 = \$40(50) + \$60(40)$]; 50; 40

   d. Since the new capital level is fixed at 40 units, the new short-run expansion path is shown in the figure above as the horizontal line at $K = 40$.

Chapter 10: Production and Cost Estimation

1. a. Total product: $Q = -0.002(10)^3L^3 + 6(10)^2L^2 = -2L^3 + 600L^2$

   Letting $A = -2$ and $B = 600$,
   $$AP = AL^2 + BL = -2L^2 + 600L$$
   $$MP = 3AL^2 + 2BL = -6L^2 + 1,200L$$

   b. $L_m = -B/3A = -600/-6 = 100$ units of labor

   c. $AP_{10} = -2(10)^2 + 600(10) = 5,800$
   $$MP_{10} = -6(10)^2 + 1,200(10) = 11,400$$

d. Total product: $Q = -0.002(20)^3 L^3 + 6(20)^2 L^2 = -16L^3 + 2,400L^2$

Letting $A = -16$ and $B = 2,400$,

$$AP = -16L^2 + 2,400L$$
$$MP = -48L^2 + 4,800L$$

e. Marginal and average product increased for all levels of labor usage. When $K = 20$ and 10 units of labor are employed,

$$AP_{10} = -16(10)^2 + 2,400(10) = 22,400$$
$$MP_{10} = -48(10)^2 + 4,800(10) = 43,200$$

As expected, AP_{10} and MP_{10} are higher when $K = 20$ than when $K = 10$, $L_m = -B/3A = 2,400/48 = 50$.

2. a. $A = -0.002$ and $B = 0.40$

$$TP = -0.002L^3 + 0.40L^2$$
$$AP = -0.002L^2 + 0.40L$$
$$MP = -0.006L^2 + 0.80L$$

b. Yes, signs are correct. Both A and B are statistically significant at the 1 percent level of significance since both p-values are less than 0.01.

c. $L_a = -B/2A = -0.40/2(-0.002) = 100$ units of labor

d. $Q_{AP\ max} = -0.002(100)^3 + 0.40(100)^2 = -2,000 + 4,000 = 2,000$ units of output

e. $AP_{L=100} = -0.002(100)^2 + 0.40(100) = -20 + 40 = 20$

$AVC_{Q=2,000} = w/AP_{L=100} = \$200/20 = \$10$

$MP_{L=100} = -0.006(100)^2 + 0.80(100) = -60 + 80 = 20$

$SMC_{Q=2,000} = w/MP_{L=100} = \$200/20 = \$10$

f. $TP = -0.002(120)^3 + 0.40(120)^2 = -3,456 + 5,760 = 2,304$

$AP_{L=120} = -0.002(120)^2 + 0.40(120) = -28.80 + 48 = 19.20$

$AVC_{Q=2,304} = w/AP_{L=120} = \$200/19.20 = \$10.42$

$MP_{L=120} = -0.006(120)^2 + 0.80(120) = -86.40 + 96 = 9.60$

$SMC_{Q=2,304} = w/MP_{L=120} = \$200/9.60 = \$20.83$

g. Repeat the procedure in parts e and f for all levels of output.

3. a. Yes, all three coefficients have the correct sign. All three coefficients are statistically significant at the 5 percent level of significance because all three p-values are less than 0.05.

b. $Q_m = -b/2c = 0.079952/2(0.000088) = 454.27$

c. $SMC = a + 2bQ + 3cQ^2 = 30.420202 - 0.159904Q + 0.000264Q^2$

d. $SMC_{700} = 30.420202 - 0.159904(700) + 0.000264(700)^2 = \$47.85$

e. $AVC = a + bQ + cQ^2 = 30.420202 - 0.079952Q + 0.000088Q^2$

f. $AVC_{700} = 30.420202 - 0.079952(700) + 0.000088(700)^2 = \$17.57$

Chapter 11: Managerial Decisions in Competitive Markets

1. The firm's demand is a horizontal line at $20, the price at which supply and demand intersect in the left-hand graph.

   a. The firm's demand is perfectly (or infinitely) elastic at every quantity.

   b. $MR = \$20$ at every level of output.

2. a. 1,500 units will maximize profit.

   b. $2, $4; increase, $2

   c. $7, $4; increase, $3

3. a. MR is a horizontal line at $7; 600

   b. $ATC_{600} = \$5$; $TC_{600} = \$5 \times 600 = \$3,000$

   c. $TR_{600} = \$7 \times 600 = \$4,200$, so $\pi = TR - TC = \$4,200 - \$3,000 = \$1,200$

   d. 500. Producing 500 units does *not* maximize profit because $MR(=P) > SMC$ at 500 units. Notice that profit at 500 units is (approximately) $1,100 [= ($7 - $4.80) \times 500]$, which is *less* than the maximum profit of $1,200.

   e. MR curve is a horizontal line at $3; 400

   f. $TR_{400} = \$3 \times 400 = \$1,200$; $TR_{400} = ATC_{400} \times 400 = \$5 \times 400 = \$2,000$; loss = $800.

   g. $TVC_{400} = AVC_{400} \times 400 = \$2 \times 400 = \$800$; $TR - TVC = \$400$ to apply to fixed cost.

   h. $1.90. When $P < 1.90$, the firm loses less by shutting down than it would lose if it produced where $MR = SMC$.

4. a. The firm is not producing the profit-maximizing level of output. At the current level of output (50 units), $P (= MR) = \$12 < SMC = \$15$. The firm can increase profit by producing less. The firm should reduce output until $P = SMC$.

   b. When ATC is at its minimum point, $ATC = SMC$. Thus, at the current level of output (10,000 units),

$P (= \$25) = SMC (= \$25)$. The firm is making the profit-maximizing decision; producing any other level of output would reduce the firm's profit.

5. Values for the blanks a through e in the figure:

a. $-\$60,000$. Profit equals $-TFC$ when output is zero. TFC can be calculated at 400 units since both ATC and AVC are given: $\$60,000 = (ATC - AVC) \times 400 = (225 - 75) \times 400$.

b and e. 1,000. This is the profit-maximizing output, since $P = MR = 225 = SMC$ at this output level in the figure. From the profit figure, $\$90,000$ is the maximum profit at the peak of the profit curve. Since the profit margin or average profit at this output is $\$90$ per unit ($= P - ATC = \$225 - \$135$), quantity must be 1,000 units to produce a total profit of $\$90,000$.

c. 80,000. This is the profit when 800 units are produced. Since profit margin or average profit is $\$100$ per unit ($= P - ATC = \$225 - \$125$), total profit must be $\$80,000$.

d. 100. The slope of the profit curve at 800 units equals $MR - SMC$. Since $MR = \$225$ and $SMC = \$125$, producing the 800th unit must add $\$100$ to profit.

e. Same answer as part b above.

6. a. The firm's demand $= MR = P$ is a horizontal line at $\$40$. The firm will produce 8,000 units of output where $LMC = \$40$. Economic profit $= (P - LAC)Q = (\$40 - \$25)8,000 = \$120,000$.

b. $P = $ minimum $LAC = \$20$. Economic profit $= 0$.

7. a. If the price of a substitute good decreases, market demand will decrease.

b. Initially market supply will be unaffected.

c. Market supply is unchanged and market demand has decreased: market price will decrease.

d. Market output will decrease.

e. A profit-maximizing firm's output will decrease.

f. At the original price, economic profit was zero. Now the firm suffers economic losses.

In the long run, firms will exit in response to the losses. Exit will reduce market supply, thus increasing market price. Exit will continue until the market returns to equilibrium, i.e., until each firm earns only a normal return.

8. a. Industry output does not affect any input prices and therefore does not affect costs. At each point on long-run competitive supply, price equals each firm's minimum long-run average cost, which does not change as industry output changes.

b. As industry output increases, some input prices increase, which causes costs to increase. At each point on long-run competitive supply, price equals each firm's minimum long-run average cost, which rises as industry output increases, causing long-run competitive supply to be upward-sloping.

9. a. $\$10; 0$

b. zero

c. $\$7,800; \$2,800 [= (\$10 - \$6) \times 700$ units$]$

10. a. and b. Your table should be:

(1) Units of labor	(2) Output	(3) Marginal product	(4) MRP	(5) SMC (= 10/MP)	(6) Profit
1	5	5	$10	$2	-$50
2	15	10	20	1	-40
3	30	15	30	0.67	-20
4	50	20	40	0.50	10
5	65	15	30	0.67	30
6	77	12	24	0.83	44
7	86	9	18	1.11	52
8	94	8	16	1.25	58
9	98	4	8	2.50	56
10	96	-2	-4	—	42

c. Profit is maximized by hiring 8 units of labor. If more than $8L$ are hired, $MRP < w (= \$10)$ and profit falls. If fewer than $8L$ are hired, $MRP > w$ and increasing L will increase profit.

d. See column (5) of table above.

e. 94, because $MR (= \$2)$ will be less than SMC if output is increased by hiring the ninth worker.

f. See column (6) of table above.

g. $8L$ or $94Q$ both result in a maximum profit of $\$58$. It doesn't matter whether the manager chooses L or Q to maximize profit. $MR = SMC$ and $MRP = w$ are equivalent rules for profit maximization.

h. $6L; \pi = -\$16; MP_6 = 12 < 12.83 = AP_6$. If $AP < MP$, the firm would shut down in the short run.

11. a. $SMC = 10 + 2(-0.03)Q + 3(0.00005)Q^2 = 10 - 0.06Q + 0.00015Q^2$

b. $Q_{min} = -(-0.03)/2(0.00005) = 300$ units

c. $AVC_{min} = 10 - 0.03(300) + 0.00005(300)^2 = \$5.50$

d. $P = \$10 > AVC_{min} = \$5.50$; $SMC = P$: $10 - 0.06Q + 0.00015Q^2 = 10$

$Q^* = 0.06/0.00015 = 400$ units

e. $AVC_{400} = 10 - 0.03(400) + 0.00005(400)^2 = \$6$; $TVC_{400} = AVC \times Q = \$6(400) = \$2,400$; $TR = P \times Q = \$10(400) = \$4,000$

$\pi = TR - TVC - TFC = \$4,000 - \$2,400 - \$600 = \$1,000$

f. $P = \$7 > AVC_{min} = \$5.50$; $SMC = P$: $10 - 0.06Q + 0.00015Q^2 = 7$; solve $0.00015Q^2 - 0.06Q + 3 = 0$

$Q^* = \dfrac{0.06 + \sqrt{0.0018}}{0.0003} = 341$ units

g. $AVC = 10 - 0.03(341) + 0.00005(341)^2 = \$5.58$

$\pi = TR - TVC - TFC = \$7(341) - \$5.58(341) - 600 = -\$116$

h. $P = \$5 < AVC = \$5.50$; $Q^* = 0$ units

i. $\pi = -TFC = -\$600$

12. a. $AVC = 80 - 0.05Q + 0.000033Q^2$

b. $SMC = 75 \Rightarrow 80 - 0.1Q + 0.0001Q^2 = 75 \Rightarrow 5 - 0.1Q + 0.0001Q^2 = 0$. Solving with the quadratic formula:

$Q_1, Q_2 = \dfrac{0.10 \pm \sqrt{0.1^2 - 4 \times 0.0001 \times 5}}{0.0002}$

$Q_1 = 53$ and $Q_2 = 947$

c. $AVC_{Q\,=\,53} = 80 - 0.05(53) + 0.000033(53)^2 = \$77.44 > P = \$75 \Rightarrow$ shut down.

$AVC_{Q\,=\,947} = 80 - 0.05(947) + 0.000033(947)^2 = \$62.24 < P = \$75 \Rightarrow$ produce 947 units.

Chapter 12: Managerial Decisions for Firms with Market Power

1. a. Strangely enough, it may well be that the much smaller Texas bank has fewer good substitutes in its area than the huge Chase Manhattan Bank and hence has more market power. Chase Manhattan competes worldwide with many other large international banks.

b. There was not nearly as much foreign competition in the U.S. auto market prior to 1970. Thus the Big Three would have less market power now.

c. They probably have about the same market power, although the regional phone company may have better substitutes and hence less market power. Both are generally regulated.

2. As international markets have expanded, new sources of raw material have come onto the world market, making control of a raw material much more difficult for a single company.

3. a. Neither are barriers to entry for toothpaste. Although consumers may develop a brand loyalty for a particular brand, they do not incur high switching costs to find or learn how to use other brands. And the value of brushing with Crest is not enhanced when other consumers brush with Crest.

b. LPs did pose a consumer lock-in problem when CDs came along because you couldn't play LPs on a CD player. It was costly to switch audio technologies. There might also be some network externalities with LPs if consumers like to swap LPs with friends.

4. a. and b.

P	Q	$TR\ (= PQ)$	$MR\ (= \Delta TR/\Delta Q)$
$20	200	$4,000	—
15	300	4,500	$500/100 = \$5$
10	500	5,000	$500/200 = \$2.50$
5	700	3,500	$-1,500/200 = -\$7.50$

c. Demand is elastic. $\$5 \times 200 = \$1,000$ lost revenue. $\$15 \times 100 = \$1,500$ added revenue. The added revenue is $\$500$ more than the lost revenue. Divided by the added sales, $MR = \$500/100 = \$5$.

d. Demand is elastic. $\$5 \times 300 = \$1,500$ lost revenue. $\$10 \times 200 = \$2,000$ added revenue. The added revenue is $\$500$ more than the lost revenue. Divided by the added sales, $MR = \$500/200 = \$2.50$.

5. a. $15

b. 200 units

c. $MR = \$10$; elastic (because $MR > 0$)

d. 400 units. $MR = 0$, so $E = -1$

6. a. $Q^* = 9$. The ninth unit of output should be produced because it adds more to TR than to TC ($MR > SMC$), but producing the 10th unit would decrease profit ($SMC > MR$).

b. $P^* = \$18$

c. $\pi = (\$18)(9) - (\$54) = \$108$

7. a. $9

b. 30

c. $270; $240; $30

8. A profit-maximizing monopolist produces the level of output at which $MR = MC$. In general, $MC > 0$, so $MR > 0$ also, and thus a monopolist operates in the elastic portion of the demand curve. A monopolist will never operate in the inelastic region of demand. When demand is inelastic, $MR < 0$, and by decreasing output the firm can increase TR, decrease TC, and thus increase profit. If costs were zero, then $MC = 0$, and a monopolist would produce the level of output at which $MR = 0$. Demand is of unitary elasticity when MR is zero and TR is at its maximum.

9. *a.* 2,000 units; $P = \$50$

   b. Profit $= (P - ATC)Q = (\$50 - \$60)2,000 = -\$20,000$

   c. $TR = \$50 \times 2,000 = \$100,000$; $TVC = AVC \times Q = \$40 \times 2,000 = \$80,000$

   d. It loses $TFC = TC - TVC = \$60 \times 2000 - \$80,000 = \$40,000$.

10. *a.* $Q^* = 500$ ($MR = SMC$)

    b. $P^* = \$7$

    c. $\pi = Q(P - ATC) = (500)(\$7 - \$6) = \$500$

    d. $Q^* = 700$, $P^* = \$6.50$ ($MR = LMC$)

    e. When $Q = 500$, $MR > LMC$; as the firm increases output, the addition to TR will exceed the addition to TC—profit will increase.

    f.

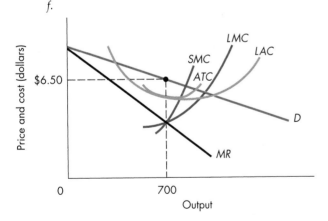

11. *a.*

L	Q	P	MP	MR	MRP
9	50	$21	—	—	—
10	100	20	50	19.00	950
11	140	19	40	16.50	660
12	170	18	30	13.33	400
13	190	17	20	8.50	170
14	205	16	15	3.33	50
15	215	15	10	-5.50	-55

b. If the wage rate is $60, the monopolist will employ 13 units of labor. Through the 13th unit, each unit of labor adds more to TR than to TC ($MRP > w$); employing the 14th unit of labor would decrease profit ($MRP < w$). If the wage rate falls to $40, the 14th unit of labor now adds more to TR than to TC and so should be hired. Regardless of the wage rate, no more than 14 units of labor will be employed—the firm will never hire a unit of labor with negative MP.

12. *a.* $L = 120$ at $\$20 = MRP$

    b. $L = 140$ at $\$10 = MRP$

    c. zero. (At $\$40 = MRP$, ARP is less than MRP.)

13. *a.* Monopolistic competition is similar to monopoly in that both types of firms have market power (face a downward-sloping demand). But the source of a monopolist's market power is the fact that the firm is the only seller in the market; a monopolistic competitor has market power because the firm produces a differentiated product—that is, the products of rival firms are not perfect substitutes.

    b. Monopolistic competition is similar to perfect competition in that there are many firms and unrestricted entry and exit in both types of markets.

    c. In the short run, a monopolistic competitor produces the level of output at which $MR = SMC$, as long as price at that output is greater than or equal to AVC. If $P < AVC$, the firm will shut down. Monopolistic competitors, like all other firms, can earn positive, zero, or negative economic profit in the short run. Although the source of the firm's market power differs, the short-run analysis of monopolistic competition is identical to that of pure monopoly.

    d. In the long run, a monopolistic competitor produces the level of output at which $MR = LMC$, charges the price associated with that level of output, and earns zero economic profit (i.e., $P = LAC$).

Thus, in the long run, a monopolistic competitor's demand curve is tangent to its LAC curve.

e. Unrestricted entry and exit drive economic profit to zero in the long run in a monopolistically competitive market. If firms earn positive economic profit in the short run, the subsequent entry will increase the number of substitutes for a firm's product: The firm's demand will decrease and become more elastic. Entry will continue until economic profit is zero. Losses in the short run will lead to exit, which will reduce the number of substitutes for the remaining firms. Long-run equilibrium occurs when there is no incentive for entry or exit (i.e., when economic profit equals zero).

14. a. In the short run, with demand curve D_S and marginal revenue curve MR_S, the monopolistic competitor will produce Q_S and charge price P_S.

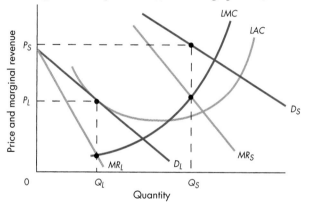

b. The long-run demand curve is D_L: the firm will produce Q_L and charge price P_L.

c. In order for the *firm* to be maximizing profit, MR_L must equal LMC. If $MR_L \neq LMC$ at the point of tangency, the firm will have an incentive to change its output, and thus the point where $P_L = LAC$ would not be equilibrium.

d. In the long run, for the monopolistically competitive firm, equilibrium price is higher ($P >$ min LAC) and output lower ($Q < Q_{min\ LAC}$) than they are for a perfectly competitive firm.

15. a. $Q = 2,600 - 100P + 0.2M - 500P_R = 2,600 - 100P + 0.2(20,000) - 500(2) = 5,600 - 100P$

b. $P = 56 - 0.01Q$

c. $MR = 56 - 0.02Q$

16. a. $SMC = 20 - 2(0.07)Q + 3(0.001)Q^2 = 20 - 0.14Q + 0.0003Q^2$

b. Set $MR = SMC$: $56 - 0.02Q = 20 - 0.14Q + 0.0003Q^2$. The solution is $Q^* = 600$ units.

c. $P^* = 56 - 0.01Q^* = 56 - 0.01(600) = \$50$

d. The firm should produce. For $Q^* = 600$, $AVC = 20 - 0.07(600) + 0.0001(600)^2 = \$14$, so $P^* = \$50 > AVC = \$14$.

e. $TR = P^* \times Q^* = (\$50)(600) = \$30,000$; $TVC = AVC \times Q^* = \$14(600) = \$8,400$; $\pi = TR - (TVC + TFC) = \$30,000 - \$8,400 - \$22,500 = -\$900$

Chapter 13: Strategic Decision Making in Oligopoly Markets

1. a. False. There is no need to know the decisions that perfect competitors will make because they are too small to have any effect on each other's profits.

b. False. While strategic thinking does involve rational decision making, managers employ strategic thinking to make decisions to maximize their *individual* profits based on what they believe their rivals will do. This does not generally maximize *total* industry profit.

c. True. Managers of firms in all types of market structures seek to maximize profit.

2. True. Even though they know the payoffs from taking certain actions, they do not know what action or strategy their rival is going to choose.

3. a. Not a prisoner's dilemma. Neither manager has a dominant strategy.

b. Not a prisoner's dilemma. The dominant strategies result in both managers deciding to cooperate instead of choosing the less desirable decision not to cooperate. There is no dilemma here; the dominant strategy equilibrium is the best Gates and Dell can do individually.

c. This is a prisoner's dilemma. Both Dell and Gates have dominant strategies and the dominant strategy equilibrium makes them both worse off than if they cooperated in making their decisions.

4. a. For firm Small, a low price dominates, because Small makes more profit going low for either choice made by Large.

b. Firm Large has no dominant strategy. If Small chooses high, Large makes more with a low price.

If Small chooses low, Large makes more with a high price.

c. Small would be expected to set a low price, which is its dominant strategy. Large will likely set a high price because Large knows Small's dominant strategy is a low price, and a high price is the best decision for Large given it believes Small is very likely to choose its dominant strategy and set a low price. Both firms end up earning $600 in profit.

5. In the prisoners' dilemma situation, each suspect has a dominant strategy: confess. Don't confess, then, will never be chosen, so it is a dominated strategy for both suspects. Eliminating don't confess from a row and a column in the prisoners' dilemma payoff table leaves the unique dominant strategy equilibrium: (**Confess**, *Confess*).

6. a. Yes, Coke's dominated strategy in the original payoff table is high. Regardless of whether Pepsi chooses low, medium, or high, Coke's best strategy would never be high.

   b. Yes, Pepsi's dominated strategy in the original payoff table is low. Regardless of whether Coke chooses low, medium, or high, Pepsi's best strategy would never be low.

   c. The reduced payoff table is constructed by deleting from the original payoff table the row corresponding to Coke's dominated strategy (row high) and the column corresponding to Pepsi's dominated strategy (column low). In the reduced payoff table, only one of the firms (Pepsi) has a dominant strategy (medium).

   d. The likely pair of decisions for Coke and Pepsi is (**Medium**, *Medium*).

   e. Pepsi is not likely to choose high for its advertising budget because Coke must be expected to choose high in order for high to be Pepsi's best decision. Since high is a dominated strategy for Coke, Pepsi would be foolish to believe Coke will choose high.

7. a. In cell D, neither Jane nor Bill can unilaterally improve her or his payoff by changing his or her individual decision. Given that Bill confesses, Jane's best outcome is to confess also. If she unilaterally decides not to confess, given Bill's decision to confess, she gets 12 years in prison instead of 6 years. She cannot benefit from a unilateral change in her decision to confess. Also, given that Jane decides

to confess in cell D, a unilateral decision by Bill to not confess only makes Bill worse off. Cell D is strategically stable because neither Bill nor Jane has an incentive to change his or her decision given the other's decision.

   b. Small and Large's likely decision pair, (**Low**, *High*), is strategically stable, since a unilateral decision by Small to choose high given Large chooses high will make Small worse off (its payoff would fall from $600 to $400), and a unilateral move by Large to low will make Large worse off (its payoff would fall from $600 to $500).

   c. Coke and Pepsi's decision pair (**Medium**, *Medium*), which can be found by eliminating dominated strategies in the original payoff table, is strategically stable, and thus is a Nash equilibrium. Neither cola firm can improve its payoff with a unilateral change in decision. With Pepsi's choosing a medium ad budget, Coke can do no better than $450 in Nash equilibrium, and with Coke's choosing a medium ad budget, Pepsi can do no better than $525.

8. Substitute P_B = $200 into Arrow's demand to get Q_A = 6,400 − 25P_A [= 4,000 − 25P + 12 × 200]. Next take the inverse of demand, P_A = 256 − 0.04Q_A, so MR_A = 256 − 0.08Q_A. Then solve MR_A = LMC_A for Q_A: 256 − 0.08Q_A = 160 and thus Q_A = 1,200. Firm A's best response to Firm B's price of $200 is $208 [= 256 − 0.04 × 1,200].

9. Arrow has no reason to price at $184, because $184 is only a best price for Arrow if Bravo chooses $100. Since point R is not on Bravo's best-response curve, Bravo's best response to Arrow's price of $184 is for Bravo to set some price other than $100 (in this situation, *higher* than $100). So if Bravo will not set price at $100, Arrow has no reason to set its price at $184.

10. a. Q_A = 4,000 − (25 × 230) + (12 × 235) = 1,070; Q_B = 3,000 − (20 × 235) + (10 × 230) = 600; π_A = (230 − 160) × 1,070 = $74,900; π_B = (235 − 180) × 600 = $33,000. Both airlines individually earn higher profit at point C than at point N.

    b. Q_A = 4,000 − (25 × 229) + (12 × 235) = 1,095; π_A = (229 − 160) × 1,095 = $75,555. Yes, cheating increases Arrow's profit.

    c. Q_B = 3,000 − (20 × 234) + (10 × 230) = 620; π_B = (234 − 180) × 620 = $33,480. Yes, cheating increases Bravo's profit.

11. *a.* Substitute P_B = \$60 into Firm A's demand to get $Q_A = 312 - 4P_A$. Next take the inverse of this demand, $P_A = 78 - 0.25Q_A$, so $MR_A = 78 - 0.5Q_A$. Then solve $MR_A = LMC_A$ for Q_A: $78 - 0.5Q_A = 2$, and thus $Q_A = 152$. Firm A's best response to Firm B's price of \$60 is \$40 [$= 78 - 0.25 \times 152$]. Point H and the graph of BR_A are shown in the accompanying figure.

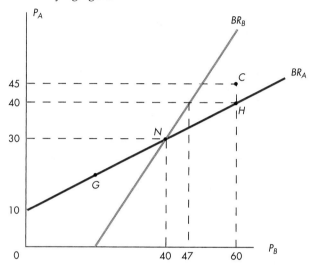

b. In a simultaneous decision when demand and cost are common knowledge, the managers can be expected to set the Nash prices found at the intersection of BR_A and BR_B. See point N in the figure. Point N allows each firm to do the best for itself given the (best) price set by its rival.

c. $Q_A = 72 - 4(30) + 4(40) = 112$; $Q_B = 100 - 3(40) + (30) = 100$

$\pi_A = (30 - 2)112 = \$3,136$; $\pi_B = (40 - 6.67)100 = \$3,333$

d. Manager A does *not* believe manager B will set its price at \$60 when Firm A sets its price at \$40. Both mangers know that manager B's best response to A's price of \$40 is to lower price to approximately \$47.

e. $Q_A = 72 - 4(45) + 4(60) = 132$; $Q_B = 100 - 3(60) + 4(45) = 100$

$\pi_A = (45 - 2)132 = \$5,676$; $\pi_B = (60 - 6.67)100 = \$5,333$

Both firms make greater profit at point C than at point N. Since the firms are making simultaneous decisions and cannot cooperate, point C will not be chosen, and point N is the expected outcome.

12. *a.* The game tree and decision path are shown in the figure below:

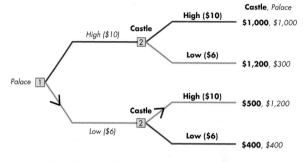

b. Yes, the equilibrium decision path shown in the game tree above is a Nash equilibrium because both Castle and Palace are doing the best they can given the best decisions made by the other. Neither firm has an incentive to change its decision given the other's decision.

13. The technology choice game when Sony goes first is shown below. The solution path is shown in light-blue color with arrowheads. The solution is (**Digital, Digital**). Since Sony makes greater profit when it goes first (\$11.875 million > \$10 million), it experiences a first-mover advantage.

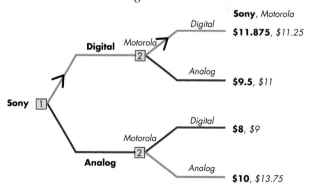

14. *a.* No. Sony ignores Motorola's threat because it is not credible: If Sony chooses digital technology, Motorola's best response is to choose digital technology also.

b. No, Motorola's statement is not a strategic promise because it does not alter the play of the game. Sony already knows Motorola will choose analog if Sony chooses analog, so the promise offers nothing to Sony it did not already have. Sony ignores the statement by Motorola and the game ends with both firms choosing digital technology.

15. *a.* Yes. Both Alpha and Beta have dominant strategies (price low) that lead to a profit outcome that is less desirable for both of them than the cooperative outcome (price high).

b. The cooperative outcome is cell A, where both firms price high. The noncooperative outcome is cell D, the Nash equilibrium. Notice that in cell A *both* firms are better off than in the noncooperative Nash equilibrium cell D.

c. When Alpha cheats by pricing low while Beta prices high: cell B is the cell in which Alpha cheats on Beta. When Beta cheats by pricing low while Alpha prices high: cell C is the cell in which Beta cheats on Alpha. So cells B and C are the cells in which cheating occurs.

d. The cooperative outcome in cell A is not likely to occur if the decision is made just one time. In one-time decisions, there is no way to punish cheating and no future consequence from cheating. Consequently, both firms expect the other will cheat by pricing low. Remember, pricing low is the dominant strategy in a one-time decision; it is the best decision no matter what the rival decides to do.

16. AMD can make a credible threat to punish Intel with a retaliatory price cut only if cutting price is the best decision for AMD to make when Intel cheats; that is, cutting price must increase AMD's profit when Intel cheats. In Table 13.5, cell C represents the situation in which Intel cheats. Since AMD can increase its profit from $0.5 million per week to $1 million per week by cutting price and moving the outcome of the decision to cell D, AMD's threat to cut price is indeed credible.

17. Since Alpha can increase its profit from $150,000 per month to $200,000 per month by cutting price and moving the outcome of the decision from cell C to cell D, Alpha's threat to cut price is indeed credible. Since Beta can increase its profit from $50,000 per month to $75,000 per month by cutting price and moving the outcome of the decision from cell B to cell D, Beta's threat to cut price is indeed credible.

18. *a.* $100,000 (= $300,000 − $200,000) per month;

$$PV_{\text{Benefits of cheating}} = \$194,156 = \frac{100,000}{(1 + 0.02)^1} + \frac{100,000}{(1 + 0.02)^2}$$
$$= 98,039 + 96,117$$

b. $125,000 (= $200,000 − $75,000) per month;

$$PV_{\text{Costs of cheating}} = \$233,271 = \frac{125,000}{(1 + 0.02)^3} + \frac{125,000}{(1 + 0.02)^4}$$
$$= 117,790 + 115,481$$

c. Since $PV_{\text{Costs of cheating}} > PV_{\text{Benefits of cheating}}$, Beta will choose not to cheat and will cooperate.

d. Beta will choose to cheat, because using a 30 percent discount rate lowers the present value of the costs of cheating (relative to the benefits) sufficiently to make cheating optimal:

$$PV_{\text{Benefits of cheating}} > PV_{\text{Costs of cheating}}$$
$$\frac{\$100,000}{(1 + 0.30)^1} + \frac{\$100,000}{(1 + 0.30)^2} > \frac{\$125,000}{(1 + 0.30)^3} + \frac{\$125,000}{(1 + 0.30)^4}$$
$$\$76,923 + \$59,172 > \$56,896 + \$43,766$$
$$\$136,095 > \$100,662$$

19. *a.* Less likely to cooperate. The present value of the benefits of cheating increases since the stream of benefits lasts for more months (i.e., N gets larger).

b. More likely to cooperate. As long as Beta believes Alpha is committed to matching its price cuts immediately, Beta will view cell C as an impossible outcome. Thus Beta will view its own cheating as leading immediately to cell D. There can be no benefit from cheating, so Beta will choose to cooperate.

c. More likely to cooperate. Beta will expect punishment to last for more than two months; that is, P (the number of periods of punishment) is expected to increase.

d. May increase or decrease the likelihood of cooperation. Product differentiation both decreases the benefit of cheating and decreases the cost of cheating. If Alpha's new product design lowers the $PV_{\text{Benefits of cheating}}$ by more (less) than it lowers the $PV_{\text{Costs of cheating}}$, then the increase in product differentiation will make cooperation by Beta more (less) likely.

Chapter 14: Advanced Techniques for Profit Maximization

1. *a.* $MC \Rightarrow Q_T = 50$ dishwashers per week

b. $P = \$550$ when $Q_T = 50$ (from the demand curve)

c. $MR = MC_T = MC_1 = MC_2 \Rightarrow Q_1 = 10$ and $Q_2 = 40$

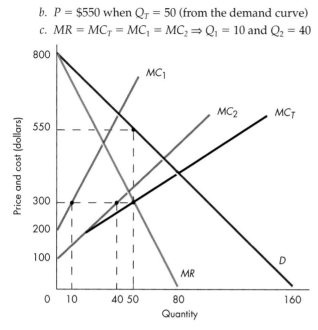

2. a. $Q_A = -1,000 + 100\ MC_A$

   $Q_B = -133.33 + 33.33MC_B$

b. $Q_T = (-1,000 - 133.33) + (100 + 33.33)MC_T = -1,133.33 + 133.33MC_T$

c. $MC_T = 8.50 + 0.0075Q_T$

d. The output at which the kink occurs is found by setting MC in the *low*-cost plant equal to the minimum value of MC in the *high*-cost plant:

   $4 + 0.03Q = 10$

   So $Q = 200$ at the kink. At total output greater than 200 units both plants are used.

e. At 700 units in each plant, $MC_A = \$17 < MC_B = \$25$. Therefore, the manager should produce more in plant A and less in plant B, until $MC_A = MC_B$. To find equal values of $MC_A = MC_B$ that produce 1,400 units at least cost, substitute 1,400 into MC_T:

   $MC_T = 8.50 + 0.0075(1,400) = \$19$

   Now find Q_A and Q_B such that $MC_A = MC_B = \$19$. Use the inverse MC functions:

   $Q_A = -1,000 + 100(19) = 900$

   $Q_B = -133.33 + 33.33(19) = 500$

   Note that $Q_A + Q_B = 1,400$.

f. See the following figure:

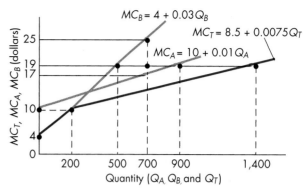

3. a. $P = 32 - 0.008Q$

b. $MR = 32 - 0.016Q$

c. Set $MR = MC_T$: $32 - 0.016Q = 8.5 + 0.0075Q \Rightarrow Q^*_T = 1,000; P^* = \$24 = 32 - 0.008(1,000)$

d. MC_T at 1,000 units $= \$16$. Set $MC_A = MC_B = 16$

   $Q^*_A = -1,000 + 100(16) = 600$

   $Q^*_B = -133.33 + 33.33(16) = 400$

   Note: $Q^*_A + Q^*_B = Q^*_T$ (600 + 400 = 1,000)

e. $MC_T = MR$ at $Q_T < 200$, which is the kink in MC_T. Thus only plant B should be operated; plant A shuts down. Set $MC_B = MR$ to find Q_B. To find MR, find inverse demand and apply the rule:

   $P = 10 - 0.0125Q$

   $MR = 10 - 0.025Q$

   $MR = MC_B \Rightarrow 10 - 0.025Q_B = 4 + 0.03Q_B \Rightarrow Q^*_T = 109$ units

f. $Q_A = 0$ and $Q_B = 109$ (see part e).

4. a. When costs are constant and the markup is set optimally: $m^* = -1/(1 + E^*)$, where E^* is the point elasticity of demand at the profit-maximizing price.

b. $m^* = -1/(1 + -1.5) = 2$, or 200 percent markup

c. $m^* = -1/(1 + -3) = 0.5$, or 50 percent markup

5. a. $MR = 36 - 0.0016Q = \$6 = SMC \Rightarrow Q^* = 18,750 \Rightarrow P^* = \$21 = 36 - 0.0008(18,750)$

b. According to the discussion in Section 14.2, the president of Markast Foundry always uses a 100 percent markup ($m = 1$). The cost-plus price will be $\$16 = (1 + 1)\$8$. The firm will likely sell 25,000 bearings ($= 45,000 - 1,250 \times 16$). Profit is $\$168,750 = (\$16 - \$8)25,000 - \$31,250$.

c. $E^* = -1.57143 = 1 + 36/[0.5(8 - 36)] = 1 + (36/-14); m^* = 1.75 = -1/(1 + -1.57143); P^* = \$22 = (1 + 1.75)\$8; Q^* = 17,500 = 45,000 - 1,250(22)$

d. $\$213,750 = (\$22 - \$8)17,500 - 31,250$. Yes, this is more profit than in part *b*. Cost-plus pricing, even when costs are constant, does not generally maximize profit because it ignores demand conditions.

6. *a.* Profit is maximized when $MR_T = MC = \$20$ at a total quantity $Q_T^* = 250$. For the business market: $MR_B = \$20 \Rightarrow Q_B = 150$ business travelers. For the vacation market: $MR_V = \$20 \Rightarrow Q_V = 100$ vacation travelers.

b. From their respective demand curves, $P_B = \$50$ and $P_V = \$30$. Revenue from vacation travelers is $\$3,000 = \$30 \times 100$, and revenue from business travelers is $\$7,500 = \$50 \times 150$. Combined total revenue is $\$10,500$.

c. You must construct the horizontal sum of the two demand curves and read off the price for 250 units. The precise answer is $\$36.67$, which you should be close to if your lines are carefully drawn. The total revenue when only a single price is charged is $\$9,167 = \$36.67 \times 250$.

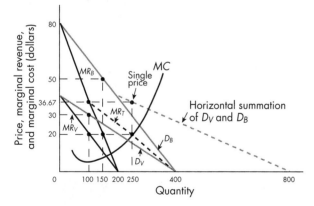

7. *a.* First find inverse demands:

$$P_A = 20 - 0.0125Q_A \qquad P_B = 24 - 0.01Q_B$$

Then the marginal revenues are:

$$MR_A = 20 - 0.025Q_A \qquad MR_B = 24 - 0.02Q_B$$

Finally take the inverses:

$$Q_A = 800 - 40MR_A \qquad Q_B = 1,200 - 50MR_B$$

b. Set $MR_A = MR_B = MR_T$ and add Q_A and Q_B:

$Q_T = Q_A + Q_B = (800 - 40\,MR_T) + (1,200 - 50MR_T) = 2,000 - 90MR_T$

Next take the inverse to get $MR_T = f(Q_T)$:

$$MR_T = 22.22 - 0.0111Q_T$$

c. See the figure top of next column:

d. $MR_T = 22.22 - 0.0111(650) = \$15$

Setting $MR_A = MR_B = \$15$,

$Q_A = 800 - 40(15) = 200$

$Q_B = 1,200 - 50(15) = 450$

Note: $Q_A + Q_B = 200 + 450 = 650$.

8. *a.* Set $MR_T = MC$: $22.22 - 0.0111Q = 4.5 + 0.005Q \Rightarrow Q_T^* = 1,100$ units.

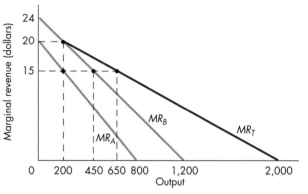

b. At $Q_T^* = 1,100$, $MR_T = 10$, so the profit-maximizing allocation between the two markets is such that $MR_A = MR_B = 10$:

$Q_A = 800 - 40(10) = 400$

$Q_B = 1,200 - 50(10) = 700$

Note: $Q_A^* + Q_B^* = Q_T^*$, or $400 + 700 = 1,100$

c. $P_A^* = 20 - 0.0125Q_A^* = 20 - 0.0125(400) = \$15$

$P_B^* = 24 - 0.01Q_B^* = 24 - 0.01(700) = \$17$

d. $E_A = P/(P - a) = 15/(15 - 20) = -3$

$E_B = P/(P - a) = 17/(17 - 24) = -2.43$

Note: The higher price ($P_B = \$17$) is charged in the market with the less elastic demand ($E_B = -2.43$) in profit-maximizing equilibrium.

9. If a firm produces two products that are unrelated, then the marginal revenue function for each product depends only on the level of output of that product. In order to maximize profit, the firm will produce the level of output for each product at which $MR = MC$. If a firm produces two products that are related in consumption, the profit-maximizing rule is the same:

Produce the level of output for each product at which $MR = MC$. But in this case, the marginal revenue function for each product depends on the levels of output of *both* products. The profit-maximizing levels of output for two products related in consumption thus must be determined jointly.

10. *a.* Set up the two $MR = MC$ conditions for profit maximization:

$$70 - 0.001Q_X - 0.00125Q_Y = 27 + 0.0005Q_X$$
$$80 - 0.002Q_Y - 0.00125Q_X = 20 + 0.00025Q_Y$$

Solving these equations simultaneously for Q_X and Q_Y, the profit-maximizing outputs are $Q_X^* = 12,000$ and $Q_Y^* = 20,000$. Using these outputs, the profit-maximizing prices for X and Y are $P_X^* = 70 - 0.0005(12,000) - 0.00075(20,000) = \$49$ and $P_Y^* = 80 - 0.001(20,000) - 0.0005(12,000) = \$54$.

b. $TR_X = \$588,000 = \$49(12,000)$; $TR_Y = \$1,080,000 = \$54(20,000)$; $TC_X = \$360,000$ and $TC_Y = \$450,000$; $\pi = TR_X + TR_Y - TC_X - TC_Y = \$858,000$

11. *a.* $MRP_T = 240 - 12H_T = MC = 150 + 3H_T \Rightarrow H_T^* = 6$

b. $H_T^* = 6 \Rightarrow MRP_T = MC = \$168$

$MRP_X = \$168 \Rightarrow H_X^* = 4.5$

$MRP_Y = \$168 \Rightarrow H_Y^* = 1.5$

c. $Q_X^* = 2H_X = 9$; $Q_Y^* = 4H_Y = 6$

d. $P_X^* = \$120 - 2(9) = \$102$; $P_Y^* = 60 - 1.5(6) = \$51$

10. *a.* $MR_J = 290 - 0.003Q = MR_X + MR_Y = 200 - 0.002Q_X + 90 - 0.001Q_Y$

b. Setting $MR_J = MC$ and solving for $Q \Rightarrow Q^* = 60,000$ drums of joint product.

c. $P_X^* = 140 = 200 - 0.001(60,000)$; $P_Y^* = \$60 = 90 - 0.0005(60,000)$

d. $Q_X^* = 94,000$ drums; $Q_Y^* = 90,000$ drums. *Note:* $MR_Y = 0$ at 90,000 drums.

e. $P_X^* = \$106 = 200 - 0.001(94,000)$; $P_Y^* = \$45 = 90 - 0.0005(90,000)$

Chapter 15: Decisions under Risk and Uncertainty

1. *a.*

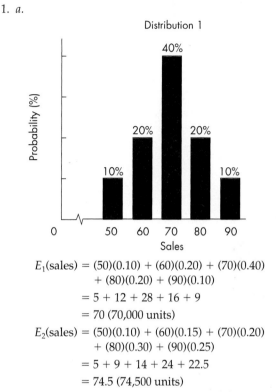

Distribution 1

$E_1(\text{sales}) = (50)(0.10) + (60)(0.20) + (70)(0.40) + (80)(0.20) + (90)(0.10)$

$= 5 + 12 + 28 + 16 + 9$

$= 70 \ (70,000 \text{ units})$

$E_2(\text{sales}) = (50)(0.10) + (60)(0.15) + (70)(0.20) + (80)(0.30) + (90)(0.25)$

$= 5 + 9 + 14 + 24 + 22.5$

$= 74.5 \ (74,500 \text{ units})$

b. Distribution 2 has a higher variance and thus is more risky than distribution 1:

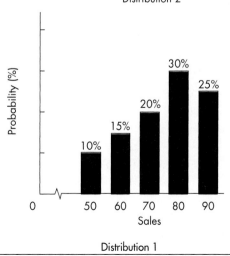

Distribution 2

Distribution 1

Sales (X_i)	Probability (P_i)	$[X_i - E(X)]^2$	$[X_i - E(X)]^2(P_i)$
50	0.10	400	40
60	0.20	100	20
70	0.40	0	0
80	0.20	100	20
90	0.10	400	40
			$\sigma^2 = 120$

Distribution 2

Sales (X_i)	Probability (P_i)	$[X_i - E(X)]^2$	$[X_i - E(X)]^2(P_i)$
50	0.10	600.25	60.0250
60	0.15	210.25	31.5375
70	0.20	20.25	4.0500
80	0.30	30.25	9.0750
90	0.25	240.25	60.0625
			$\sigma^2 = 164.75$

c. $\sigma_1 = \sqrt{120} = 10.95$

$\sigma_2 = \sqrt{164.75} = 12.84$

$v_1 = 10.95/70 = 0.16$

$v_2 = 12.84/74.5 = 0.17$

Distribution 1 has the smaller coefficient of variation ($0.16 < 0.17$), and thus distribution 1 is less risky relative to its mean than distribution 2.

2. *a.* Expected value of option A = $0.4(-\$3,750) + 0.6(\$31,770) = \$17,562$.

Expected value of option B = $0.4(-\$8,000) + 0.6(\$34,000) = \$17,200$.

Option A has the higher expected value.

b. Variance of option A = $0.4(-3,750 - 17,562)^2 + 0.6(31,770 - 17,562)^2 = 302,800,896$

Variance of option B = $0.4(-8,000 - 17,200)^2 + 0.6(34,000 - 17,200)^2 = 423,360,000$

$\sigma_A = \sqrt{302,800,896} = 17,401$

$\sigma_B = \sqrt{423,360,000} = 20,576$

Option B is more risky since its variance (or standard deviation) is higher than option A's variance.

c. Option A is chosen since it has a higher expected payoff and a lower variance.

d. $v_A = 17,401/17,562 = 0.99$

$v_B = 20,576/17,200 = 1.20$

Based on the coefficient of variation rule, option A is chosen.

3. *a.* Expected value of option A = $0.6(-\$3,750) + 0.4(\$31,770) = \$10,458$

Expected value of option B = $0.6(-\$8,000) + 0.4(\$34,000) = \$8,800$

Option A has the higher expected value and would thus be chosen if only expected value is used in decision making.

b. Variance of option A = $0.6(-3,750 - 10,458)^2 + 0.4(31,770 - 10,458)^2 = 302,800,896$

Variance of option B = $0.6(-8,000 - 8,800)^2 + 0.4(34,000 - 8,800)^2 = 423,360,000$

$\sigma_A = \sqrt{302,800,896} = 17,401$

$\sigma_B = \sqrt{423,360,000} = 20,576$

Option B is more risky since its variance (or standard deviation) is higher than option A's variance.

c. Option A is chosen since it has a higher expected payoff and a lower variance.

d. $v_A = 17,401/10,458 = 1.66$

$v_B = 20,576/8,800 = 2.34$

Based on the coefficient of variation rule, option A is chosen.

To find the probabilities that make the two expected values equal, solve the following for p:

$p(-3,750) + (1 - p)(31,770) = p(-8,000) + (1 - p)(34,000)$

After combining terms and simplifying:

$p = 0.34$

Thus expected values are equal when the probability that price is \$15 equals 0.34, and the probability that price is \$20 equals 0.66.

4. *a.* $E(\pi) = 0.05(-\$10,000) + 0.45(-\$2,000) + 0.45(\$4,000) + 0.05(\$20,000) = \$1,400$

b. $E[U(\pi)] = 0.05\ U(-\$10,000) + \cdots + 0.05\ U(\$20,000) = 0.05(-200,000) + \cdots + 0.05(400,000) = 28,000$

c. $MU_{profit} = \Delta U/\Delta \pi = 20$ since $U(\pi)$ is linear.

d. neutral; constant

5. *a.* $E(\pi) = \$3,250 = 0.05(\$1,000) + \cdots + 0.50(\$4,000)$

b. $E[U(\pi)] = 160.69 = 0.05U(\$1,000) + \cdots + 0.05\ U(\$4,000)$

c. 13.86; 8.11; 5.75 (in the three blanks)

d. averse, decreasing

6. *a., b., c.* Professor Thomas derived his own utility index for this answer:

Profit outcome	Utility index	Marginal utility of profit
$1,000	0.0	—
$2,000	0.70	0.000700
$3,000	0.90	0.000200
$3,200	0.93	0.000150
$4,000	1.0	0.000093

   d. Professor Thomas is risk averse because his marginal utility for profit is decreasing as profit rises.

7. *a.* $U[E(\pi)] = U(\$1,400) = 20(1,400) = 28,000$

   b. $U[E(\pi)] = 28,000 = E[U(\pi)]$. The two decisions yield the same expected utility since the expected utility of receiving $1,400 with certainty is 28,000.

   c. You found the manager to be risk neutral in problem 4. You would expect two decisions with exactly the same expected value to yield exactly the same expected utility for risk-neutral decision makers because they ignore risk.

8. *a.* $U(\$3,200) = 161.42 = 20 \ln(3,200)$

   b. The expected utility of receiving $3,200 with certainty is 161.42. The expected utility of the project was calculated to be 160.69 in part *b* of Technical Problem 5. Thus the manager maximizes expected utility by choosing to receive $3,200 with certainty.

   c. The manager is shown to be risk averse in Technical Problem 5. By the definition of risk averse, the manager chooses the less risky of two alternatives that have the same expected value, which is the decision reached by maximizing expected utility of profit (thank goodness . . .).

   d. The decision made by maximizing expected utility would also have been reached using mean–variance rules; pick the decision with lower risk when the expected values are equal.

9. *a.* Option B

   b. Option A

   c. Option A, because potential regret for A is $2,230 while potential regret for B is $2,270.

   d. Option A ($14,020 > $14,000).

INDEX